MW00997532

# Controlling with SAP S/4HANA®: Business User Guide

Janet Salmon and Stefan Walz

# Controlling with SAP S/4HANA®: Business User Guide

**Editor** Megan Fuerst
**Acquisitions Editor** Emily Nicholls
**Copyeditor** Melinda Rankin
**Cover Design** Graham Geary
**Photo Credit** iStockphoto.com: 866599566/© eclipse_images, 628856458/© malerapaso
**Layout Design** Vera Brauner
**Production** Kelly O'Callaghan
**Typesetting** III-satz, Husby (Germany)
**Printed and bound in** Canada

**ISBN 978-1-4932-2098-4**

1st edition 2021

**Library of Congress Cataloging-in-Publication Data**
Names: Salmon, Janet, author. | Walz, Stefan, author.
Title: Controlling with SAP S/4HANA : business user guide / Janet Salmon, Stefan Walz.
Description: 1st Edition. | Boston : Rheinwerk Publishing, 2021. | Includes index.
Identifiers: LCCN 2021009237 | ISBN 9781493220984 (hardcover) | ISBN 9781493220991 (ebook)
Subjects: LCSH: Corporations--Accounting--Handbooks, manuals, etc. | Business enterprises--Data processing--Handbooks, manuals, etc. | Controllership--Handbooks, manuals, etc. | SAP HANA (Electronic resource)
Classification: LCC HF5686.C7 S2663 2021 | DDC 338.7/616570285--dc23
LC record available at https://lccn.loc.gov/2021009237

# Contents at a Glance

# Dear Reader,

The best way to learn a new city is from someone who lives there.

I experienced this first-hand when I moved to Boston several years ago. With Google Maps and some online recommendations, I could identify the major sites, navigate to work, and locate the nearest Dunkin' for coffee. However, it wasn't until my friend, a native Bostonian, came to visit that I truly appreciated what my neighborhood had to offer. From unexpected music venues to unique coffee shops, a map alone can't do the city justice.

Similarly, in the world of controlling operations in SAP S/4HANA, a simple map of the system to navigate to the data you need won't suffice; you also need to understand how it can be leveraged to improve decision making and, ultimately, profitability for your business. So with this business user guide, you'll learn from experts who know the system best. SAP finance professionals Janet Salmon and Stefan Walz will take you on an in-depth tour of controlling in the new suite. Following step-by-step—or click-by-click—instructions, you'll discover new developments like the Universal Journal, navigate both the classic SAP GUI transactions and new SAP Fiori apps to arrive at your data, and analyze each view with practical examples. You'll make stops at key system landmarks and unexpected points of finance interest!

What did you think about *Controlling with SAP S/4HANA: Business User Guide*? Your comments and suggestions are the most useful tools to help us make our books the best they can be. Please feel free to contact me and share any praise or criticism you may have.

Thank you for purchasing a book from SAP PRESS!

**Megan Fuerst**
Editor, SAP PRESS

*meganf@rheinwerk-publishing.com*
*www.sap-press.com*
Rheinwerk Publishing · Boston, MA

# Contents

## Appendices 561

# Foreword

Digital transformation impacts all industries. Success depends on getting people, processes, technology, and data right. Worldwide crises such as the current pandemic amplify the pressure on that transition. To be successful, companies have to be flexible, extensible, and adaptable. An intelligent, flexible, and comprehensive finance solution is the key enabler for digital transformation. Customers want to get rid of painful, manual steps. They expect the support of new business models and intelligent and fully integrated business processes across the whole enterprise. Automation supported by intelligent technologies is key. It's all about rethinking business processes.

For our customers, SAP S/4HANA is the gateway to this digital transformation.

SAP HANA provides the new foundation for our finance applications. Based on the potential and power of the SAP HANA database, we drive application innovations toward an intelligent enterprise. In the past, finance was mainly transaction-based and acted as the integration hub for logistical processes. It was about collecting figures and crunching numbers. Finance in SAP S/4HANA is no longer just about integration: it is about intelligent finance.

The Universal Journal provides a comprehensive and state-of-the-art base layer for our finance applications. It is the single source of truth that ensures data integrity by design and makes reconciliation obsolete. Dispensing with aggregates and building analytics upon individual journal entry items, it allows 360-degree reporting and unprecedented insights. And more than that, the Universal Journal is the enabler for business innovations such as margin analysis, event-based revenue recognition, and predictive accounting.

As head of the SAP S/4HANA Finance and Risk development team, I am particularly pleased that, with this book, we get the opportunity to present the innovations, advantages, and business value within management accounting as a cornerstone of SAP S/4HANA Finance. In this book, we present the building blocks of management accounting and provide a deeper insight into organizational structures and master data.

The book aims to provide a comprehensive picture of management accounting within SAP S/4HANA Finance, giving detailed insights into overhead controlling, production controlling, customer project controlling, margin analysis for products and services, investment controlling, and intercompany processes. The authors, Janet Salmon and Stefan Walz, describe and explain the basic ideas and help you to understand how SAP S/4HANA management accounting improves your day-to-day processes and adds value to your overall business across the enterprise.

I am really pleased that Janet and Stefan joined forces for this book. Both have many years of experience in management accounting and understand integration within the intelligent enterprise in depth. They are connected and in a continuous exchange with a huge number of customers and partners. Janet and Stefan are role models in looking at the processes from end to end to drive innovations within SAP S/4HANA Finance and Risk.

I hope you will enjoy reading this book and that you get a lot of inspiration as to how you can benefit from SAP S/4HANA management accounting and intelligent finance in your day-to-day business and on your journey to the digital business of the future.

**Judith Pistor**
Head of SAP S/4HANA Finance and Risk

# Preface

*Controlling* has been a familiar term in the German-speaking world for at least 80 years, but it's less established in the English-speaking world. The idea is to put a management control system in place for your organization by establishing financial targets for each area, monitoring performance against the plan, analyzing variances, and looking at the root cause of these variances in order to improve future performance and improve the plan in the next iteration. These targets might be the costs to serve a customer, to manufacture a product, or to deliver a service and will usually involve a mixture of those costs that can be directly associated with the aforementioned goals, such as the raw materials used to manufacture a product and the indirect costs, like marketing and administration costs, that must be allocated. These targets can also refer to departments within the organization and their ability to use resources efficiently to achieve their goals.

Put like this, we seem to be talking about internal or management reporting. Historically, there has been a difference between the German-speaking world, which has traditionally separated internal and external reporting, and the English-speaking world, which has generally viewed them as one and the same. With the arrival of SAP S/4HANA, the traditional separation of financial accounting for external reporting and controlling for internal reporting vanishes; the two approaches become just different ways of looking at the same set of numbers, whether it's by account in the financial statements presented externally or by cost center or market segment for internal management purposes.

But let's not get ahead of ourselves. Understanding controlling is not about subscribing to one way of doing things but about driving business decisions by understanding what is happening in sales, procurement, production, and so on. This means following how the business transactions captured in these operative processes are shown as T-accounts in financials and cost objects in controlling.

This book describes a new product, but those old goals still apply. SAP S/4HANA Finance was released in March 2015 and has undergone many refinements. Throughout this book, we'll walk you through what SAP S/4HANA Finance is and how it relates to controlling. We've worked through mainframes, client servers, and now the arrival of SAP HANA; we've worked with companies large and small, large multinationals, and single manufacturing plants; we've answered a lot of questions about controlling; and we want to share our knowledge with you, whether you just qualified as a cost accountant or have been in the business for forty years.

## Target Audience

This book is for all those people who work in controlling, whether you're the *financial controller* working closely with the CFO, or a *plant controller*, a *sales controller*, or indeed any other kind of specialist controller responsible for overseeing the cost impact of the business operations running in your area. We're assuming that you have a configured system before you and need to understand how to create master data, run business transactions, manage the financial close, and report on the various business processes as part of your daily work. Perhaps you are a *cost center manager* or a *project manager* who wants to get a better understanding of the financial key figures within your responsibility and how your decisions can influence these figures. Of course, we can't know exactly what business you are in or how your company chose to implement SAP, but we hope that by the end of this book you'll feel more confident in your daily work and can ask better questions of those around you.

We are also writing for the *consultants* and *IT specialists* who set up your system and want to go deeper than the scope item descriptions to understand how the various business processes relate to one another so that they understand what they are doing when they make certain settings or extend a report. This book isn't a configuration guide, but we will discuss settings when we feel they are needed to explain the posting logic.

Although we often talk to people who have been in the SAP space for as long as we have, we're also noticing a generational change in the workplace. We're now also working with people who are fresh out of college and need to be up and running quickly. Hopefully this book will help you to learn fast, however much experience you bring to the table.

## Objective of This Book

The objective of this book is quite simply to explain controlling for business users. We want you to feel that we are at your desk beside you helping to explain the journal entries inherent in every posting, whether it's a consultant booking time or travel to a project, an employee buying a laptop for a cost center, or a major project to refurbish one of your manufacturing sites. We want you to understand the market segments by which you can analyze your business and the cost objects that capture the manufacturing and service activities for your core business and the supporting activities that keep these operational activities running. We want you to understand the various structures, whether it's the difference between a plant, a sales organization, and a division, or a cost center, a profit center, and a functional area. We know that you didn't always make those key decisions about how to structure the organization or which market segments made sense, but we want you to be able to make sense of these structures in your daily work. We want you to know where to find the reports that will help you see what's happening and prepare budgets. We'll take you step by step through the tasks of reporting, budgeting, and what needs to happen at period close or to make a correction. We also want to help you to understand where SAP is going in controlling. We won't always be able to predict the future, but we can tell you about the major developments that might change the way you approach controlling. You might find this challenging if you're using an older version of the software or your organization has chosen not to use certain functions for the time being, but we want you to know what's out there and to be able to facilitate a conversation about the direction in which controlling is moving.

## How to Read This Book

If you're new to the world of controlling with SAP S/4HANA, then you'll probably want to start at the beginning and read to the end of the book. We've assumed basic accounting experience and tried to explain any terms that we don't think you will have met before. With each chapter, we'll build on what you have learned in the previous chapter until we've gradually given you the information you need to do your job.

However, we also know that if you're working, you may not actually have the time to start at the beginning and read to the end. You may already have worked with SAP ERP and know the difference between a cost center and a profit center or standard costs and actual costs. In this case, we suggest you look at the headings and dip into those areas that have changed significantly, or start at the back with the list of SAP Fiori applications and then read through the referenced chapters to understand how SAP S/4HANA doesn't just change the look of your system but also changes the approach to profitability reporting and how new visualizations may help show connections that were previously far from obvious.

Now, we'll provide an overview of the chapters in this book.

### Chapter 1: Introduction to SAP S/4HANA

If you are a controller, then you probably didn't make the decision about whether to implement SAP S/4HANA Finance in the cloud or on-premise. But you do need to understand which deployment option your organization has chosen, because cloud software offers a *restricted scope*, controlled by the various scope items that you activate, whereas on-premise software gives you access to the full implementation guide and allows modifications, so you can be far more flexible in your approach. We'll reference the scope items where appropriate and tell you if a function is only available on-premise or, in the case of some newer functions, in the cloud first.

We'll then explore the idea of the *Universal Journal* as the place where all your financial data, both internal and external, comes together and the impact of this simplified model on controlling. Because we assume that you spend a significant part of the day working in the system, we'll also explain the difference between the classic transactions and the SAP Fiori applications so that you can navigate through the system. When we explain a business process, we'll explain whether the function is only available in SAP Fiori or only as a legacy transaction, and where both options are available, we'll provide enough information for you to perform the task either using a classic transaction or the equivalent SAP Fiori application. We're writing this book at a time when SAP Fiori applications are being added regularly, so we'll also show you how to keep abreast of changes.

### Chapter 2: Controlling in SAP S/4HANA

If you're a controller, then you need to understand the Universal Journal and the merger of financial and management accounting in SAP S/4HANA. This chapter puts many of the basic ideas in place that we'll explore in more detail later in the book. We'll use T-accounts to explain various business processes and the associated journal entries. We'll introduce the topic of planning and predictive accounting and then focus on management accounting and margin analysis, explaining what happens in terms of cost center planning and reporting, product cost planning and reporting, and profitability planning and reporting before introducing the controlling roles and some of the reports that will accompany us through the book. The idea is to give you a grounding in the big ideas before walking you through the mechanics of the organizational structures and master data. We'll return to most topics in subsequent chapters to cover them more thoroughly.

### Chapter 3: Organizational Structures

If controlling is about managing your organization properly, then it makes sense to start with the organizational structures that will shape the way you set targets and report on your business. This chapter covers financial structures, such as affiliated companies, company codes, profit centers, and functional areas, and it explains topics such as controlling areas and operating concerns that are unique to SAP. We'll also look at plants, purchasing organizations, and sales organizations and their impact on finance. Finally, we'll look at the structures that impact your financial reporting, including the options for ledgers, accounting principles, and currencies. When we find organizations going through a financial transformation, it's often because the organizational structures that they chose at the beginning no longer fit their purpose. Mistakes in this area can be expensive to fix.

### Chapter 4: Master Data

It's also important to get your master data right if you are to manage your organization properly. Getting the account structure correct is about making sure that everybody is speaking the same language and classifying their business transactions according to the same basic rules. In terms of responsibility accounting, it's equally important to get the cost center structure right because that's the level at which management responsibility for individual spending sits. Too many cost centers and you won't be able to see the forest for the trees; too few and you won't have enough transparency into who is spending what where. Then comes the question of how costs flow from these cost centers, either as activities, such as manufacturing hours or consulting hours, or based on drivers such as headcount or square footage of office space. It's unusual for all costs to be assigned to cost centers. Usually orders and projects are used either to manage individual operations, such as production, maintenance, service, and so on, or simply to refine the costs on a cost center so as to manage the individual trade fairs handled by a marketing cost center as different orders. Finally, we'll look at the market segments available for margin analysis and how to add your own to segment the market to meet your organization's unique requirements.

### Chapter 5: Overhead Controlling

Every organization has some form of overhead controlling, though you might call it by a different term. It's all about monitoring costs and understanding how to learn more by drilling down to the associated assets, purchase orders, travel, and so on. Overhead controlling is also about putting a plan in place to explain what you intend to spend and establishing limits beyond which spending should stop.

Overhead controlling is all about understanding cost flows, whether these are simple allocations of heating and energy to the shop floor or the process of valuing the work supplied by the people on the shop floor or the consultants working on customer projects. In this sense, a plan is not just a framework for spending, but a charge rate for any services provided internally by your organization or to be billed externally, as in the case of consulting work.

We'll then show you the various business transactions that are used to trigger these cost flows, from a simple reposting to correct a wrongly assigned travel expense through the various allocations to settlement to move costs once work on an order or project is complete.

### Chapter 6: Controlling for Manufacturing Organizations

You'll only need this chapter if you manufacture your own products. We'll describe how master data in production, such as the bills of materials (BOMs), routings, and work centers, are key to product costing and setting a standard for the product to be manufactured. We'll then walk you through the process of procuring raw materials and of make-to-stock and make-to-order production to understand the associated cost flows. We'll explain work in process (WIP) and production variances and how to use actual costing if you need to assign all purchase price variances and production variances to your finished products. We'll show both the classic process, whereby WIP and variances are calculated at period close, and the new approach, whereby journal entries for WIP are generated as soon as raw materials are issued and production activities confirmed. We'll wrap up by looking at asset maintenance costs as a way of supporting the manufacturing process.

### Chapter 7: Margin Analysis for Products and Services

This chapter will begin with the master data behind your market segments and the guiding principles for margin reporting in SAP S/4HANA. We'll explore simple sales scenarios and more complex customer project scenarios in terms of the associated journal entries, planning, and revenue recognition. We'll then explore the new customer service scenario as a new way of managing the associated business transactions and reporting. We'll then take a deeper look at event-based revenue recognition, which supports multiple controlling features.

### Chapter 8: Investment Controlling

With investment controlling, we'll look at a completely different type of project that is used internally to manage capital expenses for building machinery and developing new products. We'll look at how to prepare and monitor budgets in this context and how to capitalize the associated expenses, first as assets under construction and later as asset costs.

### Chapter 9: Controlling in an Intercompany Environment

When we began our work at SAP, intercompany transactions were relatively rare. But as companies have become more global in scope, intercompany trade between affiliated companies in the same group has increased enormously, and the controller has to deal with this complexity. Alongside intercompany goods movements, we also see many intercompany cost allocations, whether for a shared service center in a low-cost land or consulting services being provided across the world. This is probably the area that has seen the most changes in the last thirty years, and many organizations have complex workarounds in place that they are now trying to unravel in order to move to a standard approach.

### Chapter 10: Reporting in SAP S/4HANA

We'll use reports to illustrate the relevant journal entries and key figures throughout the book, but in this chapter, we'll go behind the scenes to explain the virtual data model behind the many SAP Fiori applications. We'll explain how to set up hierarchies for reporting and how to set up key figures. We'll also show you where you can continue to use the existing reports from SAP ERP if you aren't ready to move to the new approach.

### Chapter 11: Conclusion and Outlook

Finally, we'll review the main lessons from each of the chapters and briefly look at roadmap topics that stand to impact some of the chapters.

### Appendices

We'll close with two appendices for quick reference. Appendix A lists the key controlling transactions that we cover throughout the book, and Appendix B lists the relevant SAP Fiori apps.

## Acknowledgments

We'd like to invite you to join us on this journey through controlling. It's now been nearly thirty years since Stefan and I met. In those days, I was a young translator, and Stefan would tell me all about his product costing customers. We've worked together for many years and recently shared an office where we would bounce ideas off each other between meetings. The pandemic changed our workspace. As we've written this book, we've hardly seen one another, but we've talked a lot. This different form of collaboration feels like my take on the world. I wrote my first book in airports, on planes, in hotel rooms—indeed, anywhere where I could find ten minutes to jot down an idea or make a note of an explanation. This book has been written almost entirely at home between any number of virtual meetings.

And with that, I'd like to thank my husband, Nick, for his patience as he's looked at the back of a laptop for months on end, and my children, Martin and Lucy.

*—Janet Salmon*

I would like to add to Janet's words that we have both been carried along in our writing by our enthusiasm for the new controlling in SAP S/4HANA. We hope that we have been able to convey that. I would especially like to thank my wife, Anja, and my daughter, Saskia, for their understanding of my limited time during this project.

Together, we also thank our editor, Megan, for her varied, very helpful feedback. As you read this, know that we are looking forward to seeing you again somewhere and hoping to be greeted with a smile and the words, "I read your book and was able to gain some ideas."

*—Stefan Walz*

# Chapter 1
# **Introduction to SAP S/4HANA**

*Before we deal with the functionalities and application areas of controlling, let's take a look at SAP S/4HANA. SAP S/4HANA provides its users with a completely new look and feel and has made groundbreaking innovations possible for controlling, for which we are giving an initial introduction.*

The aim of this introduction is to explain the major changes with SAP S/4HANA to both readers coming from SAP ERP and those who are new to the SAP world. The goal is to give you direction and guiding principles now before we go into detail later.

We introduce SAP S/4HANA from the user's perspective, explaining the deployment models and the new financials architecture based on the Universal Journal. This architecture enables simplifications, new features, and improved reporting capabilities compared to SAP Business Suite. This chapter ends by showing the new user interface experience with SAP Fiori.

## 1.1 Deployment Models in SAP S/4HANA

SAP offers its SAP S/4HANA solutions with different options, which can be operated in different ways, and different license models given by different providers. Because it isn't always easy to distinguish these options, we want to give you some orientation in this chapter.

The on-premise or cloud deployment model defines the responsibilities between the customer and the service provider. There are multiple criteria to consider; for example, the option to enable customer-specific development is only available in an on-premise scenario.

All members of the SAP S/4HANA product family are based on the same program code. Therefore, a combination (in the sense of parallel operation) of both versions, and their combination with other cloud solutions (SAP and third party), is possible: this is a hybrid model.

In the following sections, we'll take a closer look at each of these three possible solutions.

### 1.1.1 On-Premise

This has been the most common deployment model for SAP software. With the on-premise edition, you can operate SAP S/4HANA in your own data center and in your own system landscape. The customer is then responsible for purchasing the hardware, installing and administering the software, and maintaining the software by importing software changes, especially legal changes.

Because the on-premise edition is always operated either by the customer or by a provider on behalf of the customer, this solution also offers a certain degree of flexibility for a customer's individual process setup, customer-specific developments, and the rhythm of applying the SAP release updates.

Many industry-specific solutions are available here, which can also be activated to cover extensive customer requirements. Extensive localization is also available.

**Note**

With the on-premise edition, SAP follows an annual innovation cycle. As of the time of writing, the latest release is 2020, which is what will be covered in this book.

### 1.1.2 Cloud

Based on the on-premise code line and its extensive solution offerings, there is a private cloud edition available. You can run on-premise SAP S/4HANA in a private cloud within your own data center or hosted by a vendor. The system and IT infrastructure management you can outsource to a service provider. As with the on-premise version, the system is flexible with regard to a customer-specific process setup.

SAP S/4HANA as a public cloud offering is a totally different story. SAP S/4HANA Cloud is operated and maintained by SAP itself. You access SAP S/4HANA Cloud via a browser from multiple devices via the internet and with a unique, customer-specific URL. There is no need to worry about system and infrastructure management on the customer side.

With this, the total cost of ownership (TCO) is dramatically reduced—and the total cost of implementation (TCI), too. After you've selected a business scope, based on several scope items, the best practice content of the scope items is deployed, and the selected business scenarios are available out of the box. Thus, the implementation effort is dramatically reduced. One example is the professional service scope, of which we show parts of in Chapter 7. With activation, there is an end-to-end scenario available from the project's creation, including updating financial project planning by system for revenue recognition and margin analysis.

The look and feel are also totally different as access to the applications is mainly provided via SAP Fiori apps. (For more information on SAP Fiori, see Section 1.3.)

Automatic updates of legal changes are ensured by quarterly software updates—the same updates that ensure you can use the latest innovations.

Further features of this solution are as follows:

- There is a subscription licensing model in place.
- System and infrastructure maintenance is done by SAP.
- To ensure a simple and transparent solution and an easy software upgrade implementation, there is no option to change SAP code to be customer specific. But there are self-configuration activities in place and substitution and extensibility, which we discuss in Chapter 4.
- For the same reason, the complete on-premise scope isn't available, nor the same flexibility.
- Upgrades and support packages are managed by SAP.

**Note**

With SAP S/4HANA Cloud, SAP follows a quarterly innovation cycle. At the time of writing, the latest release is 2102, which is what this book will address. We will show single cloud functionality for applications that are not yet available in the on-premise version but are planned on the roadmap. We will also show the customer project scenario, tailored for professional service, as an example of a typical, simplified cloud application.

### 1.1.3 Hybrid Models

You can adopt different deployment models at the same time: on-premise, private cloud, and public cloud. You also can integrate solutions from other providers. This leads to a mixture of deployment models, which we call a hybrid landscape, as shown in Figure 1.1.

As on-premise SAP S/4HANA and SAP S/4HANA Cloud use the same program code and are basically on the same development level, these solutions can operate very well with each other. In a typical application scenario, subsidiaries operated in SAP S/4HANA Cloud can be connected with the parent company's data center operated in an on-premise environment.

However, hybrid solutions are particularly suitable if further cloud applications are to be combined either with the on-premise edition or with SAP S/4HANA Cloud. This applies in particular to SAP's complementary cloud applications: SAP Ariba, SAP Concur, and SAP Fieldglass. To ensure that these solutions work together seamlessly and easily, extended SAP standard integration functionality is available.

Another very common hybrid example is the integration of SAP Fiori apps in SAP Business Technology Platform (SAP BTP) with SAP S/4HANA. You can build your own applications also—for example, to give employees access via SAP Fiori apps to enter data that is stored in the SAP S/4HANA backend system.

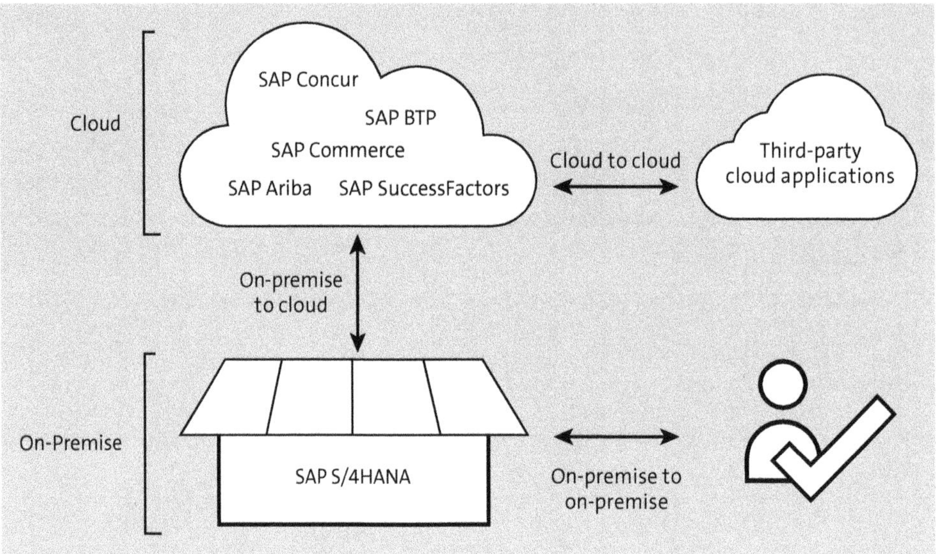


**Figure 1.1** Hybrid Landscape

## 1.2 Universal Journal Innovations

Now let's come to the major driver for innovation from a controlling perspective: the Universal Journal.

From the controller's and accountant's view, the Universal Journal can undoubtedly be described as the heart of SAP S/4HANA. It allows a drastic simplification of the processes in controlling, reduces period-end activities, and at the same time enables new functionalities and completely new, fascinating reporting insights.

The differences from SAP ERP are major: New worlds have opened up. Figure 1.2 illustrates the historical evolution of the controlling and accounting applications.

Although the various management and financial accounting tasks in SAP R/3 were taken over by special modules with their respective data structures, the new general ledger in SAP ERP already offered a certain degree of simplification and consolidation. SAP S/4HANA accounting is now taking the radical step of integrating all controlling and accounting applications and their requirements into a common data model.

Before we take a closer look at its impacts on controlling, Figure 1.3 gives an overview of the various features of the Universal Journal.

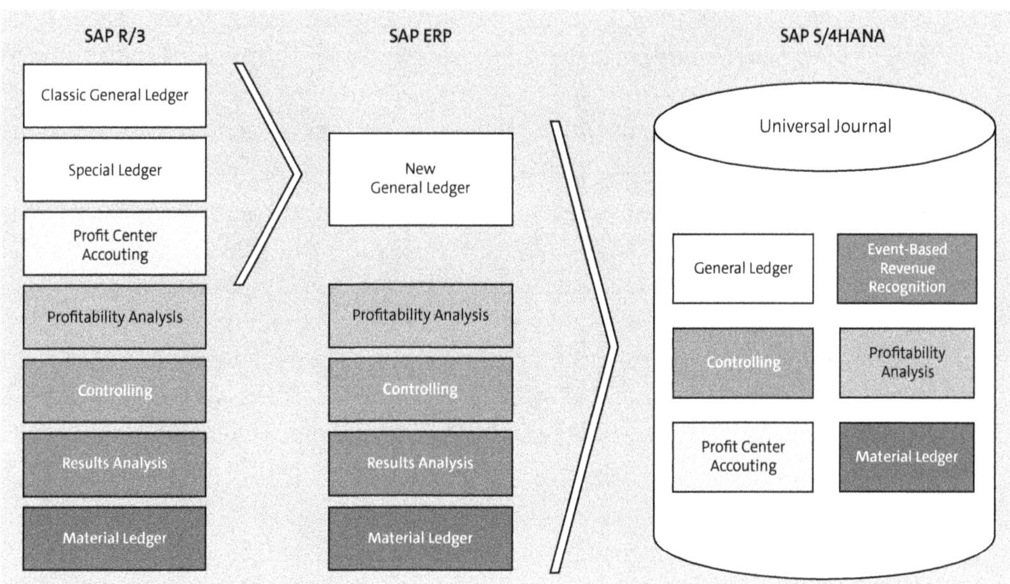


**Figure 1.2** Evolution of Controlling in SAP

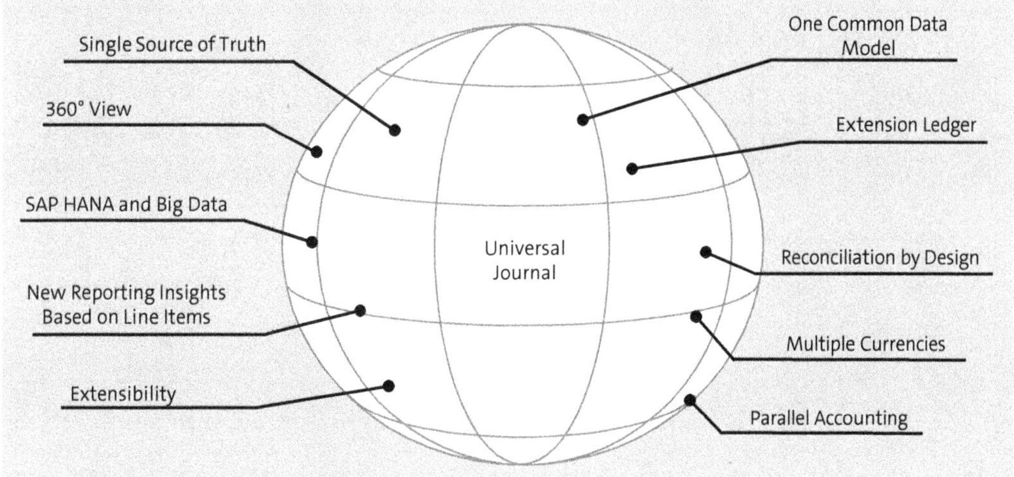


**Figure 1.3** Key Characteristics of Universal Journal

We'll explain the individual features of the Universal Journal in this section and also discuss its specific effects on particular areas of controlling throughout this book. Now, let's first look at what *single source of truth* means for controlling.

### 1.2.1 Single Source of Truth

Conventional ERP systems had data tables for all the individual accounting applications and different data structures adapted to the requirements of each application.

This required reconciliation work, which is very time-consuming due to the multiple data structures and kinds of posting logic. The ultimate goal of a modern system is to achieve a single source of truth for the data from controlling, financial accounting, and revenue recognition. With the Universal Journal, this goal has already been reached at the starting point—with no additional reconciliation work needed.

This pays off, for example, when analyzing the margin analysis on the basis of customer projects, as we'll discuss in Chapter 7. The revenues and the margin are based on journal entries, which also include revenue recognition. You will get the same values when you look at a financial statement or at the revenue recognition values. Reports from different applications deliver no longer different key performance indicators (KPIs) because the data may have been written at a different point in time or even with different values. Thus, the confidence in the data grows and it becomes more meaningful.

Regardless of whether you analyze the costs of a project, determine the profitability of a market segment, analyze the revenue recognition, or start analyzing the general ledger in the financials statement, these are different views and aggregations on the same journal entries.

With the single source of truth, common structures naturally go hand in hand.

### 1.2.2 Single Data Model for Accounting

Figure 1.4 shows the different views of the general ledger, cost object controlling, and margin analysis on a journal entry item based on the Universal Journal. The journal entry reflects the invoicing of a service order to a domestic customer. The document covers all the requirements of the different financial applications, while each application has a different view based on different fields of the document.

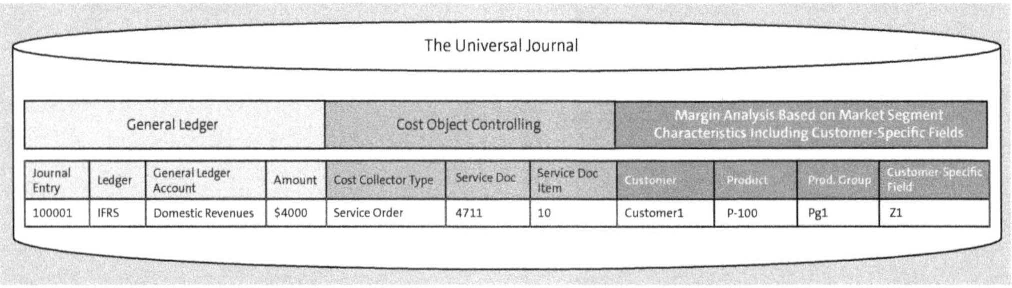

The Universal Journal

| General Ledger | | | | Cost Object Controlling | | | Margin Analysis Based on Market Segment Characteristics Including Customer-Specific Fields | | | |
|---|---|---|---|---|---|---|---|---|---|---|
| Journal Entry | Ledger | General Ledger Account | Amount | Cost Collector Type | Service Doc | Service Doc Item | Customer | Product | Prod. Group | Customer Specific Field |
| 100001 | IFRS | Domestic Revenues | $4000 | Service Order | 4711 | 10 | Customer1 | P-100 | Pg1 | Z1 |

**Figure 1.4** One Data Model for All Accounting and Controlling Applications

This common structure offers the following benefits:

- There is one data model for all applications. For example, now the general ledger account specifies the type of expense only; no value fields (costing-based profitability analysis) or revenue recognition secondary cost elements (result analysis) are used any longer. Secondary cost elements are now general ledger accounts.

- The applications inherit attributes and functionalities from each other. The following are some examples:
  - The parallel currencies of the general ledger—with more freely definable ones now possible—are also available to controlling, margin analysis, and revenue recognition.
  - The same applies to the parallel ledgers and the associated parallel valuations per accounting principle. This allows you, for example, to use different valuations in parallel in the event-based revenue recognition for local Generally Accepted Accounting Principles (GAAP) and International Financial Reporting Standards (IFRS) (see Chapter 7).
  - General ledger fields like the functional area can be now used in controlling and margin analysis reports to define the contribution margin structure.
  - Margin analysis and controlling fields are now available for general ledger reporting. This allows, for example, drilling down into the work in process (WIP) account by project, product, or customer (see Chapter 7).
- When you activate an extensibility field, it's available in all financial applications.

### 1.2.3 Advanced Analysis and Reporting Options

The rapid performance gains of SAP S/4HANA's in-memory database, SAP HANA, and the new structural innovations of the Universal Journal enable completely new reporting. This leads to a fundamental paradigm shift. Let's look at the most important aspects:

- **All accounting applications read from the same source**
  The reports of all financial accounting applications read from journal entries and their reporting views (see Chapter 10). The applications only have a different view on the journal entries.
- **All reports are based on journal entry line items**
  SAP S/4HANA can aggregate millions of rows very efficiently on the fly, so you don't need aggregated persisted data any longer. You can report on Universal Journal line items. This means that in principle all fields of the Universal Journal—including the customer-specific extensibility fields—are available in every report. For example, you can determine the data for any market segment attribute for your company. For this purpose, in addition to the standard SAP ERP reports that are still available, there are new SAP Fiori apps that query the Universal Journal and thus enable a much more flexible way of evaluating data. There is no need to define the reports beforehand. They are now live and allow users to include additional fields. They can use any combination of filter criteria from the Universal Journal to narrow down the result. There is no longer a need to define and access a database index or even aggregate data into separate database tables, as was previously the case in SAP ERP.
- **Real-time data**
  You now always report on real-time data. When you start any report, it's always up

to date. There's no need to replicate data asynchronously into a data warehouse. As far as the data from SAP S/4HANA is concerned, a business warehouse is obsolete.

- **Increased transparency**
  The Universal Journal also opens up improved analysis options for tracking. This is important for explaining the data and an aid for external and internal auditors. For example, if you analyze a WIP value in the balance sheet, you can drill down directly to the revenue recognition document, not a settled value like in SAP ERP. You can even track the link to the prima nota. Or if you want to further analyze a cost of sales KPI in the margin analysis, you can break it down directly to the prima nota.
- **A 360-degree view for cost objects and market segment**
  The integration of the various accounting applications in the Universal Journal also opens up extended evaluation options. Information that could not previously be made available in SAP ERP is now available directly and in great detail. One example is the detailed breakdown of balance sheet lines such as WIP by controlling attributes and market segments. An example of WIP drilldown by project and market segments can be found in Chapter 7.
- **Extensibility**
  To include custom fields, SAP S/4HANA provides three tools: coding block extension, journal entry extension, and market segment extension. We will discuss these in Chapter 4. With the publishing of the extension fields, they are available in the central line item table ACDOCA of the Universal Journal. Because you're reporting on journal entry line items and these extension fields are also released for the reporting views, they are available in the reports of all accounting applications. In conventional ERP systems, these extensibility fields were initially only available locally in a certain application—and because the reports were based on aggregated records, the fields were not initially available in the standard reports.
- **General ledger entities are available for controlling**
  As mentioned in the previous section, the general ledger entities are now in controlling and margin analysis is available too, so now you can structure your controlling reports by functional area. You can analyze your controlling data per ledger, and there are multiple currencies available. You are also able to analyze your product and cost object costs by profit center.

### 1.2.4 Impact on Controlling Postings and Margin Analysis

With the merging of the accounting applications, there is a paradigm shift for controlling. Controlling no longer takes place in an independent subledger. This has the huge advantages of reconcilability, simplification, and a gain in analysis options, as we mentioned previously.

However, it places new challenges on the controller, and familiar processes from an ERP system have to be adapted. This is what we want to address here.

As mentioned, the Universal Journal provides a common data model for the accounting applications. This concerns the general ledger account in particular. It's now used by all applications, and there is a central maintenance app and transaction. The decisive change for controlling is that cost elements—including the controlling internal/secondary ones—are created as general ledger accounts. (We'll discuss this further in Chapter 4, Section 4.1.)

This is accompanied by another paradigm shift: the controlling allocations are now also posted in the general ledger. This affects activity allocation as well as cost center allocation and others (see Chapter 5). There have always been a variety of controlling processes that were initially posted locally in controlling and then had to be followed up on in the general ledger at the end of the period, such as through settlement. You now simplify these steps by posting them directly in the general ledger. The following are some examples use cases, which show the relevance of controlling postings for the general ledger:

- The controlling transactions may well lead to a change in profit center, segment or functional area.
- Controlling transactions that are posted to cost objects that have to be capitalized, such as the production order (see Chapter 6), or are relevant for revenue recognition, such as a customer project (see Chapter 7), have an impact on the balance sheet and profit and loss (P&L) statement.

The biggest paradigm shift, however, is certainly in margin analysis. The widely used costing-based profitability analysis, which continues to be available in parallel, is a powerful application that uses its own persistence and data models. To make this functionality available in the Universal Journal–integrated margin analysis as well, SAP has provided a variety of new features:

- **Display contribution margin**
  As just mentioned, reporting takes place on journal entry line items. Thus, the contribution margin for market segments is shown on the original accounts instead of value fields. Each KPI can be traced back to the original prima nota.
- **Providing cost component split for cost of sales**
  To determine a multilevel contribution margin for sales of manufactured products, you evaluate the product cost estimate in costing-based profitability analysis to split the cost of sales by cost components. You also use this to detail the cost of sales in the margin analysis by posting individual journal entry items for each cost component item (see Chapter 7, Section 7.3.2).
- **Update market segment in journal entry item**
  You can assign the market segment and corresponding profitability object with manual postings (see Chapter 4), just like you do for, say, postings to a cost center or project. However, there are use cases in which the posting is assigned to a different cost object and the market segments are derived in parallel and stored in the journal entry

by the system. This is applied for customer project and service scenarios. In this way, the original posting to the project also carries market segments such as the product and the customer information. You save the settlement and get your market segment margin analysis based on the original postings to the project in real time. We'll deal with this in Chapter 7 and show an evolution example in the next section.

- **Write market segment attributes for balance sheet line items**
  It's also now possible to write market segment attributes for balance sheet line items as in the WIP postings (see Chapter 7).
- **Market segment realignment**
  All market segment attributes are persisted in the journal entry. There are use cases in which you want to change them subsequently, like when dependent attributes have changed, such as the product group in the material master, or if not enough information was available at the time of posting and you now want to update the information. For this purpose, there is a realignment in place, which we introduce in Chapter 7. With this, you can change journal entry fields subsequently. Of course, this is limited to fields that aren't relevant to the general ledger.

Because you no longer have a separate application and persistence for controlling, the question remains as to where you store specific controlling data that isn't relevant for legal reporting, such as deviating costs, additional costs, calculation costs, or commitments.

### 1.2.5 Extension Ledger for Management Accounting

In SAP S/4HANA, there is now a new type of ledger available, the *extension ledger*. It covers management accounting requirements. An extension ledger is always assigned to a standard ledger: while the standard ledger contains journal entries for all business transactions for legal purposes, the extension ledger contains management-relevant journal entries only. The extension ledger only stores delta entries to the underlying standard ledger. This setup assumes that all postings in the underlying standard ledger are part of the exension ledger reporting. With this, you avoid redundant data storage.

For management accounting purposes, there are two different ledger types available:

- The management accounting ledger, used to post additional costs like statistical sales conditions or manual adjustment postings. We'll show an example in Chapter 7.
- The commitment ledger, to post, for example, order entry or purchase order commitments. We'll cover this in Chapter 5.

Extension ledgers can also be stacked; we discuss how this is set up in Chapter 3, Section 3.3.1.

Figure 1.5 shows a possible setup, which is provided in SAP S/4HANA Cloud by default. It can be configured in on-premise systems too. Extension ledger OC is assigned to standard ledger OL. Ledger OE is assigned to extension ledger OC.

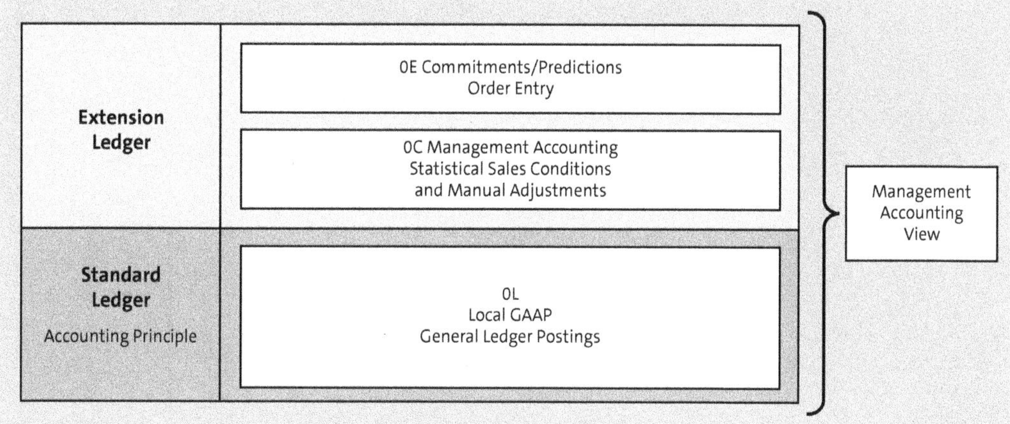


**Figure 1.5** Extension Ledger for Management Purposes

You can post management adjustments directly in the extension ledger with no update in a legal standard ledger as these postings are not relevant for legal reporting.

When you run a report for an extension ledger, the journal entries of the extension ledger and the underlying standard ledger are always displayed aggregated. So, when you run a report for ledger OE, you get a report with the commitments posted in ledger OE and the actuals as an aggregation of the management adjustments in ledger OE, plus all the journal entries posted in the legal ledger OL.

To include statistical sales conditions in a product profitability report, you need to start it with extension ledger OC; we'll walk through an example in Chapter 7, Section 7.1.

### 1.2.6 The Evolution of Controlling in SAP S/4HANA

In this section, we want to illustrate the evolution of controlling in SAP S/4HANA. The functional and architectural effects should be easy to understand based on the evolutionary steps. Our guiding principles are the simplification of the processes and the gain in transparency and analysis options.

As an example, let's consider the SAP S/4HANA implementation project at a company. In a first step, you post costs to the implementation project by time confirmation. Because the project is billable, you apply revenue recognition to get the matching realized revenue and the WIP/accrued revenue. The goal in this example is to have the results of the revenue recognition available in the general ledger and a margin on the project and the associated market segment (here the customer and the product, which is the SAP S/4HANA implementation) can be shown.

Now let's look at the processes that got us started: the SAP ERP functionality, as shown in Figure 1.6.

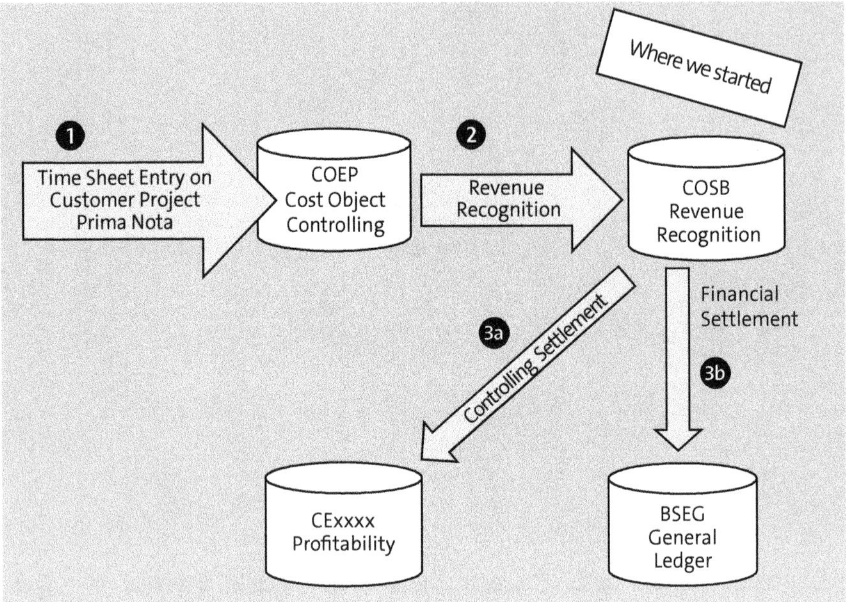


**Figure 1.6** Controlling Setup in SAP ERP

You can see that each process step has its own database per application, which meet different requirements. The time recording is initially only persisted in the controlling table, so the costs are visible for the project. At the end of the period, there is a results analysis run, which determines the matching revenue and the WIP. The result is stored in separate results analysis tables. Another periodic job is started: the settlement. It consists of two parts: the settlement to the general ledger, to update the balance sheet and income statement, and the settlement to costing-based profitability analysis to provide the costs and revenues for the market segments involved.

With this setup, you face the following challenges:

- The combined content of several tables represents the truth. Reconciliation efforts are enforced by design.
- There is a need for a periodic transfer of data (a settlement) to the appropriate table for reporting and subsequent processing. As a consequence, there is no current data in the different applications. You see data in the general ledger first at the period end.
- The structure divergency of the applications leads to deviating reporting entities. So, you have the general ledger account in the general ledger, the cost element in controlling, a special cost element in result analysis, and a value field in profitability. At the same time, there are different reporting capabilities and entities in the different applications. So the ledger as a reporting entity is only available in general ledger; there are deviating currencies in the different applications and availability of market segment attributes only in costing-based profitability analysis.

With the introduction of SAP S/4HANA, you get the general ledger, controlling, and margin analysis integrated in one database: a first simplification. Results analysis is still an application that the Universal Journal does not include. Thus, there is still a settlement required to update the other applications. Figure 1.7 provides our example with specific amounts.

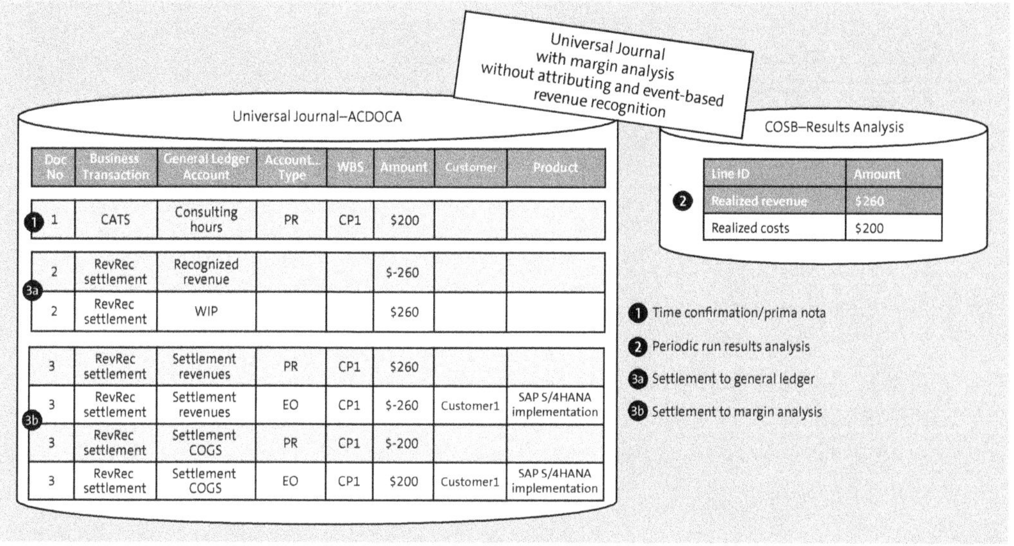


**Figure 1.7** First Steps with Introduction of Universal Journal

In step ❶, the time recording is now persisted in the Universal Journal and thus in the general ledger. The project reporting can be done based on Universal Journal. We still need the periodic runs. In step ❷, the result analysis still stores the realized revenue, matching it to the posted costs, and the WIP in separate results analysis tables.

The settlement now posts in the Universal Journal in step ❸. In step 3a, there is a settlement with document 2 to the general ledger, to update the balance sheet and income statement. In step 3b, you post document 3, which credits the project and debits the profitability segment. The first two lines settle the realized revenue; the next two line items settle the costs.

Margin analysis is now done in the Universal Journal. When you start a report for the SAP S/4HANA implementation project, you'll see two line items:

1. SAP S/4HANA implementation settlement revenue ($260)
2. SAP S/4HANA implementation settlement cost of goods sold ($200)

And with the aggregation, you get a margin of $60.

This is a first step to bringing the applications together and running them on one data model. But to further simplify, to provide data in real time and to improve the analysis capabilities, there are two additional features: event-based revenue recognition and attribution of the market segments.

Figure 1.8 shows how the preceding example is reflected in the system with the new cost management approach.

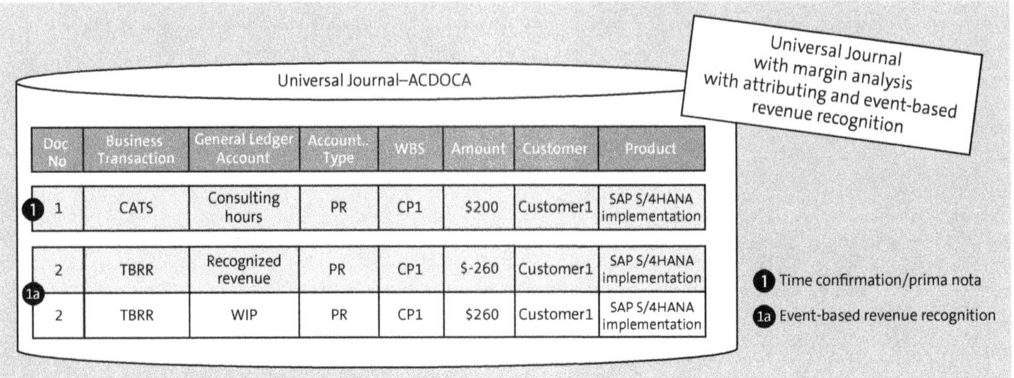


**Figure 1.8** New Cost Management Approach in SAP S/4HANA

This is a dramatic simplification. The event-based revenue recognition is triggered by the cost posting. This immediately posts the realized revenue and the WIP. The legal general ledger reporting is up to date with the cost entry.

You write the market segment on both the cost line and the revenue recognition lines. A further settlement to profitability is obsolete. Here too, you already have the market segment reporting available with the cost postings.

The leads to the following benefits:

- No reconciliation efforts between different tables required
- Real-time reporting provided for all applications
- Simplified period-end close (no settlement required any longer)
- Enhanced reporting insights:
  - Drilldown is available for general ledger accounts like WIP by project and market segment.
  - Margin reporting is done on the original postings and general ledger accounts. In our example, the cost of sales is determined by the consulting hours, and the revenue is determined by the realized revenue and not by settlement accounts anymore.

We'll discuss event-based revenue recognition, market segment attribution, and the new reporting insights in detail in Chapter 7.

Using this example, we want to draw your attention to another innovation: it's now possible to store several controlling objects on one journal entry item. So, depending on the business process, the system can enrich journal entry items and derive additional account assignment information. We make a distinction between the following:

- **The real account assignment**
  There can only be exactly one per line. It is identified by the **Account Assignment Type** field. For example, KS stands for cost center, OR stands for order, PR stands for project, and so on. Follow-up processes such as surcharges, revenue recognition, and settlement can only run on the real account assignment.
- **The attributed account assignments**
  These are only available for reporting purposes. There are no follow-up processes running on them. There can be several attributed controlling objects on one journal entry item.

In the example in this section, the posting on a customer project, the project is the real account assignment. You attribute the sales order item, to which the project is assigned, and the profitability segment, which you derive from the sales order information. We'll come back to this in Chapter 7. There are also some additional scenarios to consider:

- **Service order scenario**
  The real account assignment is the controlling object for service order items, new in SAP S/4HANA. You attribute the profitability segment based on information provided by the service order, like the customer and product sold. We cover this in Chapter 7.
- **Intercompany scenario**
  You credit the cost center in the supplying company, which is the real account assignment, and attribute the project of the receiver company. We cover this in Chapter 9, Section 9.2.

## 1.3 The New User Interface

Some user interfaces are already known from SAP ERP. SAP GUI, which has to be installed locally on the computer, is the classic user interface that is still available for SAP S/4HANA users. Another classic option is the web GUI, which is an easier and more flexible alternative to access the system. Here you only need a browser and the right URL to access the system with your user login. This access is also possible via mobile devices.

Figure 1.9 shows an example for SAP GUI. This is Transaction KB21N (Enter Direct Activity Allocation), which is included in the menus for the controlling applications under **Actual Posting**.

But with SAP Fiori launchpad, SAP S/4HANA now enables a completely new user experience. This replaces the traditional transaction codes of SAP GUI with a web-based user interface. With SAP Fiori, SAP has created a user interface that is significantly more convenient and user-friendly than the previous design. It can be used on an office computer, but also on the road, and even with various mobile devices—from smartphones to tablets. SAP Fiori launchpad is the entry point through which every user accesses his or her SAP Fiori apps. SAP Fiori can be personalized and enables role-based access: the right information is available to every user at the right time via different user interfaces. SAP Fiori applications provide a holistic view and facilitate integration between different applications. For example, in some apps, views of different applications are provided, or links are available for jumping into another application.

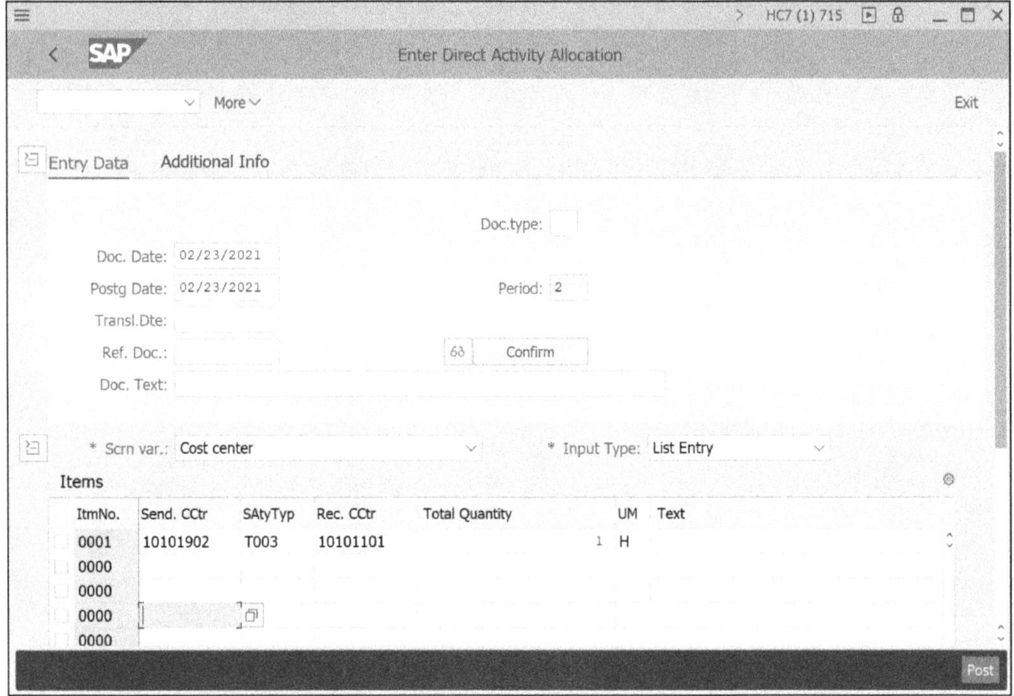


Figure 1.9 Activity Allocation via SAP GUI Application

Let's briefly outline the important elements here.

**SAP GUI versus SAP Fiori**

Within this book, we'll provide instructions for SAP GUI, but also, when available, for SAP Fiori applications. In the latter case, we'll refer to the SAP Fiori ID to help you to implement the SAP Fiori applications that you need. Also, we'll reference the transaction code that will give you access via SAP GUI and tips so that you can follow along, no matter your user interface.

You access SAP Fiori launchpad via your browser and the system URL, as shown in Figure 1.10.

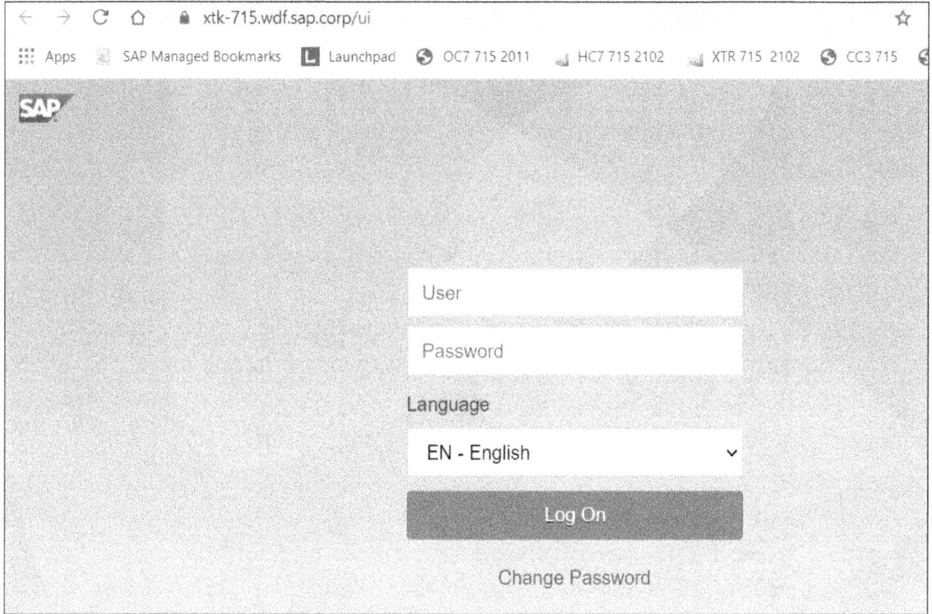


Figure 1.10 Accessing SAP Fiori via Browser

After logging in, you're immediately greeted by your home page, as shown in Figure 1.11.

Figure 1.11 SAP Fiori Launchpad Homepage

SAP Fiori is role-based. Each user is assigned to roles—for example, an overhead accountant role. The apps are linked to the roles. A user has access to all apps that are assigned to his or her assigned roles. The home page can be personalized on the basis of these apps.

Four roles are relevant for controlling:

- **Cost accountant—overhead** (SAP_BR_OVERHEAD_ACCOUNTANT)
  We'll show many of the applications delivered for this role in Chapter 2 and Chapter 5, including those for managing budgets and predictions, reassigning costs and revenues, and managing allocations. We'll also discuss their limits when using transactions carried over from SAP ERP to show the target costs and variances on the various cost centers, because an equivalent SAP Fiori application is not yet available.
- **Cost accountant—inventory** (SAP_BR_INVENTORY_ACCOUNTANT)
  We'll show the applications to manage inventory valuation in Chapter 6, when we explain how prices are stored in the material master and how to calculate standard costs. Again, we'll continue to use legacy applications from SAP ERP to view the various cost estimates and to view the results of the costing run for both the standard costs and the actual costs.
- **Cost accountant—production** (SAP_BR_PRODN_ACCOUNTANT)
  Chapter 6 also includes the new applications for managing the costs on production orders and work centers and for managing the calculation of WIP and variances, but uses the classic transactions to display detailed variances on the production orders and product cost collectors.
- **Cost accountant—sales** (SAP_BR_SALES_ACCOUNTANT)
  We'll show many of the applications delivered for this role in Chapter 7, including those for margin analysis, event-based revenue recognition, and the analysis of project profitability.

In on-premise SAP S/4HANA, these roles act as a delivery mechanism to structure the various SAP Fiori applications, but you can copy them and adjust them to meet the needs of your own controllers as you see fit. In SAP S/4HANA Cloud, roles are the only way to access the various applications, and each role is delivered with the required set of authorizations.

The apps are grouped by topic. You can jump to a topic by selecting a tab in the header or by selecting the down arrow. There is also a user action menu available. You can access it by clicking the icon or photo on the right-hand side of the shell bar, as shown in Figure 1.12.

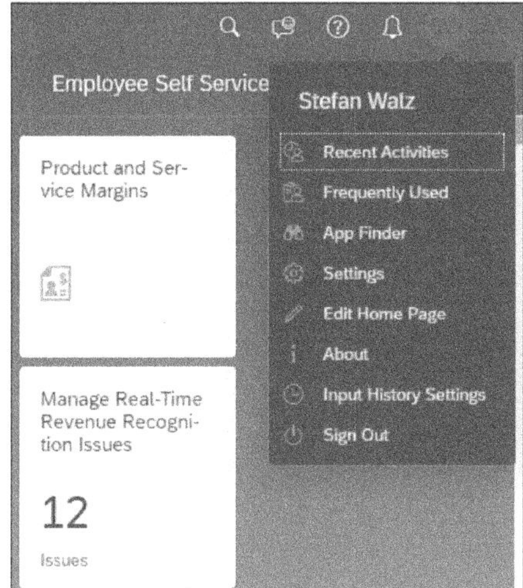


**Figure 1.12** User Action Menu

Here you can personalize your launchpad in the following ways:

- **Settings**
  Here you'll find general settings and preferences, like appearance or default values for elements such as company code or cost center.
- **App Finder**
  You can switch to available apps via the **App Finder**.
- **Frequently Used**
  Here you'll see objects and apps that you've recently visited or used.
- **About**
  This dialog contains details about the SAP Fiori launchpad or app version.
- **Sign Out**
  Select the **Sign Out** option to log off the SAP Fiori launchpad.
- **Edit Home Page**
  Here you can jump to the maintenance of the launchpad home page to personalize its content.

On the shell bar, you can click the magnifying glass icon and then type in the **Search** field, as shown in Figure 1.13. The enterprise search function searches across all apps and business objects. You can narrow the results by different filters, like employee, cost center, or activity type.

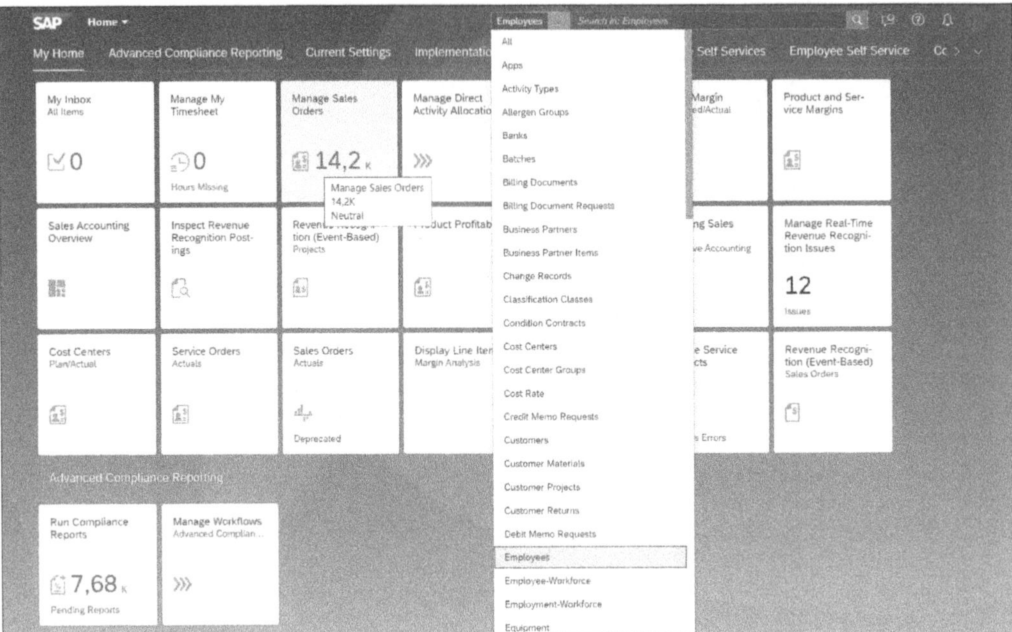


**Figure 1.13** Enterprise Search

Within the apps, context-sensitive jumps to other apps are possible. For example, you can mark individual lines in the product and service margin report in Figure 1.14. With the parameter defined this way, it's possible to jump to an extended line item view or to customer master data, or you can also trigger follow-up activities, such as the maintenance of open posting periods.

**Figure 1.14** App to App Integration

Within the applications themselves, the SAP Fiori user experience provides appealing new graphical representations, like in the Incoming Sales Orders app, shown in Figure 1.15.

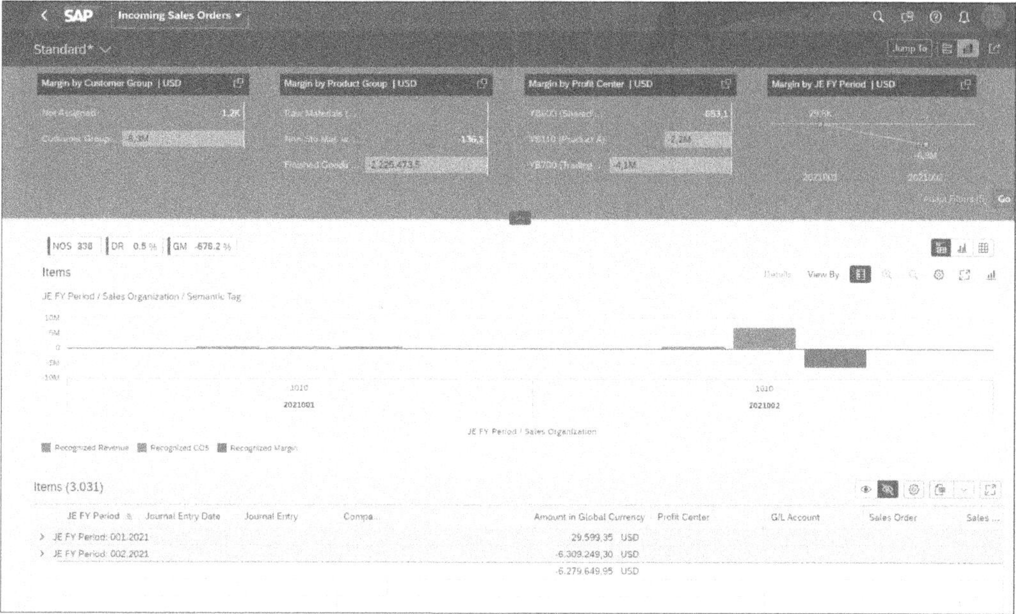


**Figure 1.15** Incoming Sales Orders App

In addition to the visualized KPIs, the bottom area shows the basis for the same: the posted line items from the Universal Journal. We'll discuss this further in Chapter 7.

With the SAP Fiori apps reference library, you get an overview of the existing apps, their key features, and their role assignments. The number of apps is constantly growing and available for many purposes and applications. You can access the library at *http://s-prs.co/v528200*. This site provides details of every SAP Fiori application from business and implementation points of view. When we introduce an SAP Fiori app in this book, we will provide the SAP Fiori ID to help you to access the relevant information in the library.

## 1.4 Summary

We hope that this chapter has given you a first impression of the innovations of SAP S/4HANA, and the new controlling options in particular. We touched on the various deployment options, innovations made possible by the Universal Journal, and the new SAP Fiori user interface.

There has been a paradigm shift for controlling in SAP S/4HANA. SAP's goal is to dramatically simplify processes, shorten the period-end closing, and provide real-time evaluations and new, advanced analysis options. These goals will accompany us on our journey through the next chapters.

Next, we'll give you a first insight into controlling in SAP S/4HANA.

# Chapter 2
# Controlling in SAP S/4HANA



*In this chapter, we'll explain how the key processes in controlling run from an end-to-end perspective and give examples of both new SAP Fiori applications and classic SAP GUI transactions when the transition to the new user interfaces isn't yet complete. We'll outline how controllers can implement a system of management reporting and support their businesses so they can make the right decisions.*

In the previous chapter, we introduced the Universal Journal as the key change of a move to SAP S/4HANA and explained how it delivers a single data model for finance and the single source of truth for all your reporting needs. The general ledger, management accounting, margin analysis, and profit center accounting are the various elements that are combined in the Universal Journal. In this chapter, we'll focus on controlling in SAP S/4HANA and explain the new data model and the merge of financial and management accounting in more detail. We'll use the Trial Balance app to explore the differences between those business transactions, such as invoices, goods movements, payroll postings, and so on, that originate as business transactions in financial accounting but are assigned to cost centers, orders, projects, and so on for the purposes of management accounting, as well as those business transactions, such as allocations, order and project settlements, overhead calculation, revenue recognition, and so on, that originate in management accounting but impact financial accounting.

If you work as a controller, you'll know that the job of controlling goes beyond simply collecting transactional data and involves putting this data into perspective in order to steer the business. This means setting up plans for the various units and goals for all stakeholders, including the cost center managers and project managers responsible for remaining within an established budget and authorizing spending by their team members, the commercial managers responsible for setting goals in terms of revenues and volumes, and, depending on the industry, the plant managers responsible for the associated production costs and the service managers responsible for the associated costs to serve.

One of the key differences between management accounting and financial accounting is that financial accounting records the information needed for external reporting, which can mean that the business transactions are recorded late in the process, when goods and invoices are received. Management accounting captures financial data for these business transactions earlier to deliver predictions, in terms of the anticipated margins for the sales orders received or the costs associated with any outstanding purchase orders. This is needed because there is often a time lag between placing a purchase order and receiving the goods and the predicted costs must be recorded as a *commitment* that reduces budget even though the goods have yet to be received. Similarly, it may not be feasible to fulfil a sales order on the day that it is received but the revenues and associated costs can be predicted to give an idea of the associated business impact. However, it's important to separate these predictions from the journal entries that are reported externally. This is achieved by storing them in a separate ledger and gradually reducing the predicted values as the various business transactions are fulfilled.

In this chapter, we'll revisit some of the concepts discussed in the previous chapter in terms of management accounting and margin analysis in Section 2.1. In Section 2.2, we'll look at the role of planning in setting targets for controlling, and in Section 2.3 we'll look at the role of predictive accounting in anticipating the impact of future business. In Section 2.4, we'll introduce the daily work of the controller in the various areas. Finally, in we'll end the chapter with Section 2.5 on reporting and analytics because this is where controllers are likely to spend the lion's share of their time, explaining variances and adjusting plans as business situations change.

We'll revisit many of these topics with detailed instructions on how to set up master data and perform the various tasks mentioned in the chapters that follow, but for now the focus is on the big picture and what you can expect from controlling in SAP S/4HANA.

## 2.1 The Merge of Financial and Management Accounting

In Chapter 1, we looked at how the various reporting entities are brought together in the Universal Journal to support the goals of multidimensional reporting. Now, in this section, we'll expand that knowledge and look at various types of journal entries within this single source of truth. In financial accounting, you typically select journal entries from the Universal Journal by company code (a high level of aggregation). Management accounting is typically more granular; you select journal entries by cost center, order, project, or market segment. The underlying data is the same, but in financial accounting you're seeing the salary costs for a legal entity, while in management accounting you're seeing the same salary costs for each cost center within that legal entity. Profit center accounting sits between the two, providing aggregated management information about the costs collected on the cost centers, orders, projects, and so on, and often crossing company codes to deliver a management view of the performance of various business units or divisions within the larger organization. We'll explore these organizational structures in more detail in Chapter 3.

The *general ledger account* is the common element for financial accounting, management accounting, and profit center accounting, structuring the company's business transactions to reflect the type of transaction: accounts payable, accounts receivable, assets, inventory, cash, salaries, benefits, travel expenses, and so on. Financial accounting has traditionally distinguished between *balance sheet accounts*, such as accounts payable, accounts receivable, assets, inventory, and cash, and *profit and loss* (P&L) *accounts*, such as revenues, costs, and expenses. As their name implies, balance sheet accounts deliver the balance for each of the key elements at year end. The P&L accounts, by contrast, reflect the costs and revenues in a period.

Now, let's take a closer look at journal entries for both primary costs and revenues and secondary costs.

**SAP GUI versus SAP Fiori**

In this chapter, we mostly use SAP Fiori applications to illustrate the various journal entries because accountants will be familiar with the idea of representing journal entries as T-accounts from their studies. There aren't equivalent SAP GUI transactions, but if your organization has yet to implement SAP Fiori, simply imagine the debits and credits in the T-account as separate posting lines. We also show several views of the Trial Balance app, which is an accounting rather than a controlling app, but we wanted to show how the internal and external world come together in SAP S/4HANA. We'll also use SAP Analytics Cloud to show the planning process. Again, your organization may not yet have made the move, so we'll provide the equivalent classic planning transactions. When it comes to target costs and cost center variances, we don't yet have equivalent SAP Fiori applications, so we show the classic transactions.

### 2.1.1 Journal Entries for Primary Costs and Revenues

To get a sense of the basic logic in financial accounting, we'll look at some simple journal entries and then explain how these are extended to include the reporting dimensions needed for management accounting. We'll see how journal entries for primary cost and revenues are displayed, and how account assignments are linked to primary costs and revenues.

#### Display Journal Entries

Figure 2.1 shows the Display Journal Entries—In T-Account View app (SAP Fiori ID F3664) and a journal entry with items for domestic receivables (accounts receivable in the balance sheet) and revenue from domestic products (revenues in the P&L statement). With SAP S/4HANA, there is no change to the journal entry item for the receivables, which continues to represent the open item to be collected from the customer who has been invoiced. The change (unless you were already using account-based profitability analysis in SAP ERP) is to the journal entry item for the revenue because the revenue assigned to this account can now be assigned to the market segment for the customer who placed the sales order, together with the product or service billed, the region, the sales office, and so on. We essentially have the basis for margin analysis in the account assignment associated with the posting line in the P&L account.

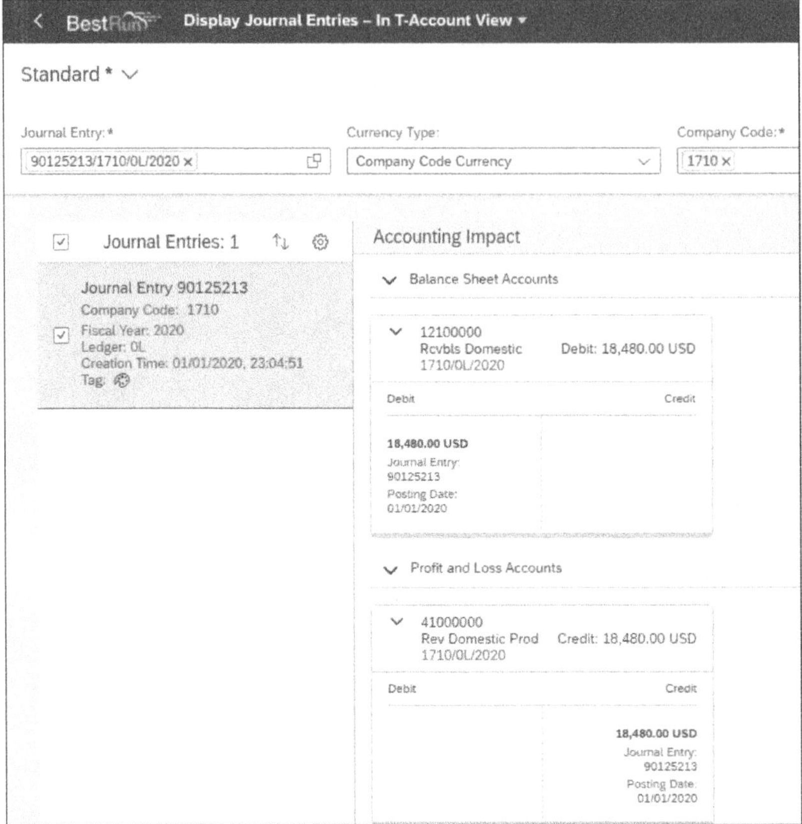


**Figure 2.1** Display Journal Entries—In T-Account View App for Revenue Posting

**Note**

For nonaccountants, a *T-account* is a graphical way of representing double-entry bookkeeping using a T-shape for each account. The account title appears above the T-shape, and debit postings are shown on the left and credit postings on the right (British accountants "drive" on the left and "crash" on the right). The debits and credits will always total to zero to balance the posting lines in any given document.

In this example, we're looking at a single posting line, but in a real invoice, we would typically go from having one line for the revenues in the legal entity in financial accounting to hundreds of lines for each product sold in management accounting. In SAP S/4HANA, we have hundreds of posting lines and users selecting from these lines with a different focus. For example, the general ledger accountant selects from these lines using the legal entity when looking at the financial statements, while the sales accountant selects from these using the product sold when looking at product profitability, and the division accountant selects using the profit center when looking at the financial statement for a division.

We can imagine the same journal entry in reverse, with an open item to the clearing account for the goods receipt and invoice receipt on the balance sheet side (accounts payable) and a raw material consumption on the P&L side (raw material consumption). Again, the change would be the assignment of the raw material consumption to the cost center, order, or project in a single document rather than a separate document in cost center accounting. The account type for these postings will force the assignment of an account assignment, such as a cost center, order, or market segment. Of course, you might also have P&L accounts that shouldn't be assigned to an account assignment, so there is a separate account type for gains or losses on the foreign exchange market that have no connection with the internal business of the organization but obviously belong in the company's financial statements. We'll explore the account types in more detail in Chapter 4.

Figure 2.2 shows a journal entry for the procurement of office supplies to a cost center, again in the form of T-accounts.

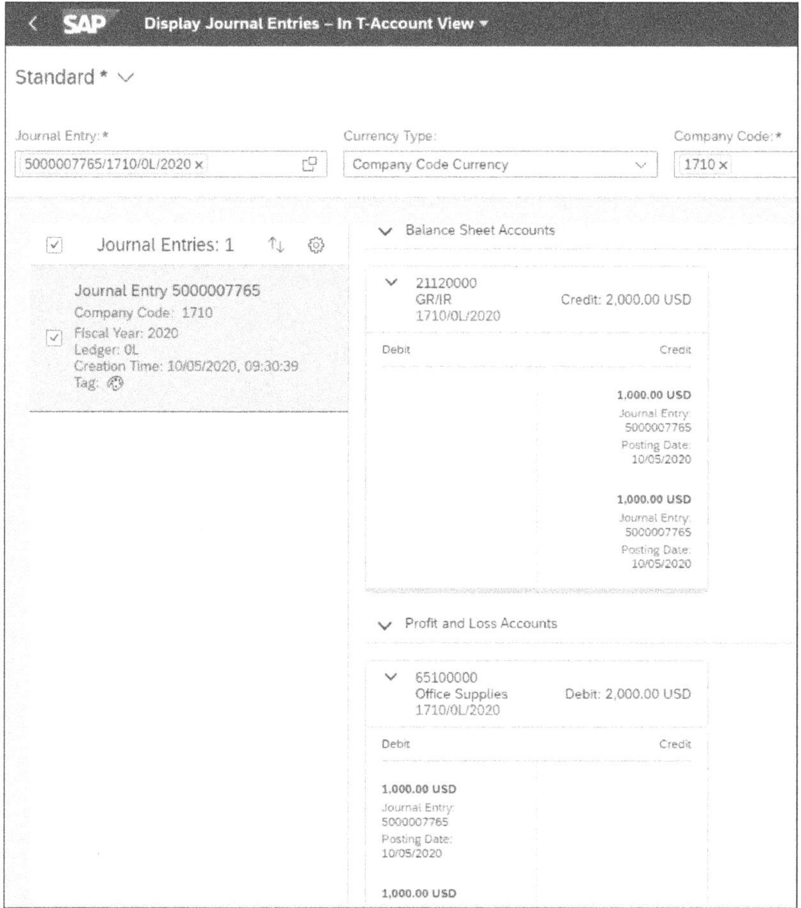


**Figure 2.2** Display Journal Entries—In T-Account View App for Purchase of Office Supplies

In SAP S/4HANA, you can select the relevant journal entry and view the details of the cost center (**Cost Center 17101101**) for which the supplies have been procured, plus the associated profit center (**Profit Center YB600**) and segment (**Segment 1000_C**), as shown in the Manage Journal Entries app in Figure 2.3.

**SAP ERP versus SAP S/4HANA**

In SAP ERP, the link between financial accounting and management accounting for the raw material costs was made using a *primary cost element* that was only available in management accounting. Just as we saw for the invoice on the revenue side, the granularity of the line items was often different, with the postings to financial accounting being highly aggregated, whereas the postings to management accounting were typically more granular. Now, we have one document, but the general ledger accountant sees the raw material costs per legal entity, the overhead accountant and cost center manager see these costs by cost center, and the divisional accountant sees the costs for the assigned profit center.

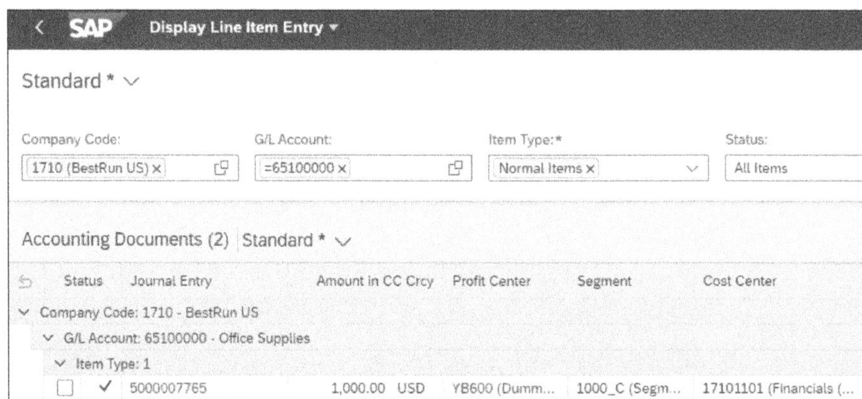


**Figure 2.3** Manage Journal Entries App, Showing Assignment to Cost Center, Profit Center, and Segment

### Account Assignments

While exploring, the general ledger accounts will help you to understand the financial statements from an external point of view; however, the purpose of management accounting is to understand how these revenues and costs are impacted from an internal point of view and to provide the information needed to steer the business. To do this, we switch from *accounting* to a related term, *accountability*. To put an efficient controlling system in place, it's not simply a question of classifying business transactions (accounting) but also of relating these transactions to the needs of the business (accountability). It's the controller's task to ensure the accountability of the relevant managers for their spending on each cost center, order, or project and to ensure their commercial success by providing and selling profitable products and services.

The *general ledger account* classifies business transactions as wages and salaries (to record the costs associated with your workforce), materials and services (to record the costs associated with the goods you buy and sell), depreciation (for recording the costs associated with your assets), and utility costs (to record the costs of energy, water, and so on), but this does not provide the whole story. To drive accountability, we must link the account with the *account assignment*: the cost center, order, or project for which these costs are incurred. With this combination of the account (e.g., consumption of raw materials) and the account assignment (e.g., the purchasing cost center), we are holding the manager of the purchasing cost center accountable for all these expenses (you'll sometimes hear this idea referred to as *cost stewardship*).

To give a sense of how the worlds of financial accounting and management accounting merge, we'll look at the Trial Balance app (SAP Fiori ID F0956A), shown in Figure 2.4. In this initial view, we're focusing on the account structure and the opening balance for each account, but what's special about the Trial Balance app in SAP S/4HANA compared to the view in SAP ERP is the number of drilldown options that allow you to explore the account assignments and the assigned profit centers, functional areas, and so on.

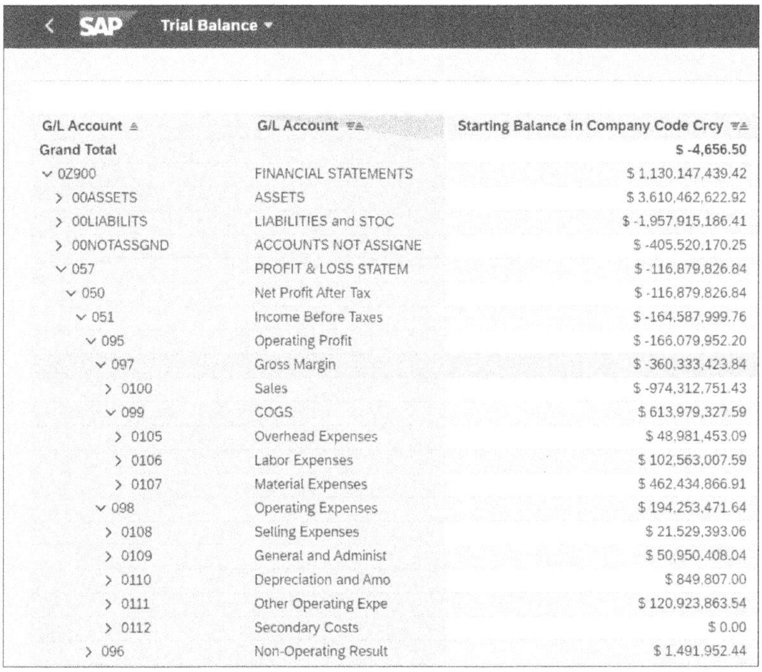

< SAP Trial Balance ▾

| G/L Account | G/L Account | Starting Balance in Company Code Crcy |
|---|---|---|
| Grand Total | | $ -4,656.50 |
| ˅ 0Z900 | FINANCIAL STATEMENTS | $ 1,130,147,439.42 |
| › 00ASSETS | ASSETS | $ 3,610,462,622.92 |
| › 00LIABILITS | LIABILITIES and STOC | $ -1,957,915,186.41 |
| › 00NOTASSGND | ACCOUNTS NOT ASSIGNE | $ -405,520,170.25 |
| ˅ 057 | PROFIT & LOSS STATEM | $ -116,879,826.84 |
| ˅ 050 | Net Profit After Tax | $ -116,879,826.84 |
| ˅ 051 | Income Before Taxes | $ -164,587,999.76 |
| ˅ 095 | Operating Profit | $ -166,079,952.20 |
| ˅ 097 | Gross Margin | $ -360,333,423.84 |
| › 0100 | Sales | $ -974,312,751.43 |
| ˅ 099 | COGS | $ 613,979,327.59 |
| › 0105 | Overhead Expenses | $ 48,981,453.09 |
| › 0106 | Labor Expenses | $ 102,563,007.59 |
| › 0107 | Material Expenses | $ 462,434,866.91 |
| ˅ 098 | Operating Expenses | $ 194,253,471.64 |
| › 0108 | Selling Expenses | $ 21,529,393.06 |
| › 0109 | General and Administ | $ 50,950,408.04 |
| › 0110 | Depreciation and Amo | $ 849,807.00 |
| › 0111 | Other Operating Expe | $ 120,923,863.54 |
| › 0112 | Secondary Costs | $ 0.00 |
| › 096 | Non-Operating Result | $ 1,491,952.44 |

**Figure 2.4** Trial Balance App Showing P&L Accounts

In Figure 2.5, we've added the **Cost Center** to the drilldown for the rows and selected **Cost Center 17101201**. What you now see are the general ledger accounts associated with the cost center (consumption of raw materials, consumption of trading goods, and so on). The idea of accountability is important in the sense that the selected cost center is not just an anonymous pool of costs, but an entity for which one person is responsible.

The purchasing cost center has a manager who is responsible for all the journal entries, the spend, being assigned to that cost center. Accounting is effectively being used to drive accountability; we'll see in the sections that follow how to plan for these expenses and monitor the effect of purchase costs that have yet to show in the financial statements.

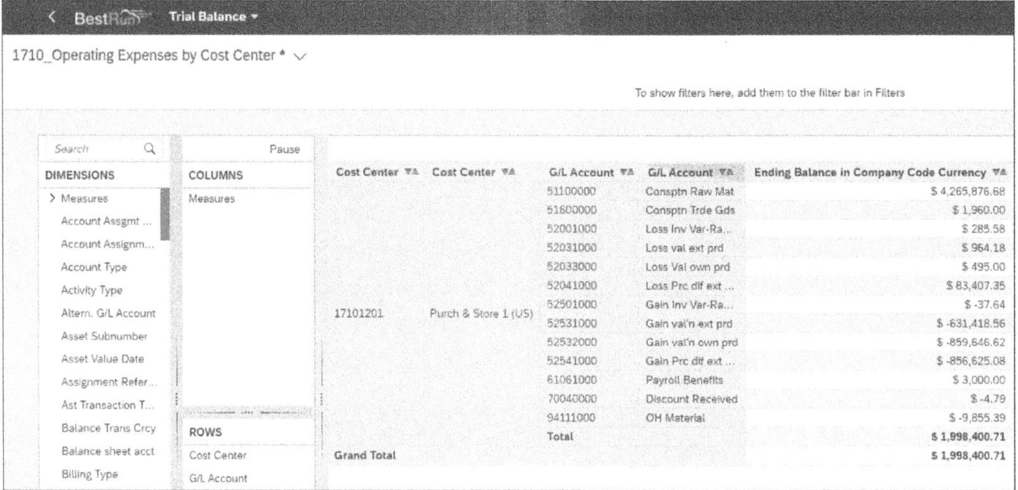


**Figure 2.5** Trial Balance App Showing Accounts Linked with Purchasing Cost Center

For many cost centers, the management tasks go beyond simply monitoring spending, and they make each manager responsible for the cost of the resources used by the cost center (assets, people, and so on) in order to perform the activities that the cost center provides. In Figure 2.6, we've added the **Object Type KL** to the drilldown for the rows in order to select those cost centers that are providing activities either to other cost centers or to orders and projects. Notice that the cost center can supply a single activity, as is the case for the consulting cost center for unit B, or several activities, as shown for the production cost centers and the consulting cost center for unit A. This view represents the cost flow through the organization via activity usage: there is a *supply* of activity from the sending cost centers and a *demand* for activity from the projects or orders to be supported. It's the controller's job to ensure that a workable structure is in place that supports the reporting needs of each cost center manager and the receiving managers, but also rolls up to support the business needs of corporate reporting when activity flows cross organizational boundaries. We'll explain the role of the cost centers in more detail when we look at the associated master data in Chapter 4.

Of course, the idea of accountability in SAP S/4HANA does not just refer to spending. The controller will also work with a network of commercial managers who are responsible for the revenues and costs for various market segments. These might be products and product groups, customers and customer groups, regions, and so on, depending on how you have chosen to set up the operating concern for margin analysis.

Figure 2.6 Trial Balance App Showing Activities Provided by Cost Center

Figure 2.7 shows the same Trial Balance app with a drilldown by the various elements that make up the market segments for a sample bicycle company. We are now looking at the revenues and costs of goods sold assigned to the **Customer** (**Performance Bikes**), the **Segments** (**RACING**, **MOUNTAIN**, and so on), and the **Products** (**MZ-FG-R100**, **MZ-FG-R200**, and **MZ-FG-R300**). We'll explore the master data used for margin analysis in more detail in Chapter 7.

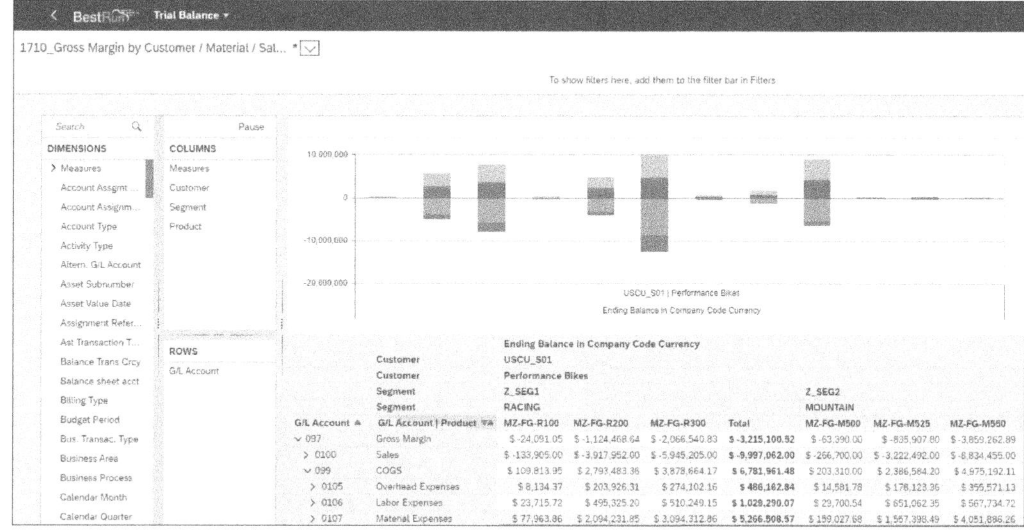


Figure 2.7 Trial Balance App Showing Accounts Linked with Customers, Segments, and Products

When you look more closely at Figure 2.7, you can see that the market segments are assigned not just to the revenues resulting from billing (the topic shown previously in Figure 2.1) but also to the *cost of goods sold* resulting from the delivery of the goods. For a trading good in a retail environment, the costs of goods sold are usually derived from the purchase price. In the case of a product that has been manufactured in house, the costs of goods sold are more complex.

The value flow can be illustrated as shown in Figure 2.8. It begins with the acquisition of raw materials by the procurement department. These goods are delivered to inventory (and held on the balance sheet) and then issued to production. When the production order is complete, the finished goods are delivered to inventory (and again held on the balance sheet) before being issued to the sales order for delivery to the final customer. We'll look at the process of calculating the costs of goods manufactured in detail in Chapter 6. There can be many steps in the manufacturing process and several semifinished goods delivered to inventory and issued to production, but for now, it's enough to understand that the cost of goods manufactured comprise the cost of the raw materials issued to the production order and the costs of the activities to convert these raw materials into a finished product. These costs are assigned to *cost components* (material costs, internal activities, overhead, and so on) to explain the various resources used in manufacture. This assignment to cost components drives the general ledger accounts that explain the cost of goods sold in SAP S/4HANA.

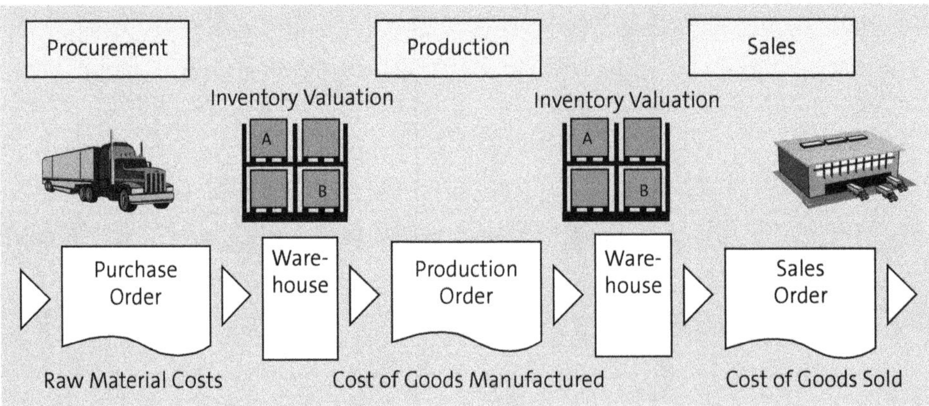


**Figure 2.8** Value Flows in Manufacturing Environment

The cost of goods sold account that we showed in Figure 2.7 is associated with the market segment at the time of delivery. The total costs of goods sold are then broken down by cost component. Figure 2.9 shows the breakdown of the total cost of goods sold, with separate cost of goods sold accounts for each of the cost components (direct materials, material overhead, personnel time, production overhead, setup time, machine time, and so on).

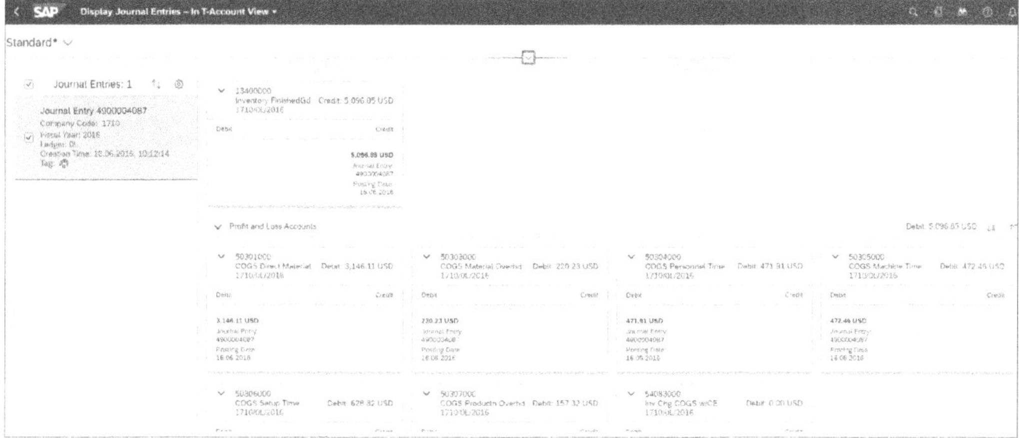

**Figure 2.9** Journal Entry for Cost of Goods Sold, Showing Cost of Goods Sold Accounts for Various Cost Elements

**SAP ERP versus SAP S/4HANA**

In SAP ERP, one of the fundamental differences between account-based and costing-based profitability analysis was the ability to separate out the cost of goods sold. In account-based profitability analysis, the costs of goods sold were assigned to a single account. In costing-based profitability analysis, the cost components could be assigned to separate value fields to provide a more detailed view. In SAP S/4HANA, the cost of goods sold can be assigned to separate accounts, as shown in Figure 2.9.

The timing of the cost recognition is also different on account of the time gap between the shipping of the goods and the billing. In SAP ERP, the goods issue to the customer was recorded in financial accounting at the time of delivery, and the costs of goods sold were included in the costing-based profitability analysis document at the time of invoicing, with many organizations recording the difference on a shipped but not billed account. In SAP S/4HANA, there are two documents. The delivery document at the time of shipping assigns the cost of goods sold to the market segment, and the invoice document at the time of billing assigns the revenue to the market segment. We'll look at the topic of revenue recognition in more detail in Chapter 7.

We've looked so far at how to link revenues and primary costs with account assignments in controlling. If you refer now to Figure 2.10, you'll see the business transactions (payroll, travel, asset accounting, procurement, materials management, sales and distribution, billing, and so on) that result in cost and revenue postings. Each of these business transactions is associated first with an account, so there are payroll accounts, travel accounts, and so on in varying degrees of detail. These accounts are then linked with an *account assignment*: payroll and travel expenses are linked with a cost center, material consumption with production orders, and revenues with market segments (the multidimensional cube at the bottom).

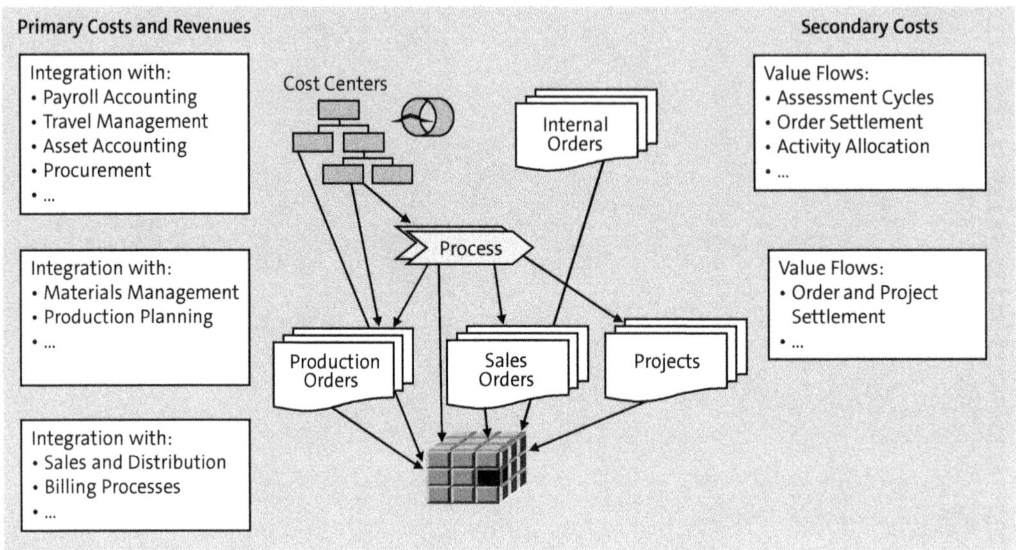


**Figure 2.10** Value Flows in Controlling

### 2.1.2 Journal Entries for Secondary Costs

As we showed previously in Figure 2.6, this initial assignment to an account assignment is not the whole story; controlling also involves building up a charge model to move the costs captured as primary costs to other objects in controlling. The right side of Figure 2.10 shows how costs flow using assessment cycles, order settlements, or activity allocation, and so on. The costs captured on the left flow by means of these mechanisms from the cost centers to the production orders, from the internal orders to the market segments, or from the cost centers to the market segments. There are many potential flows, as indicated by the number of different arrows.

A distinction is often made between *costs by nature* (wages, salaries, depreciation, operating supplies, and so on), which indicate the type of spending, and *costs by function* (marketing, sales, production, and so on), which indicate where the spend occurred and, more importantly, pass this classification on, as the various value flows shown in Figure 2.10 are recorded. So, you might see wage costs (cost by nature) being assigned to the sales cost center (sales function) and then allocated to the market segment bicycle sales to reflect the costs associated with selling the bicycles. Those wage costs might pass through several functions before finally being part of the cost of goods sold or a capital expense item. We'll explore the impact of these flows in more detail when we look at the impact of the various organizational structures in Chapter 3.

From the perspective of management accounting, costs can be transferred using a simple allocation, in which electricity or other utility costs are captured for a single cost center when the utility company sends its invoice and then assigned to other cost centers by means of an allocation, based on the relative amount of energy used or the relative headcount. The same mechanism can be used to transfer the costs incurred by the sales cost center to the market segments using an allocation based on the relative volume of goods sold in each segment. In both cases, this allocation will be stored under a *secondary cost element* for utility usage or sales costs. In SAP S/4HANA, you'll find a general ledger account for each of these secondary cost elements, meaning that the flow can be shown in T-account form, just like a journal entry that originates in financial accounting. If you compare the figures in Figure 2.11 with those shown previously in Figure 2.1 and Figure 2.2, you'll see that the credits for the sender (the cost centers in this example) will always net to zero with the debits for the receiver (the receiving cost centers or market segments in this example).

Profit and Loss Accounts
Debit: 0.00 USD

94220000
COPA Assessment
1710/0L/2020
Credit: 0.00 USD

| 94222000 COPA assessments-Mar 1710/0L/2020 Debit: 0.00 USD | | 94223000 COPA assessments-R&D 1710/0L/2020 Debit: 0.00 USD | | 94224000 COPA assessments-Adm 1710/0L/2020 Credit: 0.00 USD | |
|---|---|---|---|---|---|
| Debit | Credit | Debit | Credit | Debit | Credit |
| 131,889.80 USD Journal Entry: 2300001812 Posting Date: 01/31/2020 | 131,889.80 USD Journal Entry: 2300001812 Posting Date: 01/31/2020 | 351,123.10 USD Journal Entry: 2300001812 Posting Date: 01/31/2020 | 351,123.10 USD Journal Entry: 2300001812 Posting Date: 01/31/2020 | 116,004.73 USD Journal Entry: 2300001812 Posting Date: 01/31/2020 | 116,004.73 USD Journal Entry: 2300001812 Posting Date: 01/31/2020 |
| 293,155.44 USD Journal Entry: 2300001812 Posting Date: 01/31/2020 | 293,155.44 USD Journal Entry: 2300001812 Posting Date: 01/31/2020 | 780,451.93 USD Journal Entry: 2300001812 Posting Date: 01/31/2020 | 780,451.93 USD Journal Entry: 2300001812 Posting Date: 01/31/2020 | 257,847.22 USD Journal Entry: 2300001812 Posting Date: 01/31/2020 | 257,847.22 USD Journal Entry: 2300001812 Posting Date: 01/31/2020 |
| 269,465.24 USD Journal Entry: 2300001812 Posting Date: 01/31/2020 | 269,465.24 USD Journal Entry: 2300001812 Posting Date: 01/31/2020 | 717,382.79 USD Journal Entry: 2300001812 Posting Date: 01/31/2020 | 717,382.79 USD Journal Entry: 2300001812 Posting Date: 01/31/2020 | 237,010.32 USD Journal Entry: 2300001812 Posting Date: 01/31/2020 | 237,010.32 USD Journal Entry: 2300001812 Posting Date: 01/31/2020 |
| 166,951.28 USD Journal Entry: 2300001812 Posting Date: 01/31/2020 | 166,951.28 USD Journal Entry: 2300001812 Posting Date: 01/31/2020 | 444,465.41 USD Journal Entry: 2300001812 Posting Date: 01/31/2020 | 444,465.41 USD Journal Entry: 2300001812 Posting Date: 01/31/2020 | 146,843.35 USD Journal Entry: 2300001812 Posting Date: 01/31/2020 | 146,843.35 USD Journal Entry: 2300001812 Posting Date: 01/31/2020 |

**Figure 2.11** Display Journal Entries—In T-Account View App for Allocation Posting

If you now look at the Trial Balance app shown in Figure 2.12, you'll see that the credits to the senders and the debits to the receivers balance one another out and that the **Grand Total** for the secondary cost elements is always zero from an accounting perspective.

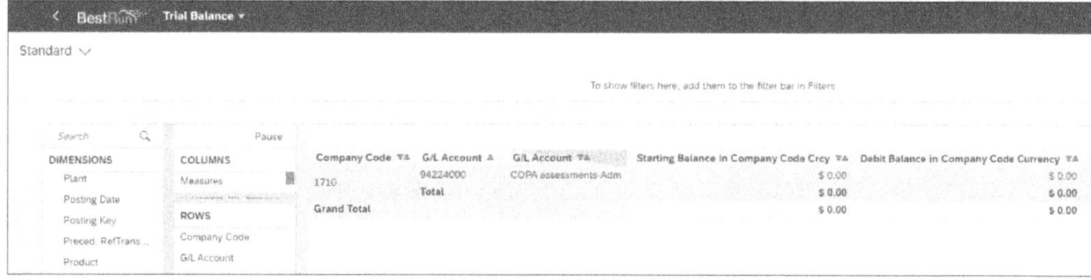


**Figure 2.12** Trial Balance App Showing How Values on Secondary Cost Element Net to Zero

This zeroing out of the senders and receivers leads to the fallacy that secondary cost elements are only visible in management accounting. With SAP S/4HANA, the secondary cost elements are also accounts, and the shift from sender to receiver can result in a change to the functional area, a change in the profit center, and sometimes even an intercompany posting. You can see this easily in Figure 2.13, in which you're looking at the same journal entries as in Figure 2.12, but we've selected **Profit Center** and **Partner Profit Center** to show how the costs have flowed between the various profit centers as a result of the allocation. The grand total continues to be zero, but you can see how the costs have flowed from profit center to partner profit center. You could perform the same drilldown for **Functional Area** and **Partner Functional Area** or indeed between any of the sender and receiver objects shown in the list of dimensions on the left. We'll explain the use of profit centers and functional areas in more detail in Chapter 3.

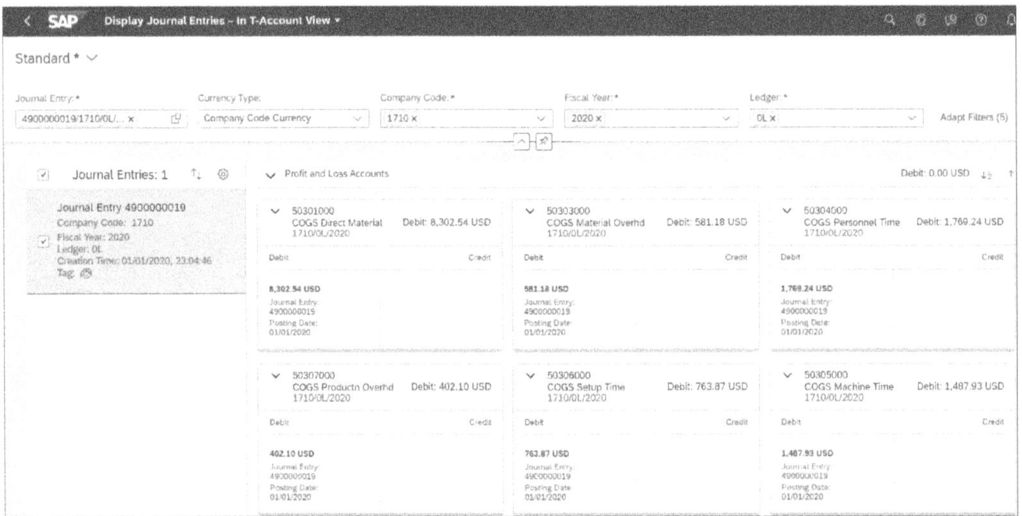

**Figure 2.13** Trial Balance App for Secondary Cost Element Showing Impact of Allocation on Profit Centers and Partner Profit Centers

In many cases, it's possible to go beyond such simple allocations in which all costs are passed from the sender to the receiver, moving to an allocation based on *usage*. In the case of a production cost center, we have a cost center that receives depreciation costs, payroll costs, operating supplies, and so on (the *input*) and provides machine time to the factory (the *output*). It was the cost flow associated with this output that you saw in Figure 2.6. In the case of a consulting cost center, we have a department that receives payroll costs, utility costs, and so on, and provides consulting hours to external clients. In both cases, the output of the cost center is represented as an *activity type*: machine time for the manufacturing plant or consulting hours for the consulting house. What's important is that usage of this activity is measurable. We'll look at the master data for the activity types in more detail in Chapter 4.

The activity allocations are triggered by order confirmations or backflushing on the shop floor in the case of the production cost center and time recording for the consulting work in the case of the consulting department. There is again an allocation that credits the sender cost center and debits the receiving order or project, but because the allocation is based on usage, you'll often find that not all costs are passed from the sender to the receiver at period close as the capacity of the cost center may have been under or overutilized. We'll look at this idea in more detail in Section 2.4.1.

In SAP ERP, it often felt like the task of management accounting was all about allocation. Things have started to change in SAP S/4HANA with the realization that allocations are not needed in all cases. This is particularly so in project accounting, in which you used to collect revenue and costs and then use results analysis to determine the recognizable revenue and then settle this at period close. Now you can use a derivation function that reads the sales order item associated with the work breakdown structure (WBS) and immediately assigns the revenues and costs not just to the project but also to the market segments as they're posted. Figure 2.14 shows the Project Profitability app (SAP Fiori ID F2764), showing that the revenues and costs are assigned not just to the WBS element (**Project** column) but also to the market segment (**Product Sold** column). The remaining three columns are not the result of settlement but are calculated in real time as the activity is confirmed for the project. We'll explain how to set up these postings and the impact of event-based revenue recognition in Chapter 7.

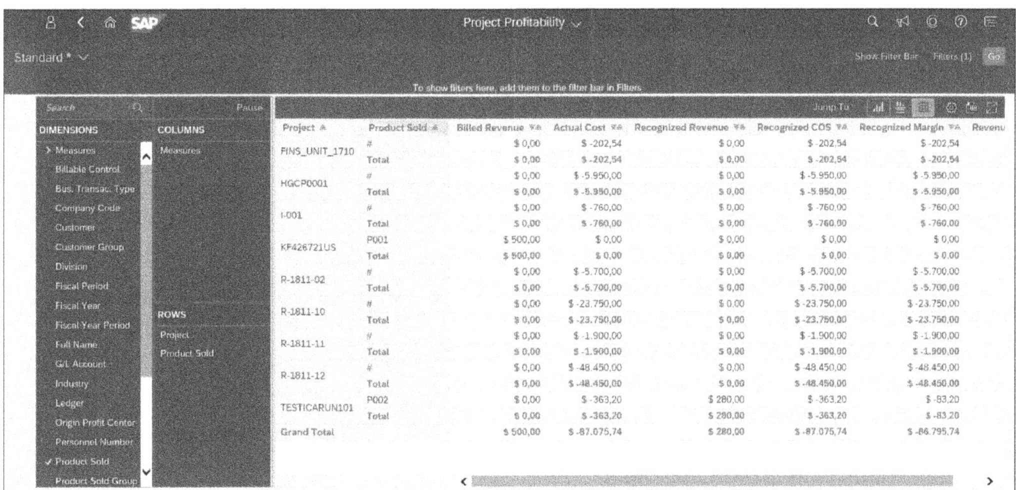


| Project | Product Sold | Billed Revenue | Actual Cost | Recognized Revenue | Recognized COS | Recognized Margin |
|---|---|---|---|---|---|---|
| FINS_UNIT_1710 | # | $ 0,00 | $ -202,54 | $ 0,00 | $ -202,54 | $ -202,54 |
| | Total | $ 0,00 | $ -202,54 | $ 0,00 | $ -202,54 | $ -202,54 |
| HGCP0001 | # | $ 0,00 | $ -5.950,00 | $ 0,00 | $ -5.950,00 | $ -5.950,00 |
| | Total | $ 0,00 | $ -5.950,00 | $ 0,00 | $ -5.950,00 | $ -5.950,00 |
| I-001 | # | $ 0,00 | $ -760,00 | $ 0,00 | $ -760,00 | $ -760,00 |
| | Total | $ 0,00 | $ -760,00 | $ 0,00 | $ -760,00 | $ -760,00 |
| KF426721US | P001 | $ 500,00 | $ 0,00 | $ 0,00 | $ 0,00 | $ 0,00 |
| | Total | $ 500,00 | $ 0,00 | $ 0,00 | $ 0,00 | $ 0,00 |
| R-1811-02 | # | $ 0,00 | $ -5.700,00 | $ 0,00 | $ -5.700,00 | $ -5.700,00 |
| | Total | $ 0,00 | $ -5.700,00 | $ 0,00 | $ -5.700,00 | $ -5.700,00 |
| R-1811-10 | # | $ 0,00 | $ -23.750,00 | $ 0,00 | $ -23.750,00 | $ -23.750,00 |
| | Total | $ 0,00 | $ -23.750,00 | $ 0,00 | $ -23.750,00 | $ -23.750,00 |
| R-1811-11 | # | $ 0,00 | $ -1.900,00 | $ 0,00 | $ -1.900,00 | $ -1.900,00 |
| | Total | $ 0,00 | $ -1.900,00 | $ 0,00 | $ -1.900,00 | $ -1.900,00 |
| R-1811-12 | # | $ 0,00 | $ -48.450,00 | $ 0,00 | $ -48.450,00 | $ -48.450,00 |
| | Total | $ 0,00 | $ -48.450,00 | $ 0,00 | $ -48.450,00 | $ -48.450,00 |
| TESTICARUN101 | P002 | $ 0,00 | $ -363,20 | $ 280,00 | $ -363,20 | $ -83,20 |
| | Total | $ 0,00 | $ -363,20 | $ 280,00 | $ -363,20 | $ -83,20 |
| Grand Total | | $ 500,00 | $ -87.075,74 | $ 280,00 | $ -87.075,74 | $ -86.795,74 |

**Figure 2.14** Project Profitability App Showing Assignment to Project and Product Sold

## 2.2 Financial Planning

If you consider management accounting to be about accountability and making managers responsible for revenues and costs, then the next stage of understanding is not just that the managers should be accountable for their costs, but that they also should have targets in the form of *budgets* for spending on cost centers or projects or plans for the business, whether these are production plans, sales plans, or investment plans. We can take the idea shown previously in Figure 2.10 and use it to illustrate the planning process, as shown in Figure 2.15. The detailed planning process starts at the top with the commercial plan for the various market segments or at the bottom with the expense plans for the various cost centers, projects, and so on. In both cases, the detailed plans roll up into the P&L plan shown on the far right.

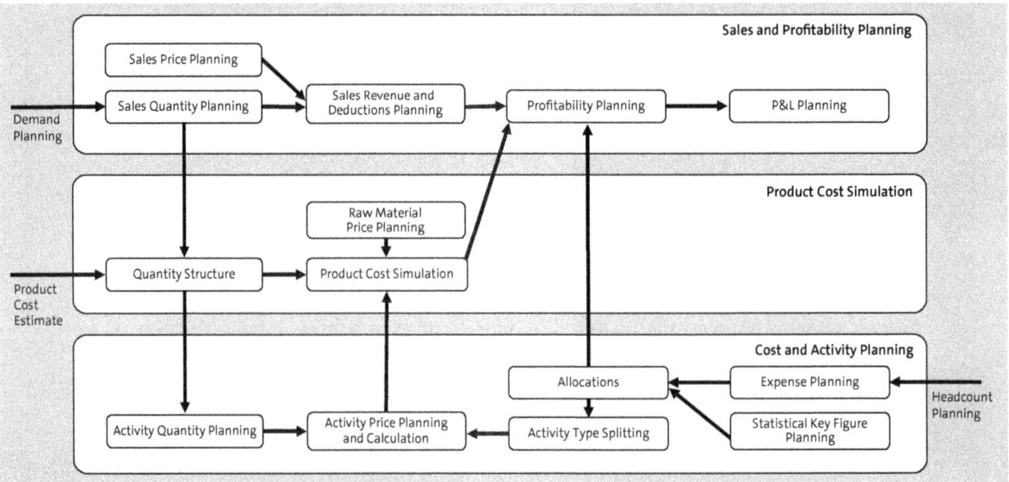


**Figure 2.15** Process of Business Planning

We'll now work through the high-level scope of such an integrated plan and explain how it relates to the accounts we discussed in Section 2.1. We'll then explore the plan/actual reporting process in the system.

### 2.2.1 High-Level Planning Process

If you begin at the top of Figure 2.15, with *sales and profitability planning*, you could simply plan the revenues anticipated for the various market segments as dollar values for the main product groups or customer groups or regions. The challenge with a dollar value, however, is that it does not explain how the planner intends to achieve this target. This is more readily achieved by planning the volumes of product to be sold, in the form of a *sales quantity plan* that describes the target volumes to be sold in the relevant market. This can then be combined with sales prices to deliver a sales revenue for the goods or services to be sold in that market. In many cases, the sales prices won't be the whole story, and it's also possible to plan the typical discounts that will be offered as part of the sales package. What you're doing in these steps is preparing targets in terms of how much business you anticipate for the market segments, shown at the bottom of Figure 2.15.

Moving into the next box, for *product cost simulation*, you're planning the operational business represented by the production orders, sales orders, and projects in the middle of Figure 2.15 and Figure 2.8 (shown previously). In this case, the plan is to sell products that involve the purchase of raw materials and the use of production activities to convert the raw materials into finished goods for sale. Most organizations have bills of materials (BOMs) or recipes that describe the raw materials needed to manufacture the finished product and routings that describe the operations to be performed to make the conversion, and this information is used in the planning process to determine the cost of goods sold for the products in the sales quantity plan. The combination of a BOM and a routing (or the master recipe in the process industries) is known as the *quantity structure*. This quantity structure is combined with price information in terms of the costs of the materials to be consumed and of the production activities to be performed in the production process to deliver a cost estimate. The cost of goods sold resulting from this cost estimate is linked with the quantities and revenues planned in sales and profitability planning to deliver the *planned profitability*, combining the planned sales revenues and cost of goods sold.

Moving into the next box, for *cost and activity planning*, you plan two sorts of costs:

1. General overhead to support the operational cost centers
2. Activity costs to convert the raw materials into finished goods

You begin on the far right with the planning of headcount-related costs, asset-related costs, travel, and so on for each of the cost centers. In the case of production, maintenance, and service cost centers, it's usually possible to plan output in the form of an activity type, such as machine hours, maintenance hours, or service hours. In other cases, it isn't possible to plan such output; allocations must then be made using statistical key figures, such as the number of workers or the square footage of the floorspace, to establish ratios between the various cost centers in order to allocate the costs fairly.

In many cases, the output of a production cost center will not be a single activity type, but rather several, such as setup time, machine time, and labor time. If this is the case, the costs for that cost center must first be split to the activity types in relation to the relative amount of activity provided. The activity quantity can be planned based on the amount of production quantity needed to deliver the quantity of goods to be sold that the commercial planner estimated in the upper box. The controller can then plan the activity rates by dividing the costs for the cost center/activity combination by the planned activity quantity.

We've illustrated the process by starting at the top and working downward, but the actual planning process is generally iterative, with targets being set at a higher level and detailed plans being drawn up by every department; regardless, the idea of a plan is important for management accounting. The standard setting is an important part of the cost accounting approach, providing a standard for the provision of a given level of activity by a cost center or a standard for the production of a given lot size of a product.

In both cases, variances with respect to this standard are analyzed at period close to explain the source of the variance (price change, quantity change, substitution of a raw material, and so on). Variance analysis is initially the controller's task, but for high variances or scrap this typically involves discussions with the relevant plant managers to understand the underlying cause of the variance and where it indicates problems on the shop floor.

### 2.2.2 Plan/Actual Reporting

When we introduced the Universal Journal in Chapter 1, we discussed how the formerly separate applications are combined in the Universal Journal. The table for planning shown in Figure 2.16 follows the same idea, combining fields for financial and management accounting and for margin analysis. The idea is that the plan data captured using the process shown in Figure 2.16 should be stored by cost center, order, project, market segment, profit center, and so on, just like the associated master data, and that any changes to the market segments in the Universal Journal will be immediately reflected in the planning table.

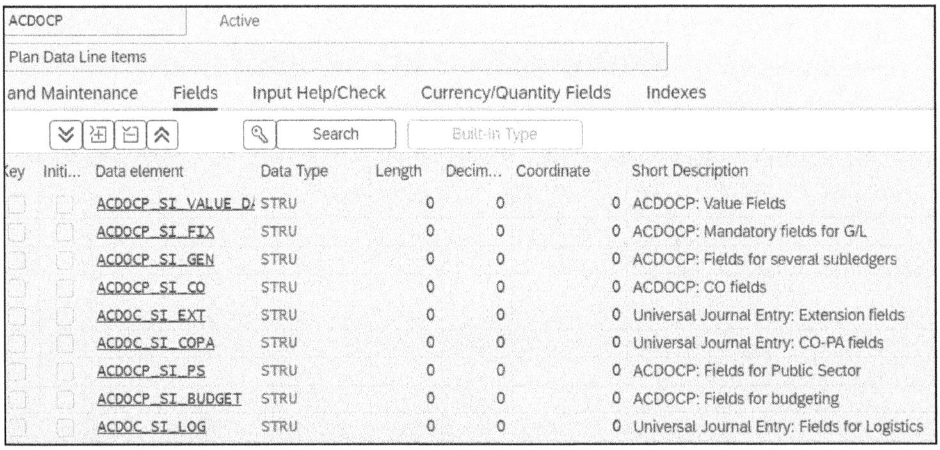

ACDOCP Active

Plan Data Line Items

and Maintenance | Fields | Input Help/Check | Currency/Quantity Fields | Indexes

Search | Built-In Type

| Key | Initi... | Data element | Data Type | Length | Decim... | Coordinate | Short Description |
|---|---|---|---|---|---|---|---|
| | | ACDOCP_SI_VALUE_D | STRU | 0 | 0 | 0 | ACDOCP: Value Fields |
| | | ACDOCP_SI_FIX | STRU | 0 | 0 | 0 | ACDOCP: Mandatory fields for G/L |
| | | ACDOCP_SI_GEN | STRU | 0 | 0 | 0 | ACDOCP: Fields for several subledgers |
| | | ACDOCP_SI_CO | STRU | 0 | 0 | 0 | ACDOCP: CO fields |
| | | ACDOC_SI_EXT | STRU | 0 | 0 | 0 | Universal Journal Entry: Extension fields |
| | | ACDOC_SI_COPA | STRU | 0 | 0 | 0 | Universal Journal Entry: CO-PA fields |
| | | ACDOCP_SI_PS | STRU | 0 | 0 | 0 | ACDOCP: Fields for Public Sector |
| | | ACDOCP_SI_BUDGET | STRU | 0 | 0 | 0 | ACDOCP: Fields for budgeting |
| | | ACDOC_SI_LOG | STRU | 0 | 0 | 0 | Universal Journal Entry: Fields for Logistics |

**Figure 2.16** Line Item Table for Planning

There are many similarities in the architecture, but there are also differences. Possibly the most fundamental is the use of a *plan category* to represent the different assumptions behind the plan (optimistic, pessimistic, and so on) and to flag certain plans as providing the basis for budget checks when actual data is posted against a cost center or WBS element. By storing the plan data in a structure that is easy to combine with the actual line items in the Universal Journal, it's easy to build reports like the Cost Center Budget Report (SAP Fiori ID F3871) shown in Figure 2.17, which combines plan data, budget data, commitments (see Section 2.3), and actual costs to deliver an overview of where cost center spend is on track and where the plan is not being followed. The columns for planned costs and budgets may sound like synonyms, but in SAP terms, a *plan* is simply a plan (and there can be several plans), but a *budget* is the ceiling for spending on a cost center or project and will be checked whenever a relevant posting is to be made.

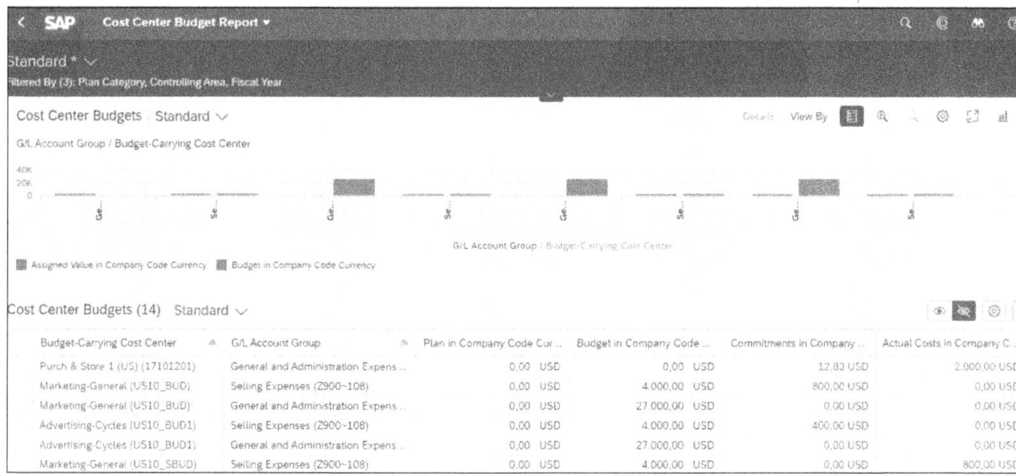


| Budget-Carrying Cost Center | G/L Account Group | Plan in Company Code Cur... | Budget in Company Code ... | Commitments in Company ... | Actual Costs in Company C... |
|---|---|---|---|---|---|
| Purch & Store 1 (US) (17101201) | General and Administration Expens... | 0,00 USD | 0,00 USD | 12,83 USD | 2.000,00 USD |
| Marketing-General (US10_BUD) | Selling Expenses (Z900~108) | 0,00 USD | 4.000,00 USD | 800,00 USD | 0,00 USD |
| Marketing-General (US10_BUD) | General and Administration Expens... | 0,00 USD | 27.000,00 USD | 0,00 USD | 0,00 USD |
| Advertising-Cycles (US10_BUD1) | Selling Expenses (Z900~108) | 0,00 USD | 4.000,00 USD | 400,00 USD | 0,00 USD |
| Advertising-Cycles (US10_BUD1) | General and Administration Expens... | 0,00 USD | 27.000,00 USD | 0,00 USD | 0,00 USD |
| Marketing-General (US10_SBUD) | Selling Expenses (Z900~108) | 0,00 USD | 4.000,00 USD | 0,00 USD | 800,00 USD |

**Figure 2.17** Cost Center Budget Report

**Classic Planning Transactions in SAP S/4HANA**

If you've moved to SAP S/4HANA from an SAP ERP environment, you can continue to use the classic planning transactions even though they are no longer in the SAP Easy Access Menu. However, be aware that these transactions do not update the planning table shown previously in Figure 2.16, but rather the former totals tables (COSP and COSS), and they are not accessed by SAP Fiori applications such as Cost Center Budget Report, shown in Figure 2.17. They are offered to ease the transition to SAP S/4HANA and because some valuations, such as results analysis, continue to read from the legacy tables rather than the planning table shown previously in Figure 2.16. From SAP S/4HANA release 2020, there is a copy function to transfer data between the new planning table and the legacy tables. SAP S/4HANA Cloud does not provide access to the classic transactions.

## 2.3 Predictive Accounting

Management accounting traditionally captures financial data for external business transactions earlier than financial accounting to deliver predictions that include the anticipated margins for the sales orders received or the purchase orders outstanding and the associated costs. You might like to think of predictive accounting as sitting between the plan and the actual journal entry from a timing perspective. Not that predictive accounting as such is new. *Commitments* existed in SAP ERP, as did records for incoming sales orders in costing-based profitability analysis, but these postings are being rearchitected in SAP S/4HANA in order to store them in the Universal Journal alongside the Generally Accepted Accounting Principles (GAAP)-relevant journal entries that we looked at in Section 2.1. The difference is that predictive journal entries are stored in a separate ledger to separate them from the GAAP-relevant postings needed for accounting purposes.

You can imagine the role of predictive accounting by looking at Figure 2.18. In any given period, you'll have posted material movements, invoices, and so on (the actuals), but you'll also have contractual information in the system for purchase orders that indicate that a goods receipt and invoice receipt are expected on the procurement side or sales orders that indicate that a goods issue and invoice are expected on the sales side. The contractual information also indicates when these business transactions are expected, with the journal entry date being used to determine the value of the incoming sales order and the posting date the value of the predicted revenues. You may not yet have made a GAAP-relevant posting, but you already have information that can indicate what the state of the business will be at the end of the next month or quarter. Of course, there are still other outstanding items, as indicated by the other items for recurring entries, close tasks, and so on, but being able to include the values for open sales orders and open purchase orders in the reporting already indicates the value of future business transactions for which a contractual obligation has already been recorded.

As you look at Figure 2.18, it's important to understand that the figures shown in the second column will gradually move into the first column as costs and revenues are incurred. If you've worked with commitments before, you'll know that this commitment is gradually reduced as goods are received and canceled when the final invoice is posted. The same process takes place in reverse for incoming sales orders, when the prediction is reduced as the customer is billed for each delivery.

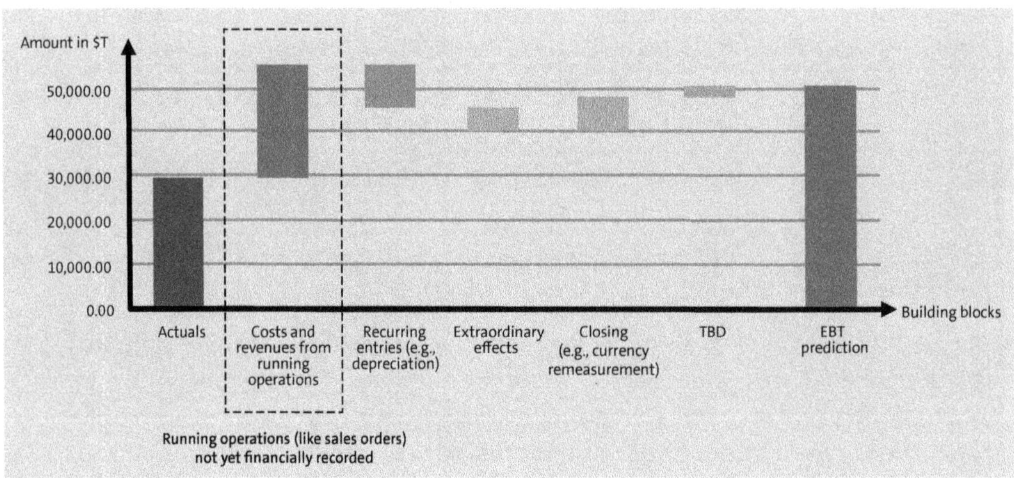


**Figure 2.18** Predictive Key Performance Indicators (KPIs)

Let's begin by looking at the Commitments by Cost Center app (SAP Fiori ID F3016) in Figure 2.19, which shows the open purchase orders and travel requests that a cost center manager is responsible for. The predicted costs are considered commitments because they represent an obligation to pay for the goods or services ordered. This analytical list page shows spend over time for the associated costs centers. This allows managers to monitor what they have already spent and what part of their budget is already committed to cover purchases that have not yet been received. These commitments will be reduced as the goods are received. This is important from an accounting perspective as the goods receipt and invoice receipt will result in actual costs on the cost center, as shown previously in Figure 2.5, and it's important not to count the same transaction twice.

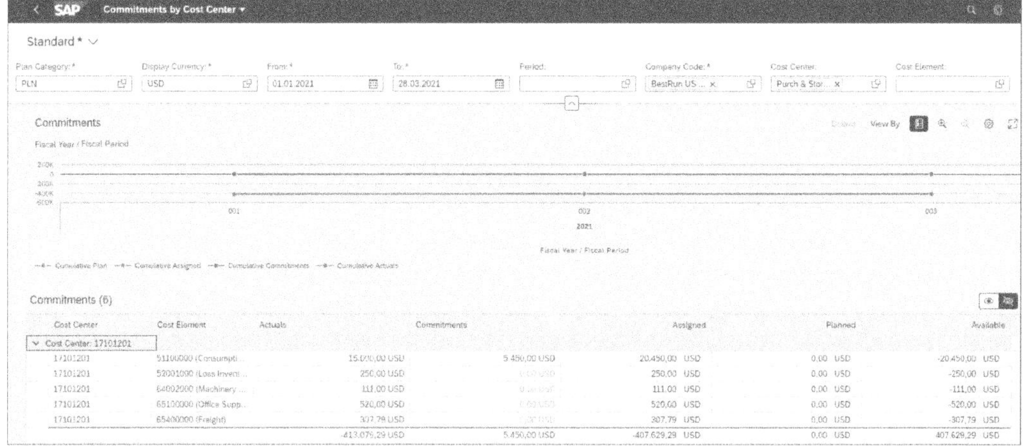


**Figure 2.19** Commitments by Cost Center

We introduced the Cost Center Budget Report previously in Figure 2.17 as a passive way to monitor spend against plan, but you can take the idea of budget monitoring further and have the system issue warnings or even errors when managers try to initiate spending that will result in them exceeding the budget set for the cost center. Notice the term *budget-carrying cost center* in Figure 2.17. Cost centers that carry budget are assigned to a *budget availability control profile*, and checks are performed for these cost centers. You can also decide which journal entries should be included in the check. Typically, you will be looking to include external purchases, travel expenses, and so on, but exclude the result of allocations and settlements. You might then define that an error will be issued when the budget is completely used up for that cost group (100%) and that a warning is issued once more than 80% of the budget has been used. We'll explain this process in more detail in Chapter 5.

It's also possible to create commitments and perform budget availability checks against WBS elements in SAP S/4HANA. At the time of writing, it isn't yet possible to create commitments for orders, and so this function only makes sense for WBS elements that do not work together with networks, maintenance orders, production orders, and so on. For this reason, we'll explain the legacy approach in more detail when we look at investment controlling in Chapter 8.

**SAP ERP versus SAP S/4HANA**

SAP ERP included two solutions for commitments, the one designed for all customers that made purchases and an extended version that supported the more complex requirements of the public sector. Both solutions continue to be supported. From a controlling perspective, the cloud solution described previously can only handle WBS elements, not any assigned orders or networks. For this reason, you should continue to use the existing solution if you work with project structures that include assigned orders.

If you now consider the sales situation, predictive journal entries are created for incoming sales orders when the sales order item is created in SAP S/4HANA. The key date for incoming sales orders is the date on which the order was captured, or the *journal entry date*, as shown in Figure 2.20 in the Incoming Sales Orders app (SAP Fiori ID F2964). This is an analytical list page, allowing the user to select by customer group, product group, and profit center and then see the associated items either graphically or in list form. These journal entries can easily be audited by following the link to the associated sales order items. Notice how all the reporting dimensions in the Universal Journal are filled using the same derivations as for the revenue and cost of goods sold postings later. As well as the extension ledger itself, the prefix **PA** for the journal entry alerts the user to the predictive nature of the posting.

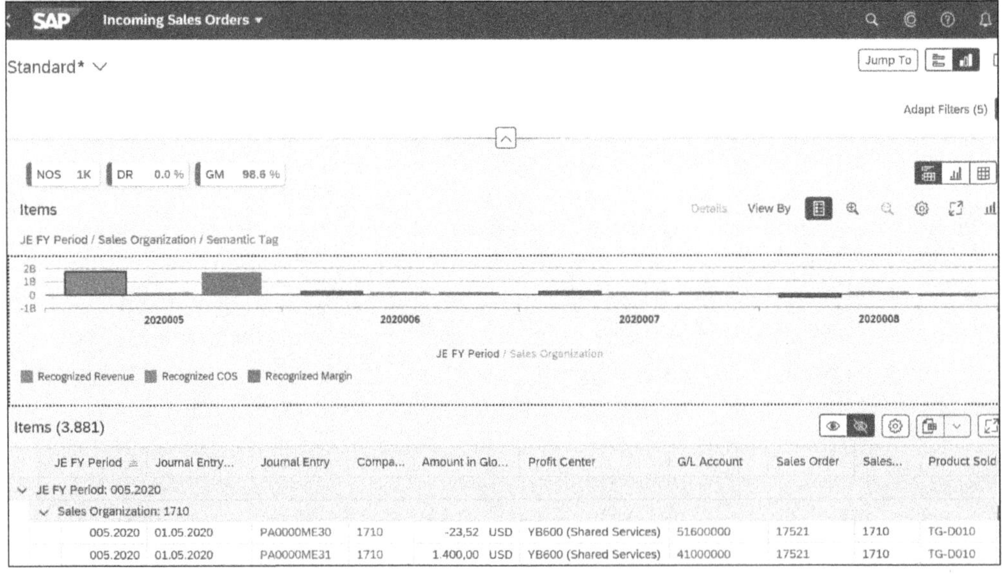


**Figure 2.20** Incoming Sales Orders

A similar app exists for predictive revenues, but this uses the *posting date* as the key date to reflect when the revenue is expected to be earned, as in Figure 2.21, showing the Gross Margin app (SAP Fiori ID F3417). In both cases, if the sales order is changed, the journal entry shown in Figure 2.20 will be flagged as obsolete and a new item created to reflect the change. An important idea behind predictive accounting is that the predictions are gradually reduced as the orders are fulfilled and invoices sent out.

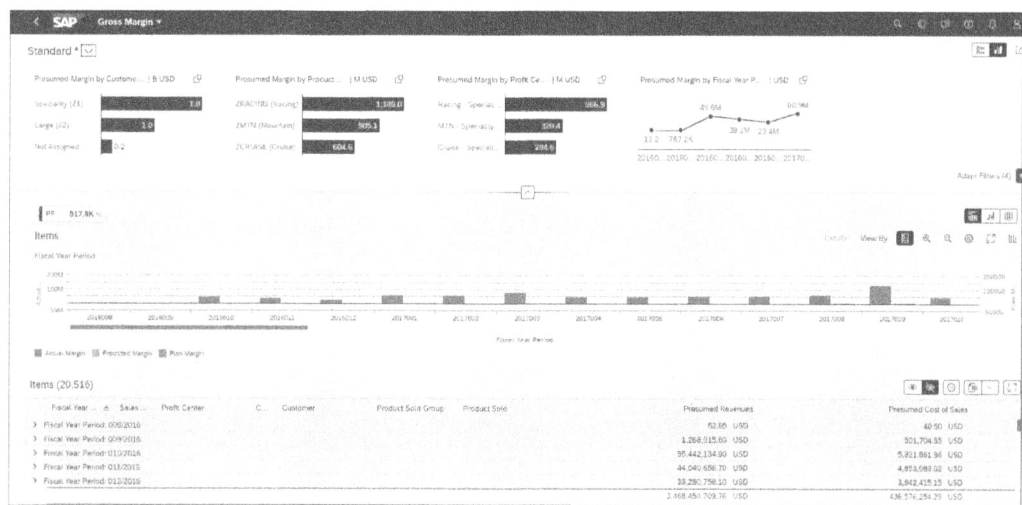


Figure 2.21 Gross Margin

As you think about predictive accounting, it's important to understand that these predictions are tightly integrated with the relevant sales and purchasing processes. The predictive journal entry is subject to all the checks that a normal journal entry in accounting would face. If there are errors in accounting, the system will prevent users from posting the material movement or invoice. In predictive accounting, the system allows the user to post the sales order, but documents with accounting errors will be stored in an error log and fixed using the Monitor Predictive Accounting app (SAP Fiori ID F3828), shown in Figure 2.22.

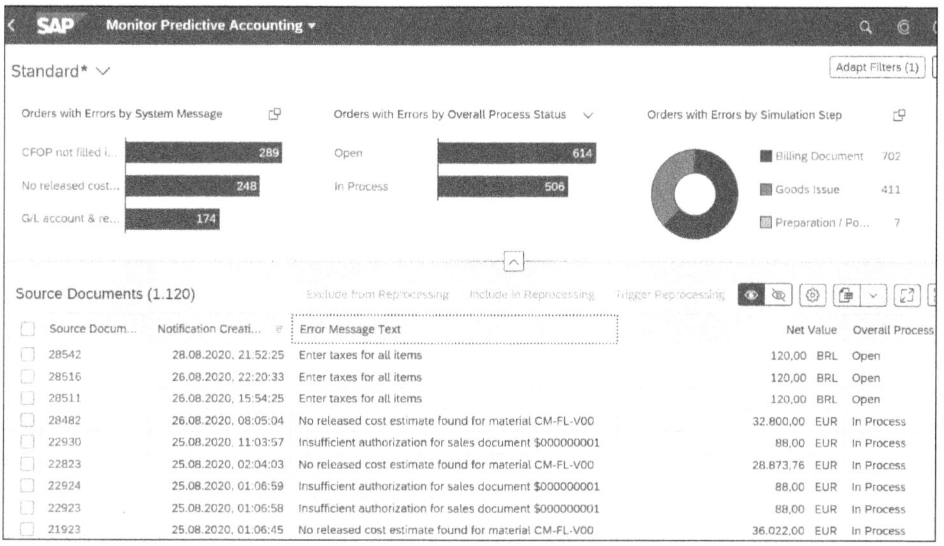


| Source Docum... | Notification Creati... | Error Message Text | Net Value | | Overall Process |
|---|---|---|---|---|---|
| 28542 | 28.08.2020, 21:52:25 | Enter taxes for all items | 120,00 | BRL | Open |
| 28516 | 26.08.2020, 22:20:33 | Enter taxes for all items | 120,00 | BRL | Open |
| 28511 | 26.08.2020, 15:54:25 | Enter taxes for all items | 120,00 | BRL | Open |
| 28482 | 26.08.2020, 08:05:04 | No released cost estimate found for material CM-FL-V00 | 32.800,00 | EUR | In Process |
| 22930 | 25.08.2020, 11:03:57 | Insufficient authorization for sales document $000000001 | 88,00 | EUR | In Process |
| 22823 | 25.08.2020, 02:04:03 | No released cost estimate found for material CM-FL-V00 | 28.873,76 | EUR | In Process |
| 22924 | 25.08.2020, 01:06:59 | Insufficient authorization for sales document $000000001 | 88,00 | EUR | In Process |
| 22923 | 25.08.2020, 01:06:58 | Insufficient authorization for sales document $000000001 | 88,00 | EUR | In Process |
| 21923 | 25.08.2020, 01:06:45 | No released cost estimate found for material CM-FL-V00 | 36.022,00 | EUR | In Process |

Figure 2.22 Monitor Predictive Accounting App

**SAP ERP versus SAP S/4HANA**

In costing-based profitability analysis in SAP ERP, you could capture the revenues and costs associated with incoming sales orders using record type A for incoming sales orders and include them in your profitability reporting. The main difference was that they are never reduced, so users had to be careful to select documents of the correct record type in reporting.

## 2.4 Management Accounting and Margin Analysis

We introduced management accounting and margin analysis in Chapter 1 and explored the high-level journal entries in Section 2.1. We'll now focus on cost center planning and reporting (a topic that we'll return to in Chapter 5), product and service planning and reporting (a topic that we'll return to in Chapter 6), and profitability planning and reporting (a topic that we'll return to in Chapter 7).

### 2.4.1 Cost Center Planning and Reporting

If you return to the Trial Balance app, shown previously in Figure 2.4, the role of the cost center manager can be thought of as monitoring the costs for the cost centers on which the operating expense is initially collected (cost stewardship) and ensuring that it flows correctly either to another cost center or to form part of the product costs or the sales, marketing, or administrative overhead in margin analysis. Depending on the type of cost center, the role changes in the following ways:

- For supporting cost centers, this means ensuring that the costs flow correctly to the operational cost centers.
- For manufacturing cost centers, this means not just monitoring and authorizing the incoming expenses but also ensuring that the resource costs are assigned properly to the activities that the cost center provides and charged to the production line correctly.
- For other operational cost centers, this means monitoring and authorizing the incoming expenses and ensuring that the resource costs are assigned properly to the services that the cost center provides and charged accordingly.
- For the cost centers responsible for sales, marketing, general administration, and so on, this also means monitoring the incoming expenses and making sure that they are charged to the appropriate market segments.

In Section 2.1, we discussed the importance of holding cost center managers responsible for the costs incurred by their cost center, in Section 2.2 the need for planning and target setting, and in Section 2.3 the need to monitor commitments on the cost center. We'll now look in detail at how to set up that plan and what business decisions are taken with reference to this plan. We'll illustrate the planning process using the planning stories delivered as business content with SAP Analytics Cloud. The integration with SAP S/4HANA is documented as a best practice in scope item 4RC (Integrated Financial Planning).



### Planning Cost Center Expenses

To access the planning content, select **Menu • Browse • Files • Public** and choose the planning story **SAP_FI_BPL_IM_COSTCENTER_EXPENSES** to plan the cost center expenses and perform some simple allocations. Notice the **Actuals**, **Expenses**, and **Reporting** tabs, as shown in Figure 2.23. You can use these to switch between the actual data selected as reference data, the data entry layout for the expenses, and the allocation view.

In Figure 2.23 we've chosen the **Expenses** view and planned payroll and travel costs for various cost centers, using reference data from the previous year as a baseline for the plan. Notice also the *data action* buttons (beneath the **Plan Cost Center Expenses** heading) to copy the actual costs from the previous year as an aid to planning or to set more complex control parameters to determine how last year's values will be reflected in your cost center planning. If you previously worked with the classic planning transactions, you had to navigate to a separate transaction, Transaction KP98, to copy cost center costs from the previous year to your current plan, but now the copy function and the associated parameters are integrated into the planning story.

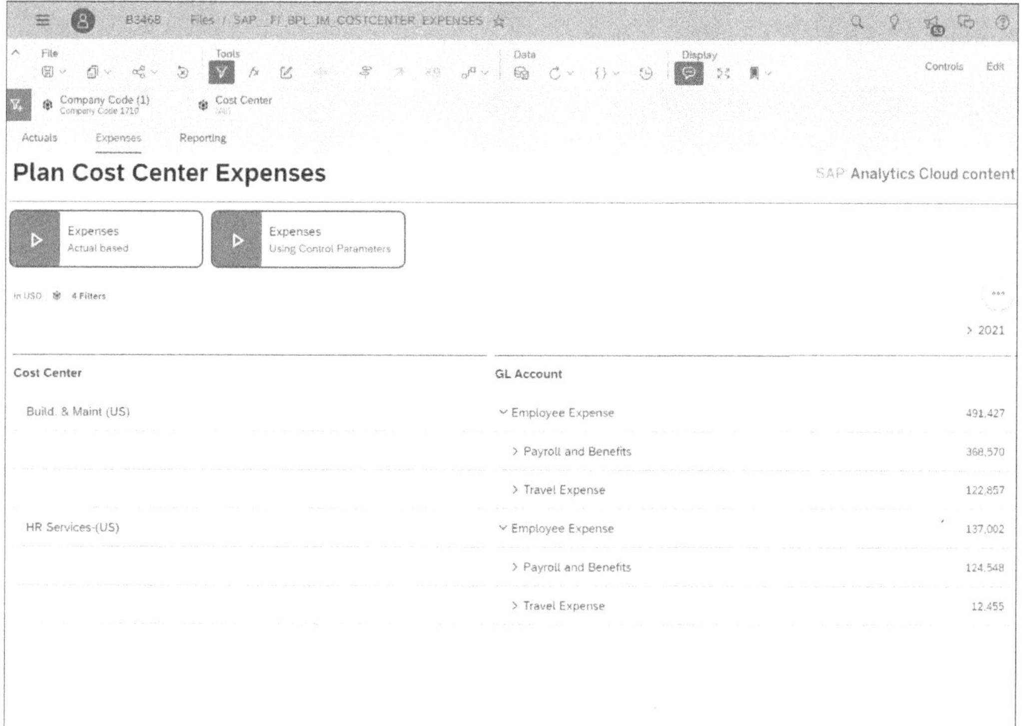


**Figure 2.23** Planning Cost Center Expenses (Primary Costs)

In Section 2.1, we explained how actual expenses can be allocated as secondary costs. The simplest form of allocation is a *distribution* (where the costs are split to the various receivers, but the account remains unchanged), but *assessments* (where the costs are allocated under a secondary cost element, as in Figure 2.12) are equally common. In Figure 2.24, we've switched to the **Reporting** view, taken the payroll and travel expenses planned in Figure 2.23, and used an assessment function to transfer them to two manufacturing cost centers. Again, notice the data action buttons to trigger the distribution (**Expenses • Distribute**) or assessment (**Expenses • Assessment**). These use a scripting language to perform the allocation and, in the case of the assessment action, to set the secondary cost element to which the allocated costs have been credited in this example.

**Classic Planning Transactions in SAP S/4HANA**

If you prefer not to move to SAP Analytics Cloud for the moment, you can plan the primary costs for your cost center using Transaction KP06 and Transaction KP97 to copy the actuals from the previous year. You can perform an allocation of the primary costs for your cost centers using Transaction KSVB for planned distribution and Transaction KSUB for planned assessment. Remember that these will not update the plan table shown in Figure 2.16 but rather the totals records tables COSP (primary costs and the results of the planned distribution) and COSS (secondary costs and the results of the planned assessment).

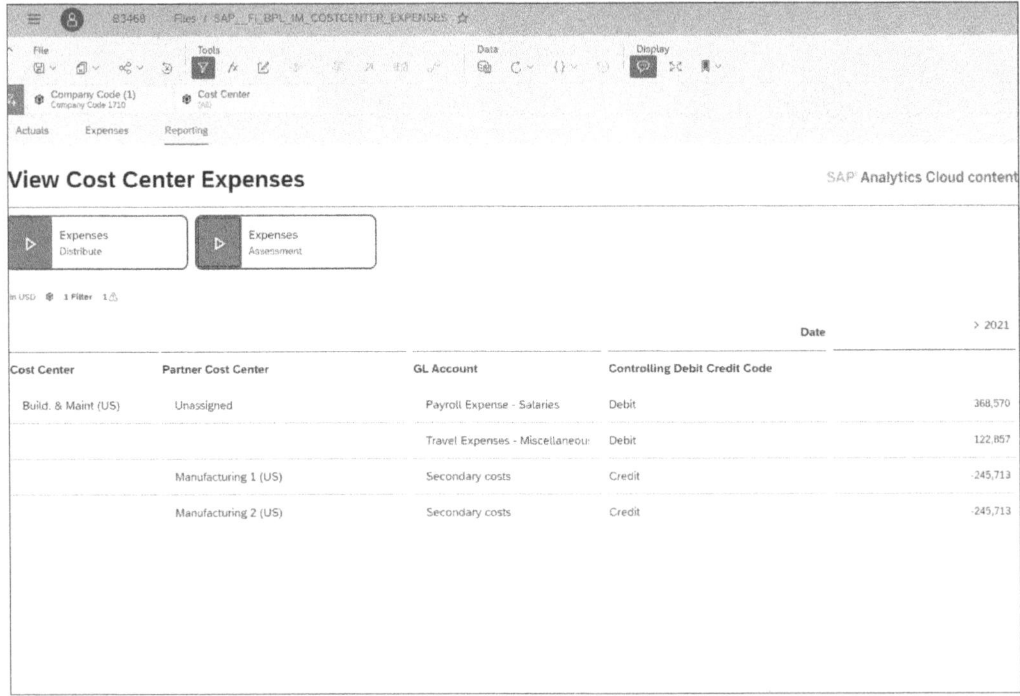


**Figure 2.24** Allocating Cost Center Expenses Using Distribution or Assessment

The planning story **SAP_FI_BPL_IM_COSTCENTER_EXPENSES** supports the simplest of cost scenarios, where costs are collected by cost center and then charged further with a net debit and credit between the senders and receivers, as in Figure 2.11. In many cases, you'll want to go beyond this simplistic model and reflect on how the various costs behave in your planning activities. To take a simple example, energy costs are *variable*, rising as the output of the cost center rises, but rent costs are *fixed*, remaining constant irrespective of how much work the cost center performs. You might plan the rent costs using the planning story shown in Figure 2.23 and allocate them as shown in Figure 2.24, but to plan any activity-dependent (variable) costs, you need to use a different planning story.

#### Planning Activity Usage

In Section 2.1, we introduced the idea of an *activity type* as the way to charge costs based on activity usage, such as consumption of machine time, consulting hours, and so on. Instead of charging all costs from the senders to the receivers and netting to zero, as shown previously in Figure 2.11 and Figure 2.12, using an activity type means that you will charge the costs from the cost center based on *usage* of that activity. The nature of planning usage is that usually some costs will remain on the cost center at the end of the period because the actual activity consumed is not the same as what was planned (over or under utilization of the cost center). The idea is that you are planning the resources associated with delivering 24,000 hours of production activity in the course of the period, but you may deliver more or fewer hours of this activity, and this will affect resources, such as the energy used, even if the costs for the rent on the building remain unchanged.

In Figure 2.25, we have chosen the planning story **SAP_FI_BPL_IM_COSTCENTER_ACTIVITYPRICE_INPUT** to link the back office, consulting unit, manufacturing 1, and manufacturing 2 cost centers with the personnel hours and machine hours activity types, all of which are charged at an hourly rate (unit **H**). We've also entered a manual activity rate for each of the cost center/activity type combinations. Again, you can base the plan on the reference data for the previous year using **Actual Quantities & Cost Rates • Actual Based**.

The next step is to plan the amount of *activity output* that can be provided by these cost centers. In Figure 2.26, we've planned the total output for the activities service, machine hours, and personnel hours from the selected cost centers. While this total output generally represents the capacity of the cost center to provide certain activities, you saw previously in Figure 2.16 that activity output can be determined by the required production output, which is determined in turn by the required sales output. Capacity and activity output won't always be equal, as the demand for the output of a cost center can vary considerably, and it won't always be possible to use the full capacity of the cost center.

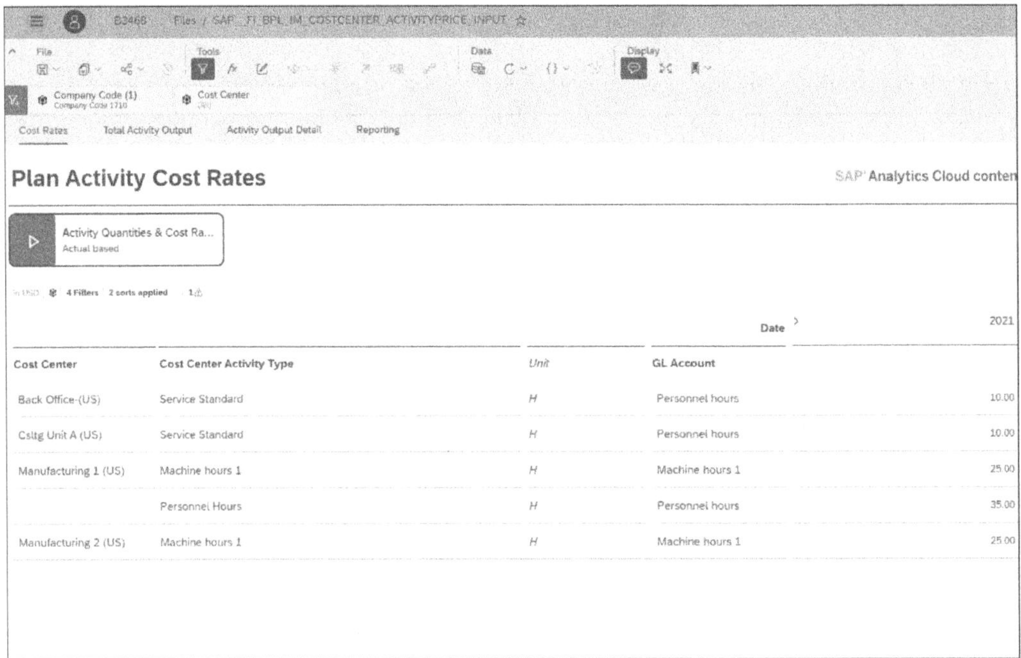


**Figure 2.25** Plan Activity Cost Rates

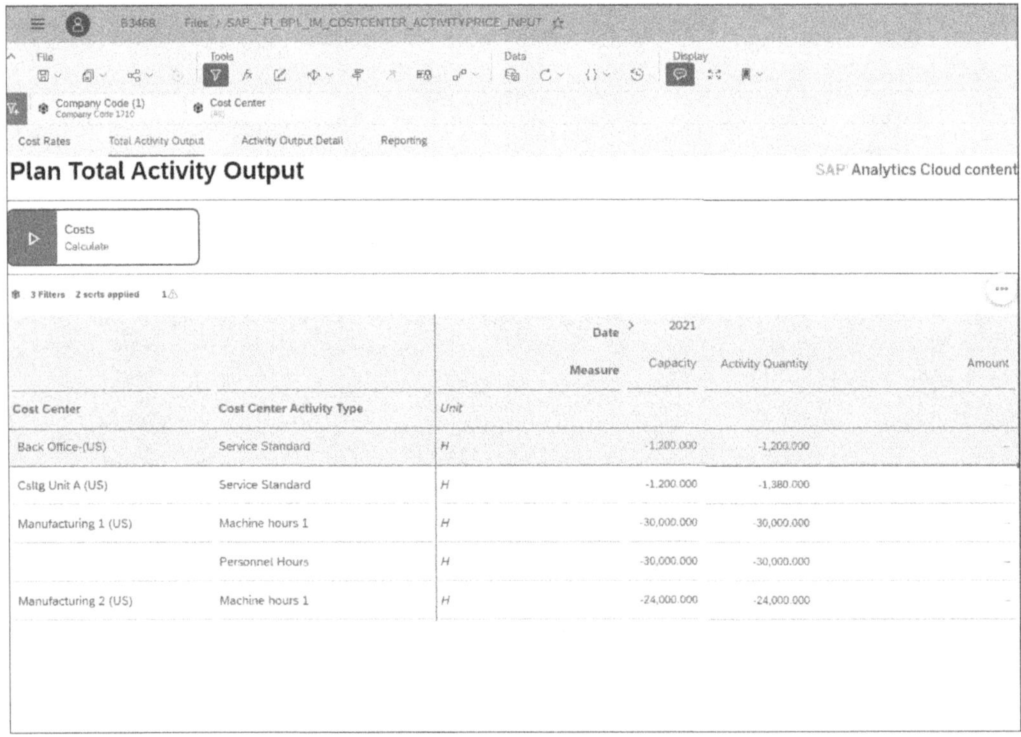


**Figure 2.26** Plan Activity Output

While the planning figures entered in Figure 2.26 reflect the potential of the cost center to deliver activity, you haven't yet planned how this activity will be used. In Figure 2.27, we have planned the amount of activity that the back office and consulting cost centers are able to provide to production. Notice that the back office in Figure 2.26 has a capacity to provide 1,200 hours of service activity and that the receiving cost centers in Figure 2.27 are planning to use 240 hours, 240 hours, 480 hours, and 240 hours. Similarly, the consulting unit has a capacity to provide 1,200 hours of service activity and the receiving cost centers are planning to use 300 hours, 600 hours, 240 hours, and 60 hours (the last line is missing).

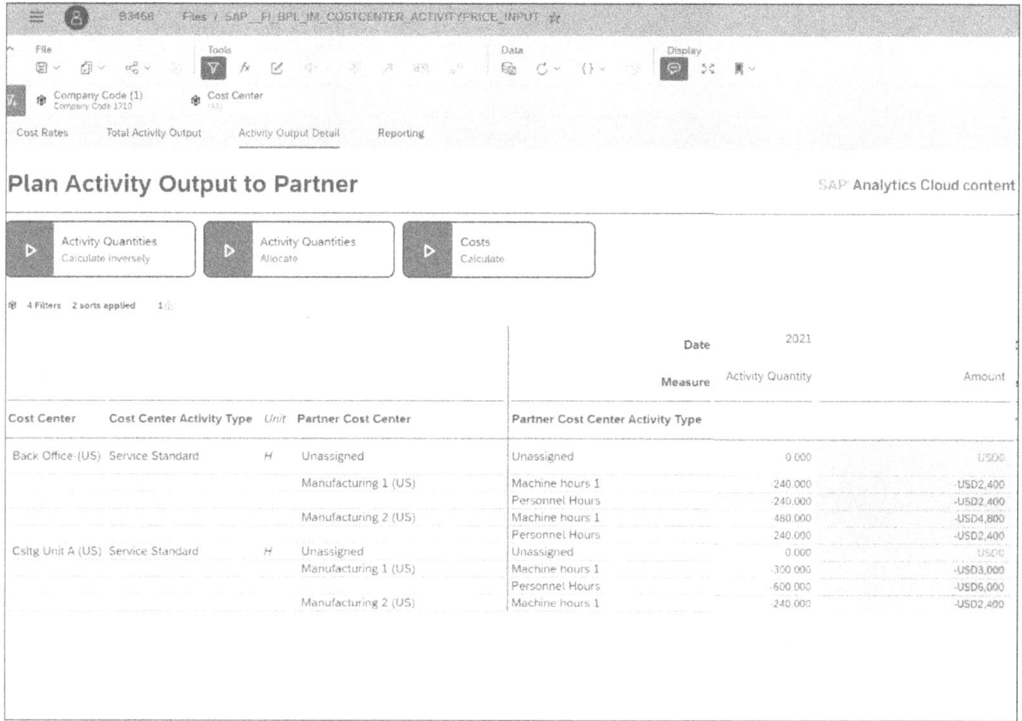


**Figure 2.27** Plan Activity Usage

Again, we've worked with data actions to make these assignments. We've used the **Activity Quantities • Allocate** data action to charge the activities from the back office to the manufacturing cost centers and the **Activity Quantities • Calculate Inversely** data action to charge the activities from consulting to the manufacturing cost centers. The final step of this process is to use the **Costs • Calculate** function to calculate the activity rates for each of the cost center/activity type combinations shown in Figure 2.27.

**Classic Planning Transactions in SAP S/4HANA**

If you prefer to work with the classic planning transactions, Transaction KP26 allows you to combine the cost center and activity types and enter a manual activity rate. You can also enter a different account/cost element for each combination and year. Transaction KP26 also allows you to enter the capacities and activity output for each cost center. Again, these will update the classic tables COST (activity rate) and COSL (activity quantities). You can also use Transaction KP06 with an appropriate layout to plan the activity usage and Transaction KSPI to calculate the activity rates automatically. At the time of writing, the SAP Analytics Cloud planning stories allow you to calculate the activity rates but do not offer the ability to break out the activity rates into their component parts (primary cost component split).

### Cost Centers in the Trial Balance

We offered several examples of cost center reporting when we explored the Trial Balance app previously (Figure 2.5 and Figure 2.6). We also showed reports that allow the manager to ensure that external spending remains within a budget in Figure 2.17 and Figure 2.19.

You can also use the Trial Balance app to drill deeper for some items, so in Figure 2.28 we've included the **Fixed Asset** in the drilldown to show how the depreciation flows from the fixed asset to the cost center. This is particularly important in manufacturing, where the value of the assets for the machinery used can be a significant part of the cost center expenses, but it can also be important where employees use smaller items, such as laptops and phones, and these are assigned to the cost center as assets.

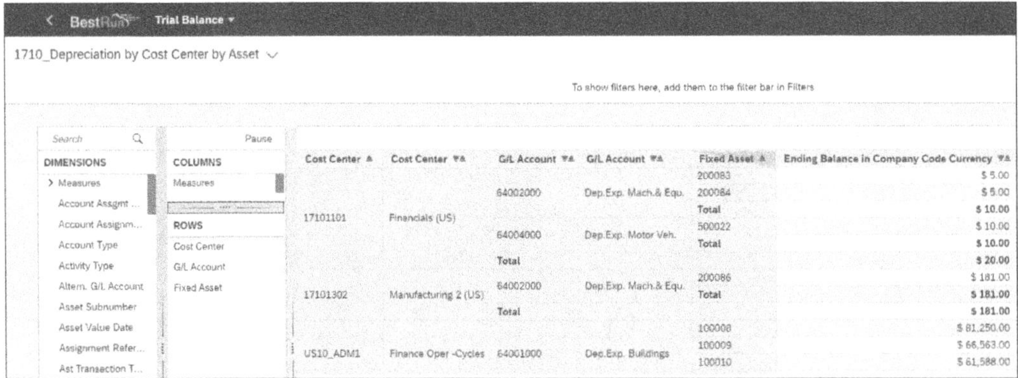


**Figure 2.28** Trial Balance App Showing Cost Center, General Ledger Account, and Fixed Asset

### Cost Center Utilization Reports

We're now going to explore the reports that support effective cost center utilization. These aren't yet available as SAP Fiori apps, so we'll use the classic reports delivered in Report Writer instead.

Figure 2.29 shows the plan/actual reports for a group of cost centers, where the comparison of the **Plan costs** (planned costs) column and **Act. costs** (actual costs) column results in absolute and percentage variances. More importantly, the bottom of the report shows that the actual quantity of quality hours supplied differs from the planned quantity. This leads us to a key concept in controlling: *target costs*.

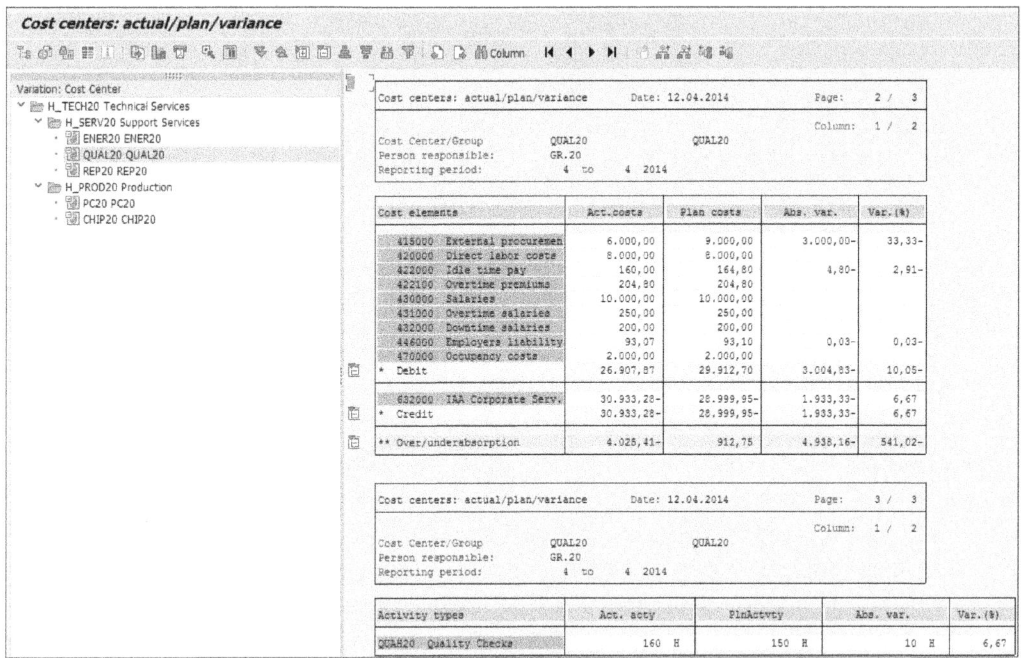


Cost centers: actual/plan/variance Date: 12.04.2014 Page: 2 / 3

Column: 1 / 2

Cost Center/Group QUAL20 QUAL20
Person responsible: GR.20
Reporting period: 4 to 4 2014

| Cost elements | Act.costs | Plan costs | Abs. var. | Var.(%) |
|---|---|---|---|---|
| 415000 External procuremen | 6.000,00 | 9.000,00 | 3.000,00- | 33,33- |
| 420000 Direct labor costs | 8.000,00 | 8.000,00 | | |
| 422000 Idle time pay | 160,00 | 164,80 | 4,80- | 2,91- |
| 422100 Overtime premiums | 204,80 | 204,80 | | |
| 430000 Salaries | 10.000,00 | 10.000,00 | | |
| 431000 Overtime salaries | 250,00 | 250,00 | | |
| 432000 Downtime salaries | 200,00 | 200,00 | | |
| 446000 Employers liability | 93,07 | 93,10 | 0,03- | 0,03- |
| 470000 Occupancy costs | 2.000,00 | 2.000,00 | | |
| * Debit | 26.907,87 | 29.912,70 | 3.004,83- | 10,05- |
| 632000 IAA Corporate Serv. | 30.933,28- | 28.999,95- | 1.933,33- | 6,67 |
| * Credit | 30.933,28- | 28.999,95- | 1.933,33- | 6,67 |
| ** Over/underabsorption | 4.025,41- | 912,75 | 4.938,16- | 541,02- |

Cost centers: actual/plan/variance Date: 12.04.2014 Page: 3 / 3

Column: 1 / 2

Cost Center/Group QUAL20 QUAL20
Person responsible: GR.20
Reporting period: 4 to 4 2014

| Activity types | Act. acty | PlnActvty | Abs. var. | Var.(%) |
|---|---|---|---|---|
| QUAH20 Quality Checks | 160 H | 150 H | 10 H | 6,67 |

**Figure 2.29** Cost Center Report Showing Plan/Actual Costs and Activity Output

Notice in Figure 2.30 that the cost center planned to provide 150 hours of quality checks but actually provided 160 hours of quality checks. As you look at the associated costs, remember that some of the costs are activity-independent (salaries, overtime salaries, downtime salaries, occupancy costs) and some are activity-dependent (external procurement, direct labor, idle time pay, overtime premiums, employer's liability). To calculate the target costs, the planned costs for the activity-dependent items in the list are adjusted to reflect the higher level of output (160 hours instead of 150 hours). This means that the planned costs of 9,000 euros for external procurement have been adjusted to give target costs of 9,600 euros to reflect the extra ten hours of activity provided. Similarly, the planned costs of 8,000 euros for direct labor have been adjusted to give 8,200 euros. The activity-independent costs remain the same regardless of the activity produced. This kind of detailed analysis can help you understand the effect of the amount of work provided on the amount of resources used by your cost center.

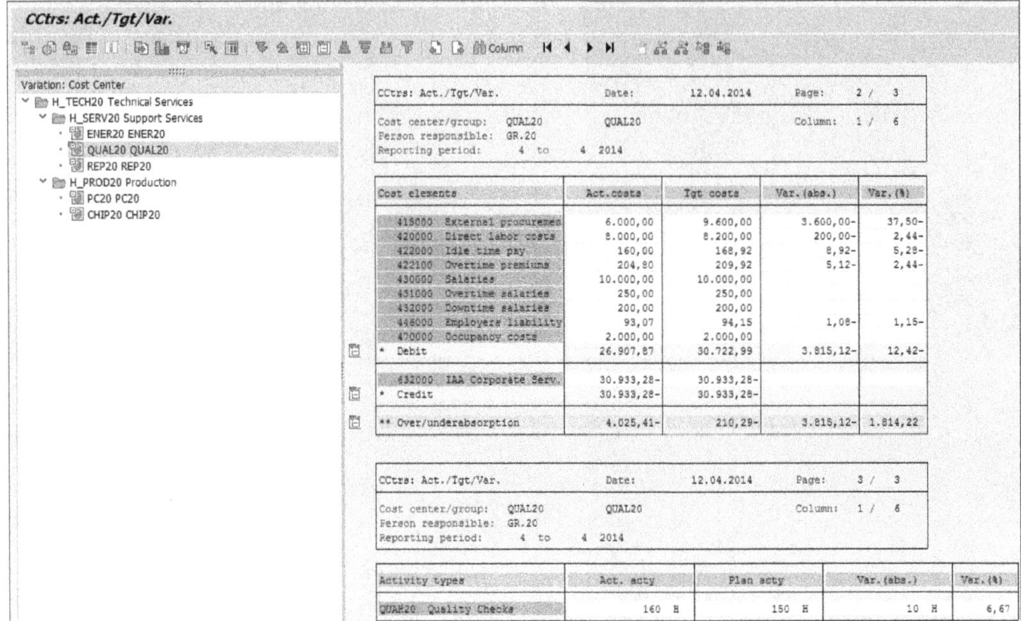


**Figure 2.30** Cost Center Report Showing Target/Actual Costs and Activity Output

An *operating rate* is calculated for each cost center to determine how effectively it worked in each period. Figure 2.31 shows that the production cost center **PC20** performed the setup activity 100% to target, but all the other cost centers worked at a different rate. The second production cost center, **CHIP20**, worked less efficiently than the target, performing at an operating rate of only 91.43%, while quality (**QUAL20**), energy (**ENER20**), repairs (**REP20**), and machine hours on **PC20** performed at a higher than planned efficiency.

**Variance Calculation for Cost Centers: List**

Cost Elements | Variance Categories

Period 4 Fiscal year 2014 Messages 1 Currency EUR
Version IDES Europe (0) Controlling area currency

| Cost Center | Description | ActTyp | Op Rate | Target Costs | Actual Costs | Allocated Actl Costs | Variance | Var.(%) |
|---|---|---|---|---|---|---|---|---|
| REP20 | | REPH... | 140,00 | 25.451,13 | 23.000,00 | 29.400,00 | 6.400,00- | 25,15- |
| PC20 | | MAH20 | 120,00 | 155.394,02 | 155.524,89 | 161.319,96 | 5.795,07- | 3,73- |
| ENER20 | | ENH20 | 114,29 | 27.607,78 | 26.750,63 | 23.714,29 | 3.036,34 | 11,00 |
| QUAL20 | | QUAH... | 106,67 | 30.722,99 | 26.907,87 | 30.933,28 | 4.025,41- | 13,10- |
| PC20 | | SETH... | 100,00 | 39.273,97 | 38.049,75 | 37.500,00 | 549,75 | 1,40 |
| CHIP20 | | MAH20 | 91,43 | 69.321,40 | 69.323,63 | 75.004,48 | 5.680,85- | 8,19- |

**Figure 2.31** Cost Center Variance Calculation

We'll return to the topic of overhead controlling to explain how to perform the steps you'll need for your daily work in Chapter 5.

## 2.4.2 Product and Service Planning and Reporting

We'll begin this section by looking at another view of the Trial Balance app. In Figure 2.32, we've selected the *production variances* for the products and product groups sold. Production variances occur on the shop floor, where components become damaged, operations take longer to perform than planned, finished goods have to be scrapped, and so on; these variances are a natural part of the production process. For this reason, they are also considered part of the cost of goods sold as they can result in gains or losses in production.

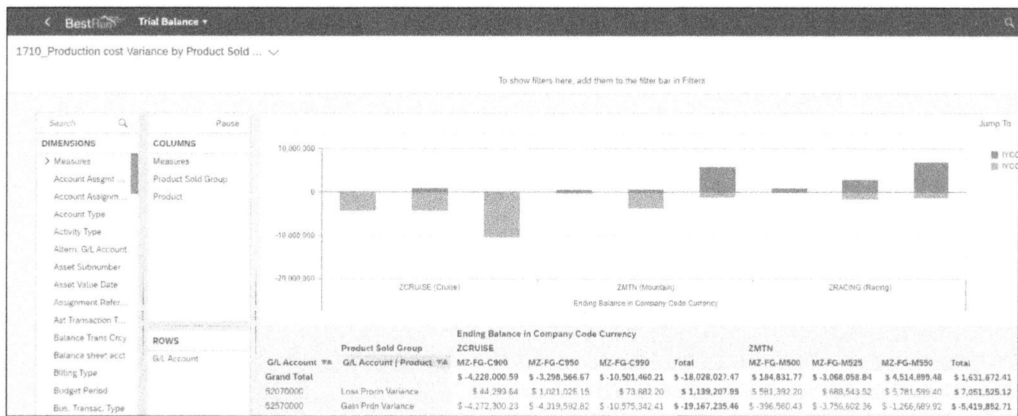


**Figure 2.32** Trial Balance App Showing Variances per Product Sold Group and Product

We'll walk through the planning process to address these production variances in the following sections.

### Production Cost Analysis

Before we explain how these variances come about, it's worth taking a minute to reflect on the nature of managing a manufacturing organization. Whereas the controller is often initiating the transactions that happen in the cost center space, whether it's reassigning travel expenses that have been posted to the wrong cost center or performing the period close transactions, in the manufacturing space outside of the period close the business transactions are being performed with little or no interaction on the part of the plant controller. Production orders are created on the shop floor, materials issued, operations confirmed, and finished goods delivered back to inventory with little or no interaction from the controller.

For this reason, you might start with the Production Cost Analysis app (SAP Fiori ID F1780), shown in Figure 2.33, which in this example lists all the open production orders in plant **1710** for material **MZ-FG-C900** within a selected period. From there you can navigate to the detail of the costs on the various production orders. Actual costs are assigned to the production order as raw materials are issued to the order, operations confirmed, and overhead assigned. To understand whether these costs are within the expected framework, they are compared with the target costs to manufacture the same lot size. This is important both as the starting point for the calculation of production variances and as an explanation of the difference between the standard costs used to value the delivery of the finished goods to inventory and the actual costs resulting from the manufacturing process. If your organization isn't yet using SAP Fiori, then you'll find a similar report as Transaction S_ALR_87013127 or by following **Accounting • Controlling • Product Cost Controlling • Cost Object Controlling • Product Cost by Order • Information System • Reports for Product Cost by Order • Summarized Analysis • Object List • Order Selection.**

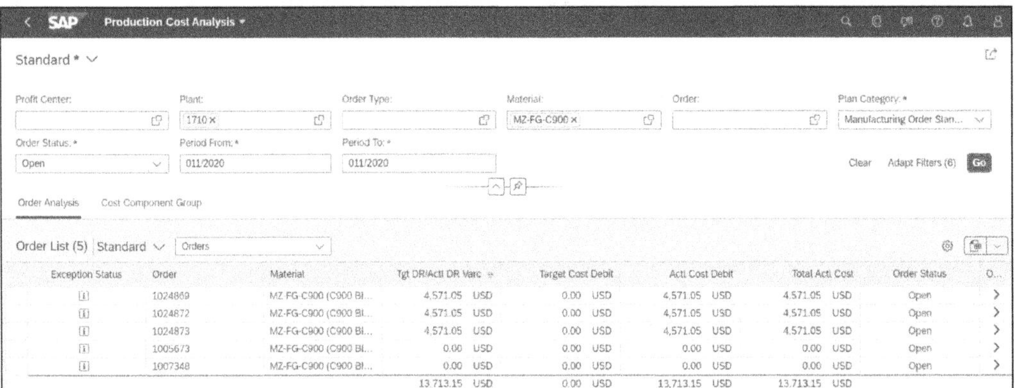

**Figure 2.33** Production Cost Analysis App

To understand the nature of the target costs, reflect on the nature of planning. Just as for the cost centers in the previous section, the target cost has been adjusted to reflect the actual lot size of goods manufactured. But in the case of production orders, there are two sets of target costs (represented by the different plan categories shown in Figure 2.33):

- The first target costs are the result of the overall planning process described previously in Figure 2.8. This process delivers a standard cost for the manufacture of the goods irrespective of any actual orders, using only the BOMs and routing for the product. The order lot size may be different from the costing lot size used in planning, giving rise to *material requirements planning (MRP) variances* as a result of the lot size changes.
- The second target costs are based on a cost estimate created automatically when the production order is created and includes the material components in the order and the operations to convert them into a finished product. Any variances against this target will reflect what changed between releasing the order to the shop floor and delivering the finished goods to inventory.

When the plan described previously in Figure 2.8 is created, the purchase orders, production orders, and sales orders that are used to manage the everyday business do not exist. Just as we discussed how the sales managers make assumptions about the sales quantities that they intend to sell, the purchasing managers make assumptions about the raw material quantities that they intend to buy, resulting in raw material costs that are stored either in the material master or in purchasing info records concerning the agreements with each supplier. The links among what is bought, what is made, and what is sold are established using the BOMs and routings that make up the quantity structure for costing. This master data forms the basis for the assumptions about material usage and activity usage needed for the planning process.

### Material Cost Estimate

Figure 2.34 shows a sample cost estimate for the manufacture of a bicycle. It's not yet possible to create a cost estimate in SAP Fiori, so here we're using Transaction CK11N. On the left of the screen, under **Costing Structure**, you can see the BOM—the list of components needed to manufacture the bicycle and the costs for each component. On the right of the screen, under **Itemization in Company Code Currency**, you can see the costs for the raw materials, the semifinished product, and the three activity types. We'll look at the master data that needs to be in place for product cost planning in more detail in Chapter 6, Section 6.1. Because of the tight integration with the master data, the creation of the itemization has to take place in SAP S/4HANA rather than in SAP Analytics Cloud for planning. If you want to use this detailed costing data as part of the planning process, you must first extract this information to SAP Analytics Cloud for planning.

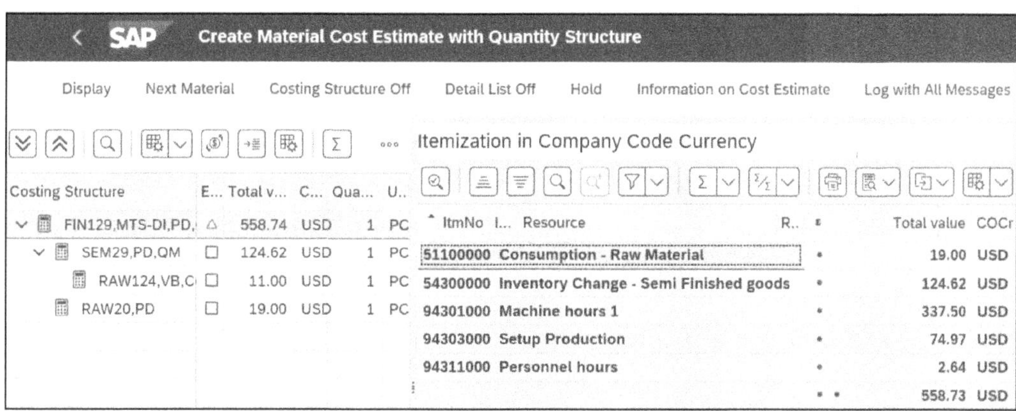


**Figure 2.34** Material Cost Estimate for Bicycle Manufacture

In Figure 2.35, we're using the planning story **SAP_FI_BPL_PRODUCTCOST_RATES** to display the quantity structure for the manufacture of one product. This uses the information shown in Figure 2.34. During the process of moving the cost estimate into SAP Analytics Cloud for planning, the BOM structure shown on the left of Figure 2.34 has been flattened to remove the semifinished material SEM29, leaving only the raw materials RAW124 and RAW20 in the quantity structure. The general ledger accounts shown aren't those for the consumption of the raw material and semifinished goods and the machine time, setup time, and personnel hours shown in Figure 2.34, but the cost of goods sold accounts that will be posted at the time of delivery.

The activity usage of the machine hours and personnel hours provides the link to the activity rates discussed in the previous section when calculating the rates for usage of each of these activity rates using the **SAP_FI_BPL_IM_COSTCENTER_ACTIVITYPRICE_INPUT** story.

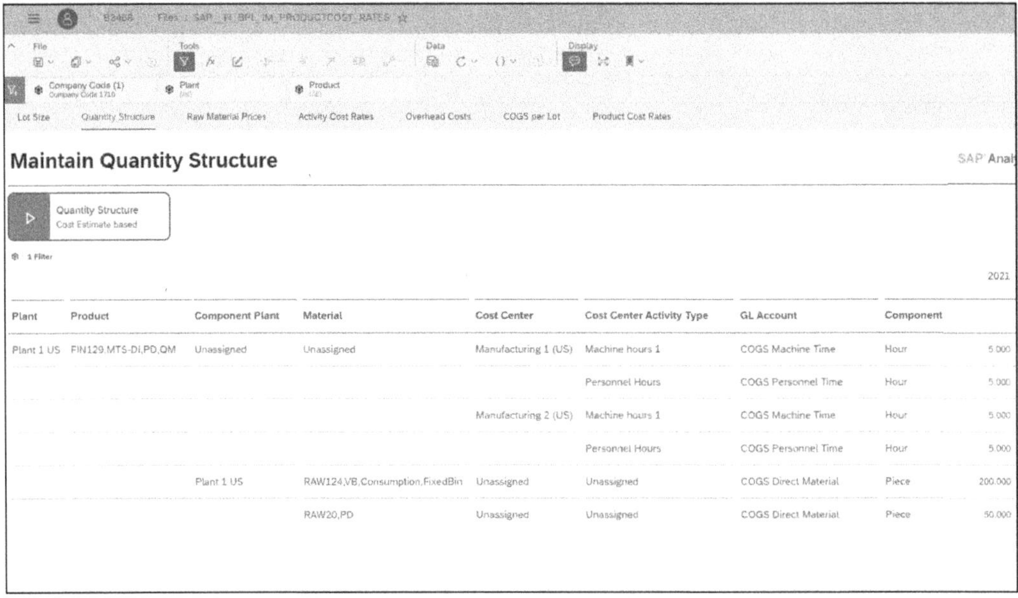


| Plant | Product | Component Plant | Material | Cost Center | Cost Center Activity Type | GL Account | Component | |
|---|---|---|---|---|---|---|---|---|
| Plant 1 US | FIN129.MTS-DI,PD,QM | Unassigned | Unassigned | Manufacturing 1 (US) | Machine hours 1 | COGS Machine Time | Hour | 5.000 |
| | | | | | Personnel Hours | COGS Personnel Time | Hour | 5.000 |
| | | | | Manufacturing 2 (US) | Machine hours 1 | COGS Machine Time | Hour | 5.000 |
| | | | | | Personnel Hours | COGS Personnel Time | Hour | 5.000 |
| | | Plant 1 US | RAW124,VB,Consumption,FixedBin | Unassigned | Unassigned | COGS Direct Material | Piece | 200.000 |
| | | | RAW20,PD | Unassigned | Unassigned | COGS Direct Material | Piece | 50.000 |

**Figure 2.35** Quantity Structure for Product Costs, Including Cost of Goods Sold Split

**Classic Planning Transactions in SAP S/4HANA**

If you used account-based profitability analysis in SAP ERP, it wasn't possible to break out the cost of goods sold according to the underlying cost components. However, if you used costing-based profitability analysis, Transaction KEPM allowed you to value the sales quantities with the standard costs by linking the various cost components with the relevant value fields. Figure 2.35 shows the equivalent process in SAP Analytics Cloud, where the inputs from the cost estimate are reflected in the cost of goods sold for a unit of product.

### Standard versus Planned Costs

The standard costs shown in Figure 2.34 and Figure 2.35 for a bicycle deliver the target costs for production using the standard lot size and standard manufacturing procedures. However, when the time comes to create a production order to manufacture the bicycle, there may be minor changes; for example, assembly may have to be moved to a different machine as a result of capacity shortages or components may be temporarily unavailable and have to be replaced. For this reason, a second cost estimate is created when the production order is created using the operations and material components specific to that particular order. Both cost estimates are stored in the planning table under different plan categories.

Figure 2.36 shows the Production Cost Analysis app and the switch between the costs based on the standard costs and the planned costs for the order. The basic approach is the same in each case, but a comparison between the standard costs and the planned order costs will reveal those differences incurred on account of changes due to short-term MRP.

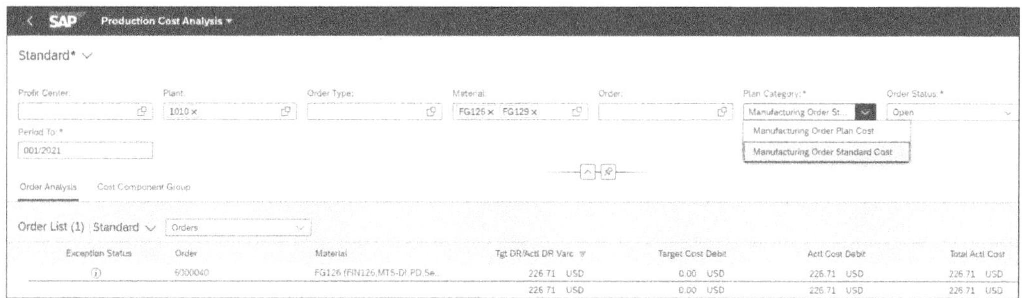


**Figure 2.36** Cost Estimate for Production Order

In SAP ERP, the costs per operation view is only available for the planned costs. One of the key changes with SAP S/4HANA is that new fields have been added to the Universal Journal for the operation and the work center so that the actual costs are also available by work center and operation. If you record your confirmations by operation and assign the material components to the correct operation, you'll be able to see the production costs by work center via the Analyze Costs by Work Center/Operation app (SAP Fiori ID F3331), shown in Figure 2.37. Here you can see the costs for the assembly work center and the line items for the materials consumed and the activities performed there.

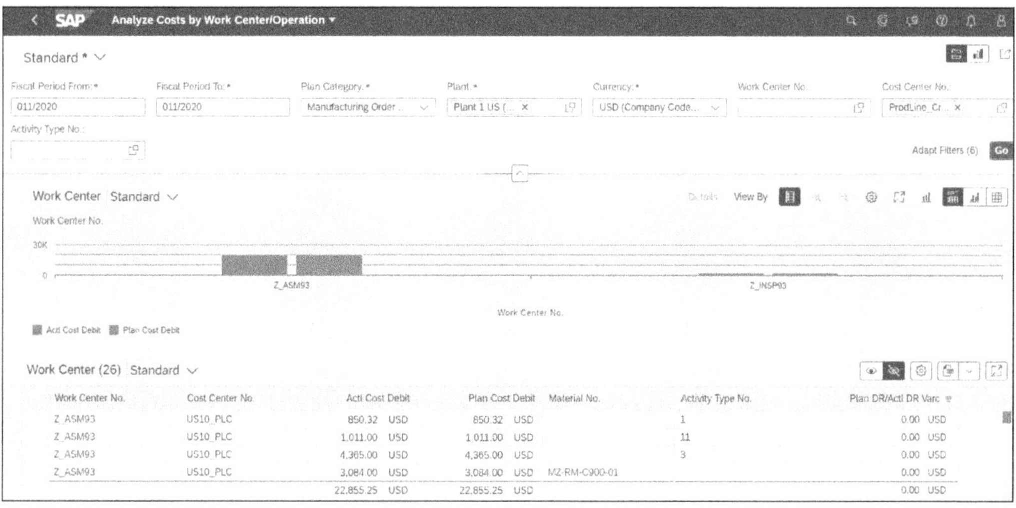


**Figure 2.37** Analyze Costs by Work Center/Operation App

### Variance Calculation

Like for the cost centers, variance calculation plays a significant role in the analysis of what's happening on the shop floor. Figure 2.38 shows a sample report for a production order with the target costs, actual costs, work in process (WIP), scrap, and variances. Detailed variance calculation is the heart of production controlling, relying heavily on standard-setting using a careful planning process; we'll explore the many variance categories in detail in Chapter 6.

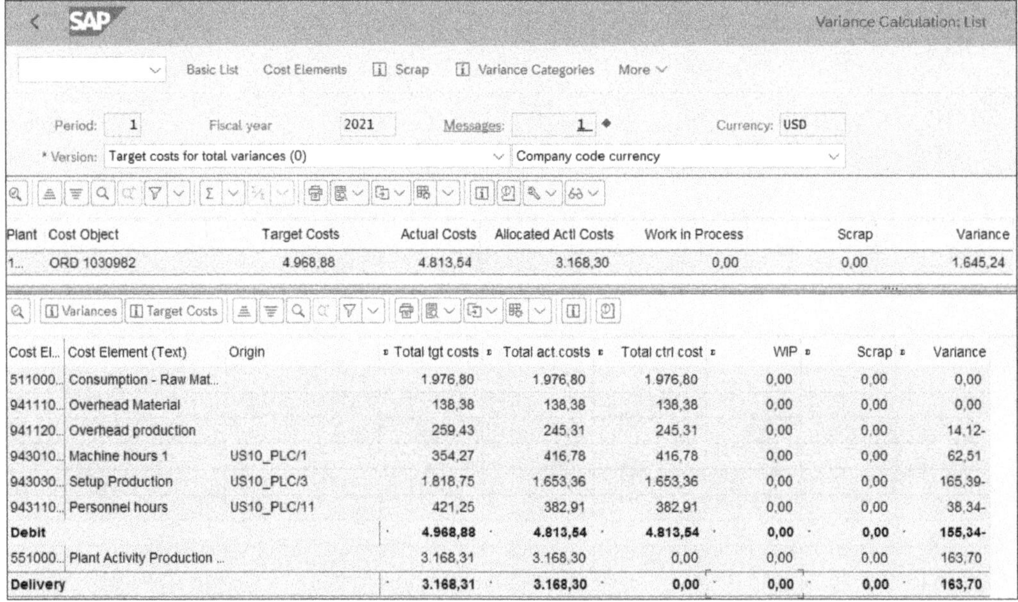


**Figure 2.38** Variance Calculation for Production Order

### Work in Process

Because it's rare for all production activities to be complete at period close, the calculation of WIP is another significant part of the work of the production controller. In Chapter 6, we'll explain the two fundamentally different approaches to WIP in SAP S/4HANA. The traditional approach involves calculating WIP for all the open production orders at period close, while the new approach creates a document for WIP immediately as soon as the underlying goods movements and order confirmations are posted.

Figure 2.39 shows the Event-Based Work in Process app (SAP Fiori ID F3498) and the documents resulting from the new process in which WIP is calculated as soon as the underlying goods movements and confirmations are posted. The WIP is reversed as soon as the finished goods are delivered to stock.

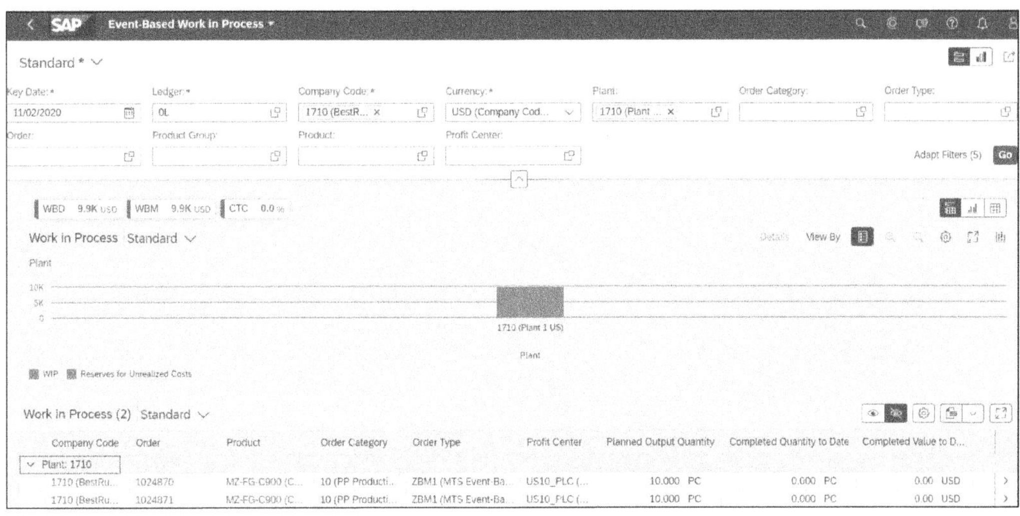

**Figure 2.39** Event-Based Work in Process App

### Actual Costing

Some organizations don't stop at analyzing their production variances but use *actual costing* to assign all purchase price variances, exchange rate variances, and production variances to the finished goods. This approach has gained massively in popularity in recent years due to fluctuations in commodity prices and in the foreign exchange markets and due to the general distrust of standard costs that comes with highly volatile business conditions.

True actual costs are calculated not by the production order as shown previously in Figure 2.33 and Figure 2.38 but rather by performing a costing run at period close that takes account of all the materials purchased, manufactured, sold, or moved in the period. The result of this calculation is a material value chain, as shown in the Material Value Chain app (SAP Fiori ID F4095; see Figure 2.40). In this app, you'll see the raw materials and production activities used to manufacture a finished product. This gives an idea of how the costing run pushes the variances through the process, picking up cost center variances for the activities and purchase price variances for the raw materials and passing them on to the finished goods. This can be a multistage procedure covering many manufacturing levels until all variances have been assigned to the cost of goods sold.

We discussed earlier that some manufacturing processes may be incomplete at period close, resulting in the need to value WIP. Others will have delivered goods to stock that have yet to be used in another manufacturing level or sold to the final customer. Actual costing adjusts not just the cost of goods sold, but also any inventories impacted by the variances. It's also possible to set up this process to handle intercompany goods transfers and value any stock in transit between legal entities.

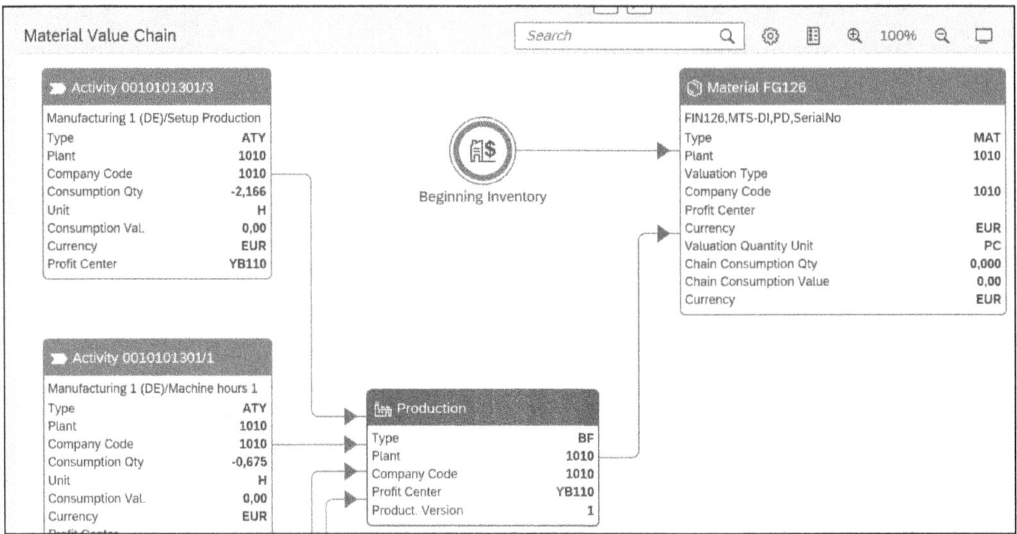


**Figure 2.40** Material Value Chain App for Actual Costing

### Other Cost Objects

Once you understand the basic logic of how to assign material costs and activity costs to production orders, you'll find that the same basic mechanisms are used to calculate costs for any work order with a task list. So, *process orders* are like production orders, but they use *recipes* instead of BOMs and routings to describe the materials and activities used. *Maintenance orders* are used to manage the repair activities performed on a piece of equipment. They use their own task lists to describe the maintenance activities to be performed and any spare parts needed. *Inspection orders* describe the activities performed to ensure quality control on a product or service. *Networks* are used to describe the production or maintenance activities performed in association with a project in which it's important to describe the *dependencies* between the various activities to ensure correct scheduling of the various parts. In each case, a plan is created automatically, as we discussed for the production order when the work order is created.

### Project Planning

In some cases, such automated planning is simply not possible. In Chapter 6, we'll explain how the cost estimates are created in make-to-order production when the sales order process begins with the configuration of the product to meet the specific needs of the customer and the selected components and activities are transferred to the production order prior to costing. In Chapter 7, we'll look at the various options for planning services and commercial projects. Where there isn't a quantity structure available for the order or project, you can use an account-based plan like we showed for the cost centers to enter the various costs for each element in the WBS. This is shown in Figure 2.41, in which we're using the **SAP_FI_BPL_IM_PROJECT_PLANNING_AND_BUDGETING** planning story to capture the costs expected for a project.

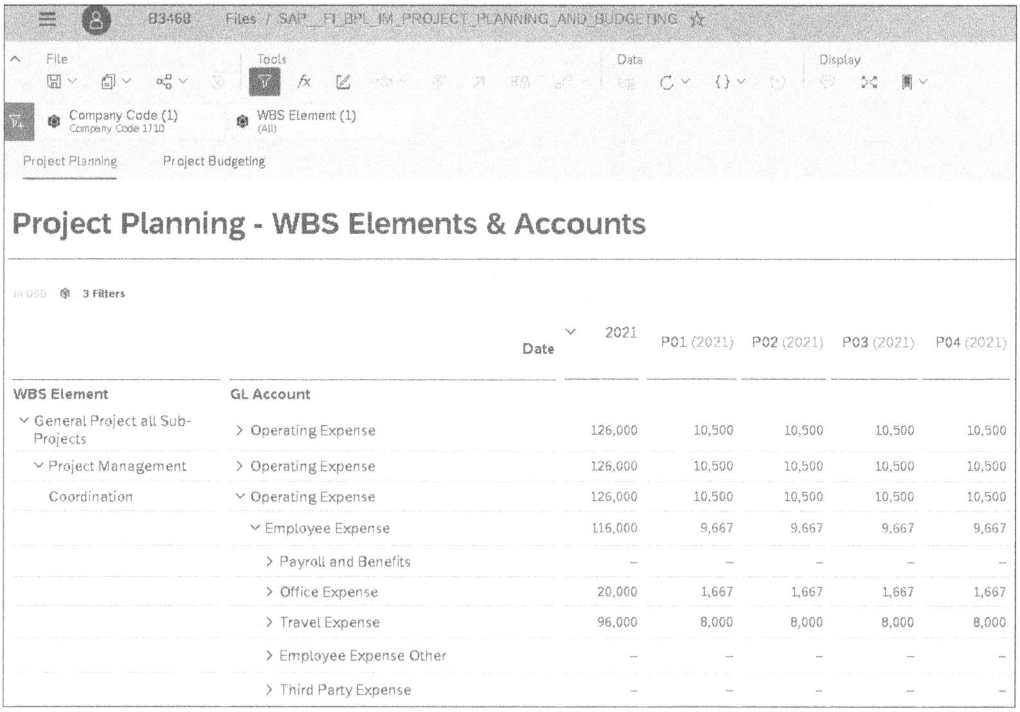

Project Planning - WBS Elements & Accounts

| WBS Element | GL Account | 2021 | P01 (2021) | P02 (2021) | P03 (2021) | P04 (2021) |
|---|---|---|---|---|---|---|
| General Project all Sub-Projects | > Operating Expense | 126,000 | 10,500 | 10,500 | 10,500 | 10,500 |
| Project Management | > Operating Expense | 126,000 | 10,500 | 10,500 | 10,500 | 10,500 |
| Coordination | Operating Expense | 126,000 | 10,500 | 10,500 | 10,500 | 10,500 |
| | Employee Expense | 116,000 | 9,667 | 9,667 | 9,667 | 9,667 |
| | > Payroll and Benefits | – | – | – | – | – |
| | > Office Expense | 20,000 | 1,667 | 1,667 | 1,667 | 1,667 |
| | > Travel Expense | 96,000 | 8,000 | 8,000 | 8,000 | 8,000 |
| | > Employee Expense Other | – | – | – | – | – |
| | > Third Party Expense | – | – | – | – | – |

**Figure 2.41** Project Planning

### 2.4.3 Profitability Planning and Reporting

Now, let's once again look at a different view of the Trial Balance app. In Figure 2.42, we've chosen a similar view to the one shown previously in Figure 2.7, but this time we've selected different market segments to give a sense of the multidimensional nature of the operating concern, which can contain up to 60 different reporting dimensions. Typically, a commercial manager will be responsible for the various market segments and will be given goals, either in monetary or volume terms. These are established as part of the planning process.

Figure 2.43 shows the **SAP_FI_BPL_IM_PROFITABILITY_PROF_INPUT** planning story with the units of product to be sold to various customers. Again, you can use the **Quantities • Actual Based** data action button to reference information about previous volumes sold before you start planning. These sales quantities will drive the production quantities and associated raw material quantities and activity quantities to be used in production, as you saw in the quantity structure shown previously in Figure 2.35.

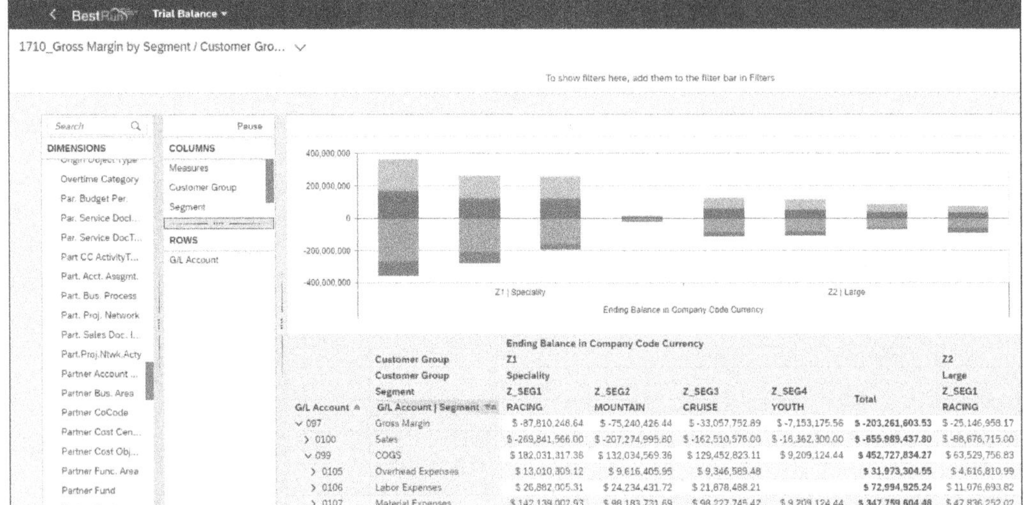


**Figure 2.42** Trial Balance App Showing Revenue and Cost of Goods Sold by Customer Group and Segment

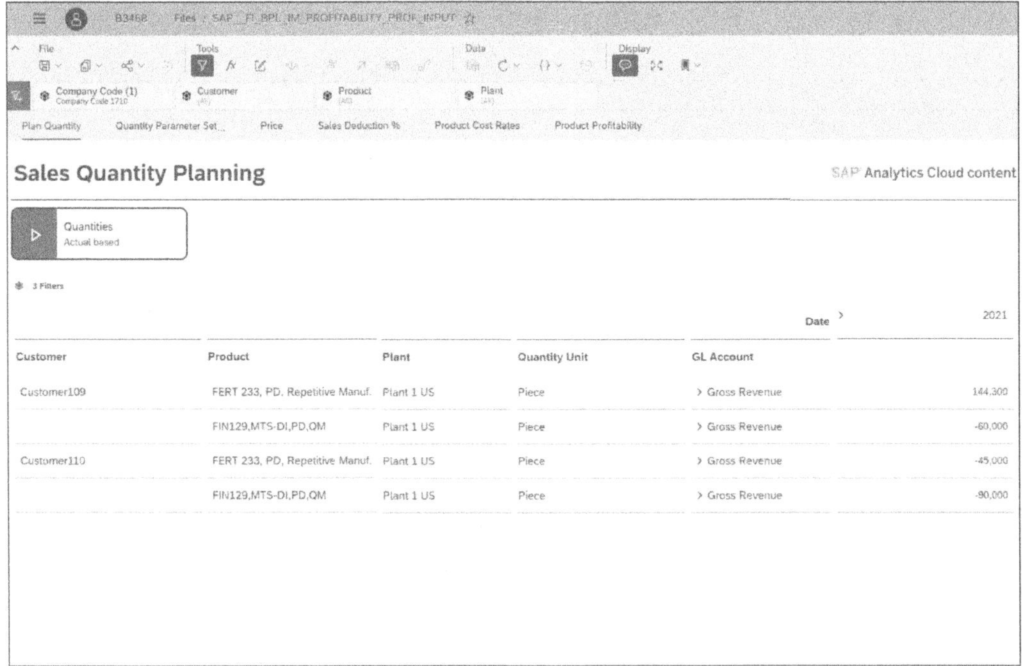


**Figure 2.43** Sales Quantity Planning

In Figure 2.44, the sales quantities are associated with the quantities from the cost estimate shown initially in Figure 2.35. Here you could adjust the assumptions about the quantities to be consumed to calculate the planned product profitability.

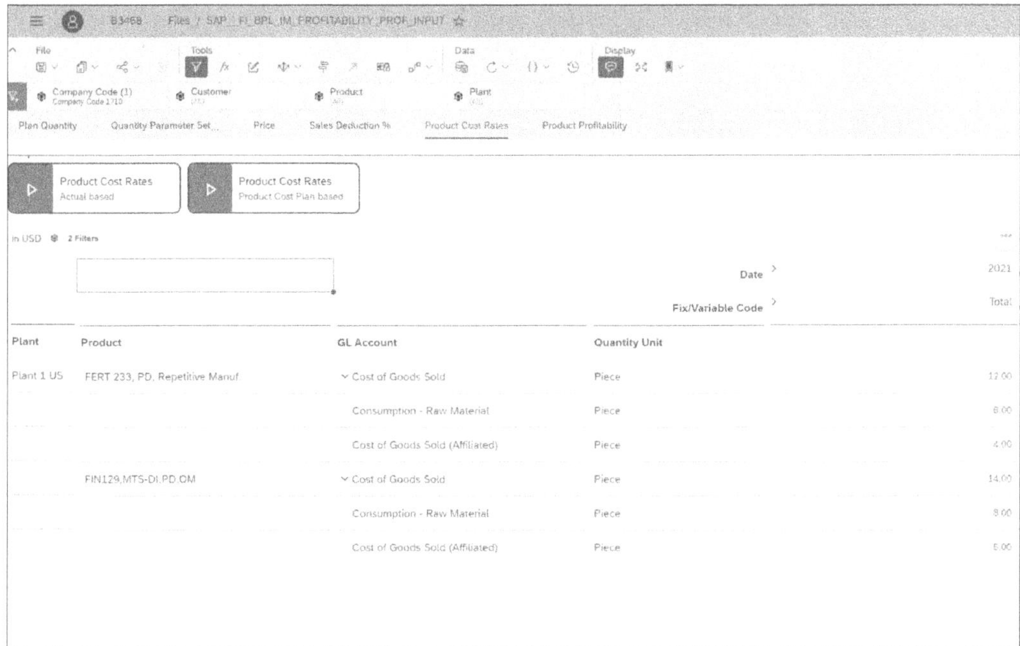

Figure 2.44 Product Quantities Relating to Sales Quantities

Although product profitability is clearly monetary, there is always a quantity associated. In the Product Profitability app (SAP Fiori ID F2765) shown in Figure 2.45, you can see the various contribution margins but also the billed quantity, which represents the numbers of bicycles sold in each category. This report differs from the Trial Balance app in that instead of showing accounts it shows *measures*: billed revenue, recognized revenue, cost of goods sold—variable, and so on. These measures are calculated using *semantic tags*, which are delivered with the report and group the various accounts for reporting purposes.

You can easily return to the account view from the Trial Balance app by choosing a general ledger account on the right. We'll look at how to assign your accounts to the delivered semantic tags and create your own tags in Chapter 10.

While Figure 2.45 is aggregating the data from the various revenue and cost of goods sold accounts and secondary cost elements to calculate the product profitability, the Display Line Items—Margin Analysis app (SAP Fiori ID F4818), shown in Figure 2.46, allows the controller to search for and analyze the line items behind the revenue, cost of goods sold, and so on. If your organization isn't yet using SAP Fiori, the equivalent transaction is Transaction KE24N or **Accounting • Controlling • Profitability Analysis • Information System • Display Line Item List • Actual**.

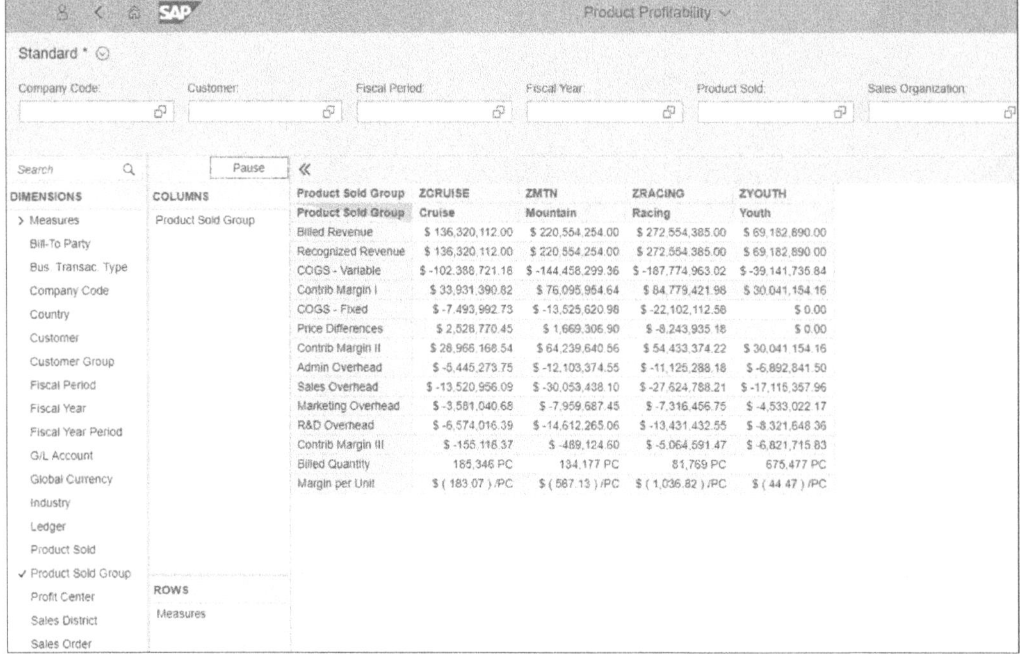


**Figure 2.45** Product Profitability

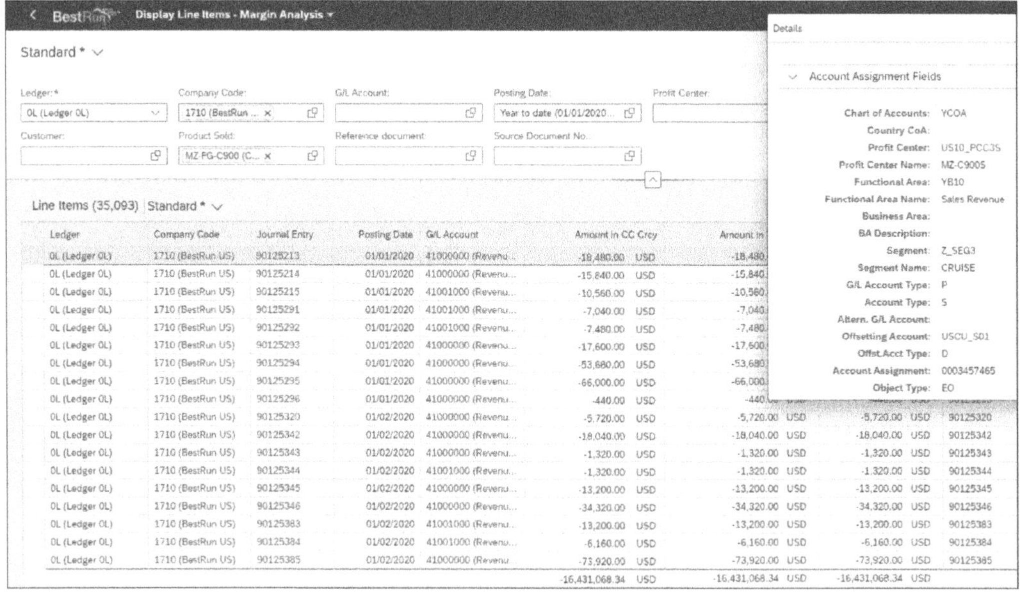


**Figure 2.46** Display Line Items—Margin Analysis App with Account Assignment Details

We'll return to the topic of margin analysis in Chapter 7.

## 2.5 Reporting and Analytics

We've used reports throughout this chapter to explain how the controlling values are captured in the Universal Journal and how they flow by means of allocations and settlement. In this section, we'll take a look at the bigger reporting picture, a topic that we'll return to in Chapter 10.

### 2.5.1 Role-Based Reporting

One of the fundamental ideas behind SAP Fiori is that it should be role-based. The activities we've looked at so far have been covered by the following roles:

- The cost accountant—overhead role covers the activities that we looked at in Section 2.4.1.
- The cost accountant—production role covers the activities that we looked at in Section 2.4.2.
- The cost accountant—sales role covers the activities that we looked at in Section 2.4.3.

Each role comprises a series of business catalogs, and the various SAP Fiori apps are assigned to these catalogs, an example of which is shown in Figure 2.47.

**Figure 2.47** SAP Fiori Launchpad with Selection of Analytical Apps

The goal is to deliver an overview of the main KPIs for each role, as shown in the Sales Accounting Overview app (SAP Fiori ID F3228) in Figure 2.48—but this roadmap item is not complete, so there isn't yet an equivalent overview for overhead accounting and production accounting.

The various cards included in this app illustrate the focus on data visualization that you saw in the T-accounts apps that accompanied us through Section 2.1 or in the Material Value Chain app in Figure 2.40. Figure 2.49 shows how the Allocation Flow app (SAP Fiori ID F4022) transforms the traditional lists of senders and receivers resulting from an allocation into a view that shows how the costs flow from the US10_M1 sender cost center to the many receiver cost centers, while offering the ability to navigate to the associated journal entries as required.

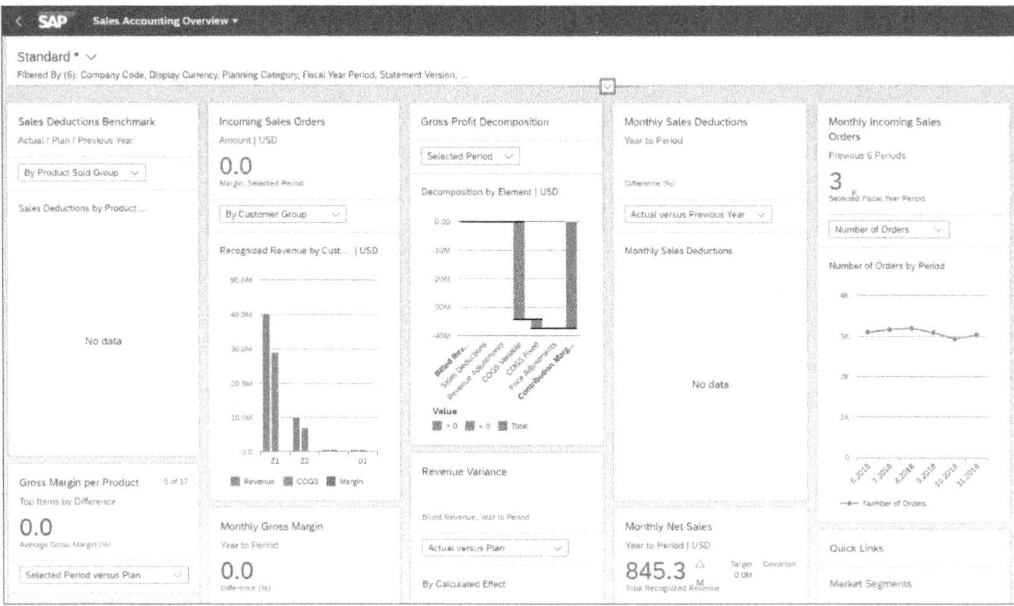


Figure 2.48 Sales Accounting Overview

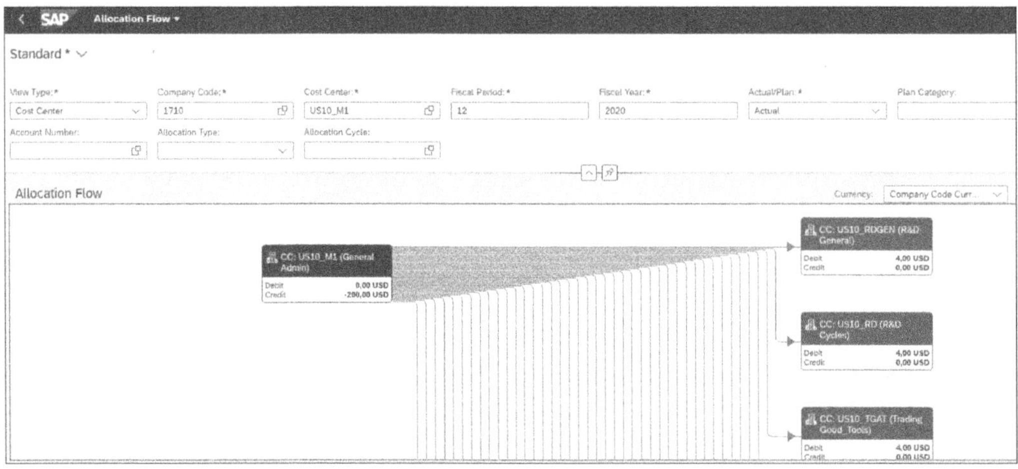


Figure 2.49 Allocation Flow App

Figure 2.50 shows the traditional document flow that provides the link between the goods movements in logistics and the associated accounting documents transformed into a visualization in the Display Document Flow app (SAP Fiori ID F3665). This app shows the purchase order, goods receipt, and invoice receipt in the upper part of the screen and the associated journal entries in the lower part of the screen.

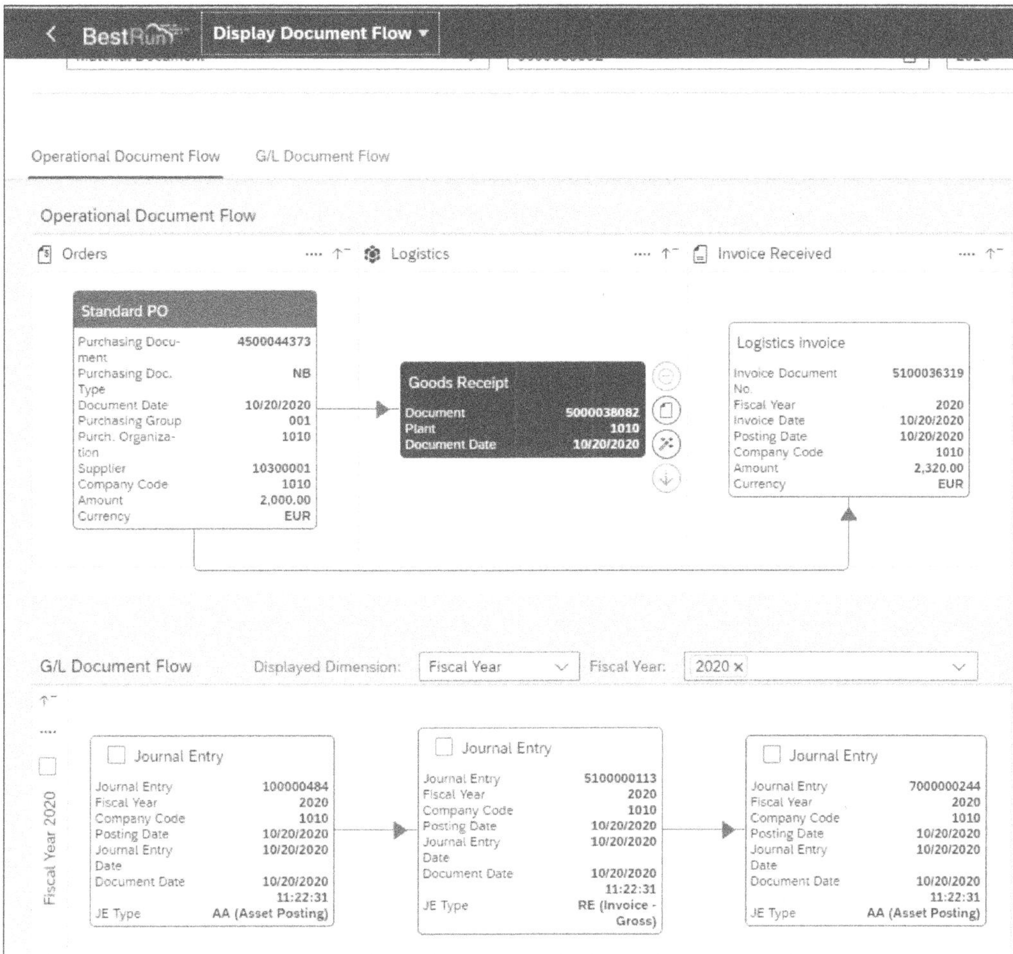


**Figure 2.50** Document Flow App

Aside from the many pure reporting apps we have shown throughout the chapter, there is a focus on apps that help the controller to fix problems caused by missing configuration, such as the Monitor Predictive Accounting app shown in Figure 2.22 or the equivalent apps for monitoring problems in the calculation of WIP or event-based revenue recognition that we will cover in more detail in Chapter 6 and Chapter 7.

What these apps have in common is that they rely on a *virtual data model* to translate the tables storing the costs and revenue and the associated master data into *core data services (CDS) views* that can be consumed in SAP Fiori. The virtual data model delivers a far greater flexibility than was possible with the legacy tables. We'll explain how to add further market segments in Chapter 4 and how to extend the master data in Chapter 10.

### 2.5.2 Compatibility Views

While we've tried to walk you through the big ideas in controlling using SAP Fiori apps, this wasn't possible in some areas, so we used classic reports to show target/actual costs and variances on the cost centers and production variances on the production orders. This is because there is not yet a virtual data model for the target costs and variances. There may also be situations in which the SAP S/4HANA functionality is not yet mature enough for your purposes and you need to use the classic functionality, as we mentioned for budget availability control on WBS elements with assigned orders or networks.

In other cases, your organization may have made a conscious choice not to implement SAP Fiori yet, and in those cases, you'll be working with the classic line item reports (Transaction KSB1 for cost center line items, Transaction KOB1 for order line items, Transaction CJI3 for project line items, and Transaction KE24 for margin analysis line items), as shown in Figure 2.51, instead of using the new reports. To work with these reports, you should know that the system is translating the information in the Universal Journal back into the old form, so you'll see cost elements instead of general ledger accounts, and you'll only be able to display the fields that were part of the old controlling tables (table COEP in the case of the line item reports).

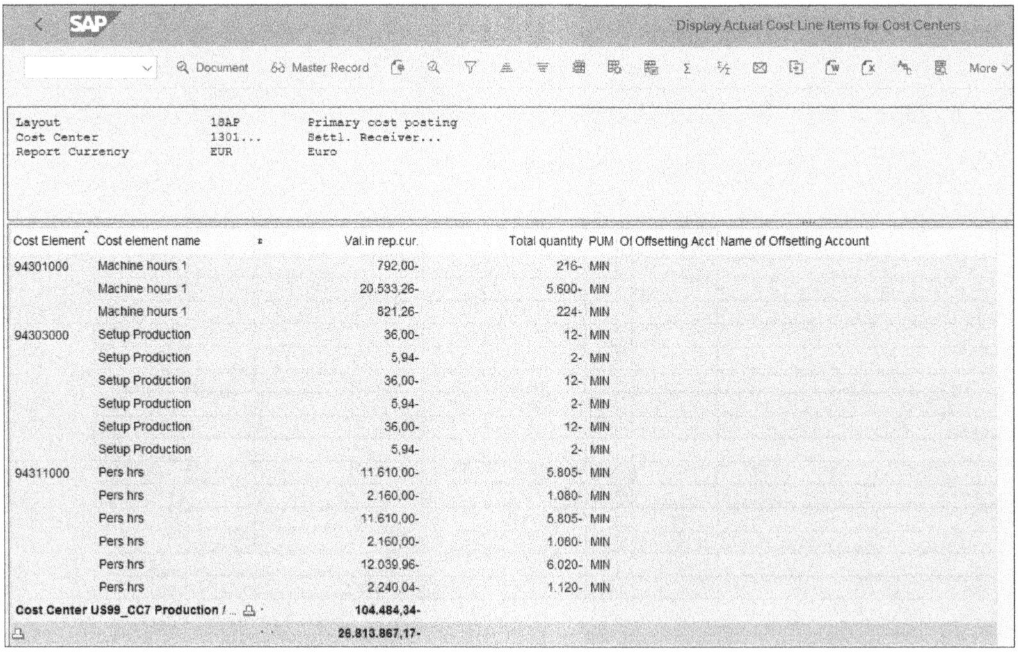

Display Actual Cost Line Items for Cost Centers
Document
Master Record
More
Layout 1SAP Primary cost posting
Cost Center 1301... Settl. Receiver...
Report Currency EUR Euro

| Cost Element | Cost element name | Val.in rep.cur. | Total quantity | PUM | Of Offsetting Acct | Name of Offsetting Account |
|---|---|---|---|---|---|---|
| 94301000 | Machine hours 1 | 792,00- | 216- | MIN | | |
| | Machine hours 1 | 20.533,26- | 5.600- | MIN | | |
| | Machine hours 1 | 821,26- | 224- | MIN | | |
| 94303000 | Setup Production | 36,00- | 12- | MIN | | |
| | Setup Production | 5,94- | 2- | MIN | | |
| | Setup Production | 36,00- | 12- | MIN | | |
| | Setup Production | 5,94- | 2- | MIN | | |
| | Setup Production | 36,00- | 12- | MIN | | |
| | Setup Production | 5,94- | 2- | MIN | | |
| 94311000 | Pers hrs | 11.610,00- | 5.805- | MIN | | |
| | Pers hrs | 2.160,00- | 1.080- | MIN | | |
| | Pers hrs | 11.610,00- | 5.805- | MIN | | |
| | Pers hrs | 2.160,00- | 1.080- | MIN | | |
| | Pers hrs | 12.039,96- | 6.020- | MIN | | |
| | Pers hrs | 2.240,04- | 1.120- | MIN | | |
| Cost Center US99_CC7 Production / ... | | 104.484,34- | | | | |
| | | 26.813.867,17- | | | | |

**Figure 2.51** Classic Cost Center Line Items

If you navigate from the legacy reports to the list of accounting documents, as shown in Figure 2.52, you'll find that the information in the Universal Journal has been chopped up into the old document structures, so it will look like you have a separate accounting document, controlling document, and Material Ledger document, even though the information shown is actually being sourced from the same document.

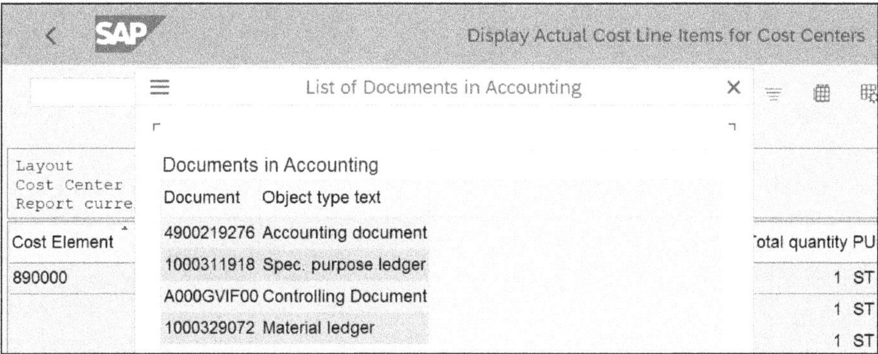


**Figure 2.52** Accounting Documents in Compatibility View

## 2.6 Summary

We've now explained the impact of merging financial accounting and management accounting in SAP S/4HANA and the effect on the different cost postings. We also looked at planning, predictions, and the objectives of the controller when working in management accounting and margin analysis. We'll return to many of these ideas as we work through the remaining chapters and return to the topic of reporting in detail in Chapter 10.

We'll now look at the organizational structures that are relevant to controlling applications in the next chapter.

# Chapter 3
# Organizational Structures

*Setting up the organizational structures correctly is essential for financial accounting and controlling to interact properly with each other and with the other applications. Mistakes in your system design can be expensive later, so it's important to set up the system correctly and have a clear understanding of the implications of each of your design choices.*



Almost all ERP business processes are integrated into financial accounting and controlling, and it's the role of controlling to valuate these processes and assign them to the correct controlling object, just as we discussed when we looked at the link between the purchasing cost center and the operating supplies in the previous chapter. This link ensures that controlling provides a reliable view of the company's costs and revenues and margin by controlling objects or market segments.

As a controller, you need to decide on the fundamental settings of the organizational structures that we'll discuss in this chapter. They need to be set up in the SAP S/4HANA implementation phase. They have a high impact on the operational processes, and they can't be changed easily later.

Our main focus in this chapter is on the entities that are important for controlling. However, we'll also explain generic general ledger and logistic organizational settings. In Section 3.1, we discuss the basic controlling-relevant organizational elements and central settings that you need to understand when setting up a system or dealing with an existing system. Then in Section 3.2, we come to the organization integration to the logistic applications. Finally, in Section 3.3 we explain reporting-relevant entities. We'll dive deeper into all these settings in the following chapters.

These necessary system settings can be found in the Implementation Guide (IMG) and can be accessed via Transaction SPRO.

## 3.1 Organizational Structures in Finance

The organizational structures that are relevant for financial accounting and controlling are defined in the IMG via menu path **Enterprise Structure • Definition • Financial Accounting** and **Enterprise Structure • Definition • Controlling**. We'll walk through each one in the following sections.

### 3.1.1 Company

The *company* organizational element in SAP S/4HANA describes a legal entity for which legal reporting requirements can be covered from the perspective of group reporting. To this extent, it's best understood as an affiliated company or trading partner within that group.

It shouldn't be confused with the company code, which we'll look at next. The focus of the company is to act as a financial entity for the purpose of group reporting and to track the intercompany relationships.

The consolidated financial statement can primarily be understood as the consolidation of legally independent companies. In SAP S/4HANA, the company entity supports the consolidation. It's also called a *trading partner* in reports, which makes the role of this legal entity clearer.

You can check the defined companies by following IMG path **Enterprise Structure • Definition • Financial Accounting • Define Company.** After selecting a company, and clicking **Details**, you'll arrive at the screen shown in Figure 3.1, here showing the information for company **1010**.

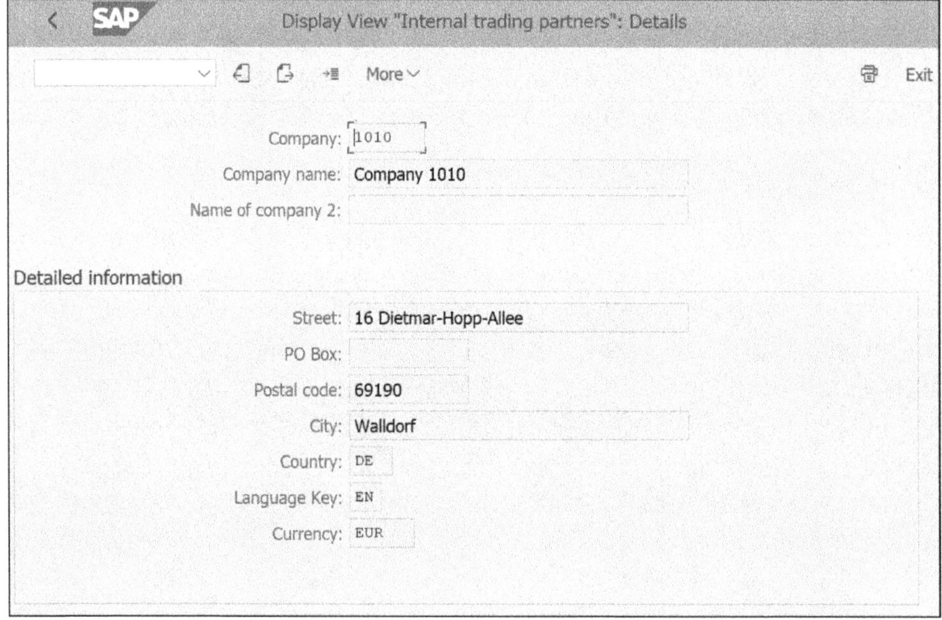


**Figure 3.1** Trading Partner Definition

The six-character **Company** field represents the company ID. To record the processes between two companies and make them analyzable for group reporting, it's stored as a trading partner attribute in the journal entry line item for the relevant postings.

Some of the associated processes will be discussed in Chapter 9, in which we'll explain intercompany stock transfers, intercompany billing, and intercompany controlling allocations. In these business processes, the trading partner is stored in the journal entries to make the cross-company relationship transparent, and it serves as a base for consolidation and group reporting.

### 3.1.2 Company Code

The *company code* reflects the legal organizational entity, for which you provide your balance sheet and income statement reporting. On the company code level, you define your chart of accounts, currencies, and applicable accounting principles, with which the business process valuation is defined. Period-end closing is also done on the company code level.

There can be a 1:*n* relationship defined between a company and company code. But all company codes within a company must use the same chart of accounts and fiscal year. The currencies can be different.

To check the defined company codes, follow menu path **Enterprise Structure • Definition • Financial Accounting • Edit, Copy, Delete, Check Company Code**, then select **Edit Company Code Data**. You'll arrive at a list with company codes and company names. You can select a **Company Code** to arrive at the screen shown in Figure 3.2—here, showing the details for company code **1010**.

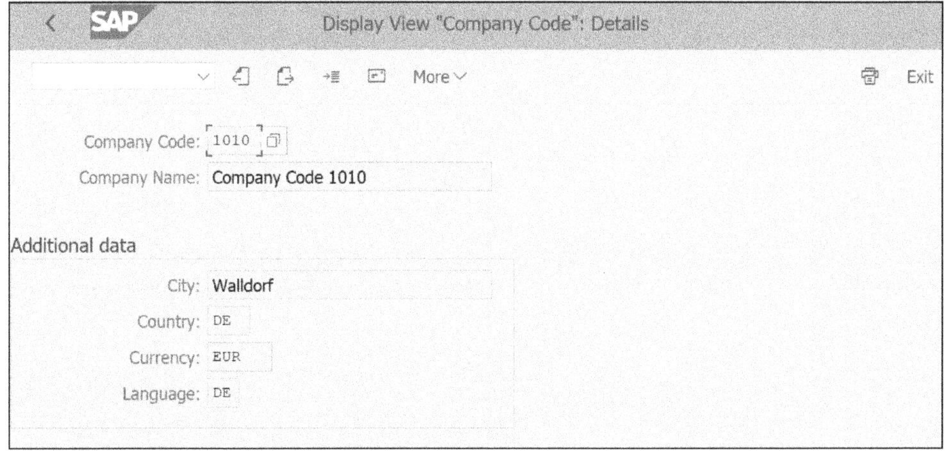


**Figure 3.2** Definition of Company Code

You see here the **Company Name**, **City**, **Country**, **Currency**, and **Language** defined for a **Company Code** ID.

For every company code, you need to control the settings for the financial postings, which you can maintain in the company code parameters. Therefore, follow IMG menu path **Financial Accounting • Financial Accounting Global Settings • Company Code • Enter Global Parameters** (or use Transaction OBY6). You'll get a list of the maintained company codes. Now double-click the relevant company code. You'll arrive at the screen shown in Figure 3.3.

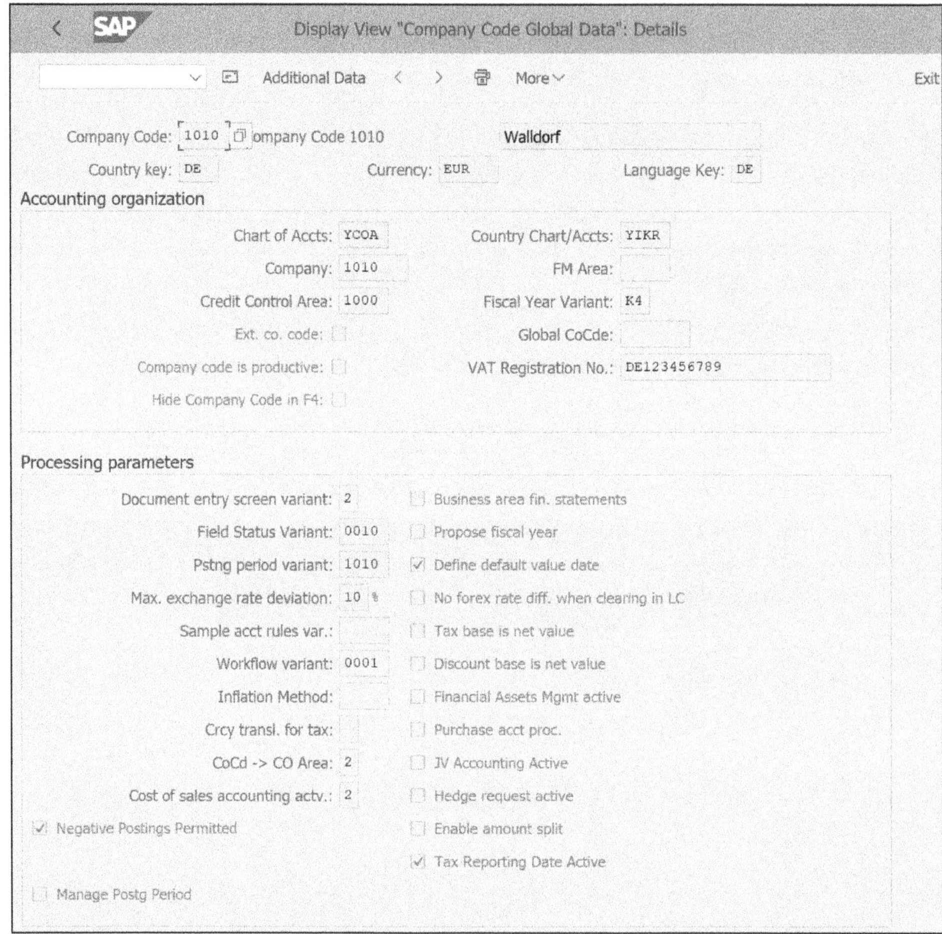


**Figure 3.3** Central Parameters of Company Code

You can see here the main parameters that determine the postings in financial accounting and—based on the Universal Journal integration—in controlling. Let's focus on some key parameters that are important for controlling.

The company code is linked with other organizational elements of the accounting organization: company and controlling area. In the top section, you see the assignment

**Company Code 1010.** The **CoCd -> CO Area** field in the lower section, defined as **2**, shows that there are multiple company codes assigned to one controlling area. We'll discuss this further in the next section.

With the **Chart of Accts** field, the general ledger accounts are defined, as are the cost elements because of the integration of controlling and the general ledger in the Universal Journal that we explored in the previous chapter. You can also define an alternative chart of accounts in parallel for local reporting requirements with the **Country Chart/Accts** field.

The **Fiscal Year Variant** defines the number of posting periods in a fiscal year, the number of special periods, and the posting period dependent on the posting date, which allows a posting period different from a calendar month. Because the fiscal year variant is defined on the level of the company code and ledger, you can work with different calendars in parallel if you define multiple parallel ledgers for your company codes. You maintain the fiscal year variants by following IMG menu path **Financial Accounting • Financial Accounting Global Settings • Fiscal Year • Maintain Fiscal Year Variant**.

You enable cost of sales accounting with the **Cost of sales accounting actv** parameter. We'll explain how this affects controlling reporting in Section 3.1.6, which discusses the general ledger reporting attribute functional area.

**SAP ERP versus SAP S/4HANA**

The company code is the central organizational element of financial accounting in SAP S/4HANA. Each posting must be assigned to a company code. On the company code level, you provide your legal reporting. The entity company code is the connector between financials and other applications. In SAP ERP, it was possible to decouple the controlling settings from the company code, but this is no longer possible in SAP S/4HANA and all controlling postings must be assigned to a company code.

### 3.1.3 Controlling Area

The *controlling area* is the central organizational unit defining cost accounting settings. It can be maintained in the IMG by following **Controlling • General Controlling • Organization • Maintain Controlling Area**, then selecting the **Maintain Controlling Area** activity.

You'll arrive at the screen shown in Figure 3.4, on which the basic settings for the controlling area are shown.

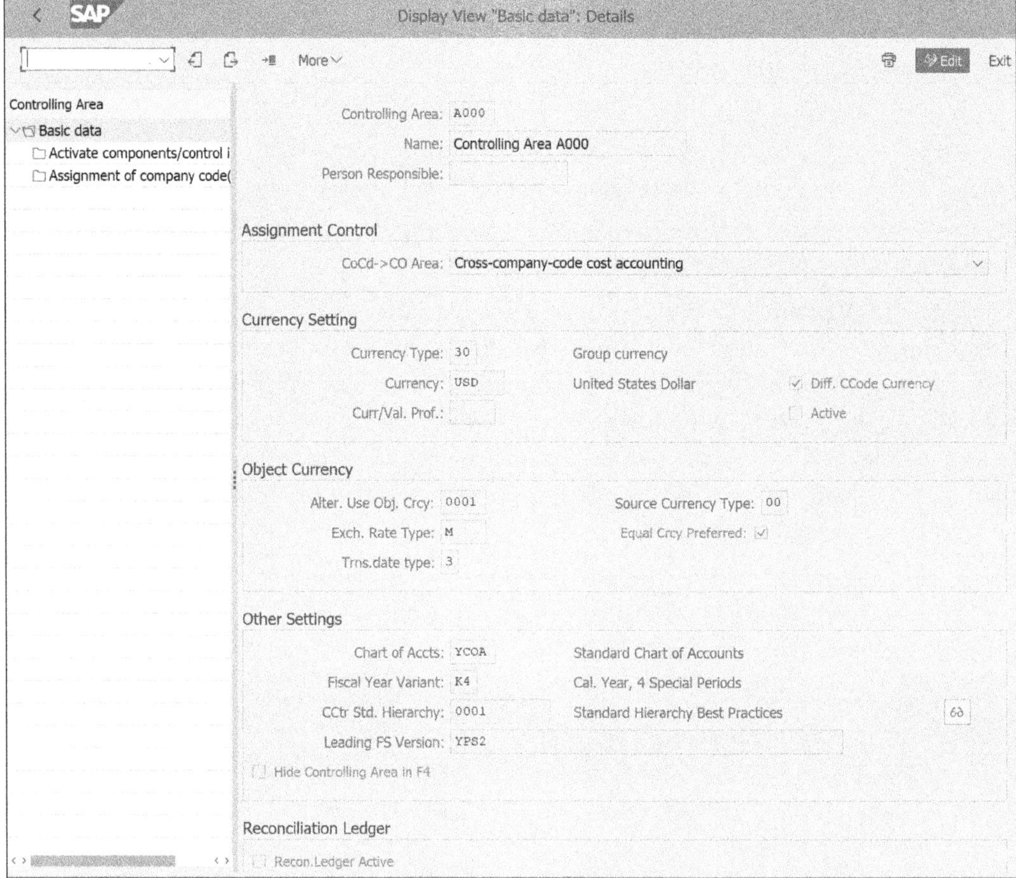


**Figure 3.4** Customizing for Controlling Area: Basic Settings

Let's go through these sections briefly.

### Assignment Control

This is a very important area that influences intercompany processes. It has a heavy impact on the setup of all assigned company codes. If **Cross-company-code cost accounting** is active—like in the example here—and multiple company codes are assigned, several settings need to be aligned for the assigned company codes.

The fiscal year variant and the chart of account must be the same in the controlling area and all assigned company codes and the currency control must be aligned. The group currency for the assigned company codes is defined by the controlling area currency (see Section 3.3.2).

You must be aware of this when several company codes are assigned to one controlling area. This is the case in the current example (see Figure 3.5). You get to this screen by marking the controlling area—here, **Controlling Area A000**—and then selecting **Assignment of company code(s)** in the activity tab on the left.

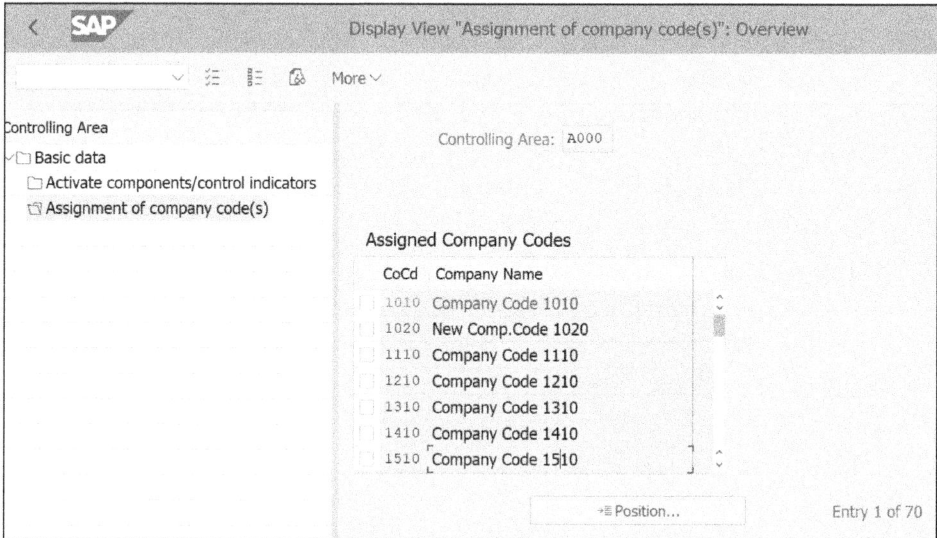


**Figure 3.5** Customizing for Controlling Area: Company Code Assignment

It's important to know that this setup for a cross-company-code controlling area is the prerequisite for the cross-company cost allocations, as we'll explain in Chapter 9.

### Currency Setting

The **Currency Setting** section (shown previously in Figure 3.4) defines the controlling area currency. In this example, **Currency Type 30** allows a company-code-independent group currency, which is defined in the line below as **USD**.

Here you assign company codes with different company code currencies—for example, EUR, GBP, and USD—to one controlling area. To enable a uniform currency across company codes, you can use the setup shown previously in Figure 3.4. You also define your own group currency—here, **USD**—which is the valid group currency for all assigned company codes.

### Object Currency

A controlling object, such as a cost center or work breakdown structure (WBS) element, can have its own object currency, which is defined in its master record. In the **Object Currency** section, you can define with which rate (**Exch. Rate Type**), with which date (**Trns.date type**), and from which currency (**Source Currency Type**) the currency conversion takes place.

#### Other Settings

In the **Other Settings** section, you define the fiscal year variant and the chart of accounts, as described in the previous section.

Then you define at controlling area level a cost center standard hierarchy (**CCtr Std. Hierarchy**). All cost centers within the controlling area—in all assigned company codes—need to be assigned to this standard hierarchy. This ensures that all cost centers and their costs can be selected with one hierarchy. Of course, you can define as many alternative hierarchies as you want—for example, for different reporting requirements. We'll explain how to set up the various hierarchies for reporting in Chapter 10.

With the financial statement version, you typically structure your financial statement reports. This allows you to create a hierarchy of general ledger accounts. For the nodes, a summary line item is created in the reporting. For example, you can define a node named **Revenues** and then assign all revenue general ledger accounts to this node to get a revenue summary line in your reporting.

When you work with the Universal Journal, all cost elements are created as general ledger accounts so that you can use financial statement versions for controlling reporting in addition to their more familiar use in financial accounting. This makes a lot of sense as it can also be used to report balance sheets accounts. This applies for 360-degree reporting for, say, customer projects and sales order reporting showing, say, work in process (WIP) with controlling and profitability attributes. We'll talk more about this in Chapter 7.

Here in the controlling area parameters, you can define a leading controlling financial statement version (**Leading FS Version**). With this setting, you ensure consistent data for the different applications. We'll discuss this setting again when we look at budget controlling in Chapter 5, product and service margin reporting and event-based revenue recognition in Chapter 7, and at the controlling reports in Chapter 10.

> **One Controlling Area**
>
> We highly recommend using exactly one cross-company code controlling area in SAP S/4HANA. This setup enables additional functionality, like intercompany cost accounting postings (see Chapter 9). It will also help to further align cost accounting and financial accounting for your group reporting. In this case, all your company codes will be assigned to one controlling area.

### 3.1.4 Operating Concern

We looked at how to assign revenues and cost of goods sold to your controlling area in the previous structure. The structure that controls your market segment reporting is the operating concern. How you set up the structure of your operating concern depends of course on your business. With the market segment reporting, you get answers to questions about the profitability of your company: What margin do I achieve for my products? What's the margin of my line of service? What's my margin in different industries?

The organizational unit for margin analysis in SAP S/4HANA therefore is the *operating concern*. This is defined in Customizing by following IMG menu path **Controlling • Profitability Analysis • Structures • Define Operating Concern • Maintain Operating Concern** (or Transaction KEA0). You'll see the screen shown in Figure 3.6.

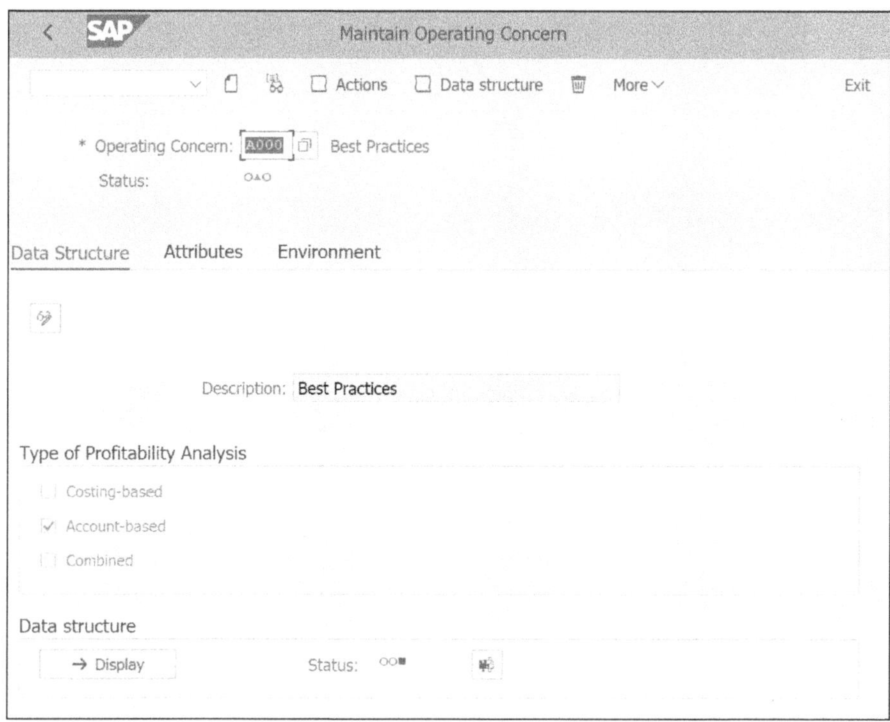


**Figure 3.6** Customizing for Maintaining Operating Concern

First you need to decide for your operating concern on the method that you will use to store your market segment data. There are two very different profitability analysis solutions available in SAP S/4HANA, which you can select in the **Type of Profitability Analysis** section. The **Costing-based** profitability analysis has its own database and assigns costs and revenues to value fields (as does combined profitability analysis, which is a variant of the costing-based method). The **Account-based** profitability analysis is integrated into the Universal Journal and assigns costs and revenues to accounts as we discussed in the previous chapter. In on-premise SAP S/4HANA, both methods are available. You can activate both in parallel too. In SAP S/4HANA Cloud, only account-based profitability analysis is available.

The operating concern is assigned to a controlling area. You can check it by following IMG menu path **Enterprise Structure • Assignment • Controlling • Assign Controlling**

**Area to Operating Concern** (see Figure 3.7). There can be only one operating concern per controlling area.

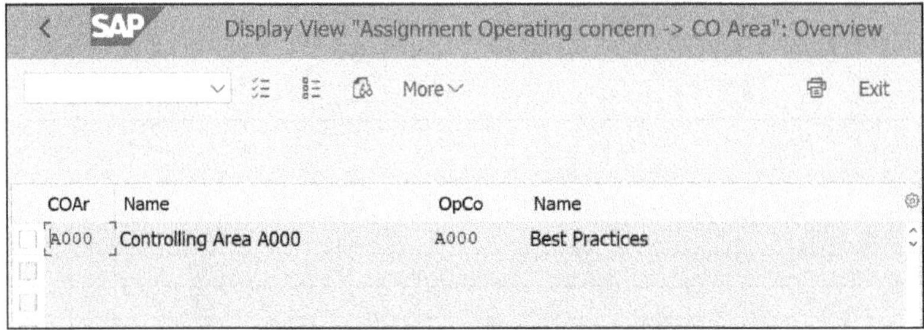


**Figure 3.7** Assignment of Operating Concern to Controlling Area

If you follow our recommendation to use exactly one cross-company controlling area for your system setup, you will only define one operating concern.

With the Universal Journal, we simplify processes but increase reporting insights, as discussed in Chapter 1 and Chapter 2. So, we get rid of period-end closing steps. We can work on one data model for all applications and there are no reconciliation efforts between the applications by design.

The Universal Journal's integrated profitability follows this approach. There is no longer any reconciliation effort required, making the lives of accountants and controllers easier. At the same time, it gifts new insights. SAP invested in this application in the last releases and will focus on it in future.

**SAP ERP versus SAP S/4HANA**

In SAP ERP, companies running SAP mainly used costing-based profitability analysis. However, to benefit from the innovations of the Universal Journal, process simplifications, and additional reporting insights, we recommend the activation of account-based profitability analysis, now known as margin analysis in the Universal Journal's integrated profitability.

It's important to recognize that when you migrate from SAP ERP using costing-based profitability analysis to SAP S/4HANA using the Universal Journal and integrated margin analysis, it will lead to significant changes. We'll discuss margin analysis in detail in Chapter 7.

With this background, we will focus in this book on the Universal Journal's integrated profitability. We'll handle costing-based profitability analysis only in side notes.

Based on the operating concern, you define your own market segment attributes that reflect your business. You define the relevant market segment attributes by following IMG menu path **Controlling • Profitability Analysis • Structures • Define Operating Concern • Maintain Characteristics** (or Transaction KEA5).

Now, select **All Characteristics** and press **Display** to arrive at the screen in Figure 3.8.

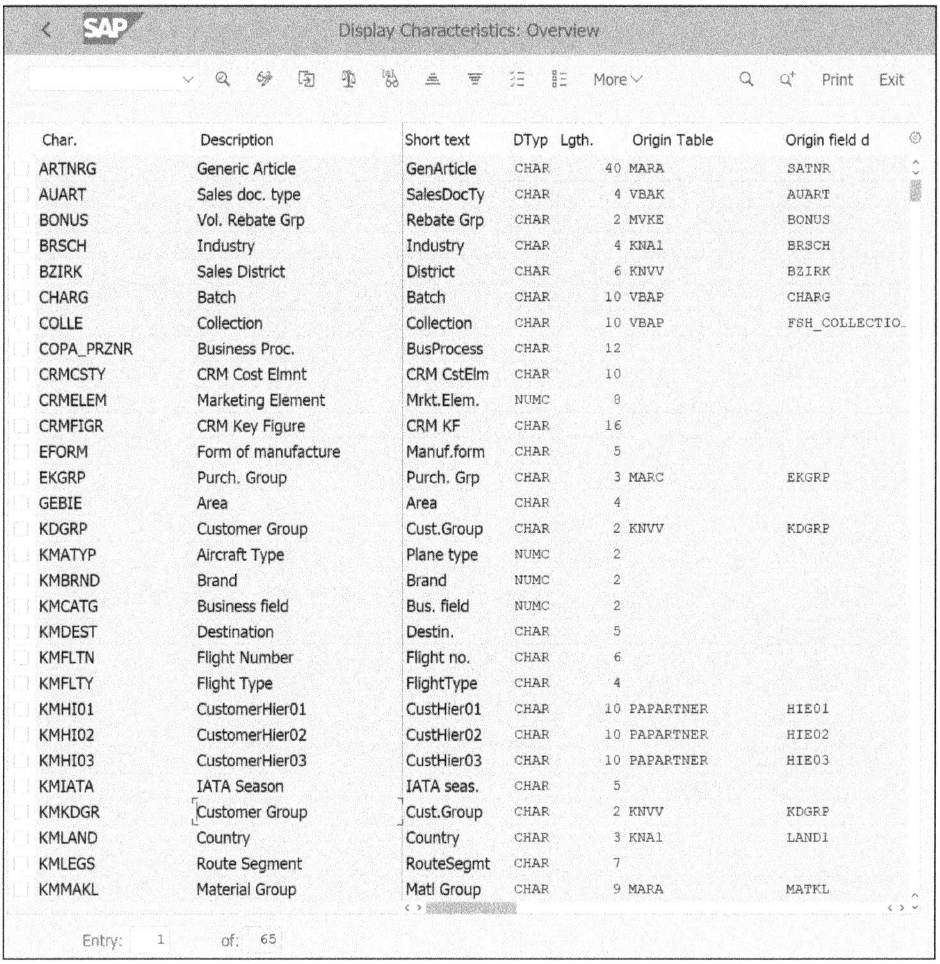

Display Characteristics: Overview

More Print Exit

| Char. | Description | Short text | DTyp | Lgth. | Origin Table | Origin field d |
|---|---|---|---|---|---|---|
| ARTNRG | Generic Article | GenArticle | CHAR | 40 | MARA | SATNR |
| AUART | Sales doc. type | SalesDocTy | CHAR | 4 | VBAK | AUART |
| BONUS | Vol. Rebate Grp | Rebate Grp | CHAR | 2 | MVKE | BONUS |
| BRSCH | Industry | Industry | CHAR | 4 | KNA1 | BRSCH |
| BZIRK | Sales District | District | CHAR | 6 | KNVV | BZIRK |
| CHARG | Batch | Batch | CHAR | 10 | VBAP | CHARG |
| COLLE | Collection | Collection | CHAR | 10 | VBAP | FSH_COLLECTIO_ |
| COPA_PRZNR | Business Proc. | BusProcess | CHAR | 12 | | |
| CRMCSTY | CRM Cost Elmnt | CRM CstElm | CHAR | 10 | | |
| CRMELEM | Marketing Element | Mrkt.Elem. | NUMC | 8 | | |
| CRMFIGR | CRM Key Figure | CRM KF | CHAR | 16 | | |
| EFORM | Form of manufacture | Manuf.form | CHAR | 5 | | |
| EKGRP | Purch. Group | Purch. Grp | CHAR | 3 | MARC | EKGRP |
| GEBIE | Area | Area | CHAR | 4 | | |
| KDGRP | Customer Group | Cust.Group | CHAR | 2 | KNVV | KDGRP |
| KMATYP | Aircraft Type | Plane type | NUMC | 2 | | |
| KMBRND | Brand | Brand | NUMC | 2 | | |
| KMCATG | Business field | Bus. field | NUMC | 2 | | |
| KMDEST | Destination | Destin. | CHAR | 5 | | |
| KMFLTN | Flight Number | Flight no. | CHAR | 6 | | |
| KMFLTY | Flight Type | FlightType | CHAR | 4 | | |
| KMHI01 | CustomerHier01 | CustHier01 | CHAR | 10 | PAPARTNER | HIE01 |
| KMHI02 | CustomerHier02 | CustHier02 | CHAR | 10 | PAPARTNER | HIE02 |
| KMHI03 | CustomerHier03 | CustHier03 | CHAR | 10 | PAPARTNER | HIE03 |
| KMIATA | IATA Season | IATA seas. | CHAR | 5 | | |
| KMKDGR | Customer Group | Cust.Group | CHAR | 2 | KNVV | KDGRP |
| KMLAND | Country | Country | CHAR | 3 | KNA1 | LAND1 |
| KMLEGS | Route Segment | RouteSegmt | CHAR | 7 | | |
| KMMAKL | Material Group | Matl Group | CHAR | 9 | MARA | MATKL |

Entry: 1 of: 65

**Figure 3.8** Market Segment Attributes of an Operating Concern

You see here an example for market segment attributes. It's possible to add your own customer-specific attributes by using an extensibility tool, as we'll discuss in Chapter 4.

Central attributes like customer (technical field **KNDNR**) or the sold product (**ARTNRG**) are determined by the business process when, for example, you sell a product or service to customer. Other attributes are derived. Some come from master data, like the product group from the product sold (**ARTNRG**) master or the industry (**BRSCH**) from the customer master. You can define your own derivation logic for the determination of the attributes. We'll cover this in Chapter 4.

If you use costing-based profitability analysis, you need to define value fields. You do this by following IMG menu path **Controlling • Profitability Analysis • Structures • Define Operating Concern • Maintain Value Fields** (or Transaction KEA6).

**Note**

All defined attributes in the operating concern will be added to the Universal Journal and will be potentially available for every journal entry item. We'll explain in detail how to do this in Chapter 4.

### 3.1.5 Profit Center

The profit center differs from the organizational entities that we've looked at so far in that it isn't considered a configuration setting, but rather defined as master data in your productive system. The *profit center* is an organizational accounting unit that structures your company in a management-oriented way. The purpose of a profit center is to be a control unit, for which you can analyze profit and loss (P&L). It's independent of legal requirements and can be defined group-wide; as a consequence, profit centers can be used cross-company.

When profit center accounting is activated, the profit center is derived and stored for every P&L line item. But it's also derived for balance sheet postings that allow, for example, the reporting of open receivable and payable items or the WIP and material stock by profit center.

We look here at the relevance of the profit center for your internal management reporting. You can use the profit center to break down the legal accounting view according to internal management reporting criteria. The product and service relationships between the companies can be analyzed too.

**Example**

Professional service companies typically structure their profit centers in a vertical way by line of service or region to get the margins for different types of services and regions.

In a production company, a horizontal structure is an option. Purchasing, production, and sales margin will be reported by profit center. Alternatively, the profit center structure can be driven by the different product lines.

For the profit center, there is master data available, as shown in Figure 3.9, which you can access with Transaction KE51 (to create it) and Transaction KE52 (to change it). This makes it different from the settings that we have looked at so far, which are always defined in the configuration client.

As you can see, each profit center is assigned to a **Controlling Area**, and there is also an assignment to a **Segment**, an organizational unit of accounting. **Name**, **User Responsible**, **Person Responsible**, and **Department** are attributes, which do not control any processes and do not influence the postings but are available in reporting as master record attributes.

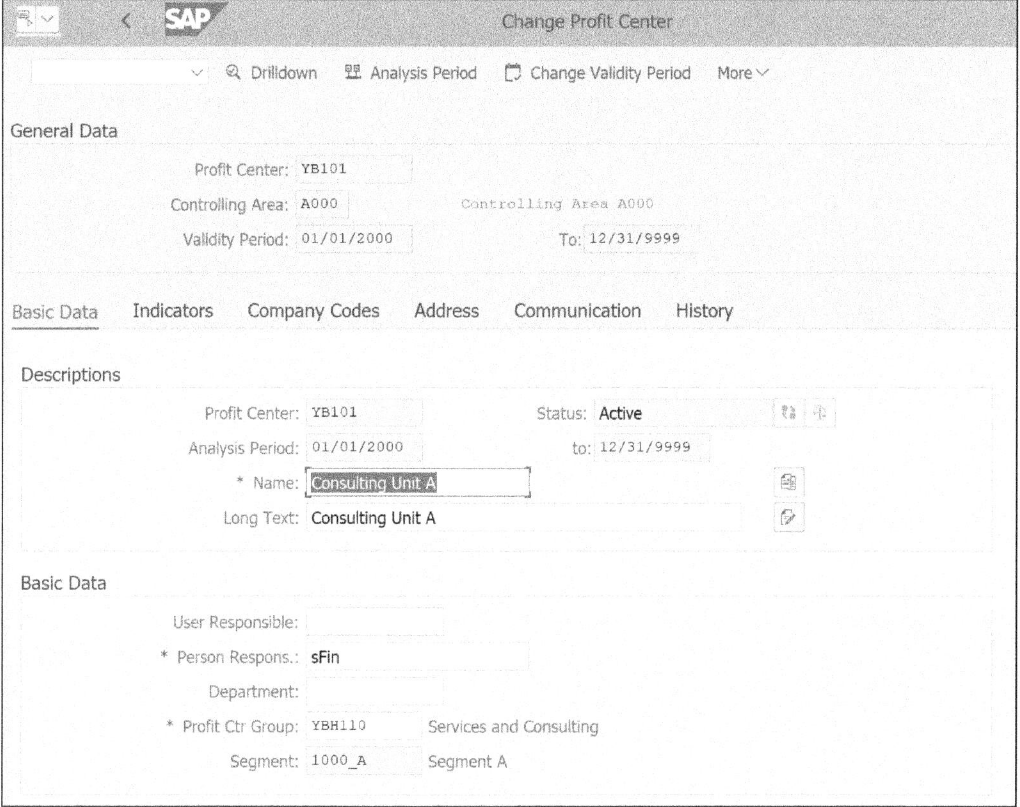


**Figure 3.9** View of Profit Center Master

You need to assign every profit center to a profit center group (**Profit Crt Group**), which is part of the standard profit center hierarchy. There is one standard hierarchy per controlling area specified. The mandatory assignment of every profit center to this hierarchy ensures that for this hierarchy you always select all profit centers. Of course, you can maintain additional hierarchies flexibly in parallel.

You can define which of the attributes shown in Figure 3.9 should be time-dependent. Time dependency is useful if you need to change the assignment of the profit center manager or the address if you move your premises. You define it via IMG under the menu path **Controlling • Profit Center Accounting • Master Data • Profit Center • Specify Time-Dependent Fields for Profit Center** (or Transaction OKE7), arriving at the screen shown in Figure 3.10.

You can now define a validity period by clicking the **Change Validity Period** button and maintaining different attributes for the time-dependent attributes for this period—for example, **Department**. Then its own period for the profit center will be created, which you can view by clicking the **Analysis Period** button.

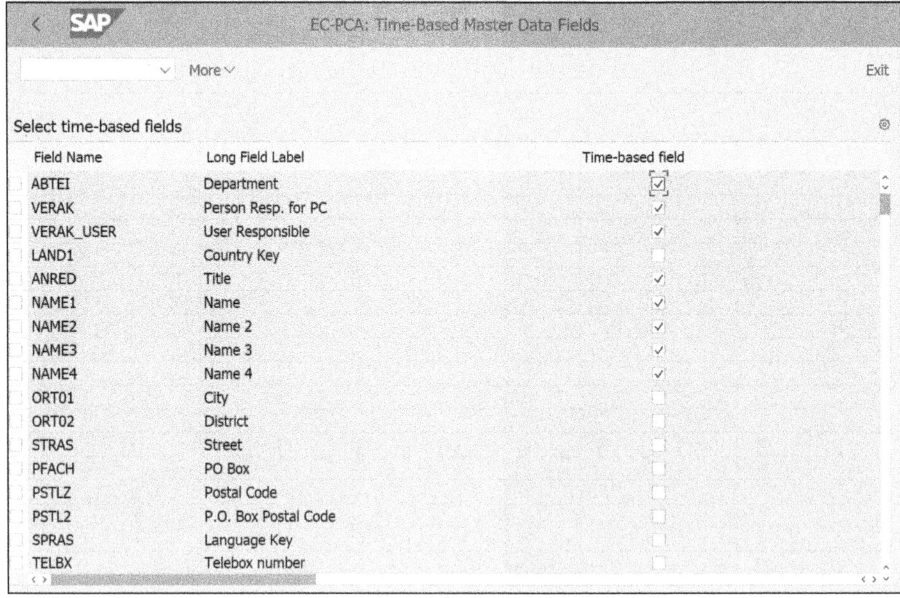


**Figure 3.10** Definition of Time-Dependent Profit Center Fields

As mentioned, the profit center can be used cross-company. The assignment to the company codes if found by selecting the **Company Codes** tab. You'll see the screen shown in Figure 3.11.

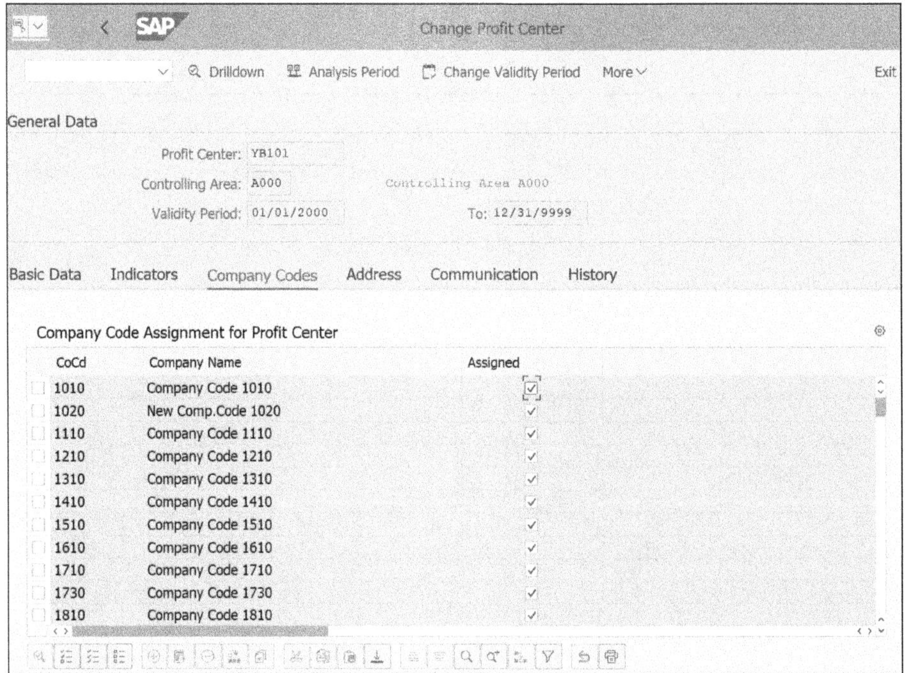


**Figure 3.11** Assignment Profit Center to Company Code

You can mark here for which company codes the profit center can be used. By default, all company codes assigned to the controlling area are active.

Within the **Indicators** tab, it's possible to lock the profit center for postings. In the **Address** and **Communication** tabs, you can provide some attributes for profit centers. In the **History** tab, you can view the history of the profit center changes.

### 3.1.6 Functional Area

You use the functional area to provide reporting according to the cost of sales format. But this isn't only relevant for your legal reporting; you can use it now for controlling analysis, too, as it's offered by the Universal Journal for all accounting applications and no longer restricted to the general ledger.

In Chapter 2, we discussed the difference between costs by nature and costs by function, and it's the functional area that drives the cost by function view. A *functional area* is a financial accounting characteristic, stored in the Universal Journal, that allows classifying expenses according to functions. To view the functional areas, follow IMG menu path **Enterprise Structure • Definition • Financial Accounting • Define Functional Area**. You'll arrive at the screen shown in Figure 3.12.

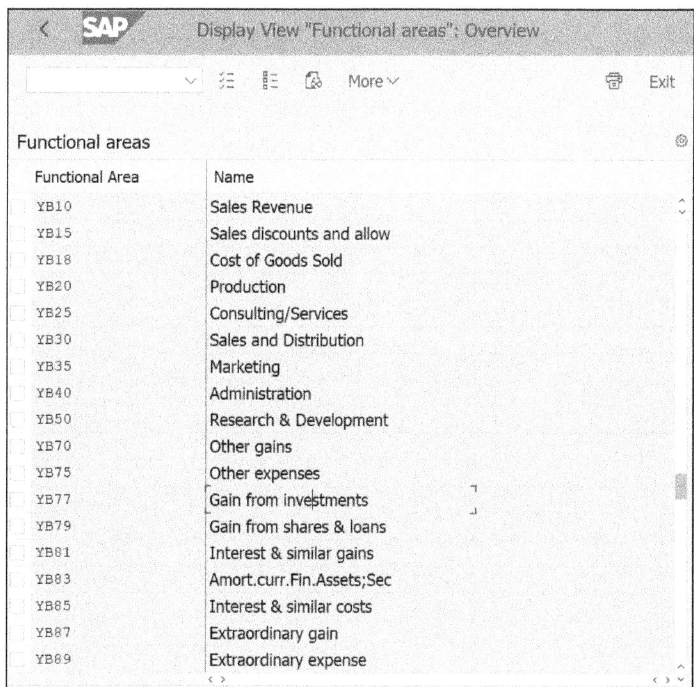


**Figure 3.12** Examples for Functional Areas Defined in Customizing

Whereas a general ledger account describes the nature of the costs, the functional area explains for which function or area the expenses were incurred.

**Example**

As a service company, you post travel expenses on a customer project or customer service order. These travel costs you want to classify as cost of sales. Travel expenses posted on an administration cost center you want to classify as administration costs. You get this distinction with the functional area, which separates the travel costs depending on the associated function.

The functional area is derived during accounting document creation for P&L line items. There are three derivation options possible, with the following access sequence:

1. The functional area is taken from the general ledger account master if one is assigned.
2. The functional area is taken from the account assigned cost object. There are rules for every object to derive a functional area. For example, for projects it's defaulted by the project profile and for cost centers by the cost center category.
3. There is a substitution in place, via which you can apply customer-specific rules for the functional area derivation.

In case of manual postings, the functional area can be manually assigned.

When implementing SAP S/4HANA, you first need to define the required functional areas. Then you need to ensure that they are process-dependently derived by assigning them to the cost objects: projects, production orders, make-to-order sales orders, cost centers, and internal orders.

## 3.2 Organizational Units of Logistics and Assignment to Accounting

As mentioned, the logistic business transactions have touch points with financial accounting. We need to ensure that the structural elements in logistics are meaningfully connected with accounting. In the following sections, we'll briefly explain these organizational elements and their assignments in and integrations with accounting. These applications trigger the cost and revenue postings and therefore are important for accounting and controlling. Of course, there is a best practice integration available, but some settings still need to be decided dependent on your business processes. All these assignments you can access via **Enterprise Structure • Assignment** in the IMG. We'll walk through the relevant organizational units in logistics and how they intersect with controlling in the following sections.

### 3.2.1 Plants

The *plant* is the organizational unit for material management. In this physical location, manufacturing takes place and products and services are provided. The company is thus structured by the plant for production, procurement, maintenance, and material planning purposes, and all logistics orders (production orders, maintenance orders, and so on) are created with reference to a plant.

The plants can be defined via IMG menu path **Enterprise Structure • Definition • Logistics—General • Define, Copy, Delete, Check Plant.** Figure 3.13 shows the attributes of a plant: address, language, and country. The impact on the business processes takes place in context with other business objects.

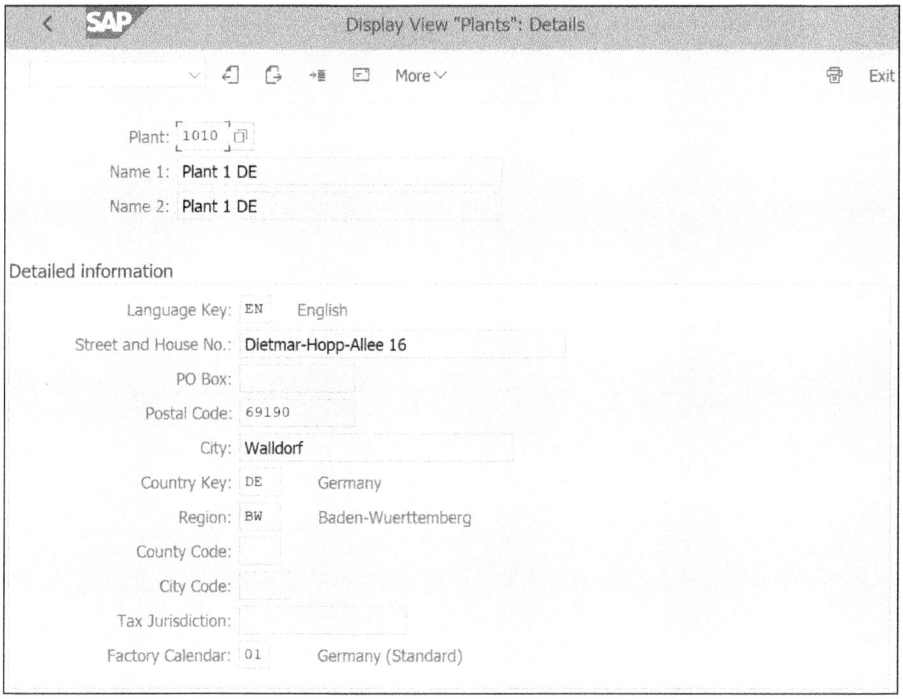

Display View "Plants": Details
More
Exit
Plant: 1010
Name 1: Plant 1 DE
Name 2: Plant 1 DE
Detailed information
Language Key: EN English
Street and House No.: Dietmar-Hopp-Allee 16
PO Box:
Postal Code: 69190
City: Walldorf
Country Key: DE Germany
Region: BW Baden-Wuerttemberg
County Code:
City Code:
Tax Jurisdiction:
Factory Calendar: 01 Germany (Standard)

**Figure 3.13** Definition of Plant

On the plant level, you can define the material cost rates and get your inventory valuation. Only in exceptional cases for certain industries can you define the company code as the valuation level. You can find these settings via IMG menu path **Enterprise Structure • Definition • Logistics—General • Define Valuation Level.**

In the material/product master, you define the product cost rates on the plant level, the profit center, and the general ledger account determination for inventory and consumption general ledger accounts. Inventory management and material stocks are managed within a plant. Costing is done for a product on the plant level. We'll return to this in Chapter 6.

In sales, you define in each sales order item a plant to determine prices, general ledger accounts for revenues, and profit centers. We'll return to this in Chapter 7.

The plant is an attribute in the Universal Journal and is available in Universal Journal reporting. The connection to accounting is made via the company code: each plant is assigned to a single company code, but a company code can be assigned to several plants.

The assignment is defined in IMG menu path **Enterprise Structure • Assignment • Logistics—General • Assign Plant to Company Code**. You'll arrive at the screen shown in Figure 3.14. As a controller, you may need to check this assignment.

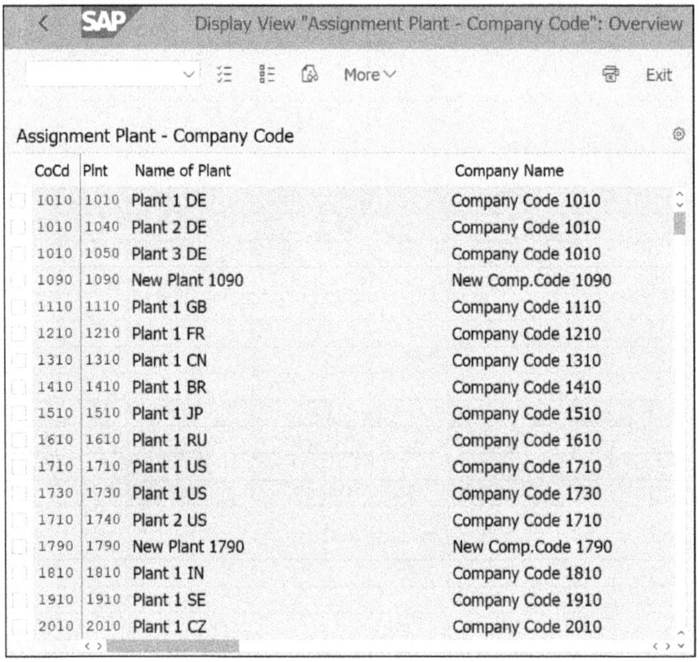

Display View "Assignment Plant - Company Code": Overview

More Exit

Assignment Plant - Company Code

| CoCd | Plnt | Name of Plant | Company Name |
|---|---|---|---|
| 1010 | 1010 | Plant 1 DE | Company Code 1010 |
| 1010 | 1040 | Plant 2 DE | Company Code 1010 |
| 1010 | 1050 | Plant 3 DE | Company Code 1010 |
| 1090 | 1090 | New Plant 1090 | New Comp.Code 1090 |
| 1110 | 1110 | Plant 1 GB | Company Code 1110 |
| 1210 | 1210 | Plant 1 FR | Company Code 1210 |
| 1310 | 1310 | Plant 1 CN | Company Code 1310 |
| 1410 | 1410 | Plant 1 BR | Company Code 1410 |
| 1510 | 1510 | Plant 1 JP | Company Code 1510 |
| 1610 | 1610 | Plant 1 RU | Company Code 1610 |
| 1710 | 1710 | Plant 1 US | Company Code 1710 |
| 1730 | 1730 | Plant 1 US | Company Code 1730 |
| 1710 | 1740 | Plant 2 US | Company Code 1710 |
| 1790 | 1790 | New Plant 1790 | New Comp.Code 1790 |
| 1810 | 1810 | Plant 1 IN | Company Code 1810 |
| 1910 | 1910 | Plant 1 SE | Company Code 1910 |
| 2010 | 2010 | Plant 1 CZ | Company Code 2010 |

**Figure 3.14** Assignment of Plant to Company Code

### 3.2.2 Purchasing Organization

The *purchasing organization* is the organizational unit responsible for all business processes tied to purchasing activities. Purchase requests and orders are entered with reference to a purchasing organization, and the same is true for price conditions, purchase info records, and the supplier master data.

The integration into accounting is done based on the relationship between a purchasing organization and a company code. It can be assigned to exactly one company code, or several purchasing organizations can be assigned to one company code. The last setting you will implement is important in case you have a group-wide, central purchasing organization. To realize more decentralized and company-specific purchasing, a one-to-one-relationship between a company code and a purchasing organization is possible.

The assignment is done via IMG menu path **Enterprise Structure • Assignment • Material Management • Assign Purchasing Organization to Company Code**. You'll arrive at the screen shown in Figure 3.15.

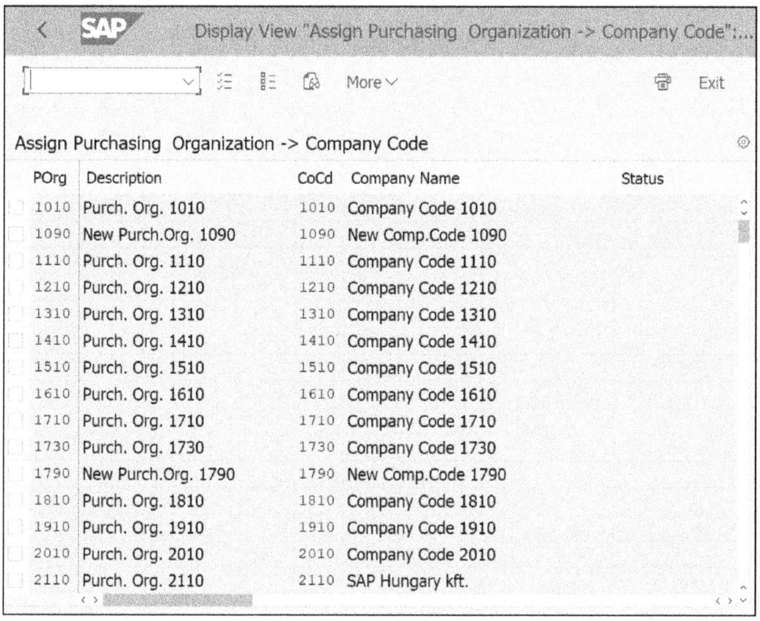

Display View "Assign Purchasing Organization -> Company Code":...

More Exit

Assign Purchasing Organization -> Company Code

| POrg | Description | CoCd | Company Name | Status |
|---|---|---|---|---|
| 1010 | Purch. Org. 1010 | 1010 | Company Code 1010 | |
| 1090 | New Purch.Org. 1090 | 1090 | New Comp.Code 1090 | |
| 1110 | Purch. Org. 1110 | 1110 | Company Code 1110 | |
| 1210 | Purch. Org. 1210 | 1210 | Company Code 1210 | |
| 1310 | Purch. Org. 1310 | 1310 | Company Code 1310 | |
| 1410 | Purch. Org. 1410 | 1410 | Company Code 1410 | |
| 1510 | Purch. Org. 1510 | 1510 | Company Code 1510 | |
| 1610 | Purch. Org. 1610 | 1610 | Company Code 1610 | |
| 1710 | Purch. Org. 1710 | 1710 | Company Code 1710 | |
| 1730 | Purch. Org. 1730 | 1730 | Company Code 1730 | |
| 1790 | New Purch.Org. 1790 | 1790 | New Comp.Code 1790 | |
| 1810 | Purch. Org. 1810 | 1810 | Company Code 1810 | |
| 1910 | Purch. Org. 1910 | 1910 | Company Code 1910 | |
| 2010 | Purch. Org. 2010 | 2010 | Company Code 2010 | |
| 2110 | Purch. Org. 2110 | 2110 | SAP Hungary kft. | |

**Figure 3.15** Assignment of Purchase Organization to Company Code

In this view you see a company code assigned for every purchasing organization.

The purchasing organization assignment to a company code is relevant for controlling and accounting for several business processes. In Chapter 6, we'll discuss how to create a purchase order for the supply of goods and services and then record goods and service receipts and supplier invoices, which are posted in accounting to inventory or expense general ledger accounts. These expenses can be account assigned to, for example, a production order (see Chapter 6) or to a customer project. On the purchase order level, you calculate commitments (see Chapter 5).

### 3.2.3 Sales Organization and Sales Area

With a *sales organization*, you organize your business processes for the sale of products and services. Based on the sales organization, you can, for example, define master data like customer and product, define prices, and define sales document types.

The definition of a sales organization is done via IMG menu path **Enterprise Structure • Definition • Sales and Distribution • Define, Copy, Delete, Check Sales Organization** (see Figure 3.16).

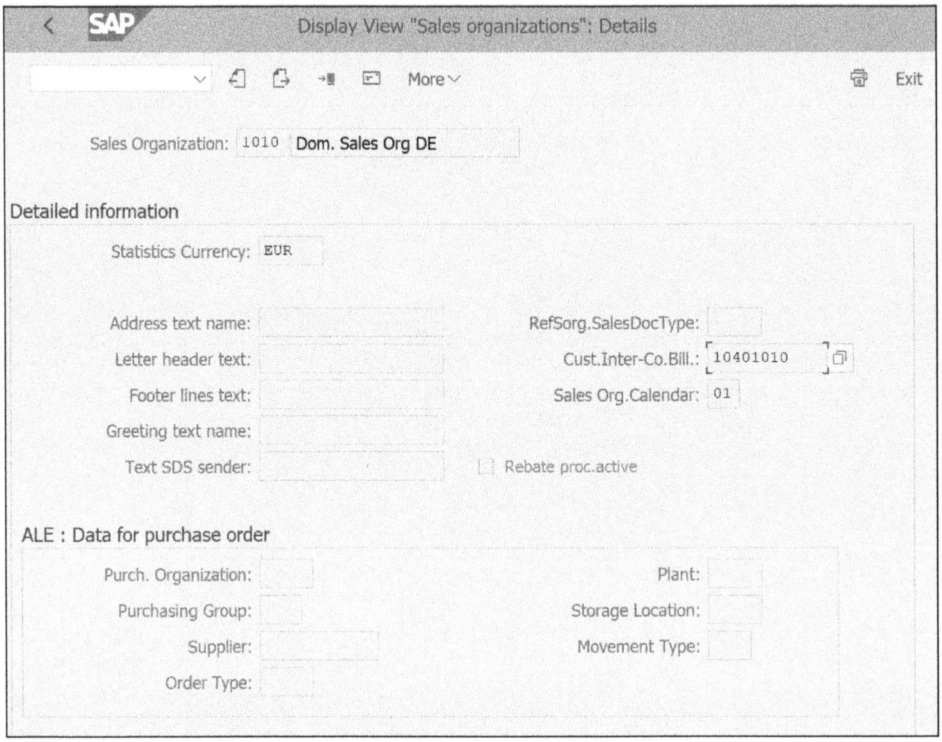

**Figure 3.16** Definition of Sales Organization

You can assign an intercompany customer for the sales organization, which we'll discuss further in Chapter 9. In an Application Link Enabling (ALE) scenario, you can define a mapping here to a purchase organization in another SAP system. (ALE is SAP middleware technology that can link two SAP systems.)

The integration into accounting is done via company code assignment: a sales organization is assigned to exactly one company code.

You can check the assignment of the sales organization to the company code by following IMG menu path **Enterprise Structure • Assignment • Sales and Distribution • Assign Sales Organization to Company Code.** You'll arrive at the screen shown in Figure 3.17.

In addition to the sales organization, the division and the distribution channel are important parameters in the sales business process:

- The *distribution channel* defines the channel, through which the product or service reaches customers. Examples are direct sales or wholesale channels.
- The *division* is an option to organize your sales organization by responsibility for product and services groups.

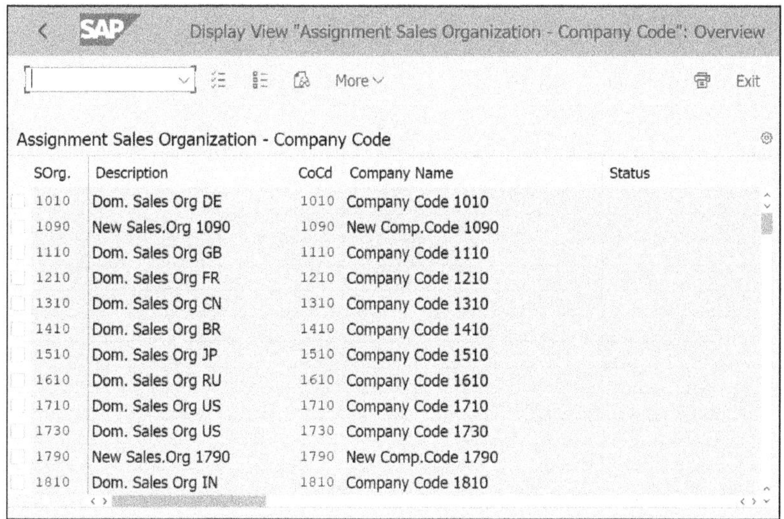

Display View "Assignment Sales Organization - Company Code": Overview

Assignment Sales Organization - Company Code

| SOrg. | Description | CoCd | Company Name | Status |
|---|---|---|---|---|
| 1010 | Dom. Sales Org DE | 1010 | Company Code 1010 | |
| 1090 | New Sales.Org 1090 | 1090 | New Comp.Code 1090 | |
| 1110 | Dom. Sales Org GB | 1110 | Company Code 1110 | |
| 1210 | Dom. Sales Org FR | 1210 | Company Code 1210 | |
| 1310 | Dom. Sales Org CN | 1310 | Company Code 1310 | |
| 1410 | Dom. Sales Org BR | 1410 | Company Code 1410 | |
| 1510 | Dom. Sales Org JP | 1510 | Company Code 1510 | |
| 1610 | Dom. Sales Org RU | 1610 | Company Code 1610 | |
| 1710 | Dom. Sales Org US | 1710 | Company Code 1710 | |
| 1730 | Dom. Sales Org US | 1730 | Company Code 1730 | |
| 1790 | New Sales.Org 1790 | 1790 | New Comp.Code 1790 | |
| 1810 | Dom. Sales Org IN | 1810 | Company Code 1810 | |

**Figure 3.17** Assignment of Sales Organization to Company Code

The sales organization, division, and distribution channel units define a sales area.

You can check the allowed combinations for the sales area via IMG menu path **Enterprise Structure • Assignment • Sales and Distribution • Set Up Sales Area**, as shown in Figure 3.18.

Display View "Assignment Sales Org. - Distribution Channel - Division"

More Exit

Assignment Sales Org. - Distribution Channel - Division

| SOrg. | Description | DChl | Description | Dv | Description |
|---|---|---|---|---|---|
| 1010 | Dom. Sales Org DE | 10 | Direct Sales | 00 | Product Division 00 |
| 1090 | New Sales.Org 1090 | 10 | Direct Sales | 00 | Product Division 00 |
| 1110 | Dom. Sales Org GB | 10 | Direct Sales | 00 | Product Division 00 |
| 1210 | Dom. Sales Org FR | 10 | Direct Sales | 00 | Product Division 00 |
| 1310 | Dom. Sales Org CN | 10 | Direct Sales | 00 | Product Division 00 |
| 1410 | Dom. Sales Org BR | 10 | Direct Sales | 00 | Product Division 00 |
| 1510 | Dom. Sales Org JP | 10 | Direct Sales | 00 | Product Division 00 |
| 1610 | Dom. Sales Org RU | 10 | Direct Sales | 00 | Product Division 00 |
| 1710 | Dom. Sales Org US | 10 | Direct Sales | 00 | Product Division 00 |
| 1730 | Dom. Sales Org US | 10 | Direct Sales | 00 | Product Division 00 |
| 1790 | New Sales.Org 1790 | 10 | Direct Sales | 00 | Product Division 00 |
| 1810 | Dom. Sales Org IN | 10 | Direct Sales | 00 | Product Division 00 |

**Figure 3.18** Definition of Sales Area

These sales area attributes influence sales functionality like pricing. They're important characteristics of a sales order item, and so these organizational units are part of the profitability segment. We'll return to these settings when we look at the business processes in Chapter 4 and Chapter 7.

## 3.3 Financial Reporting Structures

Now, let's discuss the accounting entities that are important for accounting and controlling reporting. With the bringing together of the controlling and management accounting applications in the Universal Journal, the functionalities of general ledger accounting are available in controlling (and vice versa).

First, let's look at the ledger, which enables parallel valuations for a company code. We can also use this in controlling by showing a parallel value flow based on different valuations—for example, for depreciation or revenue recognition. Both are dependent on the underlying accounting principle. And then we have an innovation: the *extension ledger* enables you to enter different and additional costs based on the Universal Journal structure, and it contains commitments, as we discussed when we introduced predictive accounting in the previous chapter.

Then we come to the currencies. Based on Universal Journal, you now have a set of parallel currencies in every single journal entry, which is identical by design in the general ledger and controlling.

Another important reporting attribute is of course the general ledger account. Its master record will be discussed in Chapter 4, and in the following chapters we will see how the general ledger account controls the postings and serves as the basis for reporting—in particular, for contribution margin reporting.

### 3.3.1 Ledger

In general ledger accounting, the *ledger* is the entity via which all business transactions are recorded and in which all general ledger accounts are systematically kept. Based on the ledger, you get your financial statement. You can manage several parallel general ledgers—for example, to be able to get financial statements according to different accounting principles, like local Generally Accepted Accounting Principles (GAAP) and then International Financial Reporting Standards (IFRS) as the common accounting principle.

The ledgers and their parameters per company code are defined in the following Customizing menu path: **Financial Accounting • Financial Accounting Global Settings • Ledgers • Ledger • Define Settings for Ledgers and Currency Types**. You'll arrive at the screen shown in Figure 3.19.

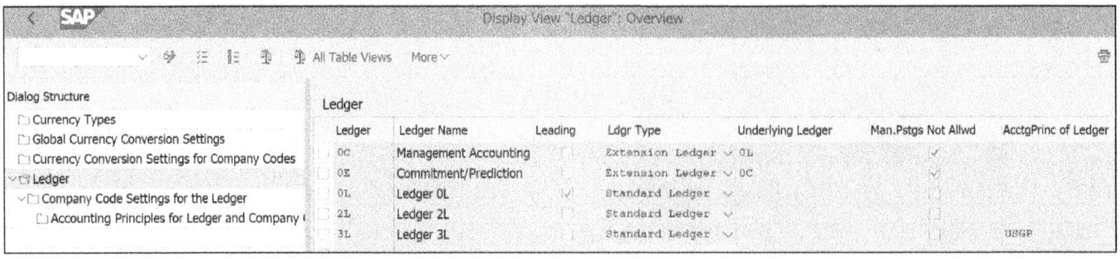

**Figure 3.19** Ledger Definition in IMG

There are two ledger types, which we'll discuss next: the standard ledger and the extension ledger.

### Standard Ledger

The standard ledger is relevant for general ledger reporting. Figure 3.19 shows three parallel ledgers: 0L, 2L, and 3L. There is always exactly one ledger marked as leading (with a checkmark in the **Leading** column). In our example, **Ledger 0L** is the leading ledger.

The postings in the leading ledger are regarded as primary and are the default for postings in other ledgers if there is no own/different valuation in this ledger. All company codes are assigned to this leading ledger per default. Especially the logistic applications rely on the leading ledger—for example, when they read actual costs for a cost object like a project to calculate a percentage of completion (PoC) or if the customer billing is based on the expense postings to the customer project (see Chapter 7).

Further parameters are defined in the same IMG activity. You mark a ledger—0L in this example—then select **Company Code Settings for the Ledger**, then double-click company code **1010**. You'll arrive at the screen shown in Figure 3.20.

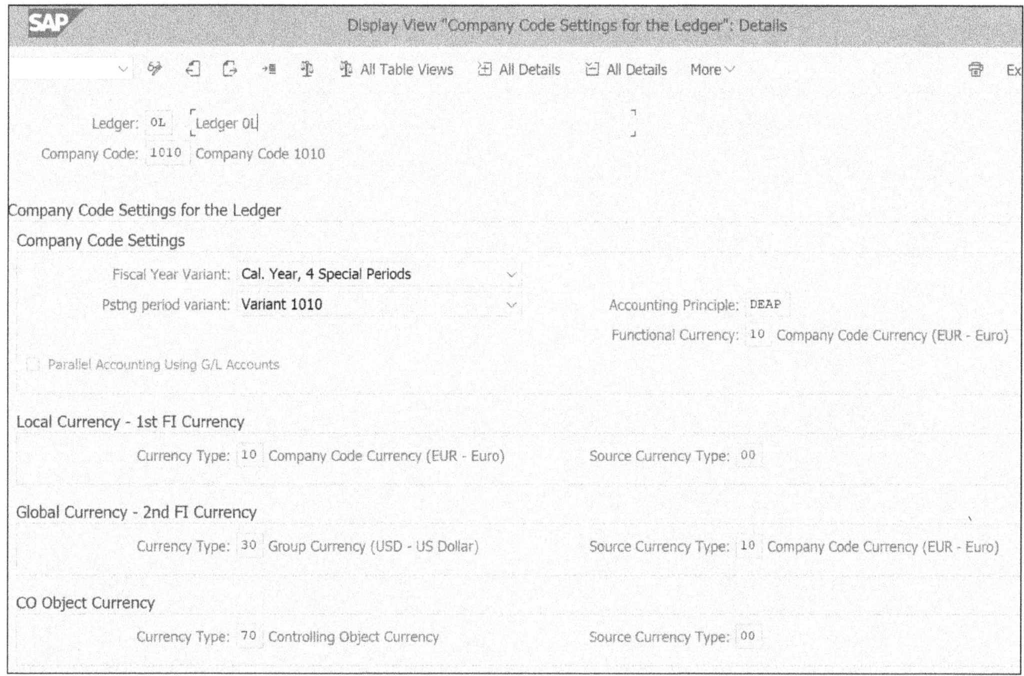


**Figure 3.20** Company Code- and Ledger-Dependent Accounting Parameter

Here you can specify the following:

- **Fiscal Year Variant**
  We discussed the fiscal year variant in Section 3.1.2. Remember the restriction: For a

cross-company-code controlling area assignment, it must be equal in all assigned company codes.

- **Pstng period variant**
  This describes the posting period (e.g., the beginning and end dates of the period).
- **Accounting Principle**
  The accounting principle can be assigned on the ledger level or on the ledger company code level. If you maintain it generally on the ledger level, you need not maintain it here.
- **Functional Currency**
  You also can define several currencies, which are stored in parallel in the Universal Journal. We discuss this further in the next section.

When you create a ledger, the system automatically creates a ledger group with the same name. To simplify work for general ledger accounting processes, you can group standard ledgers together in a ledger group. With this ledger group, you can enter one manual journal entry and it will be posted in all assigned ledgers at the same time in parallel.

With the *accounting principle*, you control the valuation in several financial applications—for example, foreign currency valuation, asset deprecations, WIP, and revenue recognition.

You can display the accounting principle by following IMG menu path **Financial Accounting • Financial Accounting Global Settings • Ledgers • Parallel Accounting • Define Accounting Principle**. You'll arrive at the screen shown in Figure 3.21.

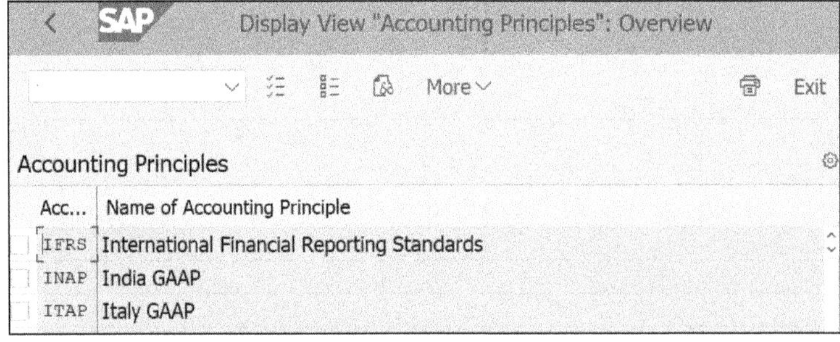


**Figure 3.21** Definition of Accounting Principles in IMG

Where you have a common accounting principle such as US-GAAP or IFRS, this accounting principle can be used for every posting by assigning the accounting principle directly to a ledger (see **USGP** to **Ledger 3L** in Figure 3.19). But you don't need a ledger for every accounting principle that you support. You can meet the financial reporting needs of your local subsidiaries by assigning the accounting principle to the combination of company code and ledger (see German local GAAP **DEAP** to **Company Code 1010** and **Ledger 0L** in Figure 3.20).

### Extension Ledger

Next to the standard ledger in SAP S/4HANA, there is now a new type of ledger available: the *extension ledger*. It covers management accounting requirements.

When you work with the Universal Journal, the postings for controlling and legal reporting are both stored in the general ledger. On the one hand this is, as already mentioned, a big advantage because there's no reconciliation needed. On the other hand, for some business processes you want to apply different figures or additional information in your internal controlling view. For this, you have the extension ledger.

Here you can enter controlling-specific journal entries in addition to the legal bookkeeping: other costs or additional costs. These journal entries are only relevant for cost accounting reporting; they do not influence the legal reporting, which is exclusively based on the standard ledger.

While the standard ledger contains the different journal entries for all business transactions, the extension ledger contains management-relevant journal entries only. The extension ledger only stores the delta entries that are posted specifically to the extension ledger. This setup assumes that all postings in the underlying standard ledger are part of the exension ledger reporting, thus avoiding redundant data storage.

For every extension ledger, you need to assign a standard ledger. For example, in Figure 3.19, shown previously, ledger 0C is assigned to standard ledger 0L, or to another extension ledger, and ledger 0E is assigned to extension ledger 0C. The extension ledger setup in our example is visualized in Figure 3.22.

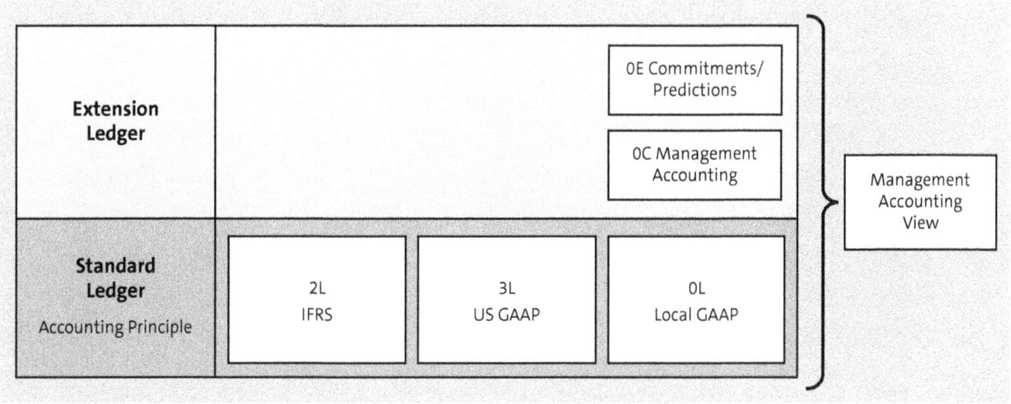


**Figure 3.22** Extension Ledger Setup

When you run a report for an extension ledger, the journal entries of the extension ledger and the underlying standard ledger are always displayed together. So when you run a report for ledger 0E, you get a report with the commitments posted in ledger 0E and the actuals as an aggregation of the management adjustments in ledger 0E, plus all the journal entries posted in the legal ledger 0L.

There are several controlling purposes covered with the extension ledger:

- **Provisioning of controlling reporting**
  For your internal controlling reporting, you want to apply different values or enhanced cost component information:
  - First you can post delta values in the extension ledger to adjust the costs or margins for specific management objects. An example could be to transfer revenues between profit centers or to add costs to a cost center.
  - You want to include statistical sales conditions in a sales scenario in your contribution margin reporting. We'll return to this in Chapter 7.
  - You use for these use cases an extension ledger of type **Management Accounting**—in our example, ledger 0C.
- **Commitments**
  If you activate commitments, they are now persisted in an extension ledger of type **Commitment/Prediction**—in our example, ledger 0E. Commitments are triggered when a purchase order or a purchase requisition is created. We'll return to this in Chapter 5.
- **Prediction**
  With predictive accounting, you want to enable the prediction of future financial data based on available operative documents already in the system, like sales orders or purchase orders. For example, for a sales order prediction you might create the journal entries for the goods issue and billing expected in the future in the prediction ledger of type **Commitment/Prediction** (ledger 0E here). We'll return to this in Chapter 5.

**Extension Ledgers and the Universal Journal**

With the extension ledger, you continue following the approach that all documents are stored in the Universal Journal and thus have the same fields and structures. With this, comparability and transparency are ensured because prediction and commitment documents have the same structure as the actual values.

The same is true for management adjustment postings, which are posted as deltas to the legal postings in the underlying standard ledger.

### 3.3.2 Currencies

In financial accounting, in addition to the transaction currency, the local currency (the company code currency) and the group currency (defined by controlling area) is calculated by default for every journal entry. There are eight freely definable currencies also available.

For an example of what this looks like for a company code, see Figure 3.23. The local currency, derived from the country, Germany, is defined as euros. The global currency,

USD, is derived from the controlling area because in this example the organization has its headquarters in the US.

You can check the currency setup for all processes and functions in financial accounting in Customizing by following menu path **Financial Accounting • Financial Accounting Global Settings • Ledgers • Ledger • Define Settings for Ledgers and Currency Types.** Then select **Company Code Settings for the Ledger** in the dialog structure. You'll arrive at the screen shown in Figure 3.23.

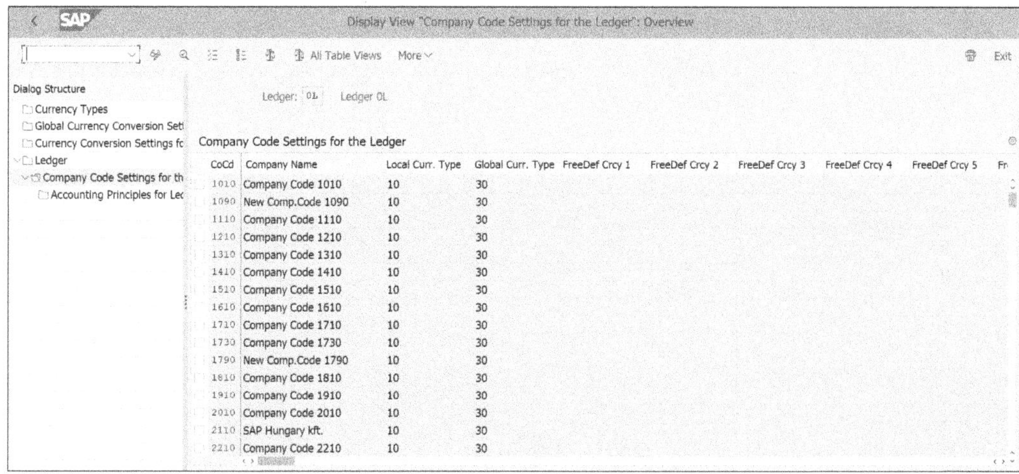


**Figure 3.23** Currency Settings for Company Code

With the integration of controlling and financial accounting in the Universal Journal, the currency setup is the same for all postings and thus available for controlling too. This means that if you purchase goods in a local currency, you'll see the same document in the transaction currency, local currency, group currency, and any other currencies entered on the screen shown in Figure 3.23, and the conversion will be made at the time of posting.

The challenge comes when you enter transactions for allocations, settlements, and so on because the secondary cost postings originally only supported the controlling area currency (usually the group currency) and object currency (usually the local currency). Work is in progress to ensure that the currencies are used consistently in financial accounting and controlling. When we look at assessment and distribution cycles, universal allocation, overhead calculation, and settlement in Chapter 5, you'll see that these processes all support multiple currencies from SAP S/4HANA release 2020. However, the activity rates are still only available in two currencies, so any additional currency will be converted at the time of posting. Top-down distribution and allocation to margin analysis using universal allocation also support multiple currencies, but the legacy transactions, Transactions KE28 (Execute Top-Down Distribution) and KEU5 (Execute Assessment), currently only support two currencies. Asset accounting, the Material Ledger, and actual costing currently support three currencies.

## 3.4 Summary

In this chapter, we covered the organizational elements relevant for financial accounting and controlling and their mapping to the logistical organizational units. We've also shown you the main settings to cover your controlling requirements.

You now know that it's a necessity to coordinate your setup with other applications so that the business processes are mapped correctly in financial accounting and controlling.

With the introduction of the Universal Journal, the level of integration within the financials applications has increased even further—and with it the need to align the design of the business processes via system setup. The benefits are unique structures within accounting and additional options for controlling reporting.

The organizational structure of financial accounting and controlling and their integration into other applications will be further explored in the following chapters. We'll now move on to discuss the controlling master data.

Chapter 4
# Master Data

*Now that we've looked at the organizational data that structures your controlling activities, it's time to discuss the master data of controlling. This data gives you a tool to define areas of accountability, for which cost and margin analyses can be provided. It also gives you capabilities to organize and control the value flow between these areas.*

As we discussed in previous chapters, the objective of controlling is to provide a cost and margin analysis for each individual area of responsibility within a company. The idea is that a person should be responsible for each of the objects considered master data and able to deliver the following insights:

- The project manager delivers insights about the current margin and outlook for his or her customer projects.
- The production manager delivers insights about production cost variances.
- The product manager delivers insights about the margin for the products that are his or her responsibility.
- The customer key account manager delivers insights about the margin and the revenue volume of the customers that are his or her responsibility.

Every company has its own entities for which it wants to show a margin. These are defined in the market segments, which we introduced in Chapter 3 and will explore further in this chapter.

In controlling, we have a number of cost objects at our disposal to collect costs and revenues and assign them to the areas of responsibility to allow a breakdown of accountability. Figure 4.1 shows an overview of the cost flow within controlling, showing the involved cost objects that we'll walk through in this chapter.

We'll also explain the master data that controls the costs and the revenue flow. The general ledger account is the master data that provides information about the nature of the costs. It also controls the cost flow between the different cost objects.

The values flow from revenues and primary expenses on the left to the margin analysis for the market segment on the right. Revenues generated by customer invoices can be assigned directly to the product and customer or to a customer project. The direct expenses can be posted as direct costs to the controlling object, which defines the area of accountability. In the production scenario, this is the production order or the product cost collector. These objects and the maintenance order will be covered in Chapter 6. In Chapter 7, we'll discuss the direct costs of the outbound delivery and the postings to the customer project. We discuss the posting of expenses for investment projects in Chapter 8.

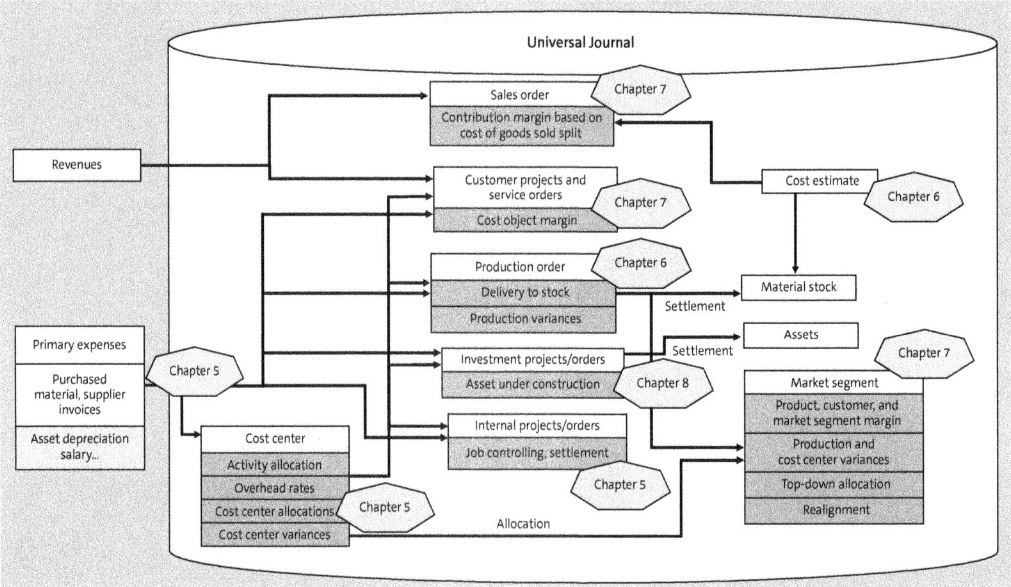


**Figure 4.1** Controlling Value Flow

But some expenses can't be directly allocated to a specific area when they occur—for example, periodic expenses such as salaries or asset depreciation, which are posted to cost centers first. How these costs are allocated to the other cost objects is shown in Chapter 5, as is the posting of expenses for internal orders or projects.

From these cost objects, they are ultimately assigned to the market segments using various allocation methods. In the end, all costs and income should be allocated to the margin analysis. We'll discuss this in Chapter 7.

Now let's start by looking at the general ledger account, and then we'll move on to other key master data: cost centers, activity types, statistical key figures, internal orders, projects, and market segments.

## 4.1 General Ledger Accounts and Cost Elements

The general ledger account provides the information about the nature of expense and revenues, but also about the balance sheet. For the accountant, it's the fundamental element to provide legal reporting in form of a trial balance and income statement, as we illustrated with examples of the Trial Balance app throughout Chapter 2.

In controlling, the goal is to analyze cost and revenues by area of accountability from an internal point of view in order to steer the business. Each of the business transactions triggered by external applications, such as purchasing and sales, is associated with a general ledger account.



To control the flow into and within controlling, we add some attributes to the controlling-relevant general ledger accounts, like the account type, which forces the assignment of an account assignment, such as a cost center, order, or market segment.

Now let's take a deeper look at how the general ledger account is reflected in the system.

**Note**

The master data and IMG settings are part of the SAP S/4HANA Cloud scope item J58, Accounting and Financial Close.

### 4.1.1 Structuring Financial Accounting Using General Ledger Accounts

There is one central general ledger account master maintenance transaction in place. You get there via Transaction FS00 or in SAP Fiori with the Manage G/L Account Master Data app (SAP Fiori ID F0731). We'll discuss the key tabs for general ledger account settings in the following sections.

**SAP ERP versus SAP S/4HANA**

With SAP S/4HANA and the integration of the accounting applications in the Universal Journal, there is one general ledger account master for general ledger and controlling purposes. The controlling entity, the cost element, is now part of the general ledger account master data. The SAP ERP transactions to create, change, and display cost elements (Transactions KAO*) are now replaced by general ledger account maintenance, Transaction FS00.

#### Type/Description

Now let's look at an example of a general ledger account (see Figure 4.2). The general ledger and controlling share the same master record, so we'll look at the controlling-relevant settings. Start Transaction FS00 and select general ledger account **61008000 Travel Expenses—Miscellaneous**. The general ledger account needs to be created separately for every company code for which you want to use it. And the general ledger account must be assigned to the chart of accounts that's relevant for the company code (see Chapter 3, Section 3.1.2).

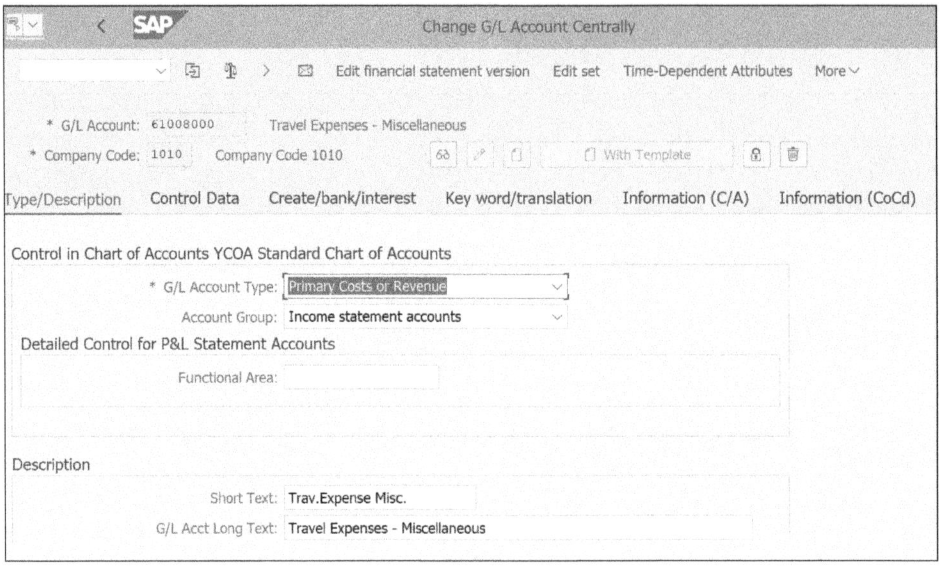

Figure 4.2 General Ledger Account Master: General Settings

Important for the use of the general ledger account is the general ledger account type. It defines in which area the general ledger account is used within the general ledger. There are five different types available:

- **Balance Sheet Account**
  Balance sheet accounts are used for any kind of assets, liabilities, and equity. We don't need to take a deeper look at it for controlling purposes. We'll touch on these general ledger accounts with the material stock, accounts payable, and goods receipt/invoice receipt (GR/IR) clearing (see Chapter 6), the assets (see Chapter 8), and the receivables and work in process (WIP) (see Chapter 7).
- **Nonoperating Expense and Income**
  These are profit and loss (P&L) accounts, which are not related to the original product and service provisioning of the company but belong in the financial statement. These general ledger accounts are only used in financial accounting. They are not part of the controlling value flow shown in Figure 4.1. For example, consider gains or losses from a foreign exchange market.
- **Primary Costs or Revenue**
  As we showed in Chapter 2, Figure 2.10, and mentioned earlier, controlling is completely integrated into financial accounting. These expenses are relevant for the controlling value flow. Primary costs are costs like material expenses, salaries, asset depreciation, and energy expenses. The revenue is posted by selling products and services.
- **Secondary Costs**
  With these general ledger accounts, you post the allocations between the cost objects and control the value flow within our controlling circle. Examples are the

allocation of costs from the cost center to customer projects, production orders, or market segments, or from internal projects to cost centers and market segments.

- **Cash Accounts**
  Cash accounts are used in the context of payments: for bank reconciliation or petty cash. They are not relevant for controlling purposes.



We'll focus in this book on primary costs or revenue and secondary costs, and we'll occasionally discuss balance sheet accounts.

The **Account Group** is a classification of the general ledger accounts; for example, it defines the number range.

The **Functional Area** was discussed in Chapter 3, Section 3.1.6. You use this an additional reporting attribute to identify the costs by function. If you maintain the functional area here, it will be used for all postings, irrespective of the receiver cost object. The functional areas for travel expense postings should be derived using the receiver object, so the field is left blank.

In each report, you can select the **Description** length. The descriptions can be defined here.

### Control Data

The next tab in the master data, shown in Figure 4.3, covers the **Control Data** of the general ledger account.

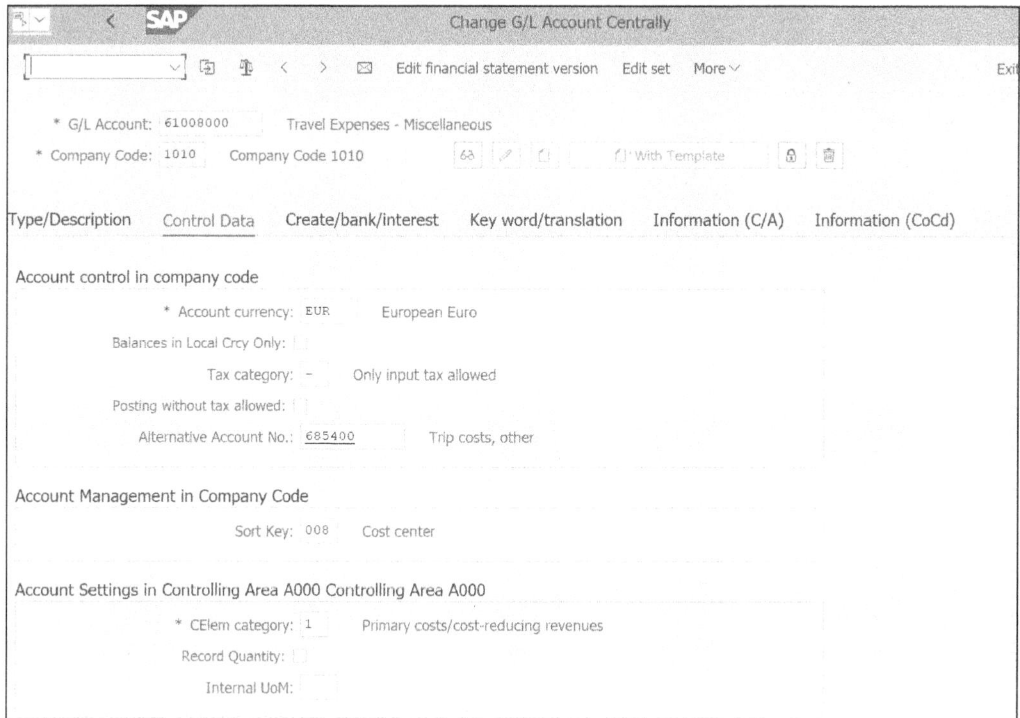


**Figure 4.3** General Ledger Account Master: Controlling Settings

Important from a controlling point of view is the **Account Settings in Controlling Area A000** section.

> **Note**
> The system examples in this book are based on controlling area A000 (see Chapter 3, Section 3.1.3).

The cost element category (**CElem category**) defines the nature of the cost element and has a clear assignment to the underlying business process. The category determines the transaction in which the general ledger account may be used. There are several categories available for primary cost or revenues and for secondary cost elements, which we'll discuss further in the next two sections.

The **Record Quantity** and **Internal UoM** settings have no influence on the quantities provided in actual postings by the prima nota. If you mark them, you get warnings for actual postings without quantities. You should select these only in special scenarios.

You can define an alternative account number, which, for example, also allows financial reporting based on general ledger accounts, which are part of a local chart of accounts.

### Create/Bank/Interest

Now let's look at the third tab, **Create/bank/interest**, shown in Figure 4.4. This is the section in which you control the document creation in your company code.

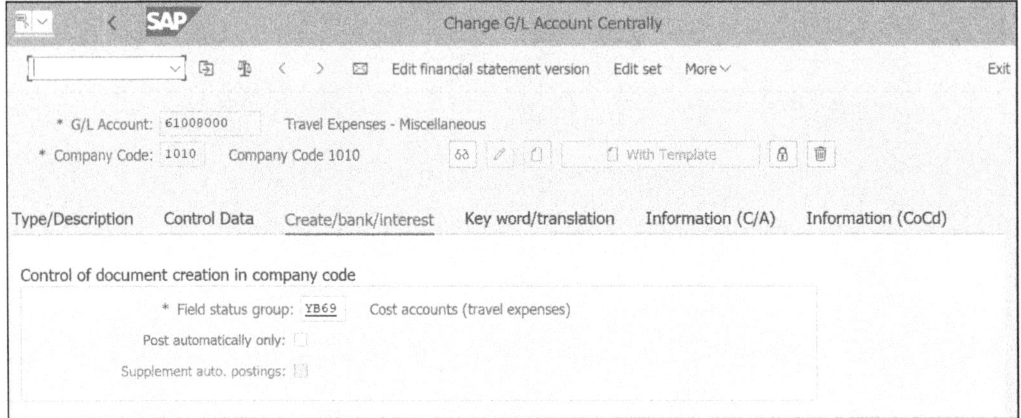


**Figure 4.4** General Ledger Account Master Data: Control of Document Creation

The **Post automatically only** flag indicates that this general ledger account can only be used by automatic account determination. It can't be manually posted—for example, by the Post General Journal Entry app (SAP Fiori ID F0718) or Transaction FB01 and Transaction FB50. Examples of general ledger accounts for which this flag is set include the material inventory accounts, which can only be used by goods movements.

**Field status group** defines which attributes are allowed in the journal entry line items in which this general ledger account is used.

> **Field Status Group**
>
> The *field status group* is the medium through which you implement an account assignment directive in your company. You define for every general ledger account to which cost object it can be—or even must be—account-assigned.

You can define the field status groups in IMG by following menu path **Financial Accounting • Financial Accounting Global Settings • Ledgers • Fields • Define Field Status Variants**. The field status variants group together field status groups. The field status variant is assigned to the company code (see Chapter 3, Section 3.1.2).

Mark your field status variant and select the **Field status groups** activity. Figure 4.5 shows the settings for the field status groups delivered in SAP S/4HANA Cloud.

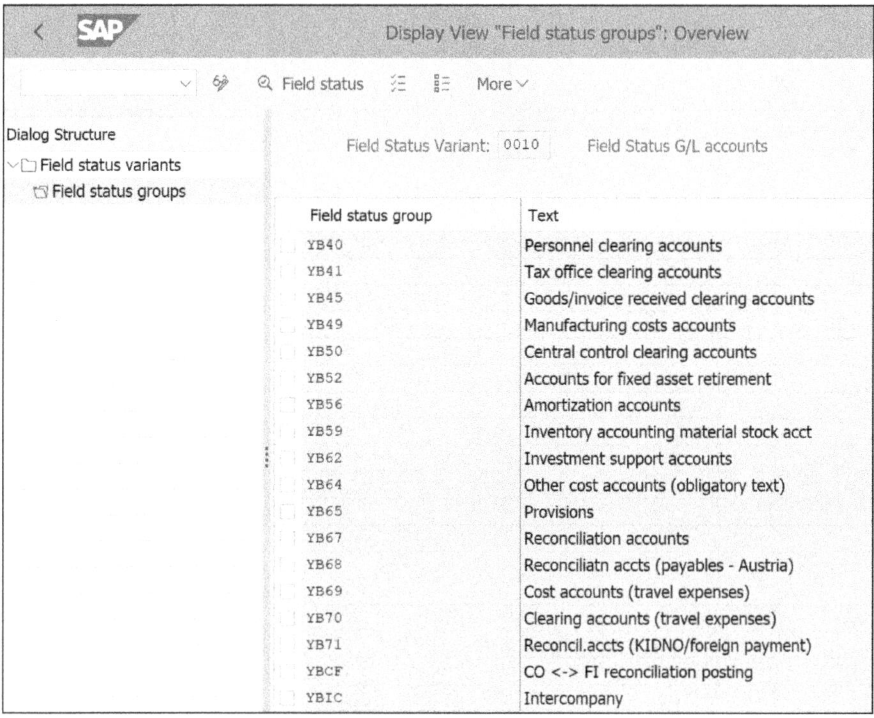


| Field status group | Text |
|---|---|
| YB40 | Personnel clearing accounts |
| YB41 | Tax office clearing accounts |
| YB45 | Goods/invoice received clearing accounts |
| YB49 | Manufacturing costs accounts |
| YB50 | Central control clearing accounts |
| YB52 | Accounts for fixed asset retirement |
| YB56 | Amortization accounts |
| YB59 | Inventory accounting material stock acct |
| YB62 | Investment support accounts |
| YB64 | Other cost accounts (obligatory text) |
| YB65 | Provisions |
| YB67 | Reconciliation accounts |
| YB68 | Reconciliatn accts (payables - Austria) |
| YB69 | Cost accounts (travel expenses) |
| YB70 | Clearing accounts (travel expenses) |
| YB71 | Reconcil.accts (KIDNO/foreign payment) |
| YBCF | CO <-> FI reconciliation posting |
| YBIC | Intercompany |

**Figure 4.5** List of Field Status Groups

You get here the list of available field status groups. The more finely you want to control the processes, the more different variants are necessary.

Now let's look how the controls are organized. Double-clicking the example group **YB69** will open the **Display Field Status Group: Overview** screen, as shown in Figure 4.6.

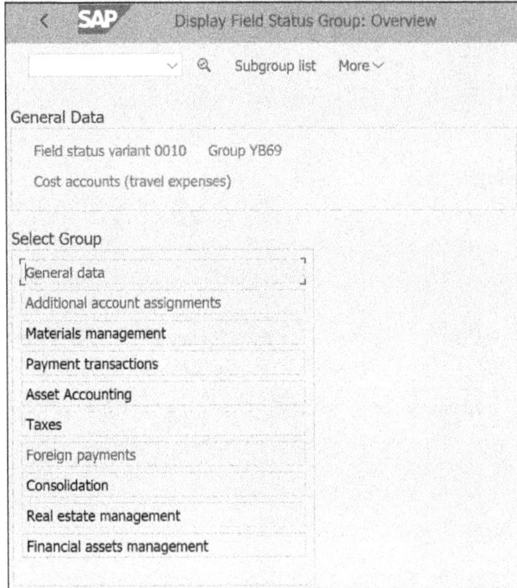


**Figure 4.6** Field Status Group: Application Area Overview

Here you see the single groups or areas to which the control can be applied. The example here deals with travel expenses and controlling to which cost objects they can be account-assigned.

This can be done by selecting **Additional account assignments**. Double-click it to open the screen shown in Figure 4.7.

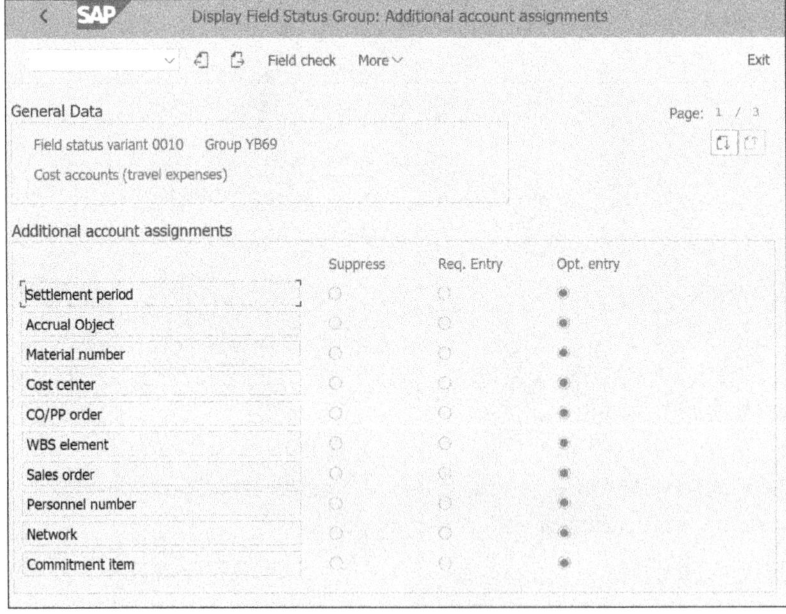


**Figure 4.7** Field Status Group: Additional Account Assignment

Here you'll see the first page of a list of allowed account assignments and controlling-relevant attributes. For each cost object, you can decide if it's not allowed (**Suppress**), if an entry is required (**Req. Entry**), or if an entry is optional (**Opt. entry**). If the entry is required and the business process doesn't provide the attribute, the posting will fail.



If you want to allow the posting of the general ledger account to several cost objects—as in this travel expenses example—then you need to mark all cost objects as optional. The business background here is that normally a travel expense is posted to the cost center of an employee, but in some cases, it will be assigned to a project or internal order. So, you need to allow several receiver cost objects to be optional.

The list of additional account assignments is the relevant group within the field status group for controlling purposes. This way, you can control the value flow within your controlling area.

### 4.1.2 Primary Cost Elements

One very basic control to determine if a general ledger account is relevant for controlling or not is the general ledger account type. The P&L accounts, which are classified as primary or secondary cost elements, are part of the controlling value flow. You further classify them by cost element categories: they determine for which processes the general ledger accounts can be used. Let's take a deeper look at this process.

P&L accounts that are posted from other applications and are determined to be controlling-relevant are referred to as *primary cost elements* (shown on the left back in Figure 4.1). Examples include the following:

- Material costs arising from material goods issues from the warehouse into production
- Salaries
- Energy costs
- Asset depreciation
- Travel expenses, initiated by an employee's expense report or an external incoming invoice
- The same for the revenues, initiated by customer invoicing

When classifiying a general ledger account with the primary costs or revenue general ledger account type (refer back to Figure 4.2), you force the assignment of these expenses and revenues to a controlling object and thus set the reflection in the controlling value flow. Without a cost object assignment, these business transactions would fail.

With the field status group, you control the permitted account assignments/cost objects.

You further classify the primary cost elements with cost element categories (IDs followed by descriptions), as shown previously in Figure 4.3:

- **01 Primary costs/cost-reducing revenues**
- **03 Accrual/deferral per surcharge**
- **04 Accrual/deferral per debit = actual**
- **11 Revenues**
- **12 Sales deductions**
- **22 External settlement**

We discussed categories 01 (primary costs) and 11 (revenues) already. They're mainly posted by other applications. Category 12 (sales deductions) is posted with customer billing—for example, discounts and rebates.

Categories 03 and 04 are posted by accrual calculation in cost center accounting. You use these, for example, when an expense occurs once per year, but the service is relevant for the whole year. An example of this is an insurance policy that is only paid annually. The insurance expenses are therefore only posted in one period, but you want to see the costs distributed equally to the cost centers every month, so a twelfth of the total is accrued every month and posted as a cost.

Category 22 (external settlement) is used when you settle costs from a cost object that bears capitalizable costs to a balance sheet account. An example is the settlement of costs from a production order to inventory. We'll discuss this in Chapter 6.

There is an additional category 90 cost element for balance sheet accounts in financial accounting. You can use this for balance sheet general ledger accounts to get them into cost object reporting and to be able to use them in results analysis (revenue recognition). As an example, you would use this category to show valuated project stock in the project report and recognize it as a kind of WIP for the project. With the Universal Journal and the attribution logic, you don't need this category for many scenarios. Instead, you write the project information process depending on the balance sheet accounts (see Chapter 7).

### 4.1.3 Secondary Cost Elements

The secondary cost elements are used for the cost allocation to enable the value flows between the cost objects.

We further classify the secondary cost elements by the cost element categories, as follows (refer back to Figure 4.3):

- **21 Internal settlement**
  Use this for the allocation/settlement of costs from an internal order or internal project to another cost object. We'll cover settlement in Chapter 5, Section 5.4.6.

- **31 Order/project result analysis**
  With this cost element, you post the results of the results analysis, the revenue recognition for, say, projects. So, for example, this might include realized cost of goods sold, realized revenue, and WIP for a project. This general ledger accounts/cost elements are not posted in the general ledger but in a different table, the results analysis table. There is now a new revenue recognition tool in place with event-based revenue recognition, which no longer uses these accounts but primary cost elements/general ledger accounts. We'll cover this in Chapter 7.
- **41 Overhead rates**
  With this general ledger account, we post the overhead surcharges on cost objects. This is relevant for nearly all cost objects: internal orders (see Chapter 5), production orders (see Chapter 6), customer projects (see Chapter 7), and investment orders/projects (see Chapter 8).
- **42 Assessments**
  The allocation of costs from one cost center to others and to profitability segments is posted with this general ledger account (see Chapter 5).
- **43 Internal activity allocation**
  This is the quantity activity allocation. It's always posted with the quantity and activity type (see Section 4.3). It's relevant for all business processes and is used, for example, for confirmation of machine hours for a production order (see Chapter 6) or time confirmation of a consultant for a customer project (see Chapter 7). It's also used for indirect activity allocation, which we discuss in Chapter 5.

There are additional categories, 50, 51, and 52, used for general ledger accounts/cost elements. These update projects with statistical cost and revenue information derived from assigned incoming sales orders. These postings are not reflected in the Universal Journal and general ledger. There is also category 66, used for a variant of costing-based profitability analysis called *combined*, which we mentioned briefly in Chapter 3, Section 3.1.4. These cost element categories are not covered any further in this book.

### 4.1.4 Grouping and Hierarchies of Cost Elements

To group cost elements, there are cost element groups available. They come into play if you want to create flexible subtotals in the lines of a report (e.g., for personnel costs in a cost center report). This is achieved by a hierarchical arrangement of the cost element groups. We discussed this in cost center reporting in Chapter 2, Section 2.4 for line item structuring.

In Customizing, you'll see these groups in many places where you want to define a rule for a group of cost elements and don't want to list all of them individually. You'll see that with settlement and with surcharges in Chapter 5.

You can create/edit and change cost element groups with Transactions KAH1/KAH2 and KAH3. Now let's look at it in the system.

Start with Transaction KAH2 (Change of Cost Element Group) and enter the **Cost Element Group** "1900_CE". After pressing Enter, you'll arrive at the screen shown in Figure 4.8.

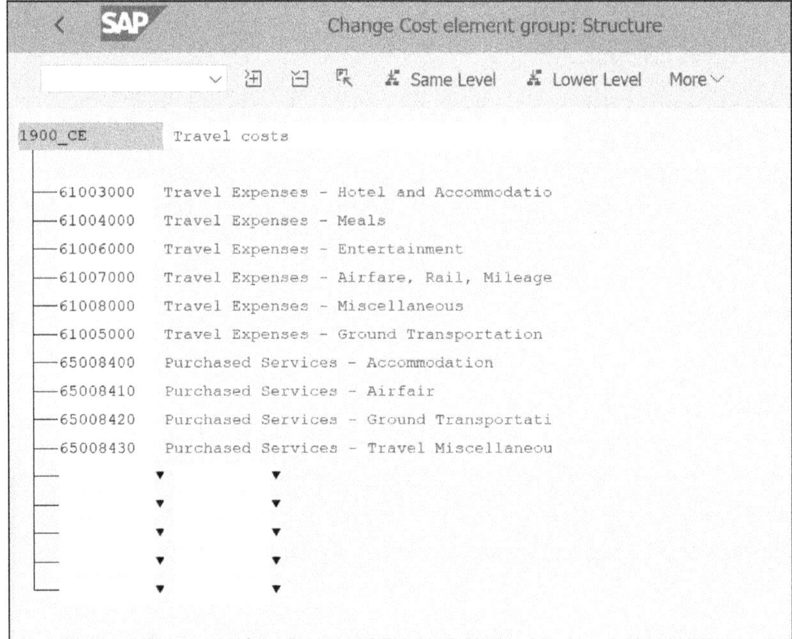


**Figure 4.8** Maintenance of Cost Element Group

You'll see the **Travel costs** cost element group and the assigned cost elements. By selecting **More** and a cost element, you can add further cost elements. Only general ledger accounts that are primary or secondary cost elements are allowed (see the general ledger account types in Section 4.1.1). You can delete assignments as well.

To provide a reporting structure for, say, cost center reporting with subtotals for individual cost categories, you need to bring the individual groups together in a hierarchy, as shown in Figure 4.9.

You see here a hierarchy of cost element groups. It's organized by grouping together all primary expenses and all secondary costs. Both again are summed up in the cost totals reflected in cost element group **10_CE**. You can create as many groups as you like in order to process your reporting requirements.

We'll show you a new option to set up these hierarchies with the Manage Global Hierarchies app in Chapter 10.

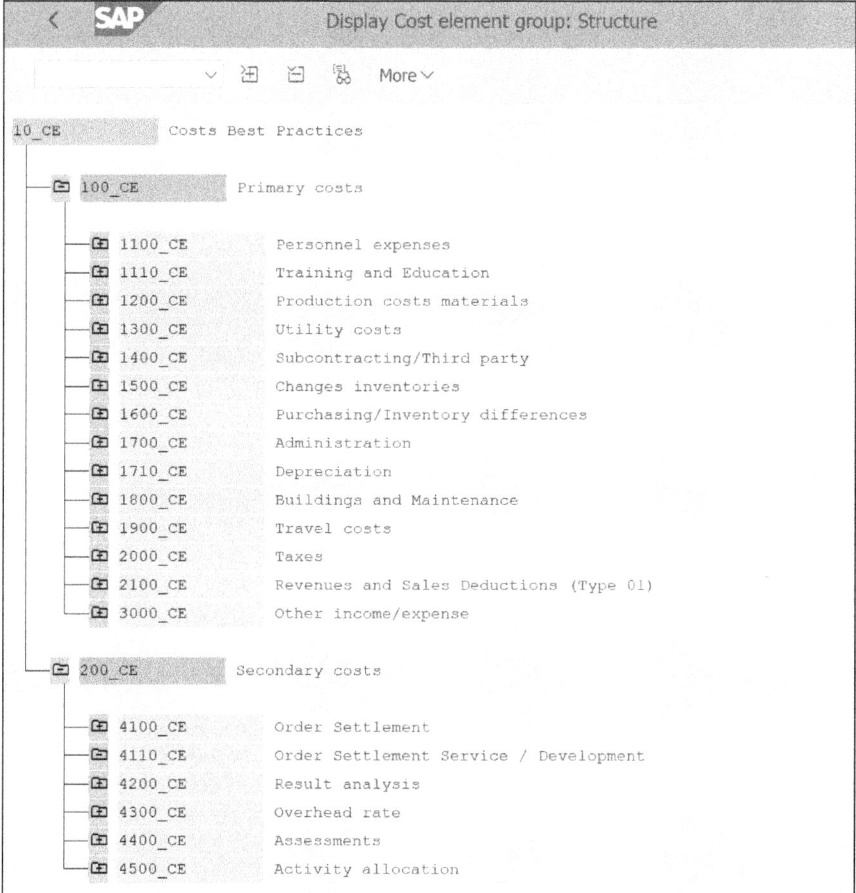


**Figure 4.9** Cost Element Groups: Hierarchy View

Another option to group general ledger accounts is with financial statement versions, with which you can manage all general ledger accounts of the assigned chart of accounts. This means that you can add balance sheet accounts too; that isn't possible in a cost element group, which allows you to group cost elements only. With the Universal Journal, there is now a 360-degree view of cost objects like customer projects (see Chapter 7). Hence, you also need to include balance sheet accounts in your controlling reporting.

Let's look at grouping general ledger accounts with financial statement versions. Start the Manage Financial Statement Version app (SAP Fiori ID OB58), which is a web GUI app and thus similar to SAP GUI Transaction OB58. Select financial statement version **YPS2**, which is the leading financial statement version that we introduced in Chapter 3, Section 3.1.3, in which we discussed the controlling area settings. Click the **Financial Statement Items** button to arrive at the screen shown in Figure 4.10.

**Figure 4.10** Financial Statement Version

Here you see the leading financial statement version for controlling area AOOO (refer back to Chapter 3, Section 3.1.3). A multilevel contribution margin calculation is shown here.

## 4.2 Cost Centers

The cost center is an important area of responsibility in the company. We introduced the role of the cost center in Chapter 2, Section 2.4.1, but in this section, we'll elaborate on its function as master data.

The *cost center* is the level at which the period costs are assigned and budget responsibility set and where the cost center manager is accountable for ensuring the correct spend. It's also where the service is provided to fulfill the corporate purpose.

Let's take a closer look how the cost center is embedded in the value flow before discussing the master data attributes and hierarchical organization.

### 4.2.1 Integration of the Cost Center into Other Applications

When you look again at the controlling value flow shown previously in Figure 4.1, you can see that the cost center is where costs are collected and a service is provided. This value flow is ensured by integrating the cost center into the master data, where the costs are incurred and the service is provided. The cost center is assigned to the employee master.

In SAP Fiori (there is no SAP GUI equivalent), you can access the employee fact sheet (see Figure 4.11) by searching **Employee** and entering the employee name.

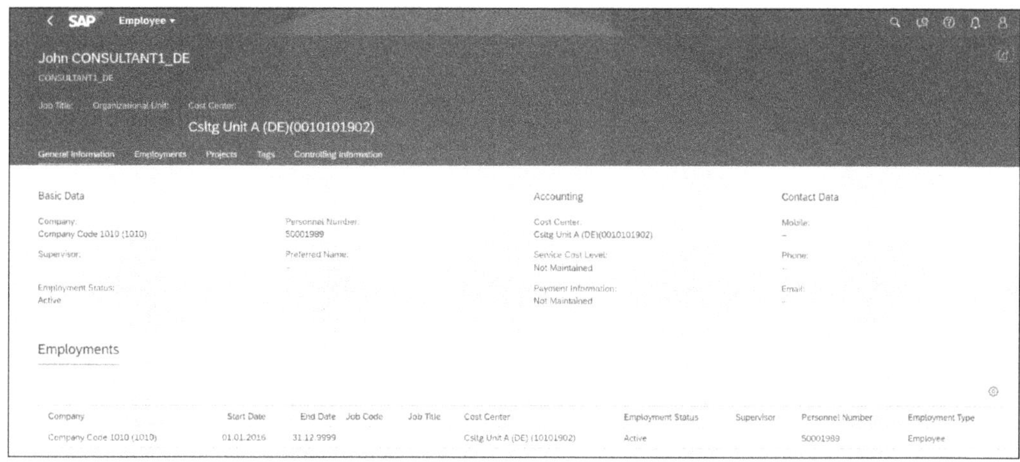


**Figure 4.11** Cost Center Assignment in Employee Master

For an employee, there can be different **Employments** defined per different periods. The employment is assigned to a cost center—here, cost center **10101902**.

The assignment of an employee to a cost center ensures that the periodic salary expenses are posted to the assigned cost center. On the output side of the cost center, the cost center is credited with the service confirmation of an employee. This will be triggered by any time confirmation of an employee. In Chapter 7, we'll look at some examples: a time confirmation to a customer project in which the employee is a staff member and a confirmation of a service order item.

The cost center is assigned to the work center in production. You can access the work center with transactions for creating (Transaction CR01), changing (Transaction CR02), and displaying (Transaction CR03) the data. The work center is in turn included in the routing, which defines the production steps to produce a manufactured product. If a service is provided at the work center, then this leads to a credit of the assigned cost center. We'll show the master data used in production in detail in Chapter 6.

The cost center is assigned to the fixed asset master. You can access it via the Manage Fixed Asset app (SAP Fiori ID F1684), shown in Figure 4.12, or Transactions AS01 to AS03.

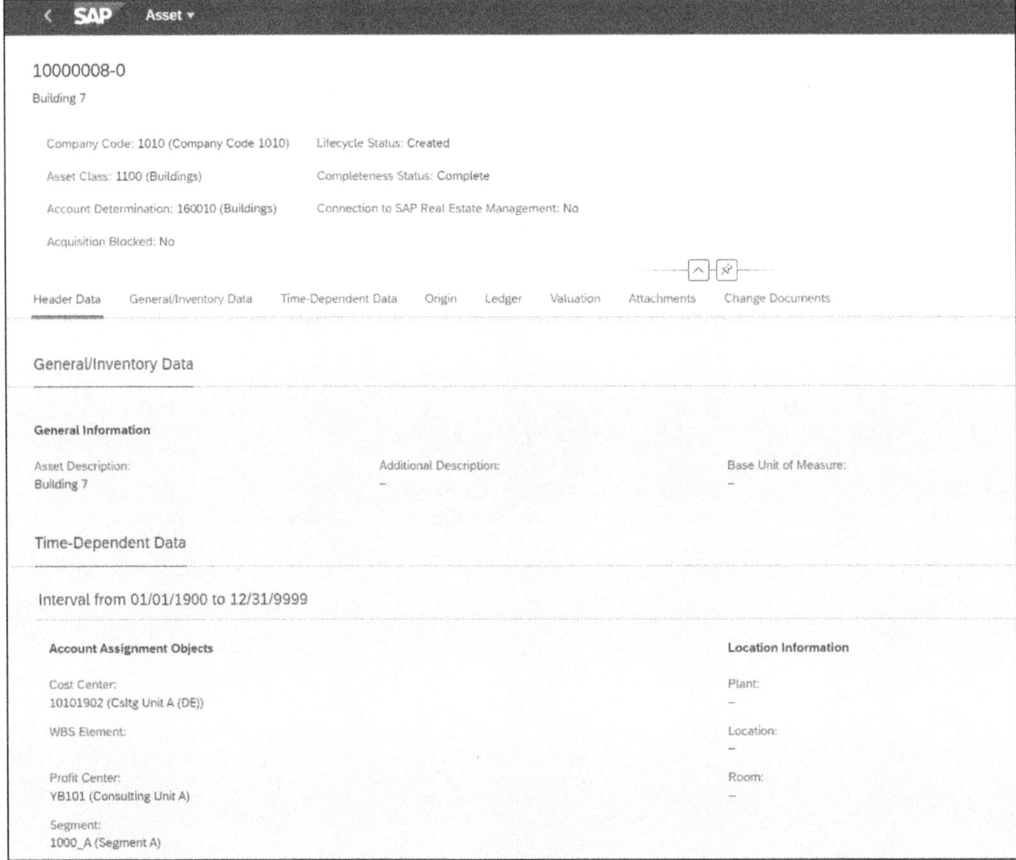


**Figure 4.12** Cost Center Assignment in Asset Master

Within the **Time-Dependent Data** section, you can assign the cost center. The **Profit Center** and **Segment** are derived from the cost center.

With the periodic depreciation run, the depreciation is posted to the assigned cost center. We'll show an example of such a posting in Chapter 5.

### 4.2.2 Cost Center Master

The cost center master you can access with Transactions KS01/KS02 and KS03 for creating/changing and displaying the cost center or via the Manage Cost Centers app (SAP Fiori ID F1443).

Let's look at an example. Execute Transaction KS02 and enter **Cost Center** "10101902". You'll arrive at the **Change Cost Center: Basic Screen**, shown in Figure 4.13.

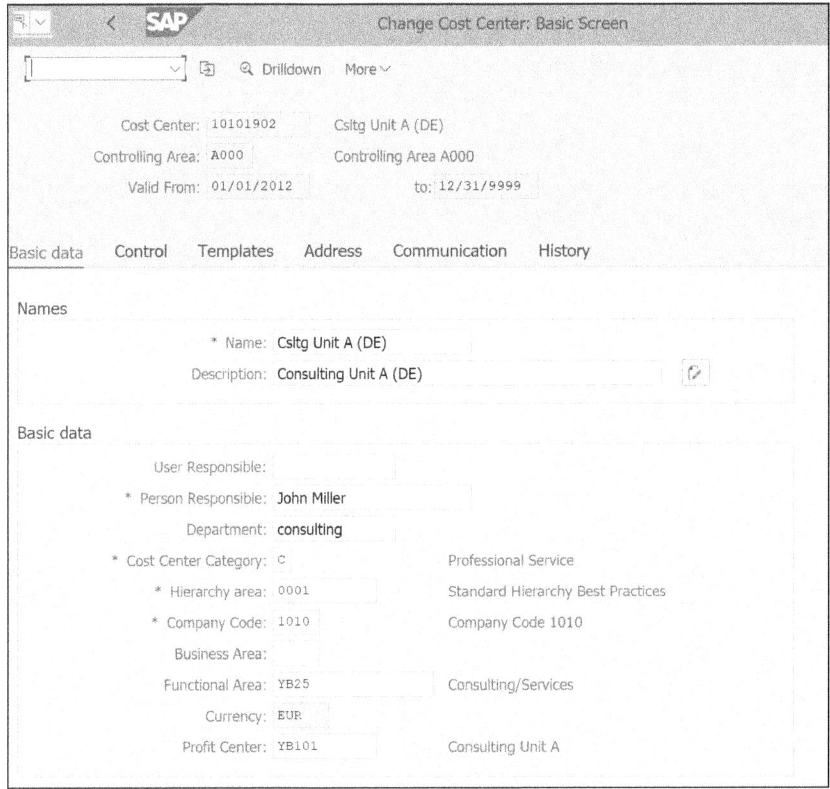


**Figure 4.13** Cost Center Master: Basic Data

Let's go now through the single attributes.

At the top of the **Basic data** tab, you'll see **Valid From** and **To** dates; the cost center master data elements are time-dependent. You can create time slices for a cost center for specific attributes. You can define the attributes for which this is supported in Customizing by following menu path **Controlling • Cost Center Accounting • Master Data • Cost Centers • Define Time-Based Fields for Cost Centers.** A use case could be that you change the assignment to a **Profit Center** from one period to another or change the **Person Responsible.** The **User Responsible, Person Responsible,** and **Department** are attributes of the cost center that do not control any functionality but can be shown in cost center reporting (see the discussion of cost center reports in Chapter 2, Section 2.4).

With the **Cost Center Category**, it's possible to classify the cost centers. There are controls enabled by default. You define the categories and their default parameters in IMG by following menu path **Controlling • Cost Center Accounting • Master Data • Cost Centers • Cost Center Categories.** Every cost center must be assigned to a cost center group: the **Hierarchy area** shown in Figure 4.13, which is part of the standard hierarchy. The standard hierarchy is defined per controlling area (see Chapter 3, Section 3.1.3). As mentioned, this is to ensure that every cost center is assigned in this special hierarchy. Then a cost center must be assigned to a **Company Code**. A cost center can't be defined across company codes; all postings on a cost center are assigned to the assigned company code. But a cost center can receive allocations from another company code or allocate costs to another company code (see Chapter 9).

The **Business Area** is a financial organizational unit that can be defined in IMG. Like the profit center, it represents an area of accountability. Because SAP now focuses on profit centers and not on business areas, we won't cover business areas further in this book.

Each cost center can be assigned to a **Functional Area**. As described in Chapter 3, Section 3.1.6, this allows you to classify costs posted to the cost center by functions. In this example, all costs debited and credited to this cost center will be attributed to the **Consulting/Services** functional area.

The **Currency** field reflects the company code currency. It's derived when you assign the company code and can't be changed.

If profit center accounting is active, you must enter a **Profit Center** as well. To allow a breakdown of the company P&L according to internal areas of responsibility, you need to assign a profit center to all cost objects (see Chapter 3, Section 3.1.5). As a result, you need to assign cost centers to profit centers too.

The next tab in the cost center master, **Control**, shows the business transaction controls (see Figure 4.14).

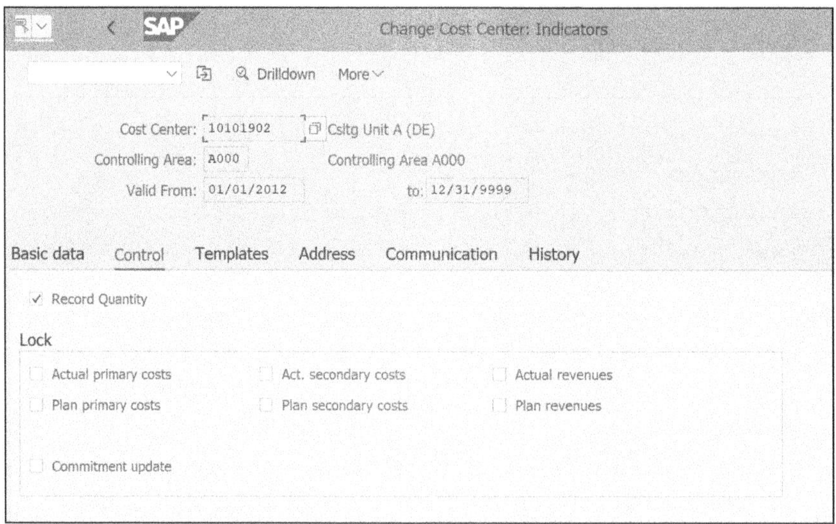


**Figure 4.14** Cost Center Master: Business Transaction Control

By flagging **Record Quantity**, you enable the quantity to be registered for postings to the cost center that carry a quantity. An example is a goods issue from stock to the cost center.

Then you have the following options to **Lock** the cost center for single business transactions:

- For **Actual primary costs** (see Section 4.1.2)
- For actual secondary costs (**Act. secondary costs**; see Section 4.1.3)
- For **Actual revenues**

You have the same three types of locks for cost center planning, and you can lock commitments, too (see Chapter 5 and Chapter 8 for more details).

In the **Templates** tab, you can activate template allocations and overhead rates by assigning costing sheets. However, this isn't widely used, so we'll cover it only briefly in Chapter 5, in which we also discuss costing sheets for orders and projects.

In the **History** tab, you can see when the cost center is created and the change documents for the cost center master.

### 4.2.3 Cost Center Hierarchies

For grouping of cost centers, there are cost center groups available, as shown in Figure 4.15. They come into action in these cases:

- In Customizing, you'll see them in places where you want to define a rule for a group of cost centers and you don't want to list all of them individually. Examples are the different periodic cost allocations, where you want to address a group of cost centers as the sender or receiver of an allocation cycle. We'll discuss this in Chapter 5.
- If you want to get your cost center data for a group of cost centers, you can add a cost center group as a parameter when you start the report.
- You can build hierarchies on these cost center groups. Thus, you can show flexible subtotals for your cost center areas in your cost center report. We showed an example for cost center reporting in Chapter 2, Section 2.4.

You can create/edit and change cost center groups with Transactions KSH1/KSH2 and KSH3. Now let's take a look at it in the system.

Start Transaction KSH2 (Change of Cost Center Group) and enter the **Cost Center Group** "1010". After pressing `Enter`, you'll arrive at the **Change Cost Center Group: Structure** screen, shown in Figure 4.15.

You see here a hierarchy for the center in Germany, with areas of accountability to which the single cost centers are assigned. You can enhance this hierarchy in the following ways:

- You can add additional groups. To do so, mark the group and select **Same Level** or **Lower Level**.
- You can assign additional cost centers. To do so, mark the group and select **Cost Center**.

You can change the standard hierarchy with Transaction OKEON.

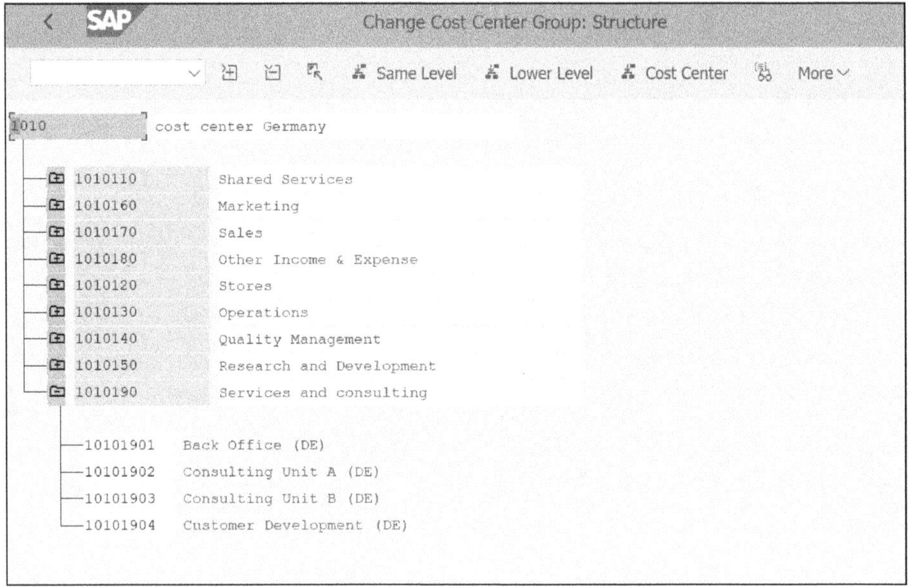


**Figure 4.15** Cost Center Group

## 4.3 Activity Types

We'll now explain how the service provided by the cost center is defined by the activity types for its output. We already showed sample reports that included the activity types for the cost center in Chapter 2. The activity types are a central tool to establish the cost flow within a controlling area. They're used to allocate costs from a cost center to other cost objects, like projects or production orders (refer back to the bottom left part of Figure 4.1).

It's important to know that the allocation is done based on quantities. The allocated amount is calculated by multiplying the quantity by a cost rate.

The activity type describes the kind of service provided by a cost center. There can be multiple services provided by a cost center and so there can be multiple activity types assigned to a cost center. Examples include the following:

- In a professional service scenario, the consulting cost center receives payroll costs, asset deprecations, and other periodic costs. Here the activity type describes the service that's planned and required for the customer project. There can be different services, like junior consulting, senior consulting, or platinum consulting. As an example, the consultant confirms the time worked for the customer project and the system posts the activity type senior consulting with the provided hours. The amount is calculated by multiplying the provided hours by the cost rate of the activity. We'll dive deeper into this scenario in Chapter 7.

- In a production scenario, a cost center can reflect a work center to which energy, asset depreciation, and salary are posted. An activity type assigned to this work center can be machine hours or labor hours, and the service consumption will be measured by hours or minutes (see Chapter 6).
- If the output of a cost center is the number of solved customer tickets, then the activity type will be the customer ticket and the unit of measure will be pieces.

Now let's have a look in the system at how the activity type is set up.

### 4.3.1 Activity Type Master

You can access the activity type master with Transactions KL01 (create), KL02 (change), or KL03 (display), or via the Manage Activity Types app (SAP Fiori ID F1605A), which is shown in Figure 4.16. The functionality and provided fields are similar to those of the SAP GUI transactions.

**Figure 4.16** Activity Type Master

The activity types are planned and allocated by recording the quantities. For these quantities, there is exactly one unit of measure defined in the activity master: the

**Activity Unit**. In this example, it's **H** for *hours*. It's also possible to enter an activity in minutes as minutes can be converted automatically into hours.

The assignment to a cost center is restricted by the allowed **Cost Center Categories**. In this example, the activity type **T002** can be only used for centers of type **C (Professional Service)**. If you enter an asterisk (*), all cost center types are allowed.

With the **Activity Type Category**, you define how the actual and plan quantities are determined and if there are quantity requests for potential receivers, how they impact these output quantities. There are the following options for activity type categories:

- **1: Manual entry, manual allocation**
  The planned activity quantity is entered manually for the cost center. There may be deviations from these plan quantities to the planned quantities requested by potential recipient objects. The actual activity allocations are entered manually, as in the examples mentioned earlier. We'll see examples of this type of allocation in Chapter 5 through Chapter 7.
- **2: Indirect determination, indirect allocation**
  These activity types support the use case of the complete pull principle, wherein the quantities performed cannot be determined in plan and actual forms. Plan and actual quantities are determined by the indirect activity allocation by the requests of the receiving cost objects. We'll show an example of this type of allocation in Chapter 5.
- **3: Manual entry, indirect allocation**
  The activity quantities are entered in plan and actual manually, but you don't enter a receiver. The receiver is determined based on the planned sender-receiver relationship.
- **4: Manual entry, no allocation**
  Here the activity quantities are planned manually for the cost center. An allocation to other objects isn't possible.

**Note**

SAP S/4HANA Cloud supports only category **1, Manual entry, manual allocation**. This is the most common method. We'll focus on this category in this book but will mention the other ones in Chapter 5.

You need to define a general ledger account, **Allocation Cost Element**, via which the allocation is posted in Universal Journal. With this general ledger account, the cost center is credited and the receiving object, such as a production order or customer project, is debited. This general ledger account must be a secondary cost element with the cost element category 43 (see Section 4.1.3).

With the **Price Indicator**, you define how the cost rate for an activity type is determined. It can be set manually or automatically calculated by the system. There are three indicators available:

- **1 Plan price, automatically based on activity**
  The cost rate is calculated by dividing the planned costs by planned quantities for the fixed and the variable components.
- **2 Plan price, automatically based on capacity**
  Here the variable component of the cost rate is calculated as for indicator 1: planned variable costs divided by planned quantity. The fixed component is calculated with fixed planned costs divided by planned capacity for the activity type of the cost center.
- **3 Determined manually**
  Here you define the cost rate manually.



With the **Actual Price Indicator**, there can be a different method determined for the actual postings. As we discussed in the context of how costs behave in Chapter 2, the cost rate has a fixed and variable component. We'll discuss the cost rate definition in next section. With the **Lock** button, you can lock the activity type for usage. Within the activity type planning process, you can have the system calculate an additional **Output Unit** in parallel. The calculation of the additional output of a cost center is based on the following formula:

*Additional output = Planned output of the activity type unit of measure x Output factor*

In the **Change Log**, you can see who created the activity type and when, as well as all changes to the master data.

Activity type groups are also available. They can be used in the cost center planning, some places in Customizing, or the definition of the assessment. You can create/change/display them with Transactions KLH1/KLH2 and KLH3.

### 4.3.2 Cost Rates

Activity types describe the quantitative output of a cost center. For every activity type of a cost center and service of a cost center, you need to define a cost rate per activity unit—for example, $50 per hour. The activity allocation with this activity type is then valuated with the cost rate multiplied by the quantity.

There are several ways of setting this rate. If the aim is to distribute the costs on the cost center to the receivers as accurately as possible, the cost rate is determined manually or automatically by the system via a simple calculation: planned costs divided by planned output quantity. An example of this calculation is shown in Table 4.1.

You may also want to charge the service receivers with fixed prices, which are defined internally by the company. This is the case in a professional service company, where consultants provide services for different customer projects in different areas. This naturally leads to an over- or underabsorption in the cost center at the end of the period and thus to a profit or loss for the assigned profit center.

| Production Cost Center Planning | | | |
|---|---|---|---|
| **Activity Type: Machine Hours** | **Output Planned: 1,000 h** | | |
| | **Planned Costs** | **Fixed Costs** | **Variable Costs** |
| | Asset depreciation | $50,000 | $20,000 |
| | Energy | $30,000 | |
| Calculated activity type rate | $100/h total | Therefore, $80/h fixed | Therefore, $20/h variable |
| **Activity Type: Person Hour** | **Output Planned: 1,000 h** | | |
| | Salary | $90,000 | $10,000 |
| | Allocation canteen | $5,000 | |
| | Allocation HR | $5,000 | |
| Calculated activity type rate | $110/h total | Therefore, $100/h fixed | Therefore, $10/h variable |

**Table 4.1** Cost Center Activity Type Rate Calculation

Table 4.1 shows an example for a production cost center, which provides two services: machine hours and personal hours. For these activity types, you need to define a planned output in a dedicated plan period. Related to the activity types, you then plan the costs, for which you can define if they are fixed or variable (i.e., whether the service is dependent on the output quantity). For example, energy costs normally are defined as variable as they only occur when the machine produces.

In SAP S/4HANA, you can plan the cost rates manually with Transaction KP26 or in SAP Fiori with the Manage Cost Rates—Plan app (SAP Fiori ID F3162; currently only available in SAP S/4HANA Cloud). The difference between the two options is that you can plan with SAP GUI for different plan versions, but with SAP Fiori, you can only plan for version 0.

Figure 4.17 shows four activity types planned for cost center **10101301**. The cost rates are always valid from a certain period—here, 001/2020. You see the total rate and the fixed and variable components. On the far right, you see the reference quantity for the cost rate: the cost rates are defined per one hour.

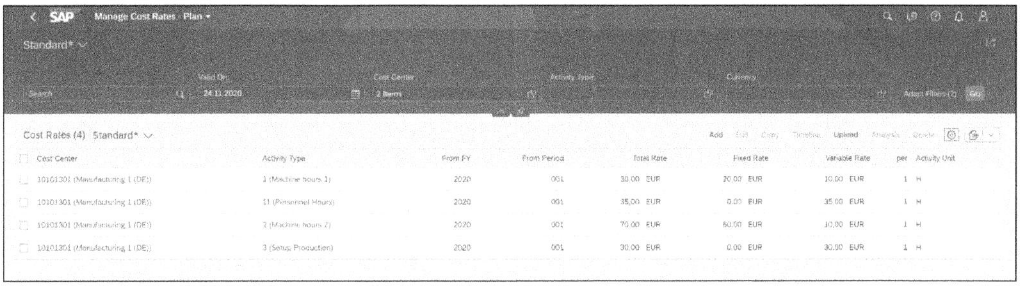

**Figure 4.17** Manage Cost Rates—Plan App

If you want to get the cost rates calculated by the system based on your planning, you can use Transaction KSPI (Execute Plan Price Calculation) or SAP Analytics Cloud. For more information, see Chapter 5.

Now let's look at SAP S/4HANA Cloud. You've already seen the cost rate depending on cost center and activity type. SAP S/4HANA Cloud also provides an app with which you can define the cost rates very flexibly: the Manage Cost Rates—Professional Services app, as shown in Figure 4.18.

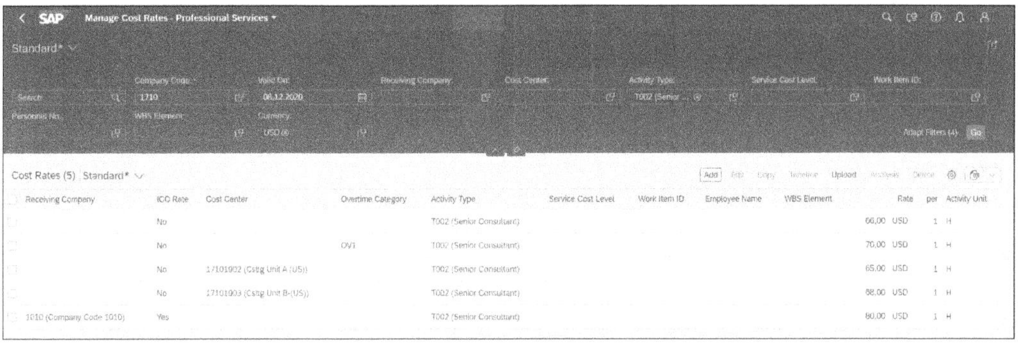

**Figure 4.18** Manage Cost Rates—Professional Services App

Here it's possible to derive the cost rate from several parameters:

- **Activity Type**
  The cost rate can be defined now by **Activity Type** only (line 1). This can simplify the maintenance of the cost rates.
- **Overtime Category**
  The cost rate can be defined dependent on the **Overtime Category** (line 2). The **Overtime** parameter can be entered by the employee when they confirm their time in the time sheet. So you can indicate that work performed on the weekend, for example, is at a higher rate than work performed during normal working hours.

- **ICO Rate**
  You can defined your own intercompany cost rate. We'll discuss this functionality in Chapter 9.
- **Service Cost Level**
  The cost rate also can be dependent on single employees or their grades via the **Service Cost Level**. This is an attribute in the employee master.

> **Note**
> SAP plans to provide this app in on-premise SAP S/4HANA, too. For more information about the app and new functionalities, visit *http://s-prs.co/v528201*.

## 4.4 Statistical Key Figures

Similar to activity types, statistical key figures can assign quantities to cost objects. But different from activity types, they describe not costs and quantity flow from one controlling object to another but a quantity directly on the object. No cost element is assigned to them and they are not represented in the general ledger.

Typical use cases are as follows:

- The number of employees assigned to a cost center
- The vacation days taken by employees of the cost center
- The incoming sales orders per sales department

The statistical key figures are available in the controlling reporting and can be used as a basis for the allocation of costs in the following ways, as we'll discuss in Chapter 5:

- The costs of the canteen cost center can be allocated to the individual cost centers according to the number of employees assigned there.
- Based on the number of vacation days taken and respectively still open per cost center, vacation provisions can be allocated.
- Costs of sales support can be allocated to the sales departments on the basis of their incoming sales orders.

Now let's look at them in the system.

### 4.4.1 Statistical Key Figure Master

You can create/change/display statistical key figures with Transactions KK01/KK02 and KK03 or the Manage Statistical Key Figures app (SAP Fiori ID F1603A). Figure 4.19 shows the **Change Statistical Key Figure: Master Data** screen, which appears after you execute Transaction KK02 for key figure **1001**.

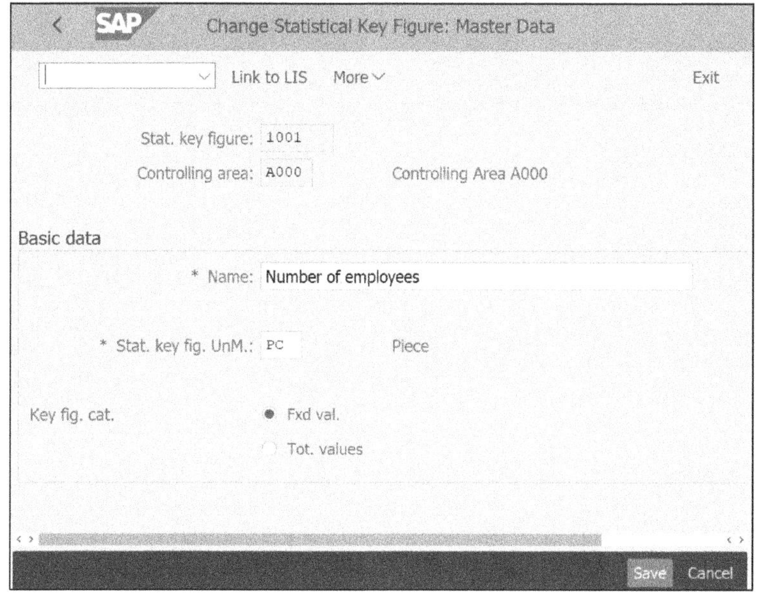


**Figure 4.19** Statistical Key Figure Master

The statistical key figure master record is assigned to the controlling area. Otherwise, you need to define a unit of measure for the statistical key figure in the **Stat. key fig. UnM** field. With this unit, the statistical key figure is recorded when you apply it to a cost object. It cannot be changed by recording.

There are two key figure categories (**Key fig. cat.**) available:

1. **Fixed values (Fxd val.)**
   With this category, you determine one fixed value per period. You use this, for example, for the number of employees. If you add for a period another value, it will replace the old value. The last entered value is always valid.
2. **Total values (Tot. values)**
   With this category, the recorded values are added up. Examples include the incoming sales orders and vacation days taken. If you add another value in a certain period, it will be added to the existing value.

Statistical key figure groups are also available. You can create/change/display them with Transactions KBH1/KBH2 and KBH3.

### 4.4.2 Entry of Statistical Key Figures

You can record the plan and actual data for statistical key figures with Transactions KB31N (create) and KB33N (display) or with the Manage Statistical Key Figure Values app (SAP Fiori ID F3915), which is shown in Figure 4.20. With the SAP Fiori app, you can select the available fields with greater flexibility.

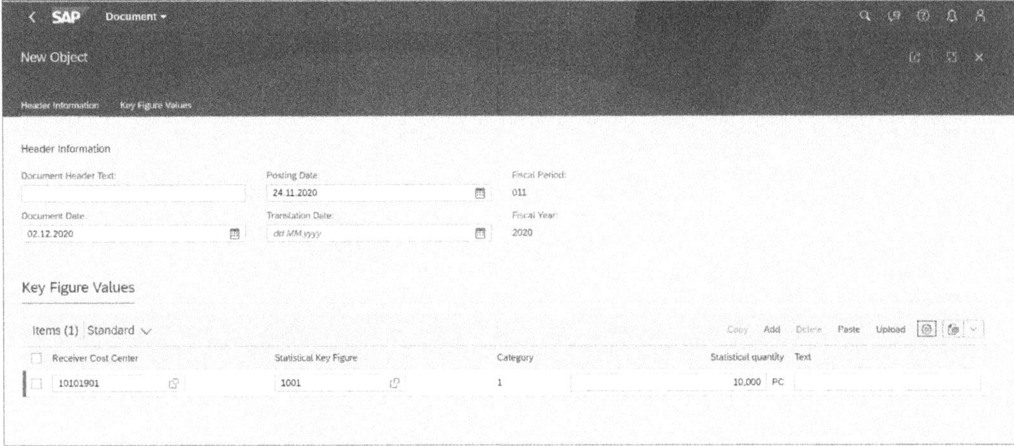


**Figure 4.20** Manage Statistical Key Figure Values App

As in journal entries, the posting date defines the **Fiscal Period**—here, **011**. Here we record the statistical key figure **1001**, which is the number of employees for cost center **10101901**. **Category 1** is derived from the statistical key figure master and reflects fixed values.

You can record statistical key figures for several controlling objects in the line items section.

Now let's look at the statistical key figure-focused reporting. Start in the Statistical Key Figures – Actuals app (SAP Fiori ID F2766), shown in Figure 4.21. Here you can see the values for cost center **10101901**.

Statistical Key Figure Items

Jump To

| | | | | Category | 1 | 2 | Grand Total |
|---|---|---|---|---|---|---|---|
| | | | | Category | Fixed values | Totals values | |
| Cost Center | Cost Center | Statistical Key Figure | Statistical Key Figure | Fiscal Period | Quantity | Quantity | Total |
| 10101901 | Back Office (DE) | 1001 | Number of employees | 7 | 8 PC | | 8 PC |
| | | | | 8 | 8 PC | | 8 PC |
| | | | | 9 | 8 PC | | 8 PC |
| | | | | 10 | 8 PC | | 8 PC |
| | | | | 11 | 8 PC | | 8 PC |
| | | | | 12 | 10 PC | | 10 PC |
| | | | | Total | 10 PC | | 10 PC |
| | | EE_ADM | Non-project relevant working times | 7 | | 0 H | 0 H |
| | | | | 8 | | 0 H | 0 H |
| | | | | 9 | | 0 H | 0 H |
| | | | | 10 | | 19 H | 19 H |
| | | | | 11 | | 0 H | 0 H |
| | | | | 12 | | 20 H | 20 H |
| | | | | Total | | 39 H | 39 H |
| | | Total | | | 10 PC | 39 H | * |

**Figure 4.21** Display Statistical Key Figures Actuals App

In the first section, you see the **Number of employees** based on category fixed values and with a fixed value per period. Note that the totals line item is a sum up not of all values but of the last values of the rows. The next section shows the administration hours, **Non-project relevant working times**, of the employees of the cost center.

If you don't use SAP Fiori, there are alternative reports available in the SAP menu below the submenus for cost element accounting and cost center accounting.



**Note**

There are additional business processes in place that update the statistical key figures. For example, statistical key figures are used in time sheets, like for posting administration hours, training hours, or vacation hours.

## 4.5 Internal Orders and Projects

With internal orders and projects, you can assign costs to your areas of accountability for certain jobs or for measurement of corporate activities. With a very flexible tool of cost allocation, the settlement, you can pass on the costs in the sense of the controlling internal value flow. Let's look back one more time at Figure 4.1, which shows that there are several receivers possible. The costs are further specified as in margin analysis and forwarded in the controlling internal value flow by posting to a cost center or even being capitalized as in asset accounting.

Both orders and projects are important controlling objects to control the internal processes of a company. They can be used for a variety of purposes to keep track of costs and in some cases revenues for the controlling job. They offer functions for planning, monitoring, and allocating costs and revenues, as well as status management.

There are four general categories:

1. **Overhead controlling**
   To monitor overhead costs incurred for a specific purpose, such as for a marketing or employee education measure or product development work. Variants within the overhead objects are statistical orders or projects. Here the statistical object is recorded in addition to the real account assignment. The costs are only available on the statistical object for reporting purposes and cannot be used for follow-up processes, which happens on the real account assigned object.
2. **Investment orders and projects**
   Used to monitor the costs incurred in creating fixed assets, such as when building a warehouse.
3. **Revenue carrying objects**
   Especially used by assignment to sales order items, but also if sales isn't in use. Thus, both costs and sales can be tracked.
4. **Accrual orders**
   Used to build accruals for periodic expenses.

**Internal Orders versus Projects**

There are several considerations when deciding between internal orders and projects. Projects provide additional functionality as you can create a hierarchical structure of project elements. Projects also are more deeply integrated into logistic processes; for example, they are integrated with networks or production orders. Seen in this way, the internal order is a simple project.

In on-premise SAP S/4HANA, you can work with both. In SAP S/4HANA Cloud, you can only use projects. Because the SAP roadmap focuses on the project, in this book we discuss only the project and its integration with assets (see Chapter 8) or connection to the sales processes (see Chapter 7).

### 4.5.1 Internal Order Master

You can access the internal order master with the Transactions KO01 (create)/KO02 (change) and KO03 (display) or with the Manage Internal Orders app. The functionality is similar.

**Note**

With this transaction, you can access the master data of production and maintenance orders too. We'll discuss them in Chapter 6.

Start the app, as shown in Figure 4.22, and create a new internal order covering overhead costs.

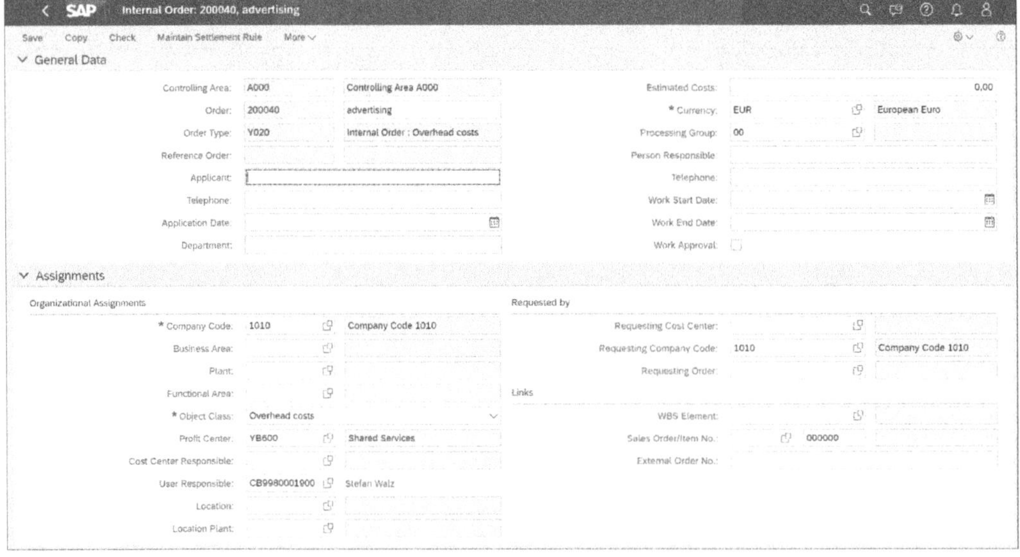


**Figure 4.22** Internal Order Master: General Data and Assignments View

With the **Order Type**, you can classify your customer orders. This is also available as a parameter in reporting. You can create your own order types in Customizing by following menu path **Controlling • Internal Orders • Order Master Data • Define Order Types**, arriving at the **Display View "Order Types": Details** screen shown in Figure 4.23.

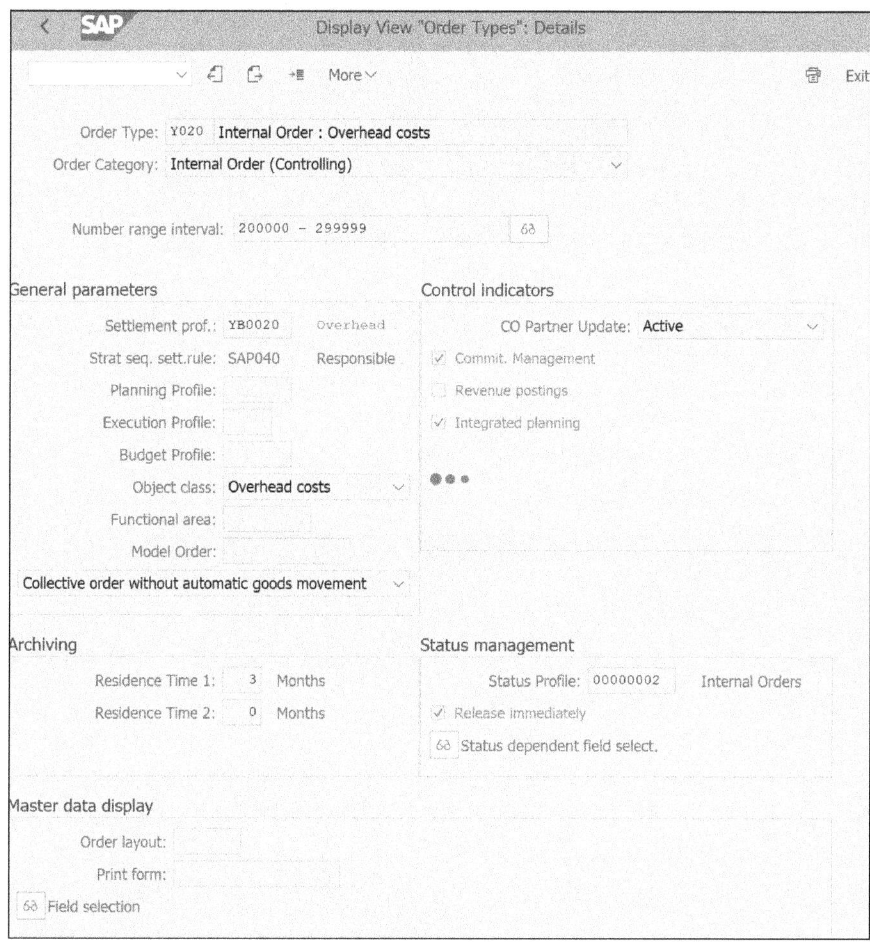


**Figure 4.23** Customizing of Order Types

With the **Order Category**, there is functionality linked. It defines the purpose of the internal order type, which we'll discuss next. Then there is a list of **General parameters**, which are defaulted using the order type. Finally, you get **Control indicators** for archiving and an option to assign a **Status Profile**. You can define your own status profile, to which you can add a customer-specific status.

Now let's return to Figure 4.22 and discuss the most important attributes:

- **Company Code**
  It's required to assign an internal order to exactly one **Company Code**. All postings on the internal order are within the same company code.

- **Functional Area**
  As mentioned in Chapter 3, if you use cost of sales reporting, it's recommended to assign the internal orders to a **Functional Area**.
- **Object Class**
  With the **Object Class**, you distinguish the purpose of the order overhead costs, investments, production, and profit analysis. This field is stored in the Universal Journal and you can report on it. When we look at settlement in Chapter 5, we'll show how the type of order determines the receiver of the settlement.
- **Profit Center**
  You assign one **Profit Center** to the internal order. All costs and revenues posted on the internal order will be assigned to this profit center.
- **WBS Element**
  You can assign an internal order to a work breakdown structure (WBS) element. In this case, the costs on the internal order can be taken into account for processes running on the project, like budgeting and availability control.

When you scroll down, you'll see the next section of the internal order master, as shown in Figure 4.24.

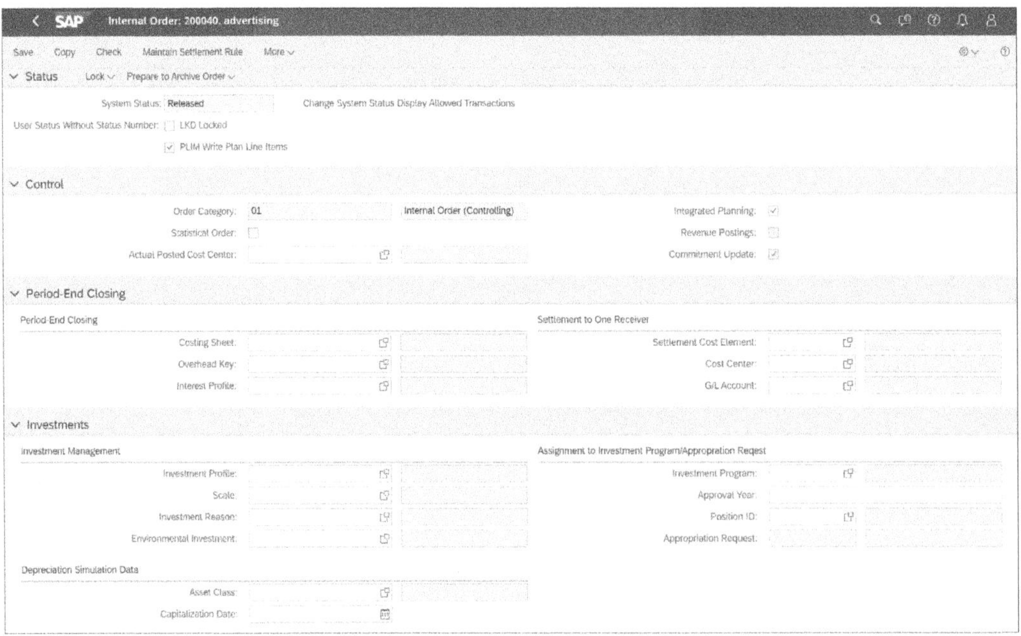


**Figure 4.24** Internal Order Master: View of Order Control, Period-End Closing, and Investment Integration

In the first section, you'll see the status control. The status determines the business transactions that can be carried out for an order. A status can permit a business process, trigger a warning message, or prohibit a business process.

The system provides four standard statuses that an order passes through:

1. **Created**
   In this phase, an actual posting on the order isn't possible.
2. **Released**
   When an internal order is released, all business transactions are allowed.
3. **Technically Complete**
   No planning-related changes are permitted in this phase. If revenue recognition is active, all actual costs and revenues are realized, and balance sheet amounts are cleared.
4. **Closed**
   With this status, no cost-relevant business transactions are permitted.

A new custom status can be created to control when certain business transactions are allowed. A user-defined status extends and updates the standard system status. You can do this in IMG by following menu path **Controlling • Internal Orders • Order Master Data • Status Management • Define Status Profiles.**

The **Control** section provides the following controls for the internal order:

- **Order Category**
  Describes the usage of the internal order and is defined by the system:
  - **01 Internal Order**
    Used for overhead controlling and controlling the corporate value flow. We will discuss this in Chapter 5.
  - **02 Accrual Calculation**
    You can use accrual orders to accrue costs for the correct periods when expenses are relevant for several periods. We explained this with the primary cost elements in Section 4.1.2.
  - **03 CO Production Order**
    A pure controlling object for production processes for which no integration with the production module exists.
  - **05 Product Cost Collector**
    Used for production processes as a kind of aggregation of production orders. We'll cover this in Chapter 6.
  - **10 Production Order**
    Primarily an instrument for logistical production processes, but it also covers all controlling requirements. We'll discuss this in Chapter 6.
  - **20 Networks**
    A logistical quantity structure can be covered with networks. They're highly variable and used in connection with projects.
  - **30 Maintenance Order**
    These are orders that cover internal service processes (see Chapter 6).

  - **40 Process Order**
    This object covers the production processes of the process industry.

  Although these orders are used in very different areas of the company and trigger very different processes, we map them to one order controlling object and provide similar functionality for, say, reporting, planning, surcharges, and settlement.

- **Statistical Order**
  If flagged, then the order cannot be used to capture real cost postings. The internal order can only be account-assigned if there is a real cost object like the cost center in parallel. If an internal order is statistical, there are no subsequent business transactions possible on this order, like settlement or revenue recognition. This order is only for reporting.
- **Integrated Planning**
  If **Integrated Planning** is flagged, the order participates in the integrated overhead planning. Planned activities on the order update the output planning of the respective cost center.
- **Revenue Postings**
  If **Revenue Postings** are allowed, select this checkbox.
- **Commitment Update**
  A checkbox to determine whether commitments are calculated and updated.

The next section controls the **Period-End Closing** transactions:

- **Costing Sheet**
  By applying a **Costing Sheet**, you activate overhead costs on the internal order.
- **Overhead Key**
  The **Overhead Key** can be used to determine order-specific overhead rates.
- **Interest Profile**
  By applying an **Interest Profile**, you activate interest calculation. An interest profile contains the rules governing the interest calculation.
- **Settlement to One Receiver**
  If you use a very simple **Settlement to One Receiver**, you can maintain here the settlement **Cost Element**, the receiver **Cost Center**, and the settlement **G/L Account**. We'll explain how to create settlement rules in Chapter 5 and explain the specifics of settlement to assets in Chapter 8.

Next, there are two sections about **Investments** covering the integration with assets. We'll take a deeper look at this in Chapter 8.

For very flexible cost allocation to different cost objects, use the settlement option, which you can go to by selecting the **Maintain Settlement Rule** button. We'll show this in more detail in Chapter 5, Section 5.4.6 and in Chapter 8.

### 4.5.2 Project Master

You can use projects to control more complex customer-related projects, internal projects, and capital expense projects. The WBS elements form flexible hierarchy levels, the nodes of which can describe a project phase. A much more complex cost control is possible.

The projects are integrated with logistical objects such as networks and production orders, which provide a quantity structure that can be used for planning and that can trigger the actual costs.

You can access the project master with Transactions CJ01 (create), CJ02 (change), and CJ03 (display) or with the Project Control app. There is also a kind of cockpit for the project master available: the Project Builder app, or Transaction CJ20N.

Let's start with the Project Builder, as shown in Figure 4.25.

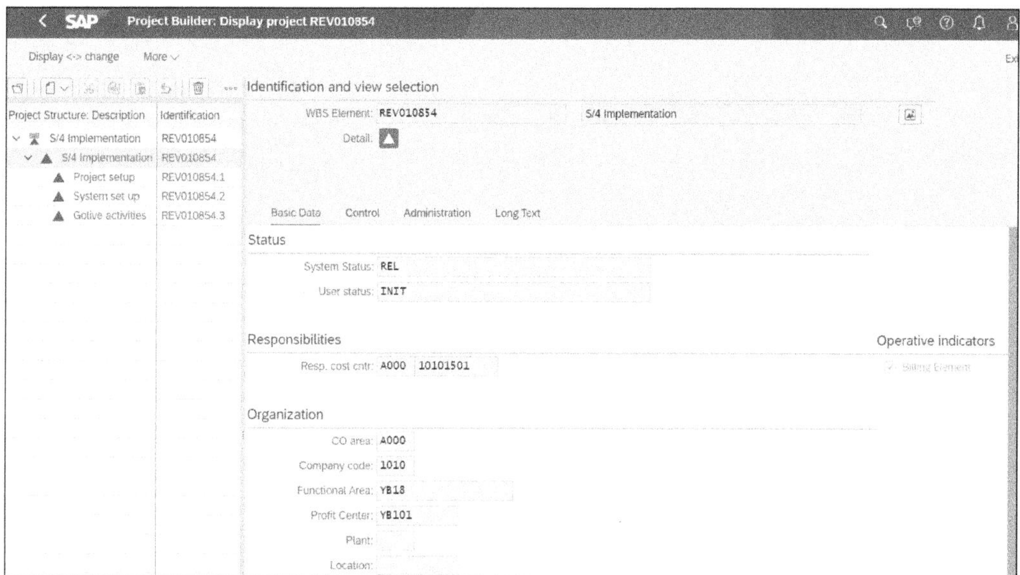


**Figure 4.25** Project Master with Structure

On the left, a two-level project hierarchy is shown in this example. The top node includes the phases of an SAP S/4HANA implementation (in the **S/4 Implementation** folder). These phases are listed on the lower hierarchical level. In the right section are the basic assignments. Like for internal orders, there's custom specific **Status** management available in the **Basic Data** tab. And like for orders, the **WBS Element** must be assigned to a company code and can be assigned to several other attributes like the functional area in the **Organization** section. The operative indicator **Billing Element** is also important. Only if it's active can you post revenues on the project and assign it to sales processes; we'll cover this in Chapter 7.

Now switch to the **Control** tab, shown in Figure 4.26.

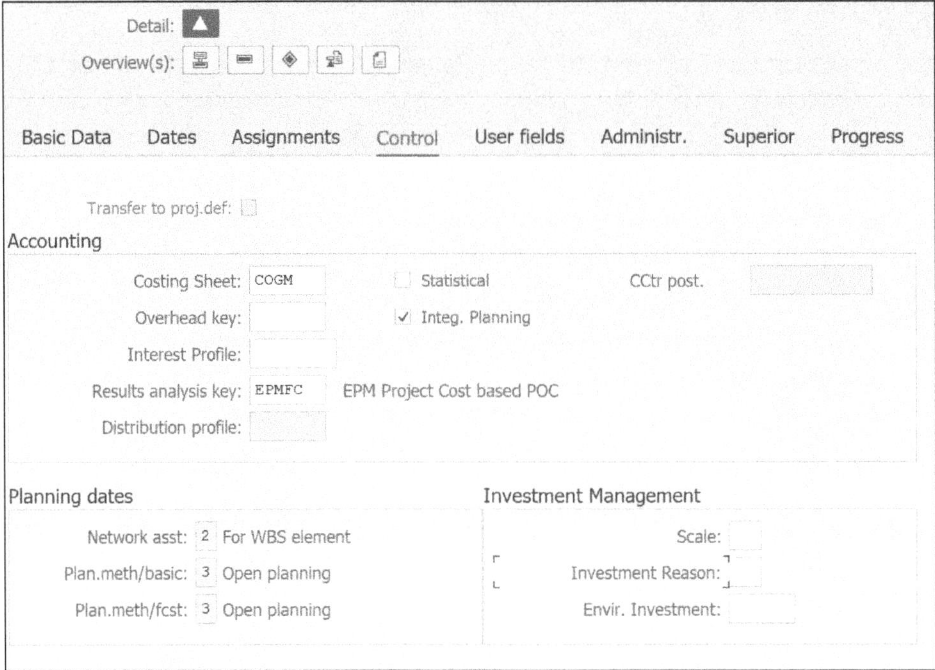


**Figure 4.26** WBS Element Control Data

Like for an internal order, you can assign a **Costing Sheet** to calculate overheads and a **Results analysis key** for revenue recognition; we'll discuss this in Chapter 7.

In the next section, you'll see one aspect of the integration with networks. As mentioned, we'll show the usage of the project within the customer project scenario and the investment projects later in this book (Chapter 7 and Chapter 8, respectively).

## 4.6 Profitability Object in Margin Analysis

Now let's look at the technical integration of the margin analysis in the Universal Journal. We discussed the market segment in Chapter 3, Section 3.1.4, reflected by the operating concern. With this you define the characteristics that are relevant for you to steer your business.

The market segment consists of fields predefined by SAP and can be extended by additional customer-specific fields. When you look again at the controlling value flow previously shown in Figure 4.1, note that the aim is to ultimately allocate all costs and revenues to a market segment and thus also to an area of responsibility. How you support this technically and how you can control market segment creation and thus your areas of accountability we'll show in the following sections.

### 4.6.1 Market Segment in the Universal Journal

As mentioned in Chapter 3, Section 3.1.4, the market segment is now part of the Universal Journal. There is no separate data store for the margin analysis application. The values we get from the journal entries and its characteristics are all part of the Universal Journal.

Let's start with an example of how the market segment is determined and stored in the Universal Journal, shown in Figure 4.27, which we'll come back to frequently in this chapter to explain how it works. The business scenario is the sale of an inventory-managed product. In this example, we post the goods issue for a customer delivery.

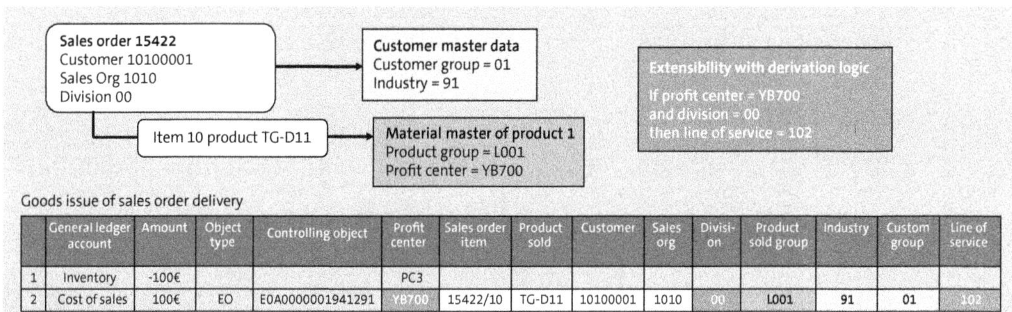


**Figure 4.27** Derivation of Market Segment in Sales Process

Relevant for profitability in this example is journal entry line item 2, which posts the cost of sales.

**Terminology**

From a business point of view, we call the combination of reporting attributes such as customer, product, sales organization, or profit center a *market segment*. Technically, this is an account assignment object in the system that is synonymous with a cost center or project, which we call a *profitability object* or, in some user interfaces, a *profitability segment*; it's often abbreviated as PSG or EO.

The market segment derivation can be done by the system via the following steps:

1. With the creation of a sales order item, there are already primary market segment attributes defined: the sales organization, the distribution channel, the division, and of course the customer and product.
2. The market segment application reads the customer master to derive additional attributes like the customer group, country, and industry of the customer.
3. From the material master you get the material group and profit center.
4. Additional extensibility fields may be derived: here in the rightmost **Line of service** column, as explained in the next section.

5. From these characteristics, a profitability segment is created, which serves as the account assignment object. As you learned in Section 4.1, controlling-relevant general ledger accounts must be posted to cost objects. The type of the account assignment object is reflected in the journal entry as an object type. Here it's EO for profitability object, followed by the technical controlling object number. This profitability object is derived with the sales order creation and stored in the sales order item. It is used in all subsequent processes of the sales order, for example, delivery and billing. In Section 4.6.3, this number will be used for the posting of the goods issue for the delivery.

There are other processes in which we can derive the market segments by system, like for customer projects and service documents (see Chapter 7).

In the following business processes, the market segment can be defined manually via an account assignment popup in which all characteristics can be maintained (for an example, see Figure 4.33 in Section 4.6.2):

- Financial business transactions. For example, in the Post General Journal Entry app, or Transaction FB01, shown ahead in Figure 4.33.
- Settlement rules for a WBS element or internal order.
- Using an allocation with a target profitability segment.

Let's now go into more detail on how the profitability object is managed.

Each combination of the attributes defines a market/profitability segment and results in a profitability object number. The number and its characteristic vector are stored in table CE4xxxx_ACCT for the Universal Journal integrated margin analysis, where xxxx is determined by the key of the operation concern. If you use costing-based profitability analysis, it's stored in table CE4xxxx.

Let's look at an example. Start Transaction SE16 or SE16H and select table CE4A000_ACCT, as shown in Figure 4.28, since the operating concern key is A000. In the next section, we'll post some examples in the system with the **Line of service** extensibility field set to attribute **102**. To allow later reference, we'll filter on this value.

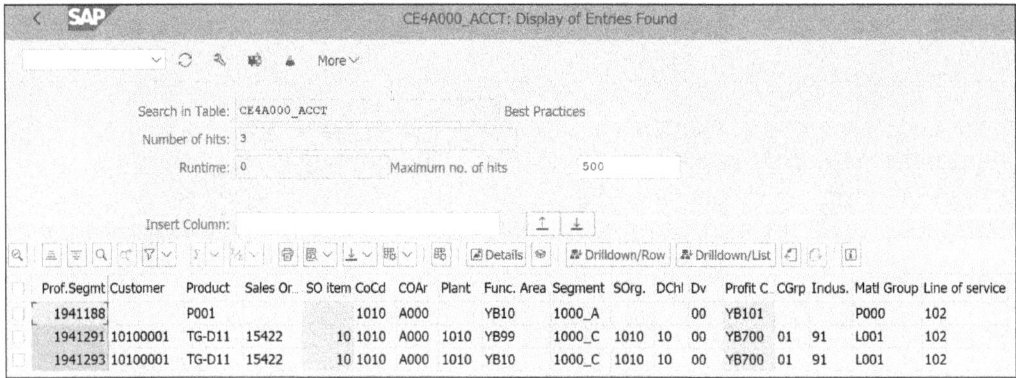


| Prof.Segmt | Customer | Product | Sales Or... | SO item | CoCd | COAr | Plant | Func. Area | Segment | SOrg. | DChl | Dv | Profit C... | CGrp | Indus. | Matl Group | Line of service |
|---|---|---|---|---|---|---|---|---|---|---|---|---|---|---|---|---|---|
| 1941188 | | P001 | | | 1010 | A000 | | YB10 | 1000_A | | | 00 | YB101 | | | P000 | 102 |
| 1941291 | 10100001 | TG-D11 | 15422 | 10 | 1010 | A000 | 1010 | YB99 | 1000_C | 1010 | 10 | 00 | YB700 | 01 | 91 | L001 | 102 |
| 1941293 | 10100001 | TG-D11 | 15422 | 10 | 1010 | A000 | 1010 | YB10 | 1000_C | 1010 | 10 | 00 | YB700 | 01 | 91 | L001 | 102 |

**Figure 4.28** Database View for Table CE4A000_ACCT

For every new combination of the market segment characteristics, you get a different number. These three line items reflect the manual posting on the profitability segment (line 1; see Figure 4.34 ahead) and the substitution example, in which we post a goods issue (see Figure 4.42 ahead). The two lower lines are used for the same sales order item **15422/10** but created with a different profitability object number as the functional area differs.



With this profitability segment object number, the technical controlling object is now created to which the account assignment of the line item is then made. It is preceded by EO, which stands for profit segment, followed by the operating concern, A000, and then the profitability segment number.

This leads in the case of the goods issue to the controlling objects EOA00000001941291 and EOA000001941293. You can check this in Section 4.6.3.

**Profitability Objects**

Just like a cost center, project, or internal order, the profitability object is a valid account assignment object in the Universal Journal. It has a technical controlling object number. Its special feature is that all market segment attributes associated with it are persisted in the Universal Journal.

If you work with your own areas of accountability and reporting entities to steer your business, you can enhance the operating concern.

**Example**

Say you want to add the line of service as your custom field for market segment analysis. It is its own area of responsibility, which isn't reflected in the standard organizational units and characteristics. This field should be derived when a sales order item is created by the system and should be manually selected to post manual costs and revenues on it or post allocations. You need it in all profitability reports.

There are the following three options to enhance the Universal Journal and thus your reporting structure with additional fields, which are identified by choosing a business context:

1. **Journal entry extensibility**
   You use this if you can derive the field or it's provided from preceding applications. There is a process extensibility in place, for example, with which you define an extensibility field in a sales area. You enter it in a sales order and it will be routed through to the journal entry.
2. **Coding block extensibility**
   Use this if you need to enter fields manually for some transactions, like Transaction FB01 (Post General Journal Entry) or Transaction KB21N (Activity Allocation).

3. **Market segment extensibility**
   Here you can enter the field manually in the account assignment view for profitability or you can derive it. The advantage is that you can use the field in subsequent transactions like top-down allocation or realignment (see Chapter 7). We'll discuss market segment extensibility further in the next section.

### 4.6.2 Market Segment Extensibility

To allow margin reporting for your specific market segment characteristics, you create your own fields and add them to the market segment. In on-premise SAP S/4HANA, there are two options to create the fields:

1. With the Custom Fields and Logic app (SAP Fiori ID F1481). After publishing, it's part of the market segment and Universal Journal. This is also available for SAP S/4HANA Cloud.
2. With Transaction KEA5, which is only available on-premise.

After the new fields are created, you need to take an additional step in on-premise SAP S/4HANA to assign it to an operating concern and activate the field. This is done via Transaction KEA0. You need this step in on-premise as there could be different operating concerns active. In SAP S/4HANA Cloud, there is only one, as is recommended. You also need this step on-premise if costing-based profitability analysis is active. By generating the operating concern via Transaction KEA0, you enhance the Universal Journal and the costing-based profitability analysis structures.

**Note**

Activating the new field for margin analysis will enhance the Universal Journal structure and will be part of the journal entry and thus potentially available for all business transactions reflected in the general ledger.

Because Transaction KEA5 is available on-premise only and we focus on our development roadmap on the SAP Fiori app functionality, we cover only the Custom Fields and Logic app in this book.

We'll walk through the Custom Fields and Logic app and the analysis process in the following sections.

#### Custom Fields and Logic

Now let's look at an example in the system. As a key user, start the Custom Fields and Logic app, as shown in Figure 4.29.

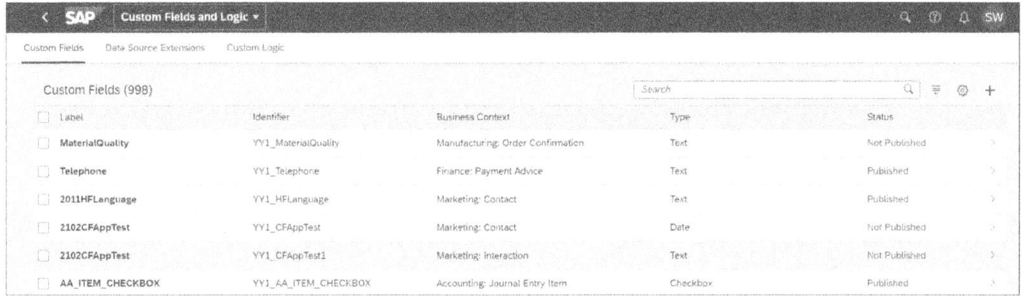


**Figure 4.29** Custom Fields and Logic App: Overview

You first get an overview of all existing extensibility fields. To create your own field, go to the **Custom Fields** tab and click the **+** button at the top right. You'll get a popup with the required parameters for the new extensibility field, as shown in Figure 4.30.

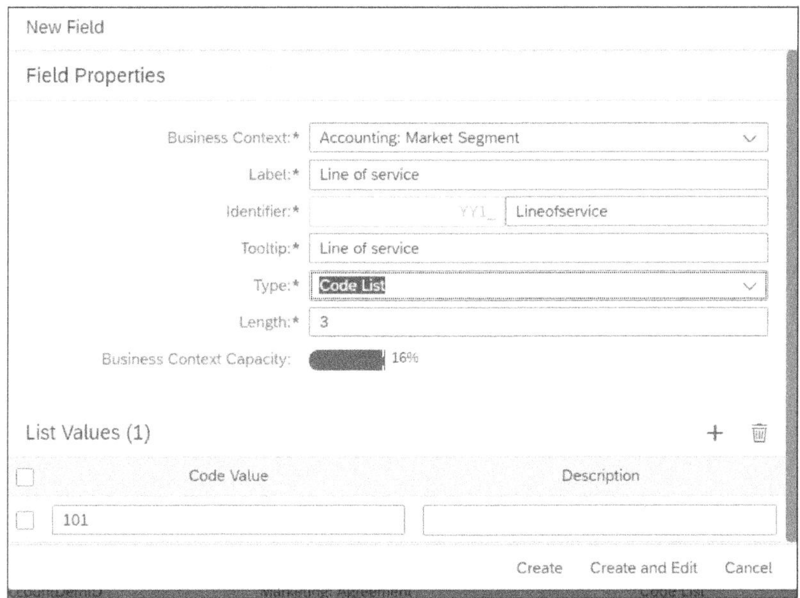


**Figure 4.30** Extensibility Field Parameter

Follow these steps to create the field properties:

1. First, select the **Business Context** (**Accounting: Market Segment**). As mentioned previously, beside it there are two additional accounting business contexts available—**Coding Block** and **Accounting: Journal Entry Item.**
2. Next, define a **Label**. For this example, create the **Line of service** market segment field.

3. Then define the **Type** field. There are three types available for this context: code list, text-field, and numerical text. We select here **Code List** with a **Length** of **3** for the code list characteristics.
4. Now define which characteristics are allowed for this field by clicking **Create and Edit**, arriving at the screen shown in Figure 4.31.

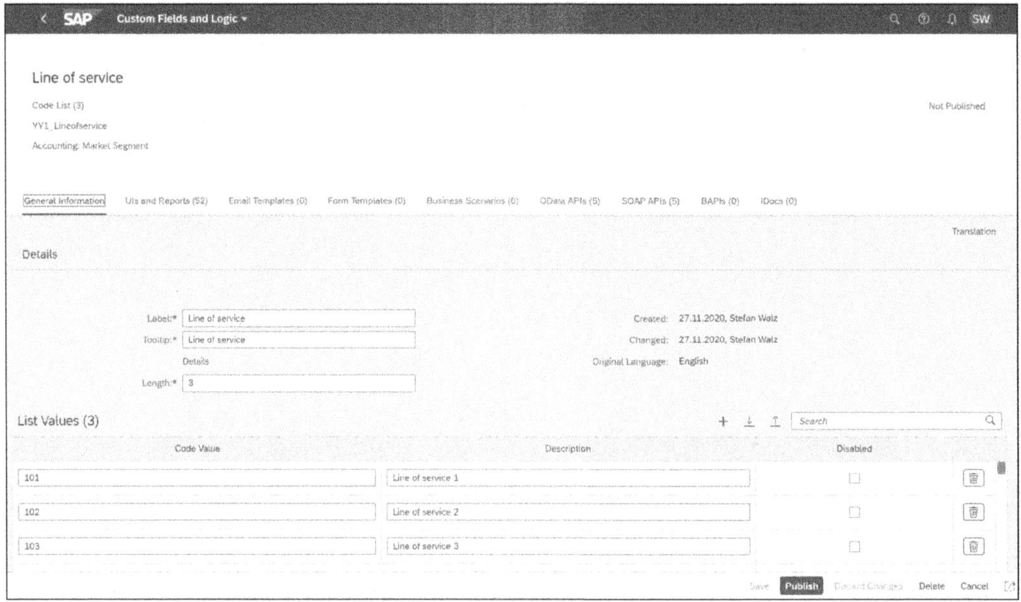


**Figure 4.31** Allowed Code List for Extensibility Field

5. Define here **101**, **102**, and **103** as allowed characteristics; these stand for line of service 1, 2, and 3.
6. Navigate to the **UIs and Reports** tab to define where the new field is available, as shown in Figure 4.32. On this page, you can define exactly in which UI the new field is available. Enable it for the **Product Profitability**, **Product and Service Margin**, **Project Profitability**, **Display Line Items in General Ledger** (not shown), and **Journal Entry Item** reports. You can enable it also for business transactions like the Post General Journal Entries app.
7. Then click the **Publish** button. The field will immediately be part of the journal entries and of the margin analysis in SAP S/4HANA Cloud. On-premise, as mentioned, you need to assign it to an operating concern with Transaction KEAO.

Let's check how this field is populated in the Post General Journal Entries app. Enter the revenue general ledger account "41000000" in the first line item and click the **View Profitability Segment** button to get a popup with the market segment characteristics, as shown in Figure 4.33.

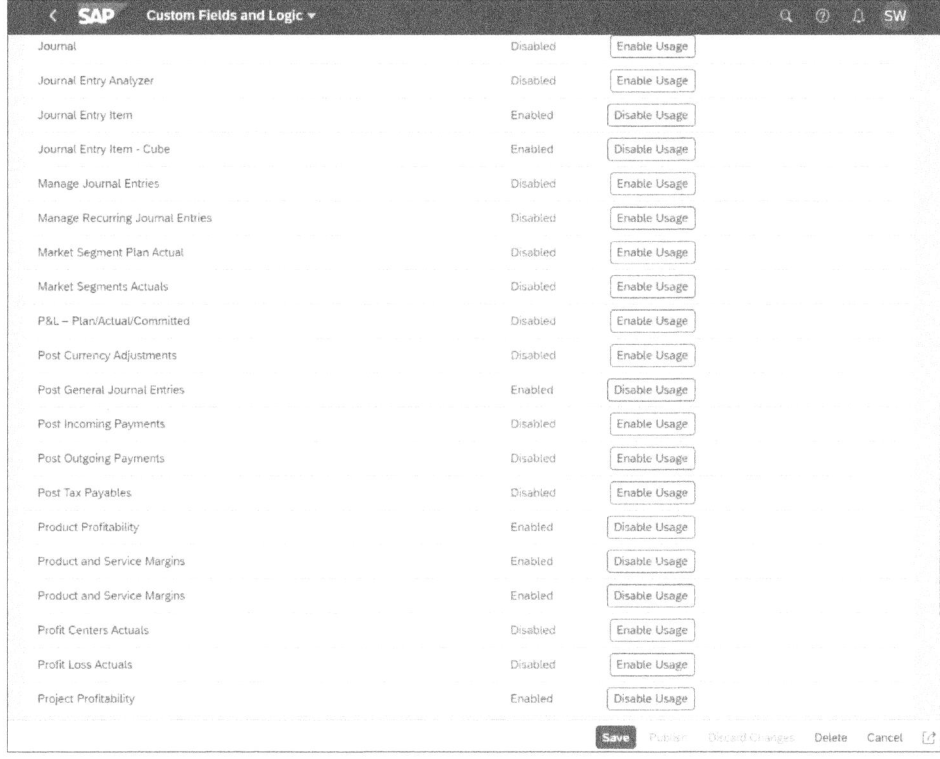


**Figure 4.32** List of Allowed UIs and Reports for Extensibility Field

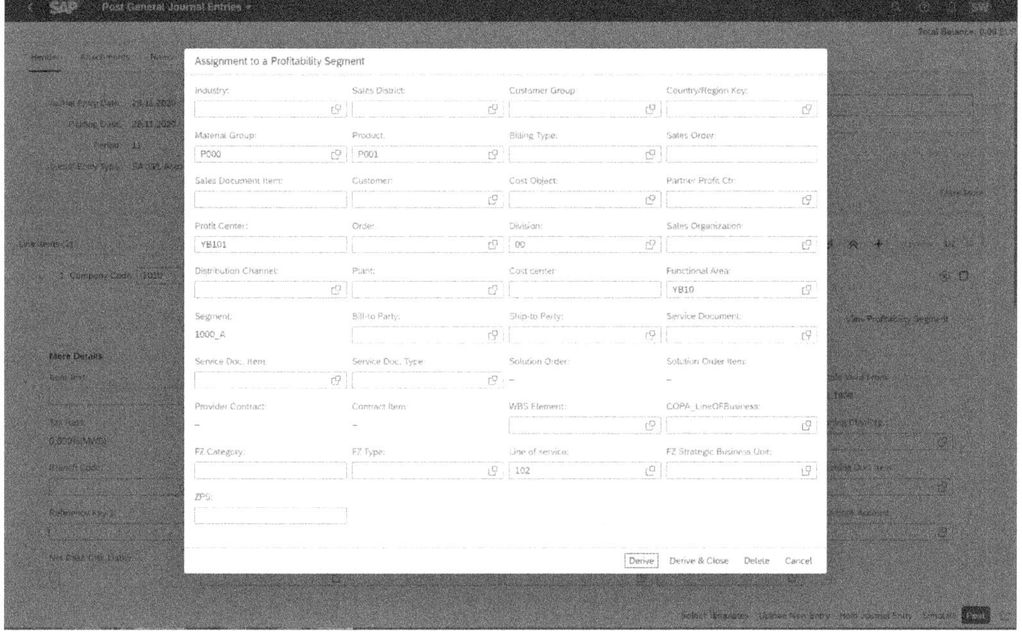


**Figure 4.33** Profitability View with Extensibility Field in Post General Journal Entries

When you select the value help for the **Line of service** profitability characteristic, you get the three items you defined previously. Select **Line of service** characteristic **102** here. Also enter the **Product** sold, **P001**. After clicking **Derive**, the **Material Group P000** is derived by the system by reading the material master.

Close the popup with the **Derive & Close** button. Then **Post** the document, and journal entry **100001096** in company code **1010** is created.

### Display Line Items in General Ledger

Analyze the document with the Display Line Items in General Ledger app (SAP Fiori ID F2217), as shown in Figure 4.34.

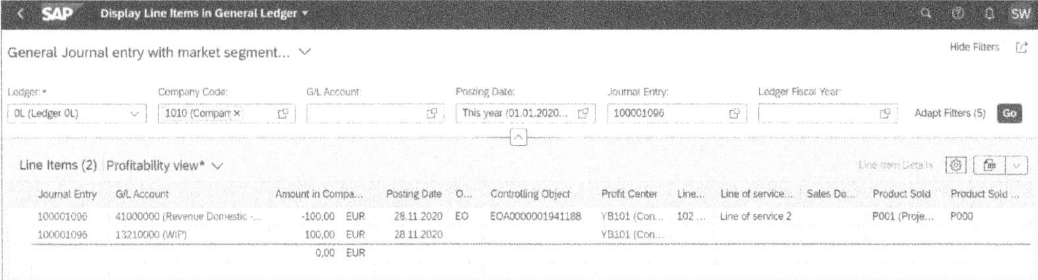


**Figure 4.34** Line Items of Journal Entry with Manual Line of Service Entry

Because you've also extended this app with the new **Line of service** field, you can select it as a column. For the first line item, the revenue line item, you see that **Line of service 2** is provided as you've entered it previously (in Figure 4.33).

The Universal Journal now includes a new market segment attribute, the **Line of service.**

You see the cost object type (**O...**) **EO** in the first line item. This shows that you have the market segment as an account assignment object. The revenue general ledger account 41000000 has an account type equal to the primary costs or revenue assigned. As you learned in Section 4.1, you must assign a cost object for such line items. In this case, it's the profitability segment (see the **Controlling Object** column).

## 4.6.3 Substitution and Derivation Logic

That you can enter the custom field manually is already an important step. But you also want it to be derived from the system in the logistic processes. There are two options available to apply derivation logic for margin analysis: the Manage Substitution/Validation Rules—Journal Entries app with a business context market segment, or Transaction KEDR. In SAP S/4HANA Cloud, only the app is available. We'll discuss both options in the following sections.

### Manage Substitutions/Validation Rules—Journal Entries App

Let's use the Manage Substitution/Validation Rules—Journal Entries app to define a rule for the derivation of the **Line of service** extensibility field by system, as shown in Figure 4.35.

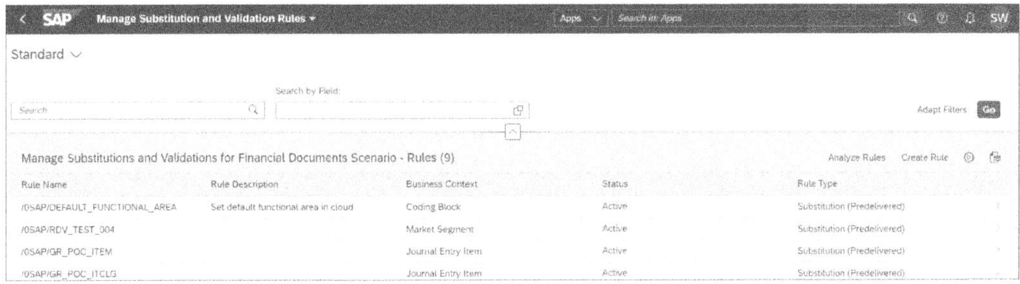


**Figure 4.35** Substitution and Validation: Start Screen

On the start screen, you see the existing rules. There can be rules created for the **Business Context Market Segment**, **Journal Entry Item**, and **Coding Block**, which are the three types of extensibility in place. An essential distinguishing feature of the different rules is the point in time when the substitution takes place. In addition to the substitution, there is an option available to validate the **Journal Entry Item** and **Coding Block** business contexts. With these business contexts, it's possible to prevent the posting by entering the document depending on defined conditions.

Click the **Create Rule** button and to get the popup for defining the parameter for the rule, as shown in Figure 4.36.

**Figure 4.36** Parameter for Market Segment Substitution Tool

The **Event** describes at what point in time the substitution/derivation rule is executed by the system. For market segment substitution, this is always the case when a profitability segment is created.

Click **Create** to arrive at the next screen, shown in Figure 4.37.

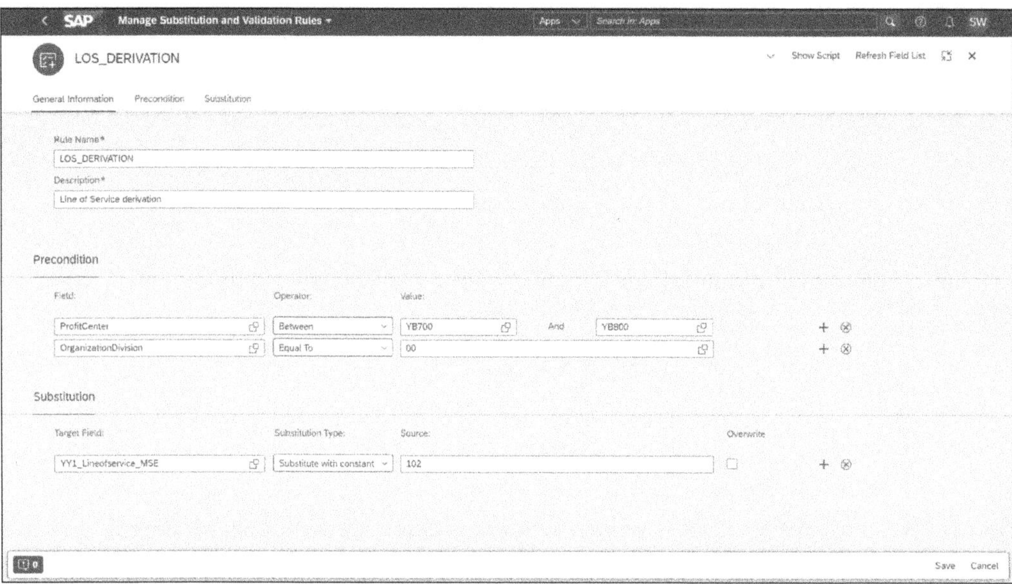


**Figure 4.37** Definition of Substitution Rule for Business Context Market Segment

This screen describes the logic for a substitution/derivation rule for a market segment business context. On the top, you define the **Rule Name** and **Description**.

The next section defines the **Precondition** for executing this rule. Every line is a condition that must be fulfilled. In this example, the profit center must be in the range between **YB700** and **YB800** and the sales division must be **00**. If one of the conditions isn't fulfilled, the rule won't be executed. There are many fields that can be used as conditions: all fields from the profitability segment, including extensibility fields, fields from sales orders, and journal entries.

The lower section defines the **Substitution** itself. As target fields, you can use fields from the profitability segment, including the extensibility field. Note that not all fields can be substituted due to requirements for legal reporting, such as company code, general ledger, account, or profit center. Figure 4.38 shows all allowed target fields. You can see them with the value help for target fields.

Click **Save** to save the rule and then click the **Activate** button.

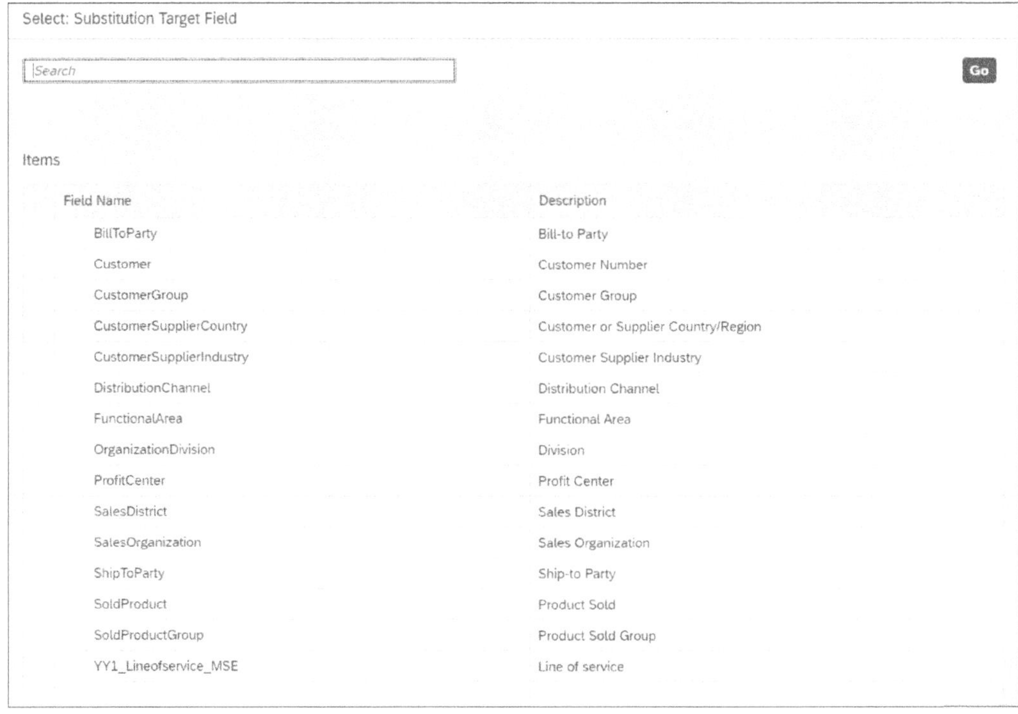


**Figure 4.38** Allowed Target Fields for Market Segment Substitution

### Transaction KEDR

Another tool to derive fields for margin analysis is Transaction KEDR, which you can access in on-premise SAP S/4HANA as shown in Figure 4.39. Currently there's additional functionality provided in this transaction, like incorporation of customer-specific enhancements. But per the roadmap, SAP intends to extend the SAP Fiori application.

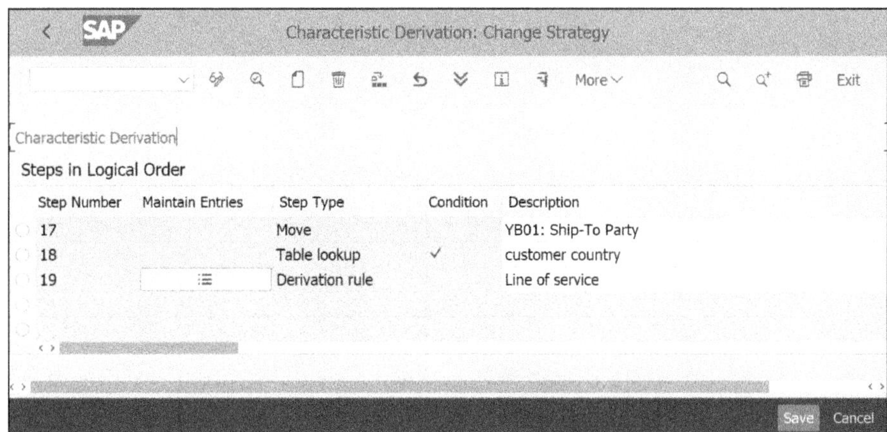


**Figure 4.39** Derivation of Market Segment Attributes with Transaction KEDR

You can define several derivation steps here, which are executed in the order of the **Step Number**. The **Step Type** defines how the field is derived. Here are the three examples:

1. **Move**
   The ship-to party field is derived from the customer field if the customer is provided by the process.
2. **Table lookup**
   The customer master is read from the customer field to derive the country (see Chapter 7, Section 7.2.1).
3. **Derivation rule**
   You derive the extensibility field from the profit center and division parameters. For this, you need to maintain derivation rules, which you can access via the three lines in the **Maintain Entries** column.

### Integration in Accounting Documents and Margin Analysis

Let's now look at how the **Line of service** extension field and the derivation logic maintained previously affect the example of a delivery in a sales transaction process. Create a sales order with division 00 and assign a product in the sales order item, which derives a profit center, YB700. Figure 4.40 shows the **Account assignment** tab of the sales order item.

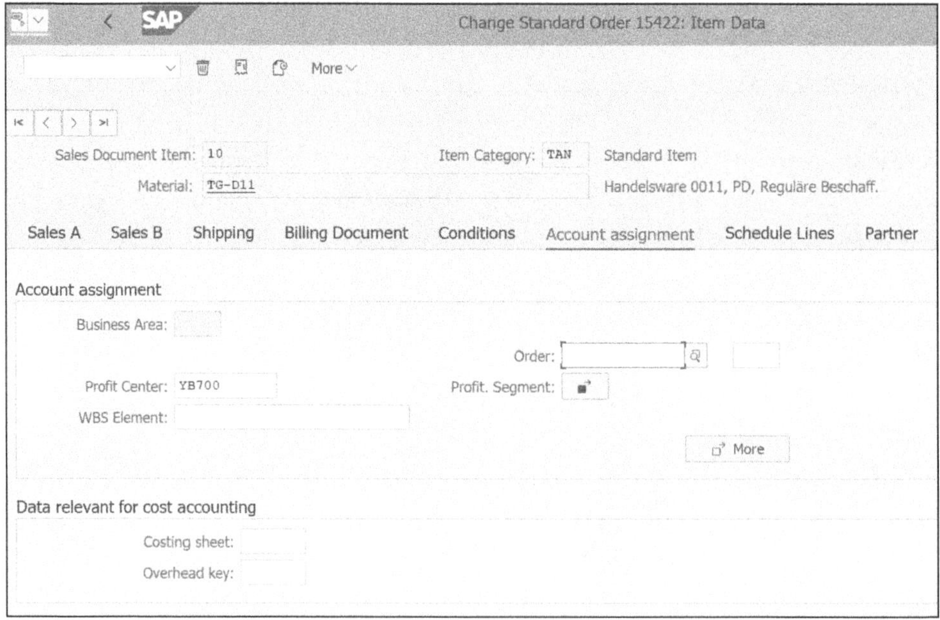


**Figure 4.40** Account Assignment Tab in Sales Order Item

When you click the **Profit. Segment** button, you'll see the system-derived market segments, as shown in Figure 4.41. At the bottom, you'll see **Line of service 102**, derived by the system using your rule.

| Assignment to a Profitability Segment | | |
|---|---|---|
| Characteristic | Char. value | Text |
| Service Document | | |
| Service Doc. Item | | |
| Solution Order | | |
| Solution Order Item | | |
| Contract | | |
| Contract Item | | |
| Customer Group | 01 | Customer Group 01 |
| Bill-to Party | 10100001 | Inlandskunde DE 1 |
| Ship-to Party | 10100001 | Inlandskunde DE 1 |
| Ctry/Reg. | DE | Germany |
| Industry | 91 | Trading |
| Material Group | L001 | Trading Materials |
| Sales District | | |
| TestLengthCE | | |
| Line of service | 102 | Line of service 2 |

**Figure 4.41** Profitability Segment Created by System for Sales Order Item

Now post a delivery for this sales order item with Transaction VL01 and post a goods issue. You'll see the accounting document shown in Figure 4.42.

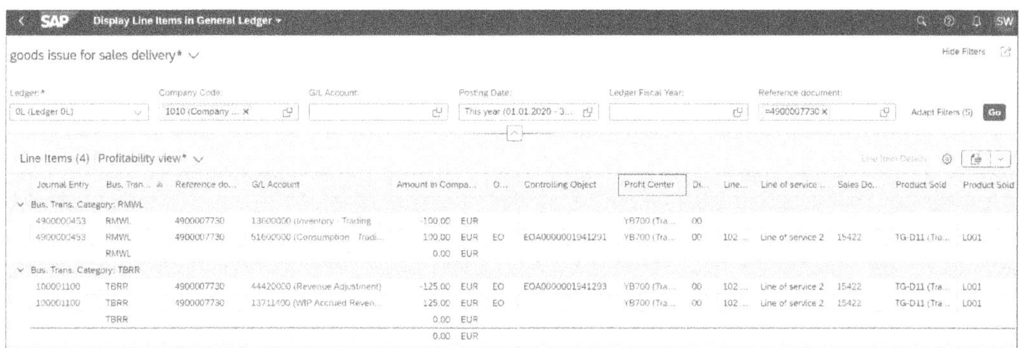


| Journal Entry | Bus. Tran... | Reference do... | G/L Account | Amount in Compa... | | O... | Controlling Object | Profit Center | Di... | Line... | Line of service ... | Sales Do... | Product Sold | Product Sold |
|---|---|---|---|---|---|---|---|---|---|---|---|---|---|---|
| Bus. Trans. Category: RMWL | | | | | | | | | | | | | | |
| 4900000453 | RMWL | 4900007730 | 13600000 (Inventory - Trading | -100.00 | EUR | | | YB700 (Tra... | 00 | | | | | |
| 4900000453 | RMWL | 4900007730 | 51600000 (Consumption Tradi... | 100.00 | EUR | EO | EOA0000001941291 | YB700 (Tra... | 00 | 102 ... | Line of service 2 | 15422 | TG-D11 (Tra... | L001 |
| | RMWL | | | 0.00 | EUR | | | | | | | | | |
| Bus. Trans. Category: TBRR | | | | | | | | | | | | | | |
| 100001100 | TBRR | 4900007730 | 44420000 (Revenue Adjustment) | -125.00 | EUR | EO | EOA0000001941293 | YB700 (Tra... | 00 | 102 ... | Line of service 2 | 15422 | TG-D11 (Tra... | L001 |
| 100001100 | TBRR | 4900007730 | 13711400 (WIP Accrued Reven... | 125.00 | EUR | EO | | YB700 (Tra... | 00 | 102 ... | Line of service 2 | 15422 | TG-D11 (Tra... | L001 |
| | TBRR | | | 0.00 | EUR | | | | | | | | | |
| | | | | 0.00 | EUR | | | | | | | | | |

**Figure 4.42** Accounting Document for Goods Issue for Delivery

The first journal entry reflects the goods issue. Line 1 is the credit of the stock and line 2 reflects the cost of sales. Expense account **51600000** is a primary cost element and thus needs an account assignment. This is the profitability segment, which you can identify with the object type **EO** (refer back to Figure 4.34) and the **Controlling Object** for the market segment (refer back to Figure 4.28). The derivation and assignment of a profitability segment to the line item leads to the update of the **Line of service**, **Sales Document**, **Product Sold**, and **Product Sold** group (and further fields not shown here).

The second journal entry is the revenue recognition posting, which is created with the goods issue by the system to provide the realized revenue for the goods issue as long there is no billing; we'll cover this in Chapter 7.

You can see that the same profitability attributes are provided as in the goods issue journal entry line item, including the line of service.

> **Note**
> Event-based revenue recognition is not yet available in on-premise systems for the sales scenario, but it's planned in SAP's roadmap.

How does the margin reporting look now for the line of service? To find out, start the Product and Service Margins app (SAP Fiori ID W0164) and filter on **Line of service 2**, as shown in Figure 4.43.

**Figure 4.43** Product and Service Margin Reporting for Line of Service

Based on the manual journal entry and several sales order processes, you get a margin for **Line of service 2** of 3,439.20 euros. You also see for **Line of service 2** WIP/accrued revenue, posted by event-based revenue recognition of 3,652.55 euros.

We'll explore these new, fascinating reporting insights further in Chapter 7, when we discuss the sales, service, and customer project scenarios.

## 4.7 Summary

In this chapter, you got to know the main controlling objects in SAP S/4HANA to define your areas of accountability and organize the value flow within your controlling area. Then we discussed the general ledger account/cost element combination as the central piece of master data, which provides information about the nature of the costs and controls the cost flow within a controlling area. For providing margins for the customer-specific accountability areas, the functionality of margin analysis and its option for extensibility is very important.

You now have the master data foundation you need to dive further into the cost objects in Chapters 5 through 8.

Let's now move on to discuss overhead controlling.

# Chapter 5
# Overhead Controlling

*In the previous chapter, we discussed the master data used in controlling. We'll now explain the general tasks associated with overhead cost controlling and look at how the role of overhead controlling is evolving in terms of how controllers collaborate with other stakeholders and as a result of changes in SAP S/4HANA. We'll explain the business transactions that make up the daily work of the overhead controller.*



Overhead controlling applies to all industries as all organizations need to monitor and control their *operational expenses* and assign costs to the products and services with which they earn their revenue, irrespective of whether these are physical or financial products and irrespective of the nature of the service provided. We introduced the master data used for overhead controlling and explained the role of the cost centers and how to use statistical key figures and activity types to allocate costs from the cost centers to products, services, and ultimately to margin analysis in the previous chapter. In this chapter, we'll focus on how the primary costs are captured and then on the business transactions used to allocate them, explaining the prerequisites for the various types of allocation and settlement.

The idea behind overhead controlling is the need to explain *why* certain costs were incurred. As we discussed in the previous chapter, travel expenses are only part of the story. It's important to understand *why* employees are traveling. The account alone will only tell you the *type* of costs (wages, salaries, operating supplies, etc.), but not why they were necessary. Taking wages and salaries as an example, the workers assigned to a manufacturing cost center are paid in exchange for performing work on the production line to manufacture certain goods, the technicians assigned to a service cost center are paid in exchange for performing maintenance work, and consultants are paid for performing work that will be billed to the customer. We are thus not looking at payroll costs in isolation but in the context of the work performed by these employees. Their activities also necessitate the use of fixed assets, whether in the form of laptops and phones or complete production lines with the associated operating supplies, as we discussed when we looked at the link between the cost center and asset in the previous chapter. Overhead costs thus cover not just payroll costs, but also the costs of the assets employed on the production line, the tools used by the maintenance technicians, and the laptops and phone used by the consultants in their daily work as all these costs impact the cost of delivering a product or providing a service. If you work with SAP Best

Practices, the settings for this approach are delivered with scope item J54 (Overhead Cost Accounting).

In this chapter, we'll focus on the idea of *responsibility accounting* and on the dialogue between the controller and the cost center manager responsible for the costs incurred for his or her cost center or the project manager responsible for the costs associated with his or her project. For small projects, you may not even need a project in SAP S/4HANA but may find that you can manage with an internal order instead. You'll sometimes find this idea referred to as *cost stewardship*, but the idea is the same: somebody must ensure that all these costs are in line with the goals of the organization. This responsibility goes beyond simply authorizing costs and covers the proper utilization of these resources to deliver the relevant activities. Thus, the manager of a consulting cost center is responsible not just for the costs associated with the employees assigned to the cost center but also for their delivery of consulting services.

We talked about primary and secondary cost elements in Chapter 4, and here we'll look at how the postings in cost accounting differ from those in financial accounting. We are not simply capturing costs and revenues, but rather making business decisions about how costs should be allocated and what represents fair usage of shared service costs. While all this might be familiar to anyone working in the controlling space, SAP S/4HANA sees the introduction of the Universal Journal, which also has an impact on how costs are recorded, in the sense that a shift from sender to receiver also potentially triggers a shift in profit centers, functional areas, and even trading partners.

We introduced the idea of planning in Chapter 2, but we'll now explain how it relates to overhead controlling and cost management. The simplest way to make a manager take responsibility for spending on a cost center or project is to give them a *budget* as a ceiling for that spending. That budget should not be an arbitrary number but rather one derived from a robust planning process in which all stakeholders agree to common goals.

We'll then walk through the various business transactions used in overhead controlling and finally look at the reports available to ensure that these tasks have been performed correctly.

## 5.1 Cost Stewardship and the Role of the Cost Center/Project Manager

In Chapter 2, we discussed the relationship between (a) the financial statements and the need to satisfy external stakeholders and (b) management accounting and the need to understand how revenues and costs are impacted in order to steer the business. The word *accounting* is related to *accountability*, and it's the job of the controller to put a system in place that ensures the accountability of the various managers. It's rare for organizations to have managers for specific general ledger accounts, but almost all organizations have cost center and project managers who are responsible for monitoring all transactions that will have a cost impact; authorizing travel requests, external purchases, and so on; and ensuring that resources are used appropriately.

We can extend the idea behind the simple expense posting described in Chapter 2, Section 2.1.1, where a cost center manager authorizes the purchase of office supplies, to the idea of overhead controlling in general and specifically to the cost stewardship performed by the cost center manager. In Chapter 4, we introduced the master data for the cost centers, orders, and projects. If the cost center structure of an organization is set up properly, then all expense postings should be assigned to a cost center, order, or project, and there should be no expense postings that are not authorized by a responsible manager. One of the guiding principles of good cost center design is that a single cost center should be the responsibility of one manager. If the number of cost centers starts to approach the number of employees in the organization, the question of who "owns" each cost center can be a good way of pruning the list of potential cost centers and ensuring that each cost center has an owner.

There was a time when managers would receive briefing books showing their spending at period close, but there is now a move toward the use of self-services in this domain. One way to provide cost center managers with an easy-to-use view of their spending is to implement the My Spend app (SAP Fiori ID F0366) along with the My Unusual Items app (SAP Fiori ID F0368) (see Figure 5.1) to identify unusual items for those cost centers based on various rules. The My Spend app also allows the cost center manager to start a dialog with his or her controller if there are costs that need further explanation.

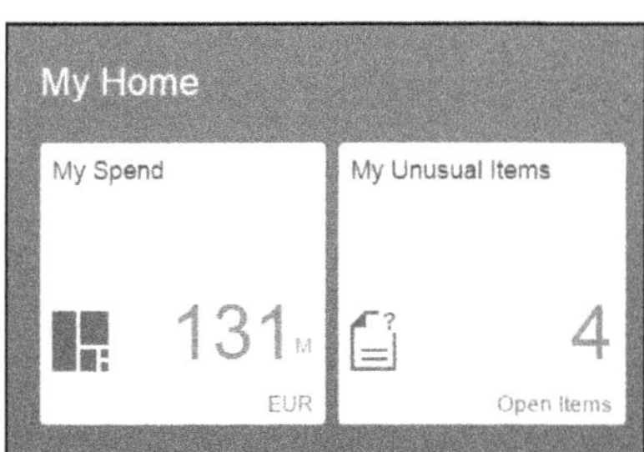


**Figure 5.1** SAP Fiori Apps for Managers: My Spend and My Unusual Items

Figure 5.2 shows the spending by department. In this example, the manager is responsible for three cost center groups: **Eastern Sales**, **Western Development**, and **Repairs Department**. These in turn comprise various cost centers. The relative size of the boxes is determined either by the budget or the spending by cost center. You can toggle between the two by using the dropdown to switch from **Budget** to **Spend**. The relative size makes it easy to see where potential problems lie. A similar view is available to explain spending assigned to internal orders.

By clicking on one of the boxes, the manager can access details of the spending, as shown in Figure 5.3, along with a visualization of where he or she is already over budget and where he or she is nearing this threshold.

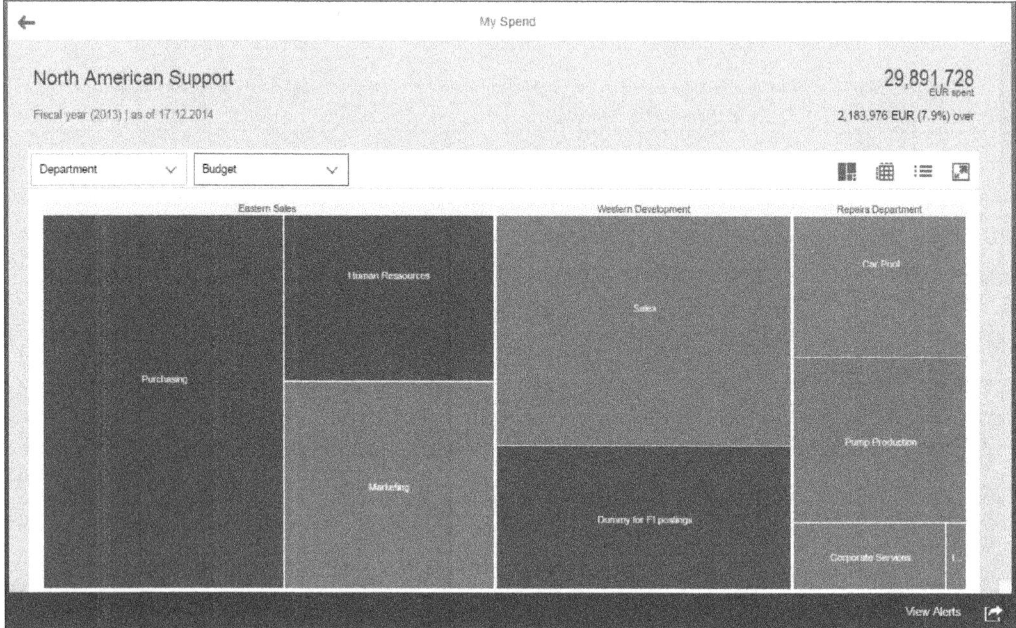


**Figure 5.2** My Spend App, Showing Spend by Department and Cost Centers That Have Exceeded Their Budgets

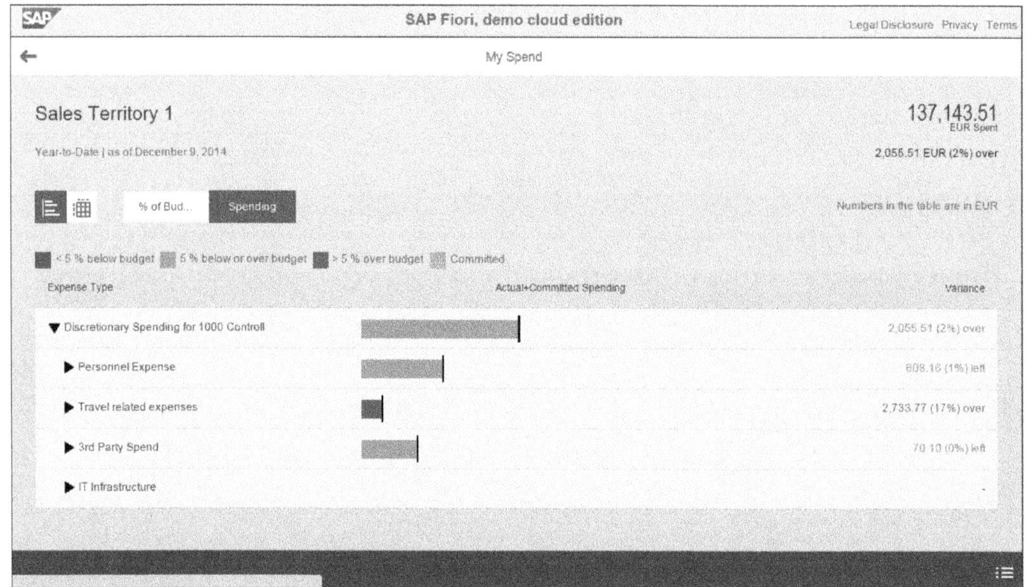


**Figure 5.3** My Spend App, Showing Spend per Account Group

Of course, the My Spend app isn't the only way to monitor the costs on a cost center or order. We'll look at some of the other options in Section 5.5, but first we'll look at how the costs we saw in My Spend are captured.

**Planned Data in My Spend**

The My Spend app predates SAP S/4HANA and therefore accesses plan data from the legacy tables COSP and COSS, rather than the newer table ACDOCP. SAP S/4HANA 2020 includes a copy function to transfer planned costs between tables ACDOCP and COSP/COSS. It also accesses commitment information from the legacy table COOI rather than from an extension ledger in table ACDOCA.



## 5.2 Postings for Cost Accounting in the Universal Journal

In Chapter 2, we explained how the Universal Journal captures both primary costs, those costs that originate outside of controlling, and secondary costs, those costs that move as a result of business transactions within controlling. In Chapter 4, we looked at the master data for the general ledger account and explained the difference between primary and secondary cost elements and the impact of various settings within the accounts. We'll now focus on the differences in the two types of posting, particularly with regard to operating expenses.

### 5.2.1 Primary Cost Postings

It's not generally the job of the controller to post primary costs as these costs are incurred as a result of material movements, invoices, and the like resulting from the integrated nature of SAP S/4HANA. Occasionally a correction will be needed to move costs between account assignments, such as wrongly assigned travel costs from one account assignment to another; we'll explain how to do this in Section 5.4.

As we explained in Chapter 4, Section 4.1.2, all primary costs will include an assignment to a profit and loss (P&L) account and to an account assignment, but it's also possible for primary costs to carry more information. You can always identify the type of account assignment from the object type in the Universal Journal: **KS** for cost center, **OR** for order, **PR** for project, **BP** for business process, **EO** for the market segment, and so on. You can use this type to filter in reports such as the Trial Balance app. In the case of the office supplies purchased in Chapter 2, you can display the material numbers of the goods purchased alongside the cost center responsible for the purchase. It's important to understand that the general ledger account, the account assignment, and the material are all stored in the same posting line of the Universal Journal. In SAP ERP, it was common to *summarize* the postings in financial accounting to remove the material numbers from an invoice but to keep this information in management accounting. In SAP S/4HANA, there is one posting line containing all the relevant information, which simplifies the task of reporting on these transactions because all the reporting dimensions are in the same posting line.

You can see the same situation if you purchase assets that are assigned to a cost center and a general ledger account, with all the relevant information in the same posting line. The same happens when the cost of this initial purchase is *depreciated* over several accounting periods as a result of the depreciation posting run. Figure 5.4 shows the Trial Balance app with the combination of the **Fixed Asset** (the assets whose acquisition cost is being depreciated), the **G/L Account** for the depreciation, and the **Cost Center** to which the asset belongs. For reasons of space, we can't show the whole story here, but the cost center is also used to derive the functional area and the profit center as additional reporting dimensions, as we discussed in Chapter 3.

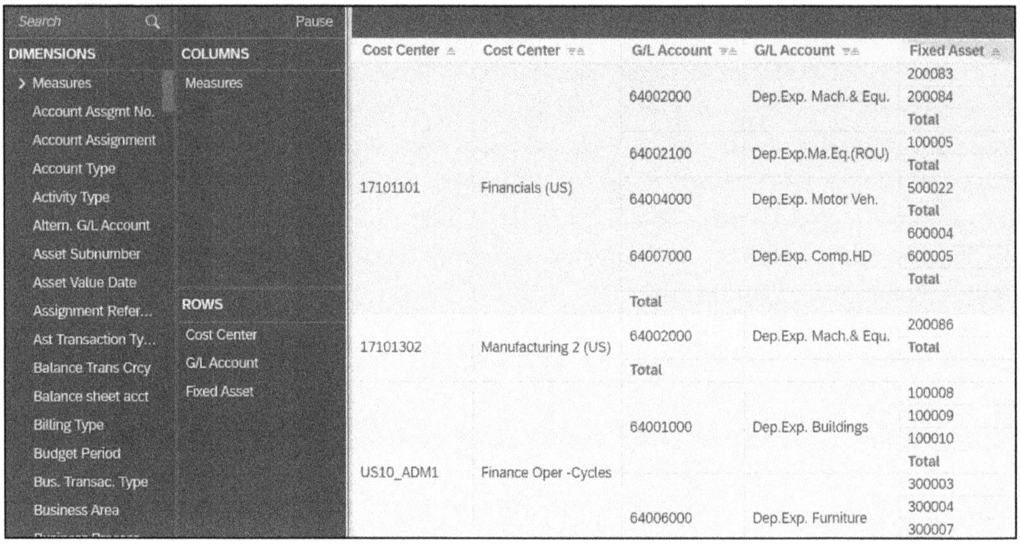
Search
Pause
DIMENSIONS
COLUMNS
Measures
Measures
Account Assgmt No.
Account Assignment
Account Type
Activity Type
Altern. G/L Account
Asset Subnumber
Asset Value Date
Assignment Refer...
Ast Transaction Ty...
Balance Trans Crcy
Balance sheet acct
Billing Type
Budget Period
Bus. Transac. Type
Business Area
ROWS
Cost Center
G/L Account
Fixed Asset
Cost Center
Cost Center
G/L Account
G/L Account
Fixed Asset
17101101
Financials (US)
64002000
Dep.Exp. Mach.& Equ.
200083
200084
Total
64002100
Dep.Exp.Ma.Eq.(ROU)
100005
Total
64004000
Dep.Exp. Motor Veh.
500022
Total
64007000
Dep.Exp. Comp.HD
600004
600005
Total
Total
17101302
Manufacturing 2 (US)
64002000
Dep.Exp. Mach.& Equ.
200086
Total
Total
US10_ADM1
Finance Oper -Cycles
64001000
Dep.Exp. Buildings
100008
100009
100010
Total
64006000
Dep.Exp. Furniture
300003
300004
300007

**Figure 5.4** Trial Balance App Showing Cost Centers, General Ledger Accounts, and Fixed Assets

If you don't work with the SAP Fiori applications, then you'll see the same data broken down according to the SAP ERP components—so you'll see the costs grouped by general ledger account and company code in Transaction S_ALR_87012284 (Balance Sheet/P&L), by asset and cost center in Transaction S_ALR_87011966 (Asset Balances by Cost Center), and by cost center and cost element in Transaction S_ALR_87013611 (Cost Center Plan/Actual Report).

To give a sense of what's changed, Figure 5.5 shows a sample document created as a result of a depreciation run with posting lines for each asset together with the associated general ledger accounts. For each P&L line, you see the associated cost centers (**Cost Ctr** column). The functional areas (**Func. Area** column; see Chapter 3, Section 3.1.6) have been derived based on the link defined in Chapter 4, Section 4.2. You also see that the cost center assignment has been used to derive the profit center (**Profit Ctr** column; see Chapter 3, Section 3.1.5) and that this link has been used to derive the **Segment** for both the balance sheet and the P&L lines, again, using the link defined in Chapter 4, Section 4.2. What you're seeing is the combination of the information from the former subledgers (asset accounting, in this example) with the assignment to a general ledger account in the general ledger and the extension of this information to provide the basis for cost of goods sold accounting and profit center accounting in a single posting line, rather than spread across several ledgers as was often the case in SAP ERP.

Display Document: Data Entry View

| CoCd | Itm | Account | SG | Description | Amount LC | LCurr | Amount | Curr. | Tx | Ref date | Clrng doc. | Cost Ctr | BusA | Func. Area | Profit Ctr | Segment |
|---|---|---|---|---|---|---|---|---|---|---|---|---|---|---|---|---|
| 1710 | 141 | 17006000 | | 000000300014 0000 | 621,00- | USD | 621,00- | USD | | | | | | | US10_PC10 | Z_SEG0 |
| 1710 | 142 | 64006000 | | Furniture-Dep.Exp | 621,00 | USD | 621,00 | USD | | | | US10_ADM1 | | Z9400 | US10_PC10 | Z_SEG0 |
| 1710 | 143 | 17006000 | | 000000300015 0000 | 288,00- | USD | 288,00- | USD | | | | | | | US10_PC10 | Z_SEG0 |
| 1710 | 144 | 64006000 | | Furniture-Dep.Exp | 288,00 | USD | 288,00 | USD | | | | US10_ADM1 | | Z9400 | US10_PC10 | Z_SEG0 |
| 1710 | 145 | 17006000 | | 000000300017 0000 | 151,00- | USD | 151,00- | USD | | | | | | | US10_PC10 | Z_SEG0 |
| 1710 | 146 | 64006000 | | Furniture-Dep.Exp | 151,00 | USD | 151,00 | USD | | | | US10_ADM1 | | Z9400 | US10_PC10 | Z_SEG0 |
| 1710 | 147 | 17006000 | | 000000300018 0000 | 355,25- | USD | 355,25- | USD | | | | | | | US10_PC10 | Z_SEG0 |
| 1710 | 148 | 64006000 | | Furniture-Dep.Exp | 355,25 | USD | 355,25 | USD | | | | US10_ADM1 | | Z9400 | US10_PC10 | Z_SEG0 |
| 1710 | 149 | 17006000 | | 000000300019 0000 | 307,00- | USD | 307,00- | USD | | | | | | | US10_PC10 | Z_SEG0 |
| 1710 | 150 | 64006000 | | Furniture-Dep.Exp | 307,00 | USD | 307,00 | USD | | | | US10_ADM1 | | Z9400 | US10_PC10 | Z_SEG0 |
| 1710 | 151 | 17006000 | | 000000300021 0000 | 145,00- | USD | 145,00- | USD | | | | | | | US10_PC10 | Z_SEG0 |
| 1710 | 152 | 64006000 | | Furniture-Dep.Exp | 145,00 | USD | 145,00 | USD | | | | US10_ADM1 | | Z9400 | US10_PC10 | Z_SEG0 |
| 1710 | 153 | 17006000 | | 000000300022 0000 | 75,00- | USD | 75,00- | USD | | | | | | | US10_PC10 | Z_SEG0 |
| 1710 | 154 | 64006000 | | Furniture-Dep.Exp | 75,00 | USD | 75,00 | USD | | | | US10_ADM1 | | Z9400 | US10_PC10 | Z_SEG0 |

**Figure 5.5** Document Showing Depreciation Posting

Where primary cost postings are derived from an integrated business process, it's important to know that you can see them in context for controlling purposes as the journal entry simply documents that there has been a business transaction, not why it occurred. Figure 5.6 shows the Manage Journal Entries app (SAP Fiori ID F0707) for a simple asset acquisition with two posting lines, but to understand more about the acquisition of the assets, you can access six further documents by choosing the **Related Documents** tab.

**Figure 5.6** Manage Journal Entries App, Showing Asset Acquisition

Figure 5.7 shows the documents relating to the asset acquisition in Figure 5.6. Here you can see that the process began with a purchase order to acquire the asset and that this triggered two accounting documents for the asset receipt (**Asset Transaction**) and the invoice receipt (**Incoming Invoice**). To analyze this chain of documents further, choose the **Display Document Flow** button.

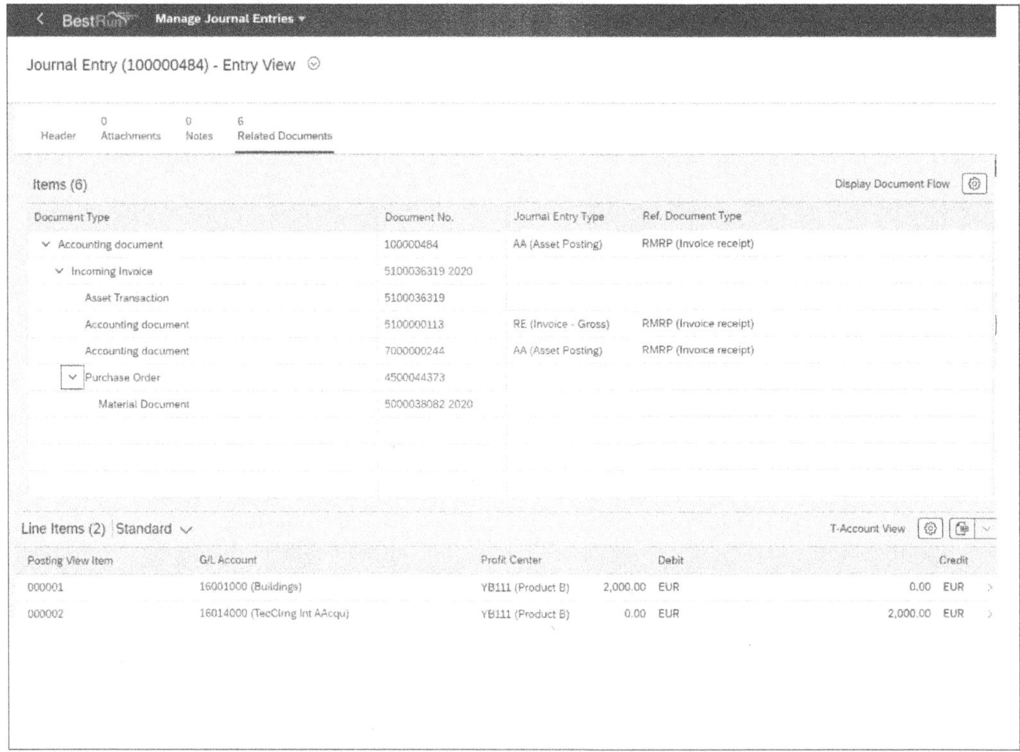

**Figure 5.7** Manage Journal Entries App, Showing Related Documents

Figure 5.8 shows the document flow for the asset acquisition, with the **Operational Document Flow** comprising the purchase order, the goods receipt, and the invoice receipt and the **G/L Document Flow** showing the associated journal entries. You can see how easy it is for the controller to explore the source of the costs and understand why they were incurred.

Primary costs don't have to be captured as part of an integrated business process. It's also possible to create a manual journal entry that assigns costs to a cost center, project, or order using either the Manage Journal Entries app or Transaction FB50. If you need to upload manual journal entries from a spreadsheet, there is also an Upload General Journal Entries app (SAP Fiori ID F2548). Figure 5.9 again shows the Manage Journal Entries app, with the balance sheet line for the payables and the P&L line for the travel expenses, but notice that this time there is only the journal entry itself without related documents.

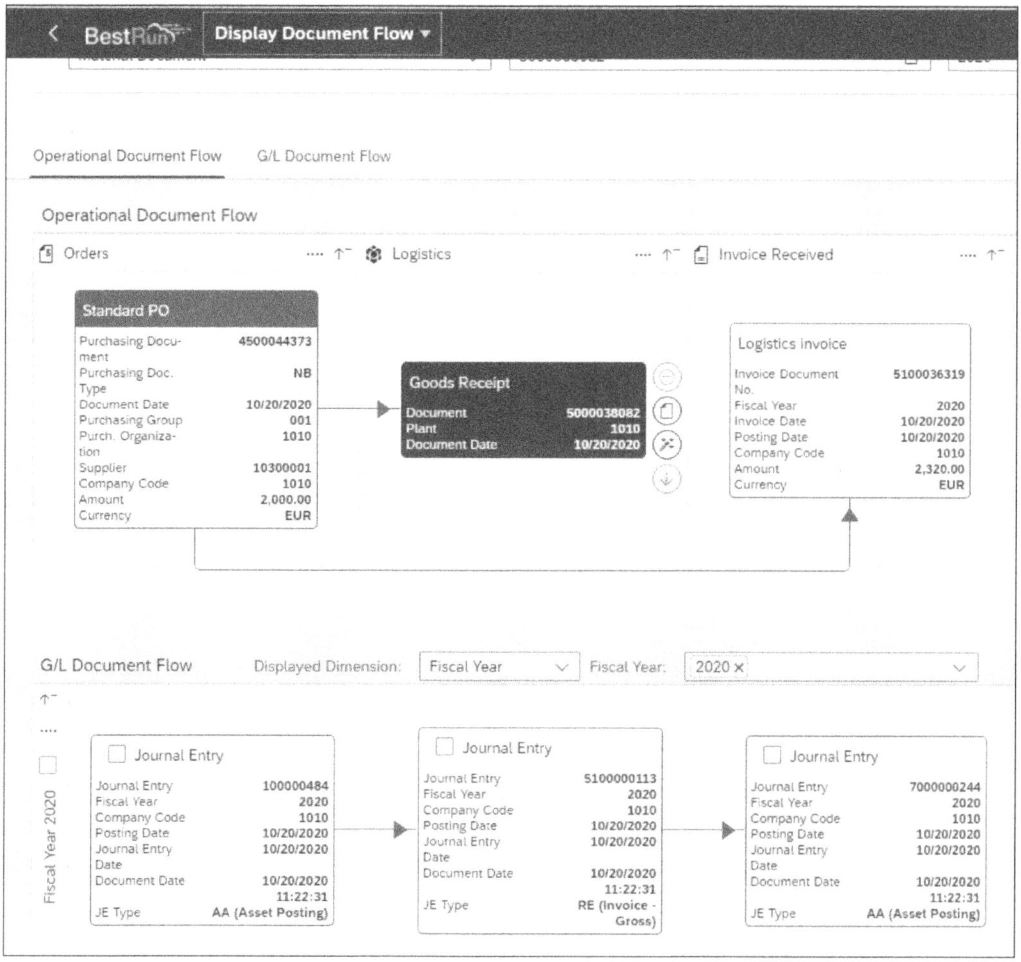

**Figure 5.8** Manage Journal Entries App, Showing Document Flow

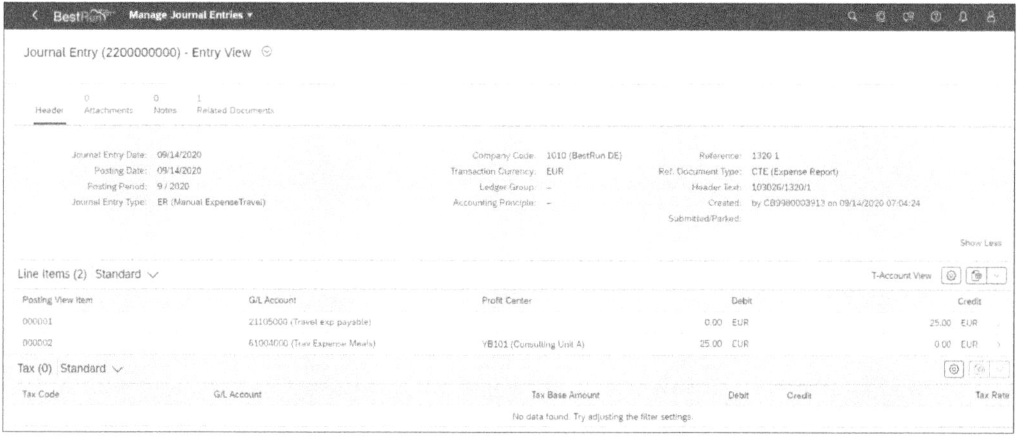


**Figure 5.9** Manage Journal Entries App, Showing Travel Expenses

Normally there's a one-to-one relationship between the P&L account and the associated costs, but *accrual costs* are an exception and use a different cost element category so that they can easily be identified, as we discussed in Chapter 4. Accrual costs are used to record costs in controlling at a different time from financial accounting. This can be the case when employees receive an annual bonus paid out at year end, but the organization chooses to spread these costs across the whole year to avoid extreme fluctuations in the monthly costs. The rules for this spread can be established by setting up an *overhead structure*. Figure 5.10 shows the accrual conditions for the allocation of yearly bonuses on the basis of the combined wage and salary costs on the cost centers. You can access the overhead structures by choosing **Controlling • Cost Element Accounting • Accrual Calculation • Percentage Method • Maintain OH Structure**.

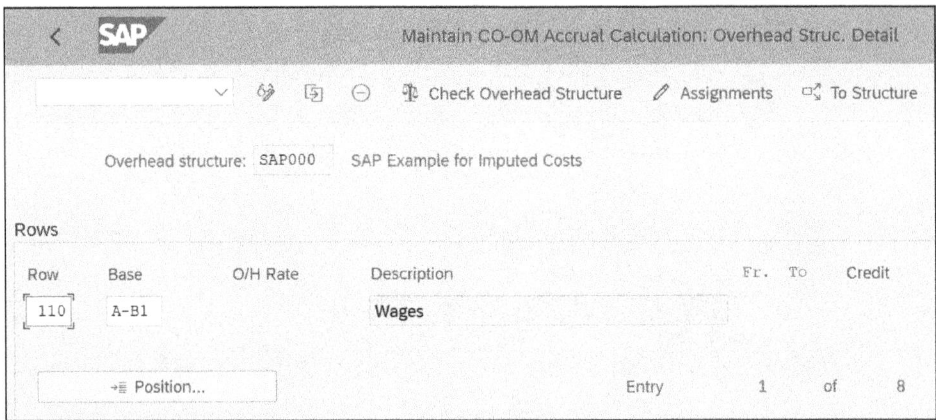


**Figure 5.10** Overhead Structure for Accrual Calculation

### 5.2.2 Secondary Cost Postings

If the focus of primary cost postings is on capturing the journal entries relating to single business transactions (the purchase of an asset, the fulfilment of an order, etc.), the focus of secondary cost postings is on the *flow* of costs through the organization. In contrast with the primary cost postings that generally arise outside of controlling, creating secondary cost postings is very much the job of the controller. It's also his or her job to trigger the various cost flows that take place at period close. We'll walk through the many business transactions that result in secondary costs in Section 5.4.

It's often thought that secondary cost postings have no impact on the financial accounts; as we discussed in Chapter 2, these postings result in journal entries that net to zero. However, a secondary cost posting will often result in switches to profit centers, functional areas, and so on, and in the case of an intercompany allocation, they can also result in journal entries on intercompany clearing accounts, as we'll show in Chapter 9.

The easiest way to think of secondary cost postings is as a set of *sender-receiver relationships*. There are many examples of such relationships in management accounting:

- Support cost centers (the sender) that provide utilities to a production cost center (the receiver)
- Sales and marketing cost centers (the sender) that provide support to a product line (the receiver)
- Research projects (the sender) that provide activity to a product line (the receiver)
- Production cost centers (the sender) that provide machine hours to a production order (the receiver)
- Consulting cost centers (the sender) that provide consulting hours to a project (the receiver)
- Technical cost centers (the sender) that provide labor hours to a project (the receiver)
- Design projects (the sender) that provide activity to a product line (the receiver)

Secondary cost postings serve to move costs within the P&L statement, but in some cases, there will be a *value added* in the sense that the costs can be capitalized within the balance sheet. We'll explore these scenarios when we look at manufacturing organizations in Chapter 6, service organizations in Chapter 7, and investment controlling in Chapter 8, but we'll first look at what these secondary cost postings have in common.

Our list of sender-receiver relationships can be considered as a list of *partners*. Every posting line for a secondary cost posting will include the object type and the key of the *sender* object (cost center, order, project, etc.), the partner object type and key of the *receiver* object (cost center, order, project, market segment, etc.) for the credit posting, and the mirror image of this sender-receiver relationship for the debit posting. This relationship can be visualized using the Allocation Flow app shown in Figure 5.11, in which we have selected cost center **10101101** and can see the flow of costs to and from this cost center as a result of allocation cycles (see Section 5.4.2) and direct activity allocations (see Section 5.4.3). The flows illustrated might be a simple flow from a production cost center to an order (one sender and one receiver) or from multiple senders to multiple receivers. The posting lines for secondary cost postings contain either the sender and its partner receiver or the receiver and its partner sender.

We showed previously in Figure 5.4 that the asset depreciation expenses were assigned not just to a cost center but also to a functional area, a profit center, and a segment. The allocation of these costs from the sender account assignment to the receiver account assignment can also result in a shift in functional areas, profit center, and segment, and reports such as the Trial Balance app shown in Figure 5.12 offer a drilldown to these partner objects. If you're working in the public sector, you might also find a shift between funds or grants as a result of an allocation.

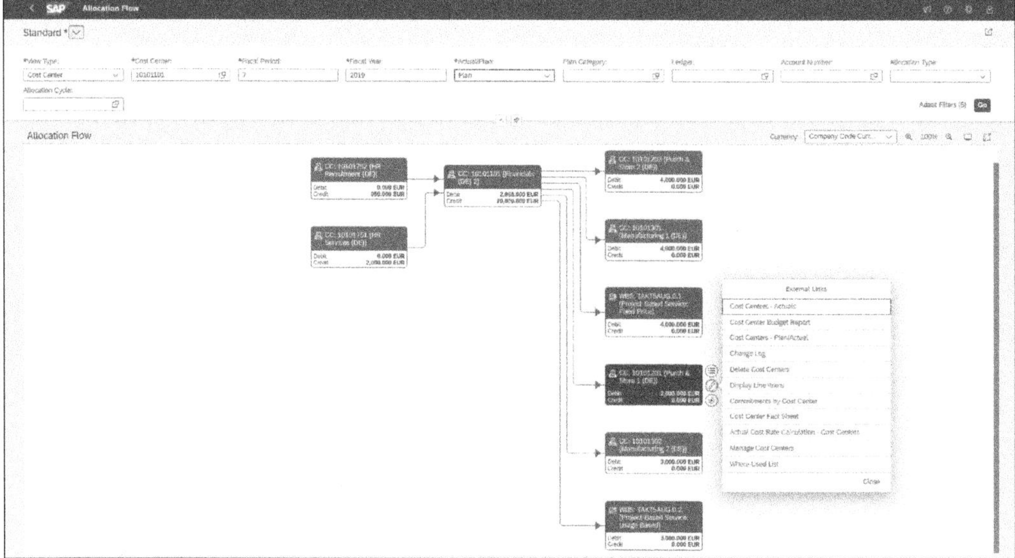


**Figure 5.11** Allocation Flow

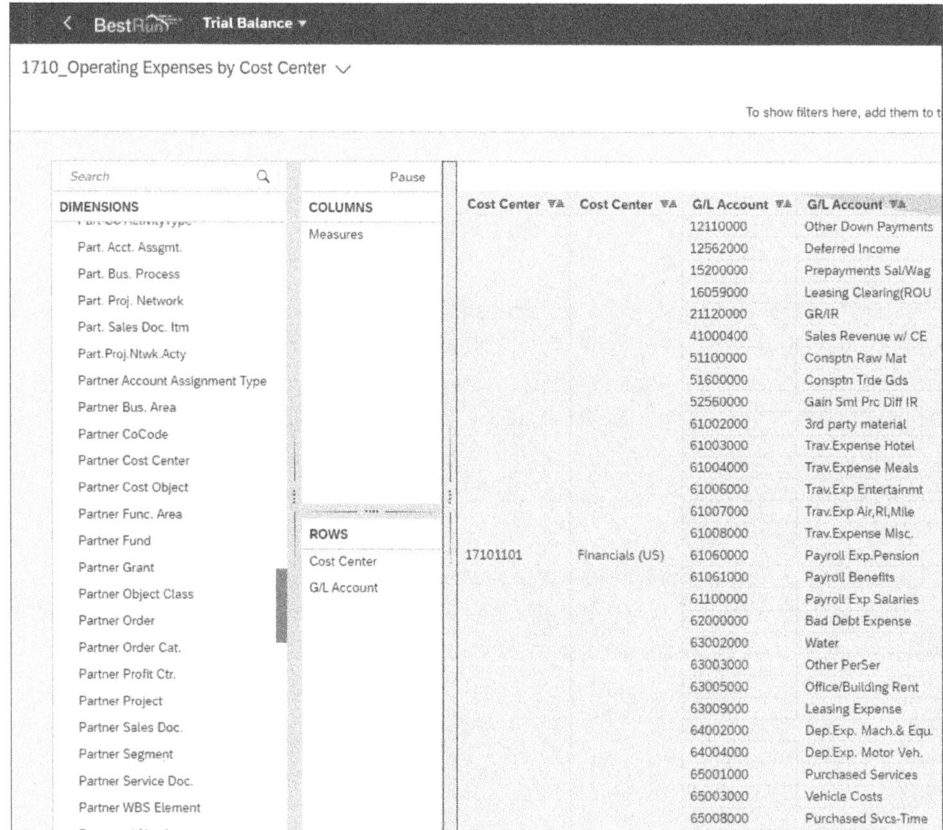


**Figure 5.12** Trial Balance Showing Partner Objects (Under Dimensions)

In SAP S/4HANA, the default document type for secondary cost postings is CO, but you can change the configuration to create separate document types for each type of posting to give you more transparency. To define new document types, choose the following path in the IMG: **Financial Accounting • Financial Accounting Global Settings • Document • Document Types • Define Document Types.**



Of course, the partner information isn't just available in the Trial Balance app. You can see the same information in the Display Line Items—Cost Accounting app (SAP Fiori ID F4023) and the Display Line Items—Margin Analysis app (SAP Fiori ID F4818), and in the legacy line item reports, such as Transaction KSB1 for the cost center line items, Transaction KOB1 for order line items, Transaction CJI3 for project line items, and Transaction KE24 for the line items in margin analysis. If you use the newer versions of the line item reports that were optimized for SAP HANA, such as Transaction KSB1N for cost center line items, Transaction KOB1N for order line items, and so on, then you can select either the object or the partner object in order to identify the senders and receivers of an allocation.

**SAP ERP versus SAP S/4HANA**

There are several key differences between allocations in SAP ERP and in SAP S/4HANA:

- In SAP ERP, allocations and settlements were posted under the secondary cost element in Controlling (CO) and under a reconciliation account in Financial Accounting (FI). It was also possible to activate a substitution to switch the account selection when the FI document was created as a result of an allocation. In SAP S/4HANA, there is no longer a switch from a cost element to a general ledger account. In the examples that follow, you'll see that the secondary cost element is visible as a general ledger account in all journal entries.
- In SAP ERP, one of the concerns was that only two currencies were available in CO, meaning that where the result of allocation or settlement had an impact on the financial accounts, values in the third currency were converted on the fly using the results of the allocation rather than allocated properly in that currency. With SAP S/4HANA, three currencies are available in controlling for most business transactions from release 2020. You can follow details of the progress of this functionality in SAP Note 2894297.
- In SAP ERP, all allocations took place within the leading ledger. With the next SAP S/4HANA release 2021, the plan is to offer ledger-specific allocations and settlements.

We'll explore the various business transactions used to make corrections and perform allocations in Section 5.4.

## 5.3 Planning in SAP S/4HANA

We introduced the topic of financial planning in Chapter 2, and we'll now focus on overhead controlling, where planning is used in the following contexts:

- **Budget setting**
  When you think about cost stewardship (see Section 5.1), the planned costs by cost center or project are also the *ceiling* for spending on that cost center or project. Planning is used to establish a framework within which spending is allowed and to block spending that exceeds that threshold. We'll explore this aspect of planning in Section 5.3.1.
- **Target setting**
  When you consider the goal of optimizing resource usage and of the sender-receiver relationships in Section 5.2.2, you're also setting goals for the level of activity to be provided for production, consulting, and so on. You're setting cost targets within the framework of the activity to be provided by that cost center and will later adjust the plan to reflect the actual activity delivered in that period. If the operating rate of the cost center increases, then so too do the variable costs that it can incur. This in turn will be reflected in the cost rate for the relevant activity, which can distinguish between the fixed costs for rent, insurance, and so on and the variable costs for energy, operating supplies, and so on, as we discussed in Chapter 4.
- **Determining cost rates**
  As we discussed when we looked at activity types in Chapter 4, before you can provide production hours or consulting services, you must calculate a cost rate for the provision of this service. We'll explore this aspect of planning in Section 5.3.2.
- **Providing a basis for revenue recognition**
  If you want to recognize revenue in proportion to progress (percentage of completion [PoC]), then you must use the planned costs and revenue to determine what constitutes completion and then calculate how much you've spent in comparison with the planned costs. We'll explore this aspect of planning in Section 5.3.3.

### 5.3.1 Planning, Budgeting, and Commitment Handling

We'll begin by looking at planning in the context of setting budgets and managing commitments. If you look at the reports for cost stewardship in Section 5.1, managers are being provided with information not just on the amounts that they have spent, but also on how this relates to what they planned to spend (the budget). Figure 5.3 showed the spend represented not just in terms of costs that have already been paid out but also in terms of committed spend, where there is a contractual obligation to cover the costs of a purchase order: a *commitment*. The idea behind a commitment is that from a budget point of view, these costs should already be considered to have used budget and thus prevent the manager from accidentally overspending.

**Note**

In Chapter 2, we showed how to plan the costs by cost center as a story in SAP Analytics Cloud for planning and then transfer the data to SAP S/4HANA. It's also possible to perform a Microsoft Excel upload or use an application programming interface (API) to fill the plan data table.

We distinguish between the various types of plans using a *plan category*, as shown in Figure 5.13. The various categories represent the different planning assumptions, but you can flag some categories as being relevant for budgeting purposes. You can check the plan categories by following **Controlling • General Controlling • Planning • Maintain Category for Planning** in the IMG. The budget-relevant categories are identified by the **Category Usage**. This setting determines that plan data in this category will be used as part of the budget check for the cost centers, for the work breakdown structure (WBS) elements or the public sector. Checks made against this plan will result in warnings and even error messages if the budget is exceeded, whereas entries for the other categories simply represent different planning assumptions and have no impact on the budgeting process.

Maintenance View for Category

| Plan Category | Medium description | Application Type | Category Usage |
|---|---|---|---|
| ACT01 | Actual | Periodic Planning and Consolidation | No specific usage |
| ACT_CONST | Actual at constant rate | Periodic Planning and Consolidation | No specific usage |
| BASE | Base Plan | Periodic Planning and Consolidation | No specific usage |
| BUDGET01 | Cost Center Budget | Periodic Planning and Consolidation | Cost Center Budget |
| CPP1 | Cash Pool Planning | Periodic Planning and Consolidation | No specific usage |
| FINAL | Final Consolidation | Periodic Planning and Consolidation | No specific usage |
| FORE01 | Forecast 01 | Periodic Planning and Consolidation | No specific usage |
| FORE02 | Forecast 02 | Periodic Planning and Consolidation | No specific usage |
| FORE03 | Forecast 03 | Periodic Planning and Consolidation | No specific usage |
| FORE04 | Forecast 04 | Periodic Planning and Consolidation | No specific usage |
| FORE05 | Forecast 05 | Periodic Planning and Consolidation | No specific usage |
| FORE06 | Forecast 06 | Periodic Planning and Consolidation | No specific usage |

**Figure 5.13** Sample Plan Categories

We'll look first at how to activate budget control for the cost centers. To do this, you'll need to navigate to the Manage Cost Centers app (SAP Fiori ID F1443A) and select a cost center, as shown in Figure 5.14. In this example, the budget for cost center **17101201** is carried by this cost center. But you can also enter a higher-level cost center in the **Budget-Carrying Cost Center** field to avoid having lots of small budgets on many different cost centers, which can become cumbersome if you keep having to move budget between cost centers whenever you need to authorize spending. You must then enter a **Budget Availability Control Profile** (we've entered "ZCCB01") and choose **Budget Availability Control Is Active**. These settings are only available in the Manage Cost Centers app, not in Transactions KS01–KS03 (Create/Change/Display Cost Center).

**SAP ERP versus SAP S/4HANA**

This approach is new with SAP S/4HANA. In SAP ERP, there was no budget availability check for cost centers.

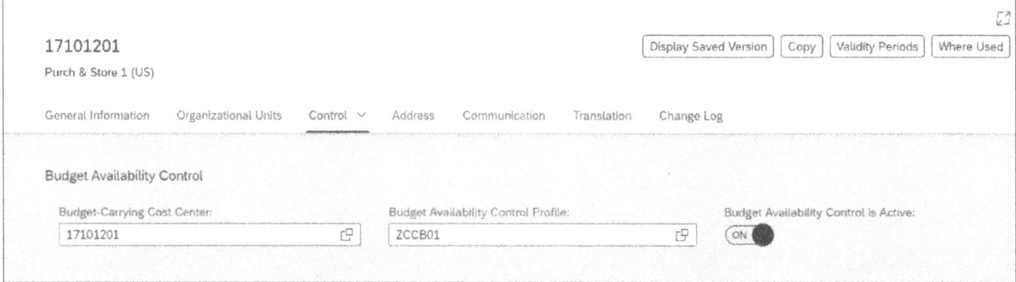


**Figure 5.14** Manage Cost Centers App, Showing Settings for Budget Availability Control

The budget availability control profile shown in Figure 5.15 determines which activities will be checked and which tolerances will be used to issue warnings and errors. To define the thresholds for budget availability control in SAP S/4HANA, choose **Controlling • Cost Center Accounting • Budget Management • Maintain Budget Availability Control for Cost Centers** in the IMG, create a budget availability control profile, assign a group of general ledger accounts, and then define the thresholds to be used to check the budget on the cost center. Notice that we're using a node of the general ledger account hierarchy (see Chapter 4) to set the rules, so you might set different rules for travel expenses and external purchases. Within the rules for that account group, you can determine when a warning is issued and when an error is issued to block the posting completely.

**Note**

In SAP S/4HANA Cloud, the settings are part of scope item J54 (Overhead Cost Accounting—Actual).

Change View "Tolerance Limits": Overview

New Entries More

Dialog Structure
Profiles
Account Groups
Tolerance Limits

Budget Availability Ctrl Prfl: ZCCB01 CC Budget Profile 01
G/L Account Hierarchy: Z900
G/L Account Group: 105

Tolerance Limits

| Activity Group | Message Type | Usage in % |
|---|---|---|
| All Activity Groups | Error | 100,00 |
| All Activity Groups | Warning | 90,00 |
| Purchase Requisition | Warning | 90,00 |

**Figure 5.15** Budget Availability Control Profile

As a result of the rules shown, whenever a user creates a purchase requisition or a purchase order with reference to a cost center, the system checks whether more than 90% of the budget has been used and, if so, issues a message that the budget tolerance limit for the cost center has been exceeded, as shown in Figure 5.16. In this example, it's only a warning, but you can see that when 100% of the budget has been used, an error is issued and the purchase blocked. We'll explain how to create a purchase order when we look at how to purchase raw materials in Chapter 6.

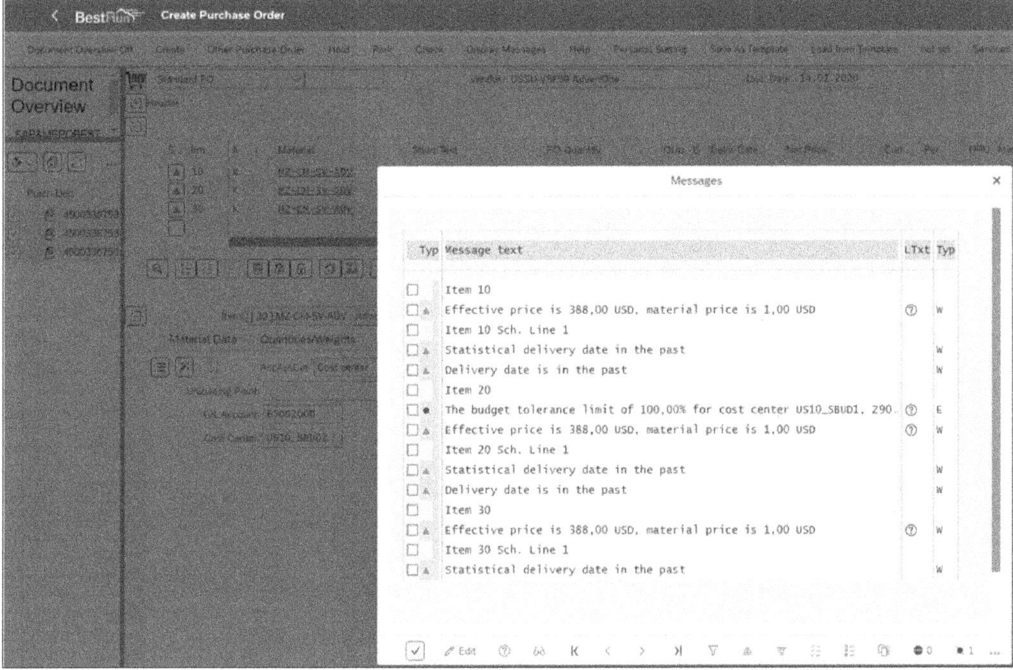


**Figure 5.16** Budget Availability Check for Cost Center

You can activate an equivalent check for WBS elements in SAP S/4HANA Cloud by using scope item 1NT (Project Financial Control). Again, you'll need to enter the budget availability control in the WBS element master data and define the relevant tolerances. The same mechanisms are available in SAP S/4HANA, but you should only use the budget availability check if you have WBS elements without assigned orders or networks as the check reads the WBS, but not the assigned orders. This gap is documented in SAP Note 2778793. We'll explain how to work with budget availability control in projects using the legacy transactions in Chapter 8.

In Chapter 2, we discussed the use of *commitment management* to track the costs of purchase orders that have been submitted but not yet delivered. The idea is that these costs reduce the available budget from the moment that the purchase order is placed, rather than when the costs are incurred. You can activate commitment management using scope item 2I3 in SAP S/4HANA Cloud and by setting up the appropriate extension ledger in SAP S/4HANA. This will ensure that the system creates a commitment for the value of the purchase order or travel request and then cancels it as the goods are received or the travel expenses posted. When the budget check is performed, the system checks against the *assigned value*, which is the sum of the actual costs and the commitments for the cost center in question.

**Budget Checks and Commitments in SAP S/4HANA**

The new budget check for cost centers uses commitments created as predictive accounting documents in the Universal Journal and is activated by assigning the budget availability control profile, as was shown in Figure 5.14.

You can also create commitments for a cost center that updates the legacy commitment table, table COOI. This is controlled by setting the **Commitment update** flag in the cost center master data (see Chapter 4, Section 4.2.2). There is no budget check for such cost centers. If you want to perform a budget check using the legacy commitment table, then you should create a statistical order that mirrors this cost center and make the budget check against the order.

### 5.3.2 Integrated Financial Planning with SAP Analytics Cloud

As you saw in Chapter 2, the process of calculating planned costs can take place in SAP Analytics Cloud for planning. Opinions on planning and analysis differ: some organizations prefer to plan in an analytical tool and access the journal entries from their operational system to check that they are on track in comparison with the plan, whereas others move the agreed plan into their operational system in order to perform active budget checks against that plan. With this in mind, SAP offers two styles of business content for financial planning (see *https://www.sapanalytics.cloud/learning/business-content/*):

1. **Financial planning and analysis**
   This business content includes planning applications and dashboards for analysis that access the actual data in the Universal Journal using core data services (CDS) views.
2. **Integrated financial planning**
   This business content includes the planning applications that we looked at in Chapter 2 and is designed with a view to moving the results of planning into SAP S/4HANA for operational use.

We already showed how to assign planned costs to a cost center using the **SAP_FI_BPL_IM_COSTCENTER_EXPENSES** planning story and to a WBS element using the **SAP _FI_BPL_IM_PROJECT_PLANNING_AND_BUDGETING** planning story in Chapter 2. You can do the same for an internal order using the **SAP_FI_BPL_IM_INTERNAL_ORDER_PLANNING** planning story. Here you're capturing the various primary costs (payroll and benefits, office expenses, travel expenses, etc.) that you expect for the different account assignments, with a view to activate a budget check for each of these items or simply monitor that the costs incurred are within the expected framework. The next step is to perform allocations to transfer costs between cost centers and to plan activity costs and cost rates. These cost rates are a prerequisite for activity allocation, as we'll discuss in Section 5.4.3, and as before you can charge machine time to a production order or consulting hours to a project you need to establish what an hour of activity will cost. This information isn't stored as a planning line item, but rather in table COST in SAP S/4HANA and table ACCOSTRATE in SAP S/4HANA Cloud, and it's accessed whenever you perform an order confirmation or time recording. At period close, you can calculate a new activity rate that reflects the actual costs for the period.



These cost rates are important in the sense that they determine the value of a machine hour or a consulting hour, but they're also part of the target setting process for the cost center. The idea behind the *target costs* is that instead of simply being responsible for the costs incurred by the cost center, the manager is responsible for the resources used to deliver a given level of activity, whether this is the number of hours worked by a production cost center or the number of hours of service provided by a consulting cost center. If the output rises, the assumption is that the variable part of the associated costs can rise too. If more machine hours are provided, it might be assumed that more energy will be consumed. If consultants provide more hours of service, it might be assumed that they will also travel more.

This brings us to the difference between *fixed* costs, such as rent or insurance, which do not change as output rises, and *variable* costs, such as energy or raw material costs, which respond to increased output. The different behavior of the costs is established in the **SAP_FI_BPL_IM_COSTCENTER_ACTIVITYPRICE_CALCULATION** planning story, where fixed costs are planned as **Expenses** and variable costs as **Expenses ActDep** (activity-dependent expenses), as shown in Figure 5.17. These costs will vary with the output planned in Figure 5.18, while the fixed costs will remain stable regardless of the output quantity, so any changes to the output in Figure 5.18 will impact the activity-dependent expenses in Figure 5.17.

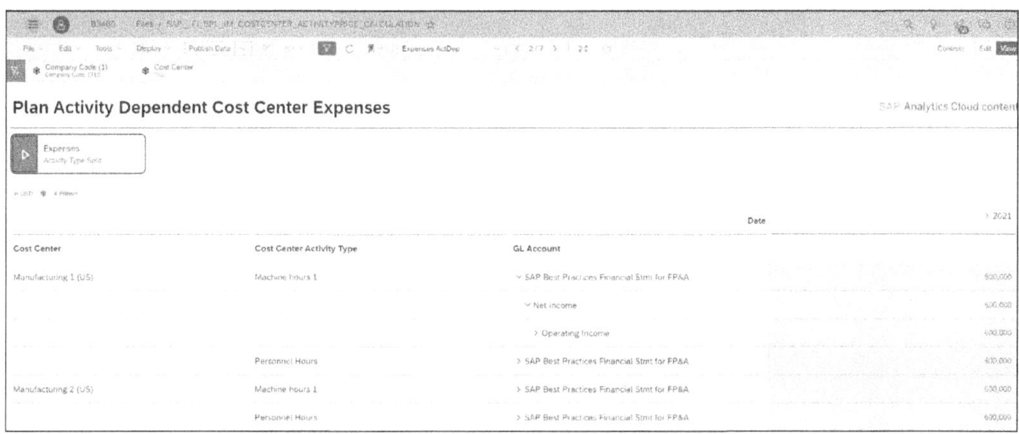


**Figure 5.17** Planning Activity-Dependent Expenses

**Plan Total Activity Output**

SAP Analytics Cloud content

Activity Quantities – Actual based

Activity Quantities – Resource Calculation based

| Cost Center | Cost Center Activity Type | Unit | Capacity (2021) | Activity Quantity (2021) |
|---|---|---|---|---|
| Manufacturing 1 (US) | Machine hours 1 | H | 30,000.00 | 30,000.00 |
| | Personnel Hours | H | 30,000.00 | 30,000.00 |
| Manufacturing 2 (US) | Machine hours 1 | H | 24,000.00 | 12,000.00 |
| | Personnel Hours | H | 24,000.00 | 12,000.00 |
| Back Office-(US) | Service Standard | H | 1,200.00 | 1,200.00 |

Figure 5.18 Planning Output

In Figure 5.19, we've used the **Activity Cost Rates • Calculate** data action to complete the process and calculated the costs to deliver a machine hour or a personnel hour using the expenses entered in the previous planning stories. This value can then be transferred back to SAP S/4HANA, where it will be used to value order confirmations on the shop floor or time sheets entered by white-collar workers.

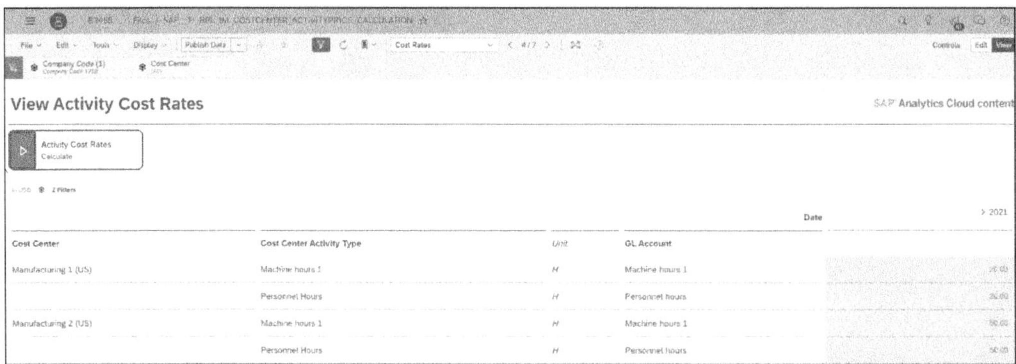


Figure 5.19 Planning Activity Cost Rates

**Planning Using the Classical Transactions**

If your organization isn't yet ready to implement SAP Analytics Cloud for planning, you can plan the activity relationships between the cost centers using Transaction KP06 and the activity rates either manually using Transaction KP26 or by running an activity price calculation using Transaction KSPI.

### 5.3.3 Using Planned Data in Operational Processes

Although many people think of planning as being an analytical process that takes place outside of their accounting system, there are many cases in which planned data is used in the operational processes in SAP S/4HANA. When we look at the business processes in Section 5.4, we'll explain that they often require planned data. For example:

- In Section 5.4.2, we'll look at how to use distribution and assessment to allocate costs between cost centers. To establish the relative weighting of the various receivers of these costs, you can use actual values, but many organizations choose to use planned values to smooth the impact of their allocations if there is a lot of volatility in the flows of actual costs.
- In Section 5.4.3, we'll show how to perform direct and indirect activity allocation. Both forms require you to calculate an activity price for the initial valuation. The activity price may be adjusted later, when the actual costs are known, but is taken as the initial basis for applying a value to the allocation.

In Chapter 7, we'll explore the topic of revenue recognition. The idea behind revenue recognition is that you realize revenue in proportion to the costs incurred for a project. To understand the progress of the project, the system compares the actual costs to the planned costs to complete the project and might determine that the project is 25% complete. If this is the case, it realizes 25% of the planned revenue as an accrual. This process continues until the project is complete, the realized revenues are the actual revenues, and any work in process (WIP) or reserves can be cancelled. Clearly this plan is not simply an assumption about future business performance but also something that is being used to determine how the project is valued in accounting.

## 5.4 Business Transactions

The business transactions in overhead controlling result in the creation of a journal entry containing a general ledger account and the relevant account assignments and derived reporting dimensions. In the case of a simple reposting of travel expenses between cost centers (see Section 5.4.1), you credit the sending cost center and debit the receiving cost center and update the impact of the switch on the functional areas, profit centers, and so on.

In Section 5.4.2, we go further and describe how to set up allocation cycles to credit multiple cost centers and debit multiple receivers. The resulting journal entries follow the same basic premises, but there are more prerequisites. Instead of simply posting the wrongly assigned travel costs from cost center A to cost center B, we need to establish the relationship between cost center A and cost center B. This involves determining the *driver* information to be used as the basis for the allocation.

In Section 5.4.3, we describe the different forms of activity allocation. Here you use the output of the cost center, whether this is kilowatt hours of energy, machine hours, or consulting hours, to describe the cost flow. This means that you've set up activity types and defined the cost rate for a unit of activity. These can then be used in a direct activity allocation, triggered by time recording for white-collar work or order confirmations for blue-collar work, or used in indirect activity allocation when the activity quantity is derived either on the sender side (splitting the total number of sales hours worked) or on the receiver side (allocating energy costs in proportion to the machine hours supplied by each production cost center).

Overhead calculation (see Section 5.4.4) can be an alternative to activity allocation in which it's possible to set up overhead rates in proportion to the underlying costs (typically raw material overhead, in proportion to the amount of raw materials used and production overhead, in proportion to the amount of production costs used). In Section 5.4.5, we'll explain how to use templates for more sophisticated activity allocation based on conditions.

Finally, in Section 5.4.6 we'll look at how to use settlement to move costs from orders and projects to the appropriate receivers. In all cases, we'll reference the cost element category (see Chapter 4, Section 4.1.3) and the business transaction that will allow you to identify the business transaction when you look at the relevant journal entries.

As you work through the allocations that follow, remember that they will only be allowed if the period is open for the relevant business transaction. With SAP S/4HANA release 2020, the approach has been extended to enable you to lock the combination of business transaction and company code using the Manage Posting Periods – Cost Accounting app (SAP Fiori ID F4684) shown in in Figure 5.20. You can check whether a period is open for postings in earlier editions by using **Accounting • Controlling • Cost Center Accounting • Environment • Period Locks • Display** or Transaction OKP2; entering the controlling area, the year, and the version; and choosing the **Actual** button.

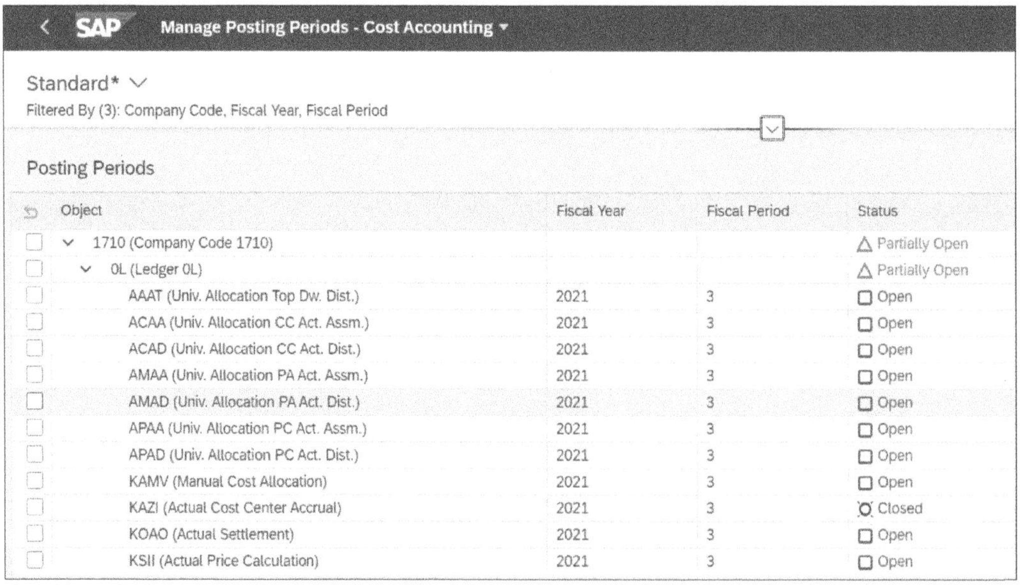

SAP Manage Posting Periods - Cost Accounting

Standard*

Filtered By (3): Company Code, Fiscal Year, Fiscal Period

Posting Periods

| Object | Fiscal Year | Fiscal Period | Status |
|---|---|---|---|
| 1710 (Company Code 1710) | | | Partially Open |
| 0L (Ledger 0L) | | | Partially Open |
| AAAT (Univ. Allocation Top Dw. Dist.) | 2021 | 3 | Open |
| ACAA (Univ. Allocation CC Act. Assm.) | 2021 | 3 | Open |
| ACAD (Univ. Allocation CC Act. Dist.) | 2021 | 3 | Open |
| AMAA (Univ. Allocation PA Act. Assm.) | 2021 | 3 | Open |
| AMAD (Univ. Allocation PA Act. Dist.) | 2021 | 3 | Open |
| APAA (Univ. Allocation PC Act. Assm.) | 2021 | 3 | Open |
| APAD (Univ. Allocation PC Act. Dist.) | 2021 | 3 | Open |
| KAMV (Manual Cost Allocation) | 2021 | 3 | Open |
| KAZI (Actual Cost Center Accrual) | 2021 | 3 | Closed |
| KOAO (Actual Settlement) | 2021 | 3 | Open |
| KSII (Actual Price Calculation) | 2021 | 3 | Open |

**Figure 5.20** Displaying Period Locks for Business Transactions

### 5.4.1 Reposting and Cost Assignment

In Section 5.2.1, we explained how primary cost postings are made in an integrated system. Just occasionally, corrections will be required when costs have been assigned to the wrong account assignment. This might happen if an employee has posted travel expenses to the wrong cost center or order or a consultant has confirmed time to the wrong WBS element. The reposting acts as a documented "undo" of the original posting, crediting the wrong account assignment to correct the error and debiting the correct account assignment. A reposting does not result in a change to the general ledger account/cost element, so you don't need to create secondary cost elements to make a correction.



There are several different types of reposting:

- **Document number**
  You know the document number and are moving the costs posted under that document number to a different account assignment. In this case, use Transaction KB61 to select the document to be changed. The reposting will be recorded under business transaction category RKU3.
- **Cost**
  You are moving costs between cost objects without reference to a document number. In this case, use Transaction KB11N to enter the sender and receiver objects manually. The reposting will be recorded under business transaction RKU1.
- **Revenue**
  You are moving revenues between cost objects without reference to a document number. In this case, use Transaction KB41N to enter the sender and receiver objects manually. The reposting will be recorded under business transaction RKU2.

In addition, the markups for intercompany service activities that we'll look at in Chapter 9 are captured as repostings, this time under business transaction KAMV.

Figure 5.21 shows the Display Line Items—Cost Accounting app and a list of travel expenses that have been reposted using business transaction type **RKU1**. Notice the document type in the **Jour...** column is **CO** for a costing document.

Let's assume that one of the employees on a cost center has just moved to another cost center. To move these costs to the correct cost center, we need to repost the line item that recorded the original expense posting using Transaction KB61 or following menu path **Accounting • Controlling • Cost Center Accounting • Actual Postings • Repost Line Item • Enter**.

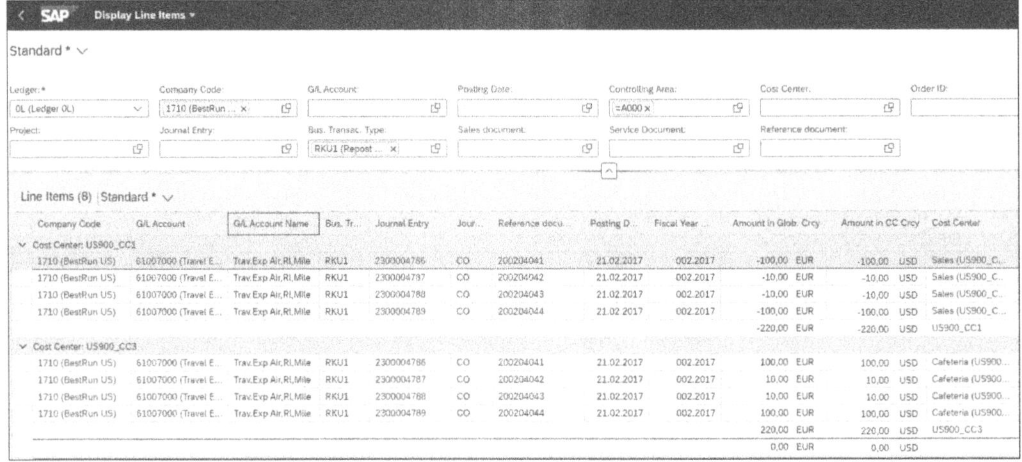

Figure 5.21 Display Line Items – Cost Accounting App

In an ideal world, you know the document number under which the travel expenses were posted and can enter it in the selection screen shown in Figure 5.22. Usually, however, finding the document that you want to repost is part of the challenge. If you don't enter a document in the selection screen, the system will select all documents that meet your selection criteria (initially, all postings to company code **1710** in **2020** in this example). To refine your selection parameters, choose **More • Change Selection Parameters.**

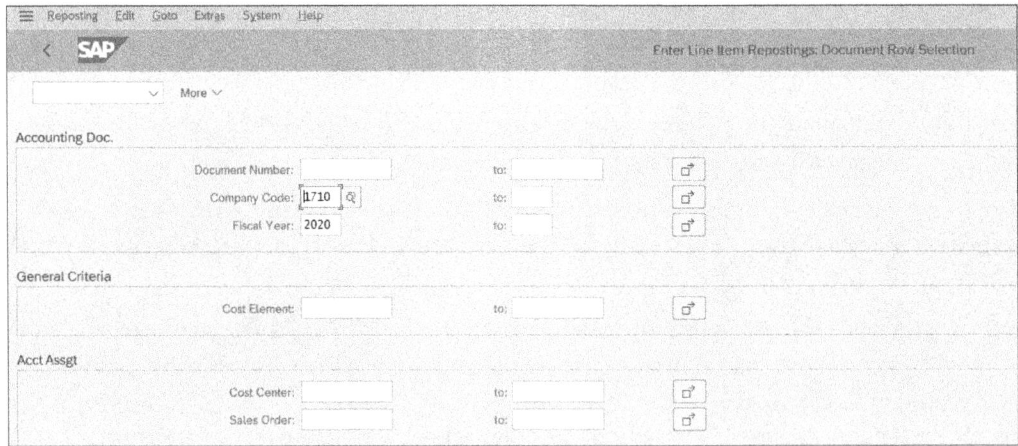


Figure 5.22 Selection Screen for Reposting

You'll arrive at the screen shown in Figure 5.23, which shows all the fields that can be used to select line items for reposting. To find the relevant travel expenses, you might add **Personnel Number** to the selection parameters by selecting it from the list on the left.

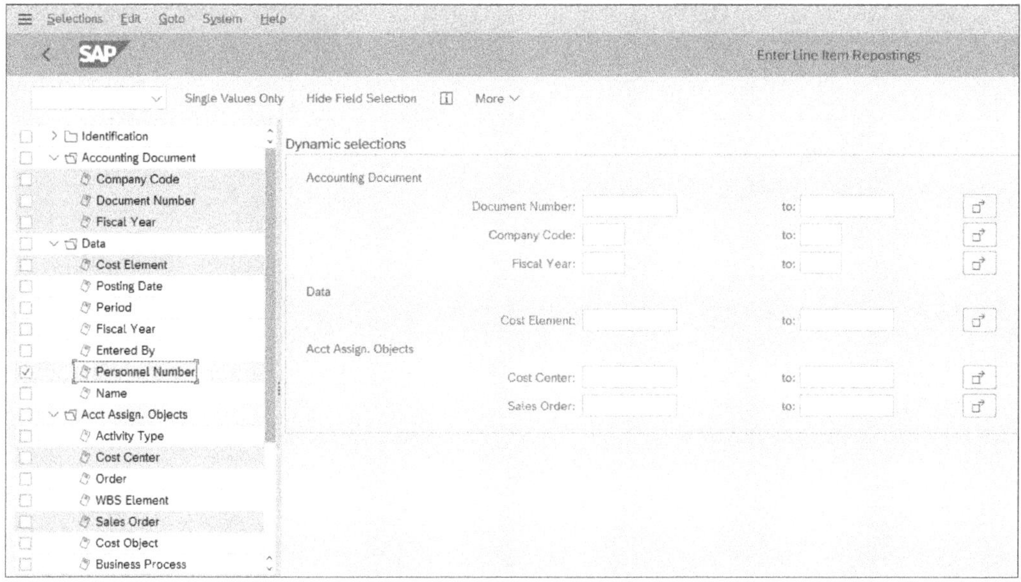

**Figure 5.23** Selection Parameters for Line Item Posting

Once you've made your selection, you have two options:

1. **List view**

   Figure 5.24 shows the list view, which is designed for mass entry of many items when mass corrections are needed (e.g., when organizations are being restructured and all postings for the period need to be moved to the new cost center). The list view requires you to choose the object type (**OTy** column) for the account assignment and then enter the new account assignment.

2. **Row view**

   Figure 5.25 shows the row view, which is designed for entering details for a single item. The row view offers a separate field for each object type.

You can switch between the two views by using the **Row** button in the list view and the **List** button in the row view.

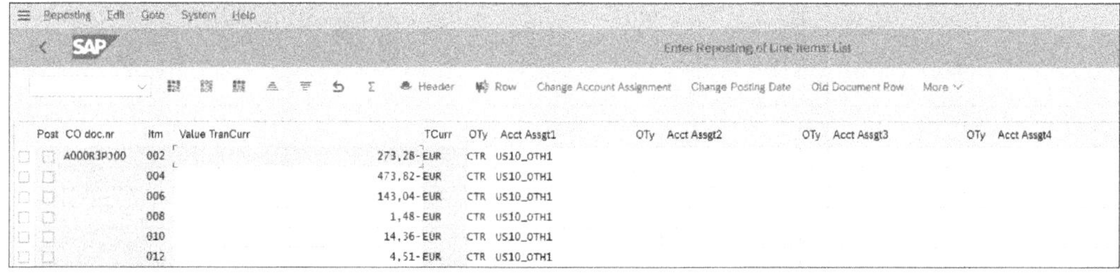

**Figure 5.24** Reposting: List View

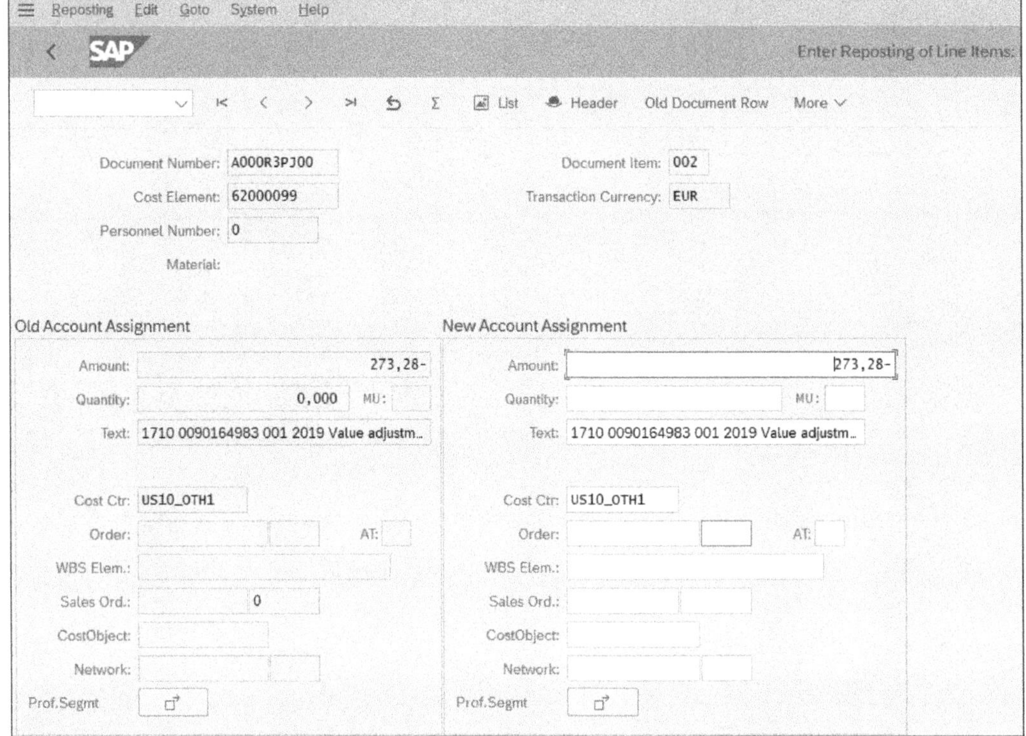


**Figure 5.25** Reposting: Row View

In the previous example, we began by selecting the original document as the basis for the reposting, but it's also possible to move costs freely from one cost assignment to another. To repost from one cost center to another, use Transaction KB11N or follow menu path **Accounting • Controlling • Cost Center Accounting • Actual Postings • Manual Reposting of Costs • Enter**. To access the relevant account assignments in this transaction, select the appropriate screen variant (**Scrn var.**), as shown in Figure 5.26, then enter the appropriate document date, the cost element, and the amount, together with the old cost center and the new cost center (or whichever account assignments you are moving costs from and to).

You can identify this reposting for auditing purposes using business transaction RKU1. If you need to repost revenues rather than costs, use Transaction KB41N or **Actual Postings • Manual Reposting of Revenues • Enter**. This time, the transactions can be identified for auditing purposes using business transaction RKU2.

Alternatively, if you have SAP S/4HANA release 2020, you can use the Reassign Costs and Revenues app (SAP Fiori ID F2009), shown in Figure 5.27, to perform the same steps. This allows you to copy and reverse existing allocations and to create new assignments. The classic transactions comprise a header and the assigned document lines, whereas the SAP Fiori app has a header, one or more assignment items, and a list of associated journal entries. The journal entries are written separately to each associated ledger, as we discussed in Chapter 3, Section 3.3.1. We'll return to this topic when we discuss the outlook for controlling in Chapter 11.

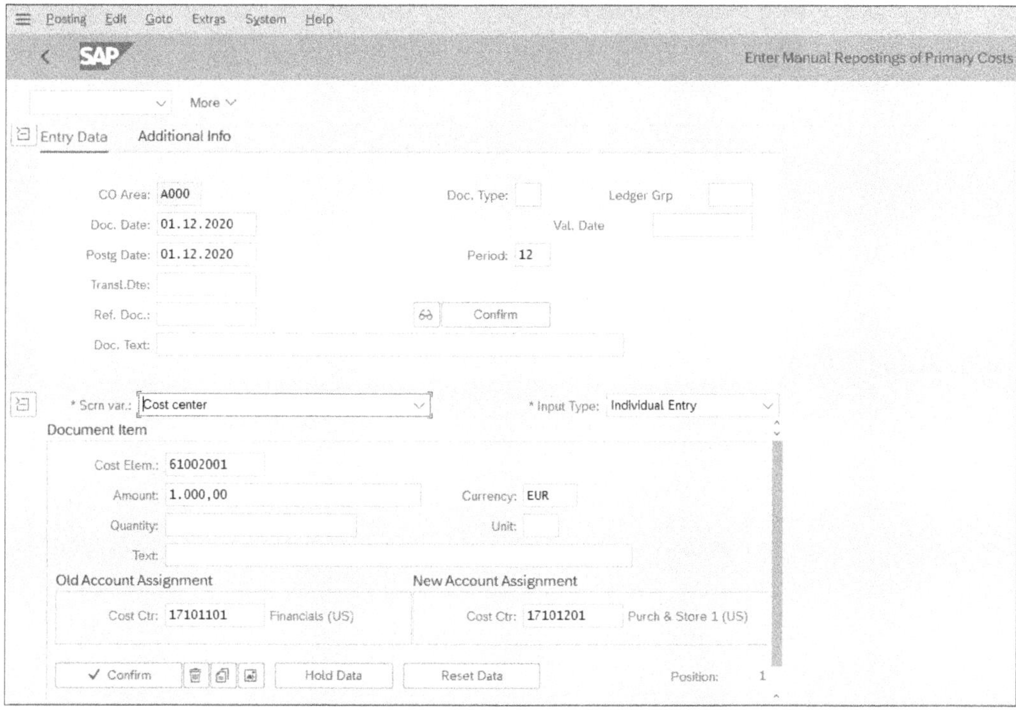


**Figure 5.26** Manual Cost Reposting

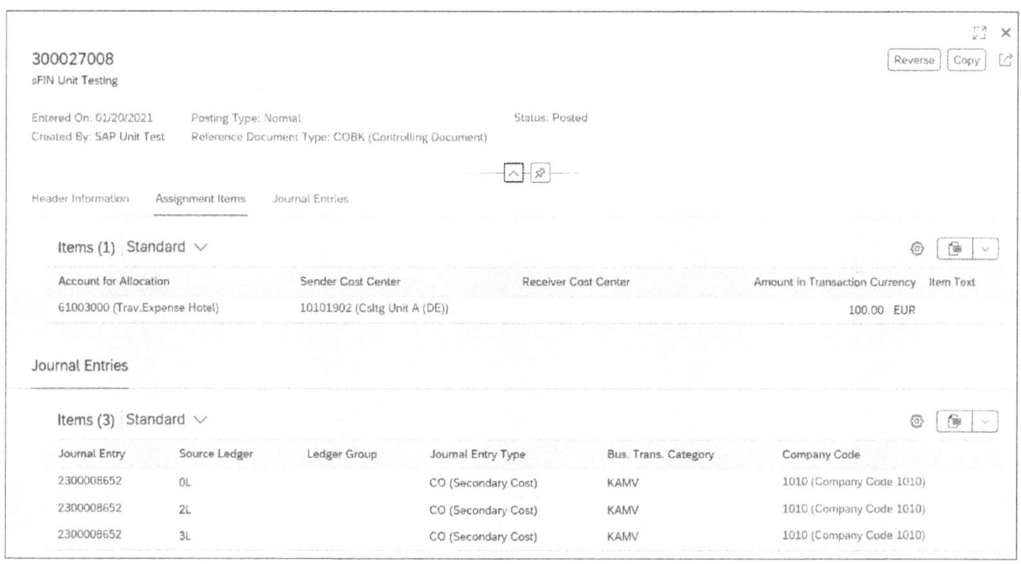


**Figure 5.27** Reassign Costs and Revenues App

### 5.4.2 Universal Allocation

In this section, we'll begin by describing how to allocate costs using the various SAP Fiori apps that are offered under the umbrella term *universal allocation*. This currently covers profit center allocation, cost center allocation, and top-down distribution in margin analysis, with allocation to margin analysis planned for on-premise SAP S/4HANA release 2021.

Before you start, it's important to think through the drivers that you will use as a basis for the allocation:

- This might be as simple as entering a percentage to split the costs to two cost centers in a 50:50 ratio. In this case, you choose the **Fixed Percentages** rule and enter the percentages manually. You can use the same approach in settlement to assign costs to several different receivers.
- You might choose to assign heating costs in proportion to the square footage of the different production lines or administrative overhead in proportion to the headcount on the various cost centers. In this case, you need to ensure that the correct statistical key figures have been created for square footage and headcount and the relevant information updated for each period. As you work through the sections that follow, make sure you understand not just what to do as part of the allocation itself, but what reference data needs to be in place in order to perform the allocation.
- You might choose to spread the costs in proportion to the relative revenues in the different market segments. If so, you need to ensure that the revenue information is being collected reliably under the proper accounts.
- Perhaps you don't want to use the same drivers for all costs but might choose to group the costs to distinguish between people-related and asset-related costs within the allocation. In this case, you need to set up general ledger account groups to separate the two types of costs, as described in Chapter 4. As you work through the allocations, remember to ask yourself whether the same rules apply to all costs to be allocated or if it's necessary to group the costs to apply different rules depending on the type of costs.

**SAP ERP versus SAP S/4HANA**

In SAP ERP, the various assessment and distribution transactions accessed the totals records to determine what costs on the sender were to be allocated and, often, which costs on the receiver would serve as drivers for the allocation, which meant that only a fairly small number of fields were available for selection. With universal allocation, you're working directly with the line items in the Universal Journal and building on the new architecture, including multiple ledgers and multiple currencies.

We described the cost center master data in Chapter 4, Section 4.2. The simplest way to move costs from one cost center to another is by means of an allocation. This is typically the case when you want to move costs from support cost centers to production cost centers. Choosing the senders and receivers is a key part of this design exercise, but it's also important to decide whether you want to perform a distribution or an assessment:

- *Distribution cycles* are generally used if a small number of general ledger accounts (such as rent costs or utility costs) are initially posted to a single cost center and then charged to many cost centers. The costs will be spread using the original general ledger account, so a distribution makes sense when you want to keep the information that you have shared rent or utility costs on the receiver. But be careful if you create a distribution cycle for a cost center with many different assigned accounts: you'll generate a high volume of posting lines, which may not give you the transparency you need.
- *Overhead allocation cycles* were known as *assessment cycles* in SAP ERP. They can be used to move costs captured under many different accounts from the sender to the receiver cost centers. The details of the accounts on the sending cost center are rolled up under a secondary cost element for assessment (see Chapter 4, Section 4.1.3).

In this section, we'll explain distribution and overhead allocation using the new collection of apps known collectively under the umbrella term *universal allocation*. This includes the following apps:

- **Manage Allocations (SAP Fiori ID F3338)**
  Use this app to define the cycle that acts as the framework for the allocation and the segments within this cycle that determine the senders and receivers of the allocation. Then define the drivers to be used to capture the relative weighting between the different receivers.
- **Run Allocations (SAP Fiori ID F3548)**
  Use this app to create a run and then trigger the allocation cycles either immediately or at a scheduled time.
- **Allocation Results (SAP Fiori ID F4363)**
  Use this app to display the result of the allocation in list form and to access the Allocation Flow app.
- **Allocation Flow (SAP Fiori ID F4022)**
  Use this app to display the flow of costs from the sender to the receivers. This differs from the Allocation Results app in that you select an individual cost center and can then see all allocations to and from that cost center, whereas the Allocation Results app shows the flow between the senders and receivers in a single allocation run.
- **Manage Allocation Tags (SAP Fiori ID F4523)**
  Use this app to tag your allocation cycles for selection later.

**Classic Allocation Transactions**

The classic transactions for distribution and assessment continue to be available in SAP S/4HANA, and you can access them using the following transaction codes:

- Create/change/display assessment cycles: Transactions KSU1–KSU3
- Run assessment cycles: Transaction KSU5
- Create/change/display distribution cycles: Transactions KSV1–KSV3
- Run distribution cycles: Transaction KSV5

At the time of writing, there are still functional gaps in universal allocation, so it isn't yet possible to run cumulative cycles that combine data from several periods or iterative cycles that take costs that build cyclical relationships in which one cost center is both the sender and the receiver in the same cycle. It's also not possible to use a source structure to distinguish the costs to be allocated by type. The allocations take place within a single company code, whereas the classic transactions can allocate between senders and receivers in several company codes, provided they all belong to the same controlling area. Going forward, SAP plans to close the gaps compared to the classic allocation transactions and use them to support new approaches, including the use of parallel ledgers and multiple currencies.

### Manage Allocations

We'll start by looking at the Manage Allocations app, shown in Figure 5.28. This app can be used to create profit center allocations, cost center allocations, and top-down distributions for margin analysis (see Chapter 7). The different approaches are represented by the **Allocation Context**. Within overhead management, we'll work with the **Cost Centers** context. We distinguish between distribution and overhead allocation using the **Allocation Type**. In SAP GUI, the two allocation types were distinguished by the transaction code, with Transactions KSV1–KSV3 being used for distributions and Transactions KSU1–KSU3 for assessment. Notice also that you can use the same mechanism to allocate planned costs and actual costs. In SAP GUI, again, cycles for planned costs had their own transaction codes, with Transactions KSV7–KSV9 being used for planned distributions and Transactions KSU7–KSU9 for planned assessments. There is a **Spreadsheet** icon above the list of cycles (not shown). You can use this button to download a template to maintain your cycles in a spreadsheet and then upload the results prior to allocation. This feature was added with SAP Fiori.

To view the segments within the cycle, select allocation cycle **ZDCRP**. Because this is a demo system, the cycle only includes one segment for the assignment of corporate overhead costs, but you can assign many different segments to a single cycle. We'll now look at the details of this segment. The same structure with one cycle comprising many segments is also used in the legacy transactions.

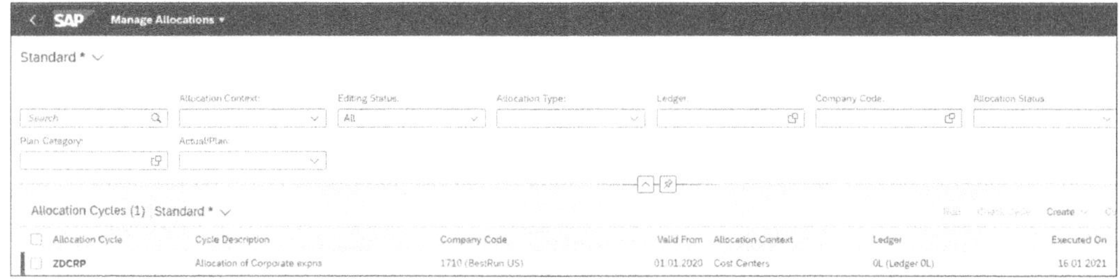


**Figure 5.28** Manage Allocations App, Showing Allocation Cycles

In Figure 5.29, we've accessed segment **1**, which determines how the corporate overhead costs will be allocated. The key entries for the segment are as follows:

- **Overhead Alloc. Acct**
  If you're performing an overhead allocation, the overhead allocation account is the secondary cost element under which the allocation will be recorded. We explained the details of the account settings required in Chapter 4, Section 4.1.3. You need to make sure that you enter a general ledger account of cost element category 42 (assessment). At the time of writing, all overhead allocations will be made under a single secondary cost element; you can't yet use a source structure to separate out the various cost blocks being allocated. If you use the legacy transactions, you can enter a source structure instead of the single cost element and then assign a different secondary cost element for each group of costs to be allocated.

- **Sender Rule**
  The **Sender Rule** determines whether you're simply going to distribute or allocate all the costs collected on the cost center for the period (**Posted amounts**, as shown here) or use a fixed amount or fixed rate. Posted amounts is by far the most common approach and requires no work in preparation for the period close because the costs on the sender cost center(s) are read during the allocation. Fixed amounts or fixed rates requires you to update the segment prior to allocation but can be useful if you want to calculate the amounts for the allocation in an external system or spreadsheet and then load them to the allocation cycle.

- **Receiver Rule**
  The **Receiver Rule** determines the basis for the allocation. Selecting **Fixed amounts** or **Fixed percentages** as shown here may seem like the easiest way to get started because it provides easy rules for everyone to understand. However, this type of rule forces you to revisit your segments once a month to make sure that the percentages for each receiver are correct, check whether new cost centers have been added to the group, and adjust the percentages accordingly. In the long term, you may be better off choosing variable portions instead and then having the system read the relative costs on each receiver cost center or the statistical key figures, such as headcount or square footage, during the allocation.

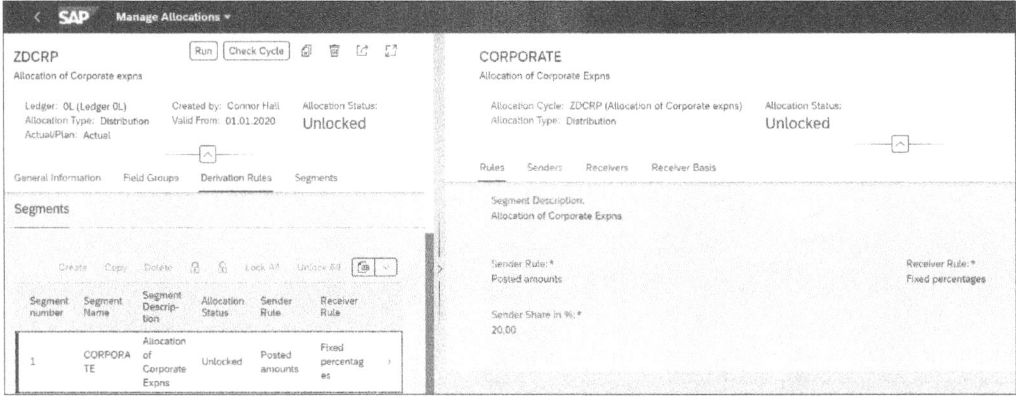

Figure 5.29 Segment Rules for Allocation

In Figure 5.30, we've navigated to the **Senders** tab to show that the costs captured under a group of cost centers and a collection of accounts are to be allocated. We explained in Chapter 4 how to set up these groups and it's important to make sure that all costs that you want to allocate are part of the grouping entered here. Of course, you don't have to allocate all the costs in one go. You can define multiple segments to allocate the people-related costs on a cost center separately from the asset-related costs. If you're using Transactions KSU1–KSU3 or KSV1–KSV3, the main difference is that instead of working with account groups, you'll be entering a cost element group for your senders. Notice also the **Spreadsheet** icon that allows you to download a template and then manually upload a list of senders. Again, this is unique to the SAP Fiori application.

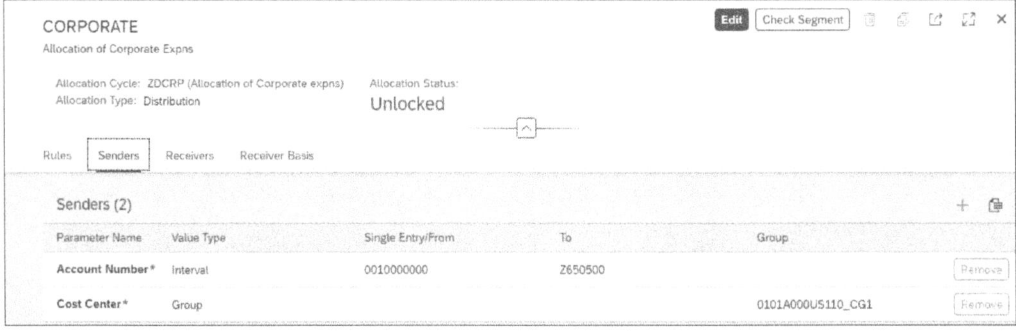

Figure 5.30 Allocation Senders

Figure 5.31 shows the group of cost centers that will receive a share of the corporate overhead costs as a result of the allocation. Again, refer back to Chapter 4, Section 4.2.3 for details on how to create such groupings. Here too you can use a spreadsheet to upload a list of receivers. To see which cost centers are assigned to the group shown in Figure 5.31, go to the **Receiver Basis** tab. Here you'll see the cost centers assigned and can assign the percentages to be used as a basis for allocation.

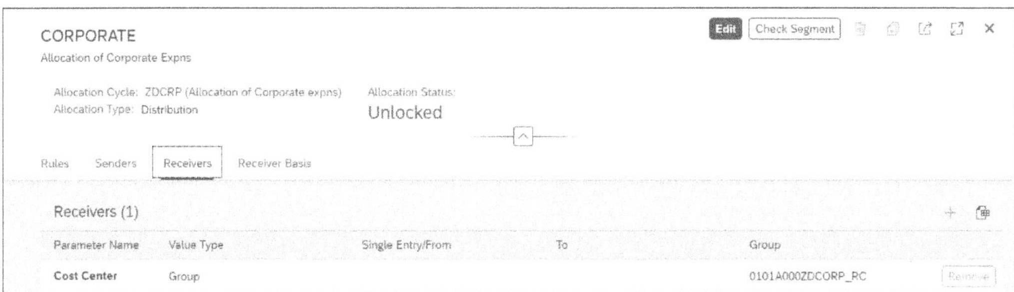


**Figure 5.31** Allocation Receivers

Figure 5.32 shows the receiver rules and the many cost centers contained in the cost center group in the previous screen. These will receive corporate overhead costs in accordance with the percentages entered here.

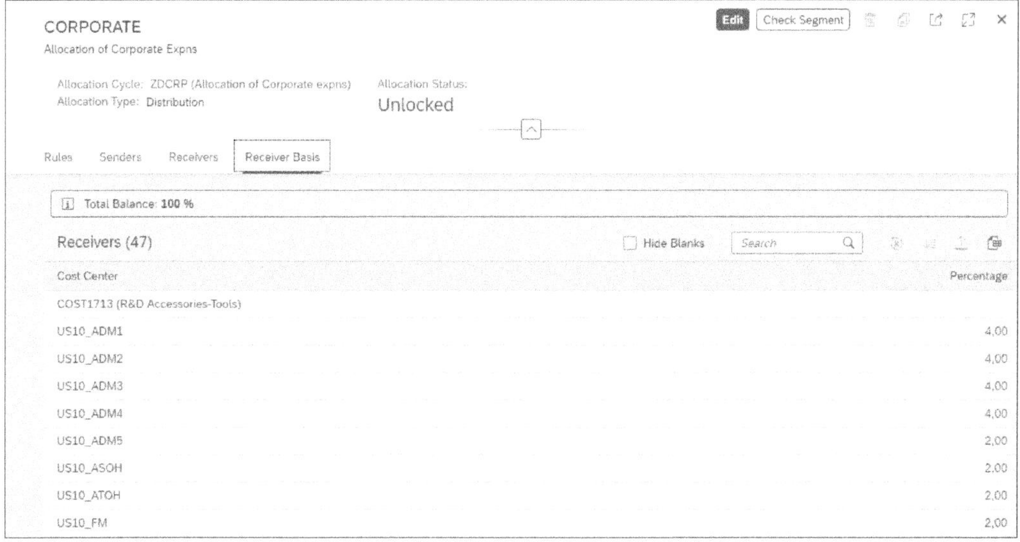


**Figure 5.32** Percentage Basis per Receiver

We've so far looked at a very simple example, in which the costs were allocated using percentages within the segment. However, the drivers for the allocations can be costs, statistical key figures (see Chapter 4, Section 4.4), or plan costs (see Section 5.3.3) instead of actuals. For this, you must change the **Var. Portion Type** from percentages (see Figure 5.29) to statistical key figures. This results in the **Receiver Basis** (see Figure 5.32) no longer containing the manual percentages but rather the link to a statistical key figure, as shown in Figure 5.33. This means that the statistical key figure entered is used to establish the ratios dynamically when the allocation is run (here, statistical key figure **1002**, square meters of floorspace) instead of relying on the figures manually entered in the cycle.

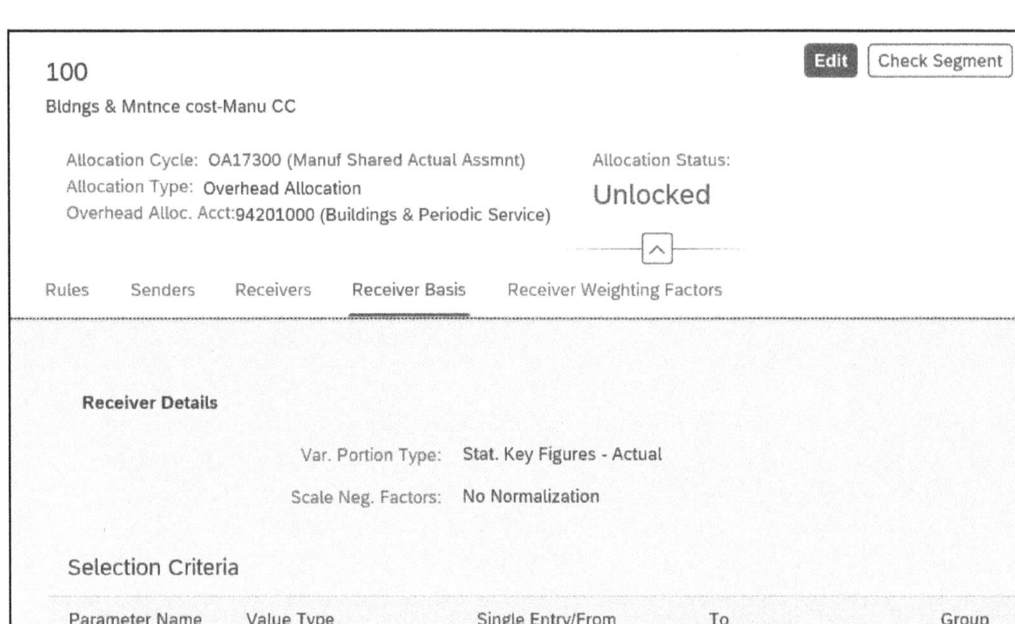


**Figure 5.33** Allocation Cycle Using Statistical Key Figures to Determine Receiver Ratios

When you allocate using percentages, the rule for the split is effectively within the allocation rule. But when you allocate based on statistical key figures, you must ensure that a figure has been entered for each cost center, either using Transaction KB31N or using the Manage Statistical Key Figure Values app (SAP Fiori ID F3915), shown in Figure 5.34. Here we've entered the number of square meters covered by each cost center as a basis for a future allocation.

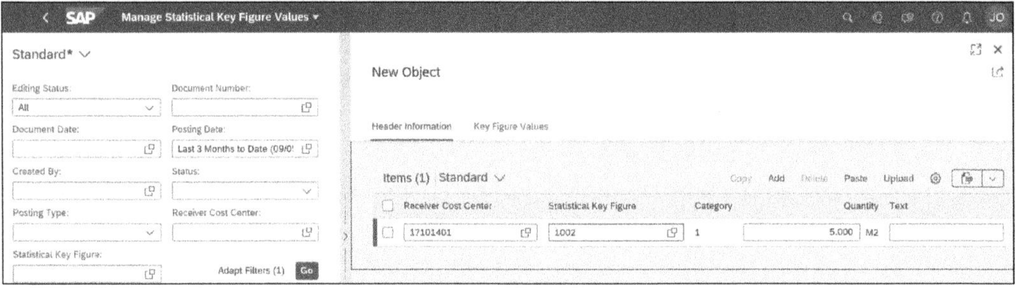


**Figure 5.34** Manage Statistical Key Figures App

If you choose to allocate using a different driver, you'll have to change the **Receiver Rule** (refer back to Figure 5.29) and then enter the appropriate **Receiver Basis** (see Figure 5.33), such as the relative costs or quantities posted to the receivers in the period. You can then add additional segments and save the whole cycle. If the allocation drivers are available, then you're ready to run your allocation.



**SAP ERP versus SAP S/4HANA**

One change in the logic between SAP ERP and SAP S/4HANA is that an allocation always takes place within one company code and one ledger. In SAP ERP, the classic transactions do not check whether the senders and receivers are in different company codes and can spread costs between any receivers in a controlling area. Where an intercompany relationship occurs, an offsetting account is updated in the affected company codes.

### Run Allocations

Now that you've established the framework for the allocation by creating a cycle, creating a segment, and entering the senders and receivers and relevant drivers within that segment, you're ready to run the allocation cycle using the Run Allocations app shown in Figure 5.35. If you're working with the legacy transactions, you can run your allocation by choosing Transaction KSU5 for an actual assessment, Transaction KSV5 for an actual distribution, Transaction KSUB for a planned assessment, or Transaction KSVB for a planned distribution.

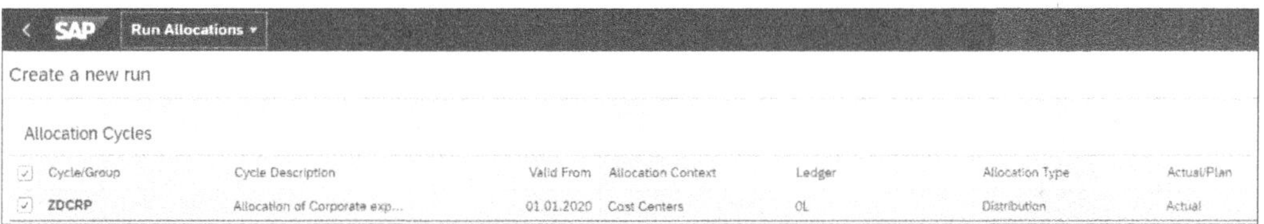


**Figure 5.35** Run Allocations App

Before you can run an allocation, you must select the allocation cycle from the list and choose **Create a new run**. Figure 5.36 shows the screen to create the run name. Here we've entered a **Run Name**, a **Journal Entry Type**, and the **Fiscal Period From** and **Fiscal Period To**. You're now ready to execute the allocation for December 2020 with reference to the run by choosing the **OK** button (not shown).

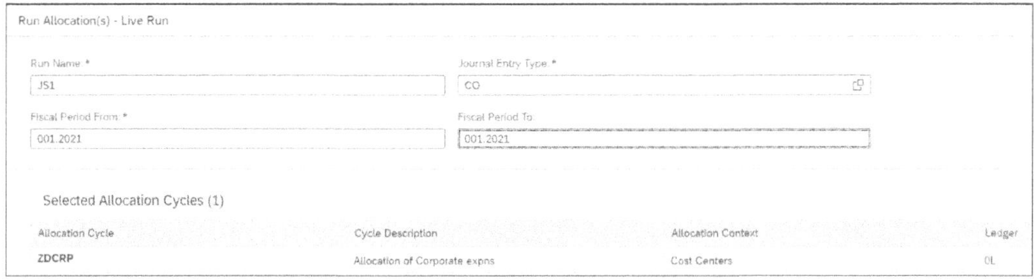


**Figure 5.36** Creating Run Name for Allocation Cycle

### Allocation Results and Flow

To check the results of the allocation, select the Allocation Result app shown in Figure 5.37. Notice that you can see allocations with multiple contexts in this screen. You can either choose **View Type Cycle** and select the cycle from Figure 5.35 or choose **Run** and select the run created in Figure 5.36 from the list.

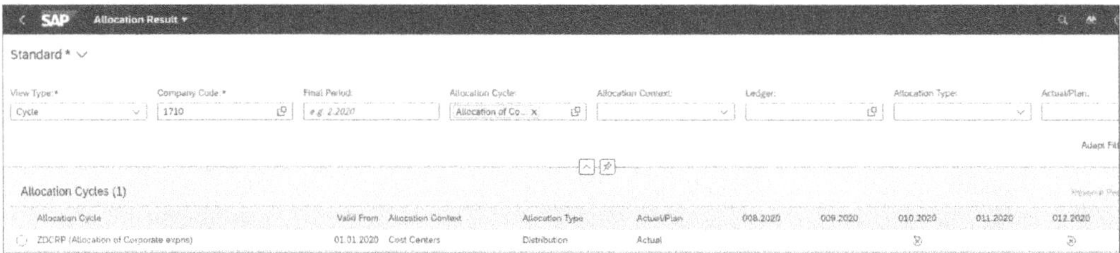

**Figure 5.37** Allocation Result App

One of the main reasons to use the new apps is the Allocation Flow app, which visualizes the flow of costs from senders to receivers, as shown in Figure 5.38. There are two ways to use this app:

1. In Figure 5.38, we've called up the Allocation Flow app directly and entered **Cost Center** "US10_M1" in the selection screen. This shows us all costs that have been allocated from or to cost center US10_M1.
2. Alternatively, you can use this app within the Allocation Result app (shown ahead in Figure 5.39), where you can switch from the traditional view that shows details of the one sender and 126 receivers in list form to a graphical list, but this is a much easier way to visualize how costs have flowed.

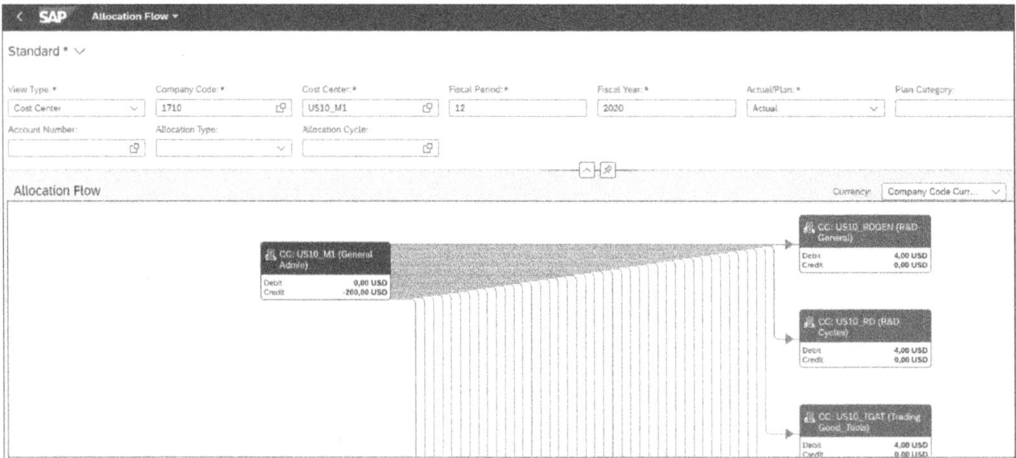

**Figure 5.38** Allocation Results: Flow

Notice also that you're only seeing the results of the simple allocation. It's common to use further allocations to move costs from these receivers to a further group of receivers in a waterfall approach, where each cost center might receive costs and send them on. The network shown here could thus extend if you executed further allocation cycles.

Finally, Figure 5.39 shows the Allocation Result app and the journal entries created as a result of the posting. Notice that this document is richer than the document created in SAP ERP in that it records not only the amounts on the senders and receivers but also details of the **Allocation Cycle**. Because the journal entries created are part of the Universal Journal, you also see the assigned profit centers, segments, and functional areas in this list. If your list looks different, click the **Settings** icon and add fields as necessary.

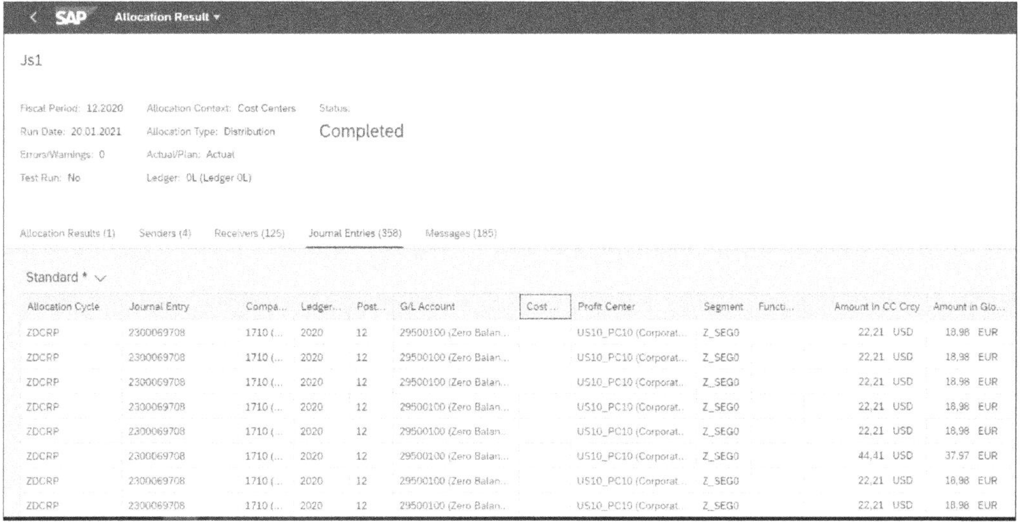


**Figure 5.39** Allocation Result: Journal Entries

### Manage Allocation Tags

As you create more and more allocation cycles, it can be difficult to find the one you need quickly. SAP S/4HANA Cloud 2011 includes a new option to create *allocation tags* to aid selection. Figure 5.40 shows the Manage Allocation Tags app, where you can create a new tag and view the existing tags. In this example, we've created the **ESI_DEMO** tag and then assigned it to the **FIN_COST**, **IT_COSTS**, **LEGAL_OH**, and **QM_COSTS** cycles.

You can then use this tag to select the associated allocation cycles as shown in Figure 5.41, where we've used the **ESI_DEMO** (Demo Webinar) tag to select the **FIN_COST** cycle for further processing.

We'll return to the topic of allocations in Chapter 7, where we'll show you how to assign overhead costs to market segments and how to perform a top-down distribution of costs to the market segments for products and customers within the framework of the universal allocation applications.

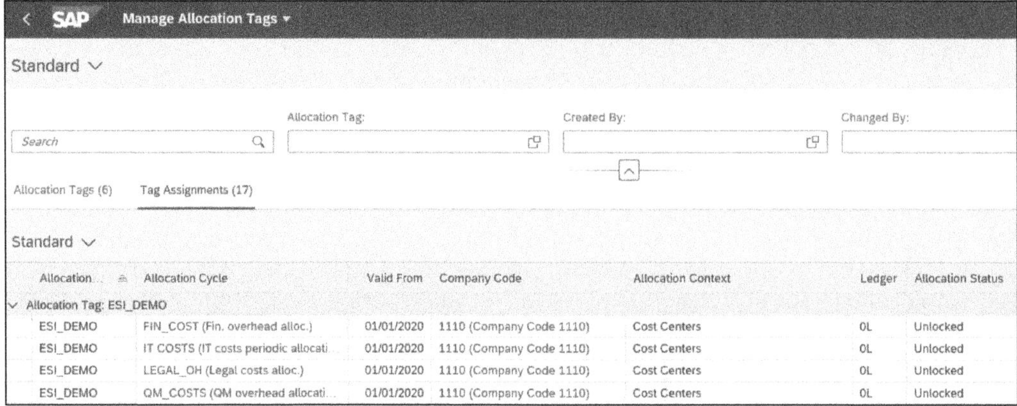


**Figure 5.40** Manage Allocation Tags App

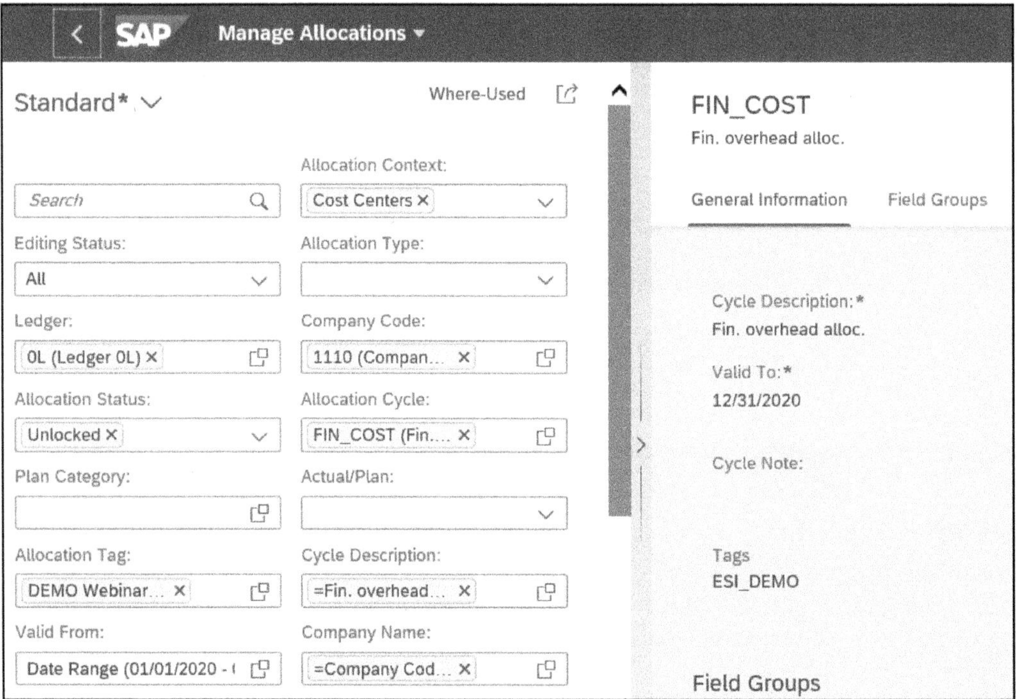


**Figure 5.41** Using Allocation Tag to Select Cycles

### 5.4.3 Activity Allocation and Cost Rates

We described the activity type master data and the relevant general ledger accounts in Chapter 4, Section 4.3, and explained the differences between direct and indirect activity allocation along with the need to calculate cost rates to charge the costs of machine time to the production line or consulting hours to a project. In terms of the involvement of the controller, the two types of activity allocation are very different:

1. **Direct activity allocations**
   *Direct activity allocations* are triggered in time recording, production, maintenance, and so on, with no involvement on the part of the controller beyond ensuring that the appropriate cost rates are available for each activity type. You'll see further examples of direct activity allocations when we look at manufacturing activities in Chapter 6 and service-related activities in Chapter 7. While direct activity allocation in manufacturing is usually triggered by order confirmations or backflush processing, direct activity allocations using time recordings require employees to fill out time sheets documenting the work that they have performed. You can also create direct activity allocations manually using Transaction KB21N or the Manage Direct Activity Allocation app.
2. **Indirect activity allocations**
   *Indirect activity allocations*, by contrast, are very much in the hands of the controller as the quantities involved are inferred rather than entered manually. These cycles make a charge based on a quantity, such as the total number of labor hours worked by a call center or the total number of kilowatt hours supplied to the production cost centers. In the first example, the total labor hours worked by the call center are entered and then spread to the various receivers, whereas in the second example the quantity of energy hours delivered to production are inferred based on the activity quantities performed by the receiver cost centers.

As we saw in planning, the cost rate can distinguish between fixed and variable costs, giving you greater transparency into the nature of the costs allocated. Both direct and indirect activity allocation will allow you to calculate the target costs and variances for your cost center, as you saw in Chapter 2 when we looked at the impact of adjusting the variable costs to reflect the actual output of the cost center. This is something that you can't do with the allocations that we looked at in the previous section, where the entire value posted to the cost centers is always transferred during the allocation, leaving a balance of zero on the cost center after the allocation. You can identify activity allocations in the Trial Balance app and similar reports by the object type **KL**, as we showed in Chapter 2, Figure 2.6.

Figure 5.42 shows the Manage Direct Activity Allocation app (SAP Fiori ID F3697), where an activity of three units has been posted from a sender cost center/activity type to a WBS element. This has resulted in journal entries in two ledgers under the **Journal Entry Type CO (Secondary Cost)** and the **Business Transaction Type RKL (Actual Activity Allocation)**. This app can be used to display direct activity allocations created manually or by using the integration with order confirmation in logistics or time sheet entry.

If your organization isn't yet using SAP Fiori, you can create a direct activity allocation by using Transaction KB21N or **Accounting • Controlling • Cost Center Accounting • Actual Postings • Activity Allocation • Enter** and choosing a screen variant containing the fields for the relevant receiver of the activity charges. You can then manually enter the cost center, activity type, quantity, and receiver of the allocation and save the allocation.

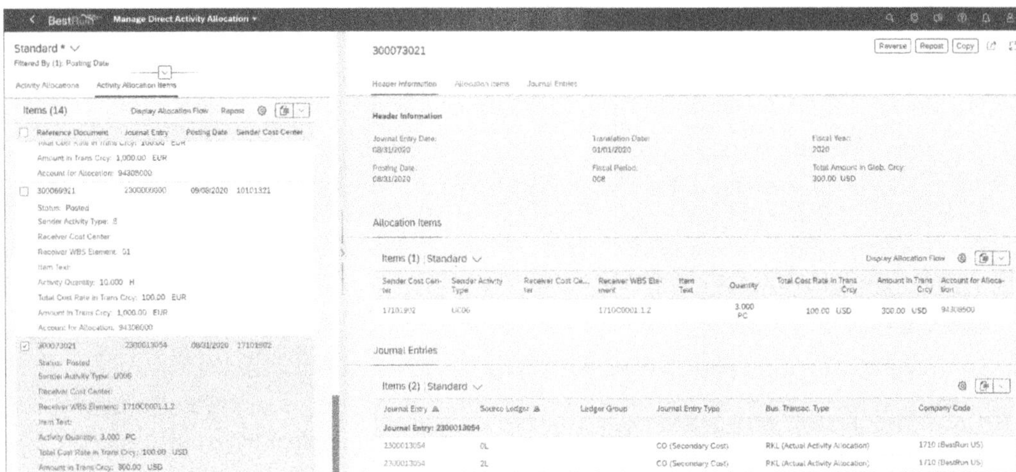

**Figure 5.42** Manage Direct Activity Allocation App

To create an indirect activity allocation cycle, use Transaction KSC1 or follow menu path **Accounting • Controlling • Cost Center Accounting • Period-End Closing • Current Settings • Define Indirect Activity Allocation**. Figure 5.43 shows the **Change Actual Indirect Activity Allocation Cycle: Segment** screen for an indirect activity allocation cycle. The main difference compared to the cycles we looked at in the previous section is that the sender rules are based on activity quantities. In the sender **Rule**, you have the following options because you are sending activity quantities rather than amounts:

- **Quantities calculated inversely**
  The **Quantities calculated inversely** option is used in combination with category 2 activity types (indirect determination, indirect allocation). The inverse calculation infers the quantity delivered by reading the quantity entered under **Receiver Tracing Factor** (in the example, this is the **Actual Activity** option) to determine how much energy has been supplied. The underlying assumption is that the more production activity the production cost centers have provided, the greater the number of kilowatt hours of energy they will have used. If the relationship between machine time and kilowatt hours of energy is not 1:1, then you need to tab to the far right and change the receiver weighting factor from 100 (the default) to a factor that better reflects your business needs.

- **Posted quantities**
  The **Posted quantities** option is used in combination with category 3 activity types (manual entry, indirect allocation). To use this option, every month you need to enter a quantity for the cost center and activity type entered in the **Senders/Receivers** tab. To enter the number of hours for the quality cost center, use Transaction KB51N

or choose **Accounting • Controlling • Cost Center Accounting • Actual Postings • Sender Activities • Enter.** Then enter the sender cost center (call center cost center), the sender activity type (call hours), and the number of hours performed in the period. The allocation then spreads the total quantity entered to the selected receivers based on whatever receiver tracing factor has been entered.

- **Fixed quantities**
  Fixed quantities are entered manually in the allocation cycle (like fixed amounts in an assessment cycle).



For each segment, you'll have to define the sender **Rule** (**Quantities calculated inversely** in this example), the **Rule** for the **Receiver Tracing Factor** (**Variable portions** in this example), and then the senders, receivers, and receiver basis just as when you created allocation cycles in the Manage Allocations app. You can then save the cycle and run the allocation once you're sure that the appropriate quantities are available for the allocation.

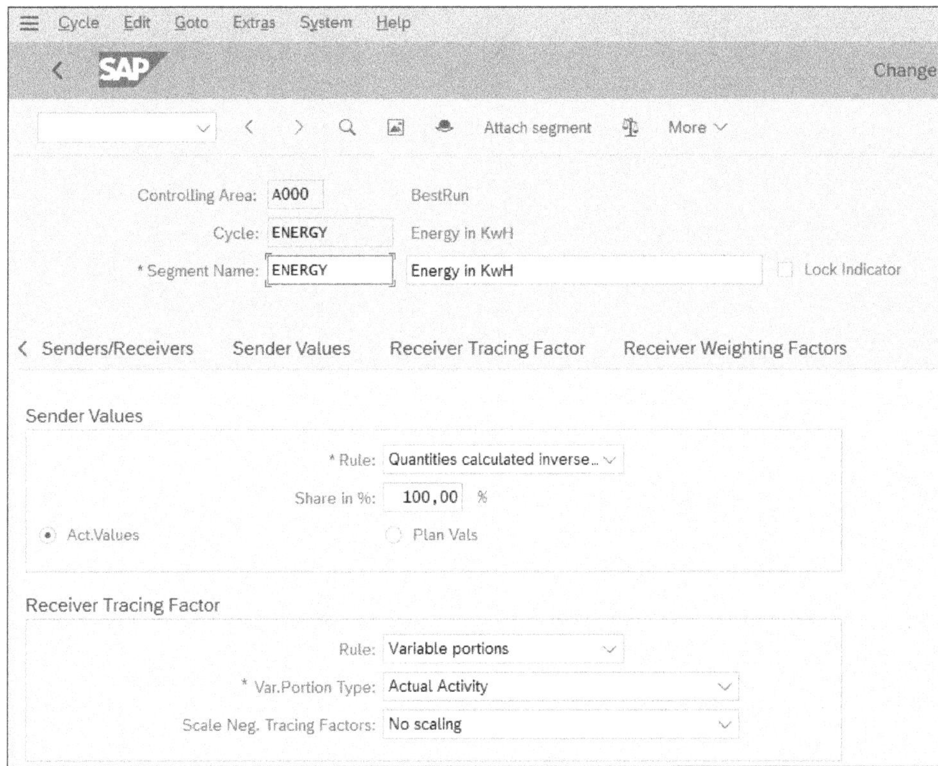


**Figure 5.43** Segment Header for Indirect Activity Allocation

To execute an indirect activity allocation cycle, follow menu path **Accounting • Controlling • Cost Center Accounting • Period-End Closing • Single Functions • Indirect Activity Allocation** or use Transaction KSC5. Enter the **Period** and **Fiscal Year** and click the

**Execute** button. Figure 5.44 shows the line items created during the indirect activity allocation. Notice that the sender is an activity (**OTy ATY**) rather than a cost center and the receivers are the production cost centers that have performed work in the period. The amounts are calculated by multiplying the number of kilowatt hours by the cost rate for one kilowatt hour. The business transaction is RKIL.

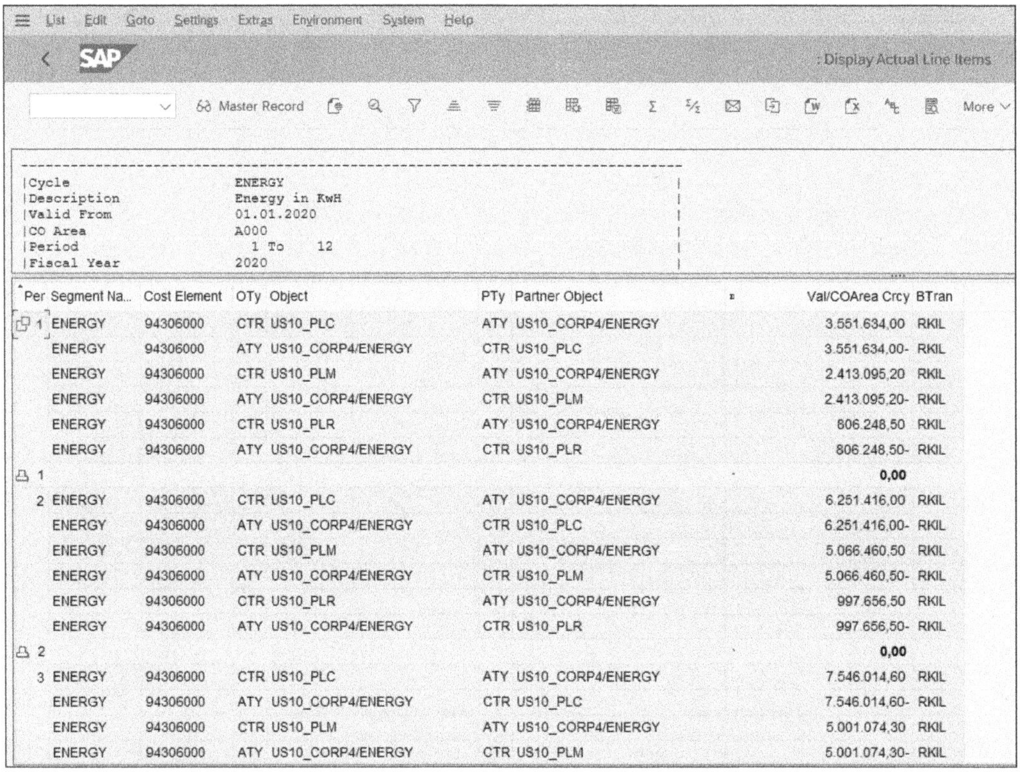

List Edit Goto Settings Extras Environment System Help

SAP : Display Actual Line Items

Master Record More

| | |
|---|---|
| Cycle | ENERGY |
| Description | Energy in KwH |
| Valid From | 01.01.2020 |
| CO Area | A000 |
| Period | 1 To 12 |
| Fiscal Year | 2020 |

| Per | Segment Na... | Cost Element | OTy | Object | PTy | Partner Object | Val/COArea Crcy | BTran |
|---|---|---|---|---|---|---|---|---|
| 1 | ENERGY | 94306000 | CTR | US10_PLC | ATY | US10_CORP4/ENERGY | 3.551.634,00 | RKIL |
| | ENERGY | 94306000 | ATY | US10_CORP4/ENERGY | CTR | US10_PLC | 3.551.634,00- | RKIL |
| | ENERGY | 94306000 | CTR | US10_PLM | ATY | US10_CORP4/ENERGY | 2.413.095,20 | RKIL |
| | ENERGY | 94306000 | ATY | US10_CORP4/ENERGY | CTR | US10_PLM | 2.413.095,20- | RKIL |
| | ENERGY | 94306000 | CTR | US10_PLR | ATY | US10_CORP4/ENERGY | 806.248,50 | RKIL |
| | ENERGY | 94306000 | ATY | US10_CORP4/ENERGY | CTR | US10_PLR | 806.248,50- | RKIL |
| 1 | | | | | | | **0,00** | |
| 2 | ENERGY | 94306000 | CTR | US10_PLC | ATY | US10_CORP4/ENERGY | 6.251.416,00 | RKIL |
| | ENERGY | 94306000 | ATY | US10_CORP4/ENERGY | CTR | US10_PLC | 6.251.416,00- | RKIL |
| | ENERGY | 94306000 | CTR | US10_PLM | ATY | US10_CORP4/ENERGY | 5.066.460,50 | RKIL |
| | ENERGY | 94306000 | ATY | US10_CORP4/ENERGY | CTR | US10_PLM | 5.066.460,50- | RKIL |
| | ENERGY | 94306000 | CTR | US10_PLR | ATY | US10_CORP4/ENERGY | 997.656,50 | RKIL |
| | ENERGY | 94306000 | ATY | US10_CORP4/ENERGY | CTR | US10_PLR | 997.656,50- | RKIL |
| 2 | | | | | | | **0,00** | |
| 3 | ENERGY | 94306000 | CTR | US10_PLC | ATY | US10_CORP4/ENERGY | 7.546.014,60 | RKIL |
| | ENERGY | 94306000 | ATY | US10_CORP4/ENERGY | CTR | US10_PLC | 7.546.014,60- | RKIL |
| | ENERGY | 94306000 | CTR | US10_PLM | ATY | US10_CORP4/ENERGY | 5.001.074,30 | RKIL |
| | ENERGY | 94306000 | ATY | US10_CORP4/ENERGY | CTR | US10_PLM | 5.001.074,30- | RKIL |

**Figure 5.44** Line Items Resulting from Execution of Indirect Activity Allocation Cycle

Both direct and indirect activity allocations use the planned cost rate initially. In the case of the direct activity allocations that are happening throughout the period, it's clear that you can't know all the cost center costs at the time of the allocation. In the case of the indirect activity allocation, you're using the cycle to determine the quantity flow first.

Once the period is completed, you can calculate a new cost rate that reflects the actual costs and output of the period. To execute activity price calculation, follow menu path **Accounting • Controlling • Cost Center Accounting • Period-End Closing • Single Functions • Price Calculation** or use Transaction KSII. Figure 5.45 shows the result of the activity price calculation with the total quantity, the actual costs, and the fixed part of those costs. These values can be used to revalue inventories and cost of goods sold as part of the actual costing process that we'll explain in Chapter 6.

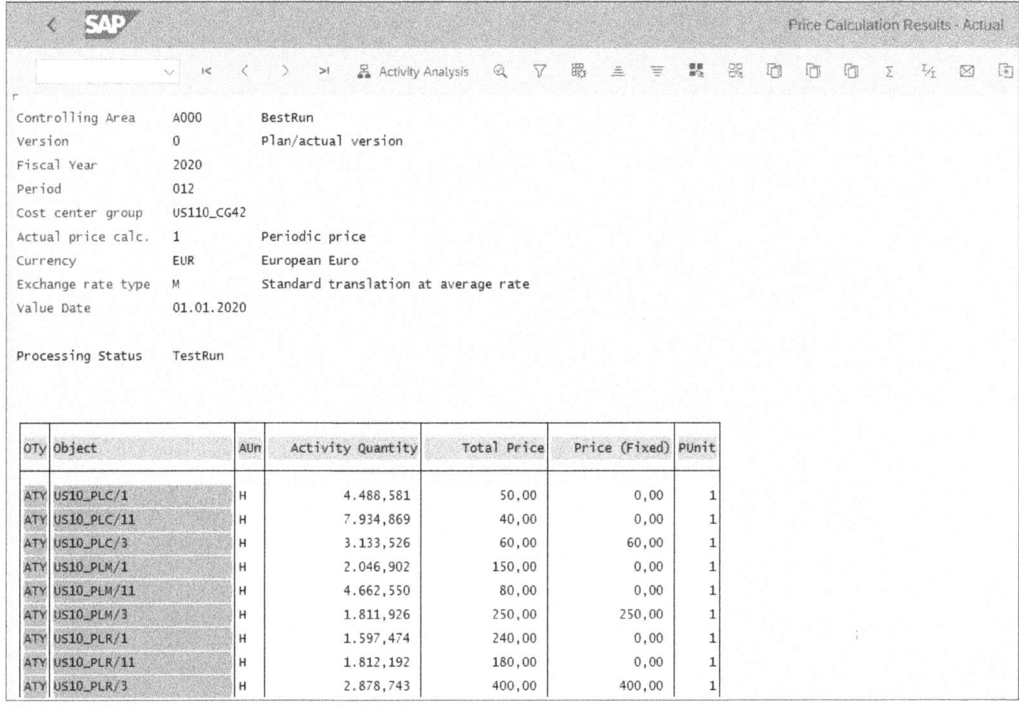


| OTy | Object | AUn | Activity Quantity | Total Price | Price (Fixed) | PUnit |
|---|---|---|---|---|---|---|
| ATY | US10_PLC/1 | H | 4.488,581 | 50,00 | 0,00 | 1 |
| ATY | US10_PLC/11 | H | 7.934,869 | 40,00 | 0,00 | 1 |
| ATY | US10_PLC/3 | H | 3.133,526 | 60,00 | 60,00 | 1 |
| ATY | US10_PLM/1 | H | 2.046,902 | 150,00 | 0,00 | 1 |
| ATY | US10_PLM/11 | H | 4.662,550 | 80,00 | 0,00 | 1 |
| ATY | US10_PLM/3 | H | 1.811,926 | 250,00 | 250,00 | 1 |
| ATY | US10_PLR/1 | H | 1.597,474 | 240,00 | 0,00 | 1 |
| ATY | US10_PLR/11 | H | 1.812,192 | 180,00 | 0,00 | 1 |
| ATY | US10_PLR/3 | H | 2.878,743 | 400,00 | 400,00 | 1 |

**Figure 5.45** Result of Activity Price Calculation

You can also assign the new activity prices to your production orders, process orders, projects, and so on using Transaction CON2 or the **Revaluate at Actual Prices** function that you'll find in every menu for the period close in cost object controlling.

> **Note**
>
> Indirect activity allocation and the revaluation at actual prices function are not available in SAP S/4HANA Cloud.

### 5.4.4 Overhead Calculation

The purpose of overhead calculation is to charge the costs from the cost center to the orders or projects based on a percentage, so you might assign the warehousing costs to a production order based on the underlying material costs. The *costing sheet* determines how the overhead will be applied and covers the following:

- The basis for the calculation (e.g., all relevant raw material costs)
- The conditions under which overhead is applied (e.g., within a particular plant or when manufacturing a particular material)
- The percentage to be applied (e.g., 10% on all raw material costs)
- The cost center that's the sender of the charge (e.g., the warehouse cost center)

To perform an allocation based on overhead calculation, you'll need to enter a costing sheet in the master data for the receiver object, as shown in Figure 5.46, which shows the production order header and the **Costing Sheet 1710PP** (we'll return to this example in Chapter 6). Normally this is defaulted using the settings for the order type (or the project type if you're working with WBS elements). To check the settings for your production order, choose Transaction CO02, enter the **Order** number and the **Plant**, and navigate to the **Control** tab. In this example, **Overhead key** is blank, but the overhead key can be used to calculate material-specific overheads by linking the overhead key with the overhead group in the material master. We'll explain these links in more detail when we look at the master data for production in Chapter 6.

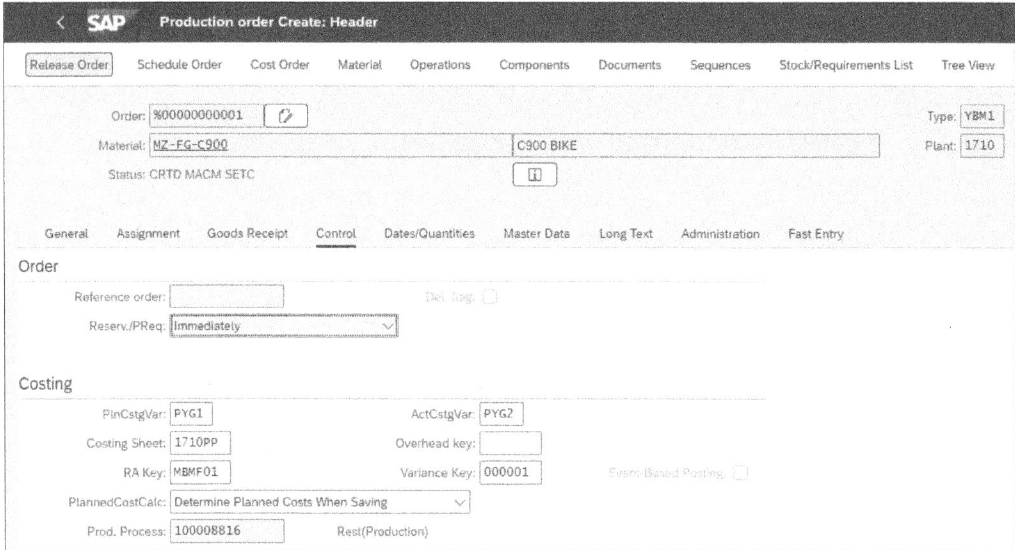


**Figure 5.46** Control Parameters for Production Order

There are two options to calculate overhead according to the costing sheet. The traditional approach has always been to calculate overhead at period close, but you can see a new flag, **Event-Based Posting**, in the control settings for the production order. If this flag is set, then the overhead will be calculated along with the related goods issues and order confirmations rather than at period close. This has the advantage that you will see your overhead costs immediately, but it will generally result in more posting documents as you'll potentially be creating a follow-on document for every goods movement and confirmation, depending on the settings in your costing sheet.

In this example, we're calculating overhead the classic way by using Transaction KGI2 or **Accounting • Controlling • Product Cost Controlling • Period-End Closing • Product Cost by Order • Overhead Calculation • Individual Processing** and entering the order number, the period, and the fiscal year. To access the results shown in Figure 5.47, choose **Dialog Display** and press [Enter]. Here we've applied a 7% material overhead and a 10% production overhead. To see the link between the costing sheet shown in

Figure 5.46 and the conditions used in Figure 5.47, choose the **Analysis** button. Figure 5.48 shows the analysis of the overhead conditions.

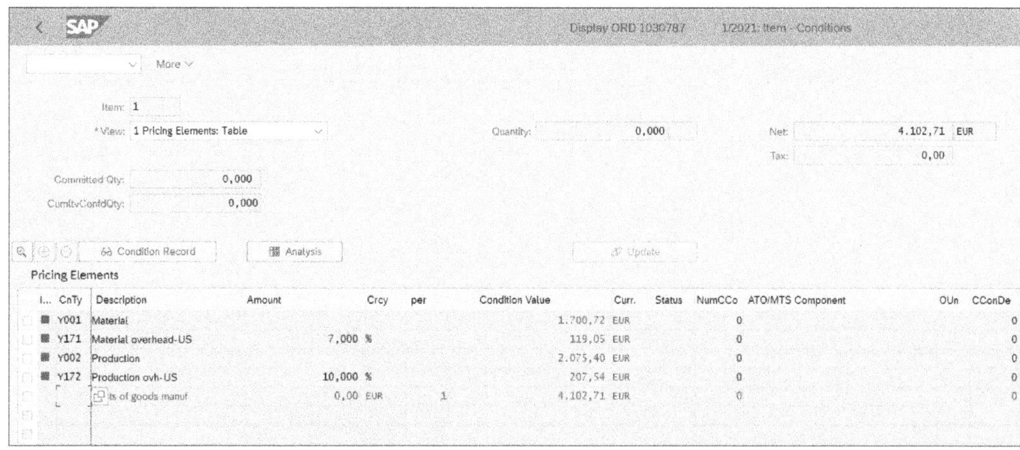

**Figure 5.47** Overhead Calculation for Production Order

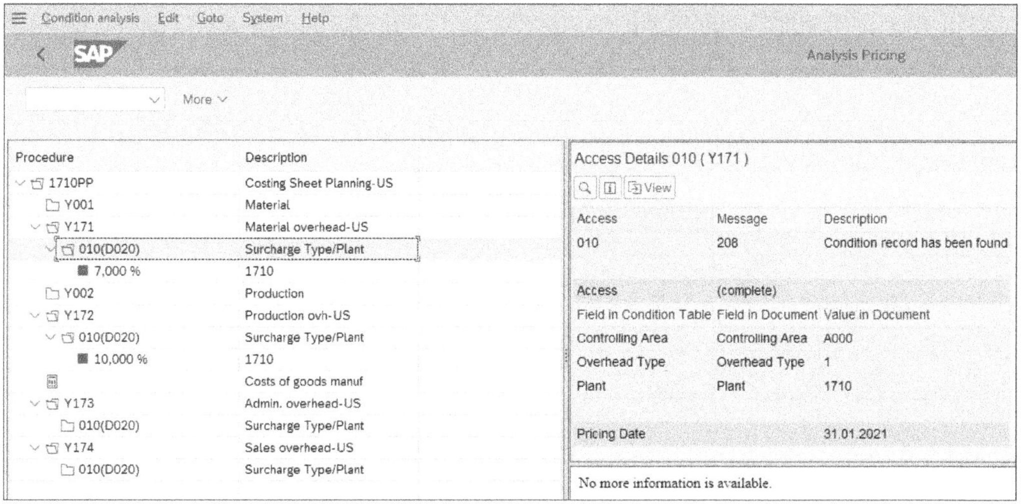

**Figure 5.48** Details of Costing Sheet for Production Order

If you now use Transaction KKBC_ORD to look at the costs for the production order in Figure 5.49, you can see postings for the raw material and the associated material overhead and postings for the confirmations (direct activity allocation) and for the production overhead. This has resulted in postings to the cost center **17101201** and the cost center **17101301**, as shown in the **Origin** column for material overhead and production overhead.

This isn't the only way to calculate overhead. It's also possible to assign quantity-based overhead and allocate overhead based on the quantity of raw material consumed or the quantity of activity confirmed. The costing sheet still controls the process, but instead of entering a percentage you enter a quantity as the condition for the overhead calculation.

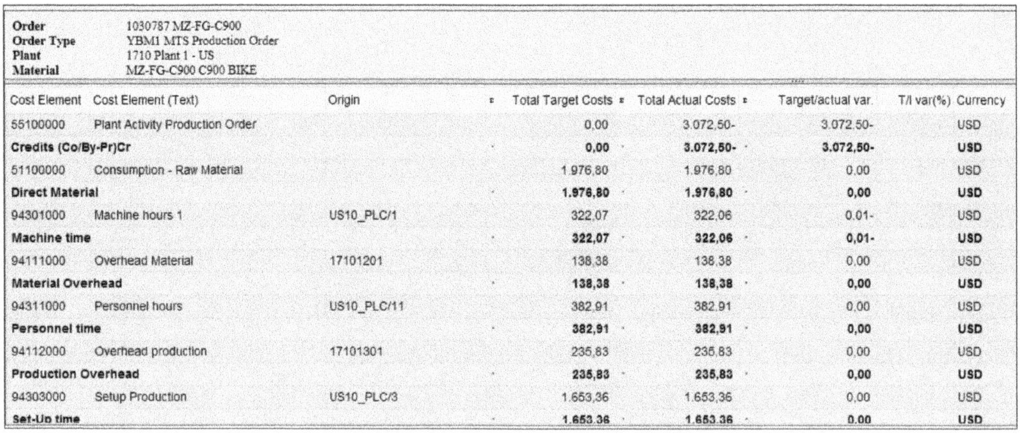

| | |
|---|---|
| **Order** | 1030787 MZ-FG-C900 |
| **Order Type** | YBM1 MTS Production Order |
| **Plant** | 1710 Plant 1 - US |
| **Material** | MZ-FG-C900 C900 BIKE |

| Cost Element | Cost Element (Text) | Origin | Total Target Costs | Total Actual Costs | Target/actual var. | T/I var(%) | Currency |
|---|---|---|---|---|---|---|---|
| 55100000 | Plant Activity Production Order | | 0,00 | 3.072,50- | 3.072,50- | | USD |
| **Credits (Co/By-Pr)Cr** | | | **0,00** | **3.072,50-** | **3.072,50-** | | **USD** |
| 51100000 | Consumption - Raw Material | | 1.976,80 | 1.976,80 | 0,00 | | USD |
| **Direct Material** | | | **1.976,80** | **1.976,80** | **0,00** | | **USD** |
| 94301000 | Machine hours 1 | US10_PLC/1 | 322,07 | 322,06 | 0,01- | | USD |
| **Machine time** | | | **322,07** | **322,06** | **0,01-** | | **USD** |
| 94111000 | Overhead Material | 17101201 | 138,38 | 138,38 | 0,00 | | USD |
| **Material Overhead** | | | **138,38** | **138,38** | **0,00** | | **USD** |
| 94311000 | Personnel hours | US10_PLC/11 | 382,91 | 382,91 | 0,00 | | USD |
| **Personnel time** | | | **382,91** | **382,91** | **0,00** | | **USD** |
| 94112000 | Overhead production | 17101301 | 235,83 | 235,83 | 0,00 | | USD |
| **Production Overhead** | | | **235,83** | **235,83** | **0,00** | | **USD** |
| 94303000 | Setup Production | US10_PLC/3 | 1.653,36 | 1.653,36 | 0,00 | | USD |
| **Set-Up time** | | | **1.653,36** | **1.653,36** | **0,00** | | **USD** |

**Figure 5.49** Costs for Production Order

### 5.4.5 Template Allocation

If you think the overhead methods described in the previous section are too simplistic for your business needs or you're having trouble calculating a percentage that will result in all costs being charged from the sending cost center to the receivers, consider using template allocation for some of your overhead. This will allow you to calculate overhead using more complex drivers and to clear all costs on the cost center at the end of the period (a legal requirement in some parts of the world).

Probably the most common usage of a template is shown in Figure 5.50, where we've specified that one unit of order processing and one unit of sales order processing should be associated with each production order. This type of template is often used to set up a quality check for every production order rather than having a dedicated operation within the routing. To create a template, use Transaction CPT1 or **Accounting • Controlling • Product Cost Controlling • Period-End Closing • Product Cost by Order • Template Allocation • Individual Processing**, then select **Extras • Template • Create**. Give your template a name and select the relevant environment (**001** in this example). The functions offered in the template depend on the environment. A number of environments are available depending on the affected object, as shown in Table 5.1.

| Environment | Object |
|---|---|
| 001 | Cost estimate/production order |
| 004 | Network |
| 005 | WBS element |

**Table 5.1** Template Environments

| Environment | Object |
|---|---|
| 007 | Internal order |
| 008 | Sales order |
| 009 | Process order |
| 010 | Product cost collector |

**Table 5.1** Template Environments (Cont.)

At period close, you can run template allocation for production orders using Transaction CPTA or **Accounting • Controlling • Product Cost Controlling • Period-End Closing • Product Cost by Order • Template Allocation • Individual Processing**. With the template shown in the example, the resulting allocation will assign one unit of order processing and one unit of sales order processing to the production orders.

**Change template 001 / COPC-10-1**

Hide editor

Template COPC-10-1 Order Processing - COGS

Environment 001 Cost estimate/production orders

Template overview : change

| Type | Description | Object | Unit | Plan quantity | Plan fix | Plan activat... | Actual qua... | Actual fix | Actual activ... | Actual alloc... |
|---|---|---|---|---|---|---|---|---|---|---|
| Subtemplate | Order Processing - Production | COPC-10 | | | | ACTIVE | | | INACTIVE | |
| Business Process | Sales order proc. | 400900 | PC | 1 | | ACTIVE | | | INACTIVE | |

**Figure 5.50** Template for Work Scheduling and Order Processing Costs

It's also possible to be more sophisticated and set up Boolean logic to determine whether the cost assignment will take place and to work with functions that read the number of work center changes to determine transport costs or the number of different bill of materials (BOM) items. Figure 5.51 shows some of the quantity functions delivered for use within the template in the production environment. To access this screen, position the cursor on the **Actual qua...** column in Figure 5.50 and double-click.

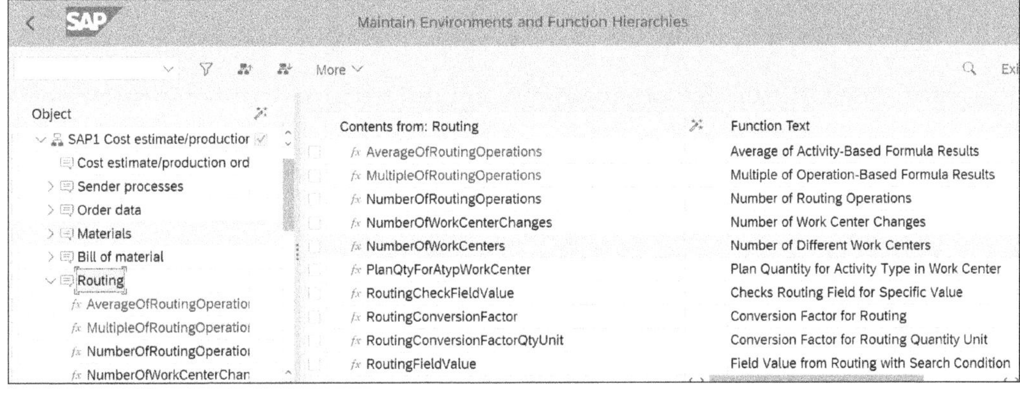


**Figure 5.51** Template: Quantity Calculation Functions

This might look complicated, but it's just a more dynamic way of triggering a direct activity allocation that doesn't tie you down to having people fill out time sheets or rely on the operations in the routing. In terms of the cost posting, the result of a template allocation looks exactly like a direct activity allocation, performed either for the combination of cost center and activity type or for a business process.

### 5.4.6 Settlement

We introduced internal orders and projects in Chapter 4, Section 4.5. When you've collected costs for orders and projects, a *settlement* is used to move these costs from the sender object to the relevant receiver. Before we look at settlements in detail, it makes sense to recall Chapter 4, Section 4.5.1 and Section 4.5.2 and the various order and project types used in your organization as this will affect how they are settled. These are the general rules, but of course there are always exceptions:

- Overhead orders/projects settle to cost centers or market segments.
- Production orders settle to inventory and any variances to market segments (see Chapter 6).
- Maintenance orders/projects settle to cost centers or projects (see Chapter 6).
- Commercial projects settle to market segments (see Chapter 7).
- Investment projects settle to fixed assets or assets under construction (see Chapter 8).

Before you can perform settlement, you need to define a settlement rule to determine the receivers of the costs. The settlement rule can never be created in isolation but is always associated with the order or project for which costs are to be settled.

In Figure 5.52, we've selected the **ALPHA-6** WBS element using Transaction CJ20N and navigated to the settlement rule using **More • Edit • Costs • Settlement Rule**. When working with projects, it's common to settle to multiple receivers—as shown here, where 90% of the costs are to be settled to the responsible cost center **10101501** (the first distribution rule) and the remaining 10% of costs are to be settled to cost center **10101601** (the second distribution rule). You can add additional distribution rules with further receivers as required, but the total percentage must add up to 100%. Notice also that the settlement rule is **PER** (periodic), meaning that settlement will be carried out at the end of every accounting period. Production orders, by contrast, normally use full settlement (**FUL**) to settle all costs on the order to inventory when the order is complete.

Settlement rules can be created automatically, as is the case with production orders, manually (as here), or by configuring a strategy to generate rules in accordance with your configuration settings. While the distribution rules associated with the settlement rule might be different for every object to be settled, the default parameters controlling settlement are defined in a settlement profile for each order type/project type to ensure consistency. You can display the settlement profile by choosing **More • Goto • Settlement Parameters**. This determines the following:

- **The types of receivers allowed**
  In the preceding example, we're settling to category **CTR** (cost center), but you might also settle project costs to an asset (as we'll show in Chapter 8) or a market segment (as we'll show in Chapter 7).
- **The type of split allowed**
  In the preceding example, we're settling percentages, but you can also define the split in terms of equivalence numbers or even enter quantities manually.
- **The validity period of the distribution rule**
  This is useful if the project lifecycle covers a long time period in which certain receivers may cease to be valid.

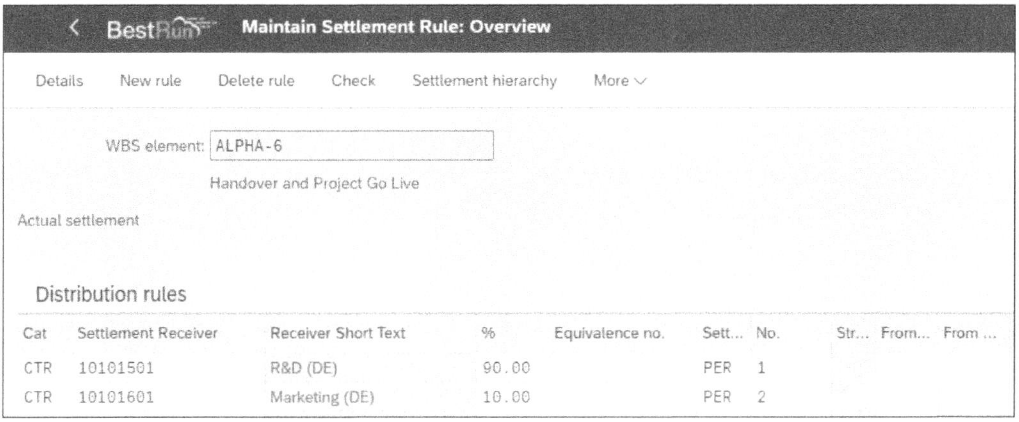

BestRun Maintain Settlement Rule: Overview

Details New rule Delete rule Check Settlement hierarchy More

WBS element: ALPHA-6

Handover and Project Go Live

Actual settlement

Distribution rules

| Cat | Settlement Receiver | Receiver Short Text | % | Equivalence no. | Sett... | No. | Str... | From... | From ... |
|---|---|---|---|---|---|---|---|---|---|
| CTR | 10101501 | R&D (DE) | 90.00 | | PER | 1 | | | |
| CTR | 10101601 | Marketing (DE) | 10.00 | | PER | 2 | | | |

**Figure 5.52** Settlement Rule for WBS Element

The settlement profile links in turn with an allocation structure. Before you can settle, you'll also need to make sure that all the general ledger accounts/cost elements posted to the sender are assigned to a source within the allocation structure and to define a settlement cost element (see Chapter 4, Section 4.1.3) for each receiver type. This is typically a configuration activity to ensure consistency. Figure 5.53 shows that the material costs on the project can settle to fixed assets (**FXA**) and other projects (**WBS**). The settlement cost element has a different category depending on whether the receiver is external (assets, general ledger account), where the cost element category is 22 for external settlement, or internal (cost center, order, WBS element, market segment), where the cost element category is 21 for internal settlement. This settlement cost element will be used to credit the sender and debit the receiver under business transaction KOAO if the receiver is a controlling object (internal) and KOAE if the receiver is a fixed asset or a material (external).

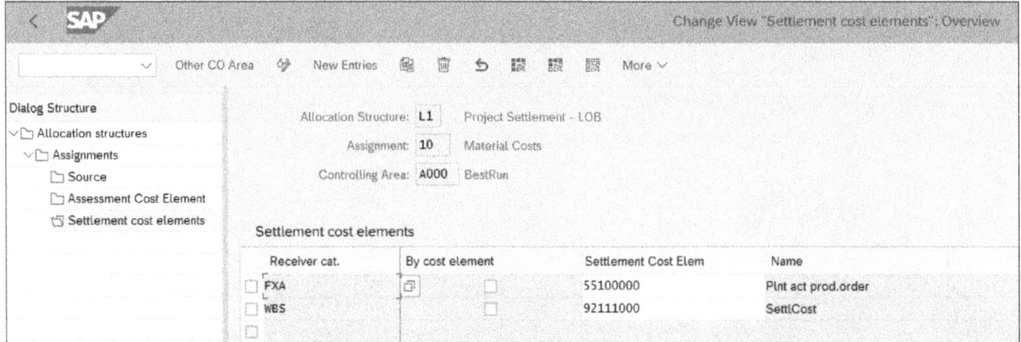


**Figure 5.53** Change Settlement Cost Elements

To avoid errors, many organizations set up strategies to generate settlement rules with the appropriate receivers automatically. Where there is a link between a field in the project, such as the requesting cost center or responsible cost center, then you can create strategies to settle to the relevant field, such as the requesting cost center or the responsible cost center, or to derive the settlement rule from the project definition or superior WBS element. Figure 5.54 shows sample strategies for the automatic generation of settlement rules for two types of projects. You can check the strategy in the IMG via **Project Systems • Costs • Automatic and Periodic Allocations • Settlement • Settlement Rule for Work Breakdown Structure Element • Determine Strategy for Settlement Rule.**

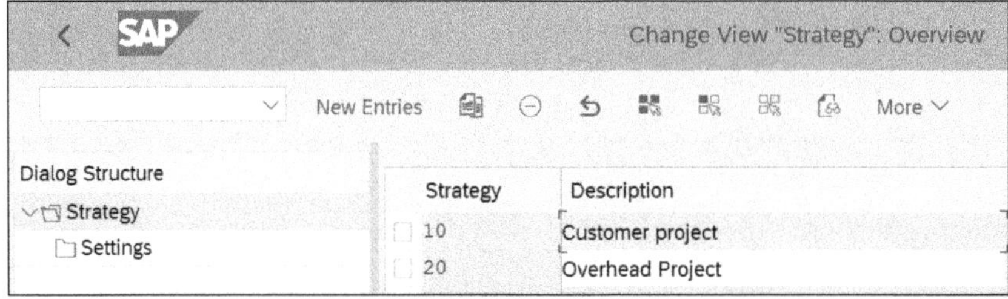


**Figure 5.54** Sample Strategies for Generation of Settlement Rules

These are then assigned to the order type or project profile. Figure 5.55 shows the controlling settings for a project profile, including the link to the default settlement profile and the settlement rule strategy **10**. You can check these settings from the IMG by going to **Project Systems • Operative Structures • Work Breakdown Structure (WBS) • Create Project Profile** and choosing the relevant project profile. Notice also the link to the costing sheet used to calculate overheads in Section 5.4.4.

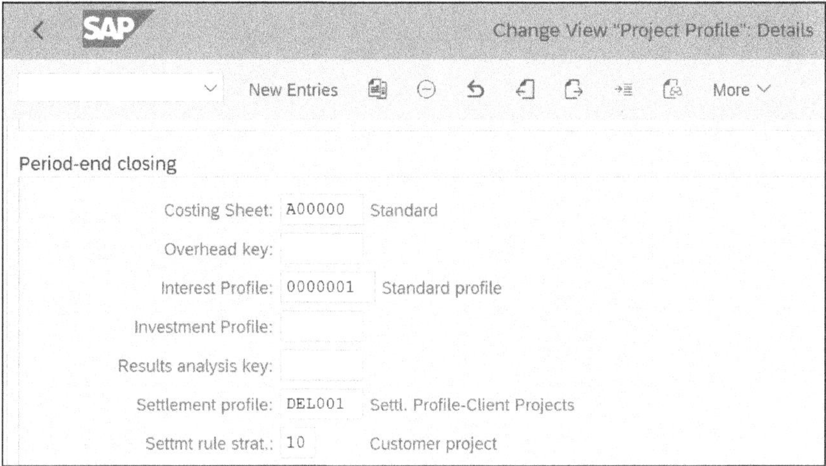


**Figure 5.55** Project Profile Showing Link to Settlement Rule Strategy

We'll come back to the topic of settlement to explain additional settlement functions used in the context of capital expenses in Chapter 8.

## 5.5 Reporting for Overhead Controlling

We already introduced some of the key reports for overhead controlling, but we'll end the chapter by showing you how to use some of the standard reports to check the flow of costs within overhead controlling. The idea is to ensure that the costs of all the supporting cost centers have flowed to the operational cost centers using distribution or assessment. From there, the costs will have flowed as activities or as overhead into production or services. Where costs have been assigned to orders and projects, settlement moves them to the next receiver. To this extent, the focus in reporting is showing that all close tasks have run and all cost centers have a balance of zero at the end of the month.

As a controller, it's important to know which business transactions have been carried out in your area. Figure 5.56 shows the Display Line Items app and the line items created as a result of the universal allocation example that we looked at in Section 5.4.2. By selecting **Bus. Transac. Type** (business transaction type) ACAD, you can view all line items associated with a distribution, and ACAA lets you see all line items associated with an overhead allocation. Alternatively, if you use the classic transactions, you'll be able to recognize the relevant flows using Transaction RKIU for assessment, Transaction RKIV for distribution, Transaction RKIL for indirect activity allocation, and Transaction RKIB for reposting. Notice that the net result is zero as costs have simply been shifted between cost centers as a result of the allocation.

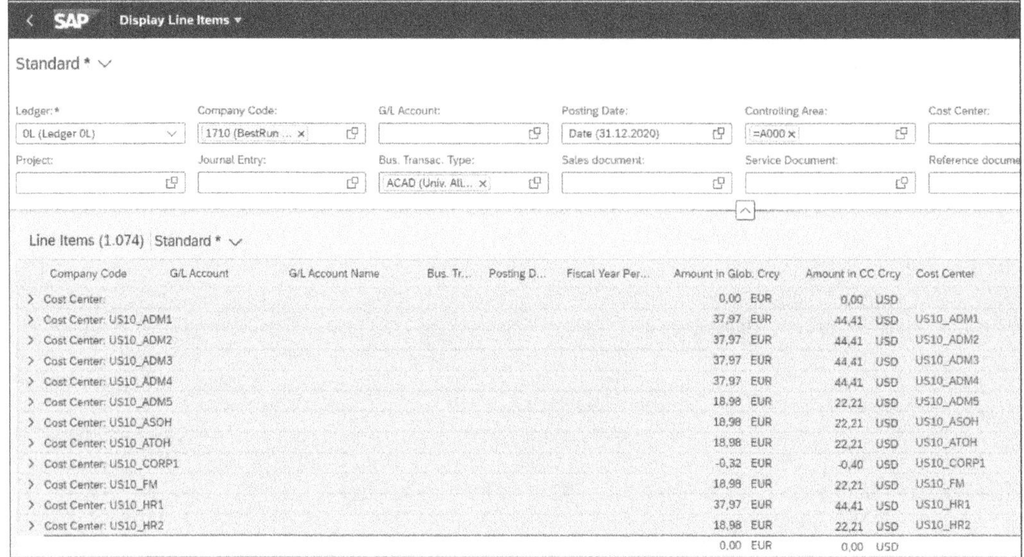

**Figure 5.56** Display Line Items, Showing Results of Universal Allocation

Figure 5.57 shows the Cost Centers—Actuals app (SAP Fiori ID F0940A), where we've selected the same business transaction, ACAD. We've run the allocations, resulting in the total value for all cost centers being zero, with credit postings to the corporate cost centers and debit postings to the operational cost centers for finance and administration, marketing, and production operations.

| Cost Center | Cost Center | Motor Veh-Dep.Exp 64004000 Amt in CO Area Crcy | Quantity | Payroll Other Exp 61010000 Amt in CO Area Crcy | Quantity | Trav.Expense Hotel 61003000 Amt in CO Area Crcy | Quantity | Total | Total | Grand Total |
|---|---|---|---|---|---|---|---|---|---|---|
| A0000001 | Standard Hierachy Be | 122,19 EUR | 0 | -135,35 EUR | 0 | 33,81 EUR | 0 | 20,65 EUR | 0 | 20,65 EUR |
| A000US000 | Velotics Bike Compan | 122,19 EUR | 0 | -135,35 EUR | 0 | 33,81 EUR | 0 | 20,65 EUR | 0 | 20,65 EUR |
| A000US000_CG10 | All Cost Centers | 122,19 EUR | 0 | -135,35 EUR | 0 | 33,81 EUR | 0 | 20,65 EUR | 0 | 20,65 EUR |
| A000US110_CG1 | Corporate | | | -169,16 EUR | 0 | | | -169,16 EUR | 0 | -169,16 EUR |
| A000US110_CG2 | Finance and Administ | 24,43 EUR | 0 | 6,77 EUR | 0 | 6,77 EUR | 0 | 37,97 EUR | 0 | 37,97 EUR |
| A000US110_CG3 | Marketing | 12,22 EUR | 0 | 3,38 EUR | 0 | 3,38 EUR | 0 | 18,98 EUR | 0 | 18,98 EUR |
| A000US110_CG4 | Production Operation | 85,54 EUR | 0 | 23,66 EUR | 0 | 23,66 EUR | 0 | 132,86 EUR | 0 | 132,86 EUR |



**Figure 5.57** Cost Center Report, Showing Result of Allocation

Where an allocation is made based on an activity price, it's important to check the activity price calculated at period close. To do this, use Transaction KSBT or **Accounting • Controlling • Cost Center Accounting • Information System • Reports for Cost Center Accounting • Prices • Cost Centers: Activity Prices**, as shown in Figure 5.58, to check the results of activity price calculation.

In addition to checking the status of the various cost centers at period close, it's also important to check the orders and projects. Again, you can use the line item report, but focus this time on business transaction RKL for direct activity allocations, business transaction category KOAO for settlement to other controlling objects, and business transaction KOAE for settlement to inventory and assets. Figure 5.59 shows all line items for project TM2102INT01, and you can see the activity allocations (**RKL**) from various cost centers and the settlement documents (**KOAO**) to various cost centers.

Activity Type Price Report: Overview Screen

| | |
|---|---|
| **Cost Center** | |
| **Activity Type** | |
| **Version** | 0 Plan/actual version |
| **Fiscal Year** | 2020 |
| **Period** | 1 To 12 |
| **Price unit** | 1 |

| Cost Center | Acty Type | Cost ctr short text | Act. type short text | CO cr... | Total Price | Price (Variabl... | Price (Fixed) | PrI |
|---|---|---|---|---|---|---|---|---|
| 1301 | ML-112 | Settl. Receiver | SP: Test Consultant | EUR | 200,00 | 0,00 | 200,00 | 1 |
| | YQ20 | Settl. Receiver | Q-Laboratory | EUR | 10,00 | 0,00 | 10,00 | 1 |
| | YQ21 | Settl. Receiver | IPC | EUR | 0,00 | 0,00 | 0,00 | 1 |
| | YQ22 | Settl. Receiver | PPC Production | EUR | 0,00 | 0,00 | 0,00 | 1 |
| 10101301 | 1 | Manufacturing 1 (DE) | Machine hours 1 | EUR | 27,50 | 9,17 | 18,33 | 1 |
| | 11 | Manufacturing 1 (DE) | Personnel Hours | EUR | 32,08 | 32,08 | 0,00 | 1 |
| | 2 | Manufacturing 1 (DE) | Machine hours 2 | EUR | 64,17 | 9,17 | 55,00 | 1 |
| | 3 | Manufacturing 1 (DE) | Setup Production | EUR | 27,50 | 27,50 | 0,00 | 1 |
| 10101701 | 11 | Plant & Maint (DE) | Personnel Hours | EUR | 10,00 | 10,00 | 0,00 | 1 |
| 11101301 | 1 | Manuf 1 (GB) | Machine hours 1 | EUR | 30,00 | 10,00 | 20,00 | 1 |
| | 11 | Manuf 1 (GB) | Personnel Hours | EUR | 35,00 | 35,00 | 0,00 | 1 |
| | 2 | Manuf 1 (GB) | Machine hours 2 | EUR | 70,00 | 10,00 | 60,00 | 1 |
| | 3 | Manuf 1 (GB) | Setup Production | EUR | 30,00 | 30,00 | 0,00 | 1 |
| 11101321 | 101 | Services/Consltg(GB) | Service Standard | EUR | 60,00 | 10,00 | 50,00 | 1 |
| | 102 | Services/Consltg(GB) | Service Specialist | EUR | 60,00 | 20,00 | 40,00 | 1 |
| | 8 | Services/Consltg(GB) | Consulting | EUR | 80,00 | 20,00 | 60,00 | 1 |
| 11101701 | 11 | Plant & Maint (GB) | Personnel Hours | EUR | 30,00 | 10,00 | 20,00 | 1 |

**Figure 5.58** Activity Price Reports

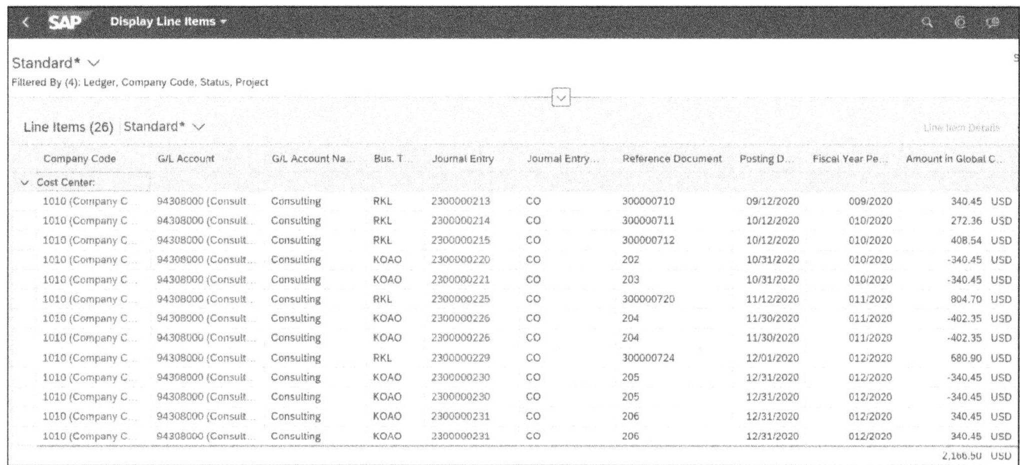

Display Line Items

Standard*

Filtered By (4): Ledger, Company Code, Status, Project

Line Items (26) Standard*

| Company Code | G/L Account | G/L Account Na... | Bus. T... | Journal Entry | Journal Entry... | Reference Document | Posting D... | Fiscal Year Pe... | Amount in Global C... | |
|---|---|---|---|---|---|---|---|---|---|---|
| Cost Center: | | | | | | | | | | |
| 1010 (Company C... | 94308000 (Consult... | Consulting | RKL | 2300000213 | CO | 300000710 | 09/12/2020 | 009/2020 | 340.45 | USD |
| 1010 (Company C... | 94308000 (Consult... | Consulting | RKL | 2300000214 | CO | 300000711 | 10/12/2020 | 010/2020 | 272.36 | USD |
| 1010 (Company C... | 94308000 (Consult... | Consulting | RKL | 2300000215 | CO | 300000712 | 10/12/2020 | 010/2020 | 408.54 | USD |
| 1010 (Company C... | 94308000 (Consult... | Consulting | KOAO | 2300000220 | CO | 202 | 10/31/2020 | 010/2020 | -340.45 | USD |
| 1010 (Company C... | 94308000 (Consult... | Consulting | KOAO | 2300000221 | CO | 203 | 10/31/2020 | 010/2020 | -340.45 | USD |
| 1010 (Company C... | 94308000 (Consult... | Consulting | RKL | 2300000225 | CO | 300000720 | 11/12/2020 | 011/2020 | 804.70 | USD |
| 1010 (Company C... | 94308000 (Consult... | Consulting | KOAO | 2300000226 | CO | 204 | 11/30/2020 | 011/2020 | -402.35 | USD |
| 1010 (Company C... | 94308000 (Consult... | Consulting | KOAO | 2300000226 | CO | 204 | 11/30/2020 | 011/2020 | -402.35 | USD |
| 1010 (Company C... | 94308000 (Consult... | Consulting | RKL | 2300000229 | CO | 300000724 | 12/01/2020 | 012/2020 | 680.90 | USD |
| 1010 (Company C... | 94308000 (Consult... | Consulting | KOAO | 2300000230 | CO | 205 | 12/31/2020 | 012/2020 | -340.45 | USD |
| 1010 (Company C... | 94308000 (Consult... | Consulting | KOAO | 2300000230 | CO | 205 | 12/31/2020 | 012/2020 | -340.45 | USD |
| 1010 (Company C... | 94308000 (Consult... | Consulting | KOAO | 2300000231 | CO | 206 | 12/31/2020 | 012/2020 | 340.45 | USD |
| 1010 (Company C... | 94308000 (Consult... | Consulting | KOAO | 2300000231 | CO | 206 | 12/31/2020 | 012/2020 | 340.45 | USD |
| | | | | | | | | | 2,166.50 | USD |

**Figure 5.59** Line Items for Activity Allocations and Settlement

## 5.6 Summary

In this chapter, we've explained the role of the cost center manager in monitoring costs in his or her area of responsibility and explained the differences between journal entries for primary and secondary postings. We then looked at the role of planning in establishing budgets and setting targets for each cost center. We also looked at the various business transactions used to move costs from sender to receiver and the reports that will help you to ensure that the correct cost flows are in place. The topics we covered here will be revisited when we look at capital expenses in depth in Chapter 8, and we'll look at intercompany allocations in detail in Chapter 9. First, however, we'll focus on production controlling and the flow of production costs to the shop floor and inventory in the next chapter.

# Chapter 6
# Controlling for Manufacturing Organizations

*In this chapter, we'll look at the controlling processes for manufactured products: the master data that needs to be in place before manufacturing starts and the various processes that result in costs, including procure-to-invoice, make-to-stock, and make-to-order scenarios. We'll finish by looking at the controlling tasks associated with asset management and maintenance.*



While the contents of the previous chapter applied to almost every organization, the contents of this chapter are only relevant if you are in a manufacturing organization. If you work for a service organization, feel free to move straight to Chapter 7.

With the manufacture of *physical products*, integration becomes a key part of your SAP S/4HANA strategy as the key information for controlling originates with the design of the product in the engineering department and then moves to the shop floor when production begins. As a controller, you have a voice in the design of your profit center and cost center structures, in setting up activity types and statistical key figures, and in choosing how to handle internal orders and projects. But when it comes to product costing, you are merely a stakeholder in a process that is owned by engineering and manufacturing. It's the engineers that drive the initial estimate of the costs to manufacture each product and source the raw materials before the start of production. Manufacturing then sets to work to optimize the production flows and manufacture in the most efficient way. To create a cost estimate, the following master data must be in place:

- Information contained in the routings and work centers is used to put a value on the activities performed during the manufacturing process.
- Information contained in the bill of materials (BOM) is used to determine the quantities of materials to be used during manufacturing.
- Information owned by purchasing is used to prepare the raw material prices.

Controlling has a shared responsibility to ensure the accuracy of this master data along with engineering and production, so we'll discuss production master data and cost estimates first in this chapter. Although it's possible to set up production master data that's only used for costing, we don't recommend this approach in the long term because it's easy for these structures to get out of sync with what's really happening on the shop floor, and you need accurate information to make the correct business decisions about which products to produce and how to manufacture them in the most efficient manner.

As we discussed in Chapter 4, controlling manages the production cost centers that perform the various activities. These cost centers and activity types must be linked with the work centers at which the operations take place. Before you can create a cost estimate, there must be a cost rate for each cost center/activity type combination that will be used in manufacturing,

We'll then discuss the procure-to-invoice process. While putting the correct master data in place is the starting point, costs only begin to flow as you procure raw materials and produce finished goods, and the purchase orders for procurement and production orders for manufacturing deliver the basis for inventory valuation. Again, controlling isn't in the driving seat, but it's important to understand how costs flow as raw materials are procured and invoices are received from the vendor in order to understand potential sources of purchase price variances and their impact on inventory valuation. It's also important to understand how costs flow as these raw materials are issued to the shop floor and converted into finished goods in order to understand the potential sources of production variances and their impact on the value of the finished goods. We'll look at the differences between manufacturing to stock and to order in terms of the different cost flows in order to understand how to capture the value of work in process (WIP) and variances. Some organizations simply write off these variances in the profit and loss (P&L) statement, while others use *actual costing* to assign both the purchase price variances and the production variances to the materials manufactured and sold in each period.

Alongside inventory valuation, it's important to understand the costs of the assets used in the production process and specifically the impact of maintenance costs in this area. As you move to SAP S/4HANA, this might be the time to consider operation-level costing, which delivers maintenance costs by operation rather than at the order level for greater accuracy. We'll close the chapter with a discussion of asset maintenance and operation.

## 6.1 Master Data Used in Manufacturing

In this section, we'll look at the prerequisites for costing. A *material master* must exist for all materials that are purchased, manufactured, or sold, and it's here that the logistics requirements (size, weight, manufacturing approach, etc.) meet the financials requirements (account determination, standard price, future price, etc.) in each plant. A *bill of materials* (BOM) must exist for all manufactured goods to describe which raw materials and semifinished goods are required to make the product. Usually, the BOM is a multilevel structure covering several manufacturing levels and sometimes crossing plants, where the manufacturing process isn't completed at a single site. A *routing* describes the manufacturing steps to convert the raw materials into semifinished and ultimately finished products, and a *work center* describes the facilities used to carry out this conversion.

Only when this master data is in place can you create a cost estimate for each of the materials in order to set a standard price prior to manufacturing. One of the challenges for the production controller is that of stakeholder management, in which engineers define the initial product structure and production planners make short-term changes that can have significant cost impact.



### 6.1.1 Material Master

The *material master* is arguably the most important master record in logistics. You'll need to create a material master for any material bought or sold on a commercial basis or used, consumed, or created in production. Materials are distinguished by *material type*. Common material types include raw materials and trading goods for purchased materials and finished and semifinished materials for manufactured materials, though there are many industry-specific variants, including the service products that we'll discuss in Chapter 7.

**Long Material Numbers in SAP S/4HANA**

With the move to SAP S/4HANA, one of the key changes is the switch from 18 characters in SAP ERP to 40 characters in SAP S/4HANA. This was previously only available for a handful of industries. To find out more about the implications of this change, refer to SAP Note 2270396.

The material master is also the best example of shared master data, with each department having its own *view* of the material master: a purchasing view for the purchasing department, several material requirements planning (MRP) views for production scheduling, accounting views for inventory valuation, costing views for controlling, and sales views for the sales department. To access the material master, you can use Transaction MM03 or go to **Logistics • Materials Management • Material Master • Material • Display • Display Current** and select the appropriate view(s). For many of the views, you'll also have to enter the appropriate organizational unit(s), so the costing, accounting, and MRP views also require you to enter a plant, and the sales view requires you to enter a sales organization and a distribution channel.

Alternatively, you can use the Manage Product Master app (SAP Fiori ID F1602) to view logistical information, including the price unit, and the Manage Material Valuations app (SAP Fiori ID F2680) to view the information from the accounting and costing views. We'll use the Manage Material Valuations app to explain the key information used for inventory valuation and costing, but you'll find the same information in the accounting and costing views of the material master.

Figure 6.1 shows the Manage Material Valuations app and the current valuation for stocks of material **MZ-FG-C900** in plant **1710**. You can also display the quantity, price, and value information by using Transaction MM03 and selecting the accounting view for the plant. To access the details behind the valuation, select the **>** arrow.

**SAP ERP versus SAP S/4HANA**

If you've worked in SAP ERP until now, the first thing that you'll notice is that material valuations in SAP S/4HANA are always available in two currencies, the group currency (here, euros) and the company code currency (here, US dollars). In the past, multiple currencies were only used if your organization chose to activate the Material Ledger for inventory valuation.

**Figure 6.1** Manage Material Valuations App

Figure 6.2 shows details of the values in US dollars (company code currency) and several key parameters for inventory valuation: the **Valuation Class**, the assignment to a **Profit Center**, the **Price Control**, and the **Price Determination**. Again, this information is also available in the accounting view of Transaction MM03. We'll begin by looking at the link to the account and the profit center to reiterate what we discussed in previous chapters and then look at the impact of the settings for price control and price determination, which are specific to product costing.

We looked at the link to the profit center when we looked at the master data for the cost centers, orders, and so on in Chapter 4. The profit center assigned to the material master represents the default for any process involving this material, whether this is a purchase order to buy a bike, a production order to manufacture the bike, or a sales order to sell the bike. This also means that any bicycle inventories will be assigned to this profit center along with any WIP.

The choice of *valuation class* determines to which *material account* the product costs will be assigned and will affect how the goods movements appear in the Trial Balance app and other financial reports. The valuation class is derived from the material type, so it's possible to assign raw material costs to a different account from finished goods inventory. If your manufacturing involves a make-to-order or engineer-to-order process, you can also set up different valuation classes for sales order stock (inventory relating to a single sales order) or project stock (inventory relating to a single project), enabling you to separate such inventory values from inventory that has been made to stock and can be issued to any sales order.

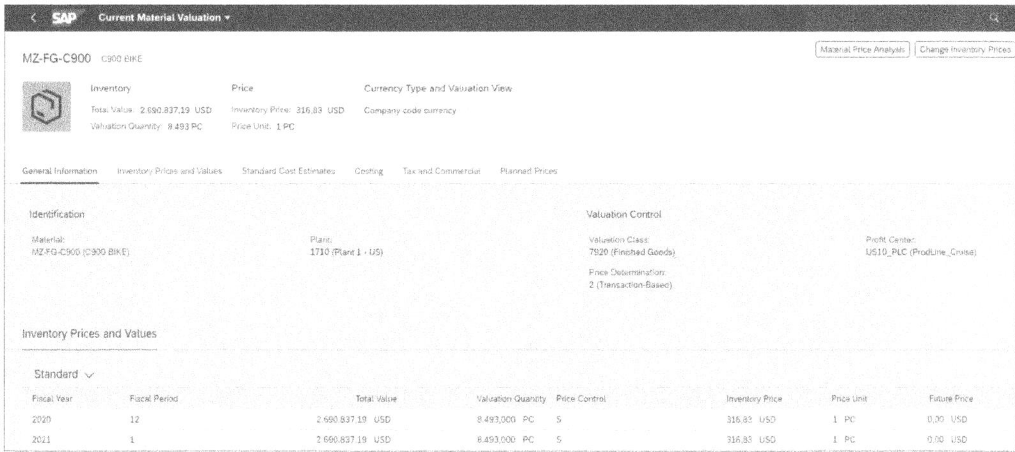


**Figure 6.2** Manage Material Valuations App, Showing General Information and Inventory Prices and Values

One of the key aspects of inventory valuation is the fact that the **Valuation Quantity** (the number of bikes in stock) and **Total Value** (the value of these bikes) are updated every time a goods movement takes place. The choice of **Price Control** affects the value of the goods in stock, allowing you to keep the material price stable (standard price) or to change it with each goods movement for the material (moving average price). In this example, the price control is **S** (for standard price), but you might choose to use price control **V** (moving average price) for raw materials. The choice of price control is arguably the most important decision for manufacturing companies from a controlling point of view. Keeping a stable standard price requires you to have a solid costing process in place to determine the standard costs for a unit of the product. Using the moving average price can seem easier as the valuation is driven by the purchasing process. But the volatility behind the moving average price can be dangerous as it's driven by the agreements with your vendors and any exchange rate differences if you purchase in a different transactional currency.

**Choosing the Correct Price Control**

The moving average price is usually used for raw materials and the standard price for manufactured materials. SAP recommends that you don't use the moving average for manufactured materials because the moving average can become distorted as a result of the timing of cost postings, settlements, and the number of orders in progress for the same material (for more information, see SAP Note 81682).

The choice of **Price Determination** will tell you whether your organization is working only with the Material Ledger (which became compulsory with SAP S/4HANA 1511) or with actual costing (which remains optional with SAP S/4HANA). In this example, the price determination is **2 (Transaction-Based)**, which means that only the Material Ledger is active. Materials with price control **S** will be updated with the standard price in multiple currencies.

If you choose to work with actual costing, then the price determination will be **3 (Single-/Multilevel)**. Instead of a moving average price, which changes in response to every goods movement and invoice receipt, valuation will be based on a *weighted average price*, which is calculated at period close using values captured during the period and thus reflects the cumulated purchase price variances and production variances. This approach can help to smooth the volatility inherent in the moving average price. We'll explain the impact of this decision in more detail in Section 6.4.5.

In Figure 6.2 and in Figure 6.3, where we've scrolled down to show the cost estimates, you can see that the standard price refers to a specific **Fiscal Period**. Some organizations choose to keep their standard costs stable for a whole fiscal year, while others will update them once a quarter or even once a month. You can access the standard cost estimate that was used to set the standard costs by selecting a **Valuation View** and clicking the **Display Cost Estimate** button. We'll explain the link to the standard cost estimate and how to update this price in Section 6.2.1.

**Figure 6.3** Manage Material Valuations App, Showing Inventory Prices and Standard Cost Estimates

In Figure 6.4, we've scrolled down to show information from the costing views of the material master. In the Manage Material Valuations app, the costing view contains control data for product costing, including the following:

- **Costing Lot Size**
  The **Costing Lot Size** is the default quantity on which any cost estimate is based and can be different from the lot size of the individual production orders. Because the choice of lot size can have a significant impact on the fixed and variable production costs, controllers are often involved in the process to determine the optimum lot size.

- **With Qty Structure**
  The **With Qty Structure** checkbox determines that the costs for the material are usually calculated using its BOM and routing (its quantity structure). This is the default for all manufactured materials.
- **Version Indicator**
  The **Version Indicator** indicates that multiple production versions are available.
- **Inventory Prices and Values**
  The values in the **Inventory Prices and Values** tab refer to the perpetual inventory that is updated with every goods movement. By contrast, the **Tax and Commercial** tab is used for balance sheet valuation. At period close, the inventory values may be adjusted to reflect the market situation (when it's no longer possible to buy or sell the material at the current price) or the usage of the product (it has been held for too long) and use to update these assumptions as tax and commercial prices.



When creating a new cost estimate, you can simply select the current inventory price, or you can configure a valuation variant to select planned prices that will become the new inventory price once the cost estimate is released. The **Planned Prices** tab contains three different planned prices that can be used to set future prices.

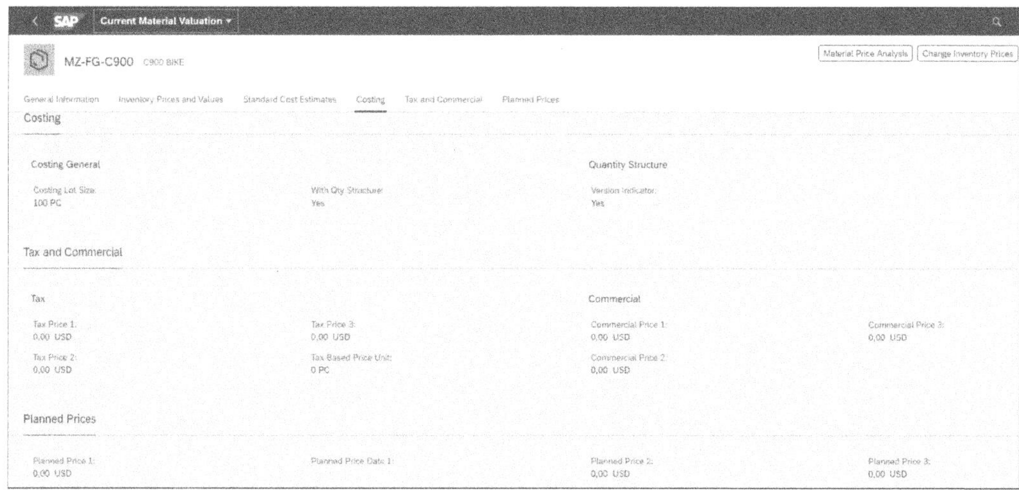


**Figure 6.4** Manage Material Valuations App, Showing Costing, Tax and Commercial, and Planned Prices Areas

### 6.1.2 Bill of Materials

The BOM is a multilevel structure that describes which raw materials are used to make a quantity of a semifinished product and which semifinished products are used to make a quantity of a finished product. Before a material can be included in a BOM, it must exist as a material master. The levels of the BOM are then built up in stages, with a BOM existing for each finished and semifinished material. Some organizations use a separate costing BOM as distinct from an engineering BOM or the production BOM to get their SAP implementations off the ground, but keeping the structures separate can be dangerous in the long term because accurate product costing should reflect the situation on the shop floor. Once the engineering process is complete and the product is ready to move into production, it's better to work with manufacturing to have a single, accurate set of master data.

To display a BOM, use Transaction CS03 or go to **Logistics • Production Planning • Master Data • Bills of Material • Bill of Material • Material BOM • Display**, and enter the material number, plant, and appropriate BOM usage. Alternatively, use the Maintain Bill of Material app (SAP Fiori ID F1813). Figure 6.5 shows a sample BOM for the manufacture of a bicycle. It consists of materials of item category **L** for materials kept in stock. Other BOMs may contain materials of category **N** for materials that have to be procured specially, items of category **R** that have to be cut to size first, and text items of category **T**.

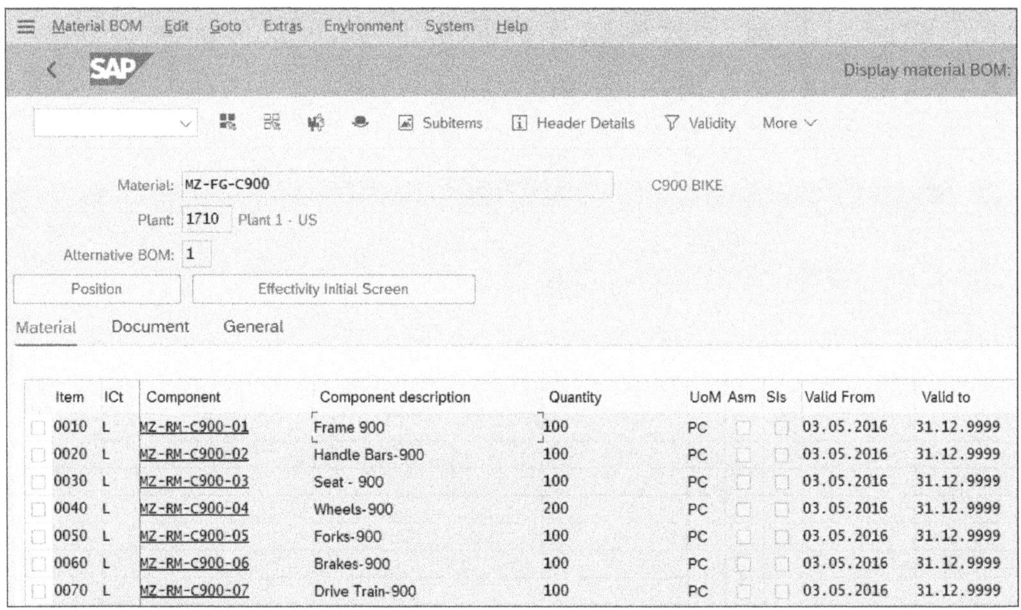


**Figure 6.5** Sample BOM

Figure 6.6 shows the cost estimate for the bicycle and lists the seven items of the BOM, together with the associated quantity and value in the **Costing Structure** section. If you're unsure which BOM was used to create this structure, go to the **Qty. Struct.** (quantity structure) tab to display the technical key of the BOM, the usage (**1** for production), and the alternative.

Notice also that the items shown in the BOM previously in Figure 6.5 are valid for a given time frame only, allowing you to substitute a raw material by retiring the existing raw material instead of creating a completely new BOM. The cost estimate selects the relevant items using the **Qty Structure Date** key date shown in the **Dates** tab of the cost estimate (see Figure 6.7). Notice also the **Costing Date From**, which determines the **Posting Period** in which the cost estimate can be released.



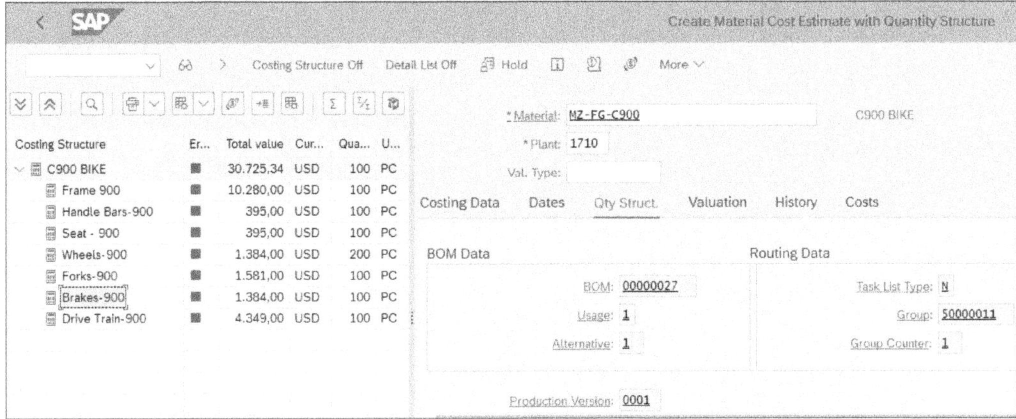


**Figure 6.6** Costing Structure and Material Components from BOM

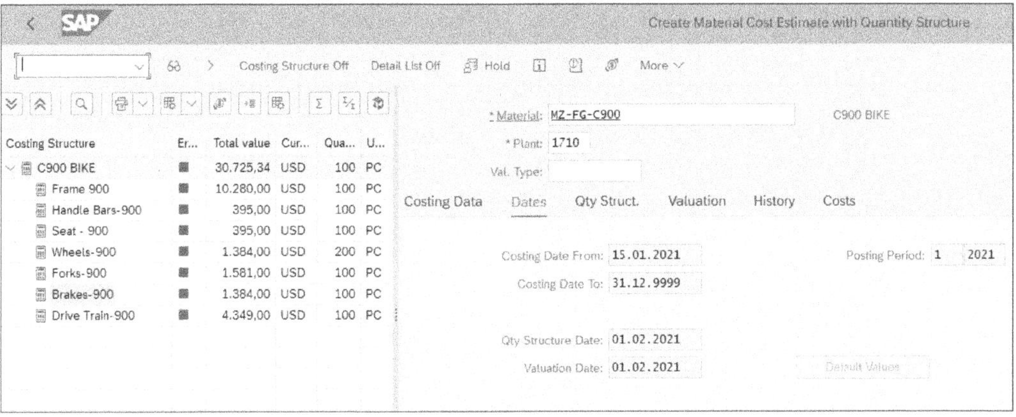


**Figure 6.7** Key Dates for Costing Items

In general, the quantities given in the BOM determine the quantities needed to manufacture a given lot size of the finished product. One exception is when spoilage is anticipated. Sometimes the manufacturing process is such that it's *never* possible to achieve the full output quantity in the order (computer chips are an example). In other cases, experience tells that there will be some loss along the way. In either case, a planned scrap percentage can be defined in the BOM. Entering 5% scrap for a component means that if 100 units are normally required to manufacture 100 units of the finished product, then 105 units are included in product costing to take account of the anticipated loss. Another exception is the handling of components for inventory costing. In this case, you can flag material costs as relevant, partially relevant, or not relevant. Partially relevant items are linked with a percentage in Customizing, allowing you to specify that, for example, only 60% of the packaging costs should be included in inventory costing for balance sheet purposes.

In our bicycle example, multiple components were used to manufacture *one* finished product. In some industries, the BOM is turned on its head, and *several* finished products may result from one production process (known as *joint production*). Meat production is an extreme example, where a single side of beef is processed to provide many different forms of meat product, but joint production is also common in the chemical and pharmaceutical industries, where several products may result from the same manufacturing process, some more valuable than others. SAP distinguishes between *coproducts* and *by-products*. Both are included in the BOM with a negative quantity, but coproducts are flagged as such in the costing and MRP view of the material master. Let's walk through each:

- *Coproducts* are considered equally valid outputs of the production process where manufacture is intentional (planned). During product costing, they're shown in the itemization with item category **A** and negative costs. During order costing, an order item is created for each coproduct. Each item is delivered to stock and has its own status. The order costs split to the order items in accordance with equivalence numbers during settlement. Variances can be calculated for each order item following settlement. The costs for the order items are then settled to stock.
- *By-products* are considered incidental outputs of the production process; their manufacture is incidental (unplanned). They differ from coproducts in that a fixed price is set in the material master. They reduce the costs of the production process and are shown in the itemization with item category **M**.
- A *fixed-price coproduct* is a mixture of the two. It's also shown in the itemization with item category **A**. The order contains an order item for this coproduct, but it's treated with a fixed price like a by-product during settlement.

In some industries, it's also common for BOM structures to be recursive (or circular). A familiar household example might be the production of yogurt, where the BOM for yogurt might include milk, sugar, and a small amount of yogurt cultures. This BOM structure is therefore a cycle as yogurt is both an input and an output. During product costing, each cycle has to be calculated separately before the next costing level is handled. The materials within a cycle are costed iteratively until they converge. Only then is the next costing level in the BOM costed.

In the automotive industry, it's common for the final product to be heavily configurable, with the customer selecting the paint color, engine size, wheels, seats, stereo system, and so on as they place their order. To handle this variability, the BOM for the vehicle includes all the possible options, together with certain rules that determine which combinations are technically feasible. Such materials that include all options are known as *configurable materials*. Another example is mill products, where the customer may request a specific grade of product to be cut to a specific size or weight.

For the controlling department, it's not possible to set a standard price for the configurable material as it contains all possible options that a customer might choose. The cost estimate is generally created from the sales order once the customer has selected his or her options and is in the process of placing his or her order. Alternatively, an order BOM can be created for the specific options requested and then costed. For selected variants, you can prepare a cost estimate in advance by defining certain "standard" options for costing. The other thing that characterizes this type of material is that it's always made to order (as you have to know what options the customer chose) before beginning manufacture.



### 6.1.3 Routing

The routing determines the processing steps to be performed in the manufacture of the material, the material components assigned to that step, and any planned scrap anticipated in the step. There are several types of routing including standard routings, rate routings, and master recipes. Further task lists exist for use in maintenance and customer service, but they all have the same basic structure. Let's walk through each:

- **Standard routing**
  The *standard routing* is the most commonly used type of routing and describes the quantities of work required to create a given number of units of the finished products. You'll find such routings wherever there is batch-oriented production, describing the steps to create each finished product or semifinished product. Our bicycle example provides a classic use case for this kind of routing. To display a standard routing, you can use Transaction CA03 or go to **Logistics • Production • Master Data • Routings • Standard Routings • Display**. If you're selecting them for use in product costing, the standard routings have type N.
- **Rate routing**
  The *rate routing* describes the throughput of the process—volume in a given time frame. Rate routings emerged with lean manufacturing and attempt to describe production as a more or less constant flow, rather than as a series of disjointed batches with deliveries to inventory for each semifinished product. To display a rate routing, you can use Transaction CA23 or go to **Logistics • Production • Master Data • Routings • Rate Routings • Display**. If you're selecting them for use in product costing, the standard routings have type R.
- **Master recipe**
  The *master recipe* is used in the pharmaceutical and chemical industries and describes the production of one or more materials in one production run. From a costing point of view, master recipes are essentially a combination of a standard routing and a BOM but include additional functions for material quantity calculation that are specific to these industries. To display a master recipe, you can use Transaction C203 or go to **Logistics • Production—Process • Master Data • Master Recipes • Recipes**

and **Material List • Display**. If you're selecting them for use in product costing, the standard routings have type 2.

Figure 6.8 shows a sample routing for the manufacture of the bicycle in Figure 6.6. This is a standard routing (as shown by **Task List Type N** previously in Figure 6.6) with the group **50000011** and group counter **1**. Again, you'll find this information in the **Qty. Struct.** tab of the cost estimate. The routing includes standard values for the setup time, machine time, and labor time, assuming a base unit of 100 bicycles.

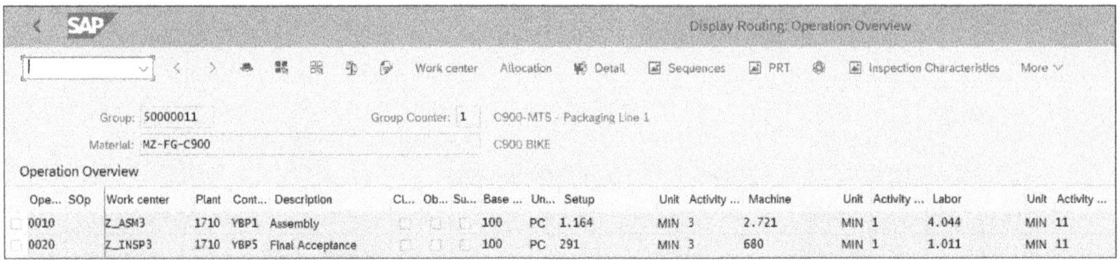

| Ope... | SOp | Work center | Plant | Cont... | Description | Cl... | Ob... | Su... | Base ... | Un... | Setup | Unit | Activity ... | Machine | Unit | Activity ... | Labor | Unit | Activity ... |
|---|---|---|---|---|---|---|---|---|---|---|---|---|---|---|---|---|---|---|---|
| 0010 | | Z_ASM3 | 1710 | YBP1 | Assembly | | | | 100 | PC | 1.164 | MIN | 3 | 2.721 | MIN | 1 | 4.044 | MIN | 11 |
| 0020 | | Z_INSP3 | 1710 | YBPS | Final Acceptance | | | | 100 | PC | 291 | MIN | 3 | 680 | MIN | 1 | 1.011 | MIN | 11 |

**Figure 6.8** Sample Routing

To display the costs for the **Assembly** and **Final Acceptance** operations in the **Costing Structure**, choose the **Materials Only/All Items** icon shown previously in Figure 6.6 and Figure 6.7 (arrow plus list of items) to activate the additional costing items. Figure 6.9 shows the costs for the **Assembly** and **Final Acceptance** operations alongside the seven BOM items in the **Costing Structure**. Notice that there are three lines in the cost estimate for each operation, and these correspond to the production activities defined in the routing for setup time (activity type **3**, on the right of the **Costing Structure**), machine time (activity type **1**), and labor time (activity type **11**). You can see this information in the **Resource** column, along with the work centers **Z_ASM3** and **Z_INSP3** and the responsible cost center **US10_PLC** used for all operations in this example. The quantities are calculated as follows:

- Setup (activity type **3**): 1,164 minutes for the assembly operation corresponds to 19.4 hours in the cost estimate and 291 minutes for the acceptance operation corresponds to 4.85 hours.
- Machine (activity type **1**): 2,721 minutes for the assembly operation corresponds to 45.35 hours and 680 minutes for the acceptance operation corresponds to 11.333 hours.
- Labor (activity type **11**): 4,044 minutes for the assembly operation corresponds to 67.4 hours and 1,011 minutes for the acceptance operation corresponds to 16.85 hours.

Notice that in this example the base unit for the operation is 100 bicycles and we have created a cost estimate for 100 bicycles. If we created a cost estimate for a different number of bicycles, the times would be adjusted to reflect the changed quantity. These quantities will also be important when we create a production order to manufacture some bicycles as the order lot size may differ from the costing lot size, and the BOM and routing quantities will be adjusted accordingly. In the past, controlling was often involved in the choice of the costing lot size to make best use of the fixed production costs, but this is becoming less important as many industries move to a lot size of one to reflect specific customer requirements.



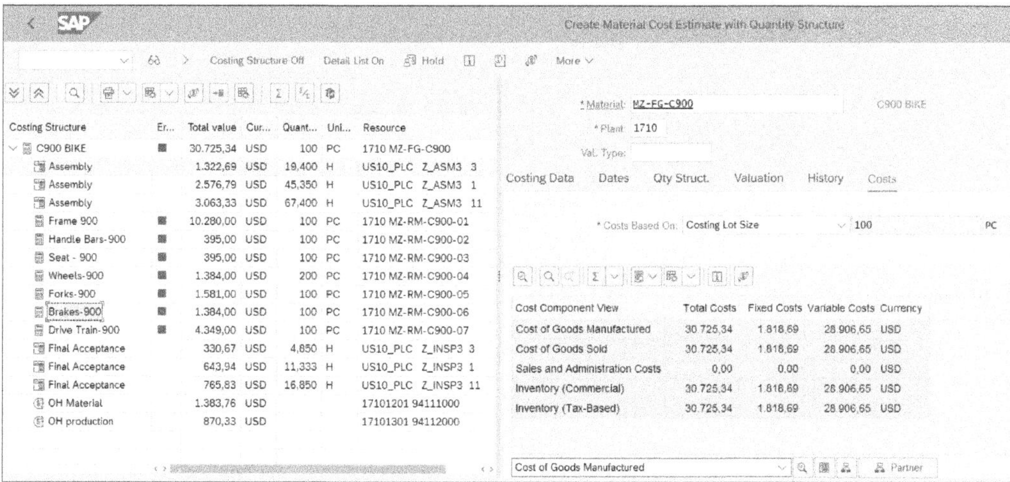


**Figure 6.9** Costing Structure with Raw Materials and Operation Costs

To adjust the reference quantity for the cost estimate, go to the **Costs** tab and change the **Costs Based On** dropdown from the **Costing Lot Size** (100 pieces) to the **Price Unit** (1 piece) or a manual entry, as shown in Figure 6.10.

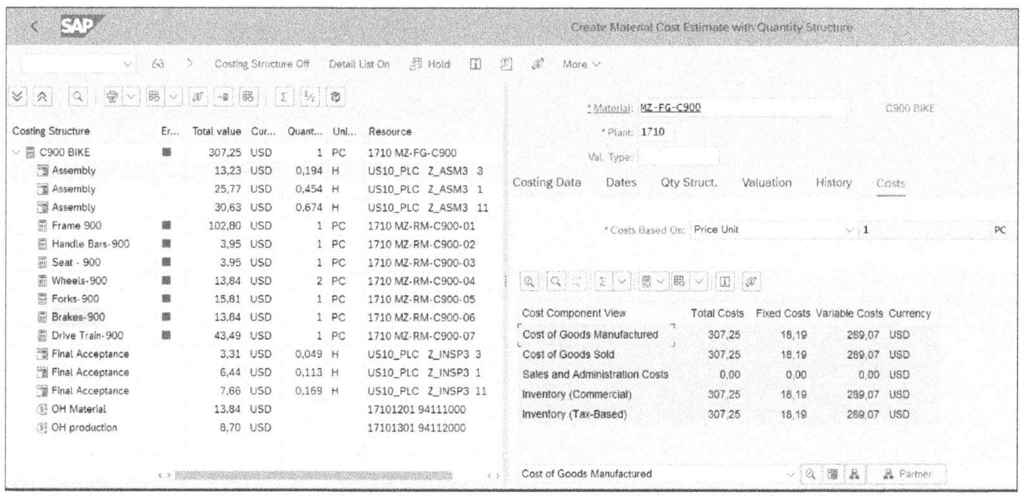


**Figure 6.10** Cost Estimate with Changed Base Unit

### 6.1.4 Work Center

Work centers and resources are used for capacity requirements planning and scheduling in logistics. Every operation in a routing must be assigned to a work center (the place where the operation is performed). The work center includes formulas that determine how each standard value in the operation is interpreted (fixed in the case of setup time and varying with the lot size in the case of machine time and labor time). You can also include an efficiency rate to take account of different efficiencies in the operation. The navigation instructions are as follows:

- To display a work center, use Transaction CR03 or go to **Logistics • Production • Master Data • Work Centers • Work Center • Display.**
- To display a resource, use Transaction CRC3 or go to **Logistics • Production—Process • Master Data • Resources • Resource • Display.**

For costing, every work center and resource must be assigned to a single cost center. This link is defined for a specified validity period as it may change over time. Figure 6.11 shows the **Cost Center Assignment** for work center **Z_ASM3**. This provides the link between the operation and work center in logistics and the cost center in finance. The **Activities Overview** shows the three activities shown previously in Figure 6.9 and Figure 6.10. The activity includes a formula key that determines how the activity quantities are calculated. For example, a setup operation may require a fixed effort of 15 minutes regardless of what lot size is in the order or cost estimate, whereas machine and labor requirements usually vary with the lot size.

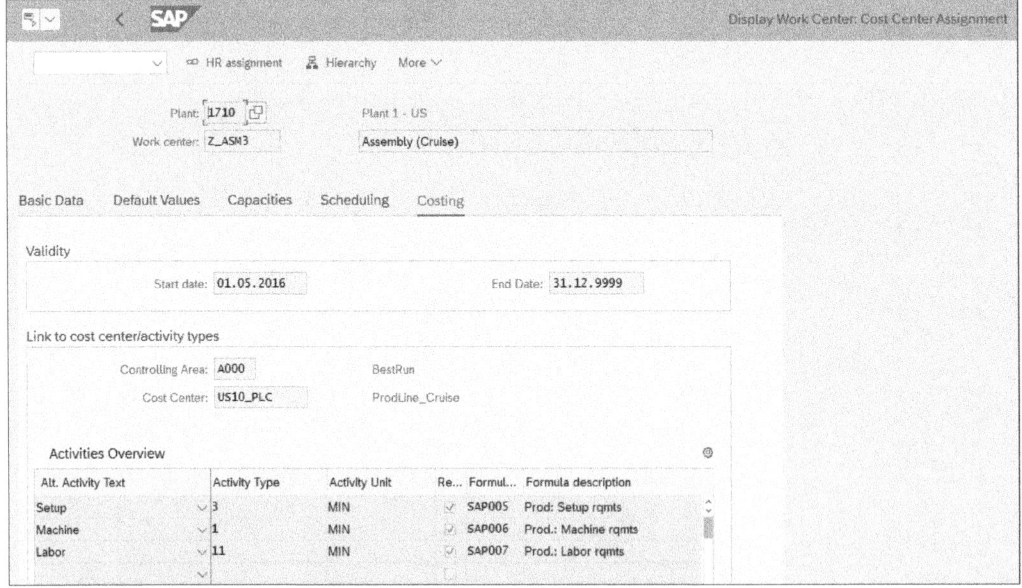


**Figure 6.11** Work Center, Showing Assignment to Cost Center and Activity Types

Notice also the **Capacities** tab for the work center. This is used during capacity requirements planning to determine how many units can be handled in each operation. When we looked at cost center planning in Chapter 5, we noted that you can also enter a *capacity* for each cost center and activity type in a given period. This is sometimes a source of confusion, but the two options are quite different:

- **Work center capacity**
  The *work center* capacity refers to the ability of a single machine to perform a given operation. It affects the activity quantity calculations in product costing because to produce a given lot size, the operation has to be performed a given number of times. For example, if the capacity of an oven is 100 units, then to deliver a lot size of 200 units, the operation has to be performed twice.
- **Cost center/activity type capacity**
  The *cost center/activity type* capacity refers to the whole period and can cover multiple work centers. It's used to define a standard quantity output over all machines assigned to the cost center in a given period.



**Activity Types per Work Center**

Confusion frequently arises about the limit of only six activity types at any work center. Why only six? The reason lies in SAP's understanding of the activity type as the *output measure* for the work center. The output measure is typically expressed in terms of drilling hours, welding hours, and so on. In other words, these are the outputs that are measured when order confirmation takes place.

When people want to use more than six activity types, they're often confusing inputs and outputs. A work center may supply welding hours, but it often uses energy hours, maintenance hours, and so on. If what you're really trying to do by using more than six activity types is see the impact of increases in energy prices, higher wage costs, or changes in depreciation on product profitability, then you should consider activating the primary cost component *split* for your activity rates. Without the primary cost component split, energy costs, wage costs, and so on are subsumed in the activity price for the welding hours. With the primary cost component split, you can break out the activity rate into its cost components, which might be wages, salaries, operating supplies, depreciation, energy, maintenance, and so on.

## 6.2 Cost Estimates

The process of setting standard costs used to be an annual undertaking to prepare cost estimates to value all stock materials prior to the new fiscal year, but more and more organizations are calculating standard costs on a quarterly or even monthly basis to keep pace with increasingly volatile markets. Normally a *costing run* is used to create a cost estimate for all materials, but during the year you may need to cost individual materials, particularly when new products are introduced. If you use SAP Best Practices, you'll find the settings for standard cost calculation in scope item BEG.

We'll begin by describing how to create a material cost estimate in Section 6.2.1 before looking at how to access more details about the costing items in Section 6.2.2 and the importance of cost components in Section 6.2.3. We'll then explain how to use a costing run to create cost estimates for multiple materials in Section 6.2.4. With these steps completed, you're ready to move onto make-to-stock production, using either individual production orders or a product cost collector. However, if you work in a make-to-order environment, there is no standard way of manufacturing your product—but there is of course a need to value inventories of products that have been manufactured to reflect customer-specific requirements. We'll explain these in Section 6.2.5.

### 6.2.1 Creating a Material Cost Estimate

We've been looking at sample screens for the material cost estimate to explain the master data used and their implications throughout this chapter. To create a material cost estimate for a new material, use Transaction CK11N or choose **Accounting • Controlling • Product Cost Controlling • Product Cost Planning • Material Costing • Cost Estimate with Quantity Structure • Create** and enter the **Material**, **Plant**, and costing variant (here, **PYC1**). Notice in the menu structure that there is no change transaction for cost estimates. This is because the master data is used to determine the *quantity structure* for costing and then material and activity prices are applied to this structure. Any errors will be displayed in the various logs for each step in the process and the assumption is that these errors will be in the underlying master data, such as a missing price, and will need to be fixed in logistics rather than by manually adding information to the cost estimate to fill the gaps.

We entered the *costing variant* in the initial screen, which controls the purpose of the cost estimate (standard costs, inventory cost estimate, etc.) and how the quantity structure and prices are selected. You will be asked to check your dates and, assuming all your master data is ready for costing, will see the information shown in Figure 6.12, with the costing lot size, the BOM structure under **Costing Structure**, and the costing items under **Itemization**. We've talked about the integration with the BOM, routing, and work center to derive the quantity structure for costing, but it's also important to understand how the price information was selected to deliver the values for each costing item. Just as we discussed the quantity structure date for the selection of the items in the BOM and routing, you should also check the *valuation date* in the **Dates** tab that determines the key date for the price selection. We'll look at how to use the **Transfer Control** and **Costing Version** fields shown in this screen when we explain how to cost an intercompany cost flow in Chapter 9.

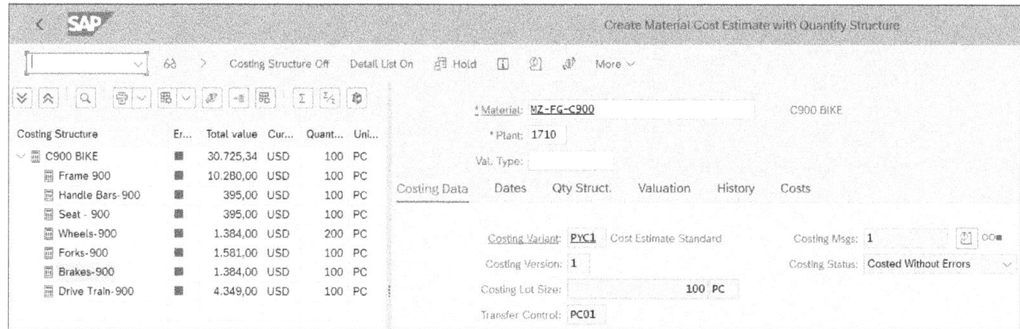

Figure 6.12 Creating Standard Cost Estimate

To check how the price information was selected for each of the material components, choose a raw material in the **Costing Structure** and navigate to the **Valuation** tab. Figure 6.13 shows that a price of USD 102.80 has been selected for the frame (**MZ-RM-C900-01**). The strategy used for material valuation is **Valuation Price According to Price Control in Mat. Master**. This means that the cost estimate is using the same approach as will be used when the frame is issued from inventory for use on the shop floor. This is the simplest approach, and variances between the standard cost estimate and the order will only occur if you are working with the moving average price, which can change with every goods movement and invoice receipt.

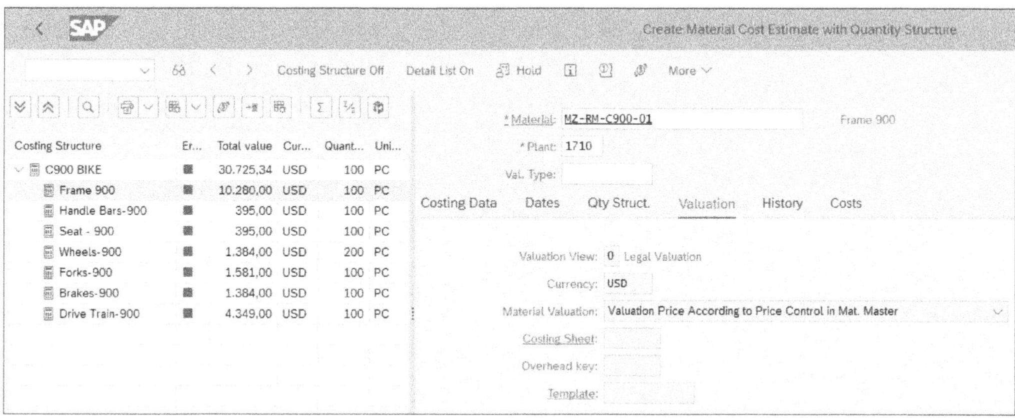

Figure 6.13 Price Selection for Raw Materials Used in Cost Estimate

If you're setting a standard price for the future, however, you may not want to deal with the potential volatility of a moving average price or take the existing standard price as your valuation. Recall that in Section 6.1.1 we showed many different material prices in Figure 6.4. Now Figure 6.14 shows the various prices that can be used during costing. The costing variant entered in the initial screen is linked with a *valuation variant* that determines the sequence of prices that the system will use for costing. The price you use depends on the purpose of the cost estimate:

- **Standard price**
  When you're setting a new standard price, as is the case here, you might prefer to use a planned price as your first option and only select the price according to the current price control if no planned price has been defined for the relevant material.
- **Inventory cost estimate**
  If you're creating an inventory cost estimate, then you shouldn't select the valuation according to the current price control, but rather the valuation price that you have filled with the relevant valuation for your tax or commercial prices. There are various ways of calculating these prices, including the lower of cost or market; range of coverage; movement rate; first in, first out (FIFO); or last in, first out (LIFO).

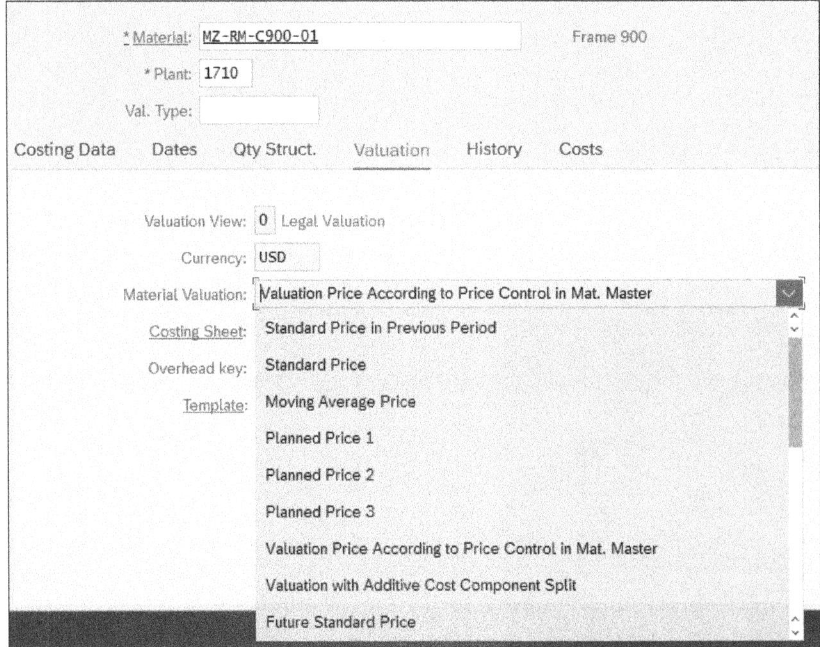


**Figure 6.14** Options for Material Price Valuation

Figure 6.12 (shown previously) gives the impression that the whole bicycle is costed in one go, but what actually happens is that the costs of each of the components are calculated separately using the costing lot size for each semifinished material and then *rolled up* to the next level (the bike in this case). The **Costing Status** determines what you'll be allowed to do with this cost estimate. If the cost estimate in this level contains errors, you won't be able to roll the costs up to the next manufacturing level or mark and release the cost estimate to deliver a new inventory value. If you're using a cost estimate to set standard costs, you should also be aware that the **Costing Date From** must be within the period for which you intend to release the cost estimate.

To activate the results of your cost estimate as a standard price for inventory valuation, you'll need to mark and release the cost estimate using Transaction CK24 or **Accounting •**

**Controlling • Product Cost Controlling • Product Cost Planning • Material Costing • Price Update.** You'll only be able to do this if your cost estimate has a valid from date in the period for which you wish to valuate inventory. Normally organizations create cost estimates in the run up to the close of the year or the quarter and release them as they move into the next fiscal year or quarter, but for testing make sure that you pick a date in the current period. Before you can release a cost estimate, you'll have to allow marking by choosing **Marking Allowance** in the entry screen of Transaction CK24. This will take you to the **Price Update: Organizational Measure** screen. Then, select your **Company Code** to open the popup shown in Figure 6.15, enter the correct **Costing Variant** and **Costing Version**, and click the **Save** icon. You're now ready to mark the cost estimate.

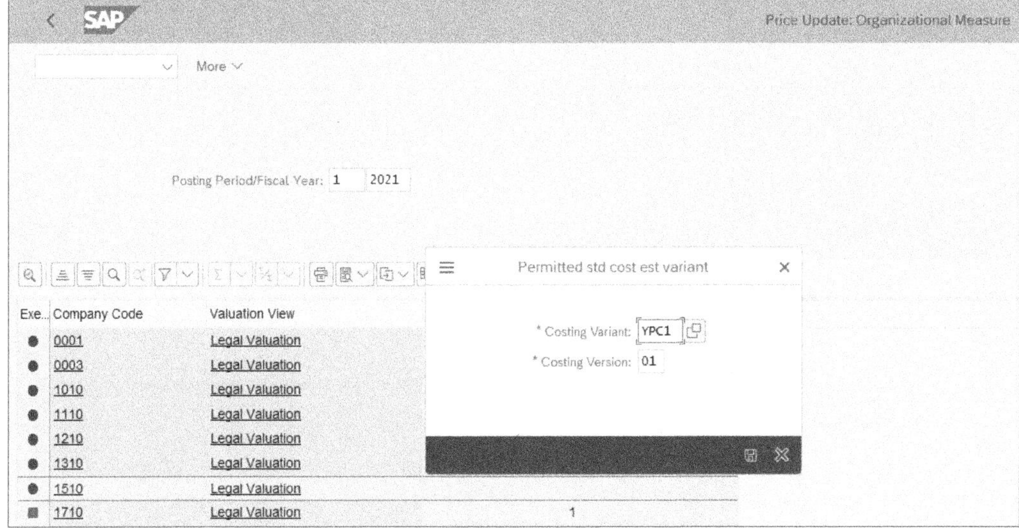


**Figure 6.15** Allow Price Update for Company Code

The release process takes place in two stages. First the cost estimate is marked, which moves the calculated price to the **Future Standard Price** field in the Manage Material Valuations app. To do this, when you have allowed a costing variant and version, return to the **Price Update** screen, choose the materials that you want to mark, and select **Execute.** Figure 6.16 shows the new costing status (**VO** means "marked") and the new standard price for the bike in two currencies.

Price Update: Mark Standard Price

More

Test run

| Exe... | Material | Plant | Valuation Type | Costing... | Fut. plnd price | Standard price | Price unit | Currency | Valuation View | With Qty S... | Description | Bas... | L... | L... |
|---|---|---|---|---|---|---|---|---|---|---|---|---|---|---|
| | MZ-FG-C900 | 1710 | | VO | 307,25 | 316,83 | 1 | USD | Legal Valuation | ✓ | C900 BIKE | PC | 0L | 10 |
| | MZ-FG-C900 | 1710 | | VO | 266,23 | 253,47 | 1 | EUR | Legal Valuation | ✓ | C900 BIKE | PC | 0L | 30 |

**Figure 6.16** Marking Standard Cost Estimate

Once you're happy that the marked cost estimate is correct, you're ready to release and adjust the inventory values to reflect the values in latest cost estimate. To do this, return to Transaction CK24, choose the **Release** button, enter the materials that you want to release, and select **Execute**. Figure 6.17 shows the result of the release, which moves the calculated price to the **Standard price** field and revalues stocks of that product if the unit price has changed as a result of the new cost estimate. Notice also the **Document Number** in the release screen that documents the revaluation of inventory as a result of releasing the standard cost estimate.

When you've released the cost estimate, you'll be able to access it from the Manage Material Valuations app (refer back to Figure 6.3) or by choosing Transaction MM03 and navigating to the **Accounting 1** tab of the material master (see Figure 6.18) as the cost estimate serves to document the business rationale behind the current material price.

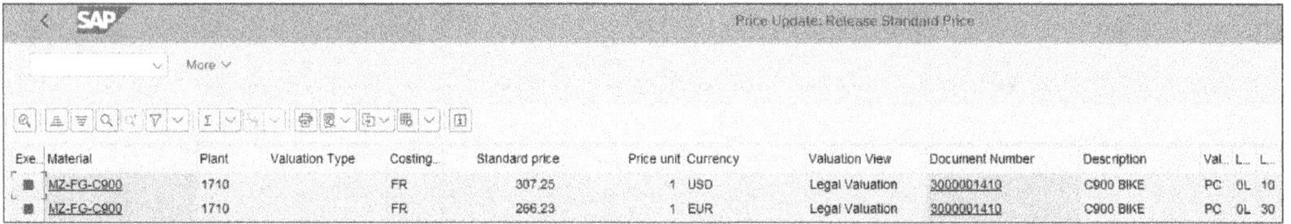


**Figure 6.17** Releasing Cost Estimate

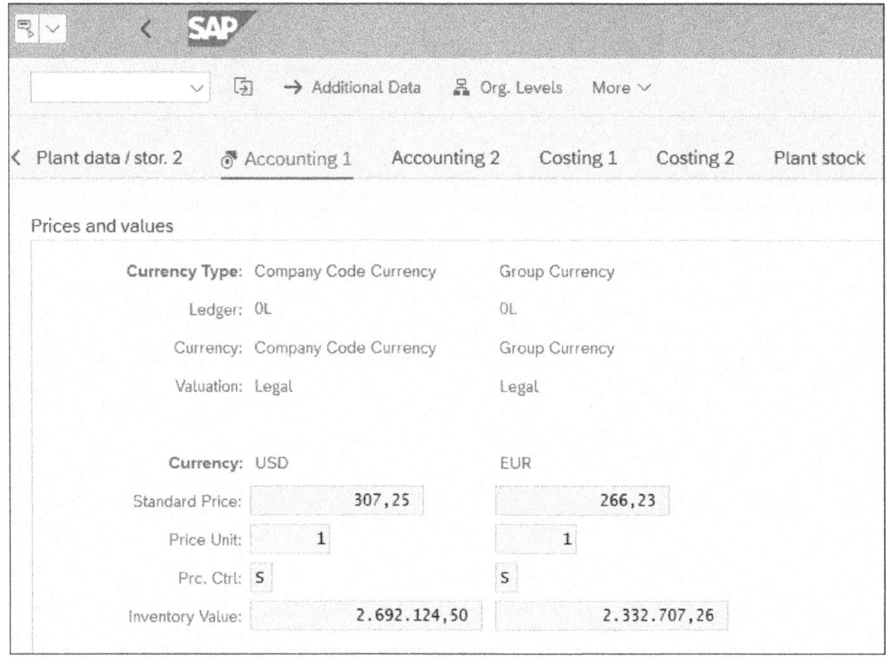


**Figure 6.18** Accounting View of Material Master for Finished Product

### 6.2.2 Using Different Layouts to View the Costing Items

In Section 6.1, we used the **Costing Structure** section of the cost estimate to explain the integration with the BOM, routing, and work centers. Figure 6.19 shows another part of the screen: the **Itemization**, the list of all costing items for the material. Because of the many different fields in an itemization, it's important to understand which information is available in which *layout*. To switch layouts, move your cursor to the detailed list part of the screen (which you can toggle on via the **Detail List On/Off** button) that shows the itemization and select the **Choose Layout** icon to access the list of layouts shown in Figure 6.19. The delivered layouts include the following:



- **Item Categories**
  Groups the items of the cost estimate by the material, internal activity, overhead, and other internal categories.
- **Costing Items**
  Lists the items of the cost estimate by their technical ID.
- **Cost Components**
  Shows the assignment of each costing item to one of up to 120 cost components (in SAP ERP, the maximum number of components was 40).
- **Assemblies/Raw Materials**
  Shows the raw materials (materials without BOMs—i.e., purchased materials) and assemblies (materials with their own BOMs—i.e., manufactured materials) used in the final product.
- **Cost Components/Cost Elements**
  Used to check the assignment of the items to cost elements and from there to cost components.
- **Operations**
  Shows the assignment of the costing items to the operations in the routing.
- **Coproducts**
  Where multiple products are manufactured in a single process (joint production), each coproduct is shown with item category A.
- **Planned Scrap**
  Normal spoilage is planned in the BOM, routing, and material master for the assembly.
- **Cost Elements**
  Shows the assignment of the costing items to the accounts/primary cost elements and the secondary cost elements.

To display the operations as part of the cost estimate, select the **Itemization** section of the cost estimate and switch the layout to **Operations**. Figure 6.20 shows the assignment of the costing items to the **Assembly** and **Final Acceptance** operations. You saw this assignment when we looked at the Analyze Costs by Work Center/Operation app in

Chapter 2, Figure 2.37, and it will be important when you calculate WIP and scrap later as you'll want to be sure the material usage is recorded at the correct operation.

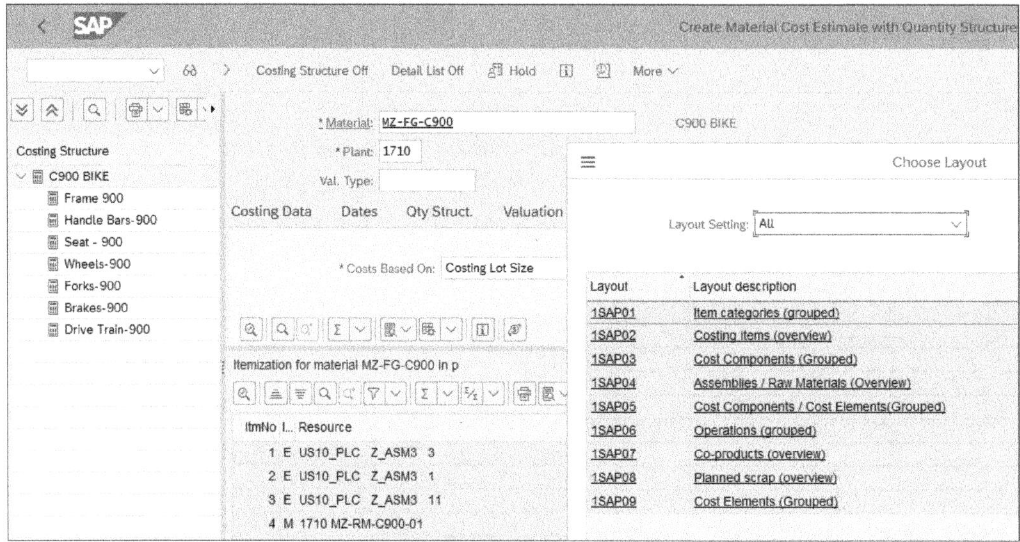


**Figure 6.19** Different Layouts to Display Cost Estimate

Itemization in Company Code Currency

| ItmNo | I... | Resource | Resource (Text) | Total Value | COCr | Quantity | Un |
|---|---|---|---|---|---|---|---|
| 1 | E | US10_PLC Z_ASM3 3 | Assembly | 1.322,69 | USD | 19,400 | H |
| 2 | E | US10_PLC Z_ASM3 1 | Assembly | 2.576,79 | USD | 45,350 | H |
| 3 | E | US10_PLC Z_ASM3 11 | Assembly | 3.063,33 | USD | 67,400 | H |
| 4 | M | 1710 MZ-RM-C900-01 | Frame 900 | 10.280,00 | USD | 100 | PC |
| 5 | M | 1710 MZ-RM-C900-02 | Handle Bars-900 | 395,00 | USD | 100 | PC |
| 6 | M | 1710 MZ-RM-C900-03 | Seat - 900 | 395,00 | USD | 100 | PC |
| 7 | M | 1710 MZ-RM-C900-04 | Wheels-900 | 1.384,00 | USD | 200 | PC |
| 8 | M | 1710 MZ-RM-C900-05 | Forks-900 | 1.581,00 | USD | 100 | PC |
| 9 | M | 1710 MZ-RM-C900-06 | Brakes-900 | 1.384,00 | USD | 100 | PC |
| 10 | M | 1710 MZ-RM-C900-07 | Drive Train-900 | 4.349,00 | USD | 100 | PC |
| **0010 Assembly** | | | | **26.730,81** | **USD** | | |
| 11 | E | US10_PLC Z_INSP3 3 | Final Acceptance | 330,67 | USD | 4,850 | H |
| 12 | E | US10_PLC Z_INSP3 1 | Final Acceptance | 643,94 | USD | 11,333 | H |
| 13 | E | US10_PLC Z_INSP3 11 | Final Acceptance | 765,83 | USD | 16,850 | H |
| **0020 Final Acceptance** | | | | **1.740,44** | **USD** | | |
| | | | | **30.725,34** | **USD** | | |

**Figure 6.20** Itemization, Showing Operations and Assigned Costs

Every item in the cost estimate will automatically be assigned to an account. We looked at the material account assignment in Section 6.1.1. The activity type is assigned to an account/cost element based on the entry in the activity type (see Chapter 4, Section 4.3). The overheads are assigned to an account/cost element based on the entries in the costing sheet (see Chapter 5, Section 5.4.6). In Figure 6.21, we've switched to the **Cost Elements** layout to show the accounts to which costs will be assigned when the associated production order is processed. These are also used to assign the costs to cost components, a topic that we'll look at next.

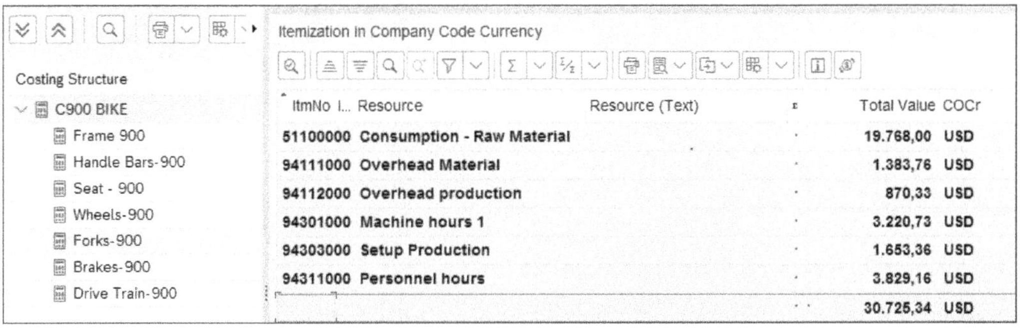

Costing Structure
- C900 BIKE
  - Frame 900
  - Handle Bars-900
  - Seat - 900
  - Wheels-900
  - Forks-900
  - Brakes-900
  - Drive Train-900

Itemization in Company Code Currency

| ItmNo | I... | Resource | Resource (Text) | Σ | Total Value | COCr |
|---|---|---|---|---|---|---|
| | | **51100000 Consumption - Raw Material** | | | **19.768,00** | **USD** |
| | | **94111000 Overhead Material** | | | **1.383,76** | **USD** |
| | | **94112000 Overhead production** | | | **870,33** | **USD** |
| | | **94301000 Machine hours 1** | | | **3.220,73** | **USD** |
| | | **94303000 Setup Production** | | | **1.653,36** | **USD** |
| | | **94311000 Personnel hours** | | | **3.829,16** | **USD** |
| | | | | | **30.725,34** | **USD** |

**Figure 6.21** Itemization, Showing Assignment to Accounts/Cost Elements

### 6.2.3 Using the Cost Component Split for Transparency

Although the account structure shown in Figure 6.21 is configured to meet general financial reporting needs, this isn't the only way to look at the product costs. An additional structure, the *cost component split*, is used to control how the various costs are to be handled by other applications and to deliver additional transparency for multilevel structures.

To switch the detail list in the lower right of the screen to show the cost components instead of the itemization, go to the **Costs** tab (behind the **Choose Layout** dialog), choose a **Cost Component View**, and select the **Cost Components** button or double-click the line for your chosen view, as shown in Figure 6.22. Each cost component is configured to control whether it's part of the cost of goods manufactured view, the cost of goods sold view, the commercial inventory view, or the tax inventory view. The idea behind the various views is that when you use the standard costs to set the inventory value for the material, the system will select only those costs that are flagged as being part of the cost of goods manufactured. For balance sheet purposes, you might want to exclude certain costs, such as packaging, from the inventory value, so you can flag these as not being relevant for commercial inventory or tax inventory.

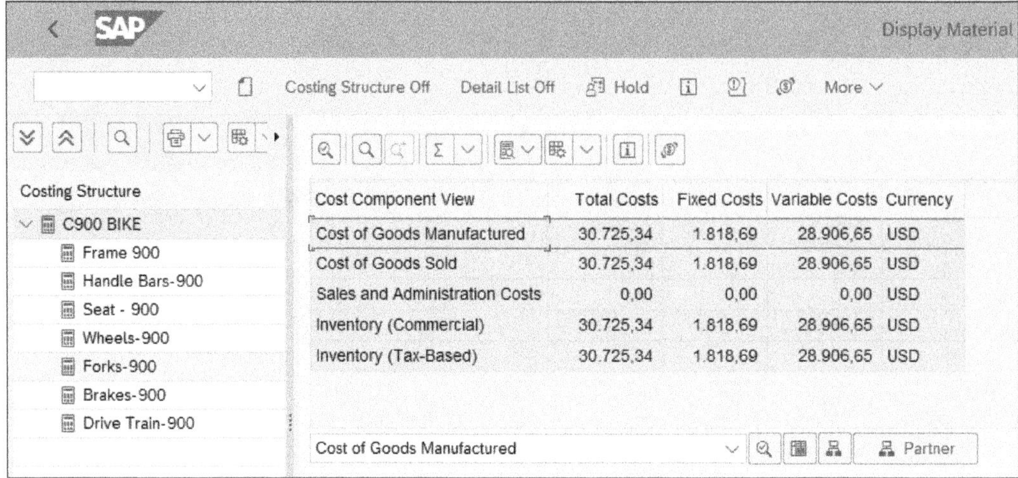


**Figure 6.22** Choosing Cost Component View

Here we'll select **Cost of Goods Manufactured** to arrive at Figure 6.23. The cost of goods manufactured reflects the account groupings coming out of the BOM and routing, so the cost of goods manufactured is usually structured by raw materials, purchased parts, and cost components for the main activities to give the cost component structure shown in Figure 6.23 with the **Direct Material**, **Material Overhead**, **Personnel time**, **Machine time**, **Set-Up time**, **Production Overhead**, and other such components. This structure is configurable, and every organization groups its costs slightly differently.

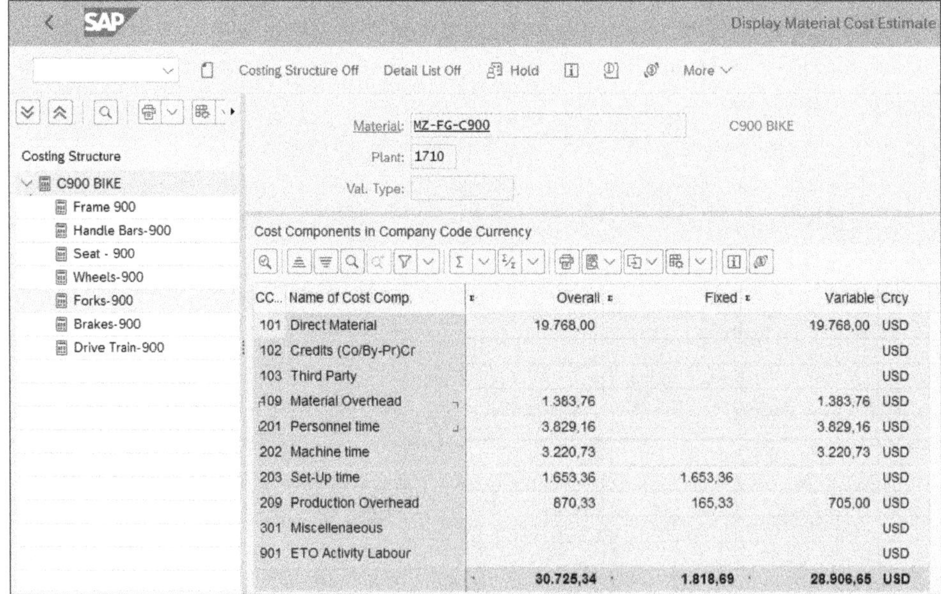


**Figure 6.23** Cost Estimate, Showing Cost Component Split

**SAP ERP versus SAP S/4HANA**

In SAP ERP, you could create up to 40 cost components (components that included fixed and variable costs counted as two), but in SAP S/4HANA you can create up to 120 cost components.



At first sight, these cost components might seem to be no more than an account grouping, showing all raw material costs, all overhead costs, and so on. The difference between the cost component view and the account view becomes apparent when we leave this simple example with its flat BOM behind to look at a multilevel costing structure. Figure 6.24 shows a costing structure with three levels (raw materials, semifinished products, and finished products). The example includes the bike components as before, but the wheel is not a purchased material here but rather an assembly with its own BOM and routing. The costs for the wheel are calculated first and assigned to cost components, so you can see that the 100 dollars includes **Direct Material**, **Machine Time**, **Personnel Time**, **Setup**, **Material Overhead**, and **Production Overhead**.

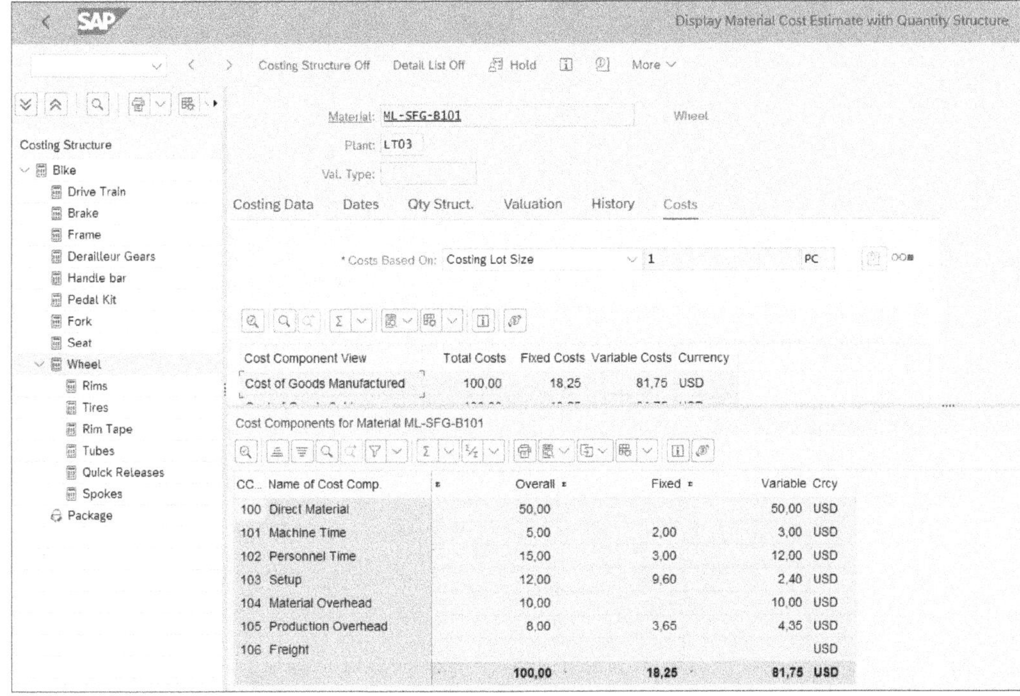


**Figure 6.24** Cost Estimate, Showing Cost Component Split for Semifinished Material

If you look at the cost components for the bicycle, as shown in Figure 6.25, you can see how the costs of the wheel have been rolled up for each cost component separately, so the costs shown for the bike under **Machine Time** represent the time worked on the wheel and on the complete bike. The costs shown under **Direct Material** represent the sum of all raw material costs for the bike, and so on through the various cost components.

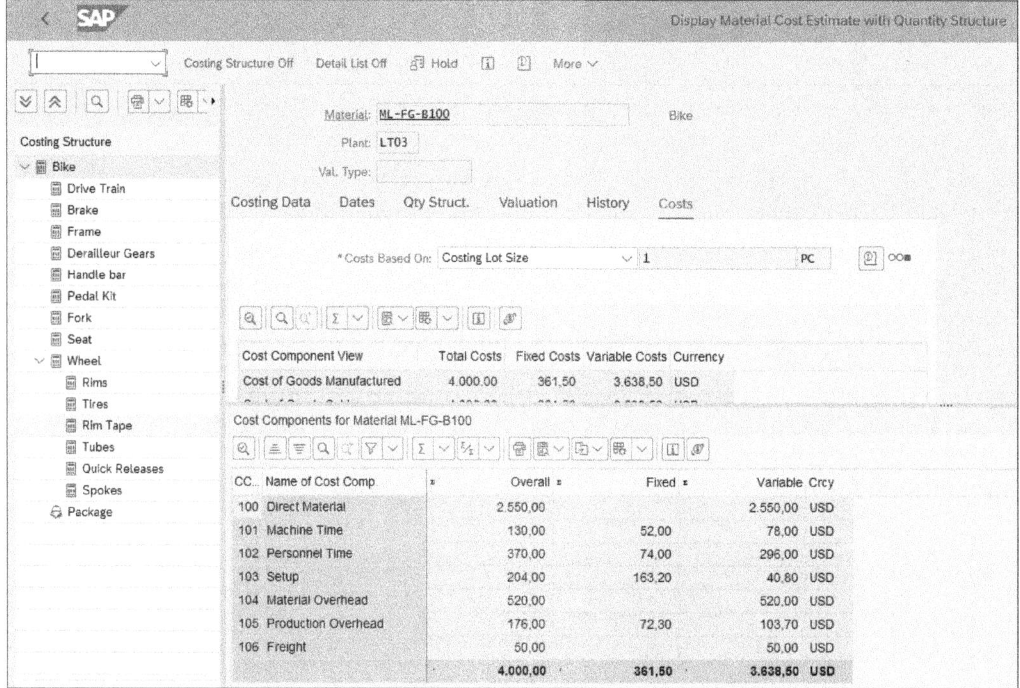


| CC... | Name of Cost Comp | Overall | Fixed | Variable | Crcy |
|---|---|---|---|---|---|
| 100 | Direct Material | 2.550,00 | | 2.550,00 | USD |
| 101 | Machine Time | 130,00 | 52,00 | 78,00 | USD |
| 102 | Personnel Time | 370,00 | 74,00 | 296,00 | USD |
| 103 | Setup | 204,00 | 163,20 | 40,80 | USD |
| 104 | Material Overhead | 520,00 | | 520,00 | USD |
| 105 | Production Overhead | 176,00 | 72,30 | 103,70 | USD |
| 106 | Freight | 50,00 | | 50,00 | USD |
| | | 4.000,00 | 361,50 | 3.638,50 | USD |

**Figure 6.25** Cost Estimate, Showing Cost Component Split for Finished Material

By comparison, if you look at the **Cost Element** layout for the bike, you see that the total costs for the bike are the same, but the costs for machine hours, production setup, personnel hours, and so on only include the work performed on the bicycle, but not on the wheel (so it's missing 5 dollars of machine time per wheel, 15 dollars of personnel time per wheel, and so on). Instead, you see the 200 dollars for the wheel under the **Inventory Change—Semi Finished goods** account in Figure 6.26. The cost component split thus gives a different view of the costs from the account view used to show the product costs in the Trial Balance app and other financial reports, where the separate cost components are subsumed in the account for semifinished goods.

You can look at the same costs from a different standpoint by setting up a separate cost component structure (the *auxiliary cost component split*) that replaces the activity costs with the costs associated with those activities, such as personnel, employee benefits, depreciation, and so on. To do this, you must first calculate the cost rate for your production activities to split out the underlying costs into their cost components, as shown in Figure 6.27, and then map the cost components for the activity type to include them in the product costs.

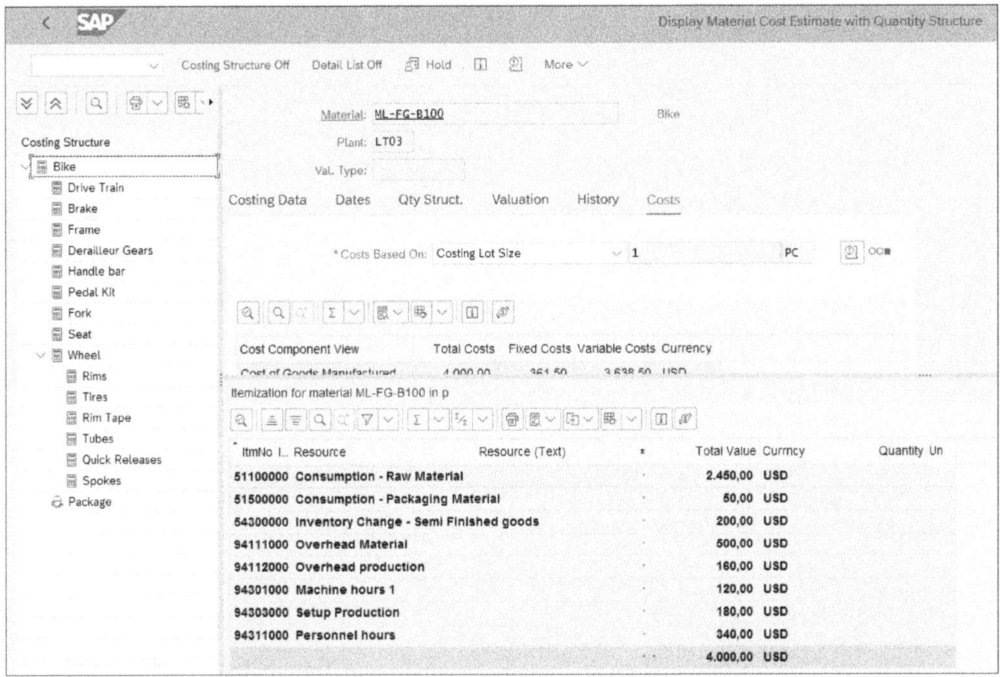


**Figure 6.26** Cost Estimate, Showing Accounts/Cost Elements for Finished Material

Activity Type Price Report: Cost Component Split

More

| | |
|---|---|
| **Cost Center** | LTP_002 Bike Production |
| **Activity Type** | ZMACHI Machine hours |
| **Version** | 0 Plan/Act - Version |
| **Fiscal Year** | 2021 |
| **Period** | 001 |
| **Price for Act.Val.** | 1 Plan price for the period |

| CC... | Name | Overall | Fixed | Variable | Crcy |
|---|---|---|---|---|---|
| 100 | Direct Material | | | | EUR |
| 101 | Machine Time | 0,29 | 0,29 | | EUR |
| 102 | Personnel Time | | | | EUR |
| 103 | Setup | | | | EUR |
| 104 | Material Overhead | 11,98- | 11,98- | | EUR |
| 105 | Production Overhead | 2,66- | 2,66- | | EUR |
| 106 | Freight | | | | EUR |
| | | **14,35-** | **14,35-** | | **EUR** |

**Figure 6.27** Primary Cost Component Split for Activity

### 6.2.4 Performing a Costing Run for Multiple Materials

It's useful to create cost estimates manually when you're testing or introducing a new product, but if you have a factory making hundreds of different products, you'll want to create cost estimates for them automatically using a *costing run*, which acts as a framework for all the cost estimates in one or more plants.

You can create and manage costing runs using **Accounting • Controlling • Product Cost Controlling • Product Cost Planning • Material Costing • Costing Run • Edit Costing Run** or Transaction CK40N (Manage Costing Run) to create a framework for the costing run, perform the various costing steps, and analyze the results. The costing run includes all the parameters that you would enter manually when you create a single cost estimate (refer back to Section 6.2.1), and you'll need to create a new one with the appropriate costing date for every period for which you set standard costs (some organizations do this annually, some per quarter, and some on a monthly basis). Figure 6.28 shows the general data for a costing run, with the same parameters for selecting dates and valuation approach as are used in a single material cost estimate. With large product structures, creating a costing run can have a significant performance impact; you may want to perform the steps by scheduling them to run in the background at a time when system load is low and specify the **Server Group** at which costing should take place.

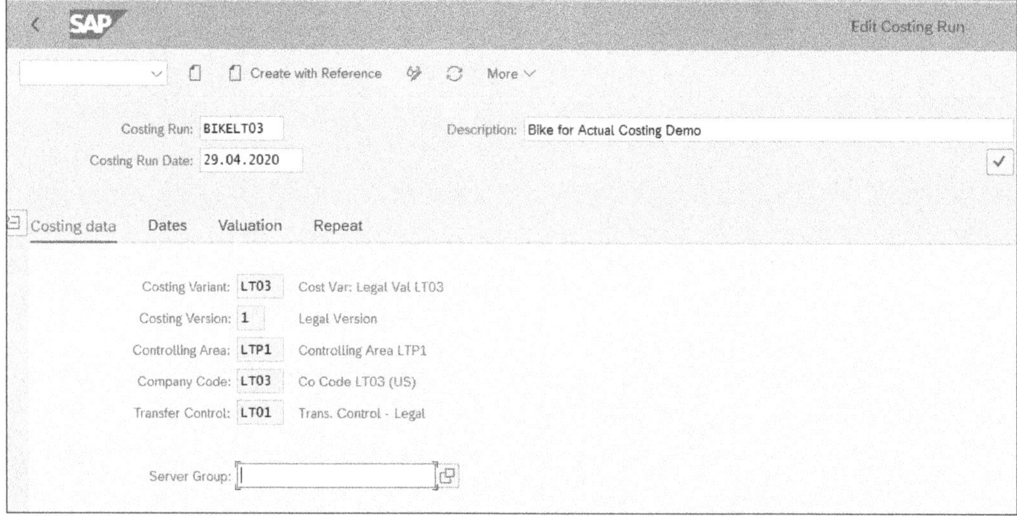


**Figure 6.28** General Data for Costing Run

In Figure 6.29, we've closed the **Costing data** section to show the **Process** flow steps in the costing run:

1. **Selection**
   Start with the **Selection** step, in which you identify the finished products that you want to include in costing. To enter the selection criteria that you want to use, select the icon in the **Parameter** column. To select all finished products in a plant, enter the plant code here and choose the **Execute** icon. When this step has run, you'll see the number of materials processed in the **Materials** column and any errors in the **Log** column.

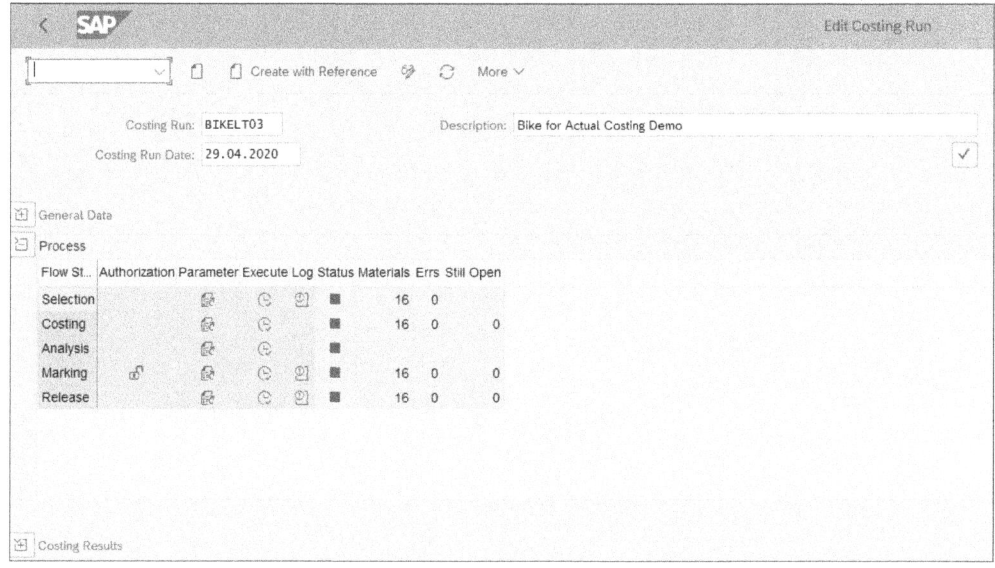


**Figure 6.29** Costing Run: Flow Steps

2. **Costing**
   Once the selection is successful, schedule the **Costing** step by entering the relevant parameters and choosing the **Execute** icon. This will create a cost estimate not just for the selected finished products, but for any semifinished products and raw materials referenced as well. In this example, we're using the bicycle from Figure 6.25 with three costing levels (the finished product, the semifinished product, and the raw materials).

3. **Analysis**
   Because releasing the cost estimate can have a significant impact on the inventory values, use the **Analysis** step to run various reports to understand the impact of the change. To ensure that everything has worked correctly, you should choose **Costing Results** after each step. This block is shown beneath the costing steps and will take you to a list showing the status for all the selected materials per costing level (see Figure 6.30). From here you can navigate to a list showing all the materials in the costing run (**Material Overview**) and an overview of the results (**Analysis**).

4. **Marking**
   When you're satisfied with the costing results, schedule the **Marking** step by entering the relevant parameters and choosing **Execute** to record the costing results as the future standard price for the selected materials. Before you do this, you'll have to allow marking for your costing variant, as we described for a single material. When marking has been performed, you'll see the unlocked icon.

5. **Release**
   Finally, schedule the **Release** step by entering the relevant parameters and choosing **Execute** to revalue the inventory with the result of the costing. With this step, you release the result of the cost estimate as a new standard price and revalue any

inventory. Again, you can access the reports to check that the changes were successful using the reports contained within the costing run (see Figure 6.31). Here you see that the status **FR** (released) has been set for all materials included in the costing run. This means that this costing run is complete.

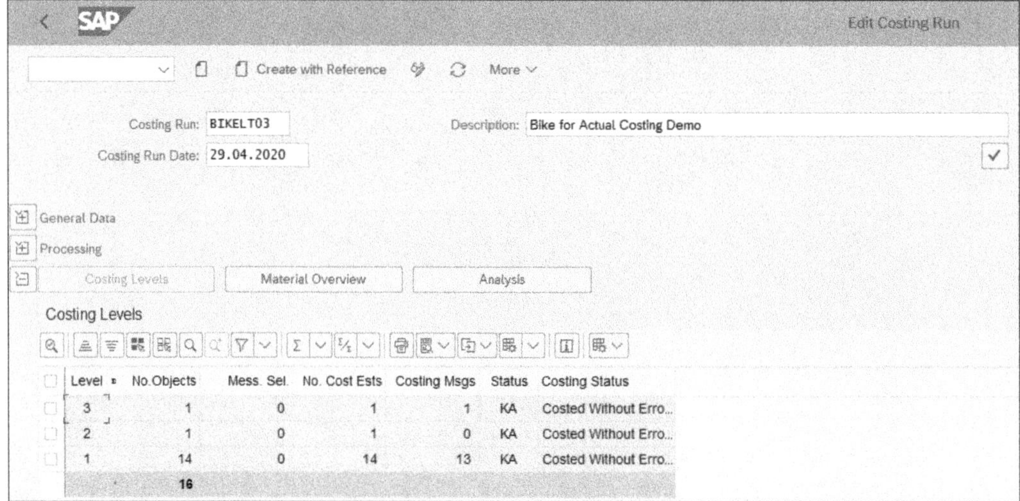


**Figure 6.30** Costing Run, Showing Results per Costing Level

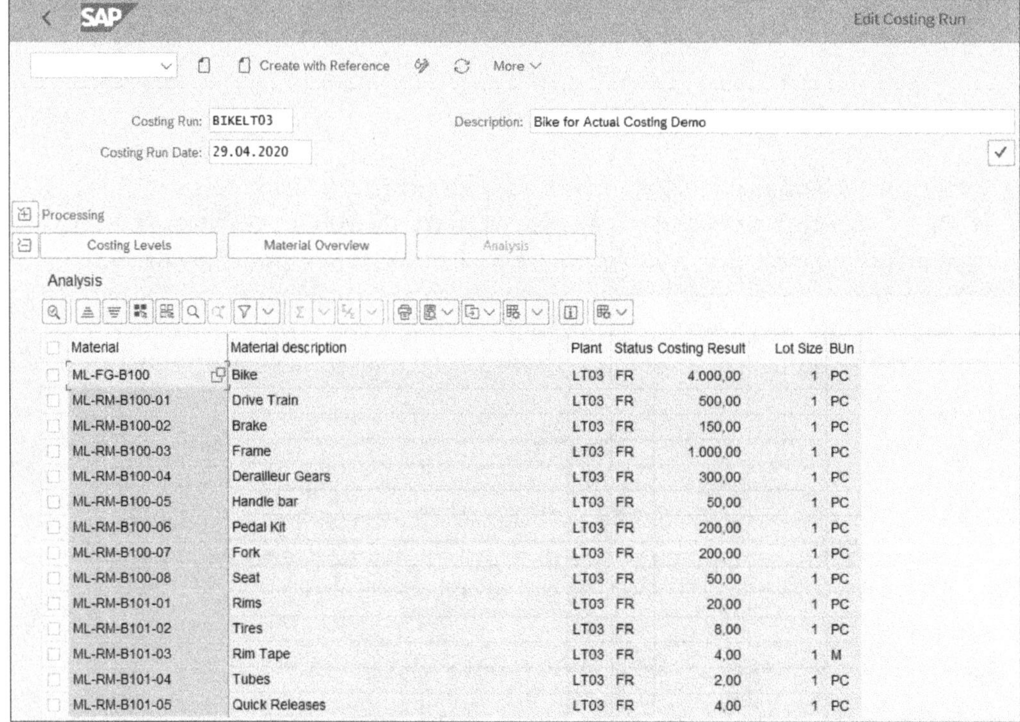


**Figure 6.31** Analysis of Costing Run

If you want to make a general selection, you can select the materials you want to include in the costing run by entering the appropriate plant and material type directly in the costing run. However, if you want to make a more specific selection, perhaps to exclude materials for which you have already created cost estimates, then you should consider using the separate *selection list*. You'll find these transactions in the **Costing Run** folder under **Create Selection List** (Transaction CKMATSEL) and **Edit Selection List** (Transaction CKMATCON).

Figure 6.32 shows the selection screen for such a selection list. This includes the same selections as in the costing run but also includes fields from the material master, such as **BOM Usage** and the **Special procurement** key, making it easier to be specific about the materials to be included and not waste system resources creating new cost estimates for materials that already have cost estimates.

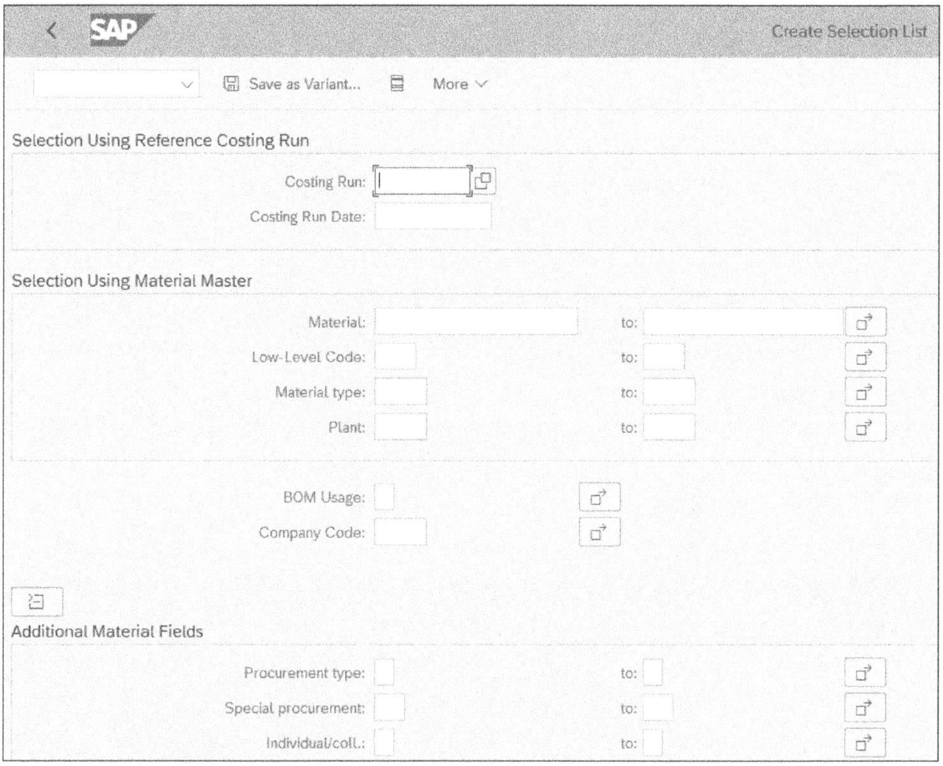

**Figure 6.32** Create Selection List for Costing

### 6.2.5 Sales Order-Specific Cost Estimates

When we introduced the BOM in Section 6.1.2, we explained that in industries such as automotive and high tech, it's common to create a BOM that includes all possible options for the product and rules that specify which combinations are technically feasible and which are not. It isn't possible to create a material cost estimate for configurable materials because the BOM contains all possible options that a customer might choose. It's only possible to create a cost estimate with reference to the sales order once the customer has specified the chosen options. You'll recognize these materials via the settings in the **MRP 3** tab of the material master (Transaction MM03), where the **Strategy Group** determines that the material can be configured and the **Configuration Allowed** flag is set for the material, as shown in Figure 6.33. You'll receive an error message if you try to create a cost estimate for a configurable material using Transaction CK11N.

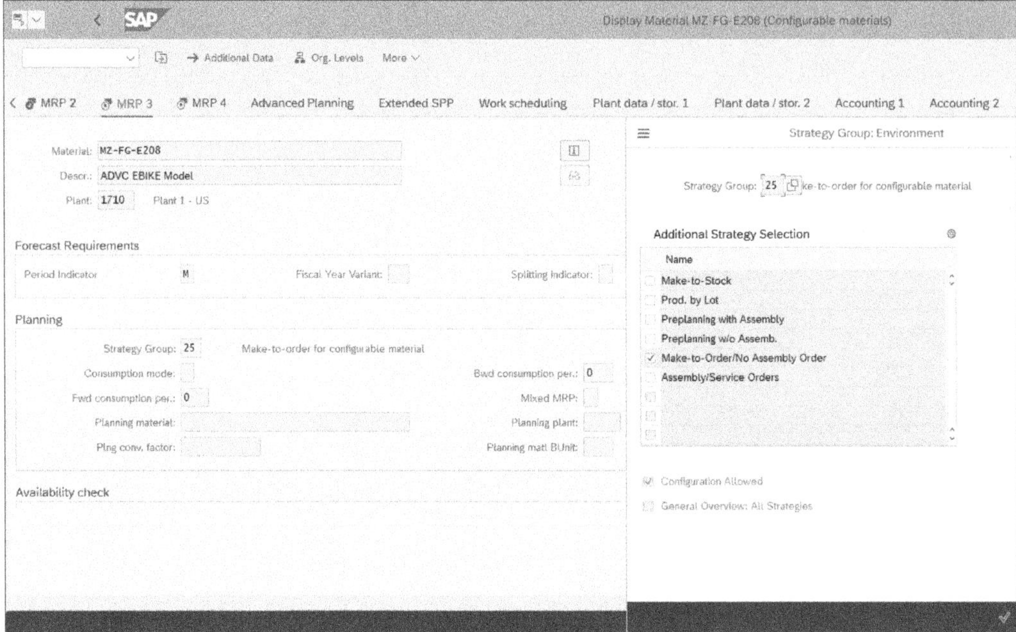


**Figure 6.33** Material Master for Configurable Material

The cost estimate for such materials can either be created by the sales representative when the sales order is created or by a specialist in controlling. To create a cost estimate within a sales order, select the sales order item and choose **Extras • Costing.** This will take you to a dialog showing a cost estimate, as in the previous sections, but one that references the sales order item. Figure 6.34 shows all the open sales orders for material **MZ-FG-E208** that are awaiting costing. To display this list, follow menu path **Accounting • Controlling • Product Cost Controlling • Cost Object Controlling • Product Cost by Sales Order • Cost Estimate • Display Sales Orders to be Costed** or use Transaction CKAPP03. You can then create cost estimates for these sales orders by following menu path **Product Cost by Sales Order • Cost Estimate • Mass Costing—Sales Documents** or using Transaction CK55.

Another option is to create a cost estimate with reference to the order BOM by following menu path **Product Cost by Sales Order • Cost Estimate • Order BOM Cost Estimate • Create** or using Transaction CK51N. Figure 6.35 shows an order BOM cost estimate. The differences compared to the standard cost estimates that we showed in Section 6.2.1 is that the estimate is assigned to the combination of material and sales order item and that the material is flagged as a **Configurable Material**. This cost estimate can be used to value inventory delivered to stock with respect to item **10** of sales order **107230**, as an alternative to creating a cost estimate within the sales order.

Display Sales Order Items to be Costed

| Sales Doc. | Item | Sold-To Party | Material | Req.Dlv.Dt | Statu... | St... |
|---|---|---|---|---|---|---|
| 107230 | 10 | USCU_L10 | MZ-FG-E208 | 14.08.2018 | | |
| 111256 | 10 | USCU-L-877 | MZ-FG-E208 | 21.09.2018 | | |
| 118662 | 10 | USCU-L-75 | MZ-FG-E208 | 04.12.2018 | | |
| 118859 | 10 | USCU-L-877 | MZ-FG-E208 | 06.12.2018 | | |
| 233245 | 10 | USCU-L-877 | MZ-FG-E208 | 21.12.2020 | | |
| 235214 | 10 | USCU-L-877 | MZ-FG-E208 | 05.01.2021 | | |
| 235218 | 10 | USCU-L-877 | MZ-FG-E208 | 05.01.2021 | | |

**Figure 6.34** List of Sales Order Items to Be Costed

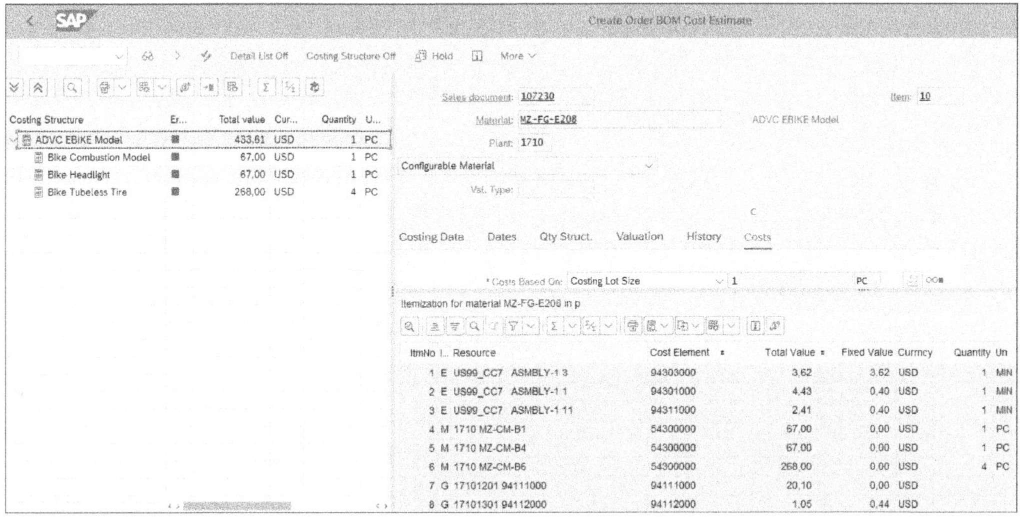


**Figure 6.35** Order BOM Cost Estimate for Sales Order 107230 and Material MZ-FG-E208

We'll explain how to create cross-company cost estimates when we look at intercompany processes in Chapter 9.

## 6.3 Procure-to-Invoice

When we looked at the cost estimate for the bicycle in the previous section, we showed a list of the various material components that need to be purchased before manufacturing of the bicycle can begin. Normally, an MRP run is used to generate purchase requisitions for the components that will be needed to manufacture the bicycles planned for a given period, and these are converted into a *purchase order* by the buyer. The purchase order is an agreement with a vendor to supply materials at a given price. This price can also be used to set the standard price in the material master, but it may change depending on the business climate. The receipt of the materials into stock and the invoice both reference this purchase order (you'll hear this process referred to as a *three-way match*). The *goods receipt* is valued initially using the price in the purchase order, and the invoice may adjust this price. The controller's concern in this process is *purchase price variances*, whether these arise as a result of exchange rate differences if the purchase is from overseas or as a result of the process itself (the price charged may depend on the quality of the material, for example).

The bicycle BOM that we showed previously in Figure 6.5 only contained stock materials, but it's also possible to include *nonstock* materials in a BOM that must be purchased specifically for a production order via a purchasing process that's triggered from the production order. In this case, the *account assignment category* in the purchase order will link the item with the production order—and of course it's also possible to purchase items with respect to a cost center, a work breakdown structure (WBS) element, an asset, and so on, as we showed in the documents relating to the purchase of office supplies in Chapter 2 and an asset purchase in Chapter 5.

In Section 6.3.1, we'll walk through the process of creating a purchase order and explain how to check the price information. We'll then show how to receive the purchased goods into stock and the associated journal entries in Section 6.3.2. Then in Section 6.3.3 we'll show how to create a vendor invoice and the associated journal entries.

### 6.3.1 Creating a Purchase Order

We'll begin by creating a purchase order to request the supply of the various bicycle components from an external vendor. To create a purchase order, use Transaction ME21N or follow menu path **Logistics • Materials Management • Purchasing • Purchase Order • Create • Vendor/Supplying Plant Known**. Then enter the vendor, purchasing organization, and company code in the header (this dialog box is closed in the example) and the **Material**, plant (**Plnt**), and quantity (**PO Quantity**) for each item (see Figure 6.36). If you work with an MRP run, this purchase order can also be created by converting the purchase requisition created during the MRP run. When you've entered all the relevant materials, choose **Save** and note the number of the purchase order for use as a reference when you create the goods receipt as the next step in the process.

Create Purchase Order

Standard PO — Vendor: USSU-VSF06 VF Vendor 06 — Doc. Date: 06.01.2021

| Itm | Material | Short Text | PO Quantity | OUn | C | Deliv. Date | Net Price | Curre... | Per | OPU | Matl Group | Plnt |
|---|---|---|---|---|---|---|---|---|---|---|---|---|
| 10 | MZ-RM-C900-01 | Frame 900 | 10 | PC | D | 07.01.2021 | 102,80 | USD | 1 | PC | Frame | Plant 1 - US |
| 20 | MZ-RM-C900-02 | Handle Bars-900 | 10 | PC | D | 07.01.2021 | 3,95 | USD | 1 | PC | Handle Bars | Plant 1 - US |
| 30 | MZ-RM-C900-03 | Seat - 900 | 10 | PC | D | 07.01.2021 | 3,95 | USD | 1 | PC | Seat | Plant 1 - US |
| 40 | MZ-RM-C900-04 | Wheels-900 | 20 | PC | D | 07.01.2021 | 6,92 | USD | 1 | PC | Wheels | Plant 1 - US |
| 50 | MZ-RM-C900-05 | Forks-900 | 10 | PC | D | 07.01.2021 | 15,81 | USD | 1 | PC | Forks | Plant 1 - US |
| 60 | MZ-RM-C900-06 | Brakes-900 | 10 | PC | D | 07.01.2021 | 13,84 | USD | 1 | PC | Brakes | Plant 1 - US |
| 70 | MZ-RM-C900-07 | Drive Train-900 | 10 | PC | D | 07.01.2021 | 43,49 | USD | 1 | PC | Drive Train | Plant 1 - US |
| | | | | | | | | USD | | | | |

**Figure 6.36** Purchase Order Showing Materials, Quantities, and Net Prices

To view how the price of each item was determined, select the item for the bike **Frame** in Figure 6.36 and select the **Conditions** tab in the lower part of the screen. In Figure 6.37, you can see that the first item (the bicycle frame) costs 102.80 dollars per piece. You can navigate to the prices for the other items using the up/down arrows. This may already be the source of a purchase price variance if the agreement with the vendor is based on a different price than that currently in the material master. The controller might also check the *account assignment*. In the example, column **A** (account assignment category) is blank (not shown), meaning the purchase order will be delivered to regular inventory and can be used by any production order that reserves it.

This document has no impact on accounting, though if the purchase is assigned to a cost center or WBS element you would see it in predictive accounting, as shown in Chapter 2, or as a commitment, as we'll discuss in Chapter 9. The next step is to record the arrival of the bicycle parts into stock.

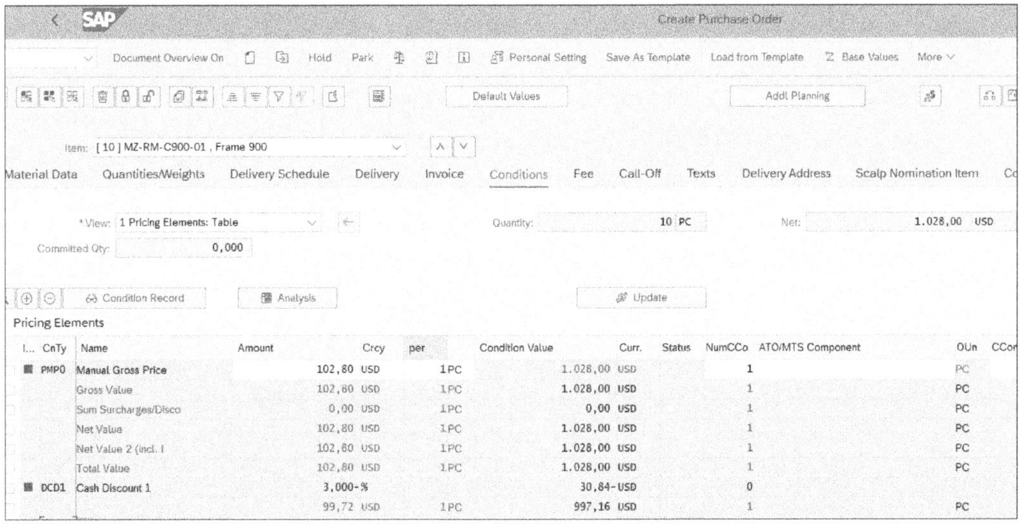

Create Purchase Order

Item: [ 10 ] MZ-RM-C900-01 , Frame 900 — Tab: Conditions — View: 1 Pricing Elements: Table — Quantity: 10 PC — Net: 1.028,00 USD — Committed Qty: 0,000

Pricing Elements

| CnTy | Name | Amount | Crcy | per | | Condition Value | Curr. | Status | NumCCo | ATO/MTS Component | OUn |
|---|---|---|---|---|---|---|---|---|---|---|---|
| PMP0 | Manual Gross Price | 102,80 | USD | 1 | PC | 1.028,00 | USD | | 1 | | PC |
| | Gross Value | 102,80 | USD | 1 | PC | 1.028,00 | USD | | 1 | | PC |
| | Sum Surcharges/Disco | 0,00 | USD | 1 | PC | 0,00 | USD | | 1 | | PC |
| | Net Value | 102,80 | USD | 1 | PC | 1.028,00 | USD | | 1 | | PC |
| | Net Value 2 (incl. I | 102,80 | USD | 1 | PC | 1.028,00 | USD | | 1 | | PC |
| | Total Value | 102,80 | USD | 1 | PC | 1.028,00 | USD | | 1 | | PC |
| DCD1 | Cash Discount 1 | 3,000- | % | | | 30,84- | USD | | 0 | | |
| | | 99,72 | USD | 1 | PC | 997,16 | USD | | 1 | | PC |

**Figure 6.37** Price Conditions for Bike Frame

### 6.3.2 Posting a Goods Receipt

Now we'll create the goods receipt for the purchase order by referencing the purchase order and the prices contained in it. The easiest way to do this is to stay in the **Purchasing** menu and select **Follow-On Functions • Goods Receipt** or Transaction MIGO. Enter the purchase order from Figure 6.36 as a reference and click **Execute**. Figure 6.38 shows the items ordered and indicates that they're to be delivered into unrestricted stock (goods movement **101** to stock segment blank). To receive the items, flag the various components as being **OK** and enter the storage location (**SLoc**) to receive them. This will result in the creation of a material document that you can also access from Transaction MIGO by choosing from the document entries shown in the overview on the left of Figure 6.38.

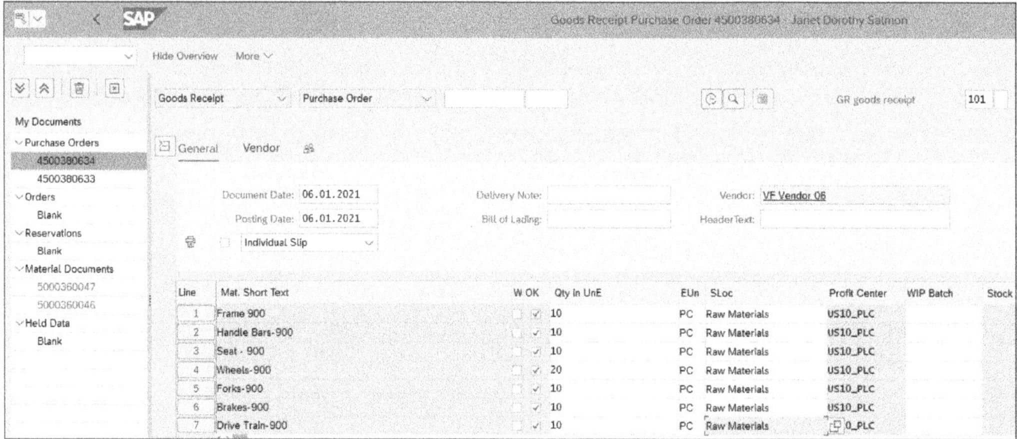

**Figure 6.38** Goods Receipt for Purchase Order

**Note**

In SAP S/4HANA, the old transactions for displaying material documents (Transaction MB03) have been removed.

We discussed the links between the various logistics steps and the related journal entries in Chapter 5. The material document for the goods receipt is recorded as a journal entry in the Universal Journal. You can display all goods movements for a material by using Transaction CKM3N or **Accounting • Controlling • Product Cost Controlling • Actual Costing/Material Ledger • Material Ledger • Material Price Analysis** and entering the material, plant, and period. From the list of goods movements in the period, choose **Source Documents** to display the material document shown in Figure 6.38 and **Accounting Documents** to show the associated journal entries. This document is integrated tightly with accounting, where many of the key steps such as the assignment of the costs to the general ledger account or any currency conversion happen within the logistics process and are then transferred to accounting. Figure 6.39 shows the accounting entries for the goods receipt, including the general ledger accounts and the associated materials. If your document shows different fields, change the layout to show some of the other fields in the document.

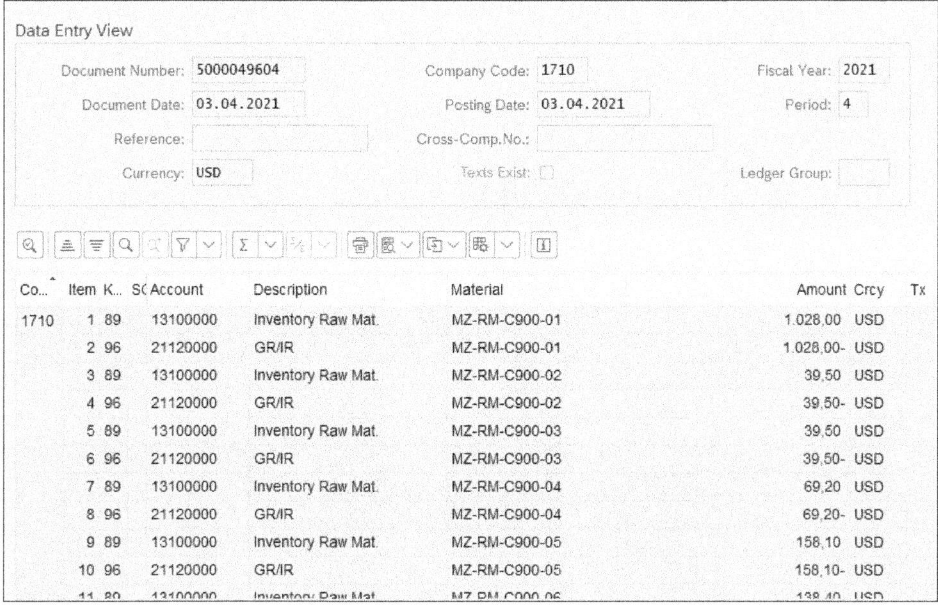


| Co... | Item | K... | SC Account | Description | Material | Amount | Crcy | Tx |
|---|---|---|---|---|---|---|---|---|
| 1710 | 1 | 89 | 13100000 | Inventory Raw Mat. | MZ-RM-C900-01 | 1.028,00 | USD | |
| | 2 | 96 | 21120000 | GR/IR | MZ-RM-C900-01 | 1.028,00- | USD | |
| | 3 | 89 | 13100000 | Inventory Raw Mat. | MZ-RM-C900-02 | 39,50 | USD | |
| | 4 | 96 | 21120000 | GR/IR | MZ-RM-C900-02 | 39,50- | USD | |
| | 5 | 89 | 13100000 | Inventory Raw Mat. | MZ-RM-C900-03 | 39,50 | USD | |
| | 6 | 96 | 21120000 | GR/IR | MZ-RM-C900-03 | 39,50- | USD | |
| | 7 | 89 | 13100000 | Inventory Raw Mat. | MZ-RM-C900-04 | 69,20 | USD | |
| | 8 | 96 | 21120000 | GR/IR | MZ-RM-C900-04 | 69,20- | USD | |
| | 9 | 89 | 13100000 | Inventory Raw Mat. | MZ-RM-C900-05 | 158,10 | USD | |
| | 10 | 96 | 21120000 | GR/IR | MZ-RM-C900-05 | 158,10- | USD | |

**Figure 6.39** Journal Entry for Goods Receipt

## 6.3.3 Entering an Incoming Invoice

Now we'll record the receipt of the invoice from the vendor for the delivery of the materials. To record the invoice, return to the **Purchasing** menu and select **Follow-On Functions • Logistics Invoice Verification** or Transaction MIRO. For invoices to be used in actual costing, it's important to use the logistics invoice verification transaction (Transaction MIRO) rather than the invoice entry transaction (Transaction FB60) in accounts payable as you need to ensure that the invoice is linked to the material purchased for actual costing.

Just as we showed for the goods receipt, the invoice also is created with reference to the initial purchase order (see Figure 6.40). Here we've created an incoming invoice with reference to the purchase order/scheduling agreement from the previous step. The system has copied over all the items from the purchase order for inclusion in the invoice. When you save the invoice, the invoice receipt is recorded as an accounting document in the general ledger, as shown in Figure 6.41. Again, you can access both the invoice and the associated journal entry from Transaction CKM3N (Material Price Analysis) as both the goods receipt and invoice receipt have an impact on the inventory valuation.

Enter Incoming Invoice: Company Code 1710
Show PO structure
Show worklist
Simulate
Help
NF
Base Values
More
* Transaction: Invoice
Diff. Posting: Not Applicable
Balance: 0,00 USD
Header
PO Reference
G/L Account
Contract Reference
Purchase Order/Scheduling Agreement
4500380634
Goods/service items
* Layout: All information
Item Amount Quantity Or... Purchase order Item PO Text
1 1.028,00 10 PC 4500380634 10 Frame 900
2 39,50 10 PC 4500380634 20 Handle Bars-900
3 39,50 10 PC 4500380634 30 Seat - 900
4 138,40 20 PC 4500380634 40 Wheels-900
5 158,10 10 PC 4500380634 50 Forks-900
6 138,40 10 PC 4500380634 60 Brakes-900
7 434,90 10 PC 4500380634 70 Drive Train-900

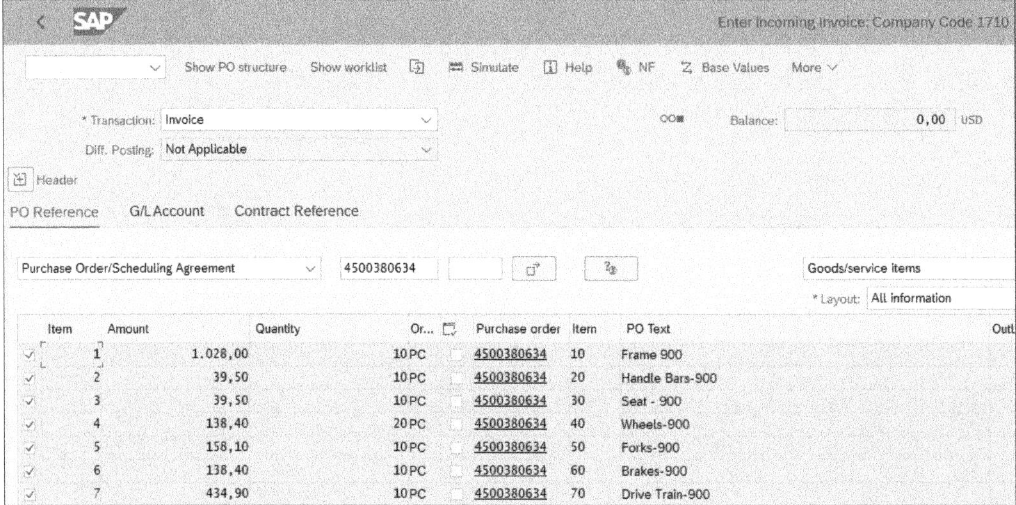

**Figure 6.40** Invoice Receipt

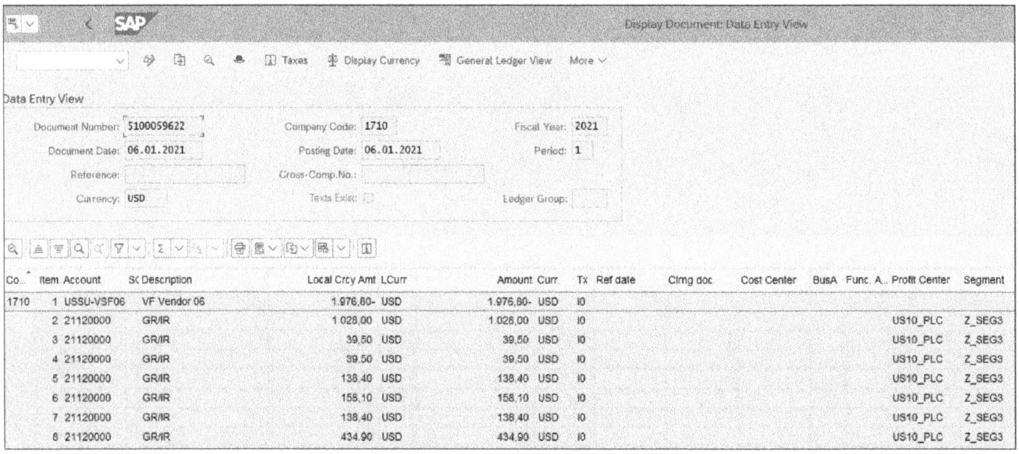

Display Document: Data Entry View
Taxes
Display Currency
General Ledger View
More
Data Entry View
Document Number: 5100059622
Company Code: 1710
Fiscal Year: 2021
Document Date: 06.01.2021
Posting Date: 06.01.2021
Period: 1
Reference:
Cross-Comp.No.:
Currency: USD
Texts Exist:
Ledger Group:
Co... Item Account S Description Local Crcy Amt LCurr Amount Curr Tx Ref date Clrng doc Cost Center BusA Func. A.. Profit Center Segment
1710 1 USSU-VSF06 VF Vendor 06 1.976,80- USD 1.976,80- USD I0
2 21120000 GR/IR 1.028,00 USD 1.028,00 USD I0 US10_PLC Z_SEG3
3 21120000 GR/IR 39,50 USD 39,50 USD I0 US10_PLC Z_SEG3
4 21120000 GR/IR 39,50 USD 39,50 USD I0 US10_PLC Z_SEG3
5 21120000 GR/IR 138,40 USD 138,40 USD I0 US10_PLC Z_SEG3
6 21120000 GR/IR 158,10 USD 158,10 USD I0 US10_PLC Z_SEG3
7 21120000 GR/IR 138,40 USD 138,40 USD I0 US10_PLC Z_SEG3
8 21120000 GR/IR 434,90 USD 434,90 USD I0 US10_PLC Z_SEG3

**Figure 6.41** Journal Entry for Invoice Receipt

Normally, the process would continue with an open item for the payables in accounts payable and a payment to the vendor, but we'll move straight to the manufacturing process to show how these components are consumed to make the bicycle. Later, the invoice receipt will clear against the goods receipt to complete the process.

## 6.4 Make-to-Stock with Order Costing

In Section 6.2, we explained how to calculate the standard costs for one or more units of product. This cost estimate is part of the planning process and is used to set *standard costs* that will be used to value the goods receipt when the finished product is delivered to stock. In general, the standard costs remain stable for some time (between one fiscal period and one year). However, the cost situation can evolve over this time, and so each order can incur costs that differ from the standard costs.

To show what can change as an order reaches the shop floor, we'll follow the production process, showing what happens when you create a manufacturing order and the impact of choosing a different lot size, substituting some components, or shifting some elements of the production process due to capacity constraints on the planned costs for the order. We'll review the main elements of this process from a make-to-stock perspective in Section 6.4.1. The *planned costs* for a manufacturing order are calculated up front before the order is released. The *actual costs* are accumulated on the manufacturing order with each step of the production process, and we'll walk through these steps in Section 6.4.2. In some organizations, every operation is confirmed separately, whereas in others only the final goods receipt is recorded, and this triggers a *backflush* of all the required material components and operations in a single event. In Section 6.4.3, we'll explain how these goods movements and confirmations provide the basis for the calculation of WIP, and in Section 6.4.4 we'll look at how to calculate production variances. We'll close in Section 6.4.5 by exploring how to use actual costing to assign variances to the finished goods inventory at period close.



### 6.4.1 Using the Material Cost Estimate to Set Standard Costs

Before you begin manufacturing, you need to be sure that there is a released cost estimate available for the material to be manufactured. This is because you will deliver this material to stock using the standard price as the most reliable basis for inventory valuation until all actual costs are known. The standard cost estimate that we showed previously in Figure 6.3 is the explanation of the standard costs used to value the inventory, and variance calculation takes place with reference to the items within this cost estimate. Before this cost estimate can be used as a basis for variance analysis, it must first be marked and released as we showed previously in Figure 6.16, Figure 6.17, and Figure 6.18.

Recall our discussion about *target costs* in Chapter 2. The released cost estimate sets a value that will be used to determine the target costs for the complete bicycle. In addition, it will be used to set the target costs for each operation when you calculate the value of any scrap or if you calculate WIP at target costs. For this reason, you should also check the operation view of the cost estimate, shown previously in Figure 6.20, to ensure that the material items are assigned to the correct operations and that any scrap includes only those material items that have genuinely been issued for use in that operation, rather than in later operations, and that your WIP is not being accidentally overstated as a result of incorrect assignments.

### 6.4.2 Monitoring the Production Process

Let's begin by understanding how your organization approaches order costing. There are two basic kinds of manufacturing orders in SAP S/4HANA:

1. *Production orders* are usually used in the discrete industry and use BOMs and routings to determine the resources used.
2. *Process orders* are usually used in the process industries and use master recipes to determine the resources used.

The two types of orders differ from a logistical point of view but are virtually identical from a costing point of view, and the reports we discuss in this section can be used interchangeably for both order types. The *order costing* approach makes sense when setup costs are significant and full traceability for each order is a business requirement. There may also be regulatory requirements concerning batch traceability in the pharmaceutical industry, meaning that each order must be considered unique to be traceable.

> **SAP ERP versus SAP S/4HANA**
>
> In terms of logistics, the main difference as you move to SAP S/4HANA from SAP ERP is that the use of *production versions* to select the BOM and routing becomes mandatory in SAP S/4HANA. From a costing point of view, the information from the BOM and routing is stored in the order in a more granular form than in SAP ERP, so the Universal Journal includes new fields for the work center and operation that did not previously exist, as we showed in Chapter 2.

As you move to SAP S/4HANA, you'll have to decide whether you are going to work with SAP Fiori or continue to use the SAP GUI transactions. If you work with production orders or process orders in SAP GUI, it will appear that not much has changed because the system is using *compatibility views* (a topic that we will return to in Chapter 10) to pull the more granular information in the Universal Journal back into the old structures for reporting. So, you won't see actual costs by work center or operation when you look at the costs in the production order transactions (Transactions CO01–CO03) or process order transactions (Transactions CR01–CR03). To see these details, you'll have to use the Costs by Work Center/Operation app.

Now, let's begin walking through the steps to monitor the value added in each stage of the production process.

#### Creating a Production Order

The basic information required to calculate the planned costs for a production order is the same as is needed to calculate standard costs. The difference is that the operations and components are included in the production order to provide the instructions for those on the shop floor.

To create a production order, use Transaction CO01 or choose **Logistics • Production • Shop Floor Control • Order • Create with Material** and enter the material to be manufactured, the plant, and the order type (this controls the selection parameters for the manufacturing process and the default settings for overhead calculation, variance calculation, settlement, etc.). The system will then use the relevant production version to select the appropriate BOM and routing for that order. To check the result of the selection, choose the **Operations** button. Figure 6.42 shows the two operations that will be performed to assemble and check the bike and the work centers at which these operations are performed. These work centers are again linked to cost centers and the activity types for the production activities. Notice the flag in the **COMP** column, which indicates that all the material components are assigned to the first operation; this is important for the calculation of scrap and WIP.



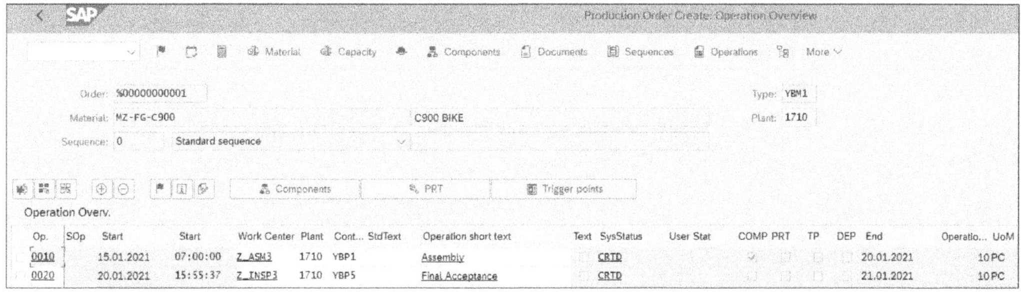


**Figure 6.42** Production Order Showing Operations

To display the components to be used at the operations, double-click the first operation (**0010** in the **Op.** column) and choose the **Components** button to access the information shown in Figure 6.43, which shows the components assigned to the first operation (the materials ordered from the supplier in the previous section). These are the materials that will have to be made available on the shop floor prior to assembly and the issue of which from stock will result in raw material costs on the order. Notice the **Bf** (backflushing) flag that means that the goods issue will be triggered by the confirmation, rather than issued as a separate goods movement.

In Figure 6.42 and Figure 6.43, we haven't yet saved the order (notice that the order number still begins with %). During order creation, the system creates the itemization view that we saw in the previous section and assigns the costing items to **Operations**, but you can create the itemization manually prior to saving by choosing **More • GoTo • Costs • Itemization** from the production order header, arriving at the screen shown in Figure 6.44. When you save the order, the system will issue an order number that you can use as a reference for all goods movements and confirmations. However, before you can assign costs to the production order, you will have to release it by choosing **More • Functions • Release** prior to **Save**.

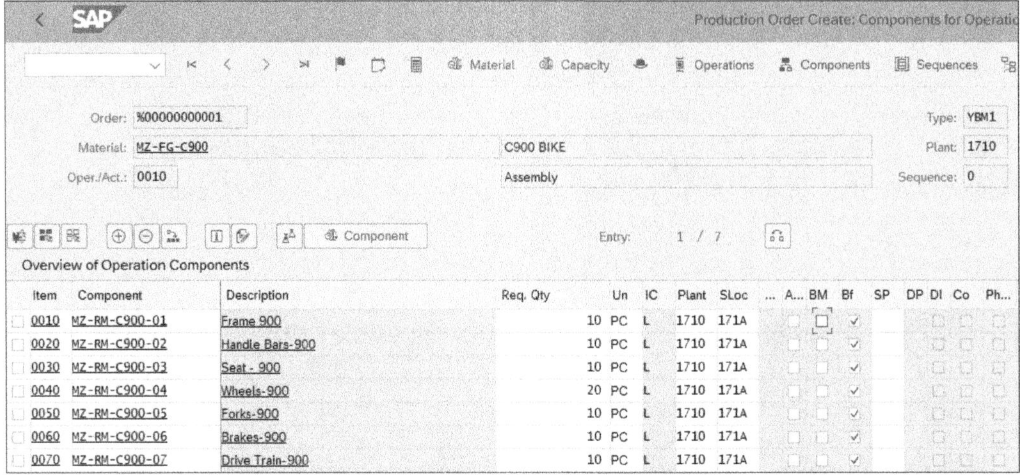


**Figure 6.43** Production Order, Showing Material Components

Operations (grouped)

**Order** %00000000001
**Material** MZ-FG-C900 C900 BIKE
**Plant** 1710 Plant 1 - US
**Lot Size** 10 ST Piece
**Cost Base** 10 ST Piece

| ItmNo | I... | Resource | Resource (Text) | Total Value | COCr | Quantity | Un |
|---|---|---|---|---|---|---|---|
| 1 | E | US10_PLC Z_ASM3 3 | Assembly | 1.322,69 | USD | 19,400 | H |
| 2 | E | US10_PLC Z_ASM3 1 | Assembly | 257,68 | USD | 4,535 | H |
| 3 | E | US10_PLC Z_ASM3 11 | Assembly | 306,33 | USD | 6,740 | H |
| 4 | M | 1710 MZ-RM-C900-01 | Frame 900 | 1.028,00 | USD | 10 | PC |
| 5 | M | 1710 MZ-RM-C900-02 | Handle Bars-900 | 39,50 | USD | 10 | PC |
| 6 | M | 1710 MZ-RM-C900-03 | Seat - 900 | 39,50 | USD | 10 | PC |
| 7 | M | 1710 MZ-RM-C900-04 | Wheels-900 | 138,40 | USD | 20 | PC |
| 8 | M | 1710 MZ-RM-C900-05 | Forks-900 | 158,10 | USD | 10 | PC |
| 9 | M | 1710 MZ-RM-C900-06 | Brakes-900 | 138,40 | USD | 10 | PC |
| 10 | M | 1710 MZ-RM-C900-07 | Drive Train-900 | 434,90 | USD | 10 | PC |
| **0010 Assembly** | | | | **3.863,50** | **USD** | | |
| 11 | E | US10_PLC Z_INSP3 3 | Final Acceptance | 330,67 | USD | 4,850 | H |
| 12 | E | US10_PLC Z_INSP3 1 | Final Acceptance | 64,38 | USD | 1,133 | H |
| 13 | E | US10_PLC Z_INSP3 11 | Final Acceptance | 76,58 | USD | 1,685 | H |
| **0020 Final Acceptance** | | | | **471,63** | **USD** | | |
| | | | | **1.541,04** | **USD** | | |

**Figure 6.44** Itemization for Production Order

**SAP ERP versus SAP S/4HANA**

In SAP ERP, this view is only available for the planned costs on the order and isn't updated when actual costs are updated to the production order during manufacturing. All that remained in SAP ERP were the accounts/cost elements and the cost centers and activity types (machine hours, setup production, and personnel hours), but no work centers or operations. For this reason, any transactions that needed information by operation to calculate the target costs for WIP and scrap had to read the information in logistics to determine the relevant costs per operation. Planned costs, target costs, and actual costs in SAP S/4HANA are all available for the operations and work centers, though you'll have to switch to the SAP Fiori applications to view them.



### Confirming the Operation

Actual costs can be confirmed either at the order level or at the operation level and your choice will depend on the production environment. In the discrete industry, it's generally possible to capture information after every operation, whereas in the process industry it can often be difficult to capture chemical processes. If you record at the operation level, every goods movement and confirmation will be captured separately as the order moves along the production line. If you record at the order level, costs are captured at the very end of the production process when the final goods receipt triggers a *backflush* of all the required components and operations.

Because the bicycle in this example is a discrete product, confirm at the operation level using Transaction CO11N or **Logistics • Production • Shop Floor Control • Confirmation • Enter • For Operation • Time Ticket**. Figure 6.45 shows the operation confirmation screen. Notice in the **Quantities** section that you will usually confirm a **Yield** (10 bicycles in the example), but it's also possible to confirm **Scrap** if one of the bicycles is damaged or **Rework** if it's possible to save the bicycle by performing extra production work. The system uses the standard values in the routing to propose the times shown in the **Activities** section, and these can be overwritten if the production activity takes longer (we've adjusted the activity times so that we can demonstrate how to analyze production variances later). Because the material components are backflushed (refer back to Figure 6.43), the system issues the material components as part of the confirmation. You can check the proposal by selecting the **Goods Movements** button. Again, if additional material is required to complete the operation, this can be recorded here.

When you check the results of the confirmation using the reports included in the production order (see Figure 6.46) or Transaction KKBC_ORD, the operation costs won't be separated but will be subsumed under the combination of cost center and activity type, meaning that you'll see single lines for **Machine hours**, **Personnel hours**, and **Setup Production**.

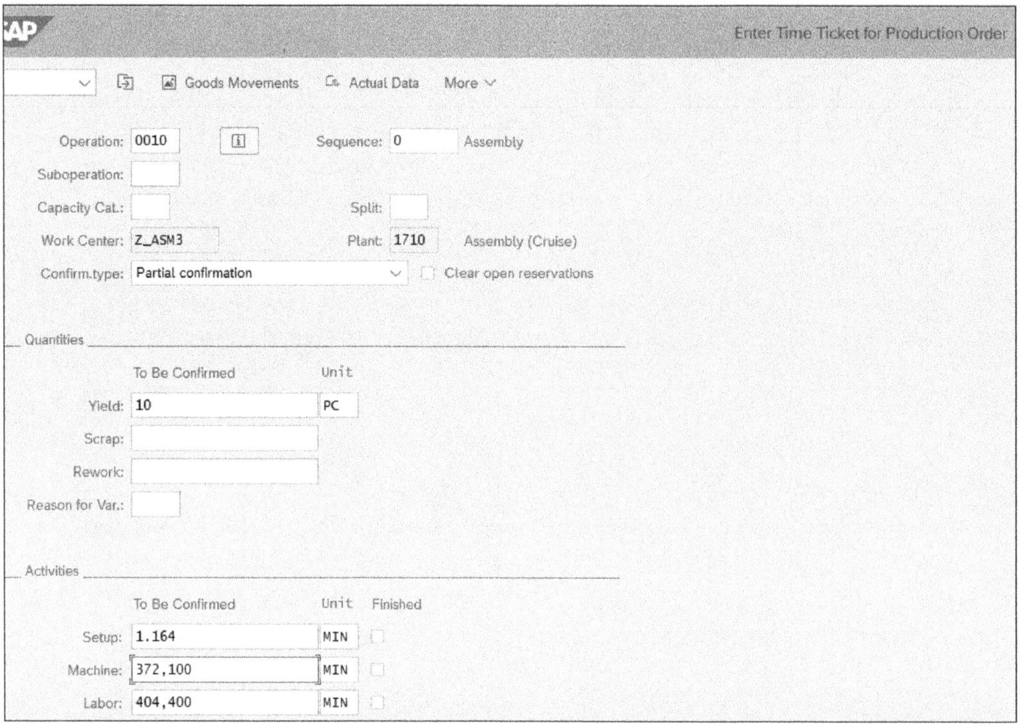


**Figure 6.45** Yield Confirmation for First Operation

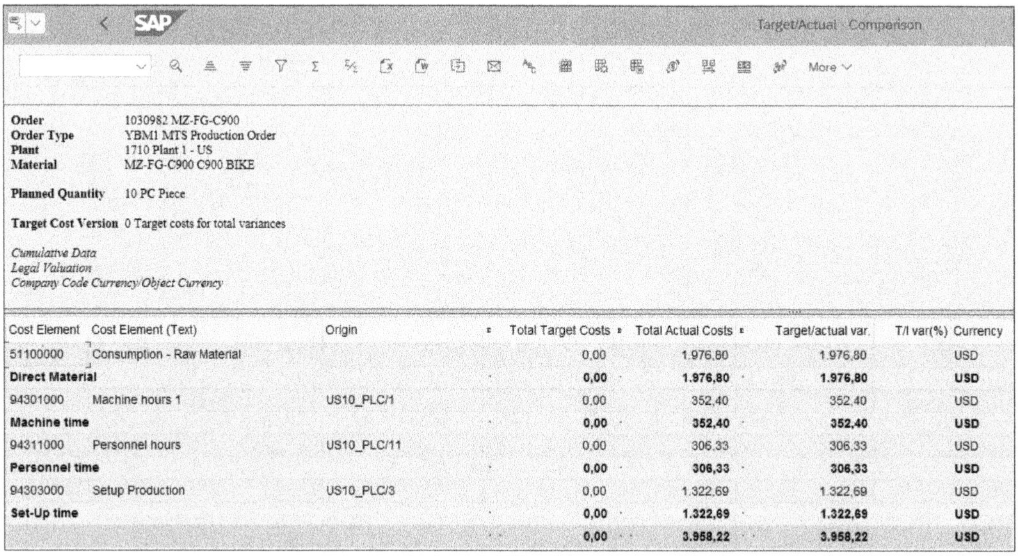


**Order** 1030982 MZ-FG-C900
**Order Type** YBM1 MTS Production Order
**Plant** 1710 Plant 1 - US
**Material** MZ-FG-C900 C900 BIKE

**Planned Quantity** 10 PC Piece

**Target Cost Version** 0 Target costs for total variances

*Cumulative Data*
*Legal Valuation*
*Company Code Currency/Object Currency*

| Cost Element | Cost Element (Text) | Origin | Total Target Costs | Total Actual Costs | Target/actual var. | T/I var(%) | Currency |
|---|---|---|---|---|---|---|---|
| 51100000 | Consumption - Raw Material | | 0,00 | 1.976,80 | 1.976,80 | | USD |
| **Direct Material** | | | **0,00** | **1.976,80** | **1.976,80** | | **USD** |
| 94301000 | Machine hours 1 | US10_PLC/1 | 0,00 | 352,40 | 352,40 | | USD |
| **Machine time** | | | **0,00** | **352,40** | **352,40** | | **USD** |
| 94311000 | Personnel hours | US10_PLC/11 | 0,00 | 306,33 | 306,33 | | USD |
| **Personnel time** | | | **0,00** | **306,33** | **306,33** | | **USD** |
| 94303000 | Setup Production | US10_PLC/3 | 0,00 | 1.322,69 | 1.322,69 | | USD |
| **Set-Up time** | | | **0,00** | **1.322,69** | **1.322,69** | | **USD** |
| | | | **0,00** | **3.958,22** | **3.958,22** | | **USD** |

**Figure 6.46** Costs Following Partial Confirmation on Production Order

However, as we discussed in Chapter 2, the Universal Journal includes new fields for the operation and the associated work center, and you'll be able to see this more granular information in the Costs by Work Center/Operation app. Figure 6.47 shows the costs at work center **Z_ASM3**, where the first operation for the assembly of the bikes was confirmed. We've added the **Order** to the selection parameters to demonstrate that the app is giving a more granular view of the costs.

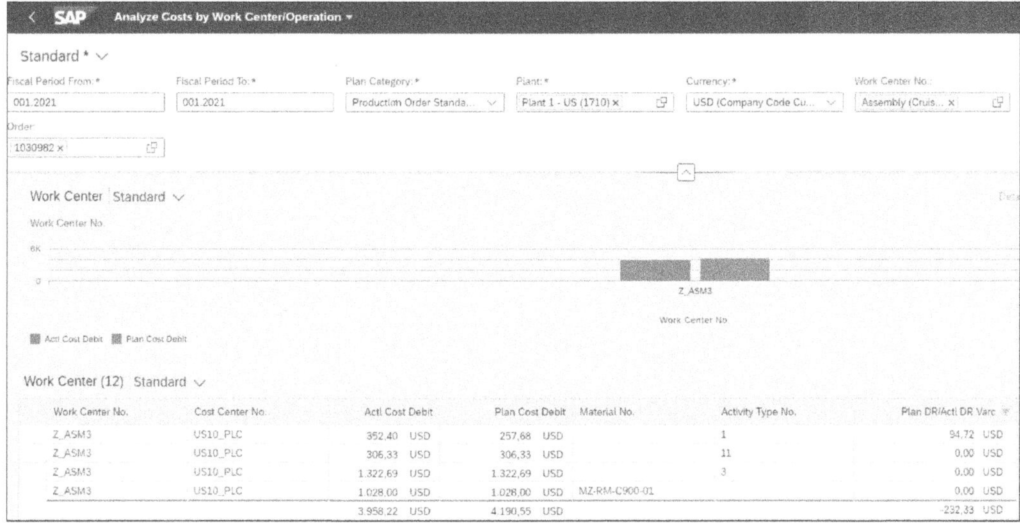


**Figure 6.47** Analyze Costs by Work Center/Operation App, Showing Results of First Confirmation

### Delivering to Stock

We'll now look at how the delivery of the finished bicycles to stock triggers the calculation of *target costs* and how the planned costs are adjusted to reflect the delivered quantity.

Figure 6.48 confirms that the last operation in the production process has been reached with a **Yield** of **10** finished bicycles. Again, this results in a goods movement, this time for the delivery of the bicycles to stock, and the assignment of production activities to the order. With the arrival of the finished bicycles to stock, the production report shows target costs, as shown in Figure 6.49. Again, you can initiate **Rework** if there are quality issues with the bicycles or report **Scrap** if there is a problem that can't be fixed. At this stage, you can also make a *partial delivery* of one or more bicycles to stock rather than the full quantity, which would result in seeing target costs for the finished bicycles, but you wouldn't yet be able to calculate variances as it would still be unclear whether the variances refer to the operations still in process for the remaining bicycles or those that have been completed for the delivered bicycles.

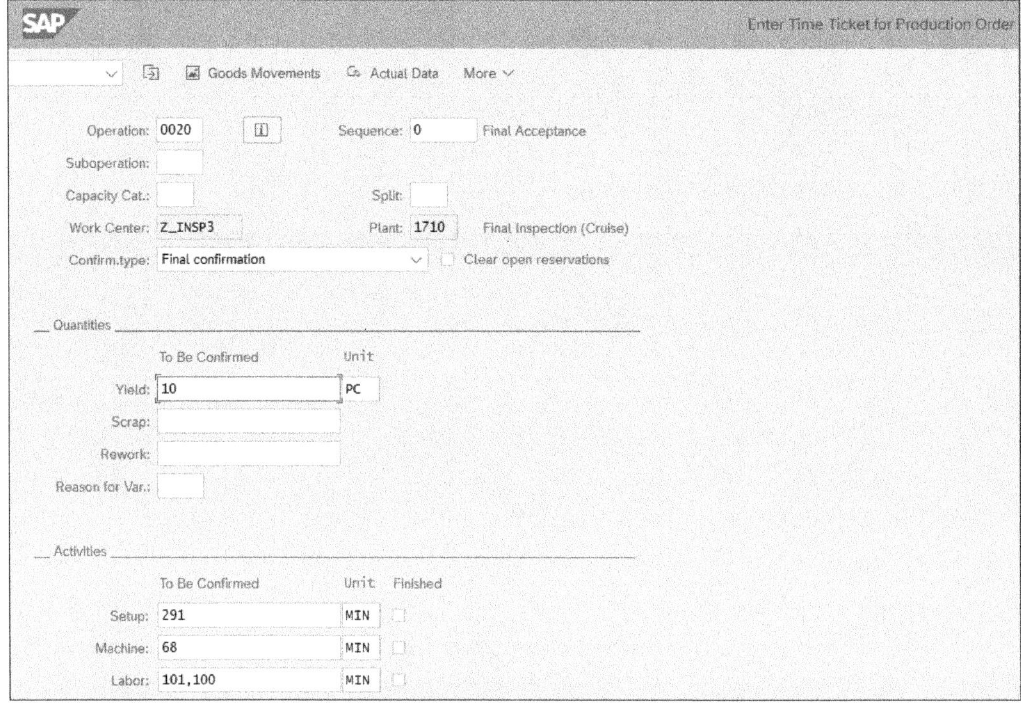


**Figure 6.48** Yield Confirmation for Second Operation

Target/Actual - Comparison

**Order** 1030982 MZ-FG-C900
**Order Type** YBM1 MTS Production Order
**Plant** 1710 Plant 1 - US
**Material** MZ-FG-C900 C900 BIKE

**Planned Quantity** 10 PC Piece
**Actual Quantity** 10 PC Piece

**Target Cost Version** 0 Target costs for total variances

| Cost Element | Cost Element (Text) | Origin | Total Target Costs | Total Actual Costs | Target/actual var. | T/I var(%) | Currency |
|---|---|---|---|---|---|---|---|
| 55100000 | Plant Activity Production Order | | 0,00 | 3.168,30- | 3.168,30- | | USD |
| **Credits (Co/By-Pr)Cr** | | | **0,00** | **3.168,30-** | **3.168,30-** | | **USD** |
| 51100000 | Consumption - Raw Material | | 1.976,80 | 1.976,80 | 0,00 | | USD |
| **Direct Material** | | | **1.976,80** | **1.976,80** | **0,00** | | **USD** |
| 94301000 | Machine hours 1 | US10_PLC/1 | 354,27 | 416,78 | 62,51 | 17,64 | USD |
| **Machine time** | | | **354,27** | **416,78** | **62,51** | | **USD** |
| 94111000 | Overhead Material | 17101201 | 138,38 | 138,38 | 0,00 | | USD |
| **Material Overhead** | | | **138,38** | **138,38** | **0,00** | | **USD** |
| 94311000 | Personnel hours | US10_PLC/11 | 421,25 | 382,91 | 38,34- | 9,10- | USD |
| **Personnel time** | | | **421,25** | **382,91** | **38,34-** | | **USD** |
| 94112000 | Overhead production | 17101301 | 259,43 | 245,31 | 14,12- | 5,44- | USD |
| **Production Overhead** | | | **259,43** | **245,31** | **14,12-** | | **USD** |
| 94303000 | Setup Production | US10_PLC/3 | 1.818,75 | 1.653,36 | 165,39- | 9,09- | USD |
| **Set-Up time** | | | **1.818,75** | **1.653,36** | **165,39-** | | **USD** |

**Figure 6.49** Costs Following Final Confirmation on Production Order

If you now look at the order in the Production Cost Analysis app (see Figure 6.50), you'll see that the order has the **Closed** status (so you would have had to change the selection parameters to see it at all) and the target costs columns now contain figures. This output figure represents the final yield of the production order (10 bicycles, in this case) and is used to adjust the two sets of planned costs to calculate target costs. Fixed costs will be proportionally higher if the final yield is lower, and variable costs will be adjusted to the yield quantity confirmed previously in Figure 6.48. If we had only made a partial delivery (five bicycles, for example), target costs would also be calculated.

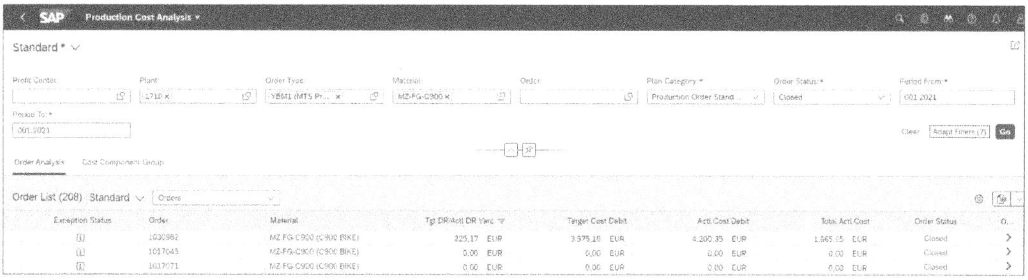

| Exception Status | Order | Material | Tgt DR/Actl DR Varc | Target Cost Debit | Actl Cost Debit | Total Actl Cost | Order Status |
|---|---|---|---|---|---|---|---|
| (i) | 1030982 | MZ-FG-C900 (C900 BIKE) | 225,17 EUR | 3.975,18 EUR | 4.200,35 EUR | 1.665,65 EUR | Closed |
| (i) | 1017043 | MZ-FG-C900 (C900 BIKE) | 0,00 EUR | 0,00 EUR | 0,00 EUR | 0,00 EUR | Closed |
| (i) | 1017071 | MZ-FG-C900 (C900 BIKE) | 0,00 EUR | 0,00 EUR | 0,00 EUR | 0,00 EUR | Closed |

**Figure 6.50** Production Cost Analysis App, Showing Results of Second Confirmation

To display the detailed order costs, select the order number **1030982** in Figure 6.50, and choose **>** in the **O...** (open detail) column. Figure 6.51 shows the delivery to stock (10 bicycles at a standard cost of USD 253.47 per bicycle), the goods issues for the seven components, and the machine time. In Chapter 5, Section 5.4.4, we introduced the idea of overhead as a way of applying additional costs to orders and projects. Here the material overhead and production overhead have been charged to this order according to the conditions defined in the costing sheet. This can take place either immediately (event-based) or at period close, depending on the settings for the costing sheet.

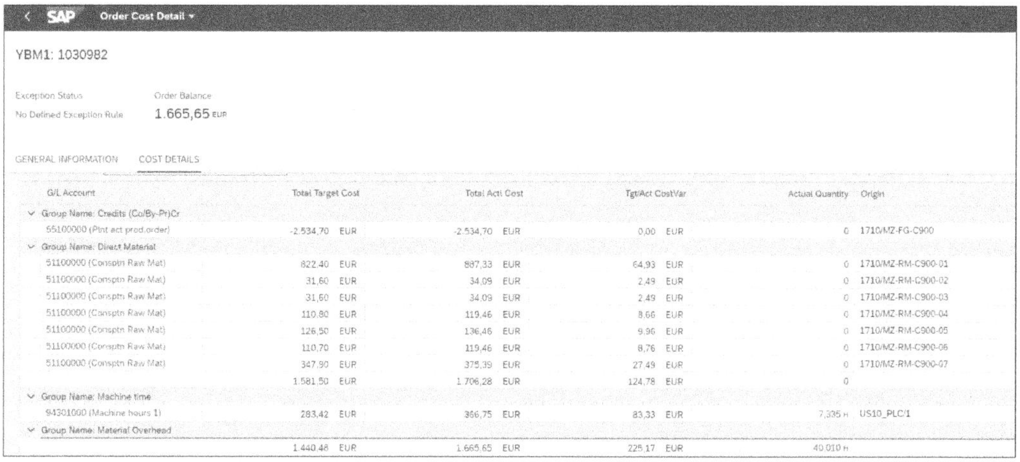

YBM1: 1030982

Order Balance: 1.665,65 EUR

| G/L Account | Total Target Cost | Total Actl Cost | Tgt/Act CostVar | Actual Quantity | Origin |
|---|---|---|---|---|---|
| Group Name: Credits (Co/By-Pr)Cr | | | | | |
| 55100000 (Pint act prod.order) | -2.534,70 EUR | -2.534,70 EUR | 0,00 EUR | 0 | 1710/MZ-FG-C900 |
| Group Name: Direct Material | | | | | |
| 51100000 (Consptn Raw Mat) | 822,40 EUR | 887,33 EUR | 64,93 EUR | 0 | 1710/MZ-RM-C900-01 |
| 51100000 (Consptn Raw Mat) | 31,60 EUR | 34,09 EUR | 2,49 EUR | 0 | 1710/MZ-RM-C900-02 |
| 51100000 (Consptn Raw Mat) | 31,60 EUR | 34,09 EUR | 2,49 EUR | 0 | 1710/MZ-RM-C900-03 |
| 51100000 (Consptn Raw Mat) | 110,80 EUR | 119,46 EUR | 8,66 EUR | 0 | 1710/MZ-RM-C900-04 |
| 51100000 (Consptn Raw Mat) | 126,50 EUR | 136,46 EUR | 9,96 EUR | 0 | 1710/MZ-RM-C900-05 |
| 51100000 (Consptn Raw Mat) | 110,70 EUR | 119,46 EUR | 8,76 EUR | 0 | 1710/MZ-RM-C900-06 |
| 51100000 (Consptn Raw Mat) | 347,90 EUR | 375,39 EUR | 27,49 EUR | 0 | 1710/MZ-RM-C900-07 |
| | 1.581,50 EUR | 1.706,28 EUR | 124,78 EUR | 0 | |
| Group Name: Machine time | | | | | |
| 94301000 (Machine hours 1) | 283,42 EUR | 366,75 EUR | 83,33 EUR | 7,335 H | US10_PLC/1 |
| Group Name: Material Overhead | | | | | |
| | 1.440,48 EUR | 1.665,65 EUR | 225,17 EUR | 40,010 H | |

**Figure 6.51** Order Cost Detail

**Process Orders**

The procedure to assign costs to a process order is very similar from a cost accounting point of view. The main differences are in terminology, where the *master recipe* represents the combination of the routing and BOM and the *resource* replaces the work center. It's also possible to have primary and secondary resources and to split operations into *phases*. The integration points with controlling remain the same, and the control key for the operation or phase determines which will be costed and thus which resource will be recorded in the cost estimate.

### 6.4.3 Work in Process

In any multilevel BOM, there are raw materials, semifinished products, and finished products. Production orders are created for each step that results in a product being delivered to *inventory*. In the classic approach, all values on the production order are considered as an *expense* until you move this expense to the balance sheet as WIP at period close. There are two basic ways of handling WIP in the classic approach in on-premise SAP S/4HANA:

- **WIP at actual costs**
  WIP is calculated by subtracting the value of any deliveries to stock from the actual costs. Some organizations configure the WIP by cost element type and capitalize only part of the conversion costs. WIP is calculated afresh in each period until the order has the status **Final Delivery** or **Technically Complete**. When you calculate the WIP in the next period, the last WIP is cancelled.

  You have to use this method if you have coproducts. If you have very long-running production orders, be aware that taking the actual costs as the basis means that variances are capitalized along with the WIP, and you will be overstating the value of the WIP.

- **WIP at target costs**
  WIP is calculated by taking the standard costs for each operation completed from either the standard cost estimate, the cost estimate for the product cost collector, or another cost estimate created for this purpose. This approach relies on the existence of detailed values per operation, so you can't use this method with coproducts (as there's only a settlement of the amounts to the coproducts). Some organizations prefer this method because it avoids an overstatement of WIP.

With SAP S/4HANA Cloud, there is a new option that allows you to calculate WIP immediately, rather than waiting until period close. The new option is currently only available for WIP at actual costs.

We'll discuss both the classic and new approaches in the following sections.

### Classic Approach

The classic approach to WIP calculation treats all costs incurred as a result of goods issues, confirmations, and overhead calculation as expenses until you calculate WIP and perform settlement to capitalize the WIP at period close. As further costs are incurred in the next period, these are again treated as expenses and the WIP increases with the next period close until the finished goods are delivered to stock and the WIP can be cancelled. The WIP will be cancelled at the latest when the *technically complete* status is set for the order as it's then assumed that this WIP will never become a finished product.



Before you calculate WIP for the first time, you should check that the production orders contain a results analysis key (see Chapter 5, Figure 5.45). The settings are Customizing activities and cannot be adjusted for reasons of consistency. When you calculate WIP, you'll be required to enter one or more results analysis versions. Normally, you only need to enter version 0 for the legal valuation of your WIP. If you use SAP Best Practices, you'll find the settings for WIP calculation at period close in scope item BEI.

To calculate WIP for a single production order, follow menu path **Accounting • Controlling • Product Cost Controlling • Cost Object Controlling • Product Cost by Order • Period-End Closing • Single Functions • Work in Process • Individual Processing • Calculate** or use Transaction KKAX. Enter the order number, the period, the fiscal year, and the results analysis version(s) and click **Execute**.

Figure 6.52 shows the result of WIP calculation for a production order. The figure in the **WIP (Cumul.)** column is the WIP for the complete lifecycle of the order. The figure in the **WIP (Period)** column is the increase/decrease in WIP in that period. In this example, the production order was created in the same period as the WIP calculation, so the two figures are identical. This process of calculating the additional WIP in each period continues until the order is complete (in other words, has the status **Final Delivery** or **Technically Complete**). When you calculate WIP in the period that follows, the WIP is cancelled and any remaining costs are assumed to be variances.

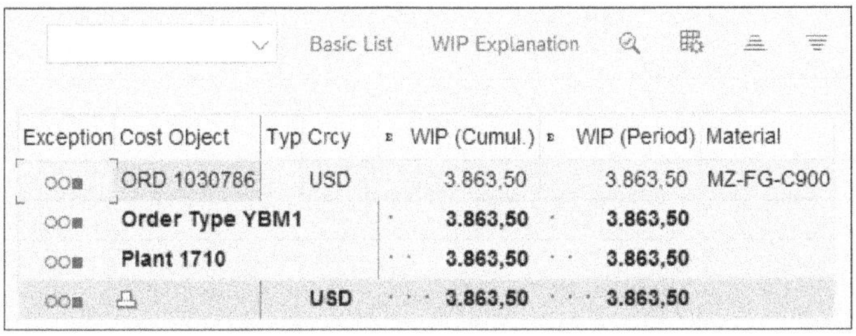

Basic List WIP Explanation

| Exception | Cost Object | Typ | Crcy | WIP (Cumul.) | WIP (Period) | Material |
|---|---|---|---|---|---|---|
| OO■ | ORD 1030786 | | USD | 3.863,50 | 3.863,50 | MZ-FG-C900 |
| OO■ | **Order Type YBM1** | | | **3.863,50** | **3.863,50** | |
| OO■ | **Plant 1710** | | | **3.863,50** | **3.863,50** | |
| OO■ | | | **USD** | **3.863,50** | **3.863,50** | |

**Figure 6.52** WIP Calculation for Production Order

Of course, it's not generally practical to calculate WIP order by order when you have hundreds or even thousands of production orders at the end of the month. The same calculations can be made for all the production orders in a given plant by following menu path **Controlling • Product Cost Controlling • Cost Object Controlling • Product Cost by Order • Period-End Closing • Single Functions • Work in Process • Collective Processing • Calculate** or using Transaction KKAO and then selecting all the orders in a given plant.

Depending on your configuration, the WIP can be separated and stored under different results analysis cost elements depending on the underlying costs, such as raw material costs, production costs, and overhead. To check how your WIP has been stored, follow menu path **Accounting • Controlling • Product Cost Controlling • Cost Object Controlling • Product Cost by Order • Information System • Reports for Product Cost by Order • Detailed Reports • For Orders** or use Transaction KKBC_ORD. Enter the order number and use the **Select Layout** button to switch the layout to **1SAP03 (WIP)**. You can access the same report from within the production order by choosing **More • GoTo • Costs • Analysis** and selecting the layout for WIP.

Figure 6.53 shows the results analysis cost elements that store these values in controlling. Notice that these all begin with **9311** in this example, distinct from the original cost elements under which the costs were first recorded in controlling. These are cost elements of category 31 and are used specifically to store the values arising for WIP or results analysis. This information is stored in table COSB, and a journal entry will be created for the WIP when you settle the order. To see WIP in this form, you'll have to use the classic reports as the SAP Fiori applications do not provide access to the legacy tables.

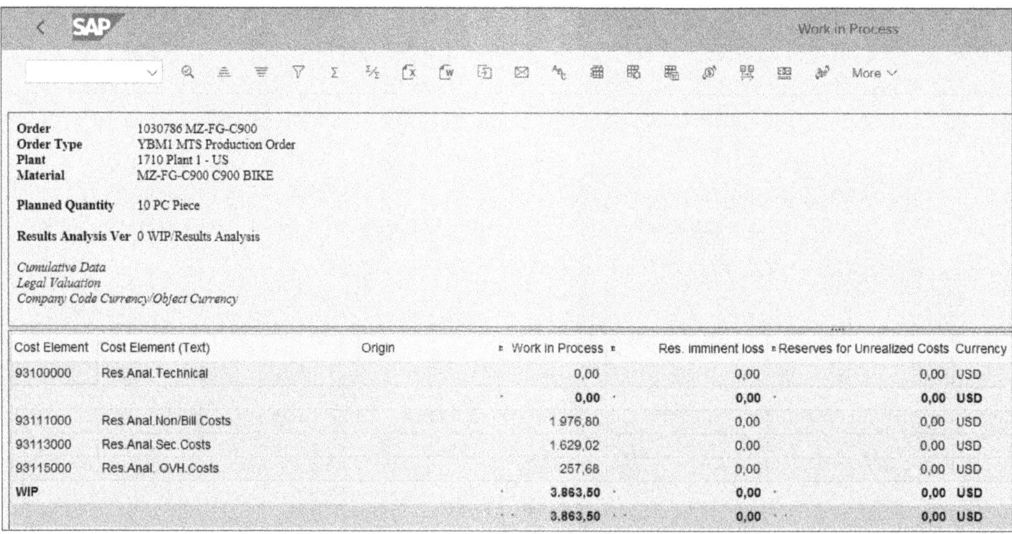


**Figure 6.53** WIP: Detail Report

### New Approach

The new approach, by contrast, doesn't require you to run a WIP calculation job at period close. Instead, the goods issues, confirmations, and overhead calculation are posted as before but this time generate an additional posting to WIP that will immediately update the balance sheet. The WIP decreases with each partial delivery. As you complete the order, either by posting the final delivery or setting the status to **Technically Complete**, this WIP will immediately be cancelled and the financial postings reversed. Real-time WIP is always calculated using actual costs. The process is activated using scope item 3F0 (Event-Based Product Cost Posting) in SAP S/4HANA Cloud or by assigning an appropriate results analysis key to the order type of your production orders. You can identify event-based production orders by the **Event-Based Posting** flag in the **Control** parameters of the production order (see Chapter 5, Figure 5.46).

Instead of running a job at period close and checking the results, as we described in the classic approach, WIP is being calculated and updated as an additional financial document whenever operations are being confirmed on the shop floor. Those working on the shop floor won't notice the difference in approach, and raw materials will be issued, operations confirmed, and finished goods delivered to stock as we described in the previous section. The controllers can use the Event-Based Work in Process app (SAP Fiori ID F3498), shown in Figure 6.54, to display the value of WIP for the production orders open at that time. We're showing the total WIP for a plant, but you can drill down to the underlying materials and orders to explore which areas have unusually high WIP by expanding the arrow beside the total for the plant to see the assigned orders. These figures will also be visible in the Trial Balance app and other financial reports without the need for settlement.

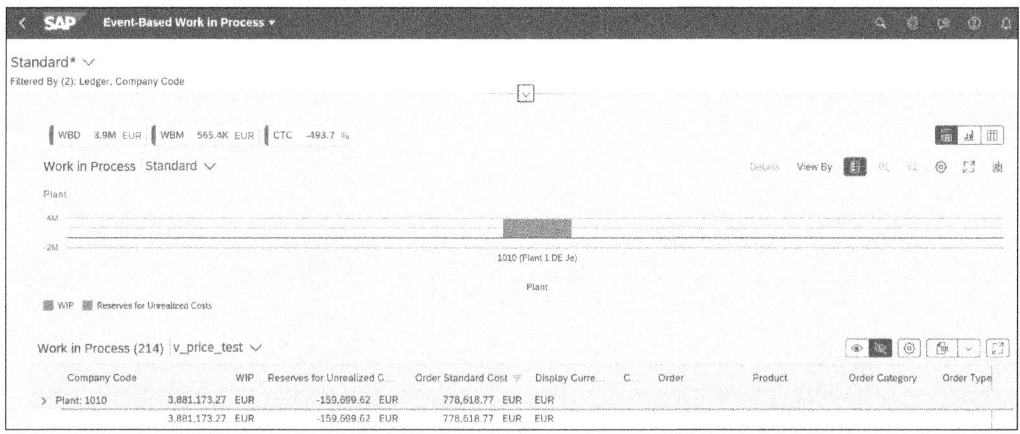


**Figure 6.54** Event-Based Work in Process App

To ensure that everything is proceeding smoothly, controllers should also use the Event-Based Solution Monitor app (SAP Fiori ID F5133), shown in Figure 6.55, and check the situation for the company code and plant for each fiscal period by entering the appropriate selection parameters and choosing **Go**. The app shows any errors that have occurred such that WIP or variances could not be posted. Production should not be held up and so goods movements and confirmations will continue, even if it isn't possible to generate WIP. For this reason, it's important that controllers check the contents of this app on a regular basis and initiate whatever corrections may be required.

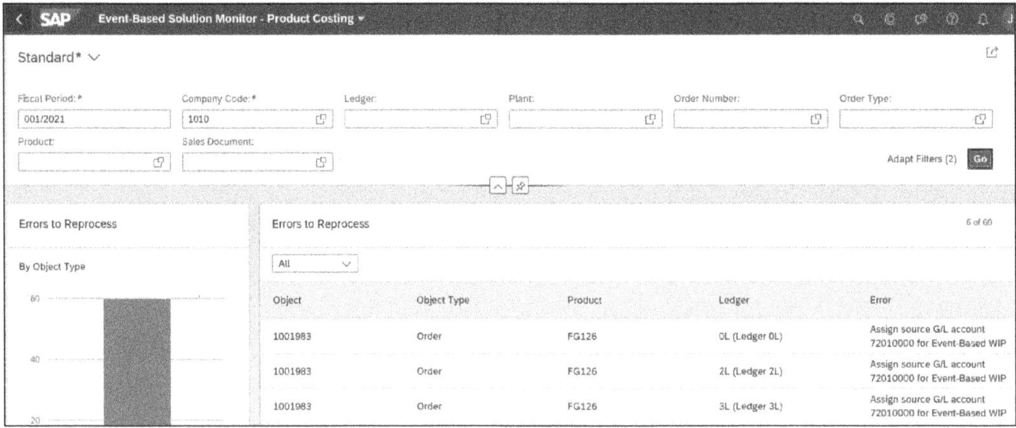


**Figure 6.55** Event-Based Solution Monitor—Product Costing App

The Manage Event-Based Posting Errors app (SAP Fiori ID F5132) allows controllers to identify and fix errors, such as a missing account for the WIP journal entry, and then repost using the Postprocess Event-Based Postings app (SAP Fiori ID F3669). It can be accessed either directly or from within the Event-Based Solution Monitor app shown in Figure 6.55 by clicking the **Errors to Reprocess** card.

WIP will be posted automatically with each goods issue and activity confirmation, but sometimes it isn't possible to generate the posting as certain configuration steps are missing. If this is the case, the material movements and activity confirmations will be updated as described in Section 6.4.2, but you'll see an error list showing the orders for which no WIP document could be created. Figure 6.56 shows the Manage Event-Based Posting Errors app and the missing account that is stopping the system from creating a journal entry for WIP on this order.

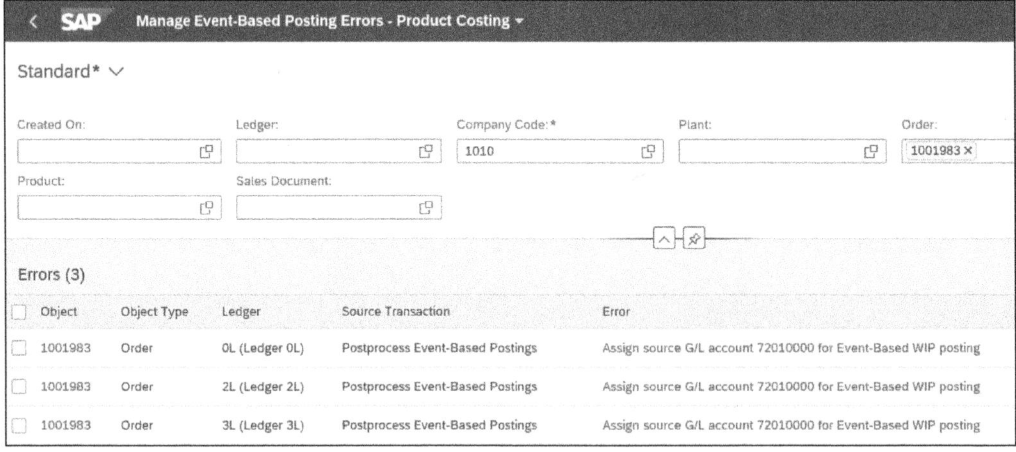


**Figure 6.56** Manage Event-Based Posting Errors—Product Costing App

Once the error is fixed, you can use the Postprocess Event-Based Postings app shown in Figure 6.57 to generate the missing postings for WIP or variances. First use the **Simulate Posting** button to determine whether the errors are fixed and then the **Post WIP/Variance** button to create the missing journal entries.

**Figure 6.57** Postprocess Event-Based Postings—Product Costing App

With the new method, there's no need to use settlement to move WIP from table COSB to the financial accounts. When you create postings that affect WIP, either automatically or using the mechanisms shown in Figure 6.57, you automatically generate the appropriate journal entries. Notice also the ledger fields in the applications for the new approach. If you need to work with multiple ledgers and accounting principles, as we discussed in Chapter 3, Section 3.3.1 and Section 3.3.2, this approach will automatically deliver different valuations into each ledger.

### 6.4.4 Variance Calculation

The difference between the original planning assumptions used to value the goods movements and production activities and reality is a *variance*, and it's the controlling department's job to work with the cost center managers and production managers to explain these variances and identify the root cause of any problems that have caused variances. There are two approaches to handling variances in general:

1. **Standard costs**
   If the raw material prices are stable and the production structures don't vary significantly, organizations tend to use *standard costs* and analyze their variances by department (purchasing, production, sales) without adjusting the value of inventory or cost of goods sold. The rationale is that if the planning assumptions were reliable, there's no need to adjust the balance sheet and any variances can simply be shown in the P&L statement.
2. **Actual costs**
   If the raw material prices are volatile or the production structures are constantly in

flux, organizations tend to use *actual costs* and push the variances through the production process, adjusting WIP, inventory values, and the cost of goods sold to reflect these variances. To do this, they run actual costing and perform an additional costing run once variance calculation and settlement are complete.

Just as we showed for WIP, SAP S/4HANA offers two approaches for variance calculation. In the classic approach, the assumption is that variance calculation runs as part of the period-close activities and determines the variances for all orders completed in the period prior to settlement. In the new approach, it's not possible to calculate variances immediately with every goods movement and confirmation as we saw for WIP, but it's possible to have the system calculate them as soon as the production order is complete and generate the appropriate journal entries in a single step. We'll discuss both in the following sections.

#### Classic Approach

When looking at the production orders, the *order quantity* provides the basis for the calculation of target costs. It's possible to calculate target costs as soon as the goods receipt of the finished goods is performed, but you'll only be able to calculate production variances once the final goods receipt has been posted or the order has the **Technically Closed** status. To calculate variances, you must enter a variance key in the **Control** parameters of the production order (see Chapter 5, Figure 5.46). You're also required to enter one or more target cost versions. If you use SAP Best Practices, you'll find the settings for variance calculation at period close in scope item BEI. The usual settings for variance calculation are as follows:

- **Version 0**
  Compares the actual costs on the order with the standard costs in the standard cost estimate. This target cost version explains the difference between the standard costs used to valuate inventory when the goods are delivered to stock and the actual costs. These values will be *settled*, meaning they'll be included in actual costing and margin analysis. The settlement profile for your production order ensures that the settlement rule automatically generates distribution rules to the correct senders.
- **Version 1**
  Compares the actual costs on the order with the planned costs calculated when the order is created. This target cost version explains the variances that occur during production.
- **Version 2**
  Compares the planned costs when the order is created with the standard costs in the standard cost estimate. This target cost version explains the variances that occur between the time of the standard cost estimate (planning) and order creation.

To calculate production variances for a single order, follow menu path **Accounting • Controlling • Product Cost Controlling • Cost Object Controlling • Product Cost by Order • Period-End Closing • Single Functions • Variances • Individual Processing** or use Transaction KKS2. Enter the order number, the period, the fiscal year, and the target cost version(s), then click **Execute**.

Figure 6.58 shows the result of variance calculation on the production order in target cost version 0. To see the details, select the order line and click the **Cost Elements** button. What you'll see is a comparison of the actual costs for the order with the standard costs to produce the delivered quantity. Because the order is complete, there's no WIP. Just like for WIP calculation, it's more common to calculate variances for all orders in the plant at period close by following menu path **Accounting • Controlling • Product Cost Controlling • Cost Object Controlling • Product Cost by Order • Period-End Closing • Single Functions • Variances • Collective Processing** or using Transaction KKS1.

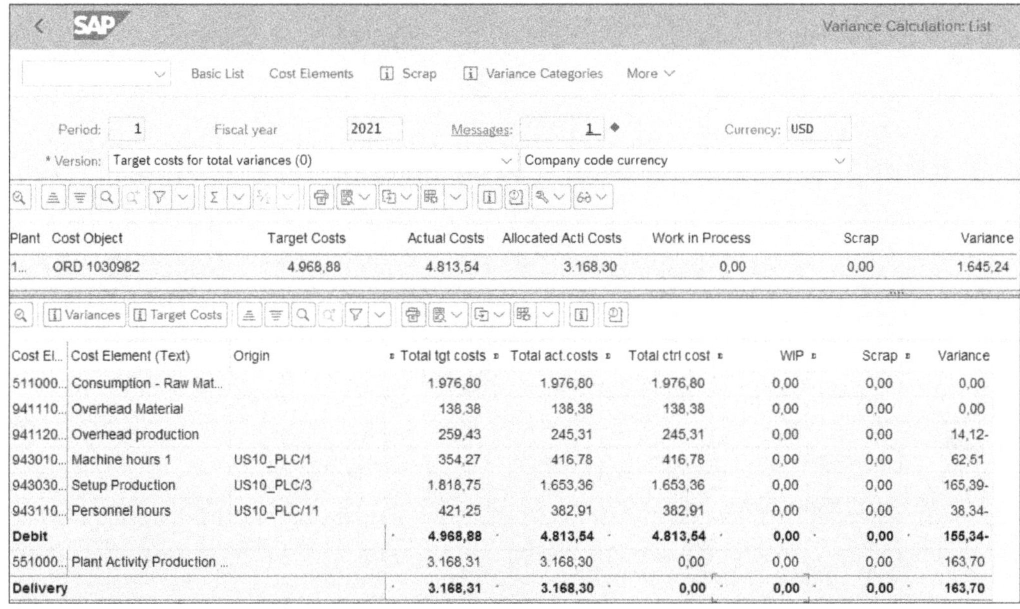


**Figure 6.58** Total Variances on Production Order

The production variances are assigned to *variance categories* that classify the sources of the variance. To display the variance categories, switch the layout for the report in Figure 6.58 by clicking the **Variance Categories** button. Figure 6.59 shows the variance categories for the production order. Notice that there are high lot-size variances because we manufactured 10 bicycles rather than the 100 bicycles in the standard cost estimate, input quantity variances owing to the different times confirmed for machine time at the first operation, and price variances for the three activity types as different cost rates were used in the standard cost estimate and during order confirmation.

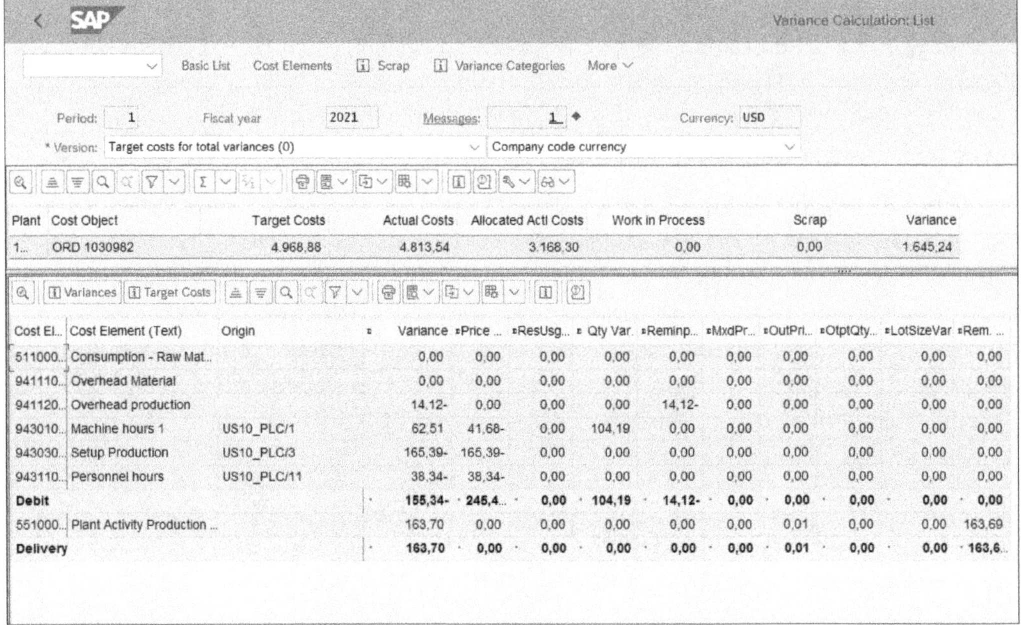


**Figure 6.59** Variance Categories for Production Order

The input variances are as follows:

- **Input price variances (Price)**
  These occur as a result of changes to the raw material prices and activity prices. Notice that we have price variances for the three activity types.
- **Input quantity variances (Qty Var.)**
  These occur as a result of using a different quantity of material or activity. Notice that we have input quantity variances for machine hours.
- **Resource-usage variances(ResUsg)**
  These occur if an operation has to be performed at a different work center or a material replaced as a result of material shortages.
- **Remaining variances (RemInp)**
  This is a catchall for any unassigned variances.

The output variances are as follows:

- **Output price variances (OutPri)**
  These occur if the standard cost isn't used for inventory valuation.
- **Mixed price variances (MxdPr)**
  These occur if the standard costs were calculated by weighting several cost estimates (we'll look at these cost estimates in Chapter 9).
- **Lot size variances (LotSizeVar)**
  These occur if the lot size for the order differs from the lot size in the standard cost

estimate. Notice that we have lot-size variances for the plant activity account as we manufactured 10 bicycles rather than 100.

- **Remaining variances (Rem)**
  This is a catchall for any unassigned variances.
- **Output quantity variances (OptQty)**
  There is also a column for output quantity variances, which is only relevant for cost center variances.

6

To analyze the input quantity variances for machine time in more detail, select the line and right-click the **Explanation of Variances** button. Figure 6.60 shows the details of this variance. Again, you can see the input quantity variance, but now you have a full explanation of how the variance calculation was performed. You can use this button to perform spot checks on any lines that seem to be unreasonably high. Like the WIP, the variances are stored in table COSB and you'll have to use the classic reports to display them as there is no equivalent SAP Fiori application.

Cost Element 94301000 Machine hours 1
Partner Object ATY US10_PLC/1

| | Total | Fixed | Variable |
|---|---|---|---|
| **Control Costs** | | | |
| Actual Costs | 416,78 | 0,00 | 416,78 |
| Scrap | 0,00 | 0,00 | 0,00 |
| Work in Process | 0,00 | 0,00 | 0,00 |
| * | 416,78 | 0,00 | 416,78 |
| **Input Side** | | | |
| Control Costs | 416,78 | 0,00 | 416,78 |
| Target Costs | 354,27 | 0,00 | 354,27 |
| Input-Side Variances | 62,51 | 0,00 | 62,51 |
| Input Price Variance | 41,68- | 0,00 | 41,68- |
| Input Qty Variance | 104,19 | 0,00 | 104,19 |
| Resource-Usage Var. | 0,00 | 0,00 | 0,00 |
| Remaining Input Var. | 0,00 | 0,00 | 0,00 |
| * | 62,51 | 0,00 | 62,51 |

**Figure 6.60** Explanation of Production Variances

We explored the general process of *settlement* in Chapter 5, Section 5.4.6 as a way of moving costs from a sender order to a receiver. In the classic approach, settlement is also used to generate postings for the WIP and production variances, taking the information in table COSB as its starting point. When you create a production order, the settlement rule will include a default rule to move the costs from the order to the material produced. However, remember that the standard costs for the finished goods were already used to value the inventory at the time of goods receipt. Settlement moves the difference, the *production variances*, to inventory.

To run settlement, choose **Accounting • Controlling • Product Cost Controlling • Cost Object Controlling • Product Cost by Order • Period-End Closing • Single Functions • Settlement • Individual Processing** or use Transaction KO88, enter the order number, the settlement period, and the fiscal year, and choose **Execute.** Figure 6.61 shows the results of settling a production order where the first rule has settled these variances from the production order to inventory. In addition, notice the second receiver, **PSG** (for profitability segment). This distribution rule is generated automatically based on the settings in the settlement profile during the first settlement and moves the variances from the order to margin analysis, where they can be analyzed as part of the contribution margin for the finished product. We'll explain how to analyze the various contribution margins for the product in Chapter 7.

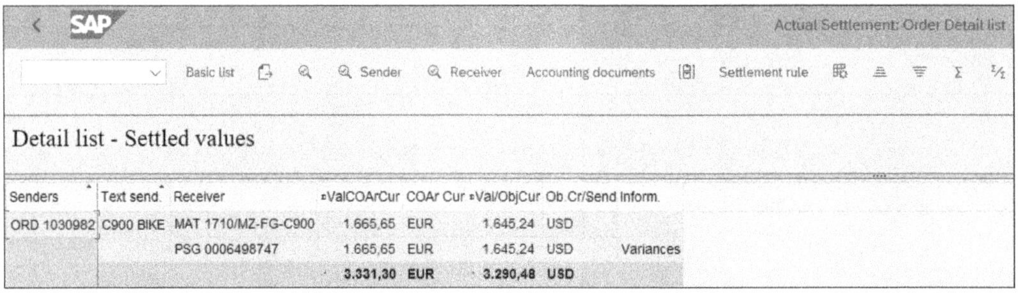

Actual Settlement: Order Detail list

Basic list | Sender | Receiver | Accounting documents | Settlement rule

Detail list - Settled values

| Senders | Text send. | Receiver | ΣValCOArCur | COAr Cur | ΣVal/ObjCur | Ob.Cr/Send Inform. |
|---|---|---|---|---|---|---|
| ORD 1030982 | C900 BIKE | MAT 1710/MZ-FG-C900 | 1.665,65 | EUR | 1.645,24 | USD |
| | | PSG 0006498747 | 1.665,65 | EUR | 1.645,24 | USD Variances |
| | | | 3.331,30 | EUR | 3.290,48 | USD |

**Figure 6.61** Results of Settling Production Order

To see the detailed figures settled to margin analysis, select the **PSG** line. Figure 6.62 shows the separate lines in margin analysis for each of the variance categories that we calculated previously in Figure 6.59. Notice again the input quantity variances (**QTYV**), input price variances (**INPV**), the lot size variances (**LSFV**), and the remaining variances (**REMV**).

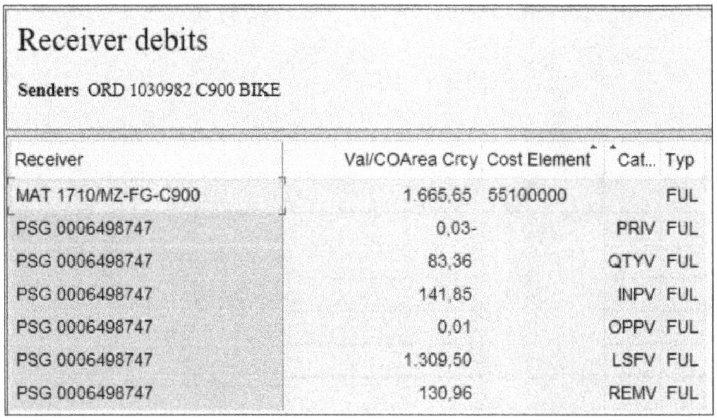

Receiver debits

**Senders** ORD 1030982 C900 BIKE

| Receiver | Val/COArea Crcy | Cost Element | Cat... | Typ |
|---|---|---|---|---|
| MAT 1710/MZ-FG-C900 | 1.665,65 | 55100000 | | FUL |
| PSG 0006498747 | 0,03- | | PRIV | FUL |
| PSG 0006498747 | 83,36 | | QTYV | FUL |
| PSG 0006498747 | 141,85 | | INPV | FUL |
| PSG 0006498747 | 0,01 | | OPPV | FUL |
| PSG 0006498747 | 1.309,50 | | LSFV | FUL |
| PSG 0006498747 | 130,96 | | REMV | FUL |

**Figure 6.62** Receiver Details, Showing Separate Lines for Each Variance Category

In SAP ERP, this settlement of the detailed production variances only impacted costing-based profitability analysis, whereas the financial accounts showed the total variance. In SAP S/4HANA, you can assign the variance categories to separate accounts, as shown in Figure 6.63, where settlement results in an initial posting of the full variance (line 1) that is then reversed (line 2) and split to different accounts for the various variance categories. We'll see these lines again in the contribution margin reports in Chapter 7. This assignment is made in the IMG by following **Financial Accounting • General Ledger Accounting • Periodic Processing • Integration • Materials Management • Define Accounts for Splitting Price Differences** and creating a **Price Differences Splitting Profile** to link the variance categories on the production order with the separate variance accounts shown in Figure 6.63. It's also possible to configure the system to make this split finer still and distinguish between the cost elements on the production order, allowing you to separate input price variances for materials and activities, and so on.



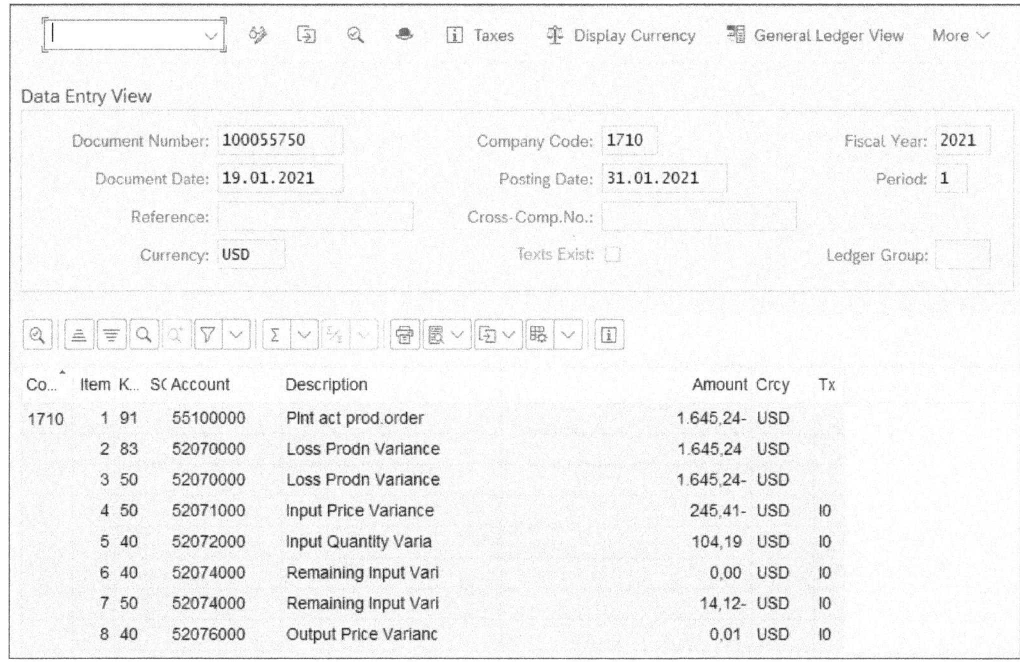


| Co... | Item | K... | S( Account | Description | Amount | Crcy | Tx |
|---|---|---|---|---|---|---|---|
| 1710 | 1 | 91 | 55100000 | Plnt act prod.order | 1.645,24- | USD | |
| | 2 | 83 | 52070000 | Loss Prodn Variance | 1.645,24 | USD | |
| | 3 | 50 | 52070000 | Loss Prodn Variance | 1.645,24- | USD | |
| | 4 | 50 | 52071000 | Input Price Variance | 245,41- | USD | I0 |
| | 5 | 40 | 52072000 | Input Quantity Varia | 104,19 | USD | I0 |
| | 6 | 40 | 52074000 | Remaining Input Vari | 0,00 | USD | I0 |
| | 7 | 50 | 52074000 | Remaining Input Vari | 14,12- | USD | I0 |
| | 8 | 40 | 52076000 | Output Price Varianc | 0,01 | USD | I0 |

**Figure 6.63** Document for Variance Split

### New Approach

Some industries are more significantly impacted by the period-based approach than others. Food companies in which production orders are generally completed in a single day were loathe to wait almost a month to understand whether they were working efficiently. Engineering companies in which production processes could run over months struggled to make sense of their production costs as the production variances accumulated as WIP over months until the orders were finally delivered to stock. Work has begun on a new option to deliver real-time variance analysis, but this is currently only available in SAP S/4HANA Cloud. Like the new approach for WIP discussed in Section 6.4.3, it is activated using scope item 3F0 (Event-Based Product Cost Posting). Partial delivery will result in the reduction of WIP and the calculation of target costs, while final delivery will result in the calculation of variances for the finished production order. Variance calculation explains the input price variances, input quantity variances, and resource usage variances, but cannot yet handle output variances and scrap.

Event-based WIP and variance calculation immediately reflect the impact of the relevant goods movements and confirmations on the shop floor. However, it's also possible to make other postings to a production order. If you use *rework orders*, these settle to the parent production order before it settles to stock. You might make manual journal entries to the production order either for expenses or to correct activities or cost assignments or include the order in an allocation (see Chapter 5). These will not be captured as WIP or variances immediately. Instead, the monitoring application will capture these journal entries, and the Postprocess Event-Based Postings app will be used to trigger either WIP or variances depending on the status of the order. To see the variances, simply scroll right in the Postprocess Event-Based Postings app shown previously in Figure 6.57.

### 6.4.5 Using Actual Costing to Assign Purchase Price Variances and Production Variances

*Actual costing* is used in industries in which the standard costing approach is not considered appropriate, such as the food industry with its volatile ingredient prices or the chemical industry with its volatile recipes, and in those countries where there is a legal requirement to assign all production-related costs to inventory at period close. A decision to activate actual costing means that additional information is recorded when the goods movements and confirmations that we looked at in Section 6.4.2 are posted. An additional document captures the inputs and outputs of each production step and of each purchase, sale, and goods transfer, and this chain of inputs and outputs is used to assign purchase price variances and production variances to each affected material using a costing run at period close.

During the period, the system still uses the standards that were established in the planning process to value all goods movements and confirmations as these assumptions are the most reliable source of data *at the time of posting*. As goods are issued from stock to production or sales, the supplier may not yet have submitted his invoice. As an operation is confirmed in production, the amount of energy used by the cost center in the period may not yet be known. Actual costing is used to *adjust* these assumptions to reflect the reality of the business situation after the fact. If you use SAP Best Practices, you'll find the settings for actual costing in scope item 33Q.

In the following sections, we'll set up actual costing and perform a costing run.

### Setting Up Actual Costing

Actual costing is activated by plant, and the material masters for every material to be included in actual costing will be flagged as having **Price Determ.** (price determination) set to **3 (Single-/Multilevel)** (refer back to Figure 6.2). This flag ensures that goods movements for the finished product and every semifinished product and material component used in its manufacture will be captured to build up the quantity structure for the product. In Section 6.2.1, we looked at how to explode the BOM and use the routing to build up the quantity structure to calculate standard costs. The difference for actual costing is that the quantity structure is built up dynamically whenever goods movements or confirmations are posted for each material and can then be displayed as an actual BOM.

You can view the quantity structure using Transaction CKM3N or by choosing **Accounting • Controlling • Product Cost Controlling • Actual Costing/Material Ledger • Material Ledger • Material Price Analysis**, entering the material number, plant, period, and year, and selecting the **Price Determination Structure** view, as shown in Figure 6.64. Here you can see the beginning inventory (10,000 pieces), the goods receipts from production for the finished pots (20 pieces), and the cumulative inventory. Actual costing involves valuing the goods movement initially with the standard costs for the pot (the figure in the **PrelimVal** [preliminary valuation] column) and then recording any price differences and exchange rate differences with respect to the initial valuation. At period close, the costing run takes these price differences and exchange rate differences and assigns them first to the material moved and then proportionately to any sales or further production processes that used the pot.

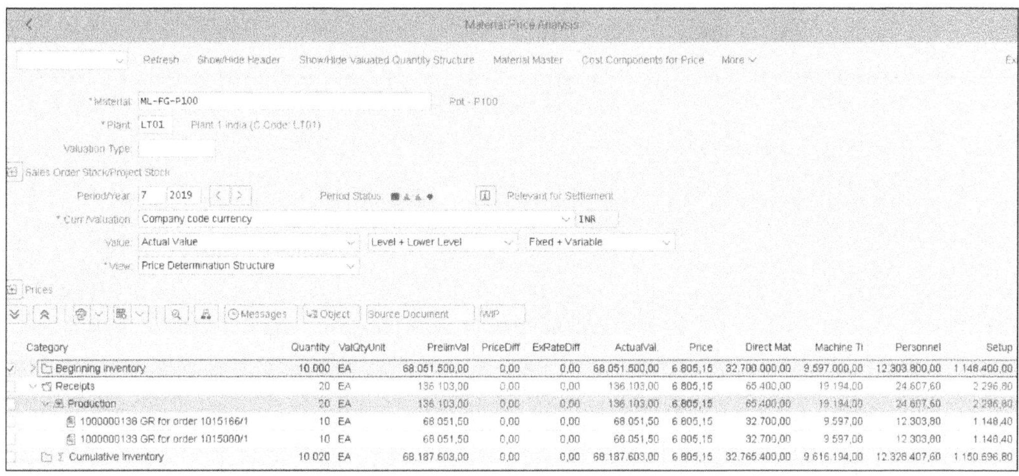


| Category | Quantity | ValQtyUnit | PrelimVal | PriceDiff | ExRateDiff | ActualVal. | Price | Direct Mat | Machine Ti | Personnel | Setup |
|---|---|---|---|---|---|---|---|---|---|---|---|
| Beginning inventory | 10.000 | EA | 68.051.500,00 | 0,00 | 0,00 | 68.051.500,00 | 6.805,15 | 32.700.000,00 | 9.597.000,00 | 12.303.800,00 | 1.148.400,00 |
| Receipts | 20 | EA | 136.103,00 | 0,00 | 0,00 | 136.103,00 | 6.805,15 | 65.400,00 | 19.194,00 | 24.607,60 | 2.296,80 |
| Production | 20 | EA | 136.103,00 | 0,00 | 0,00 | 136.103,00 | 6.805,15 | 65.400,00 | 19.194,00 | 24.607,60 | 2.296,80 |
| 1000000138 GR for order 1015166/1 | 10 | EA | 68.051,50 | 0,00 | 0,00 | 68.051,50 | 6.805,15 | 32.700,00 | 9.597,00 | 12.303,80 | 1.148,40 |
| 1000000133 GR for order 1015080/1 | 10 | EA | 68.051,50 | 0,00 | 0,00 | 68.051,50 | 6.805,15 | 32.700,00 | 9.597,00 | 12.303,80 | 1.148,40 |
| Cumulative inventory | 10.020 | EA | 68.187.603,00 | 0,00 | 0,00 | 68.187.603,00 | 6.805,15 | 32.765.400,00 | 9.616.194,00 | 12.328.407,60 | 1.150.696,80 |

**Figure 6.64** Material Price Analysis

Notice also that you can see a total value, but also the breakdown of the product costs into **Direct Material**, **Machine Time**, **Personnel**, **Setup**, and so on. These are the same cost components that we looked at when we discussed standard costing in Section 6.2.3, this time updated with the actual costs for each component.

Notice also that the folder beneath **Receipts** is called **Production**. These are procurement alternatives. When you roll up the actual costs at period close, you won't update every production order assigned to the **Production** folder, but only those at the level of the *procurement alternative* (**Production** in this example). When you create a costing run, you'll see an additional line above the individual production orders that will contain the total variances.

The material price analysis transaction shows the inputs (the goods receipt from production) and the outputs (the issue of the pot to sales or stock transfer), but if you really want to understand the value flow, choose the **Actual BOM** icon (the three boxes) to see the view shown in Figure 6.65, showing not just the material inputs and outputs but also the activities used in the production process. This is important because you aren't just assigning purchase price variances to production but will also take account of any cost center variances arising due to fluctuations in utility costs, energy costs, wage costs, and so on. Alternatively, you can use the Display Material Value Chain app (SAP Fiori ID F4095) shown in Figure 6.66 to follow the value flow from production activity and raw materials to finished goods.

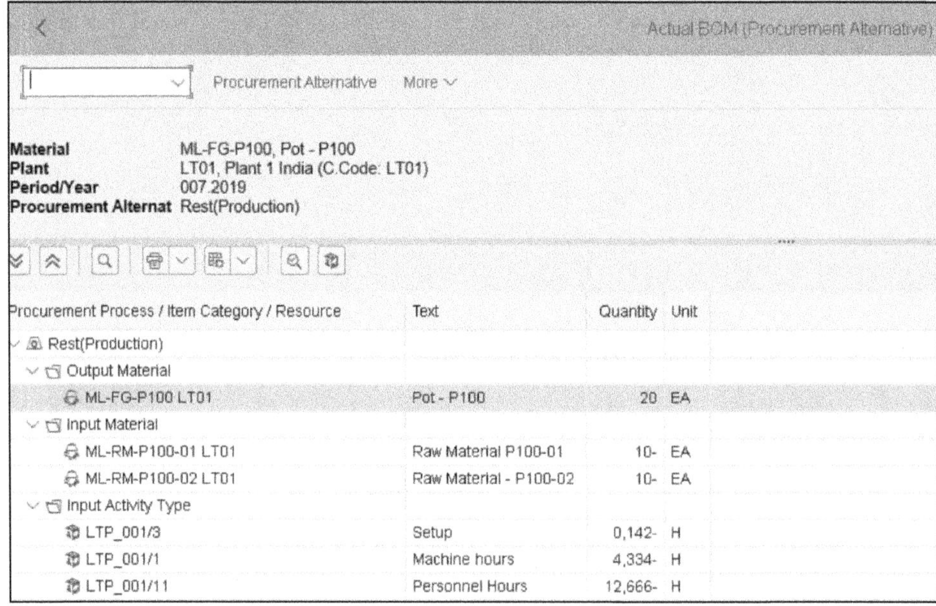


**Figure 6.65** Actual BOM

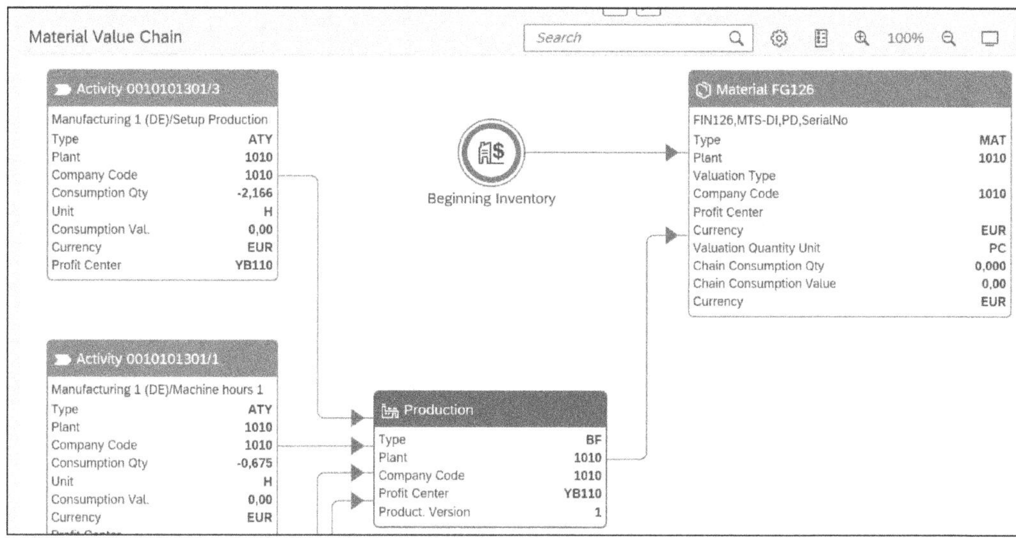


**Figure 6.66** Display Material Value Chain App

In SAP S/4HANA, two new tables have been created to store the data shown previously in Figure 6.64 and Figure 6.65. The quantity structure itself is stored in table `MLDOC` and the cost components are stored in table `MLDOC_CCS`. Both are designed for high-performance processing in combination with SAP HANA, and you'll notice a significant difference if you've been used to running large costing runs in SAP ERP.

## Actual Costing Run

During the period, actual costing simply involves monitoring material prices to make sure that there are no data quality issues, but at period close additional steps are required in the form of a costing run that assigns the follow-up costs to the materials handled in the period. To assign the actual costs to the WIP, goods in inventory, and goods sold at period close, you'll need to create a *costing run* and then perform the various steps associated with that costing run.

To access the costing run, choose **Accounting • Controlling • Product Cost Controlling • Actual Costing/Material Ledger • Actual Costing • Edit Costing Run** or Transaction CKMLCP and enter the **Costing Run**, the **Period**, and select **Actual Costing** for the **Application**. Figure 6.67 shows the **Costing Cockpit** and the plants to be included in actual costing. Notice that this is much simpler than the selection list used for standard costing as you can't exclude materials. All materials in a plant are considered relevant for costing, and the recommendation is to cost all plants belonging to one company code in one costing run.

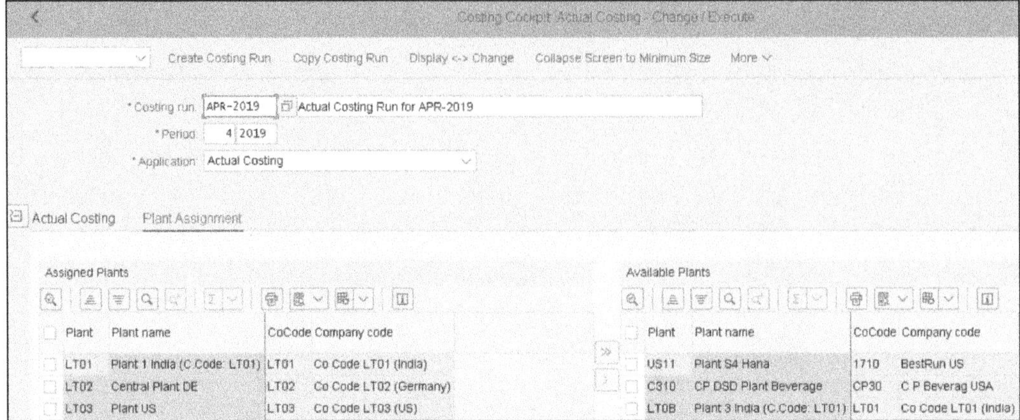


**Figure 6.67** Costing Cockpit with Plant Selection

If you're familiar with this cockpit from SAP ERP, the change you will see in SAP S/4HANA is that the periodic costing run and the alternative costing run are executed from the same transaction. The periodic costing run uses the **Actual Costing** selection from the **Application** dropdown, and the alternative valuation run uses the **Alternative Valuation** selection. The differences are as follows:

- The *periodic costing run* (**Actual Costing**) calculates a periodic unit price for the material to take account of all product-related costs in a single period and update the inventory values for the closed period.
- The *alternative valuation run* (**Alternative Valuation**) can be used to calculate costs for a different time frame (typically longer to smooth out seasonal variances) or according to a different accounting principle (such as local Generally Accepted Accounting Principles (GAAP) instead of corporate International Financial Reporting Standards (IFRS)).

**SAP ERP versus SAP S/4HANA**

In SAP ERP, the alternative valuation run was performed in addition to the periodic costing run to cumulate the result of the periodic costing run over a longer time frame and then calculate the delta to be recorded in the current period. In SAP S/4HANA, there are no delta runs. Instead, you should create an alternative run that simply cumulates for each additional month in turn without first creating a periodic costing run. In the case of different accounting principles, an alternative valuation run is used alongside the periodic costing run to perform a different valuation on the same quantity structure and take account of the requirements of inventory reporting according to a second accounting principle.

Continuing with the selection of **Actual Costing**, let's move on to the costing run process. Figure 6.68 shows the various steps that make up a costing run:

1. **Selection**
   This step selects the materials for inclusion in costing for which goods movements have taken place in the period. In some organizations, there will be many dormant stocks that haven't moved in the period and can be excluded from costing. Just as you saw for the costing run to calculate the standard costs, it's common to schedule these steps to run in the background when the system load is lower. When you're ready, enter the appropriate selection parameters and then choose the **Execute** button. When the background job is complete, you'll see the number of materials processed and any errors that occurred.
2. **Preparation**
   This step checks the material inputs and outputs of each production process and determines the number of levels in the quantity structure. This is especially important when there are cyclical production structures or costs have to be split to coproducts.
3. **Settlement**
   This step covers the single-level price determination, multilevel price determination, WIP valuation, and revaluation of consumption steps. Single-level price determination is performed for all materials to assign the price and exchange rate variances to the material in that level, and multilevel price determination rolls the variances through to the materials that used the lower-level material. WIP valuation and the revaluation of consumption steps continue to be optional and are activated by plant. If you want to value WIP, you'll have to make sure that you run WIP calculation per production order first to ensure that the WIP quantities are known. The revaluation of consumption will assign variances to margin analysis.

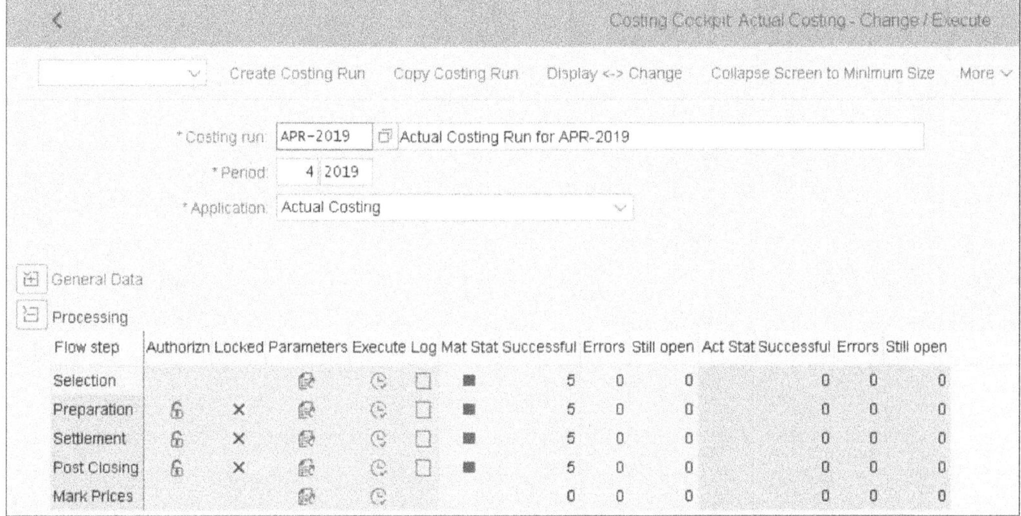


Figure 6.68 Steps in Costing Run

4. **Post Closing**
   This step updates the periodic unit price to the material master and adjusts the balance sheet value of the inventory for the period closed.
5. **Mark Prices**
   If you want to use the prices calculated using actual costing to set the standard costs for the next period, you'll need to use this step to move the prices to the material master for selection in costing.

The **Post Closing** step previously updated the inventory values in the balance sheet but had no impact on costing-based profitability analysis, relying on users to run periodic valuation (Transaction KE27) to transfer the calculated variances to costing-based profitability analysis. The procedure for margin analysis is different, and it's the costing run that triggers the update of the contribution margin with the new values. To do this, set the parameters in the **Post Closing** step to revalue the inventory for the closed period (**Revaluate Material**), revalue the cost of goods sold (**Revaluate Consumption**), and update the market segments in margin analysis (**Set CO Account Assignment**), as shown in Figure 6.69.

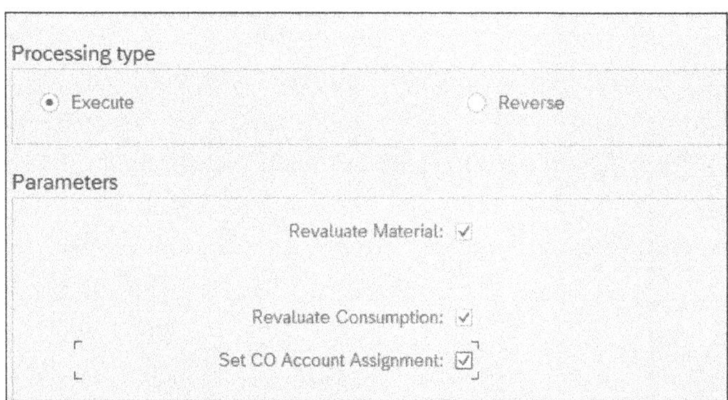


**Figure 6.69** Parameters for Post Closing Step

## 6.5 Make-to-Stock Using Product Cost Collectors

At some sites, the sheer volume of production orders is so high that it's nearly impossible to monitor costs for each order separately. In repetitive manufacturing, there's often little significant difference between the individual orders, so it makes sense to collect the costs at a higher level. In this case, instead of the production orders capturing costs, you can use a *product cost collector* to capture the costs for all manufacturing orders working with one production version. Or, you can dispense with production orders altogether and capture all production activities at the level of the product cost collector. The product cost collector is a long-living cost object that collects costs for all assigned orders. Costs are settled at period close.

This can be the case in the food industry, where the production orders can be very short lived (less than a day). It can also be the case with continuous, repetitive production with minimal setup that there is simply no requirement for individual lot-oriented controlling, and storing each production order as a separate order represents an unnecessary burden for reporting and at period close. In this case, you might report on each production version, where the production version represents a production line or a set of manufacturing cells, rather than on the individual work orders. These provide a lean controlling by period, where the goods movements and confirmations in logistics are made by production or process order, but the costs are automatically routed to the product cost collector. The output measure is then not the lot size on the individual order, but the sum of all delivered quantities in the period. Variance calculation and WIP calculation take place for each product cost collector at the end of the period. This approach is mostly used in a make-to-stock environment but is occasionally found in simple make-to-order scenarios.



**SAP ERP versus SAP S/4HANA**

In SAP ERP, it was possible to create cost object hierarchies to assign period costs, but this option has been discontinued in SAP S/4HANA.

We'll now look at how working with product cost collectors differs from working with production orders. We'll begin by looking at how to create a product cost collector and a cost estimate in Section 6.5.1. We'll then look at how monitoring a product cost collector differs from monitoring a production order in Section 6.5.2. For product cost collectors, WIP and variances usually exist in every period. We'll explain how to calculate WIP in Section 6.5.3 and variances in Section 6.5.4. Product cost collectors are captured in actual costing at the level of the production version.

### 6.5.1 Creating a Cost Estimate for a Product Cost Collector

Before manufacturing begins, you must ensure that you create product cost collectors for all relevant materials and production versions. Figure 6.70 shows the master data for the product cost collector for material **CH-6600** in plant **1710**. To create a product cost collector, go to **Accounting • Controlling • Product Cost Controlling • Product Cost by Period • Master Data • Product Cost Collector • Edit** or Transaction KKF6N. The **Header** tab shows the link to the order number for the cost collector (**700020**).

You can then create the production orders as described in Section 6.4.2, but using an order type that supports working with product cost collectors (production orders with order type PP08 in the standard configuration). For the people working on the shop floor, the production order looks completely normal, allowing scheduling, material reservations, and so on. The difference is that the order has no settlement rule, and the costing functions and cost reports are inactive. You'll recognize these production orders by the status **PCC** (**Product Cost Collector**) in the header. You can see the production orders assigned to the product cost collector by scrolling down the **Header** tab to display the various buttons shown in Figure 6.71.

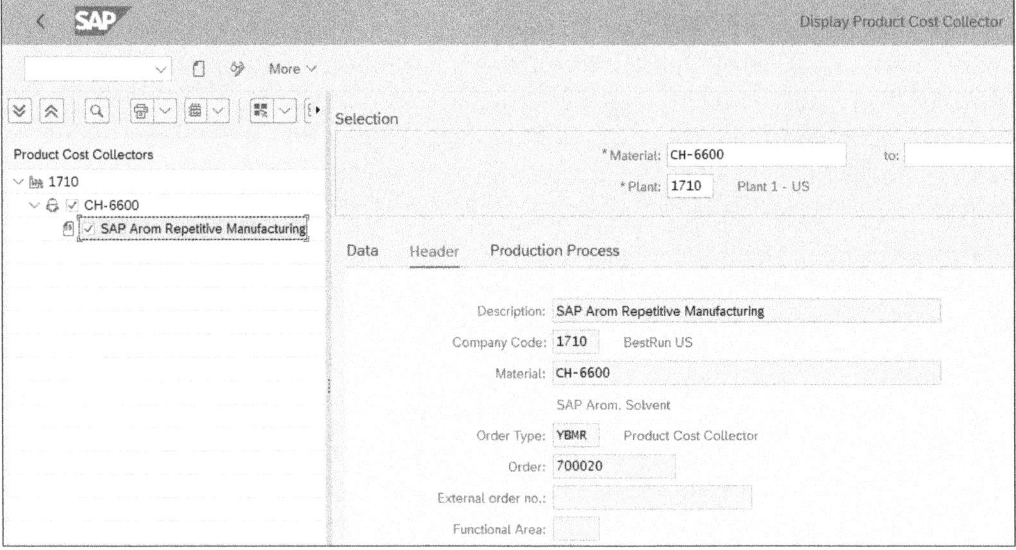


**Figure 6.70** Master Data for Product Cost Collector

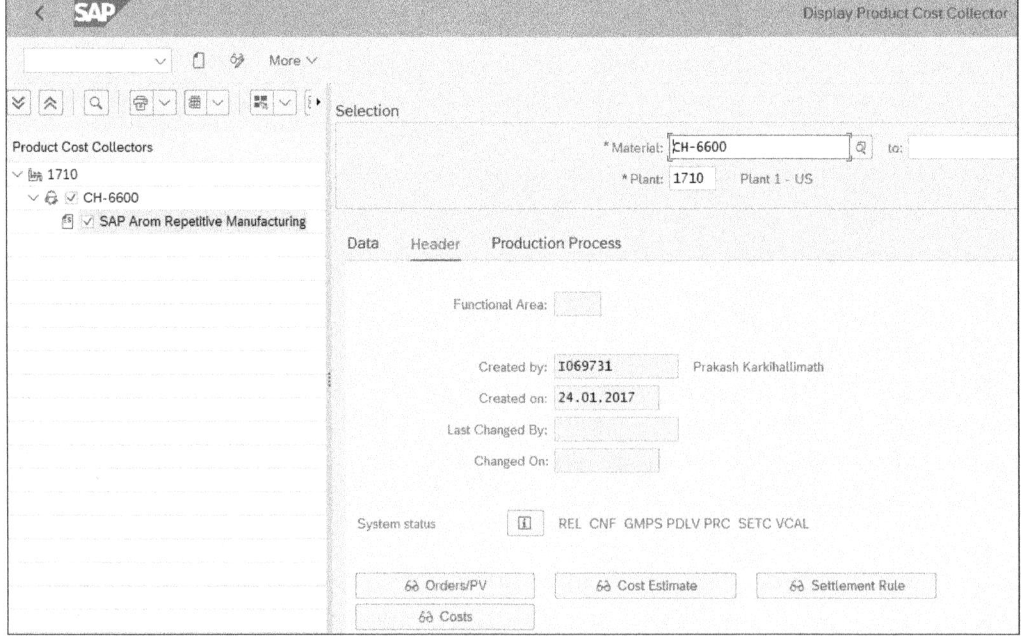


**Figure 6.71** Links from Product Cost Collector to Assigned Production Orders, Production Versions, Cost Estimate, Settlement Rule, and Costs

When you create the master data for a product cost collector, you're asked if you want to create a cost estimate for each production version. You don't have to create a cost estimate as you can use the standard cost estimate to determine the target costs for each operation to calculate the WIP and the scrap. However, if multiple production versions exist for this material or the production version includes a BOM or routing with a different structure than that used to set the standard costs, it makes sense to create a new cost estimate for the product cost collector using the BOM and routing in your production version as a starting point.

6

Figure 6.72 shows the cost estimate for material **CH-6600**. You can access it by clicking the **Cost Estimate** button in Figure 6.71. If you compare this cost estimate with the cost estimates we looked at in Section 6.2, you'll find that it's based on the BOM and the routing but also includes a link to the production version, the procurement alternative (as multiple production versions can be assigned to the product cost collector). The actual process of costing follows the same logic as the calculation of standard costs; the difference is simply in the reference.

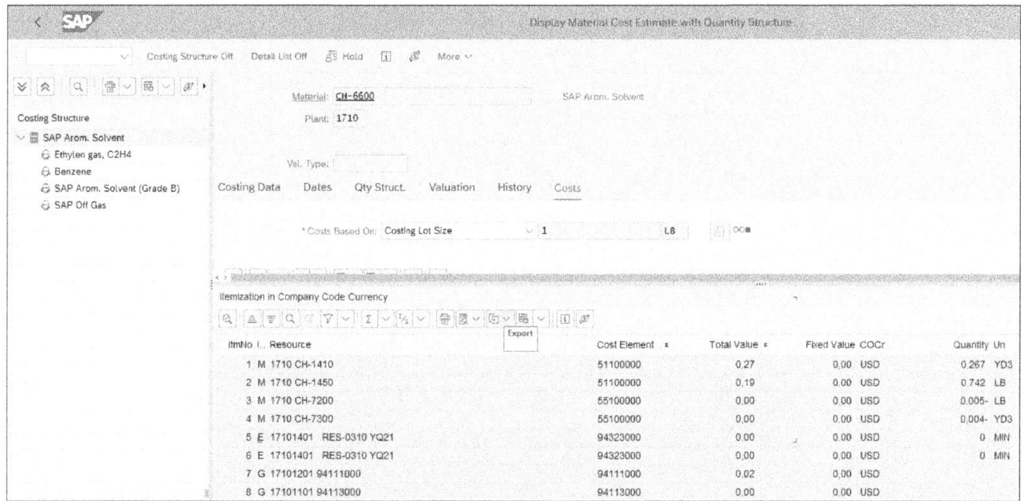


**Figure 6.72** Cost Estimate for Product Cost Collector

## 6.5.2 Monitoring the Production Process

As the production orders move through the production process and incur costs, they will be redirected from the various production orders to the product cost collector, and you can display these costs by clicking the **Costs** button shown previously in Figure 6.71. Goods issues, goods receipts, order confirmations, and so on are treated exactly the same as for a normal production order, but instead of being recorded with reference to the production order, they're recorded by material and production version. In any given period, you'll have a mixture of completed operations (finished goods inventory), incomplete operations (WIP), and scrap (recorded at the operation).

There is also an even leaner approach that dispenses with production orders altogether and uses run schedule headers. To confirm run schedule headers, use Transaction MFBF or **Logistics • Production • Repetitive Manufacturing • Data Entry • Repetitive Manufacturing • Confirmation**. To identify the product cost collector, enter the relevant material, plant, and production version, then enter the yield quantity to be confirmed in the **Conf. Qty** field, as shown in Figure 6.73. You can enter scrap by selecting the **Scrap** button and entering the quantity to be scrapped. Notice also the **Reporting Point** field in Figure 6.73. You can flag those operations in which it is possible to identify a yield or scrap as reporting points and then confirm at this level rather than at the end of the process.

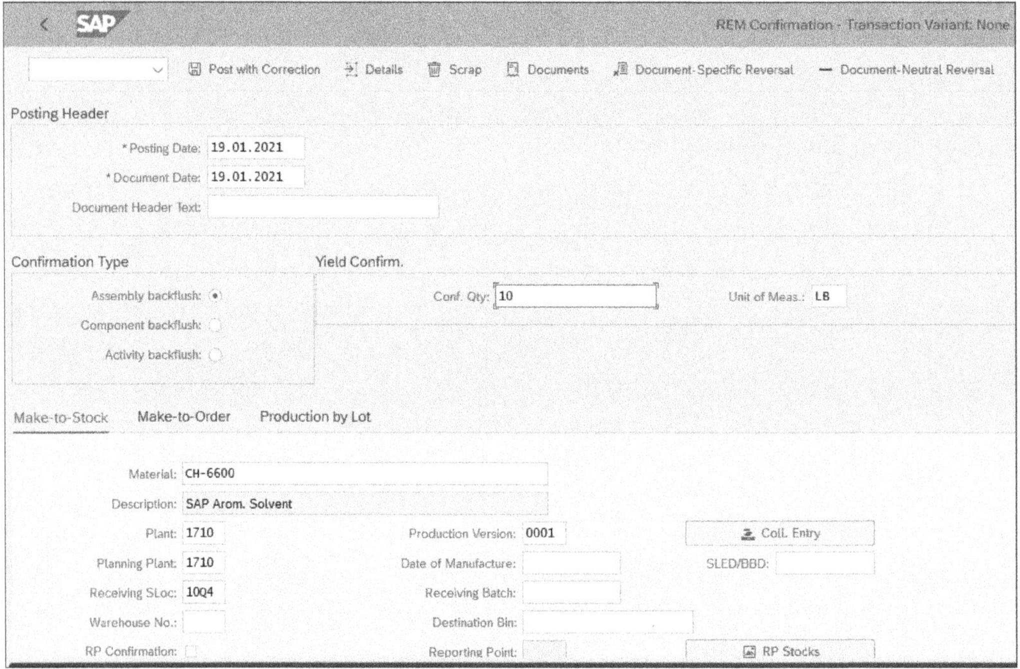


**Figure 6.73** Confirmation in Repetitive Manufacturing

### 6.5.3 Work in Process

For product cost collectors, WIP is always calculated as a target cost. This takes the standard costs for each operation completed from either the standard cost estimate, the cost estimate for the product cost collector, or another cost estimate created for this purpose and relies on the existence of detailed values per operation. The product cost collector is selected in every period and will usually have a mix of WIP, scrap, and variances as some production orders will be complete and others still in process.

To calculate WIP for product cost collectors, follow menu path **Accounting • Controlling • Product Cost Controlling • Cost Object Controlling • Product Cost by Period • Period-End Closing • Single Functions • Work in Process • Individual Processing • Calculate** or use

Transaction KKAS. Enter the material, plant, and, if multiple production versions exist for the material, the production process, along with the period, fiscal year, and results analysis version(s), then click **Execute**, as shown in Figure 6.74. Again, you'll typically also run the WIP calculation not for individual product cost collectors but for all the product cost collectors in a given plant, again using Transaction KKAO. Because we confirmed at the assembly level rather than at the operation level, there is no WIP in this example.



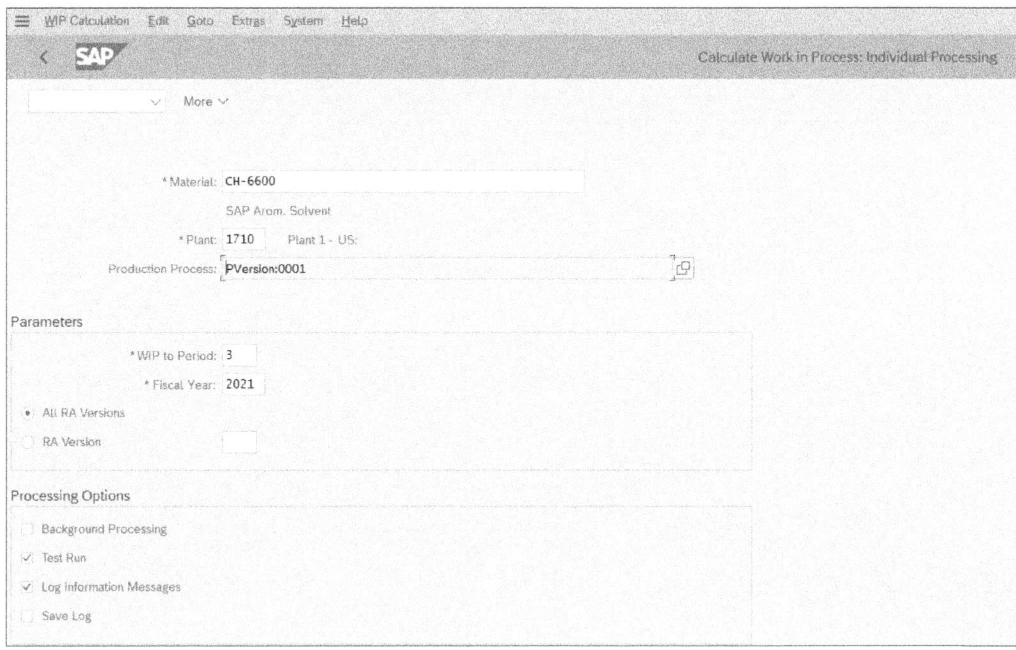


**Figure 6.74** Entry Screen for WIP Calculation

### 6.5.4 Variance Calculation

Even though most product cost collectors will have a mix of WIP and variances, you'll have to calculate WIP before you calculate variances to ensure that the open orders aren't treated as variances. To calculate variances, follow menu path **Accounting • Controlling • Product Cost Controlling • Cost Object Controlling • Product Cost by Period • Period-End Closing • Single Functions • Variances • Individual Processing** or use Transaction KKS6 (or for the whole plant, use collective processing or Transaction KKS5). Enter the material, plant, and, if multiple production versions exist for the material, the production process, along with the period, fiscal year, and target cost version(s), and click **Execute**.

The only difference compared to product cost by order is that the planned costs are calculated for the product cost collector rather than the individual production order. Figure 6.75 shows the result of variance calculation for the product cost collector. We've selected the product cost collector line and clicked the **Cost Elements** button. This time, you can see the variances and the value of the scrap. The variances are split into variance categories, as for product cost by order.



| Plant | Cost Object | Target Costs | Actual Costs | Allocated Actl Costs | Work in Process | Scrap | Variance |
|---|---|---|---|---|---|---|---|
| 1... | PCC CH-6600/1710/100... | 4,79 | 27,25 | 4,80 | 0,00 | 2,39 | 20,06 |

| Cost El... | Cost Element (Text) | Origin | Total tgt costs | Total act.costs | Total ctrl cost | WIP | Scrap | Variance |
|---|---|---|---|---|---|---|---|---|
| 511000... | Consumption - Raw Mat... | | 4,56 | 27,25 | 24,97 | 0,00 | 2,28 | 20,41 |
| 941110... | Overhead Material | | 0,23 | 0,00 | 0,11- | 0,00 | 0,11 | 0,34- |
| **Debit** | | | **4,79** | **27,25** | **24,86** | **0,00** | **2,39** | **20,07** |
| 551000... | Plant Activity Production ... | | 4,80 | 4,80 | 0,00 | 0,00 | 0,00 | 0,01- |
| **Delivery** | | | **4,80** | **4,80** | **0,00** | **0,00** | **0,00** | **0,01-** |

**Figure 6.75** Variances on Product Cost Collector

To explain the values included in the scrap, select the **Scrap** button shown in Figure 6.75. Figure 6.76 shows the cost impact of scrapping a quantity of finished goods because it didn't meet the quality standards.

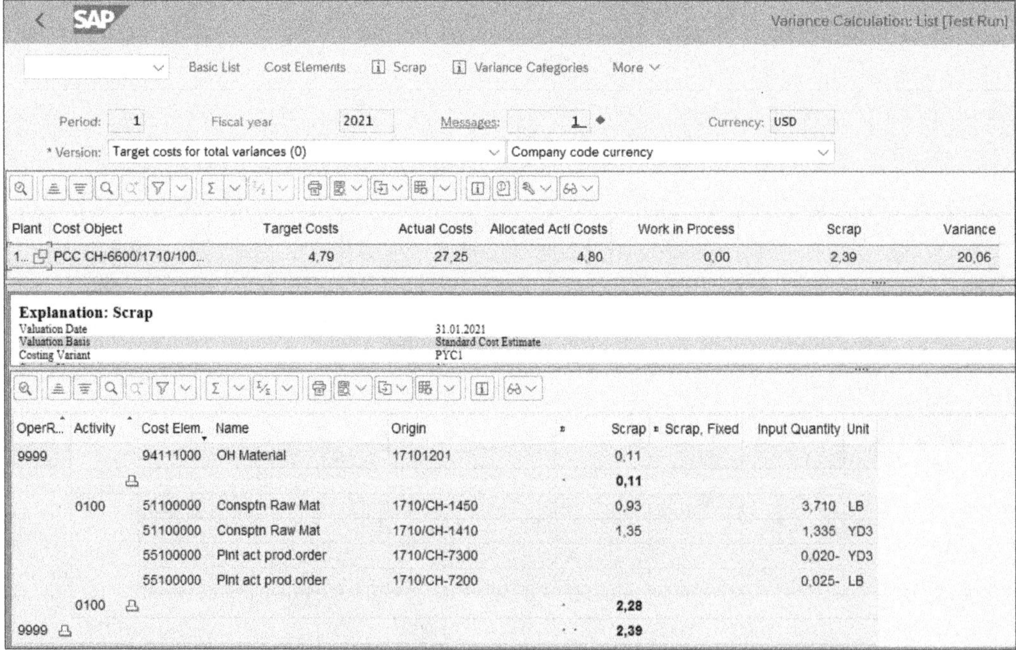


| Plant | Cost Object | Target Costs | Actual Costs | Allocated Actl Costs | Work in Process | Scrap | Variance |
|---|---|---|---|---|---|---|---|
| 1... | PCC CH-6600/1710/100... | 4,79 | 27,25 | 4,80 | 0,00 | 2,39 | 20,06 |

| OperR... | Activity | Cost Elem. | Name | Origin | Scrap | Scrap, Fixed | Input Quantity | Unit |
|---|---|---|---|---|---|---|---|---|
| 9999 | | 94111000 | OH Material | 17101201 | 0,11 | | | |
| | | | | | **0,11** | | | |
| | 0100 | 51100000 | Consptn Raw Mat | 1710/CH-1450 | 0,93 | | 3,710 | LB |
| | | 51100000 | Consptn Raw Mat | 1710/CH-1410 | 1,35 | | 1,335 | YD3 |
| | | 55100000 | Plnt act prod.order | 1710/CH-7300 | | | 0,020- | YD3 |
| | | 55100000 | Plnt act prod.order | 1710/CH-7200 | | | 0,025- | LB |
| | 0100 | | | | **2,28** | | | |
| 9999 | | | | | **2,39** | | | |

**Figure 6.76** Explanation of Scrap

To run settlement for a product cost collector, follow menu path **Accounting • Controlling • Product Cost Controlling • Cost Object Controlling • Product Cost by Period • Period-End Closing • Single Functions • Settlement • Individual Processing** or use Transaction KK87. Enter the material, plant, and, if multiple production versions exist for the material, the production process, along with the period and fiscal year, and click **Execute**.

Figure 6.77 shows the result of settlement. The variances have been posted to stock (**MAT**) as a total value and to margin analysis (**PSG**) split by the variance categories.

Detail list - Settled values

| Senders | Short text: Sender | Receiver | ΣValCOArCur | COAr Cur | ΣVal/ObjCur | Ob.Cr/Send | Inform. |
|---|---|---|---|---|---|---|---|
| ORD 700020 | SAP Arom Repetitive Manufacturing | MAT 1710/CH-6600 | 20,50 | EUR | 22,45 | USD | |
| | | PSG 0006499660 | 20,50 | EUR | 22,45 | USD | Variances |
| | | | **41,00** | **EUR** | **44,90** | **USD** | |

**Figure 6.77** Results of Settling Product Cost Collector

The make-to-stock business process ends with the delivery of the finished goods to stock, and all sales controlling activities take place in margin analysis, when the goods for the sales order are picked from neutral stock and shipped to the customer, as we'll explain in Chapter 7.

## 6.6 Make-to-Order

The most common reason to initiate *make-to-order* production is that the product requested is configurable and the customer has made certain selections that will affect the parts needed in manufacturing and sometimes the operations to be performed, as we discussed in Section 6.1. MRP triggers production with respect to a sales order rather than a neutral demand. You have two options in a make-to-order scenario:

1. **Account assignment category M: Individual customer stock without sales order account assignment**
   The production order is triggered from the sales order and delivers its completed product to *sales order stock*, from where it will be shipped to the customer. If there are no customer-specific costs for the delivery, there's no need to configure the sales order item as an account assignment as reporting and variance analysis can still take place by production order, as discussed in Section 6.4. Sales order stock is valuated, which means that goods receipts to sales order stock update the inventory value just as for make-to-stock. If necessary, you can post special sales costs directly to margin analysis, as we'll show in Chapter 7.

The two key differences compared to what we discussed in Section 6.4 is that the production order settles its costs to sales order stock and that the system is configured to pick a price for the sales order stock using a sales order cost estimate, the production order cost estimate, or occasionally the standard cost estimate (if one exists) rather than the standard price we used to value the receipt to stock in Section 6.4.

2. **Account assignment category E: Individual customer stock with sales order account assignment**
   The sales order initiates make-to-order production, and production costs are collected on the production order as before. However, the cost of performing customer-specific configuration or special delivery costs needs to be charged to the sales order. In this case, the sales order item needs to be configured as an account assignment, and sales revenue is captured as a cost element. You'll also have to perform results analysis at period close. Alternatively, post these special costs directly to margin analysis.

**SAP ERP versus SAP S/4HANA**

In SAP ERP releases prior to release 4.0, sales order stock could not be valuated, and costs for the sales order were always expensed. At period close, *results analysis* was used to determine what part of the costs related to the revenue on the sales order and could be treated as cost of goods sold and what part was WIP, awaiting the associated revenue.

We'll begin by looking at how to create a sales order cost estimate to set the initial value of the inventory in Section 6.6.1. We'll then follow the various steps in the make-to-order process in Section 6.6.2 and end by looking at the calculation of WIP and variances in Section 6.6.3.

### 6.6.1 Using the Sales Order Cost Estimate for Inventory Valuation

We talked about the need for a standard cost estimate to value the goods receipt to neutral stock in Section 6.4.1 and the need to create a cost estimate for each production version in Section 6.5.1. In make-to-order, you need to be more granular again as the material components and operations in the sales order take account of the customer's specific requirements and can differ with every sales order.

To create a sales order, choose **Logistics • Sales and Distribution • Sales Order • Create** or choose Transaction VA01, and enter the order type, the sales organization, the distribution channel, the division, the sales office, and the sales group, then press Enter. Then enter the name of the sold-to party (customer) in the order header and the material and quantity in the order item. Each sales order item can be handled differently, so you should check the requirements type for the sales order item as this determines the account assignment category and with it the type of make-to-order processing by looking at the parameters in the **Procurement** tab and specifically the entry in the **RqTy** column.

You'll recognize a make-to-order item by the special requirements type (see Figure 6.78) that controls the fact that the production order will be created with reference to the sales orders so that customer requirements can be taken into account during production. The special requirements type is shown in the **Procurement** tab in the order overview (**KEK** in this example) and also determines that the goods will be delivered to and issued to the customer from sales order stock—in other words, the inventory that belongs to the sales order rather than the general finished goods inventory. This raises the issue of how the sales order item will be valued if no standard cost estimate exists for the customer-specific configuration. Usually either a cost estimate is created for the sales order or the production order cost estimate is used to provide an initial valuation. The requirements type also determines whether the sales order item exists as an account assignment in controlling or not. In both cases, the costs and revenues for the sales order item flow into margin analysis.



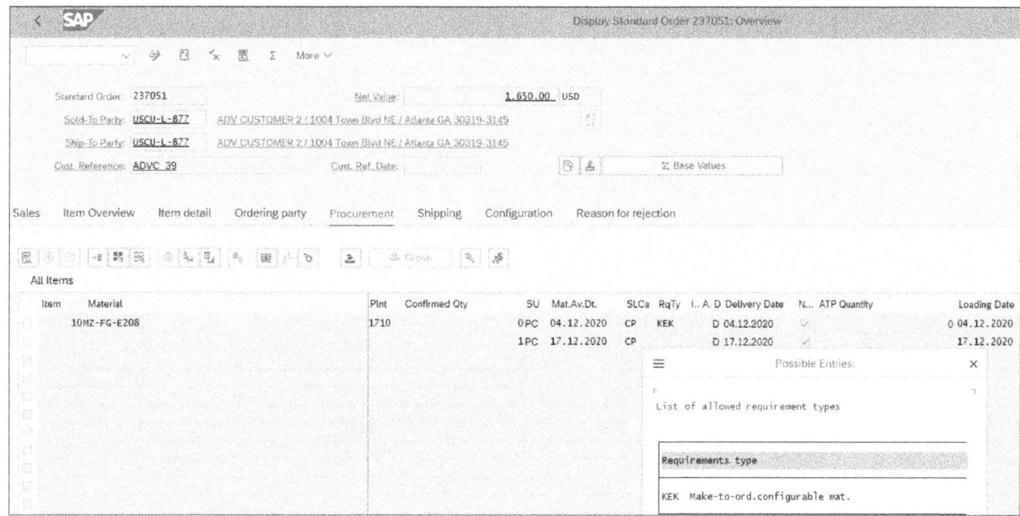


**Figure 6.78** Sales Order Item Showing Requirements Type

To create a production order to fulfill the customer requirements, you can either rely on the MRP run to link the production order with the sales order item or you can manually create a production order with reference to the sales order item. To display the link to the sales order item, create a production order (see Section 6.4.2) and note the **Sales Order** item in the **General** tab for the production order (see Figure 6.79). This link does not exist for make-to-stock orders that deliver to neutral stock.

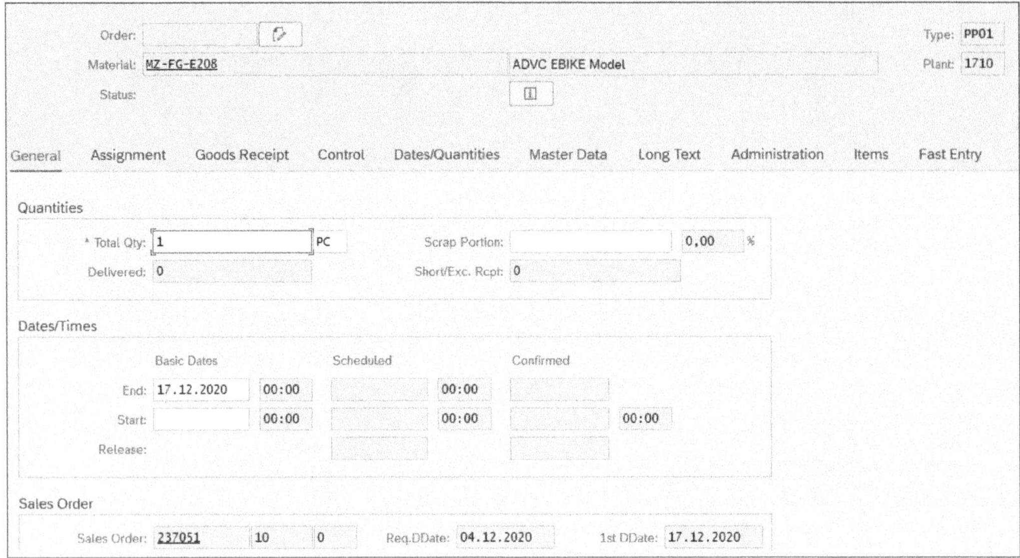

Figure 6.79 Production Order Header Showing Link to Sales Order Item

To get a sense of the sales order process, display the material components for the production order by choosing the **Components** tab from the production order header. Figure 6.80 shows the result of the configuration step for the sales order item—namely, the components that will be needed to meet the specific needs of a particular customer.

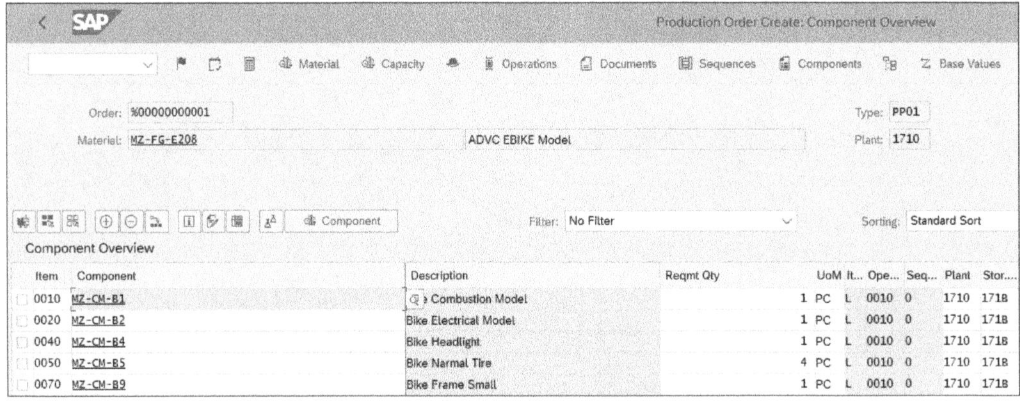

Figure 6.80 Material Components for Production Order

These material components are used in combination with the production activities for the required operations and any overhead conditions in the costing sheet to calculate the planned costs for the order. Figure 6.81 shows the planned costs for the production order. To show these, in the menu bar above the transaction title, choose **More • GoTo • Costs • Analysis**, choose the **Select Layout** icon, and switch to the **Cost Trend** layout. The values calculated here will be used to value the sales order stock when the goods receipt is performed for the e-bike.

**Order** 1030941 MZ-FG-E208
**Order Type** PP01 Standard production order
**Plant** 1710 Plant 1 - US
**Material** MZ-FG-E208 ADVC EBIKE Model

**Planned Quantity** 1 PC Piece

*Cumulative Data*
*Legal Valuation*
*Company Code Currency/Object Currency*

| Transaction | Origin | Origin (Text) | Total Plan Costs | Total Actual Costs | Plan/actual variance | P/A var(%) | Currency |
|---|---|---|---|---|---|---|---|
| Goods Issues | 1710/MZ-CM-... | Bike Combustion Model | 67,00 | 0,00 | 67,00- | 100,00- | USD |
| | 1710/MZ-CM-... | Bike Electrical Model | 67,00 | 0,00 | 67,00- | 100,00- | USD |
| | 1710/MZ-CM-... | Bike Headlight | 67,00 | 0,00 | 67,00- | 100,00- | USD |
| | 1710/MZ-CM-... | Bike Narmal Tire | 268,00 | 0,00 | 268,00- | 100,00- | USD |
| | 1710/MZ-CM-... | Bike Frame Small | 67,00 | 0,00 | 67,00- | 100,00- | USD |
| Goods Issues | | | **536,00** | **0,00** | **536,00-** | | **USD** |
| Confirmations | US99_CC7/1 | Production / Machine hours 1 | 4,25 | 0,00 | 4,25- | 100,00- | USD |
| | US99_CC7/3 | Production / Setup Production | 3,48 | 0,00 | 3,48- | 100,00- | USD |
| | US99_CC7/11 | Production / Personnel Hours | 2,32 | 0,00 | 2,32- | 100,00- | USD |
| Confirmations | | | **10,05** | **0,00** | **10,05-** | | **USD** |
| Overhead | 17101201 | Purch & Store 1 (US) | 37,52 | 0,00 | 37,52- | 100,00- | USD |
| | 17101301 | Manufacturing 1 (US) | 1,01 | 0,00 | 1,01- | 100,00- | USD |
| Overhead | | | **38,53** | **0,00** | **38,53-** | | **USD** |
| Goods Receipt | | (without origin) | 584,58- | 0,00 | 584,58 | 100,00- | USD |
| Goods Receipt | | | **584,58-** | **0,00** | **584,58** | | **USD** |

**Figure 6.81** Planned Costs for Production Order

The settlement rule for the production order settles to sales order stock (inventory that can only be delivered to the customer named in the sales order) rather than neutral material stock (which could be issued to any sales order). To display the settlement rule, return to the production order header and select **More • Header • Settlement Rule**. Figure 6.82 shows the settlement rule with the receivers: material and sales order item. You may remember that the production order we settled in Section 6.4 only included the material as a receiver. You can set up a different valuation class in the material master to assign goods movements to sales order stock to a different set of accounts from normal goods movements.

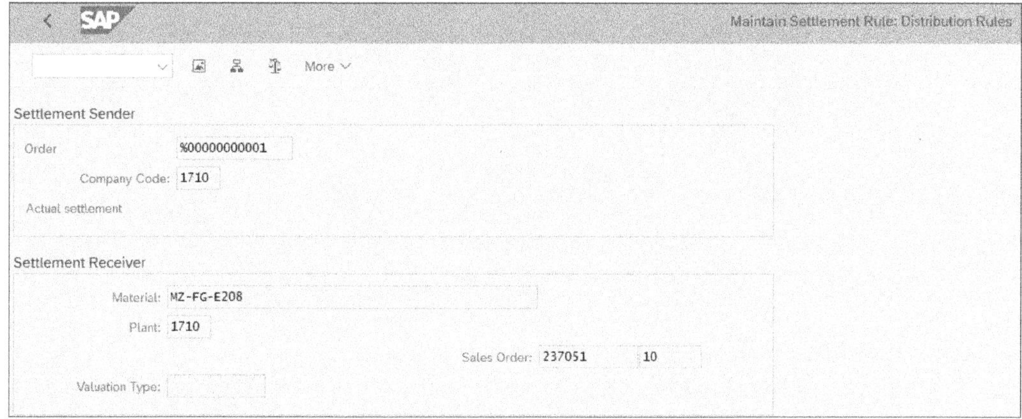


**Figure 6.82** Settlement Rule for Sales Order Stock

### 6.6.2 Monitoring the Production Process

The production process for make-to-order involves the same basic steps as in Section 6.4.2. You will still issue raw materials to the order, make confirmations, and deliver the goods to stock. The difference is that this inventory posting will update the *sales order stock*. Figure 6.83 shows the goods receipt for the finished good into sales order stock on completion of the production order. Notice that the movement type is combined with special stock type **E** for sales order stock. This means that it can only be delivered to the customer referenced in sales order **237051**, and the value of the inventory is determined by the cost estimate shown previously in Figure 6.81.

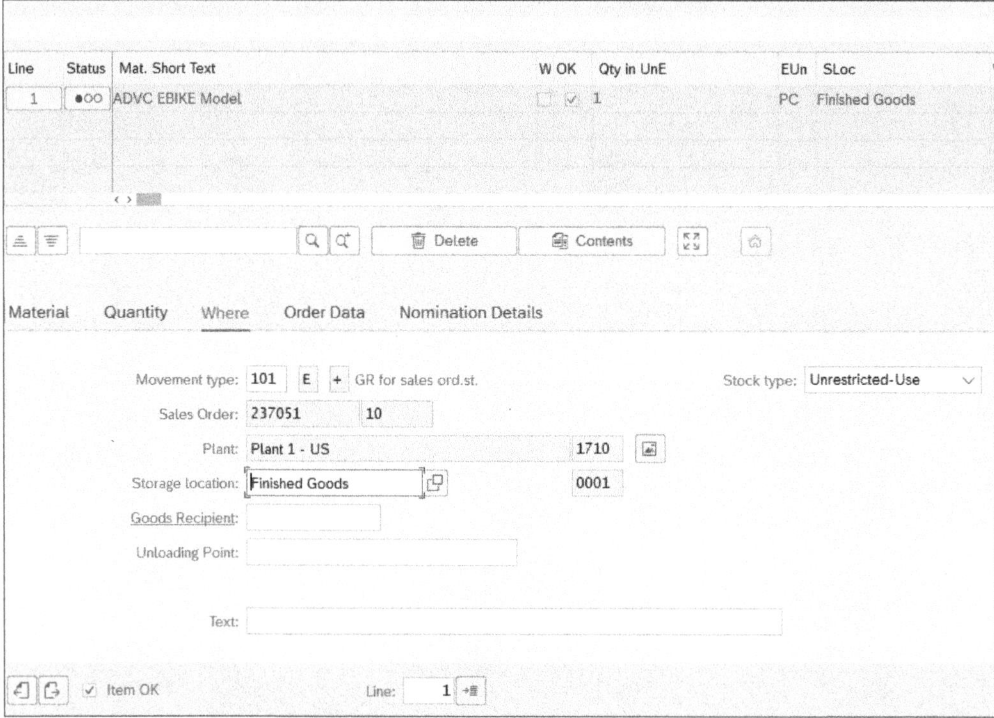


Figure 6.83 Goods Receipt to Sales Order Stock

### 6.6.3 Work in Process, Variance Calculation, and Actual Costing

One of the benefits of valuing the sales order stock, rather than using the non-valuated approach that was customary in early versions of SAP R/3, is that WIP, variances, and actual costing can take place as for make-to-stock, with the only difference being the valuation of the goods receipt to sales order stock.

In Figure 6.84, we've used Transaction KKS2 to calculate production variances for the production order assigned to the sales order. The process is the same as described for make-to-stock in Section 6.4.4. The **Target Costs** are based on the value in the production order cost estimate shown in Figure 6.81. The **Actual Costs** in this example are identical to the target costs because raw materials were issued as planned and the activities were confirmed as planned, but of course differences are possible if something changes between the initial cost estimate and order completion.

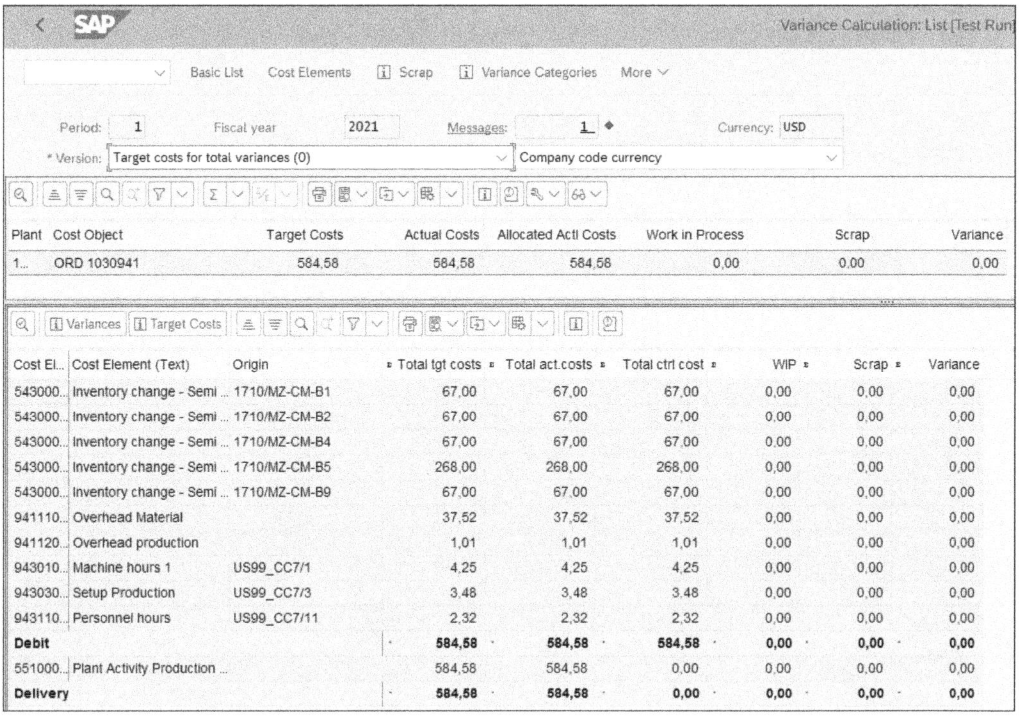

Variance Calculation: List [Test Run]

Basic List | Cost Elements | Scrap | Variance Categories | More

Period: 1 Fiscal year 2021 Messages: 1 Currency: USD

* Version: Target costs for total variances (0) | Company code currency

| Plant | Cost Object | Target Costs | Actual Costs | Allocated Actl Costs | Work in Process | Scrap | Variance |
|---|---|---|---|---|---|---|---|
| 1... | ORD 1030941 | 584,58 | 584,58 | 584,58 | 0,00 | 0,00 | 0,00 |

Variances | Target Costs

| Cost El... | Cost Element (Text) | Origin | Total tgt costs | Total act.costs | Total ctrl cost | WIP | Scrap | Variance |
|---|---|---|---|---|---|---|---|---|
| 543000... | Inventory change - Semi ... | 1710/MZ-CM-B1 | 67,00 | 67,00 | 67,00 | 0,00 | 0,00 | 0,00 |
| 543000... | Inventory change - Semi ... | 1710/MZ-CM-B2 | 67,00 | 67,00 | 67,00 | 0,00 | 0,00 | 0,00 |
| 543000... | Inventory change - Semi ... | 1710/MZ-CM-B4 | 67,00 | 67,00 | 67,00 | 0,00 | 0,00 | 0,00 |
| 543000... | Inventory change - Semi ... | 1710/MZ-CM-B5 | 268,00 | 268,00 | 268,00 | 0,00 | 0,00 | 0,00 |
| 543000... | Inventory change - Semi ... | 1710/MZ-CM-B9 | 67,00 | 67,00 | 67,00 | 0,00 | 0,00 | 0,00 |
| 941110... | Overhead Material | | 37,52 | 37,52 | 37,52 | 0,00 | 0,00 | 0,00 |
| 941120... | Overhead production | | 1,01 | 1,01 | 1,01 | 0,00 | 0,00 | 0,00 |
| 943010... | Machine hours 1 | US99_CC7/1 | 4,25 | 4,25 | 4,25 | 0,00 | 0,00 | 0,00 |
| 943030... | Setup Production | US99_CC7/3 | 3,48 | 3,48 | 3,48 | 0,00 | 0,00 | 0,00 |
| 943110... | Personnel hours | US99_CC7/11 | 2,32 | 2,32 | 2,32 | 0,00 | 0,00 | 0,00 |
| **Debit** | | | **584,58** | **584,58** | **584,58** | **0,00** | **0,00** | **0,00** |
| 551000... | Plant Activity Production ... | | 584,58 | 584,58 | 0,00 | 0,00 | 0,00 | 0,00 |
| **Delivery** | | | **584,58** | **584,58** | **0,00** | **0,00** | **0,00** | **0,00** |

**Figure 6.84** Variance Analysis for Production Order

You can also settle the production order using Transaction KO88 as in Section 6.4.4. Again, there are zero variances in this example, but you can see an assignment to the material (the sales order stock) and the profitability segment (**PSG**) in the settlement results shown in Figure 6.85. If there had been a difference, then this would impact the contribution margin for the product.

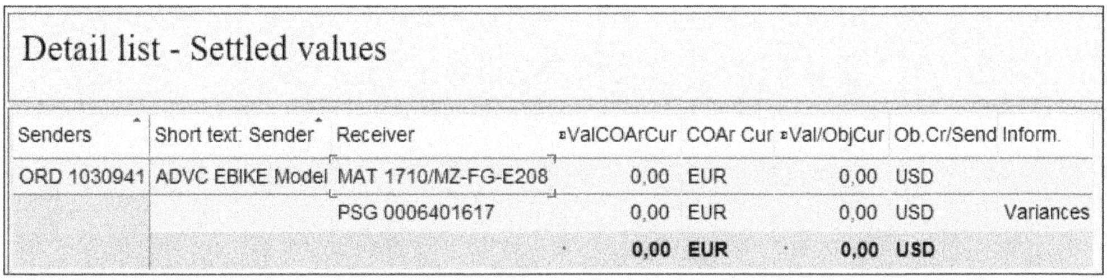

Detail list - Settled values

| Senders | Short text: Sender | Receiver | ValCOArCur | COAr Cur | Val/ObjCur | Ob.Cr/Send | Inform. |
|---|---|---|---|---|---|---|---|
| ORD 1030941 | ADVC EBIKE Model | MAT 1710/MZ-FG-E208 | 0,00 | EUR | 0,00 | USD | |
| | | PSG 0006401617 | 0,00 | EUR | 0,00 | USD | Variances |
| | | | **0,00** | **EUR** | **0,00** | **USD** | |

**Figure 6.85** Settlement of Production Order to Sales Order Stock

If you plan to use actual costing, you should also make sure that your sales order stock is valuated so that it can be treated as stock just like a standard material. Figure 6.86

shows Transaction CKM3N (Material Price Analysis), in which we've selected the material and plant in combination with the sales order item. Again, there isn't a standard cost estimate, so this special stock segment is updated with the results of the production order cost estimate at the time of the first goods movement, as shown in Figure 6.81. Any variances with respect to this cost estimate would be included in actual costing as in the make-to-stock environment.

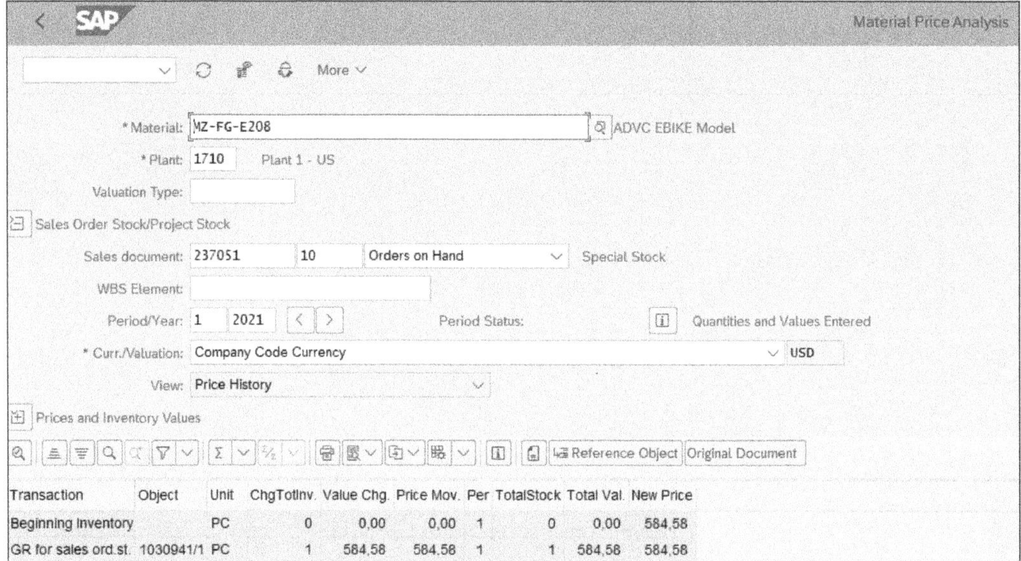


**Figure 6.86** Material Price Analysis with Sales Order Stock

## 6.7 Maintain and Operate Assets

We've now covered the main production flows and will turn our attention to maintenance as any kind of manufacturing almost also involves maintenance of the assets involved in that production process. Although maintenance orders don't generally attract as much attention as production orders, largely because their costs don't impact the balance sheet, the regulatory authorities have recently started to put them under increased scrutiny. Maintenance and service orders use exactly the same mechanisms to capture their costs as production orders. The main differences are that the task lists describe *maintenance* or *service* steps rather than *manufacturing* steps and that the orders are created with reference to a functional location instead of to a material number.

We'll begin by looking at how the planning process in maintenance differs from the planning process in production in Section 6.7.1. We'll then look at the process of capturing maintenance costs in Section 6.7.2 and end by looking at your options for analyzing maintenance costs in Section 6.7.3.

### 6.7.1 Estimating and Planning Maintenance Costs

To display a maintenance order, choose **Logistics • Plant Maintenance • Maintenance Processing • Order • Create (General)** or Transaction IW33. Like production orders, maintenance orders are created with reference to an order type, but instead of being associated with the product to be manufactured, they describe what is to be maintained (functional location, equipment). The link to costing is established via the maintenance operations. To see the operations, select the **Operations** tab. As for the production order, you see the work center (which will also provide the link to the cost center), the duration of the maintenance step, and the activity type to be used to charge the costs.



Figure 6.87 shows a sample maintenance order for the monthly maintenance of a pump, together with the three operations to capture the costs. The costs for these operations are calculated using the standard values for maintenance operations in the same way as for production operations. Notice the times in the **Work** column and **Dur.** (duration) column and the activity type in the **ActTyp** column. It's also possible to assign any materials that will be used for maintenance in the **Components** tab.

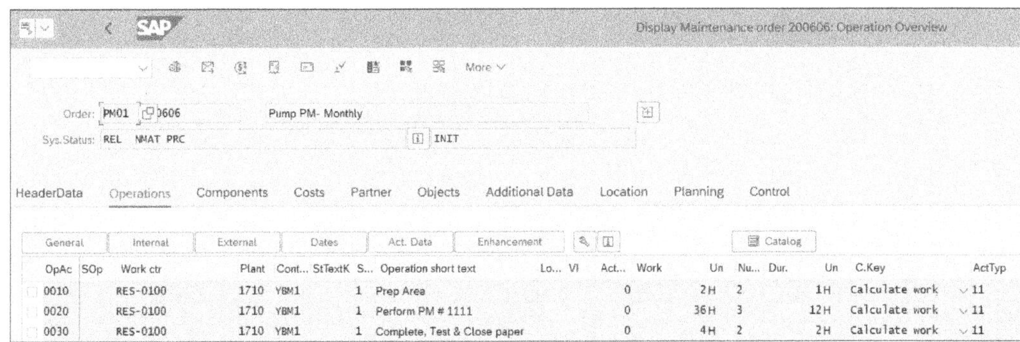


**Figure 6.87** Sample Maintenance Order

You can access the planned costs for the activities in the maintenance order by choosing **Extras • Cost Reports • Operation Cost Overview** in the order header or Transaction IW4ON (Operation Cost Overview), arriving at the screen in Figure 6.88. These planned costs were calculated using the standard values and activity types shown in Figure 6.88. It's also possible to enter estimated costs manually for the order in the **Est. costs** column to justify the need for and expected costs of the maintenance work. In maintenance, as in the project system, costs can be displayed not only by cost element but also by *value category*. The assignment to the **Internal Activity** category is simply a different way of structuring the costs and is part of the configuration effort of setting up the project system and maintenance orders.

> **Note**
>
> The assignment to value categories is not supported in SAP S/4HANA Cloud, and the SAP Fiori apps for maintenance do not show this information.

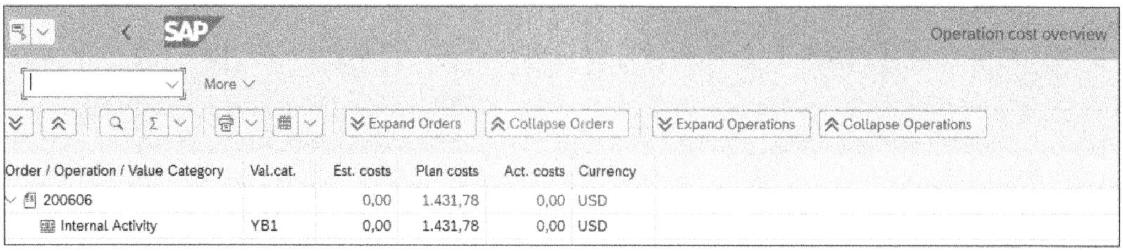

Operation cost overview

More

Expand Orders | Collapse Orders | Expand Operations | Collapse Operations

| Order / Operation / Value Category | Val.cat. | Est. costs | Plan costs | Act. costs | Currency |
|---|---|---|---|---|---|
| 200606 | | 0,00 | 1.431,78 | 0,00 | USD |
| Internal Activity | YB1 | 0,00 | 1.431,78 | 0,00 | USD |

**Figure 6.88** Operation Cost Overview for Maintenance Order

Of course, you can also view maintenance orders just like internal orders or production orders. Figure 6.89 shows the **Plan/Actual Comparison** for the maintenance order, which you can access from the maintenance order by choosing **Extras • Cost Reports • Plan/Actual Comparison.** Just as with the production orders, you're seeing a *compatibility view* here, which shows the data as it was stored in SAP ERP. We'll explain this concept in more detail in Chapter 10.

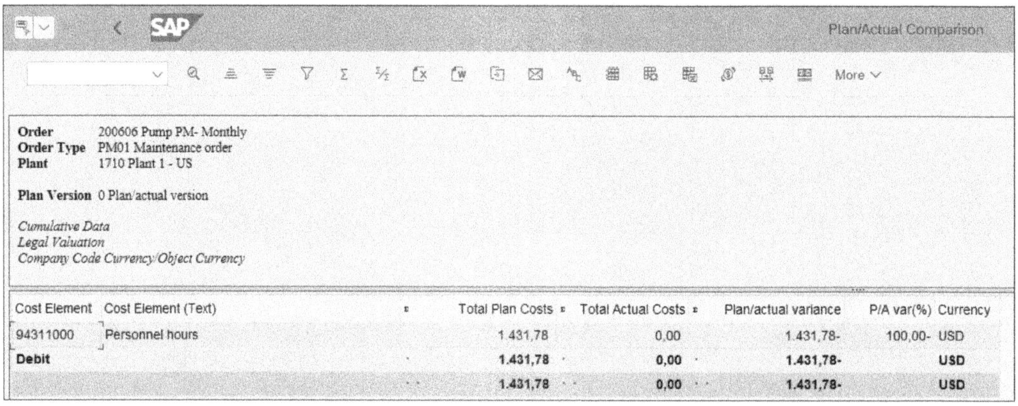

Plan/Actual Comparison

More

**Order** 200606 Pump PM- Monthly
**Order Type** PM01 Maintenance order
**Plant** 1710 Plant 1 - US

**Plan Version** 0 Plan/actual version

*Cumulative Data*
*Legal Valuation*
*Company Code Currency/Object Currency*

| Cost Element | Cost Element (Text) | Total Plan Costs | Total Actual Costs | Plan/actual variance | P/A var(%) | Currency |
|---|---|---|---|---|---|---|
| 94311000 | Personnel hours | 1.431,78 | 0,00 | 1.431,78- | 100,00- | USD |
| **Debit** | | **1.431,78** | **0,00** | **1.431,78-** | | **USD** |
| | | **1.431,78** | **0,00** | **1.431,78-** | | **USD** |

**Figure 6.89** Plan/Actual Report for Maintenance Order

### 6.7.2 Operation-Level Costing

The fields for production operations were added to the Universal Journal with SAP S/4HANA, but it's been possible to calculate maintenance costs at the operation level since SAP ERP 6.0 EHP 5 by activating the LOG_EAM_OLC business function (Operation Account Assignment). The classic maintenance order captures costs via the confirmations at the operation level but stores the costs at the header level. For the sorts of maintenance orders that are completed in an afternoon, this can be perfectly adequate. For maintenance and service orders that are more complex and have hugely different operations, consider storing the costs at the operation level instead. In configuration, the operation can be activated as an account assignment by setting a flag in the order type. You can identify orders with operation-level costing by the ACAS status (activity account assignment) in the order header. To activate operation-level costing, follow

IMG menu path **Plant Maintenance and Customer Service • Maintenance and Service Processing • Maintenance and Service Orders • Functions and Settings for Order Types • Costs at Operation Level • Define Cost Settings**.

In this context, you might wonder where the term *activity* comes from. The same coding is used to assign maintenance costs to operations as is used to assign manufacturing costs to network activities, leading to the confusion. Using the business function allows you to show costs by operation, but you don't have to change either your reporting or your period-end close processes and can continue to execute all your reports and period-close steps by order. As you do this, the system automatically selects costs for all the operations that are assigned to the order and displays or processes the costs for the multiple operations. Capturing costs by operation increases the number of objects to process at period close because each operation becomes a miniorder within the parent order, but it allows you to look at the actual costs for each operation in turn.

Once you've released the maintenance order, you can confirm the work times by using Transaction IW41 or **Logistics • Plant Maintenance • Maintenance Processing • Completion Confirmation • Individual Time Confirmation** and entering the number of hours worked in each operation.

### 6.7.3 Maintenance Reporting in the Universal Journal

The operation field was introduced for costing purposes in SAP ERP for maintenance orders, but further fields also have been added to the Universal Journal for maintenance orders, including equipment and functional location. New reports built specifically in SAP S/4HANA include the Actual Maintenance Costs app (SAP Fiori ID F3567) shown in Figure 6.90.

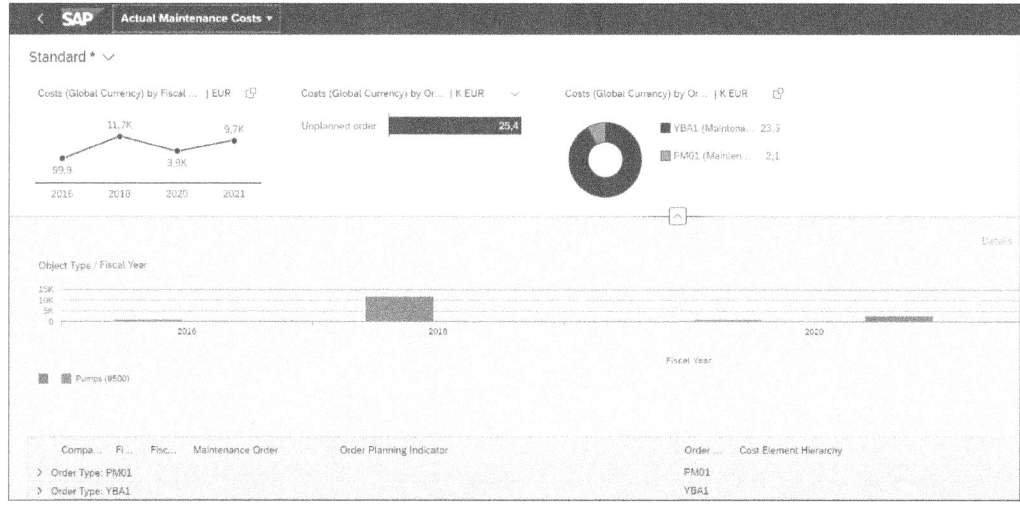


**Figure 6.90** Actual Maintenance Costs App

## 6.8 Summary

We began this chapter with a description of the master data that has to be in place prior to costing and then showed how to calculate and store the standard costs for those products manufactured in house. We then walked through an end-to-end process, from the procurement of the raw materials to the manufacture of the finished goods and the delivery to stock, to show how costs are accumulated in each step of the process, how these impact WIP and variances, and how this impacts actual costing. In addition to the production orders, we looked at the use of product cost collectors in a make-to-stock environment and the handling of customer-specific requirements in a make-to-order environment and finished by looking at the maintenance activities required to keep manufacturing running smoothly.

Now that we've shown the various ways of manufacturing goods and delivering them to stock, we'll look at how to sell the goods and monitor the profitability of each product and how to handle service processes.

# Chapter 7
# Margin Analysis for Products and Services

*In the last chapter, we looked at controlling for production processes, which enables us to analyze production accountability areas. In this chapter, we'll look at revenue-generating business processes and how SAP S/4HANA can assign revenues and their matching cost of goods sold to accountability areas and calculate margins for flexible, customer-defined market segments.*



You learned in Chapter 4 that you can define your market segment attributes very flexibly, depending on industry and customer requirements. In this chapter, we'll show you how to calculate contribution margins for products and services and how the business processes will update this market segment information. We do this with step-by-step business process examples in the system.

We start this chapter with the principles of margin analysis in SAP S/4HANA and an overview of the value flow and margin analysis functionality in Section 7.1. Then we'll show the sales scenarios in Section 7.2, including a first insight into the new prediction reporting. Based on the sales scenarios, we'll show how you can apply manual postings on profitability segments and perform management adjustment postings. We'll also demonstrate how to allocate costs from cost centers or per top-down distribution to your market segments. Next, we look at customer project scenarios in Section 7.3. We distinguish three different types: two with market segment attributes already updated with postings on the project and one that works with settlements to update market segment attributes. Then we examine the service scenario in Section 7.4, which is currently only available in SAP S/4HANA Cloud, but you'll be able to see the direction SAP is going in its roadmap in the area of the service scenarios.

We close in Section 7.5 with additional insights into event-based revenue recognition, which is an important element to provide real-time margins and ensure matching of revenue and costs of sales. We'll take event-based revenue recognition into account in our scenario examples shown in the system.

**Profitability Analysis Solutions**

There are two profitability analysis solutions in place in on-premise SAP S/4HANA. We focus in this book on the Universal Journal–based margin analysis (the new, innovative solution based on account-based profitability analysis). This solution is the focus in SAP S/4HANA and will be further enhanced per SAP's roadmap. SAP S/4HANA Cloud provides margin analysis only.

Costing-based profitability analysis continues to be available as an additional solution.

## 7.1 Guiding Principles and Overview

With the Universal Journal, the general ledger, controlling, event-based revenue recognition, and margin analysis are now integrated. All actual data for margin analysis is based on the Universal Journal.

What does this mean for margin analysis? Let's walk through the key benefits:

- Margin analysis is based on journal entries. There is no separate data store.
- All key performance indicators (KPIs), like realized revenues, cost of goods sold, or contribution margin, are calculated based on journal entry line items in the Universal Journal as the single source of truth. There is no reconciliation effort needed any longer between the financial applications.
- There is increased transparency. When you see a KPI in a report, like the margin, you can always drill down into the single journal entries from which the KPI was calculated.
- With the activation of the margin analysis and the definition of the market segment fields, and the option of additional customer-specific fields, the business processes will update the market segment information in the journal entries automatically.
- Profitability attributes are available for general ledger journal entries. You use this in business scenarios to assign them—for example, in the journal entry items for expenses, billing documents, and good issues. This enables real-time market segment and profitability reporting.
- General ledger functionalities also are now available for controlling and margin analysis. So, you can provide multiple currencies in profitability reporting, and margin analysis is supported for parallel ledgers.
- Period-end close is simplified and accelerated. Settlement between controlling, profitability analysis, revenue recognition, and the general ledger is now obsolete for most processes.

- For all margin analysis–related postings, like top-down allocation or cost center allocation, you create journal entries in the legal standard ledger because they are relevant for legal reporting. With the postings, functional area, profit center, or segment reporting could be impacted.

**Margin Analysis Data Flow**

Margin analysis is part of the Universal Journal. There is no separate data stored for margin analysis. With activation, the journal entries of the main business processes are enriched with the market segment data by the system.

Because margin analysis reporting feeds from the journal entries, in principle every profit and loss (P&L) item is relevant for profitability. Thanks to SAP HANA, you also report on the line items and not on aggregates, so every journal entry attribute can be analyzed.

Also, note that market segment attributes are updated for some balance sheet accounts to get a 360-degree view. As an example, we'll show WIP postings in this chapter.

Following the controlling value flow discussed in Chapter 4, Figure 4.1, Figure 7.1 shows how the margin reporting is triggered by the business processes and updated in the Universal Journal.

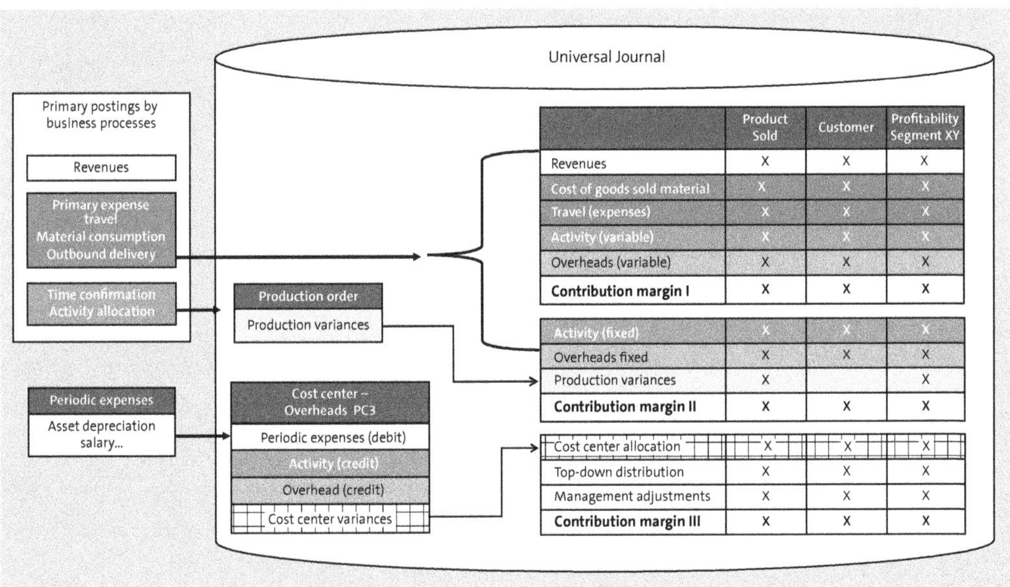


**Figure 7.1** Margin Analysis Based on Universal Journal

Figure 7.1 shows how a multilevel contribution margin calculation can be determined on the basis of the booked journal entries:

1. The revenues are generated by billing sales orders for products or services.
2. The business processes trigger the different cost types too, and you enrich them with market segment attributes. An example is the derivation logic for sales processes discussed in Chapter 4, Section 4.6.1 and in Section 7.2.
3. Activity allocation and overheads do not only debit the project or internal order but also credit the cost center. The same is true for overheads, which run based on the posted prima nota values on the projects or internal orders. On the cost center, there will be an under- or overabsorption at period end, which can be allocated to a profitability segment by a journal entry posting (see Section 7.2.5).
4. To distribute costs, which are posted with no specific market segments assigned, to more specified markets segments, there can be top-down distribution journal entries posted.
5. The production variances are settled from a production order to a profitability segment (see Chapter 6, Section 6.4.4).

The contribution margin key figures are aggregations of journal entry items. To define the reporting structure, the main basis is the general ledger account, but you also use the fixed/variable distinction provided by activity allocation and overheads in the journal entry and the functional area. To bring all these attributes together in a reporting structure, you use semantic tags (see Chapter 10, Section 10.4).

There are some business processes in which the market segment is used as real account assignment, like in the sales processes, the periodic allocation, and distribution, or when you account assign a manual posting to it. For these journal entries, the EO object type is used (see Chapter 4, Section 4.6).

There are processes in place like the customer project scenario or the service order scenario for which the main account assignment is a different object—project (object type PR) or service order (object type SV)—but the profitability segment is derived by the provided business information and also stored in in the journal entry line items. We'll show this in detail in Section 7.3 and Section 7.4.

Let's now take a look at the customer project scenario in SAP S/4HANA. In the Project Profitability Overview app (SAP Fiori ID F2794; see Figure 7.2), start by just selecting one company code.

You see here different KPIs for your customer projects—not only project-related ones like top projects or recognized margin and revenues, but also market segment data is provided, like margins for customer groups and WIP by product sold group.

Let's explore what's new in SAP S/4HANA:

- The data in the report is based on general ledger line items, which enables a drill-down on every KPI to the original journal entry in the Universal Journal as the single source of truth.

- The figures are always correct and up to date because you provide the market segment data with every posting on the customer project. There is no additional period-end close required to ensure matching of revenues with related costs and market segment enrichment.
- The settlement of customer projects is no longer necessary. All profitability and professional service–specific attributes are provided in all project-based line items, even in the revenue recognition line items. This makes settlement obsolete.
- The matching principle for cost and revenues is provided by event-based revenue recognition. Current project and market segment margins and work in process (WIP) data are always provided.



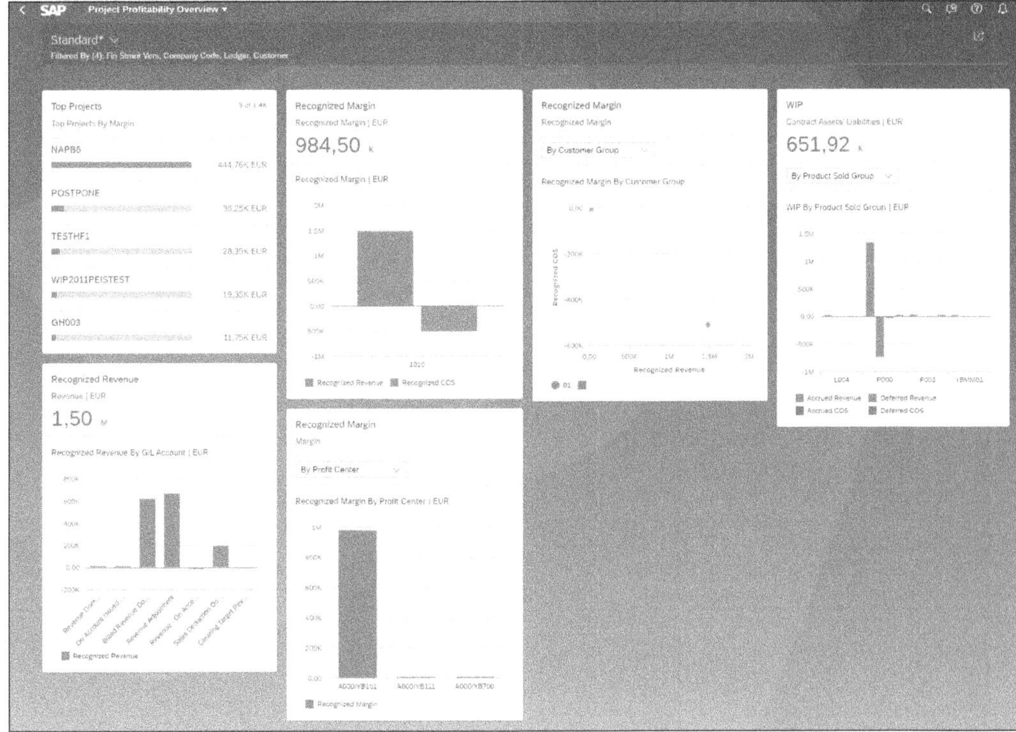


**Figure 7.2** Project Profitability Overview

Now let's look at the sales processes for manufactured goods. Here you'll see a multilevel margin based on the cost component split of the manufactured product, which we'll discuss further in Section 7.2. Start the Product Profitability app using one company code and the **Ledger OC** extension for management accounting, as shown in Figure 7.3.

You'll see the multilevel contribution margin, provided in the rows, per product group and customer, set in the columns.

| Product Sold Group | L001 Trading Materials | | | | | | | |
|---|---|---|---|---|---|---|---|---|
| Customer | 10100001 Inlandskunde DE 1 | 10100002 Inlandskunde DE 2 | S10100197 Computer Systems ... | S10100251 TechTronic Inc. (DE) | S10100252 HyperCom Inc. (DE) | S10100253 TronicTrade Inc. (DE) | S10100296 TRIMAX World (DE) | S10100298 Machattan Inc. (DE) |
| Billed Revenue Amt in Company Code Crcy | 935,10 EUR | 3.510,00 EUR | 5.246.349,00 EUR | 608.186,00 EUR | 493.667,00 EUR | 572.913,00 EUR | 443.705,00 EUR | 246.780,00 EUR |
| Sales Deduction Amt in Company Code Crcy | 0,00 EUR | 0,00 EUR | 0,00 EUR | 0,00 EUR | 0,00 EUR | 0,00 EUR | 0,00 EUR | 0,00 EUR |
| COGS - Variable Amt in CC Crcy | -927,31 EUR | -200,00 EUR | -14.697.405,82 EUR | -225.900,00 EUR | -292.780,00 EUR | -162.400,00 EUR | -271.200,00 EUR | -243.600,00 EUR |
| Contribution Margin I Amount in CC Crcy | 170,44 EUR | 3.310,00 EUR | -215.769,82 EUR | 1.537.576,00 EUR | 1.372.247,00 EUR | 1.003.261,00 EUR | 1.282.832,00 EUR | 1.039.522,00 EUR |
| COGS - Fixed Amount in CC Crcy | 0,00 EUR | 0,00 EUR | 0,00 EUR | 0,00 EUR | 0,00 EUR | 0,00 EUR | 0,00 EUR | 0,00 EUR |
| Price Differences Amount in CC Crcy | 0,00 EUR | 0,00 EUR | 0,00 EUR | 0,00 EUR | 0,00 EUR | 0,00 EUR | 0,00 EUR | 0,00 EUR |
| Contribution Margin II Amount in CC Crcy | 170,44 EUR | 3.310,00 EUR | -215.769,82 EUR | 1.537.576,00 EUR | 1.372.247,00 EUR | 1.003.261,00 EUR | 1.282.832,00 EUR | 1.039.522,00 EUR |
| Sales Overhead Amt in CC Crcy | 0,00 EUR | 0,00 EUR | 0,00 EUR | 0,00 EUR | 0,00 EUR | 0,00 EUR | 0,00 EUR | 0,00 EUR |
| Research & Dev Overhead Amt in CC Crcy | 0,00 EUR | 0,00 EUR | 0,00 EUR | 0,00 EUR | 0,00 EUR | 0,00 EUR | 0,00 EUR | 0,00 EUR |
| Contribution Margin III Amt in CC Crcy | 170,44 EUR | 3.310,00 EUR | -215.769,82 EUR | 1.537.576,00 EUR | 1.372.247,00 EUR | 1.003.261,00 EUR | 1.282.832,00 EUR | 1.039.522,00 EUR |
| Billed Quantity | 32 PC | 2 PC | 11.451 PC | 691 PC | 897 PC | 484 PC | 567 PC | 452 PC |
| Contribution Margin pUnit Amt in CCCrcy | 5,33 EUR/PC | 1.655,00 EUR/PC | -18,84 EUR/PC | 2.225,15 EUR/PC | 1.529,82 EUR/PC | 2.072,85 EUR/PC | 2.262,49 EUR/PC | 2.299,83 EUR/PC |

**Figure 7.3** Product Profitability with Multilevel Contribution Margin

That addresses the actuals, looking back at what's actually happened. Now let's address plans and predictions. Market segment planning is part of the periodic planning and is supported by SAP Analytics Cloud scenarios (see Chapter 2). This plan data is stored in table ACDOCP, with a structure matching that of the actual data. This allows a plan/actual comparison for market segments. You also have prediction data (see Section 7.2.3) based on the entered sales order. This data is stored in table ACDOCA to enable the same structure as for actual data, but in a prediction ledger (an extension ledger). To see this in action, start the Gross Margin Presumed/Actual app (SAP Fiori ID F3417), as shown in Figure 7.4.

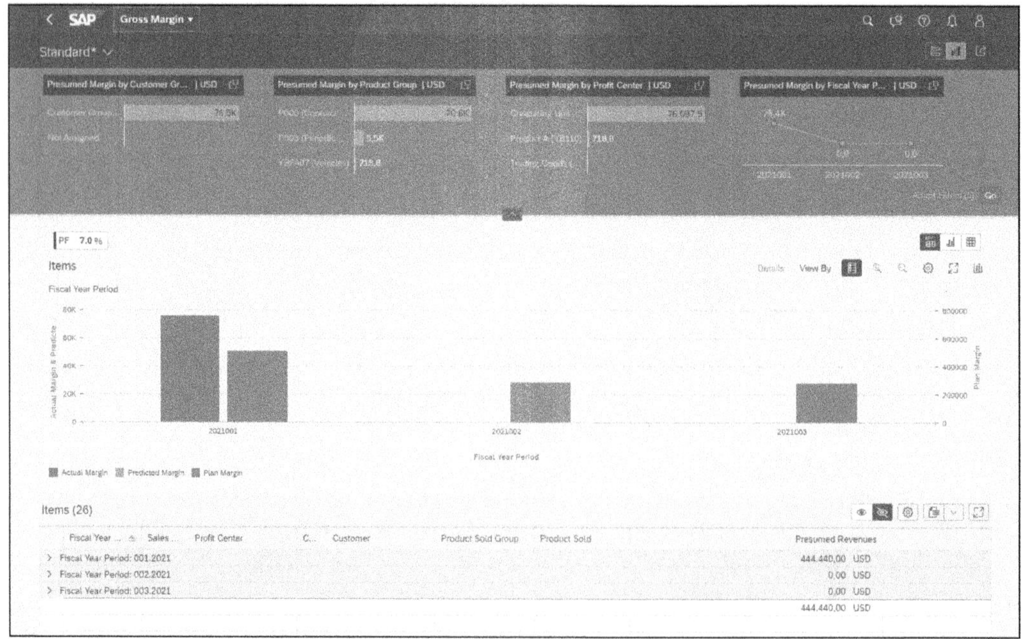


**Figure 7.4** Gross Margin—Presumed/Actual App

You see here the already realized margin by completed sales order in period 001/2021, and the predicted margin based on the entered and not yet executed sales order for the customer, product group, and profit center market segment attributes. At the bottom, you can drill down and analyze the data by the journal entries.

In Chapter 4, we discussed the master data for the margin analysis. Technically, the profitability segment is the account assignment of the margin analysis, which can be used to reflect the relevant market segment from a business perspective. The system standard already contains attributes such as product sold, customer, industry, customer and product group, profit center, and country. These are derived from the master data of the customer and the product, which we'll discuss in Section 7.2.1. The market segment can also be flexibly extended according to customer requirements. For this purpose, you have the extensibility tool in place (see Chapter 4, Section 4.6.2). To derive business process–dependent profitability objects and to enrich them for the relevant journal entry line item, you can use the derivation tool (see Chapter 4, Section 4.6.3). Based on the market segment attributes stored in the Universal Journal, you can provide margin analysis reporting.



In this chapter, we'll show the business process-related functionalities. For the sales scenarios presented in Section 7.2, we provide the following functionality:

- There is a cost component split posted to the goods issue journal entry for manufactured products. This also distinguishes between fixed and variable components to allow multilevel cross-margin reporting.
- Based on statistical sales conditions, calculatory costs such as freight charges or discounts can be reflected in multilevel cross-margin reporting. They are posted as journal entries in the management extension ledger.
- The result of actual costing for manufactured products can be used to update the costs of goods sold, as discussed in Chapter 6, Section 6.6.3.
- To be able to report incoming orders and the remaining sales order, you generate prediction data for the sales orders in the prediction extension ledger.

For the customer projects presented in Section 7.3, we enable the following:

- Derivation of profitability object and update of market segment fields for every journal entry posted to the project in addition to the account assignment on the project.
- Real-time profitability based on event-based revenue recognition.
- A simplified and accelerated period-end-close because we no longer settle in a separate profitability database.
- Project margin reporting on the prima nota and not on settlement general ledger accounts as before.
- New KPIs provided, like generated margin per employee or by origin profit center or WIP by market segment attributes.

In the service scenarios, discussed in Section 7.4, we also offer the following advanced profitability functions, currently only available in SAP S/4HANA Cloud:

- Like for the customer project scenarios, the additional derivation of market segment attributes and updates in the journal entries is enabled in addition to the account assignment on the service object.
- There is a simplified and accelerated period-end close because we no longer settle in a separate profitability database. This allows for margin reporting on the prima nota posted to the service object.

Furthermore, we provide generic margin analysis functionalities throughout the chapter:

- Special single costs can be recorded on profitability segments; for example, engineering hours or freight costs can be recorded on sales order profitability segments. We discuss this in Section 7.2.4.
- There is an option to settle costs and revenues from revenue-carrying internal orders and projects to profitability segments. We'll show an example in Section 7.3.3.
- Management adjustment postings can be recorded in the management extension ledger—for example, to allocate revenues between areas of responsibility and market segments. This is discussed in Section 7.2.4.
- For the use case of allocation with over- and underabsorption of cost centers to market segments, there is a cost center to margin analysis allocation in place, which we discuss in Section 7.2.5.
- To be able to distribute costs recorded without specific market segments, allocation to detailed market segments is used: the top-down distribution. This is discussed in Section 7.2.5.
- With the realignment tool, it's possible to new derive certain market segments and to update the relevant journal entries. We show an example in Section 7.3.2.

## 7.2 Sales Scenarios

This section is about selling products that are inventory-managed. In this scenario, there is a physical delivery process. We'll go over the sale of services later in Section 7.4. In the special case in which the product sold is manufactured in-house, you have the option to display the cost of sales according to the cost components. We'll show this scenario in the system.

First in this section, we'll explain the product and customer master data. Then we'll show the functionality via an end-to-end scenario in the system. In the example, we'll deliver and invoice a self-manufactured bike for which a cost estimate is available. Then we'll record extra direct costs. We'll activate event-based revenue recognition in the example, which is currently only available in the cloud for sales processes but is planned for on-premise. We'll then show the period-end close, which is simplified, and then look at reporting insights.

In the sales scenario, the customer and material master have an important influence on the margin analysis. Let's take a look at them.

### 7.2.1 Master Data

The material master and the customer master contain a large number of controls for many applications. Let's look at the most important ones from a margin analysis perspective.



#### Material Master

Let's first look at the product or material master, which we introduced in Chapter 6, Section 6.1.1. Start Transaction MM02 to change or Transaction MM03 to display the material master. Alternatively, you can use the Manage Product Master or Manage Material Valuations apps, as shown in Chapter 6. From a profitability perspective, you're interested in the sales and accounting data. For this example, select the MD_BIKE product, self-manufactured with a finished product material type and the following organizational units: sales org 1010, distribution channel 10, and plant 1010.

In the **Sales: sales org 1** tab, shown in Figure 7.5, the **Material Group** is defined (here, **YBFA07 Vehicles**). The product is assigned to **Division 00**. Both fields are part of the standard market segment fields and are derived when the MD_BIKE product sold is used in the process.

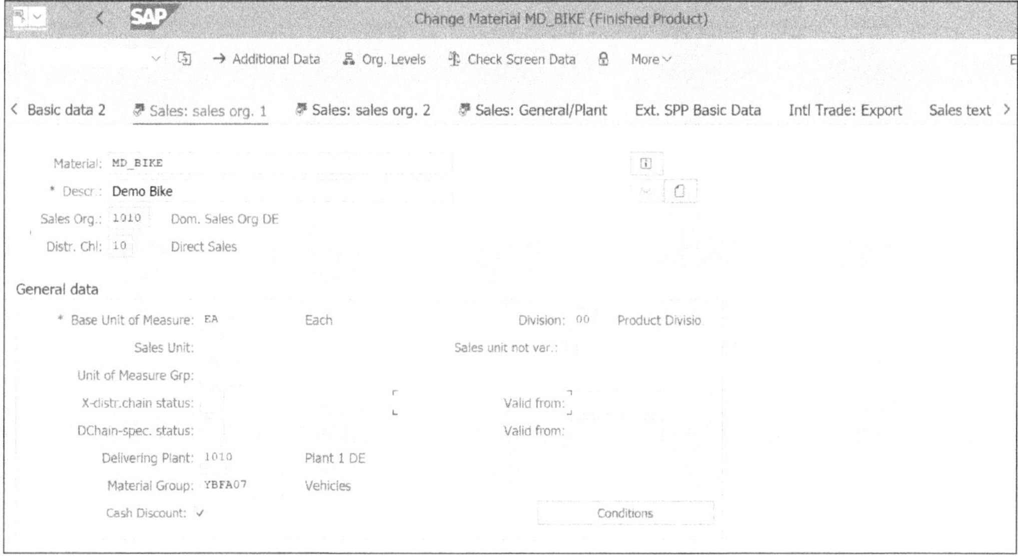


**Figure 7.5** Material Master: Sales Org Data 1

In the next tab, **Sales General/Plant, Profit Center YB110** is assigned, as shown in Figure 7.6. The profit center is defined on the plant level, and we selected plant **1010** when we started the material master transaction.

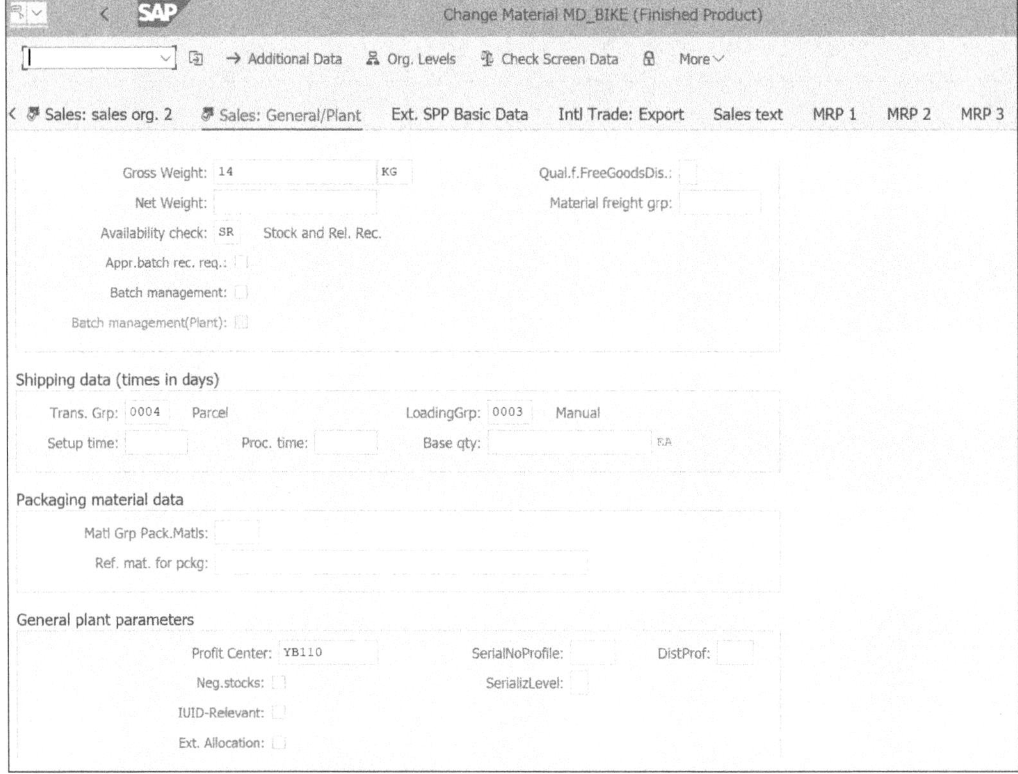


**Figure 7.6** Material Master: Profit Center Assignment

Now let's look at the controlling-relevant data and switch to the **Costing 2** tab, as shown in Figure 7.7.

In the upper section, you can see the available costing results. A **Current** cost estimate is used for the valuation of material movements (see Chapter 6, Section 6.2). For this product, there is a **Current** cost estimate with a **Standard price** of 825 EUR available.

The section at the bottom covers the **Valuation Data**:

- **Valuation Class**
  The **Valuation Class** controls the general ledger account determination for this product.
- **Price control**
  The **Price control** is defined as **S**. This means that for this product, the standard price is taken for valuation. Another valuation method could be moving average price or an actual costing method (see Chapter 6, Section 6.1.1).

Now let's see how the standard price is calculated through the cost estimation. Start Transaction CK13N to display the cost estimate. Enter the product, MD_BIKE, the plant, 1010, and the costing variant, which is relevant for the standard price update, PPC1 (see Chapter 6, Section 6.2.1). Then press F5 to arrive at the screen shown in Figure 7.8.

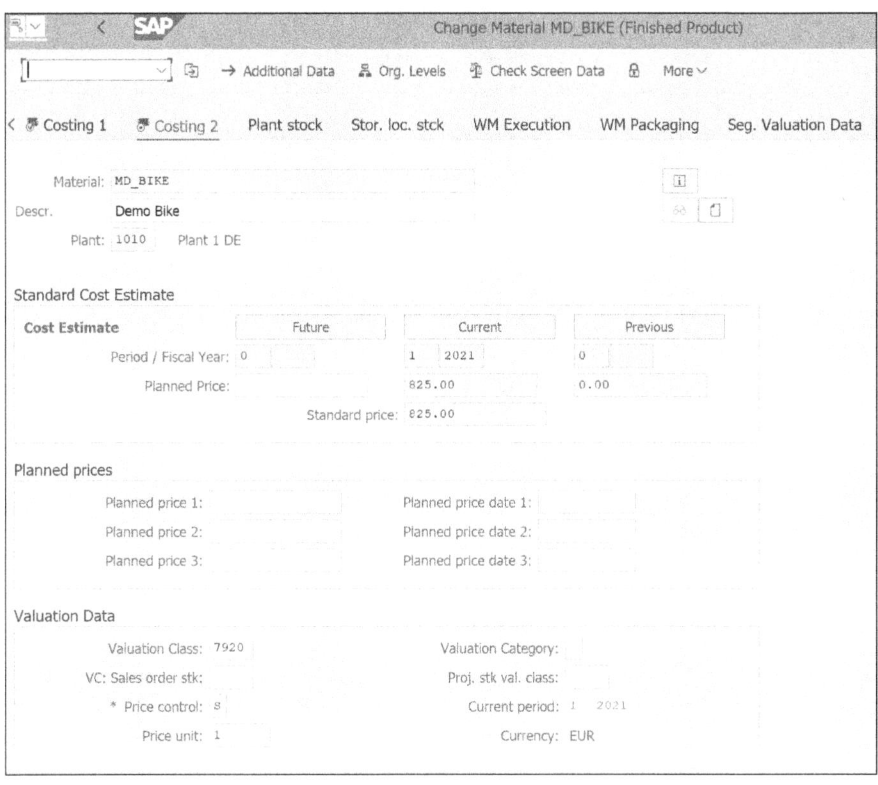


**Figure 7.7** Material Master: Controlling View

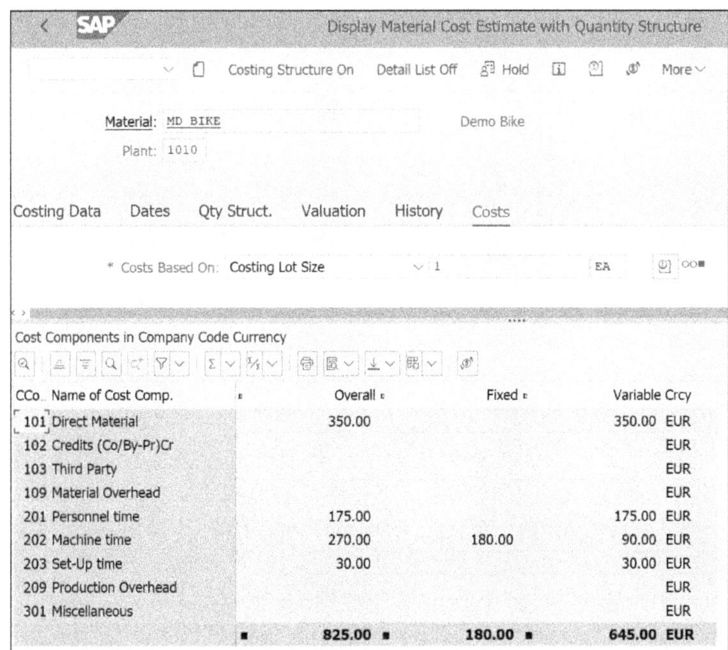


**Figure 7.8** Cost Estimation: Cost Component View

Select the cost component view (see Chapter 6, Section 6.2.3). With this view, you can see the total costs for the product: 825 EUR, of which 180 EUR is fixed. The value is split according to cost components—for example, material costs of 350 EUR. For the machine time there is a fixed portion. We'll follow up on this view in the multilevel margin reporting.

### Customer Master

Now let's look at the customer master. Start Transaction BP for maintaining business partners and arrive at a central maintenance view available for the business partner. Customer is one role of a business partner. Enter customer **10100002** in the selection screen; this is the customer we'll use in this example. Press Enter and for **Display in BP role**, select **Customer (Fin. Accounting)** to arrive at the screen shown in Figure 7.9.

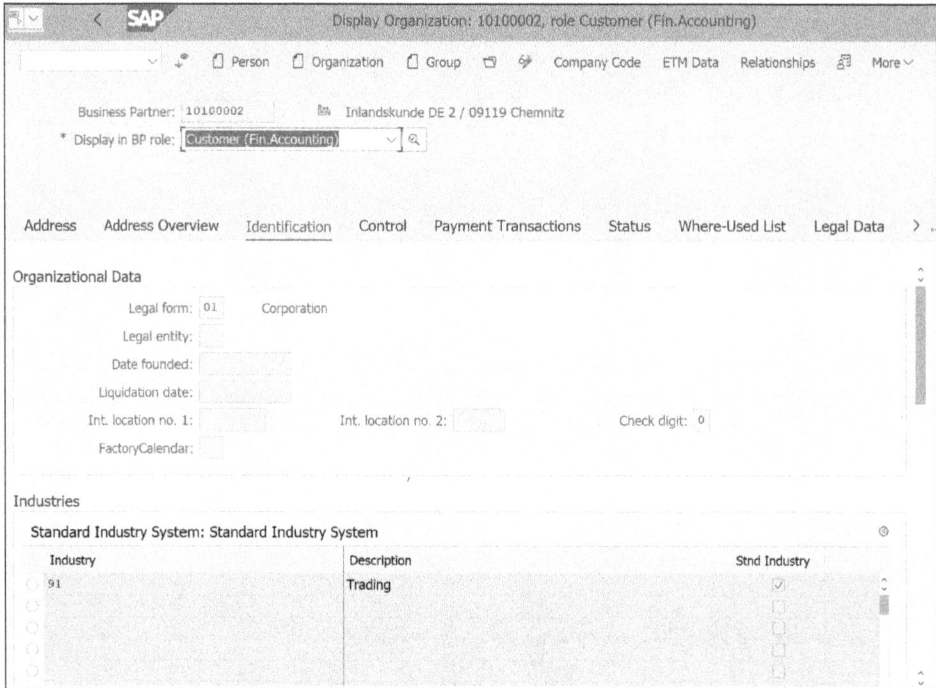


Figure 7.9 Customer Master: Industry

In the **Identification** tab, you can assign the industry to which the customer belongs. There can be multiple industries assigned. Only when you mark the **Stnd Industry** flag on the very right is it taken for the market segment.

Now switch to the **Address** tab, as shown in Figure 7.10. The defined **Country**, **DE**, will be used for the market segment derivation. Switch the **Display in BP role** dropdown to **Customer**, the sales view, and click the **Sales Area** button. Enter sales organization 1010, distribution channel 10, and division 00, then press Enter to reach the screen shown in Figure 7.11.

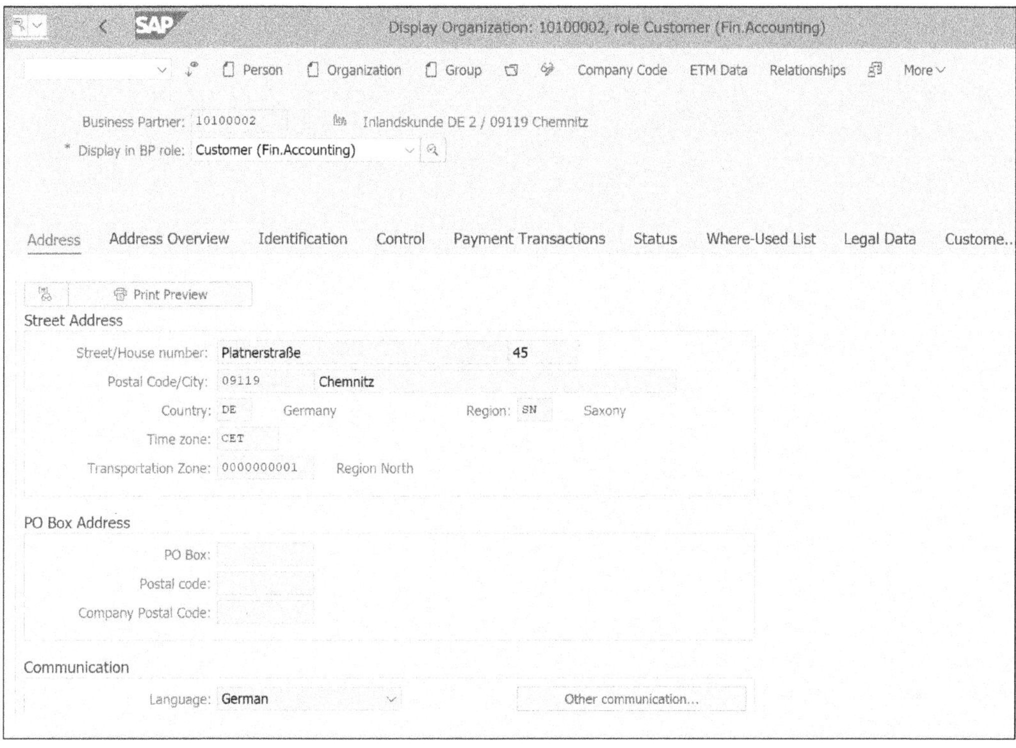


Figure 7.10 Customer Master: Address Data with Country

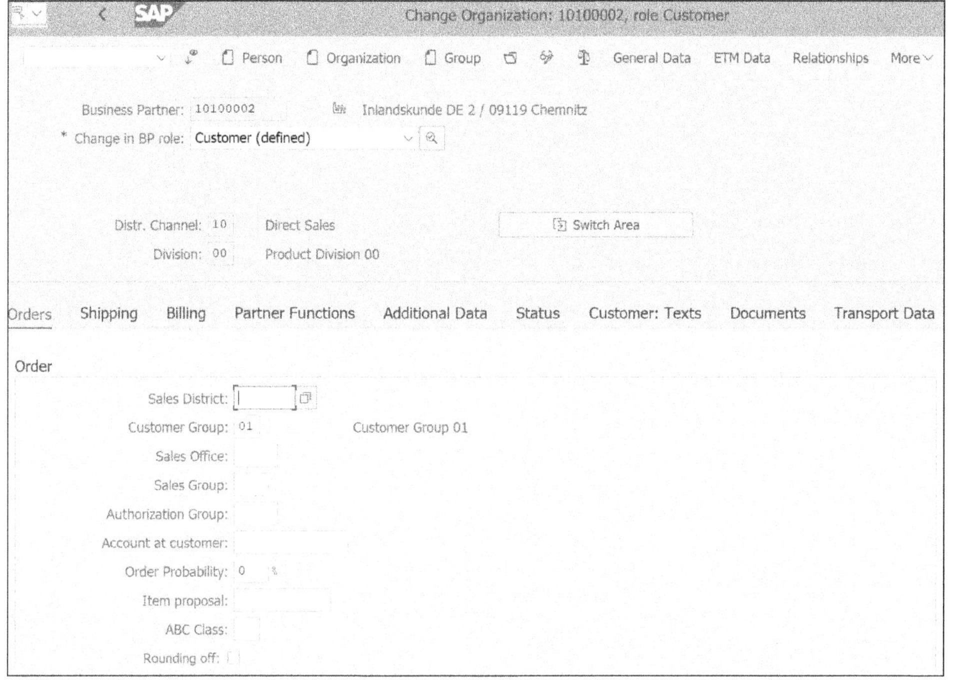


Figure 7.11 Customer Master: Customer Group

In the **Orders** tab, **Customer Group 01** is defined. Switch to the **Billing** tab, as shown in Figure 7.12.

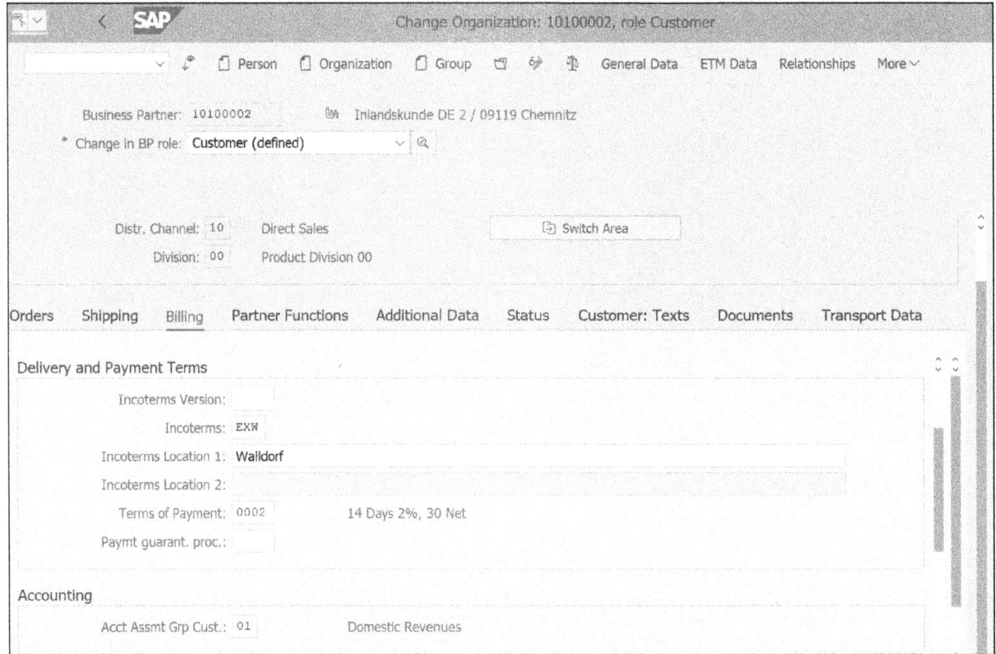


**Figure 7.12** Customer Master: Billing

The account assignment group customer (**Acct Assmt Grp Cust.**), here **01**, controls the general ledger account determination for the billing. Because the customer is based in the same country as the assigned company code, **Domestic Revenues** will be posted. The selected **Terms of Payment** (**0002**) will lead to a discount condition in sales and distribution pricing of 2%. We'll come to this later when we will post the billing.

### 7.2.2 Business Transactions

Now, let's look at an end-to-end sales scenario in the system, starting with the creation of a sales order.

#### Creating a Sales Order

Execute Transaction VA01, enter order type **OR**, and fill out the sales area as shown in the product and customer master: sales organization **1010**, distribution channel **10**, and division **00**. Press Enter to arrive at the screen shown in Figure 7.13.

For the **Sold-To Party** and **Ship-To Party**, enter the customer ID, **10100002**. Enter only one sales order item for the bike product (**MD_BIKE**) and define the **Order Quantity** as one each. Press Enter to calculate the pricing. There is a sales price maintained for this bike of 1,600 EUR.

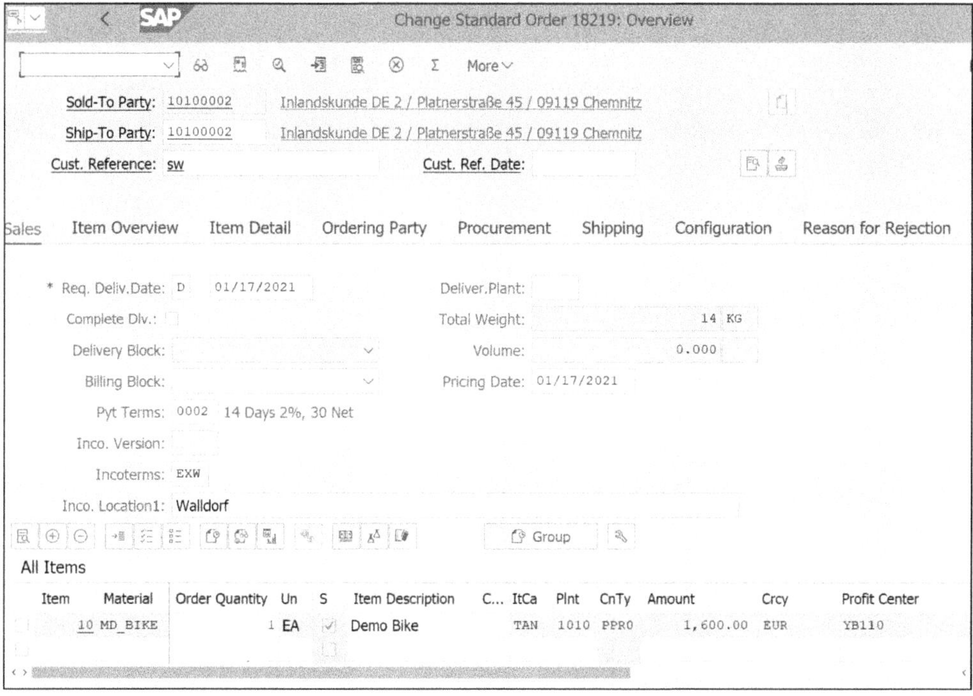


**Figure 7.13** Sales Order: Overview

Double-click the item to see the item view, then select the **Account assignment** tab, as shown in Figure 7.14.

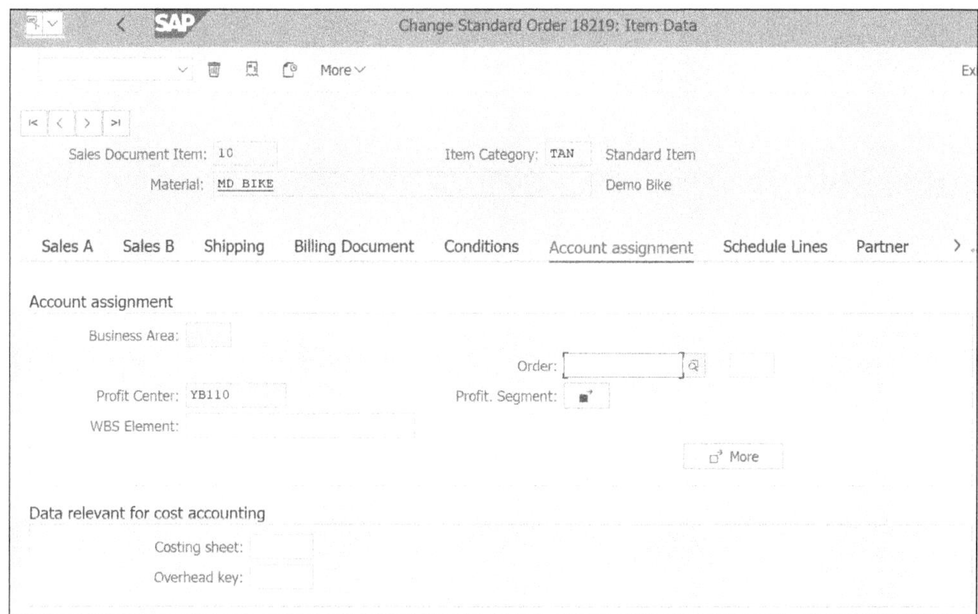


**Figure 7.14** Sales Order Item: Account Assignment View

Here, the controlling-relevant data is maintained:

- **Profit Center**
  The **Profit Center** is derived from the material master (refer back to Figure 7.6).
- **WBS Element**
  For a project-based service scenario, the work breakdown structure (WBS) element (**WBS Element**) is entered here (see Section 7.3).
- **Costing sheet**
  For make-to-order scenarios, you can also create a separate controlling object for the sales order item, to which costs and revenues are then posted. In this case, you can enter a **Costing sheet** to apply sales and administration overheads. We don't cover this scenario in this book. Instead, we'll show a scenario with the WBS element assigned, on (or for) which you can calculate overhead.
- **Order**
  Entering an internal **Order** is a special case for the single cost controlling scenario and isn't covered here.
- **Profit. Segment**
  In the product sales scenario, a profitability segment is derived and assigned on the sales order item level.

Click the **Profit. Segment** button to get to the next screen. You'll see the attributes taken from the sales order: customer, product, and sales area. When you scroll down, you see additional attributes derived from the product and customer master, as shown in Figure 7.15.

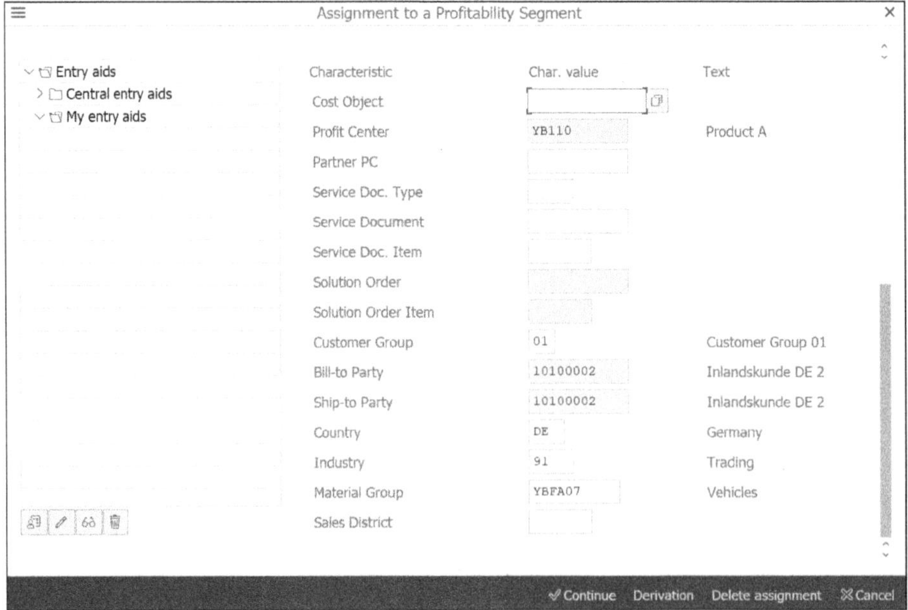


**Figure 7.15** Sales Order Item: Assigned Profitability Segment

The **Customer Group**, the **Country** of the customer, and the **Industry** are derived from the customer master (refer back to Figure 7.9). The **Material Group** is derived from the product master. With these market segment fields, all journal entry line items of subsequent business processes will be attributed.

### Creating and Analyzing an Outbound Delivery

Now create an outbound delivery for the sales order by entering Transaction VL01N. You'll arrive at the screen shown in Figure 7.16.

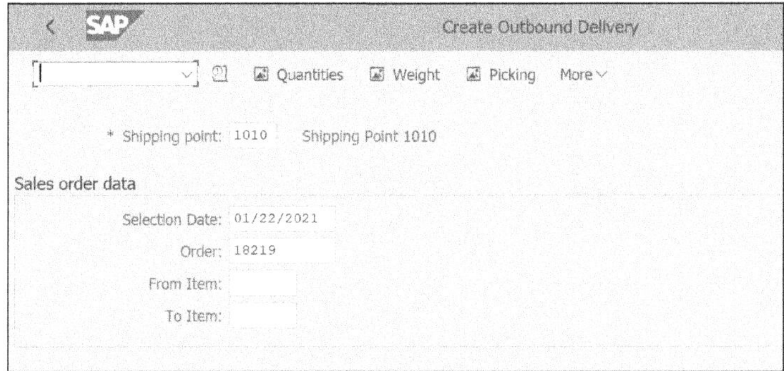


**Figure 7.16** Create Outbound Delivery for Sales Order

Enter the **1010** shipping point defined in the sales order and the sales order you created, **18219**. Press Enter and click the **Save** button at the bottom of the screen to create the outbound delivery.

Now let's analyze the created documents by entering Transaction VL03N. Enter the delivery number and press Enter to arrive at the screen shown in Figure 7.17.

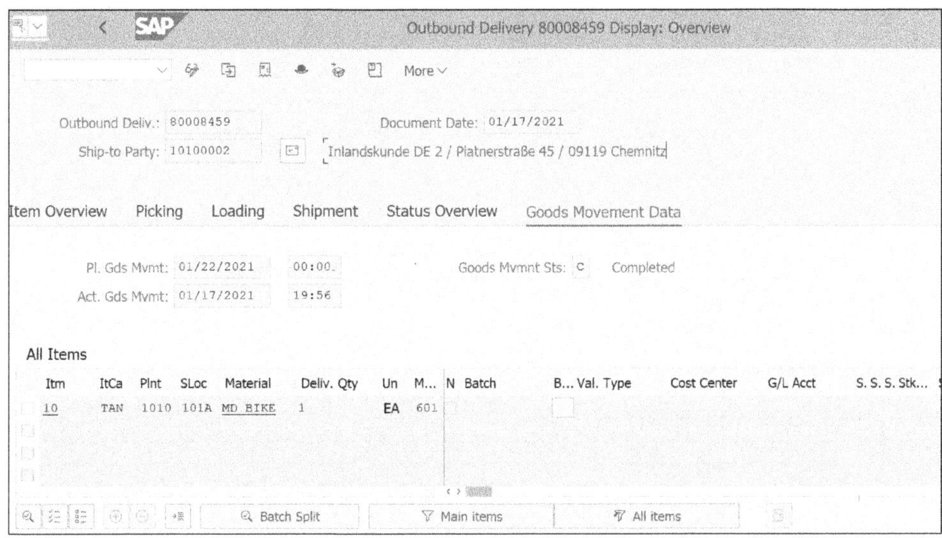


**Figure 7.17** Outbound Delivery

You see in the top section the receiving **Ship-To Party**, business partner **1010002**. There is one delivery item for the **MD_BIKE** product with a quantity of **1** each. Select the **Document Flow** icon (the third icon from the left at the top of the screen) to get to the material document shown in Figure 7.18.

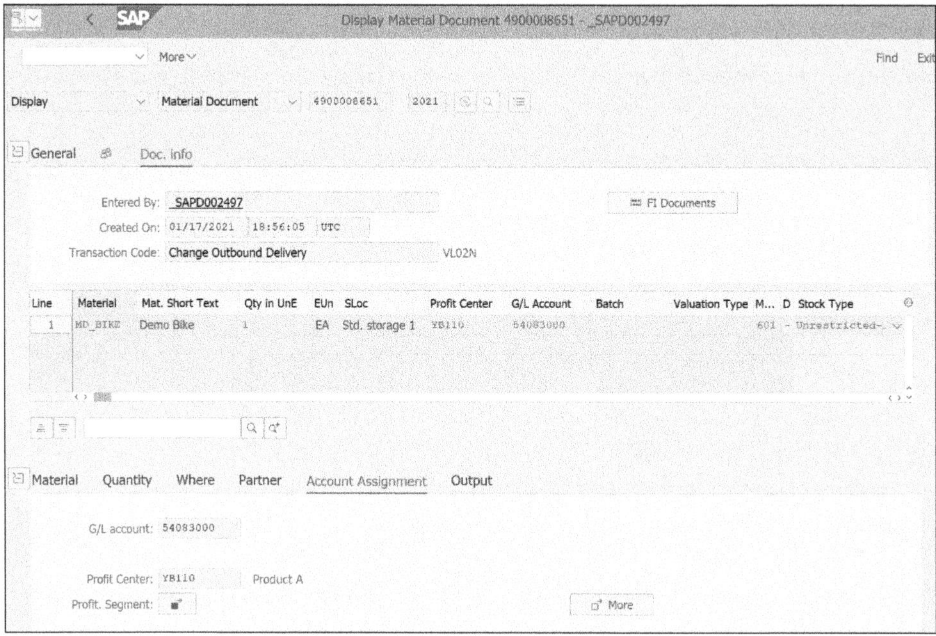


**Figure 7.18** Material Document for Outbound Delivery

There is a material document for the **MD_BIKE** product created. In the **Account Assignment** tab, you'll see the derived **G/L account 54083000** for the goods issue posting and the **Profit Center**, derived from the material master.

Click the **FI Documents** button to get an overview of all posted financial documents, as shown in Figure 7.19.

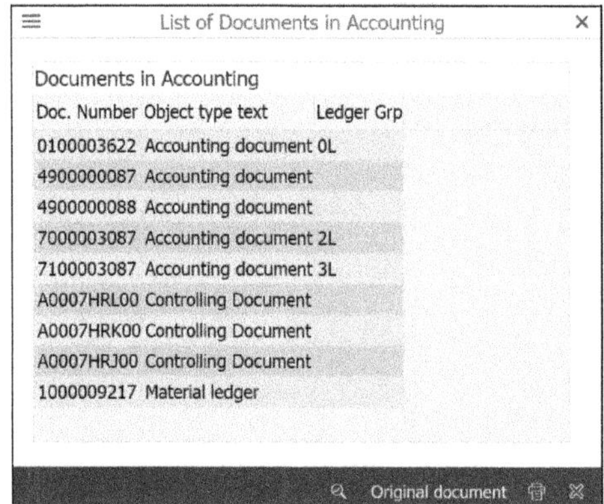
List of Documents in Accounting

Documents in Accounting

| Doc. Number | Object type text | Ledger Grp |
|---|---|---|
| 0100003622 | Accounting document | 0L |
| 4900000087 | Accounting document | |
| 4900000088 | Accounting document | |
| 7000003087 | Accounting document | 2L |
| 7100003087 | Accounting document | 3L |
| A0007HRL00 | Controlling Document | |
| A0007HRK00 | Controlling Document | |
| A0007HRJ00 | Controlling Document | |
| 1000009217 | Material ledger | |

Original document

**Figure 7.19** Overview of Posted Accounting Documents for Delivery

As you can see, a goods issue for delivery to the customer generates several documents:

- The second document is the original goods issue posting.
- The third document is driven by controlling. It provides the cost component split in the general ledger.
- The first, fourth, and fifth documents are the revenue recognition postings per ledger.
- The sixth, seventh, and eighth ones are not physical documents, but only views to provide a controlling view of the documents posted before. They do not have their own persistency. They're just a different view of the Universal Journal documents (see also compatibility views in Chapter 10, Section 10.6).
- The last document is the update of the Material Ledger as it's credited with this posting to the inventory.



Now let's look at the journal entries posted in the leading ledger 0L in detail. Start the Display Line Items—Margin Analysis app (SAP Fiori ID F4818) with the selection of the **Reference document** equal to the goods issue material document shown previously, and click **Go**, as shown in Figure 7.20.

If your organization isn't yet using SAP Fiori, you can view the same information by using Transaction KE24 or **Accounting • Controlling • Profitability Analysis • Information System • Display Line item List • Actual** and entering your operating concern and controlling area before filling out your selection parameters.

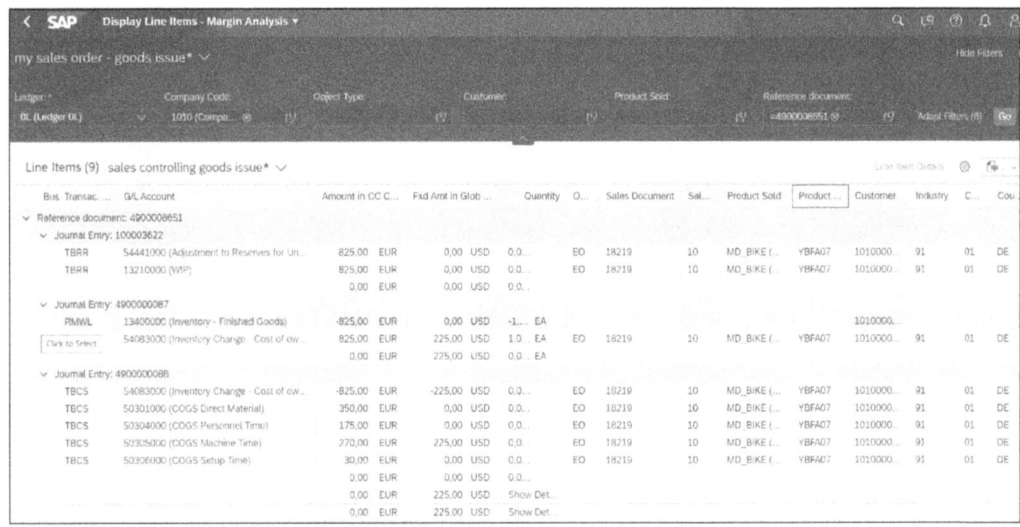


| Bus. Transac. ... | G/L Account | Amount in CC C... | Fxd Amt in Glob ... | Quantity | O... | Sales Document | Sal... | Product Sold | Product ... | Customer | Industry | C... | Cou... |
|---|---|---|---|---|---|---|---|---|---|---|---|---|---|
| Reference document: 4900008651 | | | | | | | | | | | | | |
| Journal Entry: 100003622 | | | | | | | | | | | | | |
| TBRR | 54441000 (Adjustment to Reserves for Un... | 825,00 EUR | 0,00 USD | 0,0... | EO | 18219 | 10 | MD_BIKE (... | YBFA07 | 1010000... | 91 | 01 | DE |
| TBRR | 13210000 (WIP) | 825,00 EUR | 0,00 USD | 0,0... | EO | 18219 | 10 | MD_BIKE (... | YBFA07 | 1010000... | 91 | 01 | DE |
| | | 0,00 EUR | 0,00 USD | 0,0... | | | | | | | | | |
| Journal Entry: 4900000087 | | | | | | | | | | | | | |
| RMWL | 13400000 (Inventory - Finished Goods) | -825,00 EUR | 0,00 USD | -1,... EA | | | | | | 1010000... | | | |
| Click to Select | 54083000 (Inventory Change - Cost of ow... | 825,00 EUR | 225,00 USD | 1,0... EA | EO | 18219 | 10 | MD_BIKE (... | YBFA07 | 1010000... | 91 | 01 | DE |
| | | 0,00 EUR | 225,00 USD | 0,0... EA | | | | | | | | | |
| Journal Entry: 4900000088 | | | | | | | | | | | | | |
| TBCS | 54083000 (Inventory Change - Cost of ow... | -825,00 EUR | -225,00 USD | 0,0... | EO | 18219 | 10 | MD_BIKE (... | YBFA07 | 1010000... | 91 | 01 | DE |
| TBCS | 50301000 (COGS Direct Material) | 350,00 EUR | 0,00 USD | 0,0... | EO | 18219 | 10 | MD_BIKE (... | YBFA07 | 1010000... | 91 | 01 | DE |
| TBCS | 50304000 (COGS Personnel Time) | 175,00 EUR | 0,00 USD | 0,0... | EO | 18219 | 10 | MD_BIKE (... | YBFA07 | 1010000... | 91 | 01 | DE |
| TBCS | 50305000 (COGS Machine Time) | 270,00 EUR | 225,00 USD | 0,0... | EO | 18219 | 10 | MD_BIKE (... | YBFA07 | 1010000... | 91 | 01 | DE |
| TBCS | 50306000 (COGS Setup Time) | 30,00 EUR | 0,00 USD | 0,0... | EO | 18219 | 10 | MD_BIKE (... | YBFA07 | 1010000... | 91 | 01 | DE |
| | | 0,00 EUR | 0,00 USD | 0,0... | | | | | | | | | |
| | | 0,00 EUR | 225,00 USD | Show Det... | | | | | | | | | |
| | | 0,00 EUR | 225,00 USD | Show Det... | | | | | | | | | |

**Figure 7.20** Journal Entries Posted by Outbound Delivery

You can see that a prima nota, the delivery (visible in reference number **4900008651**), generates three journal entries:

- The first line item is the event-based revenue recognition posting. To provide a matching principle with the revenues posted later in the process, cost of goods sold is deferred. You need to ensure cost of goods sold and revenues are realized in the same period. When you can't ensure that the billing is done in the same period as the goods issue, you need to activate event-based revenue recognition.
- The second journal entry is the goods issue, which credits the inventory and posts the cost of goods sold.
- The third journal entry provides the cost component split of the product in the Universal Journal. In the first line item, the cost of goods sold line item of the goods issue posting is reversed. The other line items post to general ledger accounts reflecting the cost components. Their values are taken from the cost estimation of the product (refer back to Figure 7.8). Note the fixed amount (**Fxd Amt in Glob...**) column: the fixed portion of the cost component split is updated here. There can be fixed portions for the activities and the overheads. In this example, there was a fixed portion for the machine time of 225 USD; the fixed amount is provided in the global currency.

Except for the inventory line item, all line items are account-assigned to the profitability segment (object type **EO** in the **O...** column). We explained how this derivation works in Chapter 4, Section 4.6.1. You'll see multiple market segment fields derived and stored in the line items:

- The sales order item.
- The **Product Sold**, from the sales order item. **Product Sold Group YBFA07** is derived from the product master shown previously in Figure 7.5.
- The **Customer** from the sales order. **Industry 91**, **Customer Group 01**, and **Country DE** are from the business partner shown previously in Figure 7.9.
- If you had extensibility in place, the fields would be provided here too (see Chapter 4, Section 4.6.2).

With this enriched information, you have the basis for the multilevel margin reporting for product and market segments.

#### Customer Billing

Now let's move to the next business transaction, customer billing. Start Transaction VF01 and enter as a reference document the outbound delivery (**80008459**), shown previously in Figure 7.17. Press Enter to see the invoice proposal, as shown in Figure 7.21.

There is one item created for the delivered bike. For the **Reference Doc.**, you see the outbound delivery ID, **80008459**. For the **Net Value**, 1,600 EUR is determined.

Let's look at the condition scheme. Double-click item **10** and select the item **Conditions** tab, arriving at the screen shown in Figure 7.22.

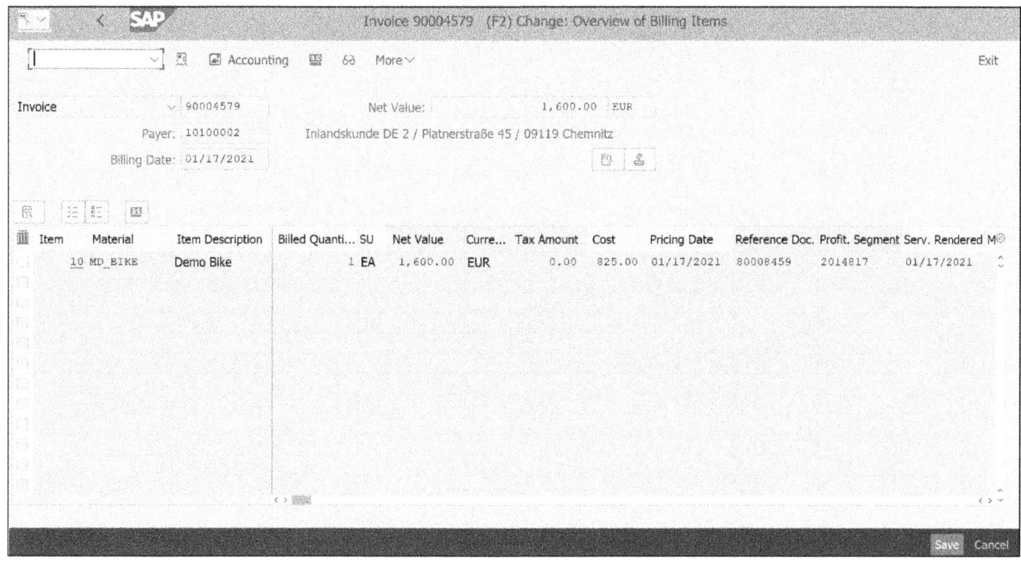

Figure 7.21 Billing Document

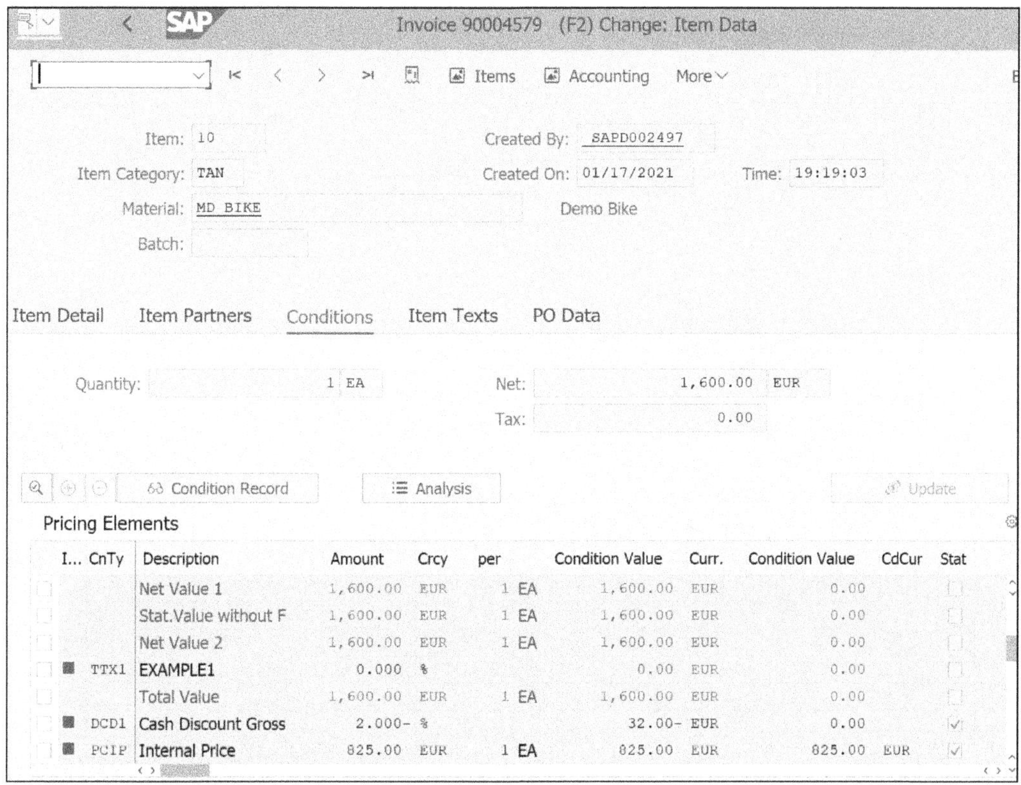

Figure 7.22 Billing Document: Pricing Scheme

In the condition scheme, you see two statistical condition types at the bottom; they have the statistical (**Stat**) column flagged. Statistical conditions do not influence the sales price determination. They're used for additional information and can be used in margin analysis reporting. Let's look in detail at these conditions:

- **DCD1** is a cash discount offered to the customer. In this case, the condition is triggered by the **Terms of Payment** business partner attribute (refer back to Figure 7.12). You expect the customer to take advantage of this when paying, but it doesn't affect the total invoice price. You'll see this 32 EUR value in the margin reporting.
- The **PCIP** internal price condition provides information about internal costs. In this example, this is the calculated costs of the product, which corresponds to the cost of goods sold amount posted with the goods issue. If costing-based profitability analysis is active, it will be transferred to a costing-based profitability analysis **Cost of Sales Value** field. For margin analysis it isn't relevant; cost of goods sold is updated already with the goods issue posting.

Click the **Save** button to save the billing document, and the data is then transferred to accounting.

### Analyzing Billing Documents

Now let's analyze the corresponding financial documents. Select the **Accounting** button at the top of the screen to see the popup shown in Figure 7.23.

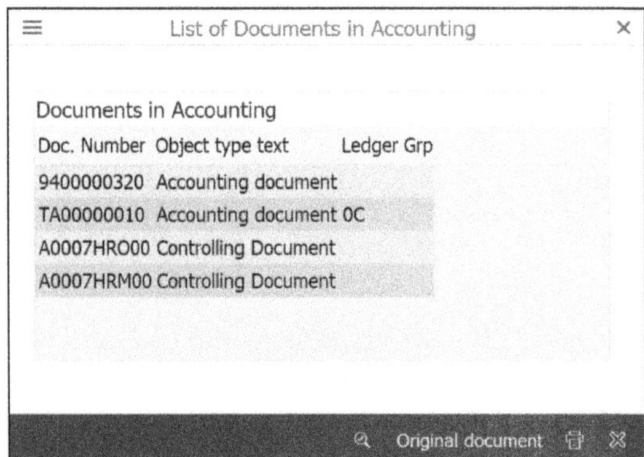


**Figure 7.23** Overview of Journal Entries Posted by Billing Document

The first document includes the prima nota of the invoice posted in the general ledger. This is the billed revenue and the receivables and tax. As the prima nota, it's posted in all standard ledgers. Documents 3 and 4 provide the technical documents needed for a controlling view.

The second document is new. It's posted in the OC extension ledger, the ledger for additional management adjustment postings. The management posting for the statistical sales condition is stored here.

Let's analyze the journal entries in detail. Start the Display Line Items—Margin Analysis app and select **Ledger 0C**. In Chapter 3, Section 3.3.1, we explained that an extension ledger is always assigned to a legal ledger. When you select data for ledger 0C, you always get the underlying legal ledger data also—here, ledger 0L. Select **Reference document** as the billing document and click **Go**. You'll now see the journal entries in ledgers 0L and 0C referenced to the billing document, as shown in Figure 7.24.

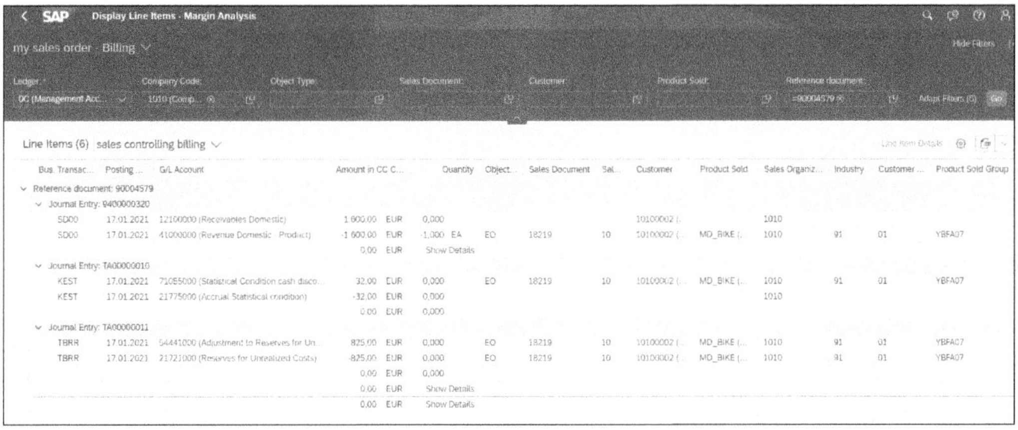

Figure 7.24 Journal Entries Posted by Billing Document

The first journal entry is the general ledger posting of the invoice, selected from the 0C ledger assigned to standard ledger 0L. You debit receivables and credit domestic revenues. Remember the attribute in the business partner shown previously in Figure 7.12, which defines (among other parameters) the account determination and leads to domestic receivables and revenues.

The second journal entry is the management posting for the statistical sales condition. It's posted in the 0C extension ledger. The first line item is the posting on the profitability object, which provides all market segment information. Posting to the **Cash Discounts** general ledger account, it will update the sales deduction in the multilevel margin reporting. As you follow the logic of double-entry accounting in the extension ledger, you need an additional line item, which balances the document to zero. The second line item posts against an accrual account without any market segment–relevant attributes.

The third journal entry is the revenue recognition posting, selected from standard ledger 0L. With the billing, you realize the revenues. To realize the matching costs of goods sold, you have to reverse the deferred costs posted with the goods issue to ensure realized cost of goods sold and revenues in the same period.

> **General Ledger Accounts for Sales**
>
> The general ledger accounts for the sales scenario—in the example, the inventory change and the domestic revenue account—are account-assigned to the profitability object. Thus, they must be maintained as primary cost elements (see Chapter 4, Section 4.1.1). If you work with costing-based profitability analysis only, these accounts must be of the nonoperating expense and income general ledger account type. So they are not created as cost elements, and thus the posting is not account-assigned to a controlling object.

### Multilevel Margin Reporting

Now let's look at how these business transactions impact the multilevel margin reporting for the market segment reporting, represented by product and customer.

Start the Product Profitability app. With this app, only journal entries that are account-assigned to a profitability segment are selected. To get the management postings included, select extension ledger 0C in the **Ledger** field. Filter on sales order **18219**. The financial statement version **YPS2**, covering controlling requirements (refer back to Chapter 4, Section 4.1.4), is defaulted. You'll see the reporting shown in Figure 7.25.

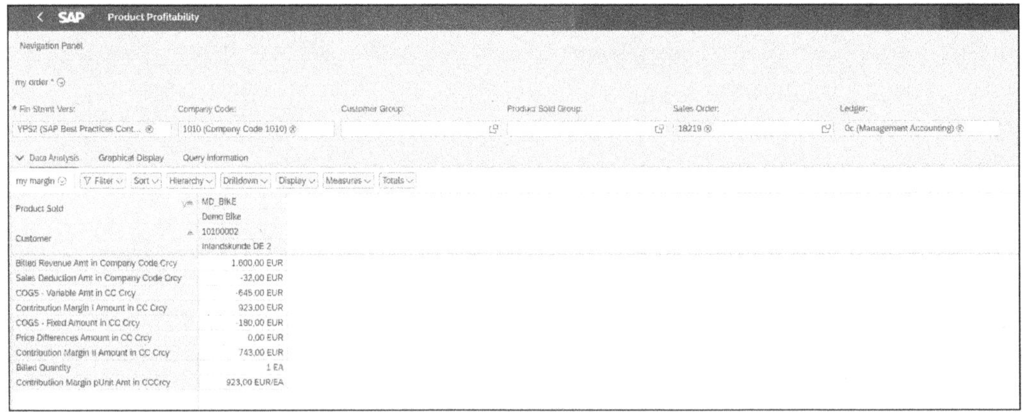


**Figure 7.25** Multilevel Product Contribution Margin

This is two-level margin reporting. The line items are semantic tags, an aggregation of general ledger accounts, taking fixed and variable costs into account. (For more on semantic tags, see Chapter 10, Section 10.4.) **Contribution Margin I** is the sum of the billed revenue, minus the sales deduction of 32 EUR posted in the extension ledger and the variable costs of the product from the cost component split. In this case, this leads to a margin of 923 EUR. **Contribution Margin II** includes the fixed price portion of the product. In this case, this is 180 EUR of the machine time (refer back to Figure 7.8 and in the goods issue posting in Figure 7.20). This leads to a margin of 743 EUR. At the bottom, the margin per billed quantity is provided. We billed one each, so we get 923 EUR each.

**Note**

If you select the extension ledger in reporting, you get always an aggregation of the management ledger postings in the extension ledger (here, 0C) and the underlying leading ledger (here, 0L).

If your organization isn't yet using SAP Fiori, there isn't a direct equivalent for the Product Profitability app, but you can use the drilldown reporting options (Transaction KE30) to build an application that will show the accounts that are used to build up the contribution margin. However, you won't have access to the semantic tags to structure the accounts in your report and will only be able to separate the fixed and variable costs in the controlling area currency as the value in company code currency is calculated using logic embedded in the core data services (CDS) view used to fill the Product Profitability app.

### 7.2.3 Sales Margin Prediction Based on Incoming Sales Order

Each time a sales order is entered, the expected cost of sales and sales revenue can be deducted in the system. The required delivery date of the sales order item (refer back to Figure 7.13) is taken as an expected posting date to determine the period for the data. You simulate the same documents as you post the actuals in the delivery and the customer invoice. In this case, the principle of double-entry bookkeeping is applied, so every journal entry is balanced to zero. Because this data has a predictive character and isn't relevant for legal reporting, it's stored in the prediction ledger, a separate extension ledger.

Now let's look at the prediction documents that were created when you created the sales order. Start the Display Line Items—Margin Analysis app and filter on the sales order. Select **Ledger 0E**, the extension ledger for commitments and prediction, and click **Go**, as shown in Figure 7.26.

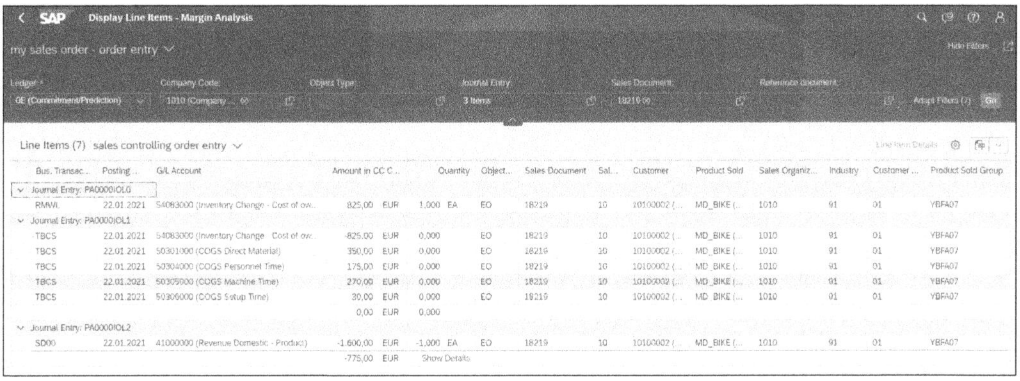

Display Line Items - Margin Analysis

my sales order - order entry

Ledger: 0E (Commitment/Prediction) | Company Code: 1010 (Company ... | Object Type: | Journal Entry: 3 Items | Sales Document: 18219 | Reference document: | Adapt Filters (2) | Go

Line Items (7) sales controlling order entry

| Bus. Transac... | Posting ... | G/L Account | Amount in CC C... | | Quantity | | Object... | Sales Document | Sal... | Customer | Product Sold | Sales Organiz... | Industry | Customer ... | Product Sold Group |
|---|---|---|---|---|---|---|---|---|---|---|---|---|---|---|---|
| Journal Entry: PA0000IOL0 | | | | | | | | | | | | | | | |
| RMWL | 22.01.2021 | 54083000 (Inventory Change - Cost of ow... | 825,00 | EUR | 1,000 | EA | EO | 18219 | 10 | 10100002 (... | MD_BIKE (... | 1010 | 91 | 01 | YBFA07 |
| Journal Entry: PA0000IOL1 | | | | | | | | | | | | | | | |
| TBCS | 22.01.2021 | 54083000 (Inventory Change - Cost of ow... | -825,00 | EUR | 0,000 | | EO | 18219 | 10 | 10100002 (... | MD_BIKE (... | 1010 | 91 | 01 | YBFA07 |
| TBCS | 22.01.2021 | 50301000 (COGS Direct Material) | 350,00 | EUR | 0,000 | | EO | 18219 | 10 | 10100002 (... | MD_BIKE (... | 1010 | 91 | 01 | YBFA07 |
| TBCS | 22.01.2021 | 50304000 (COGS Personnel Time) | 175,00 | EUR | 0,000 | | EO | 18219 | 10 | 10100002 (... | MD_BIKE (... | 1010 | 91 | 01 | YBFA07 |
| TBCS | 22.01.2021 | 50305000 (COGS Machine Time) | 270,00 | EUR | 0,000 | | EO | 18219 | 10 | 10100002 (... | MD_BIKE (... | 1010 | 91 | 01 | YBFA07 |
| TBCS | 22.01.2021 | 50306000 (COGS Setup Time) | 30,00 | EUR | 0,000 | | EO | 18219 | 10 | 10100002 (... | MD_BIKE (... | 1010 | 01 | 01 | YBFA07 |
| | | | 0,00 | EUR | 0,000 | | | | | | | | | | |
| Journal Entry: PA0000IOL2 | | | | | | | | | | | | | | | |
| SD00 | 22.01.2021 | 41000000 (Revenue Domestic - Product) | -1.600,00 | EUR | -1,000 | EA | EO | 18219 | 10 | 10100002 (... | MD_BIKE (... | 1010 | 91 | 01 | YBFA07 |
| | | | -775,00 | EUR | Show Details | | | | | | | | | | |

**Figure 7.26** Update Prediction Ledger with Sales Order Creation

You see three journal entries with a number range beginning with "PA". Because you filtered on the sales order, you won't see the line items that aren't account-assigned in this view. So, for example, in the first journal entry the inventory line item is filtered out; you only see the cost of goods sold line item. The results are filtered on the line item here, which impacts margin reporting. The second journal entry is the cost component split posting, like the goods issue posting before. Thus, you can enable multilevel margin reporting on these prediction postings. The third journal entry is the simulated customer invoice.

On the basis of these documents, prediction reporting is now possible. You analyze this kind of data with the Incoming Sales Orders—Predictive Accounting app (SAP Fiori ID F2964) and get to the selection screen in Figure 7.27. There is no equivalent report in SAP GUI. Predictive accounting requires you to work with SAP Fiori to report on the information in the extension ledger.

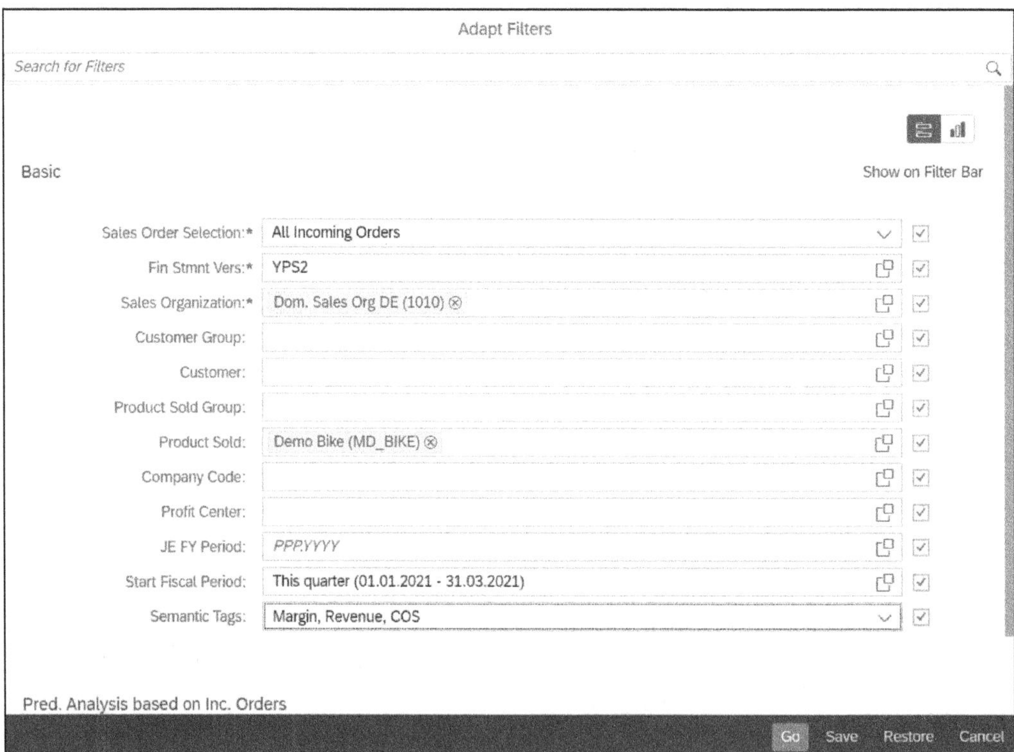


**Figure 7.27** Selection Screen for Incoming Sales Order App

For the **Sales Order Selection**, select **All Incoming Orders**. The financial statement version for defining the semantic tags is **YPS2**. Selecting the **Sales Organization** is mandatory. Select the bike (**Demo Bike**) as the filter for **Product Sold**. Start with this quarter in the **Start Fiscal Period** field to get an analysis for the periods. For **Semantic Tags**, select

**Margin**, **Revenue**, and **COS**. When you're done making your entries, click the **Go** button to arrive at the view shown in Figure 7.28.

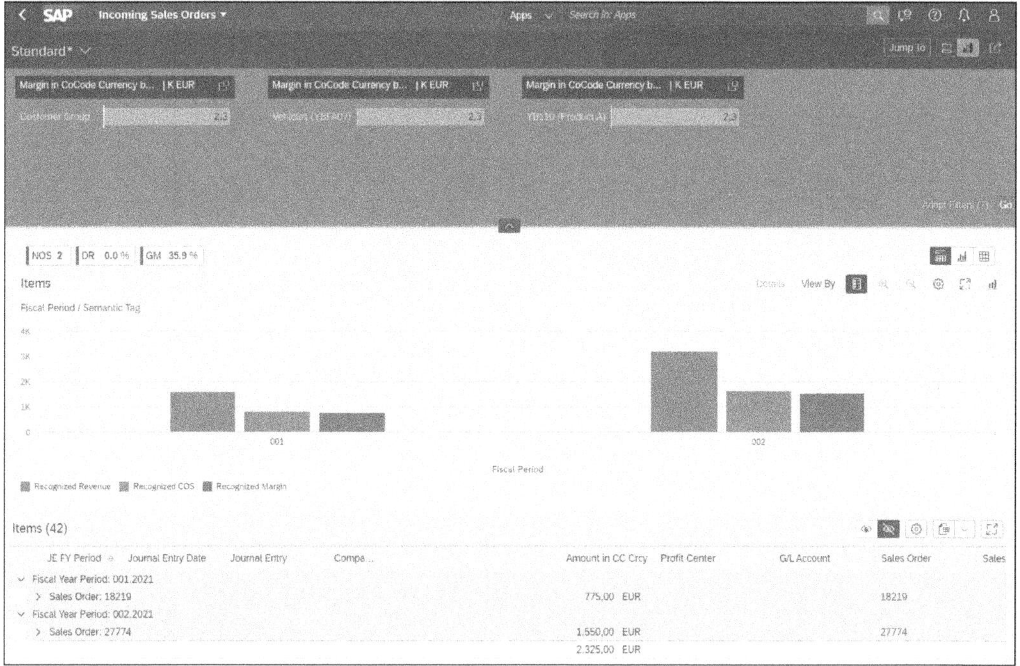


**Figure 7.28** Incoming Sales Order: Periodic View

In the top section are the KPIs for the existing sales orders. Here we've selected the predicted margin amount for the customer group, product group, and profit center. In the middle section is the predicted recognized revenue, cost of goods sold, and the resulting margin per period. At the top is the number of sales orders (**NOS**), which are based on the prediction; in this case, two are selected. You can also see the gross margin (**GM**) percentage—here, **35.9%**.

All these KPIs are based on postings in the Universal Journal in the prediction ledger and thus can be analyzed. There are line item details provided at the bottom. You see that the data are based on two sales orders: in period 001/2021, sales order **18219**; and in period 002/2021, an additional sales order, **27774**.

In the prediction ledger, the predicted journal entries are not only posted at the time of the sales order creation but also these values are reversed when the actuals are posted in the subsequent sales order–related delivery and billing:

- Reverse the predicted cost of goods sold and the cost of goods sold component split when the outbound delivery occurs.
- Reverse the predicted revenues when you invoice the sales order.

This means that in addition to the order entry, the remaining sales order amount also can be analyzed. The remaining sales order amount provides the predicted values that haven't yet been realized.

Let's look at all the postings the sales order process has created in the prediction ledger. Select the prediction journal entries by selecting **Ledger 0E**, filter on sales order **18219**, and click **Go**, as shown in Figure 7.29.

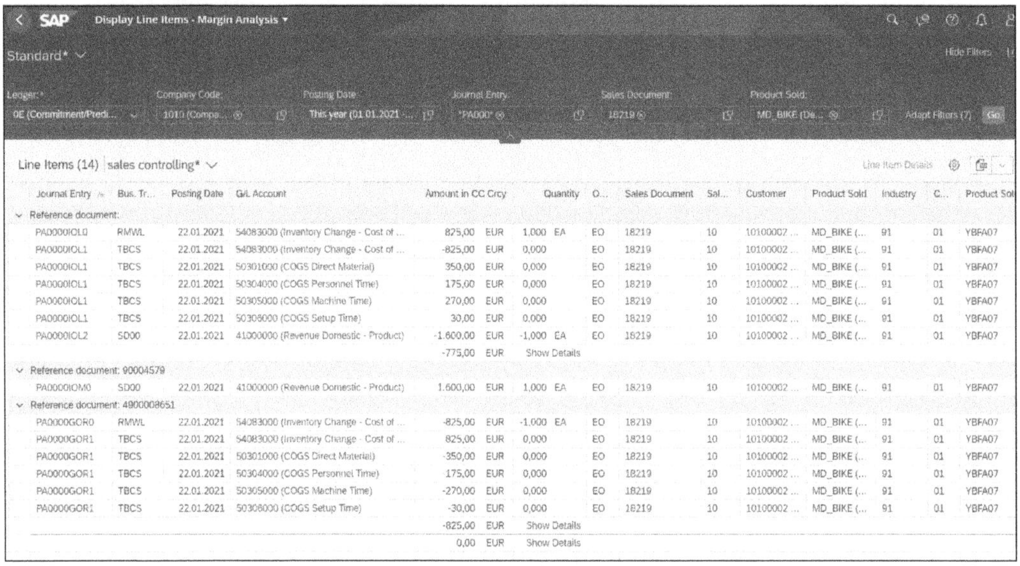

SAP Display Line Items - Margin Analysis

Standard*

Ledger: 0E (Commitment/Predi... | Company Code: 1010 (Compa... | Posting Date: This year (01.01.2021 -... | Journal Entry: *PA000* | Sales Document: 18219 | Product Sold: MD_BIKE (De... | Adapt Filters (7) | Go

Line Items (14) sales controlling*

| Journal Entry | Bus. Tr... | Posting Date | G/L Account | Amount in CC Crcy | | Quantity | | O... | Sales Document | Sal... | Customer | Product Sold | Industry | C... | Product Sol |
|---|---|---|---|---|---|---|---|---|---|---|---|---|---|---|---|
| Reference document: | | | | | | | | | | | | | | | |
| PA0000IOL0 | RMWL | 22.01.2021 | 54083000 (Inventory Change - Cost of ... | 825,00 | EUR | 1,000 | EA | EO | 18219 | 10 | 10100007 ... | MD_BIKE (... | 91 | 01 | YBFA07 |
| PA0000IOL1 | TBCS | 22.01.2021 | 54083000 (Inventory Change - Cost of ... | -825,00 | EUR | 0,000 | | EO | 18219 | 10 | 10100002 ... | MD_BIKE (... | 91 | 01 | YBFA07 |
| PA0000IOL1 | TBCS | 22.01.2021 | 50301000 (COGS Direct Material) | 350,00 | EUR | 0,000 | | EO | 18219 | 10 | 10100002 ... | MD_BIKE (... | 91 | 01 | YBFA07 |
| PA0000IOL1 | TBCS | 22.01.2021 | 50304000 (COGS Personnel Time) | 175,00 | EUR | 0,000 | | EO | 18219 | 10 | 10100002 ... | MD_BIKE (... | 91 | 01 | YBFA07 |
| PA0000IOL1 | TBCS | 22.01.2021 | 50305000 (COGS Machine Time) | 270,00 | EUR | 0,000 | | EO | 18219 | 10 | 10100002 ... | MD_BIKE (... | 91 | 01 | YBFA07 |
| PA0000IOL1 | TBCS | 22.01.2021 | 50306000 (COGS Setup Time) | 30,00 | EUR | 0,000 | | EO | 18219 | 10 | 10100002 ... | MD_BIKE (... | 91 | 01 | YBFA07 |
| PA0000IOL2 | SD00 | 22.01.2021 | 41000000 (Revenue Domestic - Product) | -1.600,00 | EUR | -1,000 | EA | EO | 18219 | 10 | 10100002 ... | MD_BIKE (... | 91 | 01 | YBFA07 |
| | | | | -775,00 | EUR | Show Details | | | | | | | | | |
| Reference document: 90004579 | | | | | | | | | | | | | | | |
| PA0000IOM0 | SD00 | 22.01.2021 | 41000000 (Revenue Domestic - Product) | 1.600,00 | EUR | 1,000 | EA | EO | 18219 | 10 | 10100002 ... | MD_BIKE (... | 91 | 01 | YBFA07 |
| Reference document: 4900008651 | | | | | | | | | | | | | | | |
| PA0000GOR0 | RMWL | 22.01.2021 | 54083000 (Inventory Change - Cost of ... | -825,00 | EUR | -1,000 | EA | EO | 18219 | 10 | 10100002 ... | MD_BIKE (... | 91 | 01 | YBFA07 |
| PA0000GOR1 | TBCS | 22.01.2021 | 54083000 (Inventory Change - Cost of ... | 825,00 | EUR | 0,000 | | EO | 18219 | 10 | 10100002 ... | MD_BIKE (... | 91 | 01 | YBFA07 |
| PA0000GOR1 | TBCS | 22.01.2021 | 50301000 (COGS Direct Material) | -350,00 | EUR | 0,000 | | EO | 18219 | 10 | 10100002 ... | MD_BIKE (... | 91 | 01 | YBFA07 |
| PA0000GOR1 | TBCS | 22.01.2021 | 50304000 (COGS Personnel Time) | -175,00 | EUR | 0,000 | | EO | 18219 | 10 | 10100002 ... | MD_BIKE (... | 91 | 01 | YBFA07 |
| PA0000GOR1 | TBCS | 22.01.2021 | 50305000 (COGS Machine Time) | -270,00 | EUR | 0,000 | | EO | 18219 | 10 | 10100002 ... | MD_BIKE (... | 91 | 01 | YBFA07 |
| PA0000GOR1 | TBCS | 22.01.2021 | 50306000 (COGS Setup Time) | -30,00 | EUR | 0,000 | | EO | 18219 | 10 | 10100002 ... | MD_BIKE (... | 91 | 01 | YBFA07 |
| | | | | -825,00 | EUR | Show Details | | | | | | | | | |
| | | | | 0,00 | EUR | Show Details | | | | | | | | | |

**Figure 7.29** Update Prediction Ledger by Different Sales Business Transactions

The first journal entries without a reference document are posted with the sales order creation, as shown previously in Figure 7.26. The second document is posted by the billing document. It reverses the revenue of 1,600 EUR. At the bottom, the journal entries are shown, posted with reference to the outbound delivery and reversing the cost of goods sold and the cost of goods sold component split. Because the sales order is completely delivered and billed, there's no remaining sales order value. This leads to the balance of zero at the bottom.

Now let's look at the remaining sales order reporting. Start the Incoming Sales Orders—Predictive Accounting app again, but now select **All Remaining Sales Orders** at the top instead of **All Incoming Sales Orders** (refer back to Figure 7.27) to get the view shown in Figure 7.30.

Now you'll see only the value of the second sales order, which is planned to be delivered in period 002/2021. The values for sales order **18219** are balanced to zero.

Figure 7.30 Reporting for Remaining Sales Order

### 7.2.4 Management Adjustment Postings

In this section, we'll show the options for handling manual special direct costs and management adjustment postings. One example use case for the special direct costs is manual freight costs or engineering costs to be entered for a sales order—especially in a make-to-order scenario, as discussed in Chapter 6, Section 6.6. With the activation of the margin analysis, this is possible because a profitability segment can be account-assigned in multiple transactions. The market segments can be manually defined as finely as desired. For example, the following transactions can be assigned to a profitability segment:

- Reassign Costs and Revenues apps (or Transactions KB11N, KB15N and KB41N)
- Manage Direct Activity Allocation app (or Transaction KB21N)
- Post General Journal Entry app (or Transaction FB01)

The postings for special direct costs have in common that they are also relevant for the legal reporting as, for example, the functional area, profit center, and segment can change. They are treated as the prima nota and posted in the legal ledger.

We'll walk through these three apps in the following sections.

#### Reassigning Costs and Revenues

Let's first assign special operating costs for the sales order and its market segments. Start the Reassign Costs and Revenues app (SAP Fiori ID F2009), as shown in Figure 7.31.

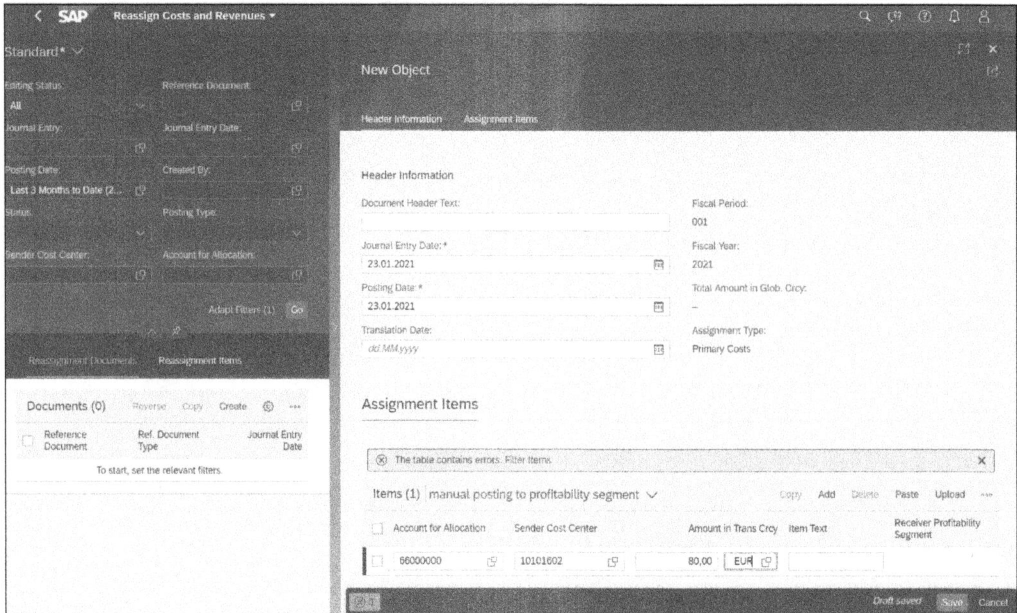


**Figure 7.31** Item Creation in Reassign Costs and Revenues App

Define the **Account for Allocation**, a **Sender Cost Center**, and an **Amount** of 80 EUR. The error message that "the table contains errors" lets you know that the receiver cost object is still missing. Select the three dots icon to open the popup shown in Figure 7.32, where you can select the receiving profitability object.

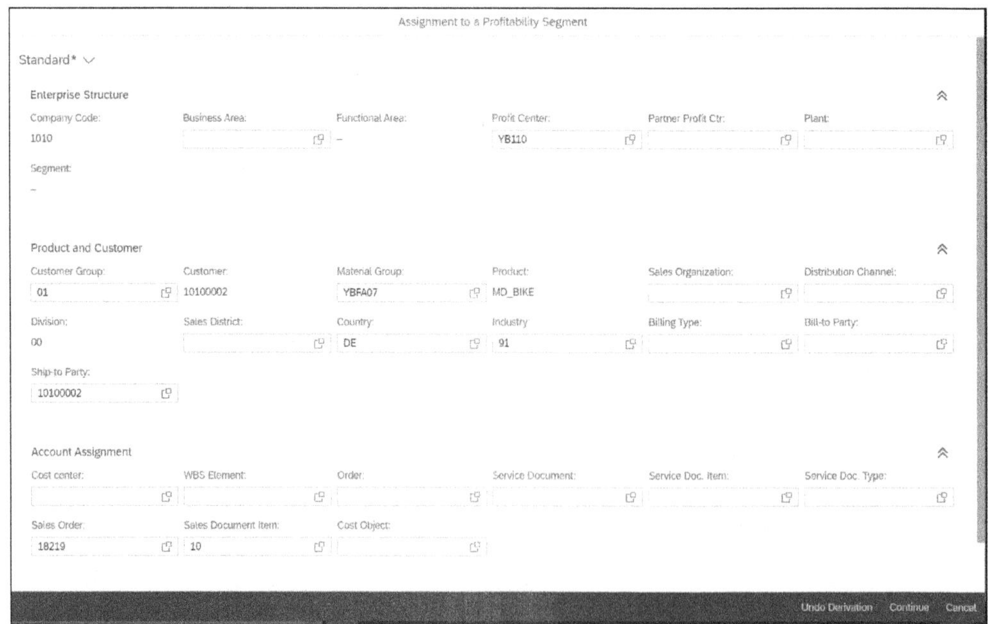


**Figure 7.32** Reassign Costs and Revenues App: Popup for Definition of Profitability Segment

You first need to define the company code. Enter the **Customer**, the **Product**, and the **Sales Order** and item, then click the **Derive** button. As a result, the **Material Group**, **Customer Group**, **Industry**, and **Country** are derived. Click the **Continue** button to return to the first screen, as shown in Figure 7.33.

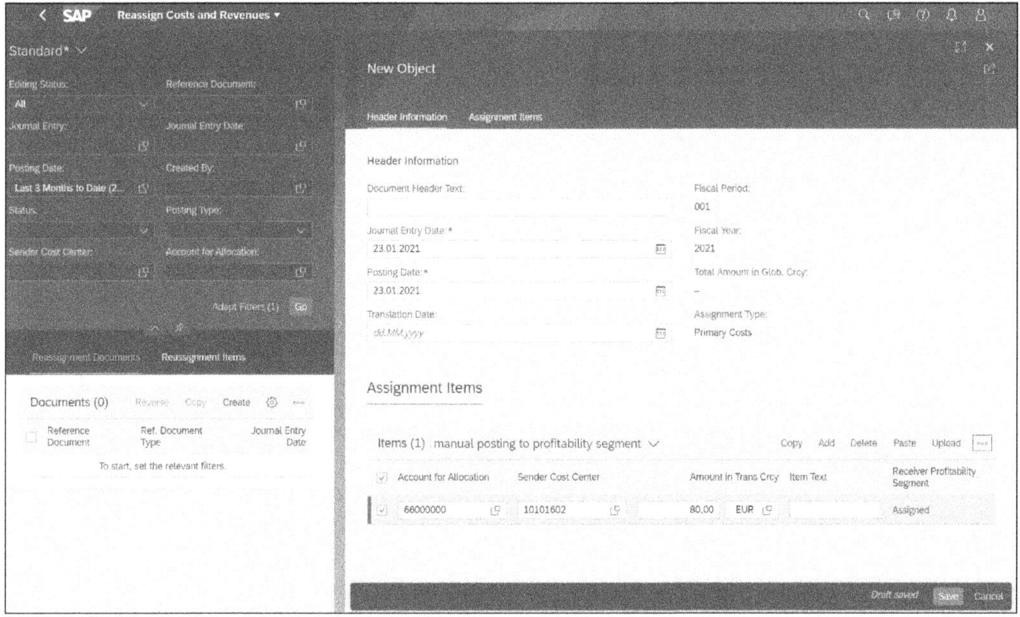


**Figure 7.33** Reassign Costs and Revenue: Item with Receiver Profitability Segment

You'll now see that the **Receiver Profitability Segment** is **Assigned**. Click the **Save** button and get the journal entry posted in ledger 0L, as shown in Figure 7.34.

If your organization isn't using SAP Fiori, you can make the same reassignment by using Transaction KB11N or **Accounting • Controlling • Cost Center Accounting • Actual Postings • Manual Reposting of Costs • Enter** and choosing the **Prof. Segment/Cost Center** screen variant to assign costs from the cost center to the chosen profitability segment. You can display the resulting journal entries using Transaction KE24N.

Display Line Items - Margin Analysis

manual posting on EO

Ledger: 0L (Ledger 0L) | Company Code: 1010 (Company ...) | Posting Date: This year (01.01.2021 - 31.12.2021) | Journal Entry: 2300002538

Line Items (2) sales controlling - manual posting

| Journal Entry | Bus. Tr... | Posting Date | G/L Account | Amount in CC ... | | O... | Sales Doc... | Customer | Product Sold | Indu... | C... | Product Sold Gr... | Profit Center | Cou... |
|---|---|---|---|---|---|---|---|---|---|---|---|---|---|---|
| 2300002538 | RKU1 | 23.01.2021 | 66000000 (Other Operating Exp... | -80,00 | EUR | KS | | | | | | | YB600 (Sh... | |
| 2300002538 | RKU1 | 23.01.2021 | 66000000 (Other Operating Exp... | 80,00 | EUR | EO | 18219 | 1010000 | MD_BIKE (... | 91 | 01 | YBFA07 | YB110 (Pro... | DE |
| | | | | 0,00 | EUR | | | | | | | | | |

**Figure 7.34** Journal Entry for Cost Allocation to Profitability Segment

The first item is the credit of the cost center without any market segment information. The second line item is the debit of the profitability segment with all profitability attributes derived.

Of course, this posting impacts the product profitability. Start the Product Profitability app again and filter on **Sales Order 18219**, as shown in Figure 7.35.

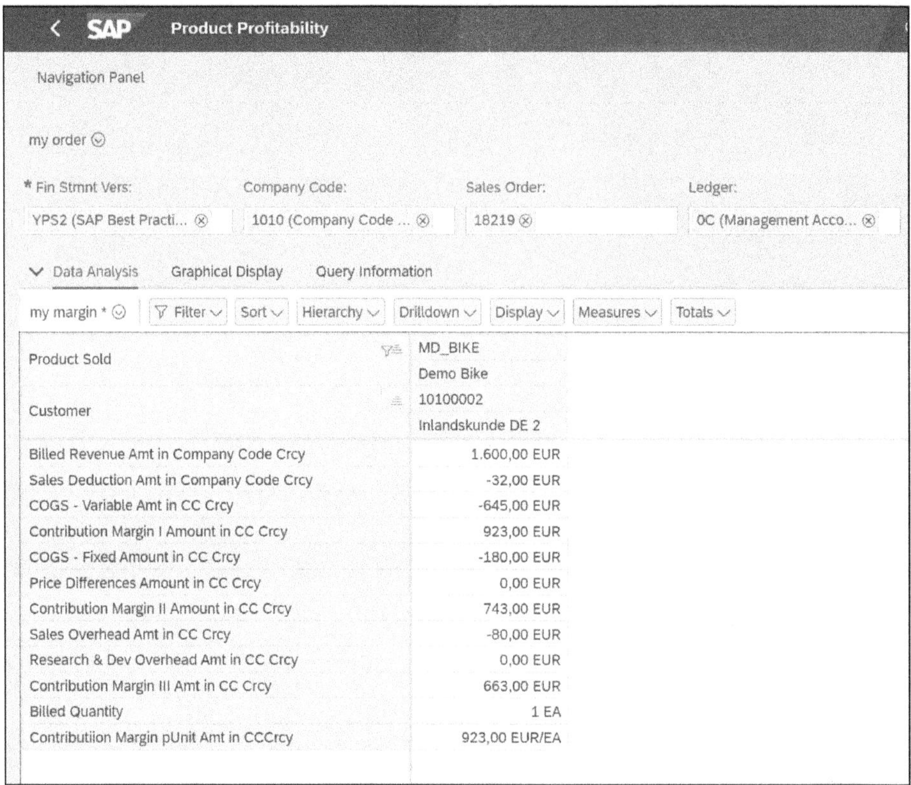


**Figure 7.35** Product Profitability Reporting after Special Cost Assignment to Sales Order

There is now a new line in comparison with the product profitability shown previously in Figure 7.25: the **Sales Overhead** line with the posted amount of 80 EUR. This leads now to a **Contribution Margin III** of 663 EUR. The **Contribution Margin** I is unchanged.

### Managing Direct Activity Allocation

Now, suppose you have a requirement to post one hour for a service technician to the sales order and the associated market segments. To do so, start the Manage Direct Activity Allocation app (SAP Fiori ID F3697).

Enter the **Sender Cost Center**, the **Sender Activity Type**, the **Quantity** of one hour, and **Profitability Segment** as the receiver. The definition of the profitability segment works the same way as for reassigning costs and revenue postings. Click the **Save** button to see the journal entry posted for all active legal ledgers, as shown in Figure 7.36.

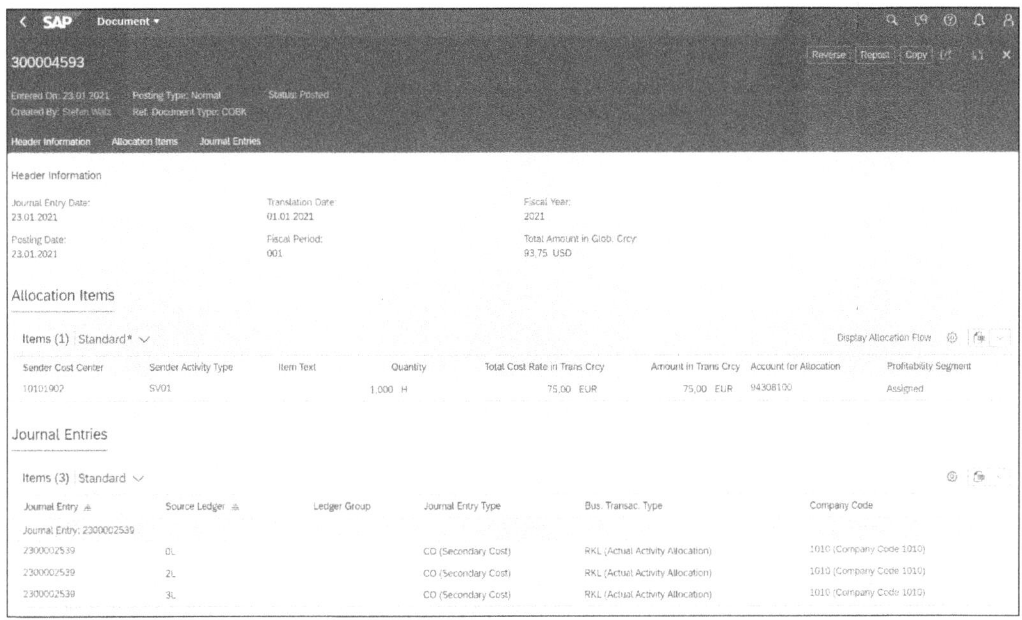


**Figure 7.36** Direct Activity Allocation to Profitability Segment

There is a cost rate of 75 EUR/h derived (see the discussion of the Manage Cost Rates—Professional Services app in Section 7.3.1).

If your organization isn't using SAP Fiori, you can make the same reassignment by using Transaction KB21N or **Accounting • Controlling • Cost Center Accounting • Actual Postings • Activity Allocation • Enter** and choosing the screen variant **Prof. Segment/ Cost Center** to assign activities from the cost center to the chosen profitability segment. You can display the resulting journal entries using Transaction KE24N.

Now let's look at the posted journal entry with the Display Line Items—Margin Analysis app. Filter on **Ledger 0L** and **Journal Entry 2300002539** and click **Go** to arrive at the view shown in Figure 7.37.

Display Line Items - Margin Analysis

manual posting on EO*

Ledger: 0L (Ledger 0L) | Company Code: 1010 (Company Code 1010) | Posting Date: This year (01.01.2021 - 31.12.2021) | Journal Entry: =2300002539 | Adapt Filters (6) | Go

Line Items (2) sales controlling - manual posting*

| Journal Entry | Bus. Tr... | Posting Date | G/L Account | Amount in CC ... | Quantity | O... | Sales Doc... | Customer | Product Sold | Indu... | C... | Product Sold Gr... | Profit Center | Cou... |
|---|---|---|---|---|---|---|---|---|---|---|---|---|---|---|
| 2300002539 | RKL | 23.01.2021 | 94308100 (Service Time) | -75,00 EUR | -1,00... H | KL | | | | | | | YB101 (Co... | |
| 2300002539 | RKL | 23.01.2021 | 94308100 (Service Time) | 75,00 EUR | 1,000 H | EO | 18219 | 10100002 ... | MD_BIKE (... | 91 | 01 | YBFA07 | YB110 (Pro... | DE |
| | | | | 0,00 EUR | 0,000 H | | | | | | | | | |

**Figure 7.37** Journal Entry for Activity Allocation to Profitability Segment

The first line item is the credit of the cost center without profitability segment attributes. The second line item is the debit of the profitability segment with the sales order and all profitability attributes updated.

Let's look at how this journal entry impacts product profitability. Start the Product Profitability app again and filter on the sales order, as shown in Figure 7.38.

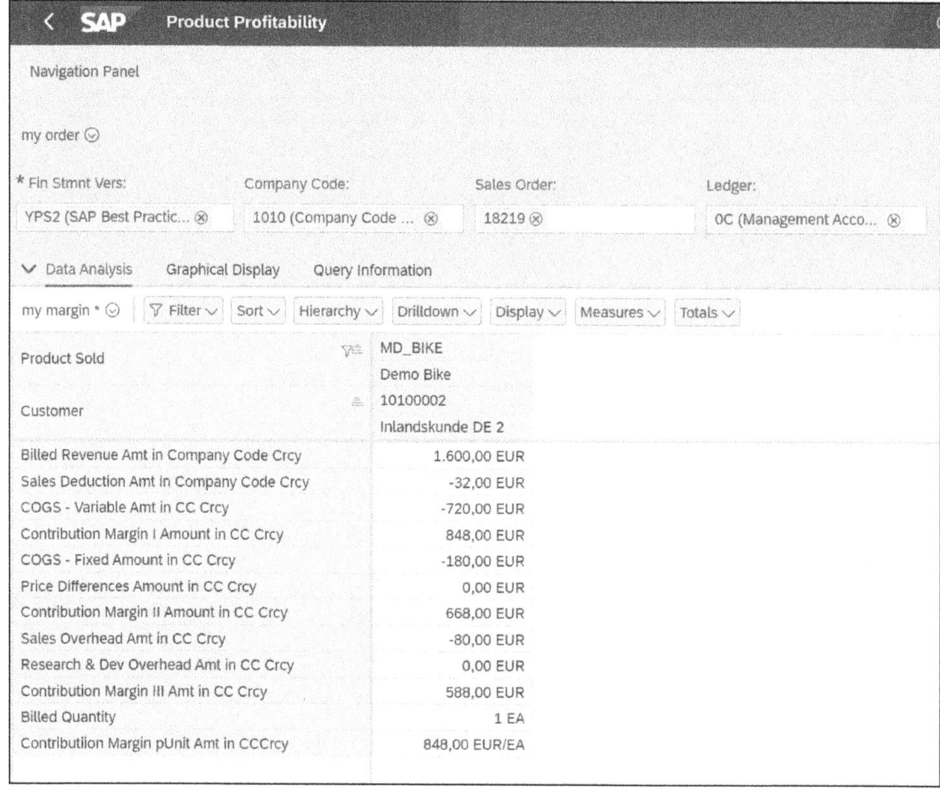


**Figure 7.38** Product Profitability after Posting Activity Allocation on Profitability Segment

The activity allocation updated the **COGS - Variable Amt** contribution margin line item with 75 EUR. Thus, the **Contribution Margin I** decreased to 848 EUR.

### Posting General Journal Entries

Now let's look at the management adjustments postings. Here you post directly in the extension ledger with no update in a legal standard ledger. Management adjustments aren't relevant for legal reporting and therefore are recorded in the management accounting ledger (the extension ledger) only.

One use case is the manual allocation of revenue or costs between certain market segments. Before you can do this, you need to allow manual postings for this extension ledger. This is done in the IMG in ledger configuration (see Chapter 3, Section 3.3.1).

You can post this with Transaction FB01L, Transaction KB11N, or with the Post General Journal Entries app (SAP Fiori ID F0718), as shown in Figure 7.39.

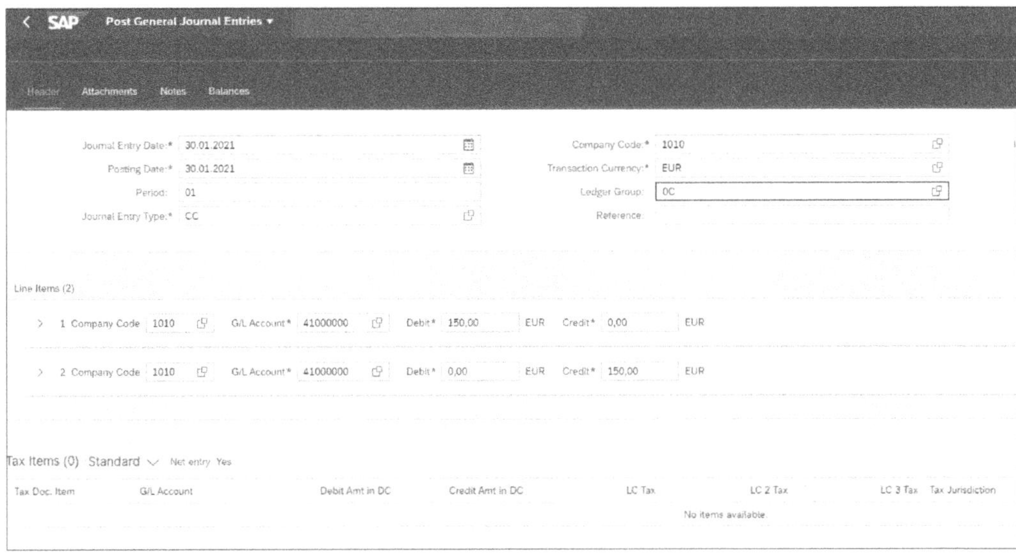


**Figure 7.39** General Ledger Posting in Extension Ledger

With this app, it's possible to select a special **Ledger Group**. Here, select the extension ledger for management accounting 0C. You can also select a P&L account—here, domestic revenue **41000000**—and repost to different account assignments, which you can assign in the detail view of the line item. This posting is reflected in the margin reporting if you start the selection with ledger 0C, as in the product profitability reporting examples shown before.

### 7.2.5 Margin Analysis Allocation Postings

In the previous section, we described how to apply mainly manual special costs to market segments and sales order items. Now we've come to the periodic, mainly job-based allocations: the cost center allocation for margin analysis and the margin analysis internal top-down distribution.

In this section, we'll show a way of specifying periodic costs and revenues more precisely and allocating them to market segments: margin analysis allocations. These are usually performed at the end of a period. For this, we come back to the universal allocation tool, which we discussed in Chapter 5, Section 5.4.2 in the cost center allocation context. There is a specific allocation context for margin analysis available. Within the margin analysis context, there are three different allocation types in place: two for cost center allocation and one for the top-down distribution.

Let's start with the underlying use case for cost allocation to the market segment. The periodic overhead costs that can't be directly allocated to a sales order, customer project, or market segment are recorded on the cost centers (refer back to Figure 7.1). Service and production cost centers are credited via activity allocation and overhead surcharges on cost objects like production orders and projects. At the end of the period, there remains an over- or underabsorption on the cost center, which can be allocated to market segments. Another use case is the allocation of sales or administration cost centers. These cost centers are not credited by business processes and are allocated completely to market segments.

Within the cost center allocation, there are two types:

1. **Overhead allocation**
   Here you use allocation general ledger accounts for postings. With this, you can see allocated sales or administration costs on the market segment.
2. **Distribution**
   Here you post the allocation with the same general ledger accounts originally posted on the cost centers.

Another method is the top-down distribution. Here, certain costs or revenues can't be assigned directly to a detailed market segment—for example, freight costs. These costs or revenues can now be distributed to market segments according to certain methods.

We'll show an overhead allocation in the system first, then the top-down distribution. As we discussed in Chapter 5, if you aren't yet using SAP Fiori, you can create an allocation cycle using Transaction KEU1 and perform top-down distribution using Transaction KE28.

### Overhead Allocations

Start the Manage Allocations app (SAP Fiori ID F3338) and click the **Create** button to arrive at the screen shown in Figure 7.40.

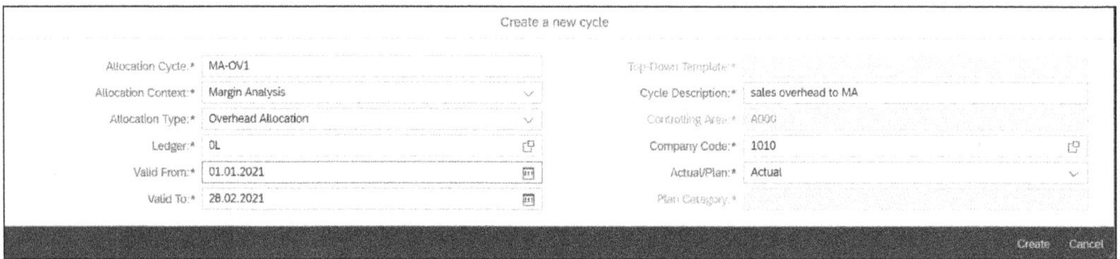


**Figure 7.40** Margin Analysis Overhead Allocation: Selection Screen for Cycle

Here you can define the parameters for the allocation cycle:

- **Allocation Cycle**
  You can freely assign the name of the allocation cycle.
- **Allocation Context**
  For the **Allocation Context**, you can select **Margin Analysis**—as we've done here—or **Cost Center** (see Chapter 5, Section 5.4.6).
- **Allocation Type**
  Under **Allocation Type**, there are the three types mentioned before. In this case, select **Overhead Allocation** for a posting with an allocation account.

- **Ledger/Valid From/Valid To**
  Define the allocation cycle per ledger and for the valid periods.
- **Company Code**
  The cycle is defined per company code.
- **Actual/Plan**
  You can define the cycle for actuals and plan data.

Click the **Create** button to reach the next screen, where you create a segment. A cycle can consist of several segments. Go to the maintenance screen of the segment, shown in Figure 7.41.

As in Chapter 5, you can create an equivalent assessment cycle and segment using Transaction KEU1 or **Accounting • Controlling • Profitability Analysis • Actual Postings • Period-End Closing • Transfer Cost Center Costs/Process Costs • Assessment** and **Extras • Cycle • Create**. As you create your cycles, make sure that the **Type of CO-PA** in the cycle header is set to **2** for account-based profitability analysis. You'll then find the same structure with one cycle comprising many segments as in the Manage Allocations app.

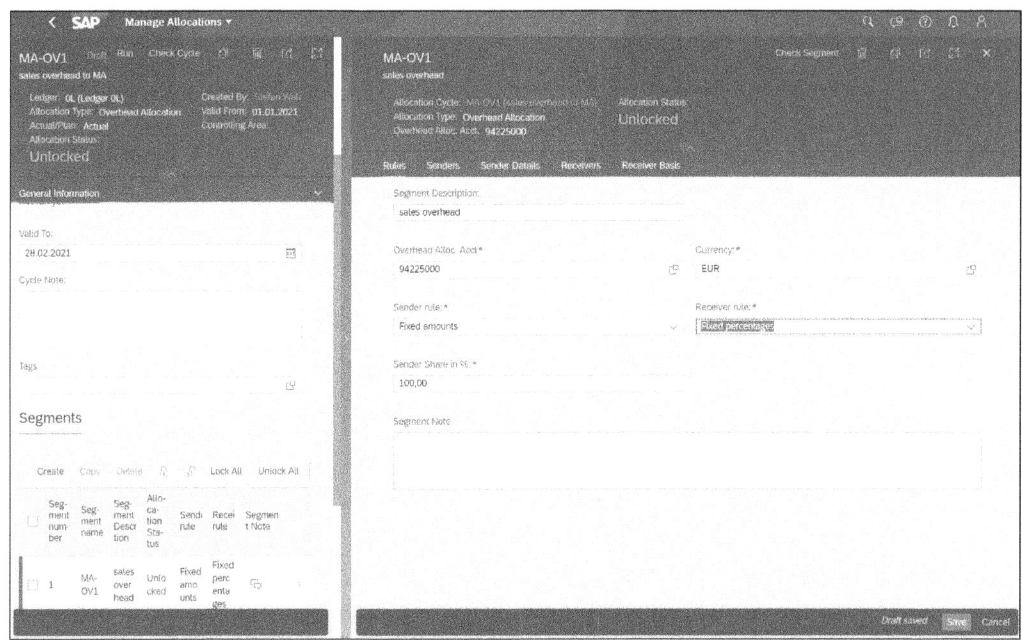


**Figure 7.41** Margin Analysis Overhead Allocation: Cycle Overview

Now define the rules for the segment in the **Rules** tab:

- **Overhead Alloc. Acct**
  Select the overhead allocation account. This must be a P&L account of type 42 (assessment account; see Chapter 4, Section 4.1.3).

- **Currency**
  You can define your own transaction currency for the allocation posting.
- **Sender rule**
  Here, select **Fixed amounts.** If you wanted to allocate the under- or overabsorption of the cost center, the use case mentioned before, you would select **Posted amounts.**
- **Receiver rule**
  Here, select **Fixed percentages.** Alternatively, you can select **Fixed** or **Variable portions**, as we'll show in the next section on top-down distribution.

Now select the **Senders** tab to specify the sender, as shown in Figure 7.42.

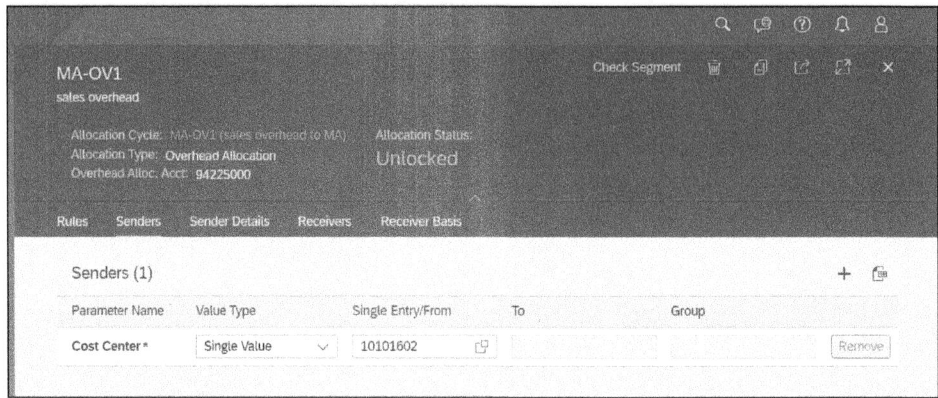


**Figure 7.42** Margin Analysis Overhead Allocation: Sender Data

Select one **Cost Center** as the sender with the **Single Value** option. Alternatively, you can use a group of cost centers by selecting **Group** from the **Value Type** dropdown.

Switch to the next tab, **Sender Details**, as shown in Figure 7.43.

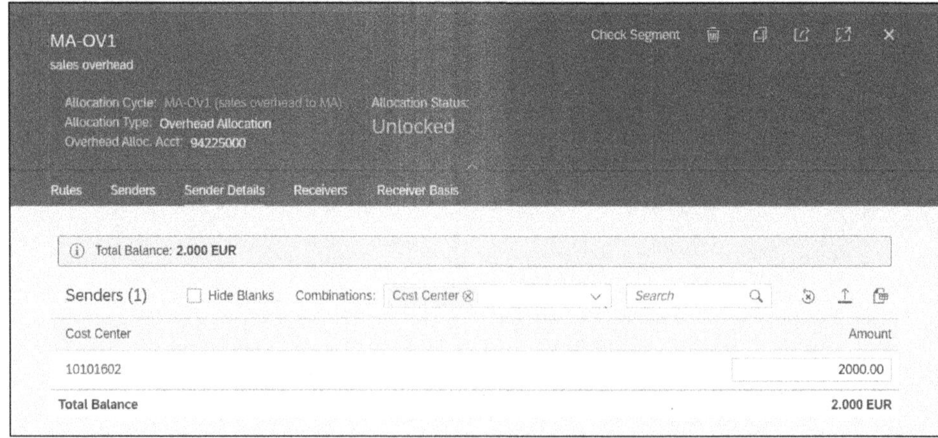


**Figure 7.43** Margin Analysis Overhead Allocation: Sender Amount

In the **Sender Details**, define the **Amount** to be allocated.

Now let's look at the market segment receiver by navigating to the **Receivers** tab, as shown in Figure 7.44.

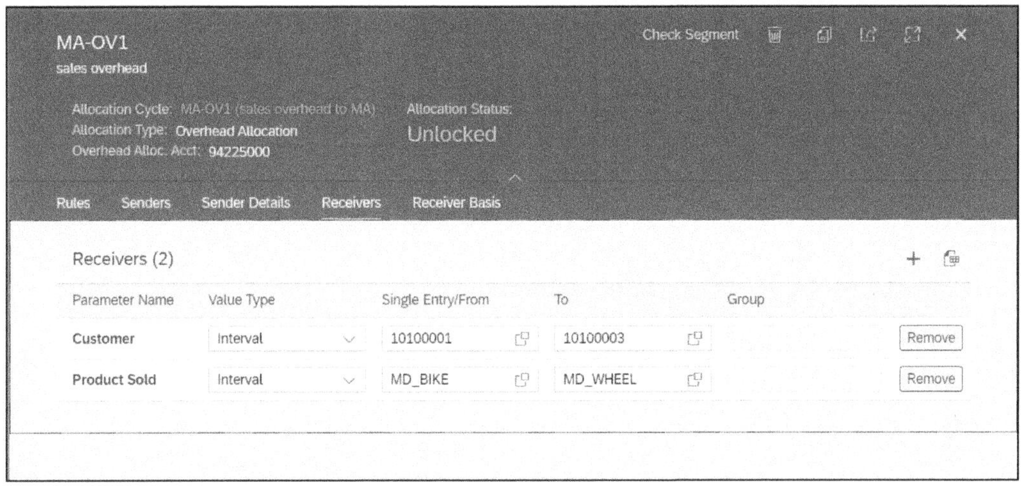


**Figure 7.44** Margin Analysis Overhead Allocation: Receiver

First, select which market segments should be updated with the allocation by clicking the plus sign (**+**). You'll see a popup with the market segment fields. Select market segments for **Customer** and **Product Sold**, nothing else; from a business point of view, a more detailed allocation, such as on the sales order level, isn't possible. Also, specify the **Customer** and **Product Sold** IDs, which are relevant. By selecting **Group** or **Interval**, there can be multiple values chosen. Here we use an interval for both fields. The customer, 10100002, and product sold, MD_BIKE, are within this range in this example.

Then define with which portion of the allocated amount the individual market segments are debited. Do this in the **Receiver Basis** tab, as shown in Figure 7.45.

The system generates a line for every attribute combination defined in the **Receivers** tab. Here we selected three customers and three products sold, so we get nine items. Enter a percentage for every receiver combination. The example here is covered in line 4 and gets a portion of 10%.

Click the **Save** button, then click the **Run** button at the top. You're forwarded to the Run Allocations app, as shown in Figure 7.46.

To run an assessment cycle using the classic approach, use Transaction KEU5 or **Accounting • Controlling • Profitability Analysis • Actual Postings • Period-End Closing • Transfer Cost Center Costs/Process Costs • Assessment** and enter your cycle, the appropriate period, and the fiscal year.

Select the allocation cycle and click the **Run** button. You'll see the parameter screen for the run, as shown in Figure 7.47.

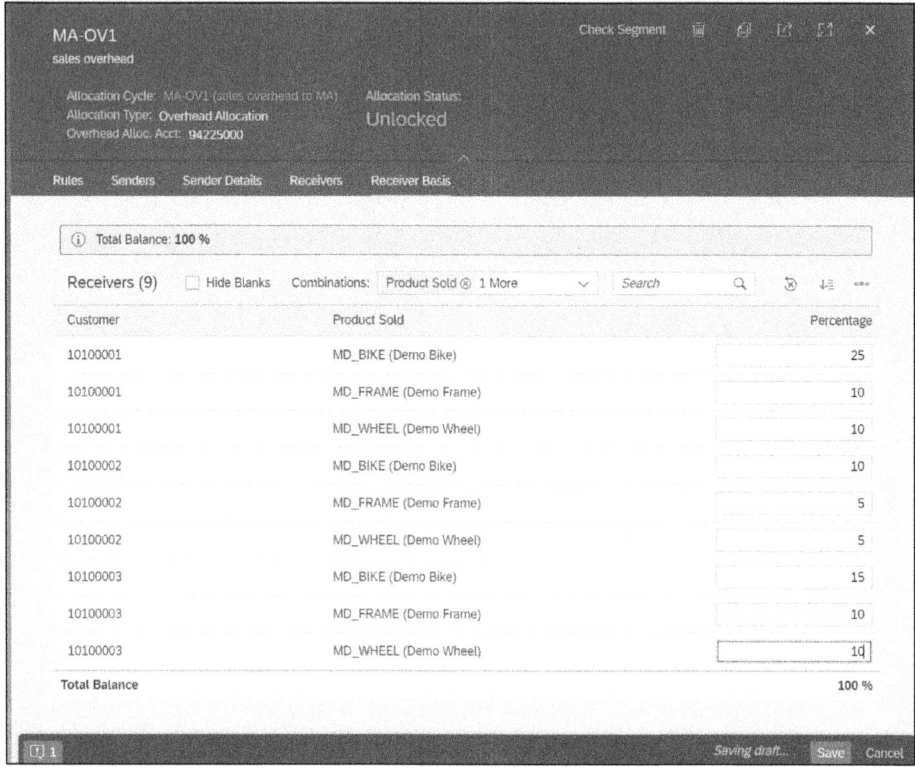


| Customer | Product Sold | Percentage |
|---|---|---|
| 10100001 | MD_BIKE (Demo Bike) | 25 |
| 10100001 | MD_FRAME (Demo Frame) | 10 |
| 10100001 | MD_WHEEL (Demo Wheel) | 10 |
| 10100002 | MD_BIKE (Demo Bike) | 10 |
| 10100002 | MD_FRAME (Demo Frame) | 5 |
| 10100002 | MD_WHEEL (Demo Wheel) | 5 |
| 10100003 | MD_BIKE (Demo Bike) | 15 |
| 10100003 | MD_FRAME (Demo Frame) | 10 |
| 10100003 | MD_WHEEL (Demo Wheel) | 10 |
| Total Balance | | 100 % |

**Figure 7.45** Margin Analysis Overhead Allocation: Ratio per Receiver Market Segment

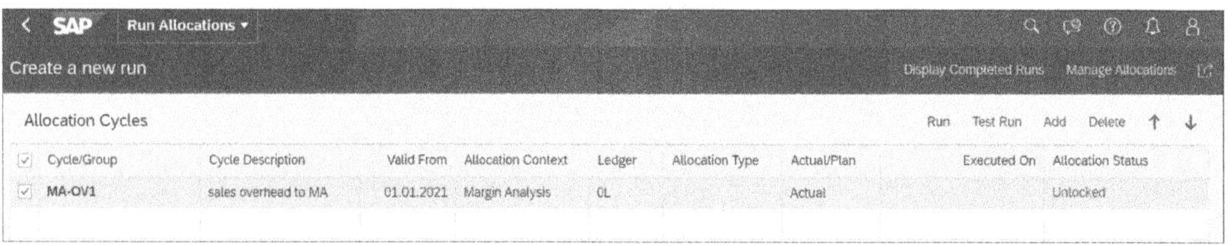


| Cycle/Group | Cycle Description | Valid From | Allocation Context | Ledger | Allocation Type | Actual/Plan | Executed On | Allocation Status |
|---|---|---|---|---|---|---|---|---|
| MA-OV1 | sales overhead to MA | 01.01.2021 | Margin Analysis | 0L | | Actual | | Unlocked |

**Figure 7.46** Run for Margin Analysis Overhead Allocation

Run Allocation(s) - Live Run

Run Name: *

sales-overhead

Fiscal Period From: *

001.2021

Fiscal Period To:

001.2021

Selected Allocation Cycles (1)

| Allocation Cycle | Cycle Description | Allocation Context | Ledger |
|---|---|---|---|
| MA-OV1 | sales overhead to MA | Margin Analysis | 0L |

**Figure 7.47** Margin Analysis Overhead Allocation: Run Parameter

Provide a **Run Name** and define the periods for which the run should be executed (**Fiscal Period From** and **Fiscal Period To**). After you click the **OK** button, the run is executed in the background.

The Allocation Result app will provide an overview of all completed runs, as shown in Figure 7.48.

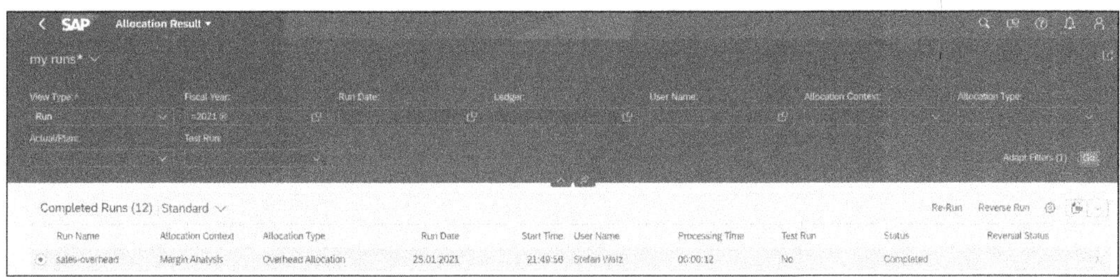


Figure 7.48 Margin Analysis Overhead Allocation: Allocation Result

Select the run and click the arrow at the far right to get the view shown in Figure 7.49.

Allocation Result

sales-overhead

Fiscal Period: 1.2021 | Allocation Context: Margin Analysis | Status: Completed
Run Date: 25.01.2021 | Allocation Type: Overhead Allocation
Errors/Warnings: 0 | Actual/Plan: Actual
Test Run: No | Ledger: 0L (Ledger 0L)

Allocation Results (1) | Senders (1) | Receivers (1) | Journal Entries (18) | Messages (2) | Technical Statistics

Standard*

| Allocation Cycle | Journal Entry | Compa... | Le... | Ledger... | Posting Period | Cost Center | Amount in CC Crcy | | Customer | Product Sold |
|---|---|---|---|---|---|---|---|---|---|---|
| MA-OV1 | 2300002760 | 1010 (... | 0L | 2021 | 1 | | 500,00 | EUR | 10100001 | MD_BIKE |
| MA-OV1 | 2300002760 | 1010 (... | 0L | 2021 | 1 | 10101602 (Sales (DE)) | -500,00 | EUR | | |
| MA-OV1 | 2300002760 | 1010 (... | 0L | 2021 | 1 | | 200,00 | EUR | 10100001 | MD_FRAME |
| MA-OV1 | 2300002760 | 1010 (... | 0L | 2021 | 1 | 10101602 (Sales (DE)) | -200,00 | EUR | | |
| MA-OV1 | 2300002760 | 1010 (... | 0L | 2021 | 1 | | 200,00 | EUR | 10100001 | MD_WHEEL |
| MA-OV1 | 2300002760 | 1010 (... | 0L | 2021 | 1 | 10101602 (Sales (DE)) | -200,00 | EUR | | |
| MA-OV1 | 2300002760 | 1010 (... | 0L | 2021 | 1 | | 200,00 | EUR | 10100002 | MD_BIKE |
| MA-OV1 | 2300002760 | 1010 (... | 0L | 2021 | 1 | 10101602 (Sales (DE)) | -200,00 | EUR | | |
| MA-OV1 | 2300002760 | 1010 (... | 0L | 2021 | 1 | | 100,00 | EUR | 10100002 | MD_FRAME |
| MA-OV1 | 2300002760 | 1010 (... | 0L | 2021 | 1 | 10101602 (Sales (DE)) | -100,00 | EUR | | |

Figure 7.49 Margin Analysis Overhead Allocation: Result Details

You'll see an overview of the results, and on the **Journal Entries** tab, you can see that 18 journal entry items have been created: nine for crediting the cost center and nine for debiting the profitability segment with a combination of product sold and customer.

Let's look at the journal entries as shown in the Display Line Items—Margin Analysis app in Figure 7.50.

You can see that there's one journal entry created with the business transaction type **AMAA** for market segment allocation. The posting date is set to the last day of the period. The amounts on the receiving profitability segment are based on the defined percentages in the cycle rule, as shown previously in Figure 7.45. The combination of customer **10100002** and the **MD_BIKE** product is debited with 200 EUR.

Display Line Items - Margin Analysis

cost-center-allocation*

Ledger: 0L (Ledger 0L) | Company Code: | Posting Date: This year (01.01.2021 - 31.1... | Object Type: | Journal Entry: 2300002760 | Adapt Filters (5) | Go

Line Items (18) sales controlling*

| Journal ... | Bus. Tr ... | Posting Date | G/L Account | Amount in CC Crcy | | O... | Customer | Product Sold | Industry | Product Sold Group | Profit Center | Cou... |
|---|---|---|---|---|---|---|---|---|---|---|---|---|
| 2300002760 | AMAA | 31.01.2021 | 94225000 (COPA -Sales. Overhead) | 500,00 | EUR | EO | 10100001 (I... | MD_BIKE (Demo Bike) | | YBFA07 | YB600 (Sh... | DE |
| 2300002760 | AMAA | 31.01.2021 | 94225000 (COPA -Sales. Overhead) | -500,00 | EUR | KS | | | | | YB600 (Sh... | |
| 2300002760 | AMAA | 31.01.2021 | 94225000 (COPA -Sales. Overhead) | 200,00 | EUR | EO | 10100001 (I... | MD_FRAME (Demo Fr... | | | YB600 (Sh... | DE |
| 2300002760 | AMAA | 31.01.2021 | 94225000 (COPA -Sales. Overhead) | -200,00 | EUR | KS | | | | | YB600 (Sh... | |
| 2300002760 | AMAA | 31.01.2021 | 94225000 (COPA -Sales. Overhead) | 200,00 | EUR | EO | 10100001 (I... | MD_WHEEL (Demo W... | | | YB600 (Sh... | DE |
| 2300002760 | AMAA | 31.01.2021 | 94225000 (COPA -Sales. Overhead) | -200,00 | EUR | KS | | | | | YB600 (Sh... | |
| 2300002760 | AMAA | 31.01.2021 | 94225000 (COPA -Sales. Overhead) | 200,00 | EUR | EO | 10100002 (I... | MD_BIKE (Demo Bike) | 91 | YBFA07 | YB600 (Sh... | DE |
| 2300002760 | AMAA | 31.01.2021 | 94225000 (COPA -Sales. Overhead) | -200,00 | EUR | KS | | | | | YB600 (Sh... | |
| 2300002760 | AMAA | 31.01.2021 | 94225000 (COPA -Sales. Overhead) | 100,00 | EUR | EO | 10100002 (I... | MD_FRAME (Demo Fr... | 91 | | YB600 (Sh... | DE |
| 2300002760 | AMAA | 31.01.2021 | 94225000 (COPA -Sales. Overhead) | -100,00 | EUR | KS | | | | | YB600 (Sh... | |
| 2300002760 | AMAA | 31.01.2021 | 94225000 (COPA -Sales. Overhead) | 100,00 | EUR | EO | 10100002 (I... | MD_WHEEL (Demo W... | 91 | | YB600 (Sh... | DE |
| 2300002760 | AMAA | 31.01.2021 | 94225000 (COPA -Sales. Overhead) | -100,00 | EUR | KS | | | | | YB600 (Sh... | |
| 2300002760 | AMAA | 31.01.2021 | 94225000 (COPA -Sales. Overhead) | 300,00 | EUR | EO | 10100003 (I... | MD_BIKE (Demo Bike) | | YBFA07 | YB600 (Sh... | DE |
| 2300002760 | AMAA | 31.01.2021 | 94225000 (COPA -Sales. Overhead) | -300,00 | EUR | KS | | | | | YB600 (Sh... | |
| 2300002760 | AMAA | 31.01.2021 | 94225000 (COPA -Sales. Overhead) | 200,00 | EUR | EO | 10100003 (I... | MD_FRAME (Demo Fr... | | | YB600 (Sh... | DE |
| 2300002760 | AMAA | 31.01.2021 | 94225000 (COPA -Sales. Overhead) | -200,00 | EUR | KS | | | | | YB600 (Sh... | |
| 2300002760 | AMAA | 31.01.2021 | 94225000 (COPA -Sales. Overhead) | 200,00 | EUR | EO | 10100003 (I... | MD_WHEEL (Demo W... | | | YB600 (Sh... | DE |
| 2300002760 | AMAA | 31.01.2021 | 94225000 (COPA -Sales. Overhead) | -200,00 | EUR | KS | | | | | YB600 (Sh... | |
| | | | | 0,00 | EUR | | | | | | | |

**Figure 7.50** Margin Analysis Overhead Allocation: Journal Entry

Let's check how this is reflected in the multilevel margin reporting in the Product Profitability app. Filter on the **MD_BIKE** product and customer **10100002** to get the view shown in Figure 7.51.

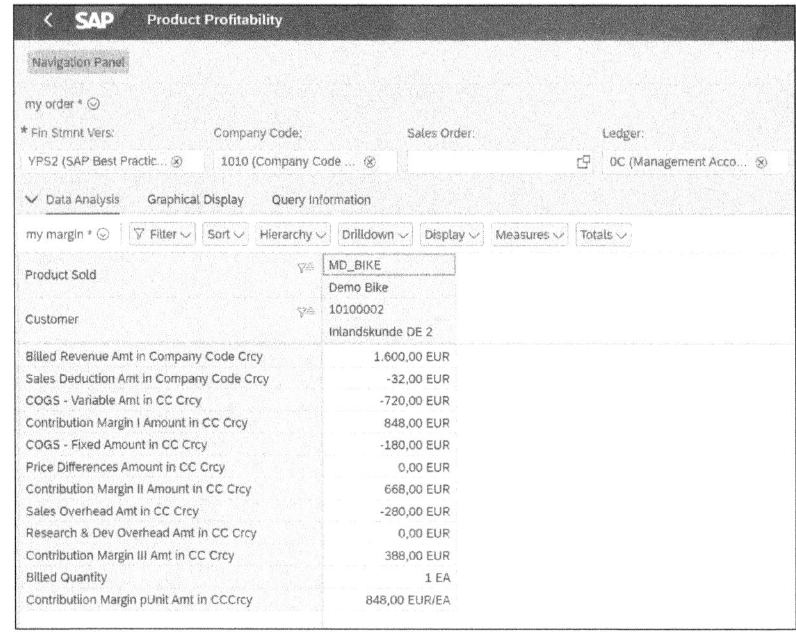


| Product Sold | MD_BIKE<br>Demo Bike |
|---|---|
| Customer | 10100002<br>Inlandskunde DE 2 |
| Billed Revenue Amt in Company Code Crcy | 1.600,00 EUR |
| Sales Deduction Amt in Company Code Crcy | -32,00 EUR |
| COGS - Variable Amt in CC Crcy | -720,00 EUR |
| Contribution Margin I Amount in CC Crcy | 848,00 EUR |
| COGS - Fixed Amount in CC Crcy | -180,00 EUR |
| Price Differences Amount in CC Crcy | 0,00 EUR |
| Contribution Margin II Amount in CC Crcy | 668,00 EUR |
| Sales Overhead Amt in CC Crcy | -280,00 EUR |
| Research & Dev Overhead Amt in CC Crcy | 0,00 EUR |
| Contribution Margin III Amt in CC Crcy | 388,00 EUR |
| Billed Quantity | 1 EA |
| Contributiion Margin pUnit Amt in CCCrcy | 848,00 EUR/EA |

**Figure 7.51** Product Profitability, Including Cost Center to Margin Allocation Posting

In comparison to the reporting results shown previously in Figure 7.38, after the activity allocation the sales overhead costs increased from 80 EUR to 280 EUR. Thus, **Contribution Margin III** decreased from 588 EUR to 388 EUR.

### Top-Down Distribution

Now let's post a top-down distribution. In this example, there are freight costs of 1,000 EUR, which are not yet assigned to a specified market segment, as shown in Figure 7.52. This is entered with the Post General Journal Entries app and assigned to a profitability segment. The only market segment attributes are **Profit Center** and **Functional Area**.

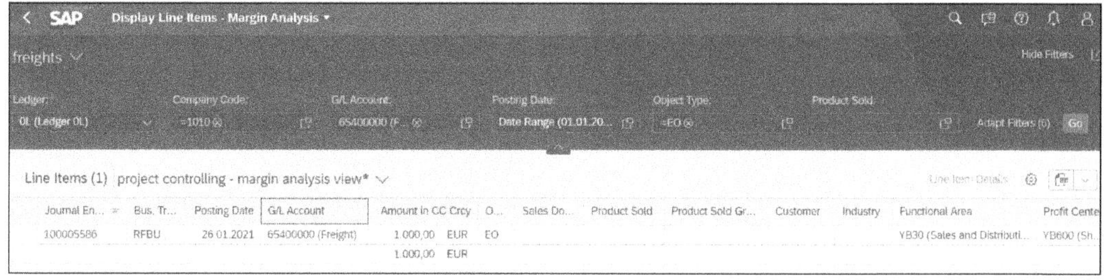


**Figure 7.52** Basis for Allocation: Freight Costs

Say that you want to allocate these costs to four products, which have been sold to two customers, and you want to allocate based on the revenues earned from these customers. In particular, you want to allocate based on the amounts posted on revenue general ledger account 41000000. You can analyze these amounts in the Display Line Items—Margin Analysis app, as shown in Figure 7.53.

SAP Display Line Items - Margin Analysis

domestic revenues by product sold

Ledger: 0L (Ledger 0L) | Company Code: =1010 | G/L Account: =41000000 | Posting Date: Date Range (01.01.2... | Object Type: =EO | Product Sold: !(<empty>)

Line Items (4) sales controlling billing*

| Journal Entry | Bus. Transac... | G/L Account | Amount in CC C... | | Object... | Customer | Product Sold | Profit Center |
|---|---|---|---|---|---|---|---|---|
| Product Sold: MD_BIKE | | | | | | | | |
| Customer: 10100002 | | | -1.600,00 | EUR | | 10100002 | MD_BIKE | |
| Product Sold: PRO_S417 | | | | | | | | |
| Customer: 10100001 | | | -3.200,00 | EUR | | 10100001 | PRO_S417 | |
| Product Sold: TG-D11 | | | | | | | | |
| Customer: 10100002 | | | -6.400,00 | EUR | | 10100002 | TG-D11 | |
| Product Sold: TG-D12 | | | | | | | | |
| Customer: 10100001 | | | -4.800,00 | EUR | | 10100001 | TG-D12 | |
| | | | -16.000,00 | EUR | | | | |

**Figure 7.53** Reference Data Posted on Profitability Segment

In Figure 7.53, the results are filtered on revenue account **41000000** and the journal entry line items grouped by **Product Sold** and **Customer**. As an example, you can see that for the **MD_BIKE** product and customer **10100002**, you've realized 1,600 EUR. This is 10% of the complete realized amount of 16,000 EUR. Note that the allocated share is not fixed, but based on variable shares, the booked revenue.

When you now distribute the 1,000 EUR freight weighted with the realized revenue, you would expect 100 EUR freight posted to the combination of **MD-BIKE** for **Product Sold** and **Customer 10100002**. To see this, start the Manage Allocations app, as shown in Figure 7.54.

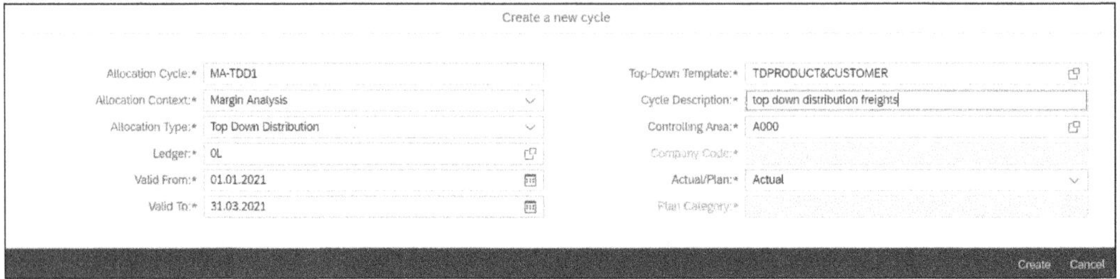


**Figure 7.54** Top-Down Distribution: Parameter Screen

Select **Margin Analysis** for the **Allocation Context**. But for the **Allocation Type**, select **Top Down Distribution**. You also need to select a **Top-Down Template**, which you can define in Customizing. With the top-down template, you specify the market segment attributes that should be part of the receiving profitability segment. These attributes will define the portion of the allocated amount the specific profitability segment will get. Here we're using a template that specifies a customer and product.

Click the **Create** button and go to the allocation cycle overview, where you create a segment, as shown in Figure 7.55. The rule of the segment is defaulted by system. The sender will always allocate the posted amount, and the receiver profitability segments will get variable portions.

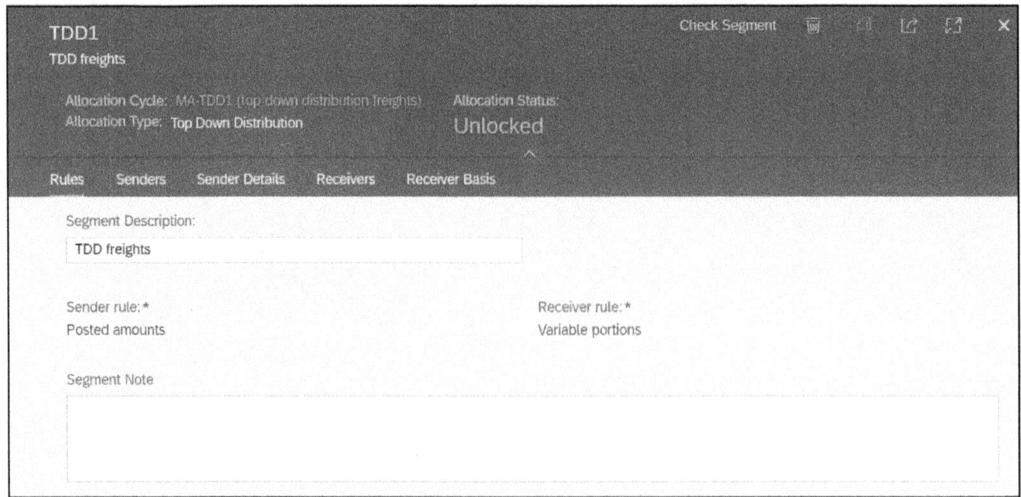


**Figure 7.55** Top-Down Distribution: Defaulted Rules

In the **Sender Details** tab shown in Figure 7.56, specify which journal entries should be selected. Filter only on the company code and the general ledger account **65400000** freights.

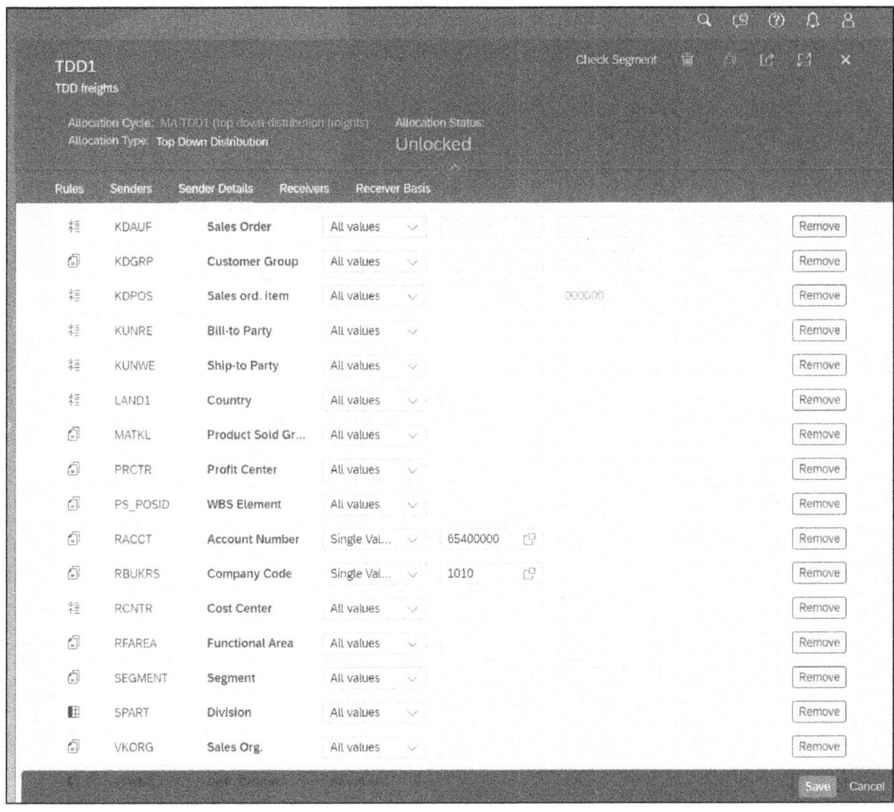


**Figure 7.56** Top-Down Distribution: Sender Details

Then define the receivers by switching to the **Receivers** tab. You automatically see two entries: one for **Customer** and one for **Product Sold**, as shown in Figure 7.57. This is defined by the template, in which you defined **Product Sold** and **Customer** as receivers.

TDD1
TDD freights

Check Segment

Allocation Cycle: MA-TDD1 (top down distribution freights)
Allocation Type: Top Down Distribution
Allocation Status: Unlocked

Rules Senders Sender Details Receivers Receiver Basis

Receivers (2)

| Type | Field Name | Parameter Name | Value Type | Single Entry/From | To | Group |
|---|---|---|---|---|---|---|
| | KUNNR | Customer | Interval | 10100001 | 10100002 | |
| | MATNR_COPA | Product Sold | Interval | MD_BIKE | TG-D12 | |

**Figure 7.57** Top-Down Distribution: Definition of Receivers

For the customer and the product sold, define a range by selecting **Interval** from the **Value Type** dropdown. All journal entries with a product sold and customer within this range will be selected as reference data and allocation receivers.

Next, define the reference data, for which you calculate the portion the receiver gets. This is done in the **Receiver Basis** tab, as shown in Figure 7.58.

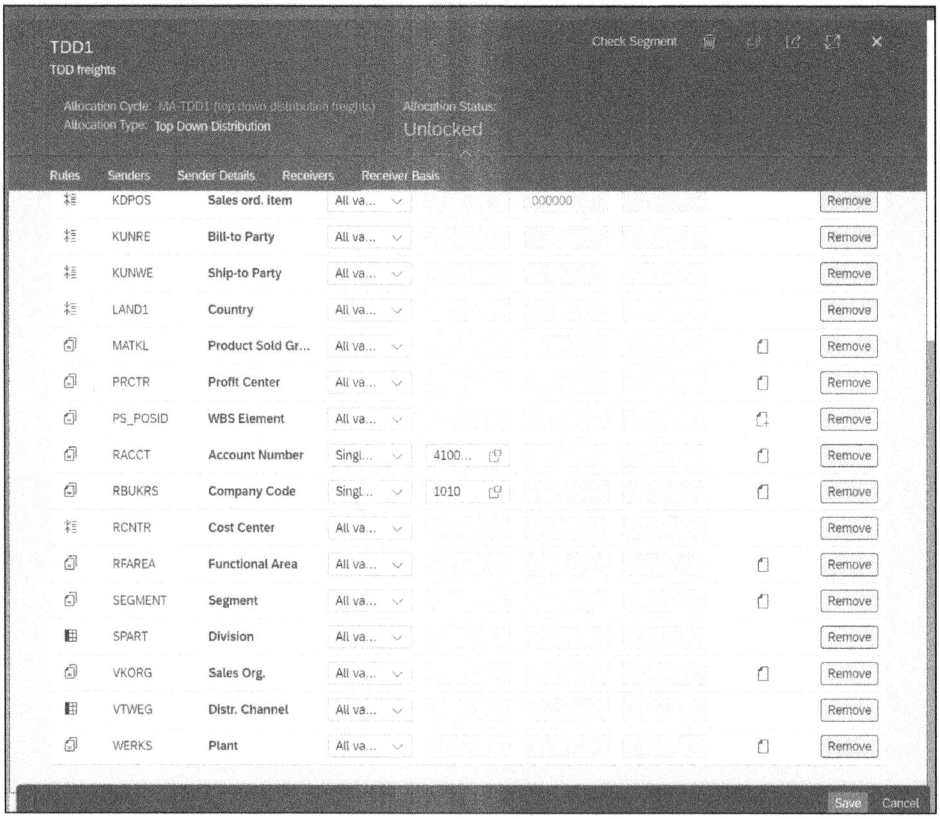

**Figure 7.58** Top-Down Distribution: Receiver Basis

Define general ledger account 41000000 as the receiver basis for the domestic revenues and specify the company code.

It's possible to calculate the portions for several attributes. This makes sense if there are multiple values for this attribute on the sender side and receiver side.

**Example**

There are amounts on profit centers 1 and 2 on the sender side. On the receiver side, there is reference data on profit centers 1, 2, and 3. You can define on which pairs the portions are calculated. For example, perhaps the values on sending profit center 1 should be only calculated for a receiver base with profit center 1, and the values of the sending profit center 2 should calculated for a receiver base with profit centers 2 and 3.

In this example, map the freights sending general ledger account to the receiver base revenue. Click the **Create** icon to the right of the general ledger account in Figure 7.58 to get to the screen in Figure 7.59.

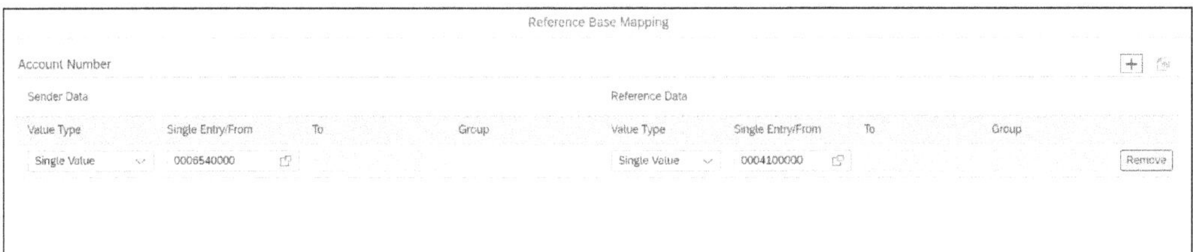


**Figure 7.59** Top-Down Distribution: General Ledger Account as Example for Reference Base Mapping

In this reference data mapping, you define that the sending general ledger account 65400000 is allocated to the receiver market segment based on the postings on general ledger account 41000000.

Click the **Save** button to save the cycle. Now, within the cycle maintenance, you can start the run. You'll see the screen shown in Figure 7.60, in which you can define the run parameters.

Run Allocation(s) - Live Run

Run Name: * TDD1

Cumulate Ref. Periods:

Fiscal Period From: * 001.2021

Fiscal Period To: 001.2021

Ref. Period From: * 001.2021

Ref. Period To: 001.2021

Selected Allocation Cycles (1)

| Allocation Cycle | Cycle Description | Allocation Context | Ledger |
|---|---|---|---|
| MA-TDD1 | top down distribution freights | Margin Analysis | 0L |

OK Cancel

**Figure 7.60** Top-Down Distribution – Run Parameter

Define the period in which the run will start, as you did for overhead allocation. You also can select multiple periods for determining the reference data. Note that we defined the allocation cycle as ledger-dependent (refer back to Figure 7.54). Thus, it runs only for ledger 0L.

After clicking **OK**, the run starts in the background. You'll see the screen shown in Figure 7.61 as the allocation run result.

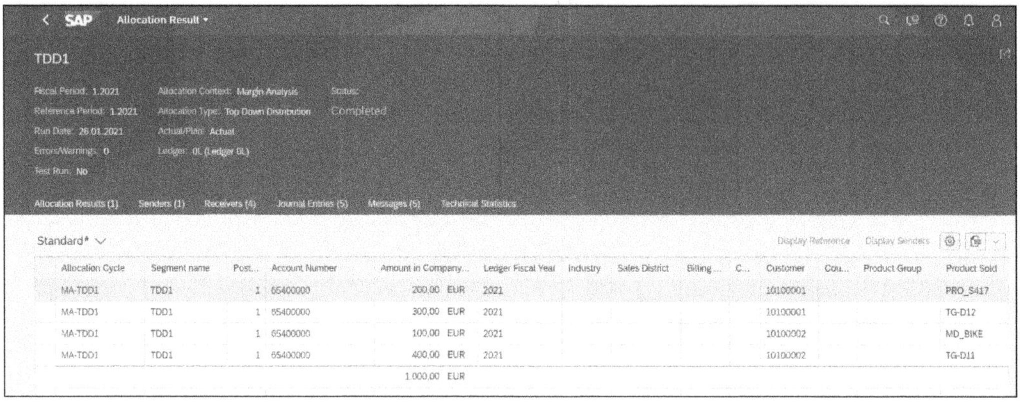

SAP
Allocation Result
TDD1
Fiscal Period: 1.2021
Reference Period: 1.2021
Run Date: 26.01.2021
Errors/Warnings: 0
Test Run: No
Allocation Context: Margin Analysis
Allocation Type: Top Down Distribution
Actual/Plan: Actual
Ledger: 0L (Ledger 0L)
Status:
Completed
Allocation Results (1)
Senders (1)
Receivers (4)
Journal Entries (5)
Messages (5)
Technical Statistics
Standard*
Display Reference
Display Senders
Allocation Cycle
Segment name
Post...
Account Number
Amount in Company...
Ledger Fiscal Year
Industry
Sales District
Billing ...
C...
Customer
Cou...
Product Group
Product Sold
MA-TDD1 TDD1 1 65400000 200,00 EUR 2021 10100001 PRO_S417
MA-TDD1 TDD1 1 65400000 300,00 EUR 2021 10100001 TG-D12
MA-TDD1 TDD1 1 65400000 100,00 EUR 2021 10100002 MD_BIKE
MA-TDD1 TDD1 1 65400000 400,00 EUR 2021 10100002 TG-D11
1.000,00 EUR


**Figure 7.61** Top-Down Distribution: Run Results

In the **Run** tab, you'll see one **Sender**, the freight posting, and four **Receivers**, the profitability segment combinations the system identified. Figure 7.61 shows the four **Receivers** with the calculated allocation amounts. The portions are defined based on the amount on the revenue accounts (refer back to Figure 7.53).

If your organization isn't yet ready to implement SAP Fiori, you can also perform a top-down distribution using Transaction KE28 or **Accounting • Controlling • Profitability Analysis • Actual Postings • Period-End Closing • Top-Down Distribution • Execute**. This transaction doesn't separate the cycle definition and the execution of the run, so you'll have to fill out the periods from which you want to select reference data in the selection screen and then use the **Processing Instructions** button to navigate to a list of market segments in which you can define the characteristics that are relevant for your distribution. From there, choose the **Selection Criteria** button to specify the data that you want to reference during distribution. Finally, use the **Value Fields** button to specify whether you're using amounts or quantities as a basis for the reference. Once you've entered all the selection data, you can start top-down distribution by choosing **Distribution • Execute**.

Now let's look at the created journal entries, as shown in the Display Line Items—Margin Analysis app in Figure 7.62.

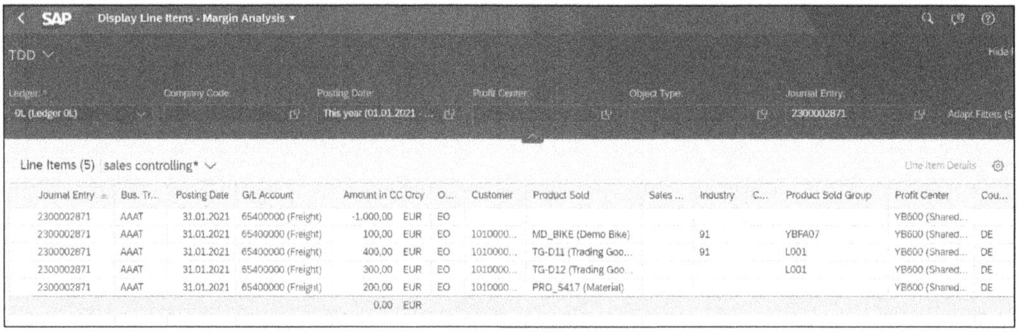

SAP
Display Line Items - Margin Analysis
TDD
Ledger:
0L (Ledger 0L)
Company Code:
Posting Date:
This year (01.01.2021 - ...
Profit Center:
Object Type:
Journal Entry:
2300002871
Adapt Filters
Line Items (5)
sales controlling*
Line Item Details
Journal Entry
Bus. Tr...
Posting Date
G/L Account
Amount in CC Crcy
O...
Customer
Product Sold
Sales ...
Industry
C...
Product Sold Group
Profit Center
Cou...
2300002871 AAAT 31.01.2021 65400000 (Freight) -1.000,00 EUR EO YB600 (Shared...
2300002871 AAAT 31.01.2021 65400000 (Freight) 100,00 EUR EO 1010000... MD_BIKE (Demo Bike) 91 YBFA07 YB600 (Shared... DE
2300002871 AAAT 31.01.2021 65400000 (Freight) 400,00 EUR EO 1010000... TG-D11 (Trading Goo... 91 L001 YB600 (Shared... DE
2300002871 AAAT 31.01.2021 65400000 (Freight) 300,00 EUR EO 1010000... TG-D12 (Trading Goo... L001 YB600 (Shared... DE
2300002871 AAAT 31.01.2021 65400000 (Freight) 200,00 EUR EO 1010000... PRO_S417 (Material) YB600 (Shared... DE
0,00 EUR


**Figure 7.62** Top-Down Distribution: Journal Entries

The journal entry of the top-down allocation has its own business transaction type **AAAT**. (If you were using Transaction KE28, then the old business transaction type was KTDA). The first line item credits the profitability segment with the freight costs without detailed market segments specified. After taking the primary posting for this freight line item into account, the freights are now balanced to zero for this low-specified profitability segment.

The other line items include the receiver with specified product sold and customer. Industry, country, product, and customer group are derived by the system if these attributes are maintained in the product and customer.



As expected, the combination of **MD_BIKE** for the product sold and customer **10100002** is debited with 100 EUR. This has an impact on product profitability, as shown in the Product Profitability app in Figure 7.63.

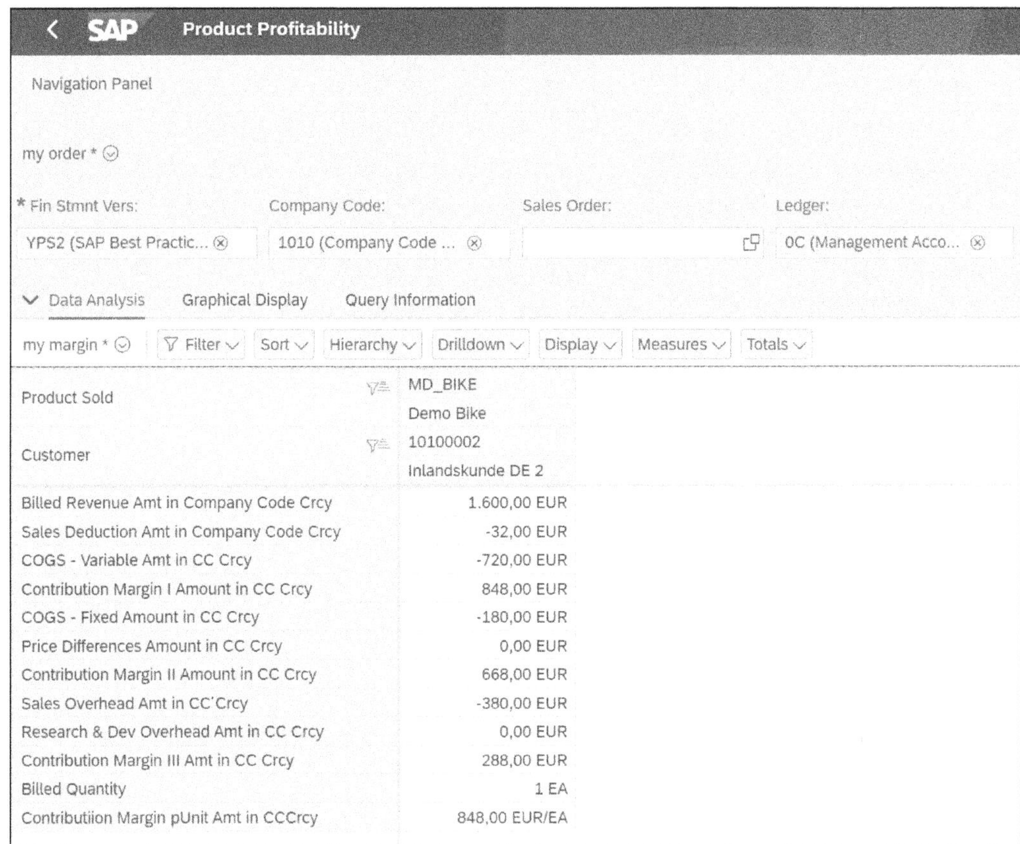


**Figure 7.63** Product Profitability after Top-Down Distribution

The freights are assigned to the semantic tag **Sales Overhead**. Thus, these costs increased now to 380 EUR. The **Contribution Margin III** decreased to 288 EUR.

**Margin Analysis Benefits from the Universal Journal**

So far, the processes we've discussed demonstrate the advantage of the inherent reconciliation between the general ledger and margin analysis—especially regarding periodic correction and equal realization of revenues and cost of goods sold. You can also see that real-time information and reporting based on the prima nota are big advantages.

## 7.3 Customer Project Scenarios

Customer projects are characterized by the fact that, in contrast to the sales scenario, you sell services, not only physical goods. There are multiple processes in place that lead to costs on the projects. The WBS of the project makes it possible to break down these costs by, for example, project phase. Because there is cost planning available, cost controlling on the basis of plan/actual comparison is enabled. The service that has been provided for the customer is invoiced via sales and distribution billing.

For these revenue-carrying projects, revenue recognition or WIP calculation is required, which is supported with event-based revenue recognition (see Section 7.5).

In this section, we'll walk through three customer project scenarios:

- A solution tailored to the professional service industry, available only in SAP S/4HANA Cloud
- The project-based service solution with integration in logistic processes—covering, for example, engineer-to-order or installation services
- Settling a revenue-carrying project to profitability analysis using planning on controlling tables, results analysis, and settlement

**Note**

The first two scenarios are identical with integration into sales and sales billing. In both scenarios, we'll work with the new architecture: table ACDOCP for plan data, event-based revenue recognition, and without settlement. In the third scenario, we'll walk through customer project scenarios using the classic functionality.

Let's start with the professional service solution in SAP S/4HANA Cloud.

### 7.3.1 Professional Service Scenario in SAP S/4HANA Cloud

The professional service scenario, available in SAP S/4HANA Cloud only, is tailored to the needs of this industry. The scenario is available out of the box via scope item J11.

In designing this scenario, SAP has pursued the goal of perfecting the integration of the business processes into accounting and controlling. This allows for complete and accurate project data to be available anytime and through all the perspectives, operationally and accounting- and controlling-wise. Thus, you can provide real-time profitability and reduce the period-end closing to a minimum. At the same time, however, there are completely new reporting insights.

In this section, we show the business processes step by step. As an example, we use a consulting project for an SAP S/4HANA implementation. We start with the project setup and the baseline planning created by the system upon release of the project. Then we post a time confirmation and travel costs on the work packages. In doing so, we show the created journal entries with the automatically created revenue recognition documents. This is followed by the billing and the periodic revenue recognition. After that, we show examples of the advanced analysis options.



Now let's look at the master data setup for this scenario.

### Simplified Project Setup

There is a new SAP Fiori app available for maintaining customer projects. Within this app, there's a guided procedure provided, which integrates all involved applications, such as sales order setup, project management, billing, staffing, and especially financials. This allows a simplified application integration and fulfills the prerequisites for the functionality gains in project accounting. In addition to this simplified customer project master data, dedicated best practice content enables all required subsequent business processes out of the box.

Within the SAP_BR_PROJ_MANAGE_COMM business role, you can access the Create Customer Project app (SAP Fiori ID F0719), as shown in Figure 7.64, which is only available in SAP S/4HANA Cloud. Let's walk through the key tabs.

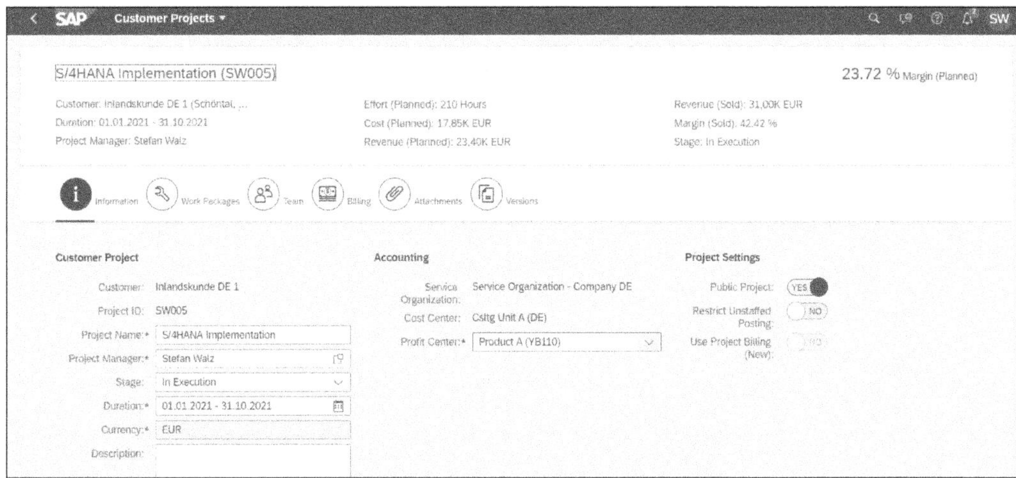


Figure 7.64 Customer Project Header Information

In the header of the customer project, the **Information** tab, assign the **Customer**, the **Project Name** and **ID**, the **Duration** of the contract, and the contract **Currency**, which is defaulted by the customer currency.

In the **Accounting** column, the organizational data is defined. The **Service Organization** is mapped 1:1 to the sales organization. It will later be transferred to the automatically created sales order. The sales organization defines the company code (see Chapter 3, Section 3.2.3). The **Profit Center** is maintained and stored as default in all assigned WBS elements.

There are five different statuses enabled by the **Stage** field:

1. **In Planning**
   Allows project work package set up and cost planning.
2. **Contract Preparation**
   Allows billing plan maintenance and assigned sales order creation by system.
3. **In Execution**
   With this status, you can post and confirm time on the project. Baseline planning also is provided.
4. **Completed**
   This status has an impact on revenue recognition. All posted costs and revenues are realized. All balance sheet values from revenue recognition are cleared, including manual accruals. Postings are still allowed on the project.
5. **Closed**
   There are enhanced checks before you can close a project; for example, there must be no remaining revenue recognition balance sheet values. With the **Closed** status set, you can't post on the project any longer and the project is no longer shown in some customer project–related apps.

In the next step, within the **Work Packages** tab, you structure the project work by creating work packages, as shown in Figure 7.65.

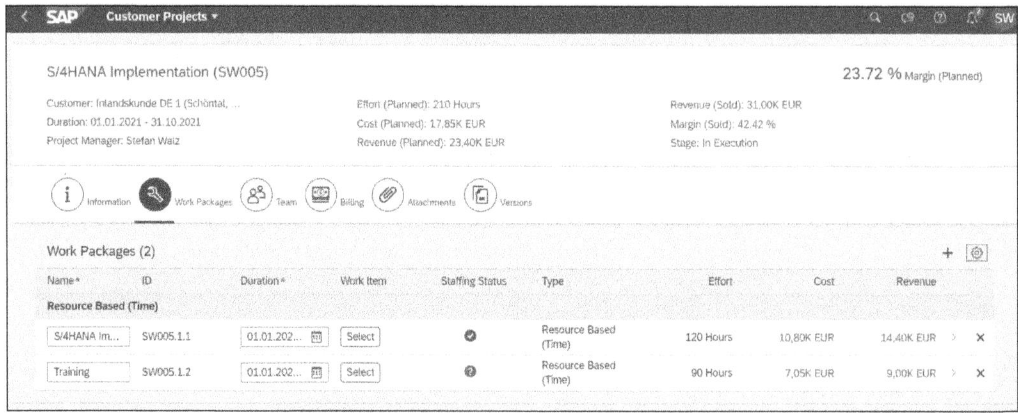


**Figure 7.65** Work Packages of the Project

Click the plus sign (+) button to create two work packages: one for the implementation work and one for the training of the business users. Note that in this scenario you can maintain all work packages of a customer project only on one level.

For these work packages, you conduct the planning of resources and expenses by clicking the arrow on the right or by selecting the **Team** tab. Select the first item to see the screen shown in Figure 7.66.

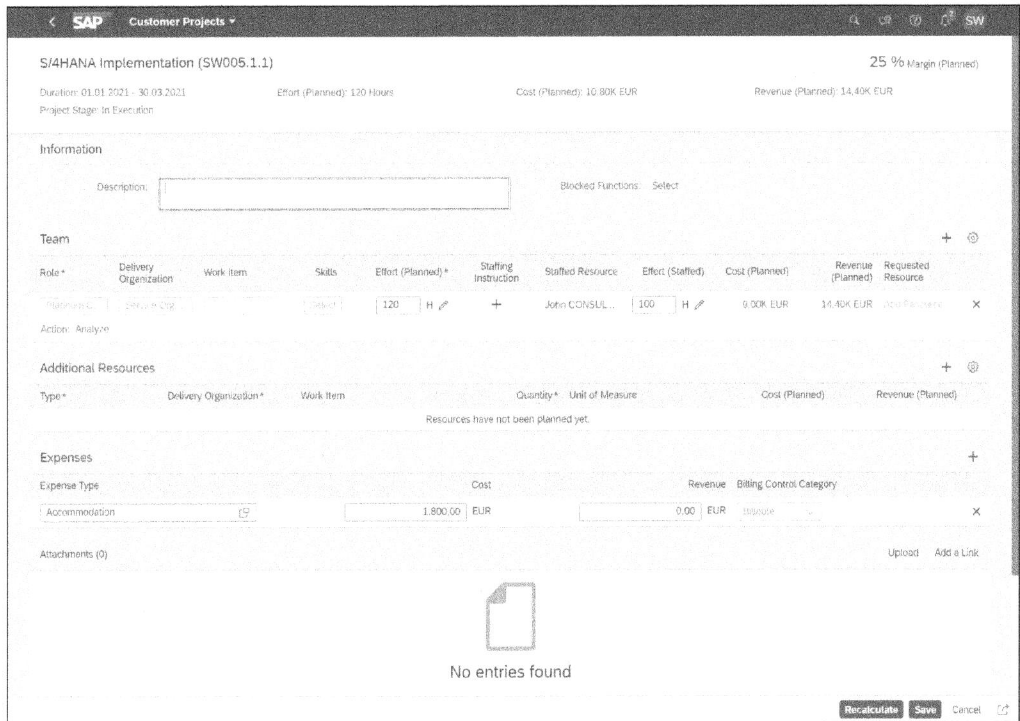


**Figure 7.66** Resource Planning for First Work Package

In the upper section, you can plan the roles and employees needed for the task. The entered **Role** is equal to the controlling activity type. Here, **Platinum Consulting** is maintained. The **Delivery Organization** is mapped to the sales organization, from which the service-delivering company code is derived. So, we can use intercompany staff, which would lead to intercompany controlling postings (see Chapter 9). With this information, a cost rate for the requested service is derived, which we'll discuss further later in this section. This rate is multiplied by the quantity maintained in the estimated **Effort (Planned)** to calculate the **Cost (Planned)**.

There is also an employee staffing application integrated into the system. Based on the selected delivery organization and the role, you'll see proposals for employees. The **Staffed Resource** chosen in this example is John Consultant1_DE. If there's an employee staffed and staffing is confirmed, this WBS element will appear in his time sheet. Thus, the staffing controls the time confirmation process.

In the lower **Expenses** section, you can plan the expenses. You can distinguish different **Expense Types**, such as **Accommodation**, **Airfare**, and **Ground Transportation**, plus the required types **Hardware** and **Licenses**. The **Expense Types** can be adapted within a self-service configuration task. In this example, plan for **Accommodation** of 1,800 EUR. When you're done, click the **Save** button.

Now let's look at the resource planning of the second work package, as shown in Figure 7.67.

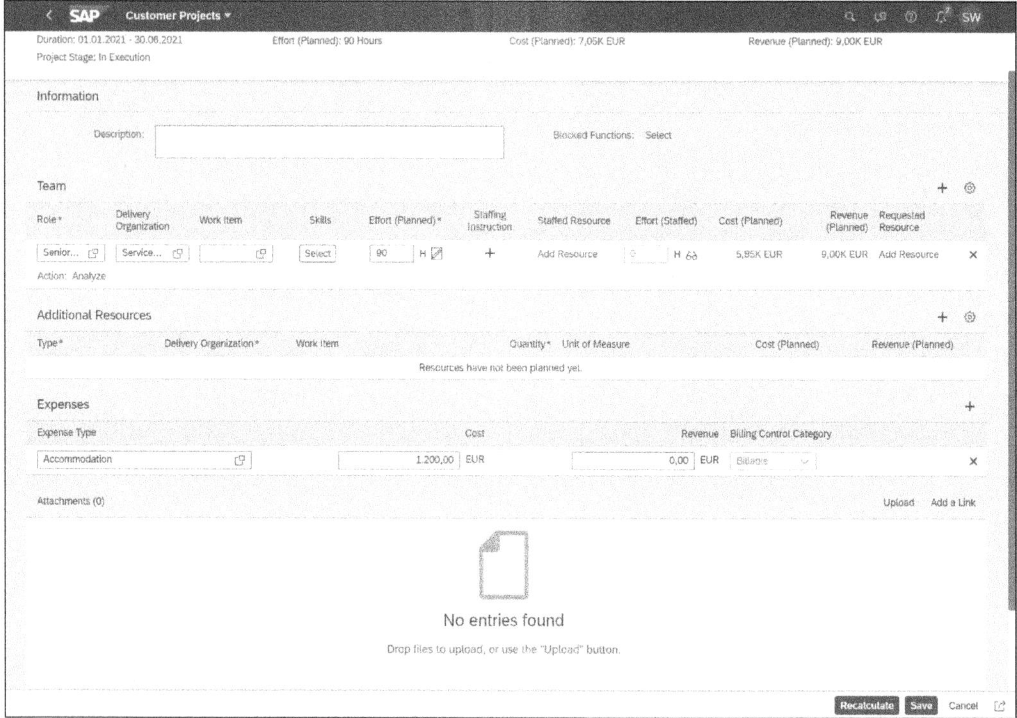


**Figure 7.67** Resource Planning for Second Work Package

There are 90 hours of senior consulting planned in the travel work package; see the **Effort (Planned)** column. By default, the planned quantity is distributed over the valid period of the work package—here, January to June 2021—in equal parts. You can adjust this with the action icon beside the **H**, hours, field to impact the cost plan per period. You'll see the popup shown in Figure 7.68.

Adjust the hours and click the **Submit** button. In the first month and last month, estimate only five hours; the largest number of hours will be required in March and April over 30 days.

Now go to the **Billing** tab, as shown in Figure 7.69. Within this tab, you can define the integration with billing and the sales order. This step is only possible if the **Contract Preparation** status or higher is set.

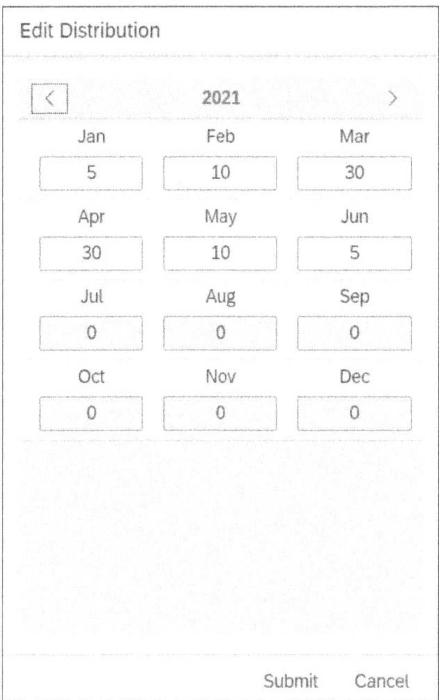


**Figure 7.68** Distribution of Planned Quantities over Periods

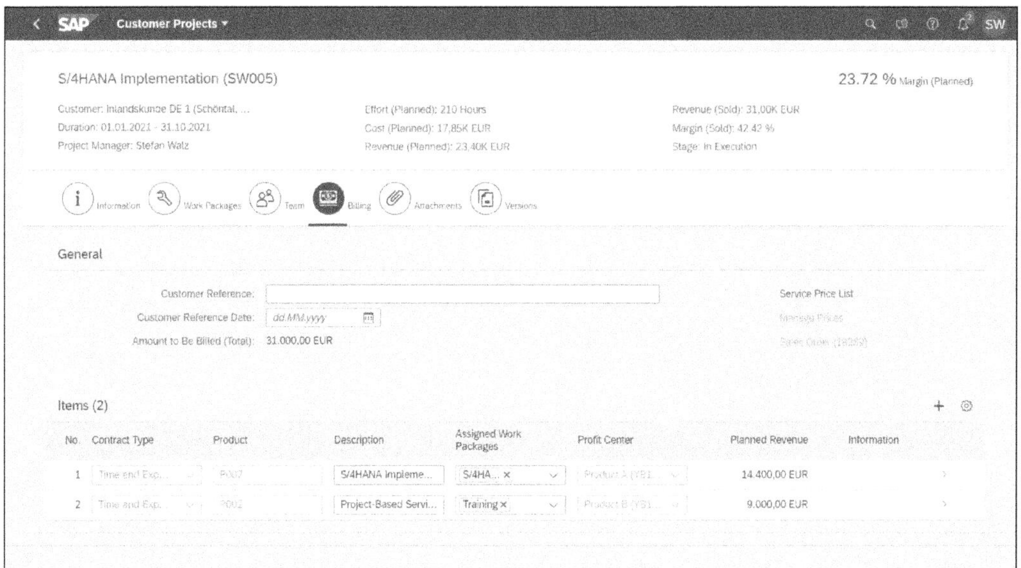


**Figure 7.69** Sales Order and Billing View for Customer Project

Every line item in the tab reflects an individual sales order item. The **Product** is stored in the sales order item and will be derived as the **Product Sold** attribute in the Universal Journal item as a margin analysis field. Add two lines here by clicking the **+** button, to enter two different products sold:

1. **P007 (S/4HANA Implementation)**
   Here, all activities that are necessary to implement SAP S/4HANA will be recorded.
2. **P002 (Project-Based Services)**
   This is where all activities for the client are recorded that have nothing directly to do with the implementation—such as user training, for example.

For every line item, you need to assign one of the work packages created previously. The **Profit Center** can be maintained for every line.

The **Contract Type** in the first column defines the billing and the revenue recognition method. There are exactly four contract types provided by SAP S/4HANA Cloud best practice content:

1. **Time and Expense (T&M)**
   This contract type enables billing based on the time and expense confirmations on the assigned work packages. This means that billing proposals are created based on the journal entries posted on the project. Billing products are determined for the different activity types, such as senior consulting or platinum consulting. For these billing products, project-specific prices can also be defined. For expenses, the expense general ledger account is mapped to billing materials. Via default billing content, expenses are billed with the same amounts. Event-based revenue recognition calculates the realized revenue for the cost postings by simulating the time and expense billing.
2. **Usage-Based**
   These contract items are quite similar to time and expenses. Usage-based billing allows you to bill your customers for services with a certain usage volume, such as the number of service tickets processed in a period or number of licenses used in a period.
3. **Fixed Price**
   For these contract items, billing is based on the planned amounts and dates maintained in the billing plan. Event-based revenue recognition can calculate the matching revenues for every confirmation based on a cost-based percentage of completion (PoC) method. The planned costs are taken from the resource planning and the planned revenue from the billing plan.
4. **Periodic Service**
   This item is used for licenses or other periodic services. The billing is here triggered based on the amount and date provided in the billing plan. You get access to the billing plan by pressing the arrow on the far right for an item in the **Billing** tab. For this contract type, for every billing plan item there is a valid period required. The realized revenues will be calculated by revenue recognition based on amount and period. This will be done with a periodic end run. We'll discuss such a revenue recognition scenario with service contracts in Section 7.4.4.

For these contract types, three different revenue recognition methods and thus revenue recognition keys are required. With the delivered content, you ensure the correct, process-driven revenue recognition key derivation. The revenue recognition keys aren't visible in this app, but you'll see them in the background master data we discuss next.

Now let's look at the master data created in the background by the system. First start Transaction CJ03 and enter the **SW005** project in the **Proj. def.** field, as shown in Figure 7.70.

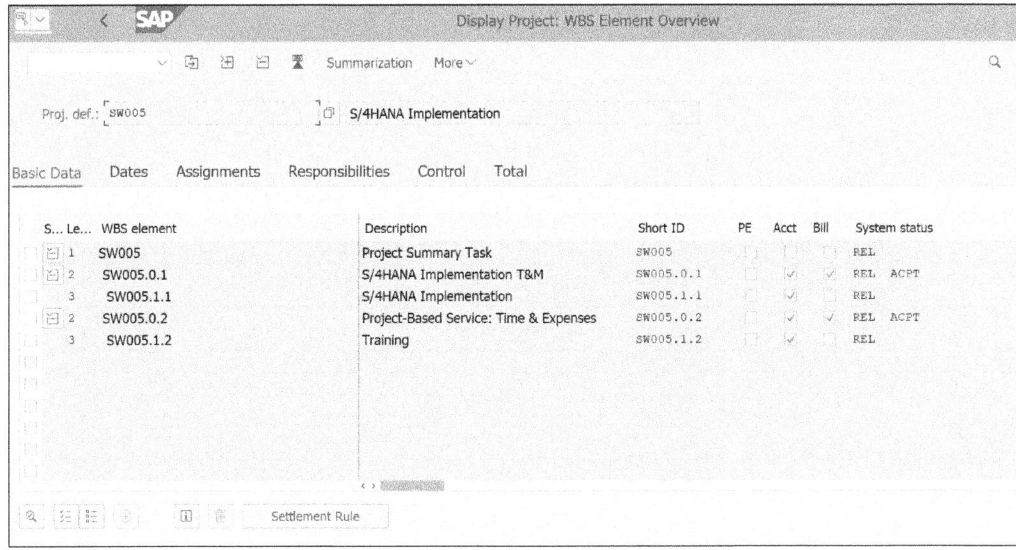


**Figure 7.70** Basic Project Data, Showing Created Structure

You see the structure of the project. On level 2 are the billing elements, as indicated by the **Bill** column. These items are created by the system. Level 3 items are the work packages you created in the customer projects app.

Now let's check the **Control** attributes, as shown in Figure 7.71.

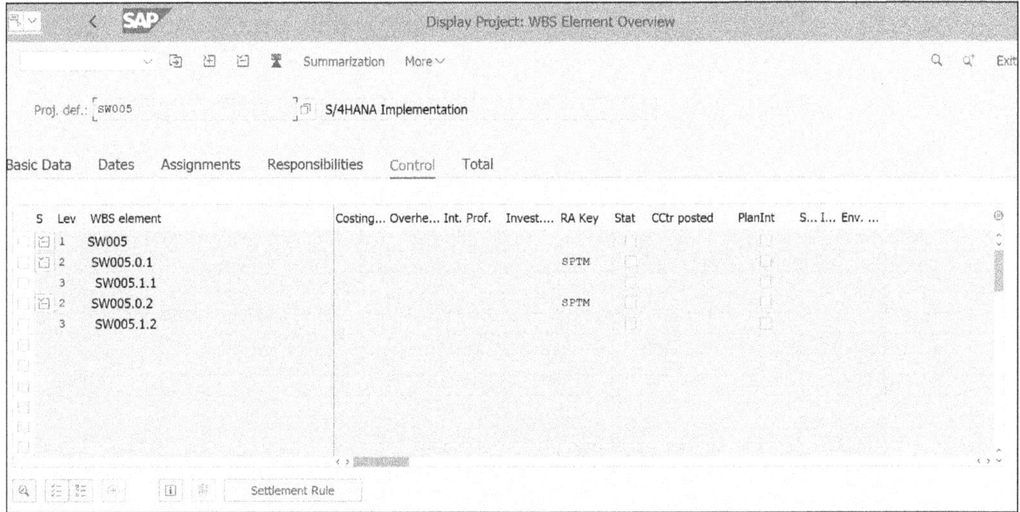


**Figure 7.71** Project Control with Revenue Recognition Key

You see the revenue recognition key **SPTM** in the **RA Key** column, indicating the method for time and material billing assigned by the system to the billing elements.

And now let's check the sales order created by system. Start Transaction VA03 and select the sales order number, **18289**, from the **Billing** tab (shown previously in Figure 7.69). Press `Enter` to arrive at the screen shown in Figure 7.72.

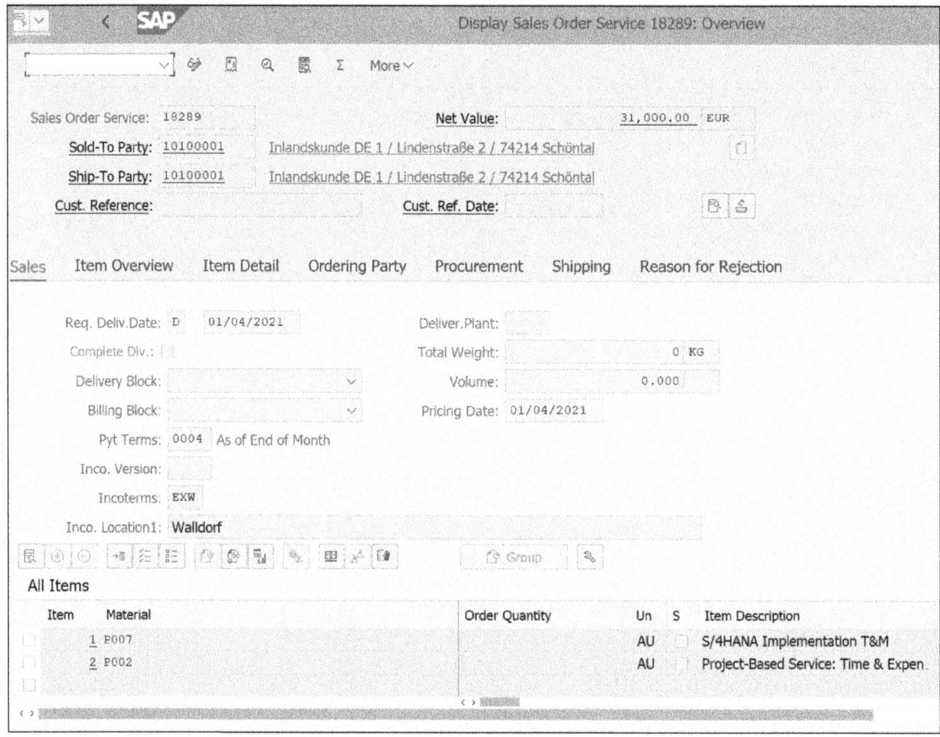


**Figure 7.72** Sales Order View for Customer Project

You'll see the two sales order items with their defined products. If you double-click an item and select the accounting view, you'll see the WBS billing elements assigned.

With the project setup complete, let's review how the customer project and sales order logistic objects work together, how revenue recognition is controlled, and how the market segment is determined, as shown in Figure 7.73.

If you're using SAP S/4HANA, you can create your project manually, provided you follow the same rules concerning the billing elements and the assignment of the results analysis key within the WBS to ensure that event-based revenue recognition can handle the values captured on the sales order items and the associated WBS elements correctly.

There is always a 1:1 relationship between sales order and project ID and project billing element and sales order item enforced by system. That is the prerequisite to allow a derivation of a unique profitability segment and to define a unique revenue recognition method on billing elements at the sales order item level.

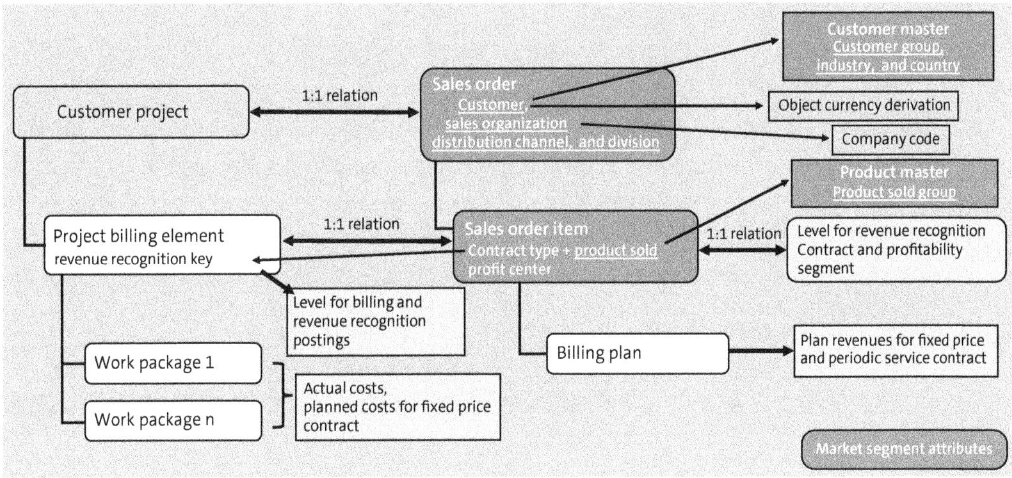


**Figure 7.73** Object Setup in Professional Service Scenario

The revenue recognition key, and thus the revenue recognition method, is derived from the contract type and optionally the product sold. The contract type defines the billing method. The revenue recognition key is stored in the WBS billing element. The profitability segment is defined by the sales order item: from here you get the sales organizational data, the customer, and the product sold. With this you read the customer master and get the customer group and industry. From the product sold you get the product sold group. The project billing element is stored in the sales order item master. The sales order item profitability attributes are valid for all assigned project hierarchy elements below the billing element. In this example, there are two sales order items and thus two profitability segments—one with the product sold as P007 and one with P002, as shown previously in Figure 7.72.

For every single posting on a work package, you derive a market segment and store it in the journal entry, parallel to the project account assignment. We'll cover this during our discussion of business transactions later in this section.

To ensure this profitability segment attribution and the event-based revenue recognition calculation, there must be a sales order item assigned to the billing element, when the postings to the project happen. Thus, postings to work packages are not allowed so long there is no billing item and sales order item assigned. The posting would be rejected by the system if no assignment exists.

**Note**

There is a unique profitability segment and a unique profit center for the sales order item, the project billing element, and all subordinated work packages. This ensures that the cost posting account assigned to the work packages, the billed revenue posting, and the revenue recognition postings derive the same profit center and profitability segment.

This setup also influences the cost and revenue planning for the customer project.

### Project Planning

Now let's look at the baseline planning created by the system. By setting the status of the project to **In Execution**, the baseline planning is created automatically by the system based on the resource planning within the customer project. The data is stored in the planning table ACDOCP, which has a similar structure to the Universal Journal for the actuals (recall Chapter 2, Section 2.2.2). You can access the plan data via the Projects Baseline/EAC/Ongoing app. Enter the **Project** and click **Go** to create the view shown in Figure 7.74.

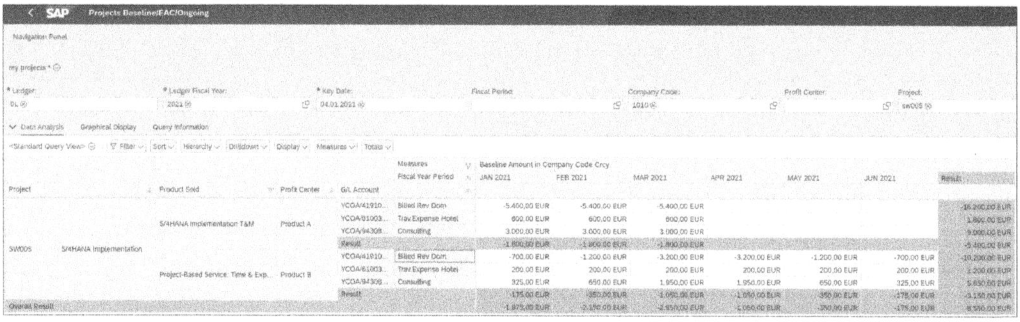

**Figure 7.74** Baseline Values after Release of Project

The plan data for the baseline is based on the project planning shown previously in Figure 7.66 and Figure 7.67. First, you see two sections with different **Product Sold** information—one for assigned work packages for the first sales order item, P007, for the SAP S/4HANA implementation, and one for the second sales order item, P002, for the training. This derivation logic works for the planning too. Thus, with the customer project planning you get market segment planning too.

The expense planning for expense type accommodation is mapped to the **Travel Expense Hotel** general ledger account. The planned hours are multiplied by the cost rate, which we'll discuss in the next section, and stored with the **Consulting** general ledger account. You can see the impact of the periodic distribution of the hours in the second work package (refer back to Figure 7.68):

- For January, the value is calculated as follows: 5 hours multiplied by the senior consulting rate of 65 EUR/h is equal to 325 EUR.
- For March, it's calculated as follows: 30 hours multiplied by the senior consulting rate of 65 EUR/h is equal to 1,950 EUR.

For the first work package, we didn't change the periodic distribution, so it's distributed equally by the system for the valid time frame from January to March.

Now let's look at the revenues: the two lines posted with the billed revenue domestic general ledger account (**Billed Rev Dom**). Their value is determined by the revenue recognition. We take the planned costs per period and simulate the time and expenses billing. In the next section, we'll explain that when journal entries are entered to the project, revenue is recognized immediately, as required by International Financial Reporting Standards (IFRS) accounting. Therefore, using the same method in the plan, we can determine a good forecast for the expected revenue.

### Business Transactions

Now we come to the business transactions and thus actual posting on the project. We'll demonstrate how every posting on a customer project immediately effects SAP S/4HANA project accounting and margin analysis. Let's start with a consultant's time recording on the SW005 (SAP S/4HANA implementation) customer project.

#### *Time Confirmation on Project*

You staffed the **John Consultant1_DE** consultant on the first work package, so the project appears automatically in his time sheet. He needs to be assigned to the `SAP_BR_Employee` business role, after which he can start the Manage My Timesheet app, as shown in Figure 7.75.

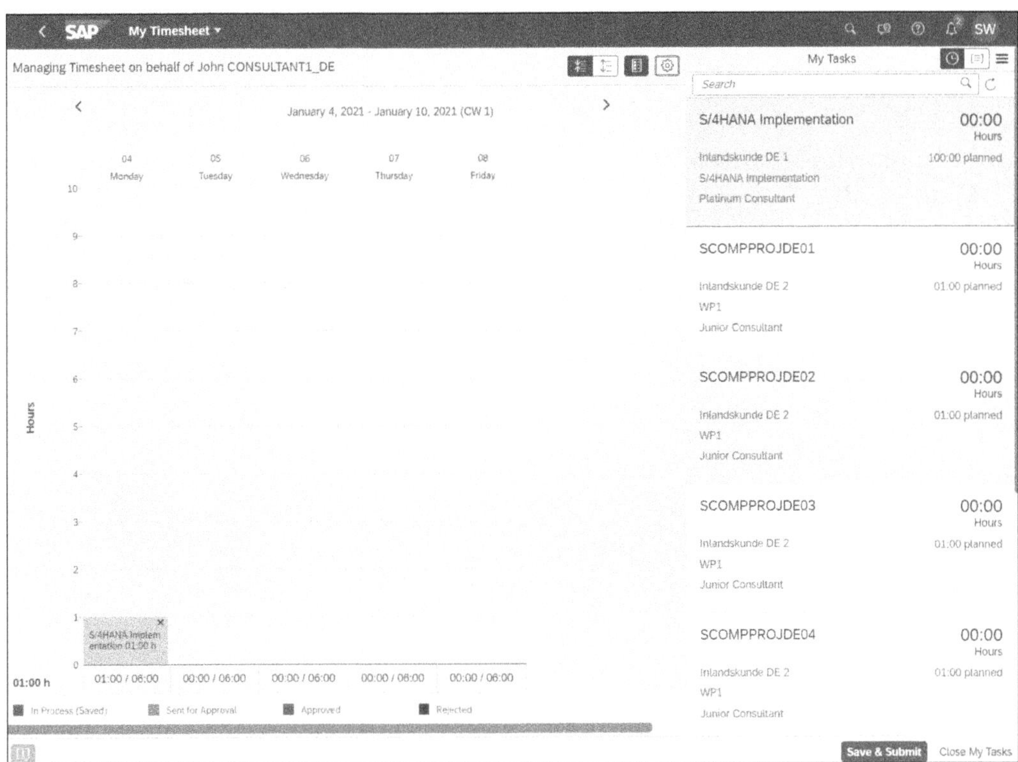


**Figure 7.75** Time Confirmation of Consultant to Customer Project

The right-hand bar shows all project tasks provided for which the employee is staffed. Select the **S/4HANA Implementation** project and capture one hour for January 4 by clicking in the time sheet. The number of hours is determined by the height of the column. Then click the **Save & Submit** button at the bottom right. Depending on the configuration, the time is automatically approved or is sent to the project's lead's inbox for approval.

With this time sheet confirmation, the following data is determined:

- The employee who rendered the service and thus the sending cost center. You get this from the employee master (see Figure 7.76).
- The type of service—in this example, **Platinum Consultant**. This is what was defined in the project plan, and you can see it in the right-hand bar below the project name. The type of service is identical to the controlling activity type.
- The quantity of hours.
- The service rendered date—here, January 4. This is the posting date by default. It deviates if the period is already closed. In this case, you can define the posting period via the Process Unposted Time Confirmation app. For more on this topic and about time confirmation for professional services, visit the blog at *http://s-prs.co/v528205*.

The financial organization data defined by the employee is shown in the fact sheet shown in Figure 7.76. You can get there with the search functionality by clicking the magnifying glass icon at the top of the SAP Fiori launchpad. Here, select **Employee**, enter "Consultant1_DE", and press Enter.

**Figure 7.76** Employee Master: Accounting Assignments

The financial assignments are done in the **Employments** section. The employments are time-dependent. There can be different employments for different periods. In this example, the employee is assigned to **Company Code 1010** and **Cost Center 10101902** with a **Personnel Number** (which is employment-dependent) of **50003243**. You'll see this number in financial reports. You could assign the employee to another cost center for 2021, in which case you'd see an additional row. The employment time frames can't be defined as overlapping. In the employee fact sheet, there is an additional section for **Controlling Information**, as shown in Figure 7.77.

**Figure 7.77** Attribute Service Cost Level in Employee Master

In this area, you can define a **Service Cost Level**, which has an impact on the derived cost rate. You can define the service cost level as time-dependent.

With this information, you can determine the cost rate. In SAP S/4HANA Cloud, you can do this with the Manage Cost Rates—Professional Services app (SAP Fiori ID F3161), as shown in Figure 7.78, which is assigned to the SAP_BR_Overhead_Accountant role. For this example, select the cost rates assigned to cost center **10101902** in company code **1010** and click **Go**.

| Cost Center | Overtime Category | Activity Type | Service Cost Level | Work Item ID | From FY | From Period | WBS Element | Rate | per | Activity Unit |
|---|---|---|---|---|---|---|---|---|---|---|
| 10101902 (Csltg Unit A (DE)) | | T001 (Junior Consultant) | | | 2020 | 001 | | 55,00 EUR | 1 | H |
| 10101902 (Csltg Unit A (DE)) | | T002 (Senior Consultant) | | | 2020 | 001 | | 65,00 EUR | 1 | H |
| 10101902 (Csltg Unit A (DE)) | | T004 (Trainer) | | | 2020 | 001 | | 65,00 EUR | 1 | H |
| 10101902 (Csltg Unit A (DE)) | | T005 (Project Manager) | | | 2020 | 001 | | 70,00 EUR | 1 | H |
| 10101902 (Csltg Unit A (DE)) | | T003 (Platinum Consultant) | | | 2020 | 001 | | 70,00 EUR | 1 | H |
| 10101902 (Csltg Unit A (DE)) | | | 7 (Service Level 7) | | 2021 | 001 | | 75,00 EUR | 1 | H |

**Figure 7.78** Manage Cost Rates—Professional Services App

You can see **Cost Center**– and **Activity Type**–dependent rates and **Service Cost Level**–dependent ones at the bottom. If the service cost level is determined in the employee master, then it has a higher priority for cost rate derivation than the activity type-based entry. So, in this case, you wouldn't the rate of 70 EUR for platinum consulting, but the 75 EUR one for the service cost level instead.

**Note**

For more on this topic and the access sequence, visit the blog at *http://s-prs.co/v528206.*

Now let's look at the created journal entry for the time confirmation with the Display Line Items—Margin Analysis app, as shown in Figure 7.79.

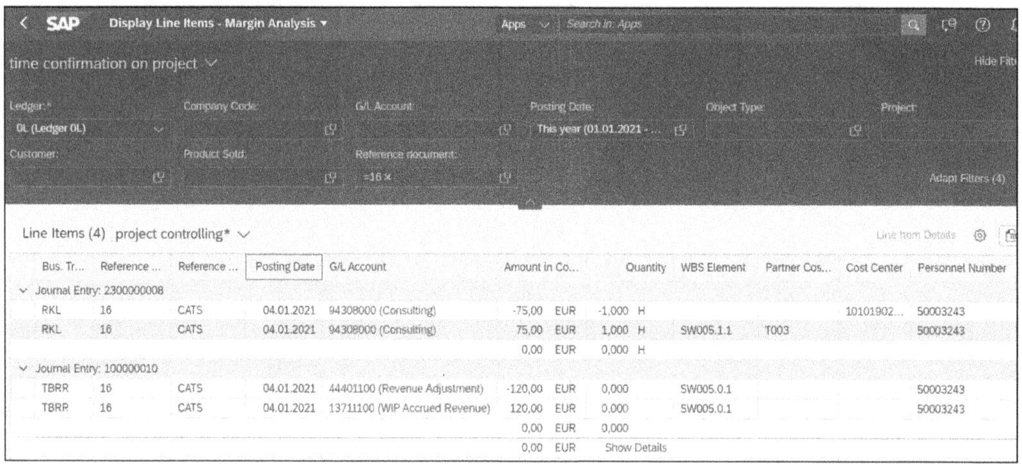


| Bus. Tr... | Reference ... | Reference ... | Posting Date | G/L Account | Amount in Co... | | Quantity | | WBS Element | Partner Cos... | Cost Center | Personnel Number |
|---|---|---|---|---|---|---|---|---|---|---|---|---|
| Journal Entry: 2300000008 | | | | | | | | | | | | |
| RKL | 16 | CATS | 04.01.2021 | 94308000 (Consulting) | -75,00 | EUR | -1,000 | H | | | 10101902... | 50003243 |
| RKL | 16 | CATS | 04.01.2021 | 94308000 (Consulting) | 75,00 | EUR | 1,000 | H | SW005.1.1 | T003 | | 50003243 |
| | | | | | 0,00 | EUR | 0,000 | H | | | | |
| Journal Entry: 100000010 | | | | | | | | | | | | |
| TBRR | 16 | CATS | 04.01.2021 | 44401100 (Revenue Adjustment) | -120,00 | EUR | 0,000 | | SW005.0.1 | | | 50003243 |
| TBRR | 16 | CATS | 04.01.2021 | 13711100 (WIP Accrued Revenue) | 120,00 | EUR | 0,000 | | SW005.0.1 | | | 50003243 |
| | | | | | 0,00 | EUR | 0,000 | | | | | |
| | | | | | 0,00 | EUR | Show Details | | | | | |

**Figure 7.79** Journal Entry Controlling View for Time Confirmation

You see two journal entries generated at the same time with the same reference document, **16** (column 2), and with the reference document type of **CATS** time sheet (column 3). In all the line items, you see information about the employee who rendered the time entry (**Personnel Number** column).

The first journal entry, **2300000008**, including two items, reflects the cost accounting posting for the time confirmation. It leads to a cost allocation between the cost center and project; we discussed this secondary controlling transaction already in Chapter 5, Section 5.2.2. It contains the following items:

- Item 1: The cost center of the employee is credited with 1 hour and 75 EUR costs.
- Item 2: The customer project is debited with the quantity of 1 hour and 75 EUR costs. The activity type **T003**, platinum consulting, is shown as a partner cost center activity type.

The second journal entry, **100000010**, is created by the event-based revenue recognition with its own business transaction type, **TBRR** (**Bus. Tr...** column). It contains the following line items:

- Item 3: The calculated recognized revenue is posted on the billing element by using the income statement **Revenue Adjustment** general ledger account.
- Item 4: Here the activation of accrued revenue or WIP is posted with reference to the billing element using the balance sheet **WIP Accrued Revenue** general ledger account.

With the **WBS Element** column, you can see that the cost accounting document and the revenue recognition document post on different WBS elements within the project. The time confirmation posts to the work package **SW005.1.1**, for which we planned the employee. The revenue recognition postings are account-assigned to the billing element **SW005.0.1**, to which the billed revenue is posted later in the process (refer back to Figure 7.73).



Now let's explain how you get the value of 120 EUR for the realized revenue. In this example, accounting principle IFRS is applied for ledger 0L (see Chapter 3, Section 3.3.1), so revenues are already recognized on a customer project with the confirmation. The method for calculating the realized revenue for this confirmation is defined by the contract type in the assigned sales order item; refer back to the derivation principle shown in Figure 7.73. In the sales order item 1, the time and expense billing **Contract Type** is assigned. In this case, the billable amount is defined by the expenses and time confirmations posted to the project and persisted in the Universal Journal. With the confirmation line item, the time and expense billing is simulated by the revenue recognition application. In this case, the provided service activity type of platinum consulting is mapped to a billing material. For this billing material, a sales price is defined; in this case, a sales price of 120 EUR per hour. Because one hour was recorded, the result is a billable amount of 120 EUR. This value is posted as recognized revenue. This ensures the recognized revenue is equal to the later posted billing amount.

As mentioned, not only the project margin can be analyzed, but also the market segment margin. Let's look again at these documents, but this time we'll use a view that defines user-specific margin analysis fields, as shown in Figure 7.80.

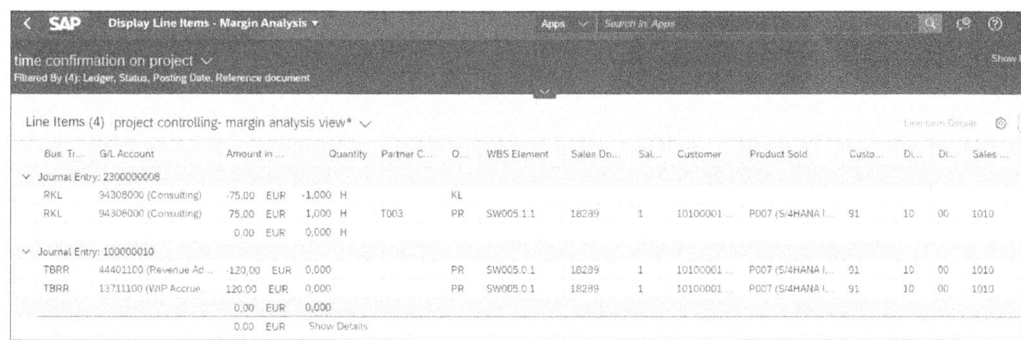


**Figure 7.80** Journal Entries with Margin Analysis Fields for Time Confirmation

Note that for the line items account-assigned to the **WBS Element**, you derive the market segment fields. This is valid for the revenue recognition postings too. With the logic explained previously and shown back in Figure 7.73, you can derive a sales order item: the **Sales Document** and **Sales Document Item** shown in the columns next to the billing element. To determine which is the real account assignment, we use the **O...** column (object type, left of the WBS element). The **PR** entry defines the project as a real account assignment. The sales order is attributed and only for additional information. With the sales order item, you get the **Customer**, the **Product Sold**, the **Industry**, the **Distribution Channel**, the **Division**, and the **Sales Organization**.

*Travel Expenses*

With the next business transaction, you post travel expenses for the project. In this scenario, the travel costs of an employee have been recorded on the employee's cost center and are now transferred from there to the project, as they were incurred as part of the project and can be billed to the customer. We'll do two postings for different employees to both of the work packages.

**Postings**

The posting to the project in this example looks like the postings from SAP Concur or an external interface. There as well, you first post to the employee's cost center and from there transfer the costs to the account assignment entered by the employee in the travel recording.

Start the Reassign Costs and Revenues app (SAP Fiori ID F2009), which is assigned to the `OVERHEAD_ACCOUNTANT` role, and click the **Create** button. You'll arrive at the entry screen shown in Figure 7.81.

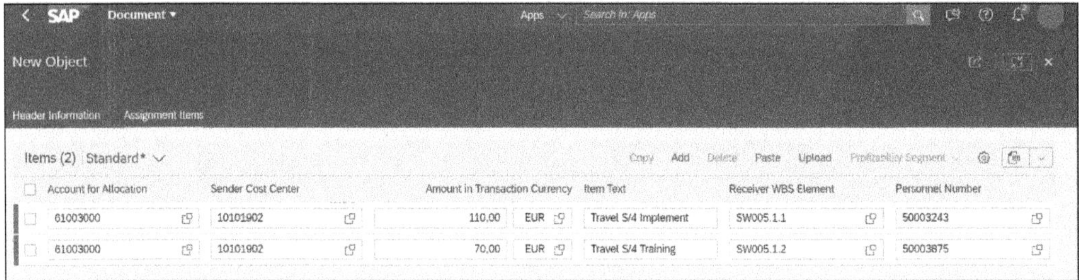


**Figure 7.81** Enter Reassignment of Travel Costs

Enter the general ledger account ("61003000" in this example) in the **Account for Allocation** field, which we will repost. Enter the sending employee's cost center in the **Sender Cost Center** column (**10101902**) and the **Receiver WBS Element**. You also can add the **Personnel Number** and **Item Text**. Both pieces of information will be stored in the journal entry and available in the customer billing.

After you click the **Create** button, the journal entries are created, as shown in Figure 7.82.

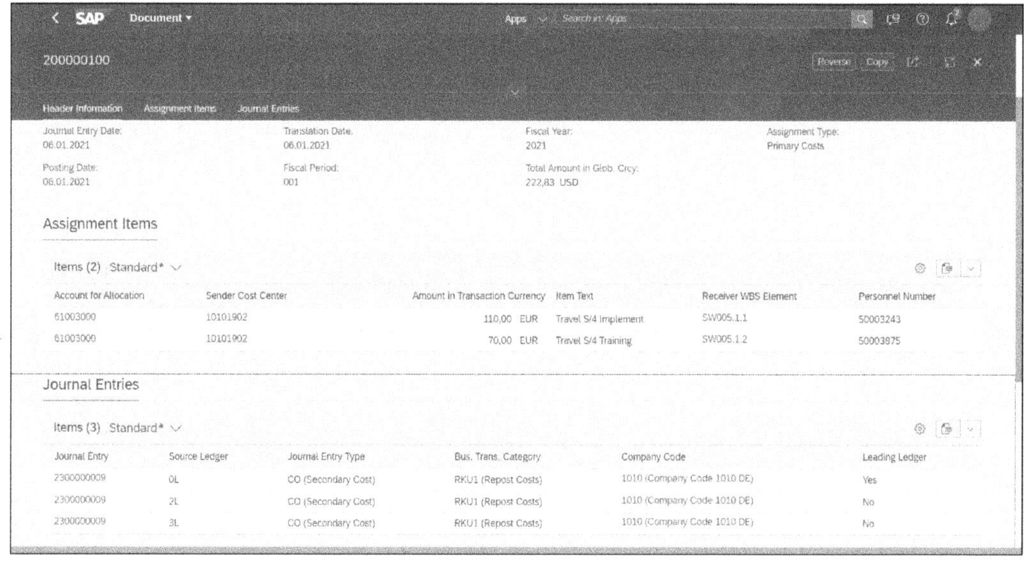

**Figure 7.82** Overview for Created Postings per Ledger for Reassignment of Travel Costs

At the bottom, you get the information about the created journal entries. For each active ledger, you get one journal entry. The reposting is handled as a prima nota and thus is relevant for every ledger.

Now let's look at the posting of ledger 0L, which is the leading ledger (see Chapter 3, Section 3.3.1), in the Display Line Items—Margin Analysis app, as shown in Figure 7.83.

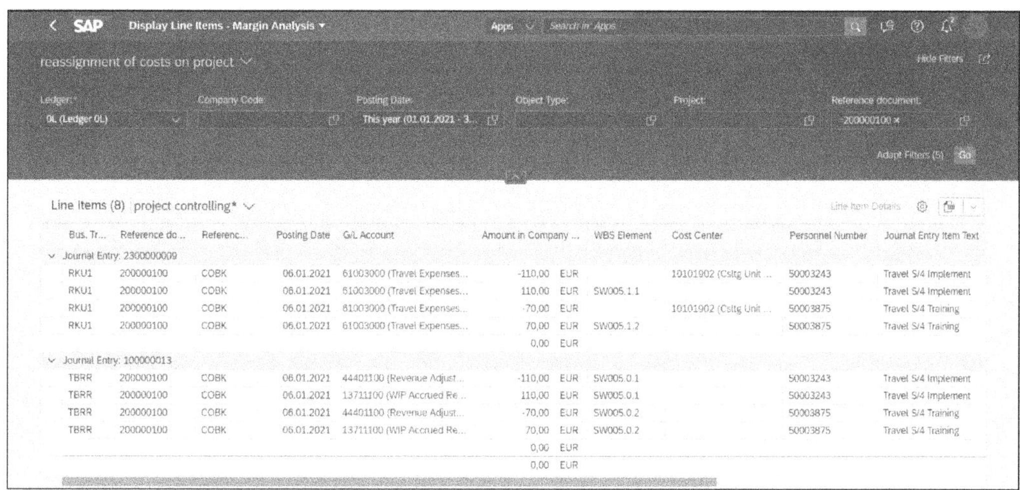

**Figure 7.83** Journal Entries with Controlling View for Reassignment of Travel Costs

Like for the time posting, in addition to the cost posting, the event-based revenue recognition document is created. Both documents have the same reference document (second column). In the upper cost posting, you see the cost center credited and the two WBS elements debited. The **Personnel Numbers** and the **Item Text** entered in the Reassign Costs and Revenues app are stored in the line item as information.

As for the time confirmation, you get the realized revenue calculated by simulating time and material billing and reading sales prices. In this example, it's defined in the sales pricing that travel expenses are billed at the cost value.

Now let's look at the provided market segment information in these postings. Switch again to the user-specific **project controlling—margin analysis view** to arrive at the screen shown in Figure 7.84.

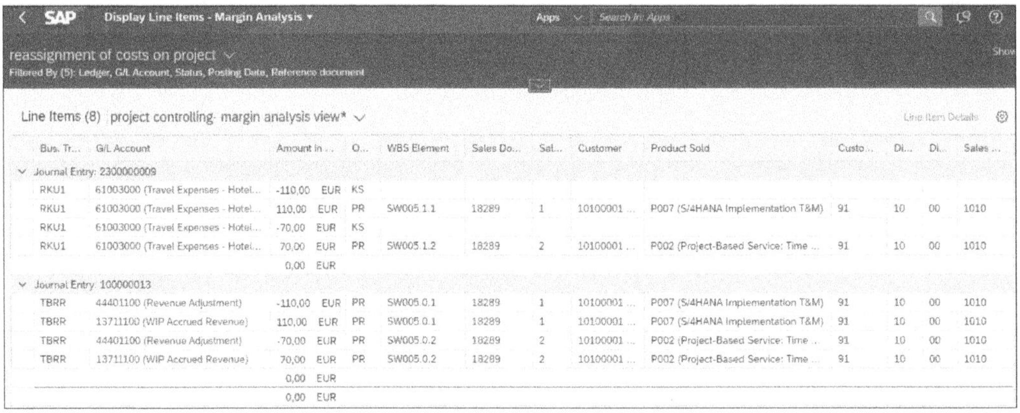

**Figure 7.84** Journal Entries with Margin Analysis Fields for Reassignment of Travel Costs

Like for the time confirmation postings, you derive the market segment fields for all the journal entry items that are account-assigned to the **WBS Element**. Because you're posting in this example to both work packages, you derive **Sales Document Item 1** and **2**. Then you get the two different products sold from the sales order items derived: **P007** and **P002**. **Customer**, **Industry**, **Distribution Channel**, **Division**, and **Sales Organization** are all derived and equal.

There are now two cost postings on the project, plus the matching realized revenues. For all of these postings, the market segment fields are applied. Let's look at the margin reporting. Start the Product and Service Margins app (SAP Fiori ID W0164), select projects in company code **1010**, and click **Go** to arrive at the screen shown in Figure 7.85.

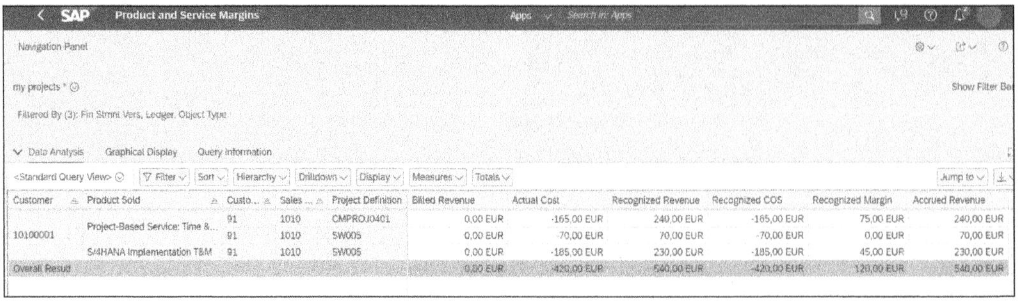

**Figure 7.85** Margin Analysis after Cost Postings, Including Event-Based Revenue Recognition

With the cost postings, in this example, we realized a margin of 45 EUR for project **SW005**, customer **1010001**, industry **91**, and the SAP S/4HANA implementation product. In the far right column, you can see the **Accrued Revenue** for the project: 70 EUR plus 230 EUR.

You can also see an aggregated amount of accrued revenue (for a service provided but not yet billed) for customer **10100001** in company code **1010** of 540 EUR.

*Customer Project Billing*

Now let's execute the customer project billing. We'll bill the consultant's time confirmation and the travel expenses we posted before.

The billing document is created by the resource-related billing method. This means that billing proposals are created based on the expenses and time confirmations posted to the project and persisted in the Universal Journal. As mentioned before, billing materials are determined for the different activity types, such as senior consulting or platinum consulting. For the derived billing material, prices, which are also project-specific, can then be defined.

Within the `SAP_BR_PROJ_Manage_COMM` business role, the project manager gets the billing items that are due in the Release Billing Proposals app (SAP Fiori ID F0780). Start the app to see an overview of all items posted to your projects and that are due, as shown in Figure 7.86.

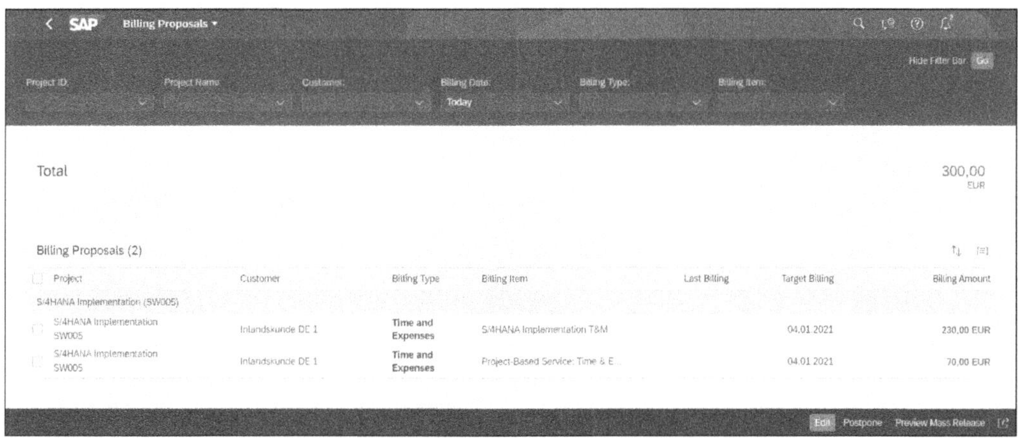


**Figure 7.86** Billing Proposals App: Overview of Items Due

Here you can select the items you want to bill. Mark the first one and select the **Edit** button in the lower right. On the next screen, shown in Figure 7.87, you'll see the single confirmation items, as shown previously in the journal entries in Figure 7.84 and Figure 7.79.

In Figure 7.87, you can see in the leftmost column that all billing item proposals are based on the journal entries posted before.

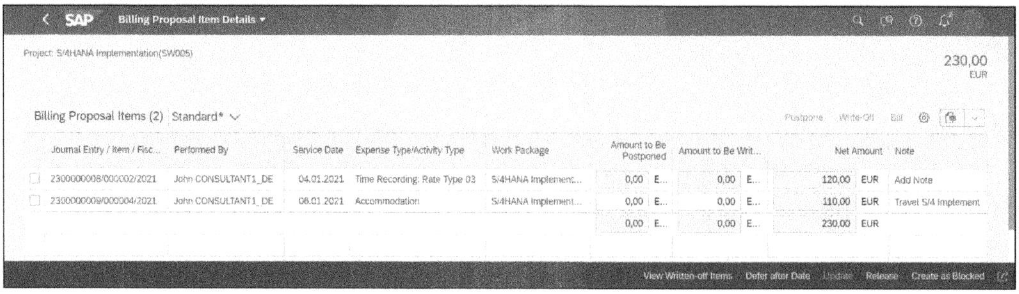

Figure 7.87 Billing Proposal Items: Detail View

In the first item, the time confirmation for the consultant is reflected, and the expense posting in the second line. The calculated **Net Amount** for both items is 230 EUR. You see here still the information about the employee who rendered the time confirmation, **John Consultant1_D**, and the travel expense and the note taken from the journal entry item text. You can include both pieces of information in the invoice that you'll send to the customer.

Select both items and click the **Release** button, and the debit memo request will be created.

Within the SAP_BR_Billing_Clerk business role, the subsequent billing processes can be performed in the Create Billing Documents app (Fiori ID F0798), as shown in Figure 7.88.

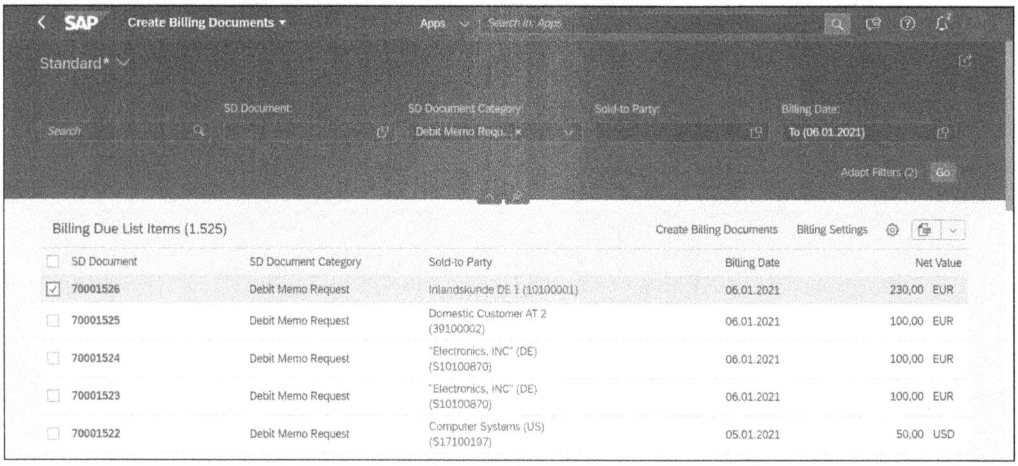

Figure 7.88 Create Billing Documents App

Start the app, select **SD Document Category** (**Debit Memo Request**), and click **Go** to see all the open debit memo requests.

Mark the line with the debit memo request created previously, **70001526**, and click the **Create Billing Documents** button. On the next screen, shown in Figure 7.89, you'll see the billing document preview.

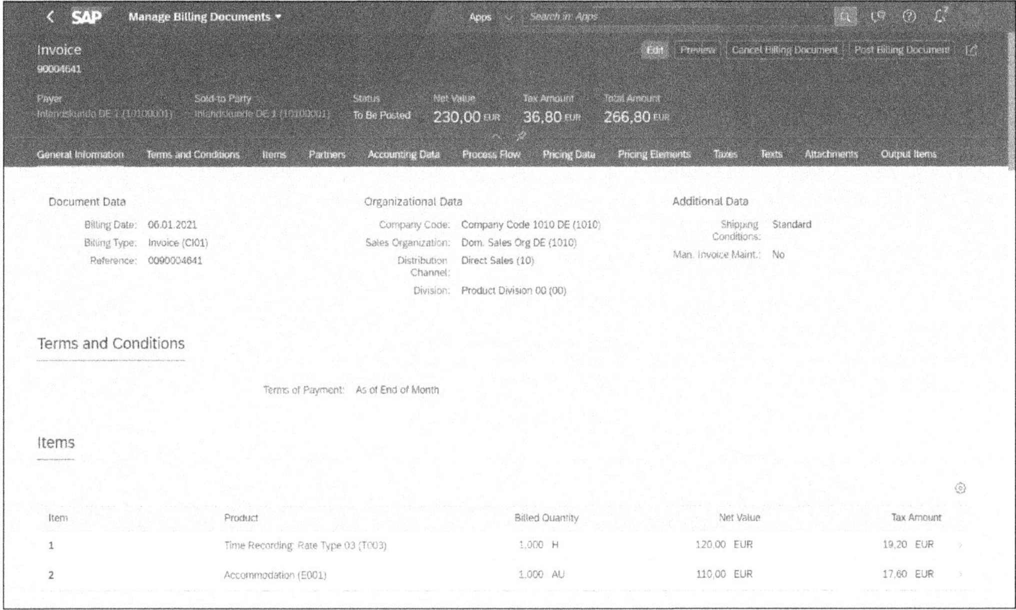


**Figure 7.89** Billing Document

We see one billing item for one hour of consulting with a net value of 120 EUR and a second item for the travel expenses with the net value of 110 EUR. After clicking the **Post Billing Document** button, you'll see a billing document and its related accounting documents created.

Analyze the created journal entries again with the Display Line Items—Margin Analysis app and filter on the reference document number **90004641** of the billing document. You'll see the view shown in Figure 7.90.

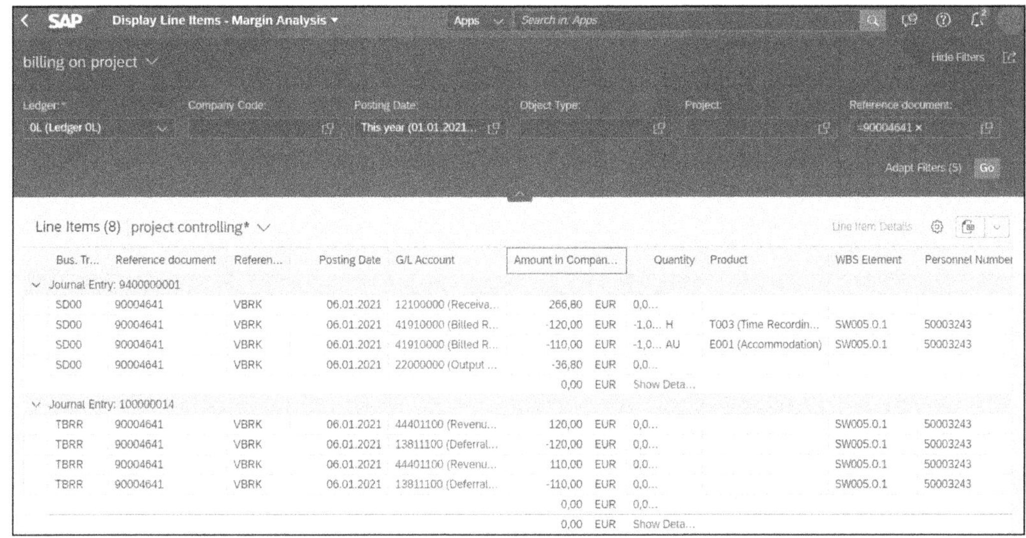


**Figure 7.90** Journal Entries for Project Billing

Like for the cost postings, with the journal entry for the billing element an event-based revenue recognition document is created. Both journal entries have the same reference to the billing document (second and third column).

The first journal entry reflects the billing element. The second and third items are the billed revenue lines posted on the project. You see different billing products, **T003** and **E001**, used, so you can distinguish what's billed on the project. And there is additional information provided about the employee who rendered the service and time, which allows you to drill down into the billed revenue by employee.

The second journal entry, **100000014**, is the matching revenue recognition document. The first two line items are referenced to the billing of time. The first line item is the debit of the realized revenue, posted on the billing element. The second line item posts on the deferral of revenues balance sheet account. The same posting logic is applied for the expense billing. In this example, the IFRS accounting principle is applied, so revenues are recognized already. With the time confirmation and the expense posting, the billed revenues need to be deferred.

Let's derive the market segment fields for the billing line items, too. This isn't visible in this view, but we'll examine it in the next section. Like for the cost postings, you'll derive the sales document and item. Subsequently, you'll see the additional market segment attributes, like product sold, customer, industry, country, distribution channel, division, and sales organization.

#### Entering Manual Accruals

There aren't a lot of period-end closing activities in this scenario. For example, as mentioned, there's no settlement needed. The only activity you need to perform is the period-end run for event-based revenue recognition. There can be several reasons that a periodic reassessment should be performed (see Section 7.5). In this scenario, the periodic run needs to clear the balances on the deferred (posted with the revenue) and accrued (posted with the costs) revenues.

With the Event-Based Revenue Recognition—Projects app, you can analyze the revenue recognition data, perform this balance sheet clearing, and create manual accruals for the project. Let's look at the use case of manual accruals in the system. Assume that you know that the customer will get a 5% volume discount in the final billing for the billing amount resulting from the time confirmation. You need to take this into account at the period-end close. With an already realized revenue amount of 120 EUR for the provided service, this is 6 EUR for the project. The revenue already realized is reduced by this amount, and a provision for expected revenue reduction is recognized in the balance sheet.

Go ahead and start the app. In the selection screen, shown in Figure 7.91, you need to define the **Display Currency**, the **Company Code** (here, **1010**), the **To Fiscal Year Period** (here, **001.2021**), and the **Ledger**. The **To Fiscal Year Period** field defines the period for which you want to adjust the revenue recognition data. Only journal entries posted until this period are selected in the following steps. The **Ledger** allows the separate valuation for different ledgers and thus accounting principles if applicable.

Further restrict the selection to the WBS **Billing Element**. After you click the **Go** button, you'll see the two billing elements.

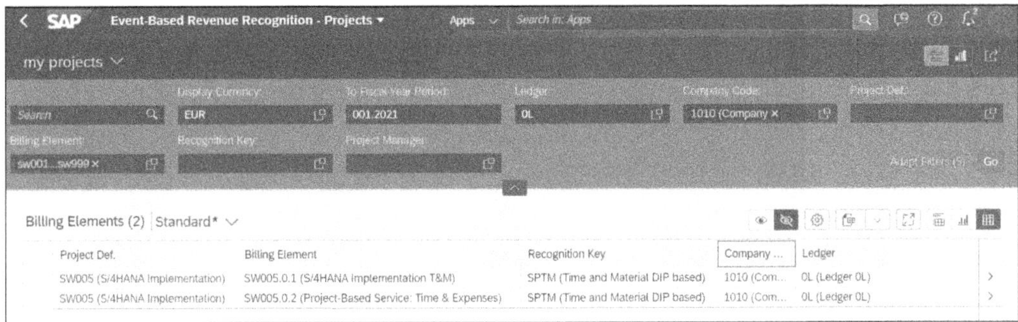


**Figure 7.91** Event-Based Revenue Recognition App: List of WBS Billing Elements

Select the first billing element for further activities. Click the arrow at the far right of this line item to see the details for this billing element (see Figure 7.92).

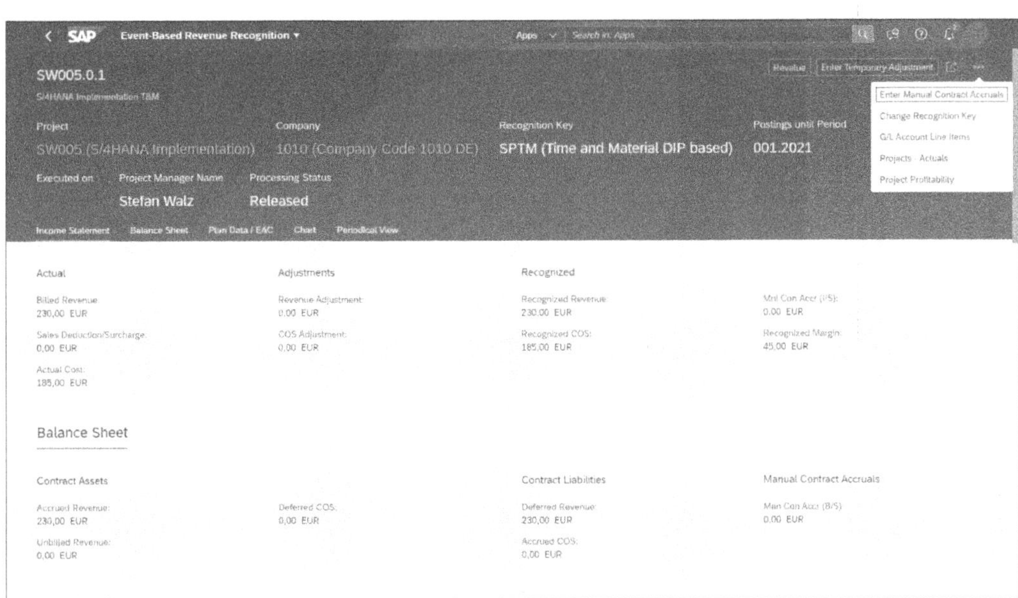


**Figure 7.92** Event-Based Revenue Recognition App: Details View

In the header of the detail screen, you can see the selected project billing element (**S/4HANA Implementation**), the assigned project manager, information about recognized **Postings until Period**, and the revenue recognition key, which defines the revenue recognition method. At the top right are links you can use to initiate follow-up activities. Under the icon showing three dots, you can find additional activities, as shown.

In the upper section, you can analyze the **Income Statement** information, which was created by the business activities in the sections before:

- The billed revenue of 230 EUR is the billed service and the expenses in the step before.
- The actual cost of 185 EUR is created by the time confirmation and travel expense posting.
- The recognized revenue of 230 EUR is the realized revenue of the revenue recognition for expense posting and service confirmation.
- The realized revenue minus margin leads to the recognized margin of 45 EUR.

In the lower section, you can see the **Balance Sheet** values:

- The accrued revenues of 230 EUR are created by the cost postings.
- The deferred revenues of 230 EUR are posted by the billing.
- At period end, both values will be cleared with each other. You can do this by clicking the **Revalue** button.

Now you can select the **Enter Manual Contract Accruals** activity at the top right, arriving at the screen shown in Figure 7.93.

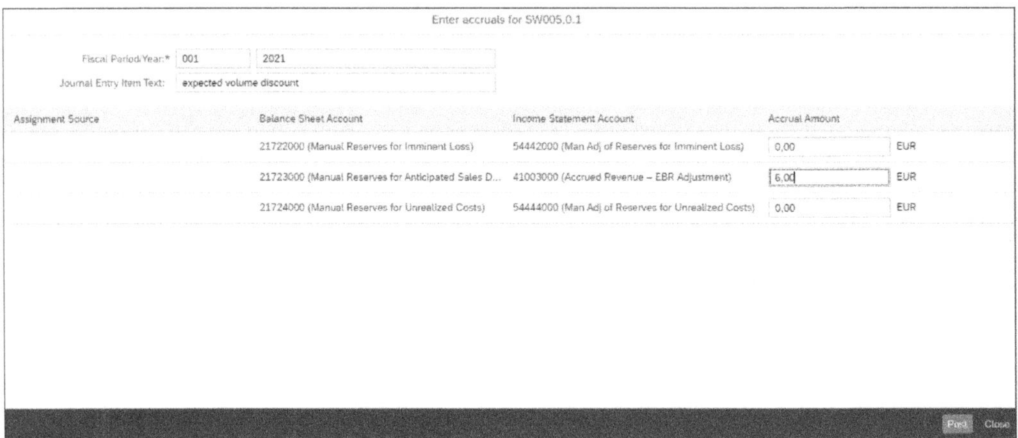


**Figure 7.93** Entering Manual Accruals

Enter a manual accrual entry for the current period, 001/2021. To allow simplified tracking and classifying of the accruals, add a note, "expected volume discount", which will be transferred in the **Journal Entry Item Text**. In Customizing, you can predefine general ledger account pairs for the balance sheet and income statement. Add 6 EUR in one line for one general ledger account pair and click the **Post** button.

A revenue recognition document is created, but before we analyze it, let's come back to the revenue recognition detail screen shown in Figure 7.94.

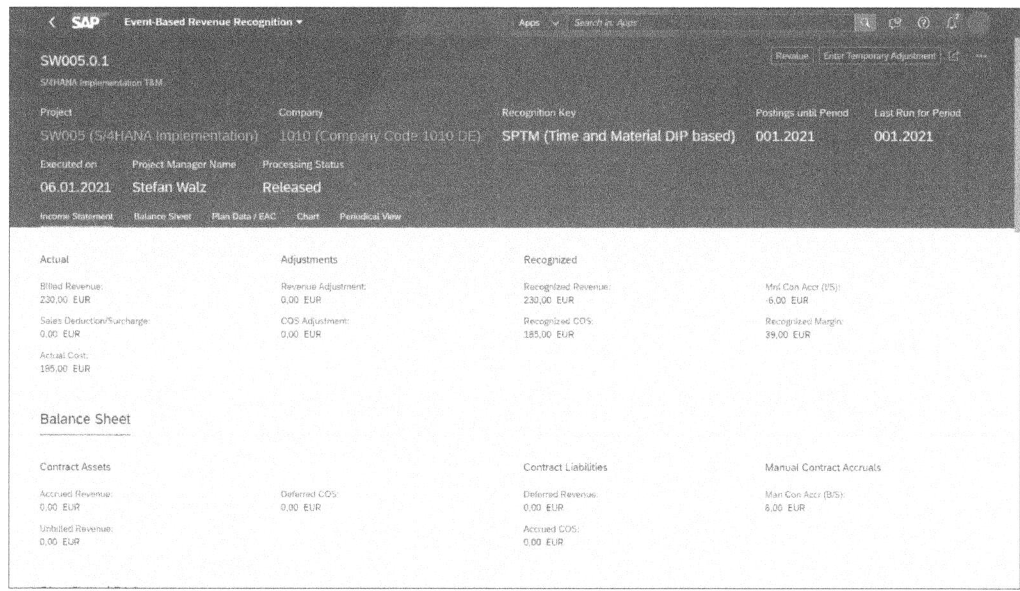

**Figure 7.94** Revenue Recognition Detail View after Balance Sheet Netting and Entering Accruals

You see in the **Income Statement** section a manual accrued revenue adjustment of -6 EUR, which reduces the margin from 45 EUR to 39 EUR. In the **Balance Sheet** section, you see the manual accrual of 6 EUR. This value stays until you complete the project or you change the accrual manual. Also note that the accrued and deferred revenue was cleared with the revalue activity.

Now, let's analyze the journal entry of the manual accrual, as shown in Figure 7.95.

Line Items (2) project controlling*

| Bus. Tr... | Posting D... | G/L Account | Amount in C... | | O... | WBS Element | Journal Entry Item Text | Sales... | Sal... | Customer | Product Sold | Custo... |
|---|---|---|---|---|---|---|---|---|---|---|---|---|
| Journal Entry: 100000015 | | | | | | | | | | | | |
| TBRR | 31.01.2021 | 21723000 (Manual Reserves for Anticipated Sales Deductio... | -6,00 | EUR | PR | SW005.0.1 | expected volume discount | 18289 | 1 | 10100001 ... | P007 (S/4HA... | 91 |
| TBRR | 31.01.2021 | 41003000 (Accrued Revenue – EBR Adjustment) | 6,00 | EUR | PR | SW005.0.1 | expected volume discount | 18289 | 1 | 10100001 ... | P007 (S/4HA... | 91 |
| | | | 0,00 | EUR | | | | | | | | |
| | | | 0,00 | EUR | | | | | | | | |

**Figure 7.95** Journal Entry for Manual Accruals

You can see two line items posted on the general ledger accounts selected in the screen shown previously in Figure 7.93. With the second line, the realized revenue is decreased by 6 EUR and, with the same amount, reserves for anticipated sales deductions are built in line one. The note entered previously is persisted in the **Journal Entry Item Text**. The **Posting Date** is the end of period date.

Both line items are account-assigned to the **SW005.0.1** project billing element. This means that the same profitability attributes are derived as for the business transactions posted before. For example, on the right you see the **Sales Order** and **Item**, and then the derived **Customer**, **Product Sold**, and **Industry**.

## Reporting

Now that we've posted some accounting documents based on project-related business transactions, let's look at how this is reflected in margin analysis and accounting reporting. Start the Product and Service Margins app again and select the project, arriving at the view shown in Figure 7.96.

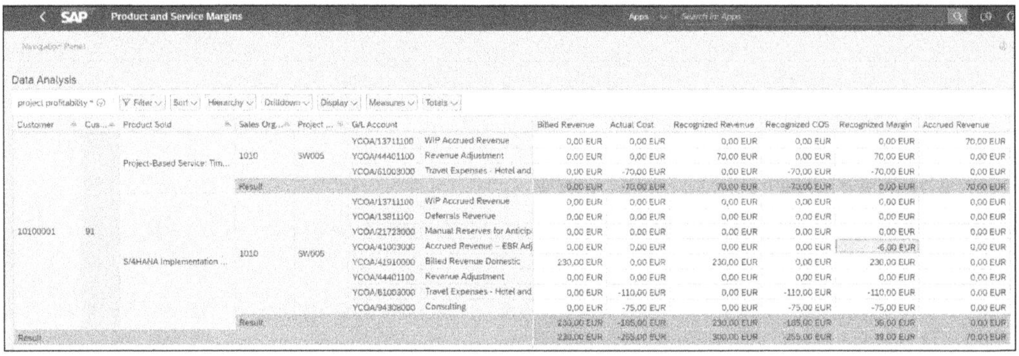

| Customer | Cus... | Product Sold | Sales Org... | Project ... | G/L Account | | Billed Revenue | Actual Cost | Recognized Revenue | Recognized COS | Recognized Margin | Accrued Revenue |
|---|---|---|---|---|---|---|---|---|---|---|---|---|
| 10100001 | 91 | Project-Based Service: Tim... | 1010 | SW005 | YCOA/13711100 | WIP Accrued Revenue | 0,00 EUR | 0,00 EUR | 0,00 EUR | 0,00 EUR | 0,00 EUR | 70,00 EUR |
| | | | | | YCOA/44401100 | Revenue Adjustment | 0,00 EUR | 0,00 EUR | 70,00 EUR | 0,00 EUR | 70,00 EUR | 0,00 EUR |
| | | | | | YCOA/61003000 | Travel Expenses - Hotel and | 0,00 EUR | -70,00 EUR | 0,00 EUR | -70,00 EUR | -70,00 EUR | 0,00 EUR |
| | | | Result | | | | 0,00 EUR | -70,00 EUR | 70,00 EUR | -70,00 EUR | 0,00 EUR | 70,00 EUR |
| | | S/4HANA Implementation ... | 1010 | SW005 | YCOA/13711100 | WIP Accrued Revenue | 0,00 EUR | 0,00 EUR | 0,00 EUR | 0,00 EUR | 0,00 EUR | 0,00 EUR |
| | | | | | YCOA/13811100 | Deferrals Revenue | 0,00 EUR | 0,00 EUR | 0,00 EUR | 0,00 EUR | 0,00 EUR | 0,00 EUR |
| | | | | | YCOA/21723000 | Manual Reserves for Anticip | 0,00 EUR | 0,00 EUR | 0,00 EUR | 0,00 EUR | 0,00 EUR | 0,00 EUR |
| | | | | | YCOA/41003000 | Accrued Revenue – EBR Adj | 0,00 EUR | 0,00 EUR | 0,00 EUR | 0,00 EUR | -6,00 EUR | 0,00 EUR |
| | | | | | YCOA/41910000 | Billed Revenue Domestic | 230,00 EUR | 0,00 EUR | 230,00 EUR | 0,00 EUR | 230,00 EUR | 0,00 EUR |
| | | | | | YCOA/44401100 | Revenue Adjustment | 0,00 EUR | 0,00 EUR | 0,00 EUR | 0,00 EUR | 0,00 EUR | 0,00 EUR |
| | | | | | YCOA/61003000 | Travel Expenses - Hotel and | 0,00 EUR | -110,00 EUR | 0,00 EUR | -110,00 EUR | -110,00 EUR | 0,00 EUR |
| | | | | | YCOA/94308000 | Consulting | 0,00 EUR | -75,00 EUR | 0,00 EUR | -75,00 EUR | -75,00 EUR | 0,00 EUR |
| | | | Result | | | | 230,00 EUR | -185,00 EUR | 230,00 EUR | -185,00 EUR | 36,00 EUR | 0,00 EUR |
| Result | | | | | | | 230,00 EUR | -255,00 EUR | 300,00 EUR | -255,00 EUR | 39,00 EUR | 70,00 EUR |

**Figure 7.96** Reporting for Project, Including Manual Accruals

You can see here the result of all the postings. You see that all postings include the margin analysis fields—even the manual accruals. The -6 EUR of the accruals, highlighted in the figure, reduces the margin.

Because the reporting is on single line items and we provide many fields for the postings in this scenario in the journal entries of the business transactions, there are several views made available by selecting specific fields. Here are some examples:

- Nonbillable confirmations per project, customer, or employee.
- Overtime spend on projects, by employee, for customer.
- Realized revenue and margin per supporting profit center. With this you can report what profit center provided the service, which can be different from the responsible profit center assigned in the WBS billing element. For more on this, visit *http://s-prs.co/v528207*.
- Realized revenue and margin per employee.

For the last example, let's look at a report based on the example scenario, as shown in Figure 7.97.

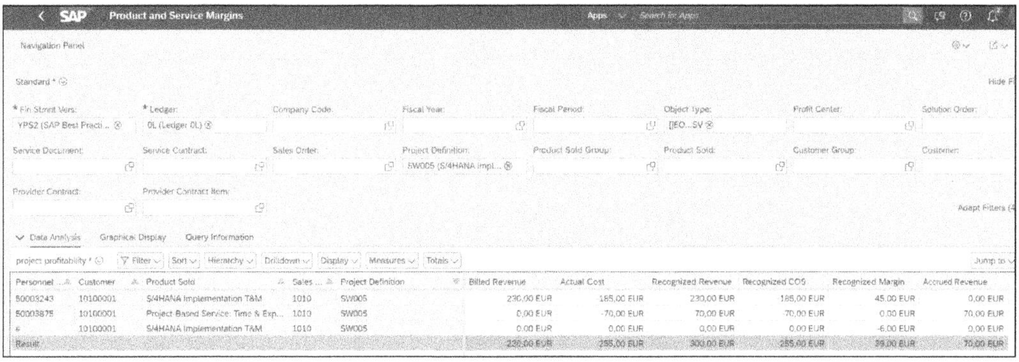

**Figure 7.97** Reporting Realized Revenue and Margin per Employee

With the time confirmation, the employee information is available in the cost journal entry item. In this scenario, we work with time and material billing. This allows us to update the employee information in the realized revenue line item of revenue recognition and in the billing line items. Only the manual accrual in the last line is without employee information. And there are of course several values added for the accountant.

Let's look at new reporting insights for the accountant. Start the Trial Balance app for company code 1010, then select the WBS element and the customer as additional attributes to reach the view shown in Figure 7.98.

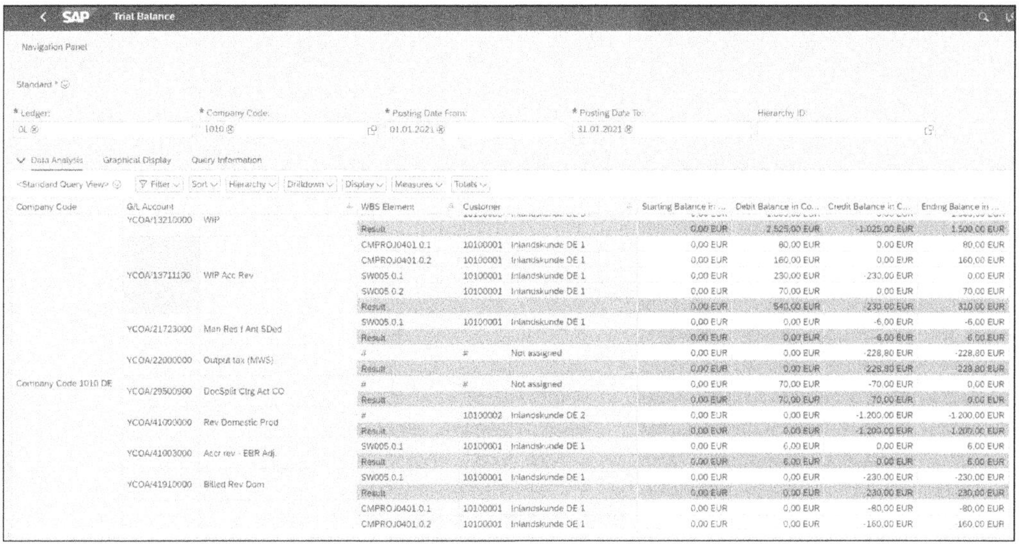

**Figure 7.98** Trial Balance App: Drilldown

It's now possible to assign the complete amounts of the balance sheet accounts' WIP/accrued revenue and manual accruals to a WBS element and customer. You can do the same for the P&L accounts' domestic billed revenues. This heavily increases the reporting insights and simplifies the tracing and auditing.

**Reporting on Journal Entry Items**

These examples demonstrate that there are entirely new reporting insights made possible through the integration of revenue recognition and profitability in the Universal Journal. Thanks to the SAP HANA database, aggregated reporting, and even trial balance reporting, is always based on single journal entry items. In principle, this allows for aggregated reporting on all Universal Journal fields.

### 7.3.2 Project-Based Sales Scenario

Now let's look at a customer project scenario that, in contrast to the professional service scenario shown before, is more determined by the delivery and sales of physical goods. This scenario includes logistic business processes such as sales from stock, delivery of free of charge items, returns, and project account–assigned procurement. In short, it covers the *engineer-to-order* scenario.

In this business scenario, a WBS element is assigned to sales order items to capture the costs and revenues of the logistical processes of a sales order. As a consequence, the outbound deliveries post cost of goods sold on the project. Delivery-based and sales order–based customer invoices and credit and debit notes post revenues on the project. There exists an option to assign several sales order items to one WBS billing element. In addition, direct costs can also be booked on this project with other transactions, such as time sheet, activity allocation, supplier invoice, goods receipt to supplier invoice, settlement from other projects or orders, post general journal entry, or goods issue from stock. Overhead surcharges can also be posted on the project. There should be a manual project planning entered, which allows for project controlling by a plan/actual comparison and revenue recognition based on PoC methods.

To achieve this simple processing and the extended reporting options, as in the professional services scenario, a few things must be taken into account during setup, which we'll discuss first in this section.

A difference from the professional service scenario is that we can't restrict to a 1:1 relation between the WBS billing element and the sales order. There will be multiple sales order items assigned. There are two options in place:

- The first solution is the determination of a leading sales order item, which is base for the market segment. This solution is currently only available in SAP S/4HANA Cloud.
- The second solution is the definition of the market segment in the settlement rule.

We'll show both, starting with the cloud solution. Then we'll go over manual planning based on the table ACDOCP database before we look at the logistic and controlling business transactions. We're using event-based revenue recognition again, so settlement as a period-end activity isn't necessary. In this scenario, however, from the margin analysis perspective, a realignment of the market segment fields in the Universal Journal may be necessary, as we'll discuss. Finally, we'll examine the reporting insights.

### Master Data Setup

Let's start with an example in a system with two customer order items, as shown in Figure 7.99. Sales order item 20 is representing a product that we deliver to the customer. Sales order item 10 is a service position for customer-specific requirements and onsite installation. The customer will only be billed for the service item that includes the total value of the contract.

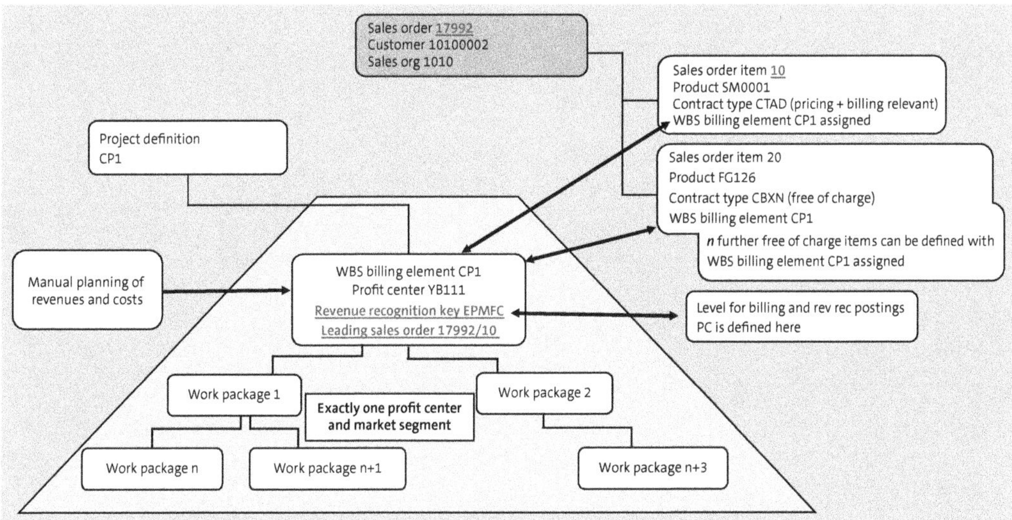


**Figure 7.99** Sales Order and Project Setup in Project-Based Sales Scenario with Leading Sales Order

As with the professional service scenario, there must be only one profit center for the WBS billing element and all multilevel assigned work packages. Also, there is only one revenue recognition key and one profitability segment. Only with this prerequisite can revenue recognition postings be automatically deducted for the cost postings and the market segments derived and updated in the journal entry.

Unlike the professional service scenario, several sales order positions can be assigned here. To be able to determine the market segment and the product sold, which are different for the two sales order items, you need to define a leading sales order. In this example, sales order item 10 is chosen by the system, the one that is relevant for pricing and billing and which is therefore also relevant for revenue recognition and derives a revenue recognition key that is stored in the project master.

**Note**

If there are multiple pricing- and billing-relevant sales order items assigned, the leading sales order can't be determined. In that case, you're in the second scenario, mentioned earlier, with the settlement rule. We'll look at that scenario in more detail at the end of this section.

Now let's look at this scenario in the system. First create the project with the Project Control app (SAP Fiori ID F3215) or with one of the SAP GUI transactions mentioned in Chapter 4 (see Figure 7.100).

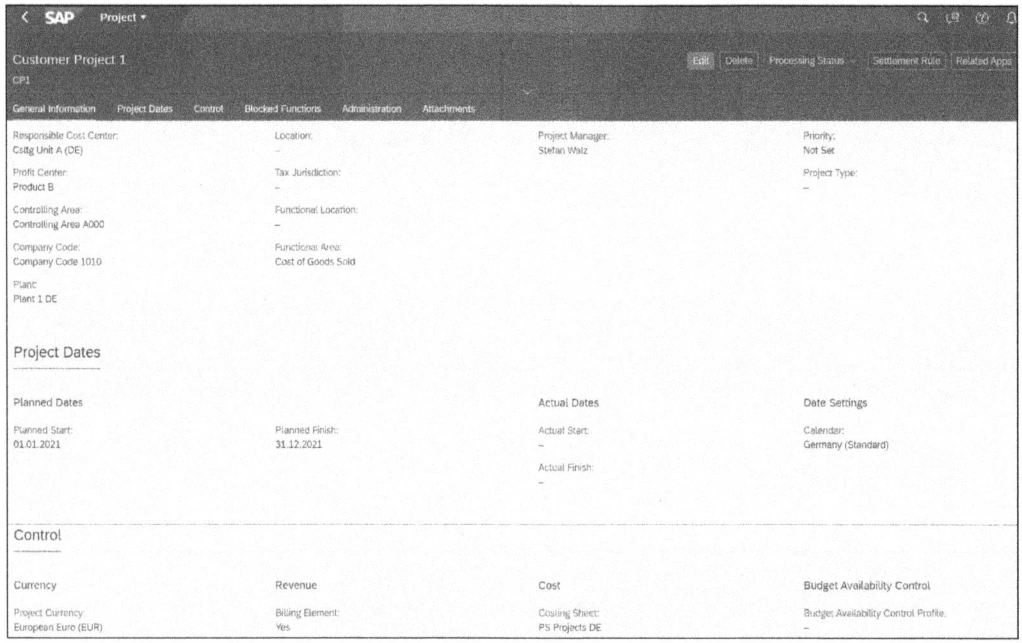


**Figure 7.100** Customer Project Master

You need just one WBS element, **CP1** (customer project 1), shown at the top of the screen, which is a **Billing Element**. Because you'll be selling to a customer, the **Functional Area** is defined with **Cost of Goods Sold**. And you want to calculate overhead, so you'll apply a **Costing Sheet**. The **Profit Center** is defined with **Product B**, ID YB111.

To follow the example in Figure 7.99, create in the next step a sales order with Transaction VA01 using order type OR and sales organization 1010, distribution channel 10, and division 00. Let's analyze it with Transaction VA02, as shown in Figure 7.101.

Here we've added two sales order items. The first item is the service item, product **SM001**, with a billing net value of 1,200 EUR. The second item is a delivery item, **FG126**, which is free of charge, with a billing net amount of zero. You see in the two right columns the assigned **WBS Element CP1** and **Profit Center**, derived from the WBS billing element.

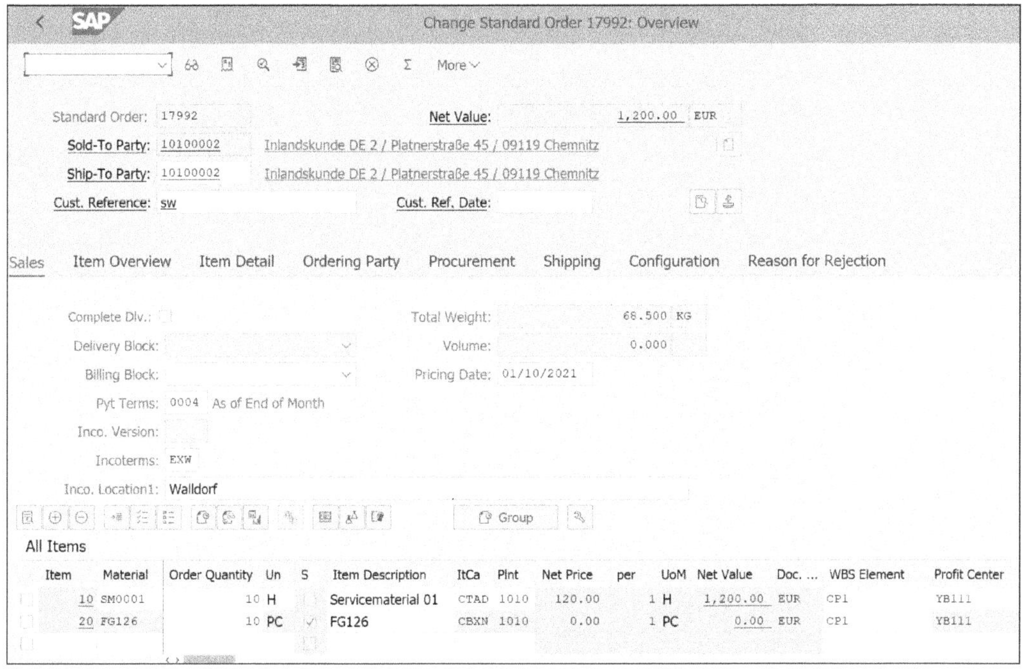


**Figure 7.101** Sales Order Master with WBS Element Assignment

## Project Planning

Now let's do the project planning. As before, use table ACDOCP and update the plan data with a file upload. An additional option could be to define the project plan in SAP Analytics Cloud and transfer it to SAP S/4HANA in table ACDOCP (see Chapter 2).

In the Import Financial Plan Data app, you can download a template for project planning. The template is shown in Figure 7.102.

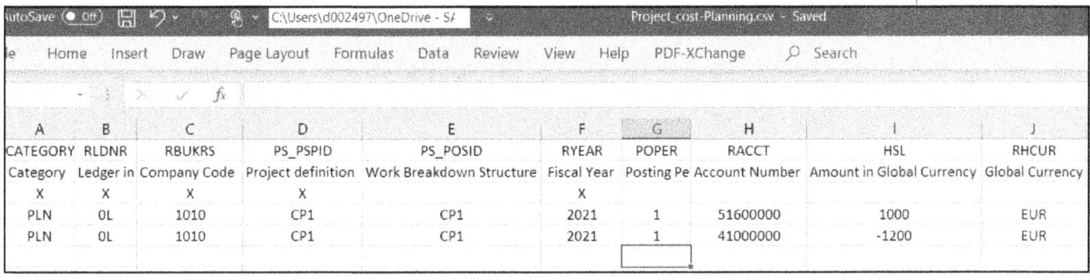

| A | B | C | D | E | F | G | H | I | J |
|---|---|---|---|---|---|---|---|---|---|
| CATEGORY | RLDNR | RBUKRS | PS_PSPID | PS_POSID | RYEAR | POPER | RACCT | HSL | RHCUR |
| Category | Ledger in | Company Code | Project definition | Work Breakdown Structure | Fiscal Year | Posting Pe | Account Number | Amount in Global Currency | Global Currency |
| X | X | X | X | | X | | | | |
| PLN | 0L | 1010 | CP1 | CP1 | 2021 | 1 | 51600000 | 1000 | EUR |
| PLN | 0L | 1010 | CP1 | CP1 | 2021 | 1 | 41000000 | -1200 | EUR |

**Figure 7.102** CSV File with Financial Project Plan Data

Enter two lines: one for revenues with general ledger account **41000000** and one for costs with general ledger account **51600000**. Use plan category **PLN**. This category is determined in revenue recognition for PoC calculation. Note that the line with the **X** entries at the top of the planning lines is very important. The **X** defines per column which data is replaced in table ACDOCA. If you don't add the **X** to the project column here, you'd delete all plan data with plan category **PLN** and ledger **0L** in company code 1010 for 2021—independent of the cost object to which it's assigned.

Save the *Project_cost-Planning.csv* file and start the Import Financial Plan Data app, as shown in Figure 7.103.

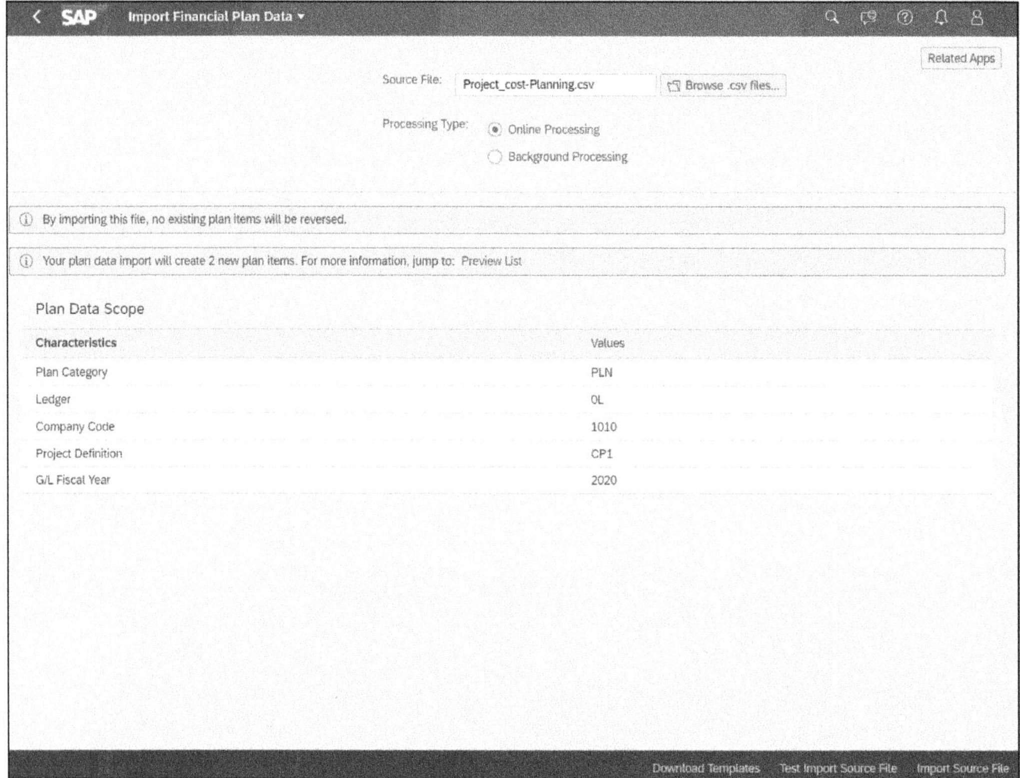


**Figure 7.103** App for Importing Financial Plan Data

Click the **Browse .csv files...** button and select the file. After you select the file, you're notified if the upload would reverse already existing plan data. In this example, you're informed that two new plan items will be created.

Click the **Import Source File** button and get the success message shown in Figure 7.104.

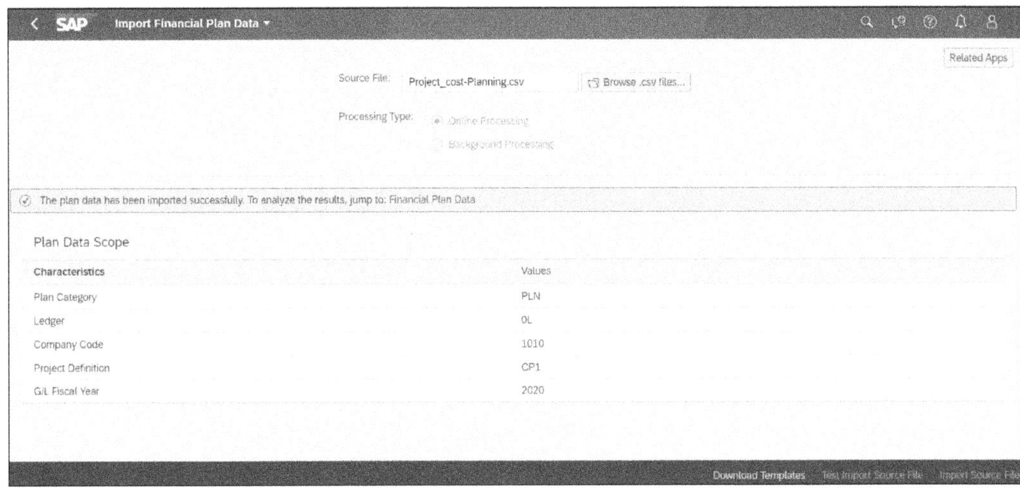


**Figure 7.104** Import of Plan Data Successful

Now let's analyze the project plan data with the Projects Plan/Actual app (SAP Fiori ID F0936A), as shown in Figure 7.105.

Project Plan Actual

| Customer | Product Sold | Product Sold | WBS Element | WBS Element | G/L Account | G/L Account | Plan Amount in CC Crcy |
|---|---|---|---|---|---|---|---|
| 10100002 | SM0001 | Service Material 01 | CP1 | Customer Project 1 | 41000000 | Rev Domestic Pr... | -1.200,00 EUR |
| | | | | | 51600000 | Consptn Trde Gds | 1.000,00 EUR |
| Grand Total | | | | | | | -200,00 EUR |

**Figure 7.105** Reporting of Project Plan Data

Here you can see both line items you entered in the file. It's important to note that for the plan data, there's also information about the customer and product sold derived. As for the actual postings, you use the assignment of the WBS billing element to the leading sales order to derive additional market segment attributes. So, if you plan a project after assignment of the project to a leading sales order item, you get the plan data on the sales order item level too.

### Business Transactions

Now let's look at the actual postings. First, you'll apply a time confirmation on the project, then you'll deliver the second sales order item. Start the Manage My Time Sheet app.

As there is no staffing set for the project, you need to assign an employee to the project first. To do this, select the icon with three lines at the top right, shown in Figure 7.106. You'll see the Manage My Tasks screen, where you click the **Create Task** button to create a task. The task includes project CP1 and the activity type. When you're done, the task is shown at the top right in **My Timesheet** screen shown in Figure 7.106.

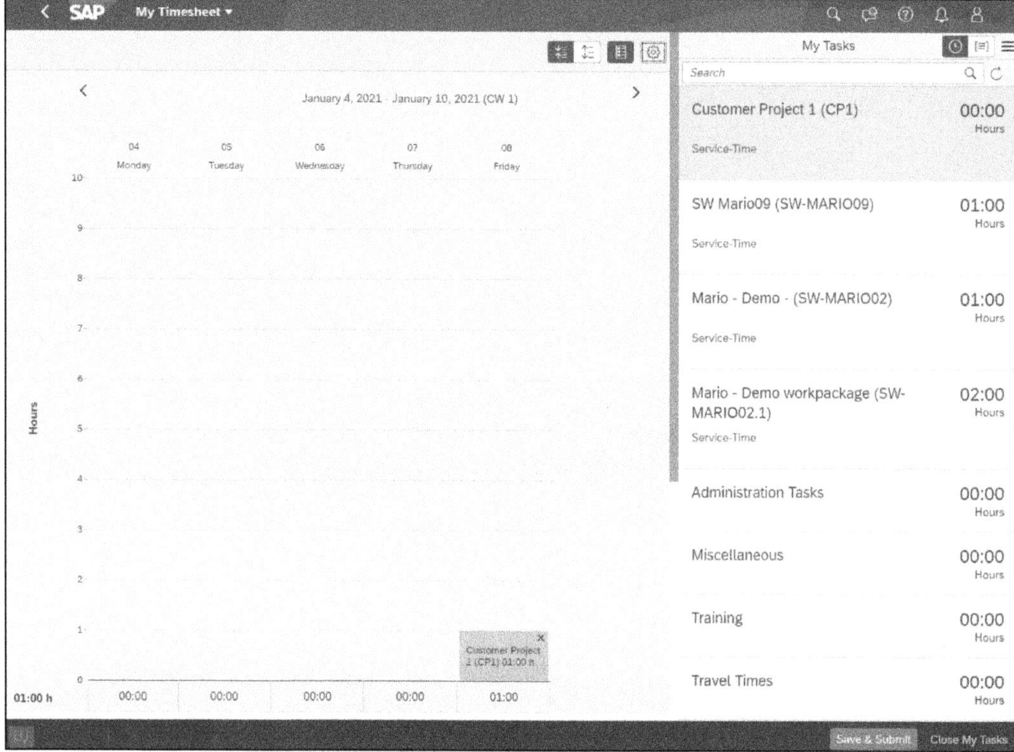

Figure 7.106 Time Confirmation on Customer Project

Select the task for the project, choose one hour for Friday, January 8, and click the **Save & Submit** button.

The journal entries posted subsequently are shown in Figure 7.107.

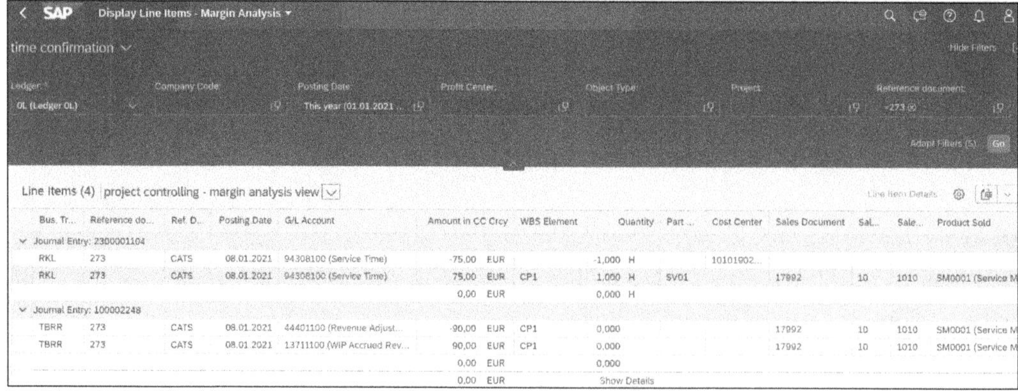

Figure 7.107 Journal Entries for Time Confirmation on Customer Project

The first two line items reflect the controlling activity allocation: the credit of the employee's cost center and the debit of the project in line item 2, in which you get the activity type used, **SV01** (see the **Part ...** column), with the confirmed one hour. The second journal entry is the revenue recognition posting. The realized revenue is calculated by the cost-based PoC method. It's posted against the balance sheet account WIP/ accrued revenue.

All line items are referenced to the time sheet entry: in column 3, the reference document type is **CATS**, and the CATS reference document **273** appears in column 2.



The PoC is calculated by actual costs divided by planned costs: 75 EUR / 1,000 EUR = 7.5%. The PoC is multiplied by the planned revenue: 7.5% * 1,200 EUR = 90 EUR realized revenue.

The activity allocation debit and the revenue recognition postings are account-assigned to the **WBS Element CP1**. As there's a leading sales order item **17992/10** defined, the system derives the sales order item and subsequent profitability attributes from the sales order item, like the **SM0001** product sold.

You can also record working time to a project manually by using Transaction CAT2 or **Human Resources • Time Management • Time Sheet • CATS Classic • Record Working Time** and entering the same working time for the chosen employee. You'll then have to transfer this information from human resources to controlling by using Transaction CATS or **Human Resources • Time Management • Time Sheet • Transfer • Project Systems • Transfer**, entering the personnel number of the employee, and executing the transfer of the working time.

Now we've come to the outbound delivery for the free-of-charge item. Start Transaction VL01 and enter "17992" for the sales order to arrive at the screen shown in Figure 7.108.

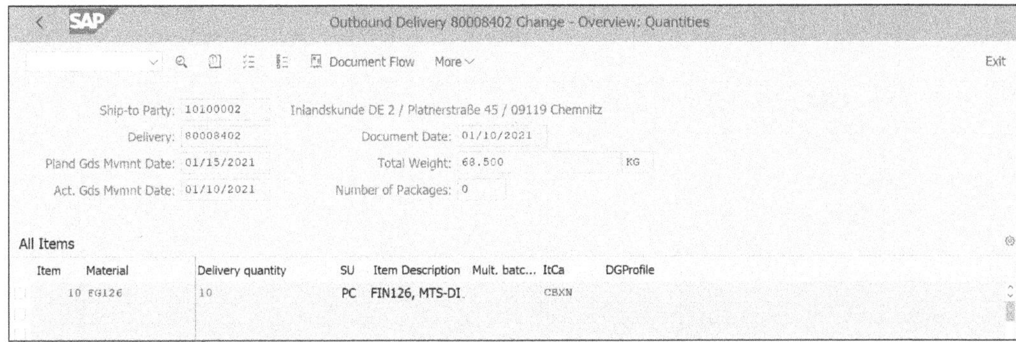


**Figure 7.108** Delivery of Sales Order Item

Click **Save** and a material document will be created, as shown in Figure 7.109.

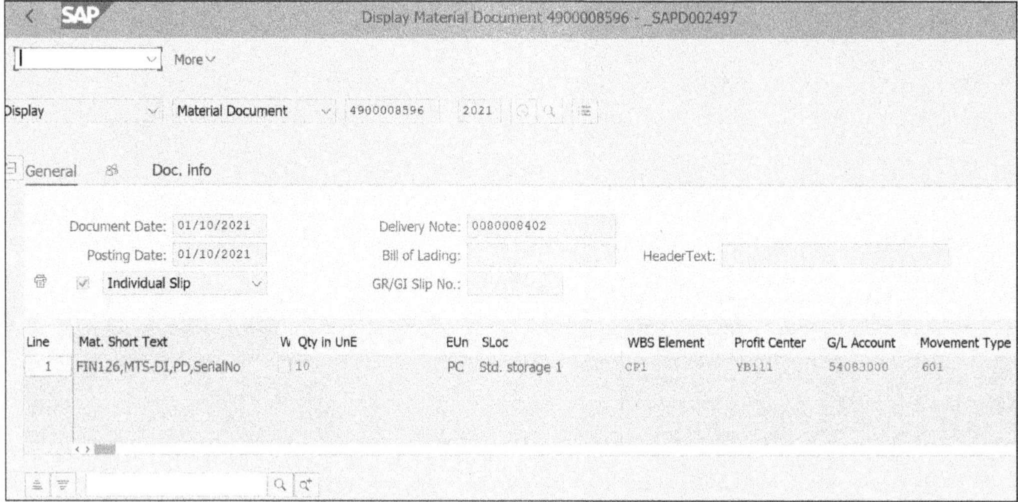


**Figure 7.109** Material Document of Delivery

You see the product of the second sales order item here, and the assignment to the **CP1** project and the profit center. Movement type **601** on the far right means this is an outbound delivery for the sales order.

Switch to the **Doc. info** tab, then click the **FI Documents** button to see the journal entries, as shown in Figure 7.110.

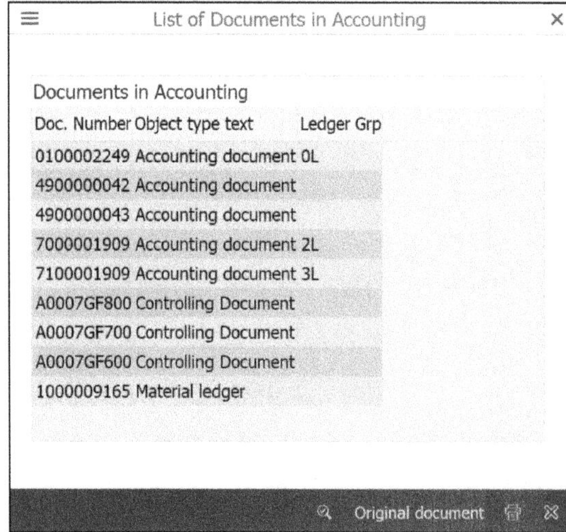


**Figure 7.110** Overview of Posted Documents of Sales Order Delivery

The second document is the prima nota, which reflects the goods issue. Then you see again the impact of parallel accounting: journal entries 1, 4, and 5 are the revenue recognition postings per active ledger in company code 1010. As mentioned, documents 7–9 are controlling views of the created journal entries.

Because we credited the inventory, a ninth journal entry was created, and it reflects the Material Ledger update.

The third journal entry is the cost component split journal entry, similar to what we showed in the sales scenario in Section 7.2. Before we can explain the values in the journal entry and the posted cost component split, let's first check the cost estimate of the delivered product. Based on its quantity structure, bill of materials (BOM), and routing, a cost estimate is performed (see Chapter 6, Section 6.2.1).



You can analyze the costing with Transaction CK13N. In the selection screen, enter the plant, the product delivered (**FG126**), and the costing variant (**PPC1**), then press Enter. You'll see the screen shown in Figure 7.111.

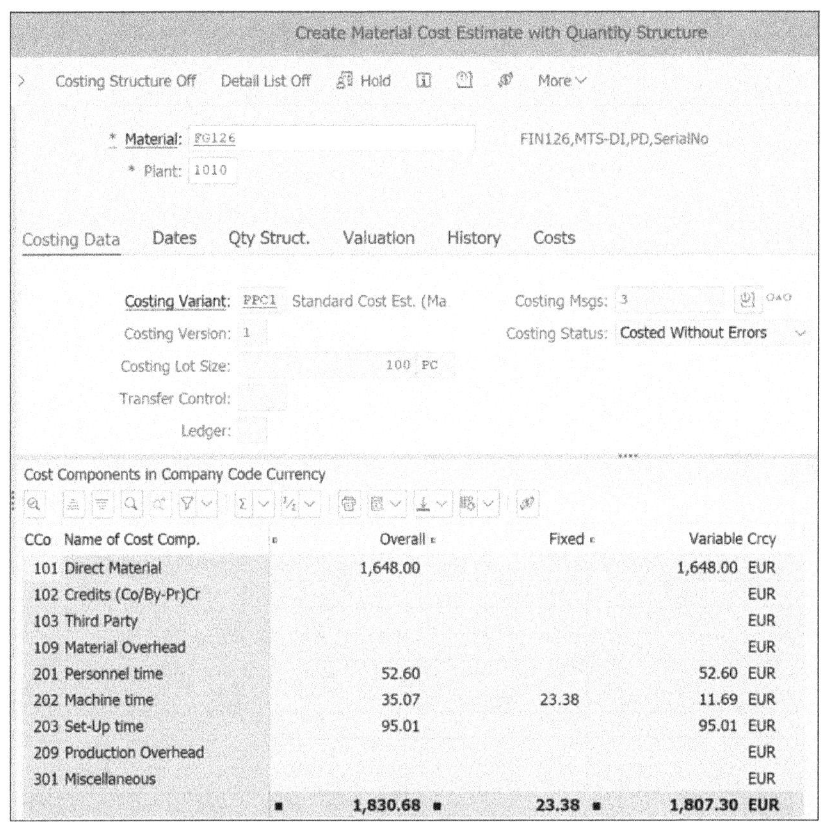


| CCo | Name of Cost Comp. | Overall | Fixed | Variable | Crcy |
|---|---|---|---|---|---|
| 101 | Direct Material | 1,648.00 | | 1,648.00 | EUR |
| 102 | Credits (Co/By-Pr)Cr | | | | EUR |
| 103 | Third Party | | | | EUR |
| 109 | Material Overhead | | | | EUR |
| 201 | Personnel time | 52.60 | | 52.60 | EUR |
| 202 | Machine time | 35.07 | 23.38 | 11.69 | EUR |
| 203 | Set-Up time | 95.01 | | 95.01 | EUR |
| 209 | Production Overhead | | | | EUR |
| 301 | Miscellaneous | | | | EUR |
| | | 1,830.68 | 23.38 | 1,807.30 | EUR |

**Figure 7.111** Cost Estimate of Delivered Product

To show the costs of the direct material and working hours on a multilevel basis, there's a cost component view available in the lower half of the screen. You can see that 100 pieces of product FG126 cost 1,830.68 EUR, including, for example, direct material expenses of 1,648 EUR, shown in the first line.

Let's analyze the journal entries for the leading ledger 0L in the Display Line Items—Margin Analysis app, as shown in Figure 7.112.

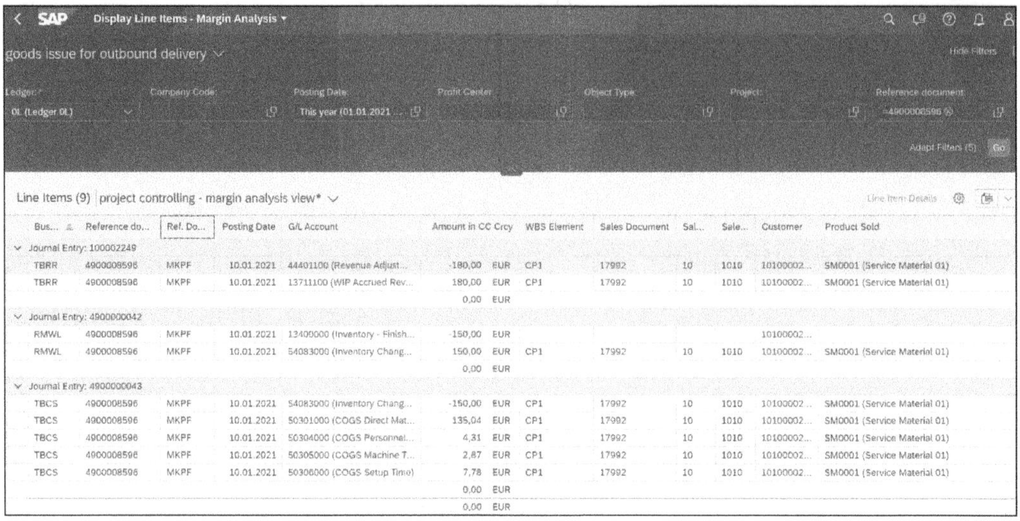

Figure 7.112 Journal Entries for Delivery

Here you can see that the goods issue of the one piece of product created three documents:

1. The first entry is posted by revenue recognition. Like for the time confirmation entered previously based on planning, a cost-based PoC is calculated. The result is posted as realized revenue and accrued revenue/WIP on the project.
2. The second journal entry reflects the goods issue posting on the project.
3. The third journal entry contains five line items representing the cost component split. As shown in the sales scenario in Section 7.2, the amounts per line are defined by the cost estimate shown previously in Figure 7.111. They are posted with the business transaction type **TBCS**. In this case, however, the cost estimate value for the product, 18.31 EUR per piece, differs from the inventory value of 15 EUR per piece, which is reflected in the journal entry items with the general ledger account inventory change—so, for example, the first line of the cost split document reverses the goods issue amount. In this case, you need to normalize the cost component split journal entry item values you see in the next four line items. The values are calculated by multiplying the values from the calculation with the factor inventory value (15 EUR divided by the cost estimate value of 18.31 EUR results in 0.8194). So, for example, for the cost of goods sold of direct materials, you get 164.80 EUR multiplied by 0.8194, resulting in 135.04 EUR, which is visible in the journal entry.

### Period-End Close

Now let's look at the period-end activity of overhead calculation. In the project master (refer back to Figure 7.100), we assigned a costing scheme, which now enables overhead calculation on the project. Start the Run Overhead Calculation Projects—Actual app (web GUI app; SAP Fiori ID CJ44), as shown in Figure 7.113.

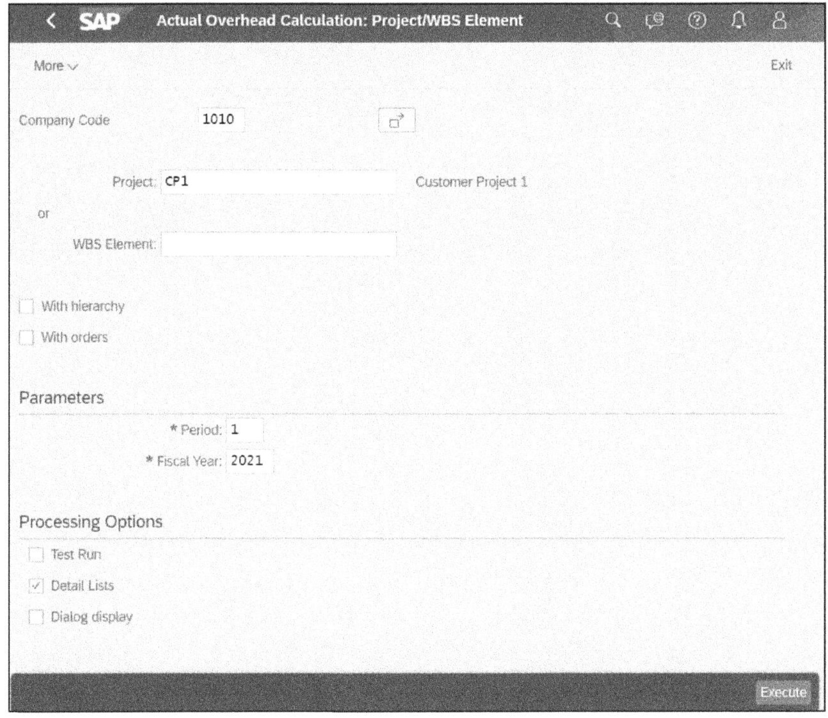


**Figure 7.113** Overhead Calculation for Customer Project: Selection Screen

Enter the **Project** and **Period** "1" in **Fiscal Year** "2021", for which you'll calculate the overhead, and click **Execute.** You'll see the detail list screen, as shown in Figure 7.114.

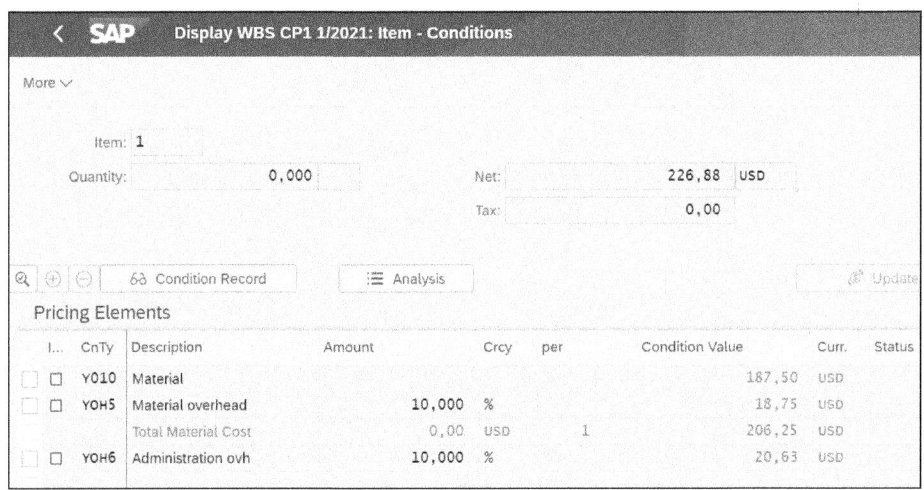


**Figure 7.114** Overhead Calculation: Costing Scheme

You see here the calculation scheme used with the posted values of the project. Note that the amounts are shown in global currency—in this example, USD. The **Material** cost base is 150 EUR (187.50 USD) for the product delivery. A material overhead of 10% is applied. The sum of both is the base for the administration overhead of 10%.

You can analyze these values in the related journal entries in the Display Line Items—Margin Analysis app, shown in Figure 7.115.

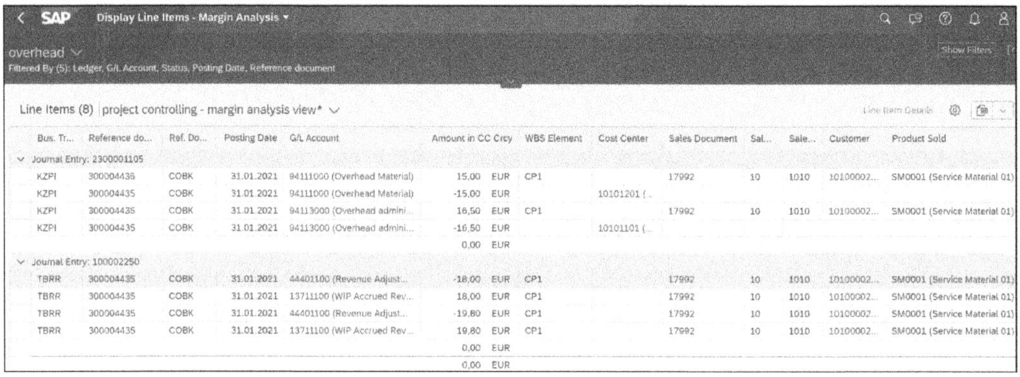

| Bus. Tr... | Reference do... | Ref. Do... | Posting Date | G/L Account | Amount in CC Crcy | | WBS Element | Cost Center | Sales Document | Sal... | Sale... | Customer | Product Sold |
|---|---|---|---|---|---|---|---|---|---|---|---|---|---|
| Journal Entry: 2300001105 | | | | | | | | | | | | | |
| KZPI | 300004435 | COBK | 31.01.2021 | 94111000 (Overhead Material) | 15,00 | EUR | CP1 | | 17992 | 10 | 1010 | 10100002... | SM0001 (Service Material 01) |
| KZPI | 300004435 | COBK | 31.01.2021 | 94111000 (Overhead Material) | -15,00 | EUR | | 10101201 (... | | | | | |
| KZPI | 300004435 | COBK | 31.01.2021 | 94113000 (Overhead admini... | 16,50 | EUR | CP1 | | 17992 | 10 | 1010 | 10100002... | SM0001 (Service Material 01) |
| KZPI | 300004435 | COBK | 31.01.2021 | 94113000 (Overhead admini... | -16,50 | EUR | | 10101101 (... | | | | | |
| | | | | | 0,00 | EUR | | | | | | | |
| Journal Entry: 100002250 | | | | | | | | | | | | | |
| TBRR | 300004435 | COBK | 31.01.2021 | 44401100 (Revenue Adjust... | -18,00 | EUR | CP1 | | 17992 | 10 | 1010 | 10100002... | SM0001 (Service Material 01) |
| TBRR | 300004435 | COBK | 31.01.2021 | 13711100 (WIP Accrued Rev... | 18,00 | EUR | CP1 | | 17992 | 10 | 1010 | 10100002... | SM0001 (Service Material 01) |
| TBRR | 300004435 | COBK | 31.01.2021 | 44401100 (Revenue Adjust... | -19,80 | EUR | CP1 | | 17992 | 10 | 1010 | 10100002... | SM0001 (Service Material 01) |
| TBRR | 300004435 | COBK | 31.01.2021 | 13711100 (WIP Accrued Rev... | 19,80 | EUR | CP1 | | 17992 | 10 | 1010 | 10100002... | SM0001 (Service Material 01) |
| | | | | | 0,00 | EUR | | | | | | | |
| | | | | | 0,00 | EUR | | | | | | | |

**Figure 7.115** Overhead Calculation: Journal Entries

The first journal entry reflects the controlling overhead posting for material overhead and administration overhead: the debit of the project and the credit of the cost center for each overhead rate. The second journal entry is the revenue recognition posting: one realized revenue line item per overhead rate. For every overhead rate, the realized revenue, calculated by the PoC, and the balance sheet activation with the WIP general ledger account is posted. All line items are referenced to the overhead document; see the **Reference do...** column.

The overhead debits and the revenue recognition postings are account-assigned to the project. As in the examples before, the profitability attributes are derived by the leading sales order item **17992/10** and stored in the journal entry line items.

Now let's look at the revenue recognition values with the Event-Based Revenue Recognition—Projects app, as shown in Figure 7.116.

You can view the following sections for key information:

- **Income Statement**
  In the **Income Statement** section, you see the total actual costs of 256.50 EUR. The matching recognized revenue is 307.80 EUR. This leads to a calculated margin of 51.30 EUR.
- **Balance Sheet**
  In the **Balance Sheet** section, you see the balance sheet values created by revenue recognition. Here you have the WIP or accrued revenue of 307.80 EUR—the offset to the recognized revenues.
- **Plan Data/EAC**
  The **Plan Data/EAC** section shows, for the revenue recognition used, the plan data: planned revenue of 1,200 EUR and planned costs of 1,000 EUR.

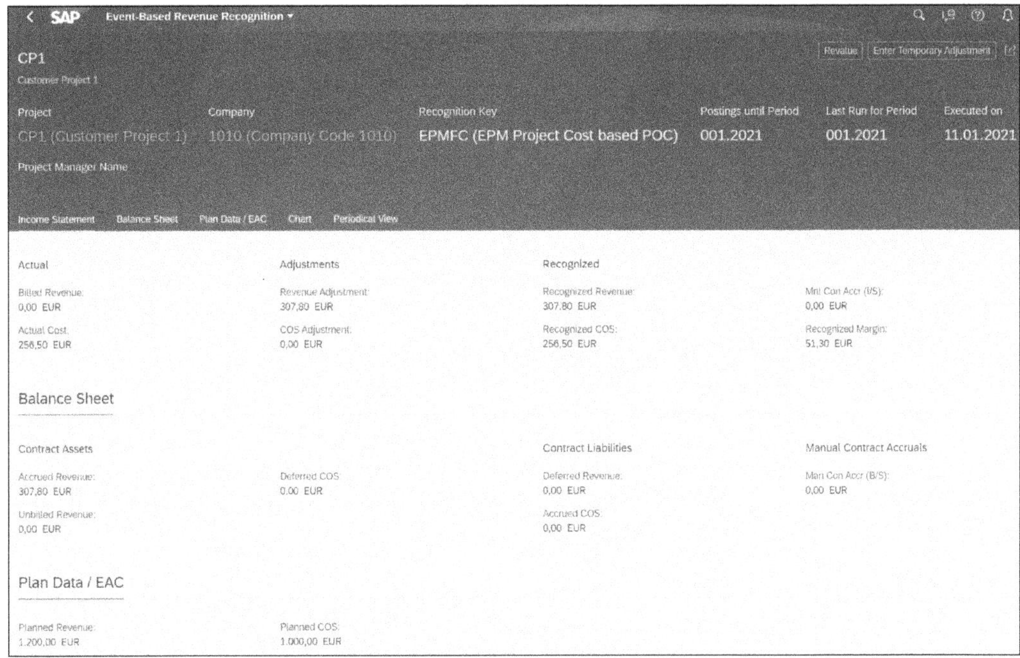


**Figure 7.116** Event-Based Revenue Recognition—Projects App: Detail View

## Reporting

Now let's look at the margin details with the Market Segment Plan/Actuals app, as shown in Figure 7.117.

SAP Market Segment - Plan/Actual

Navigation Panel

Data Analysis

<Standard Query View> | Filter | Sort | Hierarchy | Drilldown | Display | Measures | Totals

| Project | Sales Docu... | Product Sold | | Profit C... | G/L Account | | Actual Amount in C... | Plan Amount in CC ... | Difference Actual Pl... | Difference (%) CC |
|---|---|---|---|---|---|---|---|---|---|---|
| | | | | | –YPS2/015 | CM I | -51,30 EUR | -200,00 EUR | 148,70 EUR | 289,86 |
| | | | | | +YPS2/020 | Net Sales/Revenue | -307,80 EUR | -1.200,00 EUR | 892,20 EUR | 289,86 |
| | | | | | –YPS2/038 | Cost of Goods Sold | 256,50 EUR | 1.000,00 EUR | -743,50 EUR | -289,86 |
| | | | | | +YPS2/024 | Material Costs | 135,04 EUR | 1.000,00 EUR | -864,96 EUR | -640,52 |
| CP1 | 17992 | SM0001 | Service Ma... | A000/YB1... | +YPS2/027 | Labor Costs | 4,31 EUR | | 4,31 EUR | 100,00 |
| | | | | | +YPS2/028 | Manufact. costs Setu | 7,78 EUR | | 7,78 EUR | 100,00 |
| | | | | | +YPS2/029 | Manufact. costs Mach | 2,87 EUR | | 2,87 EUR | 100,00 |
| | | | | | +YPS2/030 | Overhead costs-Mater | 15,00 EUR | | 15,00 EUR | 100,00 |
| | | | | | +YPS2/047 | Time recording cost | 75,00 EUR | | 75,00 EUR | 100,00 |
| | | | | | +YPS2/050 | Overhead Cost Admin | 16,50 EUR | | 16,50 EUR | 100,00 |
| Result | | | | | | | -51,30 EUR | -200,00 EUR | 148,70 EUR | 289,86 |

**Figure 7.117** Detail Margin Reporting for Project

Filter on the project and select financial statement version YPS2 for the general ledger account attribute, which provides a hierarchical view of the costs.

With this, the costs of goods sold of 256.50 can be explained by cost components. The cost components are based on the cost component split of the product, the time confirmation, and the overhead posting. Thus, the project reporting shows not only the goods issue amount on the project but also the more detailed information about its cost components. This allows a multilevel margin reporting on the project and the customer and product market segments.

As mentioned previously, the plan data in the **Plan Amount in CC...** column is provided on the sales order item level and thus for the product and customer also. This enables a plan to actual comparison for these market segments.

This is a straightforward case when there's exactly one pricing- and billing-relevant sales order item assigned and you can use it to determine a leading sales order. This variant is currently only available in SAP S/4HANA Cloud. The next variant deals with the situation in which there are multiple pricing- and billing-relevant sales order items assigned to a WBS element. Let's look at how to cover such a project-based sales scenario in an on-premise system.

### Defining Profitability Attributes by Settlement Rule and Realignment

Now let's look at how to flexibly determine the market segments for the customer project. This is a main use case for on-premise SAP S/4HANA, in which you don't provide the leading sales order.

If you assign a settlement rule to a WBS billing element, it's used as the first priority for the derivation of the market segment. So, its maintenance is relevant for the following use cases:

- You define a customer project without assignment of a sales order item and you want to assign it to exactly one market segment.
- You use an assigned sales order item, but you want to define the market segment attributes flexibly.

> **Definition of Market Segment with the Settlement Rule**
>
> The derivation of market segments for postings on a customer project with a settlement rule works only if you define exactly one receiver in the settlement rule, and this receiver must be a profitability segment. If you add a second receiver, the system cannot derive market segment fields because they can't be determined.

Also, it's a common use case in this scenario that you want to rederive the profitability fields. The following are a few examples:

- You post to the project without a sales order being assigned or a settlement rule created. Then of course no market segments would be written into the project journal entry lines. Here you have to start the realignment as soon as the settlement rule is maintained. Thus, market segments are subsequently written for the posted lines.
- You want to change the market assignment fields, such as to add another product sold. We'll go over this scenario in this section.
- You create extensibility fields and change your derivation logic, or you change product master or customer master attributes like the industry, county, or customer and product groups.

Now let's look more closely at the second use case. Imagine that you've already derived market segment attributes for the CP1 project and now want to change the product sold.

Start the Manage Project Control app (refer back to Figure 7.100) and click the **Settlement Rule** button to arrive at the screen shown in Figure 7.118.

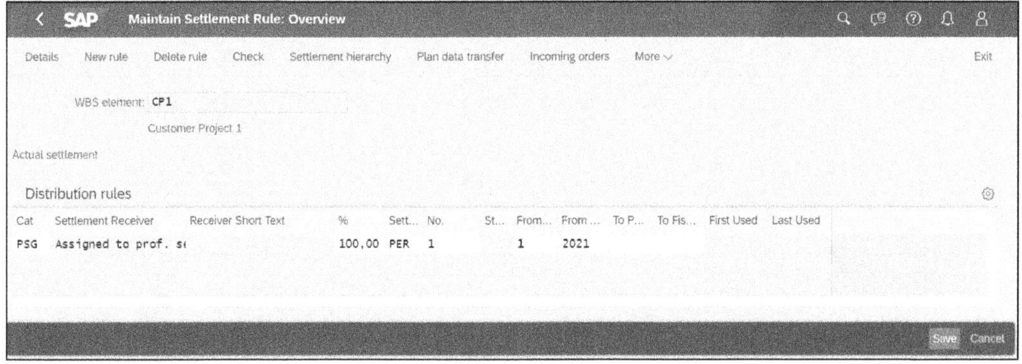


**Figure 7.118** WBS Billing Element Settlement Rule

Define a profitability segment as one receiver in the **Cat** field, indicated by **PSG**. Double-click the line to arrive at the detail screen, where you can enter the single market segment attributes into the popup shown in Figure 7.119.

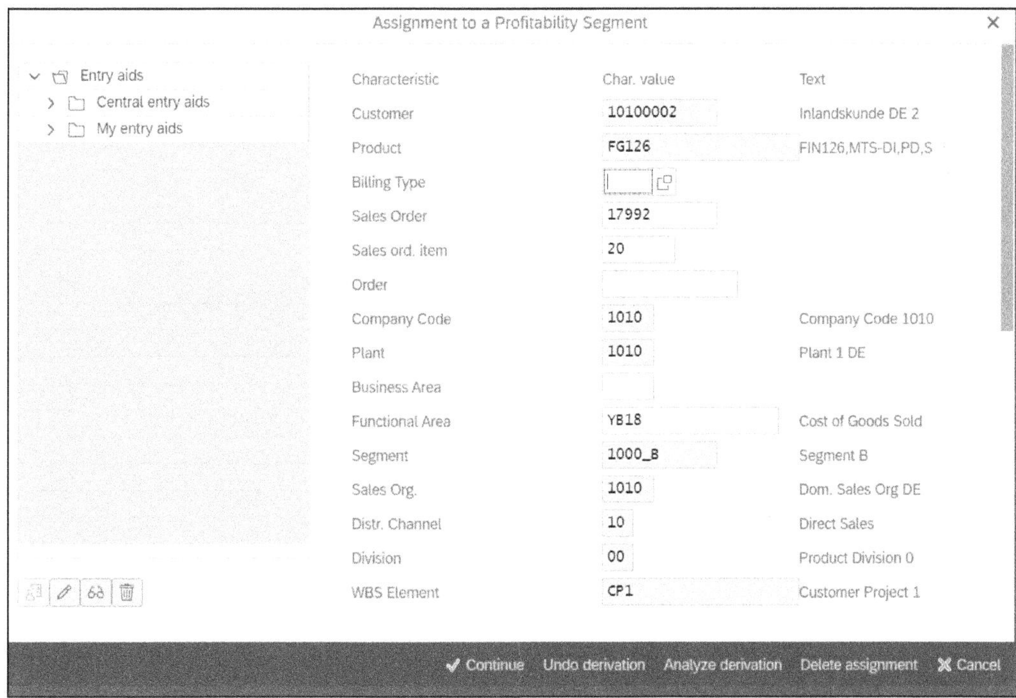


**Figure 7.119** Maintaining Profitability Segment in WBS Billing Element Settlement Rule

Enter “10100002” for **Customer** and then enter a different product sold: “FG126”. Recall that you derived the product from the leading sales order previously: SM00001. Now, enter “17992” for **Sales Order** and “20” for **Sales ord. item**. **Functional Area**, **Profit Center**, and **Segment** are derived from the project master.

Click **Continue** to return to the screen shown in Figure 7.118 and click the **Save** button. With this the settlement rule is created—but you won’t use it in this case for settlement, just for profitability attribution. In the settlement profile, it should be set as not relevant for settlement (refer to Chapter 5, Section 5.4.6).

The market segments of the project are already included in the documents previously posted. If you now want to assign the margin of the project to other market segment attributes, you have to change the journal entries.

**Market Segment Attributes in Margin Analysis versus Costing-Based Profitability Analysis**

Because we comply with the principles of proper accounting, we can only change certain journal entry document attributes that aren’t relevant for legal reporting. This is different in costing-based profitability analysis, which doesn’t have the same restrictions because of its own data persistence.

In margin analysis, for example, you can change the product sold, the industry, and the customer group from the customer master or the material group, as well as the extensibility fields.

Now let’s start the realignment. Open the Run Realignment Profitability Analysis app (SAP Fiori ID KEND). Then create a **CP1 Realignment** by clicking the **Realignment Run** button. Select the created run and click **Request CP1 Realignment**. You’ll see the screen shown in Figure 7.120.

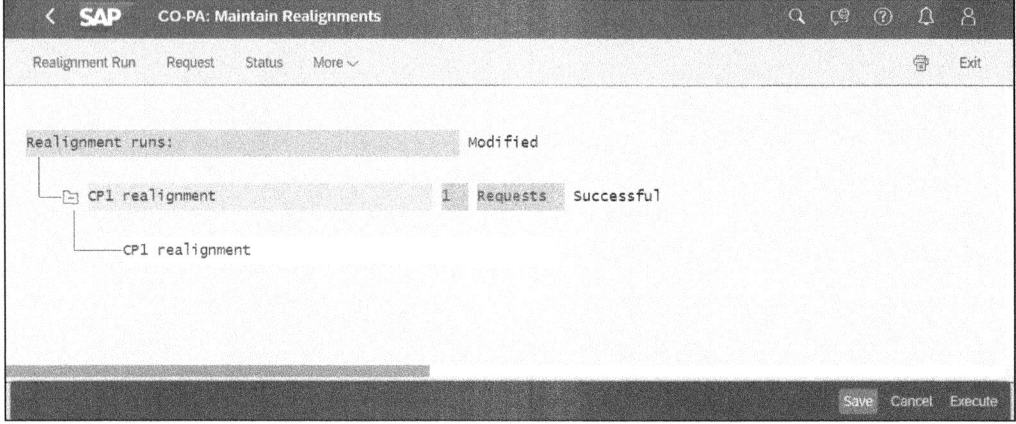


**Figure 7.120** Creation of Realignment Requests

When you create the request, you need to define which objects you want to realign and which fields. Double-click the request to get to the first screen of the realignment request, shown in Figure 7.121. Here, define the **Selection Condition**. Select the characteristic WBS element and define WBS element **CP1** as your selection.

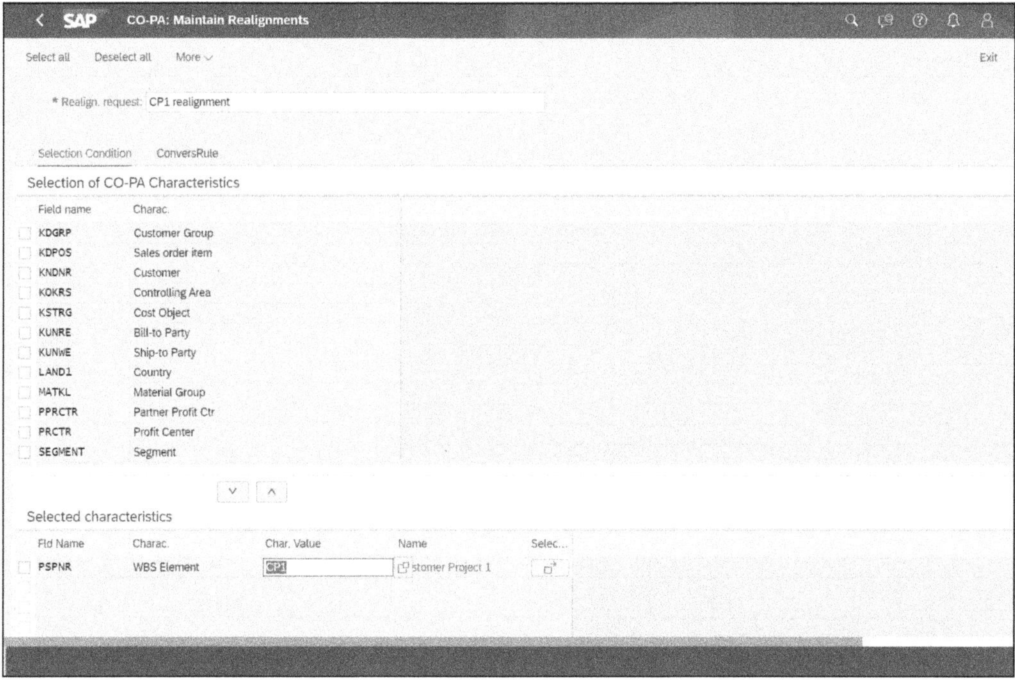


**Figure 7.121** Realignment Request: Selection Criteria

Then go the next section, the conversion rule (**ConversRule**), as shown in Figure 7.122.

Here you define which attributes you want to update. As mentioned before, you can't update fields like company code, profit center, or segment because they're relevant for legal reporting. Some fields, like sales order or customer, can only be derived if they aren't filled already; you can't overwrite them. In this example, select the product sold for realignment, showing **ARTNR** in the **Fld Name** column.

In the lower section, you can define replacement values. In this example, the aim is just to create a new derivation based on the settlement rule for a project, where the market segments are attributed. Therefore, select the **Rederivation of ACDOCA Char for Attributed Line Items** checkbox.

Return to the overview screen shown in Figure 7.120, select the run, and click **Execute**. A realignment job gets started in background. To check the result of the job, select **More • Goto • Job Overview** and arrive at the screen shown in Figure 7.123.

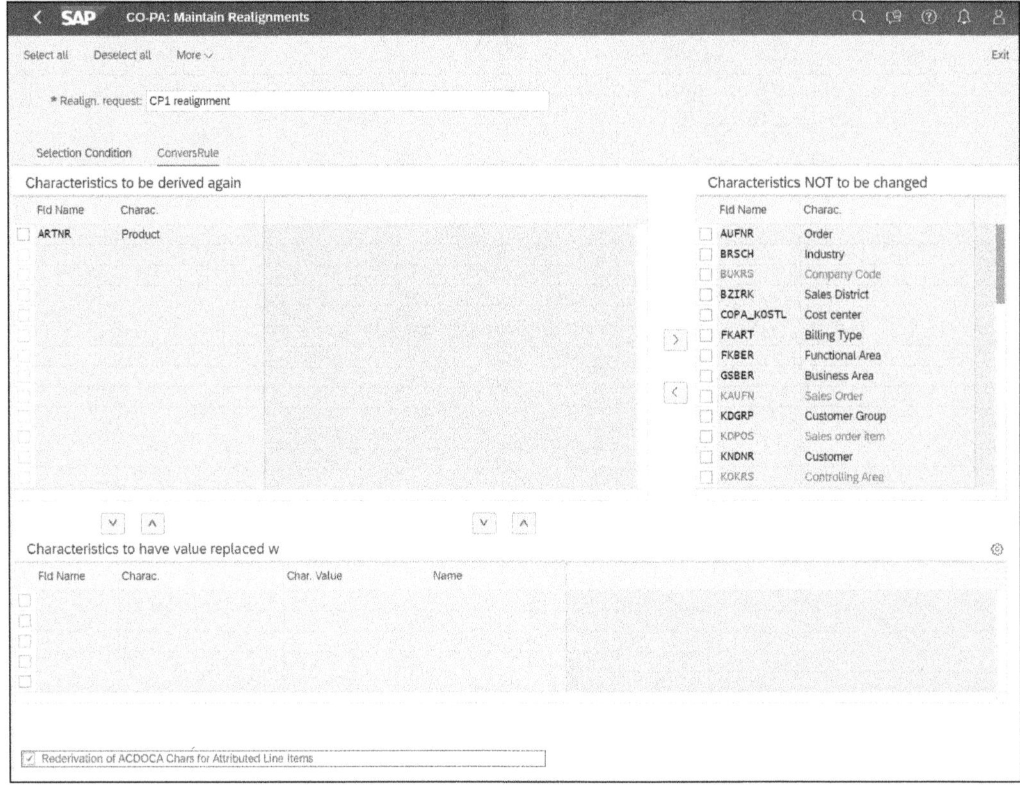


**Figure 7.122** Realignment: Definition of Attributes to Be Derived

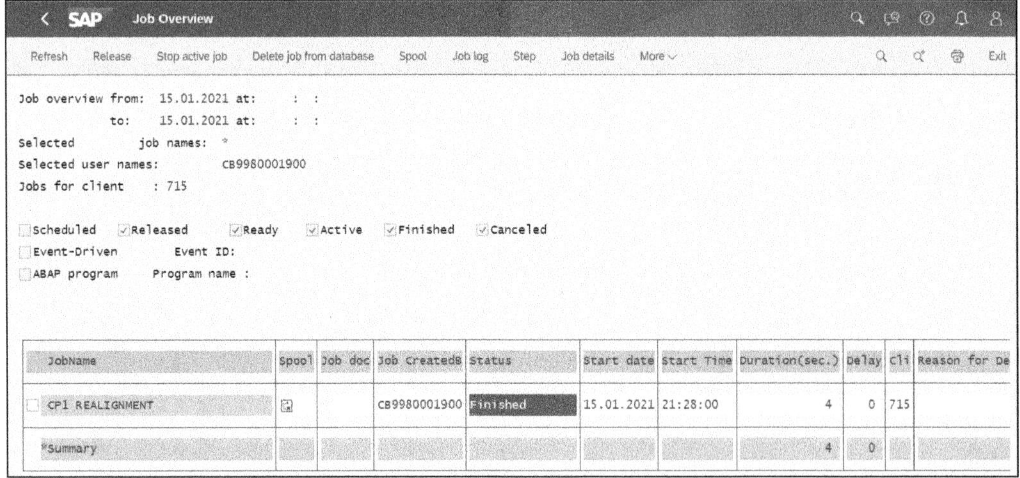


| JobName | Spool | Job doc | Job CreatedB | Status | Start date | Start Time | Duration(sec.) | Delay | Cli | Reason for De |
|---|---|---|---|---|---|---|---|---|---|---|
| CP1 REALIGNMENT | | | CB9980001900 | Finished | 15.01.2021 | 21:28:00 | 4 | 0 | 715 | |
| *Summary | | | | | | | 4 | 0 | | |

**Figure 7.123** Realignment Job Log

You'll see the job with the name **CP1 REALIGNMENT** completed successfully, as indicated by **Finished** in the **Status** column.

The results of the realignment run can be traced in the Realignment Results Profitability Analysis app (SAP Fiori ID F2549), as shown in Figure 7.124.

| Realignme... | Ledger | Posting D... | Journal Entry | G/L Account | Amount in C... | Product ... | Product Sold Group (... | Product Sold | Product Sold (Previous) |
|---|---|---|---|---|---|---|---|---|---|
| 15.01.2021 | 0L | 08.01.2021 | 100002248 | 13711100 | 90,00 EUR | L004 | YBMM01 | FG126 | SM0001 |
| 15.01.2021 | 0L | 08.01.2021 | 100002248 | 44401100 | -90,00 EUR | L004 | YBMM01 | FG126 | SM0001 |
| 15.01.2021 | 0L | 08.01.2021 | 2300001104 | 94308100 | 75,00 EUR | L004 | YBMM01 | FG126 | SM0001 |
| 15.01.2021 | 0L | 10.01.2021 | 100002249 | 13711100 | 180,00 EUR | L004 | YBMM01 | FG126 | SM0001 |
| 15.01.2021 | 0L | 10.01.2021 | 100002249 | 44401100 | -180,00 EUR | L004 | YBMM01 | FG126 | SM0001 |
| 15.01.2021 | 0L | 10.01.2021 | 4900000042 | 54083000 | 150,00 EUR | L004 | YBMM01 | FG126 | SM0001 |
| 15.01.2021 | 0L | 10.01.2021 | 4900000043 | 50301000 | 135,04 EUR | L004 | YBMM01 | FG126 | SM0001 |
| 15.01.2021 | 0L | 10.01.2021 | 4900000043 | 50304000 | 4,31 EUR | L004 | YBMM01 | FG126 | SM0001 |
| 15.01.2021 | 0L | 10.01.2021 | 4900000043 | 50305000 | 2,87 EUR | L004 | YBMM01 | FG126 | SM0001 |
| 15.01.2021 | 0L | 10.01.2021 | 4900000043 | 50306000 | 7,78 EUR | L004 | YBMM01 | FG126 | SM0001 |
| 15.01.2021 | 0L | 10.01.2021 | 4900000043 | 54083000 | -150,00 EUR | L004 | YBMM01 | FG126 | SM0001 |
| 15.01.2021 | 0L | 31.01.2021 | 100002250 | 13711100 | 37,80 EUR | L004 | YBMM01 | FG126 | SM0001 |
| 15.01.2021 | 0L | 31.01.2021 | 100002250 | 44401100 | -37,80 EUR | L004 | YBMM01 | FG126 | SM0001 |
| 15.01.2021 | 0L | 31.01.2021 | 2300001105 | 94111000 | 15,00 EUR | L004 | YBMM01 | FG126 | SM0001 |
| 15.01.2021 | 0L | 31.01.2021 | 2300001105 | 94113000 | 16,50 EUR | L004 | YBMM01 | FG126 | SM0001 |
| | | | | | 256,50 EUR | | | | |

**Figure 7.124** Realignment Results

Here, select leading **Ledger 0L** and filter on **Company Code** and **Fiscal Year** and click **Go**. You'll see all the journal entry items posted on WBS element CP1, including the event-based revenue recognition postings. The product sold has changed from SM0001 to FG126 from the settlement rule. Because of the changed product sold, there is a new product sold group derived from the new product sold master, **FG126**.

> **Note**
> A realignment run is always executed for all active ledgers.

Now let's check the impact on margin reporting. Start the Product and Service Margins app and select the project to arrive at the view shown in Figure 7.125.

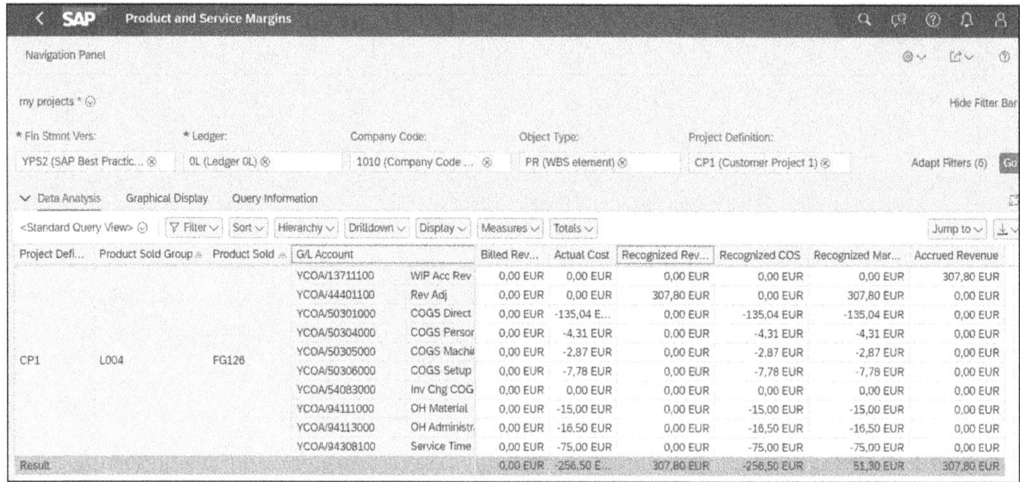


| Project Defi... | Product Sold Group | Product Sold | G/L Account | | Billed Rev... | Actual Cost | Recognized Rev... | Recognized COS | Recognized Mar... | Accrued Revenue |
|---|---|---|---|---|---|---|---|---|---|---|
| CP1 | L004 | FG126 | YCOA/13711100 | WIP Acc Rev | 0,00 EUR | 0,00 EUR | 0,00 EUR | 0,00 EUR | 0,00 EUR | 307,80 EUR |
| | | | YCOA/44401100 | Rev Adj | 0,00 EUR | 0,00 EUR | 307,80 EUR | 0,00 EUR | 307,80 EUR | 0,00 EUR |
| | | | YCOA/50301000 | COGS Direct | 0,00 EUR | -135,04 E... | 0,00 EUR | -135,04 EUR | -135,04 EUR | 0,00 EUR |
| | | | YCOA/50304000 | COGS Persor | 0,00 EUR | -4,31 EUR | 0,00 EUR | -4,31 EUR | -4,31 EUR | 0,00 EUR |
| | | | YCOA/50305000 | COGS Machi | 0,00 EUR | -2,87 EUR | 0,00 EUR | -2,87 EUR | -2,87 EUR | 0,00 EUR |
| | | | YCOA/50306000 | COGS Setup | 0,00 EUR | -7,78 EUR | 0,00 EUR | -7,78 EUR | -7,78 EUR | 0,00 EUR |
| | | | YCOA/54083000 | Inv Chg COG | 0,00 EUR | 0,00 EUR | 0,00 EUR | 0,00 EUR | 0,00 EUR | 0,00 EUR |
| | | | YCOA/94111000 | OH Material | 0,00 EUR | -15,00 EUR | 0,00 EUR | -15,00 EUR | -15,00 EUR | 0,00 EUR |
| | | | YCOA/94113000 | OH Administr. | 0,00 EUR | -16,50 EUR | 0,00 EUR | -16,50 EUR | -16,50 EUR | 0,00 EUR |
| | | | YCOA/94308100 | Service Time | 0,00 EUR | -75,00 EUR | 0,00 EUR | -75,00 EUR | -75,00 EUR | 0,00 EUR |
| Result | | | | | 0,00 EUR | -256,50 E... | 307,80 EUR | -256,50 EUR | 51,30 EUR | 307,80 EUR |

**Figure 7.125** Margin Reporting after Realignment

Now the postings on project CP1 impact the margin of the product sold, **FG126**.

**Note**

For more information about the available cloud scenarios for project-based sales, visit the blog at *http://s-prs.co/v528208*.

### 7.3.3 Project Settlement to Profitability Scenario

Now let's consider the scenario in which costs and revenues are posted to a revenue-carrying project and then settled flexibly. You need to settle and can't just attribute the market segments as before when there are several settlement receivers or when costing-based profitability analysis is active.

It doesn't matter whether the project is connected to a sales order item, as in the previous scenarios, or whether the revenues are posted via another method, such as via Transaction FB01.

In this case, you use results analysis as a revenue recognition tool to ensure matching principles for costs and revenues. This required in case you settle to profitability analysis to get the correct margin results. The data of the results analysis are stored in a separate database, not in the Universal Journal. To transfer the results to the Universal Journal—for example, the accrued revenue—and also to supply the costing-based profitability analysis, the period-end-closing step of the settlement is necessary here.

Let's walk through the master data, planning, posting, period-end, and reporting processes in the following sections.

## Master Data Setup

To create a project, start Transaction CJ01. Create only one WBS element, and mark it as billing-relevant. Enter project definition **SW009** and project profile "Project with Revenue", then press [Enter] to arrive at the screen shown in Figure 7.126.

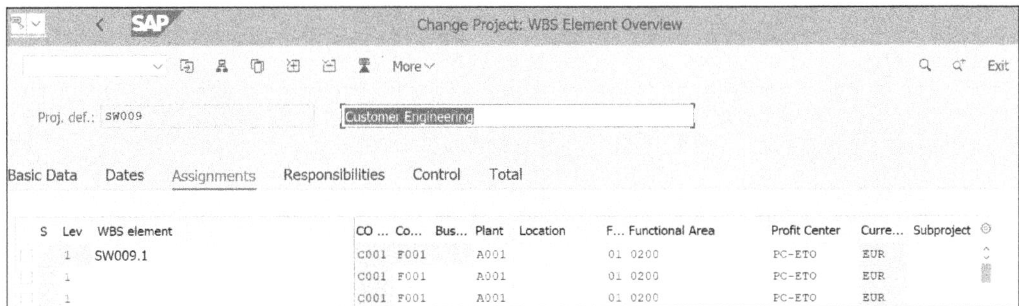

**Figure 7.126** Project Master Assignments

On the **Assignments** tab, you see controlling area **C001**, company code **F001**, functional area **0200**, and the profit center **PC-ETO** assigned. These organizational units will appear in the journal entries created ahead.

In the **Control** tab, shown in Figure 7.127, the results analysis key (**RA Key**) **000001** is defined.

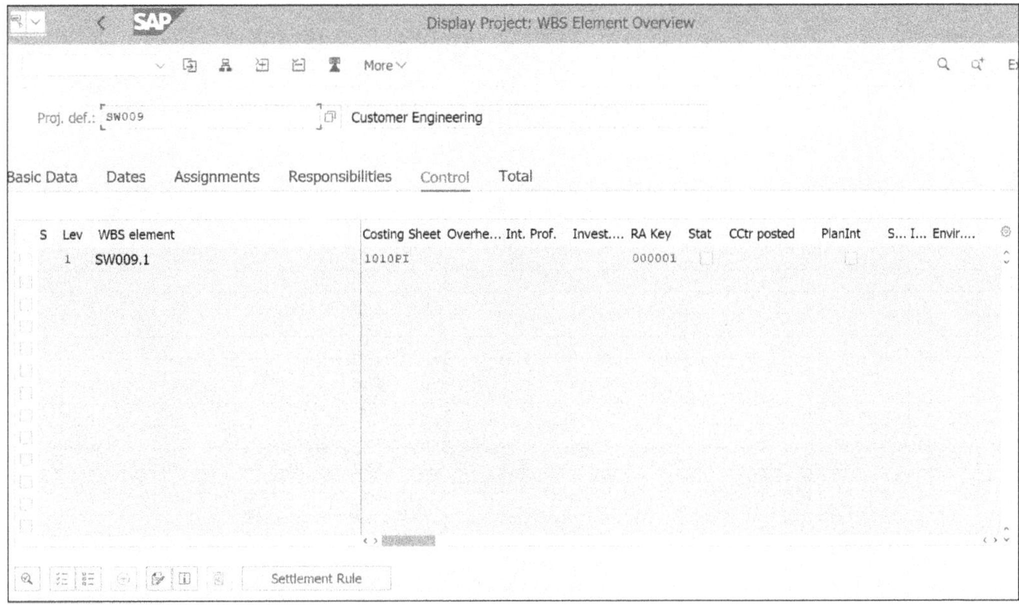

**Figure 7.127** Project Master Control with Result Analysis Key

Now create a settlement rule. Press [F7] to arrive at the screen shown in Figure 7.128.

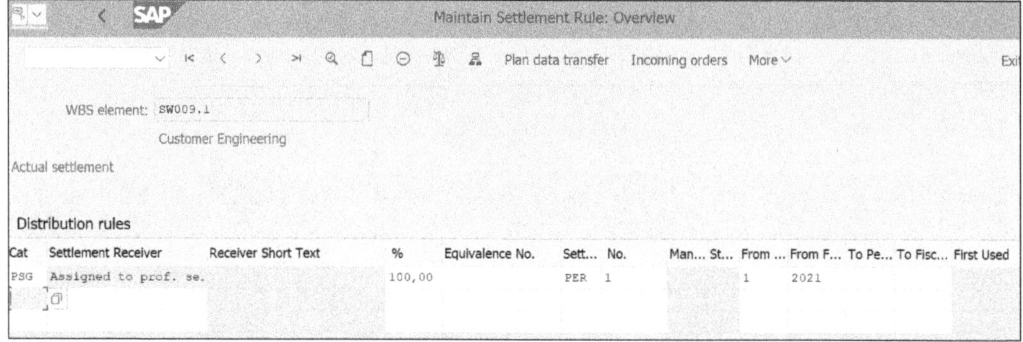


**Figure 7.128** Project Master: Settlement Rule

Define only one receiver, the profitability segment, indicated by **PSG** in the **Cat** column.

Double-click this line to go to the detail screen. You'll see a popup for defining the detailed market segment attributes, as shown in Figure 7.129.

Assignment to a Profitability Segment

Entry aids
Central entry aids
My entry aids

| Characteristic | Char. value | Text |
|---|---|---|
| Customer | CUF011001 | CUSTOMER 1 |
| Product | FG201 | FG201 |
| Billing Type | | |
| Sales Order | | |
| Sales ord. item | | |
| Order | | |
| Company Code | F001 | SAP AG |
| Plant | A001 | Tools Germany A |
| Business Area | | |
| Functional Area | 0200 | Cost of sales |
| Segment | SEG_1 | Products |
| Sales Org. | | |
| Distr. Channel | | |
| Division | | |
| WBS Element | SW009.1 | Customer Engineeri |

Continue Undo derivation Analyze derivation Delete assignment Cancel

**Figure 7.129** Project Master: Profitability Segment in Settlement Rule

Enter "CUF011001" for the **Customer** and "FG201" for the **Product** sold. **Segment**, **Profit Center**, and **Functional Area** are derived from the project master.

Click the **Continue** button to get back to the screen shown previously in Figure 7.128. Navigate to **More • GoTo • Settlement Parameters** to arrive at the screen shown in Figure 7.130.

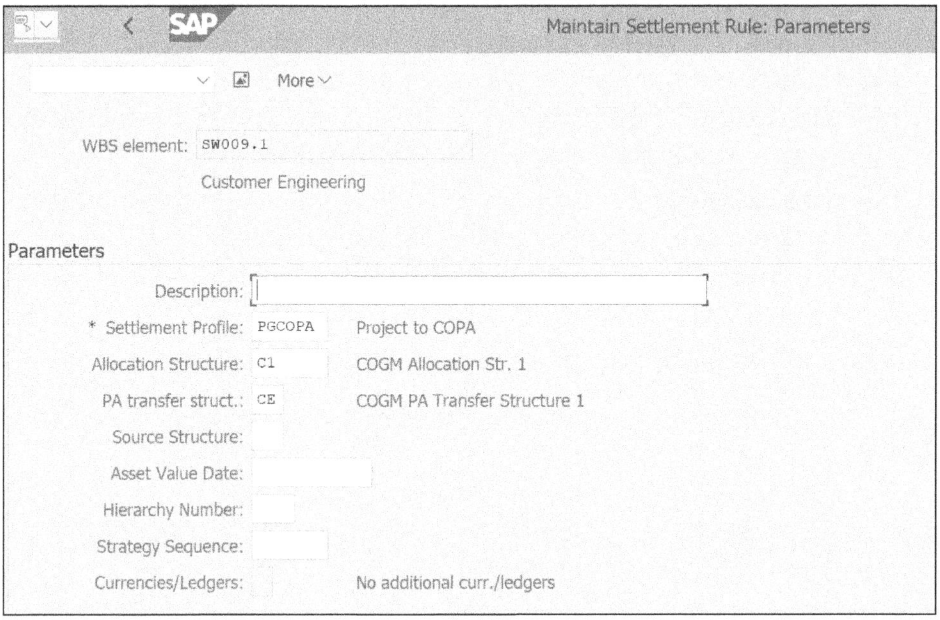

**Figure 7.130** Project Master: Settlement Parameters

The settlement parameters show how you settle the costs. They are defaulted by the settlement profile. In this profile, you define that the project costs and revenues have to be settled in full. This differs from earlier scenarios in which you didn't settle and, thus, the profile was defined as not for settlement. See Chapter 5, Section 5.4.6 for more details.

With the **Allocation Structure**, you can assign settlement cost elements to the accounts posted on the projects. In this scenario, you have to map the results analysis' own cost elements to the settlement cost elements. With these settlement cost elements, you'll post in the general ledger and will update in the Universal Journal's integrated margin analysis. In **PA transfer structure**, the integration to the costing-based profitability analysis is defined. Here you can define the value fields in which the bookings to the project are settled.

### Project Planning

As a next step, you'll provide planning on the project for plan-actual comparison and as a base for defining the percentage of completion, used by the results analysis for revenue recognition. There are several options available for entering plan data for the project:

- The manual cost element planning shown previously for the cost center. There are two transactions for projects available: Transaction CJR2 for creating and changing plan data and Transaction CJR3 for displaying it.
- If you can work with a template because you have often a similar planning structure, you can work with a manual costing application: Transaction CKECP (Easy Cost Planning). For more information about this option, visit *http://s-prs.co/v528209*.
- For high-level planning, there are two transactions in place: Transaction CJ40 for planning of costs and Transaction CJ42 for planning of revenues.
- If you can assign operational objects to the project, like networks, then the quantity structures provided by the network will be calculated and available as plan values. Similarly, you can transfer planned revenues from the billing information for assigned sales order items.

In this example, we'll use Transaction CJR2, as shown in Figure 7.131.

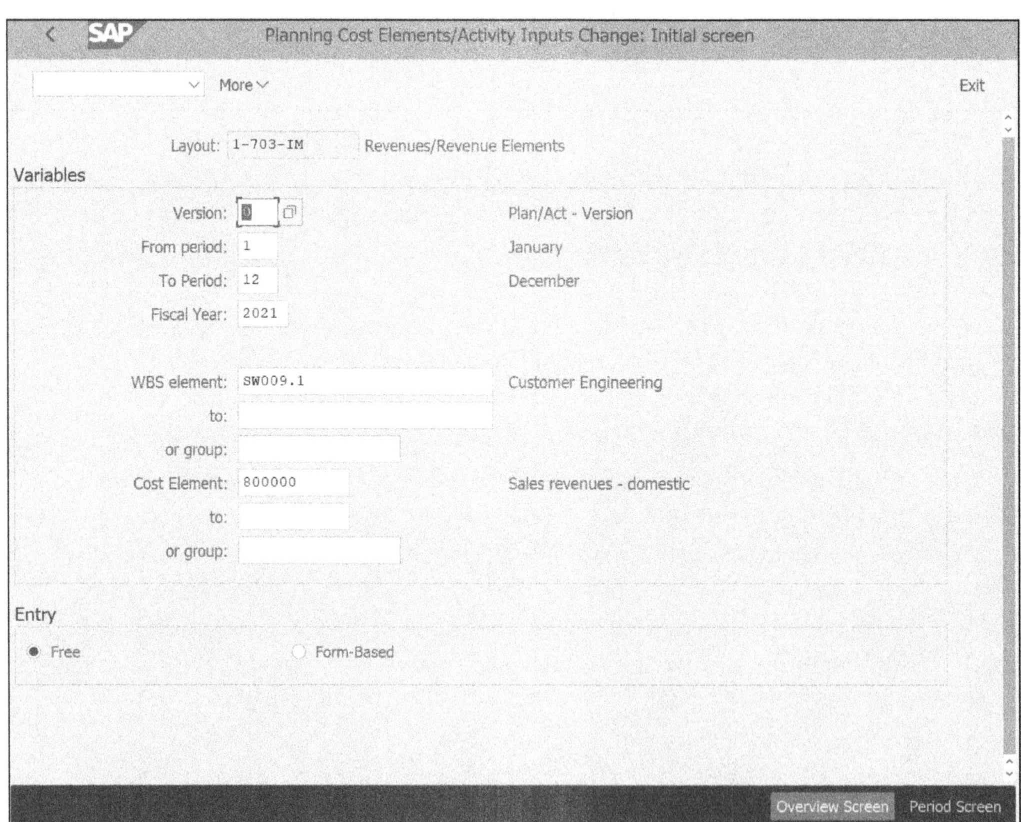


**Figure 7.131** Cost Element–Based Planning for Projects: Selection Screen

Start with the layout for revenue planning. You can select the layout with **More • Settings • Set Planner Profile**. Enter the **Version**, **From** and **To Period**, "SW009.1" for the **WBS**

**element**, and the revenue general ledger account "800000" in the **Cost Element** field, which is what you want to plan.

Click the **Overview Screen** button to go to the next screen, shown in Figure 7.132.

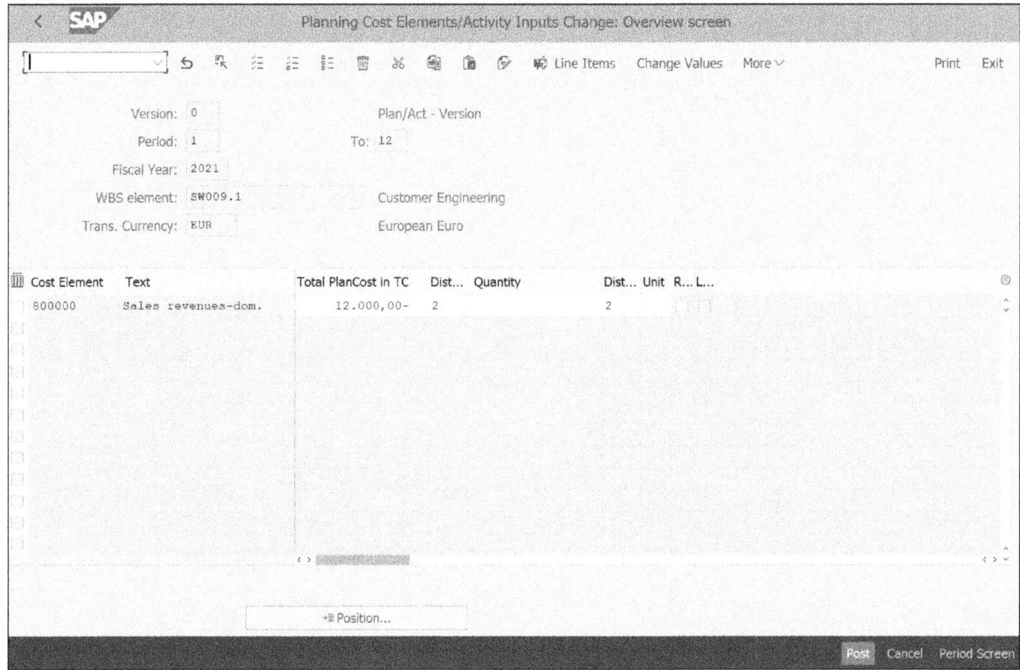


**Figure 7.132** Cost Element–Based Planning for Projects: Planning Screen

For the revenue general ledger account, enter a total plan amount of 12,000 EUR in the **Total PlanCost in TC** column. When you're done, click the **Post** button.

Do the same for the planned costs: plan 10,000 EUR for general ledger account 474210's travel expenses.

### Actual Postings and Period-End Close

Now let's move to the actual postings. Post with two business transactions on the project:

1. Activity allocation using Transaction KB21N or the Manage Direct Activity Allocation app, which we used in Section 7.2.4. This results in eight machine hours for a total amount of 800 EUR.
2. Travel expenses using Transaction KB11N or the Reassign Costs and Revenues app, which we used in Section 7.3.1, with a total amount of 100 EUR.

This leads to reporting in the Projects – Actuals app (SAP Fiori ID F0961A), as shown in Figure 7.133.

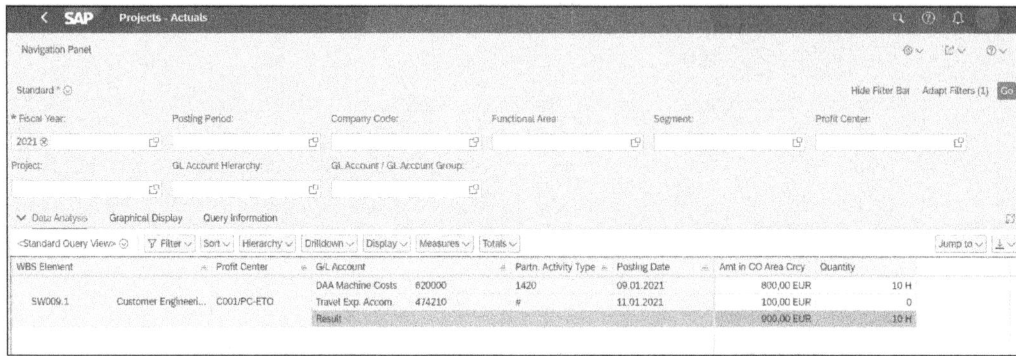

Figure 7.133 Actual Postings on Project

The 900 EUR actual value now needs to be transferred to profitability. First you need to define and post the matching revenues. So, start the results analysis with Transaction KKA2, arriving at the screen shown in Figure 7.134.

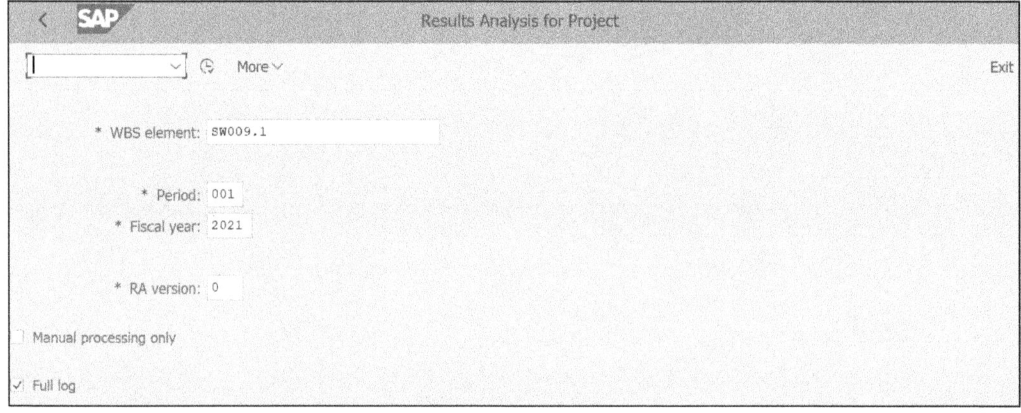


Figure 7.134 Results Analysis for Project: Selection Screen

Enter the WBS element in the **WBS element** field and the current **Period** of **001** and **Fiscal Year** of **2021** for which you want to calculate the revenue. Click the **Execute** button to arrive at the detail screen shown in Figure 7.135.

In the **Actual Data** section, you can see the posted actuals of 900 EUR. In the **Plan Data of Valuation** section, you can see the planned revenue of 12,000 EUR and costs of 10,000 EUR. The planned margin of 2,000 EUR is 20% of the planned costs.

We've assigned the IFRS accounting principle here; thus, we've already realized revenues with the cost postings based on the PoC method. The calculation results are in the **Calculated Profit/Loss** section. The calculated realized revenue is reflected in the **Revenue Affecting Net Income** line, showing 1,080 EUR.

Click **Save** to store the data in the results analysis persistence. The data isn't yet in the general ledger or the Universal Journal.

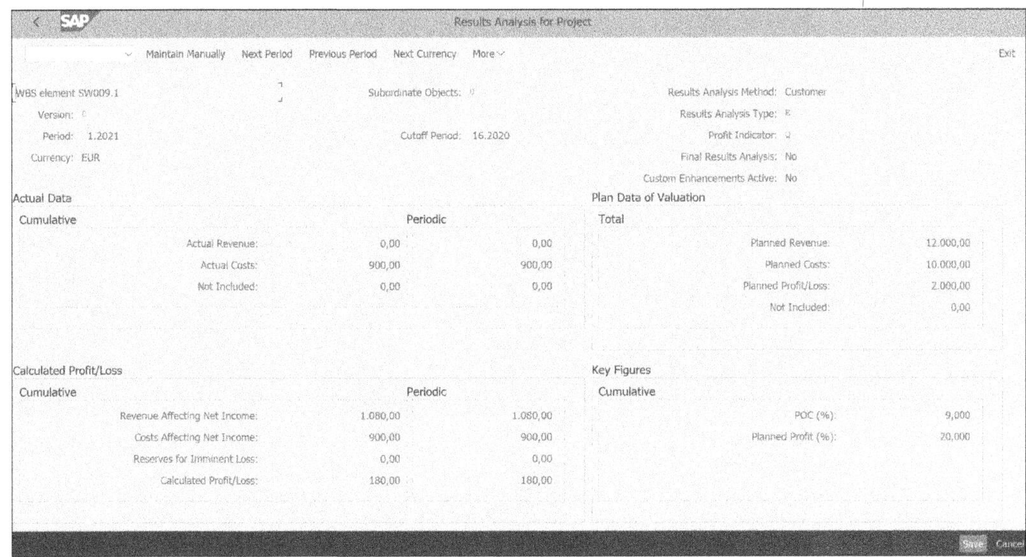

Figure 7.135 Results Analysis for Project: Calculation Results

To check the revenue recognition data, start the Report Writer–based Project Results report for the project (for Report Writer details, see Chapter 10, Section 10.6). Select the **SW009** project and click **Execute** to get the data shown in Figure 7.136.

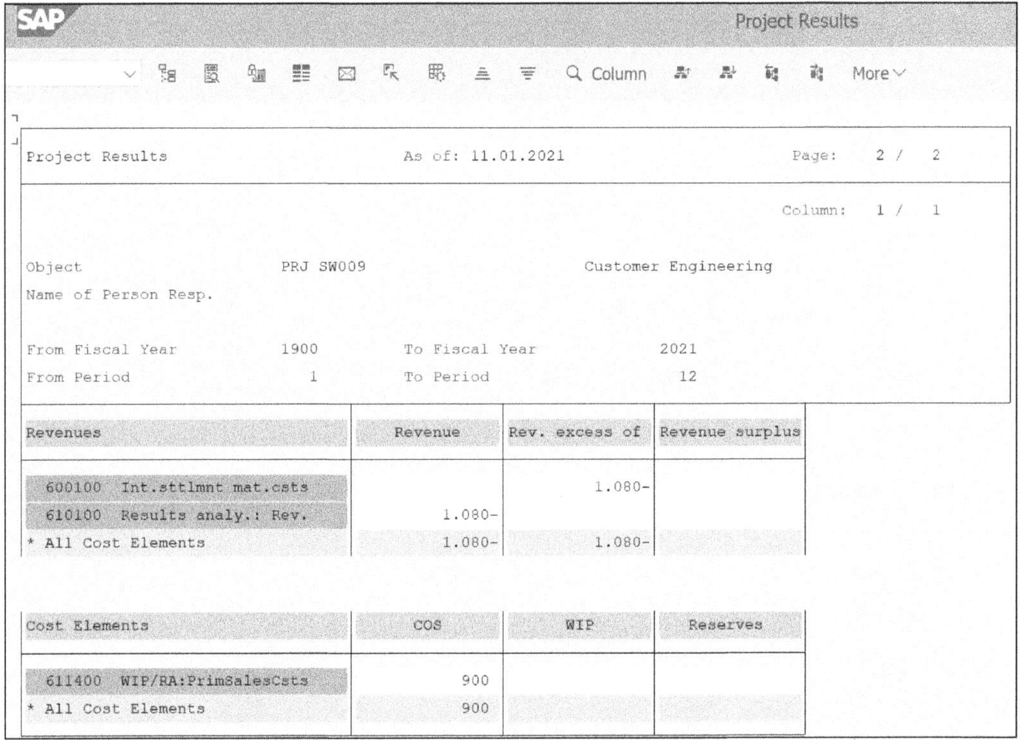

Figure 7.136 Results Analysis Data, Shown with Report Project Results

In the first column, you can see the realized revenue by the results analysis general ledger account **610100** of 1,080 EUR and the realized costs by the result analysis general ledger account **6114000** of 900 EUR.

These results analysis cost elements need to be assigned to settlement general ledger accounts. You do this in the allocation structure of the settlement profile. For the settlement profile parameter, recall Figure 7.130; for the allocation structure, see Chapter 5, Section 5.4.6.

Start the project settlement with Transaction CJ88 and arrive at the screen shown in Figure 7.137.

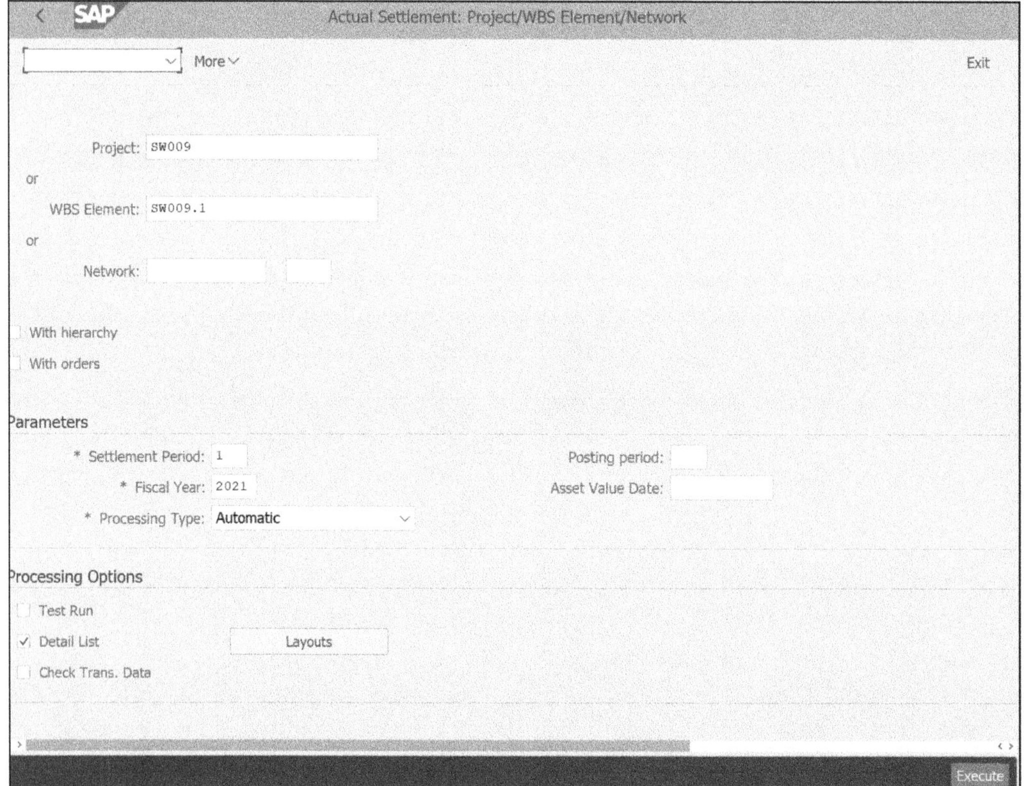


**Figure 7.137** Project Settlement: Selection Screen

Enter the **WBS Element** and the current period and year and click the **Execute** button. You can analyze the receiver as one result, as shown in Figure 7.138.

You'll see a profitability segment (**PSG**) as the **Receiver**. It's account-assigned with two lines with different cost elements:

1. The costs of the project, 900 EUR, are settled with cost element **600600**.
2. The revenues of 1,080 EUR are settled with cost element **600700**.

Actual Settlement: Project/WBS Element/Network Receiver debits

More

**Receiver debits**

**Senders** WBS SW009.1 Customer Engineering

| Receiver | Val/COArea Crcy | Cost Element | Typ |
|---|---|---|---|
| PSG 0000262844 | 900,00 | 600600 | PER |
| PSG 0000262844 | 1.080,00- | 600700 | PER |
| ■ | **180,00-** | | |

**Figure 7.138** Project Settlement Results: View of Receiver

Press F3 to access the settlement overview. Here, select the **Accounting Documents** button at the top of the screen. This takes you to the next screen, shown in Figure 7.139, which shows all related accounting documents.

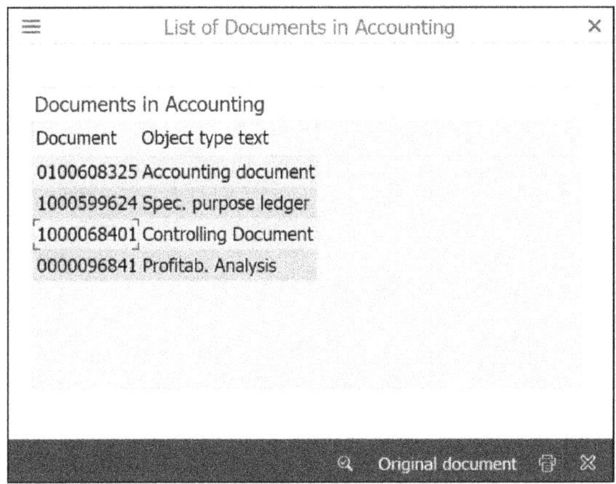


**Figure 7.139** Overview of Posted Documents for Settlement

Let's run through these posted documents:

- The first document is the settlement posting in the Universal Journal.
- The second document is the posting in the special ledger.
- The third document is the controlling document, which credits the WBS element and debits the profitability segment. As mentioned before, it no longer has its own persistency. It's just a view of the Universal Journal.
- The fourth document is the posting in the costing-based profitability analysis. There you can see the updated market segment attributes and value fields.

### Reporting

An aggregated view of all general ledger journal entries that are assigned to the project is shown in Figure 7.140 in the familiar Display Line Items—Margin Analysis app.

Display Line Items - Margin Analysis

project postings
Filtered By (5): Ledger, Company Code, Status, Posting Date, Project

Line Items (6) project controlling - margin view*

| Journal Entry | Bus. Tr... | Posting Date | G/L Account | Amount in CC Cr... | Fxd Amt in Glob Cr... | Object T... | WBS Element | Profit Center | Product Sold | Customer |
|---|---|---|---|---|---|---|---|---|---|---|
| Journal Entry: 100608164 | | | | | | | | | | |
| 100608164 | RKL | 09.01.2021 | 620000 (Dir. Int. Act. Alloc. Machine Costs) | 800,00 EUR | 800,00 EUR | PR | SW009.1 | PC-ETO (P... | FG201 (FG2... | CUF011001 ... |
| Journal Entry: 100608324 | | | | | | | | | | |
| 100608324 | RKU1 | 11.01.2021 | 474210 (Travel Expenses Accommodatio... | 100,00 EUR | 0,00 EUR | PR | SW009.1 | PC-ETO (P... | FG201 (FG2... | CUF011001 ... |
| Journal Entry: 100608325 | | | | | | | | | | |
| 100608325 | KOAO | 31.01.2021 | 600600 (settlement cogs) | -900,00 EUR | -800,00 EUR | PR | SW009.1 | PC-ETO (P... | FG201 (FG2... | CUF011001 ... |
| 100608325 | KOAO | 31.01.2021 | 600700 (settlement revenues) | 1.080,00 EUR | 0,00 EUR | PR | SW009.1 | PC-ETO (P... | FG201 (FG2... | CUF011001 ... |
| 100608325 | KOAO | 31.01.2021 | 600600 (settlement cogs) | 900,00 EUR | 800,00 EUR | EO | SW009.1 | PC-ETO (P... | FG201 (FG2... | CUF011001 ... |
| 100608325 | KOAO | 31.01.2021 | 600700 (settlement revenues) | -1.080,00 EUR | 0,00 EUR | EO | SW009.1 | PC-ETO (P... | FG201 (FG2... | CUF011001 ... |
| 100608325 | | | | 0,00 EUR | 0,00 EUR | | | | | |
| | | | | 900,00 EUR | 800,00 EUR | | | | | |

**Figure 7.140** Journal Entry Items Posted on Project

The first and second postings are the cost postings on the project. Here you can see that the market segment information is updated. This information is derived from the applied settlement rule. Note the fixed amount in the **Fxd Amt in Glob Cr...** column. The activity allocation is determined as fixed, while the travel expense is determined with no fixed portion and thus is completely variable.

The last journal entry is the settlement posting, with which we credited the project and posted to the profitability segment. The first two lines are account-assigned to the project, first for the costs and second for the revenues. The last two lines post on the profitability segment. Due to the settlement rule assignment (refer back to Figure 7.129), the WBS account assigned postings provide the market segments too.

Now let's look at how these postings on the profitability segments impacts the product profitability. Start the Product Profitability app for company code **F001** and filter on the **FG201** product. This leads to the reporting shown in Figure 7.141.

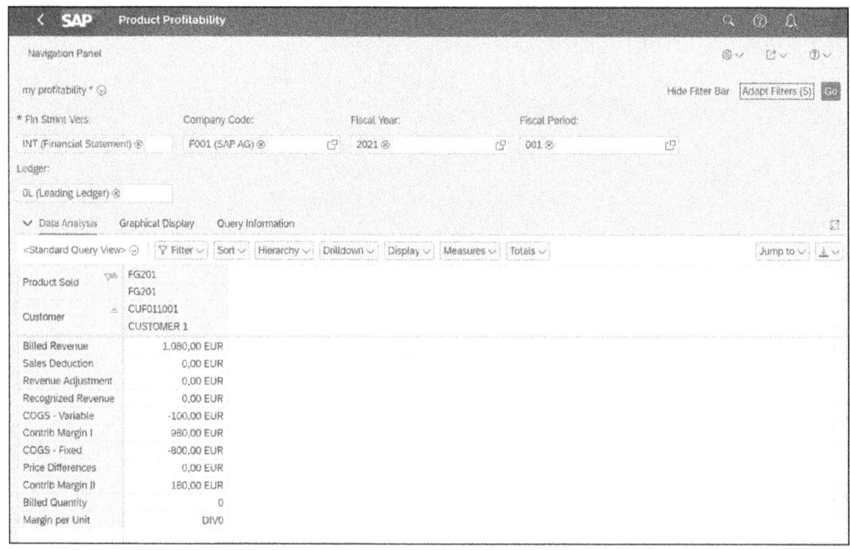


**Figure 7.141** Product Profitability Report for Settled Project

You'll see the multilevel cross-margin reporting:

- The settled revenues are reflected as recognized revenues of 1,080 EUR, and the variable costs of goods sold of 100 EUR reflects the settled travel costs. This leads to a contribution margin I of 980 EUR.
- The settled activity reflects the fixed cost of goods sold of 800 EUR. This leads to a contribution margin II of 180 EUR for the product and customer in this project.

This example shows how project costs and revenues can also be transferred to the market segment and included in margin reporting.



## 7.4 Service Scenarios

Service management is now part of SAP S/4HANA; before it was only offered in a separate system. Thus, in SAP ERP the integration of service management was only possible by mapping the service order to SAP ERP cost objects; the internal order was used primarily. In this scenario, the confirmations and the billing for the service order take place on the internal order. The entire process is coordinated by the account assignment manager and results in an internal order in SAP S/4HANA that includes additional attributes that link the order back to SAP Customer Relationship Management (SAP CRM).

In SAP S/4HANA, however, there is new integration into financials, but also into logistics, procurement, billing, and HR. There are service contracts and service orders available. Service contracts can be used to close service agreements with customers. As an example, consider a one-year maintenance contract for which an annual fee is due at the beginning of the period. The service order enables the provisioning and billing of services to a customer. An example could be a repair at customer site, spending technician hours and spare parts.

As always, SAP began development with SAP S/4HANA Cloud first.

**Cloud versus On-Premise**

The new service management scenario we show in this chapter is currently only available in SAP S/4HANA Cloud, but it's planned in the roadmap for on-premise. The scenario with the account assignment manager (where an internal order is created to represent the service order) is still available in on-premise.

In this section, we'll first introduce the new controlling object, which enables a new service order and contract-specific reporting and their assignment in multiple financial and logistic applications. We'll also explain the guiding principles we follow for this scenario. Then we'll show in the SAP S/4HANA Cloud system how the service order and its business transactions are integrated into controlling. We'll also show the special processing for the service bundle and the service contract functionality. We'll close the section by looking at some reporting insights.

### 7.4.1 New Architecture for Service Management in SAP S/4HANA Cloud

SAP has developed a number of innovations in SAP S/4HANA Cloud for the integration of service management in financials, which we'll introduce here and demonstrate in the system. The basis is the new controlling object for service order items and contract items. Via the integration into the generic controlling interface (technically, a coding block), the new service objects are available for account assignment in several financial transactions (e.g., general ledger posting or reassignment of costs and revenues) and in logistical applications (e.g., procurement or supplier invoice and goods issue posting). This now allows for financial reporting related to the service document rather than reporting on a mapped internal order. This gives new insights (see Section 7.4.5).

With the new architecture, not only can a service order margin be provided by the postings on service objects, but a real-time margin reporting on the market segments also is available. With the use of the Universal Journal's integrated margin analysis, we derive for every posting on a service object a profitability segment, similar to the customer project scenarios shown throughout this chapter.

To achieve this, in addition to the controlling object, a service document item mirror table for controlling/accounting purposes is available (table FCO_SRVDOC), which carries the financial steering attributes like profit center and revenue recognition key, but also the market segment attributes like customer and product sold, as shown in Figure 7.142. The key fields are as follows (and the scenario behind these entries will be discussed in Section 7.4.3):

1. Reporting and account assignment is on the order item level.
2. The profit center is derived by default by the responsible employee, which is maintained in the service order. In the employee master, there must be a cost center assigned. In the cost center master, there is a profit center assigned. This can be read with creation of the mirror object. But there is also derivation logic in place, with which you can derive the profit center, such as from the material master.
3. For derivation of the revenue recognition key, there is a self-configuration activity available. With the current release, only the completed contract method is available. We'll show event-based revenue recognition postings later in this section.
4. If the service order is referenced to a contract, the contract item is stored in the service order item and in the mirror table. This allows for aggregated reporting for the service order contract and its assigned service orders.
5. There's a field for the reference service document item, which is used in the confirmation-based bundle (discussed later in this section).
6. Profitability segments are derived from service orders and items and are stored in every journal entry posted to the service order.

Search in Table: FCO_SRVDOC Financials View of Service Document
Number of hits: 3
Runtime: 00:00:01 Maximum no. of hits 500
Insert Column:

| SrvDocTy | ServiceDoc | SrvDocIte | CoCd | COAr | Profit C | Func. Area | RA Key | ObCur | Object Number | Object Number | RSrvDocIt | SOrg. | DChl | Dv | Material | Customer | Bill-to Party | Ship-to Party |
|---|---|---|---|---|---|---|---|---|---|---|---|---|---|---|---|---|---|---|
| SVO1 | 8000000001 | 10 | 1010 | A000 | YB101 | YB25 | CCOCC | EUR | SV800000000100001 | SC700000000000010 | | 1010 | 10 | 00 | SRV_01 | 10100001 | 10100001 | 10100001 |
| SVO1 | 8000000001 | 20 | 1010 | A000 | YB101 | YB25 | CCOCC | EUR | SV800000000100002 | SC700000000000010 | | 1010 | 10 | 00 | SRV_02 | 10100001 | 10100001 | 10100001 |
| SVO1 | 8000000001 | 30 | 1010 | A000 | YB101 | YB25 | CCOCC | EUR | SV800000000100003 | SC700000000000010 | | 1010 | 10 | 00 | SRV_05 | 10100001 | 10100001 | 10100001 |

**Figure 7.142** Controlling/Accounting Mirror Table for Service Document Item

The new controlling object and the accounting mirror table are created when the service order and its items are released. From this point in time, confirmations and postings to the service order item can be made.

With the use of the Universal Journal–integrated margin analysis, you can derive for every posting on a service object a profitability segment based on the attributes in the accounting mirror object and can enrich the journal entry—as you do in the customer project scenario discussed in Section 7.3.

The derivation logic of the profitability attributes is shown in Figure 7.143.

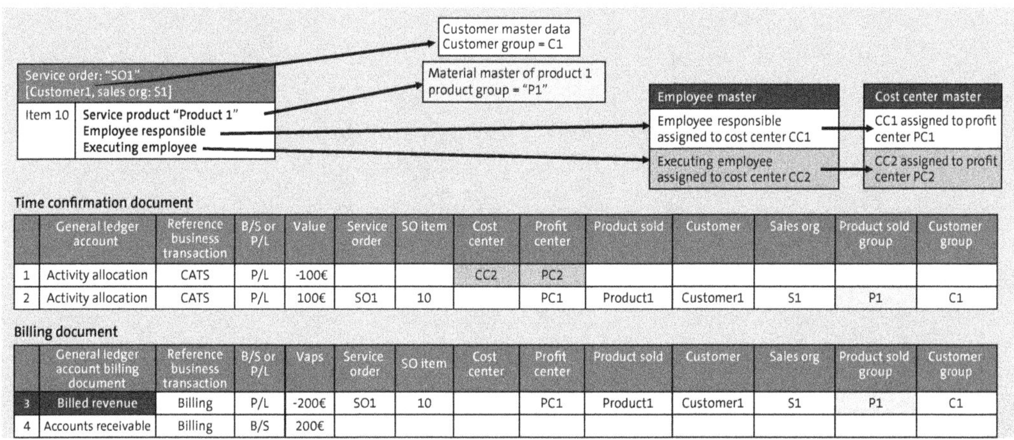


**Figure 7.143** Derivation Logic for Journal Entry Attributes Posted on Service Documents

Attributes like the customer, the product sold, or the sales organization are derived from the service order and the corresponding financial mirror object. Within the profitability segment derivation logic, additional attributes are derived by reading the master data: the product group from the product master, and the industry and customer group from the business partner. If there are profitability extensibility fields available, they will be derived and assigned to the journal entry item too.

There are rules for change management in place to ensure this architecture and avoid inconsistent data:

- The profit center assignment in the service order/contract item must not be changed if there are any postings on the service order item.
- The service contract assignment in service order items must not be changed if there are any postings on the service order item.
- If profitability attributes in the customer or product master or rules for extensibility fields change, there is a profitability realignment in place, as we showed in Section 7.3.2.

If you want to report on a service order item based not on its single items but more on an aggregated/bundled view, there are service bundle scenarios available. We have two in place:

1. **Fixed-price bundle**
   You can use the fixed-price bundle if you bill and control your margin on an aggregated level. There is one main item, which you bill for and for which you perform your margin analysis. In this case there is one controlling object created for the items, which is assigned to several service order items. An example could be inspection or oil change: you might bill a fixed amount for an inspection, such as $190, but you need additional items for the time-of-service technician, expenses, and purchased spare parts. This setup is discussed in Section 7.4.3.
2. **Confirmation-based bundle**
   Another bundle scenario is the confirmation-based bundle. Here you have a main item serving as a business bracket for several service items, which are confirmation- and billing-relevant and subitems to the main item. The main item defines the product sold. It doesn't trigger costs and revenues, but it can be used as information in the invoice output. Figure 7.144 shows an example of this architecture. As there is no confirmation and billing done for main item 10, there's no controlling object created.

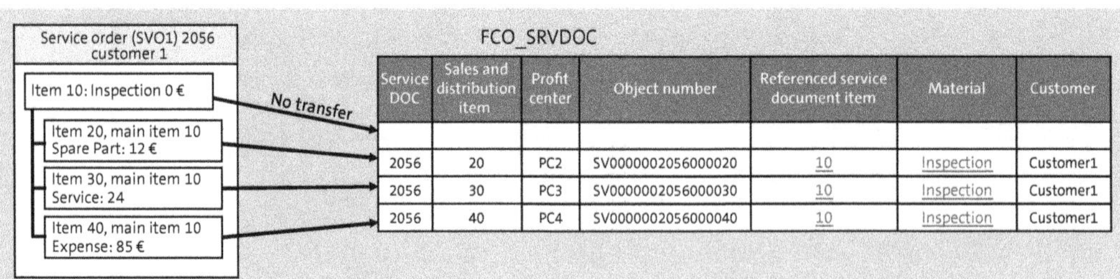


| Service DOC | Sales and distribution item | Profit center | Object number | Referenced service document item | Material | Customer |
|---|---|---|---|---|---|---|
| | | | | | | |
| 2056 | 20 | PC2 | SV0000002056000020 | 10 | Inspection | Customer1 |
| 2056 | 30 | PC3 | SV0000002056000030 | 10 | Inspection | Customer1 |
| 2056 | 40 | PC4 | SV0000002056000040 | 10 | Inspection | Customer1 |

**Figure 7.144** Architecture for Confirmation-Based Bundle

In the confirmation-based bundle, the subitems provide costs, their confirmations are sent to billing, and that leads to revenues on the subitem controlling object. There is a link in the accounting mirror table for these items to the referenced service document main item 10. The product sold is copied from the main item, so you get the margin for the inspection and not for the single items, like the service item. There can be different profit centers derived per service order item.

### 7.4.2 Guiding Principles and Financial Value Flow

You follow the same principles in the service scenario as already shown in the customer project and the sales scenarios:

- Profitability attributes are now available for general ledger journal entries. You use this in the service scenario to assign them, such as in the journal entry items for WIP, billing documents, and good issues. This provides a real-time market segment and profitability reporting.
- Settlement between the controlling and profitability applications is obsolete. You enrich the profitability attributes in the service order scenario at the time of posting on the service order item. Thus, period-end closing for service orders is simplified and accelerated.
- With the use of event-based revenue recognition (see Section 7.5), the matching principle for cost and revenues is ensured, as well as periodic revenue realization in the service contract scenario. For service orders, SAP S/4HANA Cloud release 2102 provides the completed contract method.
- Based on the Universal Journal, the new attribution of margin analysis attributes and event-based revenue recognition are possible, which we'll cover in Section 7.4.5.

Figure 7.145 shows an example for a controlling value flow including the cost centers and their under-/overabsorption. It's a detailed view of the value flow shown previously in Figure 7.1. The scenario shown here is a confirmation-based bundle without event-based revenue recognition active. However, the value flow is valid for all service scenarios.

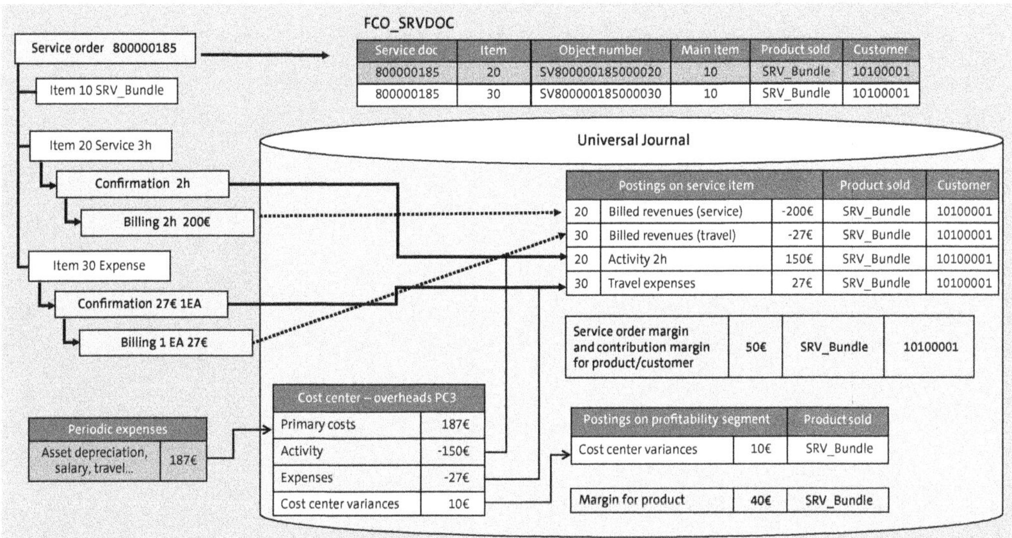


**Figure 7.145** Value Flow for Service Scenario

The confirmation of service and expense items credit cost centers and debit service orders. These costs and the billed revenue provide a margin for the service order. As we applied margin analysis attributing in parallel for these service order postings, we can provide a margin analysis for market segments, too. We used product sold and customer as example market segment fields.

The cost center is debited with periodic costs like asset depreciation, travel expenses, or salary expenses. At period end, there will be a difference in the cost center between these debits and the credits posted to service orders. These differences can be allocated to a profitability segment, as shown in Section 7.2.5. The assumption in the example here is that they can be assigned on the product level. The level of assignment depends on the customer business.

So, the margin analysis can be provided just with an aggregation of journal entries: postings on the service order and the allocation to profitability segment. There is no additional periodic step necessary, like settlement. In this example, this provides a multilevel margin for the `SRV_Bundle` product of 40 EUR.

### 7.4.3 Business Transactions

In this section, we'll discuss the service scenarios based on SAP S/4HANA Cloud release 2102.

Basically, service orders are divided into two types based on the billing method: fixed-price service orders and confirmation-based service orders. In the fixed price scenario, billing is based on the quantity and price of the service order items. In the confirmation-based scenario, the billing is triggered by the confirmations. In particular, the billing quantity is defined by the confirmations, but price-relevant attributes such as the billing indicator (billable or goodwill) can also be applied here.

Several item categories are available for the service order items, which determine the subsequent business transactions:

- **Service item**
  Used for the confirmation of technician times. This triggers the time sheet and subsequently activity allocation in controlling. In contrast to the production time confirmations in Chapter 6, the time sheet is used here to enable reporting of employee capacity utilization and operating planning, like in the customer project scenario.
- **Expense item**
  For the confirmation of expenses such as travel costs. This triggers a cost allocation from the service technician's cost center to the service order item.
- **Material stock service part**
  Triggers goods issue from the stock to the service order item.
- **Subcontractor service part for integration of subcontractor support**
  Triggers a purchase order and subcontractor time confirmation by service entry sheet.

- **Service part**
  For purchasing service order–related materials. This triggers a purchase order and subsequent goods receipt posting to service order.

As mentioned, there are two options to assign the controlling object to service order items. We start now with a service order, in which every item is assigned to a controlling object.



### Service Order Scenario with Controlling on Service Order Item Level

We'll walk through the steps for several key confirmations in this section, followed by billing and period-end close.

#### *Service Order Confirmation*

With the Manage Service Orders app (SAP Fiori ID F3571A), service orders can be maintained and confirmations created, as shown in Figure 7.146. With the creation of a service order, you determine the customer and the order type, which defines the billing method. In this example, we've selected a confirmation-based order type and the customer, which is visible in the **Sold-To Party** field (**Inlandskunde DE 1**). Click the **Save** button and then the **Edit** button to get to the screen shown in Figure 7.146.

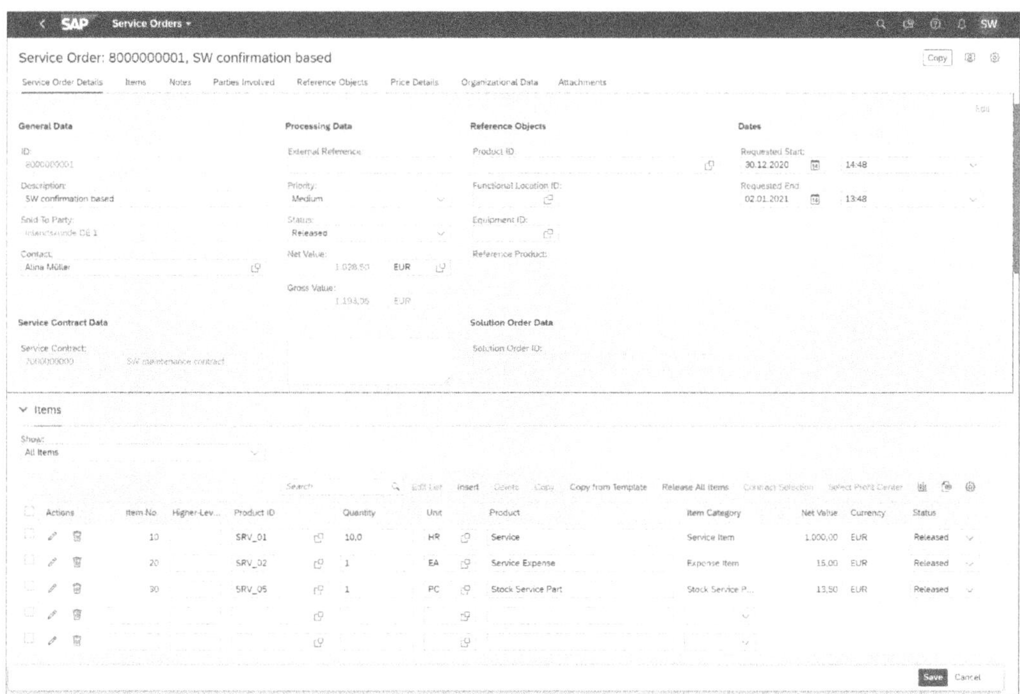


**Figure 7.146** Service Order Master with Confirmation-Based Billing Type

Then we added three items:

1. Item **10** has 10 technician hours planned, reflected as **Product ID SRV_01**, with a planned billing value of 1,000 EUR in the **Net Value** column.
2. Item **20** reflects the expected travel expense of the technician, **Product ID SRV_02**, with the planned billing value of 15 EUR.
3. Item **30** is the spare part taken from stock, **Product ID SRV_05**, which has a planned price of 13.50 EUR per piece.

In the combination of customer and product in the service order, the system checks whether there is a contract with the customer available. In this example, there is: **Service Contract 7000000000** was found and assigned. We'll revisit this later in this section.

Release the service order by selecting **Released** in the **Status** field in Figure 7.146. With this, the controlling objects are created. You can check table FCO_SRVDOC with Transaction SE16H, as shown in Figure 7.147.

| SrvDocTy... | ServiceDoc | SrvDocIte... | CoCd | COAr | Profit C. | Func. Area | RA Key | ObCur | Object Number | Object Number | SOrg. | DChl | Dv | Material | Customer | Bill-to Party |
|---|---|---|---|---|---|---|---|---|---|---|---|---|---|---|---|---|
| SVO1 | 8000000001 | 10 | 1010 | A000 | YB101 | YB25 | CCOCC | EUR | SV800000000100001 | SC700000000000010 | 1010 | 10 | 00 | SRV_01 | 10100001 | 10100001 |
| SVO1 | 8000000001 | 20 | 1010 | A000 | YB101 | YB25 | CCOCC | EUR | SV800000000100002 | SC700000000000010 | 1010 | 10 | 00 | SRV_02 | 10100001 | 10100001 |
| SVO1 | 8000000001 | 30 | 1010 | A000 | YB101 | YB25 | CCOCC | EUR | SV800000000100003 | SC700000000000010 | 1010 | 10 | 00 | SRV_05 | 10100001 | 10100001 |

**Figure 7.147** Reflection of Service Order in Table FCO_SRVDOC

For all three items, an entry is created with its own controlling object in the **Object Number** column. For all three items, there is a link to the contract with the customer in the **Object Number** column, beginning with **SC** for service contract. And there is a revenue recognition key derived in the **RA Key** column. On the right you can see the market segment fields.

Now let's start the confirmation of the service item. In the Manage Service Orders app, you can click the **Create Confirmation** button to go to the confirmation screen shown in Figure 7.148.

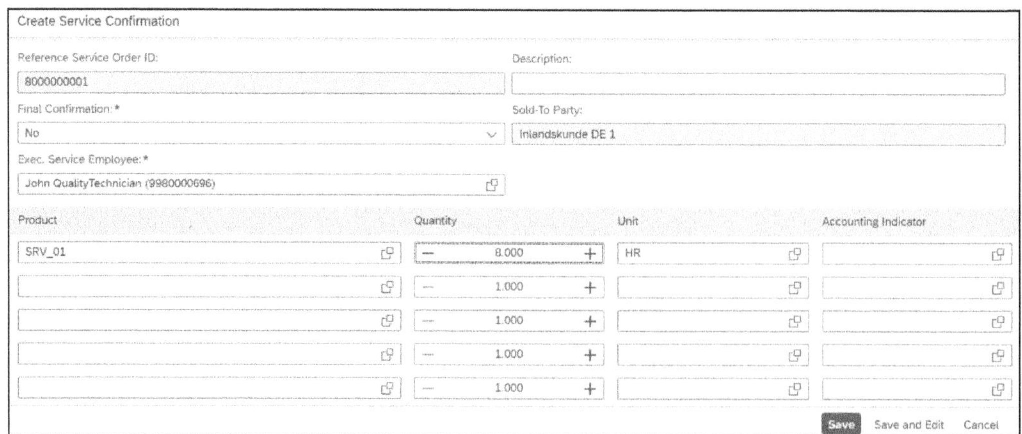


**Figure 7.148** Service Confirmation Header with Selection of Executing Service Employee

You first need to enter the execution service employee (the employee who did the work) in the **Exec. Service Employee** field. Then you need to select for which item you want to perform the confirmation via the **Product** field. You'll see a list of all three items; select **SRV_01**, which is a service product.

Click the **Save and Edit** button to arrive at the next screen, shown in Figure 7.149.

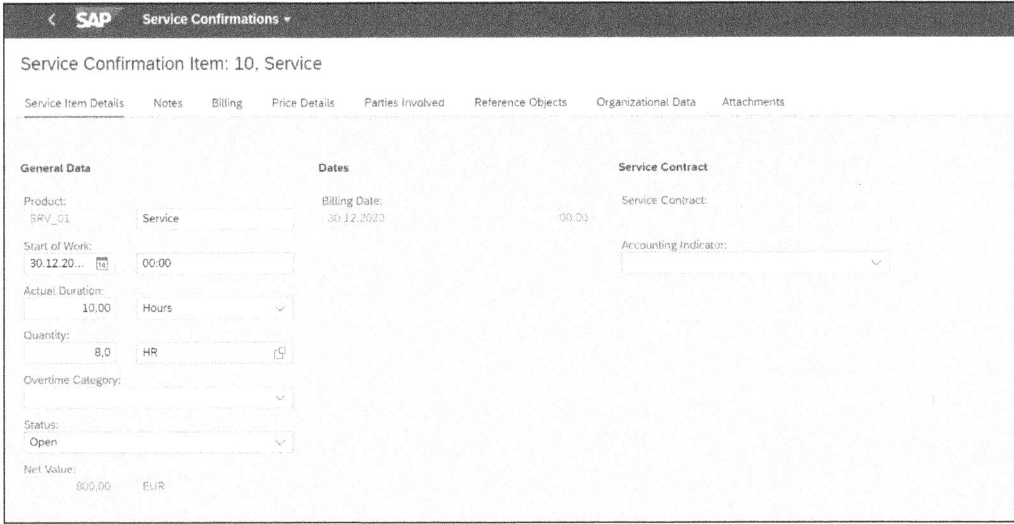


**Figure 7.149** Service Confirmation Details with Two Quantities, One for Costs and One for Billing

Two quantities can be entered:

1. The **Quantity** of eight hours is the quantity that's billed.
2. The **Actual Duration** of 10 hours is sent to the time sheet and posted in controlling as costs.

The **Accounting Indicator** is mapped to the billable control financial attribute and is provided in the cost journal entry. The **Accounting Indicator** influences the sales price of the service confirmation. So, for example, you can define in the confirmation that the item is free of charge.

For service confirmation, an **Overtime Category** can be provided. The overtime attribute needs to be enabled in HR configuration. Let's look at an example. Create an additional service confirmation for the service item and go to the screen shown in Figure 7.150.

In the confirmation, define that the two hours were provided on a weekend, indicated by the **Quantity** field and the **Overtime Category** (**work on weekend**, in this example). This impacts the subsequent processes: based on the overtime category, sales prices and cost rates can be determined. And **Overtime Category** is an attribute in the cost journal entry item, which we'll discuss next.

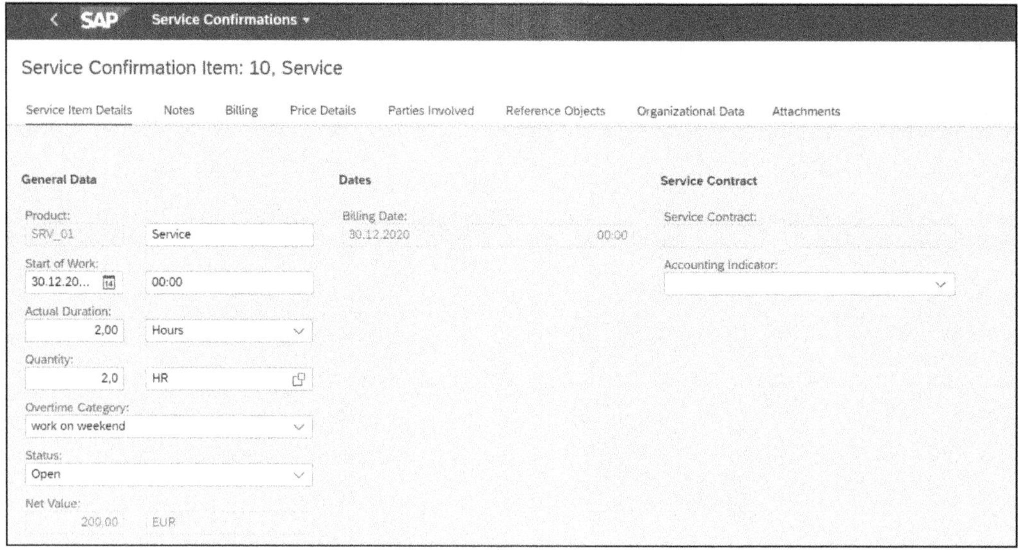


**Figure 7.150** Service Confirmation with Overtime

Let's look at the cost rate definition with the Manage Cost Rates—Professional Services app, as shown in Figure 7.151.



| Receiving Company | ICO Rate | Cost Center | Overtime Category | Activity Type | Service Cost Level | From FY | From Period | Rate | | per | Activity Unit |
|---|---|---|---|---|---|---|---|---|---|---|---|
| | No | 10101902 (Csltg Unit A (DE)) | | SV01 (Service Time) | | 2020 | 001 | 75.00 | EUR | 1 | H |
| | No | 10101902 (Csltg Unit A (DE)) | WE | SV01 (Service-Time) | | 2020 | 012 | 100.00 | EUR | 1 | H |

**Figure 7.151** Cost Rates for Services Distinguished by Overtime Category

Both lines define a cost rate in **Company Code 1010** for the **Cost Center 10101902** and the **Activity Type SV01** valid **From Period 001** in fiscal year 2020.

In this example of overtime service on weekend, attribute **WE** in the **Overtime Category** column has a higher cost rate of 100 EUR per hour than the service provided during normal working hours, with a rate of 75 EUR per hour.

As mentioned in Chapter 4, Section 4.3.2, with this app, cost rates for activities can be defined very flexibly in SAP S/4HANA Cloud. In the service scenario, this is relevant for several additional use cases:

- Rates can be defined based on *who provides*—that is, executing employee dependent—or *what is provided*—that is, activity type/service product dependent.

- The attribute service cost level can be maintained in the executing employee's master data and is taken into account for valuating time confirmation. This allows you, for example, to define a higher rate for the same service if a chief technician provides the service (refer back to Figure 7.77).
- For intercompany time confirmation, there can be specific rates. For involved technicians from affiliated companies, you can define rates with an additional markup (see Chapter 9).

7

In the Manage Service Orders app (refer back to Figure 7.146), you can set the **Status** of the two confirmations to **Completed**, after which they're transferred to accounting. Now let's look at the created journal entries in the Display Line Items—Margin Analysis app, as shown in Figure 7.152.

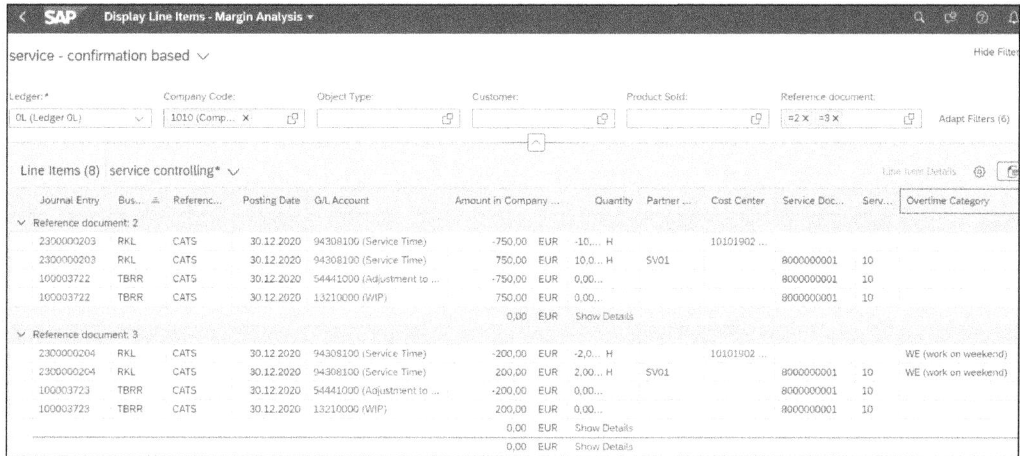


| Journal Entry | Bus... | Referenc... | Posting Date | G/L Account | Amount in Company ... | | Quantity | Partner ... | Cost Center | Service Doc... | Serv... | Overtime Category |
|---|---|---|---|---|---|---|---|---|---|---|---|---|
| Reference document: 2 | | | | | | | | | | | | |
| 2300000203 | RKL | CATS | 30.12.2020 | 94308100 (Service Time) | -750,00 | EUR | -10,... H | | 10101902 ... | | | |
| 2300000203 | RKL | CATS | 30.12.2020 | 94308100 (Service Time) | 750,00 | EUR | 10,0... H | SV01 | | 8000000001 | 10 | |
| 100003722 | TBRR | CATS | 30.12.2020 | 54441000 (Adjustment to ... | -750,00 | EUR | 0,00... | | | 8000000001 | 10 | |
| 100003722 | TBRR | CATS | 30.12.2020 | 13210000 (WIP) | 750,00 | EUR | 0,00... | | | 8000000001 | 10 | |
| | | | | | 0,00 | EUR | Show Details | | | | | |
| Reference document: 3 | | | | | | | | | | | | |
| 2300000204 | RKL | CATS | 30.12.2020 | 94308100 (Service Time) | -200,00 | EUR | -2,0... H | | 10101902 ... | | | WE (work on weekend) |
| 2300000204 | RKL | CATS | 30.12.2020 | 94308100 (Service Time) | 200,00 | EUR | 2,00... H | SV01 | | 8000000001 | 10 | WE (work on weekend) |
| 100003723 | TBRR | CATS | 30.12.2020 | 54441000 (Adjustment to ... | -200,00 | EUR | 0,00... | | | 8000000001 | 10 | |
| 100003723 | TBRR | CATS | 30.12.2020 | 13210000 (WIP) | 200,00 | EUR | 0,00... | | | 8000000001 | 10 | |
| | | | | | 0,00 | EUR | Show Details | | | | | |
| | | | | | 0,00 | EUR | Show Details | | | | | |

**Figure 7.152** Journal Entries of Service Order Service Time Confirmations: Main View

You can see that the two confirmations are reflected by two journal entries in accounting via two time sheet entries. The reference documents **2** and **3** are the time sheet documents (see also the reference document type **CATS** in the **Referenc...** column). The difference between the two entries is valuation of the costs. The second journal entry is created by the confirmation with the overtime category WE and thus with a cost rate of 100 EUR per hour. The first journal entry uses the cost rate of 75 EUR per hour.

Let's take a deeper look at the two journal entries subordinated to the **Reference document: 3** timesheet.

The first journal entry, **2300000204**, is the activity allocation: the first line item credits the cost center, which is assigned to the executing employee master, and the second line item debits service order item **800000001/10**. On the service order line item, you see the activity type derived from the service material.

There is also an additional revenue recognition journal entry created, **100003723**. Event-based revenue recognition is in place with the completed contract method. To provide the correct margin analysis at any time on the journal entries, a real-time matching principle for cost of sales and revenues is applied (see Section 7.5). Thus, the posted costs are deferred as WIP. The cost will be realized when the service order item is completed and all revenues are billed. Thus, the first line item of document **10003723** is posted with the cost adjustment P&L account and the primary costs category and the second line item activates the costs on the WIP balance sheet account. Note that both line items are account-assigned to the service order.

**Note**

If you bill the confirmation immediately within the same period and it's sufficient for you to have a period margin view after period-end close, then you can work without the event-based revenue recognition.

Let's take a second look at these journal entries and analyze the market segment view in the Display Line Items—Margin Analysis app, as shown in Figure 7.153.

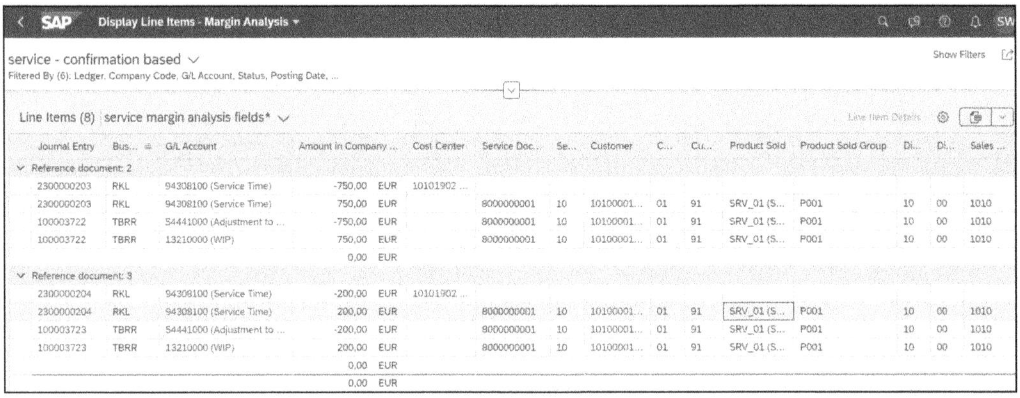

Display Line Items - Margin Analysis

service - confirmation based

Filtered By (6): Ledger, Company Code, G/L Account, Status, Posting Date, ...

Line Items (8) service margin analysis fields*

| Journal Entry | Bus... | G/L Account | Amount in Company ... | | Cost Center | Service Doc... | Se... | Customer | C... | Cu... | Product Sold | Product Sold Group | Di... | Di... | Sales ... |
|---|---|---|---|---|---|---|---|---|---|---|---|---|---|---|---|
| Reference document: 2 | | | | | | | | | | | | | | | |
| 2300000203 | RKL | 94308100 (Service Time) | -750,00 | EUR | 10101902 ... | | | | | | | | | | |
| 2300000203 | RKL | 94308100 (Service Time) | 750,00 | EUR | | 8000000001 | 10 | 10100001... | 01 | 91 | SRV_01 (S... | P001 | 10 | 00 | 1010 |
| 100003722 | TBRR | 54441000 (Adjustment to ... | -750,00 | EUR | | 8000000001 | 10 | 10100001... | 01 | 91 | SRV_01 (S... | P001 | 10 | 00 | 1010 |
| 100003722 | TBRR | 13210000 (WIP) | 750,00 | EUR | | 8000000001 | 10 | 10100001... | 01 | 91 | SRV_01 (S... | P001 | 10 | 00 | 1010 |
| | | | 0,00 | EUR | | | | | | | | | | | |
| Reference document: 3 | | | | | | | | | | | | | | | |
| 2300000204 | RKL | 94308100 (Service Time) | -200,00 | EUR | 10101902 ... | | | | | | | | | | |
| 2300000204 | RKL | 94308100 (Service Time) | 200,00 | EUR | | 8000000001 | 10 | 10100001... | 01 | 91 | SRV_01 (S... | P001 | 10 | 00 | 1010 |
| 100003723 | TBRR | 54441000 (Adjustment to ... | -200,00 | EUR | | 9000000001 | 10 | 10100001... | 01 | 91 | SRV_01 (S... | P001 | 10 | 00 | 1010 |
| 100003723 | TBRR | 13210000 (WIP) | 200,00 | EUR | | 8000000001 | 10 | 10100001... | 01 | 91 | SRV_01 (S... | P001 | 10 | 00 | 1010 |
| | | | 0,00 | EUR | | | | | | | | | | | |
| | | | 0,00 | EUR | | | | | | | | | | | |

**Figure 7.153** Journal Entries of Service Order Service Time Confirmations: Margin Analysis View

Additional journal entry fields are selected here that are relevant for margin analysis reporting. You can see the following margin analysis fields derived and stored in the journal entry: the customer group, industry **91**, product sold **SRV_01**, product sold group **P001**, distribution channel **10**, division **00**, and sales organization **1010**.

These fields are available for the costs and the revenue recognition documents. If you look at revenue recognition line item **13210000** (WIP), you can see, for example, that the service document and customer **10100001** are applied. This will allow a drilldown in the Trial Balance app (see Section 7.4.5).

For derivation of the activity type, there's a self-service configuration available. You can find this in the Manage Your Solution app within the **Service Cost Management** activity group, as shown in Figure 7.154.

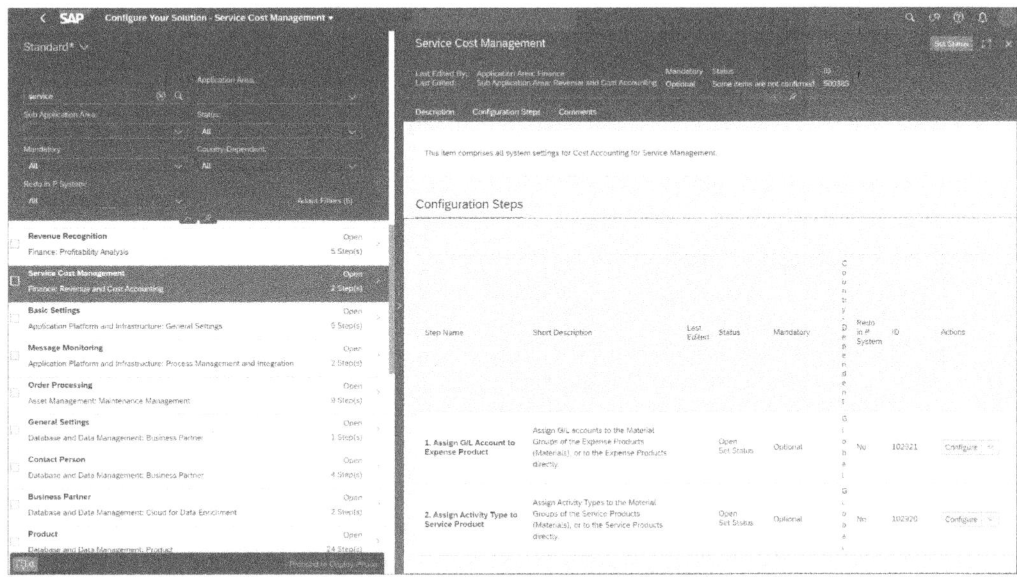


Figure 7.154 Configuration Activities for Service-Controlling Integration

There are two configuration steps available: one for expense account derivation and one for the activity type derivation. Click the **Configure** button for the second option to reach the screen shown in Figure 7.155.

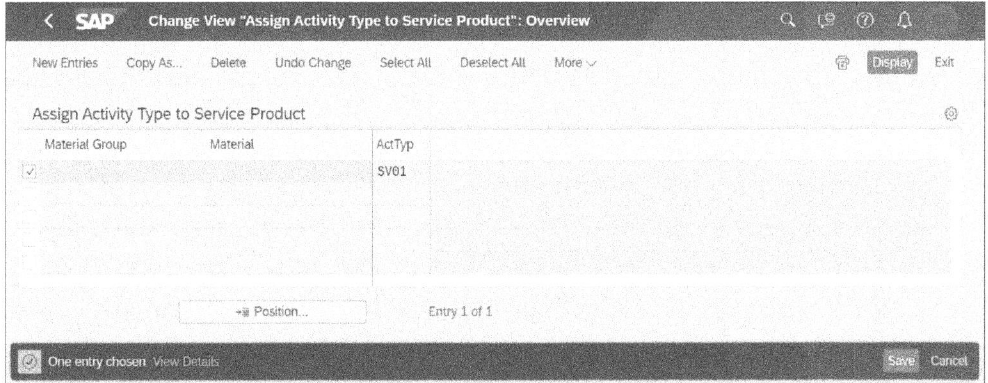


Figure 7.155 Configuration for Assignment Activity Type to Service Product

Based on the **Material Group** or a dedicated service **Material**, an activity type can be derived. In this example, activity type **SV01** is used for all materials.

> **Cost Rates per Employee Role**
>
> It's no longer necessary to define a specific activity type per employee role, like technician or chief technician, to get different cost rates. This can be controlled, as mentioned before, via the service cost level, stored in the employee master.

### *Expense Item Confirmation*

Now we come to the confirmation of the expense item. Create a confirmation in the Manage Service Orders app like for the service item; this time, select the expense item (**SRV_02**) and click the **Save and Edit** button. You'll go to the confirmation detail screen of the expense item, as shown in Figure 7.156.

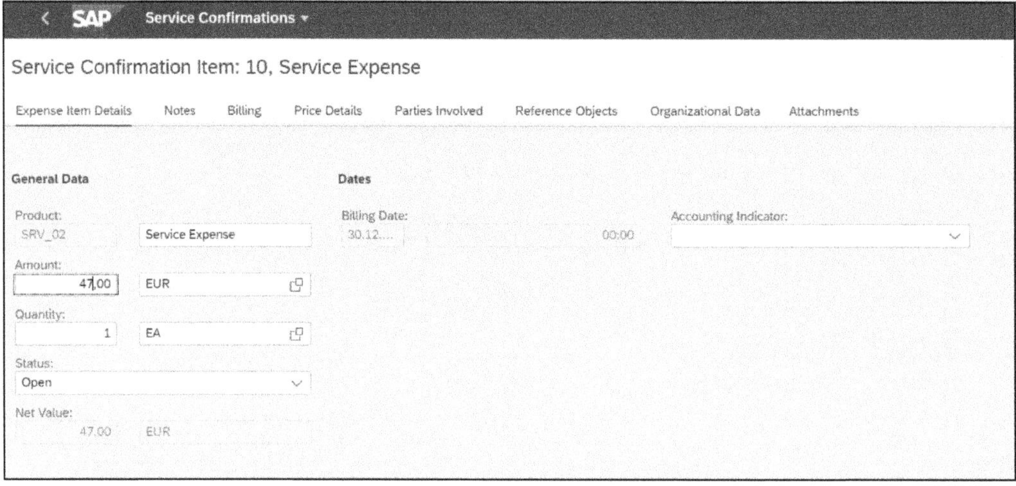


Figure 7.156 Confirmation Detail of Expense Item

Here you maintain the expense **Amount** of 47 EUR. This amount is posted as a cost and used for pricing. If required, surcharges can be maintained in the pricing scheme.

With the completion of the service confirmation, a cost reposting in controlling is triggered by the system, as we showed in the Reassign Costs and Revenues app (see the earlier example in Figure 7.31). For the reposting, you need a sending cost center—in this case, 10101902, which is derived from the executing employee. To get a general ledger expense account, the expense material of the service order item is mapped to a general ledger account via configuration with SSCUI 102921 (see Figure 7.158 ahead).

Two journal entries are created by the expense confirmation, as shown in Figure 7.157.

Ledger: * 0L (Ledger 0L) | Company Code: 1010 (Comp... 10... | Object Type: | Customer: | Product Sold: | Reference document: =200000001 | Adapt Filters (6) | Go

Line Items (4) service controlling*

| Journal Entry | Bus... | Reference ... | Referenc... | G/L Account | Amount in Compa... | | Quantity | | Service Document | Service Doc... | Cost Center | Personnel Number | Customer |
|---|---|---|---|---|---|---|---|---|---|---|---|---|---|
| 2300000205 | RKU1 | 200000001 | COBK | 61008000 (Travel ... | -47,00 | EUR | -1,000 | EA | | | 10101902... | 50002474 | |
| 2300000205 | RKU1 | 200000001 | COBK | 61008000 (Travel ... | 47,00 | EUR | 1,000 | EA | 8000000001 | 20 | | 50002474 | 10100001 (Inlan... |
| 100003724 | TBRR | 200000001 | COBK | 54441000 (Adjust... | -47,00 | EUR | 0,000 | | 8000000001 | 20 | | | 10100001 (Inlan... |
| 100003724 | TBRR | 200000001 | COBK | 13210000 (WIP) | 47,00 | EUR | 0,000 | | 8000000001 | 20 | | | 10100001 (Inlan... |
| | | | | | 0,00 | EUR | Show Details | | | | | | |

Figure 7.157 Journal Entries for Expense Confirmation

The first journal entry is the cost reposting, posted with the expense account **61008000 Travel Expenses**, which is derived by the SSCUI. The first line item credits the employee's

**Cost Center 10101902**. The executing employee is noted in the **Personnel Number** column. The second line debits the service order item.

Like for the service item, an event-based revenue recognition journal entry is created too, which defers the costs to allow matching of costs and revenues at the time of billing. Also, as for the service item, in the line account assigned to service item, the market segments are derived and stored in the journal entry; here you can see as an example the **Customer** in the far-right column.

For derivation of the expense **G/L Account** from the service material, there's a self-configuration activity available. You can click **Configure** for the first activity shown previously in Figure 7.154 to get to the screen shown in Figure 7.158.



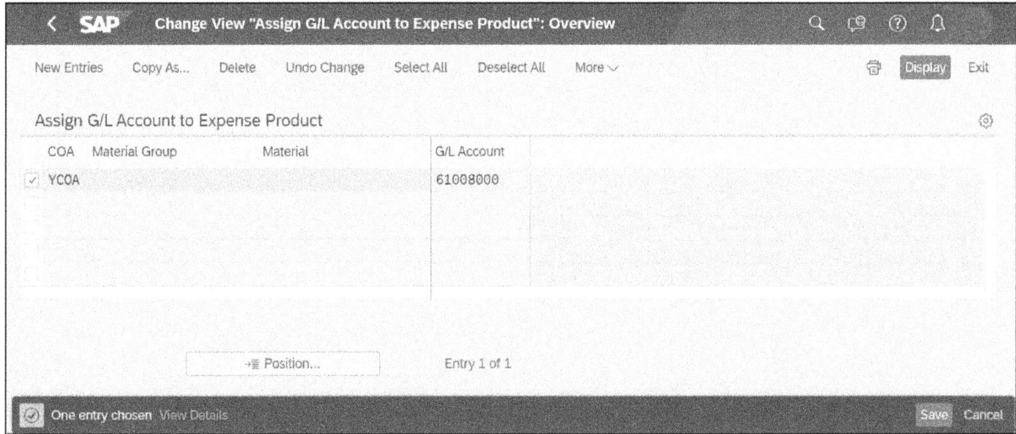


**Figure 7.158** Configuration for Derivation Expense Account for Expense Material

Based on the **Material Group** or a dedicated **Material**/product, an expense **G/L Account** can be derived. In this example, general ledger account **61008000** is used for all products.

### *Spare Part Confirmation*

Now let's do the confirmation of the spare part item. Once again, create a confirmation in the Manage Service Orders app, then select the spare part item and click the **Save and Edit** button. You'll see the confirmation detail screen of the expense item, as shown in Figure 7.159.

In the service confirmation of a spare part, the **Quantity** (here, one piece) and the **Product ID** (here, **SRV_05**) are defined.

With completion of the service confirmation, a goods movement is triggered by the system. A plant is also derived by the system based on the executing employee or service team.

Transaction MB51 will show you the material document posted by the system, as shown in Figure 7.160.

Service Confirmation: 9000000004, SW confirmation based

Service Confirmation Details Items Parties Involved Organizational Data

Service Confirmation Details

General Data
ID: 9000000004
Description: SW confirmation based
Sold-To Party: Inlandskunde DE 1
Contact: Alina Müller
Service Contract:

Processing Data
External Reference:
Life Cycle Status: Open
Net Value: 35,00 EUR
Canceled Internally:
Final Service Confirmation:

Reference Objects
Product ID:
Functional Location ID:
Equipment ID:
Reference Product:

Dates
Billing Date: 30.12.2020

Solution Order Data
Solution Order ID:

Items

Show: All Items

| Actions | Item No. | Product ID | Quantity | Unit | Product | Item Category | Net Value | Currency |
|---|---|---|---|---|---|---|---|---|
| | 10 | SRV_05 | 1 | PC | Stock Service Part | Service... | 35,00 | EUR |

**Figure 7.159** Confirmation of Spare Part Item

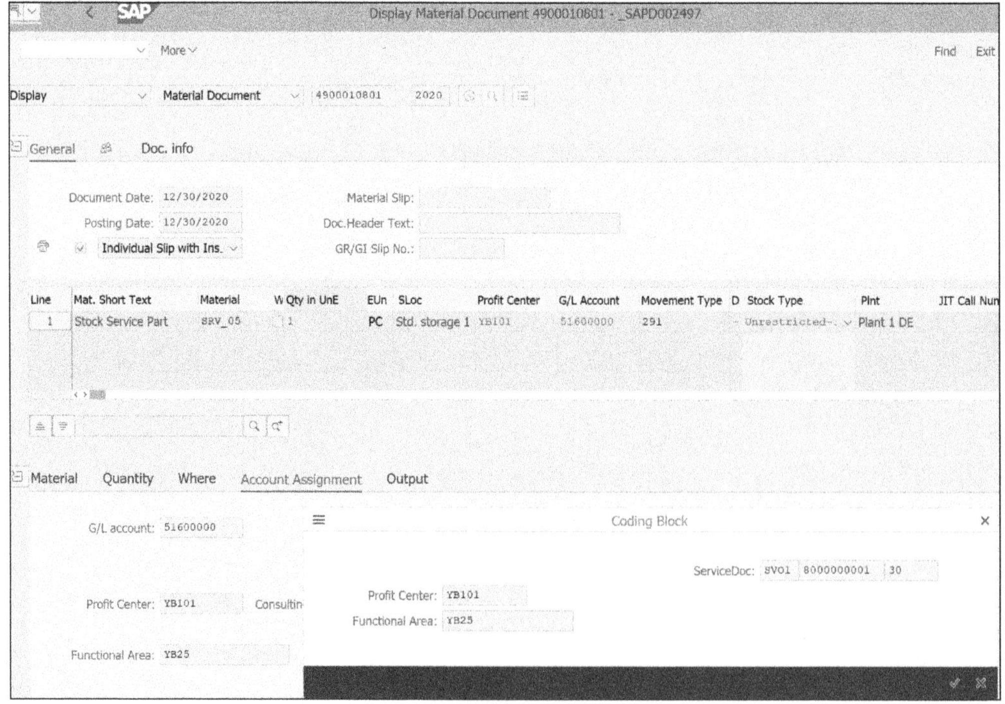


**Figure 7.160** Material Document with Transaction MB51

In the **Account Assignment** tab, you see service order item **800000001/30** assigned in the **Coding Block**. **G/L account 51600000** is derived based on the standard materials management account assignment configuration. The material movement is posted with goods **Movement Type 291** (consumption for all account assignments from warehouse) and transferred to accounting by the system. The amount for the posting is determined by the material master cost rate, here 30 EUR per piece, multiplied by the quantity. For material valuation, refer back to Figure 7.7.

Now, let's analyze the journal entries generated by service confirmation for the spare part in the Display Line Items—Margin Analysis app, as shown in Figure 7.161.

7

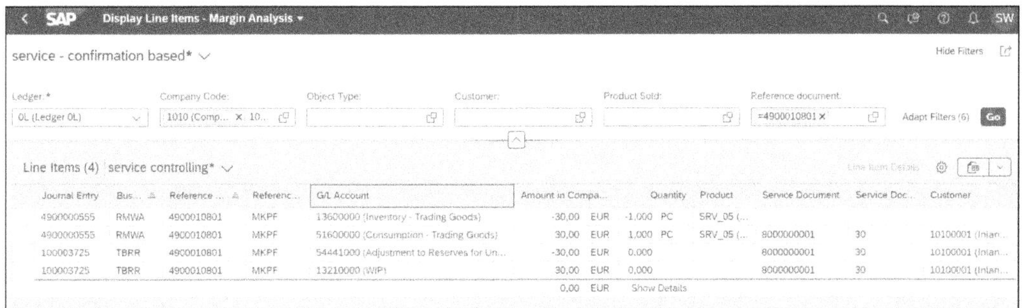


**Figure 7.161** Journal Entries for Material Consumption on Service Order

The first journal entry reflects the goods movement posting. The first line item is the credit of the inventory: the stock of material SRV_05 is reduced by one piece. The second line item is the goods issue consumption posting account assigned on the service order item.

As for the two other confirmations, an event-based revenue recognition journal entry is created too, which defers the consumption expenses to allow matching of costs and revenues at the point of time of billing.

Also, for these postings, the line items account-assigned to the service order item incorporate the market segments; here you can see as an example the **Customer** in the far-right column.

### *Service Billing*

Now let's perform the service billing based on the service confirmations. Start the Release for Billing app (SAP Fiori ID F3573) and select service order 800000001. You'll see the four items shown in Figure 7.162 that are now ready for billing.

Select all four items and click the **Release for Billing** button to create the billing document requests.

You can process these further in the Create Billing Documents app, as shown in Figure 7.163.

For the confirmations, four billing document requests are created. Select them all and click the **Create Billing Documents** button. With this, the billing document is created and you'll arrive at the screen shown in Figure 7.164.

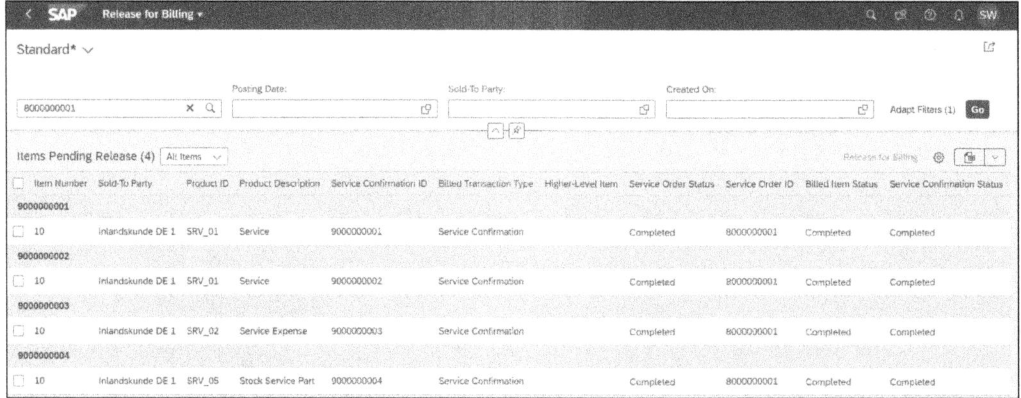

Figure 7.162 Release for Billing Service Items

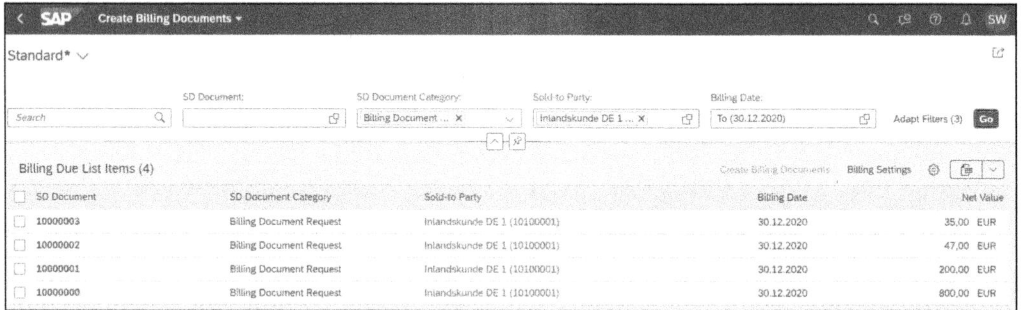

Figure 7.163 Create Billing Documents App

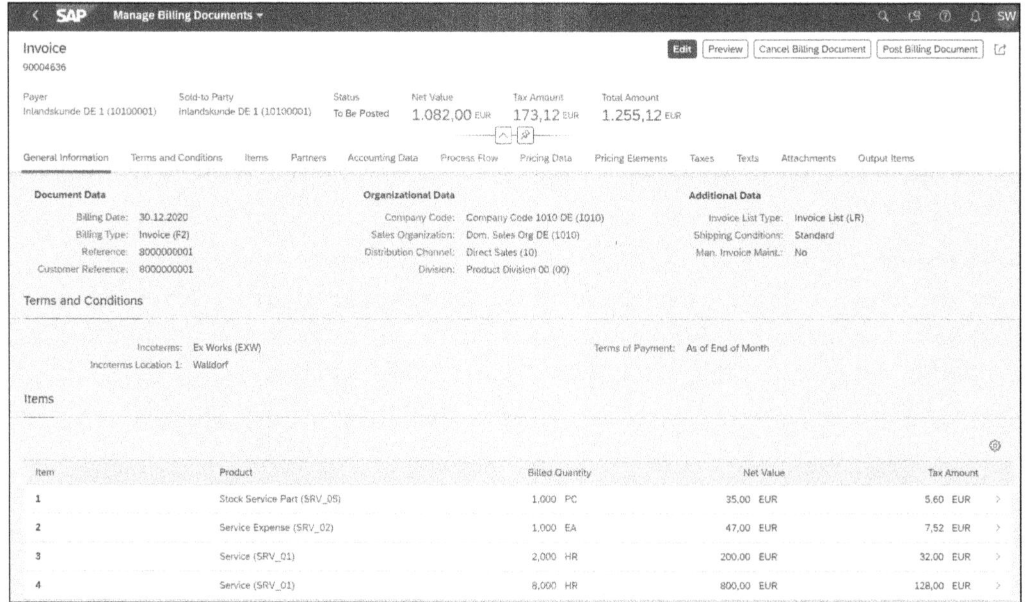

Figure 7.164 Billing Document with Four Items Reflecting Service Confirmations

After you click the **Post Billing Document** button, the journal entries are created, as shown in Figure 7.165.

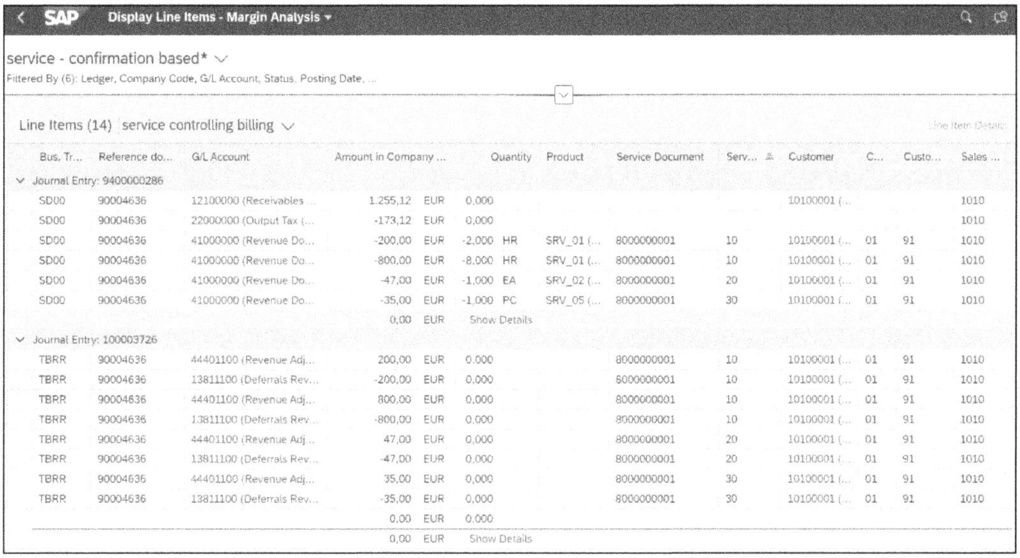

Display Line Items - Margin Analysis

service - confirmation based*

Filtered By (6): Ledger, Company Code, G/L Account, Status, Posting Date, ...

Line Items (14) service controlling billing

| Bus. Tr... | Reference do... | G/L Account | Amount in Company ... | Quantity | Product | Service Document | Serv... | Customer | C... | Custo... | Sales ... |
|---|---|---|---|---|---|---|---|---|---|---|---|
| Journal Entry: 9400000286 | | | | | | | | | | | |
| SD00 | 90004636 | 12100000 (Receivables ... | 1.255,12 EUR | 0,000 | | | | 10100001 (... | | | 1010 |
| SD00 | 90004636 | 22000000 (Output Tax (... | -173,12 EUR | 0,000 | | | | | | | 1010 |
| SD00 | 90004636 | 41000000 (Revenue Do... | -200,00 EUR | -2,000 HR | SRV_01 (... | 8000000001 | 10 | 10100001 (... | 01 | 91 | 1010 |
| SD00 | 90004636 | 41000000 (Revenue Do... | -800,00 EUR | -8,000 HR | SRV_01 (... | 8000000001 | 10 | 10100001 (... | 01 | 91 | 1010 |
| SD00 | 90004636 | 41000000 (Revenue Do... | -47,00 EUR | -1,000 EA | SRV_02 (... | 8000000001 | 20 | 10100001 (... | 01 | 91 | 1010 |
| SD00 | 90004636 | 41000000 (Revenue Do... | -35,00 EUR | -1,000 PC | SRV_05 (... | 8000000001 | 30 | 10100001 (... | 01 | 91 | 1010 |
| | | | 0,00 EUR | Show Details | | | | | | | |
| Journal Entry: 100003726 | | | | | | | | | | | |
| TBRR | 90004636 | 44401100 (Revenue Adj... | 200,00 EUR | 0,000 | | 8000000001 | 10 | 10100001 (... | 01 | 91 | 1010 |
| TBRR | 90004636 | 13811100 (Deferrals Rev... | -200,00 EUR | 0,000 | | 8000000001 | 10 | 10100001 (... | 01 | 91 | 1010 |
| TBRR | 90004636 | 44401100 (Revenue Adj... | 800,00 EUR | 0,000 | | 8000000001 | 10 | 10100001 (... | 01 | 91 | 1010 |
| TBRR | 90004636 | 13811100 (Deferrals Rev... | -800,00 EUR | 0,000 | | 8000000001 | 10 | 10100001 (... | 01 | 91 | 1010 |
| TBRR | 90004636 | 44401100 (Revenue Adj... | 47,00 EUR | 0,000 | | 8000000001 | 20 | 10100001 (... | 01 | 91 | 1010 |
| TBRR | 90004636 | 13811100 (Deferrals Rev... | -47,00 EUR | 0,000 | | 8000000001 | 20 | 10100001 (... | 01 | 91 | 1010 |
| TBRR | 90004636 | 44401100 (Revenue Adj... | 35,00 EUR | 0,000 | | 8000000001 | 30 | 10100001 (... | 01 | 91 | 1010 |
| TBRR | 90004636 | 13811100 (Deferrals Rev... | -35,00 EUR | 0,000 | | 8000000001 | 30 | 10100001 (... | 01 | 91 | 1010 |
| | | | 0,00 EUR | 0,000 | | | | | | | |
| | | | 0,00 EUR | Show Details | | | | | | | |

**Figure 7.165** Service Billing Journal Entries

The first journal entry reflects the billing document and contains the receivables line item. Next is the tax line item, and then four billed revenue line items for every confirmation. The billed revenue line items are account-assigned to service order items 10 to 30. The product is the billed product and equal to the product maintained in the service item.

An event-based revenue recognition journal entry also is created. It defers the revenue. All revenue recognition line items are account-assigned to the service order items.

As for the expense postings before, all line items account-assigned to service order items include the market segment attributes. Here, **Customer**, **Customer Group**, **Industry**, and **Sales Organization** are shown.

### *Period-End Close*

Now that the service order is completed, the period closing can take place. This consists only of event-based revenue recognition, which now recognizes costs and revenues.

Start the Event-Based Revenue Recognition—Service Documents app (SAP Fiori ID F3756) and select the service document. Click **Go** to get a list of all order items that are relevant for revenue recognition, as shown in Figure 7.166.

You see here that service order items **10**, **20**, and **30** are relevant for revenue recognition. Select the first line for service item **10** and click the arrow at the far right to go to the overview page shown in Figure 7.167.

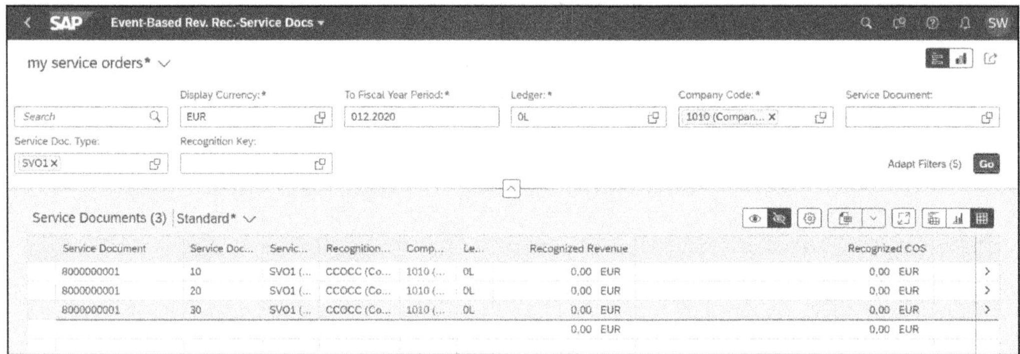


**Figure 7.166** Selection of Service Order Items in Event-Based Revenue Recognition—Service Documents App

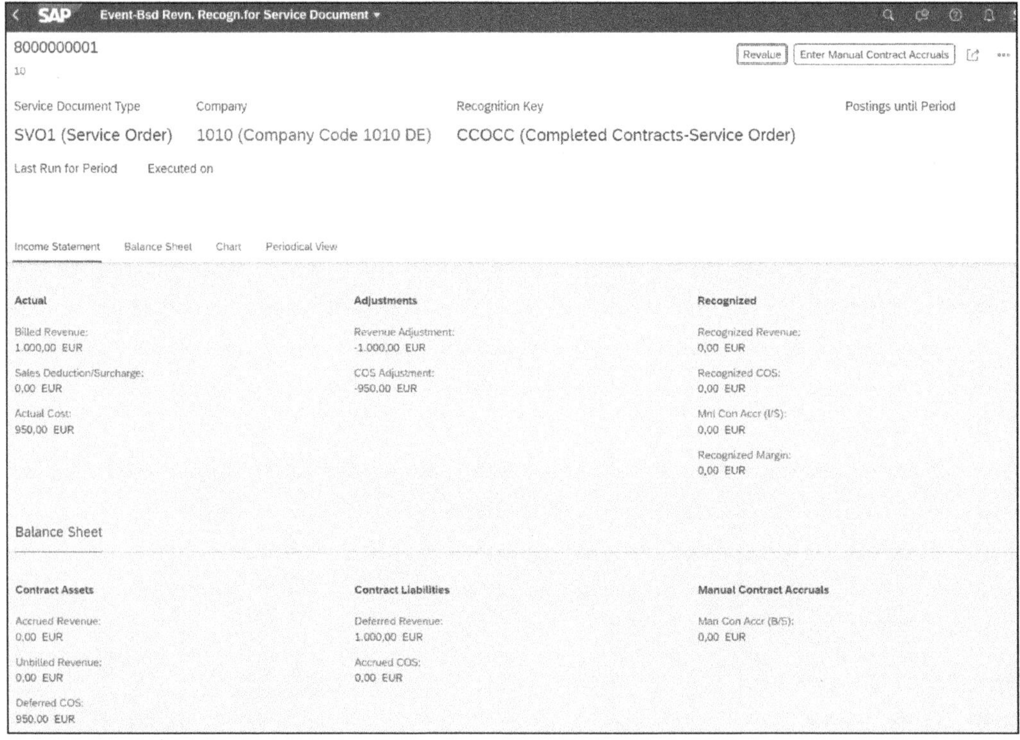


**Figure 7.167** Revenue Recognition View on Line Item 10 after Cost and Revenue Posting

In the upper section, for **Income Statement** values, you see here the **Billed Revenue** amount of 1,000 EUR and the **Actual Costs** from the time confirmation of 950 EUR. Both amounts are deferred, so the **Recognized Margin** is currently zero. The lower section covers the balance sheet values. You see the **Deferred COS** of 950 EUR and the **Deferred Revenues** of 1,000 EUR.

To realize costs and revenue, click the **Revalue** button. This has the same effect as the periodic revenue recognition run for service orders (see Section 7.5).

As the contract is now completed, all posted costs and revenues are realized and the accruals and deferrals on the balance sheet accounts are cleared. The result is shown in Figure 7.168.

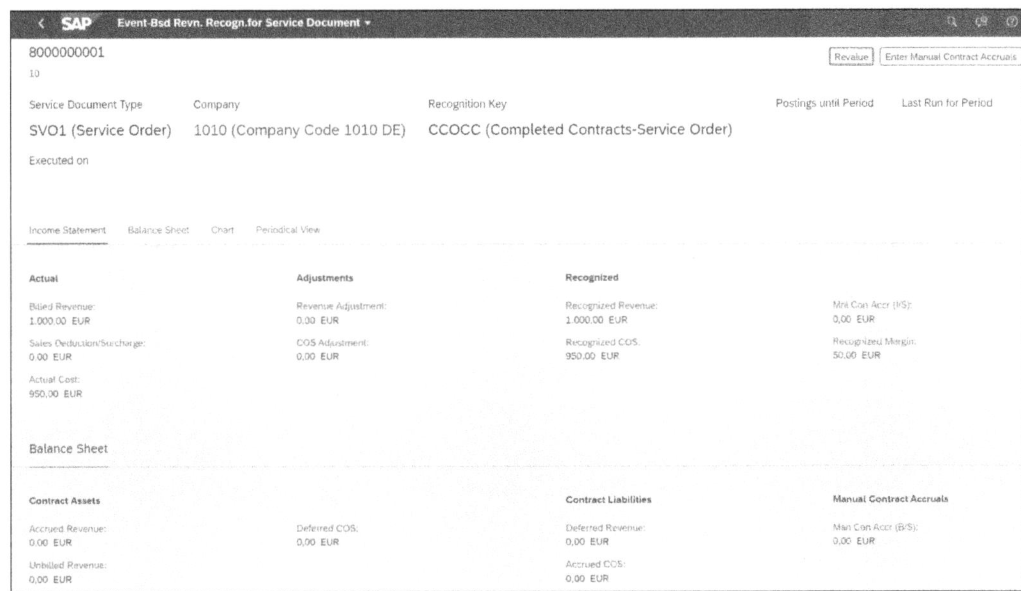


**Figure 7.168** Revenue Recognition for Service Item after Revaluation

Now you see a realized margin of 50 EUR. The balance sheet amounts are cleared to zero.

The revaluation created an accounting document, which you can see in the Display Line Items—Margin Analysis app, shown in Figure 7.169.

Display Line Items - Margin Analysis

service - confirmation based*

Ledger: * OL (Ledger OL) | Company Code: 1010 (Company... × 10... | Object Type: | Customer: | Product Sold: | Reference document: =400000000 ×

Line Items (4) service controlling*

| Journal Entry | Bus... | Reference ... | Referenc... | Posting Date | G/L Account | Amount in Company ... | | Service Document | Service Doc... | Customer | C... |
|---|---|---|---|---|---|---|---|---|---|---|---|
| 100003727 | TBRR | 400000000 | TBRR | 31.12.2020 | 54441000 (Adjust... | 950,00 | EUR | 8000000001 | 10 | 10100001 (Inlan... | 01 |
| 100003727 | TBRR | 400000000 | TBRR | 31.12.2020 | 13210000 (WIP) | -950,00 | EUR | 8000000001 | 10 | 10100001 (Inlan... | 01 |
| 100003727 | TBRR | 400000000 | TBRR | 31.12.2020 | 44401100 (Revenu... | -1.000,00 | EUR | 8000000001 | 10 | 10100001 (Inlan... | 01 |
| 100003727 | TBRR | 400000000 | TBRR | 31.12.2020 | 13811100 (Deferral... | 1.000,00 | EUR | 8000000001 | 10 | 10100001 (Inlan... | 01 |
| | | | | | | 0,00 | EUR | | | | |

**Figure 7.169** Journal Entries of Event-Based Revenue Recognition Posting after Order Completion

You see here that the cost and revenue adjustments posted before with the business transactions are reversed. Again, for all line items account-assigned to service order items, the profitability segment is derived and updated in the journal entries.

All the postings to the service order in this section lead to a final margin reporting, which you can view with the Product and Service Margins app. Select ledger **OL**, filter on service order **8000000001**, and click **Go** to arrive at the screen shown in Figure 7.170.

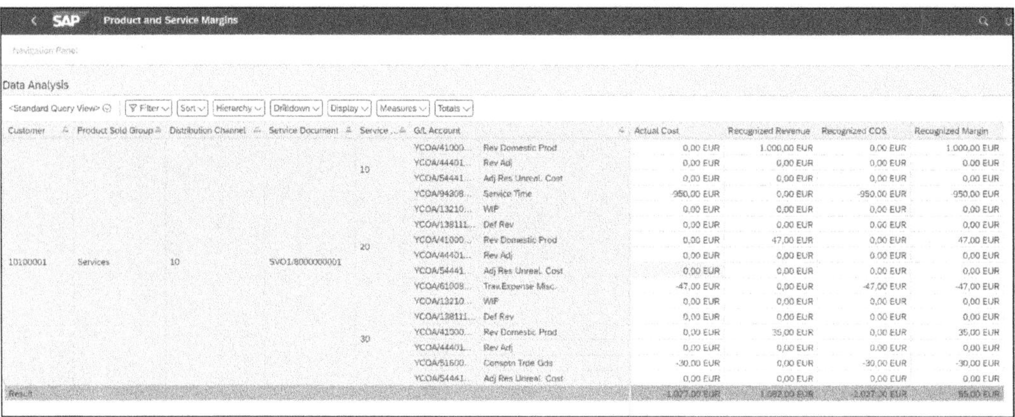


| Customer | Product Sold Group | Distribution Channel | Service Document | Service ... | G/L Account | | Actual Cost | Recognized Revenue | Recognized COS | Recognized Margin |
|---|---|---|---|---|---|---|---|---|---|---|
| 10100001 | Services | 10 | SVO1/8000000001 | 10 | YCOA/41000... | Rev Domestic Prod | 0,00 EUR | 1.000,00 EUR | 0,00 EUR | 1.000,00 EUR |
| | | | | | YCOA/44401... | Rev Adj | 0,00 EUR | 0,00 EUR | 0,00 EUR | 0.00 EUR |
| | | | | | YCOA/54441... | Adj Res Unreal. Cost | 0,00 EUR | 0,00 EUR | 0,00 EUR | 0,00 EUR |
| | | | | | YCOA/94308... | Service Time | -950,00 EUR | 0,00 EUR | -950,00 EUR | -950,00 EUR |
| | | | | | YCOA/13210... | WIP | 0,00 EUR | 0,00 EUR | 0,00 EUR | 0,00 EUR |
| | | | | | YCOA/138111... | Def Rev | 0,00 EUR | 0,00 EUR | 0,00 EUR | 0,00 EUR |
| | | | | 20 | YCOA/41000... | Rev Domestic Prod | 0,00 EUR | 47,00 EUR | 0,00 EUR | 47,00 EUR |
| | | | | | YCOA/44401... | Rev Adj | 0,00 EUR | 0,00 EUR | 0.00 EUR | 0,00 EUR |
| | | | | | YCOA/54441... | Adj Res Unreal. Cost | 0,00 EUR | 0,00 EUR | 0,00 EUR | 0,00 EUR |
| | | | | | YCOA/61008... | Trav.Expense Misc. | -47,00 EUR | 0,00 EUR | -47,00 EUR | -47,00 EUR |
| | | | | | YCOA/13210... | WIP | 0,00 EUR | 0,00 EUR | 0,00 EUR | 0,00 EUR |
| | | | | | YCOA/138111... | Def Rev | 0,00 EUR | 0,00 EUR | 0,00 EUR | 0,00 EUR |
| | | | | 30 | YCOA/41000... | Rev Domestic Prod | 0,00 EUR | 35,00 EUR | 0,00 EUR | 35,00 EUR |
| | | | | | YCOA/44401... | Rev Adj | 0,00 EUR | 0,00 EUR | 0,00 EUR | 0,00 EUR |
| | | | | | YCOA/51600... | Consptn Trde Gds | -30,00 EUR | 0,00 EUR | -30,00 EUR | -30,00 EUR |
| | | | | | YCOA/54441... | Adj Res Unreal. Cost | 0,00 EUR | 0,00 EUR | 0,00 EUR | 0,00 EUR |
| Result | | | | | | | -1.027,00 EUR | 1.082,00 EUR | -1.027,00 EUR | 55,00 EUR |

**Figure 7.170** Product and Service Margins App for Service Order

You see that the service order realized a margin of 55 EUR with its three items at the bottom of the far-right column. Because you derived all market segment attributes, this margin is visible on market segments like customer, product sold group, and distribution channel too.

### Service Bundle Scenario

The fixed price service bundle enables billing and margin analysis reporting on a main item, which is a bundle for several subordinated service order items. The subordinate items generate costs but aren't relevant for billing. Also, no margin should be reported on their products, but they contribute to the costs and thus the margin of the main item.

An example is an oil change. The oil change is offered at a fixed price and defined as a bundle item. The required components are created as subordered service items: the mechanic hours, the oil, and the filter. A margin should be shown for the oil change.

Figure 7.171 shows how a service bundle is reflected in the system with the Manage Service Orders app.

Item 10 with product **SRV_Bundle_01** is the main item. Items 20 to 40 are subordinate items, with the higher-level item **10** maintained in the **Higher-L...** column.

Figure 7.172 shows what the financial architecture and the process integration looks like in this case.

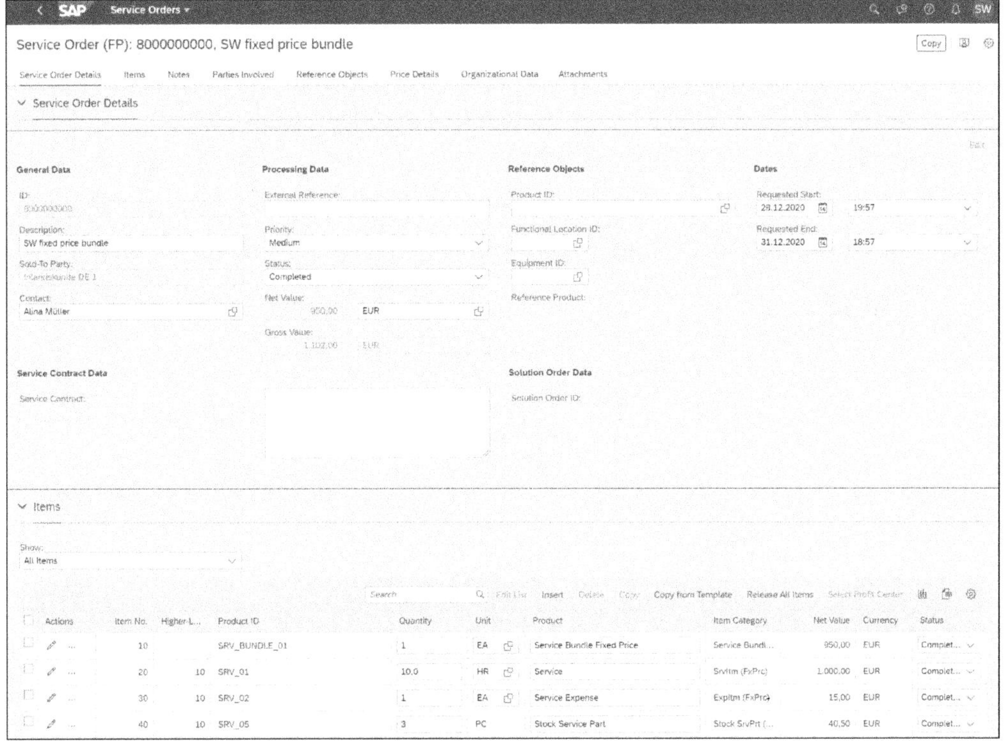


**Figure 7.171** Service Order Master in Service Bundle Case

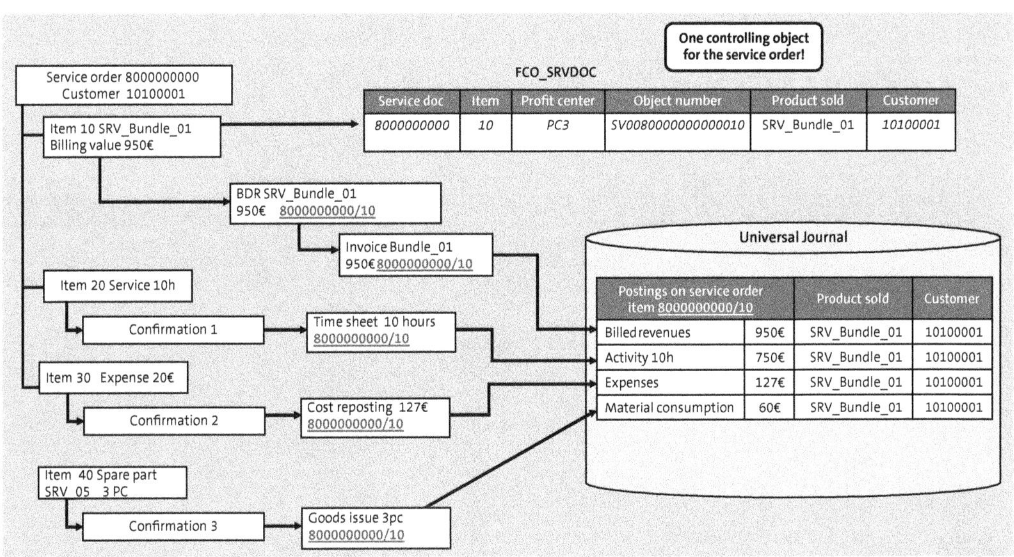


**Figure 7.172** Architecture for Fixed-Price Bundle

You see that a controlling object is created only for the main item, the service bundle. On this cost object, service order item 10, the billing of the main item and the confirmations of items 20 to 40 are posted. Of course, only the product sold of the main item is derived for all postings. This allows for the reporting of the bundle margin.

Now post all the confirmations as in the previous section: bill the main item and run the revenue recognition for item 10 like in the previous example. This leads to the report in Figure 7.173 for the service bundle. To see this view, launch the Product and Service Margins app, select the bundle service order, and click **Go**.

Product and Service Margins

Data Analysis

| Service Document | Se... | Customer | Product Sold | Distribution Channel | G/L Account | | Billed Revenue | Actual Cost | Recognized Revenue | Recognized COS | Recognized Margin |
|---|---|---|---|---|---|---|---|---|---|---|---|
| SVO2/8000000000 | 10 | 10100001 | SRV_BUNDLE_01 | Direct Sales | YCOA/13210... | WIP | 0,00 EUR | 0,00 EUR | 0,00 EUR | 0,00 EUR | 0,00 EUR |
| | | | | | YCOA/138111... | Def Rev | 0,00 EUR | 0,00 EUR | 0,00 EUR | 0,00 EUR | 0,00 EUR |
| | | | | | YCOA/41000... | Rev Domestic Prod | 950,00 EUR | 0,00 EUR | 950,00 EUR | 0,00 EUR | 950,00 EUR |
| | | | | | YCOA/44401... | Rev Adj | 0,00 EUR | 0,00 EUR | 0,00 EUR | 0,00 EUR | 0,00 EUR |
| | | | | | YCOA/51600... | Consptn Trde Gds | 0,00 EUR | -60,00 EUR | 0,00 EUR | -60,00 EUR | -60,00 EUR |
| | | | | | YCOA/54441... | Adj Res Unreal. Cost | 0,00 EUR | 0,00 EUR | 0,00 EUR | 0,00 EUR | 0,00 EUR |
| | | | | | YCOA/61008... | Trav.Expense Misc. | 0,00 EUR | -127,00 EUR | 0,00 EUR | -127,00 EUR | -127,00 EUR |
| | | | | | YCOA/94308... | Service Time | 0,00 EUR | -750,00 EUR | 0,00 EUR | -750,00 EUR | -750,00 EUR |
| Result | | | | | | | 950,00 EUR | -937,00 EUR | 950,00 EUR | -937,00 EUR | 13,00 EUR |

**Figure 7.173** Journal Entries for Fixed-Price Bundle

For all the postings, including the revenue recognition postings, account-assign only item **10**. From item **10** you get the **Product Sold SRV_Bundle_01** and the other market segment fields derived. There is a margin of 13 EUR recognized for the bundle, shown at the bottom of the **Recognized Margin** column.

### 7.4.4 Service Contract

As mentioned for the service contracts framework, service agreements can be closed with the customer, like a maintenance contract for one year. Let's look at an example in the system. To do so, start the Manage Service Contracts app (SAP Fiori ID F3763) and select the existing contract **7000000000** to arrive at the screen shown in Figure 7.174.

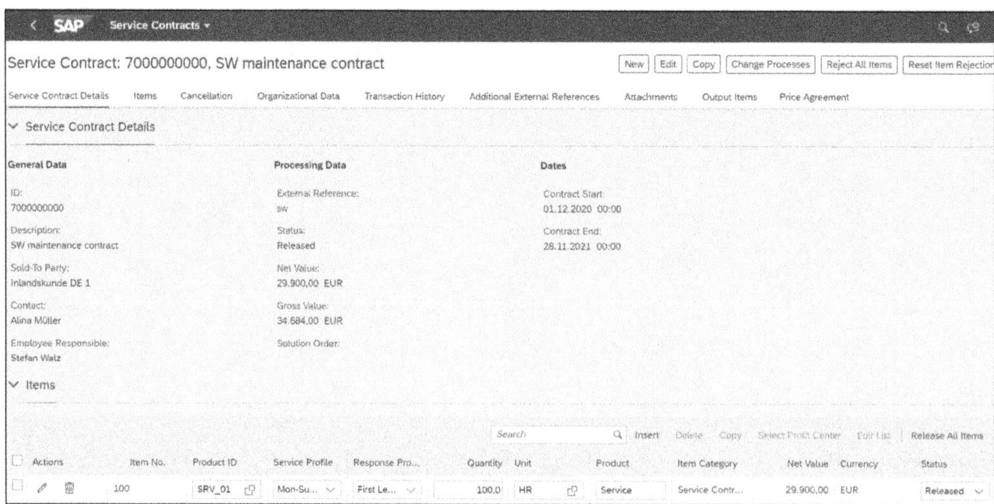


**Figure 7.174** Manage Service Contracts App

The customer is defined by the **Sold-To Party** field. It's the same as in the service orders. There is one item, **100**, with **Product SRV_01** created.

Select the item and select **Actions**, the pencil icon, in the first column. You'll go to the next screen, shown in Figure 7.175.

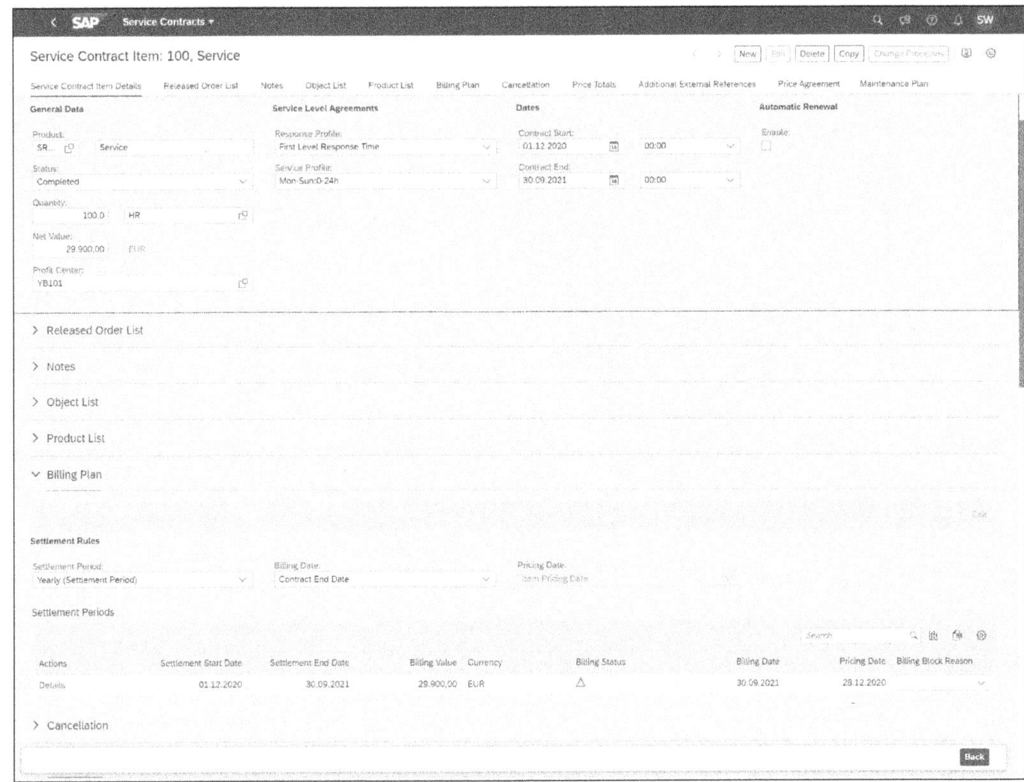

**Figure 7.175** Contract Item Detail View with Billing Plan

The **Billing Plan** is relevant for billing and revenue recognition. For this example, you can see the **Billing Value** of 29,900 EUR, which is due on the contract end date, in September 2021. The **Settlement Start Date** and **Settlement End Date** define the periods for which this service agreement is valid—here, December 2020 to September 2021, a duration of 10 months.

This is relevant for revenue recognition. Although the invoice can only be issued at the end of the contract, you have to realize a tenth of the revenue in December 2020.

So, start the Event-Based Revenue Recognition—Service Documents app again and select the contract. Revalue for December 2020 and get the results of the revenue recognition, as shown in Figure 7.176.

In the **Income Statement** section, you see that there is no invoice yet issued and the billed revenue is zero. But there is already recognized revenue of 2,990 EUR, a tenth of the billing value of the contract item. As there are no costs yet recognized on the contract, the calculated margin is equal to the realized revenues. The matching accruals to the realized revenue are shown in the balance sheet section under **Accrued Revenue**.

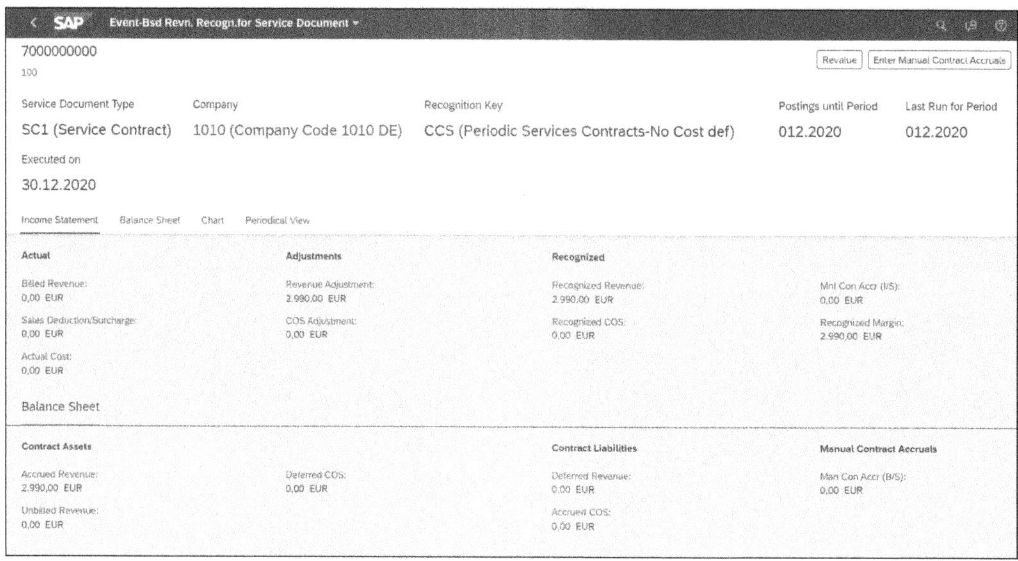


**Figure 7.176** Revalue Result for Service Contract Item

You can see the financial document generated in this process in the Display Line Items—Margin Analysis app, as shown in Figure 7.177.

SAP Display Line Items - Margin Analysis

my service contracts
Filtered By (4): Ledger, Status, Posting Date, Object Type

Show Filters

Line Items (2) service margin analysis fields*

| Journal Entry | Bus ... | G/L Account | Amount in Compa... | | Service Doc... | Se... | Customer | Cust... | Customer Supplier Industry | Product Sold | Product Sold Group | Di... | Di... | Sales ... |
|---|---|---|---|---|---|---|---|---|---|---|---|---|---|---|
| 100003730 | TBRR | 13711100 (WiP Accrued Reven... | 2.990,00 | EUR | 7000000000 | 100 | 10100001... | 01 | 91 | SRV_01 (S... | P001 | 10 | 00 | 1010 |
| 100003730 | TBRR | 44401100 (Revenue Adjustment) | -2.990,00 | EUR | 7000000000 | 100 | 10100001... | 01 | 91 | SRV_01 (S... | P001 | 10 | 00 | 1010 |
| | | | 0,00 | EUR | | | | | | | | | | |

**Figure 7.177** Journal Entries for Service Contract Revenue Recognition

The first line is the balance sheet item. The second item is posted on the P&L account. As in the service scenario, all market segment attributes are derived and stored in the journal entry items. Here you see the customer, the customer group, the industry, the product sold, the product sold group, the distribution channel, the division, and the sales organization.

The service orders, which enable the provisioning of services to the customer, can be assigned to the contract item. As mentioned, with the creation of a service order, the system checks if a contract is available for the maintained customer. In the first example, this was the case; refer back to Figure 7.146. As shown in the architecture illustrated previously in Figure 7.142, in this case the service contract item is part of the accounting mirror table of the service order item and for all postings on the service order item.

With every posting on this assigned service order item, the contract item is derived and stored in the journal entries like the profitability fields.

To get a complete view of the contract margin, including the assigned service orders, you can select **OL** for the **Ledger** and **7000000000** for the **Service Contract** and click **Go** in the Product and Service Margins app, as shown in Figure 7.178.

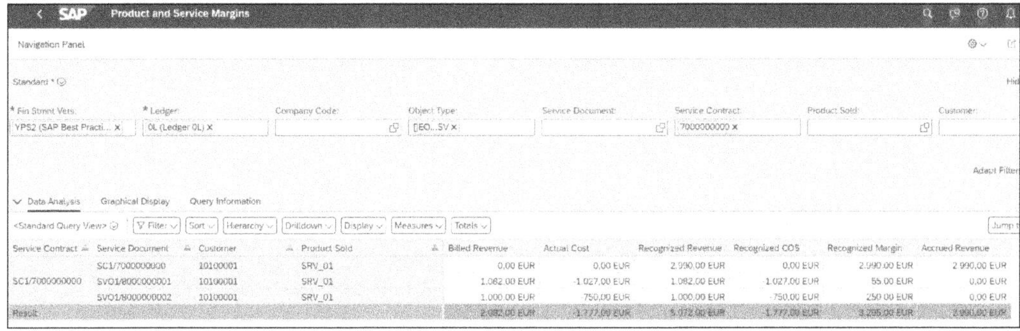

| Service Contract | Service Document | Customer | Product Sold | Billed Revenue | Actual Cost | Recognized Revenue | Recognized COS | Recognized Margin | Accrued Revenue |
|---|---|---|---|---|---|---|---|---|---|
| | SC1/7000000000 | 10100001 | SRV_01 | 0,00 EUR | 0,00 EUR | 2.990,00 EUR | 0,00 EUR | 2.990,00 EUR | 2.990,00 EUR |
| SC1/7000000000 | SVO1/8000000001 | 10100001 | SRV_01 | 1.082,00 EUR | -1.027,00 EUR | 1.082,00 EUR | -1.027,00 EUR | 55,00 EUR | 0,00 EUR |
| | SVO1/8000000002 | 10100001 | SRV_01 | 1.000,00 EUR | -750,00 EUR | 1.000,00 EUR | -750,00 EUR | 250,00 EUR | 0,00 EUR |
| Result | | | | 2.082,00 EUR | -1.777,00 EUR | 5.072,00 EUR | -1.777,00 EUR | 3.295,00 EUR | 2.990,00 EUR |

**Figure 7.178** Aggregated Reporting for Service Contract

In the report, you see in the first line the direct revenues realized on the contract by event-based revenue recognition. There are also two service orders assigned to the contract, which have costs and revenues realized. The complete margin for the contract is 3,295 EUR. In the last column, you see the **Accrued Revenue** for the contract.

## 7.4.5 New Reporting Insights for Service Management

Now let's look at a few examples of the reporting options that the new architecture enables. First, we'll show margin analysis reporting based on service documents. This is possible every time as event-based revenue recognition ensures a real-time matching principle for costs and revenues.

Start the Product and Service Margins app, select **Ledger OL** and all existing postings on the service order and service contract objects by selecting **SV** and **SC** in the **Object Type** field, and click **Go** to arrive at the results shown in Figure 7.179.

Product and Service Margins

Data Analysis

| Customer... | Customer | | Product Sold | Service Document | Billed Revenue | Actual Cost | Recognized Revenue | Recognized COS | Recognized Margin |
|---|---|---|---|---|---|---|---|---|---|
| 11 | 10100002 | Inlandskunde DE 2 | SRV_01 | SVO1/8000000010 | 1.200,00 EUR | -1.025,00 EUR | 1.200,00 EUR | -1.025,00 EUR | 175,00 EUR |
| | Result | | | | 1.200,00 EUR | -1.025,00 EUR | 1.200,00 EUR | -1.025,00 EUR | 175,00 EUR |
| 91 | 10100001 | Inlandskunde DE 1 | | SC1/7000000000 | 0,00 EUR | 0,00 EUR | 2.990,00 EUR | 0,00 EUR | 2.990,00 EUR |
| | | | SRV_01 | SVO1/8000000001 | 1.082,00 EUR | -1.027,00 EUR | 1.082,00 EUR | -1.027,00 EUR | 55,00 EUR |
| | | | | SVO1/8000000002 | 1.000,00 EUR | -750,00 EUR | 1.000,00 EUR | -750,00 EUR | 250,00 EUR |
| | | | SRV_BUNDLE_01 | SVO2/8000000000 | 950,00 EUR | -937,00 EUR | 950,00 EUR | -937,00 EUR | 13,00 EUR |
| | 10100003 | Inlandskunde DE 3 | SRV_01 | SVO1/8000000011 | 0,00 EUR | -1.500,00 EUR | 0,00 EUR | 0,00 EUR | 0,00 EUR |
| | Result | | | | 3.032,00 EUR | -4.224,00 EUR | 8.022,00 EUR | -2.714,00 EUR | 3.308,00 EUR |
| # | 17100001 | Domestic US Customer 1 | SRV_01 | SC1/7000000001 | $ 180,00 | $ 0,00 | $ 0,00 | $ 0,00 | $ 0,00 |
| | Result | | | | $ 180,00 | $ 0,00 | $ 0,00 | $ 0,00 | $ 0,00 |
| Result | | | | | * | 5.239,00 EUR | 7.222,00 EUR | -3.739,00 EUR | 3.483,00 EUR |

**Figure 7.179** Margin Analysis Reporting on Service Documents

In the columns you see the industry, which is derived from the customer master, the customer, and the product sold. The next column (**Service Document**) shows which service order provided the data.

Next, let's get an analysis for a certain period of the entered overtime and the nonbillable confirmations. Start the Service Order Actuals app (SAP Fiori ID F3591), enter period 001/2021, and click **Go** to arrive at the screen shown in Figure 7.180.

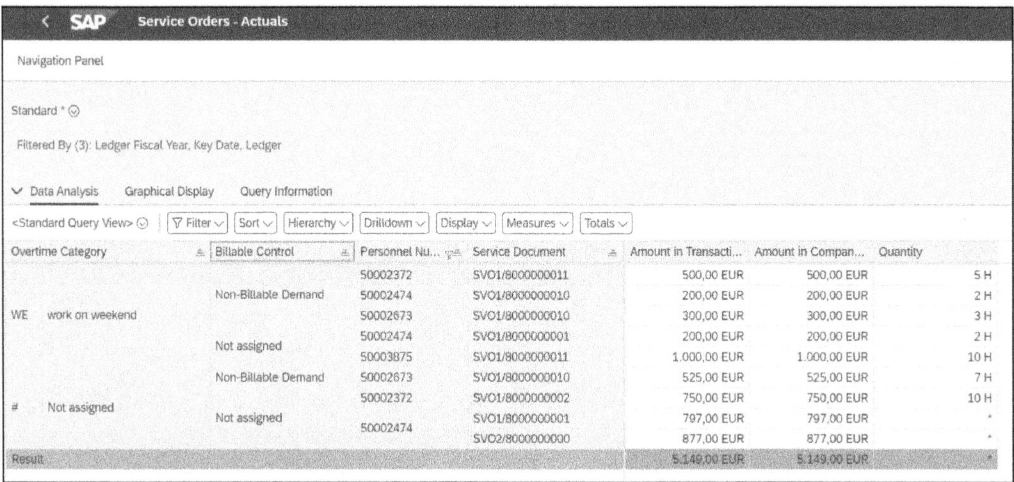

| Overtime Category | Billable Control | Personnel Nu... | Service Document | Amount in Transacti... | Amount in Compan... | Quantity |
|---|---|---|---|---|---|---|
| WE work on weekend | Non-Billable Demand | 50002372 | SVO1/8000000011 | 500,00 EUR | 500,00 EUR | 5 H |
| | | 50002474 | SVO1/8000000010 | 200,00 EUR | 200,00 EUR | 2 H |
| | | 50002673 | SVO1/8000000010 | 300,00 EUR | 300,00 EUR | 3 H |
| | Not assigned | 50002474 | SVO1/8000000001 | 200,00 EUR | 200,00 EUR | 2 H |
| | | 50003875 | SVO1/8000000011 | 1.000,00 EUR | 1.000,00 EUR | 10 H |
| # Not assigned | Non-Billable Demand | 50002673 | SVO1/8000000010 | 525,00 EUR | 525,00 EUR | 7 H |
| | Not assigned | 50002372 | SVO1/8000000002 | 750,00 EUR | 750,00 EUR | 10 H |
| | | 50002474 | SVO1/8000000001 | 797,00 EUR | 797,00 EUR | * |
| | | | SVO2/8000000000 | 877,00 EUR | 877,00 EUR | * |
| Result | | | | 5.149,00 EUR | 5.149,00 EUR | * |

Figure 7.180 Analysis of Service Order Single Postings: Overtime and Billable Control

Because you can report on single journal entry items, you can select **Overtime Category** and **Billable Control** (alias accounting indicator) values here. You can also select the **Personnel Number** to see who provided the service.

With the SAP S/4HANA reporting technology, it's possible to dynamically include service order or service order item attributes in the financial reports. This gives you more insights into the service business processes. Look again at the Product and Service Margins app, as shown in Figure 7.181.

| Customer | Product Sold | Service Doc... | Country/Region | Billed Revenue | Actual Cost | Recognized Revenue | Recognized COS | Recognized Margin |
|---|---|---|---|---|---|---|---|---|
| 10100001 | SRV_01 | SC1/7000000... | Germany | 0,00 EUR | 0,00 EUR | 2.990,00 EUR | 0,00 EUR | 2.990,00 EUR |
| | | SVO1/80000... | Germany | 1.082,00 EUR | -1.027,00 EUR | 1.082,00 EUR | -1.027,00 EUR | 55,00 EUR |
| | | SVO1/80000... | Germany | 1.000,00 EUR | -750,00 EUR | 1.000,00 EUR | -750,00 EUR | 250,00 EUR |
| | SRV_BUNDLE_01 | SVO2/80000... | Germany | 950,00 EUR | -937,00 EUR | 950,00 EUR | -937,00 EUR | 13,00 EUR |
| 10100002 | SRV_01 | SVO1/80000... | Germany | 1.200,00 EUR | -1.025,00 EUR | 1.200,00 EUR | -1.025,00 EUR | 175,00 EUR |
| 10100003 | SRV_01 | SVO1/80000... | Germany | 0,00 EUR | -1.500,00 EUR | 0,00 EUR | 0,00 EUR | 0,00 EUR |
| 17100001 | SRV_01 | SC1/7000000... | USA | $ 180,00 | $ 0,00 | $ 0,00 | $ 0,00 | $ 0,00 |
| Result | | | | * | -5.239,00 EUR | 7.222,00 EUR | -3.739,00 EUR | 3.483,00 EUR |

Figure 7.181 Including Additional Service Order Fields in Financial Reporting

You see now an additional field, **Country/Region**. This isn't a journal entry field; it's taken from the service order header. You can get this by right-clicking the **Service Doc...** column and selecting **Drilldown • Add Attribute**. Then you get a list of many fields of the service order, which you can select from, with options such as the employee responsible or several due dates. For this example, we selected **Country/Region**.

Now let's see what new analysis options are available for the accountant. Start the Trial Balance app, select **Ledger 0L**, select the example company code **1010**, and click **Go**. Then scroll to the WIP general ledger account and add the **Customer** and **Service Document** columns to see the screen shown in Figure 7.182.

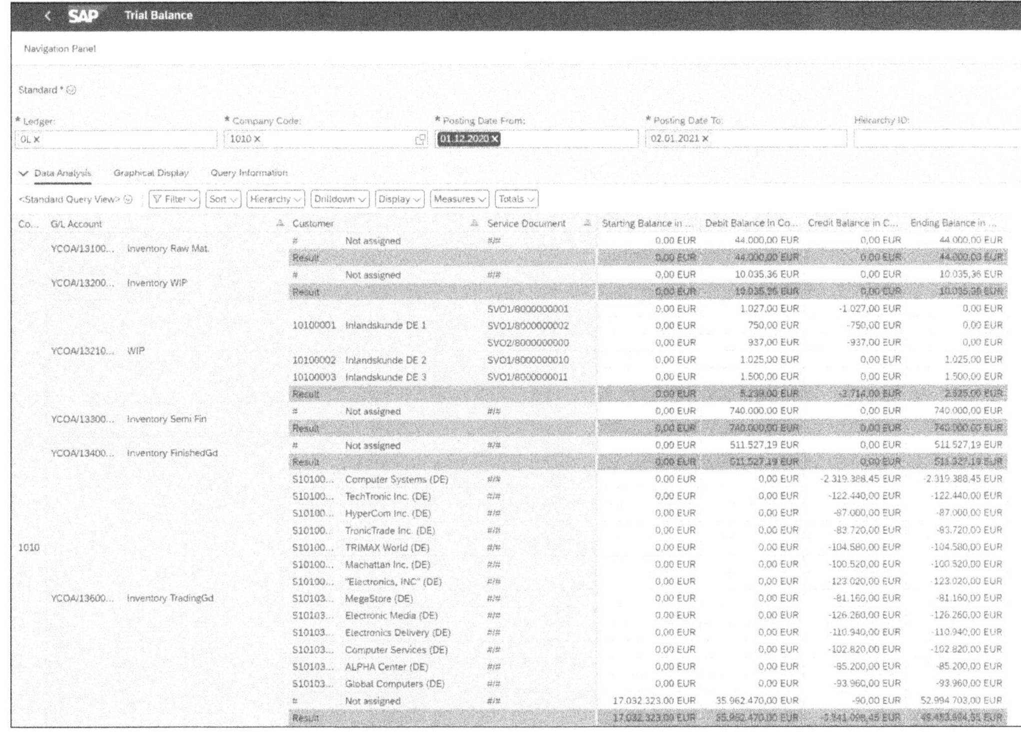


**Figure 7.182** Trial Balance with Drilldown for WIP

Note that the complete amount on the **WIP** account, the third general ledger account in the row, is assigned to service documents and thus to, for example, customers.

**Note**

For more information on service integration in financials, see the blog at *http://s-prs.co/v528210*.

## 7.5 Event-Based Revenue Recognition

Revenue recognition used to be a topic driven mostly by accountants and the balance sheet perspective, but the Universal Journal approach has given it new meaning and importance for controlling and margin analysis.

In this section, we'll discuss the purpose and the principles of event-based revenue recognition and the availability of the solution in SAP S/4HANA Cloud and on-premise. In the process, we'll take a deeper look at the special management accounting feature now available. Then we'll offer an overview of the functionality.

Let's start with the purpose and principles.

### 7.5.1 Purpose and Principles

Event-based revenue recognition was initially launched for customer projects in SAP S/4HANA Cloud. Here, in addition to the extensive requirements of the service industry for revenue recognition functionality, SAP particularly pursued the objective of an easy-to-use application. Event-based revenue recognition follows cloud principles and thus enables a simple setup, as well as a simplified period-end closing; of course, it also addresses the required legal functionality.

Until SAP S/4HANA, this functionality was covered in the SAP ERP solution with the results analysis application. This is still in use for several scenarios in on-premise SAP S/4HANA (see the example in Section 7.3.3). Here, the calculated values are stored in separate results analysis persistence and must be settled to accounting and costing-based profitability analysis at the end of the period. Additional steps are required to reconcile the different applications: general ledger, revenue recognition, and profitability analysis. Using results analysis, margin analysis information is only available after period-end closing.

In comparison, event-based revenue recognition is integrated with the Universal Journal and has no separate persistence, so no reconciliation effort or settlement is required. Calculated results are immediately available in the general ledger, along with the original entry. Together with the new Universal Journal–integrated margin analysis, the general ledger account line items of revenue recognition already contain market segment information. This simplifies management accounting, and fascinating new reporting insights can be gained, as we have seen in the processes throughout this chapter.

Consider the *sell-from-stock* process. Here companies usually don't use any revenue recognition tool, and results analysis doesn't support this scenario. The delivery generates the costs and the invoicing generates the revenue. This can be time-delayed, possibly also within different periods. We have to make sure in margin reporting that we always consider both values. Costing-based profitability analysis therefore uses a simplified approach in which revenues and costs are transferred at the time of the invoice. This ensures that revenues and costs match. However, there are periodic discrepancies with the general ledger, especially when revenues are already recognized at the time of delivery. To be able to show a correct margin at any time in the Universal Journal–based margin analysis, you need event-based revenue recognition. In IFRS, it recognizes revenue with the delivery—updating all attributes of the margin analysis—or it defers the costs and realizes costs and revenues with the invoice. This way, the matching principle is always guaranteed. Therefore, in SAP S/4HANA Cloud, only event-based revenue recognition is in use.

Based on these examples, you can see that the purpose of event-based revenue recognition is not only balance sheet valuation; there are also new management accounting functionalities provided. We'll gain an overview of the core features and principles in the following sections.



### Supported Management Accounting Features

As shown in the scenario examples, several management accounting features are incorporated into event-based revenue recognition. Let's recap them here briefly and mention those that we couldn't cover in detail in this book:

- **Event-based revenue recognition supports real-time profitability**
  Event-based revenue recognition enables real-time margin analysis for a specific cost object and derived market segments.
- **Market segment attributes derived and applied for all revenue recognition postings**
  This is what we've shown in multiple scenarios. Market segment attributes are persisted in the revenue recognition P&L and balance sheet items.
- **Real-time WIP, including market segment information**
  This is the answer to the project managers' need for an up-to-date view not only of the margin, but also of the unbilled revenue in the project. And it offers new insights for the accountant: as we showed previously in Figure 7.98, a drilldown into WIP by market segment is possible.
- **Event-based revenue recognition provides realized revenue and margin per employee**
  To cover the requirements of the service industry, event-based revenue recognition supports the inclusion of employee IDs in the revenue recognition journal entry line items. This allows reporting, as shown previously in Figure 7.97.
- **Event-based revenue recognition supports customer project plans by period and prediction**
  As shown in the customer project scenario in Section 7.3, resource planning can be distributed across periods. This provides cost planning for the project based on exact periods. Based on the costs by period, you can calculate the matching plan revenues per period with the event-based revenue recognition functionality. The transferred costs and calculated revenues are stored in plan table ACDOCP, which has the same structure as the Universal Journal. Hence, plan margins for the project are available. There also is a prediction functionality in place for the service contract, by

which the revenue is planned over periods by event-based revenue recognition based on the contract billing plan. This is stored in the prediction ledger.

- **Event-based revenue recognition calculates target revenue in fixed-price scenarios**
  In a fixed-price scenario, you calculate in parallel for a confirmation the revenue that the employee would generate in a travel and expense-based billing contract. You post the result to separate management accounts as target revenue. This has no impact on legal reporting; it's just for cost accounting purposes. For more information, refer to the following blog post: *http://s-prs.co/v528211*.

### Real-Time Matching Principle for Cost of Sales and Revenues

Now let's focus on the first principle: real-time calculation and posting of event-based revenue recognition. With event-based revenue recognition, matching of realized revenues and costs is ensured every time. For every posting on revenue-carrying objects, like customer projects and sales orders, the associated revenue recognition document is generated simultaneously and directly stored in the Universal Journal. Thus, a real-time margin reporting for the revenue carrying objects can be provided. Because market segment attributes are derived and stored for revenue recognition journal entry items too, you also get a market segment margin reporting that's always up to date.

Figure 7.183 visualizes the general posting logic of event-based revenue recognition based on the time confirmation business process executed in Section 7.3.2 as a project-based sales business process. The source document—here, a time confirmation—creates two separate journal entries: one for the initial source document—here, the time confirmation, the controlling document—and a second for the matching revenue recognition journal entry.

Depending on the contract type, the appropriate revenue recognition method is derived. In this example, the revenue is calculated based on the costing-based PoC method.

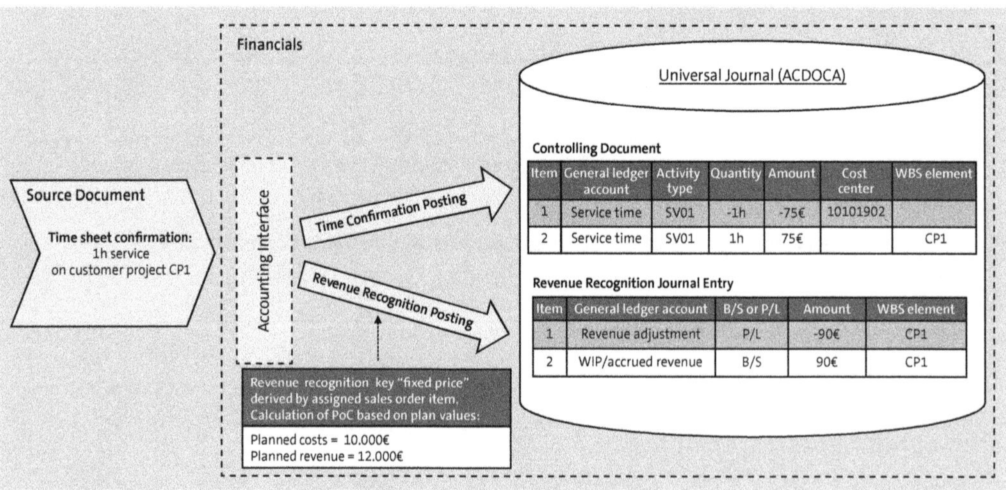


**Figure 7.183** Matching Principle Provided by Event-Based Revenue Recognition

The calculated realized revenue is posted with the P&L account revenue adjustment and activated on the balance sheet account's accrued revenue or WIP.

A posting overview for the single process steps on a customer project is shown in Figure 7.184. To highlight which general ledger accounts are account-assigned to the project, we tagged them with "PRO".

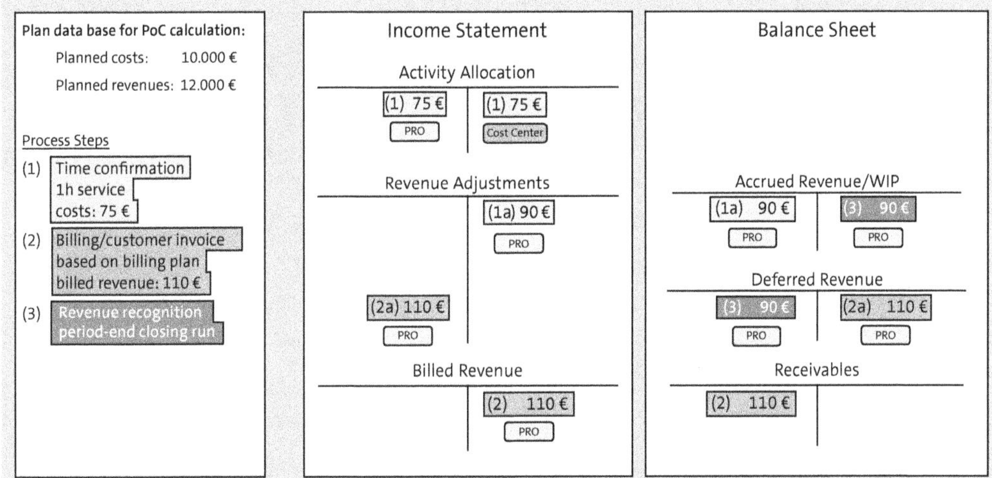


**Figure 7.184** Posting Logic of Event-Based Revenue Recognition Illustrated with T-Accounts

This posting logic is applied for all revenue recognition methods when revenues are already realized with the confirmation and cost posting. You can find this posting logic in a costing-based PoC method, for time and expense billing, or for sales from stock when you realize the revenue with the delivery.

Now, let's discuss each of the three steps for the posting logic:

1. With the time confirmation, revenues are realized on the revenue adjustment P&L account and capitalized in the balance sheet as accrued revenue.
2. The customer invoice posts billed revenue on the income statement account. The revenue recognition adjusts the balance sheet and P&L in the following way:
   - If the revenue needs to be event-based deferred because revenue realization already took place with the confirmation, then the deferred revenue balance sheet general ledger account is credited—for example, with 110 EUR, as in the posting shown previously in Figure 7.90.
   - After debiting the revenue adjustment general ledger account with, for example, 110 EUR, the value on the customer project is now a debit balance of 20 EUR. The realized revenue of the project is now shown with the billed revenue account: 110 EUR minus the 20 EUR on the revenue adjustment account, for 90 EUR.
3. The accrued and deferred revenue will be balanced at period end. Because balance sheet corrections don't influence profitability reporting, they're never performed in

real time, only with the period-end run. In this case, there will be a balance of 20 EUR on the deferred revenue account. This is equivalent to a liability as you've invoiced more than has been provided.

The revenue adjustment is a P&L general ledger account on which revenues are shown temporarily during the lifetime of a project or sales order. When the project is completed, this general ledger account will be balanced to zero, just like the balance sheet accounts for accrued and deferred revenue.

#### Incorporation into the Universal Journal

Now that we've explained the general posting logic, let's discuss the next principle of event-based revenue recognition. As shown in the scenarios in this chapter, event-based revenue recognition is fully integrated with the general ledger because the revenue recognition data is stored in the Universal Journal, just like cost and revenue data. There is no specific persistency, which would require a periodic transfer to other financial applications, like the general ledger. Thanks to this integration, you can rely on the same table structures for all the financial applications.

With this integration, you can avoid the need for any reconciliation between revenue recognition data and the general ledger. Regardless of which day of the month it is, cost and revenue information are reconciled and up to date. The same entities and semantics are used, like the general ledger account, the ledger, or currency fields. This also greatly simplifies the period-end close process.

Because revenue recognition data is stored in the general ledger, the data inherits its functionality and its line item attributes, like the ledger, currency, and profitability segment. Thus, new reporting insights are enabled.

Let's look again at the posting of the time confirmation in the project-based sales scenario in Figure 7.185. This is taken from the project-based sales scenario introduced earlier and shown previously in Figure 7.79.

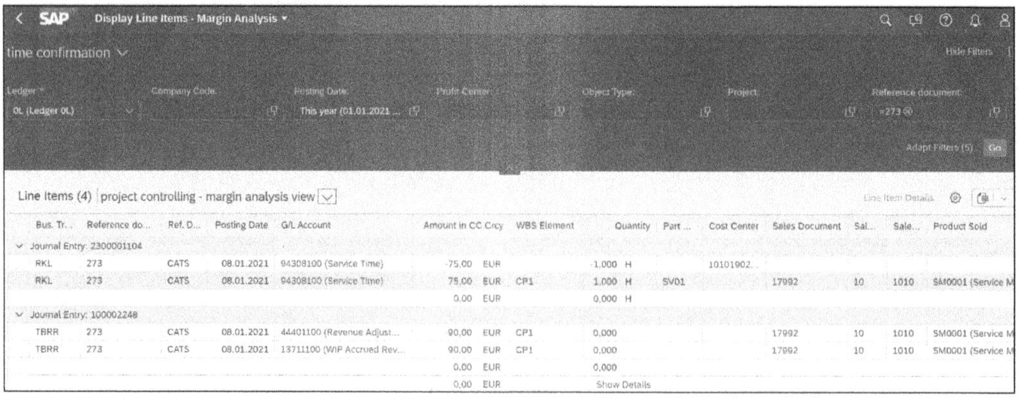

**Figure 7.185** Event-Based Revenue Recognition Posting Related to Time Confirmation with Cost-Based PoC

As shown in the postings triggered by the scenario business processes, there is a separate business transaction type (column 1, **Bus. Tr...**) used for event-based revenue recognition to identify these documents (**TBRR**).

For the revenue recognition journal entry, there is a reference document (column 2, **Reference doc...**) and a reference document type—here, a time sheet (column 3, **Ref. D...**). This provides a link from the revenue recognition journal entry to the source document and vice versa. This simplifies tracing.

The **Posting Date** is the same as the posting date of the referenced business transaction. For manual accruals (refer back to Figure 7.95) and period-end postings, the **Posting Date** is the last day of the period.

And as shown in the scenarios throughout this chapter, the revenue recognition postings are account-assigned to the cost objects: projects, profitability segment in sales scenarios, and service documents. With this, the assigned market segment can be derived and enriched in the revenue recognition journal entries. For example, you can see the **Product Sold** at the right. This allows a drilldown in the Trial Balance app into the WIP/accrued revenue by project and market segment attributes (refer back to Figure 7.98).

In Chapter 3, Section 3.3.2, we discussed currencies. The Universal Journal, and therefore event-based revenue recognition, supports multiple parallel currencies. Next to the company code currency, global currency, and transaction currency, there is also an option to activate freely defined currencies. All these currencies are also active for event-based revenue recognition due to the Universal Journal design.

And there is another important capability enabled with the integration into the general ledger: event-based revenue recognition supports parallel ledgers. There is an option to update different values based on the ledger's assigned accounting principle. We saw this in the journal entry overview for the business processes; an example was shown previously in Figure 7.19.

**Example for Parallel Valuation in Revenue Recognition**

Imagine a company in Europe dealing with customer projects. A customer works with two ledgers, one with accounting principle IFRS and the other with local Generally Accepted Accounting Principles (GAAP). The customer can assign different revenue recognition methods for the two ledgers. In the local GAAP ledger, he or she would work with a revenue-based PoC. In this case, the revenue recognition will just defer the costs and capitalize the costs to a WIP general ledger account. The revenue and costs will be realized with the billing. In the IFRS ledger, the customer would recognize revenue with the confirmation. Thus, one prima nota will lead to different valuations and postings in a particular ledger.

### Integration with Logistics Processes

First, note that you always take the revenue recognition contract data from the logistics object: the sales order item, service order, or service contract item. There is no specific revenue recognition persistence for this data. This mainly concerns the following billing information, via which the amount can be invoiced:

- In the customer project scenario, the billing method is defined by the sales order item: time and expense, periodic service, or fixed price. For the latter, the planned revenue values can be found in the billing plan (refer back to Figure 7.69).
- In the sales from stock scenario, the product and the price are stored in the sales order item (refer back to Figure 7.13).
- In the service order, you can also define whether billing is done via a fixed price or is confirmation-based. The revenue values can be found in the pricing scheme shown previously in Figure 7.146.
- The service contract contains a detailed billing plan (refer back to Figure 7.175).

The methods and the values defined in these logistic objects are the base for the revenue recognition.

In the customer project scenario, there are the following additional integration aspects:

- For the fixed-price contract type, the planned costs are taken from the resource planning on the customer project work package, and the Review Customer Projects app (SAP Fiori ID F1659) is available for the project manager to define the estimate at completion (EAC), which determines the PoC percentage of the event-based revenue recognition.
- As shown in the project scenario (refer back to Figure 7.64), there is one place to set the status: in the project header with the **Stage** field. There is no additional status option in parallel in sales or accounting that is maintainable. This customer project status is relevant for revenue recognition. With the completed status, all posted costs and revenues of assigned project elements will be realized. All balance sheet values will be cleared.

### 7.5.2 Supported Billing Methods

Let's now look at the range of functions provided. As shown before in the business scenarios, the revenue recognition needs to follow the type of contract, which is determined by the logistic sales order, service order, or service contract item. Here the method and values for billing are defined.

The following contract types are supported for event-based revenue recognition:

- **Time and expense billing, provided by the customer project scenario**
  We showed this in Section 7.3.1. This contract type enables billing based on the journal entries posted, such as by time or by expense confirmations on the project. Billing products are determined for the different postings. For these billing products, sales prices are defined. Event-based revenue recognition calculates for every posting on the project the realized revenue by simulating time and expense billing. So,

you can ensure that you get the same revenue recognition results for the confirmations as you'll get later for the billing.

- **Fixed-price billing, provided in the customer project and the service order**
If the cost-based realization method is active (which we'll discuss in the next section), you calculate for every single confirmation item the PoC based on the actual costs of the confirmation and the aggregated plan costs. This PoC is multiplied by the planned revenues of the contract item to get the matching realized revenue for this confirmation. The planned cost comes from the customer project resource planning. Plan revenues are taken out of the billing plan. The revenue-based and completed contract methods also can be applied.
- **Periodic billing, provided by the customer project scenario and service contract**
Here you realize revenue via a time-based billing plan. In this scenario, for every billing plan item, a valid time frame needs to be maintained. Based on this time frame, you distribute the realized revenues to the periods. Revenue is only realized with the periodic run. We provided an example previously in Section 7.4.4.
- **Delivery-based billing, provided by the sales scenario**
If the cost-based or delivery-based realization method is active, you calculate the realized revenue by multiplying the delivery quantity by the sales price from the sales condition scheme.



### 7.5.3 Realization Methods

The realization method defines the point in time at which revenue and cost of sales are realized. This depends on the contract agreement and the legal accounting principle. Let's go through the supported methods:

- **Cost- or confirmation-based**
Revenues are already realized with the confirmation and cost posting on the cost object. This method was applied in the customer projects in Section 7.3.1 for time and expense billing and in the fixed-price scenario in Section 7.3.2.
- **Revenue-based**
Costs are just deferred as WIP as they occur. Realized revenues are equal to the billed revenues. With the billing, revenues and the matching cost of sales are realized. If WIP existed, then it will be reduced by the realized cost of sales amount. This method was applied in the sales scenario in Section 7.2. Note a special case in the fixed-price scenario: if the WIP value was less the realized cost of sales, reserves for missing costs are accrued for the difference.
- **Completed contract**
During the lifetime of a contract (e.g., project or service order), all costs and revenues are just deferred. When the **Completed** status is set for the project or service order, all billed revenues and posted costs are realized. This method was applied in the service scenario in Section 7.3.1.

- **No revenue recognition posting**
  Costs and revenues are realized as they occur. No accruals or deferrals gets posted. In this case, matching principles for costs and revenues are not ensured.

There also can be manual accruals created, as we discussed in Section 7.3.1. Manual accruals can be posted by the Event-Based Revenue Recognition—Projects app on separate general ledger accounts. The manual accruals are automatically cleared with the completed status.

**Event-Based Revenue Recognition and IFRS 15**

The event-based revenue recognition covers the common IFRS 15 requirements for the customer project and the sales scenario:

- It supports the five-step model defined for IFRS 15.
- It includes an option for multielement arrangement within one sales order for a customer project or sales scenario.
- It differentiates accrued revenue/contract assets and deferred revenue/contract liabilities.
- It differentiates accrued revenue by contract assets and unbilled revenue.

Following event-based revenue recognition principles, the IFRS 15 functionality is highly integrated into the logistics. So, you define in the sales order items which items you want to bundle. The transaction prices and standalone selling prices are part of the sales order pricing scheme. Based on this information, allocated revenue per performance obligation is calculated and stored in an allocation table. The matching principle of cost and revenues is then based on the allocated revenues.

For more on IFRS 15 and additional information about event-based revenue recognition, visit the blog at *http://s-prs.co/v528212*.

### 7.5.4 Event-Based Revenue Recognition Apps

There are several apps available for event-based revenue recognition. They are provided with the sales accountant role. Their tiles are shown on the home page in Figure 7.186.

For every controlling object—projects, service documents, and sales orders—you can see there is an app to analyze a single object and an app to start a periodic run. There is also an app to point out possible errors if a revenue recognition document couldn't be posted: the Manage Revenue Recognition Issues app. There can be several reasons for this problem—for example:

- No plan costs or revenues could be determined in a fixed-price scenario.
- In a time and expense billing scenario, no prices are maintained for a billing material.
- There's a configuration error in the event-based revenue recognition.
- A general ledger account can't be used.

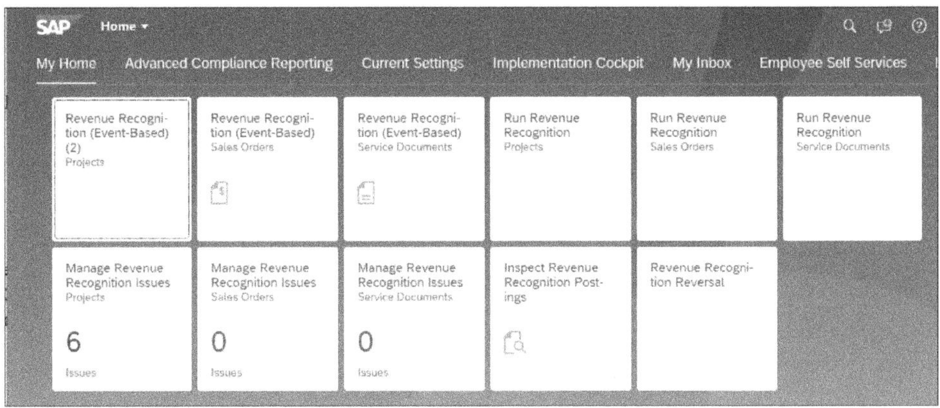


**Figure 7.186** Overview of Event-Based Revenue Recognition Apps

With the Inspect Revenue Recognition Postings app, you can analyze all postings on a revenue recognition–relevant cost object via T-accounts. Finally, you can reverse revenue recognition documents with the Revenue Recognition Reversal app.

Now, let's walk through some of these key apps.

### Event-Based Revenue Recognition—Projects

Let's look at the project from Section 7.3.1 in the Revenue Recognition Event-Based—Projects app (SAP Fiori ID F4767). Enter your project in the **Project Definition** field and click **Go** to get the list of WBS billing elements. Select the arrow for the first line to get the information shown in Figure 7.187. This is a new version of the app we showed you before.

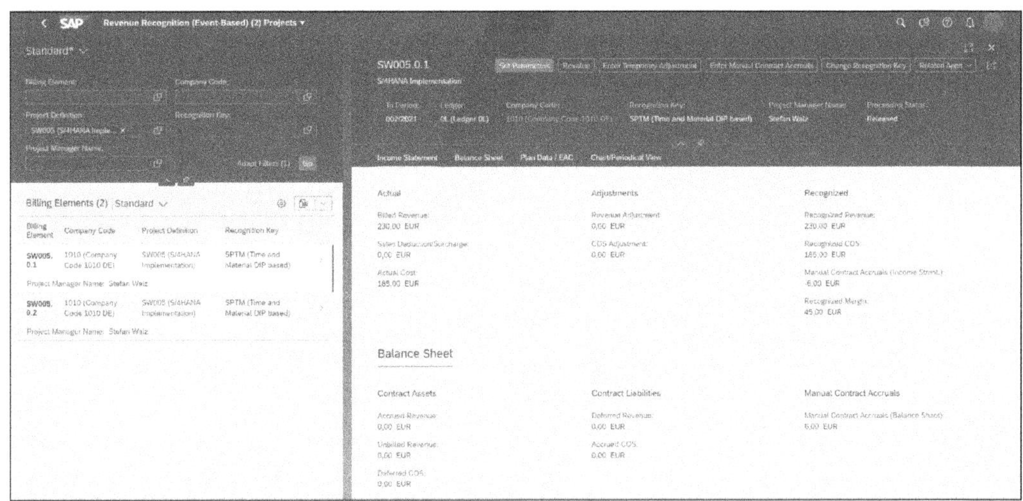


**Figure 7.187** App to Analyze Event-Based Revenue Recognition Data for Single Project

You can analyze the values for income statement and balance sheet. You'll see the possible activities at the top:

- **Set Parameters**
  With **Set Parameters**, you can set the period and the ledger.
- **Revalue**
  Revalue performs a revenue recognition posting, for which you have the option to post. It does the same as a periodic revenue recognition run.
- **Enter Temporary Adjustment**
  With **Enter Temporary Adjustment**, you can adjust the revenue recognition data for the selected period. The data will be automatically cleared with the next revenue recognition run for the next period.
- **Enter Manual Contract Accruals**
  The function of **Enter Manual Contract Accruals** was shown in Section 7.3.1. With it, you can adjust revenue recognition data. This adjustment is valid until you set the status to **Completed** or reverse it manually.
- **Change Recognition Key**
  You can also change the revenue recognition key and thus change the revenue recognition method.
- **Related Apps**
  You have the option to jump to other apps for detailed analyses of the postings via the **Related Apps** button.

### Manage Revenue Recognition Issues—Projects

Now let's start the Manage Revenue Recognition Issues—Projects app (SAP Fiori ID F4100), as shown in Figure 7.188. Here we've selected two company codes and the fiscal period.

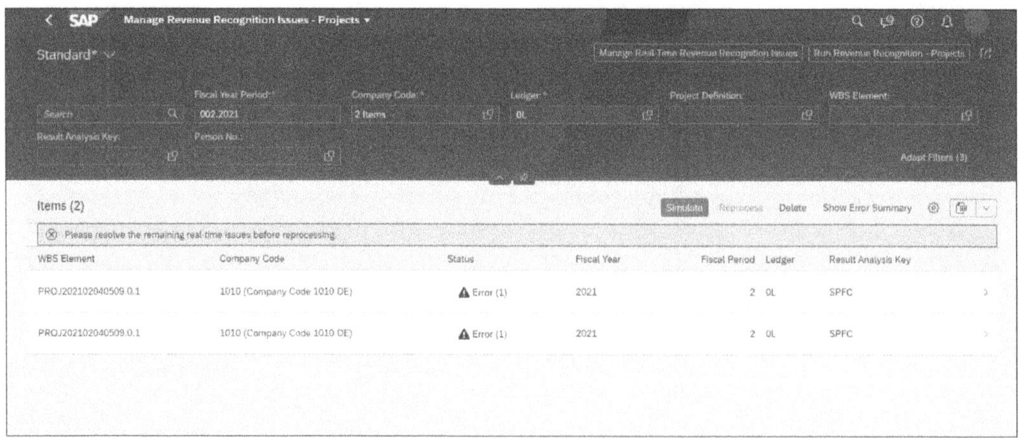


**Figure 7.188** Manage Revenue Recognition Issues—Projects App

You can see two issues for the selected company codes, **Fiscal Period 2** in **Fiscal Year 2021**, and **Ledger 0L**. You can also see the project for which the issues occurred. Select the **Error** icon in the **Status** column to see information about the root cause of the error via the log, as shown in Figure 7.189.

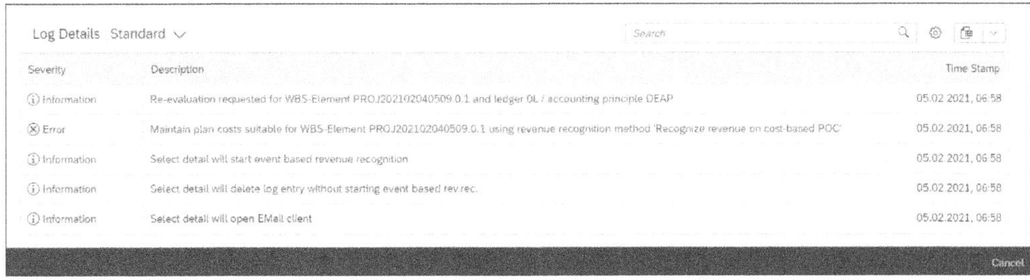


**Figure 7.189** Log for Revenue Recognition Issue

In this example, you can see that the revenue recognition failed because there is no plan data to determine the percentage of completion. You need to maintain the plan data, after which you can reprocess the data in the screen previously shown in Figure 7.188.

## Run Revenue Recognition Projects

There also are periodic run apps for every cost object available. As mentioned, the periodic run should be started at period end to take all changes during the period into account, like PoC or status change. And the netting of deferred and accrued revenue is only done by the run. Let's look at the periodic run for the projects with the Run Revenue Recognition—Projects app (SAP Fiori ID F4277), as shown in Figure 7.190.

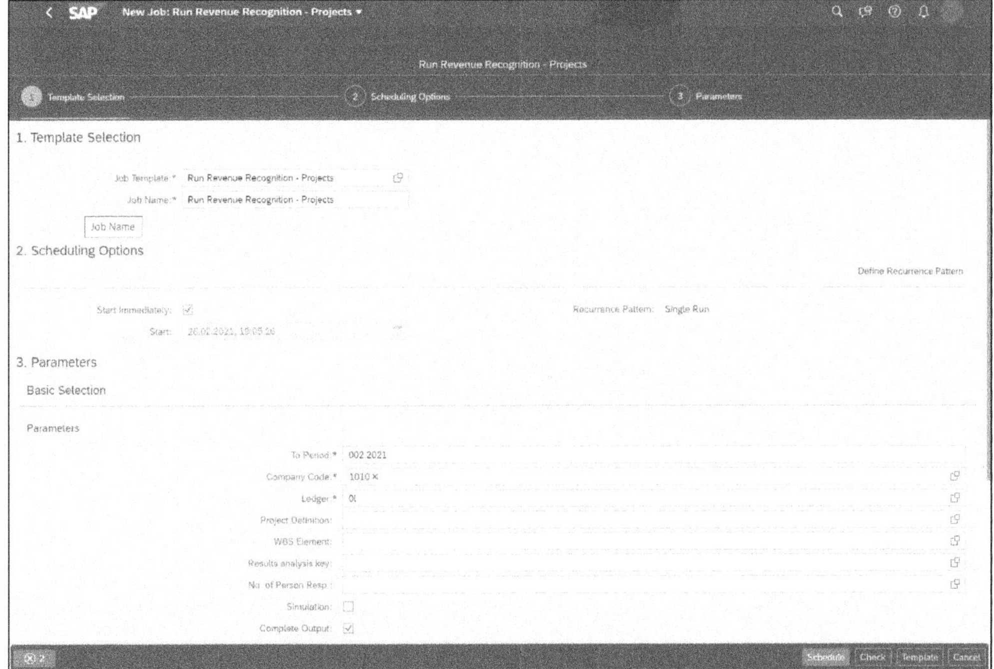


**Figure 7.190** Run Revenue Recognition—Projects App: Parameters for Run

Select the generic **Run Revenue Recognition—Projects** template in the **Job Template** field. You can use this template in accounting applications. You must specify the period (**To Period**) for which you want to calculate the data, the **Company Code**, and the **Ledger**.

> **Note**
> Before you start the periodic run, any issues must be resolved for the selected data.

### Inspect Revenue Recognition Postings

For an overview of all postings on a revenue recognition–relevant cost object, the Inspect Revenue Recognition Postings app is available. Select the WBS billing element from Section 7.3.1 as the account assignment object and click **Go** to arrive at the screen shown in Figure 7.191.

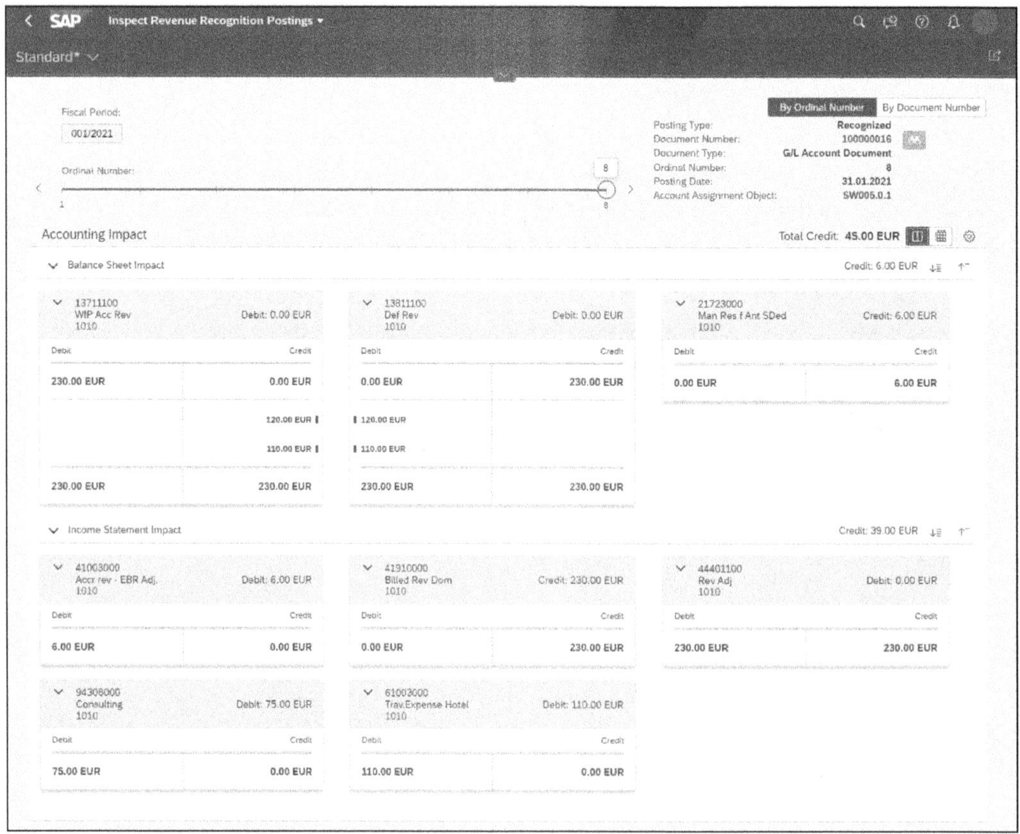


**Figure 7.191** Inspect Revenue Recognition Postings App

Based on T-accounts, you'll see the postings on the project: the travel expenses, the time confirmation, and the billed revenue and its related revenue recognition documents. You can also see the manual accrual.

### 7.5.5 Availability of Event-Based Revenue Recognition

In SAP S/4HANA Cloud, only event-based revenue recognition is in use to provide revenue recognition for cost objects. It supports the scenarios we've presented: professional service customer projects, project-based sales, sales scenarios, service orders, and service contracts. SAP plans to enhance the scope and to enable event-based revenue recognition for additional scenarios, like subscription billing.

On-premise SAP S/4HANA only supports customer projects, the project-based sales scenario, so far. The professional service scenario shown in Section 7.3.1 isn't available in on-premise systems. On the roadmap, SAP wants to expand event-based revenue recognition further and make it available in on-premise for other processes, like the sales scenario. For current availability, check SAP Note 2581947.



## 7.6 Summary

In this chapter, we discussed the goals and functionalities of margin analysis and its integration into business processes. As we visualized in Figure 7.1, the ultimate goal is to be able to apply the revenues and all costs incurred for the market segments and thus also the areas of responsibility. These market segment attributes can be very flexible and individually defined, as we discussed in Chapter 4, Section 4.6.

You've seen how closely margin analysis is integrated into the logistics business processes. We covered the sales scenario, three different versions of the customer project scenario, and the new service management scenario with SAP S/4HANA Cloud. We discussed management adjustments and the realignment tool. We also explored the margin analysis allocation tools.

The interaction of the Universal Journal's event-based revenue recognition and margin analysis opens up new analysis insights. In margin analysis, you use the same data source, journal entries, and reporting tools as those based on the Universal Journal. We'll talk about this more in Chapter 10.

But first, let's take a look at investment controlling.

# Chapter 8
# Investment Controlling

*In the previous chapters, we looked at the flow of costs to deliver products and services and their impact on profitability. We'll now look at those costs that impact future profitability in the form of investments into new products or production lines. We'll explain the idea of capital expenses and the use of investment management in SAP S/4HANA.*



Now that we've looked at overhead controlling, production controlling, and sales controlling in the previous chapters, next we'll explore investment controlling as a way of getting to grips with your *capital expenses*. The key difference between overhead controlling and investment controlling is that the costs incurred relate to *assets* rather than products and services, whether these are physical assets, such as a new production line, or intangible assets, such as the design work for a new product. The work associated with these assets isn't generally completed immediately but rather involves collecting costs over time and reporting them as *assets under construction* until the work is complete. On completion, the costs of the orders and projects are settled as the *acquisition and production costs* (APC) of the asset. Of course, an asset such as a laptop or phone can also be purchased directly and the costs capitalized immediately. Investment controlling comes into play when capital expenses are incurred over a significant length of time and a project or order is used to manage the costs incurred within this time frame, before the project is completed and the final capitalization of the asset can be reported, whereupon these costs flow back into overhead controlling as the *depreciation* of these asset costs.

Most organizations will be working on several capital projects at any given time, and *investment programs* can be used to manage budget over several different projects. If you're new to the subject of investment controlling, think of the investment program simply as a reporting layer structuring the investment portfolio, classifying the different types of investment and providing budgeting functions over and above a simple plan/actual comparison at the project or order level. It's also common to use *appropriation requests* to elaborate on investment proposals and submit detailed estimates prior to approval. The use of an investment program is optional. If you only have a few capital expense projects, you may be able to manage without any form of portfolio management and simply focus on the process of collecting and capitalizing the expenses. Once work has been approved, costs are collected on orders and projects and settlement is used to move the expenses initially to an asset under construction and later to an asset. The asset can then be written off just like a purchased asset.

In SAP S/4HANA, there are two options for managing capital expenses:

1. In on-premise, investment management is used to manage the investment portfolio, perform planning and budgeting, capture the costs on orders and projects, and settle the costs to assets. The approach is explained in SAP Note 2436714. We'll focus on the on-premise approach in this chapter.
2. Investment management isn't offered in the cloud environment. Instead, the investment portfolio is handled using SAP S/4HANA Cloud for projects and planning using SAP Analytics Cloud. The operational part of the process, involving capturing project costs, creating assets under construction, and settlement, is the same as in the on-premise environment.

Now, let's explore how to organize your investments for controlling purposes in Section 8.1, before moving on to planning and budgeting steps in Section 8.2, and finally examining the settlement and reporting processes in Section 8.3.

## 8.1 Investment Programs and Assigned Projects and Orders

Work breakdown structure (WBS) elements and internal orders are used to handle the operational part of investment controlling. We introduced the master data required in Chapter 4 and explained how to capture the costs for orders and projects in Chapters 5, 6, and 7. The difference between these projects and those that you saw in Chapter 7 is that the customer is not an external party, but the organization itself—or rather, the part of the organization that requires a new production line or design work for a new product. To this extent, the decision to approve such work is usually centralized to ensure that investment is distributed fairly between the various parts of the organization. Some organizations manage the portfolio in spreadsheets, but if multiple investment orders and WBS elements are to be handled efficiently, more structure is needed. For this reason, many organizations choose to use an investment program to structure the undertaking of creating program items for each of the investment areas, especially during planning and when assigning a budget. Once approved, investment orders or investment projects are created for the execution of the investment plans. The investment program itself can't carry costs, so you won't find any transactions that include the investment program as an *account assignment*. Instead, costs are assigned to the orders and WBS elements assigned to the investment program, as we discussed in Chapter 5. These behave exactly like any other internal orders and WBS elements, except that they settle the costs to assets rather than to materials and customers, and the costs can be reported either in isolation or via the investment program.

To display an investment program, use Transaction IM23 or go to **Accounting • Investment Management • Programs • Master Data • Investment Program Structure • Display** and enter the program (**Inv. program**) and **Approval year**, as shown in Figure 8.1. Investment programs are always created with reference to an approval year, even though the assigned projects or orders may take several years to complete. This is also different from the process of planning overhead that we looked at in Chapter 5 as it's usually assumed that the overhead budget will be consumed in one fiscal year.

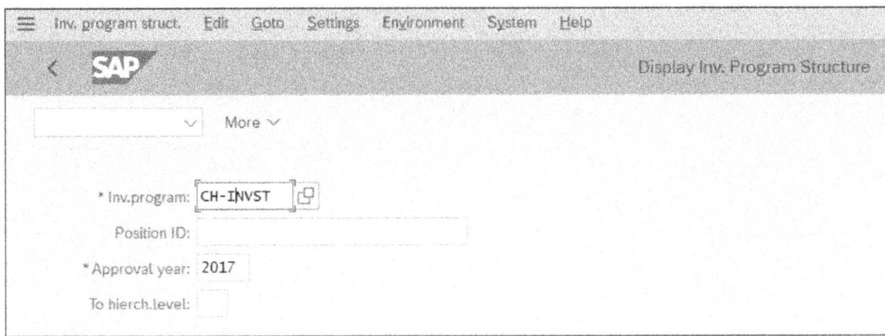


**Figure 8.1** Display Investment Program Structure

Figure 8.2 shows a sample investment program. The investment program is always assigned to a controlling area, and the structure can be derived from the cost center hierarchy we looked at in Chapter 4, either from a profit center hierarchy or created manually, as was the case here. At this stage, you're simply creating reporting nodes to structure the planned investment as you can't assign costs directly to these nodes but only to the associated orders and projects.

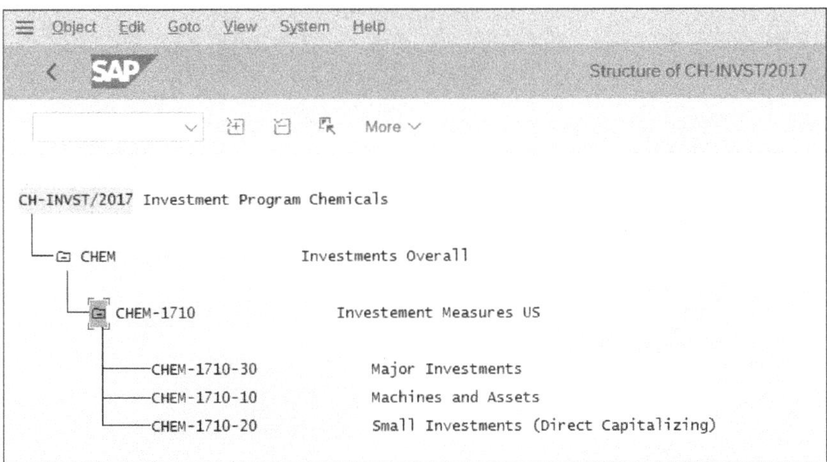


**Figure 8.2** Sample Investment Program

To view the assigned WBS elements and orders, select one of the program items shown in Figure 8.2 and then the **Assignments** button. Figure 8.3 shows the WBS element assigned to the **Major Investments** position ID. This is a WBS element just like those in previous chapters, but it's used to capture costs that will be capitalized as fixed assets in the future. In this case, all the costs are considered part of the investment program, but you can also reduce the percentage entered here.

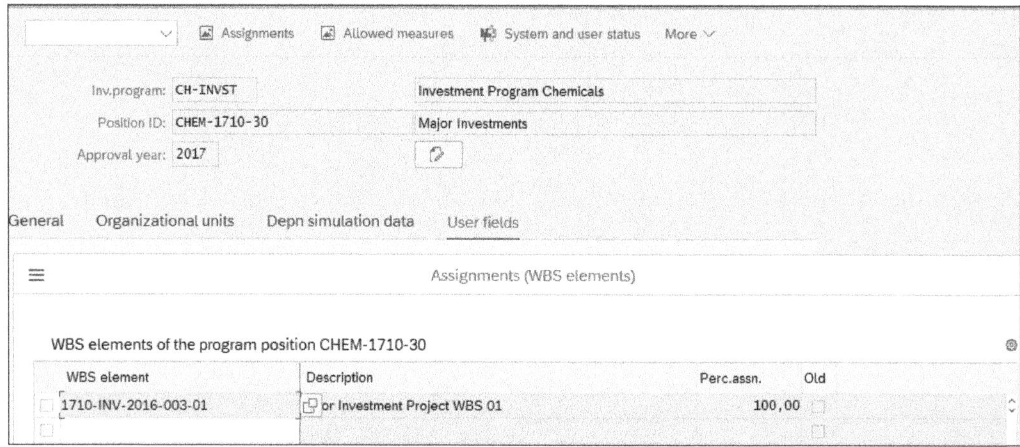

Figure 8.3 Assignments of WBS Elements to Investment Program Item

*Appropriation requests* are used to request investment as part of this investment program. The appropriation request contains details of the plan required to complete the investment. Several variants can be created that show the planning values, along with return on investment (ROI) values. Figure 8.4 shows a sample appropriation request, along with the estimate of the investment costs submitted by the requester to support his or her request. To display the appropriation request, go to Transaction IMA11 or **Accounting • Investment Management • Appropriation Request • Edit Appropriation Request • Individual Processing.** To display the planned values entered by the requestor, select the **Variants** tab at the top and the **Planned values** tab at the bottom.

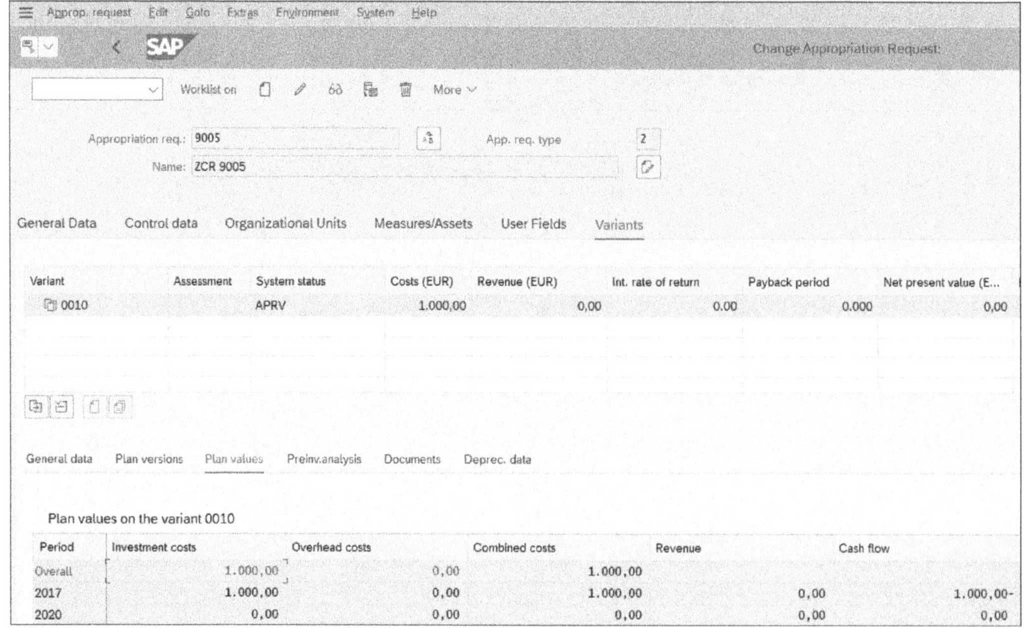

Figure 8.4 Appropriation Request

Once the framework of the investment has been approved and the individual requests checked, the next stage is to detail out the planning and set up the basis for budgeting and availability control.

## 8.2 Planning and Budgeting

Investment programs describe the organization's targets in terms of capital investment projects to replace production equipment, prepare new products for launch, or undertake major repair work. There's a link to the cost center plan that we looked at in Chapter 5 in the sense that the same organizational structure (generally the cost center hierarchy) is often used to structure the investment program. In this type of plan, however, the controller plans the investment needed to ensure the cost center output in the long term, rather than the costs of providing the output in the immediate future. This plan is subject to much greater variability than the annual operating plan. Although the costs incurred by a cost center in any period should be relatively stable, building a new production line is an inherently different undertaking.



Because of the variability in spending, it's common to set a *budget* as a ceiling for the allowed capital expenses. Variability also means that a plan can't be considered to represent a standard. This means that the variance analysis available for investment projects and orders is limited to a line-by-line comparison of the plan and budget against actual costs and commitments.

SAP currently offers two approaches to investment planning:

1. **Classic planning of overall costs with detailing by cost element**
   We'll discuss this option in Section 8.2.2 and Section 8.2.3. This option relies on the legacy tables (tables COSP and COSS) and is only available in on-premise SAP S/4HANA. Planning content is available in SAP Analytics Cloud for project planning and budgeting, as we discussed in Chapter 5, but the investment program is not covered.
2. **SAP Analytics Cloud includes dedicated planning stories for investment planning**
   We'll discuss this option in Section 8.2.4. This option can be used in both SAP S/4HANA and SAP S/4HANA Cloud.

Once we cover the planning process, we'll walk through budget management in Section 8.2.5. To begin, let's check the budget settings.

### 8.2.1 Project Planning for Capital Expense Projects

Investment planning generally starts with the items of the investment program that we looked at in Section 8.1. These items provide the framework for the planning activities. But if you don't use investment management, you can simply track your planning progress against a list of investment projects and orders and perform the same planning tasks on the individual objects. Before you start, check the budget settings for your program by going to Transaction IM03 or **Accounting • Investment Management • Programs • Master Data • Investment Program Definition • Display** and entering the program (**Inv. program**) and **Approval year**, as shown in Figure 8.5.

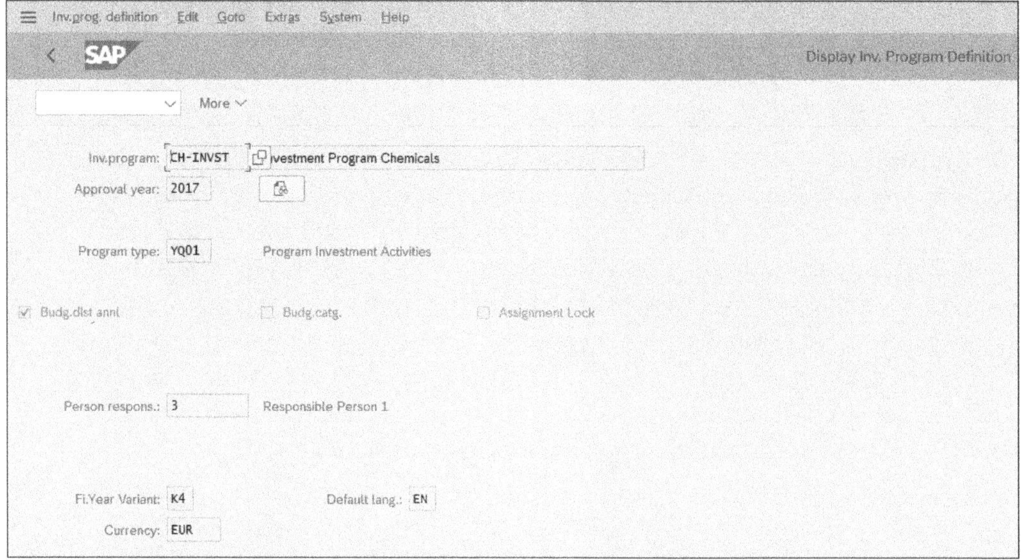


**Figure 8.5** Settings for Investment Program

**Linking Investment Program Budgets and the Underlying Orders/Projects**

In the context of investment budget planning, it's a good idea to select the **Budg.dist annl** (budget distribution annual) checkbox so that any orders or projects assigned to the program position do not receive more annual budget for the fiscal year than is available for the program position to which they're assigned. This makes it easy to ensure that each project manager keeps to his or her allotted budget during the planning process.

### 8.2.2 Overall Plan

The high-level goals for investment planning are determined by the ability of the organization to fund the investment at all. For this reason, an *overall plan* exists as a form of preplanning for orders and projects, but not for cost centers, for which the planning is inherently more predictable. The overall plan documents the high-level goal, such as the planned spending for a single project, and its refinement to a level of detail appropriate for project approval. This documents the progress toward the final project structure, breaking down the total values to the individual WBS elements, and toward an understanding of the timing of the expenses: the years in which the costs will be incurred.

To create an overall plan for a project, use Transaction CJ40 or follow menu path **Accounting • Investment Management • Investment Projects • Planning • Overall Values •**

**Change**. The transaction has been removed from the Project System menu in SAP S/4HANA, but it can still be used, as explained in SAP Note 2270407.

Enter the **Project Definition**, the **Currency**, and the **Version**. If you already know which level of the project hierarchy interests you in a large project, you can also enter a WBS element. Figure 8.6 shows a sample overall plan. You can toggle between this view (the element view), in which the leading column shows the WBS elements, and the annual view, in which the leading column shows the year, by clicking on the **Annual Overview** button. You can perform the following types of planning:

- **Top-down planning**
  The process of breaking down the project plan structurally and across the time dimension is generally known as *top-down planning*. The **Distributable** column gives an overview of the costs awaiting distribution to the lower levels. The costs that have been distributed are shown in the **Distributed** column.
- **Bottom-up planning**
  Alongside this process, you'll often find planned data being entered for individual WBS elements when the details are known (contracts with a supplier, agreements on the level of work required to perform the task, etc.). These are shown in the **Planned total** column and aggregated in a process known as *bottom-up planning*. At some point, the two value flows should meet, but the essence of the planning application is in matching the detail against the target and understanding where compromises will be needed.

We'll use this overall plan to prepare the budget for the project later.

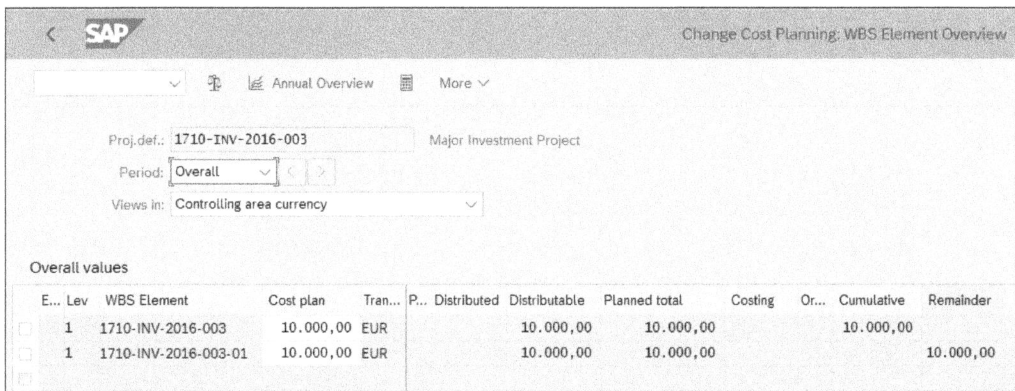


**Figure 8.6** Overall Plan for Project

### 8.2.3 Cost Element Planning

The overall plan also aggregates any other known planning data available for the project. Where assets under construction have to be capitalized for the project, it's important to distinguish the types of costs in the project (direct, indirect, material, etc.). This forces the controller to plan at the same level of detail as the inputs in the cost center.

To access the planning application shown in Figure 8.7, choose the **Annual Overview** button shown in Figure 8.6 and then click the **Primary Costs** button. This takes you into the form-based cost element plan, where you'll see a line for every cost element in your chart of accounts. Figure 8.7 shows the planning screen. This behaves the same way as cost element planning on cost centers or on internal orders.

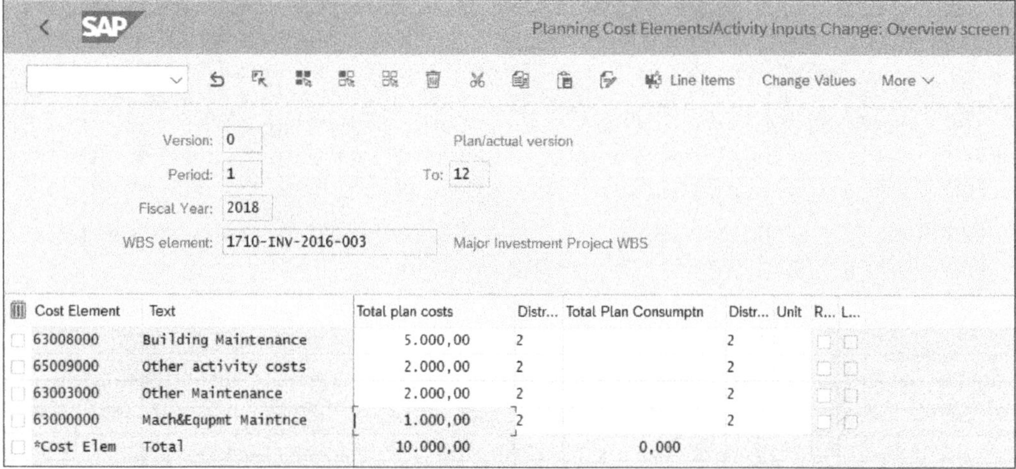


**Figure 8.7** Cost Element Plan for Project

**Including Your Own Planning Layouts in Project Planning**

If you click the **Primary Costs** button, a standard planning layout will be used that can't be switched once you're in the planning transaction. If you want planners to be able to jump to the primary costs from the overall plan but use a different planning layout, refer to the instructions in SAP Note 47207 for details on how to change the planning layout.

Alternatively, use Transaction CJR2 with layout 1-701 or follow menu path **Accounting • Investment Management • Investment Projects • Planning • Cost and Activity Inputs • Change**. Again, Transaction CJR2 is no longer part of the menu for Project System but continues to be available in SAP S/4HANA. Enter the project definition, the currency, the version, and the cost element group or interval. If you choose this route, you can choose between free planning (where you'll only see data for the cost elements you've already captured) and form-based planning (where you'll see an empty line for every cost element in the group or interval you entered in the initial screen).

Alongside the primary costs (the purchased materials and contract work) that are required to complete the project, you can also plan the work required to complete the project in the form of activity input.

If these projects are assigned to an investment program when you finish the detailed planning, you can roll up the values captured on the assigned orders and projects by going to Transaction IM34 or **Accounting • Investment Management • Program Planning • Default Plan Values**. Figure 8.8 shows the result of rolling the plan values captured for the project assigned to the research and development node into the investment program.



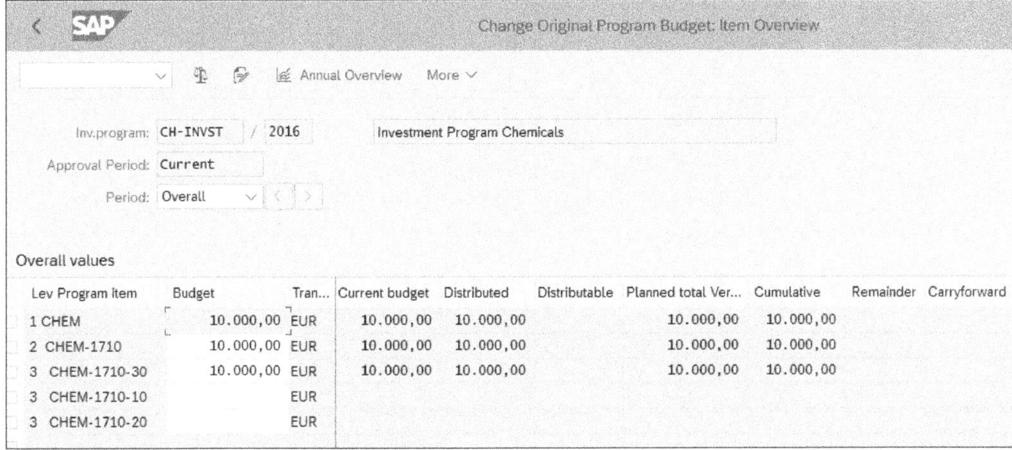


**Figure 8.8** Investment Program Planning

### 8.2.4 Investment Planning using SAP Analytics Cloud

If the screens we've looked at so far seem very tactical, you may prefer the approach to investment planning delivered as a planning story in SAP Analytics Cloud. Here you're also looking at the expenses to buy, maintain, or improve fixed assets, such as buildings or land, but the focus is on the accounts and the profit centers rather than on the individual projects as in the previous sections.

As discussed in Chapter 2, first select **Menu • Browse • Files • Public**; then, for investment planning, choose the **SAP_FI_BPL_IM_CAPEX_PLANNING** story. Figure 8.9 shows the **SAP_FI_BPL_IM_CAPEX_PLANNING** planning story, in which you're working in company code **1710** and the **Bike Parts** profit center and have copied the expenses for property, plant, and equipment for the **Buildings** and **Machinery & Equipment** general ledger accounts from the previous year. These can be adjusted as required to reflect the capital expenses expected in the next year by overwriting the figures to reflect the differences expected in this year.

The next stage is to use the rules defining the percentage depreciation to be applied to each asset class to perform the calculations shown in Figure 8.10, where we've calculated the **Depreciation Expense** for **Buildings** and **Machinery & Equipment**. These rules support both *straight-line depreciation*, where the value of the asset is reduced uniformly in each period until the end of its useful life, and *accelerated depreciation*, where the value reduction is higher in the early phases of the asset's life than the later phases.

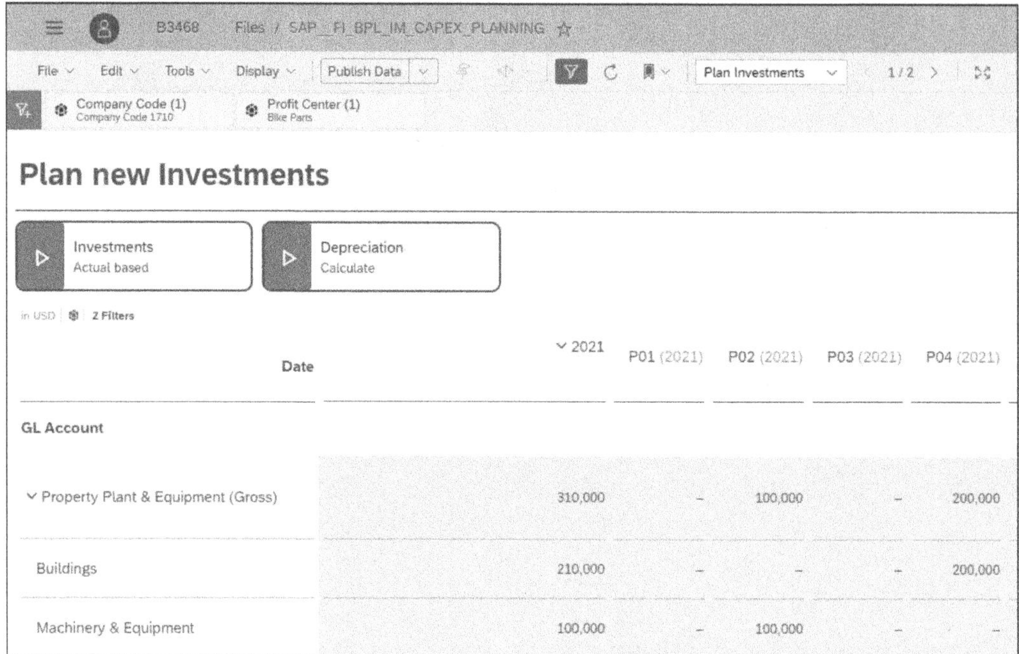


Figure 8.9 Planning Story for Capital Investments

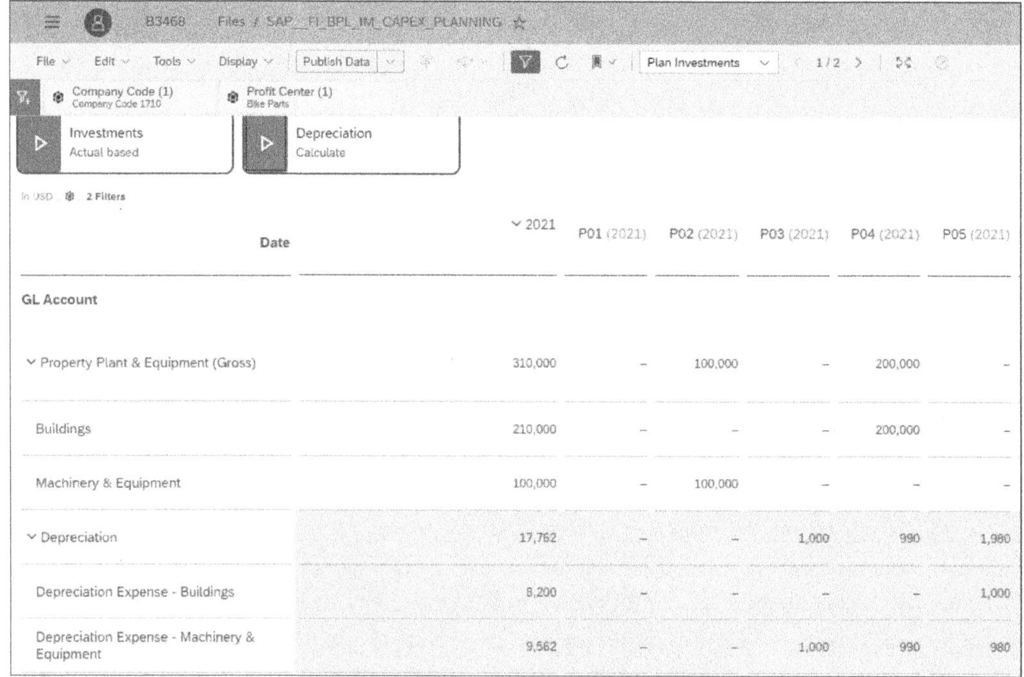


Figure 8.10 Planning Story, Showing Calculated Depreciation

The rules to calculate the depreciation shown in Figure 8.10 are defined in a planning story for the administrator (**SAP_FI_BPL_IM_CAPEX_PLAN_ADMIN**) that determines the percentage to be applied in each case and the depreciation method to be applied. Figure 8.11 shows a depreciation of 6% being applied to **Buildings** and 12% to **Machinery & Equipment** and shows that straight-line depreciation is to be used for **Buildings** and accelerated depreciation for **Machinery & Equipment**. As a controller, you might set your own depreciation percentages here to be used by the planners.



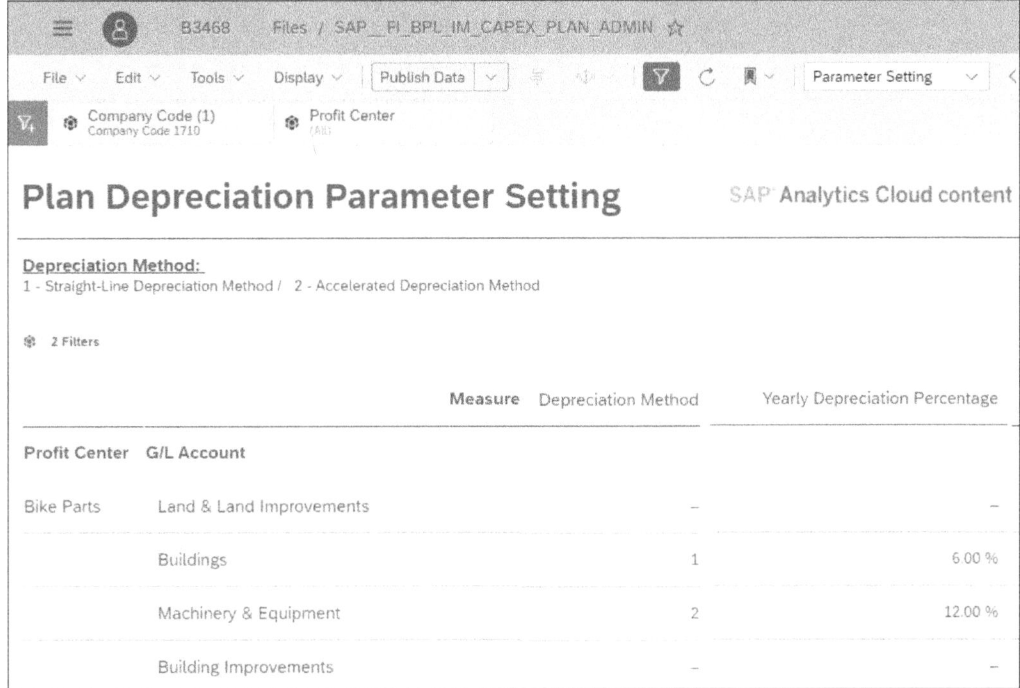


**Figure 8.11** Parameters for Depreciation of Capital Expenses

With the plan in place, we'll now look at how to set the budget in each case.

### 8.2.5 Budget Management and Availability Control

If you now assume that the project plan has been approved, the next task is the creation of the budget. The *original budget* is created using the approved plan as a guide. As we discussed in Chapter 5, the budget is more than just a plan. It's an agreement with the organization about proposed spending levels. Changing circumstances can render this ceiling inappropriate. At this stage, you can either create a *return* to give back some of the original budget or a *supplement* to document the assignment of an additional budget.

If you use investment programs, it makes sense to start your budgeting process at the highest level—namely, in the investment program. You can prepare the budget using Transaction IM32 or by following menu path **Accounting • Investment Management •**

**Programs • Budgeting • Edit Original** and entering data in much the same way as for the overall plan, as described in Section 8.2.2. If you've already prepared plan data for the investment program, you can copy this data by selecting **Edit • Copy View**, as shown in Figure 8.12.

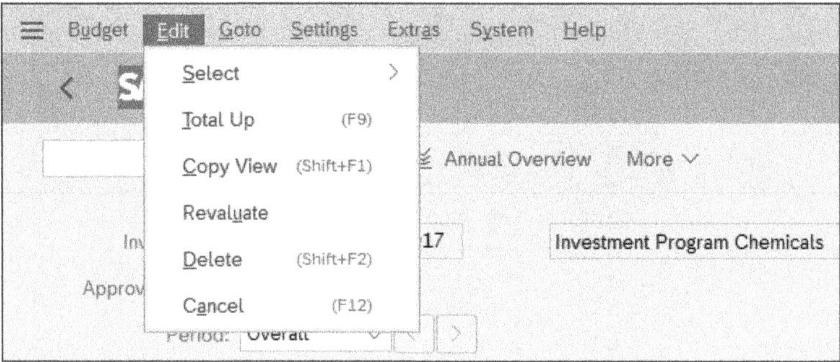


**Figure 8.12** Copy View

You can then choose the types of values that you want to copy, as shown in Figure 8.13.

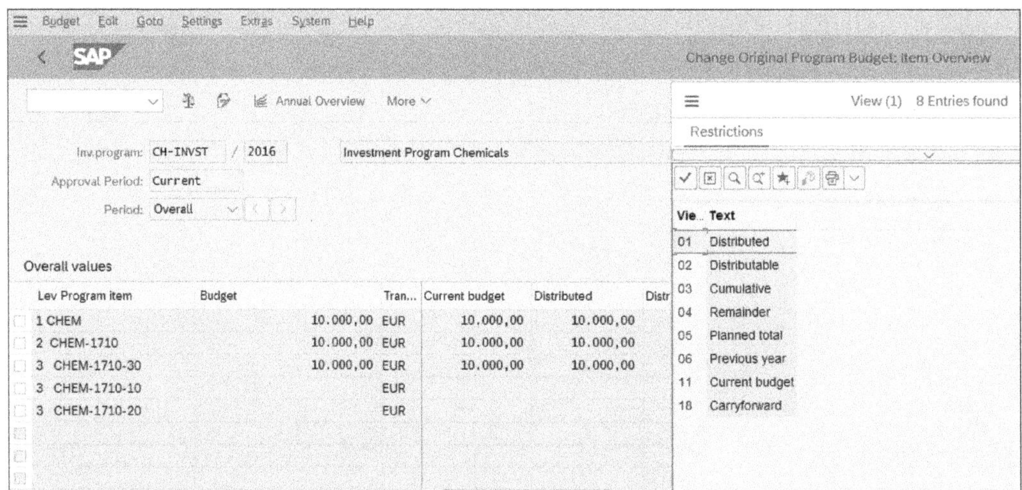


**Figure 8.13** Change Investment Programs

Once you've used the copy function to set the rough values for the items, adjust these to meet your needs by selecting **Edit • Revaluate**. When you're satisfied with your budget at the program level, you can ensure that the budget set can't be exceeded on the associated WBS elements, orders, and appropriation requests by using Transaction IM52 or by following menu path **Accounting • Investment Management • Programs • Budgeting • Budget Distribution • Edit**. Remember here the setting that we mentioned at the beginning of the chapter to ensure that the budget for the assigned items doesn't exceed the total for the year.

Figure 8.14 shows the original budget for a WBS element. You can enter the budget for a project using Transaction CJ30 or by selecting **Investment Management • Investment Projects • Budgeting • Original Budget • Change**. Notice that some of the lines in the **Budget** column don't allow entry. This is because we assigned the WBS elements to an investment program position and specified that the budget for the investment program shouldn't receive more annual budget for the fiscal year than is available for the program position by selecting the **Budget Distribution Annual** checkbox for the investment program we showed in Figure 8.2. If you want to check the connection between the WBS element and the investment program during budgeting, simply select **Extras • Investment Program**.

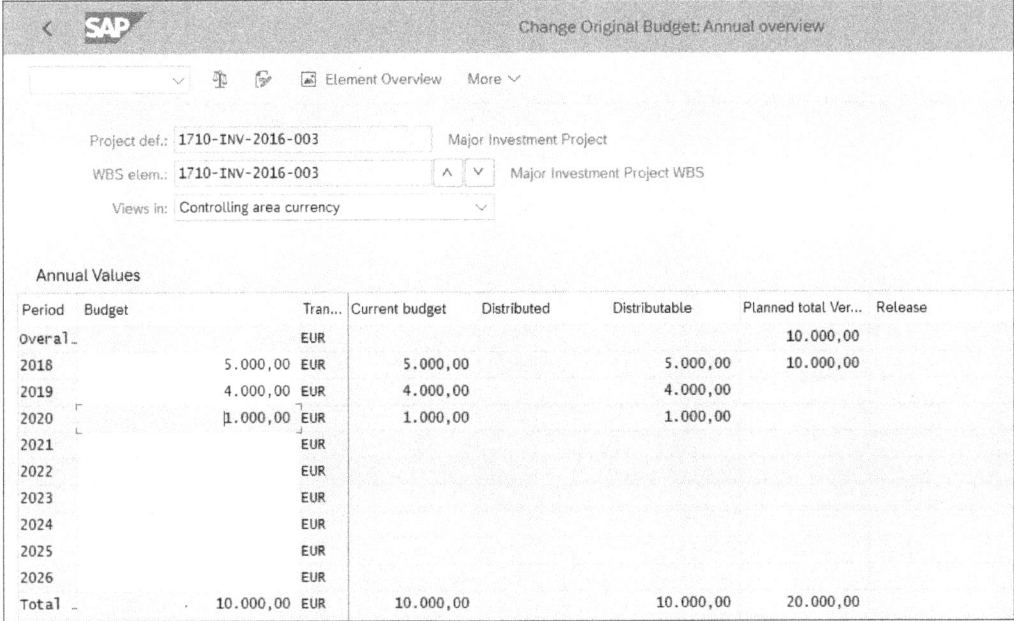


| Period | Budget | Tran... | Current budget | Distributed | Distributable | Planned total Ver... | Release |
|---|---|---|---|---|---|---|---|
| Overal_ | | EUR | | | | 10.000,00 | |
| 2018 | 5.000,00 | EUR | 5.000,00 | | 5.000,00 | 10.000,00 | |
| 2019 | 4.000,00 | EUR | 4.000,00 | | 4.000,00 | | |
| 2020 | 1.000,00 | EUR | 1.000,00 | | 1.000,00 | | |
| 2021 | | EUR | | | | | |
| 2022 | | EUR | | | | | |
| 2023 | | EUR | | | | | |
| 2024 | | EUR | | | | | |
| 2025 | | EUR | | | | | |
| 2026 | | EUR | | | | | |
| Total _ | 10.000,00 | EUR | 10.000,00 | | 10.000,00 | 20.000,00 | |

**Figure 8.14** Original Budget by Project

With the budget in place, you can perform availability checks for the projects, as shown in Chapter 5. Figure 8.15 shows the creation of a purchase order for the purchase or a material that will result in the budget on WBS element **T-20301** being exceeded and the resulting warning message. The budget check shown here uses the legacy tables BPGE for overall values and BPJA for annual values. Each time the budget is used to cover a purchase or other posting, the consumption is updated until the full budget is finally used up. This differs from the new approach we discussed in Chapter 5, Section 5.3.1, in which the budget usage is calculated dynamically by combining the actual costs and commitments on the fly.

**Note**

The budget approach just discussed is not available in SAP S/4HANA Cloud.

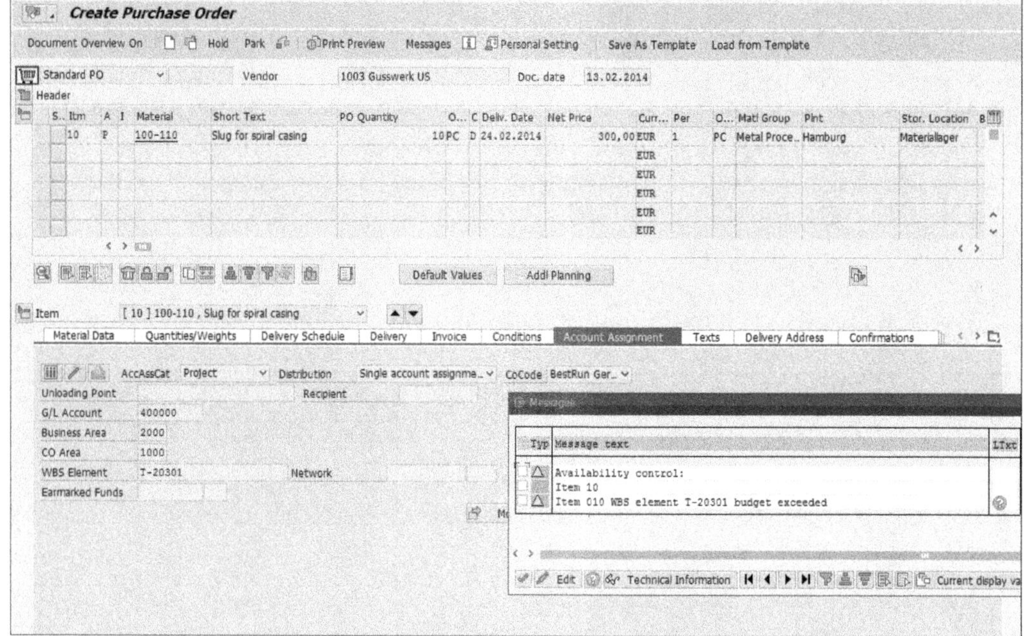


**Figure 8.15** Budget Check on Purchase Order

Now that you've planned your overall values and broken them down per year, you may wonder what happens as you go into the next fiscal year. In investment management, you need to ensure that a new approval year is created and the budget from the old year carried through into the new. To open a new fiscal year, use Transaction IM27 or follow menu path **Accounting • Investment Management • Programs • Periodic Processing • Fiscal Year Change • Open New Approval Year**. You can then copy the existing program structure and carry forward the planned values, budget values, and measures (orders and projects).

**Carrying Forward a Budget**

Remembering what you need to do to correctly move an investment program into the next fiscal year can be tricky. SAP Note 444444 tells you exactly how to proceed and how to avoid any pitfalls.

With the budget in place for the projects and orders, the process of collecting investment costs is the same as we described in Chapter 5.

## 8.3 Settlement and Reporting

If the process of capturing costs on WBS elements and orders is identical for operational expenses and capital expenses, the settlement process can be substantially different. First, the lifecycle of the project determines whether settlement is to the asset under construction or to the fixed asset. The project costs will be considered assets under construction until the project is complete, whereupon the final capitalization of the costs as fixed assets can take place. Second, it's common not to capitalize all project costs, but rather to settle some to the asset and the remainder to a cost center or other cost object. Decisions concerning what part of the project costs can be capitalized are made by the controller.

From a reporting point of view, there are two ways of viewing the investment costs. One is within asset accounting, where assets under construction are simply a special type of assets for which the balances and related transactions show up in the normal asset accounting reports. The second is within investment management, where the portfolio of capital projects can be viewed in their entirety and budget checks performed to determine where budget overruns are imminent. We'll discuss both methods in the following sections.



### 8.3.1 Assets under Construction

Assets under construction can be created automatically when you create the appropriate order or the WBS element providing the order type or project type is linked with the appropriate *investment profile*. This process is available in both on-premise SAP S/4HANA and SAP S/4HANA Cloud, where the settings can be activated using scope item BFH (Assets Under Construction), or scope item 1GF or 33G if you work with different ledgers.

Projects and orders that are linked to an asset under construction have the **AUC** (assets under construction) status. Figure 8.16 shows a sample investment project that we've accessed using Transaction CJ20N or **Accounting • Investment Management • Investment Projects • Master Data • Project Builder**. Notice also the **SETC** (settlement rule created) status. The system will automatically create a settlement rule to assign the costs to the assets under construction when the first settlement is performed.

Figure 8.17 shows the control parameters for the investment that you can access by switching to the **Control** tab. The **Investment Profile** determines whether an asset under construction will be created at the level of the WBS element or order or for each *source structure* in order to create different assets under construction depending on the type of costs collected. The investment profile also determines whether the costs will be settled at the summary level or line item by line item. As part of the portfolio process, it's also possible to categorize the investment in terms of its scale and rationale by choosing from the entries in the **Scale**, **Investment Reason**, and **Envir. Investment** (environmental investment) fields. You can see these sample parameters under **Investment Management**.

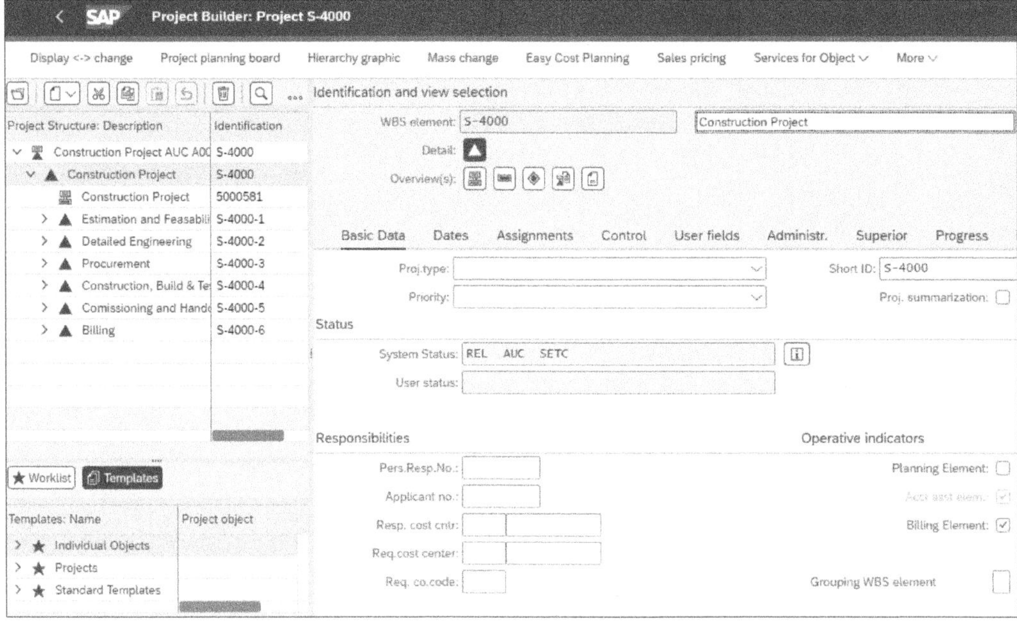

**Figure 8.16** Project Structure for Assets under Construction

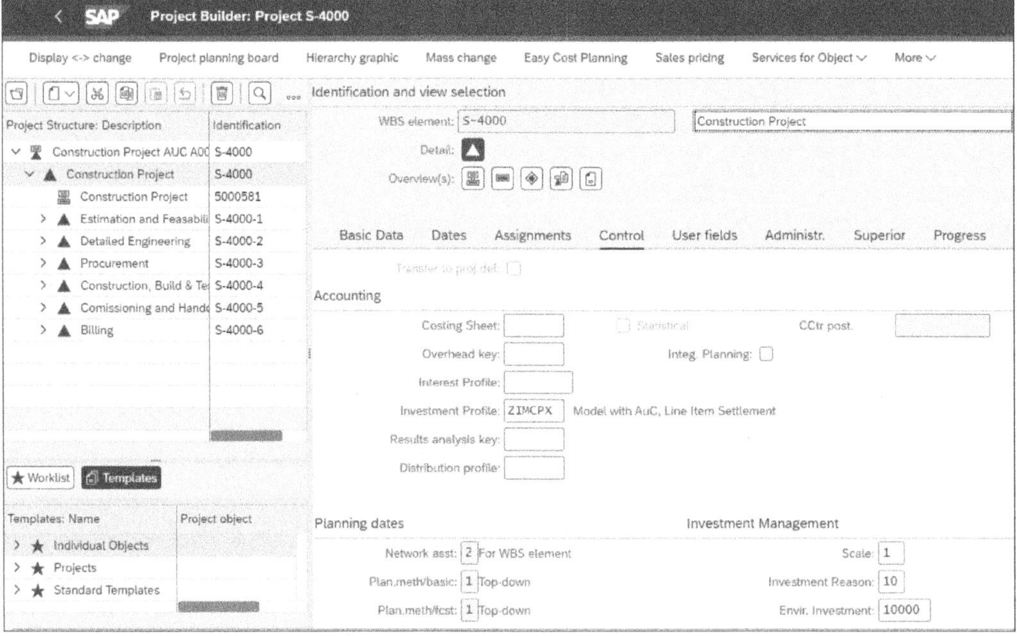

**Figure 8.17** Control Parameters for Investment Controlling

Figure 8.18 shows a sample asset under construction. The link to the project/order is via the **Investment Profile**. You can display the asset under construction by navigating to the settlement rule shown in Figure 8.19 and double-clicking the entry in the asset field, or by following menu path **Accounting • Financial Accounting • Fixed Assets • Asset • Display Asset** or using Transaction AS03 and entering the **Asset** number and the **Company Code**. Notice the asset **Class, 4002**, which separates this asset from the fixed assets that are already in use.

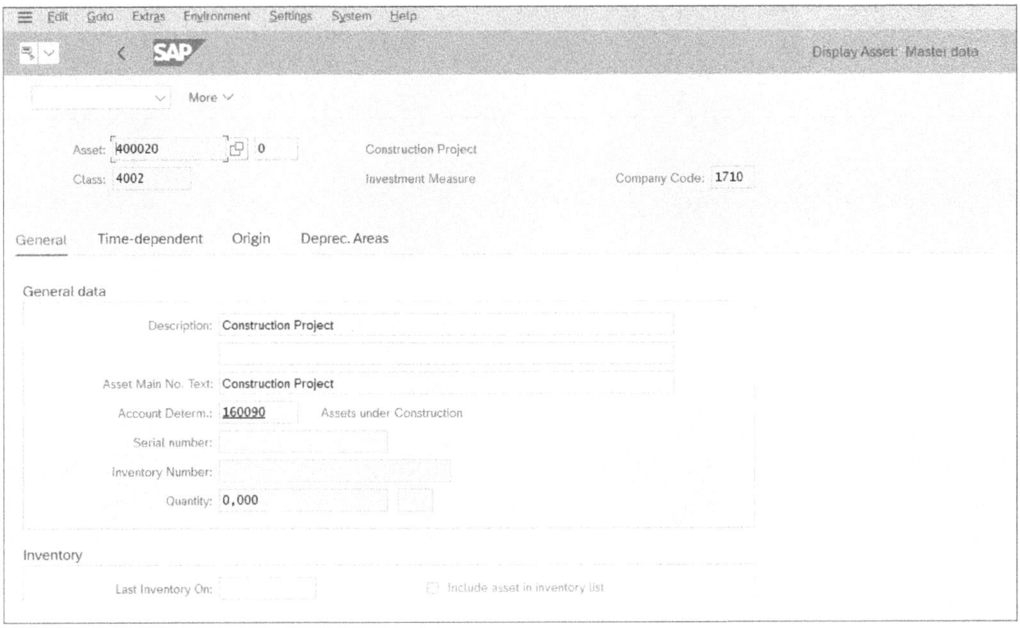

**Figure 8.18** Asset under Construction: Master Data

When we looked at settlement in the previous chapters, there was generally one receiver of the costs: in the case of overhead projects the costs were settled either to a cost center or to a market segment, and in the case of a commercial project they represented the cost of goods sold. With investment controlling, by contrast, the project costs represent either assets under construction or asset acquisition costs, depending on whether the project is complete or not. For this reason, settlement of capital projects takes place in two stages: first to assets under construction, and on completion to the fixed asset. The switch comes when the project is assigned the **Technically Completed** status. This doesn't mean that no additional costs can be captured for the project, but only that any subsequent costs flow to the fixed asset.

We introduced the role of the *settlement rule* in Chapter 5, Section 5.4.6. In the case of investment projects and orders, the settlement rule is created automatically during the first settlement to assign the project costs to the asset under construction, as shown in Figure 8.19. This first *distribution rule* (settlement type: **AUC**) can't be changed. If you need to assign some of the costs to another cost center, create an additional distribution rule of settlement type **PRE** (preliminary settlement) and assign a percentage of the costs to a cost center. The remainder will then be assigned to the asset under construction.

When the project is complete, the status is set to **Technically Completed** and the costs are moved from the asset under construction to the final asset via settlement using a second distribution rule of settlement type **FUL** (full). At this stage, you can also use a percentage to determine that some costs are capitalized as the final assets and the rest written off to a cost center.

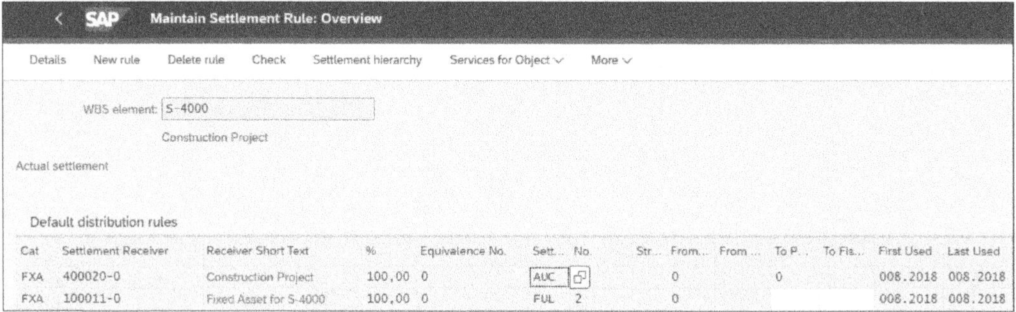


**Figure 8.19** Settlement Rule for Asset under Construction

In many countries, there are legal requirements concerning which costs can be capitalized and which can only be treated as overhead, and this simple percentage split doesn't provide sufficient flexibility. In this case, you can define a *source assignment* for each of the different types of costs in the IMG and assign the various cost elements to these source assignments. It's then possible to set up different distribution rules within the settlement rule to assign costs for the first source to the asset and for the second source to a cost center or to settle costs from one WBS element to several assets. To define a source assignment, choose **Project System Costs • Automatic and Periodic Allocations • Settlement • Settlement Profile • Create Source Structure** and define the appropriate groupings for your settlement. Then assign the accounts used to collect the costs on the project to each of these groupings prior to settlement.

If these buckets don't give you enough flexibility, it's also possible to perform *line item settlement*, where every posting line can potentially be assigned to a different receiver. This is the most powerful method of settlement as it allows you to settle every document to a different receiver, depending on its origin, but it also represents a larger workload for the controller, who must decide where to assign every posting line. Figure 8.20 shows a list of line items that have been posted to the project. To reach this view, choose **Accounting • Investment Management • Investment Projects • Period-End Closing • Single Functions • Settlement • Investment Project Line Items** or Transaction CJIC. To define the receivers for each line, choose **More • Edit • Enter Distribution Rule**.

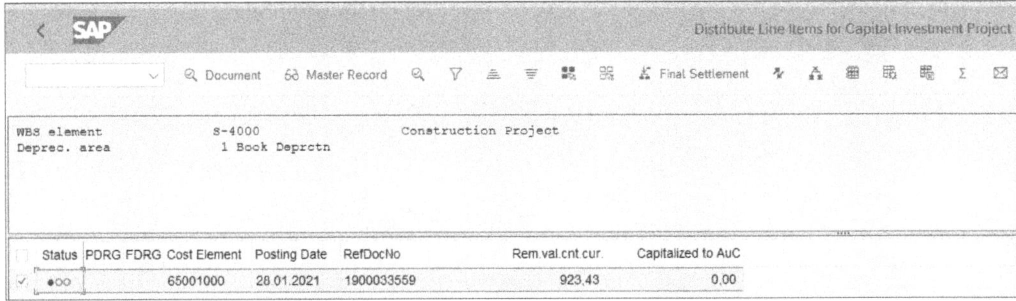


Figure 8.20 Line Item Settlement



In Figure 8.21, we've assigned 80% of the costs to **FXA** (fixed asset) **200088** and the remaining 20% to **CTR** (cost center) **17101301**. The settled costs are then considered as the acquisition and production costs of the fixed asset, while the remainder are an operational expense.

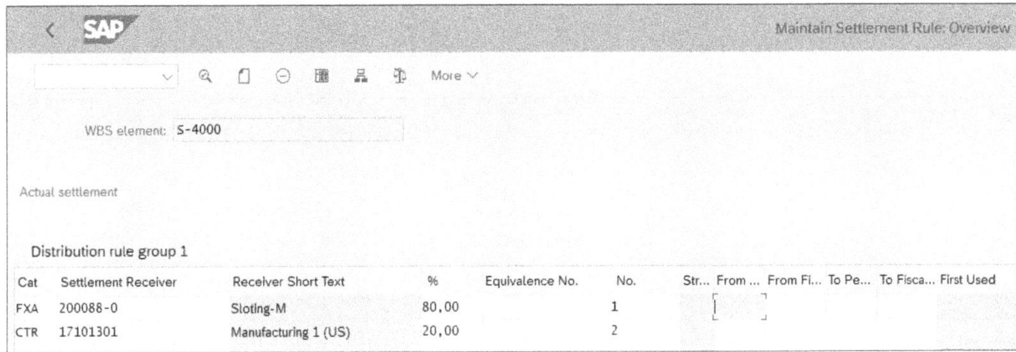


Figure 8.21 Settlement Rule to Fixed Assets and Cost Center

## 8.3.2 Investment Reporting

Now that you've planned budgets, managed them, and performed settlement for assets under construction, it's time to report on your investments. We'll walk through key reports in this section.

### View Assets

From a reporting point of view, assets under construction appear in the Asset Accounting Overview app (SAP Fiori ID F3096) shown in Figure 8.22, alongside purchased assets. The main difference, other than the transitory nature of the asset from the business perspective, is the asset class and the fact that the asset under construction is linked with a WBS element or internal order, as shown earlier.

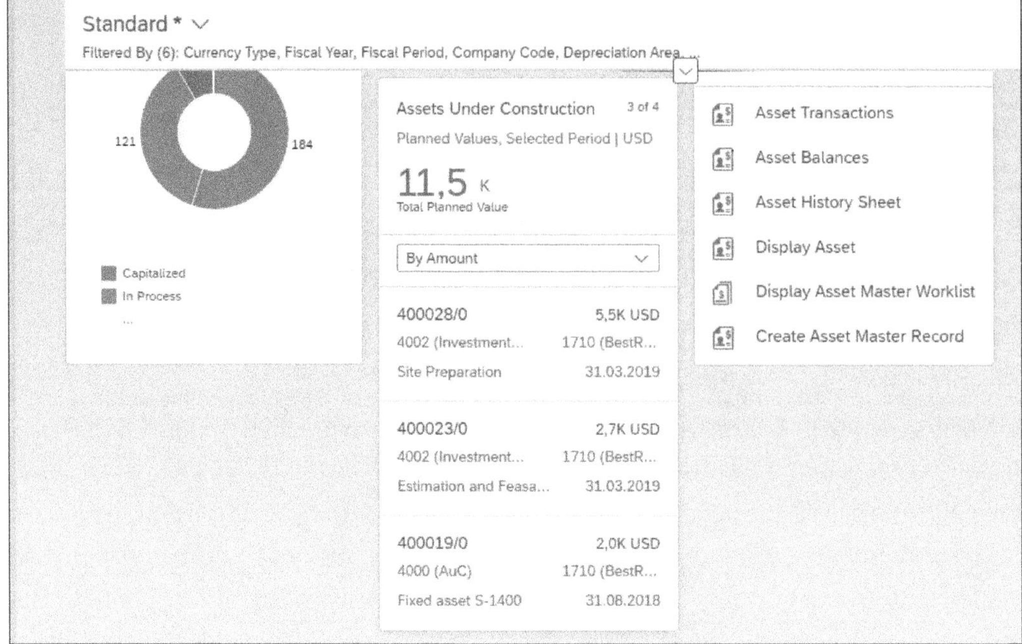


**Figure 8.22** Asset Overview, Showing Origin of Assets and Assets under Construction

Figure 8.23 shows the Asset Balances app (SAP Fiori ID F1617A). You can focus on the assets under construction as shown here by right-clicking on the asset class column and choosing **Filter By**. These costs have been settled from the underlying WBS element as the APC.

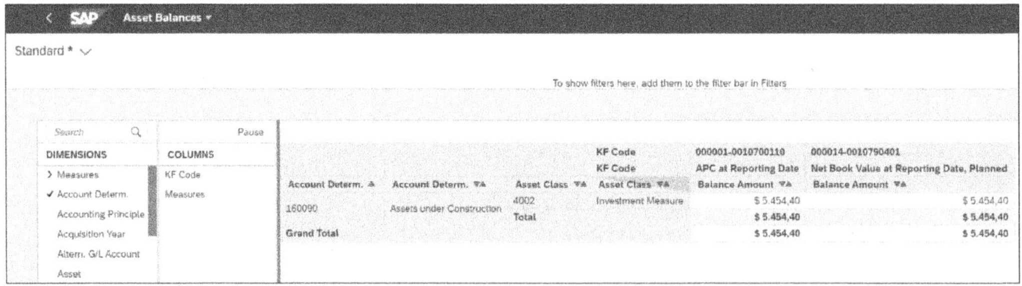


**Figure 8.23** Asset Balance Report, Showing Asset Class for Assets under Construction

Figure 8.24 shows the Asset Transactions app (SAP Fiori ID F1614), which lists all asset transactions and shows the settlement for assets under construction as a separate transaction type.

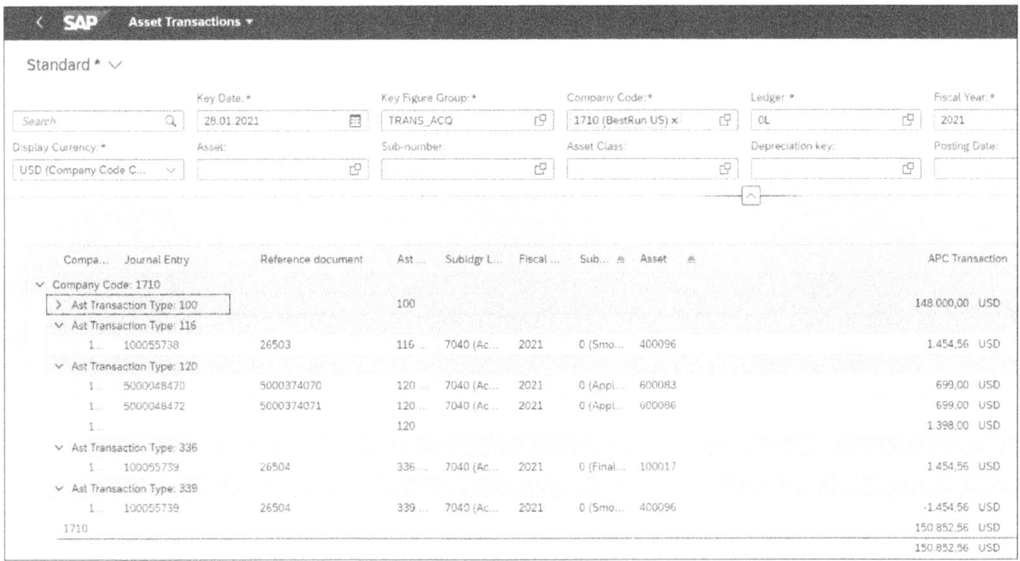

Figure 8.24 Asset Transactions Report, Showing Transaction Type for Settlement to Assets under Construction



## Budget Availability Check

When we looked at the master data earlier, we looked at the way an investment program acts as an umbrella for the various internal orders and WBS elements assigned to the program. In Section 8.2, we looked at how to plan and assign budget to an investment program and the associated orders and WBS elements and at how an active availability check is performed every time you post expenses to an order or a WBS element. As a controller, you need to be able to check the budget for each item, the part of that budget that has already been assigned, and the part of the budget available for further spending. For large investment programs, this was typically done via a long-running report that would read the budget for each of the items in the program, read the assigned orders and WBS elements to determine what had already been assigned, and calculate what budget remained.

To use the Budget Availability Check report, choose **Accounting • Investment Management • Programs • Information System • Investment Management Reports • Programs – Current Data • Monitor Availability Control for Investment Programs** or Transaction IM_AVCHANA. Figure 8.25 shows the selection screen for the availability control report introduced with SAP S/4HANA. Enter the name of the investment program, the approval year, and whether you're looking at overall values (multiple years) or values for a single year. Don't forget to make the appropriate settings for your status. Click the **Execute** icon.

The result of executing the transaction is shown in Figure 8.26. A status is set for each investment program item, and you can expand the nodes of the investment program to understand where budget is running short and clarification is required. Finally, you see the internal orders that are assigned to these program items. This report responds such that it can be run in dialog mode rather than in batch mode as was common in the past. To find out more about this report, refer to SAP Note 1652021.

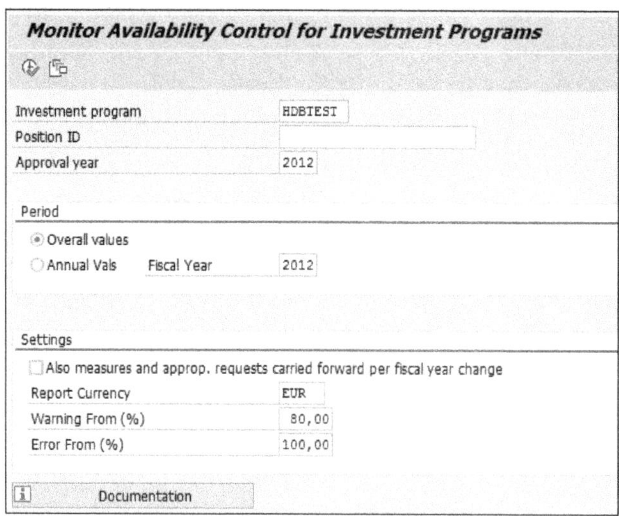


Figure 8.25 Selection Screen for Budget Availability Control

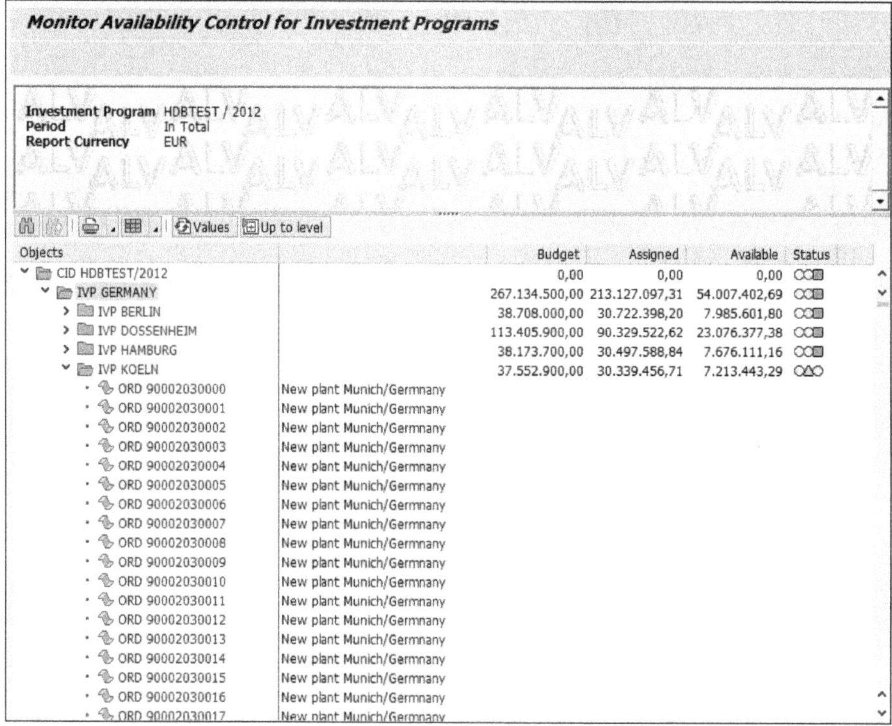


Figure 8.26 Investment Program with Status Information

In a similar vein, two new transactions allow you to monitor budget availability for WBS elements and internal orders: Transaction IM_AVCHANA_WBS for WBS elements and Transaction IM_AVCHANA_ORD for internal orders. A further transaction, Transaction IM_AVCALRT_EXEC, allows you to assign additional budget automatically when a budget ceiling is exceeded. Similarly, you can report on budget depletion using Transaction IM_AVCALRT_ORD for budget on internal orders and Transaction IM_AVCALRT_WBS for budget on WBS elements.

## 8.4 Summary



With investment controlling, we've completed our journey through the main areas of controlling. Because organizations become ever more global these days, we'll now look at how controlling works in an intercompany environment, where the corporate controllers can have very different requirements from the local controllers.

In the next chapter, we'll look at how to create cost estimates in an intercompany environment and how to perform allocations that cross company barriers.

# Chapter 9
# Controlling in an Intercompany Environment

*As organizations become more global, it's becoming more common for the sales company, the manufacturing company, and the distribution center to belong to different company codes. We also see service companies with employees located across the world, delivering services to customers managed by a different company code and organizations setting up shared service centers that share their costs with the internal companies they serve. In this chapter, we'll look at the challenges of controlling in this environment.*

9

In previous chapters, we've looked at general overhead, manufacturing, sales, and capital investment in isolation, focusing on what happens in the various business processes rather than looking at what happens when these business processes interact in an international organization. What happens in these organizations is that the sales process connects not only with the external customer buying the product or service but also with the other companies in the group that are needed to execute the contract. Typically, organizations will set up *selling companies* to deal directly with their customers in the major countries that they operate in. They have *manufacturing companies* that are producing goods that will ultimately be sold to the external customers; however, they don't deal directly with these customers but rather with the selling companies in their own group that handle the relationship with the final customers. Where the supply chain is complex, you'll also find distribution centers storing the goods that manufacturing has completed but sales has not yet sold, and you'll also find manufacturing taking place in several stages at different plants around the world. What this means is that the *material value chain* gets longer. We aren't just looking at how raw materials are bought and converted into finished goods for sale as we did in Chapter 6 but at a complex logistics process to move goods around the world and store them as they await sale.

From a controlling point of view, the stakeholders are less the accountants in the individual legal entities and more the corporate accountants who prepare the *consolidated financial statements* for the group as a whole and also help to make strategic decisions about where to manufacture and how to distribute the company's products. But it's not simply a matter of delivering key information to the corporate accountants as the companies involved must deliver their local financial statements and submit local tax returns, and these tasks are in the hands of the local accountants. This leads to a need for two different ways of looking at the value flows: the one is the local *legal view*, which supports all the legal requirements of doing business in that country/region, and the other is the *group view*, which looks at the value flow from a corporate perspective.

The first thing to establish in these processes are *trading partners* for the various affiliated companies, as we discussed when we looked at the various organizational structures in Chapter 3, as this provides the structure for the elimination of *intercompany profit* later. This intercompany profit arises because the manufacturing company has sold its goods to the distribution center and the distribution center has sold its goods to the selling company dealing with the final customer, and each of these entities has applied a profit margin. From a legal perspective, these profits must be reported by the manufacturing company or distribution center, but from a group perspective these profits must be removed and only recognized for the final sale to the customer. The process of eliminating intercompany profits normally takes place in consolidation or group reporting, but you can also activate a second management view in controlling that values these flows *at cost* without the intercompany markup.

In this chapter, we'll look at how to handle the multiple flows for intercompany goods movements in Section 9.1. Of course, it's not just goods that flow in these kinds of organizations. There will also typically be services, whether in the form of a shared service center handling payroll and accounts payable and receivable for multiple company codes or the selling of supporting services to install a product on-site or to provide consulting services or product support. We'll explore these cost flows in Section 9.2.

## 9.1 Intercompany Goods Movements

In this section, we'll look at a simple example in which a product is manufactured in India, moved to Germany, and then sent to a selling company in the United States, which then handles the sale to the final customer. From a logistics point of view, there is no difference between an external sale and an intercompany sale. The customer and vendor master records for affiliated companies are assigned to a *trading partner* company so that business transactions performed in these companies can be identified for group reporting. The material sold exists in the United States, Germany, and India and carries standard costs in each of these countries. These prices are visible in the accounting view of the material master, as shown in Chapter 6.

From a sales perspective, things become interesting when the product leaves the manufacturing plant in India. From a legal and tax perspective, a sale has been made from India to a customer in Germany, even if the customer is an affiliated company, and this sale must be recorded as revenue in the local financial statements, together with any profit realized on the sale. In Germany, this transaction is recorded at the agreed *transfer price* for the sale from India. From a group perspective, however, Germany is simply one of the affiliated companies in the value chain, and intercompany profit arising from this transaction must be eliminated as part of the consolidation process. Moreover, the organization would like to make business decisions based not on the transfer price for the sale of the product from India to Germany but on the *cost structure* across the value chain, including all manufacturing costs and the *landed costs*, for freight, duty, insurance, and so on.

To get this transparency, you can define an additional costing variant for *group costing* that treats the value chain from India to Germany to the United States as one flow and rolls up the detailed cost components as if the company boundaries did not exist. When the goods movements between the companies are recorded, any intercompany sales and intercompany stock transfers use two sets of prices: the first representing the transfer price agreed between the trading partners and the second accessing the detailed standard costs for each party in the value chain. This in turn means that material prices are stored with two views: *legal valuation* for the intercompany transfer price and *group valuation* for the internal costs.



**Availability in SAP S/4HANA**

Group valuation is currently only available in SAP S/4HANA, but not in SAP S/4HANA Cloud. You can implement it in SAP S/4HANA in a greenfield implementation and migrate from SAP ERP if you're already using it there. But if you already have journal entries in the Universal Journal, you can't activate group valuation retroactively in SAP S/4HANA. You'll find full implementation details in SAP Note 2882025.

We'll begin by explaining how to create a cost estimate to provide transparency in an intercompany environment in Section 9.1.1 and explain how to use the calculated material prices in the sales and stock transfers in Section 9.1.2. We'll then explore how to build a quantity structure that crosses all the involved companies in Section 9.1.3 and how to roll up these costs across the affiliated companies in Section 9.1.4. We'll then explain how to perform actual costing in Section 9.1.5 and how to work with stock in transit in Section 9.1.6.

### 9.1.1 Intercompany Processes in Costing

We'll start by looking at a product that is manufactured in India (company code LT01), sold to Germany (company code LT02), and then sent to the United States (company code LT03). The US company makes the final sale to the external customer.

To display a material cost estimate, use Transaction CK13N or choose **Accounting • Controlling • Product Cost Controlling • Product Cost Planning • Material Costing • Cost Estimate with Quantity Structure • Display** and enter the material, plant, and costing variant. Figure 9.1 shows the cost estimate in the manufacturing plant. The **Qty Struct.**

(quantity structure) tab in India shows the bill of materials (BOM) and routing that describe how to manufacture the product. The itemization shows the detailed costs for the material components and activities, which is built up the same way as we showed for the bikes manufactured in Chapter 6.

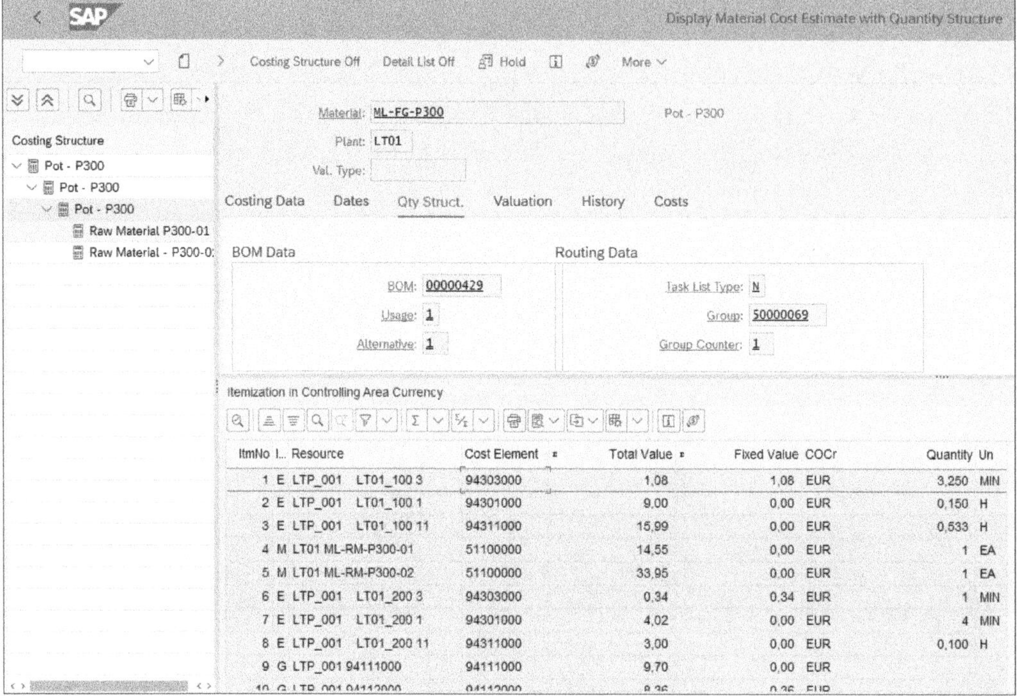

**Figure 9.1** Material Cost Estimate in Manufacturing Company

By contrast, in Figure 9.2, the **Qty Struct.** (quantity structure) in Germany and in the United States show the plant from which the product is procured. In this example, you can see the cost estimate in the United States and see in the **Special Procurement Data** area that the standard approach is to procure the product from the plant in Germany (**LT02**). You can then scroll down to the cost estimate in Germany to see the link to the plant in India and finally to the plant in India with its BOM and routing. What's important in the **Costing Structure** is that you're building up a value chain across several legal entities. It shows the value flow from India (**LT01**) to Germany (**LT02**) and to the United States (**LT03**). This cost estimate is based on a special costing variant that defines the purpose of costing as being group valuation. This setting was made in the costing type and is the prerequisite for the update of the second material price, representing the group view of the product costs.

In the group costing, you can also view the detailed cost structure from the Indian manufacturing plant and any value added by the other plants by switching to the **Cost Component View** in the **Costs** tab, as shown in Figure 9.3.

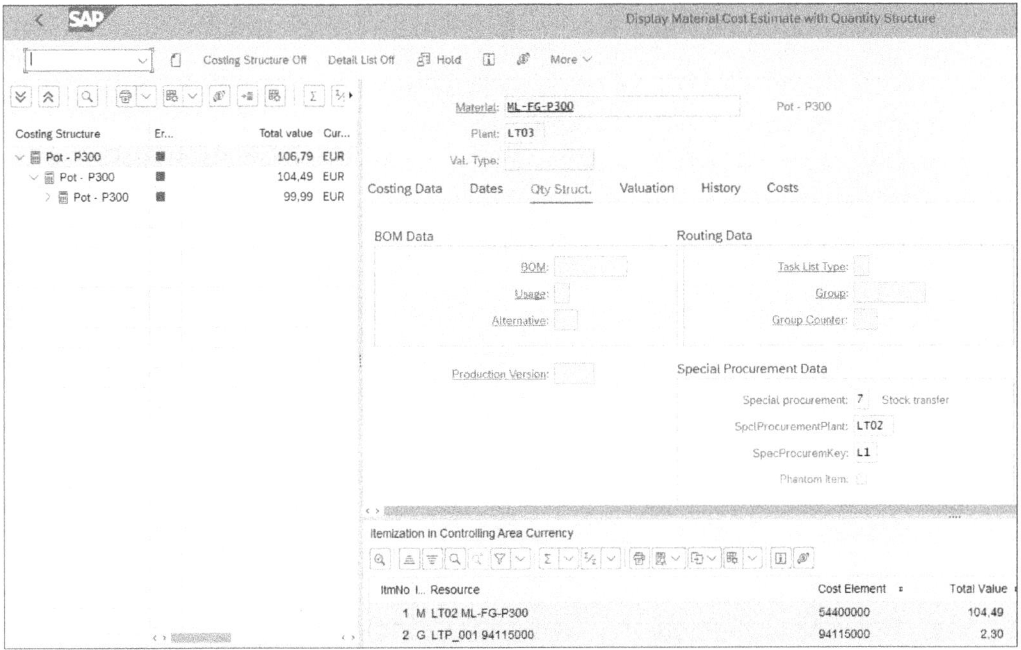

Figure 9.2 Material Cost Estimate, Showing Intercompany Goods Flow

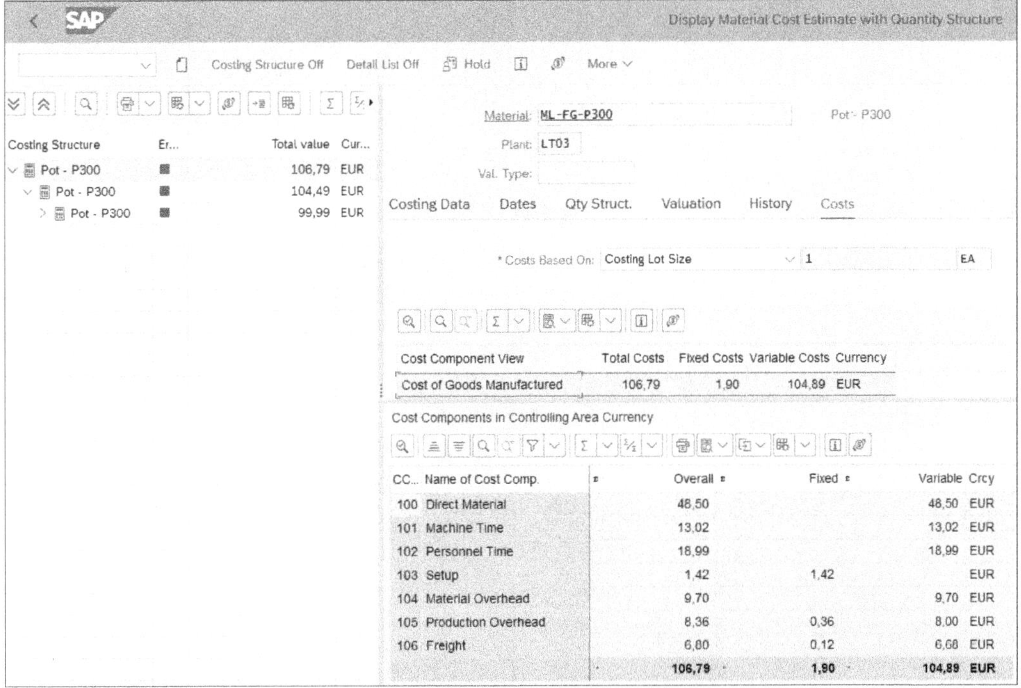

Figure 9.3 Cost Component Split, Showing Costs of Goods Manufactured Across All Plants

By contrast, if you look at the cost estimate used for legal valuation in the US in Figure 9.4, you can only see that the pot has been procured from Germany; you can't drill down further into the **Costing Structure**. The **Itemization** shows only the transfer price for the procurement of the goods from Germany and provides no transparency into the manufacturing costs from India. What you're seeing in the cost estimate is *arm's-length trading*, where each subsidiary behaves as if the goods were being purchased from an external vendor (the German distribution center).

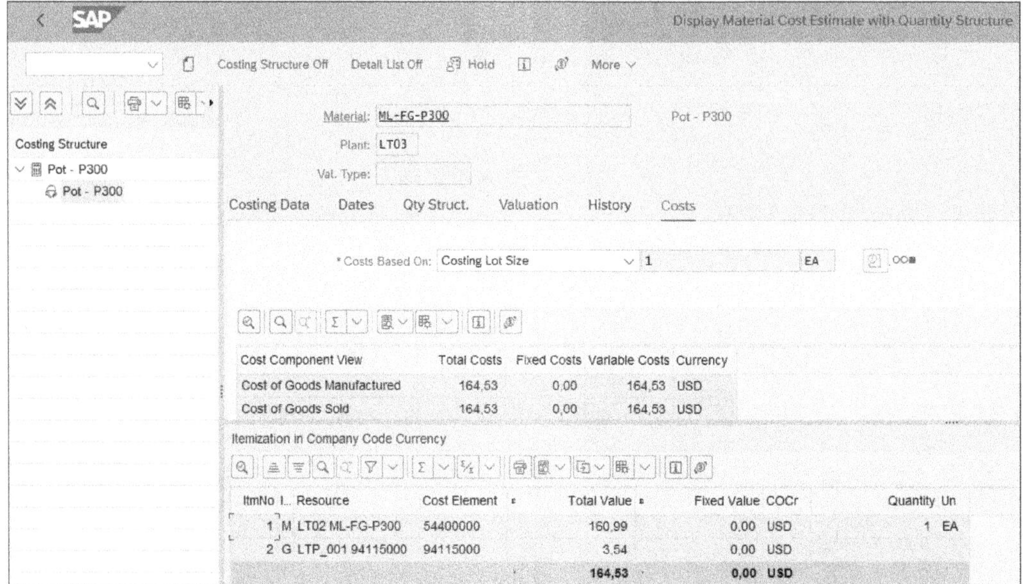


**Figure 9.4** Material Cost Estimate, Showing Only Intercompany Stock Transfer

Figure 9.5 shows what happens when the material is sold. You can view the quantity structure using Transaction CKM3N or by going to **Accounting • Controlling • Product Cost Controlling • Actual Costing/Material Ledger • Material Ledger • Material Price Analysis.** Here you can see the sale to the final customer in the **Consumption** folder. The procurement of this product is not from an external supplier but rather from the German subsidiary, so the **Receipts** folder contains a folder called **Purchase order (grp)** as distinct from the receipts from an external vendor. Notice the values in the **IntercProf** column, where the intercompany profit is rolled up for the sale from India to Germany and from Germany to the United States. In this view, all costs appear in the **Direct Mat** column (direct materials) and there is no transparency into the underlying price structure. Again, this is the idea of *arm's-length trading*, where each subsidiary behaves as if the goods were being purchased externally rather than from an affiliated company.

If you now switch the **Curr./Valuation** from **Company Code Currency** to **Group Currency, Group Valuation**, as shown in Figure 9.6, you'll see that the **I/C Profit** column is now empty and the costs shown in the **Direct Mat** (direct material) column are lower as they now only represent the cumulated raw material costs across the value chain. The other costs (machine time, personnel time, setup time, material overhead, production overhead, and freight) are now shown as separate cost components under the proper columns, giving the corporate controller complete transparency into the product costs across the value chain.

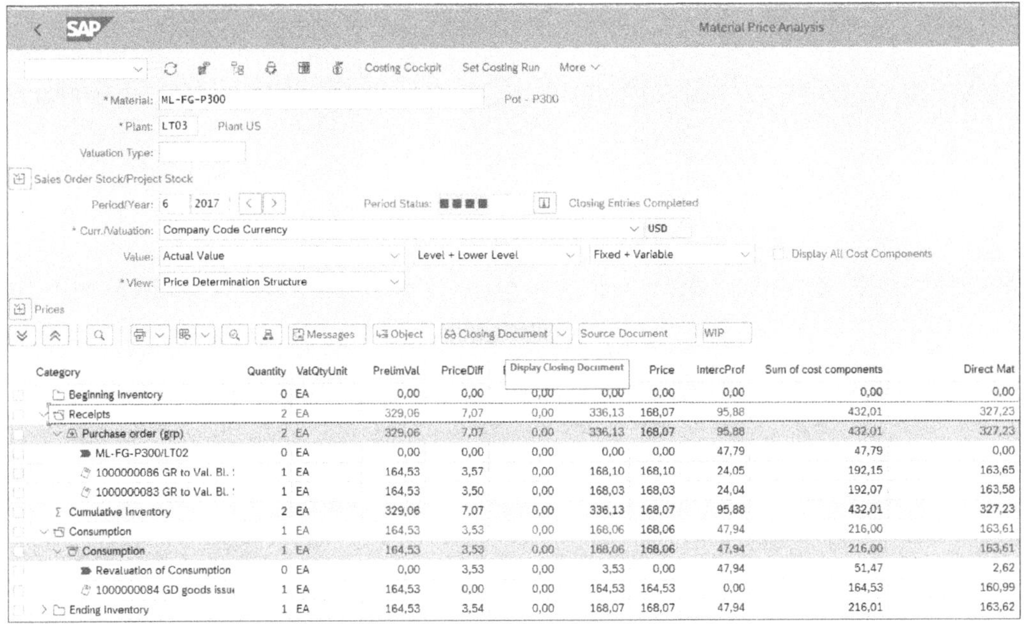


| Category | Quantity | ValQtyUnit | PrelimVal | PriceDiff | | | Price | IntercProf | Sum of cost components | Direct Mat |
|---|---|---|---|---|---|---|---|---|---|---|
| Beginning Inventory | 0 | EA | 0,00 | 0,00 | 0,00 | 0,00 | 0,00 | 0,00 | 0,00 | 0,00 |
| Receipts | 2 | EA | 329,06 | 7,07 | 0,00 | 336,13 | 168,07 | 95,88 | 432,01 | 327,23 |
| Purchase order (grp) | 2 | EA | 329,06 | 7,07 | 0,00 | 336,13 | 168,07 | 95,88 | 432,01 | 327,23 |
| ML-FG-P300/LT02 | 0 | EA | 0,00 | 0,00 | 0,00 | 0,00 | 0,00 | 47,79 | 47,79 | 0,00 |
| 1000000086 GR to Val. Bl. | 1 | EA | 164,53 | 3,57 | 0,00 | 168,10 | 168,10 | 24,05 | 192,15 | 163,65 |
| 1000000083 GR to Val. Bl. | 1 | EA | 164,53 | 3,50 | 0,00 | 168,03 | 168,03 | 24,04 | 192,07 | 163,58 |
| Cumulative Inventory | 2 | EA | 329,06 | 7,07 | 0,00 | 336,13 | 168,07 | 95,88 | 432,01 | 327,23 |
| Consumption | 1 | EA | 164,53 | 3,53 | 0,00 | 168,06 | 168,06 | 47,94 | 216,00 | 163,61 |
| Consumption | 1 | EA | 164,53 | 3,53 | 0,00 | 168,06 | 168,06 | 47,94 | 216,00 | 163,61 |
| Revaluation of Consumption | 0 | EA | 0,00 | 3,53 | 0,00 | 3,53 | 0,00 | 47,94 | 51,47 | 2,62 |
| 1000000084 GD goods issu | 1 | EA | 164,53 | 0,00 | 0,00 | 164,53 | 164,53 | 0,00 | 164,53 | 160,99 |
| Ending Inventory | 1 | EA | 164,53 | 3,54 | 0,00 | 168,07 | 168,07 | 47,94 | 216,01 | 163,62 |

**Figure 9.5** Material Price Analysis Showing Total Intercompany Profit

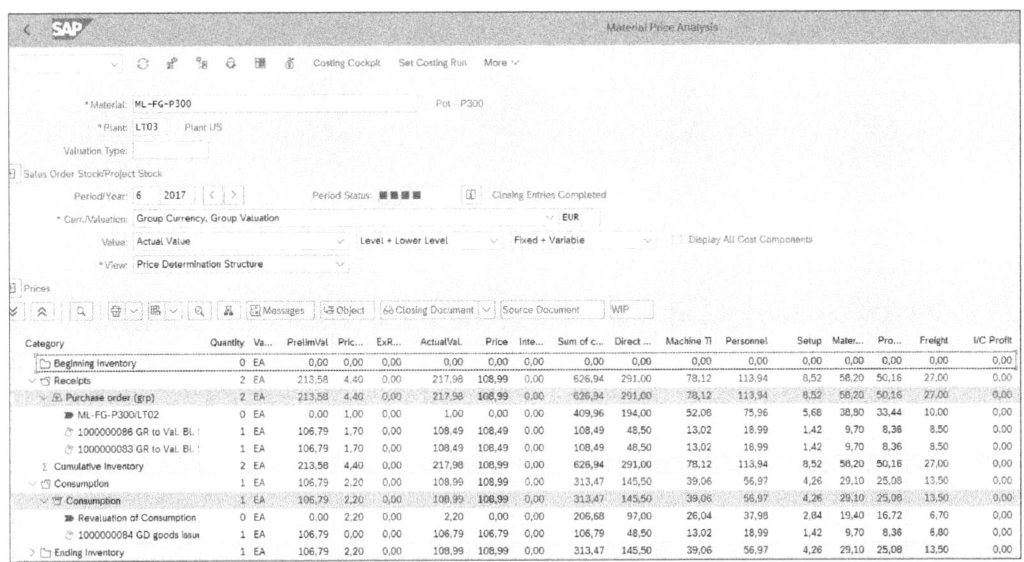


| Category | Quantity | Va... | PrelimVal | Pric... | ExR... | ActualVal. | Price | Inte... | Sum of c... | Direct ... | Machine Ti | Personnel | Setup | Mater... | Pro... | Freight | I/C Profit |
|---|---|---|---|---|---|---|---|---|---|---|---|---|---|---|---|---|---|
| Beginning Inventory | 0 | EA | 0,00 | 0,00 | 0,00 | 0,00 | 0,00 | 0,00 | 0,00 | 0,00 | 0,00 | 0,00 | 0,00 | 0,00 | 0,00 | 0,00 | 0,00 |
| Receipts | 2 | EA | 213,58 | 4,40 | 0,00 | 217,98 | 108,99 | 0,00 | 626,94 | 291,00 | 78,12 | 113,94 | 8,52 | 58,20 | 50,16 | 27,00 | 0,00 |
| Purchase order (grp) | 2 | EA | 213,58 | 4,40 | 0,00 | 217,98 | 108,99 | 0,00 | 626,94 | 291,00 | 78,12 | 113,94 | 8,52 | 58,20 | 50,16 | 27,00 | 0,00 |
| ML-FG-P300/LT02 | 0 | EA | 0,00 | 1,00 | 0,00 | 1,00 | 0,00 | 0,00 | 409,96 | 194,00 | 52,08 | 75,96 | 5,68 | 38,80 | 33,44 | 10,00 | 0,00 |
| 1000000086 GR to Val. Bl. | 1 | EA | 106,79 | 1,70 | 0,00 | 108,49 | 108,49 | 0,00 | 108,49 | 48,50 | 13,02 | 18,99 | 1,42 | 9,70 | 8,36 | 8,50 | 0,00 |
| 1000000083 GR to Val. Bl. | 1 | EA | 106,79 | 1,70 | 0,00 | 108,49 | 108,49 | 0,00 | 108,49 | 48,50 | 13,02 | 18,99 | 1,42 | 9,70 | 8,36 | 8,50 | 0,00 |
| Cumulative Inventory | 2 | EA | 213,58 | 4,40 | 0,00 | 217,98 | 108,99 | 0,00 | 626,94 | 291,00 | 78,12 | 113,94 | 8,52 | 58,20 | 50,16 | 27,00 | 0,00 |
| Consumption | 1 | EA | 106,79 | 2,20 | 0,00 | 108,99 | 108,99 | 0,00 | 313,47 | 145,50 | 39,06 | 56,97 | 4,26 | 29,10 | 25,08 | 13,50 | 0,00 |
| Consumption | 1 | EA | 106,79 | 2,20 | 0,00 | 108,99 | 108,99 | 0,00 | 313,47 | 145,50 | 39,06 | 56,97 | 4,26 | 29,10 | 25,08 | 13,50 | 0,00 |
| Revaluation of Consumption | 0 | EA | 0,00 | 2,20 | 0,00 | 2,20 | 0,00 | 0,00 | 206,68 | 97,00 | 26,04 | 37,98 | 2,84 | 19,40 | 16,72 | 6,70 | 0,00 |
| 1000000084 GD goods issu | 1 | EA | 106,79 | 0,00 | 0,00 | 106,79 | 106,79 | 0,00 | 106,79 | 48,50 | 13,02 | 18,99 | 1,42 | 9,70 | 8,36 | 6,80 | 0,00 |
| Ending Inventory | 1 | EA | 106,79 | 2,20 | 0,00 | 108,99 | 108,99 | 0,00 | 313,47 | 145,50 | 39,06 | 56,97 | 4,26 | 29,10 | 25,08 | 13,50 | 0,00 |

**Figure 9.6** Material Price Analysis, Showing Actual Cost Components for the Value Chain

To see the complete chain of affiliated companies, rather than only the movements for a single material in actual costing, use the Display Material Value Chain app (SAP Fiori ID F4095) shown in Figure 9.7. This relies on actual costing (see Chapter 6) to build up the flow of goods between the affiliated companies. Notice that you can zoom in and out of the production structures by choosing **Plant**, **Company Code**, or **Profit Center** to see the associated plants, company codes, and profit centers in a complex structure.

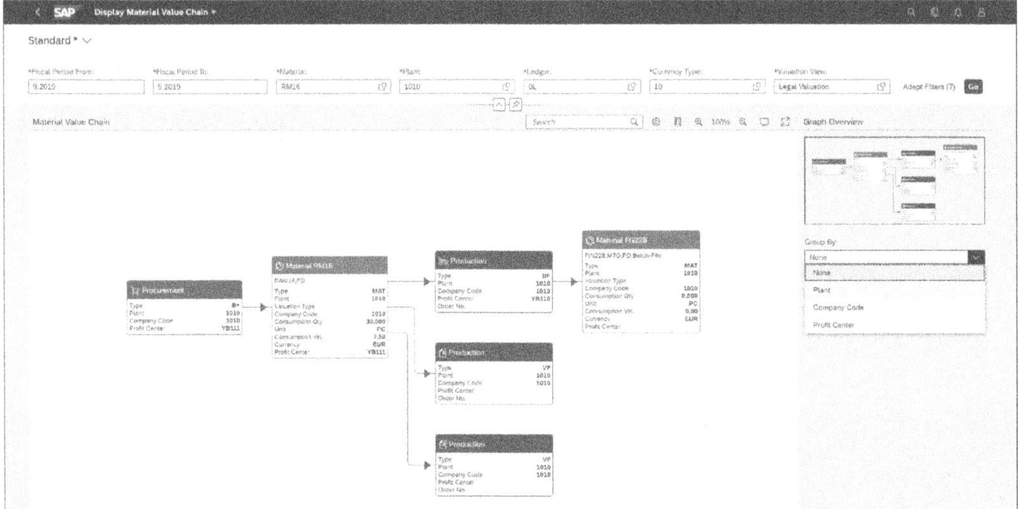

**Figure 9.7** Display Material Value Chain App

### 9.1.2 Setting up Intercompany Processing

Before you can perform goods movements in an intercompany process that reflects this double view, you need to activate group valuation by assigning a currency and valuation profile to the controlling area (refer back to the **Curr/Val.Prof** setting shown in Chapter 3, Section 3.1.3) and making the relevant settings for the associated currencies in the appropriate ledgers. Once the currency and valuation profile is in place, you'll be able to enter material prices not only in different currencies but also in different valuations.

Figure 9.8 shows the material master for the material ML-FG-P300 in the US. The value of the material in company code currency (USD) has been converted into group currency (euros). There is a second value in euros that represents the value of the material at cost (the sample company is headquartered in Europe). These prices were calculated using the cost estimate shown previously in Figure 9.2, and the release process (see Chapter 6) moved the results of both the legal cost estimate and the group cost estimate into the material master as a preparation for the valuation of intercompany sales and stock transfers.

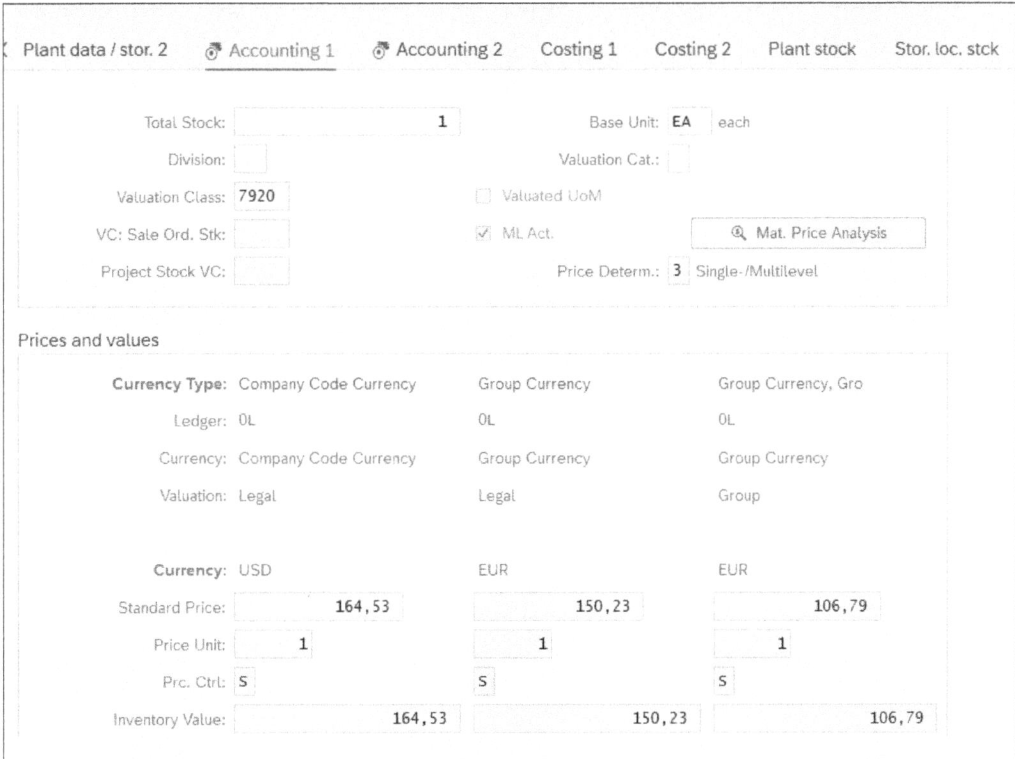


**Figure 9.8** Multiple Prices for Material ML-FG-P300



The group material prices are used in the following processes:

- **Intercompany sales**
  In an *intercompany sales process*, the selling organization takes the order from the customer and fulfills it using goods supplied by an affiliated company and delivering them to the customer.
- **Intercompany stock transfer**
  In an *intercompany stock transfer*, goods are transferred from one legal entity to another. This process is initiated by an internal purchase order that triggers the delivery and intercompany billing process.

Whenever a sales order is created, it will access the standard price and apply profit markups with the help of the various sales conditions to this price. In addition, the condition type `KW00` will be used to access the group value shown in Figure 9.8. In early editions, intercompany billing could only be performed using electronic data interchange (EDI) to transfer the group value electronically, but it's now possible to implement a business add-in (BAdI) so that a manual invoice can carry the group view in addition to the legal view. The procedure is described in SAP Note 1695310. Note also that condition type `KW00` can only carry one value, so you can transfer the group value in controlling area currency or in company code currency, but not in both. If you've activated both valuations in your ledger settings, then the second currency field will be converted from the first at the exchange rate valid at the time of posting. Which currency you take as your leading currency depends on your focus as an organization. Most choose to use the controlling area currency to provide complete transparency for steering the organization at headquarters. Others, however, choose the local currency to provide a preliminary view of their consolidated results prior to consolidation proper in group reporting.

The stock transfer is initiated using a purchase order that also carries a price condition for the legal valuation and the group valuation.

One of the challenges in an intercompany environment is the disconnect between the various sales and fulfillment processes, which focus on executing the individual business transactions rather than on the value flow as a whole. From a costing perspective, the special procurement key (**SpecProcuremKey**) shown previously in Figure 9.2 provides the link between the two plants, which belong in their turn to different company codes and trading partners. In terms of actual costing, the link for the flow shown previously in Figure 9.5 and Figure 9.6 is made during the goods movement as the material document spans both the incoming and the outgoing company code. To use this flow, you must activate the `LOG_MM_SIT` business function. We'll now look at how to create such value chains in costing.

### 9.1.3 Determining the Quantity Structure in an Intercompany Sales Process

From a planning point of view, the first thing that is needed to create an intercompany cost estimate is a link between the two plants. This link is made using the *special procurement key* (**Special procurement**) shown in Figure 9.9. You can check the special procurement keys available for you in the IMG using **Controlling • Product Cost Controlling • Product Cost Planning • Material Cost Estimate with Quantity Structure • Settings for Quantity Structure Control • Material Data • Check Special Procurement Types.**

This key must then be entered either in the material requirements planning (MRP) view, as shown here, or in the costing view of the material master, where it will impact the BOM explosion during MRP and costing. When the BOM is exploded in the first plant (LT03), instead of selecting a material price in plant LT03 (the bottom of the chain), the system uses the link in the special procurement key to access the quantity structure in the second plant (LT02). Here there is a second special procurement key, so again, instead of selecting a material price in plant LT02, the system uses the link in the special procurement key to access the quantity structure in the third plant (LT01). In plant LT01, it finds the BOM and routing that describe how the material is manufactured, assigns prices to this quantity structure, as shown previously in Figure 9.1, and then rolls the cost information through from plant LT01 to LT02 and finally to LT03, as shown in Figure 9.2.

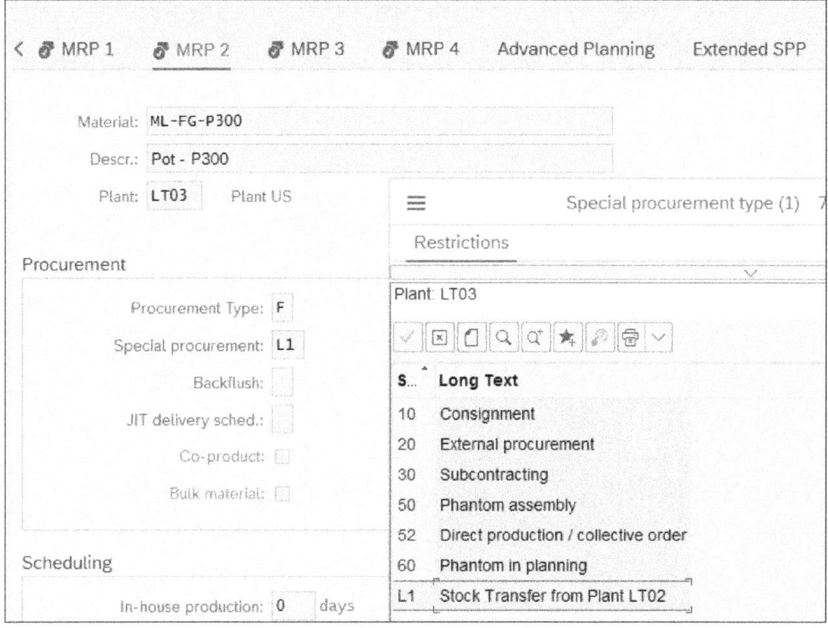


**Figure 9.9** Special Procurement Key for External Procurement via Stock Transfer



In this simple example, the quantity structure for manufacturing is in plant LT01 and is simply rolled through to plants LT02 and LT03, potentially with the addition of freight costs for the goods transfer at each stage of the journey. In a more complex scenario, manufacturing might take place in plants LT01 and LT02. If this is the case, the special procurement key is not a stock transfer for external procurement (**Procurement Type: F**) from the affiliated plant, as in Figure 9.9, but rather in-house production using production from an alternative plant (**Procurement Type: E**), as shown in Figure 9.10. This chain can be extended almost indefinitely by creating special procurement keys for each link in the chain.

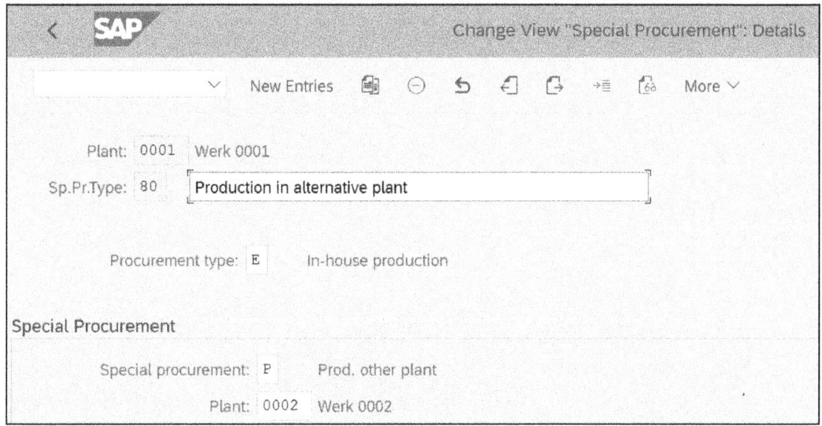


**Figure 9.10** Special Procurement Key for In-House Production from Second Plant

In a real example, such a chain can become very long and involve many materials. One trick to prevent performance issues is to reuse the separate cost estimates that already exist in the manufacturing plants so that the quantity structure is exploded only once, and group costing simply references this quantity structure and applies a new set of prices. To do this, you must define a reference variant in the IMG using **Controlling • Product Cost Controlling • Product Cost Planning • Material Cost Estimate with Quantity Structure • Costing Variant: Components • Define Reference Variant** and assign this reference variant to the costing variant used to create the group costing (refer back to Figure 9.1, Figure 9.2, and Figure 9.3).

Some organizations are happy to let the cost estimate explode the complete quantity structure across all entities and create cost estimates in all manufacturing plants. Others prefer to separate the responsibilities and have a different inventory accountant in charge of costing in each of the manufacturing plants. If this is the case, you can set up a *transfer control* strategy for movements of goods between plants. If you do this, a cost estimate might begin in plant LT02 and use the special procurement key to cross to plant LT01, but instead of creating a new cost estimate in plant LT01, it selects the one that is already there and passes the results back to plant LT02. This improves system performance as a new cost estimate is not created, and it prevents the accidental creation of new cost estimates in manufacturing plants.

You can check the strategy for transfer control in the IMG via **Controlling • Product Cost Controlling • Product Cost Planning • Material Cost Estimate with Quantity Structure • Costing Variant: Components • Define Transfer Control.** Figure 9.11 shows sample configurations for three scenarios, including **PC01** for transfer when there is a change of plant. The transfer control strategy is defined for the costing variant.

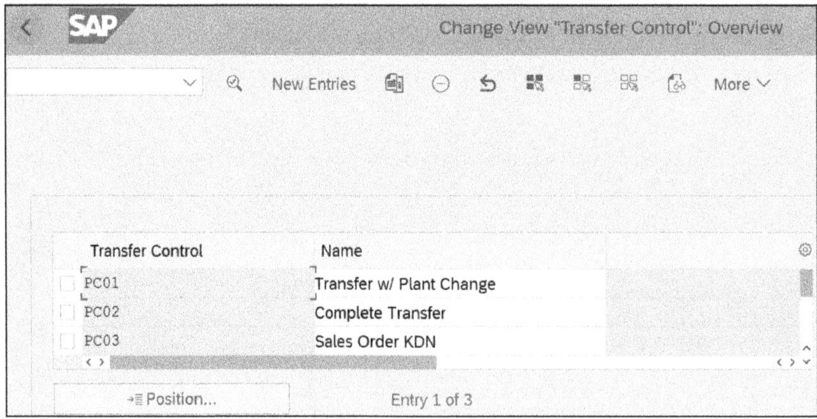


**Figure 9.11** Settings for Transfer Control

Within the transfer control strategy, you can refine the selection further to determine which type of cost estimate can be transferred (current standard cost estimate, future standard cost estimate, previous standard cost estimate, or other cost estimate).

In such scenarios, it's also common to want to represent alternative ways of procuring the same material in costing. To do this, you can create different procurement alternatives to represent the various sourcing options, including external suppliers, internal production, subcontracting, and transfers between plants, and then weight the relative use of each alternative within the product costing. To create procurement alternatives, use Transaction CK91N or go to **Accounting • Controlling • Product Cost Controlling • Product Cost Planning • Material Costing • Master Data for Mixed Cost Estimate • Edit Procurement Alternatives**, enter a material and plant, and choose **Create**. You'll then have to enter a process category (**Process Cat.**), as shown in Figure 9.12. The process category will then determine the additional entries required for the procurement alternative:



- **Purchase order**: Purchasing organization and supplier
- **Procurement** (with change of stocks): Costing lot size
- **Production**: Settings for BOM and routing
- **Subcontracting**: Purchasing organization, supplier, and settings for BOM
- **Stock transfer**: Special procurement plant

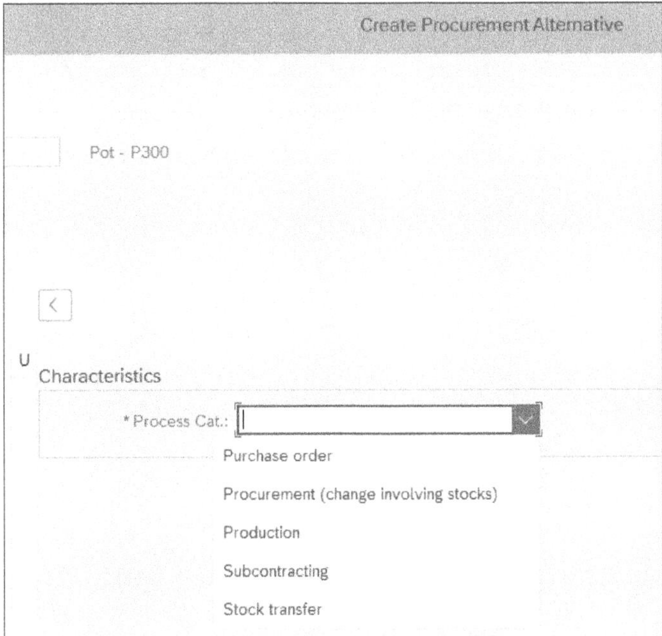


**Figure 9.12** Creating Procurement Alternative

The procurement alternatives are also used in the actual costing to separate the data for each alternative. Figure 9.13 shows a sample procurement alternative for stock transfer from plant **2700**.

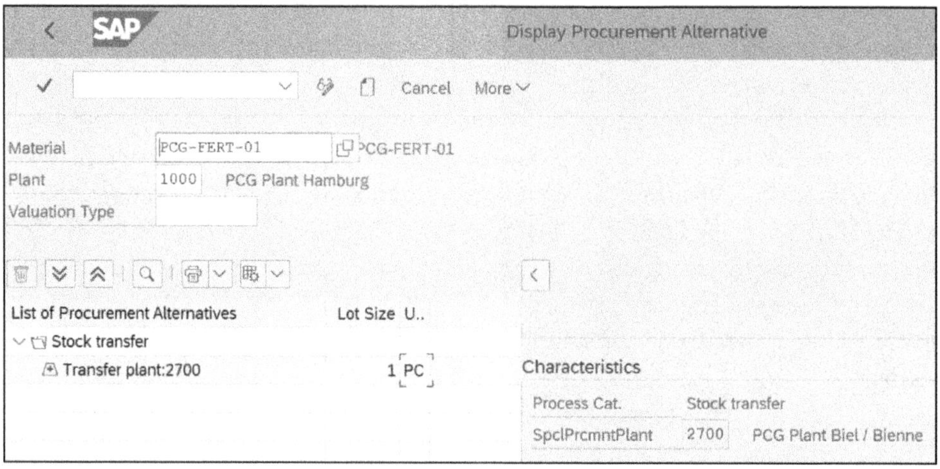

Figure 9.13 Sample Procurement Alternative

Before you can use any of these procurement alternatives to calculate standard costs, you must define mixing ratios that state what percentage of production is performed in house and what percentage is performed externally. Although the procurement alternatives are largely in the hands of production and procurement, maintaining the mixing ratios is typically a controlling task because they are only needed for product costing. During MRP, different mix factors may be used.

To create a mixing ratio or update an existing one, go to Transaction CK94 or **Accounting • Controlling • Product Cost Controlling • Product Cost Planning • Material Costing • Master Data for Mixed Cost Estimate • Mixing Ratios • Create/Change** and enter the **Material** and **Plant**. Because mixing ratios are not constant, the quantity structure type (**Qty Structure Type**) defines how long the ratio is valid. (Depending on the timescale of your standard costing, choose either a month or a year.) Then enter the relevant period and fiscal year. Figure 9.14 shows a sample mixing ratio, where 70% is manufactured in plant **CC01** and 30% in plant **0001**.

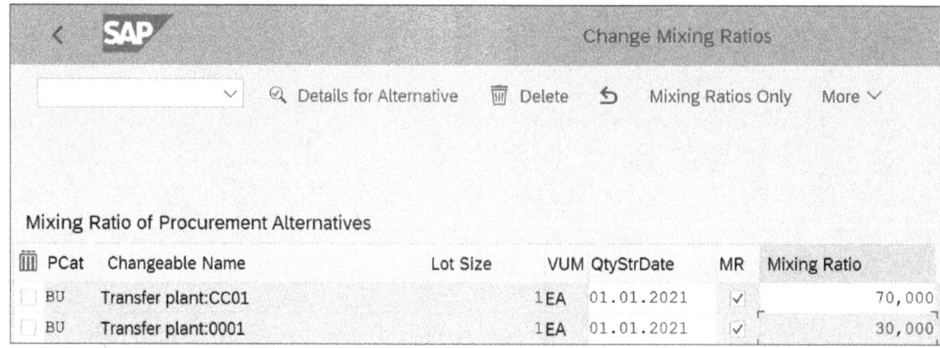


Figure 9.14 Mixing Ratios for Multiple Procurement Alternatives

### 9.1.4 Rolling Up the Costs in an Intercompany Process

In this section, we'll walk through the settings to check when rolling up the costs. We'll walk through both the cost component structure and the partner cost component split.

#### Cost Component Structure

As well as the supply chain challenges inherent in creating cost estimates in an intercompany environment, you also need to ensure that a common *cost component structure* is in place across all participating plants so that the cost components can be rolled up easily. Ideally, you will have one main cost component structure and perhaps one auxiliary cost component structure in all participating plants. But the cost component settings allow you to use different cost component structures for each plant, and many organizations have made use of this flexibility to allow them to have different cost component structures depending on the specific needs of their various manufacturing plants. If you have made use of this flexibility in the past, it won't stop you from creating an intercompany cost estimate.



To check these settings in the IMG, choose **Controlling • Product Cost Controlling • Product Cost Planning • Basic Settings for Material Costing • Define Cost Components** or Transaction OKTZ and then choose the **Assignment: Organiz. Units to Cost Component Structure** dialog structure, as shown in Figure 9.15. To define a common cost component structure for all company codes and plants participating in the group cost estimate, mask the settings for the **Company Code** and **Plant** using **++++** and create an assignment for the costing variant (**Costing...** column) for your group costs that uses one cost component structure (**01** in the **Cost Co...** column).

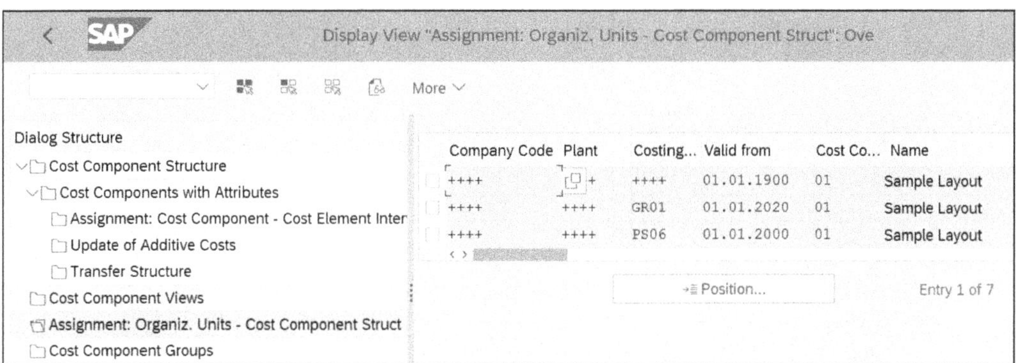


**Figure 9.15** Assignment of Organizational Units to Cost Component Structure

While you're checking the settings for the cost component structure, it's also important to ensure that the cost component structure used includes a cost component the only purpose of which is to store the profit arising as a result of the intercompany sale. To check this, in the **Dialog Structure**, navigate to **Assignment: Cost Component**. Figure 9.16 shows the **Company Code** flag for **Delta Profit for Group Costing**. This component will store the difference whenever there is an intercompany relationship between the plants used in the cost estimate.

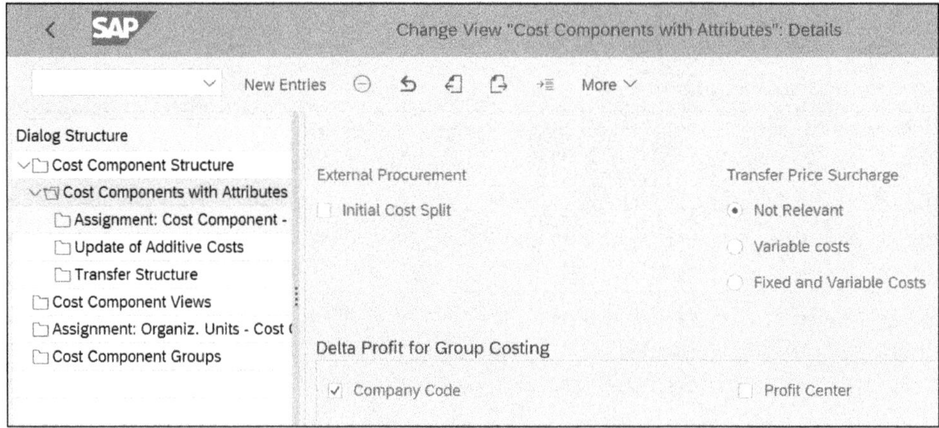


**Figure 9.16** Cost Component Attributes, Showing Flag for Delta Profit

Figure 9.17 shows the combined intercompany profit for the finished product in plant **LT03** stored under the cost component defined for the delta profit.

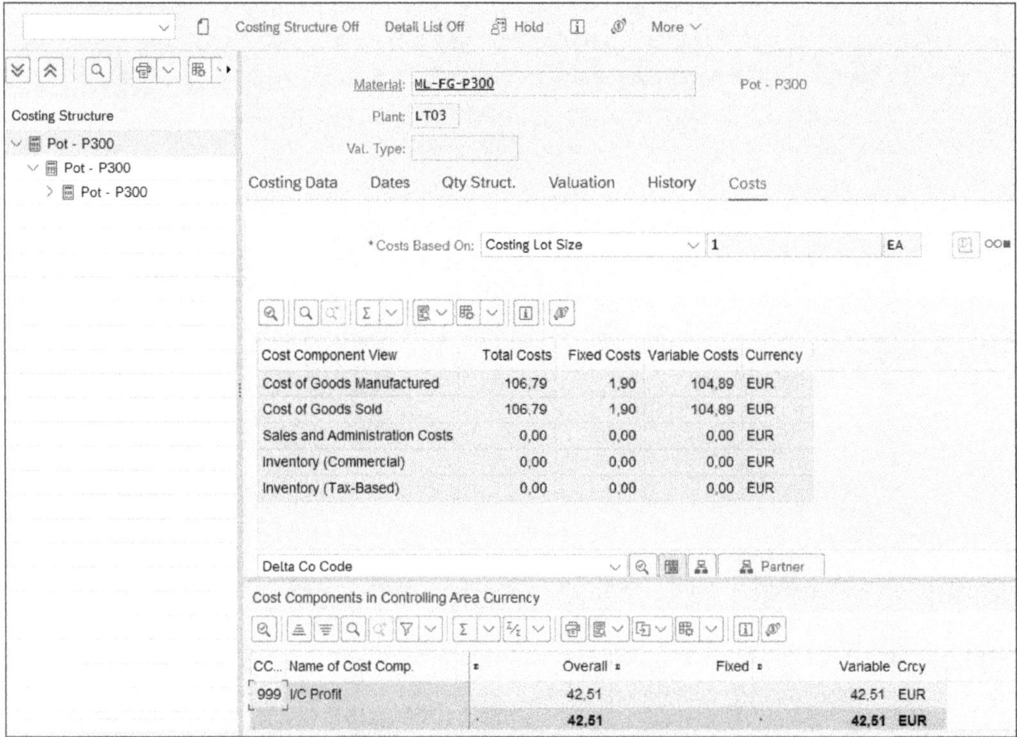


**Figure 9.17** Cost Component Split Showing Cumulative Intercompany Profit

### Partner Cost Component Split

We've focused so far on the plants participating in the process, and each of these plants will be assigned to a company code. Although we rolled the costs up across all three plants and company codes back in Figure 9.2, we haven't shown how to break them down by company code, plant, profit center, and business area. To do this, you must activate the *partner cost component split*. This is activated by assigning a *partner version* to the costing variant.

Figure 9.18 shows a sample partner version where we've activated the company code, plant, and profit center. You can check your settings in the IMG by choosing **Controlling • Product Cost Controlling • Product Cost Planning • Selected Functions in Material Costing • Define Partner Versions.** The settings per partner determine that in a cost estimate involving multiple partners, a separate line will be shown for each partner. The settings for the direct partner determine that only the immediate partner will be shown. To take effect, this partner version must be assigned to the costing type for your group cost estimate.



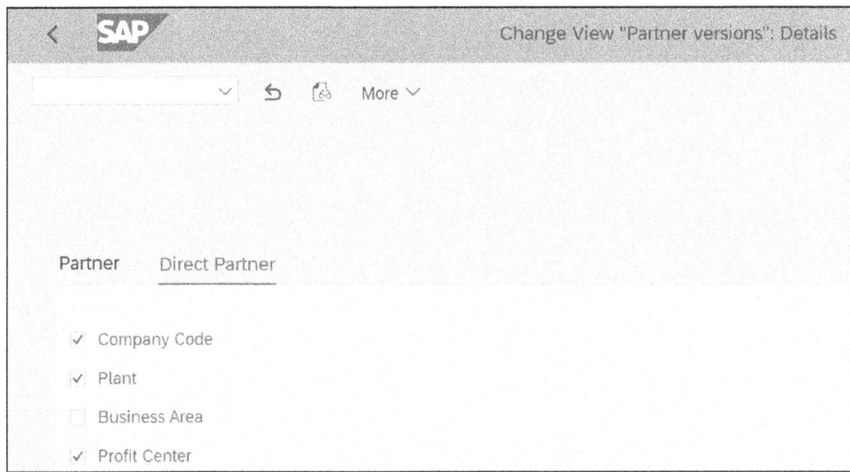


**Figure 9.18** Partner Version for Intercompany Cost Estimate

Figure 9.19 shows the partner cost component split for the finished pot. To access this, go to the **Cost Component View** and select **Partner Cost Component Split** from the **Costs Based On** dropdown, shown previously in Figure 9.3. Notice that in company code LT01/plant LT01 (India), you see the detailed manufacturing costs broken down into their cost components, together with freight costs. In company code LT02/plant LT02 (Germany) and company code LT03/plant LT03 (US), you only see the additional freight costs as no manufacturing took place at these sites. The third element in this view is the assignment to profit centers.

Partner Cost Component Split

More

**Material** ML-FG-P300 Pot - P300
**Plant** LT03 Plant US
**Costing Variant** LT02 Costing Var: Group Valuat
**Costing Version** 1 Version w/o Customizing
**Costing Date from-to** 08.06.2017 - 31.12.9999
**Lot Size** 1 EA each
**Cost Base** 1 EA each
**Cost Comp.Str.** L1 CC Structure for LTP1 (Main Cost Split)

*Cost of Goods Manufactured*
*Cost Comp. Grp 1*
*Controlling Area Currency (EUR)*

| Material/CoCode/Plant/Prof... | Description | Material | Material Overhead | Personnel time | Machine time | Set-Up time | Production Overhead | Freight | Total value |
|---|---|---|---|---|---|---|---|---|---|
| ML-FG-P300 | Pot - P300 | 48,50 | 9,70 | 18,99 | 13,02 | 1,42 | 8,36 | 6,80 | 106,79 |
| LT01 | Co Code LT01 (India) | 48,50 | 9,70 | 18,99 | 13,02 | 1,42 | 8,36 | 0,00 | 99,99 |
| LT01 | Plant 1 India (C.Code: L... | 48,50 | 9,70 | 18,99 | 13,02 | 1,42 | 8,36 | 0,00 | 99,99 |
| LTP_001 | LT01 | 48,50 | 9,70 | 18,99 | 13,02 | 1,42 | 8,36 | 0,00 | 99,99 |
| LT02 | Co Code LT02 (Germany) | 0,00 | 0,00 | 0,00 | 0,00 | 0,00 | 0,00 | 4,50 | 4,50 |
| LT02 | Central Plant DE | 0,00 | 0,00 | 0,00 | 0,00 | 0,00 | 0,00 | 4,50 | 4,50 |
| LTP_002 | LT02 | 0,00 | 0,00 | 0,00 | 0,00 | 0,00 | 0,00 | 4,50 | 4,50 |
| LT03 | Co Code LT03 (US) | 0,00 | 0,00 | 0,00 | 0,00 | 0,00 | 0,00 | 2,30 | 2,30 |
| LT03 | Plant US | 0,00 | 0,00 | 0,00 | 0,00 | 0,00 | 0,00 | 2,30 | 2,30 |
| LTP_003 | LT03 | 0,00 | 0,00 | 0,00 | 0,00 | 0,00 | 0,00 | 2,30 | 2,30 |

**Figure 9.19** Partner Cost Component Split

In the future, SAP plans to offer other segmentations to view product costs by operating division, business unit, and other entities that can be derived from the profit center.

### 9.1.5 Calculating Actual Costs for an Intercompany Process

While the special procurement type provides the link for the standard costs, to perform actual costing, you'll need to activate the LOG_MM_SIT business function. Once your administrator has activated this business function, you can create a costing run for actual costing that will cross all the plants and company codes in a controlling area. The key to building up this value chain is the existence of documents like the one shown in Figure 9.20, in which the goods leave one company code and arrive in the other company code in the same document. This also gives an impression of what works and what doesn't work. Such documents can only be created for goods movements in a single client and system. In a make-to-order process, it's the material flow that counts, and you can't perform intercompany actual costing for sales orders with nonvaluated stock.

Material Ledger Update

**Document Number** 1000000086
**User** TRANSFERPR
**Period** 006.2017
**Currency/Valuation** Company Code Currency EUR

| Item | Material | Descripti... | Plant | ChgTotInv. | Unit | Value Chg. | Crcy | It |
|---|---|---|---|---|---|---|---|---|
| 1 | ML-FG-P300 | Pot - P300 | LT02 | 1- | EA | 125,40- | EUR | UP |
| 2 | ML-FG-P300 | Pot - P300 | LT03 | 1 | EA | 164,53 | USD | UP |

**Figure 9.20** Material Ledger Document for Intercompany Stock Transfer

To perform the costing run, choose **Accounting • Controlling • Product Cost Controlling • Actual Costing/Material Ledger • Actual Costing • Edit Costing Run** or Transaction CKMLCP and enter all plants required as part of the value chain in the selection screen. The steps in the costing run are identical to those in Chapter 6. The difference is simply that the costing process can cross multiple plants and company codes. The results are organized by plant, as shown in Figure 9.21.

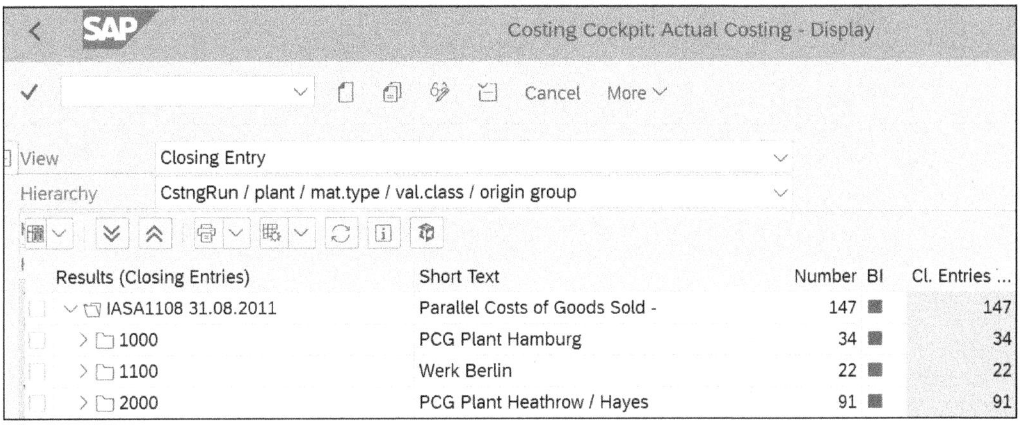

Costing Cockpit: Actual Costing - Display

Cancel More

View: Closing Entry

Hierarchy: CstngRun / plant / mat.type / val.class / origin group

| Results (Closing Entries) | Short Text | Number | Bl | Cl. Entries ... |
|---|---|---|---|---|
| IASA1108 31.08.2011 | Parallel Costs of Goods Sold - | 147 | | 147 |
| 1000 | PCG Plant Hamburg | 34 | | 34 |
| 1100 | Werk Berlin | 22 | | 22 |
| 2000 | PCG Plant Heathrow / Hayes | 91 | | 91 |

**Figure 9.21** Intercompany Costing Run for Actual Costing



### 9.1.6 Stock in Transit

We've treated the sales and stock transfer processes so far as though the move from plant to plant could be completed instantaneously and the costs simply rolled up from one plant to the next. The truth is that such goods movements generally involve international transport, which can take days, weeks, or even months to complete. In the time that the goods are under way, it makes sense to activate stock in transit as a special stock type that ensures that the goods carry a value for the full duration of their journey. For the purposes of actual costing, the stock in transit acts as a submaterial that carries not only the legal value of the goods, but also the group value (without the intercompany profit).

Figure 9.22 shows how the special stock type T (**Stock in Transit**) appears on the **Material Price Analysis** screen. You may remember from Chapter 6 how we delivered the manufactured goods into sales order stock. Stock in transit is simply another form of special stock, requiring the business to use the appropriate movement types to move the goods into and out of transit. From a controlling point of view, you can identify such stocks by selecting **Stock in Transit** in Transaction CKM3N (Material Price Analysis). There they carry a value and a cost component split just like goods in inventory. Your organization can configure at what stage of the journey these transfers are made to ensure that an ownership transfer from one company to the other is made at the proper time.

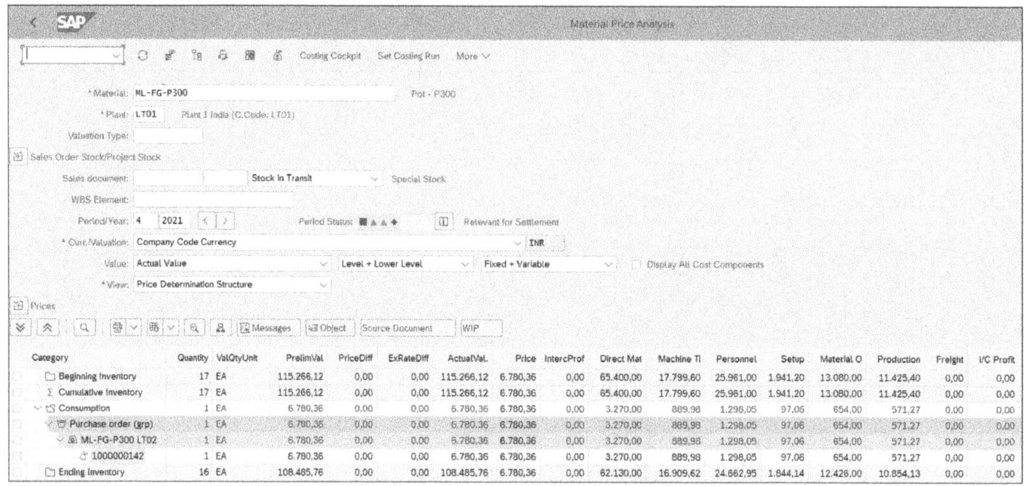

Figure 9.22 Material Price Analysis, Showing Special Stocks for Goods in Transit

## 9.2 Intercompany Cost Allocation Postings

In today's global economy, companies are intensifying their intercompany collaboration—for example, by setting up shared services. It's also increasingly the case that centralized internal projects are set up, such as development projects to which employees are assigned throughout the company. These employees then allocate their time and efforts to these projects across the company. Professional services companies in particular are familiar with this situation, as they have consultants located all over the world, just like their client projects. This requires intercompany time and travel expense confirmations. As a result, cross-company cost allocations and billing processes are on the rise.

For these processes, SAP S/4HANA provides a lean processing solution called *resource-related intercompany billing* (available with scope item 16T in SAP S/4HANA Cloud). It enables additional controlling analyses and also covers legal and group reporting requirements.

**Note**

The intercompany cost allocation only works if the allocation sending and receiving company code is assigned to the same controlling area. The cross-company-code cost accounting must be active in the controlling area (see Chapter 3, Section 3.1.3). This is different from the intercompany sales scenarios discussed in the previous section, in which this setup isn't required for all scenarios.

Not covered by the solution presented here are the following scenarios:

- It isn't possible to post intercompany material movements—like a consumption of a product in company A to a cost object in company B. The same is true for purchasing processes in which you want to account-assign a cost object of a different company code. This would lead to incorrect financial data: the expenses and the taxes would be posted in the receiving company code.

- You can post intercompany expenses with the Post General Journal Entries app. But the companies need to be not in the same tax group, and the intercompany postings aren't selected in the periodic billing. You need to manually clear the intercompany clearing accounts, which are balance sheet accounts.

We'll start this section with a process and posting overview and an explanation of the guiding principles in Section 9.2.1. Then we'll show examples of intercompany cost allocation postings with a new option to determine intercompany clearing accounts in Section 9.2.2. We'll close with a look at the resource-related intercompany billing in Section 9.2.3.



### 9.2.1 Process Overview and Posting Logic

Figure 9.23 illustrates the complete process for intercompany controlling allocation. The scenario consists of two parts: the intercompany cost postings during the period and the periodic intercompany billing.

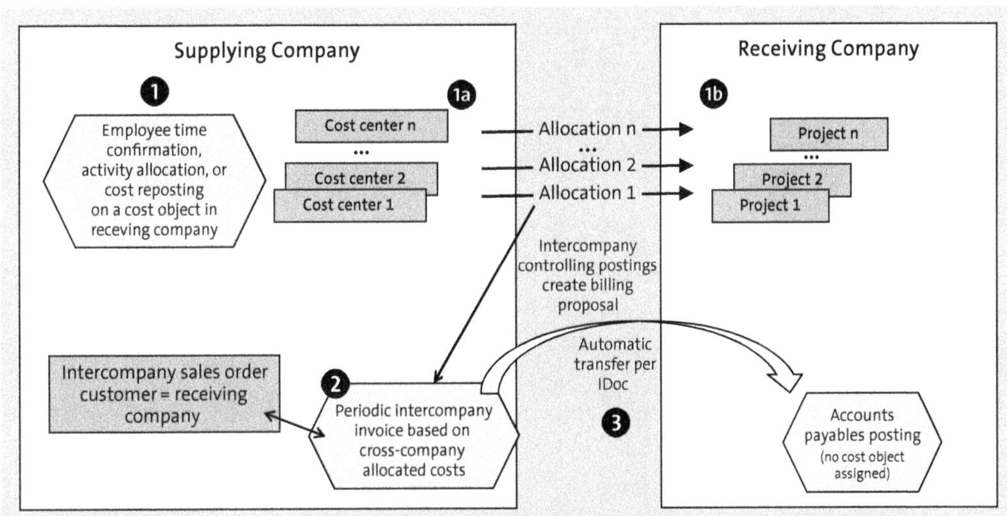


**Figure 9.23** Process Overview for Intercompany Cost Allocation

Let's first look at cross-company cost allocations in the top section. The direct cross-company code allocation enables an extended cost analysis as follows, in the sending and in the receiving company:

- The costs are immediately visible on the receiver object when they're entered. This is especially important if the receiver object is a customer project, for which time and materials are billed to a customer. The customer billing can start immediately after time or expense confirmation.

- The direct intercompany booking provides detailed information on the receiver side. If the receiver is a customer project with resource-related billing, information such as the activity type, the service rendered date, the employee, and the employee's note is transferred and available for the billing itemization list. The same is true for expenses recorded in SAP Concur.
- You can trace the receiver object expense directly to the sender object.
- There is also a wide range of partner information available on both sides of the allocation: partner profit center, partner functional area, partner cost object, and of course, partner company and trading partner.

However, cross-company cost posting doesn't post taxes, nor does it post affiliated revenues and expenses, receivables, and payables. Therefore, you also need intercompany invoicing. This is performed as a periodic job based on all intercompany cost postings incurred during the period. Invoicing is done with reference to an intercompany sales order, with the receiving company as the customer. Thus, the sending company (by sales organization) and the receiving company are determined based on the sales order.

The periodic billing items are highly aggregated. Details such as account assignments or sending and receiving profit centers aren't available here.

Figure 9.24 shows a posting example for an intercompany business scenario. The initial trigger for these postings is the time recording of a US employee company code on the left side, in which the employee assigns a controlling object of the German company code on the right side. With the transfer of the time recording to financials, two journal entries in each company code are posted.

In the supplying US company, the employees cost center is credited with (1a) the costs of the activity, \$60, plus (1b) an additional mark-up, \$20. In the receiving company code, the same amounts are posted with the same general ledger accounts on the receiving cost object, here a work breakdown structure (WBS) element. To comply with double-entry accounting rules, all journal entries are posted to an intercompany clearing account. The clearing accounts are nonoperating profit and loss (P&L) accounts. Thus, all line items are posted on P&L accounts.

To be able to show this business transaction in group reporting, the trading partner or company (see Chapter 3, Section 3.1.1) must be stored in all line items. The trading partner is derived by the company code (see Chapter 3, Section 3.1.2). In terms of value, these lines have no impact on group reporting. You see a real-time clearing here.

The periodic intercompany billing and subsequent accounts payable posting in the lower section are necessary to cover all legal requirements. These postings have an impact on group reporting and require the following group reconciliation activities:

- The intercompany billing is done by a periodic job, which takes all intercompany cost postings of a selected period into account. In this example, we assume that there was only the one controlling allocation.
- If relevant taxes are calculated and posted, they're based on the posted affiliated revenues in the supplying company and affiliated expenses in the ordering company.
- The affiliated revenue and the affiliated expense general ledger accounts are P&L accounts and impact the financial statement. There are no detailed account assignments available as the billing line items are created based on the aggregated controlling journal entries.



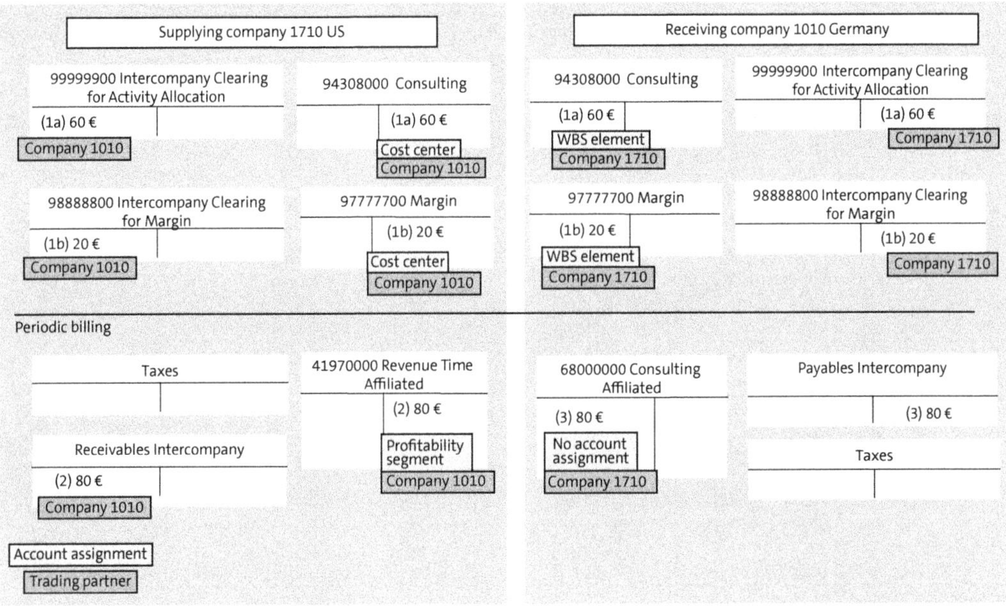


**Figure 9.24** Posting Overview for Intercompany Process

### 9.2.2 Business Transactions

There are several business processes in which intercompany cost postings are used. As shown previously, this includes the intercompany time confirmation, which is heavily used in professional service scenarios but also in the service scenario (see Chapter 7). You can post cross-company activity allocations with the Transaction KB21N (see direct activity allocations in Chapter 5). This allows you to post a variety of quantity-based allocations, like the number of solved tickets or development hours. For these, both scenario margins can be applied. You can also allocate shared service costs by a cost allocation or cost center allocation cross-company. Finally, in connection with service provisioning, employee-related intercompany (travel) expenses can also be incurred. There is a solution available for SAP Concur integration, but external travel applications also can work. For these scenarios, there's an additional intercompany cost allocation posting created by the system.

**Note**

For a detailed description of these scenarios and other additional information, visit the blog at *http://s-prs.co/v528202.*

In this book, we show the examples of intercompany activity allocation and cost allocation. Let's start with the intercompany activity allocation process.

### Intercompany Activity Allocation/Time Confirmation with Markup

For the business scenario of cross-company internal activity allocation or time confirmation, there's the possibility to apply additional markups. Let's go back to the example we have illustrated previously in Figure 9.24.

**Cloud versus On-Premise**

The shown functionality is available in SAP S/4HANA Cloud with scope item 16T. We use the Manage Cost Rates—Professional Services app here. As mentioned in Chapter 4, Section 4.3.2, this app is only available in SAP S/4HANA Cloud currently, but it's planned to add to on-premise systems in the roadmap.

In on-premise, you need to activate the `FINS_CO_ICO_PROC_ENH_101` business function. With this business function, you get the option to maintain intercompany rates with the SAP GUI Transaction CMACA02, which allows the maintenance of intercompany cost rates like in the app shown here. You also get the option to maintain your own general ledger accounts for the margin posting with the activated business function.

For applying margins on activity allocation, a prerequisite is the maintenance of intercompany activity rates. We show this with the Manage Cost Rates—Professional Services app (SAP Fiori ID F3161), as shown in Figure 9.25.

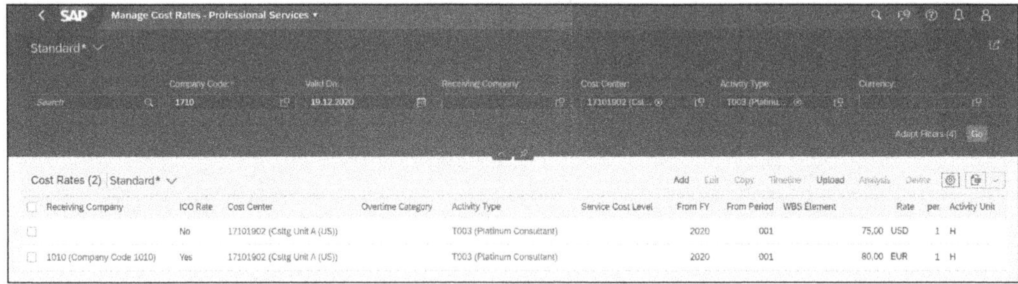


**Figure 9.25** Maintenance of Intercompany Cost Rate

There are two cost rates available for cost center **17101902** and activity type **T003**:

1. **Intracompany cost rate**
   The first type of cost rate is the intracompany rate. There is no receiving company code maintained, and the **ICO Rate** column shows **No**. This rate is used when the activity is provided within company code 1710. There is a rate maintained of 75 USD/hour for **Activity Type T003 (Platinum Consultant)**.
2. **Intercompany rate**
   The second type of cost rate is the intercompany rate. **Receiving Company 1010** is maintained, and the **ICO Rate** column shows **Yes**. This rate is used when the activity is provided from company 1710 to company 1010. There is a rate of 80 EUR/hour maintained for **Activity Type T003 (Platinum Consultant)**. This rate includes the costs plus a markup. Note that the cost rate can be defined in the company code currency of the receiving company code to allow stable prices.

Say that the John Consultant employee, working in company 1710 (US), confirms one hour for T003 Platinum Consulting to WBS element 7001 in company 1010 (DE). This leads to postings in all assigned ledgers. Let's look at the journal entries of ledger 0L in the Display Line Items in General Ledger app shown in Figure 9.26. Note that the postings are identical to the example we showed previously in Figure 9.24 in T-account form.

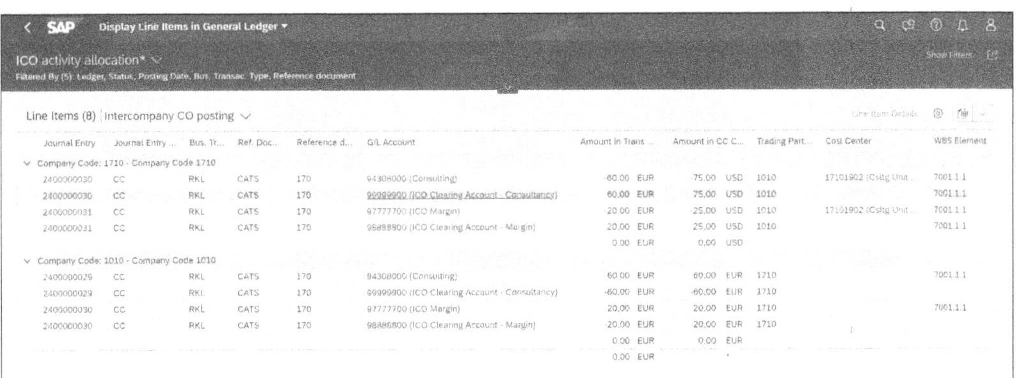


| Journal Entry | Journal Entry ... | Bus. Tr... | Ref. Doc... | Reference d... | G/L Account | Amount in Trans ... | | Amount in CC C... | | Trading Part... | Cost Center | WBS Element |
|---|---|---|---|---|---|---|---|---|---|---|---|---|
| Company Code: 1710 - Company Code 1710 | | | | | | | | | | | | |
| 2400000030 | CC | RKL | CATS | 170 | 94308000 (Consulting) | -60.00 | EUR | -75.00 | USD | 1010 | 17101902 (Csltg Unit ... | 7001.1.1 |
| 2400000030 | CC | RKL | CATS | 170 | 99999900 (ICO Clearing Account - Consultancy) | 60.00 | EUR | 75.00 | USD | 1010 | | 7001.1.1 |
| 2400000031 | CC | RKL | CATS | 170 | 97777700 (ICO Margin) | -20.00 | EUR | -25.00 | USD | 1010 | 17101902 (Csltg Unit ... | 7001.1.1 |
| 2400000031 | CC | RKL | CATS | 170 | 98888800 (ICO Clearing Account - Margin) | 20.00 | EUR | 25.00 | USD | 1010 | | 7001.1.1 |
| | | | | | | 0.00 | EUR | 0.00 | USD | | | |
| Company Code: 1010 - Company Code 1010 | | | | | | | | | | | | |
| 2400000029 | CC | RKL | CATS | 170 | 94308000 (Consulting) | 60.00 | EUR | 60.00 | EUR | 1710 | | 7001.1.1 |
| 2400000029 | CC | RKL | CATS | 170 | 99999900 (ICO Clearing Account - Consultancy) | -60.00 | EUR | -60.00 | EUR | 1710 | | |
| 2400000030 | CC | RKL | CATS | 170 | 97777700 (ICO Margin) | 20.00 | EUR | 20.00 | EUR | 1710 | | 7001.1.1 |
| 2400000030 | CC | RKL | CATS | 170 | 98888800 (ICO Clearing Account - Margin) | -20.00 | EUR | 20.00 | EUR | 1710 | | |
| | | | | | | 0.00 | EUR | 0.00 | EUR | | | |
| | | | | | | 0.00 | EUR | | | | | |

**Figure 9.26** Intercompany Activity Allocation: General Ledger View

Four documents have been posted, two in each company. The reference document **170** in column 5 shows that all four documents are based on one source document: the time sheet entry (**CATS** in the **Ref. Doc...** column).

Let's first look at the postings in the supplying company **1710**. In the first line item, you see the credit of the employee's cost center, **17101902**. It's valuated with the intracompany cost rate of 75 USD. The currency rate USD to EUR is 0.8. This leads to the transaction currency of 60 EUR. The third line item is the margin, which credits the cost center. It's calculated this way: intercompany price of 80 EUR (second line in Figure 9.25) minus the cost rate of 60 EUR, resulting in 20 EUR. As the intercompany price is maintained in EUR, the complete amount of the cost rate plus the margin will be always 80 EUR. But the costs and thus the resulting margin will have currency fluctuations.

In receiving company **1010**, you can see for the four line items the same general ledger accounts and transaction currency amounts. The consulting costs and the margin are posted on the **7001.1.1** WBS element.

The margin posting is posted with the same **RKL** business transaction type as the related activity allocation. This allows you to identify these postings—for example, when locking transactions at period-end close.

As mentioned before, the trading partner in the **Trading Part...** column shows that this document has a relation to another company and is relevant for group consolidation.

Figure 9.27 shows a controlling view of these postings:

- With the intercompany cost allocation, the same partner information is provided as in an intracompany posting. As an example, we selected here the **Partner Profit Center** field, provided in the sending and receiving company. The same information is valid for the partner cost object and functional area (not shown here).
- In the far-right column, you can see that the **Personnel Number** is provided for the cost and margin posting on the WBS element in the receiving company code. Thus, you can get information about the employee who provided the service on the receiving WBS element.
- To allow the bundling of the margin and the related activity allocation—for example, in a subsequent time and material billing to the WBS element—use the **Part CC** partner activity type. **T003** is copied in the margin posting.
- The **Quantity** of one hour is only provided in the activity allocation posting and not in the margin posting to prevent double quantities on the sending cost center and the receiving customer project for time and material billing.

Display Line Items in General Ledger

ICO activity allocation*

Filtered By (5): Ledger, Status, Posting Date, Bus. Transac. Type, Reference document

Line Items (8) Intercompany CO posting*

| Journal Entry | G/L Account | Amount in Trans ... | Amount in CC C... | Trading Part... | Cost Center | WBS Element | Quantity | Part CC... | Profit Center | Partner Pr... | Personnel Number |
|---|---|---|---|---|---|---|---|---|---|---|---|
| Company Code: 1710 - Company Code 1710 | | | | | | | | | | | |
| 2400000030 | 94308000 (Consulting) | -60,00 EUR | -75,00 USD | 1010 | 17101902 (... | 7001.1.1 | -1,000 H | | YB102 (Co... | YB111 (Pro... | 50002069 |
| 2400000030 | 99999900 (ICO Clearing Account - C... | 60,00 EUR | 75,00 USD | 1010 | | 7001.1.1 | 0,000 | | YB102 (Co... | | 50002069 |
| 2400000031 | 97777700 (ICO Margin) | -20,00 EUR | -25,00 USD | 1010 | 17101902 (... | 7001.1.1 | 0,000 H | | YB102 (Co... | YB111 (Pro... | 50002069 |
| 2400000031 | 98888800 (ICO Clearing Account ... | 20,00 EUR | 25,00 USD | 1010 | | 7001.1.1 | 0,000 | | YB102 (Co... | | 50002069 |
| | | 0,00 EUR | 0,00 USD | | | | Show Details | | | | |
| Company Code: 1010 - Company Code 1010 | | | | | | | | | | | |
| 2400000029 | 94308000 (Consulting) | 60,00 EUR | 60,00 EUR | 1710 | | 7001.1.1 | 1,000 H | T003 | YB111 (Pro... | YB102 (Co... | 50002069 |
| 2400000029 | 99999900 (ICO Clearing Account - C... | -60,00 EUR | -60,00 EUR | 1710 | | | 0,000 | | YB111 (Pro... | | |
| 2400000030 | 97777700 (ICO Margin) | 20,00 EUR | 20,00 EUR | 1710 | | 7001.1.1 | 0,000 H | T003 | YB111 (Pro... | YB102 (Co... | 50002069 |
| 2400000030 | 98888800 (ICO Clearing Account - ... | -20,00 EUR | -20,00 EUR | 1710 | | | 0,000 | | YB111 (Pro... | | |
| | | 0,00 EUR | 0,00 EUR | | | | Show Details | | | | |
| | | 0,00 EUR | * | | | | Show Details | | | | |

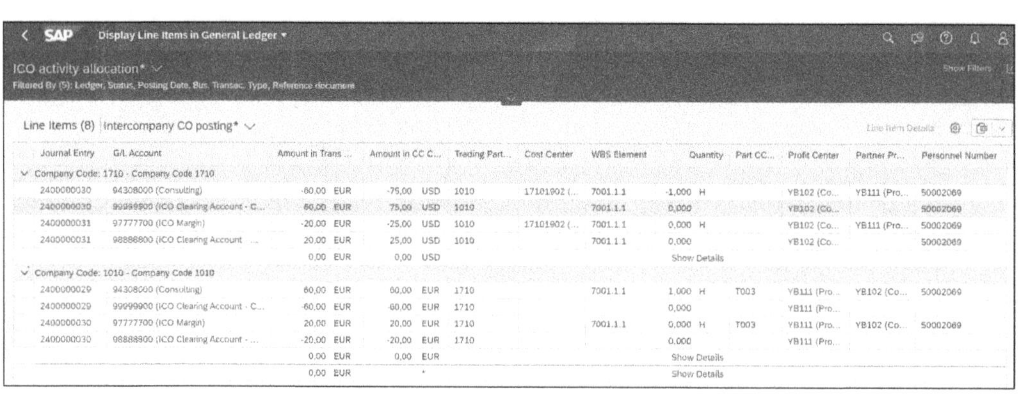

**Figure 9.27** Intercompany Activity Allocation: Controlling View

With this, you get a report on the service receiving project that shows the cost posting and the additional intercompany margin, with the option for drilldown into information about the entity providing the service.

### Intercompany Amount-Based Cost Allocation

You can allocate costs between company codes with the Reassign Costs and Revenues app (SAP Fiori ID F2009) or with Transactions KB11N or KB15N, which provide the same functionality as the SAP Fiori app and follow similar steps (see Chapter 5). Use cases for these postings are for intercompany allocation of travel expenses or shared service costs.



Now start the Reassign Costs and Revenues app and click the **Create** button. You arrive at the screen shown in Figure 9.28.

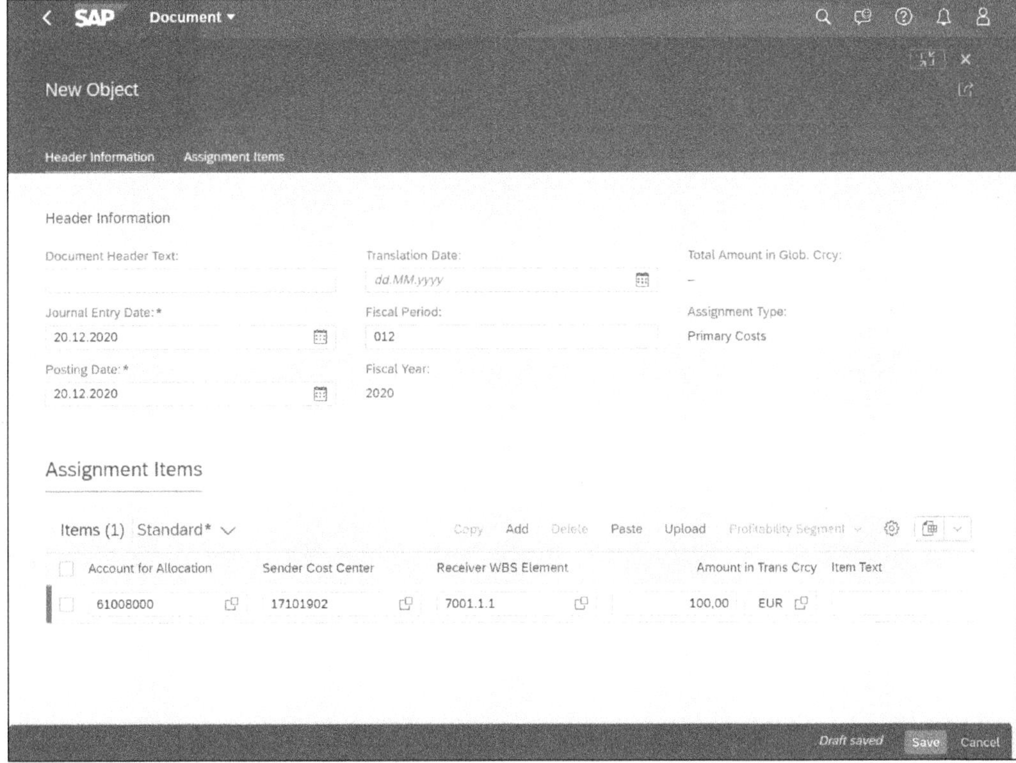


**Figure 9.28** Reassign Costs and Revenues App

Enter the travel expense account that will be allocated in the **Account for Allocation** field (**61008000** in our example). The **Sender Cost Center 17101902** is assigned to company code 1710 in US; the **Receiver WBS Element 7001.1.1** is assigned to company code 1010 in Germany. Also apply an **Amount** to be allocated of 100 EUR in the transaction currency. Click **Save** after completing your entries.

This leads to journal entry postings in all assigned ledgers. Let's look at the postings in the leading ledger OL in Figure 9.29.

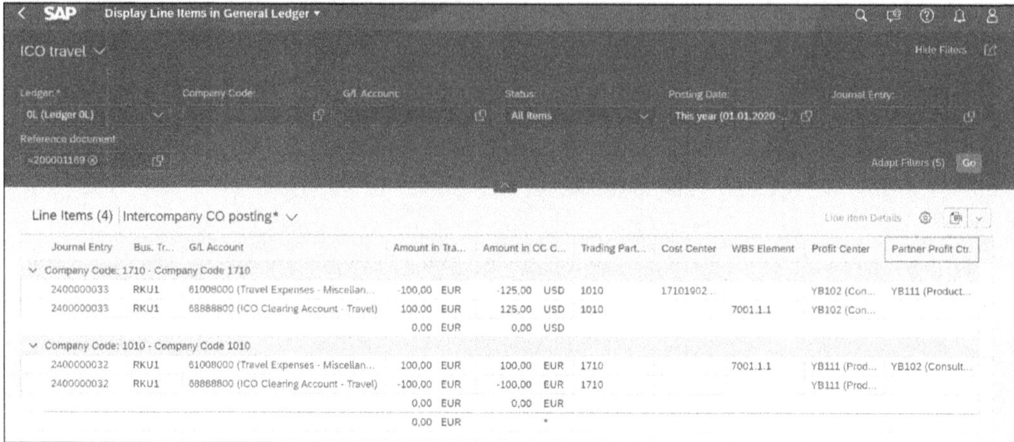

Figure 9.29 Journal Entries of Intercompany Cost Allocation

You see in every company code one journal entry posted with the business transaction type **RKU1** (repost costs). You can see the same features as for the activity allocation:

- There is a real-time intercompany clearing provided by posting on intercompany clearing accounts. Note that we assigned here a different one from the activity allocation.
- All lines are assigned to the trading partner/company to reflect all the postings in the group reporting.
- There are multiple partner information items provided, like partner profit center, partner cost object, and functional area.

This scenario offers an easy way to allocate shared service expenses.

### Additional Intercompany General Ledger Accounts

It's recommended to assign a separate intercompany clearing general ledger account for each origin general ledger account. This allows for flexibility in the financial statement reporting.

If you take the scenario of travel expense allocation in the last section as an example, you can see that the travel expenses are reduced by 100 EUR in the first journal entry line. But that isn't correct in this case. The travel expenses must not change in the sending and receiving company for legal reporting as a result of the transaction. They must remain in place but continue to be invoiced (see the discussion of intercompany billing in the next section). With the option to assign every allocated general ledger account its own clearing account, you can assign the clearing account in the same financial statement node as the allocation general ledger account. Then the intercompany allocation posting will balance to zero for this node.

There is a Customizing setting for the intercompany clearing accounts available. You can access it by following menu path **Controlling • Cost Center Accounting • Actual Postings • Assign Intercompany Clearing Accounts** in the SAP GUI or with the Manage Your Solution app. By searching for the "Automatic Account Determination" task in the app, you can reach the options shown in Figure 9.30.

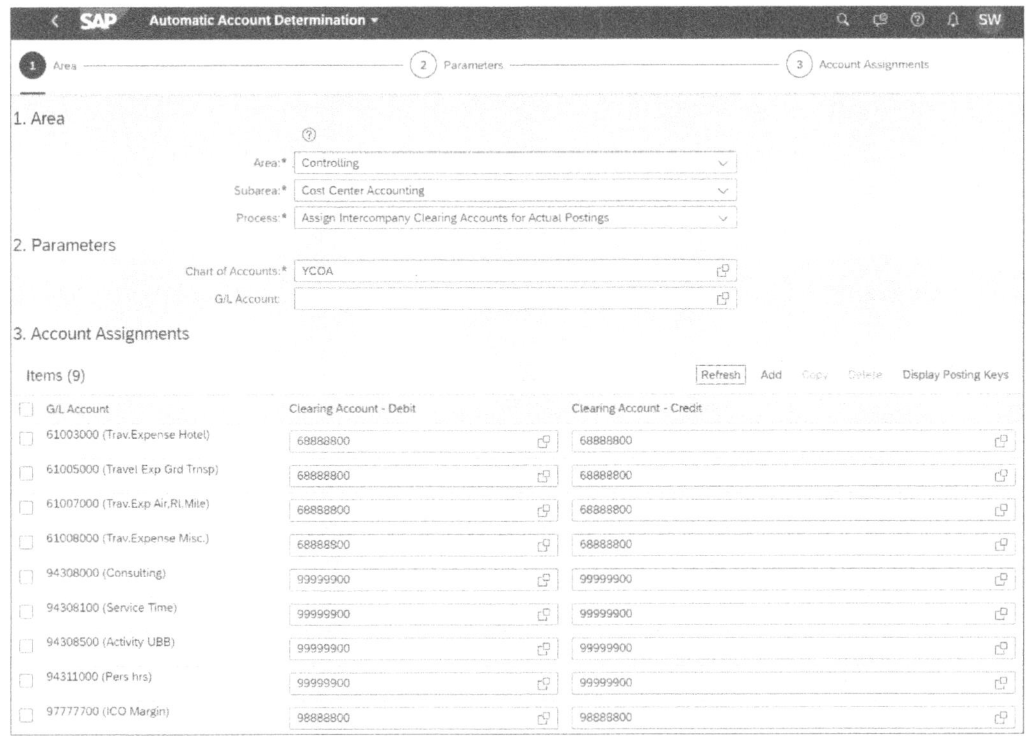


**Figure 9.30** IMG Assignment of Intercompany Clearing Accounts

Using the Manage Your Solution app, there's one activity in which we bundled all account determination Customizing. To get the intercompany clearing accounts, select the **Controlling** area, the **Cost Center Accounting** subarea, and the **Process**. As mentioned, you can define for every allocated general ledger account its own clearing general ledger account. In this example, there's a clearing account per allocation type: travel expense, activities, and the margin. The intercompany clearing accounts must be nonoperating P&L accounts.

For activity allocation, you can define a margin, posted with its own margin account (we showed an example previously in Figure 9.26). As mentioned at the beginning of this section, this functionality and its Customizing are behind the `FINS_CO_ICO_PROC_ENH_101` business function. With activation, you can define the margin accounts in Customizing by following menu path **Controlling • Cost Center Accounting • Actual Postings • Additional Transaction-Related Postings • Intercompany Margins For Activity Allocations • Assign Intercompany Margin Accounts**. You'll arrive at the screen shown in Figure 9.31.

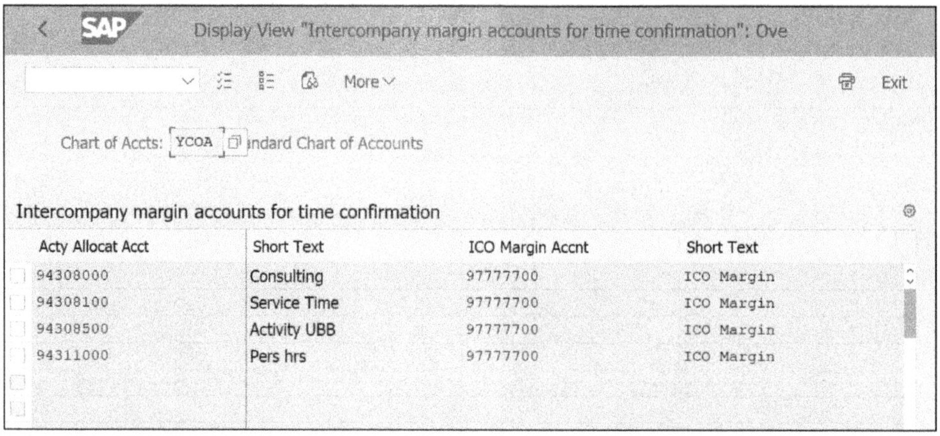

| Acty Allocat Acct | Short Text | ICO Margin Accnt | Short Text |
|---|---|---|---|
| 94308000 | Consulting | 97777700 | ICO Margin |
| 94308100 | Service Time | 97777700 | ICO Margin |
| 94308500 | Activity UBB | 97777700 | ICO Margin |
| 94311000 | Pers hrs | 97777700 | ICO Margin |

**Figure 9.31** IMG Assignment of Intercompany Margin Accounts to Activity Allocation Accounts

For every activity allocation account (**Acty Allocat Acct**), you can assign its own intercompany margin account (**ICO Margin Accnt**). The intercompany margin accounts are P&L accounts of the **Primary Costs or Revenue** type. The cost element category is **01 Primary Costs**.

### 9.2.3 Periodic Intercompany Billing

With the intercompany CO postings, some legal requirements aren't yet covered. We're still missing taxes, accounts receivable and payable, and affiliated revenues and expenses for group reporting. This is provided by the periodic intercompany billing, which we'll explain in the following sections step by step.

#### Intercompany Sales Order

The first step is the creation of the intercompany sales order. This is required for every company-to-company relationship as a basis for the intercompany billing document. You need to create these sales orders only once. You can use the same intercompany sales order for every periodic billing between the two related companies.

You can create/change/display this sales order with the sales order creation Transactions VA01/VA02/VA03 or with the Create Sales Order Intercompany app, which is a web GUI app with a similar display and functionality. With the sales order, you define the assigned sales organization, which derives the sending company code (see Chapter 3, Section 3.2.3). With scope item 16T in SAP S/4HANA Cloud, there is a separate sales order document type, SO03, available for intercompany use.

To check an intercompany sales order, start Transaction VA02 and enter the intercompany sales order **16152**. Press Enter to open the sales order master screen shown in Figure 9.32.

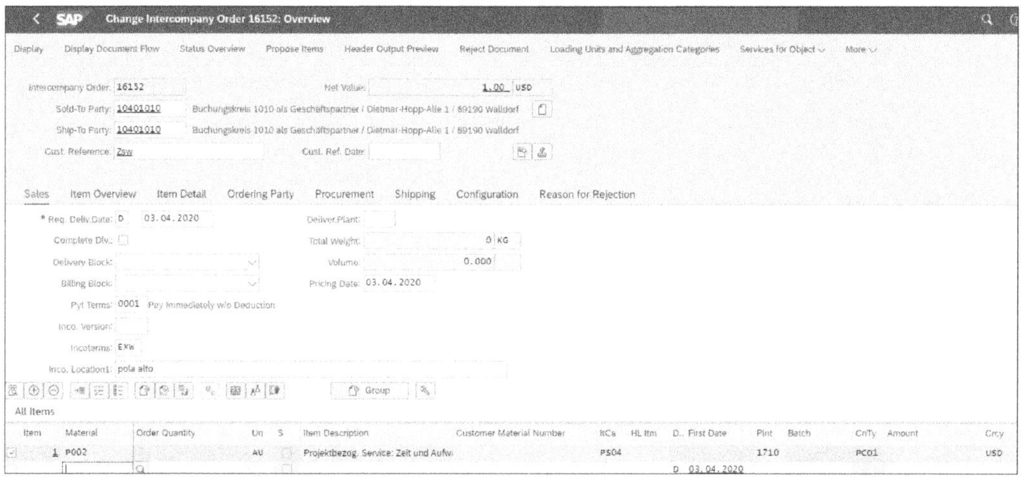


Figure 9.32 Intercompany Sales Order Master

The assigned customer, **Sold-To Party 10401010**, represents the receiving company. There is only one sales order item required and thus one product, here **P002**, to which an intercompany time and material billing profile is assigned. This profile enables the intercompany billing process.

## Billing

The intercompany controlling documents posted during the period are used for the intercompany billing.

We want to bill the services delivered from company code 1710, US, to company code 1010, Germany. Start the Display Line Items in General Ledger app (there is no corresponding SAP GUI transaction) and select all cost allocation documents in your company code (**1010** in this example) with the correct trading partner (**1710** in this example), as shown in Figure 9.33. Set April as the period in the **Posting Date** field.

Display Line Items in General Ledger

CO ICO postings received in 1010 *

Ledger: 0L (Ledger 0L) | Company Code: 1 Item | Posting Date: From (01.04.2020) | Object Type: =PR | Journal Entry: 1 Item | Trading Partner: 1 Item

Line Items (17) | ico postings *

| Company Code | G/L Account | Journal Entry | Journal Entry T... | Posting Date | Amount in Trans... | Amount in CC Crcy | Amount in Glob. Crcy | Jrnl.Entry Item Text | Trading Part... | WBS Element |
|---|---|---|---|---|---|---|---|---|---|---|
| G/L Account: 61003000 - Travel Expenses - Hotel and Accommodation | | | | | | | | | | |
| 1010 (Company C... | 61003000 (Travel ... | 2400000020 | CC | 13.04.2020 | 100.00 USD | 80.78 EUR | 91.84 USD | Hotel for workshop | 1710 | SW008.1.1 |
| G/L Account: 61007000 - Travel Expenses - Airfare, Rail, Mileage | | | | | | | | | | |
| 1010 (Company C... | 61007000 (Travel ... | 2400000002 | CC | 07.04.2020 | 10.00 USD | 8.08 EUR | 8.57 USD | | 1710 | PROJ112233.1.1 |
| 1010 (Company C... | 61007000 (Travel ... | 2400000003 | CC | 08.04.2020 | 10.00 USD | 8.08 EUR | 9.07 USD | | 1710 | PROJ202004071253.1.1 |
| 1010 (Company C... | 61007000 (Travel ... | 2400000004 | CC | 08.04.2020 | 10.00 USD | 8.08 EUR | 9.07 USD | | 1710 | PROJ202004080453.1.1 |
| 1010 (Company C... | 61007000 (Travel ... | 2400000005 | CC | 08.04.2020 | 10.00 USD | 8.08 EUR | 9.07 USD | | 1710 | PROJ202004080819.1.1 |
| 1010 (Company C... | 61007000 (Travel ... | 2400000016 | CC | 10.04.2020 | 10.00 USD | 8.08 EUR | 9.18 USD | | 1710 | PROJ202004090218.1.1 |
| 1010 (Company C... | 61007000 (Travel ... | 2400000019 | CC | 10.04.2020 | 10.00 USD | 8.08 EUR | 9.18 USD | | 1710 | PROJ202004100452.1.1 |
| | 61007000 (Travel ... | | | | 60.00 USD | 48.48 EUR | 54.16 USD | | | |
| G/L Account: 94308000 - Consulting ... | | | | | 323.10 EUR | 323.10 EUR | 400.00 USD | | | |
| G/L Account: 97777700 - ICO Margin ... | | | | | 76.90 EUR | 76.90 EUR | 95.20 USD | | | |
| | | | | | Show Details | 529.28 EUR | 641.20 USD | | | |

Figure 9.33 Intercompany Controlling Documents for Set Period

Here we've selected all intercompany postings from company code 1710 to 1010. In this view, they're grouped by general ledger account because the general ledger account will be the parameter to define the billing product and thus the certain billing line items in the periodic intercompany invoice.

### Generate Intercompany Billing

The periodic intercompany billing is done with Transaction DP93 or the Generate Intercompany Billing Request app. When you execute Transaction DP93, you arrive at the screen shown in Figure 9.34.

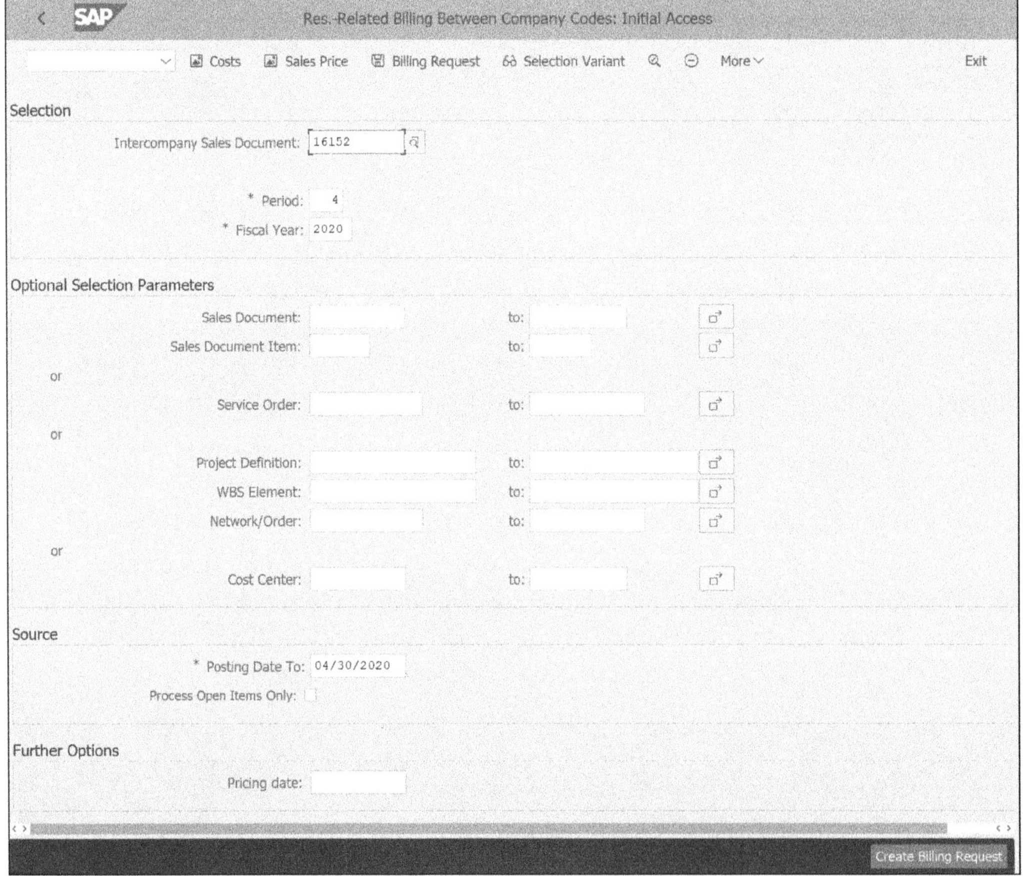


Figure 9.34 Creation of Intercompany Billing Document

As a parameter for the billing request creation, you need to input the **Intercompany Sales Document**—here, sales order **16152**—created earlier. It defines the sending and receiving company code. The time frame also needs to be defined by the **Period** and the **Posting Date To**. Here, select April 2020. You also can select the receiving cost object.

Click the **Create Billing Request** button to arrive at the screen shown in Figure 9.35.

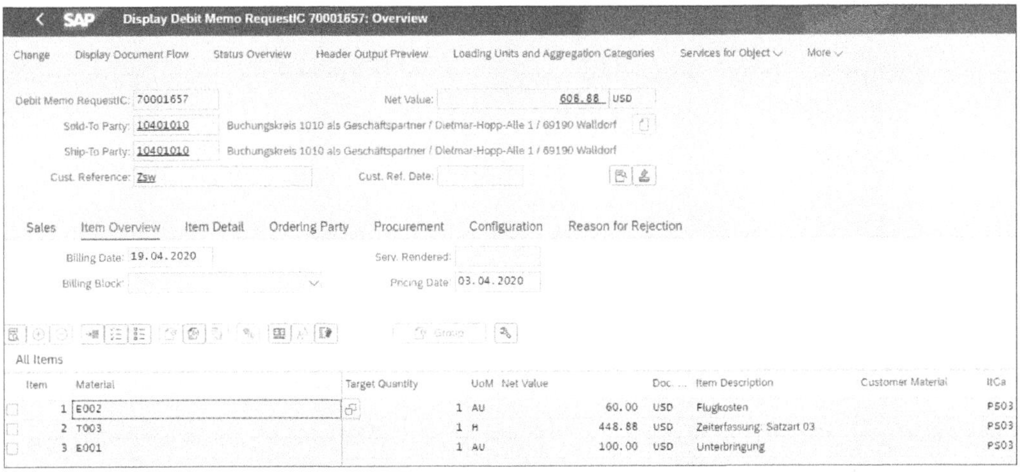

Figure 9.35 Intercompany Debit Memo Request

In the debit memo request, you see three billing line items created with different products. This grouping of the cost postings and mapping them to billing products is done by the time and expense billing functionality, which is similar to what we discussed in Chapter 7 for the customer project scenario. With this you can define specific billing products based on the allocation general ledger accounts and activity types.

All lines are derived based on the postings shown previously in Figure 9.33:

- Item 1 with product E002 with a price of 60 USD, derived by the six postings on expense account 61007000.
- Item 2 with product T003, based on the activity allocation plus the margin. Due to different currency conversion rates, there is a difference in the amounts.
- Item 3 with product E001 and price of 100 USD, based on the posting on general ledger account 61003000.

With the reference to this debit memo request, an intercompany invoice is created. In SAP S/4HANA Cloud, invoice type CI02 is used. By transferring the invoice (not shown here) to accounting, you get the journal entry shown in Figure 9.36.

The invoice creates one line for the receivables account (**Rcvbls Affiliate**) and a billed revenue journal entry item for every debit memo request item. If tax is relevant, there will be an additional tax line item created.

As an additional step, you can create the corresponding account payables document in the receiving company code 1010 using IDocs.

**Figure 9.36** Journal Entry for Intercompany Billing Document

**IDocs**

IDoc is shorthand for Intermediate Document. The purpose of an IDoc is to transfer data or information from SAP to other systems and vice versa. In this scenario, it's used to transfer data within a system.

## 9.3 Summary

In this chapter, you've learned about the various intercompany processes and how they're reflected in financials. First, variants of intercompany processing exist for inventory-managed products. Second, intercompany controlling postings are used for intercompany service allocation. Both processes share the intercompany billing that follows. The invoicing for inventory-managed materials runs for the individual logistical movement of goods, but with intercompany controlling postings, it is a periodic run that collects, evaluates, and aggregates the transactions of the period.

Next, we'll offer some deeper insights into financial reporting in SAP S/4HANA.

# Chapter 10
# Reporting in SAP S/4HANA

*We've shown many examples of controlling reports in the course of the previous chapters to illustrate how the various business processes are recorded and the related journal entries. In this chapter, we'll put reporting center stage and explain what it means to perform your financial reporting in SAP S/4HANA.*

10

It might feel like we've already shown lots of reports throughout the book, but we haven't gone behind the scenes to explain how the various SAP Fiori apps select the costs and revenue recorded in the Universal Journal for display or how the various *key figures* provide a way for internal stakeholders to compare performance between divisions, business units, plants, and so on. It's hard to think about reporting without thinking about the hierarchical structures that we introduced along with the other master data in Chapter 4 in order to group accounts, profit centers, cost centers, and so on.

The secret ingredient behind the SAP Fiori apps is the *virtual data model* that combines the transactional data in the Universal Journal with the master data for each of the reporting dimensions and the hierarchies that are used to structure information in finance. If you've generally relied on a separate data warehouse for your reporting tasks, it's important to understand how the new reporting approach might change your approach and how to extract data from SAP S/4HANA to your existing data warehouse if you need to.

Financial reporting uses many different forms of hierarchies, from financial statement versions and account groups to profit center groups, cost center groups, and so on. Here too there are changes in SAP S/4HANA, even though the various groups from SAP ERP continue to be available. We'll look at how to set up account and cost element groups for reporting and explain how these differ from financial statement versions in a *global hierarchy*. We'll then look at the reporting of cost center groups and profit center groups before introducing the idea of a *flexible hierarchy*.

In data modeling terms, there are two fundamentally different ways of looking at accounting information:

1. In business terms, financial statements, trial balances, cost center reports, and so on are based on an *account model*: it's the account and account groupings that provide

the main way of structuring the report. What's new for many users in SAP S/4HANA is that margin analysis is also structured by accounts, so you can look at the sales per region or product by selecting the appropriate revenue accounts and then drilling down by market segment, as shown in Chapter 7. However, if you have thousands of sales accounts, margin analysis by account can be cumbersome—but we'll explain how to use *semantic tags* to group your accounts for efficient analysis. It can also be the case that the account isn't the only thing you want to see. Perhaps you also want to see the quantity of goods that have been invoiced or only the variable part of the values on an account, rather than the combination of fixed and variable costs.

2. Costing-based profitability analysis, in which all amounts are mapped to value fields, is perhaps the most obvious example of a report based on a *key figure model* in SAP S/4HANA. In some cases, the value fields are just a different way of looking at the same numbers; in others, there are value fields that are not directly linked with the accounts, such as the invoice quantity, delivery quantity, and so on. In this case, we need a different way of capturing the quantities and then deriving the appropriate sales volumes. We'll look at how to capture this information in SAP S/4HANA.

Finally, if you're moving from SAP ERP, it's important to understand how much of your existing reporting continues to be available so that you can transition gradually to the new world without retraining everyone overnight. *Compatibility views* are the key here, allowing most reports to run as before but while selecting their data from the line items in the Universal Journal rather than from the various totals records that were used to preaggregate the data in SAP ERP. If you're moving from SAP ERP, these compatibility views will allow you to continue to report as before and transition gradually to the SAP S/4HANA approach, but, as shown in Chapter 7, there are also benefits to making the shift in terms of reporting on projects in combination with market segments. Also, the ability to extend the market segments that we discussed in Chapter 4 is only available in the new approach.

We'll begin in Section 10.1 by explaining the virtual data model used to collect the data to be displayed in the various SAP Fiori applications that we've shown in the course of the book. In Section 10.2, we'll explain how the global accounting hierarchy differs from the various master data groupings that we introduced in Chapter 4. In Section 10.3, we'll explain how to use flexible hierarchies to generate these structures from your master data. It's also important to understand how to define key figures. We'll explain how to work with semantic tags in Section 10.4 and how to work with other key figures, including quantities, in Section 10.5. Finally, in Section 10.6 we'll explain how the use of compatibility views allows you to keep using your legacy reports even though the introduction of the Universal Journal with SAP S/4HANA means that the underlying data model has changed.

## 10.1 SAP Fiori and the Virtual Data Model

We've used SAP Fiori applications to illustrate various business processes throughout the book. SAP Fiori was introduced as a new user experience in 2013 and delivers *role-based* user interfaces for all users in SAP S/4HANA. The first finance application was My Spend, which provided budget information to managers on the move, as shown in Chapter 5. Over time, applications have been created for specialist users in finance to meet the needs of the general ledger accountant, asset accountant, collection specialist, and so on.

What makes SAP Fiori different from SAP ERP user interfaces is that SAP Fiori can run on all devices—on smart phones and tablets, as well as on traditional desktop computers. The user interface itself runs in a browser, and the frontend is usually built using SAPUI5, which allows the user interface to respond to the space available on your smartphone or desktop. Many SAP Fiori applications use standard SAP Fiori elements (formerly known as *smart templates*), which provide a framework for the most common user interface patterns. (We've already shown many examples of analytical list pages and drilldown reports.)



The browser-based application running on a smartphone or tablet uses SAP Gateway to connect with the SAP S/4HANA system. To access data, it must transfer information about each user and their authorizations and a *query* to request the information that they want to see in the report. So when an overhead accountant calls up a cost center report, it will transfer information about the user and the cost centers they are authorized to see and a query to request the planned and actual costs on those cost centers.

In SAP Fiori, the transfer of the data between the browser and the application works using standard protocols called *OData services*. To this end, SAP has been building data services to help you to access all the information needed for financial reporting. These data services rely on core *data services (CDS) views* to gather the relevant information for reporting, so there are views to select planned costs, actual costs, predictive journal entries, and so on. The combination of views to access transactional data, master data, hierarchy information, and so on is known as the *virtual data model*.

Figure 10.1 provides a high-level view of how the analytics applications use the virtual data model to access data in physical tables, such as the Universal Journal and related master data tables. A query view for reporting might be, for example, `CostCenterPlanActualCostsQuery`, which combines all the information needed to deliver plan/actual reporting on a cost center. The contents of these views can be consumed in SAP Fiori or SAP Analytics Cloud or be used to transfer information to data warehouses and other analytical tools. If you currently move the costs from your operational system to a data warehouse, it's important to understand that you can either access the information in the Universal Journal using a traditional extractor, `0FI_ACDOCA_10`, or you can use the query views delivered in the virtual data model as shown here to select the information in the Universal Journal for transfer to the data warehouse.

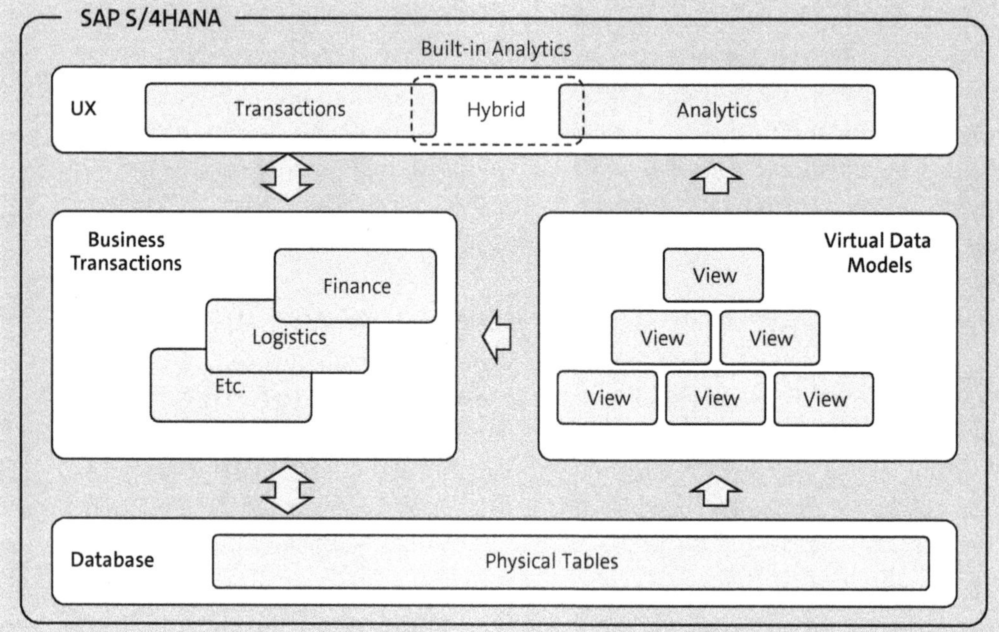


**Figure 10.1** Embedded Analytics in SAP S/4HANA

To illustrate the process of transferring information to an SAP Fiori application in more detail, we'll look at the Cost Center Budget Report app (SAP Fiori ID F3871), shown in Figure 10.2. What you see in the browser is the `FIN_COSTCBDGT` SAPUI5 application. If you think the structure looks familiar, that's because the application is built using SAP Fiori elements to deliver the standard structure comprising graphics for *visual filtering* (the selection area in the upper part of the screen), *visual content* (the graphic in the middle of the screen), and *transactional content* (the document lines in the lower part of the screen). This application uses the `FCO_COST_CENTER_BUDGET_SRV` OData service to access the virtual data model (the combination of views) used to aggregate the transactional information from the Universal Journal and to link these figures with the relevant master data. These views are delivered by SAP, but they can be extended to meet your specific needs.

**SAP Fiori Apps Reference Library**

If you want to find the applications that have been delivered for a role or application area to understand the implementation details for each of the applications that we've described so far, use the SAP Fiori apps reference library at *http://s-prs.co/v528203*. The information in the paragraph preceding this box is summarized from the entry for SAP Fiori app F3871 and describes what your technical team needs to activate before you can use the Cost Center Budget Report app in controlling. We've given the SAP Fiori IDs for each of the applications shown in the book to help you coordinate with your technical team to activate the reports that you need for your work (also, see Appendix B for a complete list).

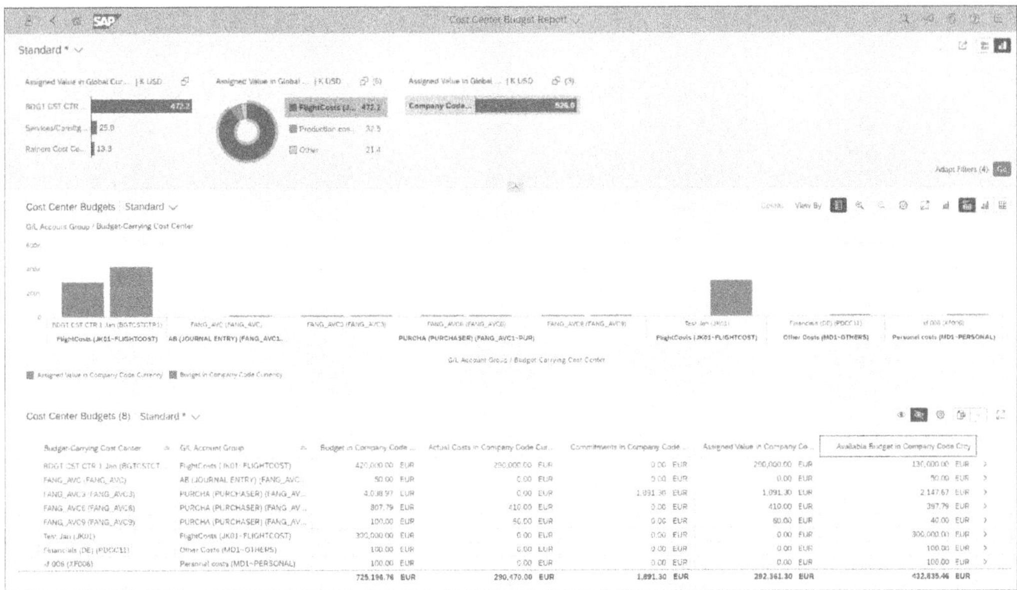

**Figure 10.2** Cost Center Budget Report App



Many organizations need the ability to add reporting dimensions based on their unique requirements. In SAP ERP, tools such as Report Writer and Report Painter offer little opportunity for extensibility. And if you've worked with some of the industry solutions in SAP ERP, you'll know that separate reports delivered for public sector accounting overlap with the existing financial reports to include the fields specific to the public sector. This is where SAP S/4HANA brings fundamental changes compared with SAP ERP. Not only can SAP extend the standard applications to include more fields, such as the work center and operation for production reporting (as shown in Chapter 6), but also, more importantly, it allows organizations to add their own reporting fields to the Universal Journal. In Chapter 4, we explained how to use the Custom Fields and Logic app (SAP Fiori ID F1481) to add your own fields to the **Market Segment** business context for use in margin analysis, and this approach is the key to your reporting as it allows you to go beyond the limits of your existing operating concern to segment your markets as you see fit.

You won't always need to extend the Universal Journal to include more information for reporting. You can use the same app with different *business contexts* to extend the cost center master data, profit center master data, and so on in order to add additional fields for display in reporting. You can use this to tag the master data for reporting purposes but also to act as the basis for creating various hierarchies, as we'll explain in Section 10.3.

## 10.2 Global Hierarchies

In Chapter 4, we explained how to create cost element hierarchies, financial statement versions, and cost center groups to structure the accounts and cost centers for reporting and to aid selection in allocations, settlement, and so on. With SAP S/4HANA, the Manage Global Hierarchies app (SAP Fiori ID F2918; previously known as Manage Global Accounting Hierarchies) provides a new option to define these structures for reporting and deliver new features that were not available in previous releases. If you feel that your hierarchies are subject to constant change and the next restructuring of your organization is always just around the corner, then it's worth looking at the global hierarchy as an alternative to the structures that we showed in Chapter 4. The new hierarchies use a different data store from the legacy transactions, one that is optimized for performance. For this reason, we'll also explain how the two structures can coexist until SAP has rewritten all the legacy transactions to select from the new hierarchies. We'll begin by looking at the financial statement version.

### 10.2.1 Financial Statement Versions

As we explained in Chapter 4, *financial statement versions* group related accounts to deliver the appropriate sections of the balance sheet and profit and loss (P&L) statement. SAP delivers many standard financial statement versions to support the various country- and industry-specific reporting requirements, and these are linked with the relevant charts of accounts. In Chapter 4, we also showed financial statement version YPS2, which is designed to deliver contribution margin reporting in a professional services environment, for product profitability and contribution margin reporting by service and product. Indeed, it's the backbone of many of the reports that we looked at in Chapter 7.

The Manage Global Hierarchies app (SAP Fiori app F2918) shown in Figure 10.3 can be used as an alternative to the transactions we showed in Chapter 4. As the name implies, you can use this app to define many different types of hierarchy for use in financial accounting and controlling, but also in group reporting and to define product groups. The *hierarchy type* is used to distinguish between the hierarchies—so to display a financial statement version, use the Manage Global Hierarchies app, select the **Financial Statement Version** hierarchy, and enter a **Hierarchy ID**, as shown in Figure 10.3. This activity should normally be performed in a Customizing client and then transported into the productive accounting system. Notice the **Timeframe** section with the **Valid From/To** field, something that wasn't an option in legacy transactions. Financial statement versions maintained using the new application can be *time-dependent* (meaning that they are valid for a limited time only) and provide the option of *status management* (marking something as a draft, active, in revision, etc.). You can only use a hierarchy in reporting if it has the **Active** status (instead of **Draft** or **In Revision**) in the Manage

Global Hierarchies app. This means that a group of master data specialists can prepare the structures prior to a reorganization, but the accountants only see the active structures in their reports.

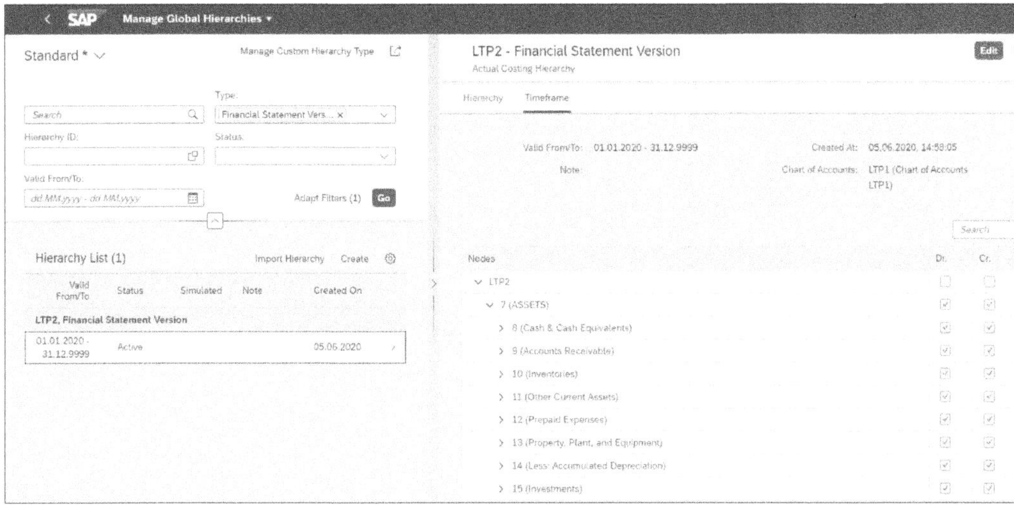


**Figure 10.3** Financial Statement Version LTP2 in Global Hierarchy App

Financial statement versions comprise financial statement items (the nodes in the tree), general ledger accounts, and functional areas (see Chapter 4). Figure 10.4 shows details of one of the financial statement version items from Figure 10.3. Here you can see the **Inventories** node for the inventory accounts, which can contain further items for raw materials, work in process (WIP), semifinished products, finished products, and so on. Note that you can determine whether the entries are considered debits, credits, or both. These flags and the **+/- Sign Change** flag are only available for hierarchies of the financial statement version type and they control the treatment of the data in the nodes and the accounts. In this example, the values on the inventory accounts will be shown in this node of the hierarchy whether they are positive or negative, but with items such as bank accounts, their position will depend on whether the balance is positive or negative. If the balance for the accounts is a debit, the accounts might be classified as *cash in bank* (an asset), but if the balance for the accounts is a credit, the accounts might be classified as *payable to banks* (a liability). This is a feature that's specific to the financial statement version as values for general ledger account groups or cost center groups can simply be aggregated.

Let's now use the P&L—Plan/Actual app (SAP Fiori ID F0297A) to show how these hierarchies are used in reporting. To select accounts from a hierarchy, select the **Hierarchy ID** used in the Manage Global Hierarchies app and then the assigned nodes, if you want to view only part of the hierarchy, as shown in Figure 10.5. The node is the financial statement version if you choose the corresponding **Hierarchy ID**.

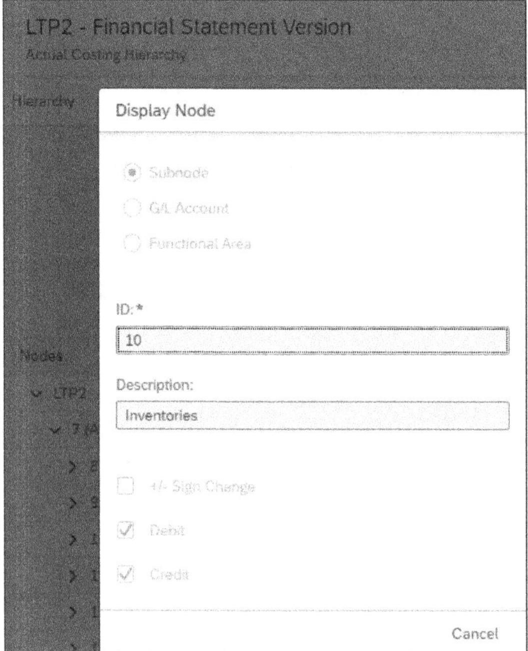


**Figure 10.4** Node Details for Raw Materials

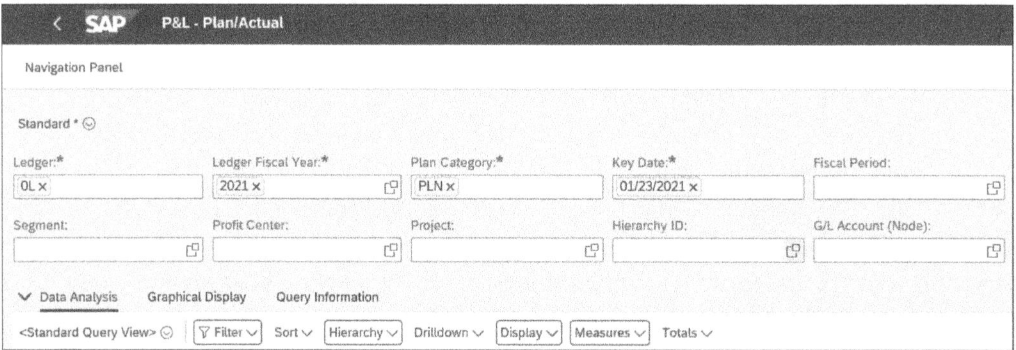


**Figure 10.5** Selection by Hierarchy ID and General Ledger Account Node

The default view lists the accounts assigned to the financial statement version entered as a flat list. To structure the selected accounts, as shown in Figure 10.6, attach a hierarchy by right-clicking the **G/L Account** column and choosing an account hierarchy. You can then expand the various nodes to reach the individual accounts and functional areas (if included).

The legacy transactions for the financial statement versions that we showed in Chapter 4 (Transactions OB58, FSE2, and FSE3) continue to be available, but you can't use the new features for financial statement versions maintained in this way. Before you can use the legacy hierarchies in reporting, you must *replicate* them to the new data store for reporting. One option is to copy classic financial statement versions into the Manage Global Hierarchies app as a draft and process further using the new app. But note that changes made using the application are not reflected in the old financial statement versions. When you change a financial statement version using the classic transactions, you'll be asked whether you wish to activate the financial statement version.

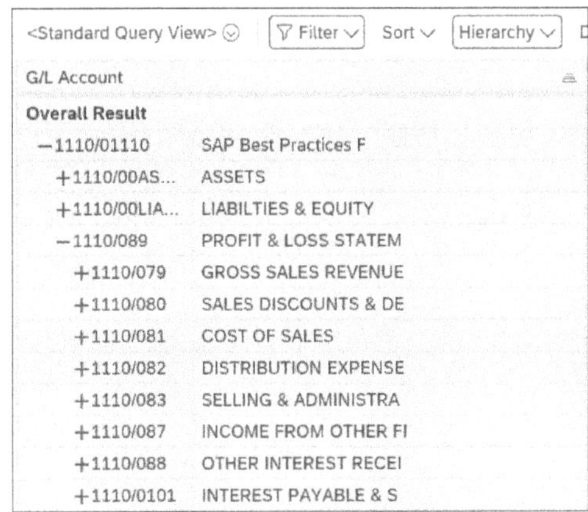


**Figure 10.6** Nodes of Financial Statement Version in P&L Report

## 10.2.2 Account and Cost Element Hierarchies

*General ledger account hierarchies* also group related accounts for reporting, but they can also be used in planning, allocations, and to set thresholds for availability checks by cost center. You saw an account hierarchy maintained in this way defining the senders and receivers for an allocation cycle in Chapter 5. Account hierarchies are also maintained using the Manage Global Hierarchies app, but this time using the **G/L Account Hierarchy** hierarchy type. Figure 10.7 shows an example. Account groups maintained using the new application are also status- and time-dependent.

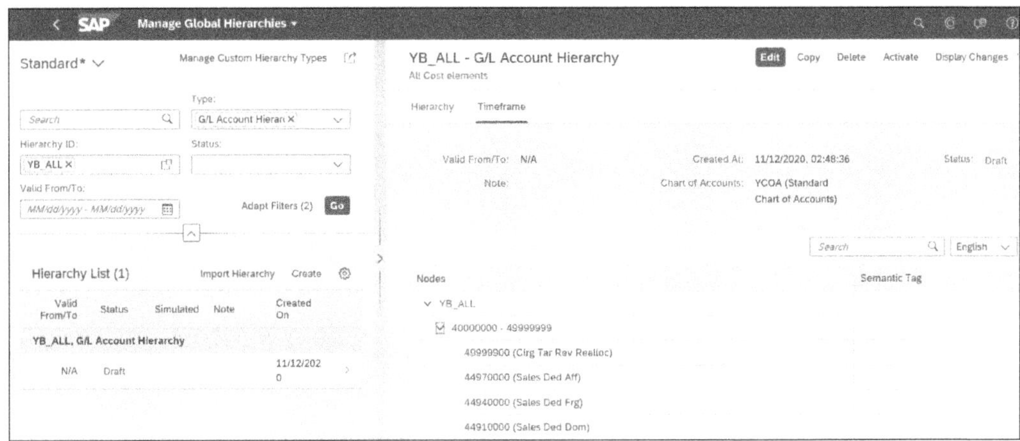


**Figure 10.7** Sample General Ledger Account Group

Figure 10.8 shows the difference between a node in the account hierarchy and in the financial statement version (shown previously in Figure 10.4). Here you can only enter an interval of general ledger accounts.

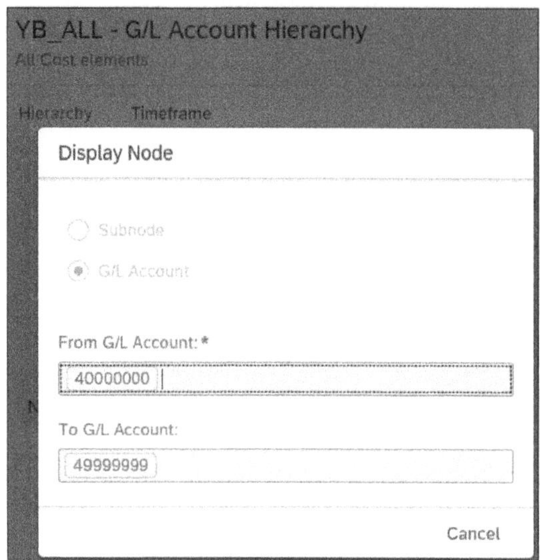


**Figure 10.8** Node Details for Account Group

Again, you can continue to maintain cost element groups using Transactions KAH1, KAH2, and KAH3 and account groups using Transactions KDH1, KDH2, and KDH3, but these transactions won't have any of the new features. You can make these classic groups available for reporting by replicating them to table HRRP.

If you've been using SAP ERP for some time, you may have defined many account groups. Before you replicate these to the new tables, use the Set Reporting Relevancy app (SAP Fiori ID HRY_REPRELEV) to flag **Set Class 0102** (cost element groups) and **0109** (account groups) as **Report Relevant**, as shown in Figure 10.9. Then use the Replicate Runtime Hierarchy app (SAP Fiori ID F1478) to perform the transfer to the new tables.

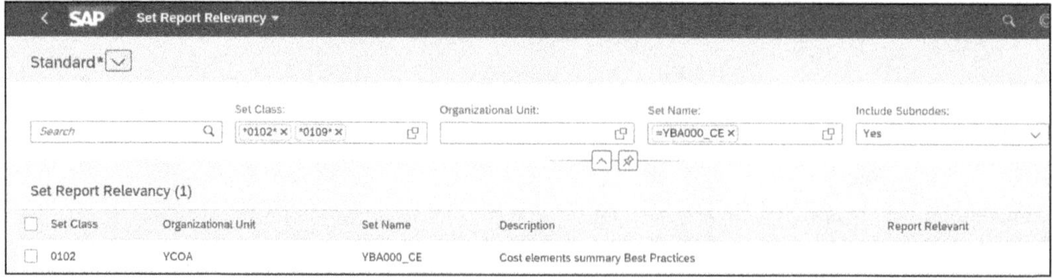


**Figure 10.9** Set Report Relevancy for Existing Account and Cost Element Groups

These hierarchies are currently only used in planning and reporting. However, cost element groups are still used extensively in the former controlling Customizing transactions, so you'll probably end up working with both structures in parallel for an interim period. If you continue to maintain your account and cost element groups using the classic transactions, you'll need to keep the two sets of data in sync by replicating them to table HRRP after each change or setting up a regular job to do so.

### 10.2.3 Cost Center Hierarchies

You can create hierarchies to report on cost centers using the Manage Global Hierarchies app in the same way by building up the tree node by node and then assigning the cost centers to the correct nodes, as shown in Figure 10.10. Alternatively, you can use the **Export/Import** button above the list of nodes to download the structure to a spreadsheet and then upload a list of your cost centers. Again, you can also use these in allocations and planning. 10

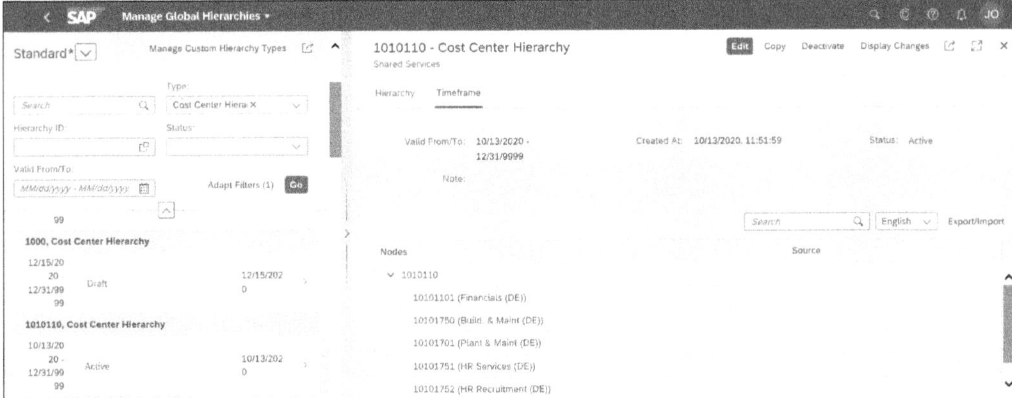

Figure 10.10 Sample Cost Center Hierarchy

As you think about the coexistence of the two hierarchies for the immediate future, consider using the Where-Used List—Cost Centers app (SAP Fiori ID F3549) shown in Figure 10.11 to see in which **Global Accounting Hierarchies** and which legacy **Groups and Hierarchy** each cost center is included.

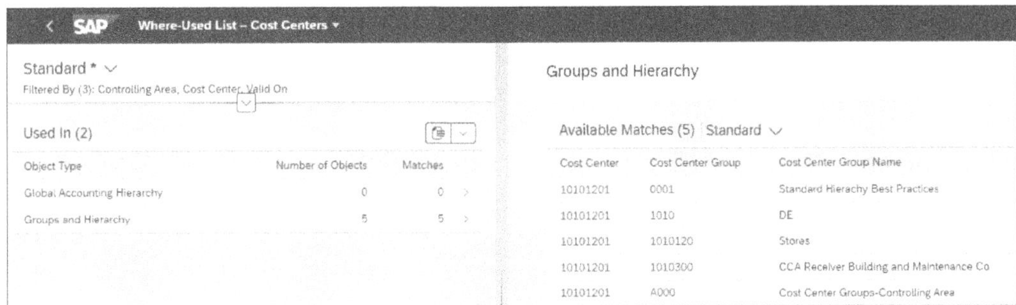

Figure 10.11 Where-Used List Showing Various Cost Center Hierarchies

You can use the same approach to create profit center hierarchies, activity type hierarchies, and statistical key figure groups. Often you want to add hierarchies to other reporting dimensions, and this is when the *custom hierarchy types* come into their own.

### 10.2.4 Custom Hierarchy Types

You can define custom hierarchy types for any dimension that you want to display hierarchically in reporting or use as a sender or receiver in universal allocation. To create such nodes, use the Manage Custom Hierarchy Types app (SAP Fiori ID F3553) shown in Figure 10.12.

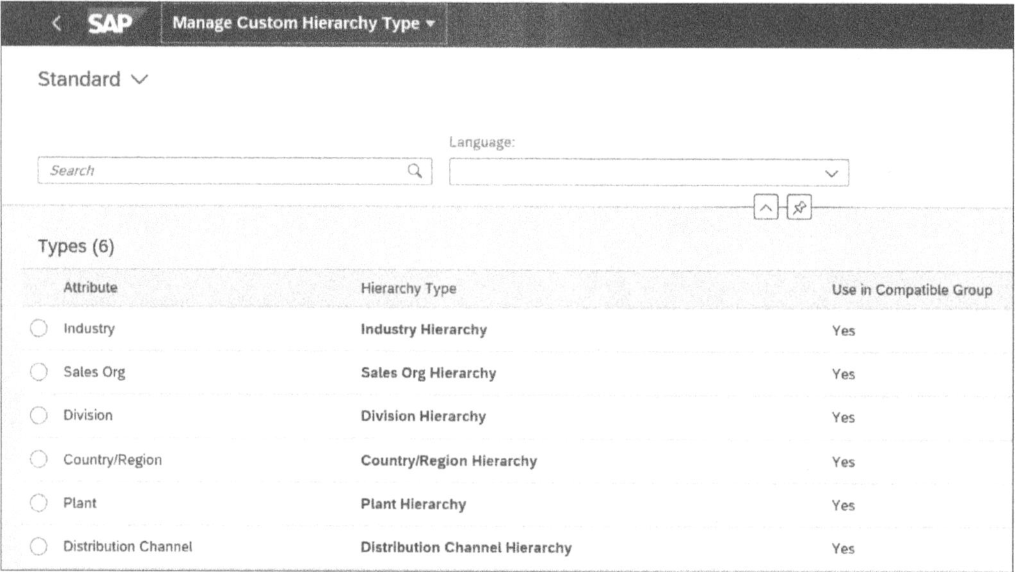


**Figure 10.12** Manage Custom Hierarchy Type App

In this example, we've created hierarchies for some of the market segments used for margin analysis, such as industry, sales organization, division, country/region, plant, and distribution channel so that they can be used to define receivers in top-down distribution (see Chapter 7). It's important to take this option into account as you build up the operating concern for margin analysis to determine which entries to store in the Universal Journal and which to keep simply as hierarchy nodes to be read when the report is run (see Chapter 4). In SAP ERP, drill-down reporting in profitability analysis required you to create characteristics for all hierarchy nodes to be used in these reports, and the hierarchy nodes were updated to the document at the time of posting, so the node was part of the journal entry along with the products, customers, industries, and so on. When you work with custom hierarchy types, only the attribute (industry, sales organization, division, and so on) is included in the journal entry; the hierarchy information is read when you run the report using the connection established through the virtual data model. This gives you greater flexibility to change your hierarchies as your organization evolves but can be slower in reporting as the report must join the hierarchy information as you run the report. Of course, writing the hierarchy information into the Universal Journal won't stop you changing your organizational structures, but you'll have to use the realignment functions that we described in Chapter 7 to bring the information in the Universal Journal up to date in the case of organizational changes.

To add your own, click the **Add** button above the list of types shown previously in Figure 10.12 and choose the market segment for which you wish to add a hierarchy, as shown in Figure 10.13. Then choose **Create** to add the hierarchy for this market segment to the list of hierarchy types.



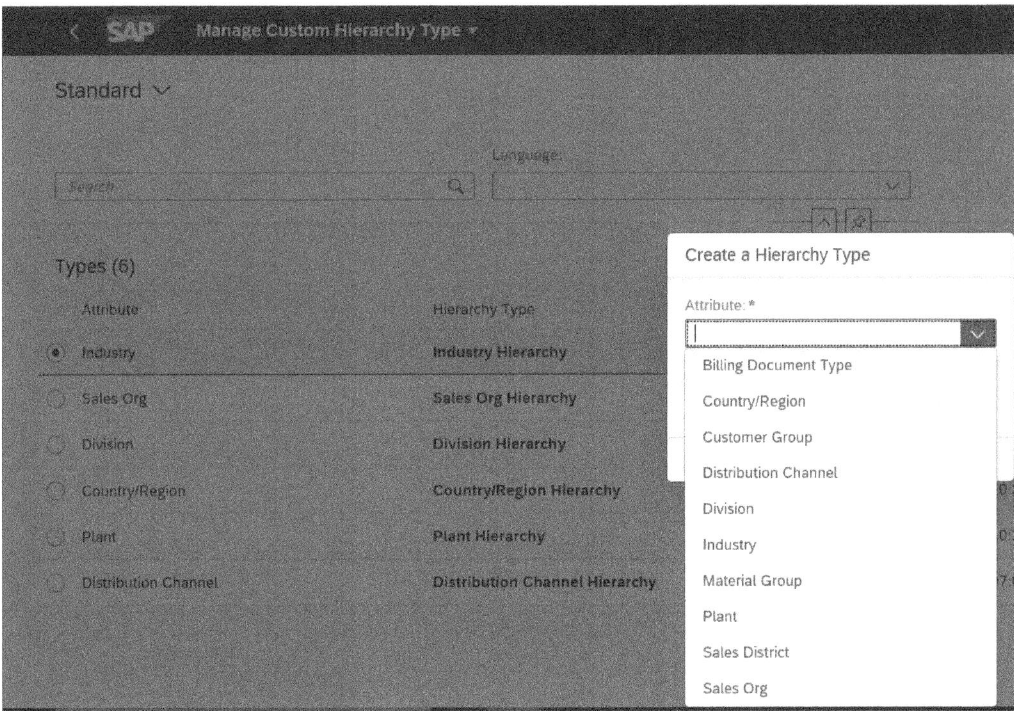


**Figure 10.13** Creating Hierarchy Type

## 10.3 Flexible Hierarchies

You can create hierarchies to report on profit centers and cost centers using the Manage Global Hierarchies app in the same way, by building up the tree node by node and then assigning the profit centers or cost centers to the correct nodes. However, many controllers have told SAP that they've struggled to keep their hierarchies in sync: they typically kept several hierarchies in parallel to provide different views of their organization, and the process of adding to or changing theses hierarchies could be cumbersome for large hierarchies.

In response to this feedback, SAP released the Manage Flexible Hierarchies app (SAP Fiori ID F2759). The idea is that you build hierarchy nodes based on fields in the relevant master data. Each node is based on a field in the cost center master record (you can have as many nodes as you need), so you might build up one node based on the company codes to which your cost centers are assigned, resulting in a grouping of cost centers in company code 1, in company code 2, and so on. To build up multilevel structures, you define the sequence of the nodes—so you might choose to separate the cost centers in company code 1 by the type of cost center, for example. Figure 10.14 and Figure 10.15 show the process of creating a simple cost center hierarchy using the **Company Code** and **Cost Center Category** fields to generate nodes first for the company codes and then for the cost center categories in order to group the cost centers for reporting. This hierarchy presupposes that all cost centers are assigned to a company code and cost center category. Any unassigned cost centers will appear at the bottom of the hierarchy in the unassigned node.

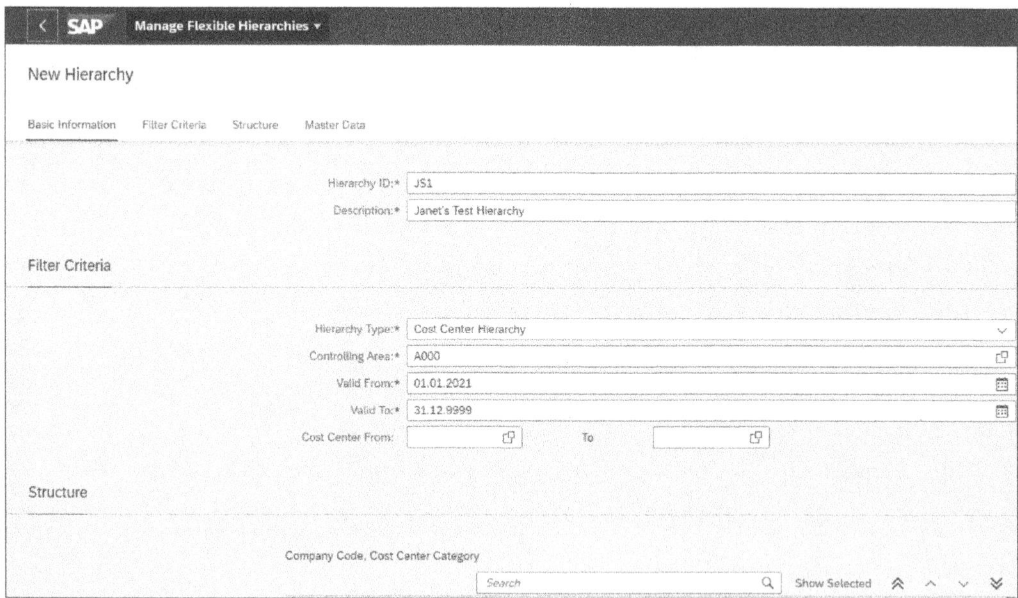


**Figure 10.14** Creating Flexible Cost Center Hierarchy

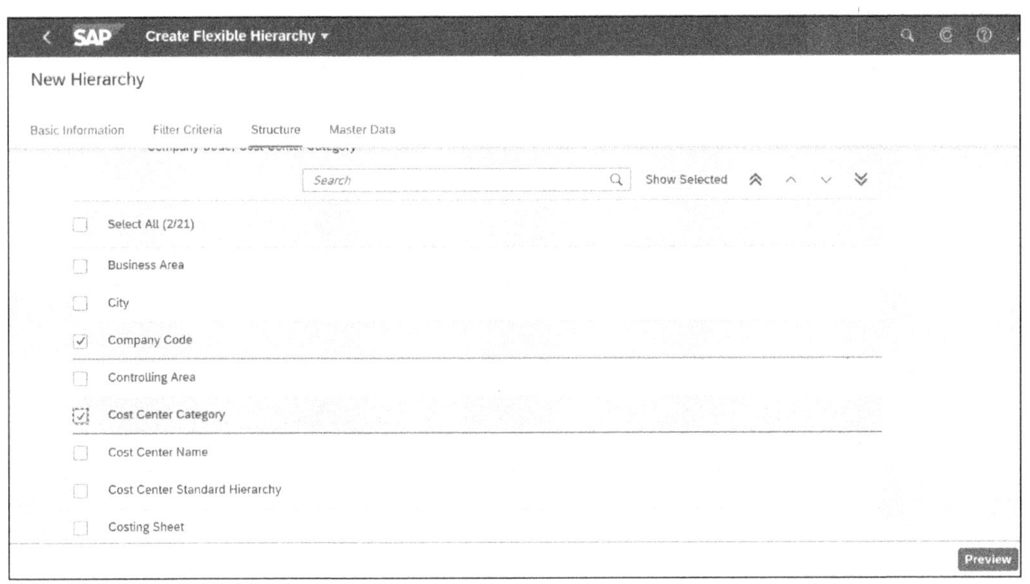


**Figure 10.15** Choosing Fields to Build Hierarchy

Figure 10.16 shows the first nodes of the resulting hierarchy, with a node for each company code in the controlling area. In Figure 10.17, the hierarchy is expanded to show the assigned cost center categories (see Chapter 4, Section 4.2) and then the cost centers in the **Administration** category.

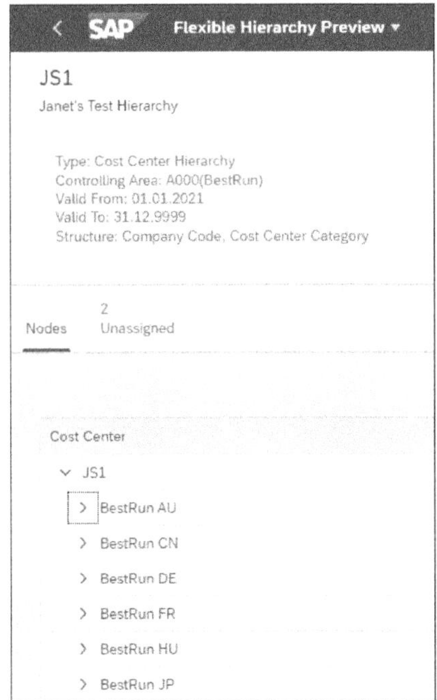


**Figure 10.16** Nodes for Company Codes

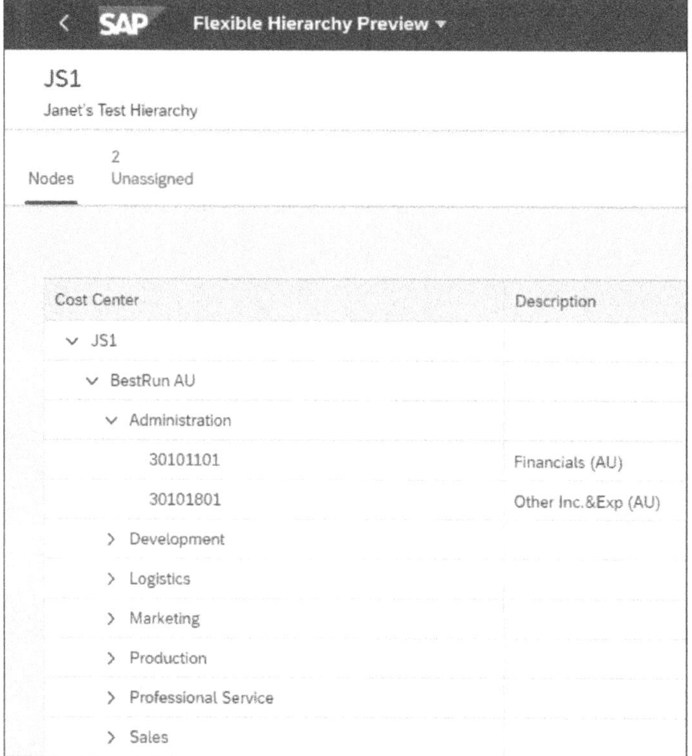


**Figure 10.17** Company Codes, Cost Center Categories, and Cost Centers

The idea isn't new; if you've worked with order or project summarization in SAP ERP, you've probably built hierarchies the same way. What's different is that orders and projects provide hundreds of fields that can potentially be used to build such structures, whereas profit centers and cost centers offer far fewer fields. Figure 10.18 illustrates the challenge of building up a new profit center hierarchy, in which fields such as **Name 1**, **Name 2**, **Name 3**, and **Name 4** may or may not contain useful information and you risk generating a hierarchy with as many unassigned profit centers as assigned ones. Instead, you should use the extensibility options to add the required fields to your profit center in order to classify them for selection in reporting. So, you might add a field for country or region, instead of using the company code, as shown in the previous example.

Figure 10.19 shows a flexible hierarchy for cost center reporting that was created using the **Country/Region Key** and **Department** fields. In general, to build these kinds of tree structures, you need to add new fields to the relevant master data and make sure that they are filled consistently. Notice in this example that there is a final node, **Unassigned**, that contains any cost centers not assigned to a country.

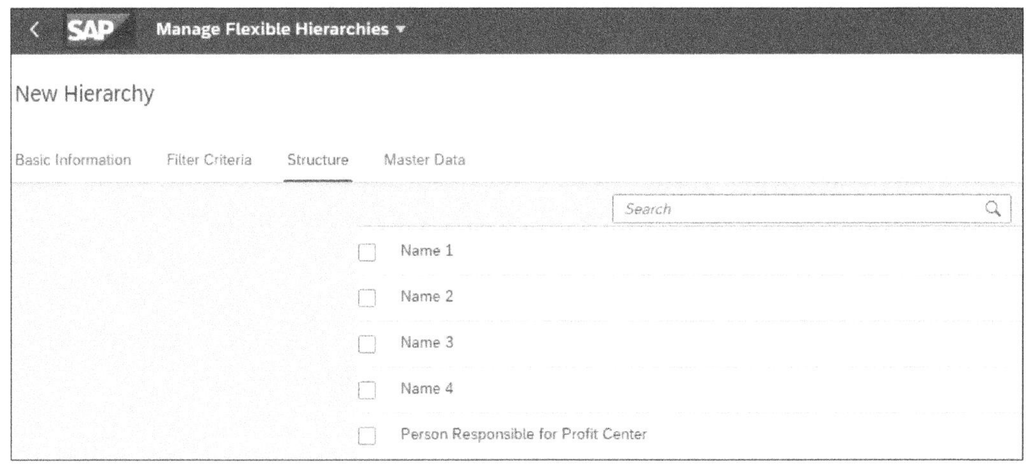


**Figure 10.18** Building Flexible Hierarchy for Profit Centers

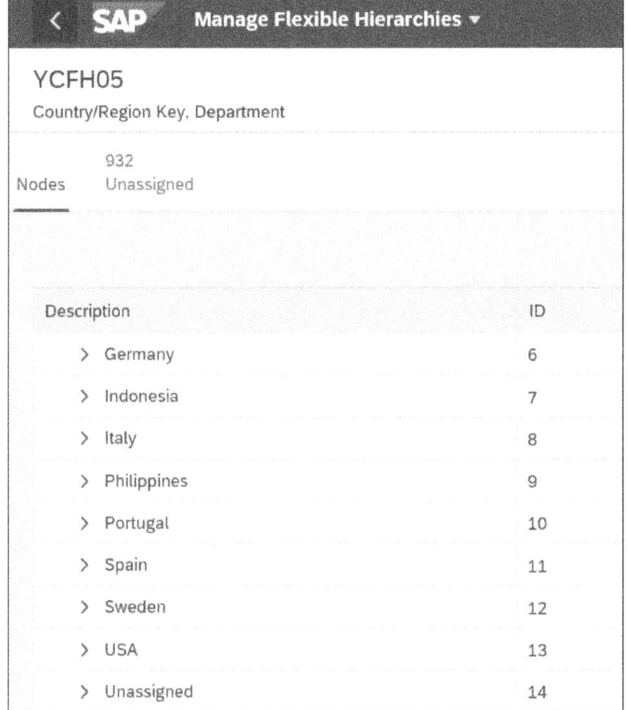


**Figure 10.19** Flexible Hierarchy Using Country/Region Key and Department

In Chapter 4, we discussed extensibility in the context of margin analysis, but it can be just as important to extend your master data using the profit center master data and cost center master data business contexts. Figure 10.20 shows the Custom Fields and Logic app, used here to create a new field for the country with **Cost Center Master Data** selected for **Business Context**.

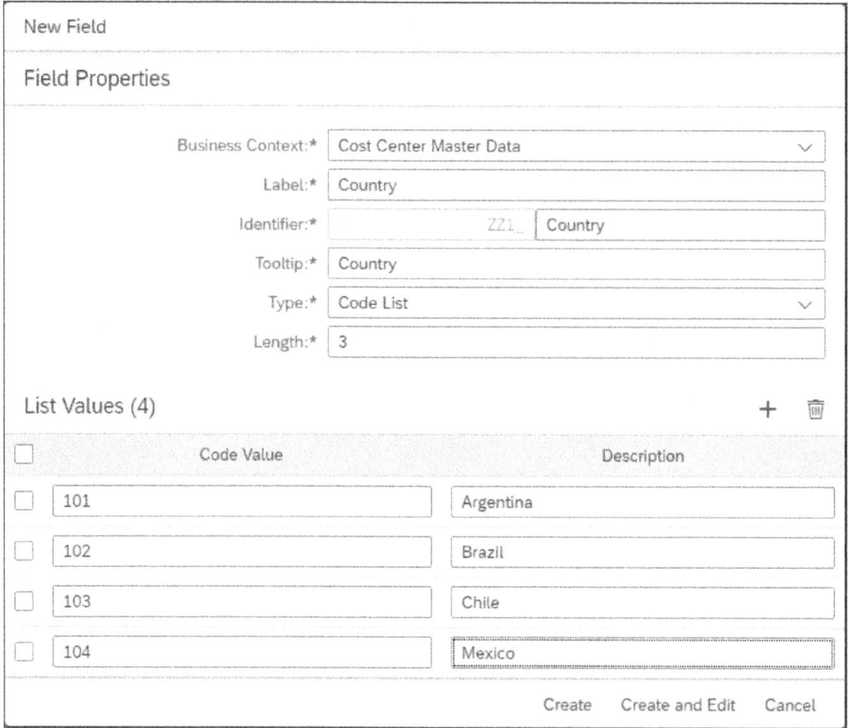


**Figure 10.20** Custom Field for Country in Cost Center Master Data

Before you publish this field, you must specify where it can be used, as shown in Figure 10.21. Here it's important to enable data entry for the country by choosing **Cost Center Master Record** and **Cost Center in Flexible Hierarchy** so that it can be used to create a hierarchy like the one shown previously in Figure 10.19.

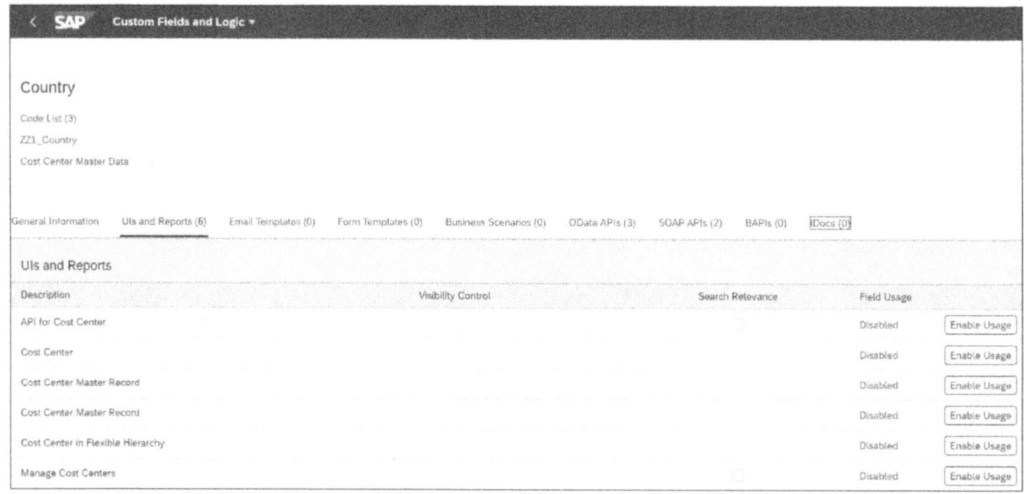


**Figure 10.21** Choosing UIs to Show Country Field

Although many controlling tasks are made easier if you can group the chosen objects in a hierarchical structure, sometimes you simply need to tag a group of accounts that will collectively deliver a key figure. We'll look at the process of creating *semantic tags* for this purpose in the next section.

**Use Case**

To read about an end-to-end use case for flexible profit center hierarchies based on profit center extensibility fields, visit the blog at *http://s-prs.co/v528204*.

## 10.4 Semantic Tags



Although the Trial Balance app introduced in Chapter 2 is the favorite demo app of many consultants, navigating through thousands and thousands of accounts to find the information you need can be cumbersome. To deliver the various layers in a contribution margin app, standard key figure definitions are used to group and aggregate information on related accounts to make the information more manageable. In this way, you can group the revenue accounts, cost of goods sold accounts, variance accounts, and so on and then calculate the various contribution margins. We already looked at two examples of such groupings. The first was the Product Profitability app shown in Chapter 7 (see Figure 7.26), where the key figures for billed revenue, cost of goods sold, price differences, and so on are calculated by linking the relevant accounts to the semantic tag used as the measure in the report. The other is the Project Profitability Overview app, also shown in Chapter 7 (see Figure 7.2), where the data shown in the **Recognized Revenue** and **Recognized Margin** cards is calculated using semantic tags. We'll now explain the use of semantic tags in more detail.

SAP delivers a set of semantic tags for product profitability and project profitability. To check the delivered semantic tags, follow the IMG menu path **Financial Accounting • General Ledger Accounting • Master Data • G/L Accounts • Financial Statement Structures • Semantic Tags for Financial Statement Structures • Define Semantic Tags for Financial Statement Structures**. Figure 10.22 shows a list of the semantic tags, including many that are familiar from Chapter 7: accrued cost, accrued revenue, actual cost, cost of sales adjustments, revenue adjustments, billed revenue, cost of goods sold, and so on. These are not part of the Universal Journal but are evaluated when the report is run by selecting the data posted to the assigned general ledger accounts.

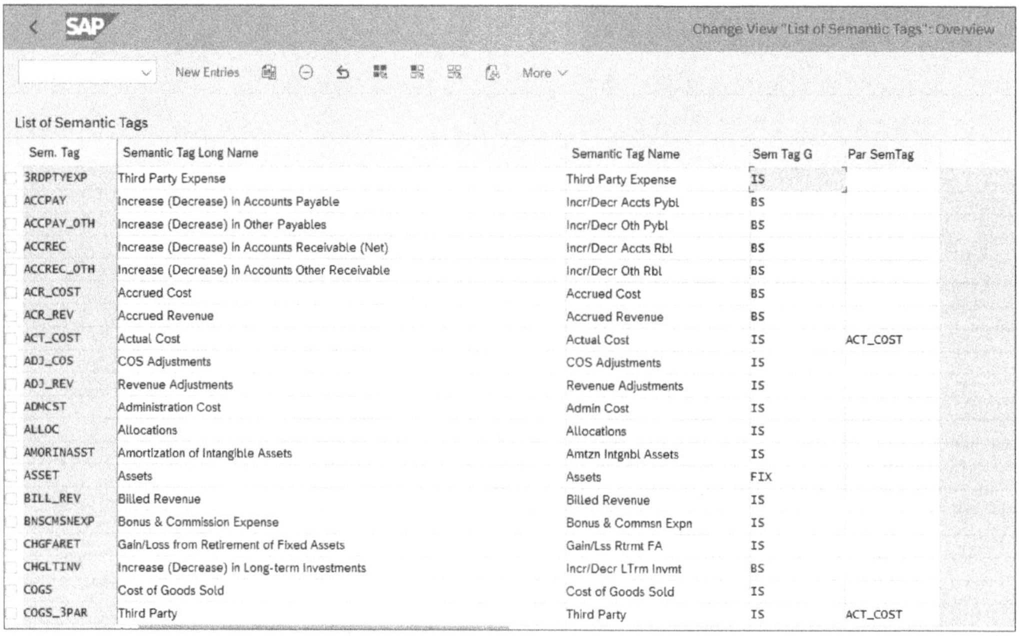

SAP Change View "List of Semantic Tags": Overview

New Entries More

List of Semantic Tags

| Sem. Tag | Semantic Tag Long Name | Semantic Tag Name | Sem Tag G | Par SemTag |
|---|---|---|---|---|
| 3RDPTYEXP | Third Party Expense | Third Party Expense | IS | |
| ACCPAY | Increase (Decrease) in Accounts Payable | Incr/Decr Accts Pybl | BS | |
| ACCPAY_OTH | Increase (Decrease) in Other Payables | Incr/Decr Oth Pybl | BS | |
| ACCREC | Increase (Decrease) in Accounts Receivable (Net) | Incr/Decr Accts Rbl | BS | |
| ACCREC_OTH | Increase (Decrease) in Accounts Other Receivable | Incr/Decr Oth Rbl | BS | |
| ACR_COST | Accrued Cost | Accrued Cost | BS | |
| ACR_REV | Accrued Revenue | Accrued Revenue | BS | |
| ACT_COST | Actual Cost | Actual Cost | IS | ACT_COST |
| ADJ_COS | COS Adjustments | COS Adjustments | IS | |
| ADJ_REV | Revenue Adjustments | Revenue Adjustments | IS | |
| ADMCST | Administration Cost | Admin Cost | IS | |
| ALLOC | Allocations | Allocations | IS | |
| AMORINASST | Amortization of Intangible Assets | Amtzn Intgnbl Assets | IS | |
| ASSET | Assets | Assets | FIX | |
| BILL_REV | Billed Revenue | Billed Revenue | IS | |
| BNSCMSNEXP | Bonus & Commission Expense | Bonus & Commsn Expn | IS | |
| CHGFARET | Gain/Loss from Retirement of Fixed Assets | Gain/Lss Rtrmt FA | IS | |
| CHGLTINV | Increase (Decrease) in Long-term Investments | Incr/Decr LTrm Invmt | BS | |
| COGS | Cost of Goods Sold | Cost of Goods Sold | IS | |
| COGS_3PAR | Third Party | Third Party | IS | ACT_COST |

**Figure 10.22** Partial List of Semantic Tags

Before you can display information related to semantic tags in SAP Fiori applications, you must link them with a financial statement version and the relevant accounts (and functional area, where relevant). To select data for the **Billed Revenue** tag, enter the accounts used to capture the relevant revenues. If you work with different charts of accounts in the various countries that you operate in, we suggest you use just one semantic tag for each key figure so that you can use the same report in every country/region. However, you should assign the country-specific accounts using the relevant financial statement versions. To assign accounts and, if necessary, functional areas to the delivered semantic tags, follow IMG menu path **Financial Accounting • General Ledger Accounting • Master Data • G/L Accounts Financial Statement Structures • Semantic Tags for Financial Statement Structures • Assign Semantic Tags for Financial Statement Structures.**

Figure 10.23 shows the assignment of the financial statement items to the semantic tags. Alternatively, you can assign the semantic tag to the account group directly in the Manage Global Hierarchies app shown previously in Figure 10.7.

To illustrate the relationship between the semantic tags and the underlying accounts, let's return to the Product Profitability app that we looked at in Chapter 7. In Figure 10.24, the rows of the report are based on the measures for the semantic tags (**Billed Revenue**, **Sales Deduction**, etc.), and we've selected the **G/L Account** dimension from the panel on the left and pulled it into the **ROWS** section to show which accounts are behind the billed revenues and sales deductions.

Mapping of Financial Statement Version to Semantic Tag

| FS Vers | FS Item | Sem. Tag | Account From |
|---|---|---|---|
| L000 | 10 | _COST | |
| L000 | 10 | COGS_SUTI | |
| L000 | 11 | ACT_COST | |
| L000 | 8 | ACT_COST | |
| L000 | 8 | COGS_DMAT | |
| L000 | 9 | ACT_COST | |
| Z900 | 1 | COST | |
| Z900 | 1 | COST1 | |
| Z900 | 10 | INVENTORY | |
| Z900 | 100 | RECO_REV | |
| Z900 | 108 | ZSELLEXP | |
| Z900 | 109 | ZGAEXP | |
| Z900 | 110 | AMORINASST | |
| Z900 | 110 | DPRTASSET | |
| Z900 | 110 | ZDEP | |
| Z900 | 111 | OOPEREXP | |
| Z900 | 112 | COST1 | |
| Z900 | 113 | CHGFARET | |
| Z900 | 114 | PROVISIONS | |
| Z900 | 13 | TANGASSETS | |

**Figure 10.23** Assignment of Financial Statement Items to Semantic Tags

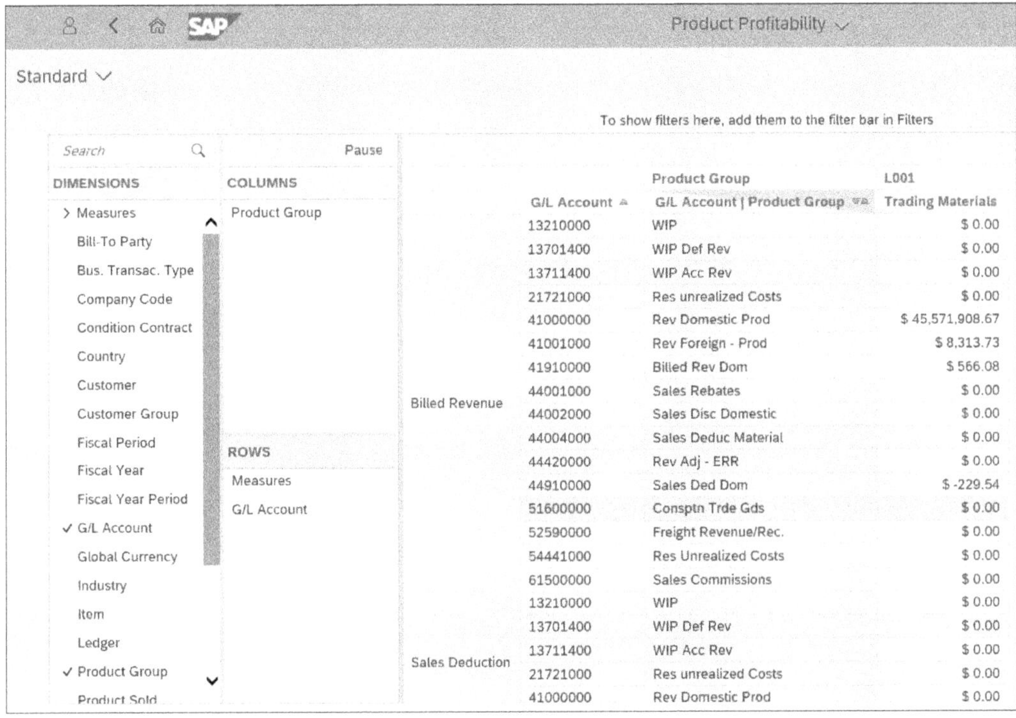


**Figure 10.24** Product Profitability App, Showing General Ledger Accounts

The idea that the semantic tags are an aggregation of the amounts on the assigned accounts holds true for many of the key figures in the Product Profitability app, which use the logic shown for **Billed Revenue** and **Sales Deduction**. However, if you refer back to Chapter 7, Figure 7.3, you'll see that there are also key figures showing the fixed and variable cost of goods sold. The fixed and variable part of the cost of goods sold is stored in the Universal Journal in group currency only. To calculate the values in local currency, the system selects the totals from the Universal Journal using the `I_GLAccountLineItemRawData` CDS view and calculates the figure in the company code currency (`FixedAmountInCoCodeCrcy`) when you run the report using the proportion between the fixed and variable costs in the group currency.

The semantic tags are also used in overview pages like the Sales Accounting Overview app (SAP Fiori F3228) shown in Figure 10.25. These apps show the performance for an individual key figure, such as the **Sales Deductions Benchmark** in the first card, or a combination of key figures, such as the **Gross Profit Decomposition** in the third card, where you can see the decomposition of the billed revenues as a result of the sales deductions, revenue adjustments, fixed and variable cost of goods sold, and price adjustments to determine the contribution margin.

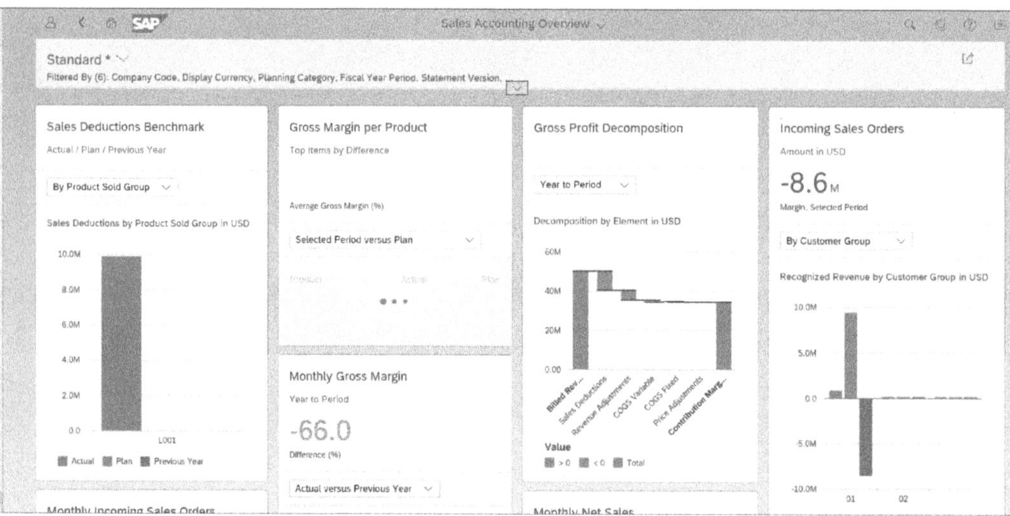


Figure 10.25 Sales Accounting Overview

Of course, the accounts and key figures are not completely unrelated. If you look at the selection parameters behind the report shown in Figure 10.25, presented in Figure 10.26, you'll see that you're still selecting by **Ledger**, **Statement Version**, and **G/L Account**.

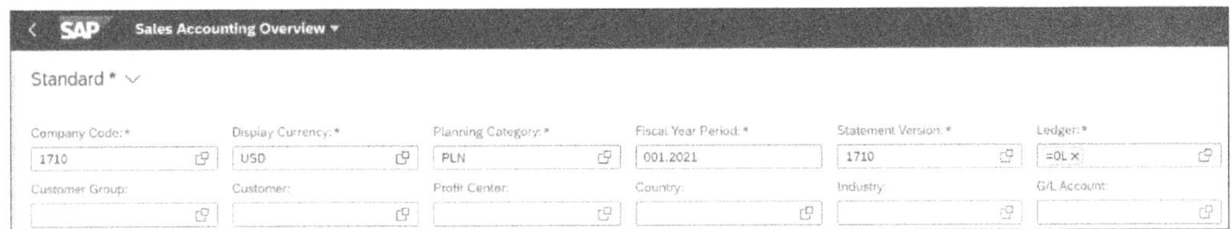


**Figure 10.26** Selection Parameters for Sales Accounting Overview

This approach works as a way of delivering easily consumable key figures for amounts that are captured by account and can then be aggregated according to the semantic tags, but you also need to consider other key figures in controlling, such as quantity information, in order to deliver the invoice quantity for product profitability reporting.



## 10.5 Key Figure Reporting

These key figures are essentially *aggregations* of the various accounts used to structure the figures in the financial statements—but margin analysis also requires the analysis of the various sales volumes. We'll turn our attention to these key figures next. Sales reporting also requires key figures that are based on *quantities* rather than amounts, such as the billed quantity in the Product Profitability app. Every time an invoice or delivery is recorded in profitability analysis, the system will update the quantity in the MSL field (**Quantity**) and the CO_MEGBTR field (**CO Valuation Quantity**) in the Universal Journal. However, many organizations find that these quantities get recorded in whatever unit of measure is needed by the logistics process, such as blister packs of drugs, boxes of washing powder, or sacks of coffee—and then they can't add blister packs to pill boxes to bottles of cough mixture to get a reliable picture of total sales volumes. To report across the whole organization, they need to convert this quantity into a unit of measure that is consistent across the organization. For this reason, SAP has provided three extra fields in the Universal Journal: **Additional Quantity 1–3**. These quantities are whatever you define them to be, so you might convert, say, all quantities into kilograms in order to be able to aggregate across the organization.

To define an additional quantity, go to **Controlling • General Controlling • Additional Amounts • Define Additional Quantity Fields**, then enter your chosen quantity and unit of measure, as shown in Figure 10.27. This will activate the **Additional Quantity 1–3** fields in the Universal Journal.

You'll then be able to use a business add-in (BAdI) to fill these additional fields using whatever logic you need to fill the appropriate quantity fields. Usually, this information can be derived from the various units of measure in the material master.

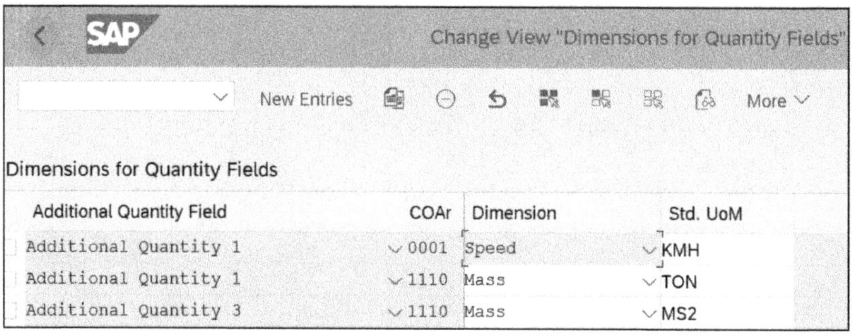

Figure 10.27 Additional Quantities in Margin Analysis

Quantity information is equally important for production and inventory reporting, with inventory quantities being recorded in apps such as the Material Inventory Values—Line Items app, shown in Figure 10.28. Material inputs and outputs are key elements in apps such as the Production Cost Analysis app and Costs by Work Center and Operation app, as discussed in Chapter 6.

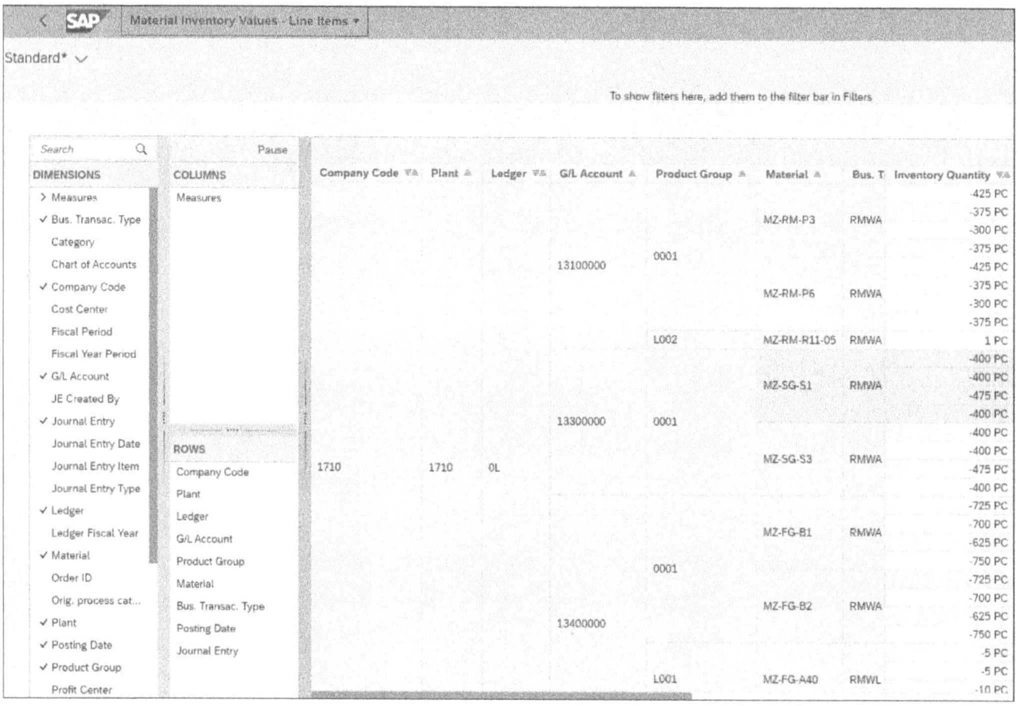

Figure 10.28 Material Inventory Values—Line Items App

Although the reporting of sales and production volumes represents the most obvious need for quantity-based reporting in controlling, statistical key figures are also commonly used to represent the number of full-time equivalents (FTEs) working on a cost center or the amount of floor space occupied by a cost center, as discussed in Chapter 4. Statistical key figures have their own master records and a series of transactions to update the relevant values so that they can be used both for reporting and as a basis for allocations. So far nothing has changed in SAP S/4HANA, so you will still be able to create statistical key figures with respect to cost centers, projects, orders, and so on using Transaction KB31N (Enter Statistical Key Figures).

**SAP ERP versus SAP S/4HANA**

In SAP ERP, statistical key figures were recorded in various different tables: the Controlling tables (COSR), the profit center tables (GLPCT), and the general ledger tables (FAGLSKF). But in SAP S/4HANA, a new table has been introduced that stores all key figures in a structure that is closer to that of the Universal Journal (FINSSKF).



The first SAP Fiori app to display statistical key figures by cost center is the Statistical Key Figure Items app (SAP Fiori ID F2766). Figure 10.29 shows the number of machines operating in three bike manufacturing cost centers and the number of employees working there.

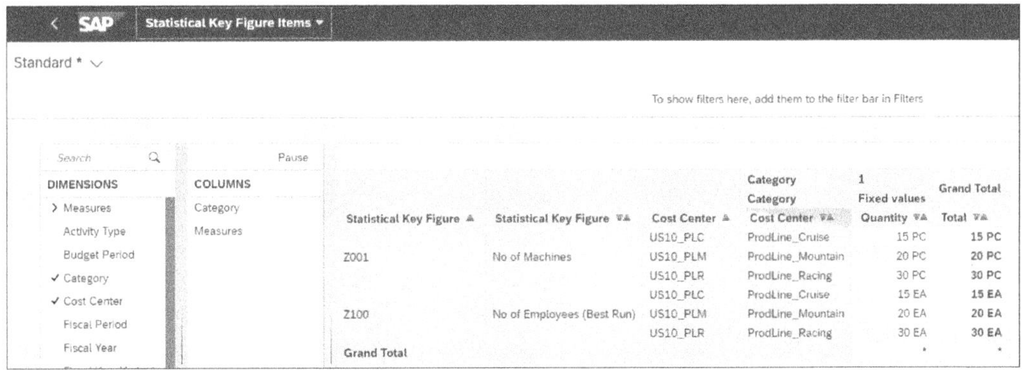


**Figure 10.29** Statistical Key Figure Items App

## 10.6 Compatibility Views: Report Writer

It's exciting to look at all the new reports on offer, but most organizations aren't starting their SAP journey from scratch and need to understand how much of their existing reporting infrastructure will continue to work as before. For this reason, we'll finish by looking at the role of the *compatibility views* to ensure backward compatibility.

In the introduction to this chapter, we said that the key to keeping your existing reports running was the existence of *compatibility views*. If you want to continue to work with the same financial statement report that you used in SAP ERP, the FAGLFLEXT view allows you to access the relevant information directly from the Universal Journal; however, you can only drill down by the account, segment, profit center, and cost center (the fields that were in table FAGLFLEXT), not by the huge number of dimensions that we showed in the Trial Balance app illustrated in Chapter 2. If you want to continue to work with your old cost center reports, order reports, project reports, and so on, then the COSP, COSS, and COEP views convert the accounts back into cost elements, chunk the line items into period blocks, and display the relevant information in the familiar format. But be aware that making these selections on the fly isn't as efficient as reading preaggregated data from the old totals reports and line item tables, and you might experience performance issues if you're selecting very large amounts of data.

Figure 10.30 shows the compatibility view for the primary cost table (COSP), and similar views exist for the secondary costs (COSS) and line items tables (COEP). If you're currently extracting information from Controlling to SAP Business Warehouse (SAP BW), then you can continue to use the old extractors, such as 0CCA_C11: CO-OM-CCA: Costs and Allocations, 0CCA_C02: CO-OM-CCA: Costs and Allocations (by Activity Type), and 0PC_C01: CO-PC: Cost Object Controlling; they will also use these compatibility views to select the data from SAP S/4HANA and move it to your data warehouse.

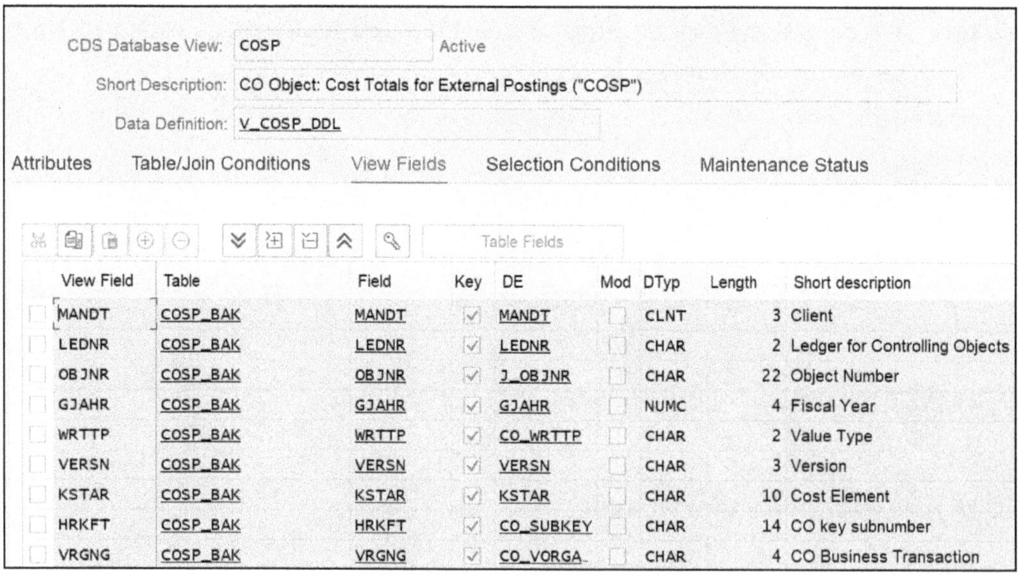

CDS Database View: COSP Active

Short Description: CO Object: Cost Totals for External Postings ("COSP")

Data Definition: V_COSP_DDL

Attributes Table/Join Conditions View Fields Selection Conditions Maintenance Status

Table Fields

| View Field | Table | Field | Key | DE | Mod | DTyp | Length | Short description |
|---|---|---|---|---|---|---|---|---|
| MANDT | COSP_BAK | MANDT | ✓ | MANDT | | CLNT | 3 | Client |
| LEDNR | COSP_BAK | LEDNR | ✓ | LEDNR | | CHAR | 2 | Ledger for Controlling Objects |
| OBJNR | COSP_BAK | OBJNR | ✓ | J_OBJNR | | CHAR | 22 | Object Number |
| GJAHR | COSP_BAK | GJAHR | ✓ | GJAHR | | NUMC | 4 | Fiscal Year |
| WRTTP | COSP_BAK | WRTTP | ✓ | CO_WRTTP | | CHAR | 2 | Value Type |
| VERSN | COSP_BAK | VERSN | ✓ | VERSN | | CHAR | 3 | Version |
| KSTAR | COSP_BAK | KSTAR | ✓ | KSTAR | | CHAR | 10 | Cost Element |
| HRKFT | COSP_BAK | HRKFT | ✓ | CO_SUBKEY | | CHAR | 14 | CO key subnumber |
| VRGNG | COSP_BAK | VRGNG | ✓ | CO_VORGA | | CHAR | 4 | CO Business Transaction |

**Figure 10.30** Compatibility View for Primary Costs

Within core SAP S/4HANA, you'll need to rely on these compatibility reports to compare the target costs with the actual costs on your cost centers or to look at cost center variances as we showed in Chapter 2, and you'll have to make a conscious choice when reporting on production orders and maintenance orders as to whether you will rely on the old reports that are part of the order maintenance transactions or move to SAP Fiori applications such as the Production Cost Analysis app and the Costs by Work Center and Operation app. You'll also be relying on the legacy reports for any Project System reports that combine information from the work breakdown structure (WBS) elements with the assigned orders, networks, and so on and to display the figures calculated in results analysis.

The reports listed under **Information System • Cost Element Accounting** are exceptions to this rule because these reports read from the reconciliation ledger (table COFI) in SAP ERP, which is no longer available in SAP S/4HANA. This shouldn't be a cause for concern as you can easily use the object type available in most financial reports to drill down to the various controlling account assignments. Figure 10.31 and Figure 10.32 show the P&L Plan/Actual app (SAP Fiori ID F0927A), in which we've drilled down from a list of accounts to the profitability segments (object type **EO**), cost center/activity types (object type **KL**), cost centers (object type **KS**), orders (object type **OR**), and projects (object type **PR**). This gives you the same information as in the old cost element reports but will require your IT team to implement the relevant SAP Fiori applications.



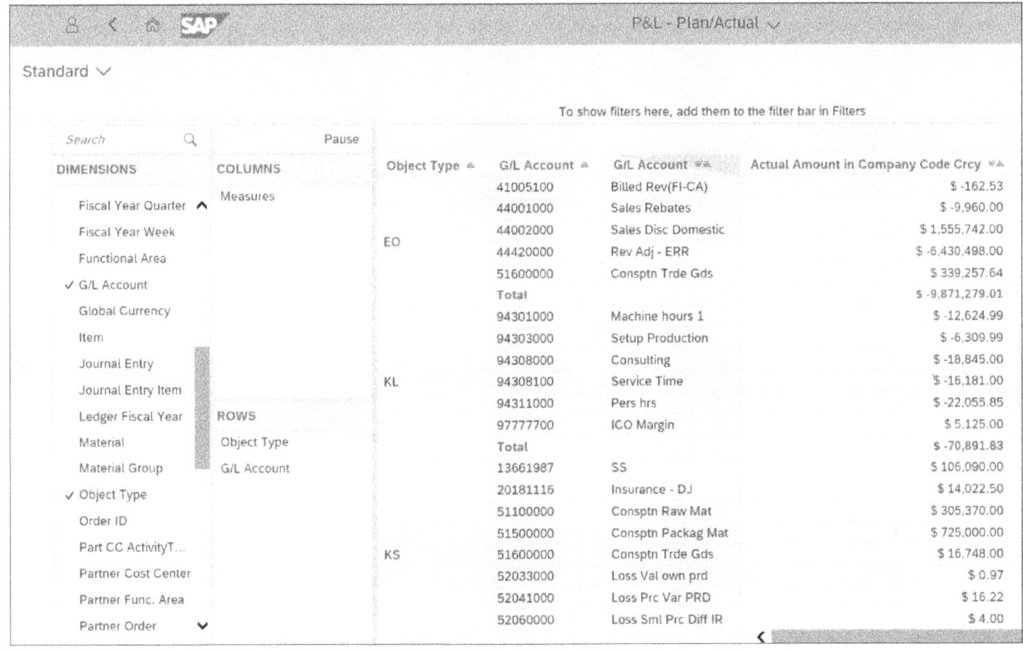


**Figure 10.31** P&L with Object Types EO, KL, and KS

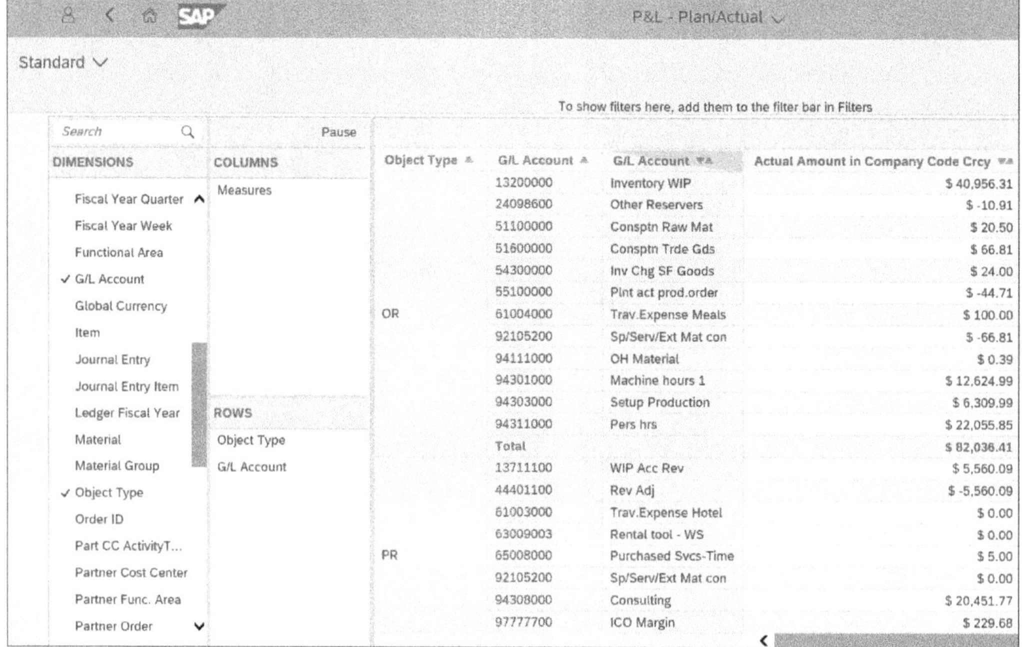


| Object Type | G/L Account | G/L Account | Actual Amount in Company Code Crcy |
|---|---|---|---|
| OR | 13200000 | Inventory WIP | $ 40,956.31 |
| | 24098600 | Other Reservers | $ -10.91 |
| | 51100000 | Consptn Raw Mat | $ 20.50 |
| | 51600000 | Consptn Trde Gds | $ 66.81 |
| | 54300000 | Inv Chg SF Goods | $ 24.00 |
| | 55100000 | Plnt act prod.order | $ -44.71 |
| | 61004000 | Trav.Expense Meals | $ 100.00 |
| | 92105200 | Sp/Serv/Ext Mat con | $ -66.81 |
| | 94111000 | OH Material | $ 0.39 |
| | 94301000 | Machine hours 1 | $ 12,624.99 |
| | 94303000 | Setup Production | $ 6,309.99 |
| | 94311000 | Pers hrs | $ 22,055.85 |
| | Total | | $ 82,036.41 |
| PR | 13711100 | WIP Acc Rev | $ 5,560.09 |
| | 44401100 | Rev Adj | $ -5,560.09 |
| | 61003000 | Trav.Expense Hotel | $ 0.00 |
| | 63009003 | Rental tool - WS | $ 0.00 |
| | 65008000 | Purchased Svcs-Time | $ 5.00 |
| | 92105200 | Sp/Serv/Ext Mat con | $ 0.00 |
| | 94308000 | Consulting | $ 20,451.77 |
| | 97777700 | ICO Margin | $ 229.68 |

**Figure 10.32** P&L with Object Types OR and PR

## 10.7 Summary

In this chapter, we introduced the virtual data model and the cluster of views that provide the basis for reporting using SAP Fiori. We looked at the various ways of structuring information hierarchically by creating global hierarchies and flexible hierarchies, and we explained how to use semantic tags to create key figures in the overview reports and for profitability reporting. Finally, we looked at how compatibility views allow you to reuse many of the reports originally delivered with SAP ERP and how to replace the reports for cost element accounting that are no longer supported in SAP S/4HANA.

Now that we've looked at reporting, we've almost completed the journey through controlling. We'll end by taking a look into the future to see some of the features that are expected to be delivered in future releases.

Chapter 11

# Conclusion and Outlook

*In this chapter, we'll briefly revisit each of the previous chapters for a recap of the main topics. We'll recall recent discussions we've had with companies about these topics and discuss some of the planned developments in each area.*



We've been on a journey that has taken us from SAP S/4HANA Finance to what makes up controlling. Within controlling, we've looked at the organizational structures and the master data that structures your activities and explored overhead controlling, production controlling, sales controlling, and investment controlling. We've looked at the move from products to services, the impact of increased globalization on the controlling function, and how reporting is changing with the new technology.

We hope you now feel more confident, but we know that there's still plenty to talk about, including topics you might think would be basics: when to use a cost center and when to use a profit center, how profit centers differ from market segments, and whether standard costs are better than actual costs. In recent years, the new conversations focus on service management and how best to set up ledgers and currencies for controlling. One of the challenges of writing a book when you're part of the development organization is that you know what's on the horizon one to two years out, but many of these things won't reach the average controller for several years. For this reason, we'll close the book by reviewing each of the previous chapters, recounting some of the major customer discussions, and introducing roadmap items when we can say with a degree of certainty that there's something coming down the pipeline.

Let's recap the chapters and take a look at what's ahead:

- **Chapter 1: Introduction to SAP S/4HANA**
  The aim of the first chapter was to explain the major concepts of SAP S/4HANA, including the Universal Journal as the new data model and SAP Fiori as the new user interface. While the impact of running a cost center report as an SAP Fiori app on your smartphone rather than on your desktop might be obvious, the implications of bringing together the formerly separate applications for general ledger accounting, profit center accounting, management accounting, and margin analysis are more significant if you're making the move from SAP ERP, in which each of these applications had its own separate data store. In the long term, this is a simplification, but in the short term it involves a degree of change management as cost elements become accounts and the market segments move into the Universal Journal. We've had

plenty of conversations about both topics, with the market segments getting particular attention as organizations move from the B2B world into the B2C world, which generally involves managing many more end customers than before.

Probably the most significant change is in the deployment options, with the choice of running your finance system in the cloud or on-premise. Running on-premise SAP S/4HANA means having your IT team upgrade your database from SAP ERP to SAP HANA, converting the core applications to run SAP S/4HANA, and then deciding whether you want to use the SAP Fiori applications rather than the more familiar SAP GUI transactions. Your IT team control the servers, the upgrade path, and the testing. Running SAP S/4HANA Cloud, by contrast, means letting SAP or another provider manage your IT system, install the quarterly upgrades, and activate the best practice content. The functional scope of your system is determined by scope items, whether these are broad items, such as J54 for Overhead Cost Accounting or J55 for Margin Analysis, or more specific items, such as 34B for Statistical Sales Conditions or 2I3 for Commitment Management. We've tried to reference the relevant scope items as appropriate in the text.

The choice between cloud and on-premise might sound like an either-or decision, but most on-premise implementations involve a degree of cloud thinking in the sense that most organizations revisit the rationale behind any modifications made in previous implementations. You may not be ready to work entirely within the constraints of the delivered scope items, but there is a quest to return to standard and reduce some of the costs associated with an upgrade by reducing the number of modifications in your system. Cloud tools are gradually becoming available in the on-premise world, so whereas you might previously have added your own fields to a cost center by activating a user exit, you might now choose to use the cloud extensibility tools. Similarly, where organizations used to extend their coding blocks and their operating concerns using tools in the IMG, now they can use the cloud extensibility tools to add fields and enable data entry in the various applications. With the current economic climate, the move from the capital expense of a major IT implementation to the operational expense of software as a service is appealing, but we advise organizations to assess their options carefully to make sure that the implementation delivers the business value that your organization needs. This book shows you what's possible as of the time of writing.

- **Chapter 2: Controlling in SAP S/4HANA**
  In the next chapter, we looked at the role of controlling within SAP S/4HANA, explaining the impact of the merge of financial and management accounting within the Universal Journal and illustrating the different journal entries for primary costs and revenues and secondary costs and the value flows that make up the cost of goods sold for a product. We then introduced the new approach to planning and explained how the plan is used to set budgets for spending and targets for business performance before looking at how to create predictive journal entries for incoming

sales orders and commitments. We then looked at the key elements of cost center planning and reporting, product cost planning and reporting, and profitability planning and reporting, ending with some more general comments on reporting and analytics using both SAP Fiori and the classic transactions.

Our aim was to introduce the main value flows in terms of how materials are bought, made, and sold and how costs flow through the organization, and to use the modern SAP Fiori applications for the allocation flows and material value chains as illustrations alongside classic reports for the analysis of cost center variances. As a new generation of controllers enters the workplace, the expert knowledge enshrined in transaction lists and cheat sheets is gradually being replaced by a set of intuitive apps that help controllers to visualize the value flows in the organization and find all related documents, but the SAP Fiori roadmap is by no means complete. Some organizations still choose to wait rather than embrace the new user interfaces to avoid confusing their end users.



If you're coming to SAP S/4HANA from a non-SAP environment, then the Universal Journal generally feels perfectly natural, while migrating users are unlearning the data silos that structured their financial thinking for so long and embracing the new approach. In the first months of SAP S/4HANA, there was often a fear that controlling had "gone away," but these fears are gone now. Most users now realize that the Universal Journal is just a different way of storing their cost center, project, and margin information, one that readily reconciles with the profit center and company code view.

We have had many conversations about the differences between planning using the classic transactions and planning with SAP Analytics Cloud for SAP S/4HANA Finance as there isn't a 1:1 link between the planning transactions in SAP ERP and the new planning applications. However, we're gradually seeing companies that are implementing SAP S/4HANA downloading the business content and exploring the delivered planning stories for integrated financial planning. If you're using a modern version of SAP S/4HANA on-premise, one compromise can be to use the transfer functionality delivered to move planned data between the transactional tables COSP/COSS and ACDOCP and the activity price tables COST and ACCOSTRATE to deliver a hybrid approach to planning during the cutover period.

Going forward, integrated financial planning has been enhanced with the addition of a simulation cockpit to simulate the impact of changed raw material costs or sales volumes on the plan. Work continues on the SAP Fiori roadmap and to deliver predictive accounting. At the time of writing, the new approach to predictive accounting doesn't yet support the make-to-order or engineer-to-order environment and you can't yet post commitments to internal orders. Stay abreast of changes by checking the information published in the SAP roadmaps at *https://www.sap.com/products/roadmaps.html*. You can then search by overhead cost management to see the various items planned for SAP S/4HANA and SAP S/4HANA Cloud over the next quarters.

- **Chapter 3: Organizational Structures**
  Whatever type of organization you work in, getting your organizational structures and your master data correct will stand you in good stead as the organizational structures are the backbone of your controlling implementation. In Chapter 3, we walked you through the various organizational structures in finance and logistics to make sure that the use case was clear for each entity, explaining the difference between an affiliated company and a company code, a profit center and a functional area, and the various organizational assignments made in logistics. You might expect these entities to remain stable, but there are plans to introduce additional business segmentations to be derived from the profit center in order to allow organizations to better structure their divisional and segment reporting and deliver an improved steering model with a structure derived, like the profit center itself, from the underlying objects in controlling. That model can exist in addition to the company codes that structure the entity close and the trading partners that structure the activities in the group close.

  We ended the chapter by introducing the link between the ledgers and the accounting principles. The basic idea was originally introduced with the SAP ERP general ledger, in which the general ledger is structured by ledgers for the different accounting principles. With SAP S/4HANA, the goal is to include the ledger as an entity not just in the general ledger but also in asset accounting, controlling, and actual costing. For groups operating in several countries, the idea is to have a common ledger in which all assigned company codes use the same accounting principle and an additional ledger that handles the different accounting principles required by each company code. In SAP ERP, only the leading ledger was linked with controlling, so only one valuation from asset accounting or financial accounting could be used to set your activity prices and value inventory. Where multiple valuations were needed in controlling, it was possible to activate an additional business function (FIN_CO_COGM) and use additional versions to handle parallel valuations in controlling. With SAP S/4HANA, the goal is to make the ledgers available in every controlling application so that you can allocate and settle differently in each ledger in overhead controlling. In the future, you'll be able to create ledger-specific cost estimates, update WIP and inventory differently depending on the ledger in manufacturing, and recognize revenue and post cost of goods sold differently for sales controlling. In SAP S/4HANA Cloud, this will be the default, with the business content being adjusted accordingly. In SAP S/4HANA on-premise, the new options will be accessed via a business function as the scope is not expected to be complete in the initial delivery. Further planned changes involve the activation of additional currencies within the ledgers and structural changes, such as the ability to handle different fiscal year variants depending on the ledger.

- **Chapter 4: Master Data**
  Master data is an area in which many organizations struggle. We often see organizations with as many cost centers as they have employees and general ledger accounts being used in an inconsistent manner. In the fourth chapter, we explained the

accounts, cost centers, activity types, statistical key figures, internal orders, projects, and market segments and what attributes are associated with each piece of master data. Getting your master data right is an essential part of your implementation, and it's important to have a clear understanding of the correct usage of each of the elements. The most significant change compared to SAP ERP is that secondary cost elements are now treated as accounts and that there is no separate reconciliation account when a secondary cost posting impacts the financial accounts. From a controlling point of view, the key point is the difference between an activity type such as machine time or consulting hours, which must be captured either during time recording or the logistics processes, and a statistical key figure such as headcount or square feet of floorspace, which is simply used to establish ratios between the various cost centers as a basis for an allocation.

With the announcement that SAP S/4HANA Cloud will only support work breakdown structure (WBS) elements and not internal orders, many customers have been concerned that internal orders will disappear from on-premise, but this isn't the case. However, if you're doing a new implementation (or starting afresh rather than migrating your existing SAP ERP setup), it makes sense to review the order types that you use today. Logistics orders, such as a production orders, process orders, maintenance orders, service orders, and so on, continue to be supported. For internal orders, it makes sense to distinguish between orders that are simply account assignments, such as those entered as default account assignments in Transaction OKB9 (default account assignment) or as senders in a costing sheet, and orders that represent simple projects. If you switch to using WBS elements instead of orders, you'll be able to perform event-based revenue recognition, as we explained in Chapter 7. But beware: if you're using internal orders that are assigned to investment program items, WBS elements, or sales order items, you'll only be able to report on these orders using the classic transactions and won't be able to use the new SAP Fiori applications.

In SAP S/4HANA Cloud, the default operating concern is hidden, and any additional market segments are added using the Custom Fields and Logic app. In SAP S/4HANA, you can choose between extending the operating concern using the classic transactions and taking the new approach, which adds fields to the Universal Journal without populating table `CE4XXXX` for the profitability segments. In the master data you have the same choices, so you can continue to add your own fields to the cost centers by activating user exit `COOMKS01` (Cost Center: Customer-Specific Additional Fields in the Master Record), or you can use the Custom Fields and Logic app to extend the cost center master data context. This doesn't mean that you have to change your master data overnight, but it's worth being aware of what's in store if you're doing a new implementation.

- **Chapter 5: Overhead Controlling**
  With the organizational structures and master data in place, we turned our attention in Chapter 5 to overhead controlling, a topic that is relevant in every industry, from

banks and retailers to manufacturers and service providers. We began by looking at the role of the cost center and project managers as stewards of the external spend required within the organization. We then showed how the cost center managers can understand the asset depreciation being transferred to the cost center and use the Document Flow app to see the details of any assets or materials they might have acquired and how to manage their budget using active availability control.

We then looked in detail at how to plan cost center costs and use them to calculate activity rates in anticipation of direct and indirect activity allocations. We turned our attention to how costs flow from the cost centers in the form of allocations, looking at the various business transactions, including reposting, universal allocation, activity allocation, overhead calculation, and template allocation. We ended by explaining how costs flow from orders and projects using settlement. The obvious roadmap item in this section concerns SAP Fiori, with universal allocation and reposting being available via SAP Fiori apps, but the other business transactions still running in SAP GUI. We discussed some of the gaps in universal allocation compared to the classic transactions and how work is underway to extend the offering to cover intercompany sender-receiver relationships and iterative cycles.

At the start of our description of the business transactions, we showed the old period lock transaction, as well as the new approach available with release 2020 that allows you to lock a combination of a company code and business transaction so that you can, for example, close company codes in Asia while keeping those in the United States open until their business day ends.

The other major changes on the horizon affect the number of currencies supported in controlling (three are planned for SAP S/4HANA Cloud and a maximum of 10 in on-premise) and the introduction of ledger-specific postings for all allocations and settlements in overhead management.

- **Chapter 6: Controlling for Manufacturing Organizations**
  In the sixth chapter, we returned to the topic of master data with a focus on manufacturing, looking at elements such as the material master, bill of materials (BOM), routing, and work centers in order to explain all the information that must be in place before you can create a cost estimate for a material to be manufactured in house. After we explained how to create a cost estimate, we looked at how raw material costs are captured in procurement and the various impacts on the purchase price variances. We then looked at three types of manufacturing: make-to-stock using production orders, make-to-stock using product cost collectors, and make-to-order using sales orders. We explained how the approach to the calculation of work in process (WIP) is changing from an after-the-fact calculation at period close to a real-time posting that is updated following every goods movement and confirmation. As we look to the future, we see make-to-stock giving way to make-to-order as consumers become ever more demanding in their requirements, and we see the large lot sizes of the past giving way to a lot size of one. The challenge for controllers

is to deal with this increased complexity while ensuring that the product purchased continues to be profitable and that margins are not being eaten away by the consumers' demand for ever more sophisticated features.

Parallel accounting will also have a major impact on product costing, bringing new tables for both the activity prices and the material prices and dedicated cost estimates for each ledger. This will in turn affect the way WIP and variances are captured and the material value chains in actual costing, which will all take the different ledgers into account. We're also seeing a move from pure product companies to companies offering services in combination with products. This doesn't just mean providing an after-sales service or returns process but a different way of delivering and paying for the products used. At one time, customers would have purchased machine tools in a hardware store, for example, but now they might lease them, pay by use, or even rent them for the short period for which they're needed.

- **Chapter 7: Margin Analysis for Products and Services**

  In Chapter 7, we reiterated the need for flexible market segments. We explained how the various sales, project, and service scenarios are handled in margin analysis and introduced generic functions for allocation and top-down distribution that can be used to assign costs in all environments.

  We then explained the master data needed for sales and used an example in which we sold the product that we manufactured in the previous chapter to show how the cost of goods sold is combined with revenues to deliver a view of the product's profitability. We extended this view to show the impact of predictive accounting in anticipating sales revenue and cost of goods sold and how this is cancelled as the order is fulfilled.

  Next, we revisited the business transactions from Chapter 5 in the context of margin analysis and showed how universal allocation can also be used in the context of margin analysis to distribute costs to more granular market segments or to allocate costs from a cost center to a market segment.

  After that, we looked at customer projects, beginning with those in the professional services industry and then looking at engineer-to-order projects. We showed how to plan these service projects, perform time recording, post travel expenses, and generate accrued revenue in association with the costs captured and what tasks are needed at period close. We then compared this with the handling of engineering projects, this time focusing on the delivery of finished goods in association with the project, and explained how the project stock is valuated.

  Then we explored generic functions, such as realigning market segments if the organizational structures change. We also looked at margin analysis in a service scenario and the new options for service confirmation, how to issue spare parts, and how to perform revenue recognition. The service scenario is new in SAP S/4HANA, so expect enhancements to the roadmap going forward as the requirements evolve in this business sector.

- **Chapter 8: Investment Controlling**
  After working through the operational processes to create goods and services to sell, we turned our attention in the eighth chapter to the costs associated with future investments and looked at how to create investment programs and assign orders and projects, how to plan capital expense projects, and how to use budget availability control to set a threshold for spending. We then looked at how the settlement of capital expense projects differs from the handling of commercial projects and the options to only capitalize some of the collected costs. We finished by looking at how to report capital expenses.

  There are currently many questions about the difference between investment management in SAP S/4HANA and SAP Project and Portfolio Management (SAP PPM). Investment management focuses on the finance side of portfolio management and handles capital expense undertakings within a single system, with all resource and timeline decisions being handled within Project System. SAP PPM offers additional functions for resource management and timeline management and manages a portfolio across multiple systems. The two approaches come together in the operational projects and orders and their link to assets under construction. SAP S/4HANA Cloud supports project management and the link to assets under construction but doesn't offer portfolio management functions. Here a new product, SAP S/4HANA Cloud for Projects, is under development. It will handle the approval and high-level planning and budgeting inherent in preparing an investment portfolio.

- **Chapter 9: Controlling in an Intercompany Environment**
  After we walked through how to manufacture products in Chapter 6 and sell them in Chapter 7, we looked at the requirements of a more complex supply chain featuring multiple trading partners in Chapter 9. We showed how to create a group cost estimate that began with a manufacturing plant in India, transported the goods to a distribution center in Germany, and delivered these to a selling company in the US for sale to the final customer. This group cost estimate used special procurement keys to link the various affiliated companies and delivered complete transparency into the manufacturing costs across the value chain. By contrast, in the legal cost estimate, each stock transfer was viewed as if the parts had been procured from an external vendor (arm's-length trading). We looked also at how this double flow with both a legal valuation and a group valuation is captured in actual costing and explained the benefits of using valuated stock in transit when there are long delays in transporting goods between the various entities.

  This area of controlling has been generating lots of interest in recent years as organizations become ever more international and start to bring their disparate ERP implementations into a common SAP S/4HANA platform. Group valuation arose out of the need to deliver a consistent steering model across the organization, with complete cost transparency in the group currency. In future releases of SAP S/4HANA, this value chain will be the focus of further developments that will eliminate intercompany markups at each intercompany border across the value chain. This will go hand in hand with new processes for intercompany sales and intercompany stock transfers that are planned to be delivered first in SAP S/4HANA Cloud.

Of course, it's not just physical goods that move around the world. Until the pandemic, consultants were moving around the world performing work for affiliated companies that would then be billed to the final customer. Even working from home, that same work is performed in a different physical company from the company that will invoice the customer for the services rendered. This process is known as *resource-related intercompany billing*, meaning that the resources (consultants, travel costs, etc.) are supplied by one company and then invoiced by the delivering company, which has the relationship with the final customer. When we looked at the delivery of consulting services in Chapter 7, the consulting hours were performed within one legal entity, but in an intercompany environment you can define different activity rates depending on the company code of the receiving entity, and this results in the posting of an additional intercompany margin. When the consultants are charging travel or materials to the receiving entity, you can also capture these expenses in the sending company and perform a reposting to charge them to the receiving company with an intercompany margin. Both the time and materials can then be invoiced to the final customer. This process is also generating a lot of interest as many consulting houses investigate SAP S/4HANA Cloud, in which it's delivered as a standard scope item.



- **Chapter 10: Reporting in SAP S/4HANA**
  Finally, in Chapter 10, we looked at the virtual data model behind the SAP Fiori applications and explained the use of global hierarchies and flexible hierarchies to structure your accounts and reporting dimensions. We then looked at the role of semantic tags to deliver stable key figures for reporting and how quantities are handled in the Universal Journal. Many organizations are gradually making the move away from the classic SAP GUI reports and embracing SAP Fiori and the new opportunities that it represents. In terms of *operational reporting*, in which the data collected is primarily stored within SAP S/4HANA, the challenge is for SAP to complete the roadmap and offer a virtual data model throughout controlling so that we no longer need to resort to using old reports to show target/actual comparisons and variance categories. There is also the broader question of the maturity of predictive accounting, which will determine whether the Incoming Sales Order app meets your needs or if you need to wait for engineer-to-order to be implemented.

  The question of data warehouses is a different one entirely. You can, of course, keep running an existing SAP Business Warehouse (SAP BW) and filling it using the existing extractors, which use compatibility views to access the old structures, or use the newer `0FI_ACDOCA_10` extractor to read directly from the Universal Journal. If you're already looking at SAP Analytics Cloud for planning as part of your planning process, then it's worth exploring its analytical capabilities. As you consider moving your operational systems to the cloud, you might also consider moving to SAP Data Warehouse Cloud, a cloud-based data warehouse.

Although the choice of data warehouse tends to be left to the IT team, with controllers mere consumers of the financial information stored within, we also see controllers moving into the realms of data science and using unstructured data sourced from data lakes to enhance their business insights. Sometimes they use sentiment analysis to anticipate trends in the marketplace and predict the kinds of products and services to be offered in the future.

# Appendices

# Appendix A
# Key Controlling Transactions

In the course of this book, we've given menu codes and transaction codes as we've introduced the various transactions. Table A.1 lists the main transactions in a quick reference guide. We've organized the list by the chapter in which the transaction is introduced.

| Chapters | Transaction Codes | Transaction Names |
|---|---|---|
| Chapter 3: Organizational Structures | OX15 | Maintain Company/Internal Trading Partner |
| | OBY6 | Create Company Code |
| | OKKP | Maintain Controlling Area |
| | KEA0 | Maintain Operating Concern |
| | OX10 | Maintain Plants |
| | OX18 | Assign Plants to Company Code |
| | OX01 | Assign Purchasing Organization to Company Code |
| | OVX5 | Sales Organization |
| | OVX3N | Assign Sales Organization to Company Code |
| Chapter 4: Master Data | FS00 | Change G/L Account Centrally (replaces cost element Transactions KA01–KA06) |
| | KAH1–KAH3 | Create/Change/Display Cost Element Groups |
| | OB58 | Financial Statement Versions |
| | OBC4 | Field Status Variants |
| | KS01–KS03 | Create/Change/Display Cost Center |
| | KSH1–KSH3 | Create/Change Display Cost Center Groups |
| | OKEON | Change Standard Cost Center Hierarchy |

**Table A.1** Transactions by Chapter

| Chapters | Transaction Codes | Transaction Names |
|---|---|---|
| | AS01–AS03 | Create/Change/Display Asset |
| | KE51–KE53 | Create/Change/Display Profit Center |
| | KL01–KL03 | Create/Change/Display Activity Type |
| | KLH1–KLH3 | Create/Change/Display Activity Type Groups |
| | KP26/KP27 | Change/Display Activity Rates |
| | KK01–KK03 | Create/Change/Display Statistical Key Figure |
| | KBH1–KBH3 | Create/Change/Display Statistical Key Figure Groups |
| | KO01–KO03 | Create/Change/Display Internal Orders |
| | CJ20N | Project Builder |
| | CJ01–CJ03 | Create/Change/Display Project |
| Chapter 5: Overhead Controlling | FB03 | Display Financial Document |
| | OKP1/OKP2 | Change/Display Period Lock |
| | KB31N–KB33N | Enter/Display Statistical Key Figures |
| | KB61 | Repost Line Items |
| | KB11N | Manual Reposting of Costs |
| | KB21N | Enter Direct Activity Allocation |
| | KB41N | Manual Reposting of Revenues |
| | KB51N | Enter Sender Activities |
| | KSU1–KSU3 | Create/Change/Display Assessment Cycles |
| | KSU5 | Run Assessment Cycles |
| | KSV1-KSV3 | Create/Change/Display Distribution Cycles |
| | KSV5 | Run Distribution Cycles |
| | KSC1–KSC3 | Create/Change/Display Indirect Activity Allocation |
| | KSC5 | Run Indirect Activity Allocation |

**Table A.1** Transactions by Chapter (Cont.)

| Chapters | Transaction Codes | Transaction Names |
|---|---|---|
| | KSII | Calculate Actual Activity Prices |
| | CON2 | Revaluate at Actual Activity Prices |
| | KSBT | Activity Price Report |
| | KGI2 | Calculate Overhead |
| | CPTA | Run Template Allocation |
| Chapter 6: Controlling for Manufacturing Organizations | MM01–MM03 | Create/Change/Display Material Master |
| | CS01–CS03 | Create/Change/Display Bill of Material (BOM) |
| | CA01–CA03 | Create/Change/Display Standard Routing |
| | CA21–CA23 | Create/Change/Display Rate Routing |
| | C201–C203 | Create/Change/Display Master Recipe |
| | CR01–CR03 | Create/Change/Display Work Center |
| | CRC1–CRC3 | Create/Change/Display Resource |
| | CK11N/CK13N | Create/Display Material Cost Estimate |
| | CK24 | Price Update |
| | CK40N | Manage Costing Run |
| | CKMATSEL | Create Selection List |
| | CKMATCON | Edit Selection List |
| | CKAPP03 | Display Sales Order to be Costed |
| | CK55 | Sales Documents: Mass Costing |
| | CK51N | Create Order BOM Cost Estimate |
| | ME21N | Create Purchase Order |
| | MIGO | Create Goods Receipt |
| | MIRO | Create Invoice Receipt |
| | CO01–CO03 | Create/Change/Display Production Order |
| | CR01–CR03 | Create/Change/Display Process Order |
| | KKBC_ORD | Display Costs for Production Order |

**Table A.1** Transactions by Chapter (Cont.)

| Chapters | Transaction Codes | Transaction Names |
|---|---|---|
| | CO11N | Enter Confirmation for Production Order |
| | KKAX/KKAO | Calculate Work in Process (Production Orders) |
| | KKS2/KKS1 | Calculate Production Variances (Production Orders) |
| | KO88 | Settle Production Orders |
| | CKM3N | Material Price Analysis |
| | CKMLCP | Create Actual Costing Run |
| | KKF6N | Create Product Cost Collector |
| | MFBF | Confirm Repetitive Manufacturing |
| | KKAS/KKAO | Calculate Work in Process (Product Cost Collectors) |
| | KKS6/KKS5 | Calculate Production Variances (Product Cost Collectors) |
| | KK87 | Settle Product Cost Collectors |
| | IW31–IW33 | Create/Change/Display Maintenance Order |
| Chapter 7: Margin Analysis for Products and Services | MM01–MM03 | Create/Change/Display Material Master |
| | BP | Create/Change/Display Business Partner |
| | VA01–VA03 | Create/Change/Display Sales Order |
| | VL01N–VL03N | Create/Change/Display Outbound Delivery |
| | VF01 | Create Billing Document |
| | KEND | Realignment of Profitability Segments |
| | KKA2 | Results Analysis for Project |
| | CJ88 | Project Settlement |
| Chapter 8: Investment Controlling | IM23 | Display Investment Program Structure |
| | IMA11 | Create Appropriation Request |
| | CJ40 | Create Overall Project Plan |
| | CJR2/CJR3 | Create/Display Project Plan by Cost Elements |

**Table A.1** Transactions by Chapter (Cont.)

| Chapters | Transaction Codes | Transaction Names |
|---|---|---|
| | IM34 | Roll Up of Plan Values |
| | IM32 | Edit Original Budget |
| | CJ30 | Create Project Budget |
| | CJIC | Perform Line Item Settlement |
| | IM_AVCHANA | Monitor Budget Availability for Investment Programs |
| | IM_AVCHANA_WBS | Monitor Budget Availability for WBS Elements |
| | IM_AVCHANA_ORD | Monitor Budget Availability for Orders |
| Chapter 9: Controlling in an Intercompany Environment | CK94 | Create Mixing Ratios |
| | DP91/DP93 | Intercompany Billing |

**Table A.1** Transactions by Chapter (Cont.)

# Appendix B
# Key SAP Fiori Applications for Controlling

We've introduced various SAP Fiori applications in this book, together with the SAP Fiori IDs that will help you to find the roles and catalogs that the application is associated with. In Table B.1, we provide a list as a quick reference guide, organized by the chapter in which the application is introduced.

| Chapter | SAP Fiori App ID | SAP Fiori App Name |
|---|---|---|
| Chapter 2: Controlling in SAP S/4HANA | F3664 | Display Journal Entries—In T-Account View |
| | F0707 | Manage Journal Entries |
| | F0956A | Trial Balance |
| | F2764 | Project Profitability |
| | F3871 | Cost Center Budget Report |
| | F3016 | Commitments by Cost Center |
| | F2964 | Incoming Sales Orders |
| | F3417 | Gross Margin—Presumed/Actual |
| | F3828 | Monitor Predictive Accounting |
| | F1780 | Production Cost Analysis |
| | F3331 | Analyze Costs by Work Center/Operation |
| | F3498 | Event-Based Work in Process |
| | F4095 | Display Material Value Chain |
| | F2765 | Product Profitability |
| | F4818 | Display Line Items—Margin Analysis |
| | F3228 | Sales Accounting Overview |
| | F4022 | Allocation Flow |
| | F3665 | Display Document Flow |

**Table B.1** SAP Fiori Transactions by Chapter

| Chapter | SAP Fiori App ID | SAP Fiori App Name |
|---|---|---|
| Chapter 4: Master Data | F2288 | Maintain Employees |
| | F1684 | Manage Fixed Assets |
| | F1443A | Manage Cost Centers |
| | F1605A | Manage Activity Types |
| | F3162 | Manage Cost Rates—Plan |
| | F3161 | Manage Cost Rates—Professional Services |
| | F1603A | Manage Statistical Key Figures |
| | F1481 | Custom Fields and Logic |
| | F2217 | Display Line Items in General Ledger |
| | F4406 | Manage Substitution and Validation Rules |
| | FIS_FPM_OVP_PROSRVMGN | Product and Service Margins |
| Chapter 5: Overhead Controlling | F0366 | My Spend |
| | F0368 | My Unusual Items |
| | F0707 | Manage Journal Entries |
| | F2548 | Upload General Journal Entries |
| | F4023 | Display Line Items—Cost Accounting |
| | F2009 | Reassign Costs and Revenues |
| | F3338 | Manage Allocations |
| | F3548 | Run Allocations |
| | F4363 | Allocation Results |
| | F4022 | Allocation Flow |
| | F4523 | Manage Allocation Tags |
| | F3697 | Manage Direct Activity Allocation |
| | F0940A | Cost Center—Actuals |
| | F4684 | Manage Posting Periods—Cost Accounting |

**Table B.1** SAP Fiori Transactions by Chapter (Cont.)

| Chapter | SAP Fiori App ID | SAP Fiori App Name |
|---|---|---|
| Chapter 6: Controlling for Manufacturing Organizations | F2680 | Manage Material Valuations |
| | F3498 | Event-Based Work in Process |
| | F5133 | Event-Based Solution Monitor—Product Costing |
| | F5132 | Manage Event-Based Posting Errors—Product Costing |
| | F3669 | Postprocess Event-Based Postings—Product Costing |
| Chapter 7: Margin Analysis for Products and Services | F2794 | Project Profitability Overview |
| | F0718 | Post General Journal Entries |
| | F0719 | Create Customer Project |
| | F2334A | Projects Baseline/EAC/Ongoing |
| | F1823 | Manage My Timesheet |
| | F0780 | Release Billing Proposals |
| | F0798 | Create Billing Documents |
| | F4767 | Revenue Recognition (Event-Based) Projects |
| | F0720 | Customer Projects |
| | F1711 | Import Financial Plan Data |
| | F0936A | Projects Plan/Actual |
| | F0925A | Market Segment Plan/Actual |
| | F2549 | Realignment Results |
| | F3571A | Manage Service Orders |
| | TBT117MCR | Create Service Confirmation |
| | F3573 | Release for Billing |
| | F0798 | Create Billing Documents |
| | F0797 | Manage Billing Documents |
| | F3756 | Revenue Recognition (Event-Based)—Service Documents |
| | F3763 | Manage Service Contracts |
| | F4008 | Inspect Revenue Recognition Postings |

**Table B.1** SAP Fiori Transactions by Chapter (Cont.)

| Chapter | SAP Fiori App ID | SAP Fiori App Name |
|---|---|---|
| Chapter 8: Investment Controlling | F3096 | Asset Overview |
| | F1617A | Asset Balances |
| | F1614 | Asset Transactions |
| Chapter 10: Reporting in SAP S/4HANA | F2918 | Manage Global Hierarchies |
| | F0927A | P&L—Plan/Actual |
| | F5295 | Set Report Relevancy |
| | F3549 | Where-Used List—Cost Centers |
| | F3553 | Manage Custom Hierarchy Types |
| | F2759 | Manage Flexible Hierarchies |
| | F3228 | Sales Accounting Overview |
| | F1423A | Material Inventory Values—Line Items |
| | F2766 | Statistical Key Figure Items |

**Table B.1** SAP Fiori Transactions by Chapter (Cont.)

# Appendix C
# The Authors

**Janet Salmon** is the chief product owner for management accounting at SAP SE and has accompanied many developments to the controlling components of SAP ERP Financials as both a product and a solution manager. She regularly works with key customers and user groups in the United States and Germany to understand their controlling challenges and requirements. Her role is to design and implement innovative controlling solutions with SAP's development teams in Germany and China.

**Stefan Walz** is the chief business process architect for SAP S/4HANA financials at SAP. He has more than 25 years of SAP financials experience through his work in consulting and financials development. He is the coinventor of Universal Journal-based management accounting and event-based revenue recognition. Today, Stefan is responsible for the process integration of the financials component to customer projects, service, and sales in SAP S/4HANA.

# Index

## B



## C

## D

## E



## F

## G



## H



## I

## J

## K



## L



## M

## Q



## R

## S

## T

## U



## V